READER'S DIGEST REPAIR MANUAL

READER'S DIGEST

Repair Manual

THE COMPLETE GUIDE TO HOME MAINTENANCE

Published by The Reader's Digest Association Limited   London   Cape Town   Montreal   Sydney

Reader's Digest Repair Manual
was edited and designed by
The Reader's Digest Association Limited, London

First edition Copyright © 1972
The Reader's Digest Association Limited
Reprinted with amendments 1981

® READER'S DIGEST is a registered trademark of
The Reader's Digest Association, Inc.
of Pleasantville, New York, U.S.A.

Printed in Great Britain

Consultant editor: Nicholas J. Frewing, Des.R.C.A., M.S.I.A.   **Building technology consultant:** John J. Scott, F.R.I.B.A.

We are grateful for assistance given by the following individuals and companies:

AC-Delco Division of General
 Motors Ltd
Airscrew-Weyroc Ltd
Aladdin Industries Ltd
Aldous and Stamp
Robert H. Andrews Ltd
Artex Products (Manufacturing) Ltd
Associated Sprayers Ltd
Avon Rubber Co. Ltd
Barking Brassware Co. Ltd
Peter Bateman
David Battie
R. W. Beach and Co. Ltd
D. G. Beard
Suzanne Beedell
Mrs J. B. Bellew
Robert Betteridge and Co. Ltd
Bissell Appliances Ltd
Black and Edgington Ltd
Percy W. Blandford
Borden Chemical Co. (UK) Ltd
Bostik Ltd
Brays Cycles Ltd
British Domestic Appliances Ltd
British Gypsum Ltd
British Insurance Association
British Knapen Ltd
British Wood Preserving
 Association
Stanley Brooks
The Building Centre
Geoffrey Burdett
Burgess Lane and Co. Ltd
Burgess Power Tools Ltd
M. E. Burrows
Stefania Cambell, Dip.Arch., A.R.I.B.A.
Caravans International, Touring
 Division
Mrs Frances Cary
Peter Chalk
Chamberlin Weatherstrips Ltd
CIBA-GEIGY (UK) Ltd
City Timber Ltd
Clam Brummer Ltd

James Clark and Eaton Ltd
W. H. Colt (London) Ltd
Cooper Pegler Ltd
The Corner Cupboard (Camden
 Passage, London)
Crompton Nettlefold Stenman Ltd
Crusader Electronics Ltd
Michael Dalrymple of Esher Ltd
W. David and Sons Ltd
Charles Deane
Dodson Brothers
Douglas Donaldson, A.I.P.D.
Dunlop Chemical Products Division
Timothy Easton
Eaton Corporation (Yale Security
 Products Division)
J. M. Edwards, R.M.R.S.H.
Ekco-Hawkins Ltd
The Electricity Council
English Abrasives (Portsmouth) Ltd
The Ever Ready Co. (Gt Britain) Ltd
Evode Ltd
The Expanded Metal Co. Ltd
Fiat (England) Ltd
Fibre Building Board Development
 Association Ltd
Fish Tanks Ltd
Ford of Britain
Patrick Forman, LL.B.
Galleon Claygate Fireplaces Ltd
The Gas Council
GEC-XPELAIR Ltd
C. Geoffroy-Dechaume
Charles H. Gilbey
J. R. Glennie
Greenhouse Erection Services
Ernest Hall
Gordon Harris
Sonia Heyworth
Highlands Water Gardens
Hillman Douglas Ltd
W. F. Holdsworth Ltd.
The House of Hardy
Humex Ltd.
W. Hurren

ICI Ltd
Imperial Machine Co.
 (Peelers) Ltd
The Independent Television
 Authority
Derek Irvine Associates
Izal Ltd
M. A. I. Jacobson, C.Eng.,
 F.I.Mech.E., M.I.Prod.E.
H. & R. Johnson Ltd
Judge International
 Housewares Ltd
Local Government Information
 Office
London Adhesives Ltd
London Association for the Blind
London Fire Brigade
Joseph Lucas Ltd
The Marley Tile Co. Ltd
Merrist Wood Agricultural College
J. W. Middleton and Co.
Midland Industries Ltd
Mullard Ltd
Mundet Cork and Plastics Ltd
B. L. Myers
G. W. Nairn
National Heating Centre
Nationwide Landscape Contractors
Newtonite Ltd
A. P. Nicholls
Oaken Lane Garden Centre
Osma Plastics Ltd
Overington Products Ltd
Overseas Spraying Machinery
 Centre, Imperial College Field
 Station
Kevin A. Page
The Parker Pen Co. Ltd
A. Parlons and Son
Philips Electrical Ltd
Polycell Products Ltd
Polycell Prout Ltd
P. Popham
Garry Porter, Dip.Arch., A.R.I.B.A.
Peter Porter, A.R.I.B.A.

The Post Office
V. Powell-Smith, LL.B.(Hons.)
The Prestige Group Ltd
Purley Pools Ltd
Qualcast Fleetway Ltd
Radiation Group Service Ltd
Radiomobile Ltd
F. G. Rayer
Redland Tiles Ltd
Rentokil Laboratories Ltd
R. S. Roberts, C.Eng., F.I.E.R.E.
Ronson Products Ltd
Ruberoid Co. Ltd
Salter Housewares Ltd
Arthur Sanderson and Sons Ltd
Scaffolding (Great Britain) Ltd
Brian Schofield
Roy Searle
Servais Silencers Ltd
Sew Fashions
Shell International Chemical Co.
Site Services (Hampton) Ltd
Sondes Place Research
 Laboratories
John Steventon and Sons Ltd
Strike One
Sunway Blinds
Charles Surridge, A.I.R.T.E.
The Sylglass Company
Thames Television Ltd
3M Co. Ltd
The Tilley Lamp Co. Ltd
Tretobond Ltd
Triang Pedigree Ltd
Trico-Folberth Ltd
Geo. Tucker Eyelet Co. Ltd
Unibond Ltd
Unitubes Ltd
Valor Heating Co.
Valor Ironcrete Ltd
Vanguard Instruments
Tony Wilkins
Wilmot Breeden Ltd
Wolf Electric Tools Ltd
M. A. Wright, Dip.Arch., A.R.I.B.A.

W. C. Youngman Ltd
Zenith Carburetter Co. Ltd

Artists:
T. G. A. Allen
W. R. Astley
Ken Baker
Alan Ball
Paul R. Burns, A.R.C.A.
Terry Collins, F.S.I.A.
Brian Craker, Saxon Artists
D.G.W.
Angela Downing
John Francis
Roger Gould
Vana Haggerty
Dennis Gosling, Peter Hawke,
 Hawke Studios Ltd
Julian Holland
Jackson Day Designs
Launcelot Jones, M.S.I.A.
Brian Watson, Linden Artists
Norman C. Lacey, A.M.I.T.A.I.
Peter North, The Garden Studio
A. W. K. A. Popkiewicz, L.S.I.A.
Garry Porter, Dip.Arch., A.R.I.B.A.
Colin Rattray
C. N. T. Rose, C.Dip., L.S.I.A.
Sherwood Designs Ltd
Les Smith
Ralph Stobart
Carole and John Tyler
Raymond Turvey
Trevor J. Hill, Venner Artists Ltd
Kenneth Vine
Christine Vigurs
Sidney W. Woods, M.P.H.
 Designers Ltd

Photographers:
John Curtis
Robert Dowling
John Vigurs
Barry Weller, Hart Associates

Contents

Replacement parts
If spares are unobtainable locally, get in touch with the manufacturers. Many firms will supply customers direct if given exact details of what is needed.

House repairs
Some repairs to the fabric and fittings of a house may be excluded by conditions in the lease or mortgage agreement. Always check the papers before starting work.

In general, it is unnecessary to apply for local council approval or planning permission to carry out replacements or repairs. If, however, the structure of the house is affected, or if, for example, a plumbing system is being adapted, seek the advice of the local council surveyor.

Renovating and restoring
Many old items of furniture, jewellery, metal, paintings and fabrics can be safely restored and repaired by an amateur. But if there is an item that could be valuable, do not attempt to repair it: take it to a specialist.

Electrical equipment
Take particular note of the safety instructions on p. 521. For repairs not covered, consult a qualified electrician or the local electricity board.

Mechanical repairs
Before beginning any job where an engine might be started by accident—sharpening mower blades, for instance—immobilise the engine by removing the spark-plug.

PART 4

IN THE GARDEN

PART 5

ELECTRICAL EQUIPMENT

PART 6

IN THE GARAGE

PART 7

REFERENCE

PART 1
HOUSE REPAIRS AND DECORATION

Boilers and central heating Construction

How central-heating systems work

Central-heating systems circulate hot water or air throughout a house from a single heat source. Many also provide the domestic hot-water supply.

Warm-air central heating
In a warm-air system, air is heated by gas, electricity, oil or solid fuel and is circulated through ducts to all parts of the house. The hot-water supply to the taps is usually provided from a separate boiler or immersion heater.

Hot-water radiators
In the most common type of central heating, water is heated at a boiler and is circulated through radiators. The system may supply the hot-water taps directly or indirectly.

A direct system has only one water circuit supplying both the taps and the radiators. Every time hot water is drawn from the taps the whole system has to be topped up with cold water from the storage tank. This frequent introduction of new water is a major disadvantage, for scaling occurs when water is heated to 71°C (160°F).

An indirect system has two water circuits. A primary circuit is heated at the boiler, circulates to a heat-exchange unit inside the hot-water cylinder and returns to the boiler to be reheated. A second, similar circuit, runs from the boiler to the radiators. These two circuits are closed and no water can be drawn from them. As a result, no scaling occurs after initial heating of the water.

The hot water to the taps is supplied by a secondary circuit, contained in the hot-water cylinder around the heat-exchange unit. As the central-heating water passes through the exchange unit, it transfers some of its heat to the tap supply. When hot water is drawn off at the taps, new cold water has to be heated in the second circuit; but it is not subjected to the intense direct heat of the boiler and so scaling is very much less. The radiators and the boiler are not affected.

In some systems the water circulates naturally: that is, hot water rises from the boiler and returns to it by force of gravity when it is cooler. Many systems, however, have a pump—usually adjacent to the boiler, on the heating return circuit—to pass the water through the pipes and radiators.

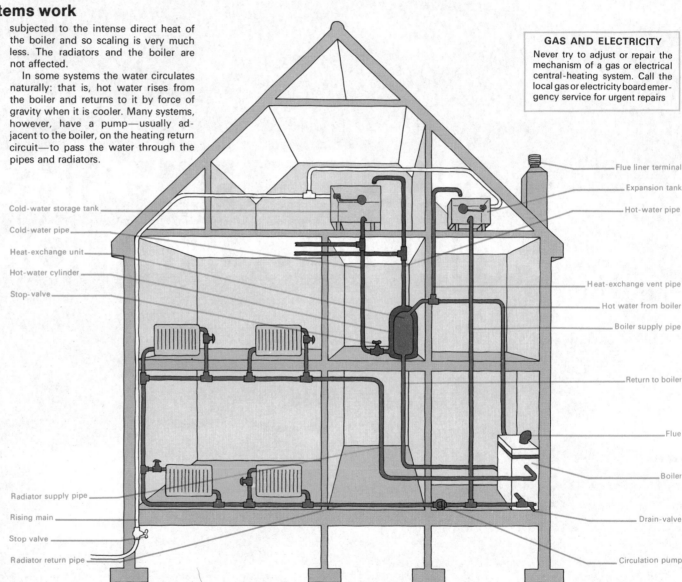

Flue liner terminal

Expansion tank

Hot-water pipe

Cold-water storage tank

Cold-water pipe

Heat-exchange unit

Hot-water cylinder

Stop-valve

Heat-exchange vent pipe

Hot water from boiler

Boiler supply pipe

Return to boiler

Flue

Boiler

Radiator supply pipe

Rising main

Stop valve

Radiator return pipe

Drain-valve

Circulation pump

Boilers and central heating

Types of fuels

Central-heating systems can be fired by solid fuel, gas or oil.

Solid fuel Suitable storage space must be provided close to the house. The boiler needs regular attention, topping up the fuel and cleaning out the ashes.

Some solid fuel systems are gravity fed; the fuel is stored in a hopper above the boiler and drops into the furnace when required.

Gas Most boilers have a safety device to cut off the gas supply if the pilot light goes out. If a gas leak is suspected, turn off the supply at the main gas cock, which is near the meter, and call the gas board emergency service to have it investigated.

Oil The siting of the storage tank is controlled by building regulations to reduce the risk of fire.

Storage tanks must be regularly maintained. Keep the oil filter clean. Make sure that the cap on the filler pipe is easy to unscrew: lubricate the threads occasionally.

Keep the vent pipe on top of the tank clear. If it becomes blocked, the fuel flow will be restricted.

Clean and repaint the tank once a year to protect it against rusting along the welded seams.

OIL STORAGE TANK

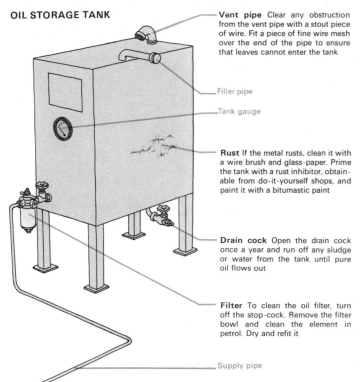

Vent pipe Clear any obstruction from the vent pipe with a stout piece of wire. Fit a piece of fine wire mesh over the end of the pipe to ensure that leaves cannot enter the tank

Filler pipe

Tank gauge

Rust If the metal rusts, clean it with a wire brush and glass-paper. Prime the tank with a rust inhibitor, obtainable from do-it-yourself shops, and paint it with a bitumastic paint

Drain cock Open the drain cock once a year and run off any sludge or water from the tank until pure oil flows out

Filter To clean the oil filter, turn off the stop-cock. Remove the filter bowl and clean the element in petrol. Dry and refit it

Supply pipe

Types of boilers

Boilers may heat only the domestic water supply or both the domestic water and central-heating systems. Domestic-water boilers are usually free-standing, and may be fired by oil, gas or solid fuel. Some open solid-fuel fires, however, also incorporate a back-boiler.

Central-heating boilers are larger than those which heat only the domestic hot water but they work on the same basic principle. They can use oil, gas or solid fuels. The burner is usually controlled automatically according to the setting of a boiler or room thermostat (see p. 12). Many can be controlled in summer to heat only the domestic hot-water supply and not the room radiators.

Maintenance for all types of central-heating boilers should be carried out only by experienced engineers: never try to adjust any of the control mechanisms. If a boiler is used during the summer, have the whole system serviced twice a year. If it is used only in winter, have it overhauled every autumn before switching on.

GAS-FIRED

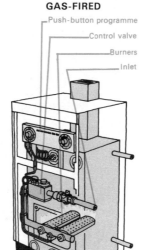

Push-button programme

Control valve

Burners

Inlet

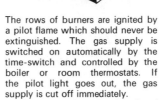

SOLID-FUEL

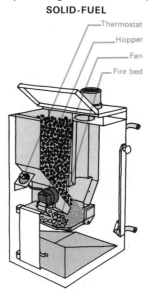

Thermostat

Hopper

Fan

Fire bed

OIL-FIRED

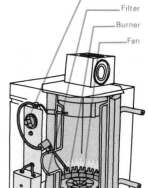

Thermostat

Filter

Burner

Fan

The rows of burners are ignited by a pilot flame which should never be extinguished. The gas supply is switched on automatically by the time-switch and controlled by the boiler or room thermostats. If the pilot light goes out, the gas supply is cut off immediately.

Water runs through tubes fitted inside the boiler furnace. Vanes on the outside of each tube are heated by the flame and the heat is then transferred to the water circulating within the tubes.

On some types there is a water jacket round the boiler.

Air may be supplied by an electric fan or by a thermostatically controlled damper.

In fan-operated solid-fuel boilers, use small anthracite only. It is available in forms known as beans, peas and grains. The hopper will need refilling about once a day in winter—every two to three days during summer. If the boiler is controlled by dampers, any kind of solid fuel can be used.

Ash from the fire drops through the fire bars to an ash-pan in the base of the boiler. Have the flue cleaned at least once a year.

There are four types of oil-fired boilers: pressure-jet, wallflame, dynaflame and vaporising.

In a pressure-jet boiler, oil is compressed to a fine spray and ignited electrically at the burner.

Wallflame and dynaflame boilers have an electric motor which rotates oil-supply jets. As the oil is thrown out against a burner ring it breaks into small drops.

In a vaporising boiler, oil is fed to the base of a burning pot where it is heated, vaporised and burnt.

Some boilers have a controlled air supply.

Boilers and central heating Boilers, pumps and thermostats

Maintenance

Clean a solid-fuel boiler every six months. If any fire-bar is damaged or worn, fit a new one. Repair kits are available from builders' merchants to repair damaged fireclay.

Have a gas-fired boiler serviced once a year by a skilled fitter. Do not try to adjust any of the jets or components. Clean and check an oil-fired boiler every six months. Always turn off the oil supply at the tank and the electrical ignition system at the master switch or mains.

Materials: petrol.
Tools: wire brush; screwdriver; tray; vacuum cleaner.

1 To clean an oil-fired boiler, remove the boiler casing and undo the screws holding the top plate

OIL FILTER UNIT

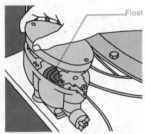

1 Remove the screws holding the filter-unit top. Check that the float moves freely

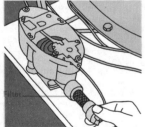

2 Lay a tray under the unit. Remove the drain nut and filter. Clean filter in petrol and refit

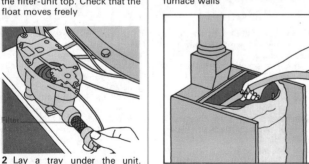

2 Cover the bearing well and burner with a clean rag. Wire brush the furnace walls

3 Remove carbon and dust with the extension hose of a vacuum cleaner. Reassemble

Adjusting a circulating pump

In most central-heating systems, the temperature of the water flowing out of the boiler should be about 7°C higher than that of the returning water in the bottom pipes. Check the temperatures every six months. If there is a much greater or smaller difference, consult a heating engineer.

If water does not circulate when the pump is running, check for air locks. If a vent key is not available, use a screwdriver to open the vent valve and bleed the air off.

Tools: screwdriver or vent key; clip-on thermometer; small spanner; regulator key.

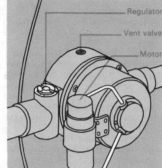

BLEEDING AIR

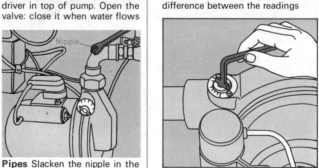

Pump Insert a vent key or screwdriver in top of pump. Open the valve: close it when water flows

Pipes Slacken the nipple in the flow pipe with a small spanner. Tighten when water flows

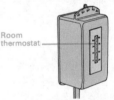

1 Clip a thermometer on bottom pipe, then on top pipe. Note the difference between the readings

2 Flow adjustment can be made by turning the regulator but this is best left to an expert

Thermostats

The heat produced by a central-heating system is controlled automatically by a thermostat fitted to the boiler and often, additionally, by one mounted on a wall.

Some radiators have thermostats fitted to regulate the temperature.

A boiler thermostat switches the boiler burner off and on to control the temperature to which the water is to be heated.

A room thermostat switches the pump off and on as the temperature in the room in which it is fitted rises or falls. Thermostats on radiators open and close a valve to control the water flow through the radiators.

Immersion-heater thermostats are fitted in the hot-water cylinder. They control the water temperature and switch on the heater when required to maintain constant heat.

The times when a heating system, and its thermostats, operate are usually governed by a time clock.

Room thermostat This must be fitted at least 5 ft (1·5 m) above floor level on a wall to minimise the effect of any draughts. Position it well away from other heat sources.

A room thermostat is connected to the circulation pump. It does not control the on-off action of the boiler. When the temperature in the room rises above the required heat, the thermostat switches off the pump.

If there is any other source of heat in the room where the thermostat is fitted, it is likely that the pump will be switched off at times when the rest of the house is not adequately heated. It is advisable to engage an electrician or central-heating specialist to move the

12 HOUSE REPAIRS AND DECORATION

thermostat to a room not affected by outside changes in temperature.

Radiator thermostats A radiator thermostat replaces the normal manual-control valve. It can be pre-set to ensure that the water flowing in the radiator maintains any temperature required.

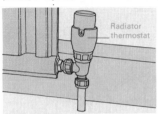
Radiator thermostat

The thermostat is controlled by a temperature-sensitive bellows. As the temperature of the air falls, the bellows contracts and allows more hot water to flow from the pipe into the radiator.

Thermostatic radiator valves can be used on one or two-pipe systems, provided they satisfy the valve manufacturer's instructions.

Immersion heaters
One of the most common methods of heating a domestic water supply is by a thermostatically controlled immersion heater set inside the hot-water cylinder. When the water reaches a pre-set temperature the heating element switches off.

Immersion heaters are inserted either into the top of a cylinder or in the side.

Some heaters have a two-way switch controlling two elements. The elements are generally rated so that on the low position only some of the water is heated and on the full setting all the water is heated.

A switch control, which should have an indicator light, must be fitted near the cylinder, but it can be an advantage to have a second switch in the kitchen where it may be seen and operated more easily.

ADJUSTING IMMERSION-HEATER THERMOSTATS
Immersion heaters, set in the hot-water cylinder, can be pre-set to operate at a required temperature. As the water reaches the temperature chosen—60, 71 or 82°C (140, 160 or 180°F)—the thermostat automatically cuts off the power supply to the heating element.

When the water is heating slowly or when heat is being lost rapidly, check the lagging round the hot-water cylinder (see p. 118). If the lagging is in good condition, turn up the temperature control on the thermostat. Always make sure that the electricity supply is switched off before adjusting a thermostat control.

Tool: screwdriver.

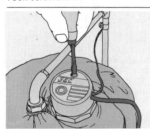

1 Undo the single screw holding the element cover and remove the cover. Prise off the regulator cap

2 Use the screwdriver to turn the regulator screw to the temperature chosen. Replace cap and cover

---

RUNNING A SYSTEM EFFICIENTLY

Any central-heating system should be serviced by qualified engineers at least once a year to ensure best performance and economy.

If a householder signs a contract to buy oil for a number of years from one of the major oil companies this may guarantee annual servicing and half-yearly visits to ensure that the system is running efficiently.

If oil is bought from a company which does not have servicing facilities, consult the manufacturer of the central-heating system—the name is usually on the inside of the boiler door—for the address of a reputable servicing-and-maintenance contractor.

Keep the boiler and oil-filter unit clean (see p. 12). Consult the gas board for gas-fired systems.

Ideal temperatures
Most heating systems are designed to keep a house warm when the outside temperature falls as low as −1°C (30°F). This usually means that living and dining-rooms are kept at a temperature of 21°C (70°F), with the temperatures of other rooms and areas proportionately lower.

In a correctly designed system each room is kept at the required temperature by a single, carefully positioned room thermostat (see p. 12) or by radiator thermostats. Once adjusted, it should not be necessary to alter the settings. The following levels of warmth suit most people:

Living-room	21°C (70°F)
Dining-room	21°C (70°F)
Bedsitting-room	21°C (70°F)
Bathroom	18°C (65°F)
Hall	15°C (60°F)
Kitchen	15°C (60°F)
Toilet	15°C (60°F)
Bedrooms	13°C (55°F)

Insulation
The costs of running central heating will be considerably higher than they need be if a house is badly insulated: 30 per cent of the heat in a house can be lost through an uninsulated roof. To insulate the floor of an attic, see p. 114; for pipework in the roof-space, see p. 115; for water-storage tanks, see p. 116.

Draughtproof badly fitting windows and doors (see pp. 63–67).

Fill gaps between floorboards which are not covered with carpet, linoleum or sheet vinyl (see p. 82). Alternatively, cover the boards with $\frac{1}{8}$ in. (3 mm) hardboard (see p. 89).

Fill gaps between skirting boards and floorboards (see p. 86).

Heat may also be lost through windows: clip-on double-glazing systems, sold at do-it-yourself shops and hardware stores, reduce heat loss, but those fitted by specialists are more effective.

Solid fuel
To ensure maximum efficiency from solid-fuel central heating use only the correct size of fuel for the boiler: solid-fuel merchants will give advice once they are told the name and type of the equipment.

Always make sure the gas poker is lit before inserting it into the fuel bed—pockets of gas may cause an explosion when ignited.

Do not let the fire die before refuelling. Always empty cold ash from the ashpan regularly.

When cleaning out the inside of the firebox, leave the ashpit door ajar to allow air to flow through and keep the interior dry.

Clean the flueway in the boiler during the summer and at least once a year, remove any deposits which have collected in the elbow at the base of the flue.

If the boiler is to be left cold for more than a day during frosty weather, drain the system and empty the boiler.

Scaling
Hissing and knocking noises in a central-heating system—especially when the boiler is stoked up—are usually an indication of hard-water scaling (see p. 17) inside the pipes, cylinder and boiler.

A check in the attic may reveal steam coming from the expansion pipe over the expansion or storage tank (see p. 10).

Although the safety valve on the boiler will lift to relieve the built-up pressure, the system should be descaled as soon as possible.

Not only will a furred system cost more to run but it could be dangerous.

Overheating
Hissing or knocking in the boiler or pipes in a central-heating system may also indicate that the water is overheating—perhaps because of a damaged thermostat, failure of the circulating pump (see p. 12), a blocked flue-way (see pp. 22–23), or lack of water in the system due to a jammed ball valve in the feed and expansion tank (see p. 141).

First cut off the supply of gas or oil. With a solid-fuel boiler, rake the fire into the ashpan and remove it from the boiler. Open the door of the boiler to cool it. Do not close the boiler damper.

If the circulation pump can be run when the boiler is not switched on, keep it operating to pump water round the system and help to lower the temperature.

When the system is cool, adjust the thermostat; if it does not click when turned either way, it is faulty. Check the flue for obstructions and also the operation of the ball valve in the header tank.

Boilers and central heating Radiators

Types of radiators

Three kinds of radiators—differing in appearance rather than in efficiency—are used in domestic central-heating systems.

Column radiators Hollow, cast-iron sections are linked together by pipes at the top and bottom.

Panel radiators These are made in one section and have a ribbed surface. The water flows through hollow webs in the metal.

Radiant panel heaters Hot-water pipes are attached to the back of a single sheet of metal, or sandwiched between two sheets with insulation on the side facing the wall.

PANEL RADIATOR

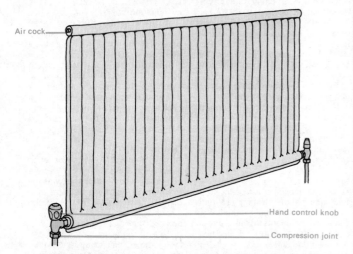

Air cock

Hand control knob

Compression joint

COLUMN RADIATOR

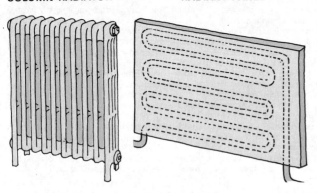

RADIANT PANEL

How radiators are fixed

Cast-iron column radiators are heavy and it is necessary for them to stand on the floor and be fitted with hooked wall brackets to steady them.

Panel radiators are much lighter and can be supported—clear of the floor—on angled brackets at the bottom and on either side.

Some are designed to allow the pipe joints to be loosened so that the radiators can be swung down from the brackets for cleaning and painting (see p. 40). When two or more radiators are linked, a coupling joint between them allows slight sideways movement to compensate for heat expansion.

Angled brackets at the side or top of the radiator are usually adjustable.

Some light-weight pressed-steel radiators have small metal bars welded to the back which rest on the hooked ends of brackets fixed to the wall.

BACK FIXINGS

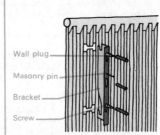

Wall plug

Masonry pin

Bracket

Screw

Hooked brackets Secured to wall with No. 12 or 14 dome-headed screws through slotted holes and with a masonry pin

Loose brackets Remove radiator (see p. 16). Fill holes and fit plugs (see p. 683). Screw on brackets and secure with masonry pin

EDGE FIXINGS

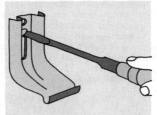

Angled brackets Screwed to wall around edges of radiator with No. 14 dome-headed screws, with a masonry pin for final fixing

Steadying brackets Tighten all side and bottom brackets. With radiator in position, tighten steadying brackets on top edge

LEAKING JOINTS

Joints between pipes and radiators may leak because of expansion and contraction. If a capillary joint (see p. 138) leaks, solder round the joint section to seal it. If a compression joint (see p. 138) leaks, tighten it with a spanner.

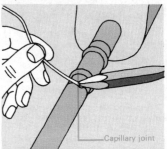

Capillary joint

Capillary joint Drain enough water from the system to empty the pipes connected by the joint (see p. 137). Use a blowlamp carefully to heat the joint, and pull out one pipe. Clean it and apply flux to the end. Insert the end into the joint and solder (see p. 692) until the joint is sealed

Compression joint Wipe the joint dry and tighten the nut on it with an adjustable spanner or grips

Draining and filling the system

Always switch off the boiler fuel supply and ignition system a few hours before draining a central-heating system, to ensure that the water is cold.

If anti-freeze or anti-rust has been introduced into the water of an indirect system (see p. 10) it is possible to drain the water into containers and pour it back into the expansion tank. On other systems, the hose must be long enough to reach an outside drain.

Materials: string.
Tools: hose; water container; spanner.

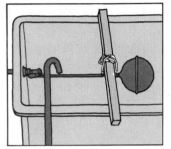

1 Close stop valve at expansion tank or tie ball valve to wood across tank (see p. 141)

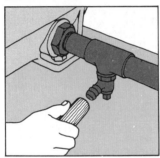

2 Attach one end of a hosepipe to the drain cock, usually located on the return pipe at the boiler

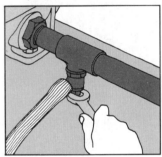

3 Take the other end of the hose to an outside drain. Open drain cock with a spanner. Allow system to empty

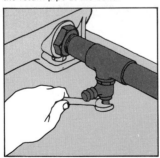

4 Before refilling the system, close the drain cock. Check it for leaks as the water flows through it

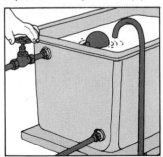

5 Release ball valve or open stop valve on expansion tank; fill slowly, so that any air can escape through vent

Removing air and fitting an air eliminator

Trapped air will reduce a radiator's efficiency. The air can be released by opening the vent valve (see below); but if this has to be done frequently it is better to replace the valve with an air eliminator. Provided that the water does not have a high alkaline content, the eliminator will release the air automatically without allowing any water to escape.

Materials: small container to collect water; PTFE tape; eliminator.
Tools: vent-valve key; spanner.

CLEARING AIR LOCKS

On most radiators a square-ended hollow key—obtainable from iron-mongers—is needed to open the vent valve to clear an air lock.

1 Insert the key and turn it anti-clockwise. Hold a jar under the valve to collect water

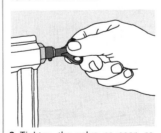

2 Tighten the valve as soon as air ceases to escape and the water flows. If necessary, repeat later

---

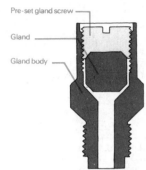

Pre-set gland screw
Gland
Gland body

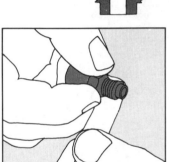

2 Cover the threads of the air-eliminator screw with PTFE tape to ensure a watertight joint

4 If filling has introduced a large volume of air, release it by undoing the eliminator

1 Drain the system. Loosen and remove the vent valve with the key provided with the system

3 Screw in eliminator finger-tight. Refill the system. If water appears, tighten eliminator with spanner

5 As soon as water appears, refit the eliminator to the radiator and tighten with a spanner

Boilers and central heating Radiators

Fitting a new radiator

To disconnect a radiator, find out how many valves it has. If it has one on each side (one will have a cover on it) close both. If it has only one, drain the central-heating system (see p. 15).

Make sure the replacement radiator is of the same size as the old one. Do not fit an old vent valve and plug on the new radiator: buy new ones.

Use a basin to collect water as the old radiator is lifted out.

Materials: radiator; vent valve; end-plug; jointing paste and hemp or PTFE tape; union connectors.
Tools: spanner or wrench; screwdriver; basin; vent-valve key; square bar.

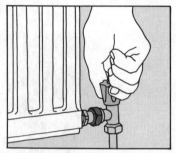

1 Lift carpets to avoid stains from any dirty water in the radiator. Close the control valve at bottom of radiator

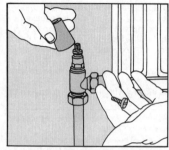

2 Remove the cover from the lock-shield valve, at the other side. Turn off the valve and count the turns

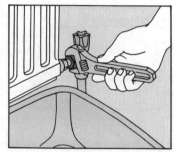

3 Place a basin under the joint at each side and undo the union nuts gently. Do not distort pipes

4 Lift the radiator off its locating bracket on the wall and tip the remaining water from one side

5 Smear the threads of two new union connectors with jointing compound, obtainable from an ironmonger

6 Wrap plumber's hemp into the sealing compound. Alternatively, use PTFE tape without compound

7 Screw the union by hand, then tighten it with a spanner. Wipe off any surplus sealing compound

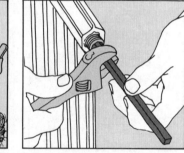

8 Spread paste and hemp on the end-plug and fit it in position at the top. Fit the vent valve in the same way

9 To tighten the end-plug, fit a square bar into the plug recess. Turn the bar with a spanner or wrench

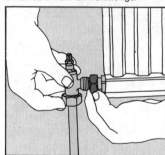

10 Spread jointing compound and the hemp round the threads of the valve unions. Position radiator and tighten

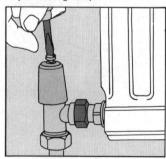

11 Open the lock-shield valve with a spanner. Turn it the number of turns which were required to close it

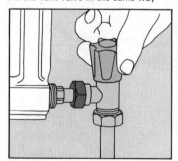

12 When the lock-shield valve has been opened correctly, fit the cap and screw it on to the valve

13 Fill the expansion tank with water if the system has been drained (see p. 15). Open the control valve

14 Hold a basin under the vent valve and open the valve with a key. Turn off when water flows

Boilers and central heating Water softeners and scale inhibitors

The effects of hard water

Before rainwater reaches a reservoir it passes through various types of earth and rock, where it absorbs chemicals and impurities. This process—especially if the water absorbs magnesium and calcium salts—can harden the water so that it becomes difficult to make a lather and leaves scum when used for washing.

It may, however, have more serious consequences. Some hard water becomes soft when it is heated above 71°C (160°F): but the chemical process which causes it to lose its hardness also results in deposits of fur or scale. This scaling, which is easily removed from kettles, is more difficult to remedy in a water-heating system: the passage for the water through the pipes gets smaller and smaller, the system becomes less efficient, and the accumulation of scale insulates the boiler walls from the cooling effect of the circulating water; eventually the walls may burn through, and the boiler will leak.

Reduction of bore by scaling

Two types of treatment are possible: to soften the water chemically or to add chemicals which reduce the amount of scaling.

Whether water is hard or soft in central-heating systems matters only if scaling occurs. If the water is difficult to lather, but no scaling is seen in kettles, it cannot damage the pipes of the heating system.

If, however, deposits of scale are found in kettles, or if the central-heating pipes are heard to knock and there are long delays in water heating, it is advisable to treat the water as soon as possible.

Specialist manufacturers, whose addresses may be given in the local classified telephone directory or by a builders' merchant, can analyse the water supply and advise on the best type of treatment.

Portable softener Connected by rubber hose to hot-water tap. Refill with common salt after every 150 gallons of water. Has no effect on other water in the house

Softening powder Can be added to small quantities of hot water as they are used. Do not use in storage tank. Available from chemists or most household stores

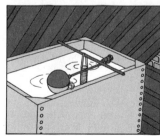

Scale inhibitor Capsules are suspended in cold-water storage tank or header tank to prevent scale forming in system. Some also soften the water

Reducing and preventing scale

There are several chemical scale inhibitors on the market which reduce boiler scale; these are available with manufacturers' instructions.

Where a hot-water system is fed from a cold-water storage tank, scale-inhibiting crystals can be hung in the tank.

Where a hot-water system is fed direct from the main, a chemical scale-inhibiting unit can be plumbed into the rising main. Install the unit as near the stop-valve as possible and fit another stop-valve with the unit so that the latter can be isolated when it has to be refilled, usually about once a year.

If the rising main is a lead pipe, engage a plumber to fit the unit.

Materials: inhibitor; stop-valve; about 24 in. (610 mm) of $\frac{1}{2}$–$\frac{3}{4}$ in. (13–20 mm) copper pipe; two pipe adaptors to suit unit (if required). Tools: measuring rod; hacksaw; adjustable spanner; PTFE tape.

SCALE INHIBITOR

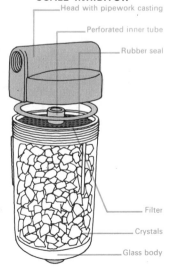

Head with pipework casting

Perforated inner tube

Rubber seal

Filter

Crystals

Glass body

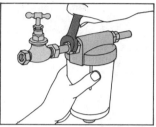

1 Turn off water at rising-main stop-valve. Fit 6 in. (150 mm) of pipe on each side of unit head with compression joints and adaptors. Fit stop-valve on arrowed side of head

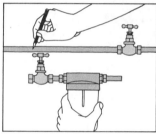

2 Hold the unit assembly at rising-main stop-valve and mark on pipe the distance required for fitting. Cut through the pipe, undo stop-valve joint and remove pipe

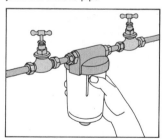

3 Position unit between mains stop-valve and cut end of pipe and secure with compression joints. With both stop-valves still closed, unscrew unit; fill with crystals

PREVENTING CORROSION

Where a central-heating system has been installed after a house was built, the water is often stored in a galvanised-iron tank and distributed to fittings through copper pipework. If these metals are in contact, the zinc coating on the tank may corrode. To prevent this, suspend a magnesium kit—a sacrificial anode—in the tank. The chemical process causing corrosion is then transposed to the magnesium and the zinc is not damaged.

Fitting an anode to a sealed tank should be done only by a plumber.

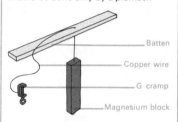

Batten

Copper wire

G cramp

Magnesium block

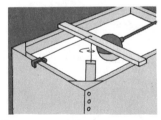

Place batten across tank and suspend magnesium block as near centre as possible but away from ball float. Adjust copper wire so that block hangs about 4–6 in. (100–150 mm) above bottom of tank. Bend wire so that G cramp can be screwed to edge of tank and scrape fixing area down to bare metal to improve contact.

Liquid inhibitors There are several chemicals that can be added to the water in the feed and expansion tank to prevent corrosion.

Removing stains from interior and exterior walls

Efflorescence on exterior brickwork

Efflorescence on a newly plastered wall

White powder or feathery crystals—similar to damp salt—often appear on the surface of new brickwork or newly plastered walls. This staining, called efflorescence, forms because rainwater, or the water used in the construction of a house, soaks the brickwork and dissolves the soluble salts in it. As the water evaporates it draws the salt to the surface.

Efflorescence does not damage exterior brickwork, but it is unattractive. Clean the walls occasionally with a stiff-bristled broom. Do not use a wire brush, which could damage the bricks and the pointing.

Neutralising the salts

The most effective permanent remedy is to brush on a neutralising liquid, obtainable from do-it-yourself shops or builders' merchants. Use a 4 in. (100 mm) brush and apply two or three coats to the affected parts of the wall. Allow about 15 minutes between applying coats.

Use the same treatment on interior walls, where efflorescence may damage the wall coverings. Leave to dry for 24 hours, then redecorate.

Never try to wash off efflorescence with tap water: it contains chemicals which accelerate the reappearance of the salts.

Vegetation stains

If brickwork has been wet for a long time, it may become stained by surrounding vegetation.

First trace the cause of the dampness and remedy it (see p. 25). Clean the brickwork with a stiff-bristled broom and apply a coat of colourless fungicide, obtainable from a do-it-yourself shop. Treat the wall in dry weather to ensure that the solution is not washed off by rainwater before it has time to take effect.

Rust

If rust appears only on the pointing of a wall, it is caused by particles of ironstone in the sand. Rake out the mortar and repoint.

Rust stains around ironwork embedded in a wall can eventually cause the brickwork to flake and crack. Dig out the mortar round the ironwork, then clean and prime the metal (see p. 37).

Repointing a brick wall

When bricks are laid, the mortar between them may be used also to finish the joints. This is called jointing. An alternative, called pointing, is to scrape out the mortar to a depth of about ⅜ in. (10 mm) before it sets. Fill to the surface of the bricks with fresh mortar after all the bricks are laid.

Pointing is also used to repair brickwork joints, both indoors and outdoors. Although the mix is the same as for laying bricks (see p. 693) it is possible to add a vegetable dye or buy a special ready-mixed coloured pointing compound to give any coloured effect required in the joints between the bricks.

If the pointing between existing brickwork has cracked or become damaged, dig it out with a hammer and chisel. When repointing, treat the vertical joints first, then move on to the horizontal joints.

Always work from the top of the wall downwards. To avoid splashing the wall below the working area, it is advisable to fix a large sheet of polythene over the brickwork. Prop stout battens against it to hold it in place. If bricks are spattered with mortar, do not try to wash it off with water: leave it to dry then scrape it off with the side of a trowel.

To trim off any surplus, hold a straight-edge along underneath the horizontal joints and cut off the overhanging mortar cleanly with the side of the trowel.

Always finish the pointing to match the original joints (see p. 19). The mortar may be flush with the brickwork or it may be indented slightly between the bricks, called keyed pointing A common alternative is struck weathered pointing, where one edge (the upper edge on horizontal joints) is set below the surface level of brickwork.

Materials: soft sand, lime, cement (see p. 693); colour additive or coloured ready-mixed mortar if necessary.
Tools: club hammer; ½ in. (13 mm) cold chisel; hawk; pointing trowel; old bucket handle or ¾ in. (20 mm) piping shaped to suit; brush; straight-edge.

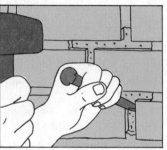

1 Chip out the damaged pointing from between the layers of bricks with a club hammer and cold chisel

2 Brush away any dust particles and soak the area to be pointed with water. Mix up the mortar required

3 Press the mortar firmly into the gap between the bricks until it protrudes beyond the brick surface

Flush pointing

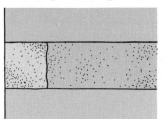

Flush pointing gives a completely flat surface over the whole area of a wall. It is often used on old brickwork where the outer corners of the bricks have crumbled and the surface of the wall is to be decorated.

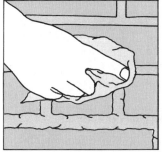

1 Apply the mortar so that it just protrudes beyond bricks. When it is almost dry, rub with sacking

2 When the mortar is completely dry, scrape over the joints with a piece of stiff plastic. Brush off dust

Weathered pointing

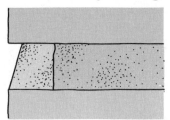

To ensure that rainwater cannot collect in a brickwork joint, the pointing mortar is often sloped downwards and outwards. Use the edge of a pointing trowel to press in the mortar $\frac{1}{8}$ in. (3 mm) at top of the joint.

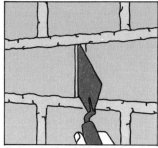

1 Start with vertical joints. Hold trowel level with the right-hand brick and press in at other side

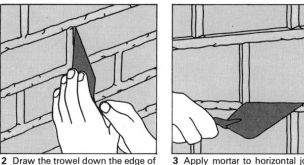

2 Draw the trowel down the edge of the right-hand brick and cut off surplus mortar with the trowel edge

3 Apply mortar to horizontal joints. Press in to depth of $\frac{1}{8}$ in. (3 mm) at top; slope to the bottom edge

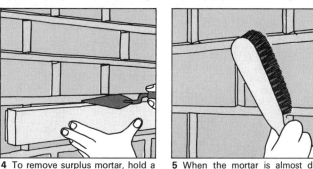

4 To remove surplus mortar, hold a straight-edge below joints and trim with the trowel

5 When the mortar is almost dry, rub the surface of the joints with a dusting brush

Keyed pointing

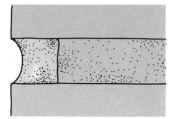

To finish brickwork joints with keyed pointing, use an old bucket handle or a piece of $\frac{3}{4}$ in. (20 mm) metal piping to press the mortar in between the bricks. Trim off the surplus mortar with the trowel.

1 Open out the hook at one end of a bucket handle. Remove the handle from the bucket

2 Cut off the handle about 9 in. (230 mm) from the end. Grip it in a vice and file smooth

3 Mark the handle 3 in. (75 mm) from one end and bend it in a vice to form a shallow curve

4 Apply mortar to the wall joints and press it in with the curved loop of the handle

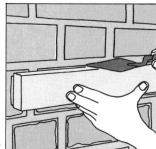

5 Use a straight-edge, or a piece of timber, as a guide and trim the edges with the side of a trowel

Brickwork Renewing

Replacing damaged bricks

When the surface of a brick wall is damaged, remove the faulty bricks and fit replacements. Do not buy new bricks: ask a builders' merchant for used ones of the same type as those in the existing wall.

If the wall is 9 in. (230 mm) thick, remove only the outside skin. If the wall has a cavity, make sure that no loose material is allowed to fall down inside the cavity and form a bridge for dampness to penetrate.

Materials: used bricks; sand, cement and lime (see p. 693).
Tools: club hammer; cold chisel; trowel; stiff brush.

1 Break and gradually remove one brick. Finish working on it before starting on the others

2 To dislodge all the other bricks in the damaged area, hammer a cold chisel along the mortar joints

3 On double-thickness brickwork, chisel off the outside half of bricks laid across the wall

4 Mix mortar (see p. 693) and fit bricks. Cut half bricks to fit where old bricks were halved

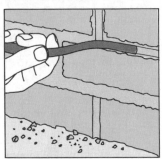

5 Match the existing pointing (see p. 18). Allow the new mortar to dry, then brush wall surface

Fitting a new airbrick

If an airbrick in the outside wall of a house becomes damaged, replace it immediately to ensure that vermin and birds cannot enter the house. Do not block the airbrick hole, even as a temporary measure.

In a cavity wall, the airbrick extends through the whole thickness. In a solid wall, the brick fits on the outside: the inside surface has a louvre. Check the type of brick required before buying a new one.

Materials: airbrick; sand and cement (see p. 693).
Tools: club hammer; cold chisel; trowel; stiff brush.

1 Cut out the old airbrick with a cold chisel and club hammer. Brush off old mortar and loose dirt

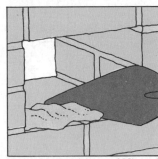

2 Mix mortar (see p. 693) and spread a ½ in. (13 mm) layer on the bottom of the hole in the wall

3 Spread a ½ in. layer of mortar on the top and sides of the new airbrick. Fit airbrick carefully in hole

4 Remove excess mortar with trowel before mortar sets. Repoint around the airbrick to match wall (see p. 18)

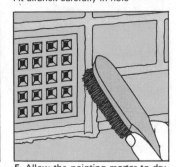

5 Allow the pointing mortar to dry, then clean the wall around the airbrick with a stiff-bristled brush

FITTING A LOUVRE

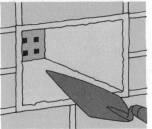

1 When a new airbrick is fitted, clean the hole made and line it with new mortar from inside

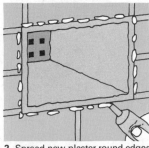

2 Spread new plaster round edges on inside wall. When dry, dab on impact adhesive (see p. 694)

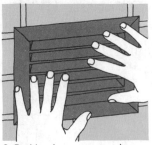

3 Position louvre accurately over the hole. Hold in position until the adhesive forms a good bond

Chimneys and Flues Pots

Always handle chimney pots with care: they are made of clay, are larger than they appear from the ground and are very heavy. Use scaffolding on high chimneys (see p. 686) and lift and lower the pots on a rope.

To find the size of pot required, remove part of the mortar: measure from top to bottom, and the internal diameter at the top. If possible, have the chimney swept before starting repair work.

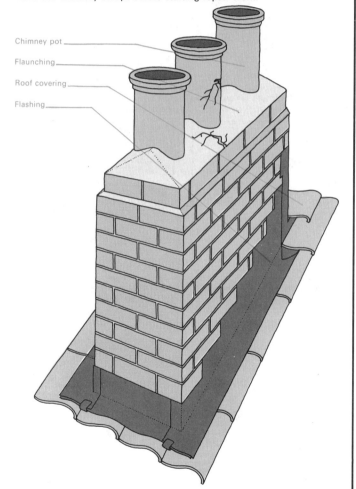

Chimney pot
Flaunching
Roof covering
Flashing

Refixing chimney pots

Damaged chimneys should be repaired as soon as possible, particularly if the cement around the base of the pot, called flaunching, is badly cracked.

If the pots are undamaged, reset them. Replace a damaged pot.

Use 3 parts sharp sand, 1 part cement and 1 part water for the flaunching: one bucket per pot is usually sufficient.

Materials: pots if necessary; sharp sand; cement; water; bucket; rope. Tools: club hammer; cold chisel; old paintbrush; wire brush; trowel; scaffolding and ladder.

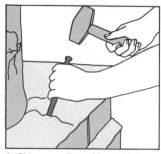

1 Chip away flaunching with hammer and chisel. Lift off pots and lower damaged ones to the ground

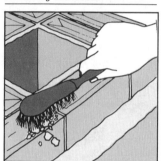

2 Remove any loose material with a wire brush. Brush away from the flue so that debris does not fall in

3 If necessary, repoint top course of bricks (see p. 18). Position chimney pots over flues

4 Mix flaunching mortar. Wet the top of the chimney stack and the bottom of the pot with an old brush

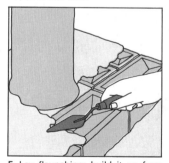

5 Lay flaunching: build it up from the edge to 3 in. (75 mm) deep around pot. Rub mortar from stack

SEALING A STACK

If a chimney is not needed after alterations in a house, remove the pot and seal the head of the flue. It is essential to insert an air brick in the flue (see p. 20).

1 Remove flaunching and pot. Clean the brickwork around edge of flue and dampen it with a brush and water

2 Lay mortar (see p. 693) 1 in. (25 mm) thick on the wet brickwork around the edge of the flue

3 Bed a slate on the mortar. Cover with more mortar and curve the surface to throw off rainwater

Chimneys and flues Asbestos

Fitting a section of flue pipe

Flue pipes are sold in 6 ft (1·8 m) lengths, with a collar at one end into which the next length is fitted.

The collar rests on a supporting clip, attached to a fixing bracket plugged and screwed to the wall.

To replace a length of pipe, loosen only the clip and lift out the faulty section: do not remove the bracket. If only the pipe collar is broken, cut it off after damping the pipe to lay any possible dust. Buy a double-collar union piece and remove the fixing bracket to accommodate it.

When working with asbestos be careful not to breathe in dust; a mask can be worn.

Materials: pipe or 4 in. (100 mm) double collar (if appropriate); mastic putty; wall plugs.
Tools: screwdriver; hacksaw; hammer; plugging tool; pencil.

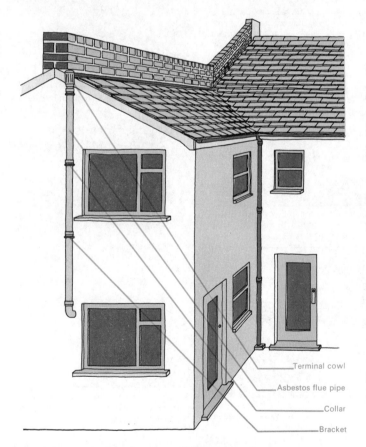

Terminal cowl

Asbestos flue pipe

Collar

Bracket

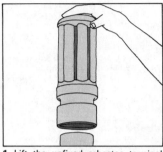

1 Lift the unfixed asbestos terminal cowl from the top of the flue and take it down to the ground

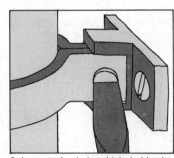

2 Loosen the bolt which holds the highest clip. Lift off and lay aside the top length of pipe

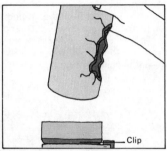

3 Unscrew clips and remove pipes until broken one is reached. Fit new pipe and replace remaining pipes

4 If only a collar is damaged, remove the pipe, dampen the end to lay any dust and cut off the collar.

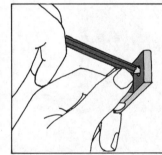

5 Unscrew the wall fixing bracket. Position new double collar and mark new position for the fixing bracket

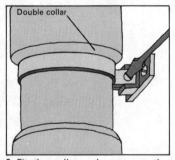

6 Fit the collar and screw on the fixing bracket. Bolt the supporting clip on to the bracket

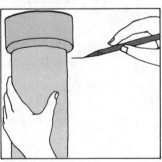

7 Hold the next length in place above and mark the new position for the bracket. Refix the bracket and clip

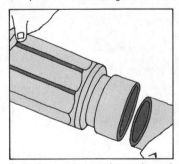

8 Fit the terminal cowl over the end of the last length before fixing that length in position

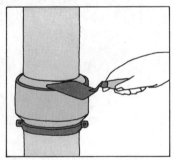

9 Seal all the joints with mastic putty. Do not seal the terminal cowl to the top length

Chimneys and flues Linings

Fitting a lining in a central-heating flue

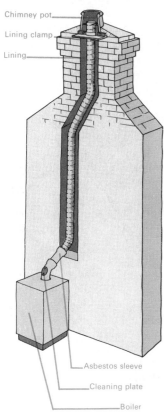

Chimney pot
Lining clamp
Lining

Asbestos sleeve
Cleaning plate
Boiler

To fit a flue lining, cut out the plaster and brickwork near the boiler outlet. If an obstruction is located in the flue, mark the approximate position and cut away the brickwork to remove it.

When a lining is fitted, taper new mortar—called flaunching (see p. 21)—from 3 in. (75 mm) above the base of the chimney pot to the edge of the stack. Replace the bricks in the wall.

Materials: lining kit; 1:3 cement-and-sand mix; asbestos sleeve; asbestos rope; heat-resistant cement; string. Tools: hacksaw; adjustable spanner; brick trowel; club hammer; cold chisel; paint tin; plastering tools (see p. 120).

1 Cut out the brickwork of the flue near the boiler outlet with a hammer and cold chisel

2 Remove mortar and pot from stack (see p. 21). Lower a weighted tin, wider than the lining, down the flue

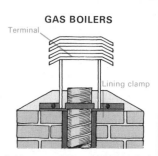

GAS BOILERS

Terminal
Lining clamp

1 Use a special terminal instead of a chimney pot. Flaunch the top of the stack after fitting (see p. 21)

3 If the tin is obstructed, tie a knot in the string to measure the distance down to the obstruction

4 Knock out bricks at obstruction point and clear the chimney. Lower the lining, nose cone first, down flue

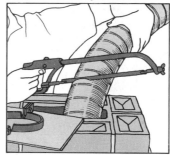

5 Place lining in asbestos sleeve at boiler. From the roof, cut off lining 6 in. (150 mm) above the stack

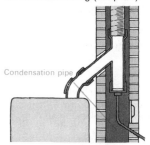

Condensation pipe

2 If the lining has an exterior condensation pipe, knock a hole in the outside wall

Acids in the fumes from gas and oil-fired boilers may discolour and affect the wall surrounding the flue. The simplest remedy is to reline the flue with a lining kit, obtainable from a builders' merchant.

For maximum safety when installing the lining, work from a sectional tower or simple scaffolding (see p. 687).

If the lining is for a gas-fired boiler, buy a louvred terminal: clay chimney pots should be used only with oil-fired and solid-fuel boilers, where less condensation occurs.

6 Place the clamp plate over lining and tighten the nuts on each side to hold it firmly in position

7 Fit chimney pot and flaunching. It is important to seal junction between lining and clamp plate

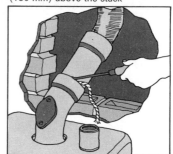

8 Connect liner and joints with asbestos string and heat-resistant cement. Replace bricks and replaster

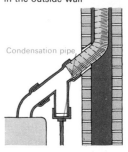

Condensation pipe

3 If the condensation pipe is inside the house, provide receptacle at floor level to collect the drips

Dampness

Sources of dampness

Dampness causes structural deterioration, leads to attack by fungus diseases, ruins internal decorations and is dangerous to health.

It is due usually to one of three main factors: the penetration of water from outside; leakages from internal pipes, storage tanks or radiators; or condensation on cold interior surfaces.

Inspection

Inspect the whole house at least once a year. If there is any evidence of dampness, trace its source and rectify the fault at the source immediately.

Inside the house

Check all pipework joints and investigate the roof from inside the loft. Lift a floorboard in each room and examine between joints with a torch. Look for the white, powdery signs of efflorescence on walls (see p. 18). Check that water is not penetrating around windows and doors—areas which are particularly vulnerable to dampness.

Outside the house

Inspect the roof, chimneys, flashings, rainwater pipes, gutters, gulleys and brick or stone pointing.

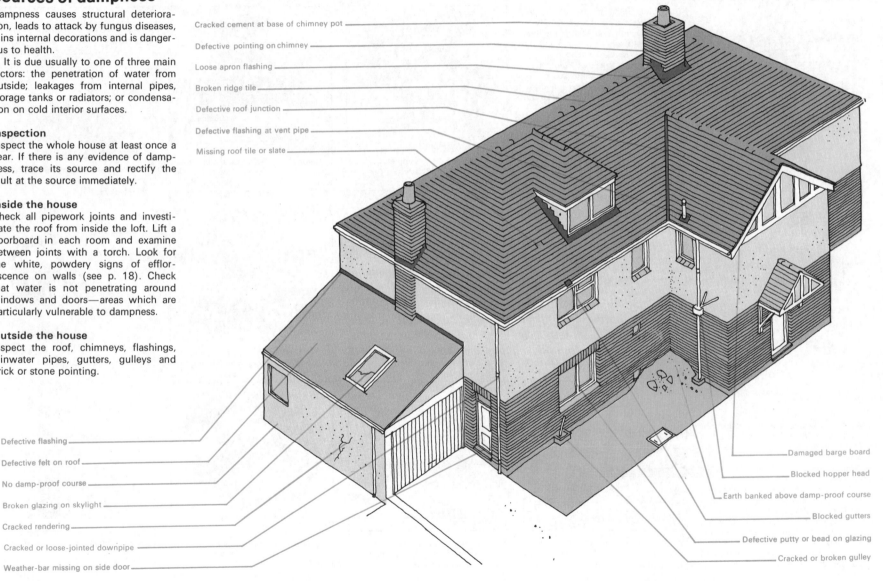

Cracked cement at base of chimney pot

Defective pointing on chimney

Loose apron flashing

Broken ridge tile

Defective roof junction

Defective flashing at vent pipe

Missing roof tile or slate

Defective flashing

Defective felt on roof

No damp-proof course

Broken glazing on skylight

Cracked rendering

Cracked or loose-jointed downpipe

Weather-bar missing on side door

Damaged barge board

Blocked hopper head

Earth banked above damp-proof course

Blocked gutters

Defective putty or bead on glazing

Cracked or broken gulley

Identification and remedy

Source	Visible damage	Cause	Remedy
Chimneys	Leaning stack Cracks and staining on stack and adjacent surfaces	Condensation in flue Fumes from boiler Deterioration of mortar Defective flue lining Defective flashings	Re-line flue if necessary (see p. 23). If stack is leaning, consult a specialist Renew flashings (consult a builder)
Condensation	Walls, floors, carpets, upholstery and bedding feel damp, even in dry weather	Warm, moist air in contact with cold non-porous surfaces Lack of ventilation	Improve insulation, provide continuous heating, and improve ventilation. Install extractor fan in kitchen (see p. 30) Apply thin polystyrene sheet under wallpaper (see p. 31). Clear any air bricks. Insulate roof space (see p. 113)
Floors	Ground-floor timber warped or lifting Coverings swell and form blisters	**Concrete floors** Damaged or ineffective damp-proof membrane **Timber floors** Inadequate ventilation	To install damp-proof membrane, consult specialist. Ensure that air bricks or vents are unblocked
Gutters and downpipes	Damp patches and stains on walls adjacent to pipes	Blocked gutter outlets Broken gutters Broken pipes	Clear gutters (see p. 101). Paint cast-iron gutters with bituminous paint Fit new pipes and gutters (see pp. 106–9)
Plumbing	Damp patches on walls and ceilings	Defective pipework Faulty ball valve in water tank Burst frozen pipes Corroded pipes and tanks Leaking tank or cylinder	Renew defective and corroded pipes (see p. 137). Renew ball valve (see p. 141). Renew tank (see p. 140) Consult builder for new cylinder
Pointing	**Outside** Mortar missing or crumbling **Inside** Stains on walls	Deterioration of mortar	Remove mortar to a depth of $\frac{1}{2}$ in. (13 mm). Repoint with 1:1:6 lime, cement and sand (see p. 18)

Source	Visible damage	Cause	Remedy
Rendering	Cracks Rendering detached from brickwork	Temperature changes Drying shrinkage Movement of building	Clean and fill with a 1:1:6 mix (see p. 197) If damage is extensive, consult a builder
Rooflights	**Outside** Broken glass, defective putty or glazing beads Shrinkage gaps **Inside** Staining	Age Timber shrinkage Defective flashings	Fit new frame. Fit new glass and putty or beads (see p. 204) Renew flashings (consult a builder)
Roofs, flat Felt and asphalt	Blisters and cracks on roof surface	Weathering Faulty installation Extremes of temperature Condensation	Repair small defects (see p. 177). If major asphalt damage, consult a specialist
Zinc and lead	Holes and cracks Defective cappings Defective upstands	Age, corrosion	Repair zinc (see p. 179) If lead, consult a builder
Roofs, flashings	Stains on ceilings Roof timbers damp	Flashing material damaged, rotted or missing	Repoint flashings (see p. 164). Renew flashings if necessary
Roofs, pitched Tiled, slated or shingled	**Outside** Slates, tiles or shingles missing, slipped, split or broken **Inside** Water stains on ceilings	Age, weathering Faulty fixing	Refit slates (see p. 169), tiles (see p. 173) or shingles (see p. 183)
Walls	**Outside** Fine white crystal growth seen on dry days **Inside** Decorations stained and peeling Mould	Failure or absence of damp-proof course Earth or plants against damp-proof course Mortar in cavity walls acting as bridge for damp	Renew damp-proof course (see p. 27). If dampness is extensive, seek expert advice Allow walls to dry before redecorating
Windows and doors	Discolouring on jambs and sills Distorted frames Flaking and blistered paintwork	No mastic sealer around door or window frame Defective putty around glass	Renew flashings (consult a builder). Clean the drip channel (see p. 198). Repoint mastic. Fit new beads or putty (see p. 204)

Dampness Outer walls

Faults and remedies for dampness

Water can penetrate directly through hairline cracks in the brickwork caused by the natural movement of a house. Repair defective rendering (see p. 197) or brickwork (see p. 18).

Note, however, that wide, extensive cracking in the brickwork, with distortion of the window and door frames, usually means that the settlement of the ground under the building has caused a structural failure. Have any such movement investigated by a surveyor immediately it is discovered.

Older buildings may have settled finally. When further movement is unlikely, repairs can be made to remedy some of the distortion.

Gaps around window and door openings can be filled with a mastic sealer (see p. 198).

If water is saturating the walls below sills, check that the groove under the sill is free of dirt; chisel out a new water channel if necessary.

Leaking from gutters and pipes is a common defect. Clean the gutters and fit new pipes and gutters if necessary (see pp. 106–109).

Dampness can penetrate a building if there are defects in the weather-proofing between roofs and walls, or where pipes and chimney stacks penetrate a roof or gutter. Inspect the junctions regularly and repair where necessary (see p. 164).

Most modern houses are constructed with cavity walls—two skins of brick or blocks with a cavity between to prevent the penetration of rain.

Between the skins are metal wall ties, shaped to prevent the passage of water from the outer to the inner skin. But if mortar is dropped on a tie during building, it becomes a bridge for damp to pass into the house. Engage a builder to clear the mortar.

To ensure that moisture cannot rise from the earth through the walls, damp-proof courses are inserted in all outside walls at a minimum of 6 in. (150 mm) above ground level. Never allow a damp-proof course to be covered with earth, plants or rendering.

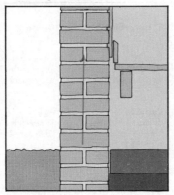

Fault The damp-proof course has deteriorated, or none was provided when the house was built, so moisture can rise up the walls from the soil below
Remedy Have a damp-proof course inserted by a firm specialising in such work. They will either insert a plastic membrane or inject a silicone solution

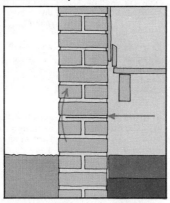

Fault The outside wall is badly pointed so that mortar covers the outer edge of the damp-proof course. Moisture gets above the course through the mortar
Remedy Carefully rake out the pointing to expose the outer edge of the damp-proof course. Do not damage the exposed edge of the damp-proof course

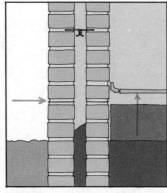

Fault No damp-proof membrane was included when the solid floor was built, so moisture is able to rise into the floor and get above the damp-proof course in the internal walls
Remedy Fit a membrane to cover the screed and unite with the wall damp-proof course. This is specialist work

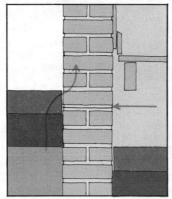

Fault An outside path or a concrete floor to an extension has been built above the damp-proof course. This can happen when a garage, for instance, has been added on the outside wall
Remedy Get a specialist to fit a water-proof link between the damp-proof course in the wall and floor membrane

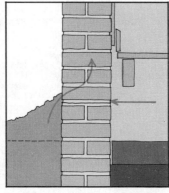

Fault Earth around the outer walls has been banked above the line of the damp-proof course, forming a bridge for dampness. In suspended floor construction (see p. 78) this may cause dry rot (see p. 185)
Remedy Remove earth to at least 6 in. (150 mm) below damp-proof course

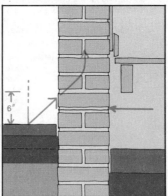

Fault The damp-proof course is too low in an outer wall, so that rainwater splashing on a path can soak the wall above it. Building regulations state that a damp-proof course must be 6 in. (150 mm) above ground level
Remedy Dig out path to at least 6 in. below damp-proof course

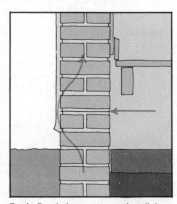

Fault Rendering on external wall (see p. 197) covers the damp-proof course, forming a path for damp to rise
Remedy If the whole wall is rendered, hack off to a line just above the damp-proof course. If only the base is rendered, cut back to a line just below damp-proof course. Slope the top edge

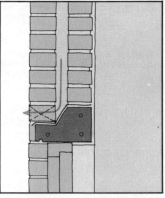

Fault The vertical joints between bricks spanning a window opening are filled with mortar, so condensation in a cavity wall cannot drain away. Moisture therefore soaks into the inner wall
Remedy Rake out the mortar between the vertical joints of two or three bricks over the window opening

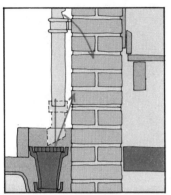

Fault A crack in the downpipe—sometimes found behind fixing brackets—allows rainwater to saturate the wall behind it. If there is no shoe on the pipe, the wall may be splashed above the damp-proof course.
Remedy Renew the pipe or the shoe, if there is one (see p. 108).

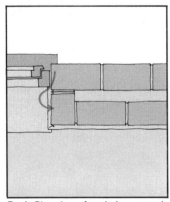

Fault Plan view of a window wrongly positioned in its opening, so allowing moisture in the outer skin of brickwork to pass over the damp-proof course—via the plaster—and saturate the inner skin of the cavity wall.
Remedy Remove the window and reposition. This is specialist work.

Tracing and stopping rising damp

When a definite tide-mark of staining appears on the inside walls of a house just above ground-floor level, moisture is penetrating the house from the soil beneath it. Such rising damp is an indication either that there is no damp-proof course (which is very common in houses built before 1875), or that the damp-proof course has deteriorated and failed.

Isolated patches of dampness—they are roughly fan-shaped or semi-circular—usually appear on a wall with a damp-proof course that has failed along its length.

First find the damp-proof course (see p. 24) and check that no earth or any growth from a surrounding garden has been banked against the walls above it. If it has been covered, dig away the soil to at least 6 in. (150 mm) below it. Brush off any loose earth or dirt from the brickwork at the course and check regularly that the soil level is not rising.

If the soil level is not above the damp-proof course, engage a specialist to discover and repair the fault.

Several methods—all of which require special equipment—can be used to remedy the fault: silicone injection, siphonage, electro-osmosis or the insertion of a new damp-proof course.

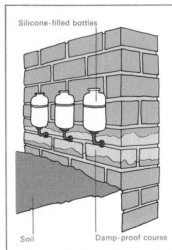

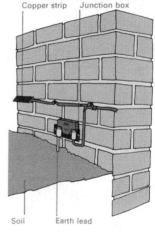

Silicone injection Holes are drilled in the walls around the outside of the house about 6 in. (150 mm) above ground level and a silicone solution is injected. The solution, which is a water repellent, spreads throughout the brickwork to provide an effective barrier against rising damp.

Specialist firms can assess the strength of the solution required and where it is needed. Most firms give a 20 or 30-year guarantee.

Siphonage Hollow tubes of porous clay about 2 in. (50 mm) in diameter and half the thickness of the wall in length, are set in a porous mortar at the level of the original damp-proof course. They are sloped downwards from inside the building, and a grille on the outside wall keeps out rainwater.

This method is sometimes used with the silicone injection. A 20-year guarantee is usually given by the firm doing the work.

Electro-osmosis Moisture rises through any wall in contact with the ground, because there is a difference in the electrical charge between the wall and the ground. This difference can be eliminated.

A $\frac{1}{2}$ in. (13 mm) copper band is attached around the house at damp-proof course level every 12 in. (305 mm). Metal rods are fitted in the ground and connected to the band to earth the electricity. A 30-year guarantee is usually given.

A new damp-proof course This requires the use of specially designed saws to cut through the mortar in solid or cavity walls in short lengths about 6 in. (150 mm) above ground level. A new damp-proof course of lead, copper, bitumen-impregnated hessian or asbestos, or polythene sheet can then be inserted.

The brickwork must be pointed above and below the course.

Specialist firms usually give a 20 or 30-year guarantee.

Dampness Inner walls

Tracing the possible sources of dampness

Dampness often does not become obvious until whatever is causing it has deteriorated into a serious condition.

If damage cannot be seen from the outside, inspect inside attics and basements and underneath staircases.

Always find and treat the source of dampness before trying to damp-proof inner walls.

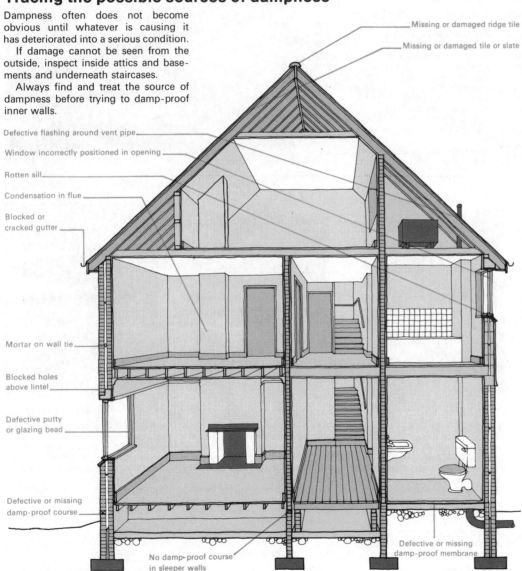

Missing or damaged ridge tile

Missing or damaged tile or slate

Defective flashing around vent pipe

Window incorrectly positioned in opening

Rotten sill

Condensation in flue

Blocked or cracked gutter

Mortar on wall tie

Blocked holes above lintel

Defective putty or glazing bead

Defective or missing damp-proof course

No damp-proof course in sleeper walls

Defective or missing damp-proof membrane

Damp-proofing a wall surface

Cover damp inner walls with an aluminium foil lining to ensure that they dry outwards, so preventing damage to wallpaper or paint.

Remove flaking paint and old wallpaper. Wash the walls with a solution of 1 part ammonia, 8 parts water and a little disinfectant. Allow to dry. Paint newly plastered or cemented walls before lining.

Materials: lining; adhesive; filler; disinfectant; ammonia; medium-grade glass-paper or pumice block; paint if required.
Tools: wallpapering brush; carpet brush; scissors; rule; plumbline.

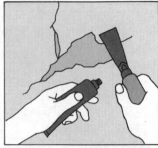

1 Clean and wash the walls. Fill any cracks or holes. Rub down surplus filler when it has set

2 Measure lining width. Deduct 1 in. (25 mm) and mark distance from corner, using a plumbline

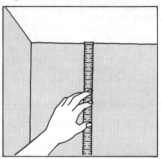

3 Measure the height of the wall from the ceiling to the top of the skirting boards

4 Add 4 in. (100 mm) to that measurement to allow for trimming, and cut lengths of lining

5 Lay lining on table and paste it (see p. 43). Use the adhesive recommended (continued)

6 Fold over both ends of the pasted lining to the centre, to make it easier to handle (see p. 44)

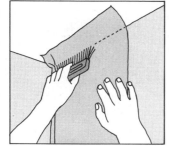

7 Hang the lining flush with the line marked on the wall. Brush into ceiling angle and corner

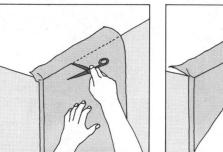

8 Score along the overlap at the ceiling angle and at the top of the skirting board

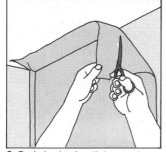

9 Peel back the lining and cut carefully along the scored lines at top and bottom of the wall

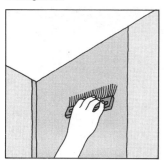

10 Brush the lining back into place. Wipe off any excess paste with a damp sponge

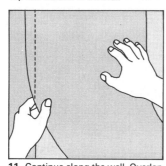

11 Continue along the wall. Overlap each length at least $\frac{1}{4}$ in. (6 mm) over the previous one

Surfacing a damp basement wall

If the damp-proof course in an outer wall becomes ineffective (see p. 26), the inner walls of a cellar or basement will become damp. Cover them with bitumen-impregnated lath, available from builders' merchants.

The lath has insulating cavities on the side fitted against the wall. It is corrugated on its outer surface to provide a key for plasterwork. If the wall is very damp, knock in wall plugs to which the lath can be secured.

Always fit new skirting boards (see p. 84) if the old ones have been affected by damp. In cellars, which do not have skirtings or damp-proof membranes in the floor, leave a 1 in. (25 mm) gap between the plaster and the floor to prevent dampness rising.

Plaster can be applied to the laths immediately but it will take some months to dry before it can be decorated. It may be advisable to fit a dry lining (see p. 135). Use the adhesive provided by the lath manufacturers.

Materials: bitumen-impregnated lath; galvanised clout nails; wooden or proprietary wall plugs if required; plaster (see p. 119); dry-lining material (see p. 135); new skirting boards (see p. 84).
Tools: hammer; trowel; bolster chisel; sharp knife; old saw.

1 Remove skirting (see p. 84). Hack off all the plaster from the wall with a hammer and bolster chisel

2 Fix a 2×1 in. (50×25 mm) soft-wood batten along the wall where the skirting has been removed

3 Butt sheets of lath against the batten along the bottom. Nail every 6 in. (150 mm) top and bottom

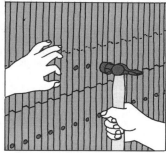

4 Work up the wall to the ceiling. Overlap each strip of lath 3 in. (75 mm) over the one below it

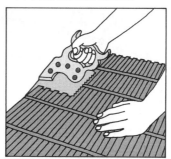

5 Measure the final width needed to reach the ceiling. Allow for overlap and cut lath with an old saw

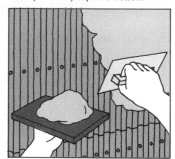

6 Apply the plaster and finishing coats (see p. 120). Remove batten when the plaster sets. Fit skirting (see p. 84)

7 If the wall is to be decorated immediately, do not plaster. Fit dry lining (see p. 135) and skirting

Dampness Condensation

Condensation occurs when water vapour in the air comes into contact with cold, non-porous surfaces. The vapour turns to water droplets which run down walls and collect on sills, skirting boards, door tops and windows. They gradually soak into plaster, and salt deposits appear on the wall surface. Wallpaper peels, and growths of mould develop.

Condensation is most common in kitchens or bathrooms because steam adds to the humidity of the air. But it is likely to develop in any house occupied after a period without heating.

Prevention Insulation and improved heating and ventilation are the best ways to stop condensation.

An extractor fan, for example, directly improves the ventilation in a room. Loft insulation (see p. 114) helps to retain warmth throughout a house. Cavity walls should have insulation, but this is specialist work: consult an insulation company.

Solid walls can be covered with polystyrene sheeting (see p. 31) or aluminium foil (see p. 28) before being hung with paper.

If a house has rising damp as well as condensation, a dry lining system (see p. 135) may remedy both faults.

When the condensation is caused by the discharge of gases from a boiler, re-line the flue (see p. 23).

Installing an extractor fan

An extractor fan can be fitted into a window pane or a wall. It is easier, however, to install one in place of an existing high-level air brick.

Do not try to connect the fan directly to the electricity supply. Wire to a fused connection unit and cut a channel to the fan. Fit a plastic conduit round the cable, bury in the channel and fill with plaster. Switch off to inspect or clean fan (see p. 534).

Materials: fan; three-core cable; wall plugs; plastic conduit.
Tools: drill with masonry bit; club hammer; bolster chisel; screwdrivers.

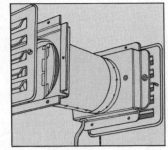

1 Remove the screws connecting the outer and inner grilles of the fan. Separate the fan sections

2 Remove air brick (see p. 20). Use a hammer and bolster chisel to cut a channel where the cable will run

3 Fit conduit over cable and feed conduit into channel. Cut cable and fill channel (see p. 132)

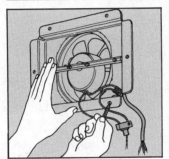

4 Position inner section of fan in the hole in the wall. Mark the wall through each screwhole with a pencil

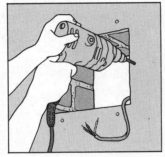

5 Remove fan section and drill holes for fixing screws provided with fan. Fit wall plugs in holes (see p. 683)

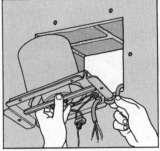

6 Thread end of cable through the rubber sleeve on the fan. Position the fan against the holes in the wall

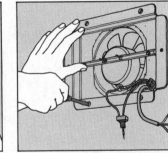

7 Fix screws securely through the flanges at top and bottom of the fan. Bare cable wire ends (see p. 526)

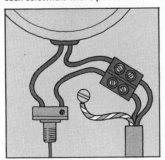

8 Fit the cable wires to the fan block terminal. Follow the manufacturer's instructions carefully

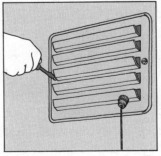

9 Thread switch cord through grille and screw grille to side flanges. Fit thumbscrew on cord

10 Outside the house, position outer sleeve. Drill holes at top and bottom, and plug and screw to wall

11 Place the outer grille over the flange and screw it home. Connect cable to terminals and switch on

Covering a wall with polystyrene

Condensation on cold walls (see p. 28) can be reduced by fitting rolls of expanded polystyrene, which is $\frac{1}{16}$ in. (2 mm) thick and can be hung like wallpaper. Cover it with vinyl paper, which is strong and washable and is sufficiently rigid to resist light pressures which could indent the polystyrene.

Ask a dealer's advice on adhesives: some pastes and resins are not suitable for polystyrene. It may be necessary to use one adhesive to fix the polystyrene and a different one to hang the wallpaper covering.

To ensure that there are no slight gaps on the wall, overlap the polystyrene strips and cut through the double thicknesses to obtain a perfect butt joint.

If any small pieces break off as the polystyrene is fitted, glue them back into place.

Never fit polystyrene on top of old wallpaper: strip the wall to bare plaster. If the wall is painted, wash off grease and dirt (see p. 39) and remove loose flakes with a pumice-stone block or medium-grade glass-paper.

Materials: expanded polystyrene; adhesive; medium glass-paper or pumice-stone block.

Tools: rule; plumb line; sharp knife; paint roller; screwdriver; straight-edge.

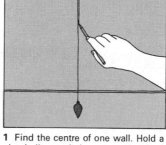

1 Find the centre of one wall. Hold a plumb line and draw a vertical line. Measure height of wall

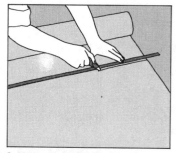

2 Mark off a length of polystyrene, about 3 in. (75 mm) longer than height of wall. Cut with a sharp knife

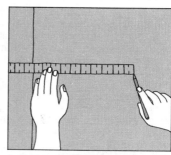

3 Mark the width of the roll from the centre of the wall. Apply adhesive as instructed by the manufacturers

4 Hang the first length of polystyrene. Smooth it down the wall with one hand. Stick on any torn pieces

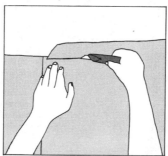

5 Use a paint roller to flatten each length of polystyrene as it is fitted. Press out all air bubbles

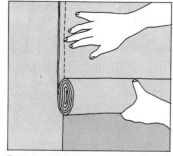

6 Trim the polystyrene at the ceiling and skirting board with the sharp knife. Do not leave ragged edges

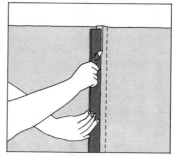

7 Mark off the area for the next length and apply adhesive. Overlap each length by $\frac{1}{2}$ in. (13 mm)

8 Cut cleanly down through both thicknesses with the sharp knife held against a straight-edge

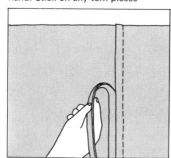

9 Gently peel off the top strip of polystyrene. Take care not to damage the cut edge

10 Lift the cut edge and peel off the strip underneath. Brush adhesive under raised edge and press it down

11 Switch off power supply. Slacken the screws on any electric fittings and apply a little adhesive behind them

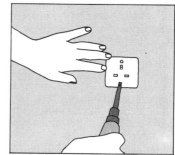

12 Cover the fitting and slit the polystyrene over it. Tuck polystyrene behind, cutting off surplus

13 Push the electric fitting back on to the polystyrene and retighten its securing screws

Decorating Painting

Equipment needed for painting

A good-quality stepladder, with a platform at the top to support paint and tools, is essential. If it is used with a scaffold board and a small two-step platform, called a hop-up, it gives comfortable access for most inside jobs.

Brushes

Always buy the best brushes you can afford: cheap brushes shed their hairs and give a poor finish. For general painting work, the best are those made with hog bristle (often referred to as 'pure bristle'). A set of 4 or 6 in., 2 in., 1 in. and ½ in. (100 or 150, 50, 25 and 13 mm) brushes will suffice for most jobs.

If you are likely to use a variety of colours, it is worth buying two sets of brushes and keeping one for use only with white paint.

A crevice or radiator brush, with a metal handle that can be bent to an angle, is useful for painting behind radiators and pipework and for reaching awkward corners.

Rollers and pads

Rollers cover large areas more quickly than brushes and are especially useful for ceilings, where brushwork can be trying and difficult. But a brush will still be necessary for corners.

Coverings of rollers include foamed plastic and natural and synthetic fibres. Mohair and synthetic short-pile coverings are better for undercoats and gloss finishes: lambswool and synthetic medium/long-pile coverings are better for emulsion and masonry paints, especially on rough surfaces. Interchangeable coverings are usually available with good-quality rollers.

To hold the paint, you will need a roller tray. For big jobs, such as exterior walls, there are special roller buckets, which can often be hired.

Paint pads may be found useful for some jobs, such as window frames. They demand less skill in application than brushes; but the method is slow, and a brush may still be required to paint in the corners. Buy good-quality paint pads: cheap ones shed hairs and disintegrate quickly.

A special tray to hold the paint is supplied with some sets of pads, but a roller tray or shallow baking tin can be used just as well.

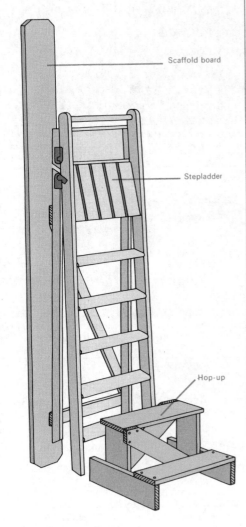

Scaffold board

Stepladder

Hop-up

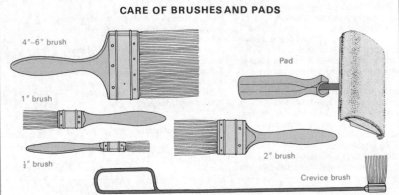

CARE OF BRUSHES AND PADS

4"–6" brush

1" brush

½" brush

2" brush

Pad

Crevice brush

A brush becomes useless if paint dries in the bristles.

For a short break, wrap the brush in a polythene bag. At the end of the day, wash off emulsion paint with warm water and soap or detergent. Rinse and shake dry. With oil-based paint, scrape the surplus off the brush with the back of a knife, wipe the bristles with newspaper, and suspend the brush from a wire through a hole in the handle in a jar of paint-brush cleaner. Before resuming work next day, rinse the brush in hot water and shake it dry.

Most paint tins give instructions about the cleaning of brushes for storage. Clean off emulsion paint, and some oil-based paints, with hot water and soap: clean off other paints with white spirit, then rinse with hot water and soap or detergent.

Dry the brush, then wrap it in polythene or greaseproof paper. Put moth repellent in the wrapping and store flat.

Paint pads In general, pads are cleaned and stored in the same way as rollers (see below). Follow instructions given by the manufacturer of the pad.

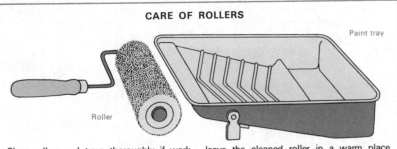

CARE OF ROLLERS

Roller

Paint tray

Clean rollers and trays thoroughly if work is to be stopped for more than 20 minutes. Use a solvent for oil paint and warm soapy water for emulsion. Rinse them several times in water. When the work is finished, leave the cleaned roller in a warm place to dry, wrap it in polythene, and store it in a dry place. With a natural covering, such as lambswool, put some moth repellent in the wrapping before storing.

STRIPPING TOOLS

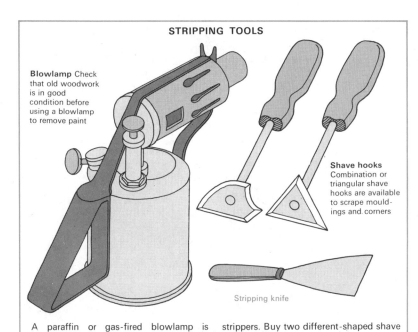

Blowlamp Check that old woodwork is in good condition before using a blowlamp to remove paint

Shave hooks Combination or triangular shave hooks are available to scrape mould-ings and corners

Stripping knife

A paraffin or gas-fired blowlamp is essential for stripping old paint which is too thick to remove with chemical strippers. Buy two different-shaped shave hooks and a flexible stripping knife to scrape off the burnt paint

ADDITIONAL TOOLS

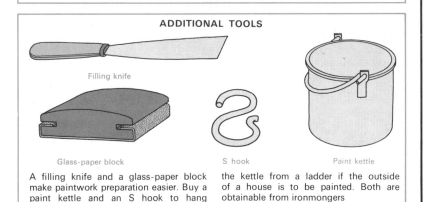

Filling knife

Glass-paper block

S hook

Paint kettle

A filling knife and a glass-paper block make paintwork preparation easier. Buy a paint kettle and an S hook to hang the kettle from a ladder if the outside of a house is to be painted. Both are obtainable from ironmongers

Choosing paint for interior and exterior work

INSIDE WORK

Surface	Paint	Finish	Special qualities
Ceilings and walls	emulsion paint	matt, mid-sheen or silk	Washable, quick-drying, no smell. Do not use in high-condensation situations
	alkyd or oil-based paint*	high gloss, eggshell or matt	Tough, hard-wearing and washable. Overnight drying between coats. Surfaces must be dry. Allow 6 months drying out for new plaster etc.
	texture paint	matt, textured	Decorative, hides surface defects. Not easily cleaned. Difficult to remove
Woodwork	alkyd or oil-based paint*	high gloss, eggshell or matt	See 'Ceilings and walls' (above)
	wood stain	matt or mid-sheen, clear or coloured	Shows grain of wood. May be varnished
	varnish	high gloss, eggshell or matt	Shows grain of wood. Easier to clean than woodstain alone
Metalwork	alkyd or oil-based paint*	high gloss, eggshell or matt	See 'Ceilings and walls' (above)

*Alkyd paints may be liquid or thixotropic (non-drip)
Some may be cleaned from brushes with hot water and detergent or soap powder

OUTSIDE WORK

Surface	Paint	Finish	Special qualities
Walls	cement paint	matt, rough	Cheap, can be applied to damp surfaces. Tends to powder in a year or two
	emulsion-based masonry paint	matt or mid-sheen. Some contain sand or fibres	Easy to apply. Quick drying. Good durability
	alkyd or oil-based gloss finish	high gloss	Very good durability. Walls must be dry. Overnight drying between coats
Woodwork	alkyd or oil-based gloss finishes	high gloss	Very good durability. Easy to clean. Overnight drying between coats. Woodwork must be dry
	exterior wood stain, preservative type	matt or mid-sheen, clear or coloured	Shows grain. Good durability if regularly maintained. Sometimes cannot be overpainted
	varnish	high gloss	Shows grain. Requires frequent recoating
	creosote	matt	Dark colour. Not easily overpainted
Metalwork	alkyd or oil-based paint	high gloss	See 'Woodwork' (above)
	bituminous or tar paint	gloss	Dark colours only. Loses gloss fairly quickly. May be difficult to overpaint
Asbestos cement cladding and rainwater goods	as for 'Walls' (above)	as for 'Walls' (above)	As for 'Walls' (above). Interior of rainwater gutters must be coated with tar paint to prevent water penetration
Asbestos cement roof sheets	bituminous or tar paint	gloss	As for 'Metalwork' (above)

Decorating Painting

The best time to paint outside is in late summer when the woodwork is at its driest. Shrinkage at wooden door and window joints during warm weather makes preparation easier.

First make any necessary repairs to the roof covering (see p. 160); gutters and pipes (see pp. 100–12); barge, fascia and soffit boards (see pp. 160–63); doors (see pp. 52–60); windows (see pp. 198–207); brick-pointing (see p. 18) and wall finishes (see p. 197).

Masking

If a wall surface beneath an area being painted is not to be decorated—for example, vertical tiling, weatherproof boarding or brickwork—cover it with canvas or polythene: oil-paint splashes are difficult to remove.

Working order

Start the preparation and painting work from the top right-hand corner of a house —if right handed—and work downwards. If there is a window which projects through a sloping roof, work on it first. Then prepare all gutters, eaves, fascia, barge and soffit boards. Continue with downpipes and wall surfaces (see p. 35), and finish with the doors and windows (see p. 36).

Safety

When erecting a tubular-frame platform or scaffolding system (see p. 686), always leave enough space between it and the wall surfaces to manipulate a brush. Make sure that ladders are properly secured (see p. 684) and avoid over-reaching from them during working. Use a crawling board (see p. 685) to paint a window which is high on a steep roof.

Never rest cans of paint on gutters, parapet walls or valley gutters; always transfer paint to a paint kettle (see p. 33) and hang the kettle with a hook from a ladder rung or gutter.

Preparing and painting woodwork and pipework

Start work from the stop end of the guttering (see p. 100). Secure a ladder to give a clear view inside the gutters.

Clean cast-iron gutters and pipes with a wire brush; wipe plastic pipes with a damp cloth and detergent. Rinse both types thoroughly. If existing pipework is coated with bituminous paint—which looks like tar—and is to be covered with ordinary paint, use aluminium primer to prevent the risk of staining.

If paint splashes on to plastic guttering, wipe it off immediately.

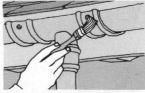

GUTTERS AND DOWNPIPES

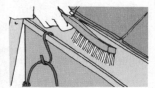

1 Remove loose dirt from gutter with a stiff-bristled brush. Clear all deposits from sides

2 Wire-brush cast-iron guttering and downpipes to remove all flaking and rusting paint

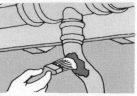

3 Treat rusted areas with rust remover. Leave to penetrate and remove. Rinse and dry

4 Touch in bare metal with metal-priming paint. Never leave metal exposed overnight

5 Paint inside guttering with bituminous paint. If it rains, allow to dry and start again

6 Apply one or two undercoats and a top coat. Use cardboard strip to avoid smudging walls

EXTERIOR WOODWORK

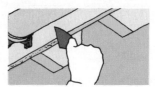
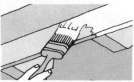

1 Wash all woodwork which is to be painted with warm water and detergent. Rinse and dry

2 Scrape and rub down flaking paint. Apply a coat of primer immediately to all bare wood

3 Apply undercoat to all woodwork. Smooth with medium-grade glass-paper before applying the top coat

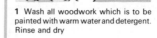

Preparing and painting outside walls

Make sure that the pointing of a brick wall is sound. If it has started to crumble, repoint before painting (see p. 18).

If a wall is clad with cedarwood boarding, finish the rest of the decoration before cleaning and resealing the wood (see p. 98). When roughcast or pebble dash is damaged, repair before painting (see p. 197).

Do not paint brickwork which has efflorescence on it (see p. 18) or a wall which is affected by rising damp (see p. 27).

PREPARING AND PAINTING TILED SILLS

1 Brush off dirt and mortar with stiff brush. Remove grit. Fill joints if necessary

2 To ensure complete resistance to water, always paint underneath the sill as well

REPAIRING AND PAINTING BRICKWORK

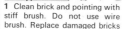

1 Clean brick and pointing with stiff brush. Do not use wire brush. Replace damaged bricks

2 Brush on paint. If brick is porous, thin paint and apply two coats. Work from top

PREPARING AND PAINTING CONCRETE

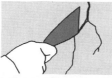

1 Remove flaking paint with wire brush. Push scraper inside cracks. Rake out loose particles

2 Fill all cracks (see p. 197) with an exterior-grade filler. Press in flush with the wall

3 Touch in repaired area with emulsion, water-based or masonry paint. Cover all filler

4 Begin painting at top right-hand corner of house (if right handed). Work downwards

Retexturing a wall

The rendering on a wall weather-proofs as well as decorates the surface. It is important, therefore, to fill all cracks and holes before painting (see p. 197). Leave for 24 hours before decorating.

Retexture with a stippling brush before the paint sets, to lift and coarsen the surface. If there is a large area, to be retextured, it is a job for two people—one to paint, the other to stipple.

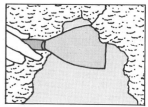

1 Scrape flaking areas and rub around the gaps with wire brush to remove paint

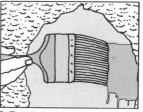

2 Touch in exposed area with alkali-resistant primer to give an even, non-porous surface

3 Brush on stucco or textured paint. If working alone, do a small area at a time

TEXTURING TECHNIQUES

Brush On textured surfaces, press and twist the paintbrush well into the crevices

Rubber stippler Pat the surface of the paint with the teeth of stippler before it sets

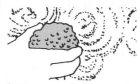

Sponge Lightly press and twist an almost dry sponge on the drying paint

Wooden stippler Rub in circular movements to score the drying paint

Decorating Painting

Preparing doors and windows

If the paintwork on a door or window has badly deteriorated it must be stripped to give a good base for new paint.

A blowlamp is quicker and more efficient than chemical strippers. Hold the nozzle of the blowlamp about 3 in. (75 mm) away from the door or window-sill and keep it moving, to avoid burning the woodwork as well as the paint.

Do not use a blowlamp, however, to strip paint from woodwork around the edges of glass. Paint on a chemical stripper instead.

If the whole of a door or window does not need to be stripped, ensure that any dents or blisters, or knots which are exuding resin, are made good before repainting.

Fill any holes with putty or a proprietary wood filler. Plaster filler mixed with paint—called Swedish putty—may also be used.

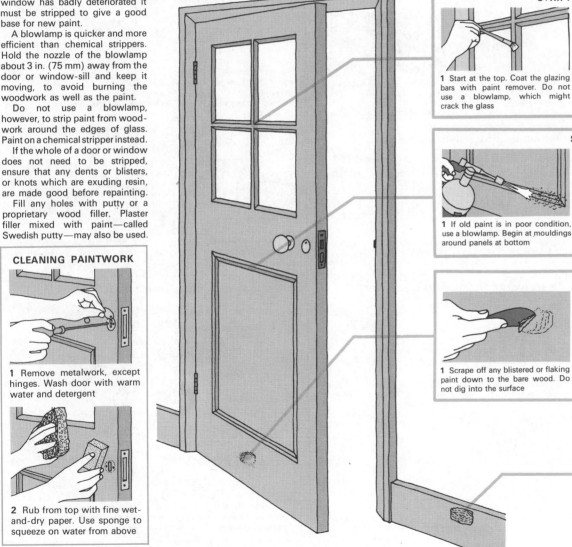

CLEANING PAINTWORK

1 Remove metalwork, except hinges. Wash door with warm water and detergent

2 Rub from top with fine wet-and-dry paper. Use sponge to squeeze on water from above

STRIPPING WITH CHEMICAL AROUND GLASS

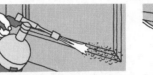

1 Start at the top. Coat the glazing bars with paint remover. Do not use a blowlamp, which might crack the glass

2 Wait a few minutes until the paint starts to bubble and blister. Scrape it off in strips with a shave hook, taking care not to damage the wood

3 Wash off all traces of paint remover with warm water. If necessary, dig out defective putty and renew (see p. 204)

STRIPPING WITH A BLOWLAMP

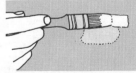

1 If old paint is in poor condition, use a blowlamp. Begin at mouldings around panels at bottom

2 Burn the paint along a quarter of a moulding length and scrape off blisters with a shave hook

3 Work from the bottom up until paint is removed. Strip paint off all mouldings first

FILLING DENTS AND BLISTERS

1 Scrape off any blistered or flaking paint down to the bare wood. Do not dig into the surface

2 Smooth with medium-grade glass-paper and fill. Rub with glass-paper when set

3 Apply undercoat. Glass-paper when dry. Feather top coat outwards to conceal edges of repair

SEALING KNOTS IN WOOD

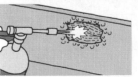

1 Burn off discoloured paint and play blowlamp gently over knot to draw resin out of the wood

2 Scrape off resin. Glass-paper surface and apply two coats of knot-sealer to cover the area

Metal window frames

Rust on a metal window frame can distort the frame and crack the glass. Inspect all metal frames regularly. If rust develops, apply a liquid rust remover until clean bare metal is exposed.

Examine old paintwork carefully before redecorating. If it is in good condition, do not strip it, but make sure that it is clean and free of grease. Wipe thoroughly with a clean cloth dipped in turpentine substitute. Remove all traces of oil at the window hinges.

Wash frames with warm water and a liquid detergent. Rinse thoroughly with clean water and rub down any irregularities in the surface with fine wet-and-dry paper.

Examine and make good any defective putty or metal clips (see p. 205). If the windows are stuck or open stiffly, because of old paint, work round the edges with a broad scraper and screwdriver until the sash is freed.

PREPARATION BEFORE PAINTING

1 Scrub rusted areas with a wire brush until rust particles and flaked paint are removed

2 Remove all cracked, crumbling and broken putty around frames with a chisel and scraping knife

3 Brush on liquid rust remover. Leave to penetrate, then wipe off and rinse with clean water

4 Paint bared areas with metal primer. Pay special attention to movable parts

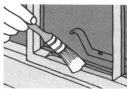

5 Prime areas where putty is missing. Take primer about $\frac{1}{4}$ in. (6 mm) on to window pane

6 Force putty into window angle with thumb and forefinger. Smooth down with a filler knife

PREPARING AND PAINTING WROUGHT IRON

Decorative ironwork is usually made of wrought iron, which rusts rapidly if it has been badly painted.

If rusting is extensive, strip off all old paintwork down to the bare metal. Use a blowlamp or a chemical stripper. Clean small areas of rust with a wire brush and wipe with white spirit. As soon as the ironwork is clean and dry, apply one coat of red lead, metallic lead, calcium plumbate or zinc chromate. When the first coat has dried, apply a second.

Paint on one undercoat of exterior gloss and apply a finishing coat when dry.

Sliding sash windows

Paint the top and bottom edges of the outer sash—the one at the top of the frame when the window is closed—with the same type and colour of paint as the outside of the window. Use the same paint and colour as on the inside of the window for the top and bottom edges of the inner sash.

The runners need be painted only at the sections which can be seen when the window is open. Paint them the same colour as the inside of the window up to the inside face of the outer beading. Do not paint the sash cords, or they will start to perish.

Hold zinc or tin strip against the glazing bars to avoid smearing the glass. Use a 1 in. (25 mm) cutting-in brush for all glazing bars and mouldings

Brush a 1 in. strip of glue size on colourfast wallpaper around the frame. If paint is brushed on the paper, the size allows it to be removed

ORDER OF PAINTING

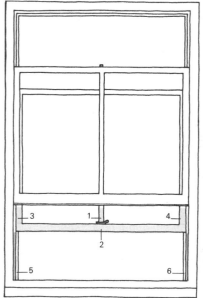

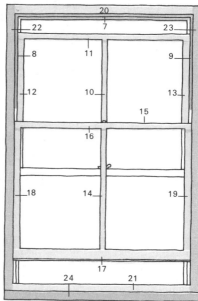

Raise bottom sash to centre of frame. Pull top sash below bottom one and paint: **1** bottom of top sash centre rail; **2** top sash bottom rail; **3, 4** bottom of top sash side rails; **5, 6** bottom sash runners.

Almost close both sashes and paint: **7–9** top and sides of bottom sash runners; **10–13** complete top sash framework; **14** bottom sash centre rail; **15** edge of bottom sash top rail; **16** top rail; **17** bottom rail; **18, 19** side rails; **20** top of window frame; **21** bottom of frame; **22, 23** sides of frame; **24** window-sill.

Decorating Painting

Casement windows

On many casement windows only one half opens. Paint an opening window first, then the fixed one and finally the frame. Start with the glazing bars and horizontal rails. On vertical surfaces, work from the top downwards. The edge of a casement window opening inwards should be painted in the same colour as the inside of the window; paint the hinge edges the same colour as the outside of the window. Paint inside and outside in the same order.

If paint is brushed on hinges, wipe off immediately.

ORDER OF PAINTING

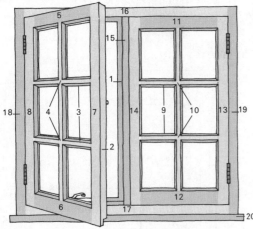

Opening window: 1 inside frame; **2** edge of stiles and rails; **3** all glazing putty; **4** glazing bars; **5, 6** top and bottom rail; **7, 8** stiles. **Fixed window: 9** all glazing putty; **10** glazing bars; **11, 12** rails; **13, 14** stiles; **15** centre frame bar; **16, 17** top and bottom bars; **18, 19** side bars; **20** window-sill.

Glass Hold a strip of tin or zinc against the glazing bars, to avoid painting the glass

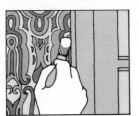

Wallpaper Apply glue size to edge of colourfast wallpaper to protect it against paint smears

Doors

Doors should be painted after windows, rails and fireplaces, but before skirting boards.

If the existing paintwork on a door is in good condition, an undercoat is unnecessary provided that the new paint is as dark as the old. If a lighter colour is to be used, an undercoat is necessary to ensure the old colour cannot show through. Use two undercoats if necessary to obscure any existing colour, and rub down each coat carefully with a medium-grade glass-paper before applying the next.

The top edge of an inside door needs to be painted only if it opens outwards and is overlooked by stairs.

To ensure a good finish, paint a panelled door in sections— about 15 in. (380 mm) square at a time; if it has glass, paint it in the same sequence as casement windows are painted.

PAINTING LARGE FLAT AREAS

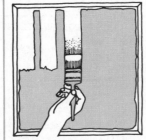

1 Using a 3 in. (75 mm) brush, make two or three separate down-strokes on one of the top quarters of the panel

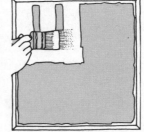

2 Without reloading the brush, fill in from the base of the down-strokes by working from side to side

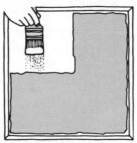

3 Still without reloading the brush, work up and down over the area again. Finish with light upward strokes

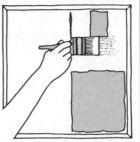

4 Paint beneath in same way, then begin again in other upper quarter. Avoid a double thickness at adjoining edges

ORDER OF PAINTING

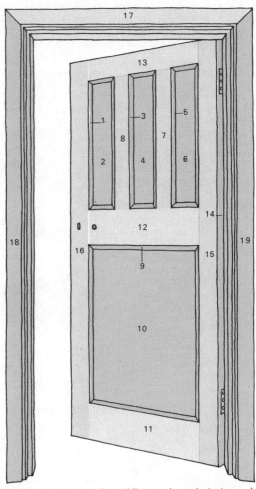

1–6 glazing bars or panel mouldings and panels (paint each panel immediately after its mouldings); **7, 8** vertical bars; **9, 10** lower mouldings and panel; **11** bottom bar; **12** centre bar; **13** top bar; **14** edge of hinge stile; **15, 16** stiles; **17** frame top; **18, 19** frame sides.

Preparing and painting staircases

If an entire staircase is to be decorated, remove the carpet and any fixings.

Staircases may be stained, varnished or painted. If the existing finish is in good condition, rub it down with fine glass-paper and revarnish or paint.

When there are some noticeable dents or knocks in the finish, wash the areas with warm soapy water and rub down with fine glass-paper. Fill any holes with putty or filler, and rub down with fine glass-paper. If the wood is to be revarnished, first touch-in areas with matching stain; but if the wood is to be repainted, first apply undercoat.

If the whole finish is in poor condition, strip with a blowlamp or a chemical paint remover (see p. 36). Begin with the balusters, strings, risers and treads. Brush away all dust and apply undercoat or stain.

Handrails, which should be finished last, are usually hardwood. If they are French polished, strip the polish (see p. 227), fill any dents and rub down. Re-stain and finish with French polish substitute, obtainable from hardware stores.

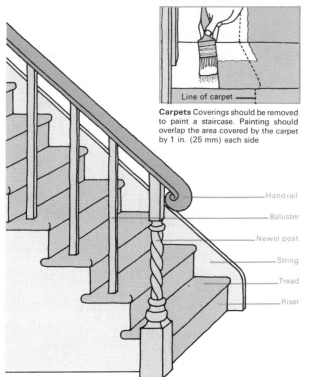

Line of carpet

Carpets Coverings should be removed to paint a staircase. Painting should overlap the area covered by the carpet by 1 in. (25 mm) each side

Hand rail
Baluster
Newel post
String
Tread
Riser

Preparing walls and ceilings

To prepare a room for painting spread plastic sheeting or brown paper over the floor. Do not use newspaper, for paint can soak through it.

Start with the ceiling, follow with the woodwork (except the skirting-boards), then the walls, and finally paint the skirting-boards. Use a soft-haired brush to remove all dust from the ceiling, cornice and walls. Restore any moulded plaster cornices (see p. 132).

Sponge the ceiling and walls with warm water and sugar soap, and rinse them with fresh water to remove all traces of soap. Scrape off any loose paint and fill all cracks and holes in the plaster (see p. 121).

If the existing walls have been painted with gloss paint, rub them down with glass-paper to score the surface and provide a key for the new paint. Wipe all surfaces with a damp, clean sponge, immediately before starting decorating.

Construct a platform to work from—using a single ladder is tiring, and frequent repositioning is necessary.

Remove lampshades to get the maximum benefit from artificial lighting when painting the ceiling or cornice.

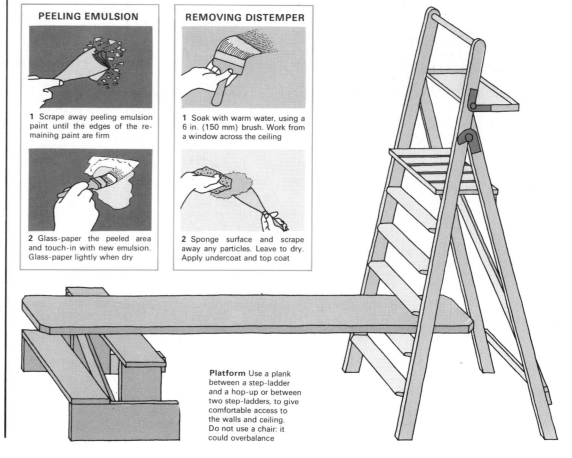

PEELING EMULSION

1 Scrape away peeling emulsion paint until the edges of the remaining paint are firm

2 Glass-paper the peeled area and touch-in with new emulsion. Glass-paper lightly when dry

REMOVING DISTEMPER

1 Soak with warm water, using a 6 in. (150 mm) brush. Work from a window across the ceiling

2 Sponge surface and scrape away any particles. Leave to dry. Apply undercoat and top coat

Platform Use a plank between a step-ladder and a hop-up or between two step-ladders, to give comfortable access to the walls and ceiling. Do not use a chair: it could overbalance

Decorating Painting

Painting walls and ceilings

Paint a ceiling or wall in one continuous operation—a stop of 20 minutes or more will result in a join line showing through the finished surface.
Ceilings Paint a ceiling in strips 24 in. (610 mm) wide. Start from the window and work across the room. Do not overlap the strips. Use the edge of the brush to paint where the ceiling and the walls meet.

To paint a ceiling with a roller, use a tray with a sloping bottom to hold the paint. Fill it about one-third of the way up the slope: do not attempt to save time or trouble by putting a greater quantity in the tray.
Walls Paint walls in sections of about 24 in. (610 mm) square. Start at the top right-hand corner of a wall (top left if left-handed) and paint as much of the wall as possible before moving the step-ladder or the platform.

PAINTING WITH A BRUSH

1 Work parallel to window. Use the edge of a 4 in. (100 mm) brush against the angle. Do not overlap on to the wall

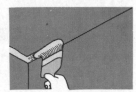

2 Paint a short way along against other wall. Do not overlap. Continue painting across the ceiling parallel to the window

3 Brush out to about 24 in. (610 mm) from wall in every direction. Brush marks do not show with emulsion paint

4 Apply a top coat of emulsion or gloss paint. Take care not to overlap the final coat on to the wall

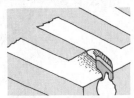

Oil paint Brush three parallel strokes in one direction, then cross-paint towards light

Walls Do not overlap at ceiling angle. Work along with first stroke, then down parallel to window

PAINTING CEILINGS WITH A ROLLER

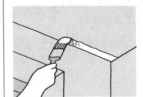

1 To start, touch-in corners and edges with a 1 in. (25 mm) brush. Do not overlap at angle

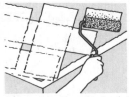

2 Cover the ceiling with diagonal roller strokes—alternate strokes in each direction

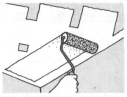

3 To finish, work with straight strokes of the roller along the ceiling towards the window

Preparing and painting radiators

The best time to paint radiators is when the walls are to be redecorated. Remove or loosen radiator (see p. 14) and decorate the wall first.

Turn off the central heating and leave the radiators to cool before working on them.

Have several rags available in case there is leakage from the joints.

To protect the floor from paint, cover the working area with brown paper or plastic sheeting. If the paintwork is in good condition, wash the surface and apply two coats of gloss of the same colour. If there is to be a colour change, an undercoat is required to obliterate the old colour.

Materials: paint (oil or emulsion); rags, brown paper or other suitable floor covering; piece of timber; clean cloth. Tools: brush; spanner; glass-paper.

1 Place rags around pipes. Loosen the retaining nuts on each side of the radiator

2 Free the radiator from wall brackets and swing it down. Rest it on a batten, and retighten nuts

3 Rub away all rough areas with fine glass-paper. Take care not to go through the primer

4 Brush off any dust and apply undercoat. Allow it to dry, then paint on the finishing coat

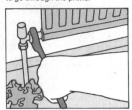

5 Loosen the retaining nuts of the radiator. Lift it back, retighten nuts, and replace brackets

6 Clean the front surface with wet abrasive paper. Apply undercoat and top coat

Cornices

If a cornice is to be painted in two colours, first paint the whole of the moulding in the colour of the raised surface. When dry, apply the second colour to the recessed parts.

Use a 24–36 in. (610–915 mm) mahlstick—a wooden dowel with a padded end—for difficult recesses. Hold it against the wall and lean the brush hand on it.

Mahlstick

Tools: 1 in. (25 mm) brush; No. 8 or No. 10 artist's brush; mahlstick.

1 Restore cornice if necessary (see p. 132). Brush on thin undercoat with 1 in. (25 mm) brush

2 Apply first colour over whole cornice. Work paint into recesses. When dry, apply second colour

3 Finish by using fine brush to touch-in details. Steady hand with the mahlstick

Summary of painting processes

PLASTER, RENDERING, BRICK AND STONE

Surface	Preparation	Number of coats
New plaster, rendering, brick and stone	1 Brush down to remove dirt and loose particles 2 Fill cracks, holes, defective pointing etc., and allow to dry 3 If alkyd or oil-based paint is to be used (dry surfaces only), apply alkali-resisting primer	Cement paint (not on plaster): 2 coats Emulsion paint: 2 coats Alkyd gloss finish: 1/2 undercoats 1/2 coats gloss Alkyd eggshell or matt: 2 coats Masonry paint: 2 coats
Painted plaster, rendering, brick and stone	1 Remove loose and defective old paint. Clean sound paint 2 Fill cracks, holes, defective pointing etc., and allow to dry 3 If alkyd or oil-based paint is to be used, prime bare areas with alkali-resisting primer 4 With other paints, apply 1 coat of finish to bare areas	As for new surfaces. Additional coats may be required if the new finishing colour differs greatly from the old

WOOD

Surface	Preparation	Number of coats
New softwood	1 Smooth with plane or scraper. Glass-paper 2 Apply knotting solution to knots 3 Apply priming coat 4 Fill in holes or dents. When hard, rub down with glass-paper 5 Brush away dust 6 Touch-in with primer	Undercoat and at least one gloss coat
Painted woodwork a) damaged	1 Burn off existing paint 2 Use glass-paper and scraper to remove any remaining paint 3 Rub down surface with glass-paper 4 Apply knotting solution where required 5 Apply priming coat 6 Fill in holes, dents and cracks. Rub down and touch-in with undercoat	Undercoat and at least one gloss coat
b) undamaged	Wash and rub with glass-paper	Two gloss coats if same colour; or 1 undercoat, 1 finish
Hardwood: cedar cladding	1 Scrape off old linseed oil or sealer. Sandpaper to remove grey powder on cedar 2 Use filler to match timber 3 Rub down with glass-paper	Two coats exterior wood stain or 4 coats (3 minimum) varnish

METAL

Surface	Preparation	Number of coats
New ferrous metal (for example, steel, cast iron)	1 Remove all traces of grease and oil with white spirit 2 Clean with wire brush and a cloth 3 Apply primer	Undercoat and two gloss coats
Rusted metal	1 Remove all rust, oil and grease 2 Prime	Undercoat and two gloss coats
New galvanised metal	1 Remove grease or oil with white spirit 2 Apply special primer—for example, calcium plumbate	Undercoat and one gloss coat
Old galvanised metal	Remove loose paint with a wire brush, but do not scratch the metal. Do not use an alkaline paint remover	Undercoat and one gloss coat
New non-ferrous metal	1 Remove grease or oil with white spirit 2 Apply primer and rub down	Undercoat and two gloss coats
Corroded non-ferrous metal	1 Remove white deposit with a scraper or wire brush. Do not scratch the surface 2 Apply primer—for example, zinc chromate or zinc phosphate	Undercoat and two gloss coats

OTHER SURFACES

Surface	Preparation	Number of coats
New asbestos	emulsion paint 1 Brush off loose particles 2 Apply sealer or thinned emulsion paint	Two coats of emulsion
	gloss paint 1 Brush off loose particles 2 Clean and apply asbestos primer	Undercoat and one gloss coat
Old asbestos	emulsion paint 1 Brush off loose particles 2 Seal with thinned emulsion	Two coats of emulsion
	gloss paint 1 Brush off loose particles 2 Fill if necessary. Touch-in with primer 3 If not previously painted, or if in bad condition, apply sealer	Undercoat and one gloss coat
New hardboard	emulsion paint 1 Remove dust 2 Apply thinned emulsion paint (1 part paint to 3 parts water)	Two coats of emulsion
	gloss paint 1 Remove dust 2 Clean and apply hardboard primer	Undercoat and one gloss coat Paint back of hardboard as sealer
Old hardboard	emulsion paint 1 Brush off loose particles 2 Seal with thinned emulsion	Two coats of emulsion
	gloss paint 1 Scrape off loose paint. Fill if necessary 2 Rub with fine glass-paper 3 Touch-in exposed areas with primer	Undercoat and one gloss coat

Decorating Wallpapering

Tools and equipment

If an entire room is to be decorated, first paper the ceiling (see p. 44) then rub down and paint the woodwork (see p. 36) and, finally, prepare and paper the walls (see p. 39).

For best results buy or hire a pasting table and two pairs of stepladders. If work is to be done more than 8 ft (2·4 m) above the floor, hire strong planking for a catwalk to stretch between the ladders. Make sure that all the tools which may be needed are available before starting work.

Lining papers

Always hang a lining paper on walls which have been previously painted or distempered. It should be hung horizontally, to prevent possible duplication of seams when the top paper is hung. Place the lengths in position with a gap of $\frac{1}{8}$ in. (3 mm) between them. This will be filled out, and will avoid the possibility of any overlapping from expansion, when the lengths are smoothed out.

When hanging lining paper, fold the lengths in concertina fashion (see p. 44).

Uneven walls

If a wall or ceiling is uneven or badly cracked, use woodchip wallpaper. Whereas ordinary papers might cling and emphasise heavily repaired breaks in plaster, woodchip absorbs moisture and becomes rigid after pasting. As a result, the surface underneath is masked evenly.

Halls and staircases

When the entire house is to be decorated, leave the staircase and hall until last. As main thoroughfares, they are more likely to be damaged when work is in progress.

When papering a staircase, place stepladders on two landings and lay a length of plank between the two to form a level catwalk.

Hang the first length of paper at the point of the longest drop from the ceiling. Fold the paper concertina fashion (see p. 44) or get a helper to hold the bottom of the paper at the foot of the stair well. The weight of a long length folded in two can distort the bottom half and cause the paper to kink—which would be emphasised as each succeeding length is hung.

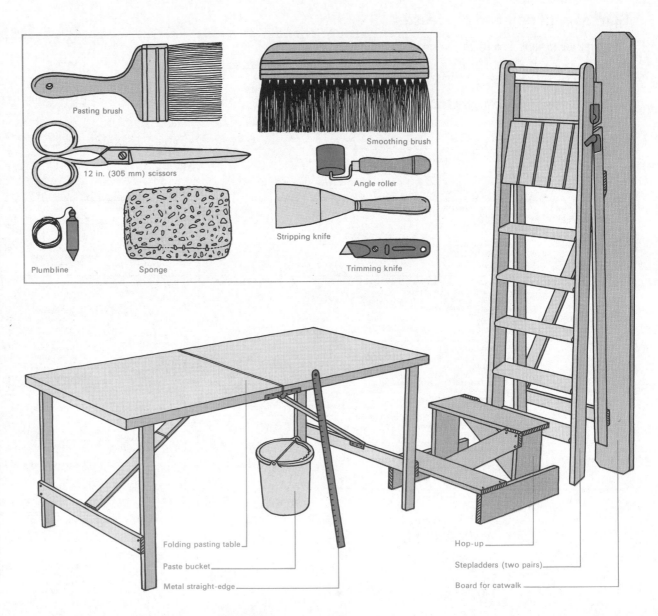

Pasting brush

Smoothing brush

12 in. (305 mm) scissors

Angle roller

Plumbline

Sponge

Stripping knife

Trimming knife

Folding pasting table

Paste bucket

Metal straight-edge

Hop-up

Stepladders (two pairs)

Board for catwalk

Paper and paste

Most wallpapers are sold in ready-trimmed rolls 33 ft × 20½ in. (10 m × 520 mm). Those with a margin at each side need trimming with a trimming knife and metal straight-edge before pasting.

Estimating the rolls
To determine the number of rolls needed:
1 Measure the height of room from the top of the skirting board to the ceiling.
2 Divide the length of the roll by the height of the room. For example, if the room is 8 ft (2·4 m) high, each roll will provide four complete lengths.
3 Measure the distance around the room, including the doors and windows, to allow for any wastage resulting from pattern matching.
4 Divide the total distance by the width of the roll.
5 Divide the figure reached in 4 by the figure in 2 to find the number of rolls needed.

When working on a staircase or in a room with different ceiling heights, measure sections with the same height separately and add totals together.

If there is any variation in the colours of the rolls, use the darkest nearest the windows. When all the lengths are cut, arrange them pattern downwards in the order they are to be used.

Buy a paste or adhesive to suit the type of wallpaper or covering being used. A wrong choice makes hanging difficult and can result in a poor finish.

CHOOSING SUITABLE ADHESIVES

Wall covering	Adhesive
All normal papers, lightweight Anaglypta, chipwood papers, backed fabrics, washable papers not in a kitchen or bathroom	Cold-water paste Hot-water paste Prepared tub paste Cellulose paste
Heavy Anaglypta panels	Dextrine paste
Lincrusta	Lincrusta glue
Vinyls, washable papers in a kitchen or bathroom	Mould-resistant adhesive (see p. 694)
Unbacked fabrics	Mould-resistant adhesive applied to the walls, not to the fabric
Small repairs to all wall coverings	Latex and multi-purpose adhesives (see p. 694)

How to cut paper

Cut all the lengths of paper needed to complete a room before starting to paste. Cut small lengths as needed to fit above doors or fireplaces and above or below windows.

Measuring each length of paper is easier if one edge of the pasting table is marked in 12 in. (305 mm) sections. The marking can be permanent for later use when any wallpapering has to be done.

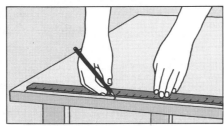

1 Mark along one edge of the pasting table in 12 in. (305 mm) sections to allow the lengths of wallpaper to be measured easily without a rule

2 Cut the first length of paper to the height of the wall plus 5 in. (125 mm) to allow for trimming and turnover at the top of the wall

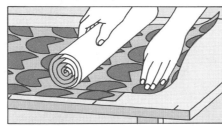

3 Match the pattern for each successive length and trim it at its top end. Cut the lengths to the size needed plus 5 in. (125 mm) for trimming

How to paste wallpaper

Position the pasting table parallel to the window. Work facing the light so that it is possible to check that there are no unpasted patches, which could cause unsightly blisters and wrinkles when the paper is hung.

Unless it is pre-mixed, paste should always be used on the day it is prepared: if it is kept longer, it may curdle. Mix the paste according to the manufacturer's instructions, in a clean plastic bucket. If the paper being used is lightweight, make the paste thin: for heavy papers mix the paste more thickly.

If any paste falls on the patterned side of the paper, remove it immediately with a dry, clean cloth.

1 Tie a length of string across the bucket so that surplus paste can be wiped from the brush before it is used

2 Roll the ends of the lengths against the curl to flatten them. Keep the top of the paper on the right of the table

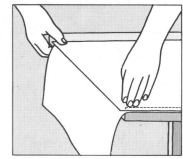

3 Align paper lengthways with the back of table. Allow it to overhang by ⅛ in. (3 mm) to keep paste off the table

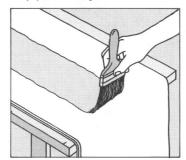

4 Paste evenly from right to left down the centre of the length of paper. Push paper to overhang the back of the table

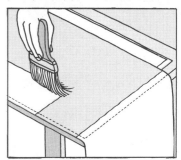

5 Brush out towards the back edge. Pull the paper to overhang the front of the table. Brush out to the front edge

Decorating Wallpapering

Preparing walls and ceilings

New wallpaper will not stick firmly to old papers. Strip walls and ceilings which have previously been papered. It is advisable to use a special stripping fluid containing a wetting agent which makes the stripping easier.

Smooth the walls with glass-paper and apply a coat of thinned adhesive to ensure that the wall cannot absorb the paste when it is applied.

Materials: water and stripping agent; detergent; filler paste; medium glass-paper; size.
Tools: 6 in. (150 mm) brush; bucket; broad scraper; sponge; filling knife.

1 Soak walls with water and wetting agent. Repeat until saturated

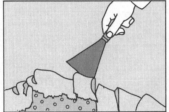

2 Scrape and peel off the old paper. Re-soak surface if it is drying

3 Scrub surface with clean water. Fill cracks with filler paste

4 Sponge the surface. If it is porous and water is absorbed, apply a coat of thinned adhesive before papering

REMOVING RELIEF PANELS

The adhesive used to fix heavy relief coverings to walls is much more difficult to remove than the paste used for ordinary wallpapers.

Materials: water; wetting agent or detergent.
Tools: scraper; brush.

1 Force the covering away from the wall with a scraper. Work in from the corner of each panel

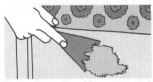

2 Brush wall with water and wetting agent. Allow to soak, then scrape off backing and glue

Papering a ceiling

Fit ceiling papers parallel to the main windows in a room, so that the joins are not highlighted unduly.

There are times, however, when this general rule should be ignored. Paper is usually sold in 33 ft (10 m) rolls, and if a room is between 11 ft (3·3 m) and 14 ft (4·2 m) long, this allows only two lengths from each roll, leaving an excess amount of unusable paper. It may, therefore, be more economic to ignore the window as a guideline and to paper across the room.

To lay the first length of paper, face the window and fit the paper from right to left (left to right if left-handed). For the remainder, face into the room and lay the lengths in the opposite direction.

To ensure comfortable working at a convenient height, arrange a catwalk between two pairs of stepladders (see p. 39).

(see p. 39)

Materials: wallpaper and paste.
Tools: pencil; string; chalk; scissors; 6 in. (150 mm) paste brush; smoothing brush; rule; 24 in. (610 mm) cardboard or wood roller; two stepladders; 1½ in. (40 mm) plank, 9 in. (225 mm) wide.

PAPERING A CEILING

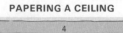
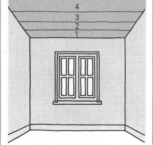

Hang ceiling paper from the window inwards. Make sure that the lengths butt against each other

1 Measure the width of the paper. Subtract ¼ in. (6 mm) to allow an overlap at the wall angle

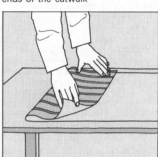

2 Measure the distance on the ceiling and mark the ceiling at both ends of the catwalk

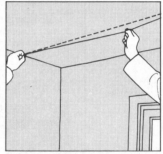

3 Chalk a length of string and use it to mark between the pencil marks on the ceiling

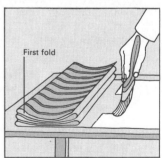

4 Cut the number of paper lengths required. Paste the first length and fold over 12 in. (305 mm)

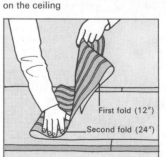

First fold (12")
Second fold (24")

5 Fold over a further 24 in. (610 mm) at the folded end. Turn back the first folded piece

First fold

6 Make another fold in the paper then pull the unpasted remainder on to the table *(continued)*

7 Paste and fold the remaining paper as before. Turn the last 12 in. (305 mm) back

8 Lay the paper over a long cardboard or wooden roller. Grip the folds with the other thumb

9 Face the wall, with eyes in line with chalk mark. Peel back last fold and press to ceiling

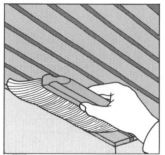

10 Walk along and release folds. Keep roller close to ceiling. Push on paper with brush

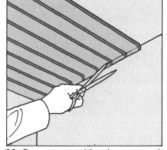

11 Score paper with scissors at end and side walls. Pull back paper and cut to leave $\frac{1}{4}$ in. (6 mm) on wall

12 Mark ceiling for second length. Make sure there is no overlap. Lay paper in opposite direction

13 At a ceiling light, find the centre of the obstruction. Push point of scissors through paper

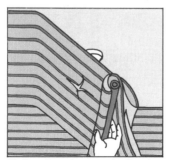

14 Cut along the paper in direction it is being laid. Make a second cut across the centre

15 Smooth paper around obstruction. Make further cuts if necessary. Pull back flaps and trim close

Starting to paper the walls

Wear overalls with pockets large enough to hold the brush, scissors and other tools. This avoids wasting time clambering up and down stepladders.

Do not overlap the wallpaper lengths if possible. When this is necessary, say at corners, overlap towards the light so that the seam does not cast a shadow. Where the overlapping is horizontal, which is advisable with lining paper, overlap upwards if the join is above eye level, and downwards if the join is below eye level.

Materials: wallpaper and paste.
Tools: plumbline; rule; pencil; scissors; smoothing brush; 6 in. (150 mm) paste brush; roller.

(continued)

ORDER OF PAPERING WALLS

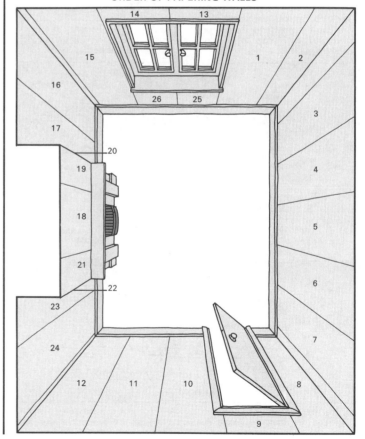

Decorating Wallpapering

(continued)

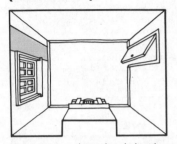

Always start at the main window in a room. Work towards the longest unbroken wall, then return to the other side of the window.

1 Hold plumbline from top corner of window frame. If frame is not parallel to it, a guideline is needed

2 Measure paper width. Subtract ⅟₄ in. (6 mm). Measure that distance from centre of frame edge and mark wall

3 Hang plumbline slightly to one side of the mark on the wall. Draw a line down wall through the mark

4 Cut and paste paper (see p. 43). Take top two corners in both hands and fold section on table in half

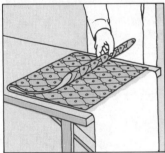

5 Check that edges of paper are in line. Fold the section once more, but keep it clear of paste

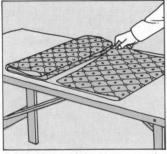

6 Pull the rest of the paper on to the table and paste. Fold the end to within 2 in. (50 mm) of other folds

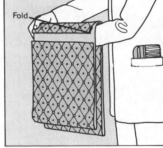

7 Fold under 2 in. (50 mm) at the first end of the paper to protect ceiling from paste. Hold paper over arm

8 Hang paper from the angle with the ceiling. Keep outer edge parallel with the guideline drawn on wall

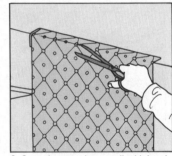

9 Smooth paper down wall with brush, then score along overlap at the ceiling angle with a pair of scissors

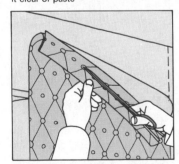

10 Peel the paper back from the ceiling angle and cut along the score line. Remove any surplus paper

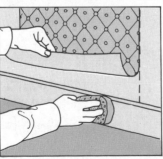

11 Score and trim the surplus at the bottom of the paper. Remove any paste from skirting board with a sponge

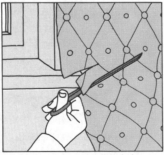

12 If there is a protruding ledge, cut from edge of paper to ⅟₄ in. (6 mm) beyond top and bottom corners

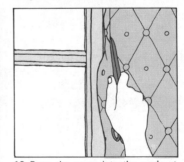

13 Press the paper into the angle at the window frame with the smoothing brush. Score down the overlap

14 Gently peel the paper back from the frame. Cut from the bottom up the scored line. Smooth paper

Papering a corner

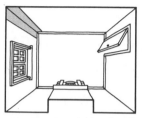

Do not attempt to fold a length of paper to fit into a corner. Instead, cut the paper so that only ½ in. (13 mm) extends round the corner. Paste this piece in position. Then cover the overlap with the adjacent piece.

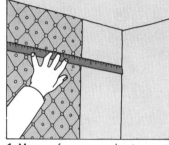

1 Measure from paper edge to corner at top, middle and bottom. Add ½ in. (13 mm) to widest measurement

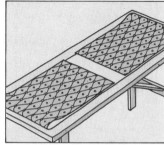

2 Paste full length of paper (see p. 43). Fold ends to within 4 in. (100 mm) of each other at middle of table

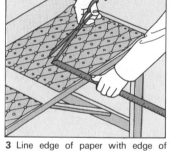

3 Line edge of paper with edge of table. Measure the width of paper required for first stage

4 Cut from one fold up through both thicknesses of paper. Take care that the cut is straight

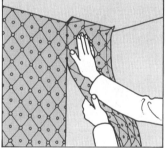

5 Hang the pasted strip on the wall and smooth the overlap round the corner down the whole length of wall

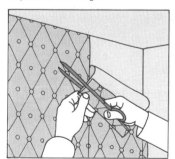

6 Score and trim the overlap at top and bottom of the paper. Remove paste from skirting with a sponge

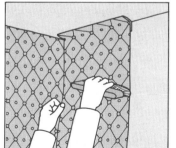

7 Hang remainder of cut length on second wall. Match pattern at top and smooth into the corner angle

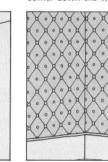

8 Hang plumbline from ceiling at centreline of paper. Adjust paper if necessary. Trim ends

Papering round a door

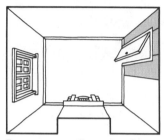

To ensure a neat fit at a door, hang a full width of paper, then cut out the door shape in two stages. Wipe all paste off the woodwork before it sets.

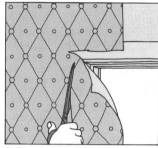

1 Paste (see p. 43), fold and hang full width of paper. Cut shape to within 1 in. (25 mm) of frame

2 Cut diagonally at top corner. Make cut about ¼ in. (6 mm) beyond the edge of the door frame

3 Press paper flat against the wall with smoothing brush. Press overlap tightly into angle with frame

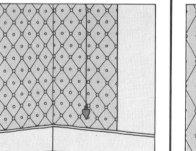

4 Score overlaps at top and bottom and round the door frame. Peel back edges of paper and trim

Light switch Push scissors through paper at centre of switch. Cut diagonally to beyond corners. Trim

Decorating Wallpapering

Papering round an obstruction

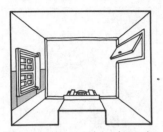

When papering round an obstruction (for example, a window) it is often impossible to avoid ending with a long strip of wall narrower than the width of the paper.

1 Measure length and the widest part of the gap between paper already hung and the window

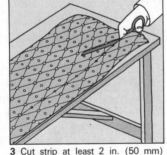

2 Lay paper at table edge. Hold ruler with scissors against its end. Score down the paper

3 Cut strip at least 2 in. (50 mm) longer than the gap on the wall to allow for pattern matching

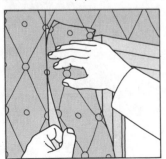

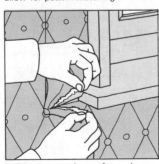

4 Paste paper (see p. 43). Match pattern and hang it against edge of paper already laid. Do not overlap

5 Trim any overlap at frame (see p. 47). Tear off excess at top and bottom to help disguise joins

Papering round a fireplace

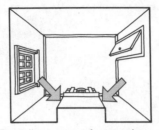

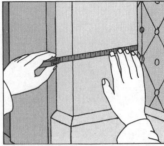

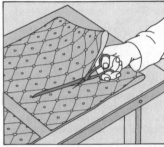

Protruding corners—for example, at a fireplace—may not be perpendicular. To keep the paper vertical and to prevent gaps, cut the corner length of paper and hang it in two sections.

1 Measure the top, middle and bottom distances between fixed paper and the corner of the wall

2 Paste and fold the paper (see p. 43). Subtract ⅜ in. (10 mm) from widest measurement and cut to width

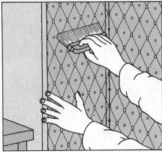

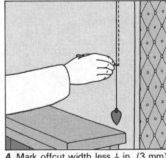

3 Butt the strip against paper already hung. This leaves ⅜ in. (10 mm) gap unpapered at the edge

4 Mark offcut width less ⅛ in. (3 mm) from paper around corner. Hold plumbline and draw a line down the wall

5 Match the offcut at top and slide the edge flush with line. Fold round the corner to overlap existing strip

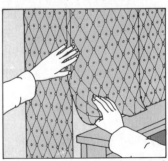

6 Hang the middle strip. At the second corner, cut a strip to jut beyond the wall by ½ in. (13 mm)

7 Paste and hang a strip to fit the wall around the corner. Smooth and trim top and bottom

8 Fold ½ in. (13 mm) overlap around corner and stick. The pattern may not match but the seam is hidden

Positioning the design at a fireplace

When a wallpaper has an obvious and dominant central pattern, random hanging can cause sections to be out of balance at important parts of a room. It is advisable to start by centring the paper on a chimney breast or on the central point of the main wall.

The method used depends on whether the centre of the pattern is at the edge of the paper or at some other point across its width.

Use a plumbline down the centre to get the pattern upright.

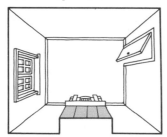

1 Measure width of wall on which the pattern is to be centred. Mark the centre of the wall

2 Hang a plumbline from the ceiling and draw a line through the mark. Prepare the paper (see p. 43)

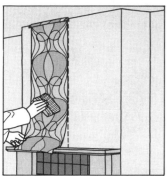

3 If pattern centre is at edge of paper, hang first length so that edge is flush with pencilled line

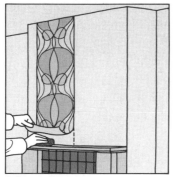

4 Trim excess and sponge off surplus paste. Hang second length on other side of centreline

---

IF THE PATTERN CENTRE IS NOT AT AN EDGE

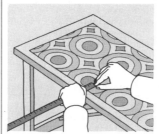

1 Measure the distance from the pattern centre to the left-hand edge of the paper

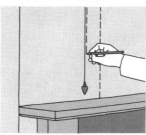

2 Mark that distance on left of centreline. Hang plumbline and draw line through new mark

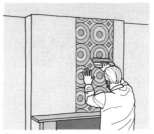

3 Hang first length on right of new line. Hang second length flush on left of new line

---

Papering a recess

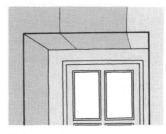

When papering a room, do the surfaces inside a bay window at the stage when the wall above the window is being covered.

1 Measure wallpaper width. Subtract ½ in. (13 mm) and mark distance around corner from inside edge

2 Draw a line and hang paper to it. Make a horizontal cut ¼ in. (6 mm) above recess top

3 Smooth first length above and round corner. Cut, paste and hang short length for top wall

4 Cut a piece for the gap, allowing a ½ in. (13 mm) overlap at the back, and 1 in. (25 mm) at the front

5 Trim overlap at back. At front, tear overlap carefully to leave ragged edge to conceal join

Decorating Wallpapering

Papering a frieze or beam

Friezes above picture rails and beams between rooms are usually covered with the same paper as the ceiling. Always allow 2 in. (50 mm) extra on the depth of paper at a picture rail, so that it can fit neatly behind the rail.

Cut the paper for a beam slightly undersize, however, so that it does not quite reach to the bottom of the beam. When the beam is between adjoining rooms, and the rooms have different papers, cover the sides of the beam with the paper to match each room. Leave the bottom uncovered—or hang plain white paper—so that the beam is not shown to be part of any one room.

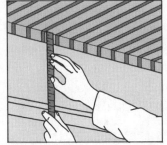

1 If paper is laid across ceiling, measure depth of the beam or frieze and count lengths on ceiling

2 Subtract ⅛ in. (3 mm) from depth for a beam; add 2 in. (50 mm) for frieze. Cut required lengths

3 Paste and fold each length. Match pattern with ceiling paper at right-hand corner. Hang and trim

WHEN PATTERN IS LAID ALONG CEILING

1 Measure between corners. Add 4 in. (100 mm) and cut length of paper. Measure depth and cut

2 Overlap the paper 2 in. (50 mm) round the corner. Smooth along and fold overlap round other corner

Hanging fabrics

Do not hang unbacked fabrics on freshly plastered walls. Leave the walls to dry for six months or more, then rub them down and treat them with an alkali-resistant primer. Wash old plaster walls thoroughly and fill any small cracks or holes (see p. 121). If the walls have been painted, wash and rub down with glass-paper to create a good key.

Lining

Always hang lining paper before covering walls with fabrics. It is advisable to use a paper of the same colour as the fabric, so that gaps are less obvious if the material shrinks. Paste the wall, not the fabric—unless it has a backing. Even then, however, take care not to soak the material.

Use a felt-covered roller to smooth each length, but do not apply heavy pressure with the roller, to avoid stretching the fabric and forcing paste out of the joins.

Matching

Slight differences in weaving patterns are common in fabric wall coverings and it may therefore be difficult to match adjacent strips along their complete length. If this difficulty is encountered, make sure that the fabric matches at eye level around the room.

1 Cut fabric to length (see p. 43). Lay a straight-edge on fabric and cut ½ in. (13 mm) from each side

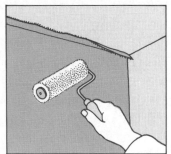

3 Hang the fabric and smooth it from the centre outwards with a felt-covered roller. Do not apply heavy pressure

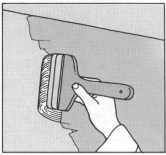

2 Prepare wall surface and spread paste (see p. 43) evenly. Cover only the width of two strips of fabric

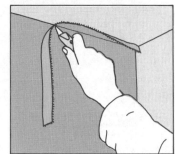

4 After 15 minutes, score the top and bottom edges. Trim with scissors or a sharp knife

VINYL AND PRE-PASTED PAPERS

Hang vinyl coverings only on dry surfaces. If the surface is absorbent, seal it with a coat of thinned adhesive, or the sealer recommended by the covering manufacturer, and let it dry before hanging the vinyl.

If it is non-porous, such as one that has been painted, hang lining paper (see p. 42) before hanging the vinyl covering.

Always use a fungicidal adhesive to hang vinyl, and use it also to hang lining paper if that paper is to be covered with vinyl.

If papers or coverings are pre-pasted, activate the adhesive by immersing cut lengths of the covering in water in the trough provided.

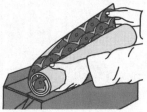

1 Cut required number of lengths (see p. 43). Place pre-pasted paper in a water tray with its pasted side outermost

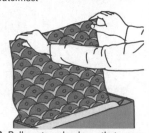

2 Pull up top slowly so that paper rubs against the lip of the tray. Allow excess water to drain back. Hang the length of paper

Repairing blistered or peeling paper

When heavy paper is pasted, it can expand by as much as $\frac{1}{4}$ in. (6 mm). If it is hung on the wall too soon, the expansion is likely to continue and the paper will blister.

If the paste used to hang wallpaper is too weak or spread too thinly, the paper may peel.

Two repairs are possible: cutting and re-pasting, or injecting paste with a syringe. Of the two, injection is the more satisfactory because it leaves only a pin mark.

INJECTING PASTE

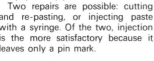

1 Half fill a syringe with suitable paste (see p. 43). Wash outside of syringe and fit plunger

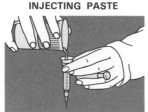

2 Inject paste into centre of each blister. Allow the paper to absorb paste for five minutes

3 Flatten blister to wall with fingers. Go over it lightly with roller until completely flat

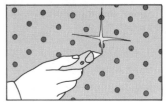

1 Cut vertically and horizontally through centre of blister with a sharp knife. Cut beyond edge of blister

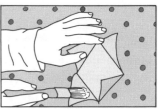

2 Pull back corners of the blister. Apply paste with 1 in. (25 mm) brush. Allow to soak

3 Push flaps back into position on the wall. Flatten the area lightly with a seam roller

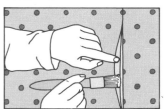

Peeling Lift back the peeled section and apply a multi-purpose adhesive (see p. 694). Roll lightly

Patching torn wallpaper

When wallpaper is torn, cut a piece of matching paper larger than the damaged area. Tear round it to make ragged edges. At the back of the patch, peel away paper so that the edges are about half the thickness of the rest of the patch.

Some wall coverings—for example vinyl, hessian or grasscloth—cannot be torn by hand. A straight-edged patch can be used, but it is more difficult to conceal.

PATCHING VINYL

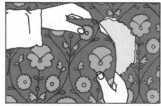

1 Match and cut a piece of replacement vinyl larger than the damaged area of wall covering

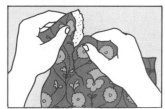

2 Hold the material firmly against the wall and cut a square shape through both layers

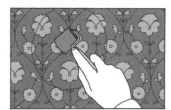

3 Peel off cut pieces of old paper. Paste and stick on patch. Press lightly with a roller

1 Tear off all damaged and loose paper. Leave only paper which is fixed firmly to the wall

2 Fit piece of paper over hole so that pattern matches surrounding paper. Paste (see p. 43)

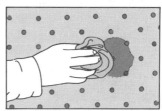

3 Tear a ragged patch from the new paper. Cut and peel $\frac{1}{8}$ in. (3 mm) strip from back around edges of patch

4 Match edge of pattern all round. Leave paste to dry for a few minutes. Roll lightly from centre to edges

Removing stains

If wallpaper is stained, test that the pattern is colourfast. Apply a cleaning agent or water to a small piece in a dark corner. If the pattern blurs, do not try to clean any noticeable area.

Heavy papers can be washed with a mild detergent in water. Work from the bottom upwards so that paper at the bottom does not get too wet before being washed. Rinse and dry.

Remove grease spots with a proprietary fluid or Fuller's earth mixed with white spirit.

Aerosol cleaner Spray stain and leave to dry. Brush off white powder lightly. Repeat if necessary

White spirit Test inconspicuous part of paper, then rub stain gently with a cloth and white spirit

Vinyl paper Lubricate greasy patches with oil or lard. Wipe off carefully with a clean dry cloth

Doors Construction

Buying a new door

Before changing a door in a flat or maisonette, consult the local council surveyor's office: the door may have to be fire-resistant to comply with the legal requirements.

Most doors are made to standard sizes and are stocked by builders' merchants and some larger do-it-yourself shops. Suppliers have illustrated catalogues showing the range of standard designs and sizes available. If the old one is a non-standard size or is unusual in design, delivery of the new door may take three or four weeks.

Most doors that are painted are made of softwood: they must be stopped, knotted (see p. 36), and given two coats of primer. Hardwood doors, which are heavier and more expensive, are usually treated with a sealer and polished (see p. 98).

Before hanging a new door (see p. 53), fit hinges, a lock or latch (see pp. 55–56) and, for an outside door, a letter plate and weatherboard (see p. 57). Fit the lock or latch keep on the frame after the door is hung.

Fit glass (see pp. 202–6) in a glazed door after it has been hung. On a glazed internal door, glass is held in place by strips of hardwood beading, or moulding, nailed to the recesses.

On an internal door frame there are strips of wood, nailed to the inner faces of the frame, for the door to butt against and reduce draughts. On an external door, the frame is rebated—the stop is cut into the frame—to provide adequate protection against the weather.

Unseasoned wood (see p. 688) may cause a frame to shrink and the door to fit badly. In this case fit a draught sealer (see pp. 63–67) or, if the door rattles, adjust the position of the lock's striker plate (see p. 56).

Gaps due to a distorted frame can often be remedied (see p. 58).

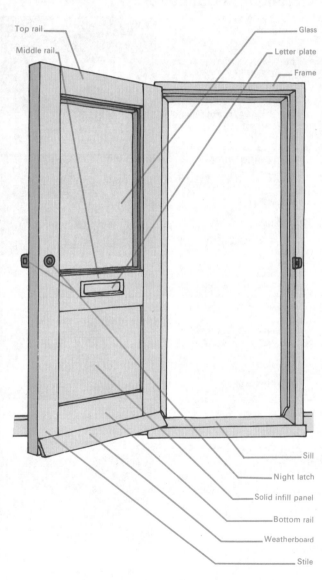

Top rail

Middle rail

Glass

Letter plate

Frame

Sill

Night latch

Solid infill panel

Bottom rail

Weatherboard

Stile

Doors Hinges

Choosing new hinges

Hinges must be strong enough to carry the weight of a door. Always give the supplier the height, width and thickness of the door to ensure that the correct size is obtained.

Hinges are measured by the height of the leaf and the overall width of both leaves when opened flat. The size range is 1–6 in. (25–150 mm). Solid hardwood doors, or heavy, glazed doors, should have three hinges. A third hinge is also advisable on new softwood doors to prevent the timber warping.

If possible, use non-ferrous metal hinges for external doors and paint them to give additional protection against corrosion.

Butt hinges are the type most commonly used for doors and windows. They are available in ferrous and in non-ferrous metals, with pins which can be removed.

Rising-butt hinges lift a door slightly when it is opened and allow it to close by itself. The door can be removed without unscrewing the hinges. They are available for left-hand or right-hand opening.

T hinges, of black japanned or galvanised steel, are used mainly for garage doors.

Spring hinges are for self-closing single or double-swing doors and are made of ferrous or non-ferrous metals.

Parliament hinges allow a door to which they are fitted to be folded flat back against an adjacent wall.

Hook-and-band hinges are generally used on heavy doors—such as solid hardwood—or external gates. They are made of galvanised steel.

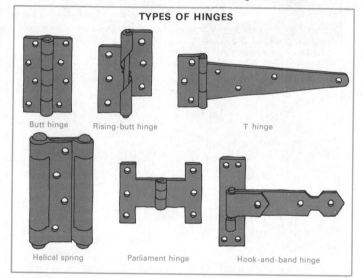

TYPES OF HINGES

Butt hinge — Rising-butt hinge — T hinge

Helical spring — Parliament hinge — Hook-and-band hinge

Lubricate metal door and window hinges occasionally with a drop of light oil at the head of the hinge. Do not use too much oil. Hold a cloth under the hinge to catch any surplus and wipe the surface clean immediately after lubrication. Oil rising-butt hinges every month: if the pin is allowed to become dry, the hinge will wear rapidly. Never try to lubricate nylon hinges: if they squeak, slacken or tighten the screw heads half a turn.

Hanging a new door

Make sure before trying to hang a door that it fits squarely into its frame with enough clearance on all sides. If there is an uneven sill, mark and cut the bottom of the door to fit (see p. 58).

Mark the hinge positions accurately and make sure that the hinges are recessed flush with the timber.

Materials: new door; three 4 in. (100 mm) hinges; 1¼ in. (30 mm) 10-gauge screws; primer; paint (see p. 33).
Tools: panel saw; long plane; mallet; 1¼ in. (30 mm) bevel-edged chisel; screwdriver; mortise gauge; swing brace and bit; paintbrush.

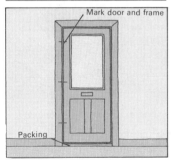

Mark door and frame

Packing

1 Press the door against the jamb on the hinge side. Mark the frame line on the top of the door with a pencil

2 Saw straight down the pencil line at the top of the door. Plane the cut edge smooth to give slight clearance

3 Again hold the door tightly against the jamb on the hinge side. Mark where the side of the door meets the jamb

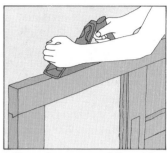

4 Shave down to pencil line with a long plane. Position door on ⅛ in. (3 mm) packing

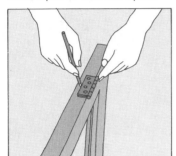

5 Mark hinge tops 9 in. (230 mm) from top of door, 13 in. (330 mm) from bottom and midway between

6 Hold hinges on the stile edge, level with the marks. Mark the hinge widths on the face of the stile

7 Set a mortise gauge to the hinge width and score that measurement on the stile and door frame

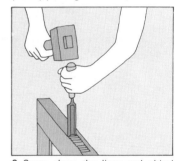

8 Lay a hinge against top line on the stile and pencil along bottom. Do the same on the frame

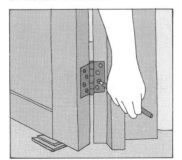

9 Score along the lines and chisel the recesses to depth of hinges on the door and the frame

10 Fix the hinges into recesses on the door stile with 1¼ in. (30 mm) 10-gauge countersunk wood screws

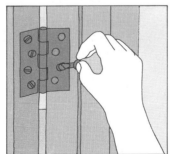

11 Stand the door open, on wedges, so that the hinges are in place on the frame. Mark screw holes on frame

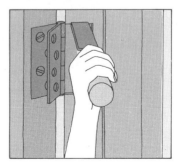

12 Drill screw holes in frame but fix each hinge with only one screw. Open and close door

13 If the door is stiff, remove each hinge screw in turn and chisel a little more from frame recesses

14 When the door opens and closes correctly, fit the other screws to the hinges and the door frame

Doors Hinges

Fitting rising-butt hinges

Rising-butt hinges (see p. 52) raise a door over a carpet and allow it to close under its own weight. They are in two sections, one with a socket and the other with a spindle. Always fit the spindle section on the door frame. Tell the supplier how the door opens so that the correct hinges can be obtained. Cut the top of the door on the hinge side to ensure that it can open without fouling the top of the frame.

Materials: hinges; screws; dowel rod. Tools: pencil; straight-edge; screwdriver; plane; panel saw; hammer; chisel; mallet; cutting gauge; combination square; bradawl.

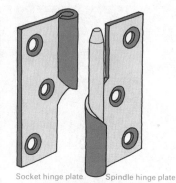

Socket hinge plate   Spindle hinge plate

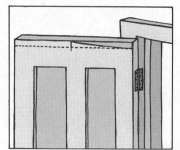

1 Close the door. Mark a line across the top where it meets the underside of the doorstop

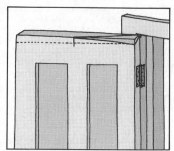

2 Open the door. Mark from the end of the drawn line at the hinge edge to the centre of the top edge

3 Draw two connecting lines on the top and the hinge edge of the door to form a bevelled section

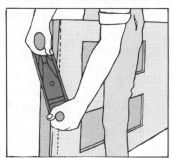

4 Remove the door and stand it on edge. Plane off the bevelled section marked at the top corner

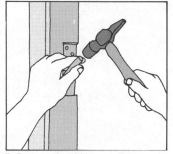

5 Remove the old hinges. Taper small dowel rods, and plug the screw holes in the door and frame

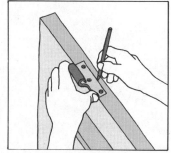

6 Hold and mark the shape of the rising-butt plates over the old hinge positions on the door edge

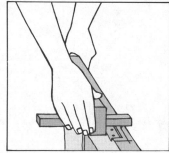

7 With a cutting gauge, score width of rising-butt plate about $\frac{1}{8}$ in. (3 mm) deep along the mark

8 Score the top and bottom marks and chisel out the recesses to take the thickness of the hinge plate

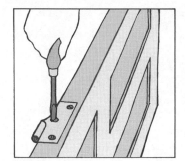

9 Hold socket hinge plate on door and start screw holes with a bradawl. Screw on plates

10 Hold door in open position. Raise it on packing pieces until top bevelled corner is level with frame

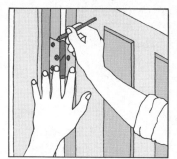

11 Get helper to hold door. Fit hinges together and mark top and bottom of hinge plates on frame. Remove door

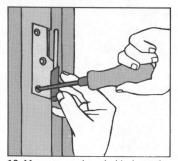

12 Measure, mark and chisel out the recesses for the spindle hinge plates. Screw the plates in position

13 Lift door and ease hinge sockets over spindles. If it is too tight, remove the door and plane the bottom

Doors Locks and latches

Fitting a mortise latch and lock

When a broken lock is to be replaced, keep the existing door plates and handles for refitting. If, however, a door is new, buy new handles and plates when obtaining the lock. Always make sure that the length of the latch spindle suits the thickness of the door.

On a new door, fit the lock casing in position but leave the handle furniture until it has been painted.

Materials: mortise latch and lock; set of lock furniture (handles and plates); fixing screws.
Tools: screwdriver; bradawl; mallet; $\frac{1}{2}$ in. (13 mm) chisel; hand brace and $\frac{3}{8}$ in. (10 mm) wood bit; padsaw.

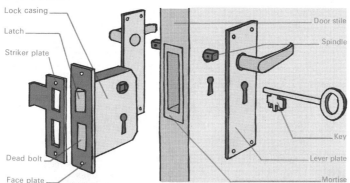

Lock casing
Latch
Striker plate
Dead bolt
Face plate
Door stile
Spindle
Key
Lever plate
Mortise

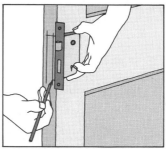

1 Hold the lock against the door. Mark height and thickness of lock casing on centre of door-rail edge

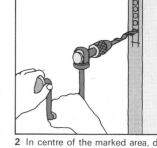

2 In centre of the marked area, drill a row of $\frac{3}{8}$ in. (10 mm) holes to the depth of the lock case

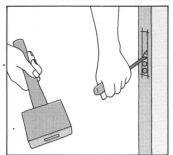

3 Cut out the mortise in the door edge with a chisel and mallet. Cut within the marked lines. Clean out mortise

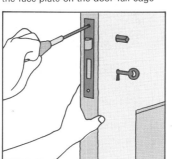

4 Push the lock casing as far as possible into the mortise. Mark around the face plate on the door-rail edge

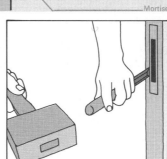

5 Remove the lock. Carefully chisel out a recess inside the pencil line to the thickness of the face plate

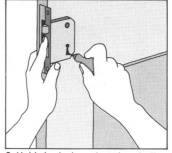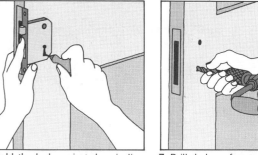

6 Hold the lock against door in line with recess. Push bradawl centrally through key and spindle holes

7 Drill holes of same diameter as keyhole and spindle. Make sure brace is at right angles to door

8 Cut the lower part of the keyhole shape with a padsaw. Make it slightly larger than the key

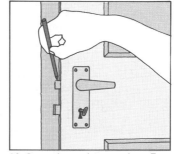

9 Push the lock case into the mortise, fit the key and spindle. Screw the face plate to door edge

10 Screw lever plates to door. Turn key. Close door and mark dead bolt and latch positions on frame

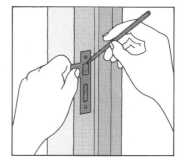

11 Hold the striker plate against the marks on the door frame and mark areas for the latch and dead bolt

12 Chisel mortises deep enough to take latch and dead bolt, and recess for striker plate. Screw on plate

Doors Locks and latches

Fitting a night latch

A cylinder night latch has a pin tumbler action operated by a key from the outside and a knob or lever on the inside.

The cylinder is secured to the backplate by two screws. Cut them to length to suit the door thickness. If the door already has a mortise latch, fit the night latch at shoulder level.

Materials: night latch; latch pull.
Tools: swing brace; 1¼ in. (30 mm) wood bit; chisel; mallet; screwdriver.

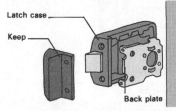

Latch case
Keep
Back plate

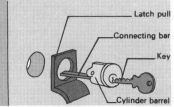

Latch pull
Connecting bar
Key
Cylinder barrel

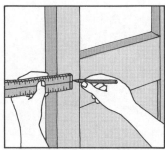

1 Measure from centre of cylinder to outside edge of latch case. Mark that distance from door edge

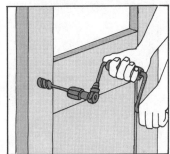

2 Block the door open and drill through the stile at the cylinder mark with a 1¼ in. wood bit

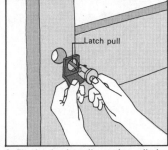

Latch pull

3 Fit the latch pull on the cylinder barrel and slide the cylinder into the hole from outside the door

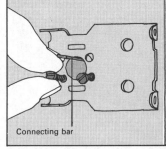

Connecting bar

4 Hold the cylinder in place and fit the back plate inside the door. Fit the two cylinder retaining screws

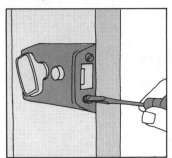

5 Fit the casing on the back plate so that the connecting bar engages in the latch. Fit the end-plate screws

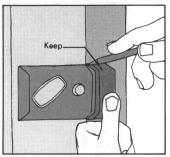

Keep

6 Shut door and mark top and bottom of latch on the jamb. Open door, hold keep in place and mark the depth

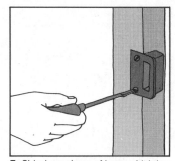

7 Chisel out shape of keep which has been marked on the jamb. Screw the keep end plate to the jamb

Mending a rattling door

If a door rattles, it is likely that the timber has shrunk across its grain and that it no longer butts tightly against the door stop.

The simplest repair is to move the latch keep slightly to compensate for the shrinkage of the wood.

To find out how far the keep should be moved, close the door and then measure the distance between the surface of the jamb and the surface of the stile.

Materials: two wooden plugs; wood filler; matching paint.
Tools: screwdriver; mallet; chisel; pencil; rule; hammer; paintbrush.

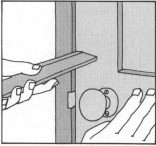

1 Close the door and push it hard against the stop. Measure distance from the jamb to the face of the door

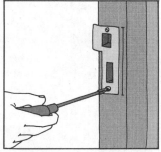

3 Undo the screws holding the striker plate on the jamb and remove it. Discard screws if they are damaged

4 Remove wood with a chisel up to the pencil line to match the depth of the existing recess

6 Hold latch plate in position and mark mortises. Chisel out extra to match depth of original holes

7 Make sure the keep plate fits flush with the jamb. Refit the plate and tighten the screws securely

Doors Letter plates

Doors Weatherboards

Fitting a letter plate

Letter plates may fit horizontally on the middle rail of a door or vertically on the stile. The method of fitting is the same in both cases.

First cut out the size and shape of opening required in the door, then drill the holes for the securing bolts. Note that they are usually very close to the letter opening: keep the drill straight so that it does not run into the cut-out area.

Materials: letter plate.
Tools: swing brace; wheelbrace; $\frac{3}{4}$ in., $\frac{1}{2}$ in. and $\frac{1}{4}$ in. (20, 13 and 6 mm) wood bits; padsaw; small spanner; chisel; glass-paper.

Fitting a weatherboard

Weatherboards for outside doors are sold only in standard sizes, but they can be cut to fit any door width.

Materials: weatherboard; 2 in. (50 mm) nails; paint and primer.
Tools: mallet; chisel; paintbrush; hammer; rule.

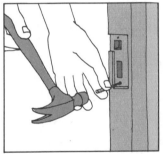

2 Open door. Draw measured distance on jamb, behind the latch keep parallel with its back edge

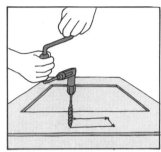

1 Hold letter plate on door and mark outline of the opening. Drill a $\frac{3}{4}$ in. hole at each corner

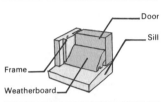

Door — Sill — Frame — Weatherboard

1 Open the door and measure its width. Cut the weatherboard to fit it exactly

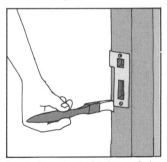

5 Cut wooden plugs to fit old screw holes and drive them into jamb. Chisel off surplus

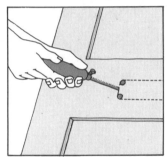

2 Cut along the marked lines from each hole with a padsaw. Clean edges with a chisel and glass-paper

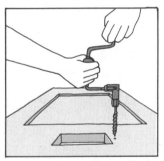

3 Hold the letter plate outside the door and mark through the bolt holes. Drill $\frac{1}{2}$ in. holes, $\frac{1}{2}$ in. deep

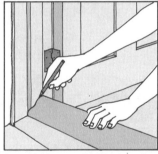

2 Hold the weatherboard against the door-frame stops and mark its outline on the stops with a pencil

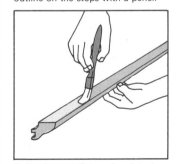

3 Carefully chisel out the shape marked on both stops, down to the main door frame

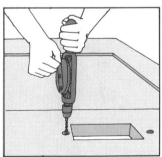

8 Fill the gap at the front of the keep plate with plastic wood. Paint to match existing finish

4 Drill through the centre of the $\frac{1}{2}$ in. holes with a bit the same size as the bolts which are to be used for fixing

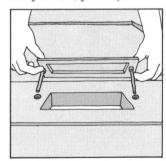

5 Fit letter plate on the outside of the door. Make sure its sockets fit in the holes. Fit and tighten the nuts

4 Brush an oil-based paint (see p. 33) on to the back of the weatherboard. Do not allow it to dry

5 Hold the weatherboard in position and close the door. Nail it to the door. Prime and paint it (see p. 36)

Doors Frames

Refitting a door in a distorted frame

Settlement may cause a door frame to distort so that a gap, up to $\frac{1}{2}$ in. (13 mm) deep, occurs above the door and the bottom rubs against the floor.

To remedy this, cut the top of the door to match the angle of the frame, add to the bottom of the door and rehang it.

Materials: batten thicker than door; $1\frac{1}{4}$ in. (30 mm) countersunk wood screws; wood plugs; PVA glue; primer; paint.
Tools: panel saw; mallet; screwdriver; wood chisel; bradawl; hand brace; $\frac{3}{16}$ in. (5 mm) wood bit; hammer; long plane; paintbrush.

1 Cut a length of $\frac{1}{2}$ in. (13 mm) batten, to match the width of the door but slightly thicker. Plane its faces smooth

2 Hold the batten against the frame at the top and mark underneath it on the door to show amount to be cut away

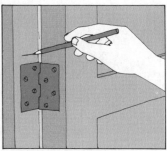

3 Draw straight lines on the door frame, $\frac{1}{2}$ in. above the top of the existing hinges

4 Remove the screws from all the hinge flaps on the door frame. Lift the door away from the frame

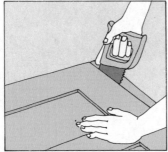

5 Cut along the marked line at the top of the door with a panel saw. Plane the edge smooth

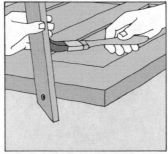

6 Drill and countersink screw holes in the batten. Coat the door bottom and the batten with PVA glue

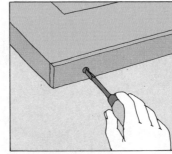

7 Fit the glued surfaces together and secure the batten with $1\frac{1}{4}$ in. (30 mm) wood screws

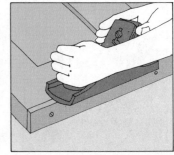

8 Plane along the edges of the batten to match the door thickness. Paint the bare wood (see p. 33)

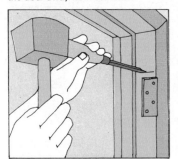

9 Chisel out the marked surplus for $\frac{1}{2}$ in. above the existing hinges on the door frame

10 Cut solid wood plugs to fit the old screw holes. Hammer them in and cut them flush with the surface

11 Support the door in its new position (see p. 53). Fit hinge screws and make sure the door swings easily

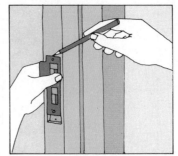

12 Remove the latch striker plate. Hold it $\frac{1}{2}$ in. above the old position and mark the frame

13 Make new recesses (see p. 53). Refit striker plate. Fill beneath hinges and striker plates with plastic wood

Fitting a new timber sill

Exposure to the weather and constant use may eventually cause the timber sill on an outside door to rot. When this occurs, remove the sill and cut a new one to fit.

Sills should always slope forwards slightly so that rainwater cannot run into the house. Make a groove, called a drip, on the underside to ensure that water cannot run underneath the sill on to the brickwork. The door frame should jut over the sill to give a weatherproof joint.

Materials: hardwood; linseed oil.
Tools: rule; planes; hammer; chisel; panel saw; pencil.

1 Buy a piece of hardwood slightly larger all round than the sill that is to be replaced

2 Cut timber to length and width. Cut a drip with a plough plane, ½ in. (13 mm) from one edge. Turn wood over

3 At each end, mark ½ in. down on drip edge. Draw curving slope at each end. Join slope marks on top

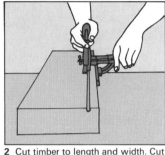

4 Join slope marks along front. Plane front and top of sill until slope lines are reached

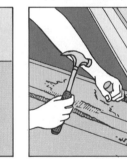

5 Prise out rotten sill from bottom of side frames with old chisel. If tenoned together, cut first with a panel saw

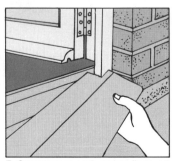

6 Hold the new sill against the door frame and mark where it is to fit round the frame posts

7 Cut recess at each end to fit round frame. Paint linseed oil on underside of sill and fit it

8 Hold a block of wood against sill and hammer it into position. Oil top and front of sill with two coats

Repairing wooden doors

A wooden door on a garage or out-building may rot or break at the bottom. Do not try to repair it by fixing a rail across the bottom. Although this may cover the damaged parts, it will also accelerate the rot by channelling water down the grooves between the boards.

Remove any outer rail, cut out the rotted sections and fit new pieces of wood.

Materials: tongued-and-grooved planks to match door; wirecut nails. Tools: hammer; chisel; tri-square; tenon saw; rule; marking gauge; rebate plane; plane; punch.

1 Mark the position of the bottom rail—at the back of the door—on the boards at the front

2 Saw carefully—with the tip of the saw—through the damaged boards between the marked lines of the rail

3 If the saw cannot cut completely through the boards, chisel along the saw line to remove damaged wood

4 Measure the height of the hole and mark tongued-and-grooved sections to fill width

5 Cut the number of marked boards to length and fit the tongues and grooves together   *(continued)*

Doors Garage

(continued)

6 If the width of the gap is smaller than the new panel, mark excess on grooved edge with a gauge

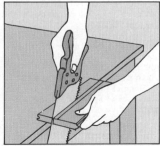

7 Mark another line ⅜ in. (10 mm) nearer groove. Hold wood firmly and saw down the second line

8 Cut a rebate with a rebate plane, from edge to gauge marking, and about half the thickness of board

9 Plane off the sharp corner of the rebate. Hold board against door and check the fit

10 Fit the cut board to the panel and position it in gap, with the rebate against the tongue of existing wood

11 Nail the boards to the rail behind with 1¼–1½ in. (30–40 mm) nails. Drive in with punch and fill holes

Maintaining up-and-over doors

Up-and-over garage doors may be made of aluminium, pressed steel or wood. They are operated by counter-balanced weights on pulleys or by a pair of springs.

In all cases regular lubricating of the moving parts is essential to ensure easy operation. Use a thin machine oil. Keep all metal channels free of dust or dirt which may cling to the oil and cause the mechanism to bind. Check and, if necessary, tighten the mounting bolts which secure the door to the metal framework and mechanism.

Aluminium doors should not be painted: wipe occasionally with a damp cloth. If the paint on a pressed-steel door is chipped, touch it in (see p. 33) as soon as possible to prevent rusting. Do not try to repair any part of the mechanism of an up-and-over door: consult the manufacturers.

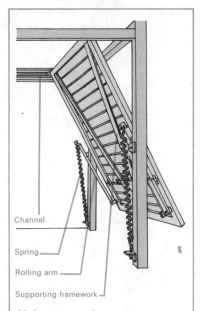

Channel

Spring

Rolling arm

Supporting framework

Maintenance Clean old oil from channels, cables and rolling arms with a cloth. Apply light machine oil. Do not oil the springs

Channels Wipe off oil. Apply new oil and open and close the door two or three times to spread the oil over the full length of the metal channels

Pulley wheels Wipe old oil from the wheels and the wire ropes. Apply new oil to each wheel and spindle from the inside. Open and close the door slowly

Lock and handle Oil the working parts of the lock and the locking-pin through the keyhole. Operate the key two or three times to spread the oil

Drainage

How a drainage system works

House drains are normally 4 in. (100 mm) internal-diameter pipes, made of saltglazed stoneware and laid in straight lines. At every point where the drain has to change direction, there is a manhole, with a channel in the bottom into which one or more drainpipes can discharge. All manholes have covers which give access for clearing blockages and to carry out annual maintenance.

Lavatory pans are connected to the drainpipes directly through soil pipes. Other fittings in the house and the rainwater downpipes (see p. 100) discharge into water-trapped gullies at the base of the wall outside the house.

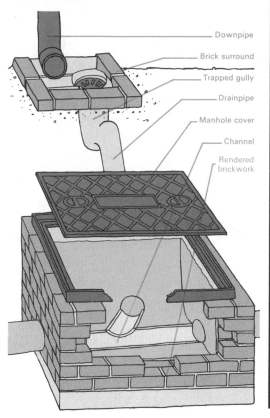

- Downpipe
- Brick surround
- Trapped gully
- Drainpipe
- Manhole cover
- Channel
- Rendered brickwork

Clearing a blocked drain

If the waste water in a lavatory pan, sink or basin runs away very slowly, or if a trapped gulley starts to overflow outside the house, it is likely that the drainpipes between the house and the sewer are blocked. Clear any blockages immediately.

Most houses have two or three manholes: the one nearest the house is at the highest level; the one nearest the boundary is lowest and has a fresh-air inlet pipe beside it.

To find a blockage, remove the cover of the manhole nearest the gulley or lavatory. If the manhole is clear, the blockage must be somewhere between the manhole and the house. If the manhole is full, remove the cover of the next one. If this is empty the blockage is in the pipe between them. If this is also full, check the third manhole.

Never use improvised tools: hire a set of drain rods from a builders' merchant or do-it-yourself shop. Always place a piece of board at the outlet end of a manhole to ensure that material causing the blockage cannot enter the next length of drainpipe.

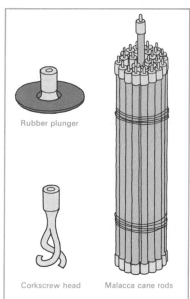

Rubber plunger

Corkscrew head   Malacca cane rods

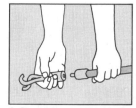

1 Fit a corkscrew head to the screw end of a drain rod

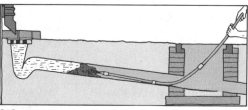

2 Screw on two lengths of rod. Push rods up drain. Keep turning clockwise to ensure that the rods stay connected

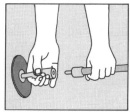

3 Pull back rods. Remove corkscrew, fit rubber plunger

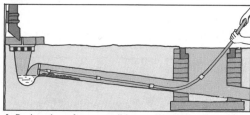

4 Push rods as far as possible up pipe. Withdraw them to remove loose material still in the pipe

5 Remove the rubbish from the channel in the manhole with a scoop or trowel

6 Push the rods and rubber plunger through any other drainpipes which enter the manhole

7 Hose down gulley or flush lavatory until clean water flows into the manhole

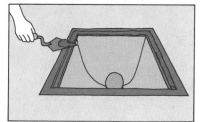

8 Clean grease from manhole rim. Apply fresh grease (see p. 62) and refit the cover

Drainage

Fitting a new manhole frame and cover

If a path or driveway is resurfaced, the manhole cover and frame should be raised at the same time. If either is rusty or cracked, measure length and width of existing cover and note any identifying number on it. Buy a matching replacement.

If a manhole is shared with neighbouring property, consult the owner so that the work can be done when lavatories and sinks are not in use.

Materials: plastic sheeting; sand and cement; cold tarmac; thick grease; 1 in. (25 mm) softwood.
Tools: straight-edge; bolster; chisel; hammer; hose; broom; trowel.

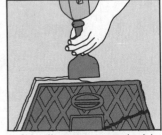

1 Chip off any tarmac covering joint between cover and frame. Chip off tarmac and concrete on top of outer edge of frame

2 Clean dirt from finger recesses and lift off manhole cover. Line manhole with plastic sheeting to catch debris. Lever off old frame

3 Chisel frame bed smooth. Brush off loose material and wet the old mortar. Lay 3:1 sand-and-cement mix around the edge

4 Position frame with straight-edge across it. Tap down until straight-edge is flush with tarmac; wedge up if necessary with brick pieces

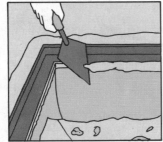

5 When frame is level, place mortar around outside to within about $\frac{1}{2}$ in. (13 mm) of the upper edge. Fill between frame and bed with mortar

6 Sweep around manhole. Remove plastic sheeting and hose inside: take care not to disturb new mortar. Grease rim and lid and fit the lid

7 After 24 hours, fill between the existing path surface and upper edge of frame with a proprietary cold tarmac (see p. 497)

8 Use a piece of softwood, about 1 in. (25 mm) thick and with a club hammer tamp down the cold tarmac. Do not strike the frame or lid

Repairing a gully channel and surround

A gully may have a brick surround, rendered on the inside, with a channel at the bottom.

If the pipe which forms the channel is damaged, or if the rendering is badly cracked, moisture can cause damp patches to appear inside the house.

The channel pipe is usually glazed earthenware. Buy a straight half-section 24 in. (610 mm) long and cut it to length.

Materials: cardboard; cement and sand; earthenware half-pipe; bricks.
Tools: rule; pencil; cold chisel; club hammer; pincers; trowel; pointing trowel.

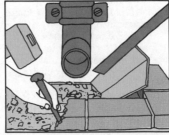

1 Cover the gully outlet with a piece of cardboard. Hack off any cracked rendering and cut out the old channel and any loose bricks

2 Measure and mark length of the new channel. Place half-pipe upside-down on sand and tap along marked line with cold chisel. Trim with pincers

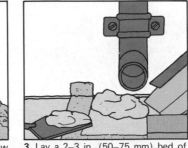

3 Lay a 2–3 in. (50–75 mm) bed of 4:1 sand-and-cement mortar (see p. 693) for the channel and slope it slightly down towards the outlet

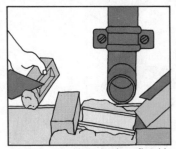

4 Lay the new bricks in place, flat side up. Slope the mortar up from each edge of the channel towards the top of the placed bricks

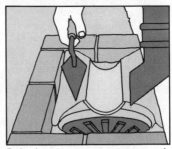

5 As the mortar starts to set, smooth the surface with a pointing trowel and a little water. Point the brickwork (see p. 18) with a flush joint

Draught-proofing

Tracing and stopping draughts

Most draughts penetrate through gaps around windows and doors. Check first that the frames and the putty round the windows are sound.

If there are gaps between the frame and the door or window, buy proprietary metal or plastic sealing strips from a do-it-yourself shop. Several types of seals are designed for particular kinds of doors or windows. Make sure that the type bought is suitable.

Do not try to draught-proof the base of an exterior door which hangs over a concrete sill. Seek professional help.

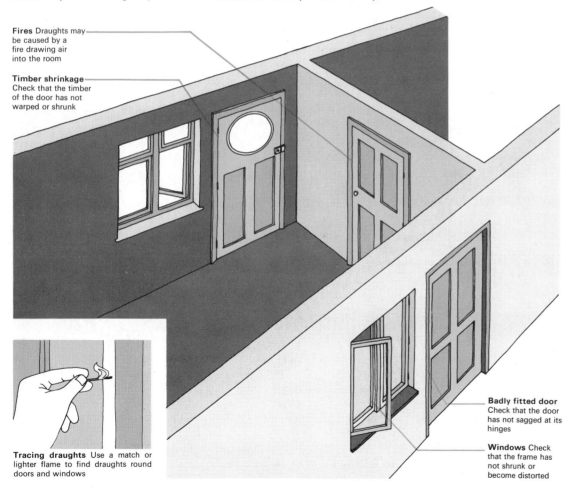

Fires Draughts may be caused by a fire drawing air into the room

Timber shrinkage Check that the timber of the door has not warped or shrunk

Tracing draughts Use a match or lighter flame to find draughts round doors and windows

Badly fitted door Check that the door has not sagged at its hinges

Windows Check that the frame has not shrunk or become distorted

---

DOOR FAULTS

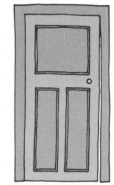

Loose hinges The top hinge may be worn, or its holding screws may have worked loose. If the hinge is worn, fit a new one. If only the screws are loose, remove them, fill the holes with a wood or fibre plug and refit them

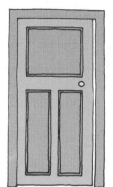

Hinge-bound The door may fit too closely against the hinge jamb, creating a gap at the other edge. Undo the top hinge. Fit a piece of card between it and the frame. Refit the hinge. Do the same at the bottom hinge

Distorted door Mark top and bottom of door parallel to the frame and floor. Remove the door (see p. 58), plane it to marked lines. On top, fit a strip of wood to leave a gap of only $\frac{1}{16}$ in. (2 mm) at top and bottom

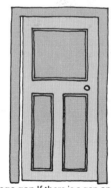

Hinge gap If there is a gap on the hinge side of the door, it may rub against the other side of the frame. Either the hinges are not recessed to fit flush with the door and frame, or the screws have not been driven fully home

Draught-proofing Doors

Fitting a V-shaped seal

Doors can be sealed against draughts with a V-shaped sprung-metal strip obtainable from do-it-yourself shops. Some types should be nailed to the frame, others require adhesive.

Before fitting the seal, check that there is a gap of at least $\frac{1}{16}$ in. (2 mm) between the top and sides of the door and the frame. If not, remove the door and rehang it on its hinges (see p. 53).

Fit a plastic strip to the bottom of the door (see p. 67).

Materials: V strip; nails or adhesive. Tools: tape measure; scissors or wire cutters; push-pin or punch; bradawl and hammer.

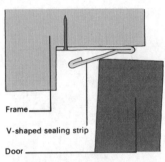

Frame

V-shaped sealing strip

Door

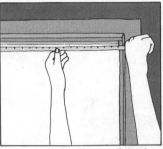

1 Measure inside the top of the door frame. Cut a length of V strip slightly longer than the frame width

2 Hold the strip in position. Trim it so that its ends just touch the frame on both sides

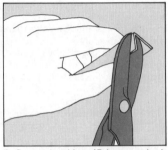

3 Cut narrow side to 45 degrees at both ends. Hold wide side on frame, with closed V edge facing the door

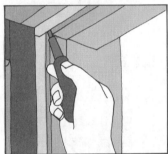

4 Load nail into push-pin. Push the nail through the wide side of the strip, $\frac{1}{2}$ in. (13 mm) from each end

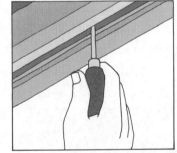

5 Fix nails through the wide side of the strip, every 4 in. (100 mm) along the width of the doorway

6 If no push-pin is available, make holes with a bradawl, and hammer in nails with a punch

7 Cut strips to fit the sides of the frame. If necessary, angle their narrow sides slightly to fit at the corners

8 Nail through the wide side, $\frac{1}{2}$ in. (13 mm) from the top corner and every 4 in. (100 mm) down the sides

9 Carefully measure the position of any protruding lock or hinge on the frame and cut just above it

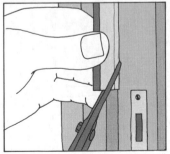

10 Cut at an angle through both sides of the strip and make a pointed end above the obstruction

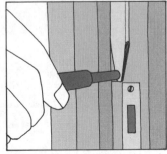

11 At the pointed ends, push a pin through the double thickness of the V strip to ensure that it cannot split

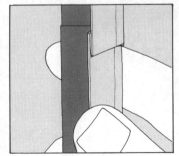

12 If a strip is too short, cut a new piece to fill the gap and overlap about $\frac{1}{4}$ in. (6 mm)

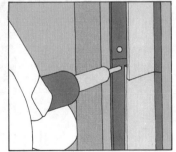

13 Fit the new piece inside the first strip and push a nail through the two wider sides of the strips

Fitting a sprung felt seal

If there is a gap of less than $\frac{3}{4}$ in. (20 mm) below an interior door, fit a felt seal with a spring mechanism.

The seal has a push rod which protrudes at one side. It must be fitted so that when the door closes, the rod is pressed against the jamb on the hinge side. When that happens the mechanism drops the felt to the floor. The felt rises when the door is opened.

The push-rod spring mechanism can be reversed inside the seal to suit the door. Undo fixing screws along metal strip. Remove spring mechanism, reverse it and refit the screws.

Materials: spring seal; glass-paper.
Tools: hacksaw; scissors or wire cutters; screwdriver; tape measure; pencil.

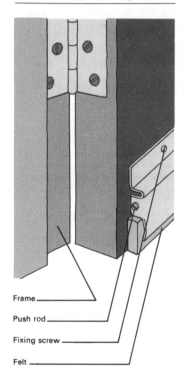

Frame
Push rod
Fixing screw
Felt

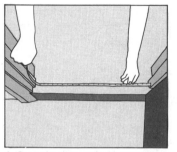

1 Open the door and measure across. Check that the push rod can be fitted at the hinge side. Reverse it if necessary

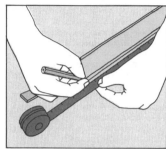

2 Mark the measurement, less $\frac{1}{4}$ in. (6 mm), on the metal felt holder. Measure from the push-rod end

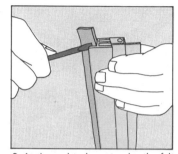

3 At the end to be cut, prise the felt holder back with a screwdriver. Pull out about 6 in. (150 mm) of felt

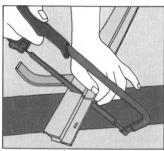

4 Hold the strip firmly on a block of wood. Cut to the required length with a fine hacksaw. Glass-paper the end

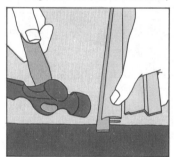

5 Push the felt back into the holder to project by $\frac{1}{2}$ in. (13 mm). Tap the holder corners to secure the felt

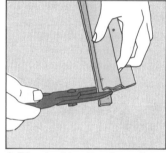

6 Trim the felt with wire cutters or strong scissors to leave only $\frac{1}{4}$ in. (6 mm) at both ends of the holder

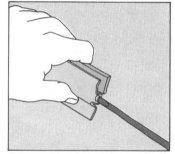

7 Loosen the screw at the end of the push rod until the rod can be moved in and out freely

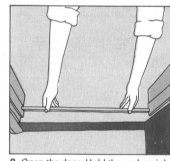

8 Open the door. Hold the seal upright in position across the frame. Check that the length is correct

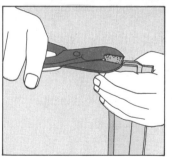

9 If the seal is too tight, trim the felt projecting at each end. Do not remove it entirely

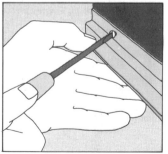

10 Close the door and hold the strip on it. Make sure that the felt is in contact with the floor. Fix with screws

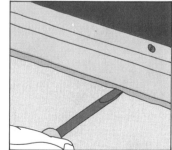

11 To check that the felt rests on the floor surface, try to press the screwdriver between the felt and floor

12 If the felt is too loose or tight, open the door and adjust the screw at the end of the push rod

Draught-proofing Doors and windows

Fitting a buffer strip

When the gap above or at the side of a door is more than ¾ in. (20 mm), fit a proprietary aluminium strip which incorporates a plastic sealing tube. Because the strip is fixed on the outside frame around the door, it is more unsightly than other draught excluders. It is recommended mainly for exterior back doors.

Fit the strip on the outside surface of the closed door. Make sure that the fixing screws are near the end of the slots in the strip.

Materials: buffer strip and screws.
Tools: tape measure; hacksaw; bradawl; screwdriver.

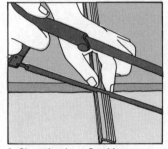

1 Close the door. Outside, measure across the top. With a hacksaw, cut a strip to the same measurement

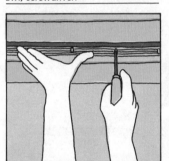

2 Push the strip against the underside of the frame and the door. Make holes for screws with a bradawl

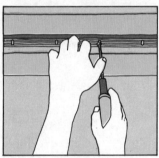

3 Insert the screws in the slots. Position the strip and drive the screws home with the screwdriver

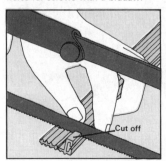

4 Remove the plastic from the side sections. Cut projecting part on side sections to fit profile on top section

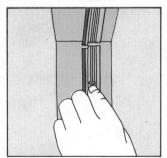

5 Fit plastic and slide side pieces into position against the top strip. Make holes and fix the screws

Fitting a plastic strip

Plastic strips are less expensive and easier to fasten than metal draught excluders and can be bought from most hardware stores. Plastic strips are more likely to discolour and perish and should be replaced every year.

Self-adhesive plastic strips which incorporate a ribbon of felt are suitable for sealing gaps at the bottom of internal doors. A foam-backed plastic—also self-adhesive—is suitable for draughtproofing the edges of doors and window frames.

Other types—which are fixed with screws—should be used for exterior doors and windows.

Materials: plastic strip.
Tools: scissors; clean rag; felt pen or wax crayon.

TYPES OF STRIPS

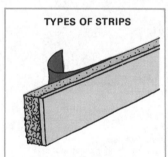

Foam-backed To fit foam-backed plastic strips, pull off the backing and stick the foam to the door or window

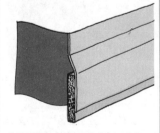

Felt ribbon Plastic strips incorporating a felt ribbon are suitable for interior doors

---

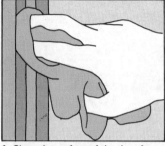

1 Clean the surface of the door frame thoroughly with a damp cloth to remove all grease, dirt and dust. Leave to dry

2 Peel back about 12 in. (305 mm) of the backing paper and press the sticky side of the foam on to the surface

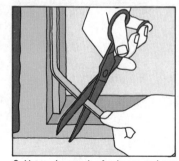

3 Use a sharp pair of scissors and cut the strip to the required length. Leave backing paper on the unused foam

FELT RIBBON

1 Clean the surface of the door. Mark the width on the seal strip with a wax crayon or felt pen

2 Cut off the surplus length of seal with a pair of sharp scissors and peel off the brown-paper backing

3 Press the adhesive side on the door so that the bottom of the felt fits snugly against the floor

Sealing a metal frame

Metal windows can be sealed with a proprietary system of pre-formed aluminium strips which snap over the outside frame. Corner clips are provided to secure the strip.

The strip is available in packs to fit 3 ft and 4 ft (915 mm and 1·2 m) windows. Make sure that the frame is free of rust before fitting the strips. Clean the surface with a wire brush and fill any bad pit holes.

To accommodate casement stays or window handles, cut a rectangular section from the flange side.

Materials: aluminium strips.
Tools: scissors or wire cutters.

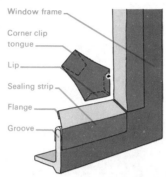

Window frame
Corner clip
tongue
Lip
Sealing strip
Flange
Groove

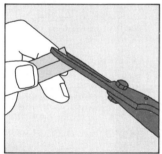

1 Measure and cut strips to fit the frame sides. Trim both ends of each strip from the middle to 45 degrees

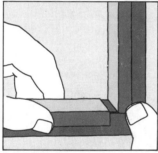

2 Push the groove of the strip over the outside frame. Fit the top piece first, then the bottom and the sides

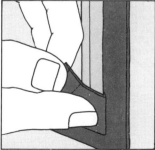

3 Push the corner clip tongues over the junctions of the sealing strips in the corners

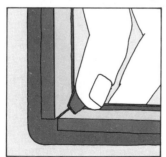

4 Turn the tongue of the corner clip over the flange. Press it down firmly to secure it in place

Fitting a seal to a wooden frame

The neatest and most lasting way to draughtproof a hinged wooden window frame is to use a V-shaped metal strip similar to that used for doors (see p. 64). Fit the wide side to the window frame. If the window opens inwards, the closed edge of the V should face inwards. This means that on pivoting windows, each length must be fitted to match the opening direction of the side at which it is fixed

Materials: sealing strip; nails (alternatively, use impact adhesive).
Tools: tape measure; scissors or wire cutters; push-pin or punch; bradawl and hammer.

1 Measure between the rebates at the top, the bottom and the sides of the window frame

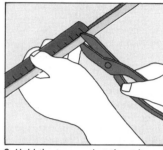

2 Hold the tape against the strip and cut to the measured lengths with scissors or wire cutters

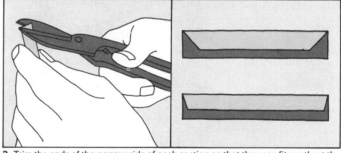

3 Trim the ends of the narrow side of each section so that they can fit neatly at the corners of the window. Cut angles of 45 degrees for the top and sill sections (top, right) 15–20 degrees for the side lengths (bottom, right)

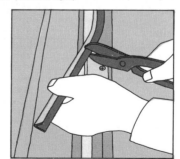

4 Fit the top and bottom lengths first. Insert nails ½ in. (13 mm) from each corner and then 4 in. (100 mm) apart

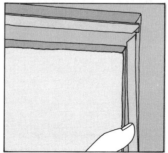

5 Slide the side lengths neatly into the top and bottom corners. Push in nails every 4 in. (100 mm)

6 If there is a hinge or catch, mark the strip just above and below it and cut squarely across the width

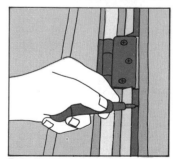

7 Fix the strip with a nail ½ in. (13 mm) from the end. Fix other nails 4 in. (100 mm) apart

Fireplaces Surrounds

Maintenance and cleaning

Fireplace surrounds may be of brick, stone, tile, metal or wood. Make sure that the correct cleaning materials are used. Never, for example, use soapy water on brick or stone. Never use a stiff wire brush on a stone, brick or polished-metal fireplace as it will scratch the surface.

Brick and tile

If a brick or tile surround is very badly stained, mix a solution of 1 part spirits of salt (hydrochloric acid) to 15 parts water. Use a soft hairbrush to apply the mixture to the dirty area. Leave the solution to soak into the stains for 20 minutes, then wash it off with clean cold water. Spirits of salt is a dangerous acid. Do not let it spill on the skin or clothes. Store safely away from children.

Stone and marble

Do not use acid on a stone surround. Mix a strong solution of water and detergent and apply it to dirty stonework with a stiff bristle brush. Use warm water to wash it off.

Detergent and warm water can also be used on marble, but apply them with a soft-haired brush. Never use stiff bristles on marble—they can scratch the polished surface.

Timber and steel

Clean timber surrounds with a soft brush and warm, soapy water. Use a good-quality furniture polish and a soft cloth to pick out the natural grain and highlights of the wood.

Many fireplaces have a stainless-steel trim round the fire opening. Clean regularly with detergent or warm soapy water. Dry and polish with a soft cloth and metal polish. Do not use any sharp tool or wire brush on steel. If dirt is difficult to remove, use a proprietary cleaning pad—for example, Duraglit.

Fire back

The fire back is made of fireproof clay. If it cracks or crumbles (see p. 76), clean the area with a stiff wire brush. Mix enough fireclay to make the repair and press it into the holes and cracks with a small trowel. Leave the clay to harden for at least 24 hours before relighting the fire.

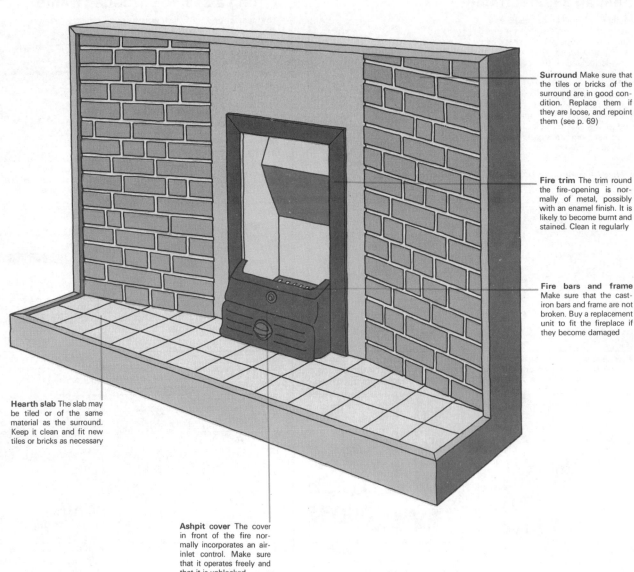

Surround Make sure that the tiles or bricks of the surround are in good condition. Replace them if they are loose, and repoint them (see p. 69)

Fire trim The trim round the fire-opening is normally of metal, possibly with an enamel finish. It is likely to become burnt and stained. Clean it regularly

Fire bars and frame Make sure that the cast-iron bars and frame are not broken. Buy a replacement unit to fit the fireplace if they become damaged

Hearth slab The slab may be tiled or of the same material as the surround. Keep it clean and fit new tiles or bricks as necessary

Ashpit cover The cover in front of the fire normally incorporates an air-inlet control. Make sure that it operates freely and that it is unblocked

Repointing a brickwork fireplace

Fumes from a coal fire can cause the mortar, called pointing, in the joints of a brick fireplace to deteriorate. Damaged areas can be filled with fresh mortar, but to improve the appearance of the fireplace, it is better to repoint all the brickwork. Prepare a mortar mixture with 1 part Portland or sulphate-resistant cement, 3 parts lime and 10–12 parts clean silver sand, which is heat resistant.

The mortar can be applied flush with the brick or be recessed.

Materials: lime mortar, with colouring agent if necessary; sacking.
Tools: pointing trowel; builder's hawk; file card (steel bristle brush with a webbing backing); hand brush or broom head; file; bucket.

MAKING A HAWK

Mix and carry the mortar on a hawk, which can be made from ½ in. (13 mm) softwood. Cut a piece 9 in. (230 mm) square. Cut a short length of broom handle and fix it with a 1½ in. (40 mm) screw through the base of the hawk

1 Scrape the old mortar out of the joints with the tang end of a file to a depth of about ½ in. (13 mm)

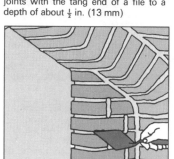

4 Press the mortar firmly into the vertical joints first, then into the horizontal joints above and below them

7 Do the same along the horizontal joints. Use a sliding stroke so that the mortar is pressed into a V shape

2 Brush dust and loose particles from the joints. Use a hand brush or broom head to soak the brickwork with water

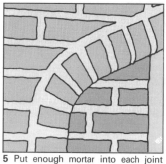

5 Put enough mortar into each joint to stand flush with the surface of the adjacent brickwork

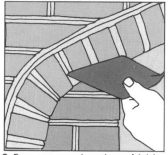

8 Face any curved sections of brickwork—for example, the edging of the fireplace—in the same way

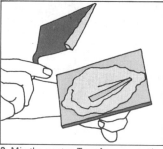

3 Mix the mortar. Transfer some to the hawk. Pick up the mortar from the hawk on the back of the trowel

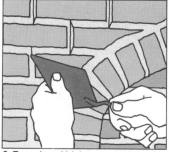

6 To make a V joint, steady the point of the trowel with one hand and draw it down the sides of the vertical joints

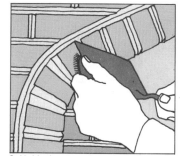

9 Hold the trowel against the soft mortar and clean the edges of the bricks with a piece of file card

JOINT VARIATIONS

1 For a recessed joint, scrape away ¼ in. (6 mm) of the new mortar with a trowel or metal hook

2 Gently draw a piece of wood, the width of the joint, along the recess until it is smooth

Flush joint When the mortar is semi-stiff, draw damp sacking across flush with the brickwork

Fireplaces Surrounds

Replacing a loose brick

If a brick in a brickwork fireplace becomes loose, clean the mortar from the surface of the brick and from the faces of the bricks which adjoin the loose one in the surround.

To refit the brick, use a 3:1 mixture of sand and quick-drying cement. Ordinary cement can be used, but it takes longer to set. Repoint the brickwork (see p. 69).

Materials: quick-drying cement; sand; lime mortar (see p. 69).
Tools: trowel; soft brush, or broom head; file card; length of wood, approximately 2 × 24 in. (50 × 610 mm); pointing trowel; bolster.

1 Clean away old mortar from the sides of the loose brick and faces of the adjoining bricks

2 Thoroughly wet the brick. Apply a ½ in. (13 mm) layer of cement mix to the back and sides of the brick

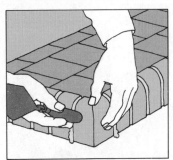

3 Position the brick. Tap it carefully and gently into place with the end of the trowel handle

4 If necessary, use a straight piece of wood to line the brick up with the existing brickwork in the fireplace

5 Use the tip of the trowel to clean out the mortar between the bricks to a depth of about ¼ in. (6 mm)

6 When the cement is set, point the joints between the bricks (see p. 69). Press the mortar in firmly

7 Use a file card (see p. 69) to clean the edges of the joints when they are set. Do not scratch the brick surface

8 To achieve a clean finish, brush lightly round the joint with a water-dampened soft brush or broom head

Fitting new tiles

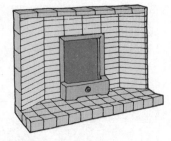

Matching ceramic and mosaic tiles are usually obtainable from a builders' merchant, gas or coal showroom, or direct from the manufacturer of the existing tiles.

But it may be difficult to obtain tiles to match those in a fireplace more than ten years old, and in such an instance the only source of supply could be the manufacturer, who may still have some discontinued designs left in stock.

The backing behind the tiles of most fireplaces is concrete faced with mortar. This usually leaves a clean gap once the damaged tile has been chipped away—which means that replacement tiles can be stuck in place with a thin adhesive.

If, however, the mortar below is pitted with holes when the tile is removed, use a thicker adhesive.

Fill the small gaps between the tiles with a fine wet mortar made from a mixture of 1 part grouting cement to 3 parts silver sand.

Tiles in front of the fire often craze badly because of heat. Replace them with heat-resistant tiles. When they are dry there may be a white smear on their surface; clean them with pure linseed oil. This also brings out the colour and texture of the tiles.

Materials: matching tiles; grouting-cement mixture; thin or thick tile adhesive.
Tools: small, sharp cold chisel; hammer; adhesive applicator or paintbrush; round-ended stick.

1 Use a cold steel chisel, and hammer, to chip out the damaged tile. Start at the centre and work outwards

4 Fit a new tile in the space. Make sure it lies flat and flush with the existing tiles

7 Place the tile carefully and squarely into the space. Press all round firmly with the fingers

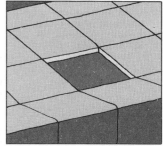

2 Gradually enlarge the hole. Take care not to damage the edges of the adjoining tiles

3 Lift out the pieces. Make sure that the edges of adjoining tiles are clean and that the base is clean and even

5 Lift out the tile and spread adhesive on its back with a paintbrush or applicator supplied with the adhesive

6 Apply adhesive to the backing. Do not spread it on the sides of the adjacent tiles

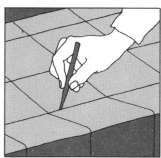

8 If any adhesive is squeezed out between the tiles, remove it with a damp cloth

9 Use grouting mixture between the tiles (see p. 196). Give a neat finish with a round-ended stick

Replacing a loose piece of marble or stone

If a stone or a piece of marble becomes loose in a fireplace, clean and refit it. Remove any loose cement from the recess that the stone has to fit and refit the stone with 3:1 mix of sand and quick-drying cement.

Replace marble blocks with a mixture of neat grouting cement. Repoint the surround (see p. 18). If the existing pointing is coloured, use a matching cement coloriser—available from builders' merchants—in the mortar mix.

Materials: mortar; grouting cement; pointing mixture (see p. 693); strips of wood ¼ in. (6 mm) thick to match the width of the joint.
Tools: trowel; hammer; chisel; paintbrush; straight-edge; spirit level; soft brush, or broom head; bucket; sponge.

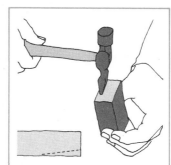

Trimming If a piece of marble or stone needs to be trimmed to fit a gap, break off the excess with the pointed back of a cross-pein hammer, or with a hammer and chisel

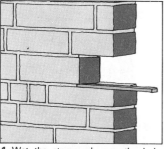
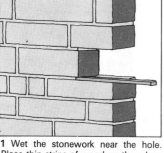

1 Wet the stonework near the hole. Place thin strips of wood on the edges of the stone below the gap

3 Press the stone firmly into position. Place wood strips above it, flush with the existing stonework

5 Mix the pointing mortar. Squeeze water on to the mixture with a sponge, to avoid over-wetting it

2 Wet the loose stone thoroughly and apply a generous amount of mortar to its back and sides

4 Use a straight-edge or a spirit level to make sure that the replaced stone is flush with the original stonework

6 Allow the mortar to set. Remove the wood strips. Prepare the pointing and apply it with a trowel   *(continued)*

Fireplaces Surrounds

(continued)

7 When the cement is set, point joints between the stones (see p. 18). Press in the mortar firmly

8 When pointing is almost dry, clean the stone surrounding it with a soft brush or broom head

9 Wipe the stones with a sponge soaked in water to remove any mortar stains from the surface

Refitting a broken piece of marble

If a piece of marble breaks, stick it back in position with an epoxy-resin adhesive (see p. 694). Clean the meeting surfaces of the broken piece and the fireplace. To provide a good key for adhesive, roughen the surfaces with glass-paper.

Epoxy resins are two-part adhesives. Always follow the manufacturer's instructions for the best results. When the two parts have been mixed they must be used within four hours.

Wipe off surplus resin as soon as the repair has been made. Make sure that the broken part is held in place until the resin has set.

Materials: adhesive; adhesive tape; glass-paper.
Tools: knife; stiff brush; paintbrush.

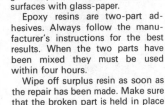

1 Clean the fireplace and broken piece with a stiff brush. Rub the meeting surfaces with glass-paper

2 Mix the two parts of the adhesive on an old tin lid, following the manufacturer's instructions

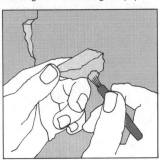

3 Use an old paintbrush to spread an even film of the mixture on both marble surfaces

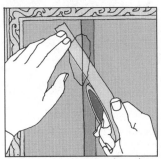

4 Press the broken piece into place. Remove surplus adhesive with a knife. Secure temporarily with tape

Filling chips in marble

Light surface scratches on marble can be removed with a piece of carborundum stone, called a slip. Chips or deep scratches should first be filled with epoxy-resin adhesive. If the fireplace is coloured, buy a matching vegetable dye from a builders' merchant.

Use a coarse slip to cut the surface to shape and a fine stone to polish the finished repair.

Materials: epoxy-resin adhesive; powdered vegetable dye, to match colour required.
Tools: spatula; carborundum slips; sponge.

1 Mix adhesive on a flat surface. Add vegetable dye gradually to produce a matching colour

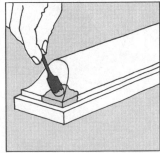

2 Use a spatula to fill the chip with the adhesive. Do not distort the contours of the marble

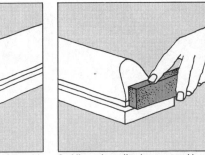

3 Allow the adhesive to set. Use a coarse carborundum slip to rub the adhesive down to shape

4 Wash marble with a sponge and clean water. Make sure all dust from the adhesive is removed

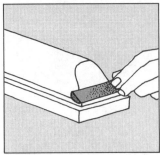

5 Polish the repaired area with fine carborundum. Check frequently that the contour is correct

Repairing timber with beeswax

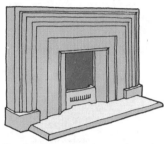

Repair a chipped or damaged wooden surround with melted beeswax, obtainable from hardware stores. Take care when melting the wax, for it gives off an inflammable, explosive gas.

It is usually necessary to colour the wax to match the wood. Use a powdered vegetable dye, and mix it after melting the wax in a tin on a gas or electric ring, or with a blowlamp. Do not let the flame touch the wax.

Beeswax can also be used to fill small holes. Polish or varnish the repair to match the existing finish.

Materials: beeswax; vegetable dye; polish or varnish.
Tools: flour-grade glass-paper; adhesive tape; tin; old spoon or fork; chisel; blowlamp or gas or electric ring.

1 Break beeswax into small pieces. Put them in a tin and melt with a blowlamp or on a cooker ring

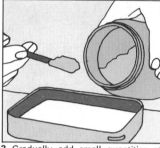

2 Gradually add small quantities of vegetable dye to the molten wax. Do not overcolour the wax

3 Mix the dye thoroughly each time it is added to the wax. Check the shade frequently

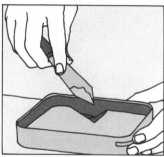

4 Leave the wax to set. When it is hard, prise it out of the tin in pieces with a putty knife

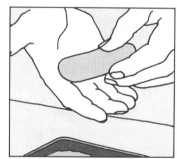

5 Roll the wax between both hands to make a long sausage shape. Check that the colour matches the wood

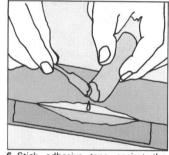

6 Stick adhesive tape against the damaged section. Warm the handle of a spoon and press it against the wax

7 Overfill the damaged area with wax, to allow for shrinkage when it cools. Support the tape if it bulges

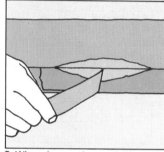

8 When the wax has cooled and set, peel off the tape. Take care not to dislodge the filling

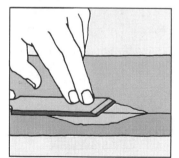

9 Hold a wide chisel flat against the surface. Shave the wax filling to a smooth and even finish

10 Rub flour-grade glass-paper gently over the edges of the wax until it blends into the woodwork

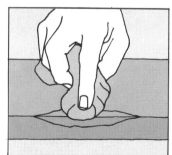

11 Wipe the repaired area with polish to match the timber. This also seals the wax filling

FILLING HOLES

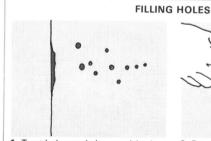

1 Treat holes made by wood-boring insects (see p. 186) with a proprietary fluid, such as Rentokil

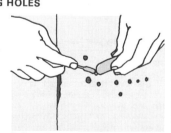

2 Press beeswax into the holes with an applicator or warm spoon handle. Smooth and polish

Fireplaces Slow-combustion stoves

Replacing buckled or cracked fire bars and grating

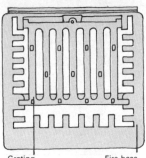

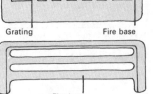

Grating   Fire base

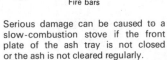

Fire bars

Serious damage can be caused to a slow-combustion stove if the front plate of the ash tray is not closed or the ash is not cleared regularly.

If the fuel burns white-hot, it can buckle the cast-iron fire grating and base and may crack the fire bricks. When dismantling the unit, make a note of how the parts fit together: in some stoves assembly can be complicated.

Materials: fire bars (base and grating); fire bricks if required.

1 Lay a sheet of hardboard on the hearth to avoid damaging the tiles. Remove the ash-tray plate

5 Take out the side fire bricks. If they are damaged, note their number or keep them to match new ones

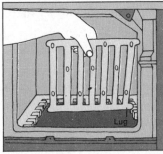

9 Fit the lugs of the new grating into the base at the back and pivot it down into position

2 Disengage the front fire bars. If they are damaged, see if there is an identification number on them

6 Lift out the fire base and take a note of its identification number. Buy the necessary new parts

10 Replace the two side bricks, or fit new ones if the old ones were cracked or damaged

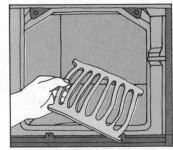

3 Lift out the grating. If it has no number, take it to a builders' merchant and get an identical one

Shaker lever

7 Clean out any ashes and dirt from the base of the stove and make sure that the shaker lever works freely

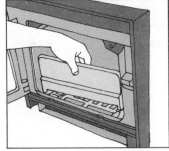

11 Slot the front fire brick back into place behind the bottom of the stove doorway

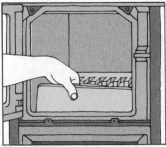

4 Lift the front fire brick from its slots at the bottom of the stove door. Lay it aside carefully

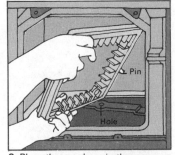

Pin

Hole

8 Place the new base in the stove, so that its pin at the back fits into the shaker hole

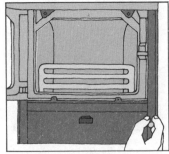

12 Refit the fire bars. Check that the shaker mechanism works correctly and refit the ash-tray plate

Fitting a glass panel

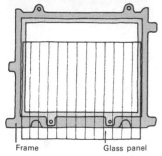

Frame   Glass panel

If the glass in the door of a stove breaks, air can get into the stove and it will not operate efficiently.

A new replacement glass panel, toughened to withstand heat, can be bought from a builders' merchant or from the manufacturer. Give the name and model number of the stove.

Rust around the screws holding the door may make them difficult to move; apply penetrating oil and turn the screws a little *tighter* to break the rust seal. Note that only replacement glass panels are sold: if the panel is mica, buy a complete new door.

Materials: glass panel, with asbestos rope.
Tools: screwdriver; spanner; blunt chisel; brush.

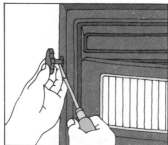

1 Remove the knob which controls the flow of air into the stove. If it is stiff, prise it off with a screwdriver

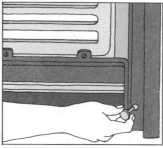

2 At the bottom of the stove unscrew the grate-shaker spindle as far as possible. Pull it out

3 Open the fire door and undo the four screws which secure the front casing to the stove

4 Lift out the ash-tray front and gently work the front casing backwards and forwards to ease it away from the stove

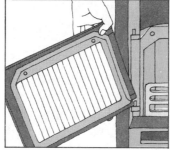

5 Lift the fire door off its hinges and lay it carefully face down on a sheet of hardboard

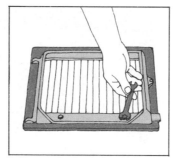

6 Unscrew the four bolts which secure the glass panel in its frame in the fire door. Keep them carefully

7 Lift off the frame, turn it over, and remove the asbestos rope from the groove. Brush out any dirt

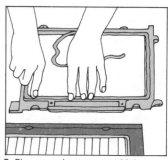

8 Fit new asbestos rope. Make sure that the join comes in the centre of one of the sides, not at a corner

9 Fit the new glass panel, which is supplied pre-taped to keep the strips intact. Do not remove tapes

10 Remove the old glass from the door front. Scrape out asbestos particles from the edges with a blunt chisel

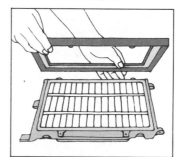

11 Brush the edges clean and fit the door front, enamel side upwards, over the frame containing the new glass

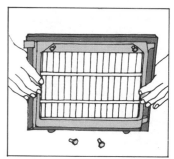

12 Hold the door front and frame together. Turn them over and refit the four securing bolts   *(continued)*

Fireplaces

(continued)

13 Tighten each bolt a little at a time. Do not overtighten: too much pressure can break the panel

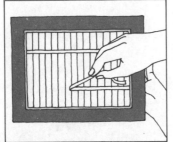

14 Pull the tape away from the new glass panel. If the panel is fitted correctly, it should move slightly

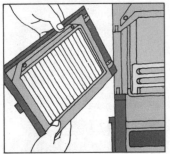

15 Lift the fire door with its new glass panel and position it on the hinge-pins of the stove

16 Refit the stove casing. Make sure that the air-control and grate-shaker spindle are properly located

17 Fit the four screws to hold the front casing to the stove, and refit the grate-shaker knob

18 Press the air-control knob firmly back into place and then refit the ash-tray front

Fireplaces Firebacks

Filling cracks in a fireback

If a fireback is cracked, smoke and heat can penetrate behind the fireplace and eventually weaken the structure of the chimney.

If the cracks are bad, fit a new fireback (see p. 77). If they are very small it may be possible to fill them with plastic fire clay, obtainable from builders' merchants. The fireback must be soaked with water to prevent it absorbing water from the filler, which would result in poor adhesion.

Materials: plastic fire clay.
Tools: pointing trowel or putty knife; wire brush; old paintbrush (to apply water).

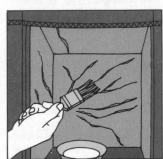

1 Brush soot and loose dirt from the fireback with a stiff brush. Look for cracks

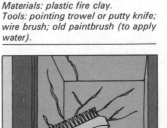

2 Rake out the cracks in the fireback with the point of a trowel or any other sharp-pointed tool

3 Clean out any loose particles from the cracks with a wire brush. Brush each side of the cracks

4 Soak the cracks thoroughly with water and an old paintbrush. Work the water well into the cracks

5 Fill the cracks with the plastic fire clay before the water dries. Use an old trowel or putty knife

6 Make sure that the fire clay is pressed as firmly as possible into the cracks. Work it in with a trowel

7 Dip a finger in water and scrape off any excess clay. Smooth the surface with a wet finger

Fitting a new fireback

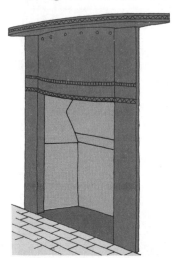

A fireback in a new house is fitted as a single unit because it goes into position before the fireplace surround is installed. If it later becomes badly damaged, however, the replacement must usually be split into two, so that it can be fitted and cemented correctly into the opening.

The cement, which fills the space behind the fireback, helps to support the fireback and prevent cracking. Use a weak mixture—1:1:9 of lime, cement and sand. Render the top of the fireback with a 1:4 mixture of cement and sand.

When a new fireback has to be fitted, take the opportunity to refix any loose tiles and to renew any broken ones in the hearth or on the fireplace surround (see p. 70).

Materials: fireback of same dimensions as existing (measure height, width and depth); lime, cement and sharp sand (see p. 693); fire cement; new tiles if required.
Tools: club hammer; cold chisel; bolster; cleaning brush; paintbrush; cementing trowel; pointing trowel.

1 Carefully break away the existing fireback with a club hammer and cold chisel. Remove all the broken pieces

2 Trim the edges near the hearth tiles. Lay aside any tiles which have been disturbed and any loose ones

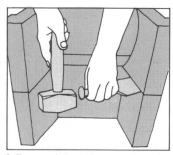

3 Tap carefully with a bolster along both sides of the joint in the new fireback. Separate the parts

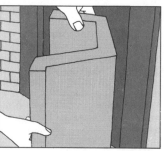

4 Fit the lower half into the fire. Make sure that it stands squarely and centrally in the opening

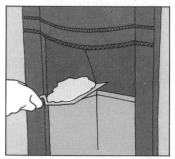

5 Pack a weak mixture of lime, cement and sand (see p. 693) into the space behind the fireback

6 Push the mixture well down with a trowel until the space behind the fireback is completely filled

7 Fit the top section of the fireback into the opening. Seat it squarely on the bottom half

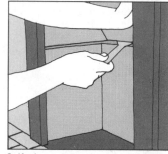

8 If the top section does not fit squarely at the first few attempts, lever it into place with a bolster

9 Pack the same weak mixture of lime, cement and sand into the space behind the top section of the fireback

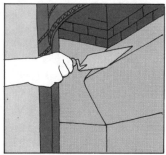

10 When the cavity is filled to the top, slope a layer of rendering cement to meet the brickwork of the chimney

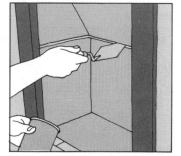

11 Wet the joint between the top and bottom sections. Fill with fire cement and smooth with a trowel

12 Remove and clean any loose hearth tiles and refix with a 1:4 cement-and-sand mixture (see p. 693)

Floors

How floors are constructed

The ground floor of a house is either suspended or solid. On houses built before 1939, the floor is almost certainly suspended—with floorboards laid on timber joists supported by open brickwork, called a sleeper wall. These walls, which rest on a concrete slab in the ground, have alternate bricks missing to allow air to circulate freely and prevent the build-up of dampness under the floor.

Solid floors—more usual in houses built after 1939—rest directly on the ground. They consist of a layer of hardcore covered with concrete, a damp-proof membrane and another layer of concrete, called screed. The floor covering—tiles or floorboards, for example—is laid on the concrete screed.

Upper floors have boards carried on timber joists, which are built into or supported by the walls. The way in which they are fixed depends on the design of the house.

CONSTRUCTION OF A SOLID FLOOR

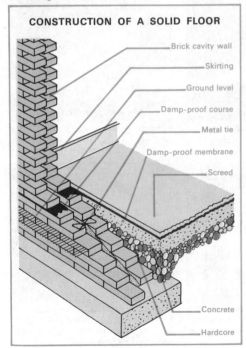

- Brick cavity wall
- Skirting
- Ground level
- Damp-proof course
- Metal tie
- Damp-proof membrane
- Screed
- Concrete
- Hardcore

WOODEN FLOORS—UPPER AND GROUND-FLOOR CONSTRUCTION

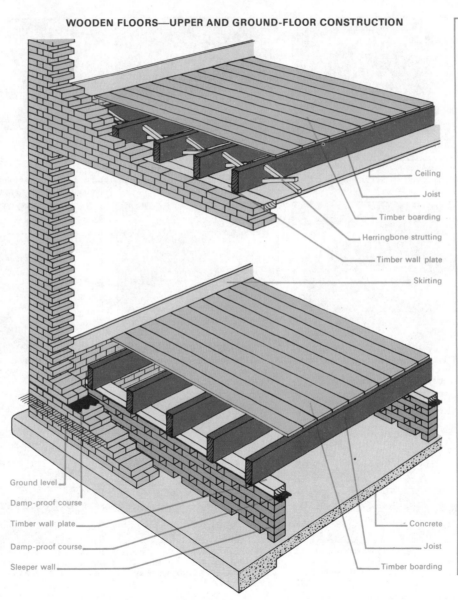

- Ceiling
- Joist
- Timber boarding
- Herringbone strutting
- Timber wall plate
- Skirting
- Ground level
- Damp-proof course
- Timber wall plate
- Damp-proof course
- Sleeper wall
- Concrete
- Joist
- Timber boarding

HOW JOISTS ARE SUPPORTED

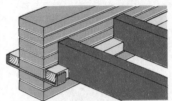

Wall plate The joists may be notched over a wooden plate held to the wall by an iron bracket

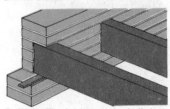

Built-in The joists may be built into the wall and bear upon an iron wall plate which spreads the load

Hanger Pressed-steel hangers may be built into the wall to carry the ends of the joists

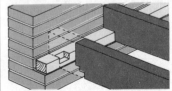

Timber plate The joist may be notched into and over a timber wall plate resting on the brickwork

Floors Joists

Fitting a new joist

When floor joists are badly damaged—for example, by woodworm or by dry rot—they must be removed and replaced as soon as possible. It is dangerous to continue using a damaged floor.

Although most joists are built into the brickwork of the house when it is erected, replacement joists can be fitted more simply by using metal hangers.

Ceilings

When the joists to be replaced are on an upper floor, it may be impossible to make the repair without damaging the ceiling underneath. In most cases it will be necessary to resurface the ceiling with plasterboard (see p. 126) after the new joists have been fitted.

To minimise the damage, look carefully for the nails which hold the ceiling to the joist. Slide a knife blade along under the joist until the nails are located. Press down very gently round the nails while a helper finds and removes them in the room below.

If there is an electricity cable passing through the joist, switch off the power at the mains before freeing the cable.

Cut a wedge in the new joist to take the cable or, if the joist rests on an intermediate support at this point, disconnect the cable and pass it through a hole drilled in the new joist.

Materials: joists to match existing ones; two hangers per joist; sand and cement; bricks; PVA adhesive.
Tools: kitchen knife; panel saw; tenon saw; claw hammer; trowel; brace and bit; chisel.

PRESSED-STEEL HANGER

Hangers are available to support joists of any size between 1½ in. (40 mm) and 4½ in. (115 mm) wide and 6–9 in. (150–230 mm) deep

---

1 While someone holds the damaged joist, cut through it about 12 in. (305 mm) in from each wall

2 Remove the joist and pull the cut ends from the walls. Do not dislodge the surrounding bricks

3 Brick up the recesses, bonding as necessary. Do not put mortar on the top joint, where the hanger will fit

4 Tap a hanger into the open joint, lining up the bottom with that of the joists. Fill joint with mortar

5 Chisel a recess in the bottom of the new joist at each end to fit over the base of the hangers

6 When the mortar around the top of the shoe is dry, fit the joist. Tap it in with a hammer if necessary

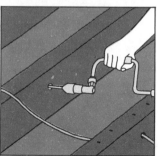

7 To replace a cable, drill a ¾ in. (20 mm) hole through the joist—about 2 in. (50 mm) from the top

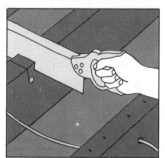

8 Make two angled cuts from the top of the joist to the hole and remove the cut wedge

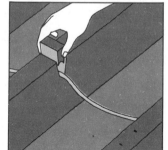

9 Lay the cable in the hole. Apply PVA adhesive to the wedge faces and press it back in position

Renewing the joists

if the floorboards in a room cannot be made to lie flat (see p. 83), the joists beneath them may be bowed or twisted. This fault is most often found in upstairs rooms where the ceiling of the room below has crazed or cracked. The reason for the twisting is usually that the joist timber was unseasoned.

Remove the floorboards and straighten the joists by nailing struts between them. Fix the struts at the centre of the span of the joists. If they are very badly twisted, it may be necessary to fix more struts every 6 or 8 ft (1·8 or 2·4 m). Place the struts in line between the joists.

Solid struts Cut the struts from a piece of 6 × 1 in. (150 × 25 mm) softwood, so that they fit tightly between the joists. Before fitting, tap 2 in. (50 mm) wire nails at an angle into the four corners of the strut. Fit the strut and drive the nails firmly home into the joists

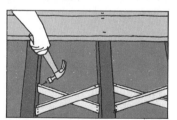

Herringbone struts Cut struts from 2 × 1 in. (50 × 25 mm) softwood battens. Saw the ends at an angle to fit flush against the joists. Tap the nails into the battens before fitting them. Fix the lower nails in the sides and top nails in the upper edge of the battens

Floors Floorboards

Lifting square-edged or tongued floorboards

If floorboards have to be lifted, first find out whether they are square-edged or tongued and grooved. Try to push a knife between two boards at several points along their length. If it can be inserted, the boards are square-edged; if the knife cannot be pushed in, they are tongued.

Square edged

Square-edged boards can be removed without sawing, provided that both ends are free. Use a tool called a bolster, which resembles a very wide cold chisel.

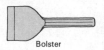

Bolster

Tongued flooring must be cut free along one side of one board. When the first tongue has been cut, the rest of the boards can be removed with a hammer and bolster.

Tongued and grooved

Always turn the power off at the mains switch before cutting through boards. It is advisable to use a special flooring saw, designed to cut without risk of contact with any under-floor cables. If no flooring saw is available, use a padsaw: but take care to turn the blade round frequently and feel with the flat edge of the saw for any cables.

Do not cut the joists under the floorboards. Look for rows of nails—called floorbrads—across the width of the floor: the joists usually extend 1–1½ in. (25–40 mm) on each side of the floorbrads.

Tools: padsaw or flooring saw; claw hammer; bolster.

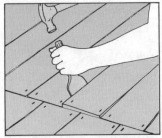

1 If the floorboards are square-edged, insert a bolster near the end of one board. Angle it away from the board and tap it down with a hammer

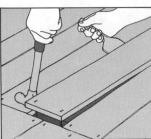

2 Prise up the end of the board until a hammer claw can be pushed in beside it. Lever with the hammer and ease the bolster along the board

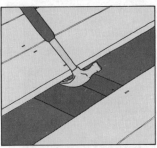

3 When the first board is lifted, use the hammer claw to lift the others. Lever each board gradually, taking care not to split the wood

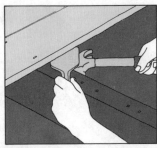

4 When a board cannot be lifted easily, push the bolster between it and the joist. Strike the bolster from underneath with the hammer

TONGUED-AND-GROOVED BOARDS

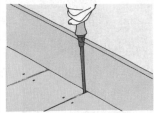

1 To cut a floorboard tongue, insert a padsaw between the floorboards close to the skirting. Saw gently for about 1 in. (25 mm)

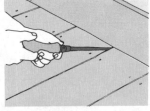

2 Lower the saw to a shallow angle and use only the tip of the blade. Feel frequently with the back of the blade for cables and joists

Cutting across a board

If only part of a floorboard has to be lifted—perhaps to repair an underfloor pipe—cut it first close to, but not on, a joist. Check that there is no cable underneath the board.

Materials: 2×1 in. (50×25 mm) softwood; 1½ in. (40 mm) No. 8 screws. Tools: tenon or flooring saw; padsaw; drill; bolster; claw hammer; screwdriver; knife.

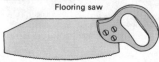

Flooring saw

3 Insert the tip of the padsaw and cut at a shallow angle across the board. Tilt the saw slightly sideways so that the cut is not made vertically

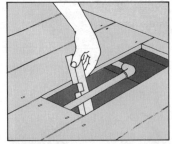

6 To replace a board, cut a piece of 2×1 in. (50×25 mm) softwood just slightly longer than its width. Notch the wood to fit around any pipework

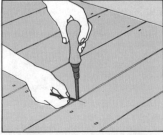

1 With a knife or padsaw find the joist nearest to where the board is to be cut. Draw a line across the board, clear of the joist

4 Insert a bolster and prise up the cut end of the board. Use a claw hammer, if necessary, to lift about 4 in. (100 mm) of board

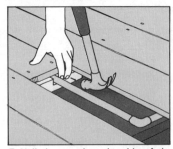

7 Nail the wood to the side of the joist at the inside end of the hole. Make sure its upper edge is flush with the top of the joist

80 HOUSE REPAIRS AND DECORATION

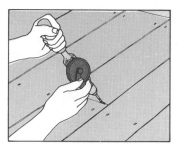

2 Drill two or three ⅛ in. (3 mm) holes close together and at an angle away from the joist to make a start hole for the padsaw

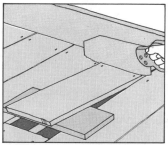

5 Ease a piece of scrap wood underneath the free end. Use a tenon saw or flooring saw to cut across on top of the joist at the other end

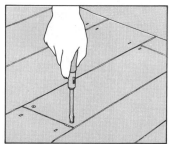

8 Replace the board. Drill two holes through the board into the centre of the softwood. Screw it to the support and to the joist at the other end

Re-laying floorboards to close gaps

The gaps created by shrinking floorboards cause uneven wear to carpets and linoleum. The most effective repair is to re-lay the boards tightly together. Fill the final gap with a length of wood the same thickness as the floorboards.

When lifting the floorboards, start close to the skirting at one side, but leave the first board in place under the skirting. If the wood is tongued, plane off the tongue on the edge of the first board when it is removed.

To make sure that boards butt tightly, cut at least four softwood wedges from wood slightly thicker than the floorboards. They should be at least 18 in. (455 mm) long and 2 in. (50 mm) deep at their thick end. If the floorboards extend for more than 6 ft (1·8 m), cut enough wedges to fit every 3 ft (915 mm).

Materials: wedges; length of floorboard; scrap wood block; scrap straight board; floorbrads.
Tools: bolster; two hammers; mallet; old wood chisel; scraper; brush; plane.

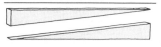

Wedges

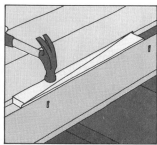

3 Start at the side lifted last and lay five boards, close together. Place a pair of wedges every 3 ft (915 mm) against the laid boards

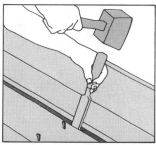

7 When all five boards are nailed, remove the scrap board. Lay and nail the other boards, pushing them together in groups of five

1 Lift all the floorboards (see p. 80). Remove all floorbrads. Use a scraper to clean the edges of each board so that they will butt together tightly

4 Push a length of scrap board tightly against the wedges. Nail it to the joists, but leave the nail heads clear so that they can be removed

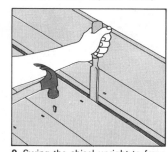

8 Tap two floorbrads into the board where it will be nailed to the joists. Drive an old chisel at an angle into the joist to lever the board

2 When all floorboards are lifted, brush the tops of the joists and remove any nails. Use a scraper to smooth any irregular patches

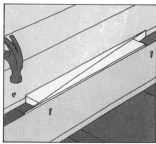

5 Use two hammers to knock the wedges together. Work on each pair of wedges alternately, so that they force the boards together evenly

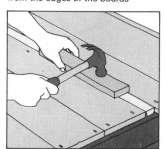

9 Swing the chisel upright to force the loose board against the last nailed one. Hold the chisel and nail the board to the joists

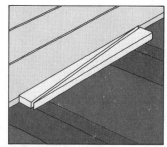

6 Start nailing to the joists at the board next to the wedges. Hammer in two floorbrads 1 in. (25 mm) from the edges of the boards

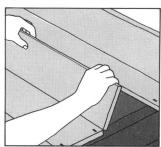

10 Cut a length of new floorboard to fill the gap. Plane its edges to slope in slightly. Tap it home and nail to each joist

Floors Floorboards

Filling a gap with a strip of wood

If the gaps between floorboards are wide—say, more than ¼ in. (6 mm)—it is possible to fill them with long offcuts of softwood. This can be laborious with smaller gaps.

Make sure that the wood used is the same thickness as the existing floorboards. If the offcuts are shorter than the floorboards, make sure that they meet on a joist.

Materials: softwood offcuts ½–1 in. (13–25 mm) wide; 1½ in. (40 mm) panel-pins.
Tools: hammer; marking gauge; panel or handsaw; nail punch; smoothing plane; pencil.

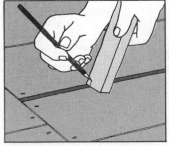

1 Hold the end of a strip of softwood against one edge of the floor gap. Mark the other edge on the strip

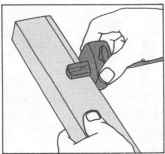

2 Set the marking gauge to the width measured. Hold the strip firmly and mark down its length with the gauge

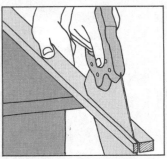

3 Saw the strip slightly oversize. Use a smoothing plane to taper it very slightly to a wedge shape

4 Lay the strip and tap it into place with a hammer. Make sure it fits tightly to allow for shrinkage

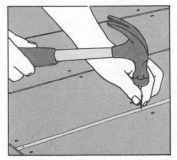

5 Secure the strip with a 1½ in. (40 mm) panel-pin at the centreline of each joist. Tap gently to avoid splitting

Filling a gap with papier mâché

When there are small gaps—less than ¼ in. (6 mm) wide—between a lot of the boards in a floor, the wood-strip method is not suitable for filling. The most effective repair is to take up all the boards and re-lay them (see p. 81), but an easier alternative is to fill the gaps with home-made papier mâché.

If the floor is entirely covered by carpet or linoleum, any kind of paper can be used to make the papier mâché. Note, however, that newspapers dry to a grey colour, which is not attractive if part of the floor is visible at the edges of a carpet. The most suitable to pulp in such a case is a soft, white and unprinted paper. Bind the paper to a thick paste with a cellulose-based wallpaper adhesive. Use too much rather than too little adhesive, to make sure that the papier mâché cannot contract.

If necessary, dye the papier mâché with a proprietary liquid dye before applying it to the floor. When it dries, it is suitable for any normal varnish or floor-sealing compound.

Materials: bucket; 2×1 in. (50×25 mm) scrap wood; paper; adhesive; boiling water; fine glass-paper.
Tools: scraper; brush; glass-paper block.

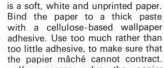

1 Use a scraper to clean paint and dirt from between the boards. Vacuum-clean the floor

2 Tear or cut paper into pieces the size of postage stamps. A bucketful covers about 80 sq. ft (7 sq. m)

3 Pour boiling water, a little at a time, over the paper and pound it with a piece of wood

4 Stir and pound the mixture until it is a thick paste. If it is too thin add more paper

5 Leave the mixture to cool for an hour. Pound in adhesive powder until the mixture is very thick

6 When the mixture is cold, force it between the boards with a scraper. Make sure it is pushed well down

7 Leave the mixture to dry for two or three days. Rub along each filled gap with glass-paper and a block

Securing loose floorboards

Loose floorboards are dangerous and cause floor coverings to wear unevenly. For safety, secure them as soon as possible.

If the boards cannot be secured by hammering in the existing floorbrads, buy some brads at least ¾ in. (20 mm) longer than the thickness of the floorboards.

When the new floorbrads are hammered in, make sure that their heads, and those of the old floorbrads, do not protrude above the surface of the floorboards.

Materials: floorbrads.
Tools: hammer; nail punch.

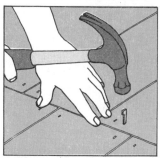

1 Position the new floorbrads about ½ in. (13 mm) from the old ones, on the centreline of each joist

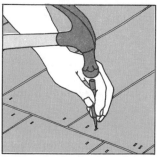

2 Drive the floorbrads well home and use a nail punch to knock the heads below the surface of the boards

---

FIXING CREAKING BOARDS

1 Punch floorbrads down just below the surface, along all the floorboards in the creaking area

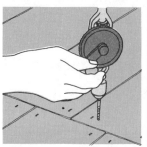

2 Next to each nail head, drill undersize pilot holes for No. 8 1½ in. (40 mm) screws

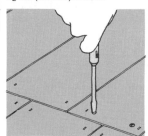

3 Drive each screw home tightly into the joist. Make sure the heads are below the surface

---

Replacing a worn floorboard

When a worn floorboard needs to be replaced, it may be difficult to buy timber of exactly the same thickness. In this event, buy timber to the nearest size thicker than the existing floorboards and cut grooves in the undersides to fit over the floor joists. For example, if the existing boards are ⅝ in. (16 mm) thick, buy ¾ in. (20 mm) timber.

Materials: 2 in. (50 mm) floorbrads; boards.
Tools: bolster; claw hammer; combination square; marking gauge; tenon and panel saw; 1 in. (25 mm) chisel; mallet; G cramps; vice.

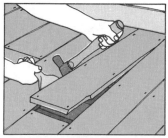

1 Lever up each worn floorboard with a bolster and claw hammer (see p. 80). If matching timber is unobtainable, buy slightly thicker boards

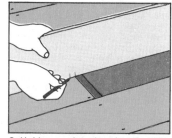

2 Hold a new board against the skirting and mark the length required on the underside. Allow an extra 1 in. (25 mm) to fit under the skirting

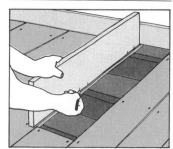

3 Cut the board. If it is too thick, hold it at right angles against the skirting and on the underside mark ½ in. (13 mm) on each side of the joists

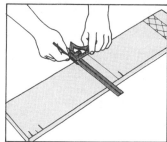

4 Allow for the 1 in. (25 mm) that will be under the skirting and mark the joist positions with a combination square. Shade in the joist areas

5 Set the gauge to old floorboard thickness. Hold the gauge against the top side of the new board and scribe both edges of the shaded areas

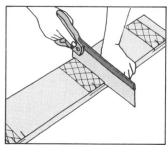

6 Use a tenon saw to cut along the joist lines to the depth of the scribe marks on the edges. Do not saw too deeply into the new board

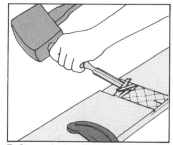

7 Cramp the board on a bench. Chisel out the unwanted wood between the saw cuts. Take care not to chisel below the lines scribed on the edges

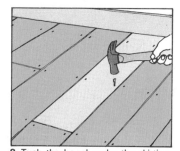

8 Tuck the board under the skirting. Make sure that its top surface is flush with the adjacent boards. Secure to the joists with floorbrads

Floors Skirting boards

Replacing a damaged board

When removing a damaged skirting board and cutting a new piece, use a mitre block and make sure that mitre angles slope out away from the wall.

Skirting may be nailed to a continuous piece of batten embedded in the wall or to small blocks of wood—called groundings—which are nailed at intervals along the wall. When groundings are used, it is usually necessary to fit new blocks behind the edges of the old and new board.

Materials: skirting board; softwood; wire or masonry nails.
Tools: hammer; saws; mitre block; rule; nail punch; crowbar.

1 Prise the damaged skirting from the wall with a crowbar. Wedge a thin board behind, to the left of the damage

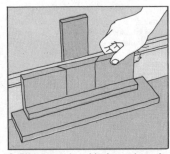

2 Place a mitre block against the skirting. Raise it on a board until it is level with the top of the skirting

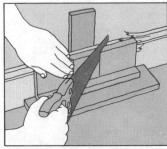

3 Make an outward sloping mitre cut on the left of the damage. The wedge allows the saw to cut the skirting

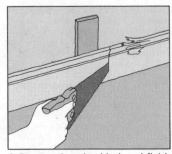

4 Remove the mitre block and finish sawing through the skirting board to the floorboards

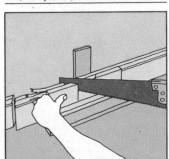

5 Jam the wedge behind the skirting on the other side of the damage and cut the opposite mitre angle

6 Remove the damaged board. If there is no batten or grounding visible, two wooden blocks will be needed

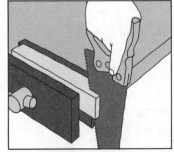

7 Measure the thickness of the plaster jutting out over the exposed brickwork. Measure the height of the brickwork

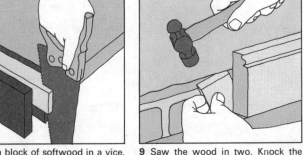

8 Hold a block of softwood in a vice. Cut it to the thickness of the plaster and the height of the bricks

9 Saw the wood in two. Knock the two pieces behind the skirting edges so that half their width is exposed

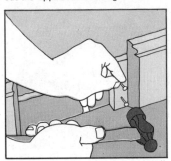

10 Nail the two pieces to the wall. Use masonry nails for brickwork, wire nails if there is a timber frame

11 Hold a new piece of skirting board on the mitre block. Cut it longer than the length required

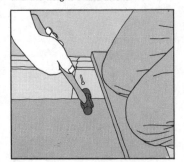

12 Place the new skirting against the existing piece. Mark the length and angle required. Cut it on the mitre block

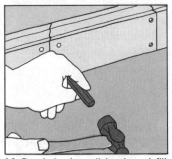

13 Fit the skirting. Place a board on top of it and kneel on it. Nail the new and old skirting to the wood behind

14 Punch in the nail heads and fill the holes. Paint the wood to match the surrounding skirting

Replacing angled skirting

When the removal and replacement of skirting boards involve an internal-angle corner, special care must be taken when cutting the new pieces of skirting board.

New boards are cut with the usual mitre angle (see p. 84) if the top of the existing skirting is square-edged. If the skirting has a shaped top edge, one of the boards must be cut with a lip on the top to overlap the top edge of the other board and make a clean joint with the shaping.

Materials: skirting board; nails.
Tools: panel saw; coping saw; hammer; nail punch.

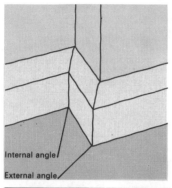

Internal angle

External angle

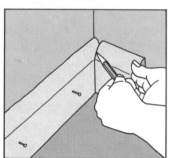

1 Temporarily nail a piece of skirting in the corner. Draw on it the profile of a second piece

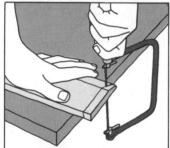

2 Remove the nailed board. Cut it with a coping saw, carefully following the drawn line

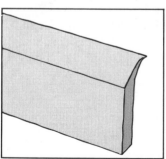

3 When it is cut, the skirting should be shaped to overlap the top corner of the adjacent board

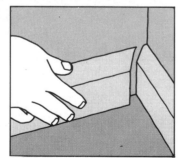

4 Butt the new pieces of skirting together. Nail to the existing groundings (see p. 84). Punch in nails

---

FITTING AN EXTERNAL ANGLE

The fitting of skirting boards to an external-angle corner is simpler than when an internal corner is involved. Cut the new boards in usual way at the centre of the wall (see p. 84). Measure to the external corner and mark the outside edge of the existing skirting. Cut to size with the mitre block.

The new boards are nailed to groundings in the usual way, but extra wire nails should be driven through the mitre-angled joint at the corner. Take care not to split the wood.

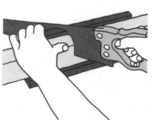

1 Remove old skirting (see p. 84). Measure and cut new boards with a 45-degree mitre

2 Nail the boards to groundings (see p. 84) and also drive nails through the joint

---

Shaping skirting to fit uneven floors

Where the floor is uneven, cut the bottom edge of a new piece of skirting board to fit the shape of the floor surface.

The new board must be at least 1 in. (25 mm) deeper than the existing skirting. Mark and cut the bottom edge to the contours of the floor. If the top edge is then higher than the skirting boards on each side of it, plane the top of the new board until it matches exactly.

Materials: skirting; nails.
Tools: claw hammer; rule; pencil; saw; saw stool; wood block; spirit level; plane.

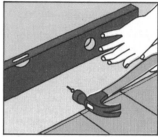

1 Cut the new skirting to length (see p. 84). Hold in position. Use a level to make sure it is straight. Fix temporarily with nails

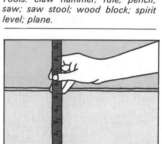

2 Measure the widest gap between the bottom of the new board and the floor. Cut a block of wood slightly deeper than that gap

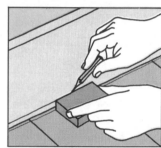

3 Hold the block—with a pencil on its top edge—against the skirting. Slide block and pencil along to mark the skirting board

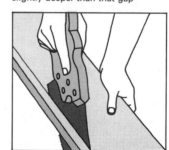

4 Cut along the line marked on the board. Angle the cut so that the front of the board is slightly deeper than the back

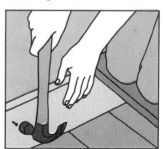

5 Hold the board in position. Lay a second board on its top edge and kneel on it to press down skirting. Nail the board

Filling a gap between skirting and floorboards

As the moisture in a new house dries out, the skirting boards often shrink, leaving unsightly and draughty gaps above the floorboards. Fix a strip of moulding to the floor, not to the skirting. This allows for further skirting movement.

Mouldings are available in many shapes. The only requirement is that they have two sides forming a right angle where they fit against the skirting and floor. If the floorboards are to be left covered with a carpet or linoleum, it is advisable to choose a moulding with a squared front edge which the covering material can butt against. When two pieces of moulding have to be fitted together at a corner, cut each piece with mitred ends.

Materials: 1 in. (25 mm) panel-pins; pencil; ¾ in. (20 mm) moulding; fine glass-paper.
Tools: tenon saw; mitre block; hammer; nail punch; coping saw; chisel.

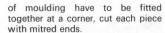

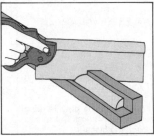

1 Measure the length of moulding needed, and if either end will butt against another piece of moulding, cut a mitre, using a mitre block

2 If adjacent walls are affected, make sure that the mitred mouldings fit together. Nail to the floor with panel-pins 6 in. (150 mm) apart

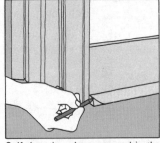

3 If there is a door surround in the wall, hold the moulding in place and mark a curve where it projects beyond the surround

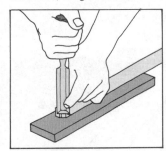

4 Lay the moulding on a scrap of wood and chisel off the corner to match the line of the curve. Smooth the curve with fine glass-paper

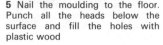

5 Nail the moulding to the floor. Punch all the heads below the surface and fill the holes with plastic wood

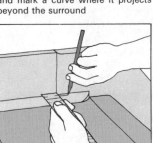

6 If the skirting butts against anything of greater thickness, such as a staircase string, measure and mark the extra thickness on the moulding

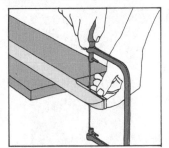

7 Cut the marked shape from the inside of the moulding with a coping saw. Chisel off and glass-paper the corner to give a smooth edge

Hiring a sanding machine

A wooden floor that is uneven and ingrained with dirt can be smoothed and cleaned with a sanding machine. This has a revolving rubber-covered drum mounted on a wheeled frame that tilts backwards to lift the drum from the floor. A sheet of abrasive material is wrapped round the drum and a removable linen bag, which is attached to an extractor fan, collects the wood dust.

Local classified telephone directories usually list agents who hire out the lighter machines suitable for do-it-yourself work. Sanders for household use are usually powered by a 1 hp electric motor. This must not be used with a 5 amp plug: a 13 amp circuit is the minimum requirement. Do not hire a heavy and more powerful machine, which would be difficult to handle and could damage the floor.

Check that the voltage marked on the sanding-machine motor corresponds to the house supply (see p. 514). Running the machine on low voltage can overheat and burn out the motor. If an extension is needed to lengthen the cable on the machine, be sure to use a heavy-duty cable.

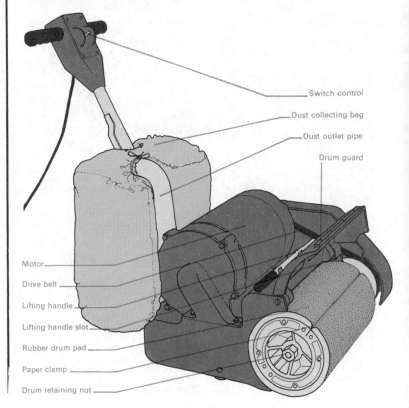

Switch control
Dust collecting bag
Dust outlet pipe
Drum guard
Motor
Drive belt
Lifting handle
Lifting handle slot
Rubber drum pad
Paper clamp
Drum retaining nut

Operating a sanding machine

Sand a floor in stages. Use coarse-grade abrasive first, to remove dirt and level the boards. For the second and later stages, fit middle and fine-grade abrasives to smooth the surface of the boards. A selection of abrasives is usually supplied with hired machines.

Never switch on a sanding machine until an abrasive sheet has been fitted. The rubber covering on the drum may be damaged if it revolves against the floor.

To use the machine, first tilt it backwards until the drum is clear of the floor. Switch on the power and gently lower the drum until it comes into contact with the floor. If the drum is lowered too quickly, the abrasive material scars the surface of the wood.

The machine sands in both directions—backwards and forwards. Keep it moving when it is switched on, with the drum in contact with the floor. The machine tends to pull away from the operator. Hold it in check so that it moves at a slow and even pace throughout the whole operation of sanding.

1 Tilt the machine and lift the drum guard. Insert the two keys in the slots in the ends of the drum. Twist them in opposite directions

3 Thread the sheet, abrasive side outwards, between the back of the drum and drum guard. Tuck one end as far as possible into the slot

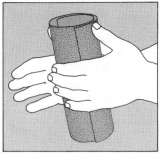

2 Gently roll a sheet of abrasive between the hands to make it flexible. If it is difficult to fit in the drum slot, roll it again

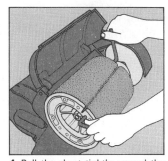

4 Pull the sheet tightly around the drum and tuck the other end into the slot. Insert the keys and twist them back to tighten the drum slot

CARRYING THE MACHINE

Never push a sanding machine across hard surfaces. A small carrying handle is usually provided. Screw it into the slot on the drum shaft.

1 Make sure the machine is switched off. Unclip the handle from its housing above the drum

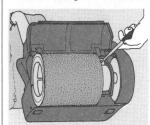

2 Tilt the machine back. Push the shaft of the small handle into the slot in the drum

3 Screw in tightly. Carry with one hand on the handle and the other on the shaft

Using a rotary sanding machine

To sand awkward corners, cupboards, stair-treads and other areas inaccessible to the larger sanding machines, it is advisable to hire a small rotary sander. This works on the same principle as the larger machines—with an abrasive disc attached to a rubber disc—but it is easier to handle. It is also possible to attach abrasive discs and polishing pads to many types of power drills.

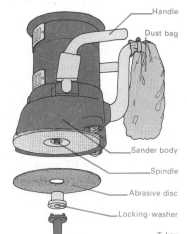

Handle

Dust bag

Sander body

Spindle

Abrasive disc

Locking-washer

T-key

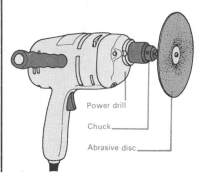

Power drill

Chuck

Abrasive disc

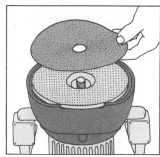

1 Switch off the machine. Turn it upside-down. Use the T-key to unscrew the paper clamp

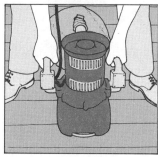

2 Fit the abrasive disc over the threaded spindle. Replace locking-washer and tighten it

3 Turn the sander over. For safety, drape the power cable over one shoulder when using the sander

Floors Sanding

Using sanding machines

Before sanding a floor, make sure that all the floorboards or tiles are securely fixed. Check floorboards at each joist and provide new boards if necessary (see p. 83). Make sure that all nail heads are punched in to avoid damaging the abrasive paper or the rubber-covered drum on the sanding machine. Loose grit will damage the floor irreparably if it is rubbed in by a powerful sanding machine. If wooden tiles are broken or loose, fit new ones (see p. 97). Allow the adhesive to dry before starting to sand.

Remove all paint with a sturdy scraper—for example, a block of wood with a plane blade bolted to it. Sweep the floor before starting to sand the surface, and repeat frequently during the sanding operation.

Tools: sanding machine; rotary sander or power tool with sanding attachment; glass-paper and block; sharp scraper; broom; brush; hammer; pincers; nail punch.

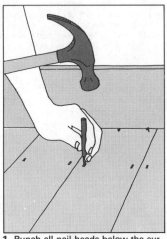

1 Punch all nail heads below the surface. Remove tacks and any remaining floor covering. Check that there are no proud nails at the skirting

2 Use a sturdy scraper to remove paint and varnish. If it is left, the sanding paper could become clogged. Sweep the floor thoroughly

3 Use a broom or brush to clear the dust and scrapings frequently. Do not tread or sand them into the surface of the floor

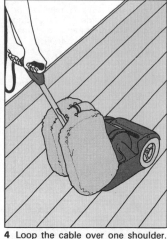

4 Loop the cable over one shoulder. Tilt the machine back, switch it on, and tilt forwards to let the drum make contact gently with the floor

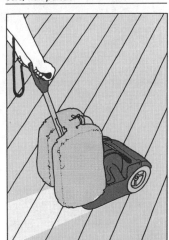

5 Start at one corner and work diagonally across the room. Pull the machine back without tilting it to re-sand the same line

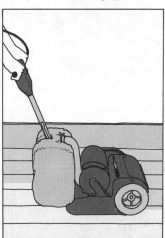

6 Overlap each sanding by about 3 in. (75 mm) until the whole floor is sanded. If necessary, repeat in the opposite diagonal direction

7 Change to a medium or fine abrasive paper. Sand the floor in the direction of the floorboards. Pull back to sand each strip twice

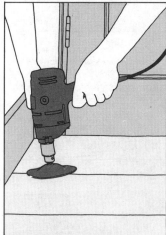

8 Use a smaller rotary sanding machine or power-tool attachment in awkward areas where the drum of the larger machine cannot be used

9 Finish with a fine abrasive paper. If possible, use a power tool and disc at the skirting. If not, rub with glass-paper and block

Floors Hardboard

Levelling the surface with hardboard

When floorboards are badly worn, they can be covered with hardboard—either as an underlay for tiles or linoleum, or as a floor finish.

If the hardboard is to be covered, lay it with its rough side upwards: if it is to be visible at any point, fit it smooth side upwards. Prepare the floor by filling gaps (see p. 81) and sanding any areas of the floor where the surface is uneven (see p. 86).

Buy 8 × 4 ft (2·4 × 1·2 m) hardboard sheets and cut them across their width to make 4 ft (1·2 m) squares. For economy, take into account the number of usable offcuts which will be produced as smaller pieces of hardboard

are fitted round the edges of the floor. In houses which have had central heating for some years, it is not necessary to condition the hardboard before it is used. Stand it on its edge in the room for 48 hours before fixing. In other cases, however, conditioning is essential.

Materials: hardboard; 2 × 1 in. (50 × 25 mm) softwood; wood block; 2 in. (50 mm) floorbrads; 1 in. (25 mm) annular nails.
Tools: hammer; nail punch; scraper; pincers; brush; bucket; hand saw; coping saw; combination square; chisel; pencil.

ORDER OF LAYING HARDBOARD SQUARES

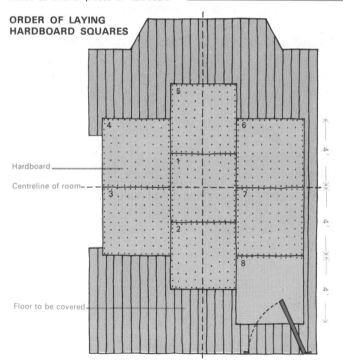

Hardboard
Centreline of room
Floor to be covered

Find the centrepoint of the room and lay the first square exactly on it. Lay the remaining squares clockwise round it. Stagger the joins in one direction only

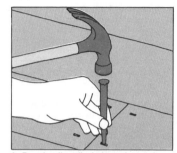

1 Punch all nails below the surface. Fill any gaps between floorboards and sweep the floor clean of all grit

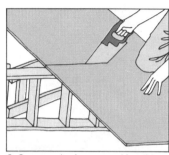

2 Open a pair of steps on either side to support hardboard sheets. Cut sheets in half to make 4 ft (1·2 m) squares

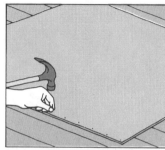

3 Lay a square exactly in the centre of the room. Nail along the edges, ½ in. (13 mm) in and 4 in. (100 mm) apart

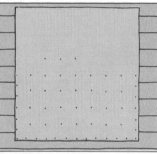

4 Hammer in rows of nails every 6 in. (150 mm). Work from the centre to the edges, with nails 6 in. apart

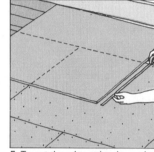

5 To cut the edge strips, lay a piece of hardboard squarely on the nailed boards and touching the skirting

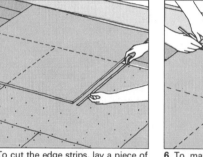

6 To mark the shape, hold a pencil against a wooden block. Push the block along the skirting

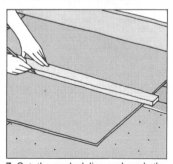

7 Cut the marked line and push the board to fit against the skirting. Mark the edge of the nailed boards on it

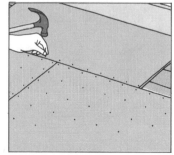

8 Cut the board to the size marked and nail it in place. Continue round the room. Use offcuts when possible

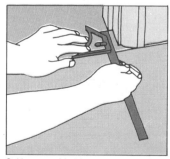

9 Use a combination square to mark on the board the distance from the door stop to the skirting edge *(continued)*

Floors Hardboard

Floors Chipboard

(continued)

10 Cut a wood block the width of the marked line. Push it and a pencil along against the skirting

11 Use the block and pencil to transfer the main points of the door frame on to the hardboard

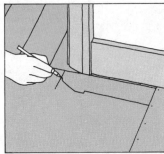

12 Join the marked points to give the door-frame shape. If there are any curves, draw them freehand

13 Mark the other side of the door frame in the same way. Use a coping saw to cut the board as marked

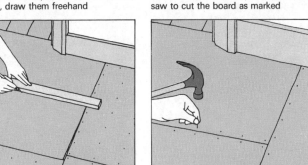

14 Lay the board in place and mark on it the edge of the adjacent nailed board. Cut new board to size

15 Fix the board with the nails in the first row 4 in. (100 mm) apart—later rows 6 in. (150 mm) apart

Replacing a damaged floor with chipboard

When an old wooden floor is badly damaged or worn, it can be covered or replaced completely with chipboard.

When floorboards are to be covered, make sure that they are smooth and sound. Buy chipboard, $\frac{1}{2}$ in. (13 mm) thick and nail it to the floorboards with $2\frac{1}{2}$ in. (65 mm) wire nails. The most convenient sheet size is 8×4 ft (2·4× 1·2 m), other sizes are available.

Use flooring grade chipboard only when it is to be fixed directly on top of the joists. It must either be 7/10 in. (18 mm) or 4/5 in. (22 mm) thick and must fit the joist pattern in the room. The heads of floorbrads in the existing floorboards indicate the position of the joists underneath. If the centrelines are exactly 16 in. (405 mm) apart, 8×4 ft sheets of chipboard are suitable—for each edge of chipboard must rest along the centre of a joist. If the floorbrads indicate that the joists are a different distance apart, the sheets of chipboard will have to be cut to fit.

Make sure that a good supply of 3×2 in. (75×50 mm) softwood is available to make supports for fitting between the joists and securing the edges of the adjacent boards at right angles to the joists. When the floorboards are removed (see p. 80) check that the joists are in good condition (see p. 79). Remove the skirting and groundings (see p. 84) to fit chipboard with $\frac{3}{8}$ in. (10 mm) gap between walls of the room.

Apply a suitable sealer (see p. 98) to the chipboard if it is to be left uncovered.

Materials: chipboard; 3 in. (75 mm) wire nails; 2 in. (50 mm) 8–10 gauge screws or 2½ in. (65 mm) wire nails. Tools: rule; claw hammer; club hammer; bolster; panel saw; wheelbrace and bit; countersink bit; screwdriver.

FLOOR PLAN OF A ROOM SHOWING HOW CHIPBOARD IS LAID

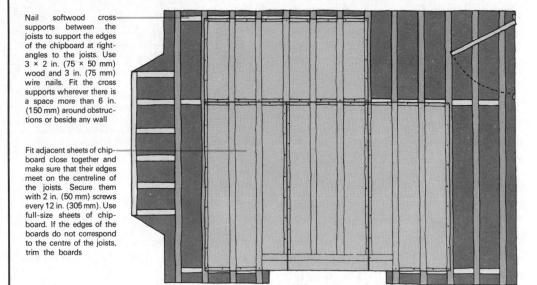

Nail softwood cross-supports between the joists to support the edges of the chipboard at right-angles to the joists. Use 3 × 2 in. (75 × 50 mm) wood and 3 in. (75 mm) wire nails. Fit the cross supports wherever there is a space more than 6 in. (150 mm) around obstructions or beside any wall

Fit adjacent sheets of chipboard close together and make sure that their edges meet on the centreline of the joists. Secure them with 2 in. (50 mm) screws every 12 in. (305 mm). Use full-size sheets of chipboard. If the edges of the boards do not correspond to the centre of the joists, trim the boards

Measure the room carefully before starting work. Draw a plan and calculate the smallest number of full-sized boards required to cover the main part of the floor. Find out what gaps will remain round the edges and calculate if they can be cut from one complete board. If not, it may be more economical to buy smaller offcuts of chipboard to cover those areas. Fix each board in place before laying the adjacent boards

1 Remove any floorbrads or screws in the upper surface of the joists. Scrape and brush off any collected dirt

2 Use a bolster and club hammer to trim any plaster which could obstruct the chipboard at the walls

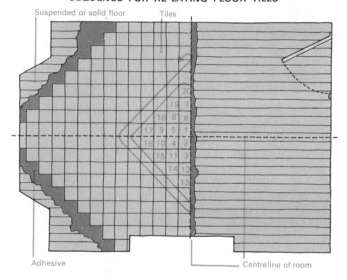

3 To support the chipboard edges, cut softwood to fit between the joists. Hammer flush with joists

4 Hammer two 3 in. (75 mm) wire nails through the joists into each of the cross supports

5 When a support is to be fitted to a wall, partly drive in nails at an angle near each end of the support

6 Position the support against the wall flush with joists. Drive the nails home into the joists

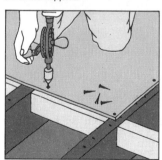

7 Lay chipboard. Drill pilot holes for 2 in. (50 mm) screws every 12 in. (305 mm) along the edges

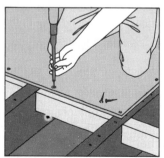

8 Countersink each hole and partly drive in all the screws round the board. Tighten all the screws

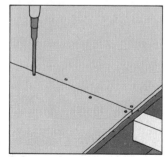

9 Stagger the position of screws in adjacent edges. Make sure their heads are flush with the boards

Repairing damaged floor tiles

Floor tiles may become loose or damaged for a number of reasons: for example, the use of the wrong adhesive when they were laid (see p. 694); the lack or breakdown of the damp-proof membrane in the floor (see p. 25); natural shrinkage of the joists and floorboards in a suspended floor (see p. 78); or—in the case of wood mosaic or parquet—the use of unseasoned timbers (see p. 688). Do not start to repair damaged tiling until the fault has been traced and corrected. Never refit tiles which have lifted. Take an old one to a do-it-yourself shop or builders' merchant and buy replacements to match the rest of the tiles.

Make sure that all old adhesive is removed before new tiles are laid. Some manufacturers produce a solvent for their adhesives: ask at a do-it-yourself shop if the type of adhesive used is known. If not, cut it away with a hammer and bolster.

SEQUENCE FOR RE-LAYING FLOOR TILES

Suspended or solid floor   Tiles

Adhesive   Centreline of room

It is usually possible to see the pattern of tiling on a floor after all the tiles have been removed, no matter how well the floor has been cleaned. Use this pattern as a guide when laying new tiles.

If the pattern cannot be seen—or if felt paper (see p. 95) was previously used on a wood floor—mark guide-lines before laying the tiles and follow them throughout.

Find the centre of the wall at each side of the room and stretch a chalked line taut between them at floor level. Snap the line on the floor, which will transfer a chalk mark across the floor. Find the centre of the end walls and mark in the same way.

Spread the adhesive on the floor, and lay about nine tiles at a time. An alternative is to spread adhesive on the back of each tile as it is laid.

Lay the first tile at the intersection of the two lines in the centre of the room and follow the numbered order in the diagram above.

Floors Coverings

Measuring and marking plastic tiles

When replacing tiles in the middle of a floor, no measurement or marking is necessary if the replacement tiles match the existing ones (see p. 91).

Where the damaged tiles are at the edge of a room, the new tiles may have to be measured and cut. It may be possible to hold a tile against the skirting and mark the distance from it to the first sound tile.

It is more likely, however, that the shape needed will be slightly irregular. Another tile is then used to make an accurate measurement.

Materials: tiles.
Tools: pencil; straight-edge.

1 Lay a new tile of the same size squarely on the first full tile next to the damaged edge piece

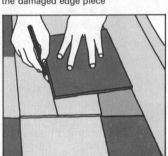

2 Lay another tile on top of the loose one. Butt it against the wall and mark its outside edge on the tile below

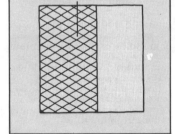

4 Remove top tile. The outer marked section on the lower one corresponds exactly to the area to be filled

3 If the shape of the tile to be replaced is angled, move upper tile along wall to complete line

Offcut Use an offcut to fill a space, provided that it can be overlapped by the upper tile when measuring

MARKING CORNERS

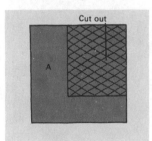

1 Lay a new tile (A) over the first whole one near the corner. Lay a second (B) on it to butt against skirting, and mark its edge on A

2 Do not turn tile A, but move it to the first whole tile around the corner. Place the second tile over it, and mark its edge on A

3 Remove the tiles. Shade the marked area and cut it out. The L shape remaining should fit into the corner exactly

Marking round obstacles

To measure and mark a tile to fit round an obstacle at the edge of a room, first cut it to the shape and size of the ordinary edge tiles. If the edge tiles vary in length, use the size which will ensure that its edges align with the joints in the second row of tiles.

For complete accuracy, always make sure that the lower tile is in exactly the right position before making a mark on it.

Materials: tiles.
Tools: pencil; straight-edge; compasses; tile or strip of wood equal to the depth of a full tile; sharp knife.

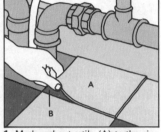

1 Mark and cut a tile (A) to the size of the one (B) at the side of the obstacle. Lay A squarely on top of B and make sure that the edges align

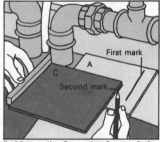

3 Move tile C to the front of the obstacle. Hold wooden strip on far side of obstacle and butt tile C against it. Mark outside edge on tile A

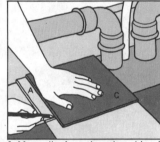

4 Move tile A to the other side of obstacle, with the lines already marked on the side nearest the obstacle. Mark in the same way

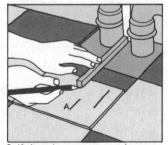

6 If there is a narrow gap between obstacles, position a strip the exact length of a complete tile against it. Mark end of strip on tile A

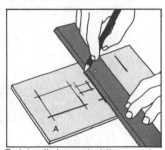

7 Join all the marked lines on the tile to show the position of each obstacle. There should be a square for each one

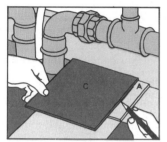

2 Lay a full tile (C) on top, so that it touches the side of the obstacle. Mark the position of the edge of tile C on tile A

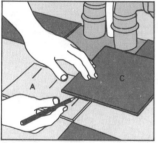

5 Lay the marked tile A on top of the fixed tile in front of the obstacle. Butt a full tile C against the obstacle and mark its edge on A

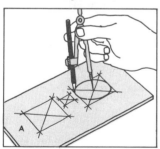

8 Draw diagonally from corner to corner to find centre of squares. Draw circle from the centre to the edges of each square with compasses

Cutting plastic tiles

Always cut a plastic tile on the waste side of a marked line, then trim it to make an exact fit.

There are three main types of plastic tiles: vinyl, vinyl-asbestos, and thermoplastic. The vinyl tile is flexible and can be cut and handled without difficulty. The others are rigid and brittle, and may require the slight heat of a low oven or a fan-heater to facilitate cutting: distortion will occur if the heat is anything more than slight.

Materials: tiles.
Tools: knife; straight-edge; oven or fan-heater.

2 Discard the waste piece of tile. Tidy the underside of the piece to be used by running the knife slowly along the edge

4 Lay the tile flat on a firm base. Carefully cut out the marked shapes, using the knife against a metal edge where there are straight lines

1 Where only one cut is needed, cut along outside marked line against a straight-edge. Bend the tile back on the cut line

3 Mark the tile for cutting. If it is vinyl-asbestos or thermoplastic, heat it *slighty* in an oven or in front of a fan-heater

5 Press out the cut areas and tidy edges. Slit the tile to its back edge where it is to be fitted round obstructions. Check fit before glueing

Laying single tiles

When replacing damaged tiles, take a piece to a do-it-yourself shop to make sure that the new tiles are the required type, colour and size.

If tiles have been laid on paper felt over timber, fit new felt and pin new tiles at each corner (see p. 92). With hardboard or chipboard backing, apply adhesive and lower the tile into position: do not slide it into place.

Materials: tiles; adhesive; sealer.
Tools: mallet; old chisel; adhesive spreader with serrated edge; dustpan and brush; old paintbrush; stripper; fan-heater.

1 Chisel out the damaged tile from the centre outwards. Do not damage adjacent sound tiles

2 Scrape off any remaining tile or adhesive with a paint stripper. Do not dig into backing. Brush off dust

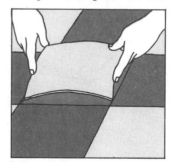

4 Heat tile if possible. Ease it down into the corners. Press down firmly all round

3 Spread adhesive on the floor. Use a spreader which has a serrated edge, to give a good key

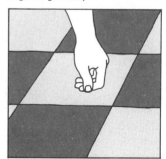

5 Rub the tile from the centre outwards to remove air bubbles. Seal to match the floor (see p. 98)

Floors Coverings

Measuring and marking cork tiles at a wall

It is sometimes difficult to measure accurately the size and shape of an awkwardly positioned cork tile—for example, one that is partially obstructed or oddly shaped.

An accurate method is to remove the damaged tile and chalk the upper edges of adjoining ones. By pressing the replacement tile smooth face down, on the chalked edges, the marks will be transferred and the corner accurately positioned.

If the space to be filled is accessible, measure with a ruler.

Materials: tiles; white chalk.
Tools: pencil; rule.

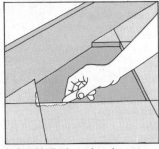

1 Rub chalk along the edges near a corner opposite the obstruction. Chalk must extend into corner

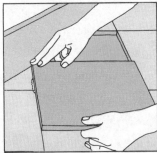

2 Press new tile, smooth side downwards, with corner against wall and edge in line with tile join

3 Turn the tile over and carefully reinforce the chalk line with a sharp pencil

4 Turn the tile round and line it against the other long edge of the hole. Chalk and mark the corner

5 Draw a pencil line between the two marks to give the shape of the tile required to fill the hole

MARKING ROUND A CORNER

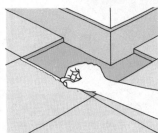

1 Chalk along the edges of the complete tiles surrounding the space which is to be filled

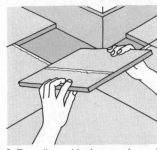

3 Turn tile upside down and round 180 degrees. Take it to the wall on the other side of the corner

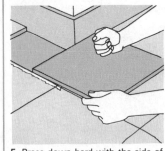

5 Press down hard with the side of the hand along the edge of the tile below to transfer the chalk marks

2 Place new tile, smooth face downwards, against wall and in line with adjacent tiles. Press down

4 Turn tile over again. Place it against wall and line its edges with tile joins

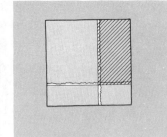

6 Mark in chalk lines with a sharp pencil and straight-edge. Shade the area to be cut from the tile

Cutting cork

Always cut cork tiles through their smooth face, not the underside. Use a metal straight-edge and a very sharp knife: a blunt knife can tear the cork and damage the edge of the tiles.

If the tiles which have been removed were tongued and grooved, cut through the tongues round the hole in the floor and use square-edged tiles as replacements. Hold the knife vertically to ensure that the cut is at right angles to the surface, so that the tiles can butt tightly against each other.

Cut tiles that are to be fitted around obstacles, such as pipework, in conveniently sized pieces which can be assembled around the obstruction like a jigsaw.

Materials: tiles to match existing floor.
Tools: sharp knife; metal straight-edge.

1 Use a sharp knife and a metal straight-edge to cut square edges

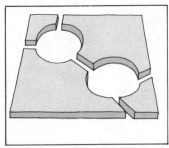

2 Cut tiles that are to fit around obstructions like a jigsaw

Laying replacement cork tiles

If a damaged or badly stained tile is surrounded on all sides, chisel it out from the centre. Do not try to fit tongued-and-grooved tiles individually: always fit straight-edged tiles as replacements instead.

Cork tiles on a timber floor often have a paper-felt underlay, which must be renewed at the same time.

Materials: replacement tiles; paper felt; 1 in. (25 mm) panel-pins; adhesive (see p. 694); sealer (see p. 98).
Tools: metal straight-edge; sharp knife; paint stripper; mallet; hammer or push-pin; old chisel; dustpan and brush; old paintbrush.

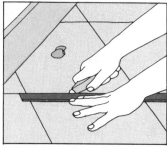

1 Cut along the edges of each damaged tile with a sharp knife. Use a metal straight-edge

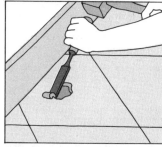

2 Use an old chisel with its bevelled side down and tap gently with a mallet to prise the tile from the floor

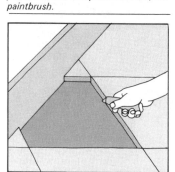

3 On a concrete floor, scrape off old adhesive. On a wooden floor, cut through felt with a sharp knife

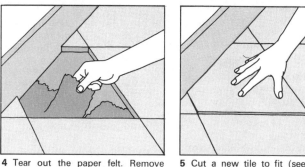

4 Tear out the paper felt. Remove the old panel-pins and brush out all loose material from the space

5 Cut a new tile to fit (see p. 94). Press it in place to check the fit before final fixing

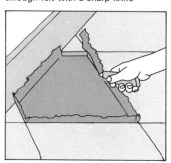

6 If the floor is wooden, press a piece of paper felt into position and trim round the edge to fit

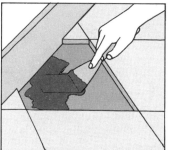

7 Apply adhesive with a paint stripper directly on to concrete or on to the paper felt if the floor is wooden

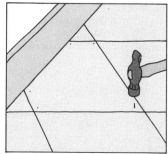

8 Fit tile. On a wooden floor, hammer a pin into each corner. Ensure pins are driven well in. Apply sealer (see p. 98)

Marking clay and quarry tiles

Quarry tiles are thick, hard and un-glazed—usually red, buff, brown, or black. They are available from $\frac{1}{2}$ in. (13 mm) thick and from 3 in. (75 mm) long and wide.

Clay tiles resemble quarry tiles, but are thinner and easier to cut. They are more readily available in two sizes—$4 \times 4 \times \frac{3}{8}$ in. ($100 \times 100 \times 10$ mm) and $6 \times 6 \times \frac{1}{2}$ in. ($150 \times 150 \times 13$ mm).

Matching coved or right-angled skirting tiles are available with internal and external angles.

Before attempting repairs to quarry or clay tiles, check that replacements are available in the same colour, size and thickness. Take a small piece of the damaged tile to a builders' merchant to obtain matching replacements.

As clay and quarry tiles are difficult to cut, replacements for awkward areas are easier to deal with if they are split into several simple square or rectangular shapes. Usually the original damaged tile gives a guide to the simplest shapes to be replaced.

Always mark the cutting lines on the underside of tiles.

Materials: replacement tiles.
Tools: pencil; straight-edge.

1 If an irregularly shaped tile is needed, mark an arrow on one edge of its top face

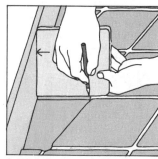

2 Hold the arrowed side of the tile against the skirting and mark width of space on the tile

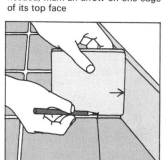

3 Hold the tile on the other side of the space with the arrow against the skirting. Mark width

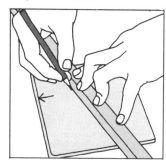

4 Join the marks with a pencil. Draw a cutting line slightly inside first line to allow for join

Floors Coverings

Cutting clay and quarry tiles

Clay and quarry tiles are dense and hard, and accurate cutting is a tedious and exacting job. Because some tiles are likely to crack during cutting, it is best to buy three or four more than required.

It may be possible to take the tiles, after measuring and marking, to an engineering workshop, to be cut with a diamond-tipped saw. Ask firms listed in the classified telephone directory if they do cutting work.

Materials: marked tiles.
Tools: hammer; small cold chisel; pincers; carborundum stone or an abrasive disc.

1 Hold the marked tile on a brick. Tap a row of indents along the line with a hammer and cold chisel

2 Hold the tile in both hands and strike it against the brick corner directly underneath the line

3 If the piece to be cut off is too narrow to hold, snap or nibble off with a pair of pincers

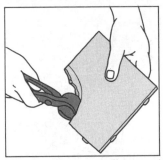

4 Do not try to snap off a curved shape. Mark and indent the tile, then nibble off the waste with pincers

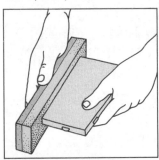

5 Smooth edges after cutting with the rough surface of a carborundum stone or an abrasive disc

Laying clay and quarry tiles

Some tiles have lugs, to ensure even spacing. If these tiles are not available, use small pieces of $\frac{1}{8}$ in. (3 mm) hardboard as temporary spacers.

When filling joints—called grouting —stand on a board 3 ft (1 m) square. This spreads the weight of the body and ensures that tiles not already grouted are not displaced.

Allow at least four days after laying the tiles before walking on them.

Materials: adhesive (see p. 694); tiles and skirtings; cement and sand.
Tools: cross-pein hammer; small cold chisel; pointing trowel; wood float; clean rag; sponge; bucket or basin.

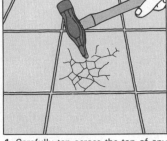

1 Carefully tap across the top of any cracked tile with a cross-pein hammer to craze and crack the whole surface

2 Work from the centre of each tile towards the edge and chip out fragments with a small cold chisel

3 Use the chisel to smooth the concrete underneath. Scrape the corners and brush the floor clean

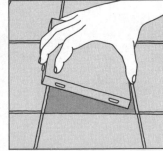

4 Place the new tile in position to check that it is level and just below the surface of adjacent tiles

5 Remove tile and spread on a thin layer of adhesive or a damp mix of 1:3 cement and sand (see p. 693)

6 Press tile into position. Straighten the joints and remove surplus adhesive with trowel

7 After 24 hours, grout the joints. Rub a 4:1 sand-and-cement mix between the tiles with a rag

8 Remove surplus grout carefully with a damp sponge. Rinse the sponge out frequently in clean water

Laying hardwood strips

Small areas of hardwood strip floor can be bought from most do-it-yourself shops. They are sold in panels 18 in. (455 mm) square and are arranged in either basket-weave or herringbone pattern, mounted on a paper or felt backing sheet.

If the strips have a felt backing, stick them felt side down. Fit paper-backed strips paper side up and sand off paper afterwards. Rub only in the direction of the wood grain.

Materials: hardwood strips; adhesive (see p. 694); serrated spreader.
Tools: chisel; old chisel; plane; mallet, glass-paper and block; brush.

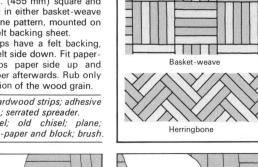

WOOD STRIP PATTERNS

Basket-weave

Herringbone

1 Cut out each damaged strip of hardwood with a sharp chisel and a mallet. Always work from the centre of a strip towards its edge

2 Scrape any old adhesive from the floor with an old chisel: brush the surface clean. Apply thin bed of adhesive with a serrated spreader

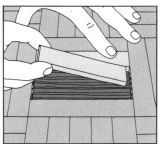

3 When the adhesive is tacky lay the strips: paper-backed strips with the paper side up, felt-backed strips the felt side down

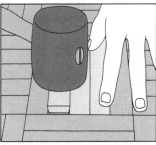

4 If the last strip is too wide, plane its depth to a slight wedge shape. Tap in position with mallet. Glass-paper surfaces clean and smooth

Cutting and laying sheet materials

Sheet materials—such as plastic or linoleum—are sold in rolls. Always spread them flat before attempting to cut or fix them in position. If a whole floor is to be re-covered, lay the material in strips—long edges butted together—and allow an extra 2 in. (50 mm) against each wall. Allow about 1 in. (25 mm) all round when making a patch. Trim after finally fixing the material.

Measure and mark the sheets which have to fit around awkward shapes before the adjacent straight strips have been laid (see p. 89).

Make sure the floor is clean and remove all old adhesive. Fill large gaps between floorboards (see p. 82), and remove any nails.

If the covering is not to be stuck to the floor, use a paper-felt underlay to cover irregularities.

If the covering is to be permanent, use an adhesive recommended by the manufacturer. Always lay each strip in position first. Pull back halfway and stick it: then stick other half.

Materials: sheet covering; adhesive (see p. 694); sealer (see p. 98) if required; softwood block.
Tools: sharp knife with straight and hooked blades; metal straight-edge; pencil; spreader; combination square.

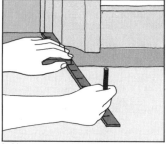

1 Use a combination square to measure and mark the sheet material to fit round obstructions (see p. 89)

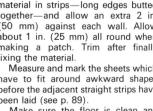

2 Transfer the shape of obstructions to the covering material with a soft-wood block (see p. 90)

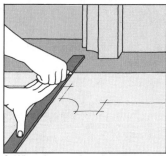

3 When the complete shape is marked, score the upper surface of the material with a sharp straight blade

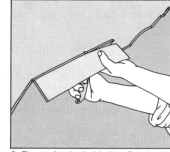

4 Fit a hooked blade. Bend the material along the scored lines and run the blade along from underneath

5 Slide the sheet into position against obstruction. Fit adjacent sheets to overlap it by about $\frac{1}{2}$ in. (13 mm)

6 Fit a straight blade. Lay a straight-edge on the double thickness and cut through both. Peel away offcuts

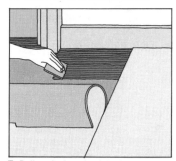

7 Pull each sheet back halfway. Apply adhesive with serrated spreader and fit sheets. Pull back and stick other halves

Cleaning and sealing methods

When buying a sealer to improve the appearance of a floor, make sure that it is suitable for the particular type of floor finish.

When sealer is correctly applied it keeps out dirt and provides a durable thin layer on the floor surface.

Make sure that the floor to be treated is completely clean and that it is free of grit, dust or grease. If sealer is brushed on to a dirty floor, stains underneath cannot be removed without stripping off the sealer. If a floor is painted, scrape it clean before sealing. The most efficient general cleaner is white spirit used with a soft cloth—or wire wool for stubborn stains. Some wax polishes, however, should be removed with a liquid wax remover. Check with a dealer. Follow the manufacturer's instructions when applying a sealer and let one coat dry before applying the next. Clean the floor and rub it down with fine wire wool and white spirit between each coat. Allow to dry before brushing on more sealer.

If the sealed finish is dull, it may be possible to brighten it with a wax polish. Consult the manufacturer's instructions, however, for in some cases wax destroys the non-slip properties of the sealing mixture.

Use sweeping powder—wax-impregnated sawdust obtainable from builders' merchants—to pick up dust and maintain the shine on wood, cork and linoleum floors.

FLOORING	PREPARATION Old	New	SEALER	MAINTENANCE
Wood (including chipboard and hardboard)	Remove paint, wax and grease with glass-paper, or wire wool, and white spirit or liquid cleaner. Rinse and allow the floor to dry	Sand and remove dust. Wash and allow to dry	Resin or polyurethane sealer	Wipe with a damp cloth. Dust, or sweep with sweeping powder. Apply a little emulsion or paraffin polish two or three times a year. Shine, before it dries, by hand or machine
Cork	Remove polish with wax remover. Use glass-paper or wire wool for stubborn marks, but use all abrasives with great care—especially if they are machine-applied	If cork is not pre-surfaced, sand with a machine. Sweep and wash	Resin or polyurethane sealer	Wipe with a damp cloth. Dust, or sweep with sweeping powder. Apply a little emulsion or paraffin polish two or three times a year. Shine, before it dries, by hand or machine
Linoleum	Remove old wax with a proprietary liquid wax remover. Remove stains with a Brillo pad. Do not use soda, caustic solution or coarse abrasives. Wash with detergent, rinse with clean water and allow to dry	Wash with liquid detergent, rinse and allow to dry	Only acrylic emulsion seals or those recommended by the manufacturer	Use a mop dampened with liquid detergent. Dust or sweep with a sweeping powder. Apply acrylic emulsion polish regularly, stripping off as specified by the polish manufacturers
Thermoplastic, asphalt and rubber	Use a liquid wax remover, not cleaners containing white spirit, turpentine or paraffin. Do not use abrasives	Wash with soapy water—not detergent. Rinse and allow to dry	Only sealers recommended by the manufacturer	Apply emulsion polish and shine by hand or machine. Do not use paraffin-based waxes

Finishing a pipe channel

When central heating is installed in a house, it is usually possible and desirable to conceal the pipework underneath the floor. On wooden floors, this involves only lifting and replacing the floorboards (see p. 80).

On a concrete floor, however, a channel about 3 in. (75 mm) deep, and wide enough to take the pipes, has to be cut into the sand-cement mixture—called screed—which covers the concrete base and damp-proof membrane to provide a smooth surface for the floor covering.

Although pipework channels are usually cut by the central-heating fitters, the job of restoring the floor finish is often the responsibility of the householder. If the existing damp-proof membrane has been damaged, it must be repaired, if it is to be effective, before the channel is filled in.

A damaged membrane consisting of bitumen can be repaired by brushing on three coats of proprietary sealing compound. If the membrane is polythene sheeting, the repair is more difficult (see p. 99).

Materials: proprietary damp-proofing compound; 3:1 sharp sand and cement.
Tools: brush; old paintbrush; bucket; wooden float; metal trowel.

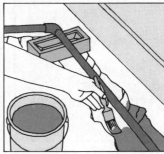 

1 Support pipe on brick. Brush out loose material. With clean water and a brush, dampen screed. Remove brick

2 Paint channel and pipe with sealing compound. Brush on three coats; let each dry before next is applied

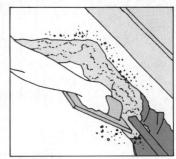 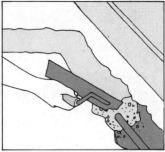

3 Fill the channel with a damp sand-and-cement mix (see p. 693). Pack the mix with a wooden float

4 Polish with a metal trowel to match up with the existing screed. Use a little extra water if it is too dry

Making a channel damp-proof

If a polythene damp-proof membrane in a floor screed has been torn or damaged during the installation of central heating or gas-fire pipework, it must be repaired before the channel is filled. A yard or two of toughened polythene, specially made for damp-proof membranes, can be bought at most builders' merchants.

Materials: proprietary bituminous sealing compound; 10-gauge polythene sheeting; 6:1 $\frac{3}{4}$ in. (20 mm) ballast; 3:1 sand and cement; 2×1 in. (50×25 mm) softwood.
Tools: knife; wooden float; metal float; old paintbrush; trowel.

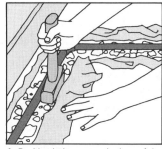

1 Peel back the exposed edges of the polythene and ram down any loose material to get a level base

2 Fill the channel to the level of the polythene with ballast and cement (see p. 693). Trowel it smooth

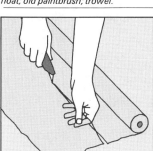

3 Cut strips of polythene to the width of the channel so that they overlap 6 in. (150 mm) lengthways

4 When dry, brush new concrete with sealing compound. Press the torn polythene back over the channel

5 Apply sealer to the old and new polythene. Press on the new strips, overlapping 6 in. (150 mm)

6 Cover the polythene with a damp mix of 3:1 sand and cement. Level it with a piece of wood

7 Pack the mix down hard. Rub it with a wooden float to get the surface smooth and level

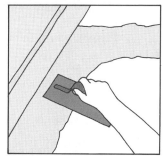

8 Polish with a trowel to match the existing concrete. Use a little water if the mix is too dry

Resurfacing a concrete floor

When tiles or wood blocks are to be laid or relaid on a solid floor, make sure that any irregularities in its surface are levelled. If this is not done, the floor finish will wear unevenly and the tiles or blocks will lose their adhesion.

Several compounds to give a smooth finish are available from builders' merchants. When the floor is pitted with holes deeper than $\frac{1}{8}$ in. (3 mm), these must be filled first.

Most smoothing compounds are in powder form. When mixed with water, they can be poured over the floor and trowelled lightly. Because they are self-smoothing, the trowel marks are not seen when the compounds dry. Note, however, that they cannot be used to level a sloping floor.

If the floor has a non-absorbent surface—for example, old quarry tiles—which is to be covered with plastic tiles or wood blocks, paint it before resurfacing with a suitable primer. This ensures that the smoothing compound can stick properly. Most smoothing compounds—unless the manufacturer's instructions state otherwise—are unsuitable for damp floors. Use them only when there is a sound, damp-proof membrane.

Leave the whole of the floor clear and work towards a doorway so that the smoothing compound can set—after about an hour—before it is walked on.

Materials: smoothing compound; detergent.
Tools: bucket; stick; stiff broom; metal trowel.

1 Sweep the floor and wash it with detergent to remove any grease or polish adhering to it

2 Mix the powder with water in a bucket according to the manufacturer's instructions. Stir it thoroughly

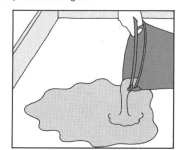

3 Start at the furthest point from the door and pour about a quarter of the mixture on the floor

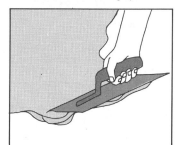

4 Use a metal trowel at an angle to spread the compound evenly to a thickness of $\frac{1}{8}$ in. (3 mm)

Gutters and downpipes Construction and maintenance

How a gutter system is constructed

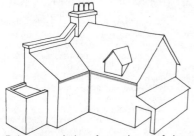

Rainwater drains from the roof into guttering attached to boards—called fascias—at the eaves. The gutter along each wall slopes to an outlet which conducts the water through the down-pipe to the house drainage system (see p. 61).

Guttering systems are made in many materials: aluminium, copper, cast iron and plastic. Complete cast-iron systems are less readily available, but parts can be obtained for replacement and repair work. To maintain watertight joints, replacements must be the same shape, size and material as the existing system.

Box gutters

Many houses also have a drainage system—called box gutters—between adjacent lean-to roofs or behind parapet walls on sloping roofs (see p. 110).

Maintenance

Inspect and clean the rainwater system once a year in good weather to make sure that leaves and silt do not collect and cause blockages.

Start from the top of the system and work downwards, cleaning gutters, outlets, swan-necks, hopper-heads and downpipes. If pipes do become blocked, clear them as soon as possible.

Warning

Use scaffolding where possible. If a ladder is used, fix it securely (see p. 684).

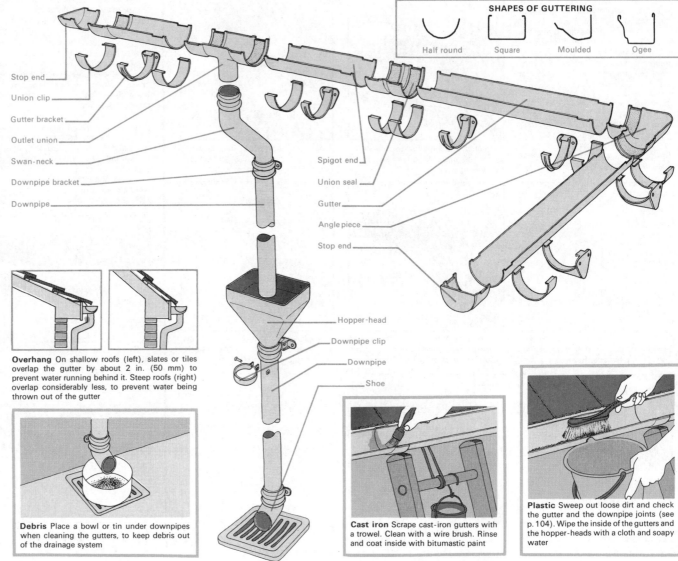

SHAPES OF GUTTERING

Half round   Square   Moulded   Ogee

Stop end
Union clip
Gutter bracket
Outlet union
Swan-neck
Downpipe bracket
Downpipe

Spigot end
Union seal
Gutter
Angle piece
Stop end

Hopper-head
Downpipe clip
Downpipe
Shoe

Overhang On shallow roofs (left), slates or tiles overlap the gutter by about 2 in. (50 mm) to prevent water running behind it. Steep roofs (right) overlap considerably less, to prevent water being thrown out of the gutter

Debris Place a bowl or tin under downpipes when cleaning the gutters, to keep debris out of the drainage system

Cast iron Scrape cast-iron gutters with a trowel. Clean with a wire brush. Rinse and coat inside with bitumastic paint

Plastic Sweep out loose dirt and check the gutter and the downpipe joints (see p. 104). Wipe the inside of the gutters and the hopper-heads with a cloth and soapy water

Clearing blockages in gutters and pipes

When a gutter has to be unblocked, it is advisable first to put a plastic bowl or large tin at the bottom of the downpipe where the rainwater discharges into the gully. This ensures that no debris flows into the gully at the foot of the downpipe where it could block the drainage system.

With metal systems, use rubber gloves to protect the hands against sharp edges during cleaning.

Materials: rag; length of cane or clothes prop; piece of hardboard; 7 ft (2·1 m) of stout wire; paint.
Tools: rubber gloves; trowel; bucket; wire brush; paintbrush.

1 Cut hardboard smaller than the gutter. Scrape debris into heaps. Do not push it down the outlets

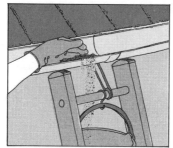

2 Hook a bucket on the ladder. Wear gloves to lift debris into bucket. Never use a trowel on plastic gutters

3 Lift debris from the hopper-head. Try not to compress it and cause a blockage in the downpipe

4 Tie rag to a cane or clothes prop and push obstructions through any downpipe fixed directly to the gutter

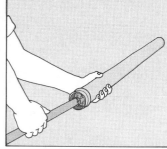

5 If an obstruction cannot be cleared, disconnect the downpipes (see p. 104) and clean them separately

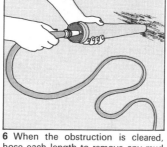

6 When the obstruction is cleared, hose each length to remove any mud inside. Refit the downpipes

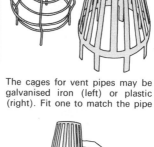

7 Push the lower arm of a swan-neck up to free it from the downpipe. Remove the other end from the gutter

8 Lay the swan-neck on the ground and push and pull wire or cane through. Hose the pipe thoroughly

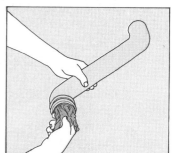

9 Wipe the ends of the pipe with a rag. If it is cast iron, remove flaking with a stiff wire brush

10 Position the swan-neck top and spring it into the downpipe. If it is cast iron, fit first into the downpipe

11 Pour water into the gutter at its highest level to swill down any particles on the inside of the pipe

see p. 104

FITTING A CAGE TO A VENTILATING PIPE

Every house has a 3 or 4 in. (75 or 100 mm) soil and vent pipe, on one wall or through the roof, to ventilate the underground drainage system. It should always be left open at the top.

To prevent birds nesting on top of the pipe, and to make sure that debris cannot enter it, fit a wire or plastic cage. They are obtainable from builders' merchants in various sizes. Measure the diameter of the existing pipe to get one to fit.

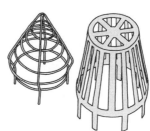

The cages for vent pipes may be galvanised iron (left) or plastic (right). Fit one to match the pipe

To fit a vent pipe cage, squeeze and ease the prongs into the neck of the pipe and push the cage down as far as it will go

Gutters and downpipes Maintenance

Fitting a new rubber seal

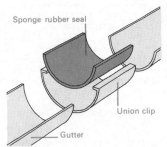

Sponge rubber seal

Union clip

Gutter

In most plastic rainwater systems, gutter sections are connected by pieces called union clips lined with replaceable sponge-rubber seals. If a joint in the gutter leaks, the seal may need replacing.

One system also incorporates a plastic silt bridge in each union. The bridge ensures that grit and dirt from the roof cannot get between the union and gutter and cause leakage.

Some of the seals for different manufacturers' systems are interchangeable, but it is generally safer to buy replacements of the same make as the existing seals.

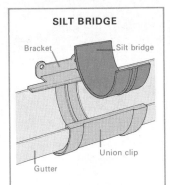

SILT BRIDGE

Bracket

Silt bridge

Union clip

Gutter

Hook one end of the silt bridge under the front lip of the union clip. Snap the other end under the lip at the back of the gutter

1 To release the clip, pull the lip at the back up over the gutter edge and squeeze the front edge

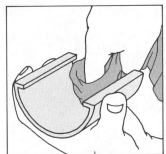

2 Peel off the old rubber seal. If necessary, use petrol to remove perished rubber and clean the union

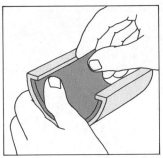

3 Fit a new seal. Squeeze the ends of the gutter slightly and snap the union clip back over each edge

Removing a cemented joint

In some rainwater systems, union joints are cemented to make them watertight. But the outlet union is never cemented, to allow expansion and contraction with temperature changes. If a joint leaks, cut out a short length of gutter and cement in a new piece with two union clips.

To get space to fit the new length of gutter, push the whole gutter along towards the outlet. It may be necessary to unhook one or two brackets.

Materials: ladder; wooden block; gutter; union clips; solvent cement. Tools: fine-toothed saw; tri-square; pencil; masking tape.

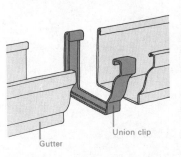

Gutter

Union clip

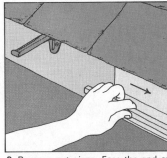

2 Cut along one line with a fine-toothed saw. Stick masking tape along the cut and cut along the second line

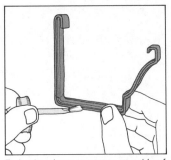

5 Apply solvent cement to one side of two union clips and fit one clip to each end of the new length of gutter

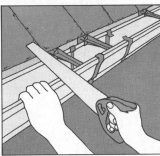

3 Remove cut piece. Ease the end of the gutter about 3 in. (75 mm) towards the outlet. Unclip brackets if necessary

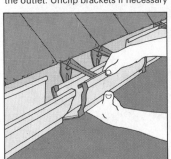

6 Apply cement to one union clip on the new gutter and fit it on to the fixed end of the existing guttering

1 Mark the gutter inside and outside about 12 in. (305 mm) on each side of the joint. Use a tri-square

4 Place a new gutter section on a block of wood and cut a length to match the part removed

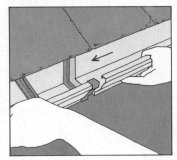

7 Push the other gutter back towards the clip. Apply cement, and push the guttering into the clip

Repairing a cast-iron joint

Cast-iron gutter sections overlap each other and are held together by a single bolt through the double thickness. The joint is sealed with putty, which can crack and disintegrate.

If a cast-iron joint leaks, remove the bolt and replace the putty sealer. If the bolt is badly corroded, take it to a builders' merchant and buy a new one of the same size.

Materials: putty; galvanised bolt and nut of correct size; bituminous paint.
Tools: hammer; screwdriver; pliers; putty knife; wire brush; hacksaw; old chisel; spanner.

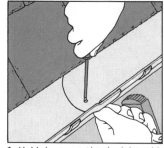

1 Hold the nut under the joint with a spanner. Loosen the bolt from above with a screwdriver

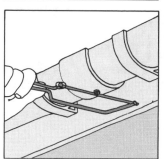

2 If the bolt is corroded, cut off the nut, flush with the underside of the gutter, with a hacksaw

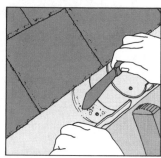

3 Prise apart the sections with an old chisel. Scrape off old putty and spread a layer $\frac{1}{4}$ in. (6 mm) thick

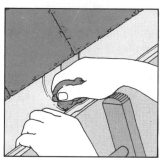

4 Press the two sections together. Squeeze out any excess putty and clean it off with a damp rag

5 Push a bolt through the hole from above. Screw on a washer and nut. Remove debris; paint both sides

Correcting a faulty gutter

Gutters are fixed at a slight slope to allow rainwater to drain to the downpipe at their lower end.

In an old house, the rafters may gradually spread and push out the fascia to which the gutter is fixed. As a result, loose dirt and leaves are likely to accumulate and eventually cause rainwater to overflow at the centre instead of running away to the outlet.

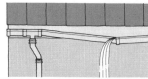

This should be remedied as soon as possible since the wall beneath may become badly saturated and, in freezing conditions, cause the surface of the brickwork or rendering to craze and flake off.

To correct the fault, first clean out the gutter (see p. 100) and then either raise the piece of gutter affected or lower the sections between it and the outlet pipe. Make sure, however, that the gutter sections are not moved more than 1 in. (25 mm) to avoid breaking the joint between sections. If a joint does break, renew it (see p. 105).

If a gutter has to be lowered by more than 1 in., remove the whole system along the wall and refit it correctly (see p. 106).

When guttering is lowered, check that there is enough play at the swan-neck to fit the new gutter level. If necessary, cut 1–2 in. (25–50 mm) from the bottom end of the swan-neck.

If there is no swan-neck, it may be necessary to loosen the downpipe and move it down the wall (see p. 104).

If a gutter has sagged for several weeks, the brackets may need refastening (see p. 104).

Materials: two 4 in. (100 mm) nails; ball of string or twine.
Tools: screwdriver; hammer; bradawl; spirit level.

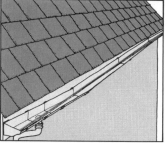

1 Stretch a length of string or twine along the top of the gutter. Make sure that it is taut

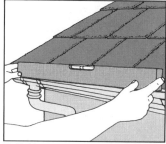

2 Hold a spirit level flush with the string and check that the gutter slopes evenly to the downpipe

3 If the gutter sags slightly, partly drive nails into the fascia near the outlet 1 in. (25 mm) below the gutter

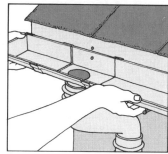

4 Undo the screws securing the brackets or gutter near the outlet. Drop the gutter to the new nails

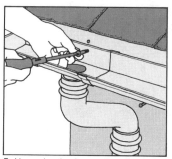

5 Use a bradawl to make pilot holes for the fixing screws. Drive in the screws and remove string and nails

6 Pour water into the higher end of the gutter to check its slope. Fill holes in the fascia; prime and paint

Gutters and downpipes Maintenance

Renewing gutter brackets

Some gutters are screwed directly to the fascia, but most are mounted on brackets. If brackets break or bend, the gutter sags and may lose its slope. It is then likely to leak and overflow and may eventually fracture.

Gutter brackets are made of metal, plastic or plastic-coated metal. They may be screwed to the fascia, on top of the rafters or on the sides of rafters. When new brackets are required, take an old one to a dealer to obtain a matching replacement.

TYPES OF GUTTER BRACKET

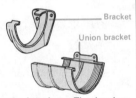

Bracket

Union bracket

Fascia brackets The brackets which support the gutters may be screwed to the fascia. Cast-iron brackets are usually bolted to their gutters. Plastic ones (as here) clip over the gutter

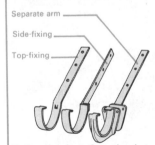

Separate arm

Side-fixing

Top-fixing

Rafter brackets Gutter brackets may be fixed to the rafters, and the slates usually have to be removed to work on them. An alternative type has a separate plate bolted to the arm which is screwed to the rafter

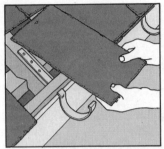

1 To remove a top-fixing rafter bracket, take off the slates. If necessary use a slate ripper (see p. 171)

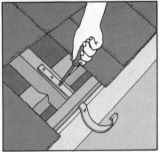

2 Make new screw holes in the rafter, or use longer screws. Screw on the new bracket

3 Paint the bracket with bituminous or rustproof paint and refit the slates (see p. 171)

Securing a loose downpipe

Downpipes are fixed to the walls with clips and brackets, and a pipe which is inadequately secured—especially a cast-iron one—is easily broken.

In many houses the joint on a downpipe is dry and unfilled. This is adequate only if the joint is clean. If dirt and leaves collect, however, water may gather and freeze—which could split the pipe. To avoid this, fill the joint with a mixture of red lead and putty or a proprietary mastic.

Materials: batten; mastic; paint.
Tools; claw hammer; plugging iron; cold chisel; screws or nails; brush; ladder.

3 Hammer two holes ½ in. (13 mm) diameter, 2½ in. (65 mm) deep in the mortar where the lugs are to fit

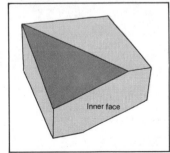

Inner face

6 Cut a 2 in. (50 mm) plug from a piece of 2×1 in. (50×25 mm) batten. Shape it as shown and fit

1 Put a block of softwood against the wall and lever nails from the lowest bracket lug with a claw hammer

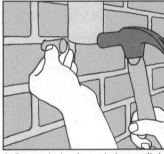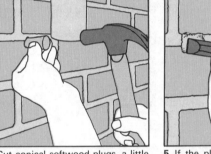

4 Cut conical softwood plugs, a little longer and thicker than the holes, and drive them home

7 When the plugs are flush with the wall, replace the downpipe and drive in the nails through the lugs

2 Lower the downpipe and lay it aside on the ground. Repeat procedure until the loose bracket lug is reached.

5 If the plugs do not hold or if the mortar is powdery, scrape out one long rectangular hole with a cold chisel

8 If joints are loose, pack them with a proprietary mastic and seal with a coat of bitumen paint

Gutters and downpipes Cast iron

Removing and fitting a cast-iron gutter section

A badly rusted cast-iron gutter is dangerous: replace it. If the whole system has eroded, fit plastic guttering (see p. 106); but a short section can be replaced with a cast-iron piece.

Guttering is in 6 ft (1·8 m) lengths of 3, 4 and 4½ in. (75, 100 and 115 mm) diameter. Make sure that the new section matches the old. Buy new brackets if necessary (see p. 104).

Materials: putty; bitumen paint; batten; bolts, washers and nuts.
Tools: spanner; hacksaw; claw hammer; centre-punch; wheelbrace and bit; putty knife; ladder; bucket; brush; pencil.

1 Brush the gutter and remove loose dirt. Protect the eyes if necessary against rusted flakes

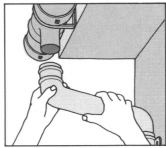

2 Remove the swan-neck (see p. 101). If there is no swan-neck, remove the downpipe section below the outlet

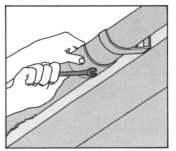

3 Undo the nut securing the damaged section. Use a penetrating oil if it is tight. Cut if necessary (see p. 103)

4 Lift the section from its brackets and take it to the ground. Handle carefully: it is heavy and brittle

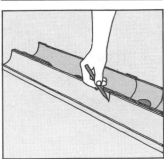

5 Place the new gutter beside the old and mark out the replacement lengths. Allow an overlap for any joins

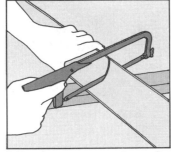

6 Rest the new gutter on a batten. Cut it with a hacksaw and turn the gutter slowly as it is cut

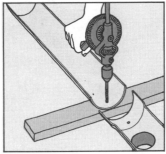

7 Lay the gutter on the batten and mark and gently centre-punch the bolt hole. Drill it $\frac{5}{16}$ in. (8 mm) diameter

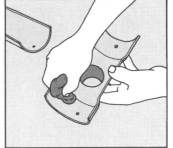

8 Knead some putty and press a $\frac{1}{4}$ in. (6 mm) layer evenly over the inside edge of the socket on the outlet union

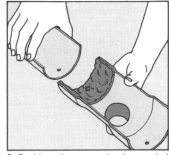

9 Position the gutter in the puttied socket. Line the fixing holes and press together. Push a pencil through holes

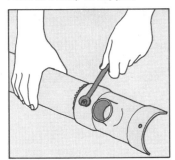

10 Push a bolt through the gutter and the outlet union from above. Attach and tighten the washer and nut

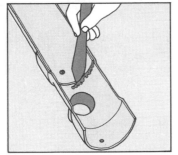

11 Use a putty knife to trim off the excess putty. Clean putty from both sides of the gutter with a damp rag

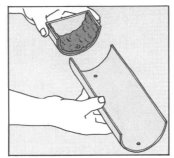

12 Measure, cut and drill an end piece. Remove the stop end from an old gutter, brush it and line it with putty

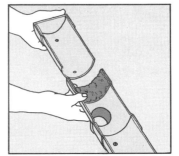

13 Bolt the stop end to the end piece and fit them to the outlet union. Paint inside the gutter with bitumen paint

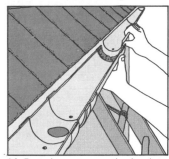

14 Rest the gutter on the brackets. Move it until the end fits the adjacent section. Line with putty and fit a bolt

Gutters and downpipes Plastic

Fitting a new plastic gutter

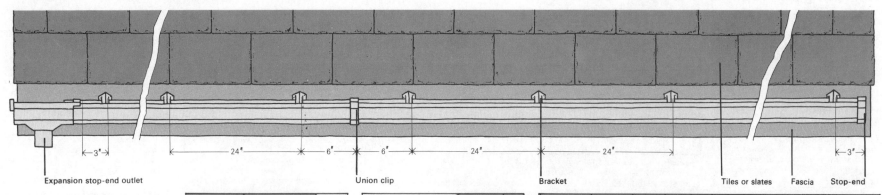

Expansion stop-end outlet   Union clip   Bracket   Tiles or slates   Fascia   Stop-end

Cast-iron rainwater systems are heavy and difficult to install. If several parts are severely rusted or hanging loose, fit a new plastic system. The method of assembly may vary slightly from one system to another. Before starting work, read the manufacturer's instructions carefully and check that the fittings ordered are correct.

Most houses use only two sections of guttering for each wall. There is no limit, however, to the number of sections or parts of sections which can be fitted.

Make sure that the timber fascia is true and level and in good condition. If it is not, renew it (see p. 160).

Every gutter should slope down from its closed end to the outlet pipe. This slope—called the fall—must be at least 1 in. (25 mm) in every 10 ft (3 m), to ensure that the gutter can drain.

It is advisable to hire and erect scaffolding for an extensive gutter repair (see p. 686). If scaffolding is not available, make sure ladders used are fixed securely (see p. 684).

Materials: gutter to fit; stop-end; expansion stop-end outlet; union clips; fascia brackets; solvent weld cement; 1 in. (25 mm) 8-gauge sherardised screws; fine glass-paper.
Tools: screwdriver; hacksaw; string; spirit level; measuring rule; tri-square.

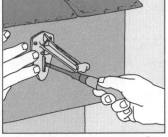

1 Screw a bracket on the fascia 3 in. (75 mm) from the end opposite to where the downpipe is to be fixed. Tie a weighted string to the bracket

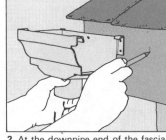

2 At the downpipe end of the fascia, hold the expansion stop-end outlet in place and make a mark 3 in. (75 mm) from it for the last bracket

3 Hold the bracket in place against the fascia, with the weighted string running over it. Use a spirit level to make sure the string is level. From the bracket position, measure down 1 in. (25 mm) for every 10 ft (3 m) of fascia. Fix the bracket at the lower level, so that water in the gutter will always flow towards the downpipe

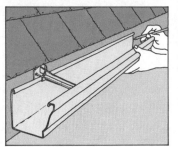

4 Hold the first length of gutter in place. Leave 5 in. (125 mm) on the outlet side of the bracket and mark the other end of the fascia

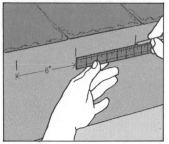

5 Remove gutter. Measure positions for two brackets—6 in. (150 mm) on each side of the marked point. Tie string between the two end brackets

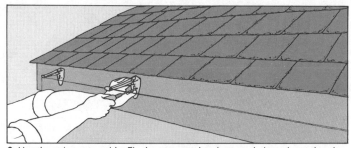

6 Use the string as a guide. Fix the two new brackets on their marks so that they just touch the underside of the string. Screw intermediate brackets every 24 in. (610 mm) along the fascia. If further lengths of gutter are needed, mark the joint position and fix a bracket each side in the same way *(continued)*

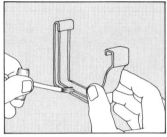

7 Apply weld cement to the left-hand slot of a union clip. Use the weld cement supplied with the gutters and follow the maker's instructions

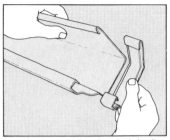

8 Coat the right-hand end of the first gutter piece with cement. Push the clip fully home along the gutter end. Leave it until the cement sets

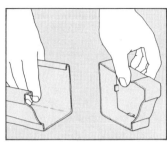

9 Take the length of gutter for the other end of the wall. Coat its right-hand end and the left side of the stop-end with weld cement. Fit together

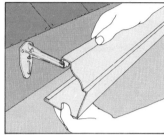

10 Fit the first section of guttering on to the brackets at the downpipe end. Hook the front edge over the turned-up ends of the bracket arms

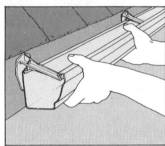

11 Press firmly upwards along the back of the gutter until its whole top edge snaps securely into place under the support brackets.

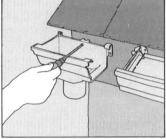

12 Hold the expansion stop-end outlet against the fascia. Move it until it is exactly in line with the guttering. Screw it directly to the fascia

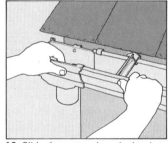

13 Slide the gutter along its brackets to overlap by 2 in. (50 mm). Do not cement it. The gutter must be free to move with expansion and contraction

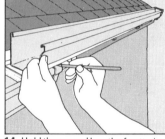

14 Hold the second length of guttering on the brackets and mark where it meets the first. If it does not, measure a piece to fill the gap

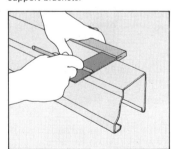

15 Take the marked piece of guttering to the ground and use a tri-square to mark the cutting line around the outside of the gutter

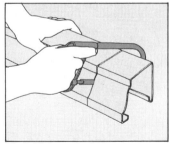

16 Hold the marked gutter firmly on a flat surface. Cut through it with a fine-bladed hacksaw. Clean the cut edge with fine glass-paper

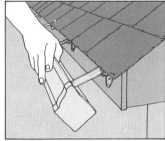

17 Coat the cut end of the gutter and the slot of the union clip already fitted with weld cement. Clip the gutter on to its brackets

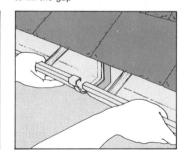

18 Push the gutter along into the clip. If more than two lengths are being fitted, cement and fix the others in the same way

FIXING ANGLE PIECES

If a gutter has to be taken round a corner, buy an angle piece—internal or external—to suit the house. The method of fixing the two types is the same. Measure the distances involved carefully to ensure that the angle piece is fitted accurately.

1 Hold the angle piece on the corner. Draw marks 1 in. (25 mm) from the end of each fascia and fix brackets at these points. Fit and hold the angle piece on the bracket

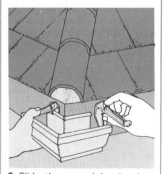

2 Slide the second bracket into position behind the angle piece. Mark the holes on the fascia with a pencil. Remove the angle piece and fix bracket. Refit angle piece

Gutters and downpipes Plastic

Fitting a new downpipe

A rainwater system should normally be of the same material throughout. If an old cast-iron gutter has been replaced with a plastic one (see p. 106), fit new plastic downpipes to suit the system.

Methods of jointing vary. Vertical joints need no cement, but for horizontal joints follow the manufacturer's instructions for mixing weld cement.

To make holes in the brickwork of the house for the fixing brackets, use either a wall-plug tool—called a jumper—or a hand electric drill and masonry bit.

Fill the holes with pieces of softwood or proprietary fibre or plastic plugs. Make sure that they are just tight enough to be hammered in easily. If they are too tight, they could shatter old soft brickwork.

If the gutter overhangs the wall, a swan-neck pipe is needed at the top of the downpipe. On some systems, however, it is possible to slot the top of the downpipe directly into the gutter outlet.

Materials: plastic pipes; bend; socket-and-spigot bend; fixing clips and brackets; outlet shoe; weld cement; 1½ in. (40 mm) screw.
Tools: claw hammer; wall-plug tool, or drill and masonry bit; hacksaw or other fine-toothed saw; spirit level; screwdriver; chisel; file.

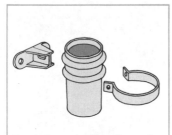

Brackets and clips Screw the downpipe brackets to the wall so that the retaining clips can be fitted round the groove of each of the downpipe sockets

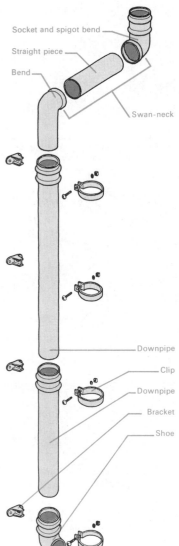

Socket and spigot bend

Straight piece

Bend

Swan-neck

Downpipe

Clip

Downpipe

Bracket

Shoe

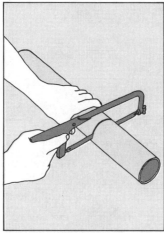

1 Measure the length of the original straight piece of pipe on the swan-neck. Allow for the ends in the sockets and cut a new piece to length

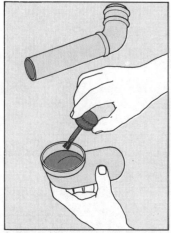

2 Brush weld cement on the joints of the two swan-neck bends and on the ends of the straight piece. Fit together and leave to dry for five minutes

3 Place the made-up swan-neck bend on the end of the gutter outlet. Mark the wall just below the pipe where the downpipe socket will be positioned

4 Hold the downpipe bracket on the mark on the wall. Use a plug tool and hammer to mark the position of the bracket holes

5 Use a power drill and a ½ in. (13 mm) masonry bit to drill the holes between the bricks. Drill deeply enough to fit a 1½ in. (40 mm) screw

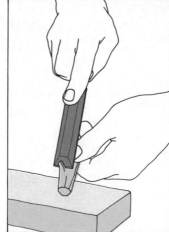

6 Make softwood plugs to fit the holes. Cut the plugs along the grain of the wood and taper them slightly with a sharp chisel *(continued)*

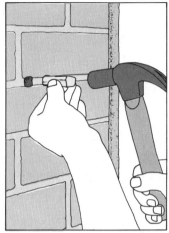

7 Drive the wooden plugs into the holes. If they do not go in completely flush with the wall, trim off the ends with a sharp chisel

8 Tap 1½ in. (40 mm) screws through the bracket holes into the plugs, then screw them fully home with a large-bladed screwdriver

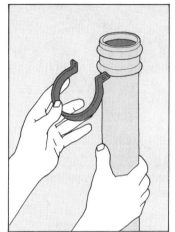

9 Spring the downpipe clip round the downpipe socket. Pull ends of the clip together round the bracket at the back of the downpipe

10 Make sure that the clip fits at each side of the wall bracket. Fit the bolt through the bracket and clip. Fit a spring washer and tighten the nut

11 Push the socket end of the swan-neck on to the gutter outlet pipe. Spring the swan-neck to fit over the downpipe socket without cement

12 Use a spirit level to check that the pipe is vertical. Mark the wall halfway down the pipe. Push pipe aside and fit a bracket and clip

13 Hold the last length of pipe upside-down just above the drain. Mark the length required to meet the downpipe already fixed

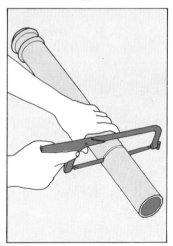

14 Cut the pipe straight across at the mark. Use a hacksaw and clean the edges of the cut with a fine file. Make sure that the shoe fits

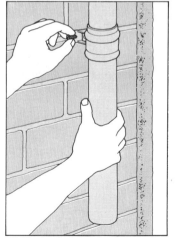

15 Fit the final length of downpipe. Screw a bracket to the wall and fit the retaining clip round the centre of the socket. Tighten the bolt

16 Fit the shoe on the end of the downpipe. Fix a bracket and clip the shoe socket to it. Make sure that all bolts are secure in their clips

Gutters and downpipes Box gutters

Relining an asphalt gutter

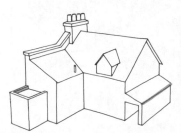

Box gutters are usually found between adjacent lean-to roofs, on boundary walls, or behind parapet walls on flat roofs. They may be lined with zinc, lead, bitumastic felt or a special pliable asphalt which allows slight movement when it is set.

Asphalt-lined gutters are constructed of timber, which is covered with chicken wire or expanded metal lathing before the asphalt surface is laid.

Damaged areas can rarely be made weatherproof in patches. The only satisfactory repair in such an instance is to lay a lining of fresh asphalt over the whole guttering.

If the gutter is beside a parapet wall, work either from a scaffolding (see p. 686) or from a well-secured ladder. Never try to balance on the parapet. If the gutter is between lean-to roofs, work from inside the roof (see p. 167).

The gutter must be dried thoroughly before new asphalt is laid. Use the flame of a blowlamp or butane burner and move it over the surface just fast enough for the heat to penetrate, but not melt, the old asphalt.

Before applying the new layer of asphalt make sure that any irregularities in the surface have been smoothed. Cut away loose pieces.

Materials: cold asphalt; $1\frac{1}{4}$ in. (30 mm) galvanised slating nails; new slates if necessary; batten.
Tools: blowlamp or butane burner; hammer; bolster chisel; trowel; filling knife; stiff brush; dustpan; bucket; slate-ripper.

1 Remove the slate nails (see p. 171) and lift out the two layers of slates overhanging the gutter edges

2 Bend back the underfelt or lead flashing to give more working space in the gutter

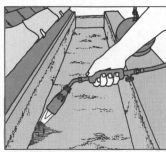

3 Use a blowlamp or butane burner to dry out the surface of the gutter. Do not allow the asphalt to melt

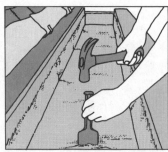

4 Use a hammer and bolster chisel to chip away any loose pieces of asphalt from the surface and sides of the box

5 If there are any irregularities, heat the asphalt to a putty-like consistency. Smooth the surface with a trowel

6 Start at the top end of the gutter, and trowel on a coating of cold asphalt, $\frac{1}{4}$ in. (6 mm) thick

7 Heat the asphalt with a blowlamp and smooth it evenly. Work on about 4 in. (100 mm) at a time

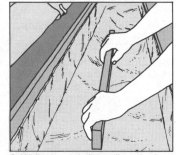

8 While the asphalt is still warm, draw a batten across it to make sure that the surface is level

9 When the asphalt has dried, pour water down the gutter to make sure that it runs away to the outlet

10 Check the gutter carefully. Look particularly for pools of water which have collected at uneven patches

11 If there are small depressions in the asphalt, heat the affected area. Fill with new asphalt and smooth it

12 Allow the asphalt to harden for two hours. Refit the slates (see p. 171) which were removed from the roof

Relining a gutter with roofing felt

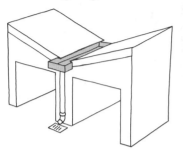

Roofing felt—which is made from bitumen-impregnated hessian—can be used to reline box gutters.

Remove top section of drainpipe and undo gutter outlet. Strip off old felt. Remove any nails which may be embedded in the framework, and smooth the surface of the timber to avoid damaging the new felt.

The long runs of felt need not be folded accurately. It is enough for them to fit the contours of the gutter approximately. The end, however, has to be carefully folded to a box shape. Fold the felt in a warm atmosphere, to avoid cracking or splitting.

When the end box is in position, carefully mark the drain hole and cut it out with a sharp knife.

Securing

The felt can be secured in the box gutter by tucking it under the roof edge. An alternative is to fix it with large galvanised flat-headed nails, called clout nails. If nails are used, hammer them in along the top of the box timber—under the roof edge—to protect them from rain. This involves removing and replacing the lower section of slates, tiles or roof covering (see p. 160).

Materials: mineral-faced roofing felt; sink waste-top; mastic sealer; galvanised nails.
Tools: steel rule; hammer; spreader for mastic sealer; sharp knife; large spanner or Stilson wrench.

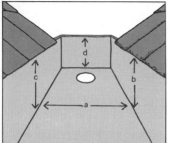

1 Measure from stop-end to a point at least 6 in. (150 mm) past drain hole. Allow for overlap with next section

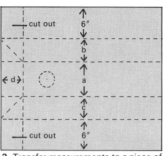

2 Transfer measurements to a piece of felt. Leave 6 in. (150 mm) each side, to tuck under the roof

3 Fold the felt in a warm room. Lay a piece of timber on the marked felt and bend up the sides

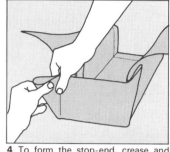

4 To form the stop-end, crease and double up the felt. Fold it round the sides. Do not cut the felt

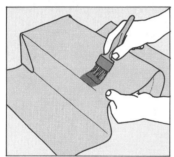

5 Turn over the stop-end and coat the underside with a thin film of mastic sealer. Fit it in the gutter

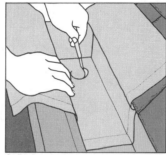

6 Feel to find the drain-hole position and press around the rim. Carefully cut out the hole with a sharp knife

7 Coat the underside of the flange of a sink-waste top with mastic sealer. Push it into the drain hole

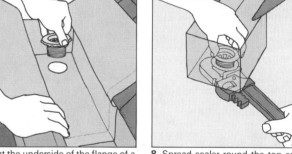

8 Spread sealer round the top end of the waste nut. Screw the nut on to the waste pipe and tighten it

9 Spread a thin layer of mastic, 4 in. (100 mm) wide, on the end of the felt where it meets the next piece

10 Overlap the next length of felt on the previous piece. Press it firmly on the sealer

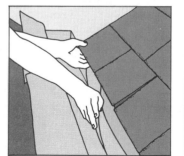

11 Tuck the edge flaps of the felt under the roof. If nails are used, remove the roof covering (see p. 160)

12 Continue along the gutter and make a second stop section for the other end. Secure with sealer

Gutters and downpipes

Relining a gutter with zinc

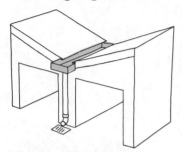

Box gutters are often fitted between two lean-to roofs. Do not stand in such a gutter to carry out maintenance work; it is unlikely to be strong enough.

To gain access to the roof, remove some of the roof covering from outside. If the roof has large panels—such as corrugated asbestos sheeting—remove every third panel of the covering to gain access to the gutter (see p. 175).

Box gutters may be lined with zinc or roofing felt (see p. 111). Before starting work, remove the top section of drainpipe and undo the gutter outlet. Clean out the gutter thoroughly and remove any damaged zinc sheets. Check that the woodwork forming the box structure (see p. 110) is sound. If any of the wood has to be renewed, creosote the new wood thoroughly before fitting the new zinc lining.

Use a sink waste-top as a drain outlet. This can be screwed into the base of the gutter or it can be soldered to the zinc plate. If it is soldered, make sure that the zinc does not overheat. If the soldering iron is too hot, it could burn or hole the zinc.

For convenience of handling make the section of lining incorporating the outlet hole about 3 ft (915 mm) long. Line the rest of the gutter with the longest lengths available.

Materials: sheet of zinc plate; solder and flux; wire wool; sink waste-top.
Tools: heavy soldering iron; tin-snips or metal shears; wooden dresser (see p. 164); steel rule; pliers; blowlamp.

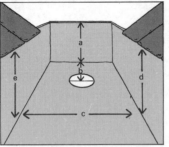

1 Measure height and width of gutter for outlet section. Measure distance from stop-end to centre of drain hole

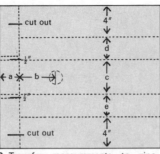

2 Transfer measurements to zinc, allowing 4 in. (100 mm) side flaps and ½ in. (13 mm) lap on end piece

3 Mark the drain hole and drill a small hole in centre. Cut from hole to marked outer circle

4 Bend back cut zinc with pliers. Snip off the bent pieces of zinc to make the hole for the waste-top

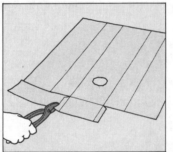

5 Heat soldering iron with blowlamp and tin zinc at the hole (see p. 692). Cut out zinc shape for the gutter

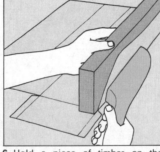

6 Hold a piece of timber on the marked lines. Hammer the zinc to shape with a wooden dresser

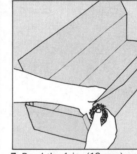

7 Bend the ½ in. (13 mm) end pieces round to meet the sides. Clean the overlap with wire wool

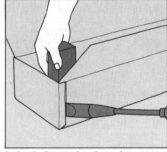

8 Apply flux to the cleaned areas and tin with solder. Solder the two edges together (see p. 692).

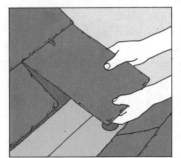

9 If the roof has tiles or slates, remove the bottom layer on one side to fit the zinc flaps underneath (see p. 160)

10 Position the zinc. Push one flap under the tiles and bend the other over the exposed roof. Refit tiles

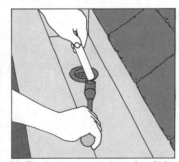

11 Fit the waste-top into the drain hole. Heat the waste rim with soldering iron. Run solder between rim and zinc

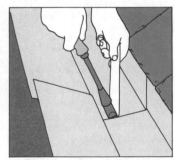

12 Trim the edge of the existing lining and run solder between the two meeting pieces

Insulation

Preventing heat loss in the attic

Because hot air rises, considerable loss of heat in a house occurs mainly through the bedroom ceilings and the roof. To prevent the heat loss and reduce heating bills, insulate the floor, pipes and tanks in the loft and, where possible, the walls.

For convenience, insulate the pipework first, then cover the tank and cylinder. Finish with the floor of the roof-space. Always use proper insulating materials: newspapers and old rags attract insects and are a fire risk.

Before insulating, check that the roof is in good repair (see p. 160).

Walls Attic walls are usually unplastered brick or breeze block, which let heat escape quickly. Cover them with insulating material (see p. 135)

Attic floor Insulation laid between the ceiling joists in the attic floor reduces heat loss to the attic as warm air rises from the rooms below (see p. 114)

Cold-water storage tank When an attic floor is insulated, the winter temperature in the attic drops and water may freeze. Insulate the tank (see pp. 116–18)

Pipework Copper or galvanised iron pipes have a large total surface area through which heat can be lost rapidly. Insulate them with lagging (see p. 115)

Hot-water cylinder A hot-water cylinder has thin walls through which heat can be lost quickly. Insulate it (see p. 118)

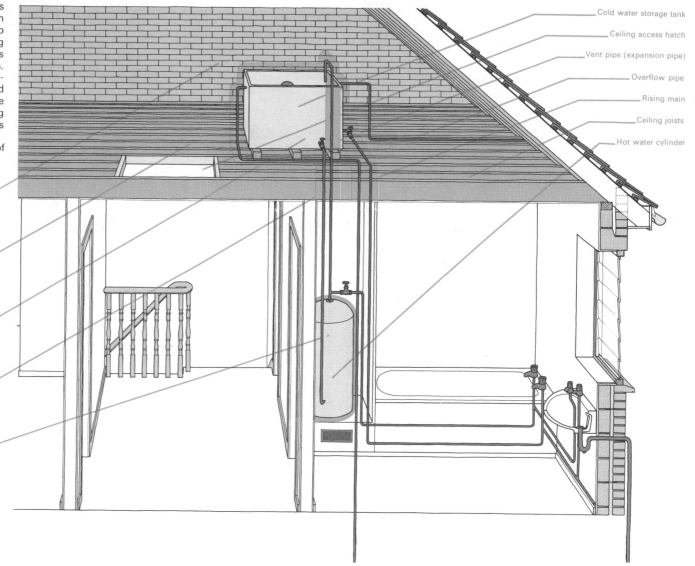

Cold water storage tank

Ceiling access hatch

Vent pipe (expansion pipe)

Overflow pipe

Rising main

Ceiling joists

Hot water cylinder

Insulation Lofts and attics

Insulating a loft with loose material

A loft can be insulated with a 4 in. (100 mm) depth of loose granulated material such as cork, expanded polystyrene, vermiculite or mineral wool. This method is ideal when joists are spaced irregularly or when the loft has awkward corners.

Insulate the hatch with a sheet of polystyrene.

Materials: insulating material; hardboard or thick card for a spreader; planks; polystyrene to fit ceiling hatch; adhesive.
Tools: dustpan and brush or vacuum cleaner with extension lead; tenon saw.

1 Rest planks on the joists and kneel on them. Sweep or vacuum away any dirt between the joists

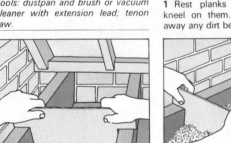

2 Cut a T-shaped spreader to leave a gap of 4 in. (100 mm) between its base and the ceiling

3 Tip insulating material from the eaves inwards. Spread it evenly with the spreader

4 Push the insulating material under any obstruction and spread it by hand to the depth required

5 If pipes are more than 2 in. (50 mm) below the top of the joists, cover with insulating material

Insulating a loft with glass-fibre

The easiest way to insulate a roof if the floor joists are regularly spaced is to use glass-fibre quilting. It is just wide enough to be laid between the joists and be tucked down to make a close-fitting cover.

If you have no insulation in the attic, lay the 4 in. (100 mm) thickness: if you have some and it is less than 4 in. thick, get a thinner quilting that will bring the thickness up to not less than 4 in.

Materials: glass-fibre quilting; PVA adhesive; planks.
Tools: batten; dustpan and brush or vacuum cleaner.

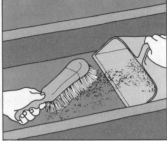

1 Sweep or vacuum dust from between the joists. Check the joists for any signs of rot (see p. 185)

2 Start at the eaves and unroll the glass-fibre carefully from the edge towards the centre of the loft

3 Push the glass-fibre well into the eaves. Do not block up gaps: air must still circulate to avoid condensation

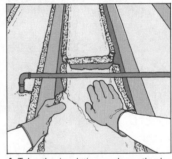

4 Take the insulation underneath obstructions, pipes or cables. Tear the roll if necessary

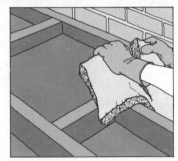

5 When the ceiling hatch is reached, tear off the roll. Continue from the other side of the hatch

6 Tear off a piece of glass-fibre wider and longer than the ceiling hatch. Stick to hatch with PVA adhesive

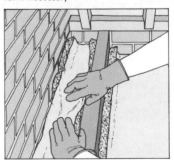

7 For narrow spaces, between a wall and a joist, tear off strips of glass-fibre and tuck them well down

8 Overlap the ends, such as those of a finished roll and a new one, or of a tear, by about 3 in. (75 mm)

Insulation Pipework

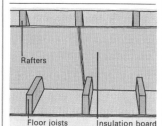
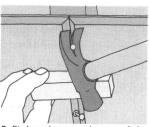
Lagging with felt

Felt strip for lagging is available in rolls 3 in. (75 mm) wide and 12 ft (3·6 m) long. Buy enough to lag all the pipework in the roof, including any small overflow pipes.

Wrap the felt round the pipework like a bandage, so that the edges overlap by about half the width of the strip. Start and finish at right angles to the pipe, and bind diagonally in between. If the material has a waterproof backing, make sure that the felt surface faces the pipes.

Materials: felt strip; ball of twine or string.
Tools: scissors or sharp knife.

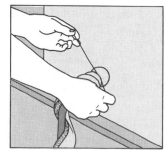

1 Start lagging at the tank. Wind felt round three times. Bind with string or twine

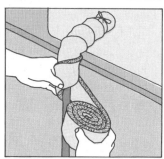

2 Wrap the rest of the strip diagonally so that the edges overlap by half the width of the felt

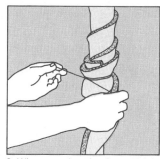

3 When one length of material is finished, overlap the next one a full turn and bind with string

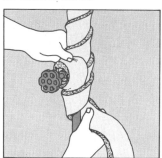

4 Wrap lagging round the neck of any valves. Overlap generously and continue down the pipe

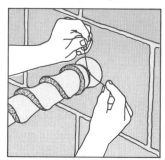

5 Lag overflow pipes. At the outside wall, wrap felt round one full turn and tie with string

Lagging with foamed plastic

Flexible foam-plastic lagging is available to fit any pipe between $\frac{1}{4}$ in. (6 mm) and 3 in. (75 mm) diameter. Do not try to fit lagging of the wrong diameter: it cannot insulate the pipes properly if it does not fit exactly.

The lagging is normally sold in 3 ft (915 mm) or 6 ft (1·8 m) lengths, which can be cut to any size with a sharp pair of scissors.

The lagging is secured with waterproof plastic adhesive tape.

Materials: foam-plastic covering; waterproof plastic adhesive tape.
Tools: scissors or a sharp knife.

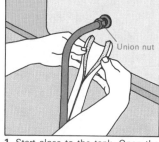

1 Start close to the tank. Open the lagging and spring it over the pipe and the union nut

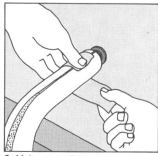
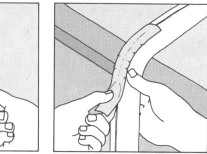

2 Make sure the edges are close together. Wrap adhesive tape round the tank end of the lagging

3 At bends, push the edges together and seal lengthways with adhesive tape to prevent it parting

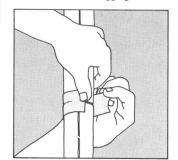

4 To seal joins between lagging sections, wrap tape around the pipe to overlap both pieces of foam

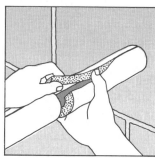

5 Cut a piece to fit between last full length of lagging and wall. Tape the join and at the wall

Insulation Cold-water tanks

Insulating a cold-water tank with loose material

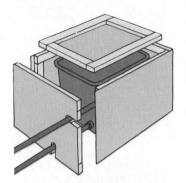

A cold-water storage tank can be insulated in several ways: with a glass-fibre blanket (see p. 118); with polystyrene slabs; or, if the floor is boarded, by surrounding the tank with a hardboard box filled with loose insulation material. Insulate the lid as well as the tank.

Materials: 2×1 in. (50×25 mm) softwood; hardboard; insulating material; plastic funnel with 3 in. (75 mm) diameter top; corrugated fasteners; panel pins; oval nails.
Tools: fine-toothed handsaw; padsaw; rule; claw hammer; wheelbrace and ⅜ in. (10 mm) bit.

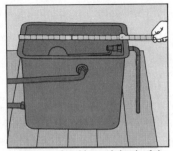

1 Measure the sides and depth of the tank. Add 4 in. (100 mm) to dimensions for a gap between box and tank

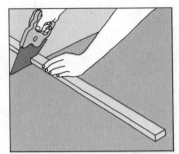

2 Measure and cut four pieces of 2×1 in. (50×25 mm) softwood to make the frame for the first side panel

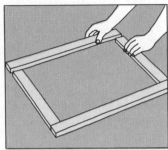

3 Lay the four cut pieces of softwood on a flat surface. Butt their corners together. Check overall size

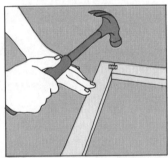

4 Hammer a corrugated fastener into each corner to pull and hold the timber pieces tightly together

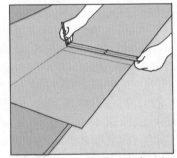

5 Measure the hardboard for the panel. Allow 2 in. (50 mm) extra on the length to cover the end panels

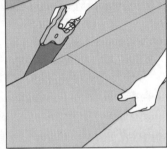

6 Lay the hardboard smooth side up and saw it. Support it with the other hand to prevent it breaking

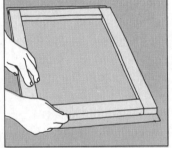

7 Lay the frame on the rough side of hardboard so that 1 in. (25 mm) of hardboard projects at each end

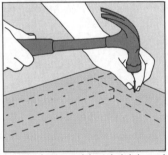

8 Hold frame and board tightly and turn them over. Nail with panel pins spaced 2 in. apart

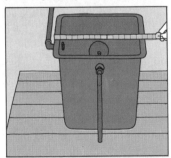

9 Make second panel, then measure width and depth for end frames. Add 4 in. (100 mm) on each dimension

10 Mark the exact dimension for the end panel on the smooth side of the hardboard sheet

11 Saw accurately. Again support the hardboard with one hand to prevent it breaking

12 Position the board and nail with panel pins every 2 in. Cut and make a second end frame

13 Fit one end panel against the hardboard projecting on one of the side panels *(continued)*

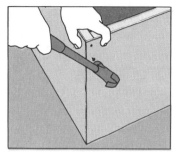

14 Pin through the hardboard overlap into the frame on the end panel. Space panel pins 2 in. apart

15 Place the two joined pieces around the tank sides without pipes. Measure pipe positions

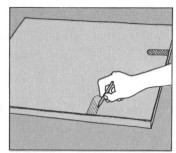

16 Measure and mark pipe positions from the outside edges of the unfitted panels. Shade pipe areas

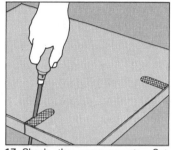

17 Check the measurements. Cut round the shaded areas with a pad-saw. Re-pin hardboard if necessary

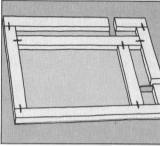

18 Measure and cut extra battens to strengthen the cut panel. Fix with fasteners and panel pins

19 Slide the cut panel into position. Ease the cut-out slots down and around the pipes at the tank

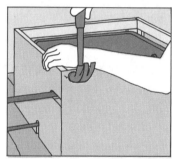

20 Position the final panel. Hold together and pin the overlaps on the side panel to the end frames

21 To keep the box in position on the tank base, nail wood off-cuts tightly against the bottom at each side

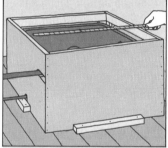

22 Measure the internal dimensions and deduct ½ in. (13 mm) from each. Cut lid-frame pieces

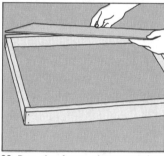

23 Butt the frame pieces together. Nail through the side pieces into the end pieces. Do not split the wood

24 Cut hardboard to fit outside measurements of the frame. Nail to frame with panel pins

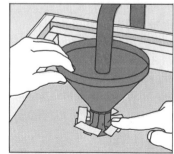

25 Fit lid, frame upwards. If there is an expansion pipe, drill a hole and fit funnel. Seal with adhesive tape

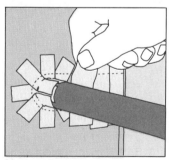

26 Use adhesive tape to seal around the slots cut for the pipes so that insulation cannot spill out

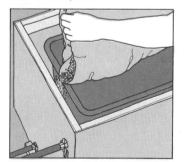

27 Remove lid. Carefully fill the gap around tank with insulating material. Make sure it does not spill into tank

28 Fit the lid with the funnel. Fill lid with insulating material until it is flush with top of frame

Insulation Cold-water tanks

Lagging with a glass-fibre blanket

The simplest way to insulate a cold-water storage tank—rectangular or circular—is with a glass-fibre blanket. Buy a type bonded with paper on one side, for easier handling. Although it is more convenient to have a helper, insulation blankets can be fitted working alone.

Try to buy glass-fibre which is at least as deep as the tank. If this is unobtainable, wrap a second layer around the tank so that it overlaps the first layer. Secure the blanket round the tank with string.

Materials: glass-fibre blanket; string.
Tool: scissors.

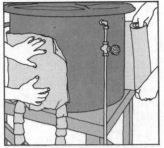

1 Start at the base and wrap glass-fibre round the tank. Overlap the ends of the roll by 3 in. (75 mm)

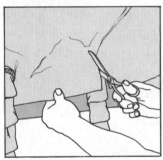

2 Cut a slit in the glass-fibre where pipes enter the tank. Tuck the cut edges under the pipes

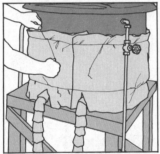

3 Secure with two lengths of string. Do not overtighten, to avoid compressing the insulation

4 If the tank is deeper than the roll, wrap a second layer round overlapping the first. Tie with string

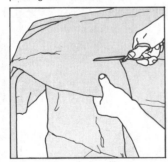

5 Lay a piece of glass-fibre to overlap the lid by about 6 in. (150 mm). Press it to shape. Do not tie it

---

POLYSTYRENE

An insulation box to surround a rectangular cold-water tank can be made from sheets of expanded polystyrene. This lightweight material is an excellent insulator and is available from builders' merchants and hardware stores in varying sheet sizes ranging from $\frac{1}{4}$ to 3 in. (6 to 75 mm) thick.

Make the box about 2 in. (50 mm) larger than each side of the storage tank. Stick the sides together with polystyrene tile cement. Make the lid of two pieces: one to match the overall dimensions of the box and another, glued to the underside, to fit within the sides of the box.

Cut holes for any pipes with a sharp knife. When the sheet is in place around the pipe, glue the access pieces back in position.

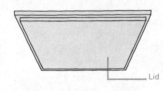

Lid

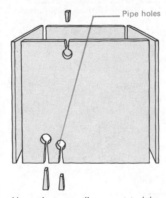

Pipe holes

Use polystyrene tile cement to join the sides; also the two lid pieces

---

Insulation Hot-water cylinders

Lagging with a jacket

When a hot-water cylinder is not insulated, heat can escape rapidly and fuel costs increase unnecessarily.

Insulating jackets to fit most types of cylinder can be bought from builders' merchants or hardware stores. The jackets usually have loose insulating material, such as polystyrene or glass-fibre, in a plastic or fabric covering.

To be effective, a jacket must fit the cylinder. Measure the cylinder's height and circumference, or find out how much water it holds, to order the correct-size jacket.

Materials: insulating kit.

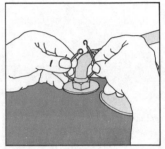

1 Pass the collar provided round the pipe at the top of the cylinder. Do not fasten it

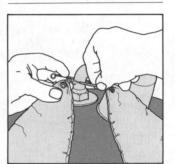

2 Thread the loops of the jacket on to the collar. Secure the collar with the hook and eye

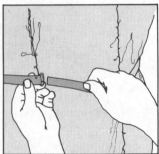

3 Smooth the jacket down over the cylinder. Wrap one of the belts around near the top and fasten it tightly

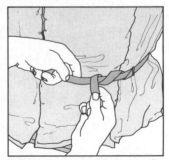

4 Fasten the second belt near the bottom. Twist the excess lengths of belt under the tightened parts

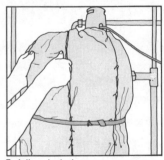

5 Adjust the jacket segments to cover any gaps between them which could let heat escape

---

Plasterwork Methods and materials

Repairing defective plasterwork

Plastering is usually beyond the scope of the amateur, and it is not advisable to attempt to replaster a large area of a wall or ceiling. Small repairs, however, can be undertaken without difficulty.

In most cases, the reason for damaged plasterwork is dampness (see p. 28). Always trace the source and repair the fault before trying to put on new plaster.

Providing a good key

Two coats of plaster are required on any wall. The first —called the undercoat or rendering—must form a good bond or key with the wall. On brickwork, dig out the existing plaster between the bricks to a depth of $\frac{3}{4}$ in. (20 mm). On other walls, roughen the surface by hacking or hammering with a sharp piece of metal, such as a cold chisel.

To give a good bond between the undercoat and the final coat, which is called the skim coat, use a scratcher (see p. 120) on the surface to make score marks about $\frac{1}{16}$ in. (2 mm) deep.

On timber-framed surfaces in old houses, the bond is usually provided by thin strips of wood, called lathing, nailed across the plaster area. If the lathing is inadequate for a bond, fit plasterboard (see p. 126).

If a white deposit appears on the plaster when it has dried, brush it off. If the deposit continues to appear over a period of more than 18 months, the probable cause is dampness (see p. 25).

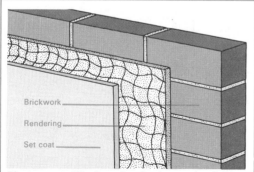

Brickwork

Rendering

Set coat

Plaster coats Wet the wall and make sure that there are no loose particles before putting on the rendering. Score the undercoat before applying the final skim or set coat

The right plaster for the job

The main constituent of plaster is gypsum— the chemical calcium sulphate—which has been partially or wholly dried by burning in a kiln. This process, and the provision of additives during manufacture, determine the type and grade of plaster, which have different setting and hardening times.

Different types and grades are usually sold under brand names. To ensure that the correct plaster is supplied, tell the dealer what repair work is being done.

Because the proportions of the constituent parts in mixing are important, it is advisable to buy pre-mixed plasters. These are available from builders' merchants for undercoats and finishing coats.

Undercoats are plaster powder to which a coarse-grained material—usually sand— has been added. The final coat is neat plaster powder. Both must be mixed with water to give a dough-like consistency for application.

For small holes and fine cracks, use a filler such as Alabastine or Polyfilla. Follow the manufacturer's instructions. To repair a large area where lath and plaster have previously been used (see p. 126) use plasterboard. One side, usually coloured cream, has a surface ready for decoration. The other, usually grey, is for finishing with a coat of plaster.

When storing plaster, make sure that it is protected from damp and cold. The material crystallises with water and cannot be remixed once that has taken place.

Plaster takes a long time to dry out completely after application. Its surface should not be sealed with non-porous materials, especially oil paint, for about six months. Use a water-based paint as a temporary decoration.

Lime

In houses that are more than 60 years old the walls are probably finished with lime plaster or with lime plaster on wooden lathing.

Lime is used mainly as an additive to cement-and-sand mixes, some gypsum plasters, and mortars for brickwork (see p. 693). Added to sand-and-cement rendering it helps to prevent cracking and crazing on outside walls (see p. 197).

Lime is alkaline: treat all surfaces which may contain it in any form with an alkali-resistant primer before using an oil paint (see p. 41) to cover them.

TYPES OF PLASTER AND THEIR USES

Plasters	Examples	Uses	Mixers	Characteristics
Hemi-hydrate	Plaster of Paris, sometimes called gauging plaster	For reproduction of decorative plasterwork, such as moulding		Sets very quickly. Difficult for amateurs to use
Retarded hemi-hydrate	Adamant; Belpite; Sirapite board plaster; Sirapite browning; Thistle	The only plaster suitable for finishing plasterboard. Can be used as an undercoat on brick, concrete and block surfaces	For undercoat, use 1 part plaster to $2\frac{1}{2}$ or 3 sand. For skim coat, use neat plaster with water	Unsuitable for use over large areas since it sets quickly
Anhydrous— moderately burnt	Sirapite	For undercoats and finishing coats. Easiest for amateur to use since it can be moistened with water when nearly set, enabling the surface to be smoothed with the trowel	For undercoat, use 1 part plaster to 3 sand. For skim coat, use neat plaster with water	Ideal for larger repairs since it dries slowly and can be given a better finish
Anhydrous—hard burnt	Keenes; Parian	Suitable for finishing coats and exposed angles	Use neat plaster with water. For the undercoat use 1 part cement to 3 sand, or 1 plaster to 2 sand. Do not use lime	Gives a hard, smoother finish

Plasterwork Tools and techniques

Choosing tools for plasterwork

Use a clean bucket, basin or bowl to mix plaster and carry water. Although some tools—for example hawks, scratchers and bats—can be made to save money, many must be bought. It is advisable, to obtain good results, to buy good-quality tools. The better the blade of a float, for example, the better the finish. Buy the lightest float available, for easy handling.

Spot board To hold the plaster within easy reach for high work, lay a piece of marine plywood or hardboard stiffened with battening on an old box or a stool.

Hawk Make a hawk to carry the plaster to the area being covered. Use marine plywood $\frac{1}{4}$ in. (6 mm) thick and nail on a handle of $1\frac{1}{2}$ in. (40 mm) diameter rod.

Trowel Buy a small one for mixing materials and repairing small areas of damage; can also be used for brickwork pointing (see p. 18).

Floats Buy two floats—one metal, one wood. Use the metal float for applying large areas of plaster and polishing skim coats. Use the wooden float to give undercoats a rough finish. Always clean them after use.

Scratcher Drive nails into a piece of wood and cut off their heads with pincers. Use it to scratch the undercoat to provide a bond for the final coat of plaster.

Brush To dampen the surface of a wall before plastering, use either an old distemper brush or a two-knot stockbrush. Always clean the brush after use to make sure that it is clean when it is next used.

Filling knife Use a filling knife to apply filler to small patches.

Bat To carry small quantities of filler, make a hardboard or plywood bat. Carry the filler on the rough side of the bat and clean off the surplus after use.

Basic methods

Remove all loose plaster with a hammer and chisel and clean the area with a wire brush.

If necessary, especially with concrete, hack the surface with a cold chisel to give a good key and apply a proprietary bonding compound.

Use a large brush to wet the wall just before applying the plaster.

Mixing the plaster
If sand is needed for the undercoat, make sure that it is clean. Never use beach sand; it contains salt which can spoil the surface.

Mix the plaster powder and sand together before adding clean water to give a dough-like consistency. Use it immediately. If a short delay is anticipated, make the mixture a little wetter. Never mix more than can be used within about half an hour.

Use of tools
Make sure that the metal float is kept wet during plastering. Hold it at right angles to the mortar, sweep the plaster on to the hawk and shake it gently so that the plaster settles.

When taking plaster off the hawk to start work, lift it with the underside of the float blade. Push the plaster firmly on to the wall and hold the blade at about 30 degrees when spreading it. If the float is held too flat, it sticks to the plaster.

As the plaster spreads, gradually release pressure on the blade so that it flattens towards adjacent surfaces.

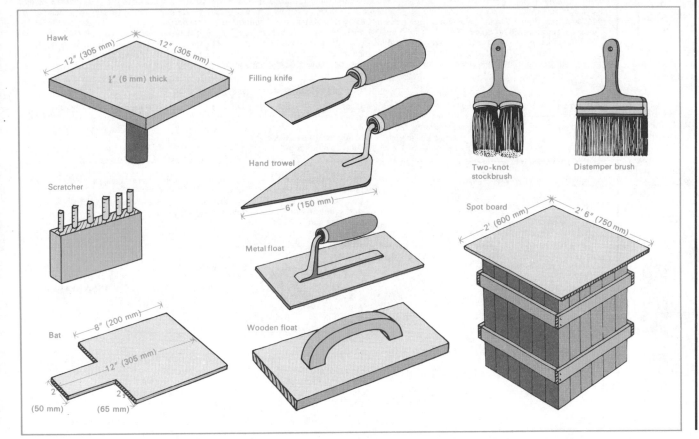

Hawk
12" (305 mm)
12" (305 mm)
$\frac{1}{4}$" (6 mm) thick

Filling knife

Scratcher

Hand trowel

6" (150 mm)

Metal float

Wooden float

Two-knot stockbrush

Distemper brush

Spot board
2' (600 mm)
2' 6" (750 mm)

Bat
8" (200 mm)
12" (305 mm)
2" (50 mm)
2½" (65 mm)

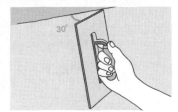

30°

Float To spread the plaster, keep the metal float at an angle of about 30 degrees to the surface

Plasterwork   Solid walls and ceilings

Filling small cracks

Hairline cracks in walls and ceilings can be repaired with a simple plaster filler. Fill wider cracks—where a stronger bonding agent is needed, or where there is heat or vibration to withstand—with a cellulose-based compound. Mix only enough filler for half an hour's working—the average setting time. The filling compound can be coloured by mixing in an emulsion paint or watercolour. Several attempts may be needed, however, to get the tint to match the surrounding area. A less satisfactory alternative is to paint the finished repair.

Materials: filler; medium-grade glass-paper.
Tools: filler knife or scraper; old paint-brush; plasterer's bat; glass-paper block.

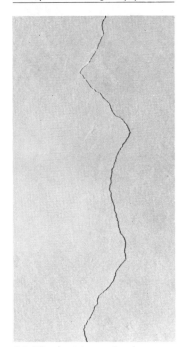

A hairline crack in a wall surface

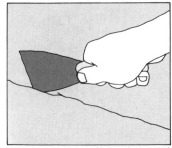

1 Scrape away any loose plaster and score a little more deeply into the crack to provide a key for the filler

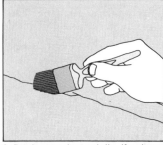

2 Brush away dust and dirt. If a plaster filler is to be used in the repair, dampen the crack slightly

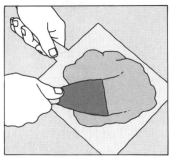

3 Mix the filler on the bat, adding water to the powder and stirring to get a fairly stiff consistency

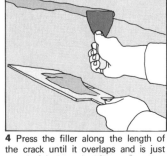

4 Press the filler along the length of the crack until it overlaps and is just proud of the sound surface

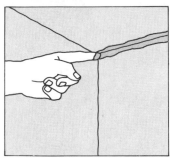

5 In an awkward corner or angle, the best way to press the filler home is with the fingertips

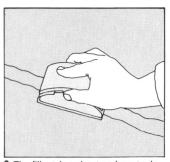

6 The filler takes about an hour to dry. Rub down with glass-paper and leave for 24 hours before painting

Repairing a chipped corner

Chipped wall corners are one of the commonest forms of plaster damage in the home. Where the damage is relatively minor, and the surrounding area is sound, the repair can be made readily with a cellulose-based filler, such as Polyfilla. It is essential to remove all loose and unsound plaster surrounding the damaged area. If, as a result, the brickwork underneath is bared, or if a very large area has to be renewed, a more substantial repair, using plaster, may be necessary.

Materials: cellulose-based filler; rubber glove; bucket; medium-grade glass-paper.
Tools: filler knife or scraper; old brush; plasterer's bat; glass-paper block.

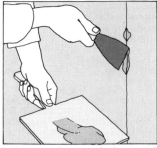

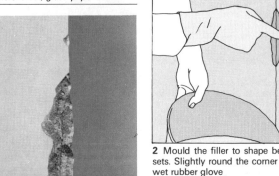

Damage after furniture removal

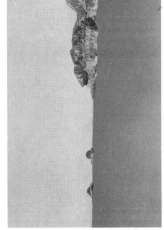

1 Remove all unsound plaster and brush clean. Apply filler until it is proud of the surrounding area

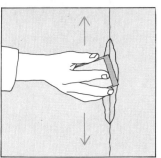

2 Mould the filler to shape before it sets. Slightly round the corner with a wet rubber glove

3 When the filler is dry, rub it down with glass-paper, matching the angle with the surrounding area

Plasterwork Solid walls

Reinforcing a corner

Extensive damage to plaster corners may occur when heavy furniture has to be moved in a confined space, such as in a narrow passageway or landing or on a winding staircase. Similar damage is less likely to occur again if metal reinforcement is included when re-plastering is done.

For right-angled corners a strip of aluminium or nylon can be used; but since this must be fixed flush with the surface of the plaster, it can be unsightly unless covered with wallpaper.

A better method is to use Expamet metal angle bead, a zinc-coated steel mesh with a firm, rounded corner which is fixed to the brickwork and covered with plaster. Since the bead serves as a straight edge, it is relatively easy to achieve a true right angle when applying the final coat of plaster. Expamet can be obtained from most builders' merchants.

Materials: metal reinforcer; rendering; plaster.

Tools: plasterer's hawk; bolster; club hammer; spirit level; metal float; straight-edge.

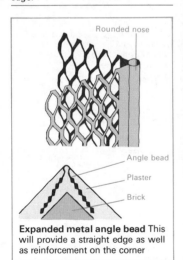

Expanded metal angle bead This will provide a straight edge as well as reinforcement on the corner

Rounded nose
Angle bead
Plaster
Brick

Damaged plaster on a brick corner

1 Cut back the plaster on both sides of the corner to expose 4–5 in. (100–125 mm) of brickwork

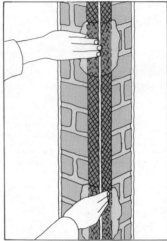

2 Apply dabs of plaster about 24 in. (610 mm) apart on each surface. Press the reinforcer wings into the dabs

3 Use a straight-edge and spirit level to adjust the reinforcer, allowing for the thickness of the finish

4 Press the wings of the reinforcer into the plaster so that they will not project through the rendering

5 Apply rendering, leaving $\frac{1}{16}$ in. (2 mm) for the final plaster finish. Do not scratch the zinc on the bead

6 Apply finishing plaster just proud of the bead and thinly over the nosing. Polish, but not excessively

Repairing a damaged corner

When part of a single wall surface has to be replaced, there is usually sound plaster on each side of the repair area. It is easy, therefore, to ensure that the new surface is level with the old. Repairs to a corner are more difficult because there is only one section of old plaster against which to judge the level of the new. To get a second guideline, cut a length of straight softwood slightly longer than the height of wall to be plastered. Nail the softwood batten against one side of the corner, so that its front edge is flush with the level of the plaster on the other. To repair the second wall, hold the batten against the first side. Do not nail it.

Materials: 2 × 1 in. (50 × 25 mm) softwood; nails; plaster (or sand and cement) and water; 3 ft (915 mm) batten; rubber glove.
Tools: bolster; club hammer; hammer; chisel; brush; bucket; trowel; wooden and metal floats; panel saw; hawk; corner trowel (optional).

GETTING THE SURFACES LEVEL

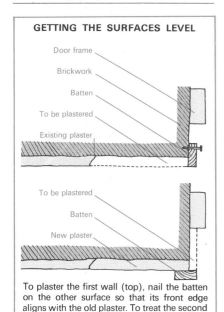

Door frame
Brickwork
Batten
To be plastered
Existing plaster

To be plastered
Batten
New plaster

To plaster the first wall (top), nail the batten on the other surface so that its front edge aligns with the old plaster. To treat the second side (bottom), hold the batten lightly against the area just covered

Plasterwork damaged at a corner where a partition wall has been removed

1 Chisel the old plaster straight. Cut a piece of softwood slightly longer than the height of the damage

2 Nail the softwood batten on the other wall so that its front edge is level with the surface of the old plaster

3 Mix half a bucket of plaster with water to give a creamy consistency, or 4:1 sand and cement (see p. 693)

4 Dampen the brickwork and edges of the remaining plaster. Use a large brush and plenty of clean water (*continued*)

Plasterwork Solid walls

(continued)

5 Apply plaster or mortar in thin layers, working from the bottom. There is no need to wait for each layer to dry

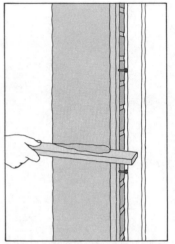

6 Scrape off the surplus with a piece of softwood held against the existing plaster and the batten

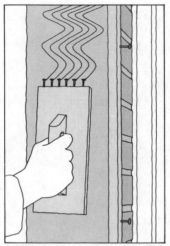

7 Hammer nails into the wooden float. Get a flat finish flush with the existing plaster, then score slightly

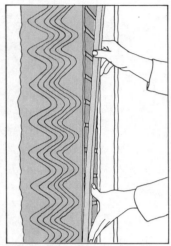

8 Remove the nails and pull the batten straight off the wall. If it is removed sideways, the plaster may crumble

9 Hold or wedge the batten against the new plaster. Undercoat the other wall, flush with narrow edge of batten

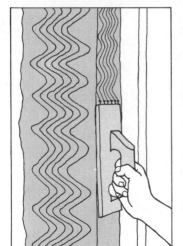

10 Remove the batten and lightly score the second surface of plaster. Leave both for 24 hours until touch-dry

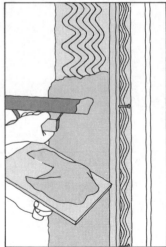

11 Mix plaster, dampen undercoats and apply skim coat flush with adjacent surfaces. Use batten as previously

12 Use the dampening brush and metal float to get a polished finish. Maintain the corner angle

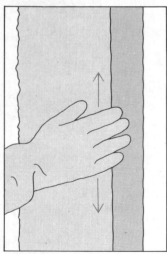

13 Before the plaster hardens, round the corner slightly by hand, wearing a wet rubber glove

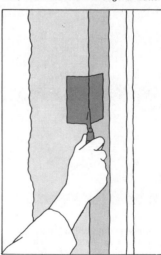

14 A corner trowel, obtainable from a builders' merchant, can simplify the job of polishing corner surfaces

Plasterwork Plasterboard

Filling nail holes

As new plasterboard dries and contracts, the nails securing it are often loosened. As a result, the skim coat of plaster covering the nail heads is pushed out and drops away. Damage of this type—where the hole in the plasterboard is no more than $\frac{1}{2}$ in. (13 mm) across—can be repaired simply with a proprietary filler. Avoid damaging the board when the nail is tapped back into position.

Materials: filler; medium-grade glass-paper.
Tools: nail punch; hammer; filler knife or scraper; glass-paper block; old paintbrush.

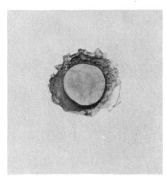

Plasterboard skim coat damaged

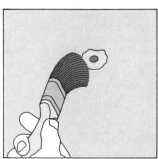

1 Use an old paintbrush to remove all the loose plaster from around the exposed nail head

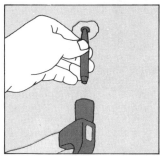

2 With a punch and hammer, lightly tap in the nail. The board can be damaged by fierce hammering

3 Press enough filler on to the cleaned area to make it just proud of the plasterboard surface

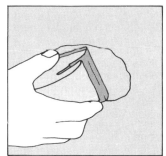

4 When the filler dries, rub it down gently with glass-paper. Avoid damaging the surrounding surface

Filling a small hole

When the damage to the plasterboard is more than superficial—say, a small hole left after a wall fitting has been removed—use plaster instead of filler to repair it. But if the hole is more than about $\frac{1}{2}$ in. (13 mm) across, plaster alone may not be enough: use plasterer's scrim cloth to provide a key. Before starting to repair, find out if there are any electricity cables running behind the damaged area. If there are, switch off at the mains and try to push the cables aside, using a blunt tool or probe that cannot damage the cable. If the cables cannot be moved, make sure they are not damaged during the repair work. Complete the repair before restoring the power.

Materials: scrim cloth; plaster; medium-grade glass-paper.
Tools: knife or old chisel; filler knife or scraper; plasterer's bat; metal float; old paintbrush; glass-paper block.

Hole after removing a wall fitting

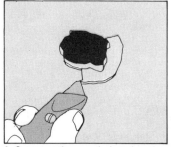

1 Cut away the sound plasterboard—about $\frac{1}{2}$ in. (13 mm) wide and $\frac{1}{4}$ in. (6 mm) deep—around the hole

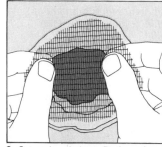

2 Cut scrim cloth to fit the enlarged hole. Two pieces, made to overlap, can be used if necessary

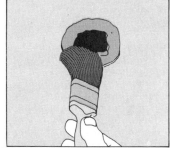

3 Dampen the bared plasterboard around the hole and apply small dabs of plaster to the exposed edges

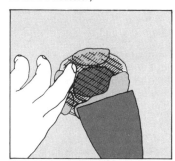

4 Press the scrim on to the dabs to hold it and apply a thin coat of plaster with a filler knife

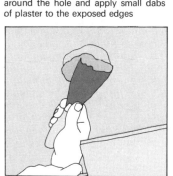

5 Let the plaster become spongy before applying further coats. Build up gradually to the surrounding surface

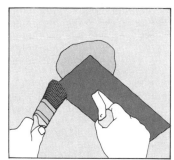

6 When the final coat is almost set, dampen the plaster and polish with the metal float. Decorate when dry

Plasterwork Plasterboard

Mending a large hole in a ceiling

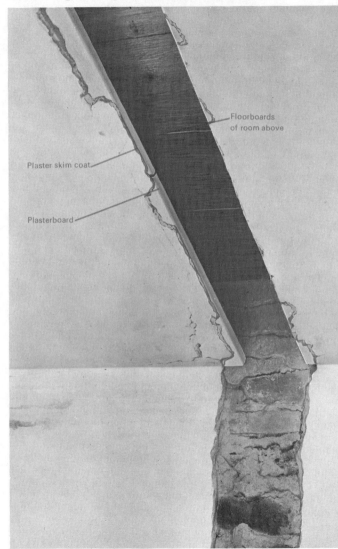

Gap left by removal of a partition wall

The removal of a wall or partition between two rooms results in a long, narrow hole in the ceiling. If the hole is at right-angles to the floorboards above, and therefore parallel with the joists, timber bearers will have to be fitted and the new plasterboard secured to them. Before starting to fill the hole, lift one or two floorboards in the room above to provide access to each end of the hole. If the hole is in line with the floorboards (see below), the plasterboard can be secured to the joists.

Materials: plasterboard (for plasterboard finish, see p. 119); scrim cloth; rough-sawn softwood to provide fixing edges for plasterboard: 2, 3 or 4×2 in. (50, 75 or 100×50 mm) depending on the length of the hole to be repaired; 2 or 3 in. (50 or 75 mm) wire nails; 1½ in. (40 mm) galvanised clout nails.
Tools: rule; pencil; Stanley knife; straight-edge; hammer; hand or panel saw; metal float; old chisel; hawk; bolster; damping-down brush; large trowel or small coal shovel.

HOLE ACROSS JOISTS

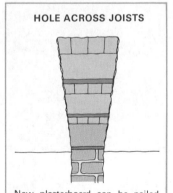

New plasterboard can be nailed directly to the joists if two or more joists are exposed by the hole. In this case, ignore the first six pictures of the sequence

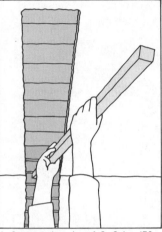

1 Cut two lengths of 2×2 in. (50×50 mm) softwood to match the long sides of the hole, allowing an extra 1–2 in. (25–50 mm) at each end

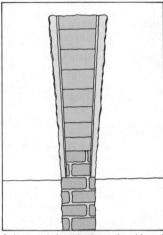

2 Lay each length along the sides of the hole, with about ½–¾ in. (13–20 mm) protruding. These will provide bearers for the new plasterboard

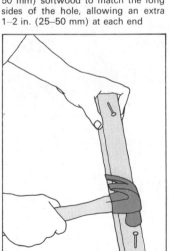

3 Cut two 2×2 in. (50×50 mm) bearer battens to go between the joists above the bearers. Tap a wire nail, at an angle, into each end

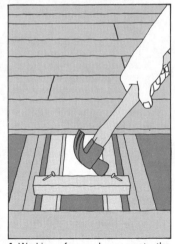

4 Working from above, rest the bearer battens on the bearers at the ends of the hole and drive the angled nails into the joists *(continued)*

5 Nail the bearers to the battens. Do this carefully, as heavy hammering may cause further damage to the ceiling on either side

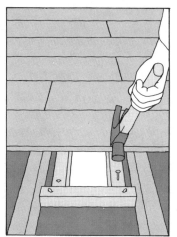

6 Alternatively, the bearer battens can be fixed between the joists at the ends of the bearers, and skew-nailed to both joists from above

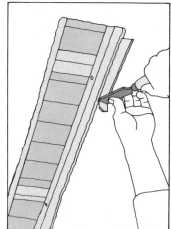

7 Chisel off the plaster skim coat from the old plasterboard for about 1 in. (25 mm) all round the edge of the hole. This is to take the scrim cloth

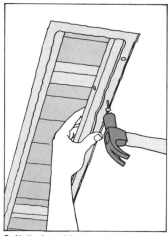

8 Nail the old plasterboard to the bearers with galvanised clout nails, supporting the bearer with your free hand. Measure the hole

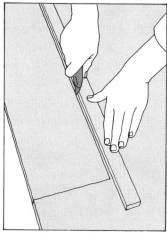

9 Score the measurements deeply on the paper side of the new board with a knife. Bend the board and complete the cut from the other side

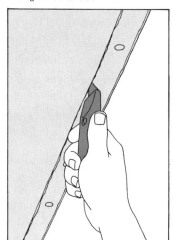

10 Dry-fit the plasterboard into position. Run a sharp knife between the edges of the new and old boards if the new one is a tight fit

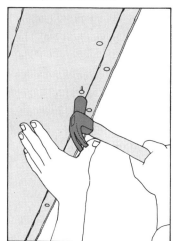

11 Nail the plasterboard to the bearers with galvanised clout nails spaced 6 in. (150 mm) apart. Cut lengths of scrim to cover all joins

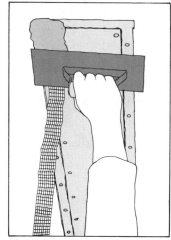

12 Fix the end of a length of scrim with a dab of plaster. When it starts to set, apply plaster sparingly to secure the rest of the scrim in place

13 Push the plaster well behind the scrim and into the join to form a key. When it is firm, but not dry (about an hour later), apply a finishing coat

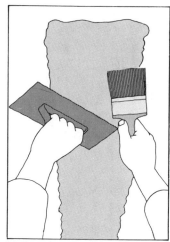

14 Smooth and polish with a metal float and a damping-down brush. Finish the new plaster flush with the surrounding surfaces

Plasterwork Plastic-surfaced ceilings

Filling a small ceiling crack

Jagged cracks at the edge of plaster-board—at the angle between a ceiling and a wall—may occur as a new house shrinks when drying out. If the ceiling is plastic-surfaced, check the damage carefully and make sure the surface is not likely to peel further. A proprietary filling mixture—especially suitable for plastic-surfaced plasterboard—is usually obtainable from most do-it-yourself dealers.

Materials: sponge; stick; Artex Cold Water Mix.
Tools: paint scraper; 1 in. (25 mm) paintbrush; bucket; small bowl.

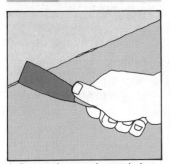

1 Remove loose and ragged plaster with a paint scraper to open the crack to $\frac{1}{16}$ in. (2 mm) wide

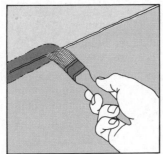

2 Lightly dampen the plaster along the crack with a 1 in. (25 mm) paint-brush and clean water

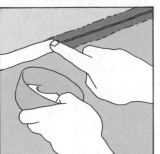

3 Mix a small quantity of Artex to a thick, creamy consistency. Press it into and along the crack

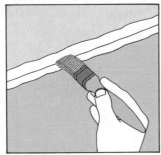

4 Allow the filling to firm. Dampen the paintbrush and clean off any excess filler

Restoring a loose surface

If a small area of a plastic-surfaced ceiling comes away from the plaster-board, remove all the loose plastic and loose surface paper before filling the hole with Artex Cold Water Mix.
  Special scrim paper tape is available to strengthen the area before finishing the repair.

Materials: Artex Cold Water Mix; Artex tape $2\frac{1}{2}$ in. (65 mm) wide; washing-down sponge; stick.
Tools: sharp knife; paint scraper; home-made applicator; paintbrushes; home-made texturing tool; clean bucket; plastic bowl (or additional bucket).

MAKING A TEXTURING TOOL AND AN APPLICATOR

Texturing tool To achieve a finish similar to the existing surface, cut plywood 6×4 in. (150×100 mm). Cut a softwood handle with two notches and nail through the board into the handle. Fit a sponge and cover it with polythene. Secure it to the handle with a stout elastic band

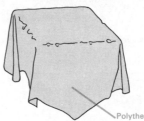

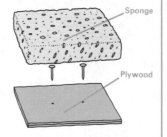

Polythene

Sponge

Plywood

Softwood

Elastic band

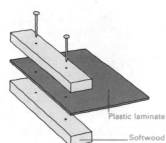

Plastic laminate

Softwood

Applicator Cut plastic laminate 8×4$\frac{1}{2}$ in. (200×115 mm). Cut two pieces of 1$\frac{1}{2}$×$\frac{1}{2}$ in. (40×13 mm) softwood, 8 in. (200 mm) long. Drill two undersized holes through the wood and laminate. Nail the laminate between the wood pieces

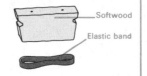

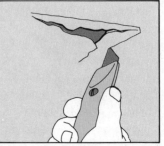

1 Use a sharp knife to cut back all plastic and surface paper which has come loose from the plasterboard

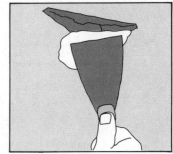

2 If the core of the plasterboard is exposed, dampen with water. Spread on a thin layer of Artex

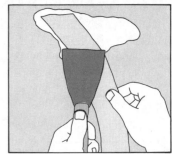

3 Soak enough lengths of scrim tape to fill the damaged area. Lay them on with the paint scraper   *(continued)*

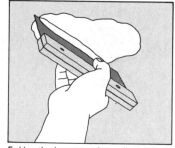

4 Leave the scrim and mix to dry for 12–24 hours. Apply a second coat of Artex Mix

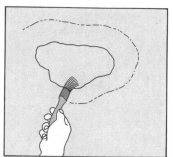

6 With paintbrush or sponge, dampen 3–4 in. (75–100 mm) of the ceiling surface around the repair

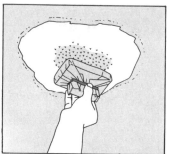

8 Use a home-made texturing tool (see p. 128) to match the new surface with the existing texture

5 Use the home-made applicator (see p. 128) to spread the mix as evenly and smoothly as possible

7 Mix a little more Artex Mix. With a brush, apply it evenly over the whole area under repair

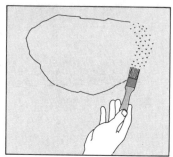

9 Remove any unwanted mix from the surface texture with a dampened 1 in. (25 mm) paintbrush

Mending a large hole through a ceiling

If a ceiling plasterboard has broken through—perhaps because of damage from an attic above—first make a frame by nailing four lengths of wood to the joists above the ceiling. This will provide a support for the old and new plasterboard.

Materials: 1½ in. (40 mm) 14 SWG plasterboard nails; Artex Cold Water Mix; Artex Kraft scrim tape; 2×2 in. (50×50 mm) wire nails; sponge. Tools: hammer; saw; paint scraper; sharp knife; 3–4 in. (75–100 mm) paintbrush; 1 in. (25 mm) paintbrush; home-made texturing tool; two buckets; plastic bowl.

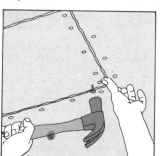

1 From above, nail four lengths of softwood flush with the bottom of the joists

2 From underneath, trim back the hole to expose about 1 in. (25 mm) of each edge of the softwood frame

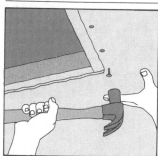

3 Nail the sound edges of the old plasterboard to the frame. Use 1½ in. (40 mm) nails to secure it

4 Cut plasterboard to give ⅛ in. (3 mm) gap all round. Nail it, cream side showing, to the frame

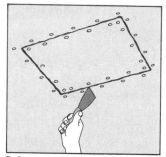

5 Scrape back the surface for about 6 in. (150 mm) all round to provide a smooth surface for the scrim

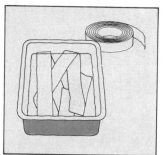

6 Cut enough lengths of scrim to cover the area. Dampen them and place in a dry container *(continued)*

(continued)

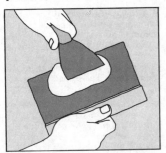

7 Mix the Artex thickly. Use a paint scraper to spread it on the edge of an applicator

8 Spread the mixture in 6 in. (150 mm) strips over the joints of the patch and any cracks

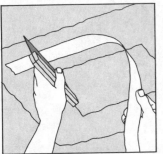

9 Use the applicator to lay the damp scrim tape evenly along the four joins of the patch

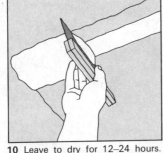

10 Leave to dry for 12–24 hours. Apply a second coat of mixture flush with the existing surface

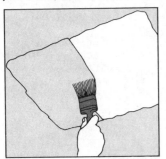

11 Dampen existing ceiling about 3–4 in. (75–100 mm) around the resurfaced area. Apply mixture

12 Finish with the texturing tool. Allow to firm, and remove excess mixture (see p. 129)

Repairing a small or medium-sized hole

The method of repairing a hole in a lath-and-plaster surface depends on whether or not the laths are broken. If they are undamaged, they will provide sufficient support or key for the new plaster; if damaged, an additional key must be provided. Where the hole is not more than 3 in. (75 mm) across, the key can be supplied by a plug of stiff paper, soaked first in water and then in plaster of a creamy consistency. Reinforce larger holes with expanded metal (see p. 131). Holes may be filled solely with filler compound or plaster; for economy, holes may be partly filled with a 4:1 sand-and-cement rendering and then finished flush with a coating of plaster

Materials: sand and cement; filler compound or plaster; medium glass-paper. Tools: pointing trowel; filler knife; hawk or plasterer's bat; damping brush; bucket; glass-paper block.

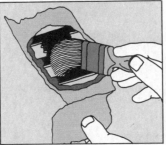

1 Peel back any surrounding wallpaper and brush away loose material in and near the damaged area

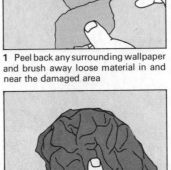

3 Push the paper into the hole until it is about $\frac{1}{4}$ in. (6 mm) below the surface of the good plaster

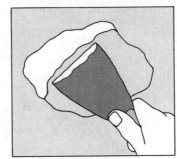

5 Damp the filling with a wet brush and apply a coat of plaster to finish flush with the surrounding surface

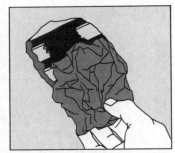

2 If the laths are broken away, prepare a plug of paper roughly the size of the hole and soak it in plaster

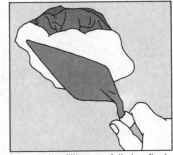

4 Apply the filling carefully but firmly with a trowel to within $\frac{1}{16}$ in. (2 mm) of the surface. Allow to dry

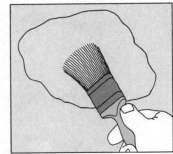

6 Brush and smooth over the repaired and surrounding area with water. Avoid leaving bristle marks

Using expanded metal to repair a large hole

To repair a hole larger than 3 in. (75 mm) across in a lath-and-plaster wall, use expanded metal as a key for new plaster. Smaller holes can be filled without the key (see p. 125).

Expanded metal is diagonally meshed steel which has a galvanised or bitumen-paint finish to ensure that it cannot rust and stain the plaster. It is usually sold in 9 × 2 ft (2·7 m × 610 mm) sheets, but most do-it-yourself shops or builders' merchants can supply smaller offcuts if necessary. Several mesh sizes are available.

The most useful for plaster work is $\frac{1}{4} - \frac{3}{8}$ in. (6–10 mm) mesh. Nail the edges of the metal every 4 in. (100 mm) to any timber uprights in the wall. If there are no uprights, hook the metal over the existing laths.

Apply plaster in small dabs and build it up in layers gradually to the required thickness. If it is applied in large amounts, plaster will fall through the mesh before it has time to set.

Materials: expanded metal; sand, cement and plaster, or proprietary plaster (see p. 119); water; 1–1½ in. (25–40 mm) galvanised clout nails. Tools: chalk; tin snips; hammer; brush; hawk; pointing trowel; metal float.

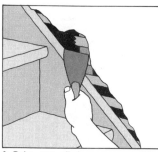

1 Rake out all loose or crumbling plaster from the hole. Cut back the plaster underneath its edges

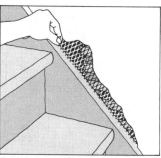

4 Push the metal into the hole. Tuck the edges between the plaster and broken laths

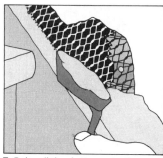

7 Dab a little plaster on to the metal with a pointing trowel. Build up plaster in thin layers

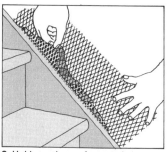

2 Hold a piece of expanded metal against the hole and mark the size with a piece of chalk

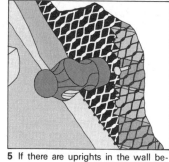

5 If there are uprights in the wall behind the laths, nail the edges of the metal to them

8 Leave plaster to dry for about 24 hours. Dampen surface and apply final coat with a metal float

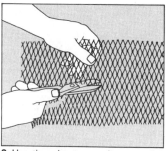

3 Use tin snips to cut the expanded metal slightly larger all round than the size chalked on it

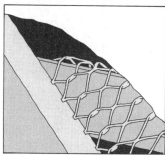

6 If there are no uprights, hook the edges of the metal over the edges of the nearest laths

9 Smooth and polish the finished surface with a metal float and a dampening brush (see p. 120)

Plasterwork **Wall fittings**

Repairing plaster at a wall socket

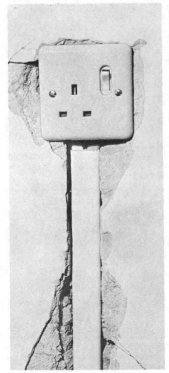

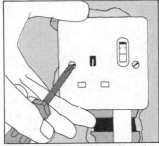

1 Switch off the power at the mains. Remove the screws securing the face-plate on the socket box

2 Brush out any loose crumbling materials round the box and dampen the plaster with clean water

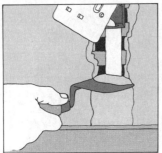

3 Apply first coat of plaster with a pointing trowel. Push the mix in around the conduit

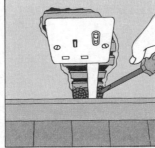

4 If plaster falls through bottom of the channel, jam a ball of chicken wire into it. Cover with plaster

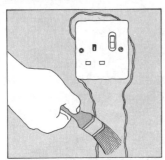

5 When the first coat of plaster has set—about two hours later—dampen it with a brush and clean water

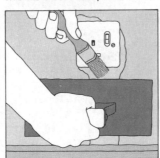

6 Screw back the face-plate. Apply the final coat. Plaster and polish the surface with the metal float

Never attempt any work on a wall near an electric socket with the power supply on; always switch off at the mains beforehand.

When a socket has just been installed, encase the new wiring in a plastic conduit, available from do-it-yourself shops and electrical suppliers. Conduits are C-shaped and just flexible enough to be opened up and clipped around the cable.

Materials: cement, sand and plaster, or proprietary plasters (see p. 119); water; chicken wire.
Tools: screwdriver; paintbrush; bucket; hawk; trowel; metal float.

Plasterwork **Cornices**

Restoring an old cornice

The appearance of an old cornice may be spoilt if paint is allowed to accumulate in its crevices.

Test a small section of cornice with a damp sponge to see if the paint can be removed with water. If it can, lay dust sheets or plastic sheeting and work on lengths of about 12 in. (305 mm) at a time. Each length dealt with will take about an hour to restore.

Restore cornices before the rest of the room is decorated: it is a messy job and can ruin existing wallpaper.

Materials: water; dust sheets.
Tools: garden spray; small screwdriver; soft-haired brush; stepladder.

1 Fill a spray with clean water and soak about 12 in. (305 mm) at a time of the surface of the cornice

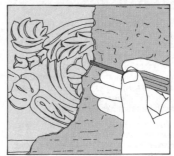

2 Leave cornice to soak for half an hour, then carefully scrape out the paint with a screwdriver

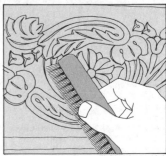

3 Brush out loose or flaking material frequently until all paint has been removed. Redecorate (see p. 40)

Fitting plaster coving

When cracks develop persistently along the angle between walls and ceiling, strengthen and conceal the damaged area with ready-made cornices, called covings. Plaster covings, available from builders' merchants, have a smoother texture than the lower-priced polystyrene covings. They are fire-resistant and easy to cut and handle. If lengths of more than 6 ft (1·8 m) are to be fitted, get a helper to hold one end while the adhesive sets sufficiently to keep the coving in position.

Coving sticks only to plaster, and any paper on the area to be covered by coving must be removed. Adjacent remaining paper is likely to be slightly soiled by adhesive when the coving is fixed. For that reason it is advisable to fit cornices when the walls are being stripped for redecorating.

Use only the adhesive supplied or recommended by the coving manufacturer. Apply it thickly to pack any small holes in the wall. If the wall surface is very irregular, fix it with 1½ in. (40 mm) alloy nails every 24 in. (610 mm). Punch in the nail heads and fill the holes.

Materials: coving; coving adhesive; fine glass-paper; nails; string; chalk.
Tools: fine-toothed saw; hammer; scraper; flexible filling knife; paintbrush; bucket; trowel; ruler; knife; old chisel; punch; mitre block.

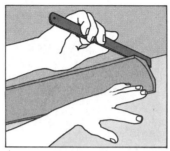

1 Hold a piece of coving against the wall and measure how far the top edge projects

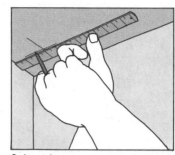

2 At each corner, measure the length of that projection from both walls and mark the ceiling

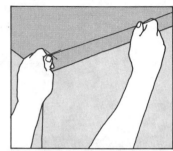

3 Rub coloured chalk along a length of string. Fix it at one corner and hold it at the other. Snap along its length

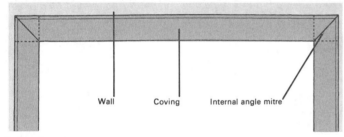

Internal angle corners Measure from one corner to the other and cut coving to fit exactly. Cut mitres at the ends of the coving. If the corner is less than 90 degrees, cut the mitres a little less than 45 degrees: if more than 90, cut a little more than 45 degrees. Fill any gap with the coving adhesive

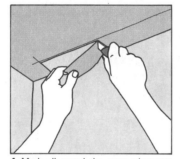

4 Mark all round the room, then cut the paper ⅛ in. (3 mm) inside the lines. Strip off the paper

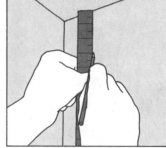

5 Mark the depth of the coving on each wall at each corner. Mark lines with chalked string

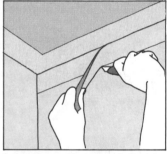

6 Cut along with a sharp knife ⅛ in. inside the marked lines. Remove the wallpaper as it is cut

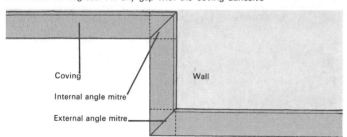

External angle corners Measure and cut coving to the length of each wall plus the width of the coving. Mitre each strip of coving at an external angle. If the corner is not exactly 90 degrees, adjust the angle of the mitre and fill any gap with coving adhesive

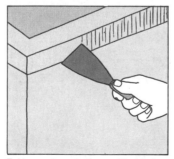

7 Use a sharp knife or old chisel to roughen the exposed wall and ceiling plaster to improve adhesion for coving

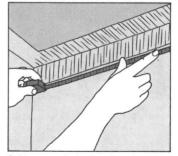

8 Measure all the lengths of wall in the room and mark the lengths of coving required

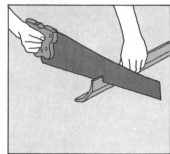

9 Cut the coving with a fine saw. To ensure a clean edge, saw from the front of the coving strips *(continued)*

Plasterwork Cornices

(continued)

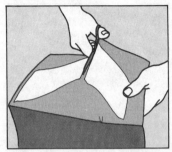

10 To mitre the corners, first cut out the paper templates supplied by the coving manufacturers

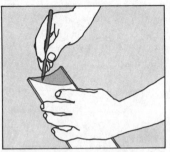

11 Check whether each mitre is internal or external. Trace the appropriate template on the coving

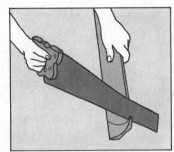

12 Cut all mitres with the fine saw. Cut from the front of the coving to ensure a clean edge

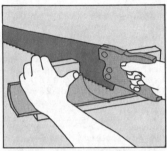

13 If the corners are exactly 90 degrees, use a 45-degree mitre block as a guide when cutting through the coving

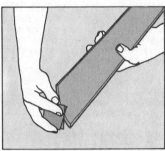

14 Smooth all cut edges with fine glass-paper. Do not distort the angle of the cuts

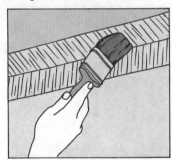

15 Wet all the exposed wall and ceiling surfaces. Apply plenty of water with an old paintbrush

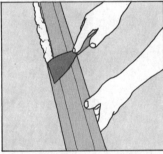

16 Mix adhesive—not more than can be used in 20 minutes—and spread it thickly on the back edges of the coving

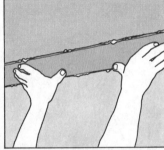

17 Press the coving firmly into place at the angle of the wall and the ceiling. Hold it in position until it sticks

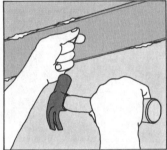

18 If the coving cannot stick because the walls are uneven, fix with nails every 24 in. (610 mm). Punch in heads

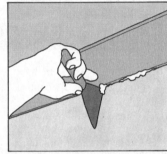

19 Use a scraper to remove all excess adhesive along the edges of the fitted coving before it dries

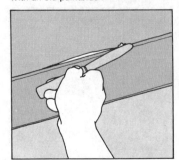

20 Use the excess adhesive as a filler to plug all the small cracks, gaps and nail-head holes

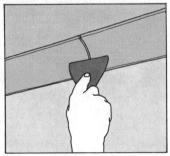

21 Leave a gap of $\frac{1}{8}$ in. between adjacent lengths of coving. Fill in with excess adhesive

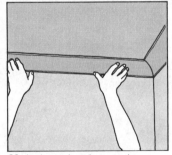

22 At internal and external corners, butt the mitred edges as tightly together as possible

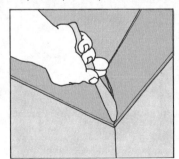

23 Fill the mitre joint with adhesive. Use a flexible knife and fill upwards towards the ceiling

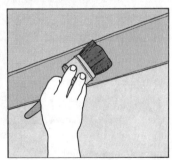

24 Remove any last traces of adhesive from the edges and face of the coving with water and a clean paintbrush

Plasterwork Dry lining

Fitting plasterboard

If an interior wall is in poor condition, a simple alternative to replastering is to fit sheets of specially prepared plasterboard, called dry lining. The technique improves the heat insulation of a room and no finishing work is needed before decorating the walls.

Dry-lining boards, which are usually 8×4 ft (2·4×1·2 m) wide with slightly bevelled edges, are not normally stocked by builders' merchants. Order the boards, jointing material and tape required in advance of the work.

Hack off old plaster and loose material and remove the skirtings (see p. 84) before trying to fix the lining. The plaster required for the fixing is first-coat plaster (see p. 119) which hardens in about an hour.

The filling material at the joints sets in about 45 minutes and cannot be softened, but the finishing material for the joints can be: its hardening rate depends upon the amount of water used. Mix it 30 minutes before use and follow the manufacturer's instructions.

Materials: dry-lining plasterboard; first-coat plaster (see p. 119); joint filler; joint finishing; jointing tape; double-headed nails; battening; sponge.
Tools: claw hammer; plumbline; pencil; straight-edge; spirit level; applicator.

1 Mark three horizontal lines on the wall: one about 9 in. (230 mm) from the top, one across the centre, and one about 6 in. (150 mm) from bottom

2 Start at one end of the wall and mark points every 18 in. (455 mm) along the top line until the other side of the room is reached

3 Temporarily secure a plumbline at each mark on the top line. Mark a vertical line downwards from each mark on the top line

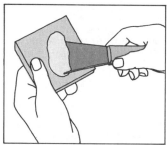

4 Cut 6 in. plasterboard squares for each of the intersection marks on the wall. Spread coarse plaster on a few of the squares

5 Place a plasterboard square—called a dot—at the ends of each line. Centre them on the line with one edge against the other wall

6 Place dots over each of the remaining line intersections. Check with a straight-edge that they are in line. Leave to dry for 24 hours

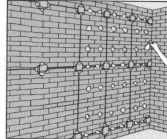

7 Place dabs of plaster, evenly spaced, in two rows between the vertical lines. The dabs should project about $\frac{1}{4}$ in. (6 mm) in front of dot surfaces

8 Use battens to make a foot lever. Rest a dry-lining board on them and lift to ceiling against corner. Bottom of board should be below skirting height

9 Keep the board in position and press it on to the dabs. Fix double-headed nails through the bevelled edges at each side of the board

10 Leave plaster to set for about an hour. Remove the nails with a claw hammer. Work carefully to avoid pulling the board from the plaster

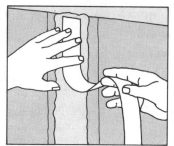

11 Press joint filler into gaps between boards. Finish with thin coat of filler across bevelled edges. Stick tape over filler. When set, apply second coat

12 When set, apply thin coat of joint finishing, about 8 in. (200 mm) wide. Use applicator (see p. 128), and smooth the edges with a damp sponge

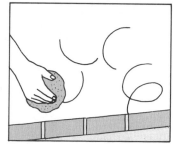

13 Apply second coat when first is dry. When dry, apply watery mix over whole surface with circular movement. Refit skirting boards (see p. 84)

Plumbing Water and waste systems

How the water and waste systems work

The cold-water supply—from the water board main—enters a house below the ground and passes through the rising main to a storage tank (see p. 140) in the roof space. The rising main has a loop (a gooseneck) for expansion and contraction.

In most houses at least one tap—fed from the rising main—provides drinking water. Pipes from the storage tank distribute cold water to the system. Other pipes distribute the hot water.

Waste from a single-stack system (shown right) is fed into a soil pipe, 3–4 in. (75–100 mm) in diameter, connected at ground level to the drainage system (see p. 61). The other end of the pipe emerges through the roof to ventilate the system.

The connection between every waste fitting and the soil pipe has a water-filled trap (see pp. 142 and 155), to prevent foul air entering the house from the drainage system.

Most older houses have a two-stack drainage system: the lavatory outlet has a separate discharge pipe, and other wastes are connected to a second pipe that drains into an open gulley. Both discharge into the same manhole.

It is illegal to make plumbing alterations (except replacement of fittings) without consulting the local authority.

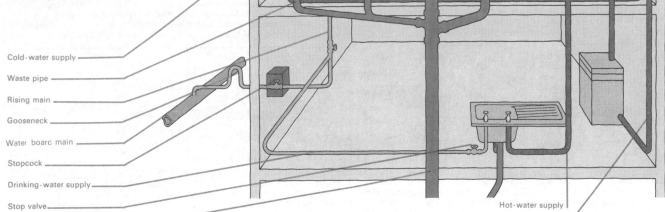

Hot-water expansion pipe
Cold-water supply
Overflow outlet and pipe
Storage tank
Hot-water cylinder
Boiler to cylinder

Cold-water supply
Waste pipe
Rising main
Gooseneck
Water board main
Stopcock
Drinking-water supply
Stop valve
Soil pipe

Hot-water supply
Cylinder to boiler

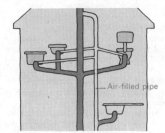
TURNING OFF THE WATER

If the rising main bursts, turn off the water board stopcock which is always near or just inside the boundary of the property.

The stopcock may be in a covered box or pit, about 2–3 ft (610–915 mm) deep. If it cannot be reached by hand, use a length of wood with a V shape cut in the end. Turn clockwise to cut off the supply.

Inside the house

If any other pipe inside the house bursts, turn off the nearest stop valve which supplies it. If there is no separate valve, turn off the valve on the rising main.

Always turn off the water supply when working on taps or fittings. If a tap is fed directly from the rising main, turn off the main valve. If a tap is fed from a tank or cylinder, turn off the nearest supply stop-valve to it. If there is none, turn off the supply at the main valve and open all taps to drain the tank.

Plumbing Pipes

Clearing an air lock

USING MAINS PRESSURE

If air spurts out of a tap with the water or if knocking noises are heard in a pipe, there is an air lock.

It may be possible to clear it by forcing water from the mains supply through the air-locked tap. The greater pressure of the mains pushes the water and air in the pipe up through the system to the storage tank.

This is a simple operation when the air lock is at the hot-water tap in the kitchen. Run a length of hose between the hot-water tap and the adjacent cold-water one, which is the mains supply.

Even when an air lock is else-where in the system, it may be possible to use a very long hose to connect the kitchen cold tap to the one that is affected.

If more than one tap is air-locked, clear the system from the lowest one.

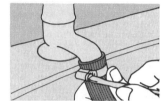

1 Fit a hose between the kitchen cold tap and the air-locked one

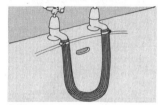

2 Turn on both taps for five minutes. Turn off affected tap first

BLOWING THROUGH THE PIPES

When a cold-water pipe is air-locked, and its tap cannot be connected to the kitchen cold tap, try to clear the air lock by blowing through the pipes. Push a length of tube into the cold-storage tank and through its outlet. Turn on all cold taps and blow down the tube.

Note that this is not possible with hot-water pipes: there is no access to the inside of the cylinder.

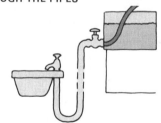

DRAINING THE SYSTEM

If an air lock cannot be cleared by flushing or blowing, drain the system. Turn off the water at the hot-water cylinder (or rising main if the cold-water pipes are air-locked) and open all the taps until water ceases to flow.

Close each tap approximately two-thirds, then turn on the supply. Adjust the taps to get a small, even flow of water.

Turn each tap in rotation—starting at the bottom of the house—until they are all half open, then all three-quarters open. When all the air has spurted free, turn off each tap in rotation until only a dribble of water flows. Close taps.

Pipes and joints used in plumbing

The pipes in a household plumbing system may be iron, lead, copper or plastic. Do not try to mend a damaged lead or iron pipe: skilled techniques are required, and it is advisable to call in a plumber.

It is, however, possible to replace lead pipe with plastic or copper. Plastic is cheap, and easy and light to handle, but most plastics are unsuitable for hot-water systems. If an iron pipe has to be replaced, always consult a plumber.

Three basic methods are used to join pipes: pressure, welding and soldering. Joints which rely on pressure are called compression joints. There are two types: manipulative and non-manipulative.

A manipulative compression joint should be fitted only by a plumber: special tools are necessary to shape the ends of the pipes that are to be connected.

A non-manipulative (Type A) compression joint is the best to use for above-ground replacement and extension work. It is easily fitted with a spanner.

The most common type of soldered connection is the capillary joint. The pipes are joined inside a metal sleeve which has two raised sections containing solder.

Capillary joints can be used only on metal pipes: compression joints are suitable for either metal or plastic.

For certain types of plastic pipes, there is a further alternative—solvent welding. The ends of the pipes are coated with a special solvent and are pushed together inside a sleeve. The solvent fuses the pipes and the sleeve together.

TYPES OF JOINTS

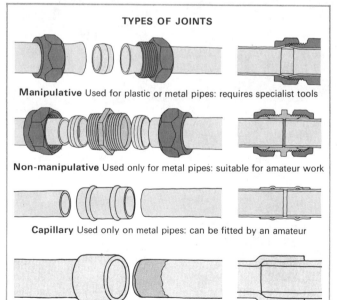

Manipulative Used for plastic or metal pipes: requires specialist tools

Non-manipulative Used only for metal pipes: suitable for amateur work

Capillary Used only on metal pipes: can be fitted by an amateur

Solvent-welded Only for plastic pipes: suitable for amateur work

Capillary joints

Capillary joints require no nuts to hold the pipes together and are most suitable for visible connections of copper or stainless steel pipes. (They cannot be used for other metal pipe connections.)

Use only a phosphoric acid flux for stainless steel joints.

Fit the ends of the pipes into the joint sleeve and heat the raised rings with a blowlamp to melt the solder inside. After cooling, the solder hardens to hold the pipes together.

Materials: capillary joint to match diameter of pipes; wire wool; flux. Tools: blowlamp; file; screwdriver.

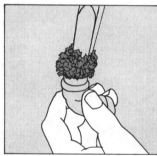

1 Clean inside both ends of the joint with wire wool held on the end of a screwdriver

2 File off any rough edges on the pipes and clean the outside with wire wool *(continued)*

Plumbing Pipes

(continued)

3 Spread a coating of flux on the pipe ends and inside both ends of the capillary joint

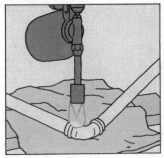

4 Push both pipes into the joint. Heat round one ring on the joint with a blowlamp

5 When solder appears at joint rim, stop heating and clean rim. Do the same at the other ring

MENDING A LEAKING CAPILLARY JOINT

If a capillary joint is leaking, it may be possible to repair it by soldering. If that is not successful, the only remedy is to remove the section containing the joint and fit a new pipe with two new capillary joints.

If a joint has to be soldered while the pipe is against a wall or floor, fix or lay in place a protective blanket of glass-fibre matting to prevent fire. Turn off the water and drain the pipe before starting work.

Materials: solder; flux; glass-fibre; wire wool.
Tool: blowlamp.

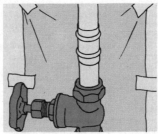

1 Turn off water and drain the pipe. Fix glass-fibre behind the capillary joint to protect the surroundings

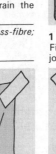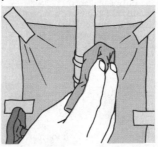

2 Clean ½ in. (13 mm) of the pipe on each side of the joint with wire wool. Make sure the pipe is dry

4 Heat the joint with a blowlamp until the solder in the joint begins to melt and run out

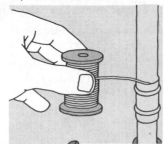

3 Spread flux on the cleaned pipe. Flux is poisonous: do not let it touch any cuts on the hands

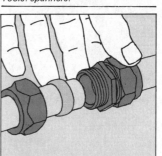

5 Take away the blowlamp and then apply wire solder round the warm joint. Allow to cool

Fitting a compression joint

A non-manipulative compression joint (see p. 137) is the easiest for an amateur to use when connecting metal or plastic pipes. Measure the external diameter of the pipes (see p. 698) and buy a joint to fit.

Each joint has two coupling nuts and two metal rings which fit over the ends of the pipes being joined. As the locking-nuts are tightened, the rings bite into the pipes and seal them together.

Materials: compression joint to fit pipework; boss white sealing compound (from builders' merchants).
Tools: spanners.

1 Fit a nut and compression ring on each pipe. Smear boss white on pipe ends and compression rings

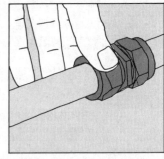

2 Push one pipe into the compression fitting and screw up its coupling nut by hand

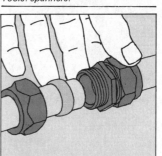

3 Push the other pipe into the fitting. Hand-tighten, then tighten both nuts fully with two spanners

MENDING A LEAKING COMPRESSION JOINT

1 Hold the joint and tighten each nut half a turn. If that is not successful, drain the pipe

2 Undo the nuts and smear boss white round the threads of the fitting. Tighten the nuts

Fitting a T junction

If an additional supply is to be taken from an existing copper water pipe, connect the old and new pipework with a compression T junction. If the existing pipe is lead, engage a plumber for the work.

The new pipe must not have a larger internal diameter than the existing pipe. The T piece should be same internal diameter as supply pipe: if new pipe is smaller than old one, buy a reducing T piece.

Materials: T junction; compression fittings; boss white; lagging.
Tools: hacksaw; wrench; adjustable spanner; file.

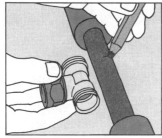

1 Hold the T piece against the existing pipe where the junction is required and mark on the existing pipe the centre of the T

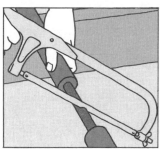

2 Hold the pipe with one hand to prevent straining and make a right-angle cut at mark with hacksaw. Smooth the burred edges with a file

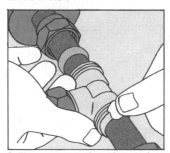

3 Fit a compression ring and a coupling nut on each cut end. Smear boss white round pipe end and ring to make joint watertight

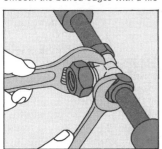

4 Tighten nuts on to the threads by hand. Finish by holding body of joint with wrench and tightening nuts with spanner. Do not overtighten

5 Fit new pipe, with its compression ring and coupling nut, in place. Lag the T piece, the extension pipe and the old pipe (see p. 115)

Replacing a lead pipe with copper

Do not try to repair a damaged lead pipe: replace the worn or broken section with a copper pipe.

Buy a length of copper pipe, with a diameter which can be inserted in the lead pipe. Make sure, however, that the diameter of the copper is large enough not to restrict the flow of water. Seek advice when buying the pipe from a builders' merchant.

Materials: length of copper pipe; thin plastic tube for siphoning water; wire wool; flux; glass-fibre; plumber's solder; glass-paper.
Tools: hacksaw; screwdriver; penknife; blowlamp; wood block.

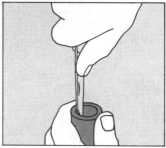

1 Turn off water and cut off damaged section with hacksaw. Scrape away some lead inside pipe with penknife

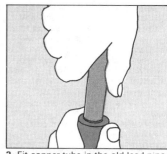

2 Fit copper tube in the old lead pipe. It should fit snugly about 1 in. (25 mm) deep. Scrape more lead if necessary

3 Remove copper pipe. Clean end with wire wool. Hold in a rag. Smear on flux and heat with blowlamp

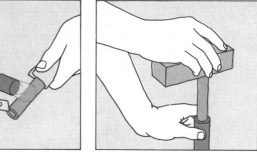

4 Keep pipe in flame and apply solder. Lay aside and apply flux to edge and inside of lead pipe

5 Heat copper pipe again. Insert it while still hot into the lead pipe. Tap firmly in place

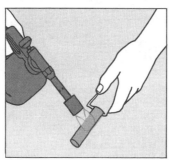

6 Apply a coating of flux to a piece of glass-paper. Lay aside. Protect wall or floor with glass-fibre

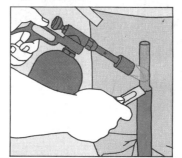

7 Apply solder to the joint. Concentrate flame on the copper pipe to avoid melting the lead

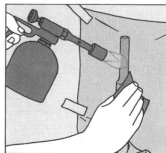

8 Build up a thick layer of solder. Wipe it with flux-coated glass-paper to make a neat finish

Plumbing Storage tanks

Fitting a new cold-water tank

If a galvanised cold-water storage tank leaks, fit a new polythene tank.

Check that the pipes can be fitted on the new tank at the same level as they are on the old. If the tank is corroded, the ball valve may need to be replaced (see p. 141). If new pipework is fitted, use copper with compression fittings (see p. 138).

Pipes and fittings are now made in metric sizes only, though fittings for connection to imperial sized pipes can still be obtained.

Materials: polythene tank, same capacity as the old one; new high-pressure ball valve; 15 mm and 22 mm copper pipe; 15 mm and 22 mm gate-valves, with compression joints; tank fittings; timber for platform if needed.
Tools: claw hammer; saw; hacksaw; file; adjustable spanner; wheelbrace; $\frac{5}{8}$ in. (16 mm) and $\frac{7}{8}$ in. (22 mm) bits.

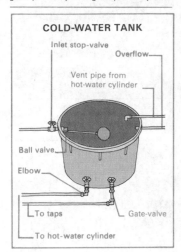

COLD-WATER TANK

Inlet stop-valve
Overflow
Vent pipe from hot-water cylinder
Ball valve
Elbow
To taps
Gate-valve
To hot-water cylinder

WARNING
Never try to install a new hot-water tank—engage a plumber for the work. A hot-water tank incorrectly installed is a potential hazard and may prove dangerous.

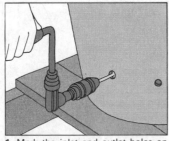

1 Mark the inlet and outlet holes on the new tanks at the correct height. Drill the inlet $\frac{5}{8}$ in. and the outlets $\frac{7}{8}$ in. diameter

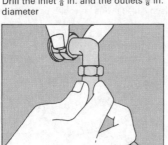

5 Fit the made-up gate-valve to the end of the inlet ball valve outside the tank. Use a compression fitting for this joint

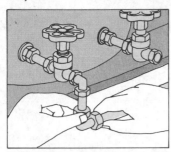

9 Cut off the old outlet pipes. Use 22 mm pipe and elbows to connect the pipes with compression joints to the new tank

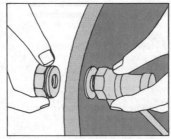

2 Fit the inlet end of the ball valve to the inlet hole at the top of the tank. Fit a nylon washer on the inlet and tighten the lock-nut

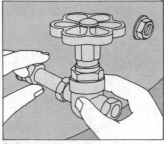

6 Cut two 6 in. (150 mm) lengths of 22 mm pipe and connect to the two 22 mm valves and elbows. Fit to the two outlet connectors

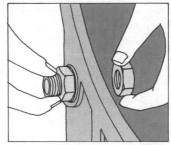

10 Cut a $\frac{1}{2}$ in. hole in the top of the tank opposite the ball valve. Fit a union piece with a nylon washer for the overflow pipe

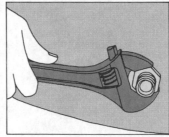

3 Fit nylon washers to compression-joint tank connectors. Push the connectors through the outlet holes at bottom. Fit nuts outside

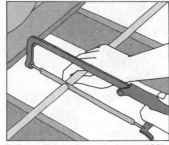

7 Turn off the rising main (see p. 136). Drain the old tank and cut the old rising-main pipe near the inlet pipe on the new tank. Remove old tank

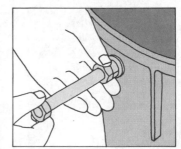

11 Cut a length of 15 mm copper tube to extend the overflow from the new tank to the old pipe. Connect with compression joints

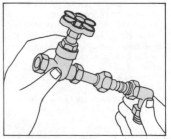

4 Cut a 6 in. (150 mm) length of 15 mm copper pipe. Fit it with a compression joint to the gate-valve. Fit elbow at other end of pipe

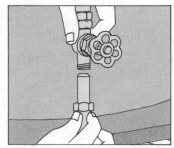

8 Use 15 mm elbows and copper pipe to connect rising main to the inlet stopcock on new tank. (If lead rising main, see p. 139 for connection)

12 If necessary, use new copper pipe and compression joints to extend the old vent pipe to discharge over the new tank

Plumbing Ball valves

Stopping an overflow

The water flow into a cistern or tank is controlled by a ball float operating a piston. As the float, which is on the end of a lever arm, rises with the water level, it moves the piston to close a valve and shut off the water.

The cistern may overflow if the piston washer is worn, if dirt obstructs the valve or if the ball float leaks.

There are two basic types of valve: the Portsmouth, which has a horizontal piston, and the Croydon, with a vertical piston.

Materials: rubber piston washer; wire wool; Vaseline.
Tools: pliers; screwdriver.

PORTSMOUTH VALVE

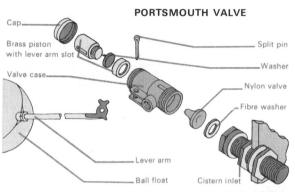

Cap
Brass piston with lever arm slot
Valve case
Split pin
Washer
Nylon valve
Fibre washer
Lever arm
Ball float
Cistern inlet

CROYDON VALVE

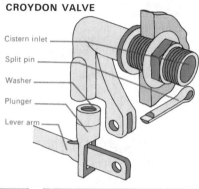

Cistern inlet
Split pin
Washer
Plunger
Lever arm

FITTING A BALL FLOAT

The ball float is screwed on the lever arm and is easily replaced if it becomes faulty. Water will enter a corroded or punctured float and the valve will close more slowly. Eventually the valve will fail to close, causing an overflow. As a temporary measure, remove the float, empty it, replace it on the lever arm and tie it in a plastic bag.

To keep a valve closed until the float can be replaced, tie the lever arm to a length of wood laid across the top of the cistern.

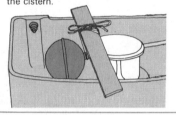

1 To replace a washer, shut off the water supply to the cistern. Withdraw the split pin holding the lever arm

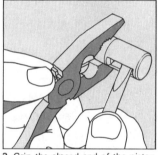

2 If there is a cap on the end of the valve case, remove it. Push out the piston with a screwdriver

3 Grip the closed end of the piston and insert a screwdriver in the slot to unscrew the two parts

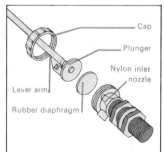

4 Prise out the rubber washer from the smaller end of the piston and replace it with a new one

REDUCING THE NOISE

The fitting of silencer tubes to tanks and cisterns is now forbidden by most water authorities because of the risk of back-siphonage.

The noise of a cistern filling up can be greatly reduced by fitting a Torbeck equilibrium diaphragm valve.

5 Screw the two parts together, clean off any burrs or scale with wire wool and smear with Vaseline

6 Turn on water briefly to flush out any dirt. Replace piston—washer end first—and lever arm. Restore supply

If the cistern overfills Bend the lever arm down slightly to lower the level of water in the cistern

Cap
Plunger
Nylon inlet nozzle
Lever arm
Rubber diaphragm

Diaphragm valve Many modern units have a replaceable diaphragm instead of a piston to control the flow

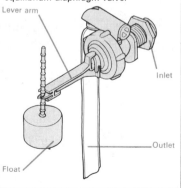

Lever arm
Inlet
Outlet
Float

Plumbing Traps and waste fittings

Fitting new washers on a waste trap

Every basin, sink and bath has a waste trap which retains a quantity of water to ensure that smells cannot enter the house from the waste pipe; it also collects waste which may block the pipe.

Traps are of lead, copper or plastic. Blockages can be dealt with in all types by the householder, but *repairs* to lead traps require the skill of a plumber.

Place a bucket under a leaking trap, unscrew the connections and remove the washers. Take the washers to an ironmonger or builders' merchant and buy new ones to match. After refitting a trap, run the water to check for leaks.

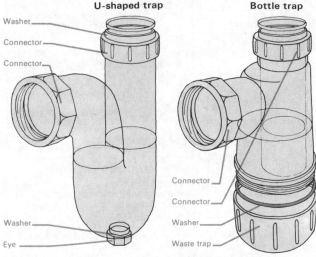

U-shaped trap   Bottle trap

Washer
Connector
Connector
Washer
Eye

Connector
Connector
Washer
Waste trap

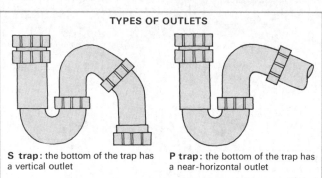

TYPES OF OUTLETS

S trap: the bottom of the trap has a vertical outlet

P trap: the bottom of the trap has a near-horizontal outlet

Sealing a waste fitting

A waste fitting is a short pipe connecting the sink or bath outlet to the trap and the waste pipe.

The flange which sits on the sink outlet and the back nut below the sink should both be sealed with a linseed oil or mastic putty. If they leak, remove and clean the fitting. Replace with new putty.

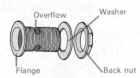

Overflow   Washer

Flange   Back nut

1 Disconnect the trap below the sink (see p. 151). Fit pliers into the grating and grip with a spanner

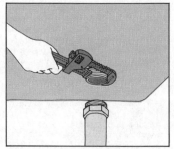

2 Hold the grating steady with the pliers. Unscrew the back nut below the sink with an adjustable spanner

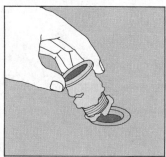

3 Lift the fitting out of the outlet. Strip off the old washer and brush the fitting clean

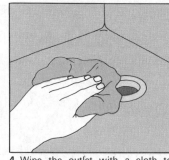

4 Wipe the outlet with a cloth to remove dirt and putty. Dry it thoroughly to ensure that new putty sticks

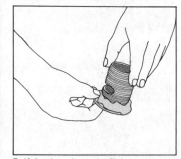

5 If the threads on the fitting are worn, buy a new one. Knead putty under the flange

6 Insert the fitting in the outlet. Put putty on washer and fit the washer and the back nut underneath the sink

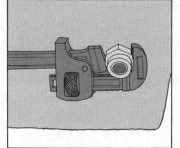

7 Hold the grating above the sink with pliers. Tighten the back nut with an adjustable spanner

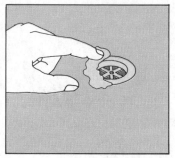

8 Remove surplus putty round the flange and above the back nut with the fingers. Check for leaks

Plumbing Taps and stop valves

Maintenance and repair

Wash and polish all taps regularly to prevent corrosion. Do not use abrasives: they destroy the chrome finish.

Maintenance and repair for ordinary taps and stop valves is the same: some others—for example, the Supatap or one with a pull-off head—need slightly different adjustments (see pp. 144, 145).

Use replacement washers that match the size of the existing ones and before fitting them make sure there are no pieces of the old washer left in place. If the old washers are leather or fibre, use rubber or nylon replacements.

Materials: washers as required—½ in. (13 mm) for sinks and basins, ¾ in. (20 mm) for baths; or washer plate (Supataps); mixer unit seals; rubber O rings.
Tools: adjustable spanner; screwdriver; small spanner for jumper nut; pliers.

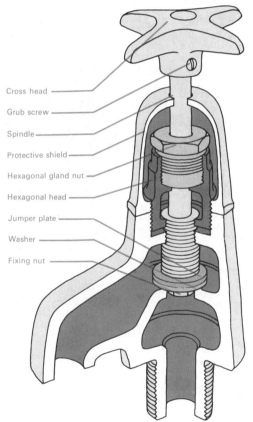

Cross head
Grub screw
Spindle
Protective shield
Hexagonal gland nut
Hexagonal head
Jumper plate
Washer
Fixing nut

STOP VALVES AND SUPATAPS

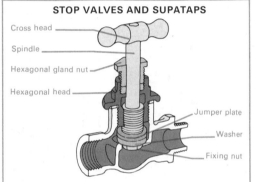

Cross head
Spindle
Hexagonal gland nut
Hexagonal head
Jumper plate
Washer
Fixing nut

Stop valves are used to control the flow of water in pipework and are often found near cold-water tanks, hot-water cylinders and lavatory fittings

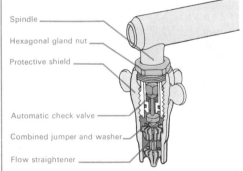

Spindle
Hexagonal gland nut
Protective shield
Automatic check valve
Combined jumper and washer
Flow straightener

Supataps prevent water vibration noises in pipework. The washers can be changed without turning off the water supply

Fitting a new washer

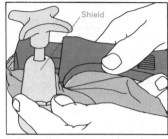

Shield

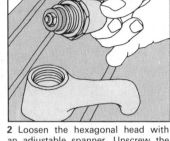

1 Shut off the water supply and open the tap or valve fully. Fit waste plug in sink. Protect shield with rag and remove it with a spanner

2 Loosen the hexagonal head with an adjustable spanner. Unscrew the loosened nut by hand and lift the top of the tap away from the body

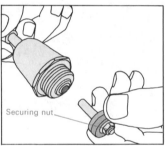

Securing nut

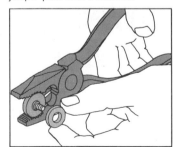

3 On some taps the jumper can be removed; on others it fits loosely. The washer is usually held against the jumper plate with a small nut

4 With either kind of tap, grip the edge of the jumper plate with pliers. If the washer is held by a nut, undo it with a small spanner

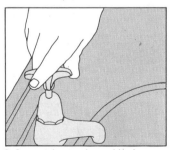

5 Remove the old washer and fit a matching new one. Fit the side of the washer bearing the maker's name so that it faces downwards

6 Secure the washer with the nut. Reassemble the tap. Turn on the water supply. Turn the tap on and off to check that it does not drip

Plumbing Taps and stop valves

Tightening the gland nut

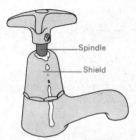

Spindle

Shield

If water oozes out between the spindle and the protective shield, the gland nut is loose. Undo the shield and tighten the nut.

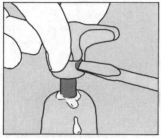

1 Open the tap fully. Do not shut off the water supply. With a small screwdriver, remove grub screw securing the cross head to spindle

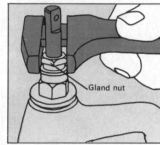

Gland nut

2 Unscrew the shield. Insert an adjustable spanner underneath the shield and lever shield up to force off the cross head

3 Remove the shield to expose the spindle. Tighten the gland nut at the base of the spindle half a turn, using an adjustable spanner

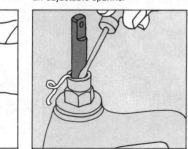

4 Temporarily replace cross head; check that the tap is easy to turn off and on. If too tight, loosen gland nut slightly. Reassemble tap

Re-packing a gland If the tap still leaks, turn water off, remove gland nut and re-pack around spindle with string rubbed with Vaseline

Pull-off head

Some taps have a head which pulls off. To gain access to the gland nut, first remove the small recessed button in the centre of the head.

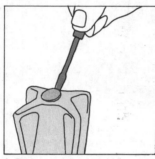

1 Push a small screwdriver under the button and lever it out of the centre of the head

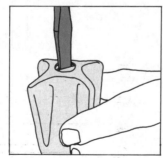

2 Undo the centre screw in the head with a small screwdriver. Remove it and pull off the tap head

Fitting a new stop-valve washer

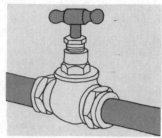

When a stop-valve tap is closed, the flow of water is stopped by the underside of the washer. Never overtighten a stop valve.

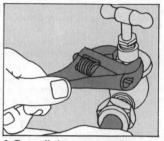

1 Turn off the water supply to the stop valve. Turn on any taps fed from the controlled supply pipe to drain pipes. Unscrew valve head

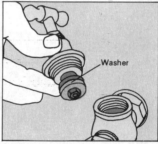

Washer

2 Lift off the head to expose the washer on its seating at the base of the head. It is held in position by a small retaining nut

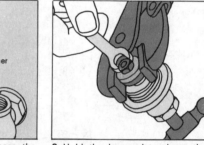

3 Hold the brass plate above the washer with a wrench, and undo the small nut. Remove the rubber washer from its seating

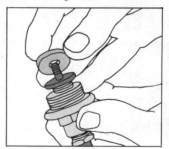

4 Press the new washer into position, and refit the retaining nut. Tighten the nut firmly with a small spanner. Do not overtighten

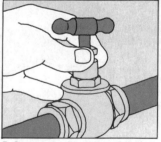

5 Screw on the head until it is finger-tight. Tighten with an adjustable spanner. Do not overtighten, to avoid damaging the tank connection

Fitting a Supatap washer

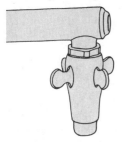

When fitting a washer on a Supatap remember it has a left hand thread. A check valve in the tap obviates the need to turn off the water.

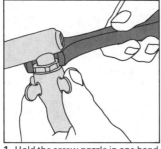

1 Hold the screw nozzle in one hand and loosen the gland nut at the top of the nozzle with a spanner

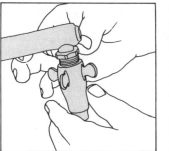

2 Hold the loosened gland nut in one hand and unscrew the nozzle anti-clockwise

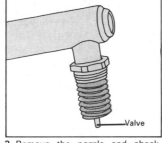

Valve

3 Remove the nozzle and check that the valve which controls the water flow drops into position

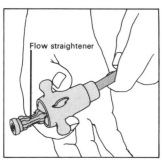

Flow straightener

4 Insert a pencil into the nozzle outlet and push out the flow-straightener unit

Washer and jumper plate

5 Clean the flow straightener with a nailbrush. Pull out the washer plate and jumper. Fit a new one

Swivel nozzles

Shroud

1 If a swivel nozzle drips, unscrew or lever up the shroud at the base. Do not shut off the water

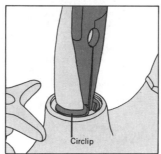

Circlip

2 Prise up the circlip and expand it with a pair of pliers so that it can be slid up the nozzle

3 Pull off the nozzle. Remove the seals in the base and fit new ones. Wet the nozzle base and refit

Fitting a shower O ring

Continuous dripping from a shower is usually caused by a perished or worn O ring.

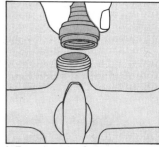

1 To replace the O ring, switch off the water at mains. Unscrew and remove the flexible shower piping

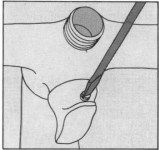

2 Undo the screw securing the shower-diverter lever. Remove the lever to expose a slotted connector

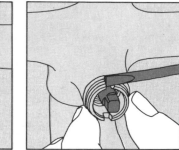

3 Hold a screwdriver sideways against slot and push to remove the connector from the tap unit

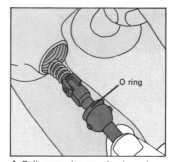

O ring

4 Pull out the mechanism from inside the tap body. Identify the O ring and slide it off the end

5 Slide a new O ring over spring end. Refit the mechanism and re-assemble the unit and connections

HOUSE REPAIRS AND DECORATION 145

Plumbing Baths

Installing a new bath

If a new bath is to be fitted without expert help, the taps and waste outlet should be in exactly the same position as those on the old bath. If they are not, have the work done by a plumber.

Buy a combined waste and overflow fitting, which drains any overflow water into the bathwater outlet pipe. Cut off the old overflow pipe at the wall, and hammer it flat to seal it.

Combined waste and overflow fitting

Materials: overflow and waste fitting; mastic sealer; pipe-jointing compound; tile cement or rubber sealer; rags; rubber washers; dome-headed screws; 2×2×4 in. (50×50×100 mm) timber blocks; 2×2×24 in. (50×50×610 mm) softwood battens. Tools: hacksaw; pliers; spirit level; adjustable spanner; basin wrench (if necessary); hammer; chisel; screwdriver; pointing trowel.

BASIN WRENCH

If access to the pipes behind the bath is difficult, buy a double-jointed basin wrench

1 Turn off hot and cold water supplies; open taps. Remove bath panels and timber framing

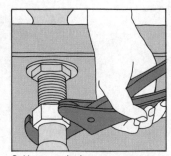
2 Unscrew the hexagon cap nuts to disconnect the pipes from the taps. Plug pipes with wads of cloth

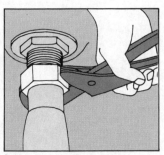
3 Unscrew the large hexagon cap nut to disconnect the waste trap from the outlet beneath the bath

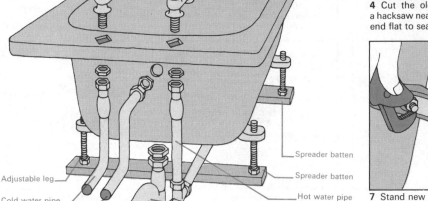
Hot water tap
Cold water tap
Spreader batten
Spreader batten
Adjustable leg
Hot water pipe
Cold water pipe
Overflow pipe
Waste outlet and trap

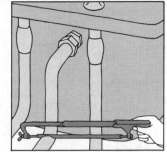
4 Cut the old overflow pipe with a hacksaw near the wall. Hammer the end flat to seal it

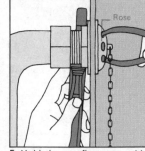
Rose
5 Hold the overflow rose with the handles of pliers. Undo the nut behind the rose. Discard pipe and rose

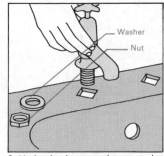
Washer
Nut
6 Undo the hexagonal nuts under the taps and remove the washers. Pull out the taps

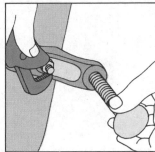
7 Stand new bath on end. Screw in the feet brackets and adjust feet to the approximate height required

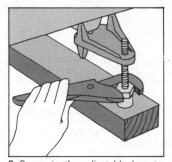
8 Screw in the adjustable legs to lower the bath and prevent damage to tiles when it is removed

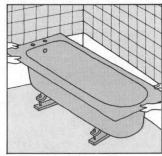
9 Remove the old bath. Fit new one in approximate position and stand it on wooden battens *(continued)*

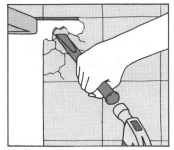

10 Chip out and replace damaged tiles where necessary with a hammer and chisel (see p. 196)

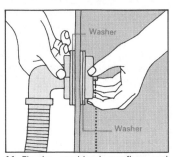

11 Fit the combined overflow and waste to the rose with the rubber washers provided. Tighten the nut

12 Spread a layer of mastic sealing compound round the waste outlet and press the waste fitting firmly on it

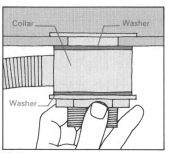

13 Spread compound under the waste outlet. Fit the rubber washers, overflow collar and nut

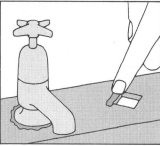

14 Spread compound on the tap holes and fit the nuts as tightly as possible on the tap threads

15 If the bath is too low for leg adjustment, position wooden blocks and lift the bath carefully on to them

16 Check that there is only a small gap between the bath and the tiles for cementing. Raise or lower if necessary

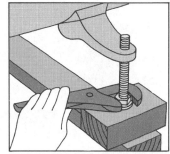

17 Check that the bath is level along its length and width with a spirit level. Adjust the feet as necessary

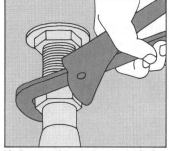

18 Remove the rag plugs and refit the water pipes to the taps. Smear on pipe-jointing compound and tighten nuts

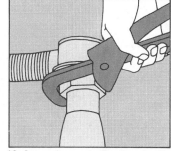

19 Smear the waste pipe thread with jointing compound and fit it to the bath outlet. Tighten the nut

20 Turn on the water. If there is a leak, tighten the nuts. If necessary, undo joint and apply more compound

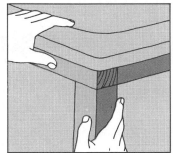

21 Fit the timber framing and alter it to fit the bath if necessary. Check that it is upright

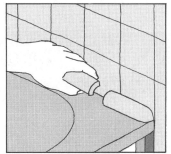

22 Fit glazed quadrant tiles (see p. 149) to cover the gap between the tiles and the edge of the bath

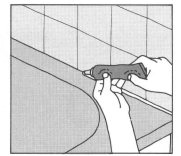

23 Alternatively, seal the gap with a mastic compound (see p. 148). Follow the maker's instructions

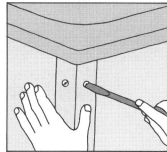

24 Cut the bath panels to size and fit them. Fix on the metal corner plates with dome-headed screws

Plumbing Baths

Re-enamelling a bath

Some modern baths are made of cast iron covered with vitreous enamel which has been baked on the metal. If the surface chips or becomes damaged, do not try to paint it. Consult a plumber.

Older baths, however, are usually cast iron painted with enamel. If they become worn or chipped, they can be repainted. When the bath is first used, always run in cold water before hot.

Materials: ½ pint bath enamel: 300-grit wet-and-dry paper; turpentine substitute; detergent.
Tools: 2 in. (50 mm) paintbrush; sponge; soft cloth; two tins.

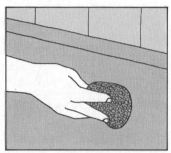

1 Remove plug and undo chain. Sponge bath thoroughly inside with hot water and detergent

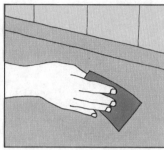

2 Rub down surface until bath is completely smooth with wet-and-dry paper dipped in clean water

3 Rinse out bath and leave to dry. Hang empty tins under taps to avoid water drips during painting

4 Wipe over surface with turpentine substitute to remove remaining traces of detergent. Dry with soft cloth

5 Paint on a coat of bath enamel with a 2 in. (50 mm) brush. Apply enamel as thinly and evenly as possible

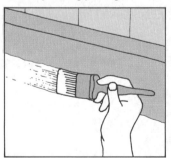

6 Paint bottom of bath first, then the sides. Use long, one-way strokes to avoid runs or drips

7 Paint the rim last. Leave to dry overnight with windows closed, door ajar. Apply second coat

8 Allow to dry for 48 hours. Fit chain and fill bath with cold water. Leave for 48 hours

Sealing a gap behind fittings

As a wash basin, sink or bath is used, slight movement may gradually cause a gap to develop between the back of the fitting and the wall.

Filling the gap with plaster or putty is only a temporary remedy, since these materials harden and crack and then become traps for dirt and moisture.

Use a rubber-based sealer, obtainable from a builders' merchant. It is easy to apply and it remains elastic to allow for further movement.

Materials: tube of sealer; detergent.
Tools: nail brush; razor blade or sharp knife; soft cloth.

1 Clean dirt and grease from the gap at the back of the bath or sink with a small nail brush

2 Wash along the gap with hot water and detergent. Wipe and allow the area to dry thoroughly

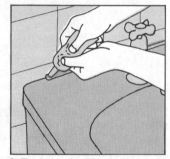

3 The lower the tube nozzle is cut, the wider the strip of sealer. Work forwards and squeeze it into gap

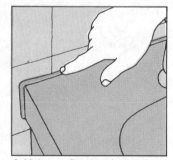

4 Moisten a finger and press down any parts of the sealer which are raised or have become bumpy

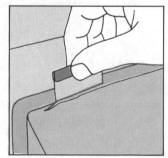

5 Trim off rough edges with a razor blade or sharp knife. Leave joint to set for 24 hours

Sealing a gap with quadrant tiles

Gaps between a wall and the side of a bath or basin can be covered with quadrant-shaped ceramic tiles obtainable from do-it-yourself shops.

Mark the centre of the length and width of the bath. Fix the tiles—one on each side of the centre mark at a time—from the ends inwards. If the gap remaining is less than a tile width, cut a tile to fit. If the gap is more than a tile width, fit two tiles of equal size.

A quadrant tile is easily cut, after scoring, to fit a shorter space.

Materials: bath trim kit; rag; white spirit. Tools: tile cutter (see p. 196); hacksaw or pincers; knife; glass-paper.

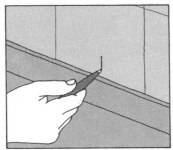

1 Dry bath and wall. Find the centre of the bath's length and width and mark them on the walls behind the bath

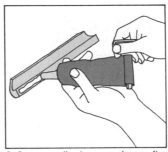

2 Squeeze adhesive on to the two flat surfaces at the back of a mitred tile. Keep adhesive away from the front edge

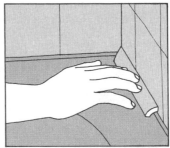

3 Fit the first mitred tile. Start in a corner and press it firmly in position against the wall and bath

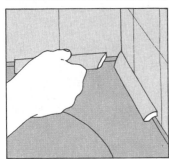

4 Apply adhesive to a second mitred tile—including angled face—and fit to butt against first mitred tile

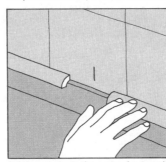

5 Fix a round-edged tile at each outer corner of the bath. Make sure that they are in line with the edge of the bath

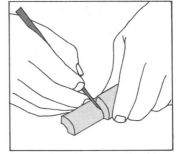

6 Work towards the centre from each corner and from each round-edged tile with full-sized tiles

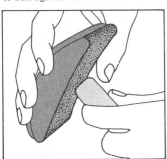

8 Cut tile and smooth the cut edge with glass-paper. Keep end flat against paper to avoid curving it

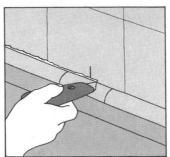

9 Check that each tile fits in place with same width joints as other tiles. Apply adhesive and secure

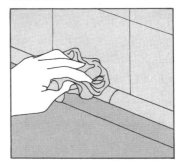

7 When there is a gap smaller than a tile length at the centres, measure it and score tile to fit

10 Trim off the surplus adhesive between the tiles with a sharp knife as soon as the last tile is laid

11 Clean the surface of the tiles with a rag dipped in white spirit or a proprietary paint cleaner

CUTTING QUADRANT TILES

Breaking Tap the tile sharply with the base of a cold chisel just behind the scored line (see p. 196)

Snapping Grip the edge of the tile with a pair of pincers and snap off the scored end

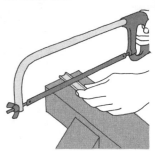

Sawing Cut halfway through the unglazed side of tile with a hacksaw, then tap sharply on glazed side

Plumbing Basins and sinks

Fitting a new basin

Before buying a new basin, make sure that the positions of its taps correspond to those on the one which is to be removed. Use metal casement putty for sealing the tap mountings.

Materials: putty; basin; fixing pins with rubber sleeves, washers, nuts; bracket; woodscrews; wall plugs; washers and nut for waste fitting; tap washers.
Tools: large adjustable spanner; screwdriver; basin wrench.

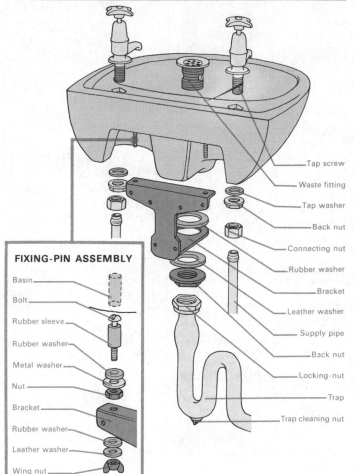

Tap screw
Waste fitting
Tap washer
Back nut
Connecting nut
Rubber washer
Bracket
Leather washer
Supply pipe
Back nut
Locking-nut
Trap
Trap cleaning nut

FIXING-PIN ASSEMBLY

Basin
Bolt
Rubber sleeve
Rubber washer
Metal washer
Nut
Bracket
Rubber washer
Leather washer
Wing nut

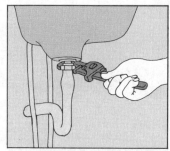

1 Turn off the water supply (see p. 136). Unscrew the locking-nut at the top of the trap

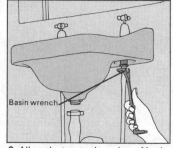

2 Allow the trap to drop clear of basin. Unscrew the connecting nuts under the taps with a basin wrench

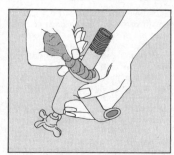

3 Remove old basin and bracket from wall. Remove taps and waste fitting. Apply putty round top of tap threads

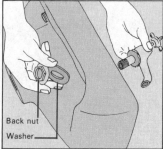

4 Fit taps into new basin and fit the leather washer and back nut on the tap screw. Tighten with basin wrench

5 Get a helper to hold the bracket and new basin so that supply pipes meet taps. Mark wall below the bracket

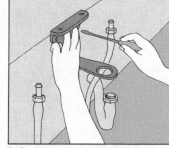

6 Fit the wall bracket on to the wall at the point marked. Drill and use wall plugs if necessary (see p. 683)

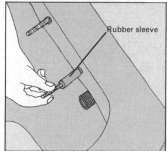

7 Fit the rubber sleeves over the bracket fixing pins and push them in the holes on the underside of the basin

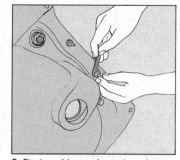

8 Fit the rubber and metal washers to the pins under the basin. Tighten the nuts. Put putty on flange of waste

9 Insert fitting in outlet, making sure that the overflow coincides with the basin overflow *(continued)*

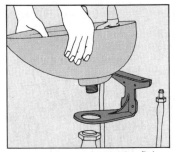

10 Fix rubber washer under fitting. Place fixing pins into top of bracket and waste fitting through bottom

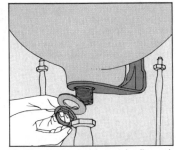

11 Fit a leather washer and a flanged back nut over the waste fitting which juts through the bracket

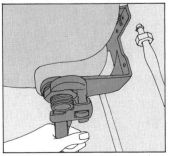

12 Hand-tighten the back nut, then tighten it fully with a spanner to compress the washers

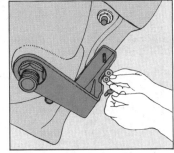

13 Fit the rubber and metal washers and the wing nuts on to the fixing pins. Tighten the nuts by hand

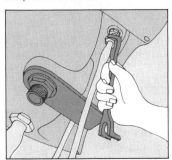

14 Connect the inlet pipes to the taps. Tighten the connecting nuts with a basin wrench

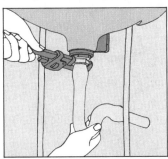

15 Fit the trap to the waste fitting and tighten the locking-nut. Turn on the water. Check for leaks

Fitting a new kitchen sink top

Replacement kitchen sink tops are available from most ironmongers and stores. When a new top is to be fitted, it makes little difference whether a right-hand, left-hand or double draining-board model is chosen. It is important to ensure that the length can be accommodated and that the tap holes will be located as before.

Materials: new sink unit with waste-outlet fittings; plug and chain; $1\frac{1}{2}$ in. (40 mm) deep-seal trap; boss white. Tools: small cold chisel; adjustable spanner; pipe grips; hacksaw; hammer.

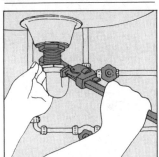

3 Undo the locking-nut between the trap and the sink outlet with a large adjustable spanner

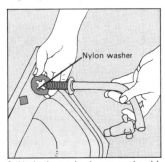

6 Undo the tap back nuts on the old sink. Remove taps, fit nylon washers and insert in the new sink top

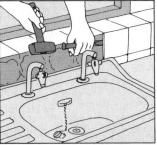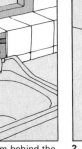

1 Remove any tiles from behind the sink with a hammer and cold chisel. Keep undamaged ones to refit later

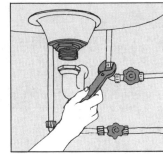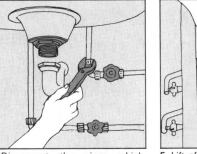

4 Disconnect the pipes which supply the water to the taps at the nearest junction to the sink

7 Put a plastic 'top hat' washer on the tails of the taps underneath the sink. Fit and tighten back nuts

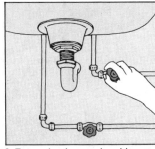

2 Trace the hot and cold water pipes back to their nearest stop-valves and turn off the supply

5 Lift off the old sink top. Stand it sideways and unscrew the lengths of pipe protruding from the taps

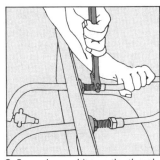

8 Smear boss white on the threads of the taps. Reconnect the pipes. Do not tighten fully   *(continued)*

Plumbing Basins and sinks

(continued)

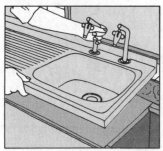

9 Position the sink top and check that the pipes meet supply pipes. Adjust angle of taps and tighten fully

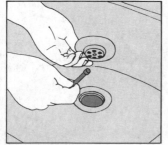

10 Fit a rubber washer in the outlet and position the waste fitting. Insert the centre bolt

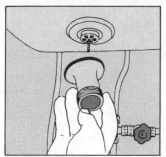

11 Place washer on the waste top and screw waste to the threaded outlet below sink

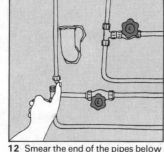

12 Smear the end of the pipes below the taps with boss white. Connect the pipes to the supply pipes

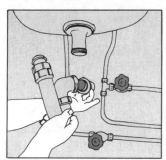

13 Check that the trap outlet is in line with the outlet pipe. Connect to the waste

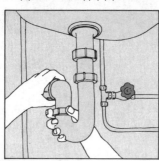

14 Join the trap to outlet pipe. Clip on chain and plug. Turn on supply. Refit tiles (see p. 196)

Fitting a new waste outlet pipe

When a new sink top is fitted, the outlet hole of the new trap may not line up with the existing waste pipe. If the waste is made of lead, there is no way of joining it to the plastic trap. Instead, cut lengths of plastic tubing and fit them between the trap and the gully outside with elbow joints for changes of direction.

Materials: length of plastic piping with diameter to fit in trap outlet; wall bracket of the same diameter; plastic elbow joints as required; welding solvent; mortar mix (see p. 693).
Tools: hacksaw; club hammer; cold chisel; file; pointing trowel.

1 Cut off the waste pipe flush against inside wall. Cut away from both sides of hole to free the rest of the old pipe

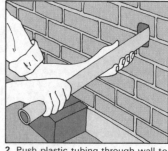

2 Push plastic tubing through wall to the sink trap and mark it about 2 in. (50 mm) from the outside wall face

3 Mark a second length of pipe to stretch from first section to gully; cut tubing and file rough edges

4 Connect both lengths of pipe with an elbow and push through from outside to check fit. Adjust if necessary

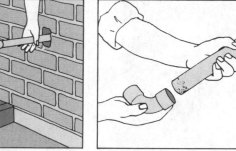

5 Disconnect the parts. Smear the ends of the pipes and inside elbow with welding solvent. Fit together

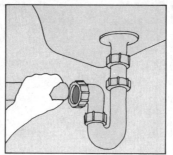

6 Push the pipe through the wall and, from the inside, connect it to the trap by tightening the threaded collar

7 Outside, fix a wall bracket near the bottom of the pipe (see p. 108) and fill hole with mortar (see p. 693)

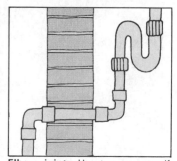

Elbow joints Use two or more if multiple changes of direction are necessary to get from trap to gully

Plumbing Lavatory pans and cisterns

(see p. 156)

CHAINS AND WASTE PLUGS

The chain attached to a sink or basin plug is linked to a metal ring, which may be part of an overflow grille or be fitted separately.

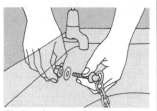

Chains Secure chain bolt with a washer and nut at the back of the sink or basin

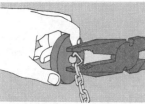

Plugs Open the ring on the chain. Fit the plug on the ring and close it with pliers

OVERFLOW SYSTEMS

Overflow

Waste outlet

Sinks and basins have a slot, just below the rim, so that water is channelled back to the waste preventing it overflowing the rim

---

It is illegal to install any new plumbing equipment without first obtaining written permission from the surveyor's department of the local authority.

It is permissible, however, to replace damaged equipment—including converting a high-level cistern to low-level (see p. 156)—provided that the replacement does not necessitate altering any existing plumbing.

Do not try to install a siphonic flushing cistern—identifiable by its silent action. It is a complicated job and is best left to a plumber.

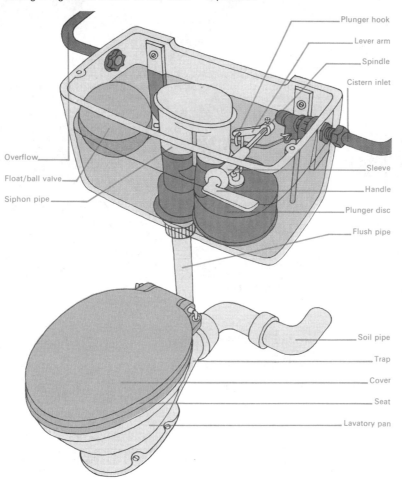

Plunger hook
Lever arm
Spindle
Cistern inlet
Overflow
Float/ball valve
Siphon pipe
Sleeve
Handle
Plunger disc
Flush pipe
Soil pipe
Trap
Cover
Seat
Lavatory pan

FITTING A NEW LAVATORY SEAT

If a lavatory seat is damaged, do not try to repair it; fit a complete new unit. Seats and lids are normally sold together but some merchants supply them separately.

Fitting instructions are usually supplied with a new seat unit. It must be bolted through the existing holes in the back of the pan rim. Tell the supplier the size of the bolt holes and the distance between them when choosing a new seat.

Materials: new seat unit.
Tools: screwdriver; spanner.

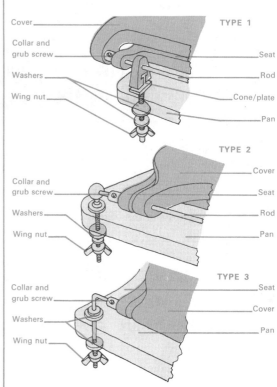

TYPE 1
Cover
Collar and grub screw
Washers
Wing nut
Seat
Rod
Cone/plate
Pan

TYPE 2
Collar and grub screw
Washers
Wing nut
Cover
Seat
Rod
Pan

TYPE 3
Collar and grub screw
Washers
Wing nut
Seat
Cover
Pan

CAUTION Wing nuts securing the hinge bolts of a lavatory seat must never be more than finger-tight

Plumbing Lavatory pans and cisterns

Removing a cracked lavatory pan

When a lavatory pan is damaged, try to buy one identical in size and pattern, so that it will fit into the existing pipe connections.

If the flush pipe is plastic, it will be connected to the pan with a simple push-in joint, covered by a rubber sleeve.

The same pipe can be connected to the new pan. If the old pipe is lead or copper, fit a plastic one.

Lavatory pans have either an S or P-trap connection to the soil pipe (see p. 155). If the pan has an S trap, it may be connected to a glazed-earthenware soil pipe. When removing the old pan, try not to damage the pipe collar in any way. If you should accidentally do so, a modern plastic push-on lavatory connector can be used directly into the drain itself without the need for a collar.

A lavatory pan with a P trap is usually connected to a cast-iron or plastic soil pipe.

Before starting to remove the pan turn off the water supply. Keep flushing the cistern until the water stops flowing and soak up any remaining water from the pan with a mop or cloth until the trap is dry.

Tools: hammer; cold chisel; hacksaw; piece of rag.

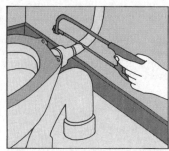

1 If the flush pipe is lead or copper, cut it with a hacksaw as close as possible to the joint at the pan

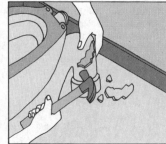

2 Hold the side of the pan to avoid straining the soil-pipe collar and break through the top of the pan bend

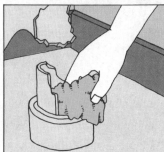

3 Hammer all round the trap. Push a rag into the soil-pipe collar to keep out debris

4 Chip out fragments from the soil-pipe collar. Wipe the rim clean and remove the rag from the pipe

5 Pull the damaged pan away from its cement bed on a concrete floor. Handle carefully: it is heavy

6 Use a hammer and chisel to chip away old cement from a wooden or concrete floor

ALTERNATIVE TYPES OF FITTINGS

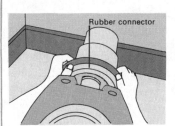

Rubber connector

Plastic pipe Peel back the rubber cone which covers the joint and pull out the end of the flush pipe

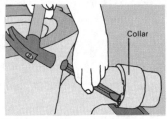

Cast-iron or plastic Chip out cement or putty from the soil-pipe collar. Do not crack pipe

Collar

Rubber connector Peel back the rubber sleeve and ease it gently over the pipe collar

Wooden floor Undo the four screws which secure the flange, at the base of the pan, to the floorboards

Fitting a pan

To ensure easy working, make sure that a new lavatory pan matches the old one in size and type of trap (see p. 155). Seats and covers are sold separately. Fit a plastic bag, with a cloth inside it, at the bottom of the pan in case anything is dropped in it during fitting.

Materials: sand-and-cement mortar; four 2 in. (50 mm) countersunk brass screws with rubber or fibre grommets for wood floor; rubber cone connector for flush pipe.
Tools: screwdriver for wooden floor; pointing trowel; spirit level.

1 Place a small mound of cement and sand on the floor and position the new pan correctly on it, with the trap meeting the soil pipe

2 Press the pan down into the cement-and-sand bed and check it with a spirit level to ensure that it is horizontal   *(continued)*

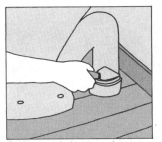

3 Use a pointing trowel to press 1:3 cement and sand firmly into the joint between the trap and the soil-pipe collar

4 If the floor is wooden, fit the securing screws carefully (see p. 157) through the base. Use brass screws that will not rust

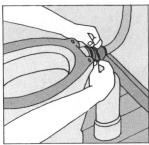

5 Fit plastic flush pipe with rubber connector to cover the joint. Fit seat (see p. 153). Turn on water supply. Flush pan

Adapting a lavatory trap

Lavatory pans are designed to contain enough water at all times to ensure that smells from the main drainage system (see p. 61) cannot enter a house.

The water is contained in a trap which—unlike that on a basin or sink (see p. 142)—is part of the pan. The outlet may be connected by an S trap to a soil pipe in the floor, or by a P trap to a soil pipe in a wall.

A P-trap pan can be adapted to connect with any soil pipe. If the pan has an S trap however, it cannot be converted. The new one must be bought to match the old one.

Materials: plastic bend; rubber connector; sand and cement.
Tools: hacksaw; pointing trowel.

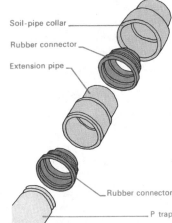

Soil-pipe collar
Rubber connector
Extension pipe
Rubber connector
P trap

TYPES OF TRAPS

Pan with S trap

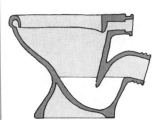

Pan with P trap

When fitting a new low-level cistern (see p. 156), moving the pan forwards can be done only with a P-trap pan

EXTENSION PIPES

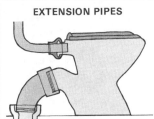

A P-trap lavatory pan can be fitted to a soil pipe in the floor by using a curved plastic extension pipe and two rubber connectors

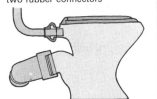

Curved extension pipes may, in some cases, be used to connect a P trap to a soil pipe which is in a wall beside a lavatory pan

1 Stand the new pan on a moist mixture of 1:3 cement and sand. Position outlet to line with soil pipe

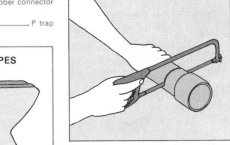

3 Cut the extension pipe with a hacksaw. Turn pipe slowly while cutting to ensure an even edge

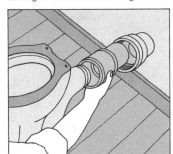

5 Fit extension piece into the rubber connector. Turn it gently to make sure that it is a tight fit

2 Hold extension piece with its collar beside pan outlet. Mark other end 2 in. (50 mm) beyond pipe

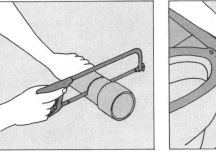

4 Push a rubber connector as far as possible into the collar of the soil pipe. Make sure it fits evenly all round

6 Push a connector into extension collar. Push pan back slightly so that connector fits over its outlet

Plumbing Lavatory pans and cisterns

Fitting a new low-level cistern

When a lavatory system is faulty or damaged, the pan or cistern can be removed and replaced with new ones of the same type. If the existing cistern is a high-level type, however, it might be better while doing major repair work to replace it with a more modern low-level one.

Low-level cisterns are available from builders' merchants. Measure the distance from the wall to the back of the existing pan: this determines the size of cistern which can be most easily accommodated. Remember to allow a few inches so that the seat and lid can rest at an angle against the new cistern when it is fitted.

To accommodate the low-level cistern a P-trap pan must be moved forwards a little, and a straight extension pipe fitted between the pan and soil pipe (see p. 155).

Fit a curved extension piece (see p. 155) if the soil pipe is in the ground. An S-trap pan can only be used with a slim cistern.

Materials: new cistern, complete with ball valve, flush and overflow pipes, extension pipes and connectors; wall plugs; sand and cement.

Tools: screwdriver; hacksaw; file; two spanners; hammer; wheelbrace and ¼ in. (6 mm) masonry drill; pointing trowel; cold chisel; spirit level.

HIGH-LEVEL CISTERN

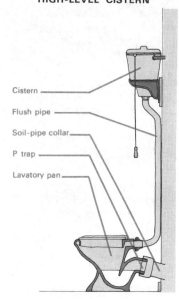

Cistern
Flush pipe
Soil-pipe collar
P trap
Lavatory pan

LOW-LEVEL CISTERN WITH S-TRAP PAN

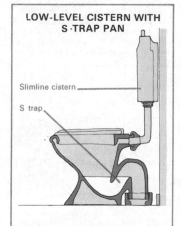

Slimline cistern
S trap

LOW-LEVEL CISTERN

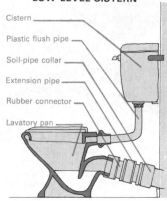

Cistern
Plastic flush pipe
Soil-pipe collar
Extension pipe
Rubber connector
Lavatory pan

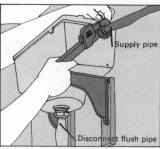

1 Turn off water supply and flush cistern. Disconnect chain, flush pipe and supply pipe to ball valve

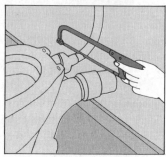

4 Cut through the lead flush pipe with a hacksaw as close to the inlet of the pan as possible

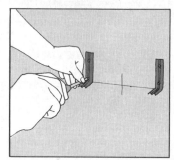

7 Drill, plug and fix the brackets to the wall (see p. 683). Check with a spirit level that they are in line

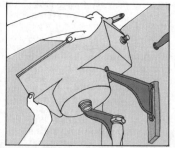

2 Lift off cistern. Handle it carefully: it will be heavy and the ball valve may fall out. Do not stand on the pan

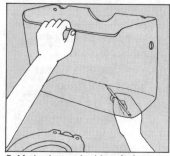

5 Mark the underside of the new cistern on the wall at the height advised in the manufacturer's instructions

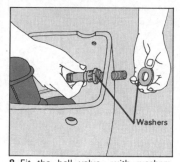

8 Fit the ball valve—with washers inside and outside—on the supply-pipe side of the cistern

3 Unscrew or lever off the brackets holding the old cistern. Repair the damaged plaster (see p. 121)

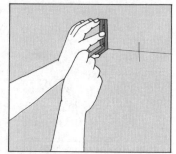

6 Mark centre of the cistern position. Hold brackets on each side of centre-line and mark for screw holes

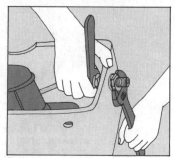

9 Use two spanners and tighten the nuts inside and outside the cistern. Screw ball float on to arm *(continued)*

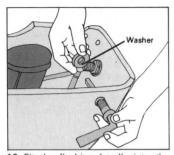

10 Fit the flushing handle into the hole at front of cistern. Fit and tighten the retaining washer inside

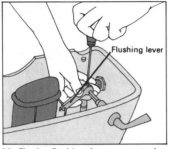

11 Fit the flushing lever arm on the end of the flush-handle spindle. Secure it with a grub screw

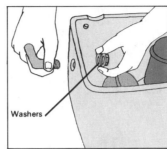

12 Fit the plastic elbow for the overflow pipe in the hole opposite the ball valve with washers and nut

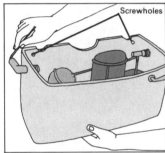

13 Hold cistern on brackets. Mark overflow position on wall and mark screw holes through back of cistern

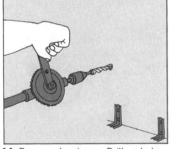

14 Remove the cistern. Drill and plug holes. Drill and knock downward hole in wall for overflow pipe

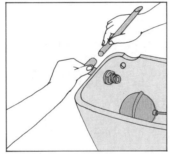

15 Connect and stick plastic pipe to the elbow to protrude 3 in. (75 mm) beyond outer wall face

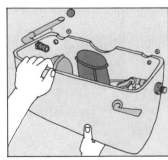

16 Position cistern with overflow pipe through its hole. Tighten screws. Move pan if necessary (see p. 154)

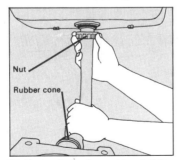

17 Secure flush-pipe nut hand-tight. Fit the pipe to the pan. Push the rubber cone over the joint

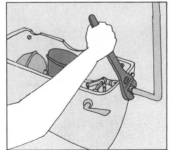

18 Fit the supply pipe to the ball valve (see p. 141). Turn on the water supply and check for leaks

Levelling a lavatory pan

If a lavatory pan tilts to one side on a wooden floor, loosen the floor fixings. Wedge the pedestal upright and pack mortar below it. The mortar should be a crumbling, dry, 1:3 cement-and-sand mixture (see p. 693). If new screws are needed, use brass ones, which resist corrosion; position the screws through grommets. Screws are not used if the floor is concrete.

Materials: cement; sharp sand; screws and grommets.
Tools: screwdriver; pointing trowel; spirit level; hardboard scraps 2 in. (50 mm) square.

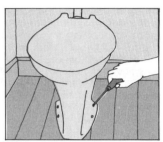

1 Take up floor covering around pedestal. Remove screws on side to be raised, and loosen those at the other side

2 Lay a batten across seat and put a spirit level on it. Jack up pedestal with hardboard scraps until the pan is level

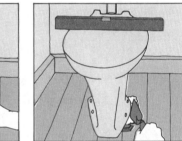

3 Push mortar below pedestal with a pointing trowel. When the hollow is filled, remove the hardboard scraps and fill the holes

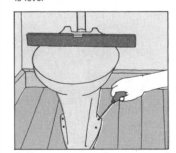

4 Fit grommets on the screws and place them in the holes in the pedestal. Do not drive the screws in at this stage

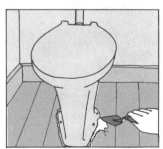

5 Trim any surplus mortar flush with the base of the pedestal. Allow to dry for at least three hours, then tighten screws carefully

Plumbing Blockages

Preventing blockages

All baths, basins and sinks should have a grid over the waste outlet to stop solids which could block the trap or waste pipe below. But small solids—for example tea leaves, hairs and vegetable scrapings—can pass the grid and trap and block the sink.

If possible, do not empty tea leaves into the sink. Always run hot water after pouring hot fat down the sink, to ensure that the fat cannot solidify in the bend of the trap. Never put disposable nappies down a lavatory pan. Although soluble, they can cause blockages. Clean out the trap under a sink regularly.

MAKING A PLUNGER TO CLEAR SINKS

Bought plungers have a rubber cup attached to a handle. When the cup is placed over a sink waste hole and moved up and down, it creates suction which can dislodge most obstructions in a pipe. Plungers can be made at home from a rubber sanding disc or rubber sponge.

Materials: 2 × 1 in. (50 × 25 mm) batten, 3 ft (915 mm) long; 8 × 4 in. (200 × 100 mm) foam-rubber sponge; cloth; string.
Tools: scissors or knife.

1 Fold a sponge in half to make a square. Position it on the end of a 3 ft (915 mm) batten

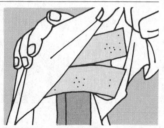

2 Hold the sponge in place and wrap a piece of cloth round the sponge and the top of the batten

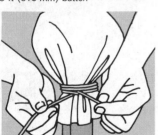

3 Wind string tightly over the edges of the rag and tie the string tightly round the batten

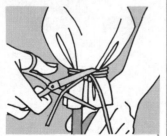

4 Check that the sponge is held firmly on the end of the batten and cut off the ends of the string

Clearing a blocked basin with a plunger

When a sink, bath or basin is blocked, it may be necessary to dismantle the trap below it; but first try to clear it with a plunger.

Note that if a lavatory pan is blocked, a special type of plunger is needed (see p. 159).

Material: rag.
Tools: plunger; cup or mug.

Plunger

Overflow hole

1 Push a rag into the basin overflow hole so that air and water cannot escape when plunger is used

2 Take out sufficient water from the basin to prevent slopping over when the plunger is used

3 Place a plunger firmly over the waste outlet hole. Work the handle vigorously up and down

4 When the blockage is dislodged, the pool of water will drain out. Turn on a tap and agitate the plunger

5 Remove rag from the overflow hole and run cold water for a minute or two to refill the trap

Clearing a trap

If a plunger does not clear a blocked sink, washbasin or bath, it will be necessary to clear the blockage from the trap or the waste pipe.

Most sinks, and some basins and baths, have a U trap fitted with a screw plug at the lowest point of the bend in the pipe. In most cases, when the screw plug of the trap is removed any blockage can be pulled free by hand or with curtain wire.

Materials: screw plug; washer.
Tools: mole wrench, pliers or adjustable spanner; metal rod or batten; wire (to reach from the basin outlet to trap); flexible curtain wire; bowl or bucket.

1 Push a length of curtain wire into the waste pipe outside the house. Move it up and down inside the pipe

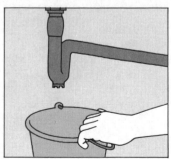

2 If the sink is still blocked, place a bucket under the trap to catch any water or dirt *(continued)*

3 Hold a timber batten firmly in the U of the pipe to counteract pressure. Undo the screw plug with a wrench

4 If the obstruction is not freed, bend the end of a piece of curtain wire and push it down the waste outlet

5 When the wire reaches the trap, work it round from the bottom and try to pull out the obstruction

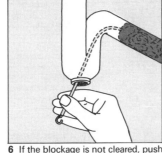

6 If the blockage is not cleared, push flexible curtain wire into the other section of waste pipe

7 When the obstruction is cleared, fit a new washer and screw on plug. Hand-tighten; do not use a wrench

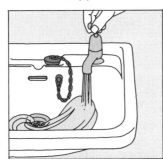

8 Run the cold tap slowly to refill the trap with water and seal off any smell from the external drain

Clearing a two-piece or bottle trap

Some sink traps do not have a screw plug at the bottom of the U pipe; instead, the whole U section of the trap can be removed. Lock-nuts join the trap section to the sink waste and the outlet pipe. An adjustable spanner or wrench is needed to slacken them.

Many modern sinks have a trap which looks like a bottle. The bottom half can be unscrewed to remove any obstruction. Always place a bucket underneath beforehand and fit the plug in the sink outlet.

Materials: bowl or bucket; flexible curtain wire.
Tools: adjustable spanner or wrench.

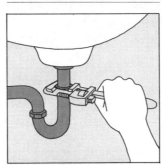

1 Place a bowl or bucket underneath. Undo the lock-nuts at both ends of the U-shaped waste trap

2 Push a curtain wire into the U section and into the ends of the waste pipe. Refit when clear

BOTTLE TRAP

1 Hold the waste pipe with one hand and unscrew the bottom of the bottle trap under the sink

2 Push a curtain wire up into the waste outlet and along the waste pipe. Clear the blockage

3 Refit screw-cap on bottle trap. Run water for a few minutes to ensure that trap is filled

Clearing a w.c.

When a lavatory pan is blocked, a plunger with a metal plate above the rubber cup is needed. The plate ensures that the cup cannot turn inside out when it is worked up and down inside the pan.

The plunger must be moved very vigorously, for there is no flat surface in the base of the pan to create effective suction. The plunger can only force short, sharp surges of water into the bend to dislodge any obstruction. Take care not to damage the pan.

When the blockage has been cleared, flush the cistern to refill the trap below.

If a plunger does not remove the obstruction, call a plumber, who can clear a blocked trap or drain with special equipment.

If tools are available to rod the drain (see p. 61), check at the first manhole to see whether the obstruction is between the manhole and the lavatory pan or further down the pipe.

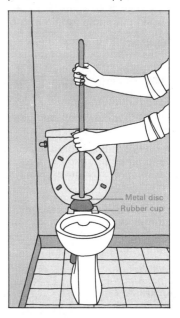

Metal disc
Rubber cup

Roofs Construction

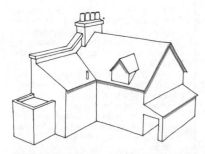

Sloping roofs have wooden rafters and beams which rest on 4×3 in. (100×75 mm) softwood beams at the top of the walls. The roof covering—tiles, slates, shingles, thatch, corrugated iron, plastic, or asbestos—is fixed to wooden battens nailed at right angles to the rafters.

Except for thatched roofs, all types have wooden boards, called fascias, to protect the bottom of the rafters and support the gutters. Additional weatherproofing is provided by wooden boards, called soffits, fixed behind and at right angles to the fascias.

At the triangular end of a roof, further weatherproofing is provided by barge boards fixed to the edge of the roof against the wall.

Most repair jobs to the rafters or beams should be attempted only by experts, because the structural strength of the roof is involved. The householder can, however, fit new slates (see p. 169), tiles (see p. 173) or shingles (see p. 183), replace bargeboards (see p. 162) and fascia and soffit boards. He can also carry out repairs to the weatherproofing between sloping surfaces or between the roof and any pipes passing through it (see p. 166). On thatched roofs, attempt only emergency repairs (see p. 181).

Most flat roofs are constructed like wooden floors, with joists fitted between the walls and covered with boards.

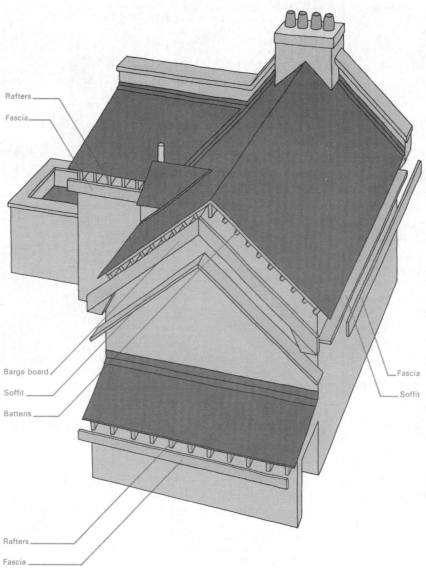

Rafters
Fascia
Barge board
Soffit
Battens
Fascia
Soffit
Rafters
Fascia

Roofs Gutter boards

Fitting fascias and soffits

The fascia boards to which gutters are fixed are nailed to the ends of the rafters and the ceiling joists. The inside face of each board is grooved at the bottom to take another board—a soffit board—to give support and seal the lower edge of the roof.

Both boards are liable to rot after some years, but they can be removed and replaced by the amateur.

Do the work only during dry weather, for until it is finished the house can have no guttering. It is a two-man job and scaffolding is essential (see p. 686).

Measure the width and thickness of the existing boards. Always allow 6 in. (150 mm) extra on each length required, and note that if the roof has sunk slightly in the centre it may be necessary to buy timber a little deeper than before.

Materials: tongued-and-grooved softwood boarding; pieces of timber for packing; string; galvanised nails; knotting sealer; lead-based wood primer.
Tools: cold chisel or crowbar; claw hammer; panel saw; mallet and chisel; combination square; spirit level; rule.

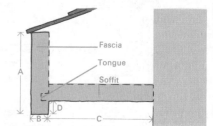

Fascia
Tongue
Soffit

A Depth of fascia
B Thickness of fascia (and soffit board)
C Width of soffit board without tongue. Allow $\frac{1}{2}$ in. (13 mm) extra on C for tongue
D Distance of groove from bottom edge of fascia

1 Remove gutter (see p. 105). Rip off the fascia and soffit with a cold chisel or crowbar. Remove any nails

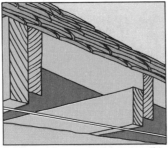

2 Tie a string as tautly as possible across the undersides of the joists between each end of the roof

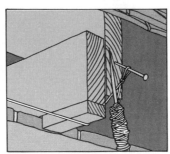

3 Check with a spirit level. Pack, if necessary, the underside of the outer joists to bring the string level

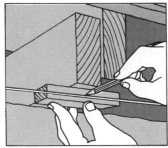

4 Hold a piece of softwood under each joist which is above the line. Mark the string's position on the wood

5 Cut these to size, as packing pieces, paint with primer and nail them to the underside of the joists

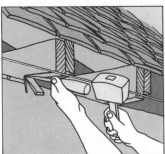

6 Make a saw cut at wall if any ends of joists project below the string. Draw line back to cut, chisel off surplus

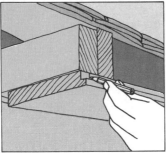

7 From one end of the wall offer up the first soffit section. Mark the centre of the joist nearest to the end

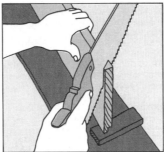

8 Take down soffit and make a 45-degree cut at the mark so that the longer face can be fitted downwards

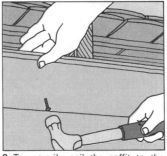

9 Temporarily nail the soffit to the underside of the joists as tightly against the wall as possible

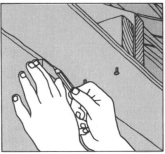

10 If there is any gap, slide a piece of wood along the wall and mark a line on the soffit board

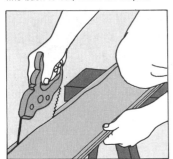

11 Remove board and cut along the marked line. Saw at an angle so that bottom edge fits tightly against wall

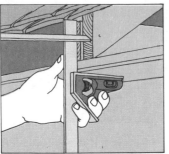

12 Replace board. Mark its edge (excluding tongue) on any joists or rafters which project. Remove board

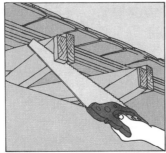

13 Cut the surplus off the marked joists and rafters. Saw carefully to avoid damaging the roof covering

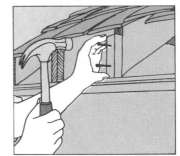

14 Measure, cut and nail packing pieces to the ends of any joists and rafters which are short

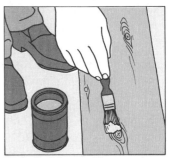

15 Seal all knots with a proprietary sealer. Allow to dry and paint the soffit board with primer *(continued)*

(continued)

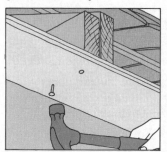

16 Push the cut edge firmly against wall and nail board to underside of joists and packing pieces

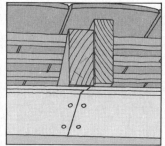

17 Cut, trim, seal and prime the second board and nail it in place, so that the angled cuts butt together

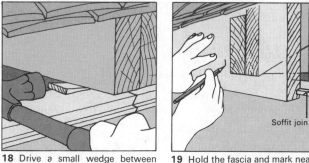

18 Drive a small wedge between the soffit board and any joists where there is a gap

19 Hold the fascia and mark near its end the centre of nearest joist, but not at same place as soffit join

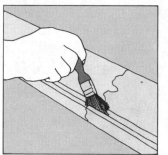

20 Take down the board and cut a mitre. Knot, stop and prime the board. Prepare second board

21 Nail the fascia with two nails—one through the soffit edge, the other through the joist or rafter

Fitting new barge boards

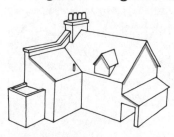

A barge board protects the roof timbers at the gable end of a house. Like a fascia, it incorporates a soffit board. Barge boards are exposed to the weather and in spite of regular painting will eventually rot or split; in this condition they are dangerous and should be replaced.

Buy new softwood to match the existing board. For the new soffit board, measure the width of the existing one and buy the next standard width above it, to allow for any cutting needed to fit it to the wall. Take a dimensioned sketch to a timber merchant who will supply the wood already tongued and grooved.

Do not try to fit a barge board from a ladder; use scaffolding (see p. 686).

Materials: tongued-and-grooved softwood; 2½ in. (65 mm) nails and screws; 4 in. (100 mm) galvanised screws; knotting sealer; lead-based primer; sharp sand; cement.
Tools: claw hammer; cold chisel; combination square; screwdriver; panel saw; plane; sliding bevel; wheelbrace; ½ in. (13 mm) bit; ¼ in. (6 mm) drill; pointing trowel; 4 in. (100 mm) paintbrush.

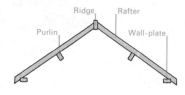

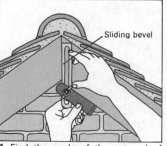

1 Find the angle of the cut end of the barge board—where it butts at the ridge or chimney—with a sliding bevel

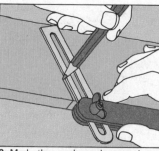

2 Mark the angle and approximate length on the new wood. Cut with a panel saw

3 Lever off the existing barge and soffit boards with an old chisel. Start at the bottom and work upwards

4 Carefully remove and lay aside for re-use any creasing or verge tiles (see p. 174) which have become loose

5 Hold the barge board in position and check that the cut end butts squarely against the ridge or stack

6 Temporarily tack the board with 2½ in. (65 mm) nails, at two points: do not drive them home *(continued)*

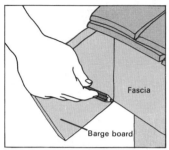

7 Mark the end of the fascia board on the inside face of the barge board. The bottom corners must align

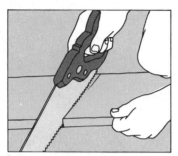

8 Remove nails, take down the barge board and cut along marked line. Check that it fits in position

9 With the bevel set at the angle used on the barge board, mark a mitre at each end of the soffit board

10 Cut the mitred ends and temporarily nail the soffit board (see p. 160) on to the ends of the purlin

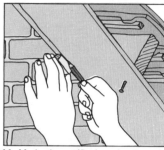

11 Mark the soffit board where it meets adjoining fascia board. Mark the wall profile on the board (see p. 161)

12 Remove the board. Cut it at the fascia mark and along the marked line of the wall face

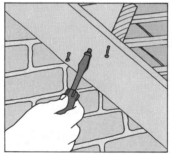

13 Prime the edges. Temporarily nail soffit in position, then fix with 2½ in. (65 mm) screws. Remove nails

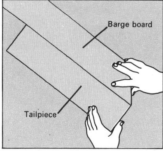

14 Lay the barge board flat. Lay an offcut for the tailpiece, 24 in. (610 mm) long, against end of barge board

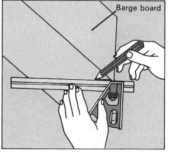

15 Use a combination square and draw a line on the offcut, at right angles to the cut end of barge board

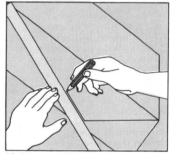

16 Measure along the line the width of the soffit. From that point draw the slope of the old tailpiece

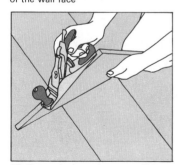

17 Cut and plane the new tailpiece. Check that it fits the barge board. Prime the edges

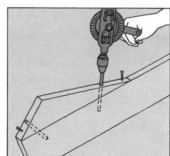

18 Temporarily nail it to the board. Drill ¼ in. (6 mm) holes at right angles through tailpiece into board

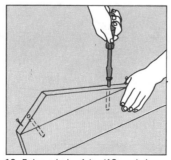

19 Enlarge holes ½ in. (13 mm) deep. Fix tailpiece with 4 in. (100 mm) screws. Remove nails. Fill holes

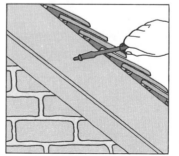

20 Fit barge board with its groove over the soffit-board tongue. Screw board to roof timbers

21 Refix slates (see p. 169) or tiles (see p. 173) and point with 4:1 sand-and-cement mortar (see p. 693)

Roofs Weatherproofing

Sealing the junction between the top of a roof and a wall

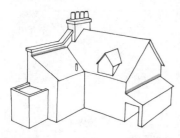

Mortar, which is often used to weatherproof the junction between a roof and a wall or chimney, cannot absorb the natural movement in the structure. If the mortar has cracked remove it and fit zinc, lead or felt flashings.

Zinc, cheaper than lead and more durable than felt, can be bought in 8 ft (2·4 m) lengths, 36 in. (915 mm) wide.

Buy a dresser, a tool made from hornbeam or boxwood for shaping metal, from a builders' merchant.

Block the gutter outlet with an old rag before removing a mortar flashing, to prevent debris entering the drainage system.

Materials: zinc sheeting; soft sand and cement (see p. 693).
Tools: pointing trowel; hawk; dresser; ½ in. (13 mm) cold chisel; tin snips; hammer; brush; sliding bevel.

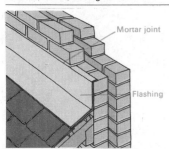

Flashings Strips of waterproof material shaped to fit the angle between the wall and the roof lap over the roof-covering material

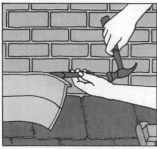

1 Lever out damaged flashing or old mortar with a cold chisel. Do not damage the roof covering

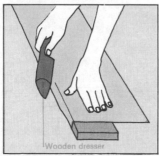

4 Cut zinc 12 in. (305 mm) wide. Lay it on board and use dresser to hammer over ¾ in. (20 mm) strip at right angles

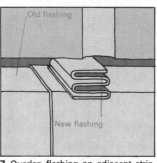

7 Overlap flashing on adjacent strip by 6 in. (150 mm). To secure, wedge in folded zinc pieces above each end

2 Rake out old mortar from the flashing joint in the wall to a depth of at least 1 in. (25 mm) with the chisel

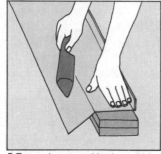

5 Turn strip over and lay it on thicker board. Hammer down centre to match the angle set on the bevel

8 Gently hammer flashing down to match slope of roof. Fill joint with 4:1 sand and cement (see p. 693)

3 Hold a sliding bevel against the wall and the roof. Set it to match the angle of the junction between them

6 Throw water with a brush into the cleared flashing joint to ensure that new mortar sticks to the wall

9 Press mortar home, then run trowel along top of flashing at the joint to remove any surplus cement

Sealing a junction betwee

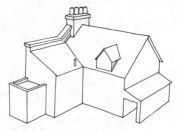

The junction between a sloping parapet wall and the side of a roof is usually weatherproofed by small sheets of zinc, lead or roofing felt, called soakers.

If the rendering cracks or the soakers become eroded, fit new ones. To make sure that the new soakers match the old, mark each damaged one, and the wall beside it, as it is removed.

Do not attempt the work without a crawling board and scaffolding (see p. 685). Work on a few feet at a time.

On some roofs the junction is sealed with a stepped flashing. Repair of this is best left to a professional.

Materials: waterproof cement; sand (see p. 693); zinc sheeting; 1¼ in. (30 mm) galvanised nails.
Tools: trowels; floats; club hammer and cold chisel; brush, bucket and water; shovel; tin snips.

Soakers Strips of zinc dressed into the shape of the wall/roof angle fit between alternate slates. Their vertical face is covered with mortar

he side of a roof and a wall

1 Wedge a small piece of wood into the gutter at foot of roof to ensure that debris cannot fall off the roof

2 Break away old cement rendering on the surface of wall above the roof with a club hammer and cold chisel

3 Rake out mortar in brick joints above roof to a depth of at least ¾ in. (20 mm). Do not damage the soakers

4 Remove any damaged slates or tiles and those covering the faulty soakers. Number and lay them aside

5 Number the damaged soakers and mark the wall where they were positioned. Keep undamaged soakers

6 Cut new zinc to match damaged soakers. Hold each new soaker on top of the old one and shape it

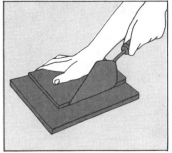

7 Cut new slates to match damaged ones if necessary (see p. 170). If roof is tiled, buy new tiles (see p. 173)

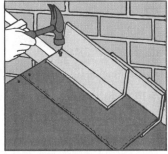

8 Fit new soakers from eave up, upper edge in line with slate beneath. Use one nail, and cover with soaker above

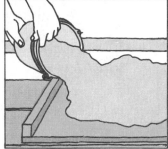

9 Mix 4:1 sand and cement (see p. 693) at ground level. Take several buckets of mix up to a board on scaffolding

10 Throw water on wall with brush. Make sure that the wall is soaked to give the new mortar good adhesion

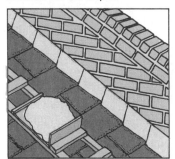

11 Fix a batten to one side of a board, 18 in. (455 mm) square. Lay board on crawling board and pile mortar on it

12 If bricks have crumbled or if joints are ragged, first fill cavities with mortar. Use a pointing trowel

13 Cover wall and soakers with a ½ in. (13 mm) layer of mortar. Use wooden float and slap mortar firmly on to wall

14 Smooth surface and score with point of a trowel to provide good key. Clean mortar droppings from roof

15 Leave for a day to dry. Spread ½ in. (13 mm) mortar with wooden float. Finish with a metal float

Roofs Weatherproofing

Weatherproofing a pipe passing through a roof

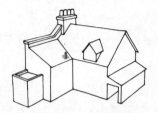

The point where a vent pipe or flue emerges through a roof must be protected against the entry of rainwater. Proprietary mastic waterproofers can be used but they will provide only a temporary seal.

The most efficient method is to cut a hole the size of the pipe in a sheet of zinc. Solder a zinc collar around the edge of the hole and fit it snugly around the base of the pipe.

It is unlikely that a faulty zinc slate and collar can be removed without damaging the adjacent slates or tiles. Buy matching ones and fit them after positioning the zinc.

Materials: zinc 2×3 ft (610×915 mm); slating battens if required (see p. 169); solder and flux (see p. 692); sealing strip or plastic sleeve; 1¼ in. (30 mm) galvanised nails; cardboard.

Tools: slate ripper; hammer; snips; trowel; soldering iron; wire wool; crayon; bradawl; compasses; scissors.

A pipe through a valley gutter (see p. 167) can also be weatherproofed with a zinc slate.

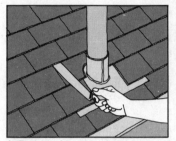

1 Remove the roof covering around the base of the pipe for an area of about 3 ft (915 mm) square. If it is slate, use a slate ripper (see p. 171)

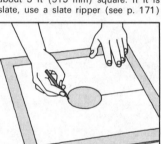

5 Lay the cardboard on a piece of zinc, approximately the size of the old slate. Draw the outline of the circle on the zinc with a wax pencil or crayon

9 Unwrap the strip, cut off the waste and wrap it around the pipe again. Score along the edge of the overlap with a bradawl

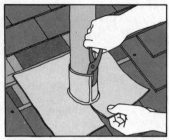

2 If there is an existing zinc slate, cut it out with snips after noting its size and shape. Renew any rotten slating or tiling battens

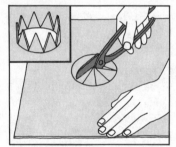

6 Dig one blade of the snips into the centre of the zinc and cut slits out to the edge of circle. Turn the slits up vertically

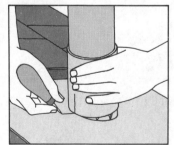

10 Scratch a line on the back of the strip, at the junction of the collar and zinc sheet. Mark a corresponding line on the flat zinc sheet

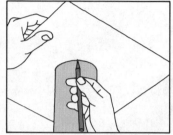

3 To find the size of the hole required in the new zinc, hold a square of cardboard on top of the pipe and trace the pipe outline with a pencil

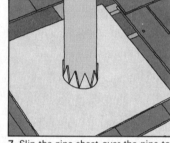

7 Slip the zinc sheet over the pipe to check that it fits. If necessary, open out the slits and bend up tabs a little more until the sheet fits

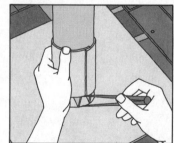

11 At the front of the pipe, measure the maximum gap between the strip and the flat zinc sheet. Use a pair of compasses or a ruler

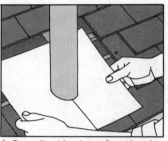

4 Cut a slit with scissors from the edge of the cardboard to the marked circle. Cut out the circle. Check cardboard in position on pipe

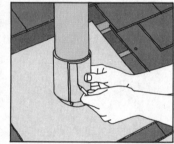

8 Wrap a 3 in. (75 mm) zinc strip around the pipe so that it touches the zinc behind. Mark where strip overlaps by ½ in. (13 mm)

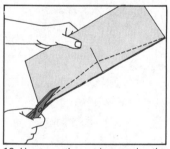

12 Unwrap the strip, mark the distance of the gap on the scored centreline and join that point to the bottom corners. Cut out *(continued)*

13 Wrap the strip round the pipe with the cutout at the back. Check that it fits accurately, and that there are no gaps at the bottom

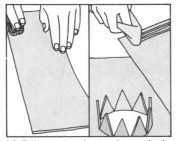

14 Rub overlapping ends on both sides of zinc strip with wire wool (left). Smear flux on overlapping edges and on outside of tabs (right)

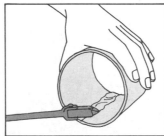

15 Overlap the collar correctly and apply flux and solder (see p. 692) inside it to make a smooth and weatherproof seam

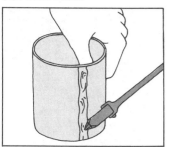

16 When first solder is set, apply flux and solder along the outside of the joint. Allow the solder to set for a few minutes

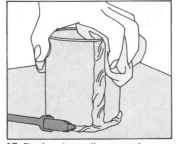

17 Fit the zinc collar correctly over the tabs of the zinc slate. Check that there are no gaps, then solder round the join

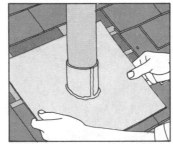

18 Fit the made-up collar and slate over the pipe. Tuck the edges of the slate if necessary under the adjacent roof covering

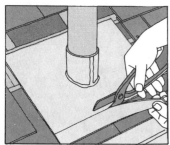

19 Trim the top edge of zinc to line up with the centre line of the nearest slating batten. Trim lower edge to line up with adjacent slates

20 Nail the top edge of the zinc sheet to the nearest slating batten to hold it in place. Do not use more than three nails

21 Replace roof covering. Seal joint between top of collar and pipe with self-adhesive strip, obtainable from builders' merchants

Re-lining a valley junction

The junction between two sloping roof surfaces is usually made of metal, which in time can corrode and become porous. The only satisfactory remedy is to re-line the junction—a two-man job which must be done from scaffolding.

If necessary, stand on the valley boards: never stand on the rafters, battens or roof coverings.

The old lining may be zinc, lead, aluminium or copper. Use zinc to re-line: it is lightweight, easier for an amateur to cut and handle, and relatively inexpensive.

Standard size sheets of zinc are 7 and 8 ft (2·1 and 2·4 m) long by 3 ft (915 mm) wide. Two sheets are usually enough for the length of the average valley gutter.

Slates and tiles

Remove any broken slates or tiles bordering the gutter. Replacement tiles of the correct size can usually be bought from a builders' merchant, but slates will have to be cut to size. Use old slates as templates and copy them exactly, including the position of the nail holes. Lay the new slates, or tiles, from the bottom upwards (see pp. 171 and 173).

Materials: 14–16 gauge zinc; slates or tiles; 1¼ in. (30 mm) galvanised slating nails; 1–1½ in. (25–40 mm) galvanised nails for zinc sheeting and battens; felt underlay (if any); softwood.

Tools: slate ripper (see p. 171); hammer; tin-snips; trowel; dresser (see p. 164); scaffolding; brush; pencil.

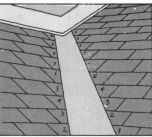

1 Remove the flashing or cement where junction butts against wall (see p. 164). Number slates, from bottom up, along edge of lining

2 Remove slates or tiles covering valley edge and lay aside for re-use. Buy new tiles where needed; cut new slates if old ones need replacing

3 Remove lining. Nail 2×1 in. (50×25 mm) softwood between rafters to support ends of battens butting valley boards *(continued)*

Roofs Weatherproofing

(continued)

4 Check that the valley boards are securely nailed to the rafters. Refix if necessary. Brush off all grit and debris from the boards

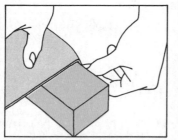

5 At ground level, lay a sheet of zinc on a thick board so that one of the long edges overhangs by $\frac{1}{2}$ in. (13 mm). Press down a corner to hold it

6 Hammer down the projecting $\frac{1}{2}$ in. with a dresser to form a right-angled bend. Work down along the whole side gradually

7 Turn the sheet over flat on the ground and place the board against the turned edge. Hammer until corner angle is sharp and well defined

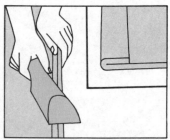

8 Remove board and hammer edge down flat to form a rigid seam (inset). Do the same with the other long side of the zinc sheet

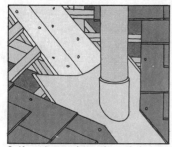

9 If a pipe projects through bottom of the valley, make and fit a zinc slate (see p. 166). Re-lay tiles or slates covering edge of zinc

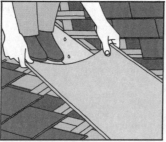

10 Lay first sheet of zinc on valley boards—seams uppermost. Allow lower end to overhang zinc slate (if any) or eaves by 2 in. (50 mm)

11 Press zinc down to fit angle of valley. Nail it sparingly to the slate battens or tiling battens to keep it in place until slates are laid

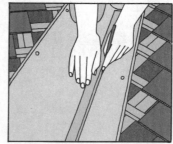

12 Use a long batten as a straight-edge and draw two lines 6 in. (150 mm) from each edge to mark where corners of tiles or slates should be

13 Re-lay the slates or tiles, starting from the eaves and working upwards. Complete each course, horizontally, before starting on the next

14 Slates inserted beneath a course of existing slates cannot be nailed; make and use a zinc clip to hold the slate in place (see p. 171)

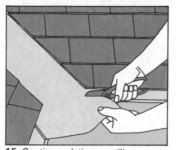

15 Continue slating or tiling up to within 12 in. (305 mm) of top of the zinc. Cut zinc at bottom to overlap the gutter by 1 in. (25 mm)

16 Bend edge down slightly. Fold the edges of a second zinc sheet and overlap first by about 9 in. (230 mm). Bend the top into approximate position

17 Use snips and cut the top of the lining to follow shape of junction of roof and wall. Allow for about 3 in. (75 mm) upright against wall

18 Nail sheet at both edges. Extend slating or tiling lines and finish re-laying slates or tiles up to the junction. Weatherproof the junction (see p. 164)

Roofs Slate

How slates are laid

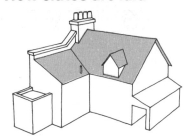

Roof slates are laid upwards from the lower edge—the eaves. Each row, called a course, overlaps the one below it, and the vertical joins between slates are staggered in adjacent rows. Thus, any one slate partly covers two below it.

The size of the main slates is determined by the design and slope of the roof and the position of the battens to which the slates are nailed. On every roof, however, two other sizes are used. The slates along the eaves and at the ridge are the same width as those used on the main part of the roof, but they are shorter. A third type of slate—called a tile-and-a-half—is half as wide again as the main slates and is used at the end of every alternate row.

Some roofs have a narrow slate—called a creasing or verge slate—at the end of each course on a gable end. It is laid underneath the main slates and tilts the edge of the roof upwards to stop rainwater running off the end of the roof and down the end wall.

The top course and the eaves course of slates are always held with two nails along their top edge. The main slates may be fixed in the same way or they may be nailed halfway down. If a slate roof requires repair, the new slates must be fixed in the way originally used.

Check all battens before starting to lay new slates or secure old ones. Cut away any rotten pieces and replace where necessary (see p. 171).

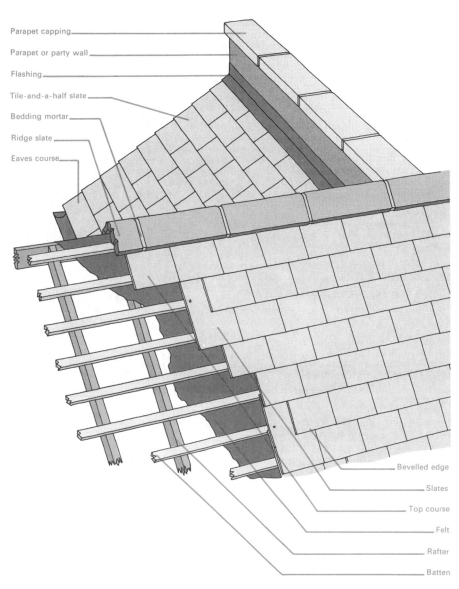

Parapet capping

Parapet or party wall

Flashing

Tile-and-a-half slate

Bedding mortar

Ridge slate

Eaves course

Bevelled edge

Slates

Top course

Felt

Rafter

Batten

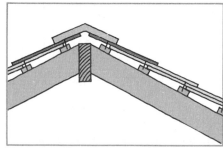

Top course Short slates are used for the course at the ridge. They partly cover the course below to give double thickness for weatherproofing

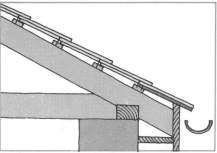

Eaves course Short slates are used for the first course above the eaves. The second row covers them completely for double thickness

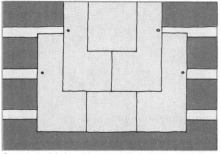

Staggered joins Slates—nailed either along their top edge or at the centre—are staggered in adjacent rows to make the roof watertight

Roofs Slate

(continued)

FIXING AND SIZES

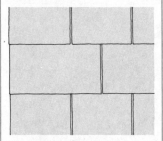

Nailing Each slate has two fixing holes—either near the top edge or across its centreline

Tile-and-a-half Each alternate course of slates has a tile-and-a-half slate at the gable end to form the bonding

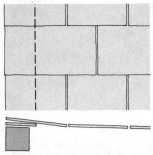

Gable ends Some roofs have narrow slates under the main slates to tilt the surface at the gable end

Buying and handling slates

Slates vary in size, shape and thickness. When new ones are fitted to a roof they must be the same as the existing slates to ensure that the roof is watertight. If the exact size required is not available, buy the nearest larger size—but the same thickness—and cut them to fit.

Slates are also available in different colours to match the roof.

New slates can be bought from builders' merchants, either singly or in bulk. A cheaper alternative, however, for repairs to the roof of an old house is to buy second-hand slates from a builder's yard or from a site where property is being demolished. They are usually only about two-thirds the price of new slates, but they have some disadvantages. For example, as slates age they flake and powder on the surface, especially near the nail holes; hairline cracks—which can be difficult to detect—develop along the grain. It is possible, however, to buy large second-hand slates which are damaged only at the edges, and trim them to the size required.

Some builders' merchants refer to slates as bests, seconds and thirds. These grades relate not to quality but to thickness and texture.

Handling slates

Slates are very brittle: if they are handled roughly they break easily. Always hold them along their longer sides and tip them from the ground before lifting. Do not try to lift them flat off a pile.

When carrying several slates at a time, wear canvas gloves and hold them on edge under one arm. If they are carried flat in a pile, they are likely to crack or break. To take slates up to a roof, stack them on edge in a canvas or plastic bag.

SECOND-HAND SLATES TO AVOID

Hairline cracks along the grain

Chipped or split edges

Surface flaking or powdering

Chipped or flaking areas around nail holes

Always check used slates before buying. If there is any fault, do not buy them. If any slates with flaking, chips or cracks are found on the roof, remove them and fit new ones

Cutting and drilling slates

Slates can be cut to any size or shape. Mark the size needed with a nail or trowel and hold the slate on a board. Make sure that the piece to be cut off is over the edge of the board. Chop with that part of the trowel blade nearest the handle.

Make nail holes in new slates before taking them to the roof. Find out which method of fixing is used and lay each slate, bevelled edge downwards, on a flat board. Make holes with hammer and nail or wheelbrace and bit.

Tools: trowel; hammer; galvanised nails; wheelbrace and bit.

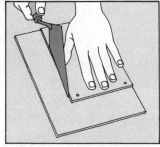

1 If new slates are too big, lay an old slate on each and trace its shape with the point of a trowel

2 Lay the marked slate over the edge of a board. Gently chop a slot halfway along the line from one edge

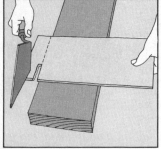

3 Turn the slate round and complete the cut from the other edge. Do not try to snap the surplus off

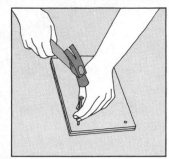

4 Lay an old slate on each new one, and mark nail holes. Lay new slate on wood and hammer nail through

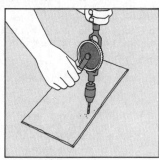

5 Alternatively, drill holes with wheelbrace and bit. Make sure the bit size matches the nails to be used

Replacing or refixing slates

As a house ages, the roof slates may crack or break; or the nails securing them may corrode, and movement in the roof structure, or a high wind, make the slates shear

Replacement slates cannot be nailed in place, because their fixing points are covered by the row above. They can, however, be secured with strips of lead.

An indispensable tool for removing slates is a ripper; buy one from a builders' merchant.

Materials: slates; lead for clips; large-headed galvanised slating nails. Tools: slate ripper; hammer.

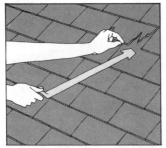

1 Slide the claw of a slate ripper under the damaged slate. Hook it round the fixing nails

2 Pull the ripper to break the nails. Pull out the old slate. Do not dislodge any of the sound slates

3 Cut a strip of lead about 9×1 in. (230×25 mm). Nail to the batten between the exposed slate nails

4 Gently lift the slates of the row above. Push the new slate into place. Keep it flat against the battens

5 When the bottom edge of this slate lines with adjoining slates, bend up the end of the lead clip to secure it

Repairing a large area of a slate roof

Roof movement or the subsidence of rotting battens may dislodge or damage a large area of slates. If the battens are unsound, fit new ones before fixing new slates. Treat the wood with a preservative.

Do not try to work from a ladder: it is essential for extensive roof repairs to erect a scaffolding system and use crawling boards (see p. 685).

Materials: battens if required; lead for clips; 2 in. (50 mm) galvanised nails to fix battens; large-headed galvanised slating nails. Tools: slate ripper; panel saw; hammer; trowel; knife; straight-edge.

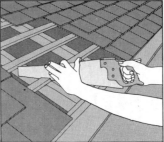

1 Remove all broken slates with a slate ripper. Cut back rotten battens to the centre of a rafter at each end

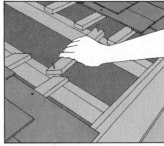

2 To provide a close fit, cut one end of the old batten diagonally. Cut new battens to match. Check their size

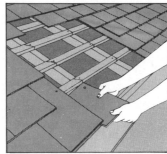

3 Fit the new battens against the edges of the old ones. Hammer in a 2 in. (50 mm) nail at each end

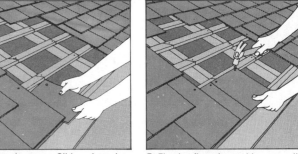

4 Start at the eaves. Slide a short slate under an adjacent full-length slate up to the batten centreline

5 Fix the first slate with one nail—because it is partly covered. Fix the others along the row with two nails

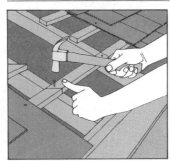

6 Check that each slate lies on the centreline, to allow the second row to be fixed to the same batten

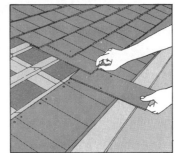

7 Lift the first existing slate in the row above and carefully slide the first new full-length slate under it

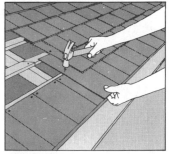

8 Make sure that the new slate comes to the centreline of the batten. Fix it with one nail   *(continued)*

Roofs Slate

(continued)

9 Lay the other slates along the same row, so that they cover the vertical joins in the row below

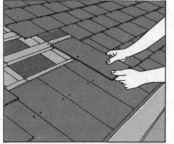

10 Continue working up the roof. Cover the previous joins and securing nails with each slate laid

11 Because the nail holes are covered by the rows above, it may not be possible to nail the last few slates

12 Use a knife and straight-edge to cut 9×1 in. (230×25 mm) lead clips to hold the remaining slate or slates

13 Fix the clips between the nails securing the adjacent slates. Make sure they are nailed to a batten

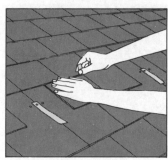

14 Fit the remaining slates so that their bottom edges are flush with the rest of the row. Bend up the clips

Fixing a loose ridge slate

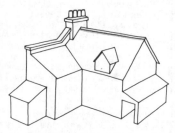

The natural settlement of a roof can cause mortar between the ridge slates on top of the roof to fall out.

A loose ridge slate is dangerous: refit it as soon as possible.

Materials: 3:1 sand and cement (see p. 693).
Tools: crawling board; ladder; club hammer; bolster or cold chisel; trowel.

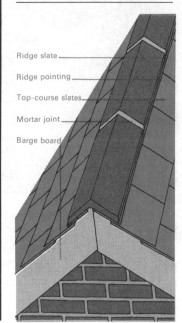

Ridge slate
Ridge pointing
Top-course slates
Mortar joint
Barge board

1 Lift off the loose ridge slate and take it to the ground. Handle it carefully to avoid breaking

2 Chip old mortar from inside the ridge slate with the edge of a trowel. Take care not to crack it

3 Use a club hammer and bolster—or cold chisel—to remove old mortar from the ridge of the roof

4 Mix 3:1 sand and cement (see p. 693). Lay it along the ridge and roughen the surface with a trowel

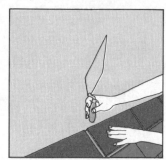

5 Position the cleaned ridge slate on the mortar. Tap it gently until it is level with the adjacent slates

6 Push mortar into the joints on each side and along the bottom of the slate. Smooth with a trowel

Roofs Tile

How tiles are laid

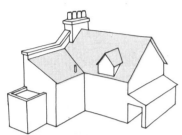

Tiles are laid in rows, called courses, from the eaves up to the ridge of a roof. Each course overlaps the one below it, and the vertical joins between the tiles are staggered in adjacent rows so that any one tile partly covers two in the row below it.

Three sizes of tile are used: a standard tile for the main covering; a tile—called a tile-and-a-half—half as wide again as the standard size at the end of alternate rows up the roof; and a shortened version of the tile-and-a-half for the course along the eaves and along the ridge of the roof.

On some roofs, there are narrower tiles—called creasing tiles—at the gable end of each course. They are laid underneath the end to tilt the edge of the roof upwards to ensure that rainwater cannot run down the gable wall.

Some tiles are nailed to the battens on the roof: others have small projections—called nibs—which fit over the battens. Although nibbed tiles may be nailed when they are first laid, it is not usually necessary to use nails when replacing a single tile or course. Tiles without nibs must always be nailed.

When removing damaged tiles, use a slate ripper carefully: the tiles may be laid on bitumenised felt, which tears easily. Always fit new felt if the existing covering is torn.

Check all tiling battens before starting to lay new tiles. Cut away any rotten pieces and replace them where necessary with pre-treated timber (see p. 185).

TYPES OF TILES

When buying replacement tiles, take an old one to a builders' merchant to ensure that the new tiles match.

There are six basic types: plain tiles, pantiles, double pantiles, interlocking tiles and Roman and Spanish tiles.

Unlike slates (see p. 170), tiles cannot be cut to size.

Most roofs have plain tiles, which are usually $10\frac{1}{2} \times 6\frac{1}{2} \times \frac{1}{2}$ in. (265×165×13 mm). They are very slightly curved to ensure that the tail end beds evenly on the tiles below.

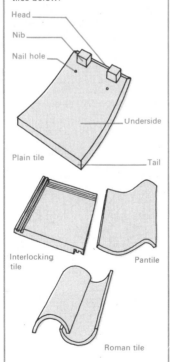

Head

Nib

Nail hole

Underside

Plain tile

Tail

Interlocking tile

Pantile

Roman tile

Replacing broken tiles

The natural settlement of a roof may cause some tiles to crack. Remove them and lay new ones as soon as possible.

Whatever type of tile is used, the method of replacement is similar: the main differences are in the spacing of the battens to which the tiles are fixed and the number of nails—if any —that are needed. Always lay new tiles in the same way as they were fixed originally.

Materials: replacement tiles; piece of softwood batten; galvanised nails. Tools: trowel; slate ripper (see p. 171); hammer; ladder.

1 Lift the tiles above those damaged and ease the broken pieces carefully away from the course

2 If the tiles are nibbed, prise the sound ones up with a trowel and lift the damaged ones over the batten

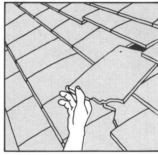

3 If the tiles are nailed, rock them gently from side to side. If necessary, use a slate ripper

4 If tiles have to be nailed, use $1\frac{1}{4}$ in. (30 mm) galvanised nails. Fit them from the eaves upwards

5 To fit the last tiles, wedge up one of those above. Lift the other and slide the new tiles in place

Mending felt

When the roofing felt underneath damaged tiles is also damaged, rain or snow can penetrate through the roof, damage interior decoration and cause wet rot (see p. 185).

To repair a tear, buy an offcut of roofing felt from a builders' merchant or do-it-yourself store and stick a patch over the hole with bitumen adhesive.

Materials: roofing felt; bitumen adhesive; galvanised nails; preservative; hardboard offcut; tiles. Tools: tenon saw; sharp knife; rule; old paintbrush; dustpan and brush; pincers.

1 Remove tiles to expose torn felt. Remove the nails which hold battens on rafters with pincers

2 Slide a hardboard offcut, smooth side down, under battens and over rafters at one side *(continued)*

Roofs Tile

(continued)

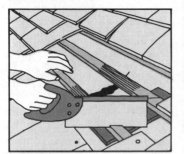

3 Cut at angle through battens on top of hardboard. Cut other side of tear in the same way

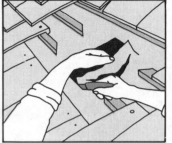

4 With a sharp knife, cut a square, slightly larger than the damaged area, out of the roofing felt

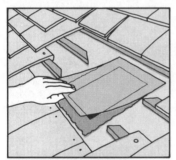

5 Cut felt patch slightly larger than the square removed. Spread adhesive round edge and stick patch

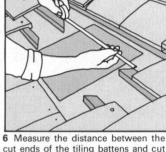

6 Measure the distance between the cut ends of the tiling battens and cut new pieces to size

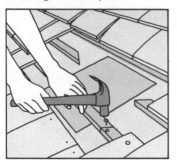

7 Brush the softwood battens with preservative (see p. 186) and nail them in place on the rafters

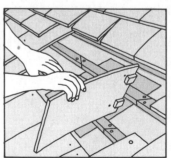

8 Replace tiles. Sweep all loose materials and debris from the repair area and from the gutters

---

TILING RIDGES AND SLOPING EDGES

The ridge of a tiled roof is covered with semi-circular or right-angled ridge tiles. The edges formed by two sloping surfaces—called hips—have semi-circular or bonnet-shaped tiles.

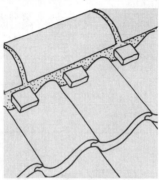

Ridge Small triangular pieces of tile are inserted into the bedding mortar before it has set

Hip hook A $\frac{1}{4} \times 1\frac{1}{2}$ in. (6×40 mm) curled piece of wrought iron is screwed to the top of the hip rafter

Bonnet hip Small triangular pieces of tile are inserted into the mortar pointing of the last tile

---

TILING EAVES AND VALLEY JUNCTIONS

The eaves course on a plain-tiled roof rests on the top of the fascia board with curved tiles filled with mortar at the outside edge. On some roofs, a valley junction (see p. 167) may be tiled.

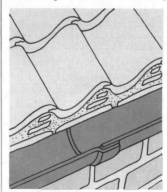

Pantile eaves Small pieces of tile inserted into the mortar help to reinforce the eaves course

Creasing tiles Narrow tiles are inserted under the main covering to tilt up the edge of the roof

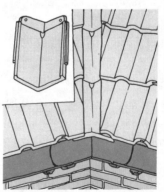

Valley junctions Specially shaped tiles, that interlock with each other, are available for tiled gutters

Roofs Corrugated sheeting

Repairing a corrugated roof

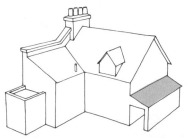

If a corrugated-iron roof needs to be replaced, fit sheets of plastic or asbestos; both are more brittle than iron but easier to cut. When cutting asbestos always be careful not to inhale any dust; it is advisable to wear a mask and to dampen the work.

When the junction between the wall and the existing iron roof has a flashing (see p. 164) still in good condition, bend it upwards carefully so that it can be used again. If a new flashing is needed, buy a special kit.

When fitting plastic or asbestos, do not kneel or stand on the sheeting. Lay a plank across it as a support where there is a roof joist.

Make sure that the new sheets butt against the wall and that they overlap each other by two corrugations. Drill holes for the fixing screws in the centre of a raised corrugation and at a point where there is a joist.

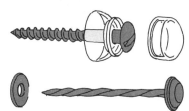

Screws Use screws with plastic washers and protective caps (top) for plastic, screw nails (bottom) for asbestos

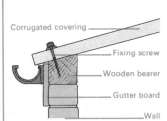

Fixing Screw through the centre of raised corrugations only

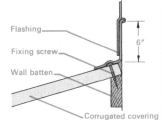

Flashing Mould flashings down over corrugations and screws

MARKING AND CUTTING

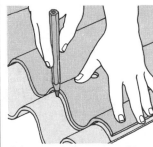

1 Lay an old sheet or an offcut on the new roof material. Mark along at the length required

2 Lay the marked sheet between two planks, so that the line is at the edge of the wood

3 Cut through raised corrugations at the edge of the wood. Turn sheet and cut the other side

4 To cut lengthways, lay the sheet between the two planks and cut through a raised corrugation

Fitting a new plastic roof

Plastic corrugated sheeting is light and easy to handle. It allows more light to enter, and is a useful replacement for corrugated iron.

Before buying plastic sheeting, consult the building inspector at the local council offices. Some brands of plastic roofing may not meet the fire-resistance requirements.

Materials: plastic sheeting and screws or screw nails; flashing kit; wall batten if necessary; cold pitch; mastic sealer.
Tools: fine tenon saw; rag; paint-brush; wheel brace and bit; drill; wire brush.

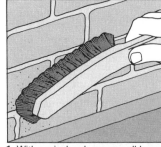

1 With a wire brush, remove all loose particles from the wall up to 6 in. (150 mm) above the roof batten

2 Thickly coat the cleaned area with cold pitch. Make sure that the top edge of the pitch is straight

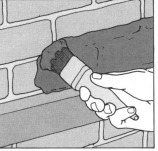

3 Apply a second coat of pitch and leave it to dry. Fill any holes or crevices with a mastic sealer

4 Measure and mark the sheeting. Allow extra 1½ in. (40 mm) if there is a gutter, 3 in. (75 mm) if not

5 Position first sheet and drill into the wood through every third raised corrugation *(continued)*

Roofs Corrugated sheeting

(continued)

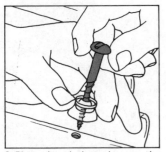

6 Place the vinyl washer on the screw and drive the screw into position. Do not overtighten

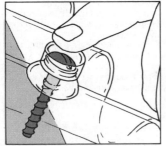

7 Push a plastic cap down on to each screw and over the lip of the washer below

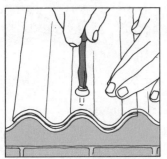

8 Fit each sheet to overlap the previous one by two corrugations. Drill and screw through both

9 Peel backing from a flashing strip. Fit adhesive side against the wall 3 in. (75 mm) above the roof

10 Wipe along the flashing with a rag, to press it tightly against the wall. Mould it into the roof corrugations

11 If there is a buttress, cut the flashing and turn corner with a new piece. Overlap by 2 in. (50 mm)

Fitting single asbestos sheets

Fix asbestos sheeting with screw nails, obtainable from a builders' merchant. Drill holes in the sheeting $\frac{1}{16}$ in. (2 mm) larger than the diameter of the nails, which have a spiral thread and should be hammered, not screwed, through the asbestos into the roof joists. Be careful not to inhale asbestos dust. Wear a mask and dampen the work.

Materials: corrugated asbestos sheeting; flashing kit; 2½ in. (65 mm) galvanised screw nails; rubber or vinyl washers.
Tools: mole wrench; hammer; wheelbrace and bit; tenon saw; planks; four 2 in. (50 mm) square softwood pieces.

1 Lay a plank down the roof near the damaged sheet. Make sure that it spans two roof joists

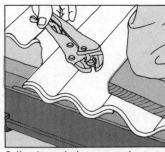

2 Kneel on plank to press sheets together near the heads of the screw nails. Remove the nails with a wrench

3 At the wall, ease the flashing up away from the asbestos. Slide out the damaged sheet

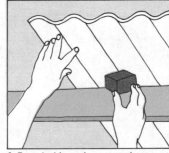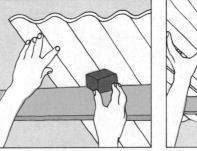

4 From inside push up one sheet next to gap. Fit blocks under the third corrugation between the sheets and joists

5 Cut a new sheet to fit and slide it under raised sheet and over the sheet on the other side

6 Check that the sheeting is fully home. Remove blocks and make sure that the sheets fit together

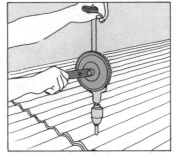

7 Drill holes through the new sheet. If it is under an old sheet, use the existing holes as a guide

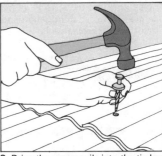

8 Drive the screw nails into the timber joists at ends and overlaps until the flexible washer is just compressed

Roofs Felt

Construction

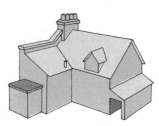

Roofing felt is a laminated material made of two or three layers of bitumen-impregnated fibres that are bonded together with a liquid bitumen to form a waterproof sandwich. The types of felt that can be used on any roof are controlled by the building regulations. Consult the local building inspector before buying or fitting new felt. A sloping roof needs one underlay and a top layer; a flat roof an additional underlay.

The felt is usually laid on softwood boarding, which is nailed to the rafters. On some roofs, sheets of manufactured boards (see p. 689) are used.

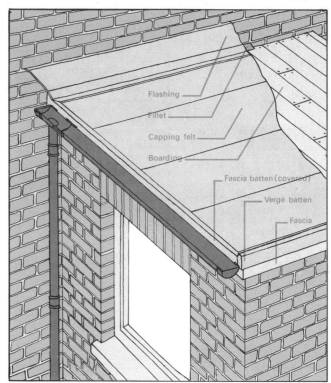

Flashing —
Fillet —
Capping felt —
Boarding —
Fascia batten (covered) —
Verge batten —
Fascia —

Repairing a felt roof

A felt roof may eventually leak because the covering has been cracked by heat or by the natural movement of the structural timbers.

If water is penetrating although the roof appears to be sound, check the flashings where the roof meets a wall or a parapet. Repoint or fit new flashing (see p. 164) where it has become necessary.

If the felt covering is damaged and allows water to penetrate, remove it. Check all the boards and fit new ones where necessary.

Wear soft-soled shoes to avoid damaging the remaining felt. When the felt is laid on a flat roof, apply a coating of cold mastic, a small area at a time, and sprinkle white stone chippings to reflect the heat.

On sloping roofs use felt that incorporates a light-coloured granular material, such as fine sand.

It is most important to ensure that joins of successive layers of felt are staggered and do not coincide.

Materials: underlay felt; capping felt; mastic bitumen; bitumen adhesive; $\frac{3}{4}$ in. (20 mm) galvanised clout nails; white stone chippings.
Tools: broom; claw hammer; plane; punch; knife; tin shears; trowel; ladder; rags; gloves.

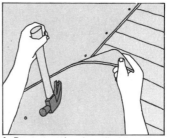

1 Remove or bend up flashings (see p. 164). Withdraw nails with claw hammer and remove the existing felt and underlay

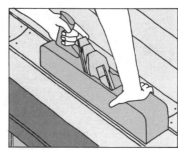

2 Check the boarding and replace any boards that are unsound. Plane flat any raised edges and punch down protruding nail heads

3 Sweep the roof. Then start at the centre of gutter edge and unroll first underlay strip. Allow for an overlap at the gutter fascia

4 Cut the first strip of underlay to length and nail it to the boarding every 6 in. (150 mm). Fix from the centre of strip outwards

5 Unroll and cut other lengths of underlay. Lay them in position so that they overlap the previous length by 2 in. (50 mm). Nail every 6 in.

6 When cutting an end piece of felt against a wall or parapet wall, make cut just short of top edge of triangular-shaped wooden fillet

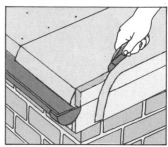

7 At an exposed edge, cut last length to fit flush with the inside edge of the verge batten. Nail felt down and sweep the roof *(continued)*

Roofs Felt

(continued)

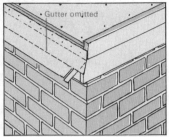

8 Cut felt for fascia 10 in. (225 mm) wide. Nail top edge to within $\frac{3}{4}$ in. (20 mm) of fascia batten top. Fold up and stick to surface of underlay

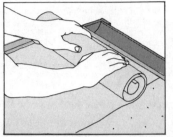

9 Make sure surface of underlay is clean. Position and unroll first strip of second underlay so that edges are 2 in. from overlap of first

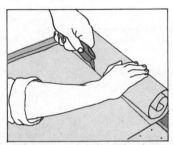

10 Cut strip to length so that lower end butts against top edge of stuck-down fascia strip. Avoid cutting through first underlay

11 Roll up the felt from both ends towards the centre and weight it down temporarily with a brick or with a block of wood

12 Spread bitumen adhesive over first underlay to a width slightly greater than that of the rolled underlay. Work from roll upwards or downwards

13 Stick down relevant roll; repeat with other. Tread down. Fix other strips with 2 in. overlaps. Repeat with top layer stuck to within 1 in. of verge

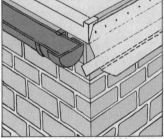

14 Cut verge felt 15 in. (380 mm) × 4 ft (1·2 m) long. Fix in the same way as the gutter felt, overlapping the lengths by 2 in.

15 Fold down the existing flashings or, if fitting new ones, rake out brickwork joint to depth of $1\frac{1}{4}$ in. (30 mm). Brush joint clean

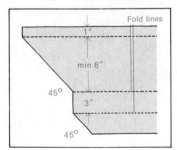

16 Cut flashing felt about 12 in. (305 mm) × 4 ft (1·2 m) long. Cut the ends to shape and fold the felt to fit against the wall length

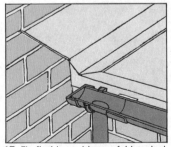

17 Fit flashing with top fold tucked into brick joint. Position adjoining lengths to lap by 2 in. with overlap on lower side of roof

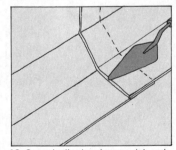

18 Spread adhesive along each length of flashing and, working from the gutter, press it into place. Repoint the joint (see p. 164)

19 Block gutter outlet with rags. Work towards ladder, spreading mastic and sprinkling stone chippings. Remove rags from gutter outlet

Corner joints

Some felt roofs may include internal and external angles—for example, where a chimney stack meets a wall. Form a lapped joint to turn the felt around corners.

Since dimensions will vary with different roofs, make paper templates before cutting the felt. The widest point of the overlap should be a minimum of 6 in. (150 mm).

Some roofs may have a triangular timber fillet at the junction of wall and roof to form a slope and help throw off rainwater.

If repairing a roof that does not have a fillet, provide a fillet from 2×2 in. (50×50 mm) softwood.

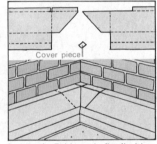

Internal Fold and fit flashing (right): overlap and stick second piece. Stick cover piece over corner joint and repoint (see p. 164)

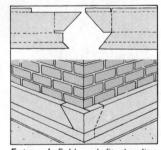

External Fold and fit the first flashing (left): overlap and stick second in place with bitumen adhesive. Repoint (see p. 164)

Roofs Zinc

How a zinc roof is constructed

A zinc roof is constructed in 33×90 in. (935 mm×2·3 m) panels, which are laid in steps called drips.

Each panel is made in the shape of a tray, with the sides and top edge bent up at right angles and solder-jointed at each corner. These three sides are called upstands. The bottom edge is folded under to form a welted joint with the top upstand of the tray immediately beneath it.

Each tray is laid between battens of timber, called rolls, which hold the tray-retaining clips in position. The rolls are nailed or screwed to the roof timbers every 21 in. (535 mm). A zinc capping is fixed with clips at the overlapped sections. The end of each capping is shaped to fit over the end of its roll.

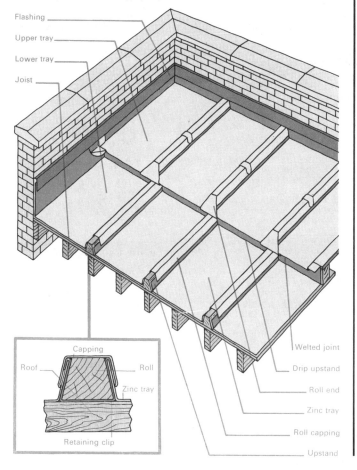

Flashing
Upper tray
Lower tray
Joist

Capping
Roof
Roll
Zinc tray
Retaining clip

Welted joint
Drip upstand
Roll end
Zinc tray
Roll capping
Upstand

Fitting a new zinc tray

Attempt only minor repair work to a zinc roof. Extensive work should be done by a builder. Make sure that any replacement zinc is of the same gauge as the existing roof covering. Take an old offcut to a builders' merchant when buying new strips.

Inspect the mortar at the zinc flashing round the roof. If it is cracked or damaged, repoint it (see p. 164).

Materials: zinc sheet; 4 ft (1·2 m) length of 2×4 in. (50×100 mm) timber; nails and screws; wire wool; solder and flux; rags.
Tools: straight-edge; pencil; hammer; tin shears; dresser; soldering iron.

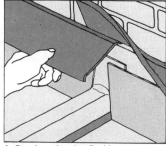

1 Bend up the zinc flashing to expose the tray upstands. If flashing or mortar is damaged, remove it

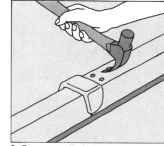

2 Remove nails in capping along the rolls beside damaged tray. Slide capping off the rolls

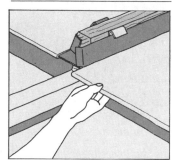

3 Open the welted joint at the top of the drip upstand and slide the damaged tray off the roof

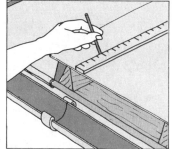

4 Start at lower tray. Lay zinc sheet over rolls and mark the width of tray with pencil and straight-edge

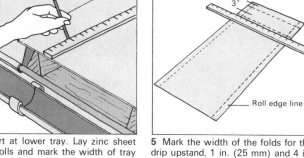

Roll edge line

5 Mark the width of the folds for the drip upstand, 1 in. (25 mm) and 4 in. (100 mm) from top edge of zinc

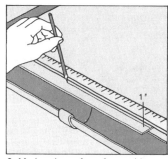

6 Mark edge of roof, or drip, on zinc. Draw line 1 in. beyond it and trim off surplus

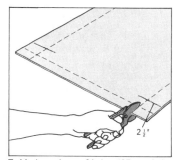

7 Mark and cut 2½ in. (65 mm) in from end of zinc side fold lines. Bend outer pieces to right angles

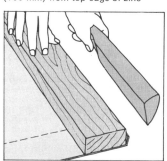

8 Hold a batten along 1 in. line at top and hammer up the zinc with a dresser (see p. 164)   *(continued)*

Roofs Zinc

(continued)

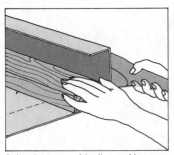

9 Lay batten on 4 in. line and hammer up zinc to make drip upstand fold. Do not distort first fold

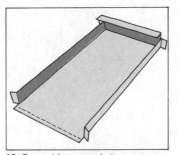

10 Form side upstands in same way. Cut off surplus to leave 1 in. (25 mm) at top and $\frac{1}{2}$ in. (13 mm) at bottom

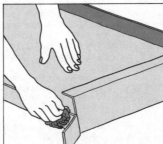

11 Clean the inner faces and the edge of each projecting piece with wire wool. Clean outside upstand

12 Bend the projections round the drip upstand at top of zinc tray. Solder (see p. 692) round the edges

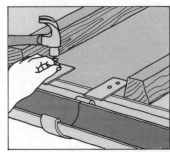

13 Cut zinc clips 6×3 in. (150×75 mm). Nail to the roof to overlap edge or drip by about 1 in.

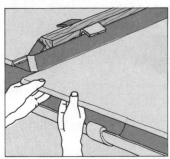

14 Slide the tray into position so that the folded end of zinc fits round the roof clips

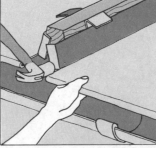

15 Bend back projections at bottom of each side upstand. Hammer against roll end. Secure retaining clips

16 Measure strips of zinc 4$\frac{3}{4}$ in. (120 mm) wide by 4 ft (1·2 m) long. Score with a knife, then cut

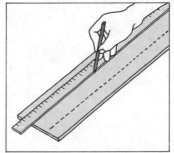

17 To make the roll cappings, mark two pencil lines 1$\frac{1}{2}$ in. (40 mm) in from each side of cut strips

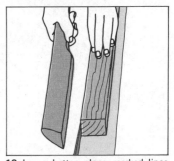

18 Lay a batten along marked lines and hammer the capping carefully to shape with a dresser

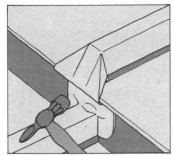

19 Lay and fold capping zinc over roll. Shape over roll end with hammer and fold end of zinc under upstand below

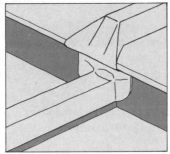

20 If opposite end of capping fits beneath roll above, cut zinc to length and hammer it flat against upstand

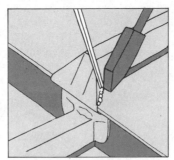

21 Solder edges of zinc on roll end where they butt against the edge of the zinc tray underneath

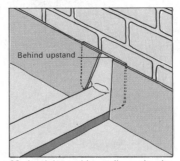

Behind upstand

22 At joint with wall, tuck the hammered end behind the upstand. Replace the cover flashing

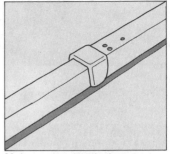

23 Insert upper length of capping into clip fold. Nail capping clips in position over capping joints

Roofs Thatch

How roofs are thatched

On a thatched roof, layers of straw or reed are laid vertically down thatching battens, nailed across the roof rafters. The thatch is held in place on the battens by metal pins. A layer of repair thatching is secured to the existing by twisted hazelwood strips, called spars.

Roofs can be thatched with three types of material: long straw, combed wheat reed, or Norfolk reed. Straw roofs last between 10 and 20 years; combed wheat reed roofs, 30 to 40 years; and Norfolk reed roofs, 50 to 60 years.

Roofs thatched with straw should always be protected with wire netting, to stop birds from nesting or burrowing in the thatch.

Thatching is a skilled job: do not try to repair a large area. Tackle only small holes or damage. If extensive work is needed, engage a professional thatcher immediately. Bear in mind, however, that skilled thatchers are in great demand, and it may be months before the repair can be carried out.

Straw is usually obtainable in lengths of 2–2½ ft (610–760 mm), and reeds in lengths of 3–7 ft (1–2 m). There are dealers who specialise in supplying these materials but in case of difficulty write to the Council for Small Industries in Rural Areas, 35 Camp Road, Wimbledon, London SW19 4UP. It can give advice on where to obtain materials and how to find a professional thatcher.

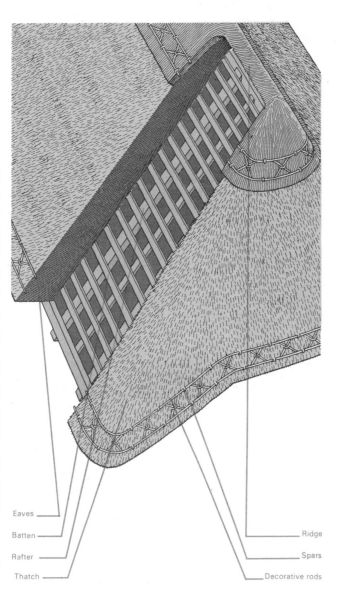

Eaves

Batten

Rafter

Thatch

Ridge

Spars

Decorative rods

Fitting new netting

The wire netting on a straw-thatch roof usually lasts for about 10 to 15 years: but check it once a year.

Replace netting only at the eaves or any part of the roof which can be reached safely from a ladder. Never stand or use a crawl board: the thatch can be damaged easily.

Use netting of the same mesh and gauge as the existing covering. If several large patches need attention, engage a thatcher to do the repair.

Materials: wire netting—usually ¾ in. mesh (20 mm)×20 gauge; 18 in. (455 mm) batten.
Tools: wire cutters; pliers; mallet.

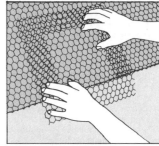

1 Cut out the damaged wire. Cut a new piece to overlap the edges of the hole by about 4 in. (100 mm)

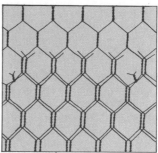

2 Tie the new netting to the old with wire every 6 in. (150 mm). Press the ends down into the thatch

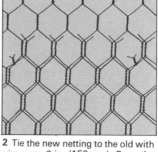

3 Hook the loose ends at the edge of the new wire around the old. Use a pair of pliers to hold it

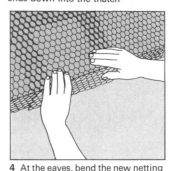

4 At the eaves, bend the new netting over the old and shape it by hand to match the angle of the eaves

5 Hold a batten on the top edge and hammer wire lightly with a mallet. Fasten new and old wire together

Roofs Thatch

Fitting rods and spars

Hazel rods are fixed at the ridge, eaves and gables to secure the thatch on a straw roof.

The rods are hazel branches split into strips about ½ in. (13 mm) in diameter and 2–6 ft (610 mm– 1·8 m) long.

The rods are held in position every 6 in. (150 mm) by spars, which are split hazelwood branches, twisted in the centre, bent in half and sharpened at each end. In time, rods may rot. If many are damaged, engage a professional thatcher.

Materials: hazel rods and spars.
Tools: mallet; hand axe; knife.

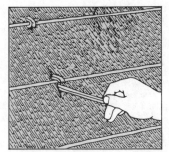

1 Pull out and discard the broken spars which may be securing any rods that are rotten

2 Cut a piece of hazel 24 in. (610 mm) long. Split it lengthwise into ½ in. (13 mm) strips

3 Sharpen the ends with a knife: the sharper the point, the easier it is to drive the spar into the thatch

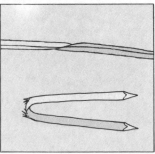

4 Hold the ends of the spar and twist it; then bend it at the middle into a U shape

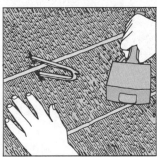

5 Hold new rods in place and hammer in the spars horizontally every 6 in. (150 mm)

Plugging small holes

Small holes in a thatched roof can be plugged with reed or with straw secured with a spar. If the hole is larger than a tennis ball, engage a professional thatcher.

A bundle of suitable straw may be obtainable from a farm: if it cannot be obtained from a local source, contact the Council for Small Industries in Rural Areas (see p. 181).

Always replace any netting after plugging the holes.

Materials: straw or reed; hazel spars; new netting (if required).
Tools: shears or sharp knife; mallet; softwood battens.

REED THATCH REPAIRS

1 Clean out loose reed from the hole and insert lengths of cut reed into it. Push the reed in tightly until hole is filled

2 Use shears to trim the ragged ends of the reed flush with the rest of the thatch

STRAW THATCH REPAIRS

1 Roll up netting. Hook a handful of straw through a spar. Pull the material back around the spar

2 Push the spar and straw by hand as far as possible into the hole. The spar must be at an angle to the thatch

3 Push a batten against the spar and hammer it home into the existing thatch. Refit the netting

EMERGENCY PATCHING

If a roof starts to sag or the thatch becomes stained and rotten where water has collected, fit a temporary patch of heavy polythene until a thatcher can be engaged (see p. 181).

Cut away any wire netting over the damaged area and remove the rotten thatching to a depth of about 6 in. (150 mm).

Materials: polythene; wire netting; 18 in. (455 mm) lengths of fencing wire.
Tools: wire-cutters; pliers; scissors.

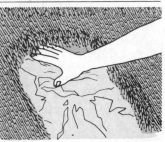

1 Remove rotten thatch. Cut a piece of polythene twice as large as the damaged area. Spread the polythene flat and tuck the edges under the sound thatch round the hole

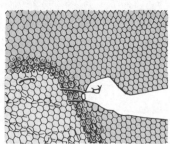

2 Fit netting (see p. 181) if any has been cut away. Bend pieces of wire and push them every 6 in. (150 mm) through the edge of the polythene. Twist ends to secure netting

Roofs Shingles

Repairing a shingle roof

Cedar shingles usually last at least 30 years—longer if they have been treated with preservative before fitting.

If shingles are damaged, attempt a repair only if the roof is less than 15 years old. After this time, the shingles are likely to be brittle, and when a defective one is removed the adjacent shingles can be damaged.

For repairs to an older roof, it is better to engage a roofing specialist.

Butt end   Feathered end

Shingles Lay the butt ends downwards, except for those on the ridge. Lay the centre ridge shingle—the highest—butt end upwards; lay side ridge shingles butt end sideways. Nail 6–7 in. (150–180 mm) from the butt end

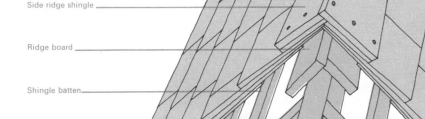

Side ridge shingle

Centre ridge shingle

Side ridge shingle

Ridge board

Shingle batten

Shingle

Rafter

Fitting ridge shingles

There is no special shingle to cover the roof ridge: the shingles are butted against each other at the top of the roof to form a weatherproof covering. Each overlapping shingle is secured with three nails, each overlapped shingle with two nails.

If more than one shingle has to be replaced, start repairs from the ends of the ridge and work towards the highest point—at the centre. Shingles can be cut with a sharp hatchet or knife.

Materials: shingles; galvanised or silicone-bronze nails, $1\frac{1}{4}$ in. (30 mm) by 15 gauge. Tools: slate ripper; claw hammer; bolster chisel; hatchet; knife; ladder; crawl boards (see p. 685).

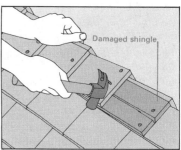

Damaged shingle

1 Remove the nails from both the damaged and overlapping shingles with the claw of a hammer

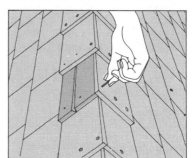

2 Remove the nail that is holding the damaged shingle from the opposite side of the roof ridge

3 Insert a slate ripper (see p. 171). Hook it round the hidden nails and withdraw it to shear the nails

4 Tap gently downwards with hammer and bolster chisel to remove shingle. Trim the new one to size with a hatchet or knife

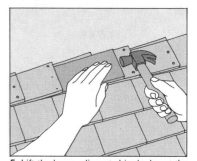

5 Lift the loose adjacent shingle. Insert the thin end of new shingle. Hammer into position and nail

Roofs Shingles

Centre ridge shingle

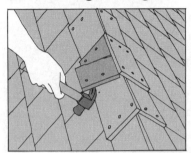

1 Prise the damaged shingle off the ridge. Do not damage existing shingles underneath it

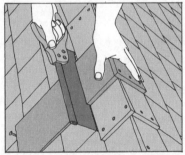

2 Trim new shingle at the feathered end to match adjacent ones. Fit it with the thicker end at the top

3 Check that width of new shingle matches old. Nail new shingle ½ in. (13 mm) in from each corner

Fitting new shingles

When fitting new shingles, always follow the pattern in which the original ones were laid on the roof. Some roofs, for example, have some shingles in each course laid ½ in. (13 mm) above those on each side of them.

To avoid splitting the shingles, fix them with two nails at least ½ in. in from the side edges.

Materials: shingles; galvanised or silicone-bronze nails, 1¼ in. (30 mm) by 15 gauge.
Tools: slate ripper; claw hammer; bolster chisel; hatchet; sharp knife; ladder; crawl boards.

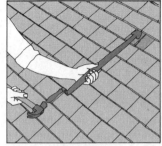

1 Insert a slate ripper under the shingle above the damaged one and hook nail with end of ripper

2 Hammer the handle of the slate ripper sharply downwards to shear through the nail

3 Use the hammer and ripper to remove the nails holding the split or damaged shingle

4 Tap gently downwards with a hammer and chisel to remove the parts of the damaged shingle

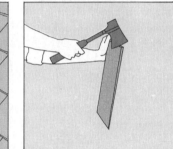

5 Measure the width to allow ⅛ in. (3 mm) gap at each side when fitted. Trim new shingle with hatchet

6 If the shingle is too long, trim along the feathered end of it with a sharp knife

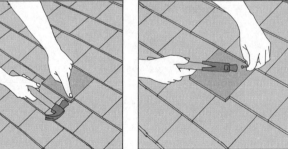

7 If two shingles are needed to fill a space, make sure that one overlaps the vertical join by 1½ in. (40 mm)

8 Allow an ⅛ in. gap at each side and push the shingle as far as possible under shingles above

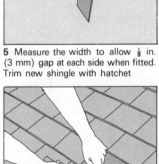

9 Gently hammer in the shingle until it projects only ½ in. (13 mm) below the adjacent ones

10 Fix the new shingle with two nails as close as possible to the edge of the shingle above

11 Tap the new shingle up gently until the nails are hidden and the shingle lines with those adjacent

Rot and woodworm

Inspecting for dry and wet rot

Dry and wet rot are two types of fungi which develop in damp conditions, usually associated with bad ventilation. Wet rot is a fungus which remains localised. Dry rot is more serious and can spread rapidly through a building.

Inspect the building regularly for damp (see p. 24). Inspect timbers in roof spaces, under stair-cases, in cellars, pipe ducts and under suspended ground floors (see p. 78). Make sure that air bricks and gratings are not blocked. Check that the damp-proof course is effective (see p. 27).

If rot is suspected, or an outbreak is obvious, seek specialist advice. If structural timbers are involved, do not try to replace them without specialist advice.

WET ROT

1 The timber splits along the grain and is usually covered with dark brown vein-like strands

Crown copyright

2 In advanced wet rot, timber splits along and across the grain, similar to dry rot

Crown copyright

DRY ROT

1 Wood surfaces become distorted and the structural timbers of a floor weaken beyond repair

3 The fruit body produced in the advanced stage contains the spores to germinate further outbreaks

2 In its advanced state, densely packed sheets of dry rot appear on the timber under the floorboards

4 As the attacked wood dries out, cracks along and across the grain produce a cubed effect

Recognising dry rot

Dry rot—*Serpula lachrymans*—causes extensive damage to house timbers. It spreads from one area to another by spores which may be airborne or carried on shoes or clothing.

The spores of dry rot settle on timber and surrounding areas, and in suitable conditions of dampness, temperature and lack of ventilation, they will germinate rapidly.

Thin white strands appear and develop into thick, cottonwool-like sheets, from which tendrils spread through the fabric of the building seeking more timber to provide moisture and nutriment to feed the fungus. Timber fibres are broken down, resulting in loss of strength and decay. Fruit bodies—grey-white masses which contain millions of spores—eventually appear and spread the disease.

Symptoms
An infestation of dry rot has a 'musty' smell like that of mushrooms.

Timber surfaces which are painted may look distorted, wavy or split. Dry rot can affect all joinery timbers—such as skirtings, frames and linings to windows, and doors and panelling—as well as structural timbers.

If a sharp tool, such as a screwdriver, can easily penetrate the surface and the timber crumbles, it is likely that the wood is infested.

In advanced cases the timber dries and splits along the grain. Sheets of white strands appear, and spores like coffee powder accumulate in enclosed spaces. Fruit bodies that glisten with water are known as 'weeping fungus'.

Treatment
Investigate and treat any suspect area immediately. To find the source of the attack, probe the timber with a penknife to determine the soft areas, which are the central points of the attack. Cut out all the affected timbers at least 24 in. (610 mm) beyond the decayed timber until sound timber is exposed. Burn all the affected timber.

Where decayed timber is adjacent to, or built into walls, cut away plaster around the affected areas until the full extent of the rot is determined. Clean exposed brickwork with a wire brush; carefully collect all dust and debris and burn it. Paint or spray (see p. 187) the wall surface, and any timber within 5 ft (1.5 m) of the exposed area, with a fungicide.

Drill ½ in. (13 mm) downward-sloping holes around the affected area and inject fungicide fluid into them with a spray-lance (see p. 187) or pour it through a funnel.

When fitting new timber, make sure that it has been treated against rot. Cut timbers should have the ends soaked in preservative overnight.

It is advisable to apply a coat of zinc oxychloride paint or plaster to the exposed wall surface to give an extra barrier against spores and strands that may still be present in the brickwork.

Recognising wet rot

Wet rot—*Coniophora puteana*—affects timber in saturated conditions, for example the bottoms of posts in soil or timbers in wet cellars.

Fruiting bodies, or evidence of spores, are seldom seen inside a building, but if rot is not confined it will spread to similar wet timber near by.

The timber affected looks charred with splits along the grain or with dark-coloured vein-like strands. Timbers are spongy when they are wet. Painted timber will show splits and flaking of the paint in early attacks of wet rot.

Treatment
Remedy the source of dampness, and if necessary improve ventilation. Check minor outbreaks by drying out the area and soaking with dry rot fluid.

Cut out affected timber and fit wood which has been treated with preservative.

Rot and woodworm

How wood-boring insects attack timber

There are 12,000 species of woodworm—the grubs or larvae of wood-boring insects—but only four cause serious damage to timber in Britain: the common furniture beetle, the powder-post beetle, the death-watch beetle and the house longhorn beetle.

An adult beetle may fly into a house or it may already be in second-hand furniture or timber. The beetle lays its eggs—possibly as many as 60—in cracks and crevices, especially in the end grain or in rough-surfaced timber. The eggs hatch into grubs which bore down into the wood, forming small tunnels which weaken the timber. The grubs eat into the wood around them

and over a period of up to six years, depending on the species, eventually become adult beetles which bite their way out. Their exit holes are the evidence that the wood is infested.

Many houses contain timber with these exit holes, but this does not necessarily mean that the woodworm is active. But if bore dust—the timber eaten by the larvae and pushed out by the adult—is seen near the holes, the wood is probably under active attack.

Make sure that any new wood introduced into the house is pre-treated against rot. Spray or paint it with one of the wood preservatives that are to be found in most stores and hardware

shops—paying particular attention to the ends. If there is any doubt that the existing structural wood in a house may not have been treated against woodworm, spray it (see p. 187) immediately.

Inspect all the house timbers each summer. Check the less-accessible areas—for example, the loft and underneath the floorboards—at least once every two years.

If woodworm is found in the attic of a terraced house, notify the neighbours: the roof timbers may be continuous and the infestation could have moved from one house to another.

Examine and, if necessary, treat any second-hand furniture before taking

it into any part of the house. If evidence of woodworm is found on any piece of furniture or in any part of the woodwork of a house, check the rest of the house thoroughly before trying to treat the area that is known to be affected.

If the damage is found to be extensive, it is always advisable to engage a specialist firm. Many firms offer free inspection and estimates, and in some cases the treatment is guaranteed for 30 years.

Furniture and small areas of woodwork can be treated without expert help. Use a proprietary woodworm killer, such as those of Rentokil and Cuprinol. The fluid can be applied to the wood with a brush, an aerosol or a sprayer.

Preparation

First remove all loose covers and any upholstery which can be detached without damaging the furniture. Use a stiff brush to clean all dust and cobwebs from the surface and apply the fluid generously.

It is possible to use a soft paintbrush, but the deeper the penetration the more effective the treatment. For that reason it is usually advisable to obtain a special aerosol with a nozzle to inject the fluid into every known exit hole. This ensures that the woodworm is exterminated.

Leave the fluid to soak in for 24 hours, then wipe off any excess with a dry clean cloth.

If furniture has to be stood on a carpet within a month of treatment, it is essential to lay protective rags under the legs. The fluids used to kill the woodworm can rot and corrode the carpet.

Valuable furniture

When valuable furniture is affected, engage a specialist firm, which can treat it without removing the upholstery. This is usually done by fumigating the furniture in a sealed chamber with a gas which does not damage the upholstery.

Insect	Timber attacked	Beetle emerges	Holes and dust type	Appearance	Other features
Common furniture beetle *Anobium punctatum*	Seasoned softwoods and hardwoods, but usually only the sapwood: plywood	May–August	Circular, about $\frac{1}{16}$ in. (2 mm) diameter The bore dust feels gritty	Brown-black. Length $\frac{1}{10}-\frac{1}{5}$ in. (2·5–5 mm) The front of the body has a hard hood which extends over the head Larvae are curved, fleshy and white	The beetle may be seen crawling on walls or window ledges on sunny days
Powder-post beetle *Lyctus brunneus*	Seasoned and partly seasoned hardwoods	May–September	Circular holes, about $\frac{1}{16}$ in. (2 mm) diameter The dust feels like flour	Reddish-brown or black Length about $\frac{1}{6}$ in. (4 mm) Body is in two distinct parts; the antennae end in enlarged joints Larvae are white with two brown spots on the end segment	The beetle flies at dusk. More usually found on timber-storage premises than in houses
Death-watch beetle *Xestobium rufovillosum*	Old hardwoods softened by damp, particularly oak	In the spring of the year after larvae attack	Circular—about $\frac{1}{8}$ in. (3 mm) diameter The dust has bun-shaped pellets	Mottled brown shell with the front segment flattened Length $\frac{1}{4}$ in. (8 mm) Larvae are curved, fleshy and white	The larvae may be seen on the surface before boring in
House longhorn beetle *Hylotrupes bajulus*	Well-seasoned softwoods, but usually only the sapwood	July–September	Oval—about $\frac{1}{4} \times \frac{1}{8}$ in. (6×3 mm) The dust is a mixture of wood fragments and small cylindrical particles	Greyish-black with two shiny spots on the head and small white marks on both wing covers. Length $\frac{2}{5}-\frac{4}{5}$ in. (10–20 mm) Larvae are grey-white and fleshy with distinct segments	Rare except in NW Surrey. Common on the Continent

Spraying roof timbers

When the woodwork damaged by rot or woodworm affects the structural strength of the house—for example, in the loft or under the floorboards—painting or aerosol application (see p. 186) is not enough: more extensive measures are required.

Protection

The fluids available are flammable, pungent and solvent, and can destroy some materials such as polystyrene and rubber. Cover any cables that are exposed with polythene sheeting, or paint them with a wood sealer before spraying. Remove any insulation material from joists, and do not replace it before the treated timbers are dry.

Take care never to bring the insecticide into contact with a water tank insulated with polystyrene. Protect it with polythene sheeting.

Wear old clothes, leather gloves, a light fume mask—which can be bought from a do-it-yourself shop—and a head covering. Keep the fluid away from the face and eyes and smear barrier cream on any exposed skin.

When working in the roof space lay planks over the joists. Do not try to balance on the joists and never step in the space between them.

Fluid and equipment

Buy 1 gal. (4.5 l) of woodworm killer for every 200 sq. ft (18.5 sq. m) to be sprayed.

Spraying equipment can be bought or hired from builders' merchants. A simple spray-lance, at least 24 in. (610 mm) long, with a hand-pump attachment, is adequate for small areas.

Hand pumping can become tiring and less easy to control on large areas, however. Obtain a pressure-operated unit which can be carried on the back or rested on a plank.

Materials: woodworm-killing fluid; polythene sheeting; planks.
Tools: spraying equipment; stiff brush; sharp knife; vacuum cleaner or dustpan and brush.

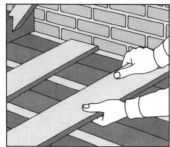
1 Lay planks across joists to give access to the areas needing treatment. Do not work balancing on the joists

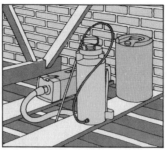
2 Stand all the equipment which is to be used on the planks. Do not stand it on or between the joists

3 Use a stiff brush to remove all dust and cobwebs so that the fluid can penetrate fully

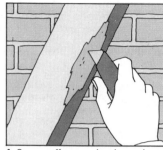
4 Scrape off any seriously weakened areas of timber to a maximum depth of $\frac{1}{2}$ in. (13 mm)

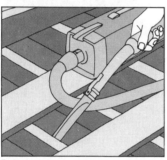
5 Remove any debris from between the joists with a vacuum cleaner or stiff brush and dustpan

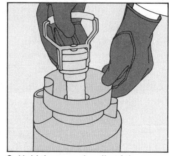
6 Hold the pump handle of the spraying unit and unscrew the top. Withdraw pump unit from cylinder

7 Pour the fluid into the cylinder. Do not overfill, to prevent spilling when the pump is replaced

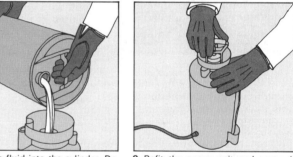
8 Refit the pump unit and screw it fully home. Check that the hose connection is secure

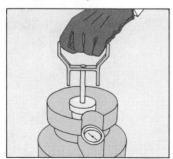
9 Work the pump handle up and down to build up pressure to the level recommended by the manufacturers

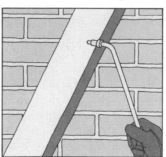
10 Hold nozzle close to the timber and spray the entire width. Make sure that no part is missed

11 Take care to direct the spray at the timber only. If fluid soaks through the ceiling, it may cause staining

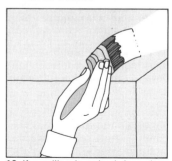
12 If a ceiling is stained, leave it to dry for two weeks. Coat with aluminium primer and repaint it

Staircases

How a staircase is constructed

The way in which a staircase is designed and built determines the ease or difficulty with which repairs can later be made. In its simplest form, a staircase consists of two pieces of wood (the strings) sloping from one floor to another, with steps fixed between them. But there are two basic types of construction, distinguished by the method of fixing the steps.

In one style, the top edges of the strings are cut out, and the steps (horizontal treads and vertical risers) are fitted on to them. This is known as open-string design.

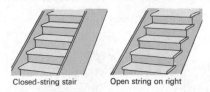

Closed-string stair   Open string on right

In the other, the edges of the strings are straight, but grooves are cut into their inside faces to accommodate the steps. This is closed-string construction.

Many staircases are made by a combination of both methods. The steps are fixed to a closed string on one side—for example, against a wall—and on the other side they rest on the edges of an open string.

When at least one side of the staircase has an open string, repairs to the steps are easily made from above. But if both sides are closed—perhaps because the staircase is between two walls—repairs must be done from beneath the stairs. This may involve stripping off a lath and plaster or plasterboard covering.

There is, moreover, a common complication. Many staircases have additional supports—called carriages—running beneath the steps. This does not affect repairs to the open-string design, but it makes the replacement of steps in a closed staircase a major structural job which should be left to a builder.

Moulding When the tread and riser are not jointed, a moulding may cover any gap caused by shrinking wood

Handrail A wooden (sometimes plastic-covered metal) rail secured to the wall by brackets

Closed string Treads and risers are glued and wedged into grooves in the sloping wooden side of the staircase

Riser The upright front of a step

Tread The horizontal part of the step

Nosing The protruding front edge of the tread is usually rounded

Newel grooves Because no string is available, the first steps are fixed in grooves in the newels

Balustrade This consists of the baluster rails, handrail and the part of the steps supporting them

Baluster rail The vertical rail supporting a handrail

Open string Treads and risers are secured to edges cut in the top of the sloping wooden side

Newel The main post on a balustrade also supports the bottom steps

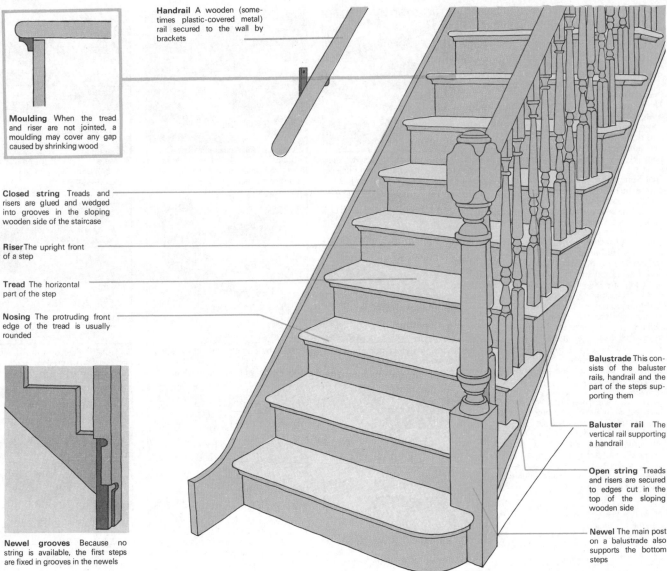

Staircases Treads and risers

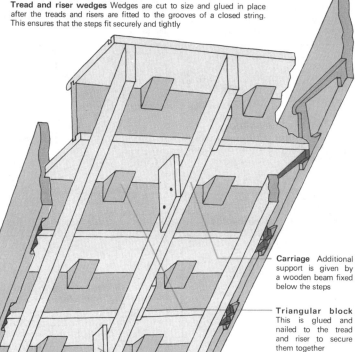

Tread and riser wedges Wedges are cut to size and glued in place after the treads and risers are fitted to the grooves of a closed string. This ensures that the steps fit securely and tightly

Carriage Additional support is given by a wooden beam fixed below the steps

Triangular block This is glued and nailed to the tread and riser to secure them together

Bracket The structure is strengthened by nailing a piece of hardwood to the tread and the carriage

Securing loose treads and risers

As a wall settles, it may pull the string (side) of a staircase away from the steps. The simplest repair is to drive wedges between the wall and the string of the staircase. But this is possible only when the gap between the string and the steps is no more than $\frac{3}{4}$ in. (20 mm) and where the wall is substantial. If the gap is wider or the wall seems weak, replace the steps (see p. 190).

On brick and breezeblock walls, wedges can usually be inserted anywhere along the gap. On a timber-framed wall with plaster covering, fit wedges only against timber uprights.

Materials: softwood; screws; oval nails. Tools: cold chisel; hammer; tenon saw; wheelbrace and bit; screwdriver.

FINDING TIMBER UPRIGHTS

Hammer Tap the wall. The approximate centre of the upright is where the highest note is heard

Drill Use a drill to make holes 3 in. (75 mm) apart with a $\frac{1}{4}$ in. (6 mm) bit to locate uprights

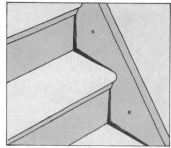

1 Remove nails and screws exposed by the movement of the string away from the treads and risers

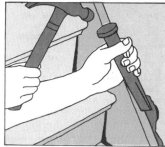

2 Chisel off the plaster near the gap between the string and the steps. On a timber wall, find the uprights

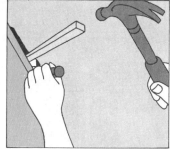

3 Ease the string off the wall, and drive in a 12 in. wedge, about $1\frac{1}{2}$ in. (40 mm) wide and 1 in. (25 mm) thick

4 Fit as many wedges as necessary to force the string against the steps. Cut the wedges flush with the string

5 Drill and countersink a hole through the string and partly into the wedge. If the wedge is narrow, use an oval nail

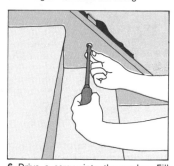

6 Drive a screw into the wedge. Fill the countersunk head in the string and repair the plaster (see p. 131)

Staircases Treads and risers

Replacing a tread from above

When a gap between a string and the steps of a staircase is more than ¾ in. (20 mm), the string is likely to split if it is forced back with wedges. Fit wider steps instead.

If the staircase has closed strings (see p. 188) on both sides, the treads and risers can be replaced only from below (see p. 192). With at least one open string, do the work from above. Slip a hacksaw blade between a tread and riser to find out how they meet.

Materials: softwood to cut new treads; nails; PVA adhesive.
Tools: hammer; panel saw; hacksaw or padsaw; mallet; plane; nail punch; marking gauge; combination square; large and small wood chisels; power saw or plough plane.

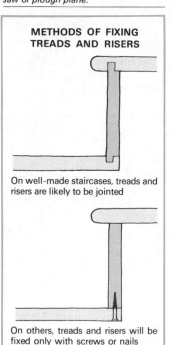

METHODS OF FIXING TREADS AND RISERS

On well-made staircases, treads and risers are likely to be jointed

On others, treads and risers will be fixed only with screws or nails

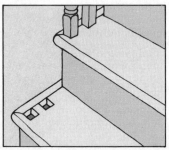

1 Remove the baluster (see p. 195) from the loose treads. Prise out any mouldings under the tread nosings

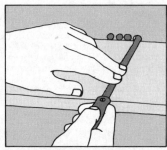

2 If treads and risers are jointed, drill a few small holes in the risers, insert a padsaw, and saw along the joint

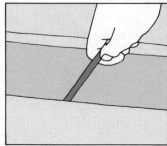

3 If the treads and risers are not jointed, use a hacksaw blade to cut the screws or nails fixing them together

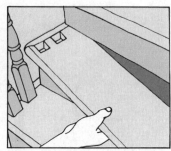

4 Remove each tread and riser. If they stick in the groove in the inner string, tap the string gently with a hammer

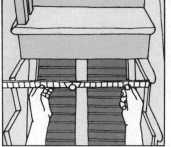

5 Measure for new treads and risers. Include depth of groove for both. For treads, add the width of side mouldings

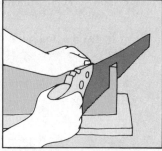

6 Cut a length of softwood for the riser. Mark its outside upright edge for a mitre (corner joint) and cut it off

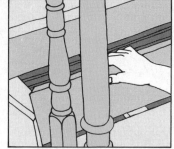

7 Position the riser with the mitre against the outer string. Cut a wedge, if necessary, to raise the riser flush

8 Glue in the wedge first, then the riser. Drive nails at an angle through the riser into the vertical string groove

9 Glue and nail the mitre joint on the outer corner. Wipe off any surplus glue and punch the nails below the surface

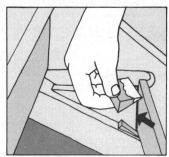

10 If a tighter fit is needed, drive a glued wedge between the riser and the inner string's vertical groove

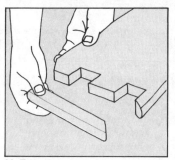

11 Take the old tread and carefully remove any side moulding. Clean the moulding for fixing to the new tread

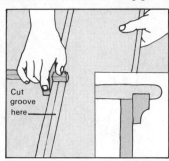

12 Cut the new tread to length. If the original had a moulding underneath, mark its groove *(continued)*

Cut groove here

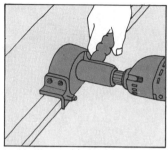

13 Measure the depth of the original groove; saw or plough-plane to that depth along and between the marks

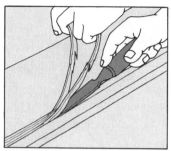

14 Chisel out the sawn wood. Take care not to deepen, or cut into, the sides of the moulding groove

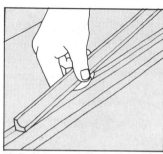

15 Test the moulding in its groove. When it fits correctly, clean the fixing surfaces ready for gluing later

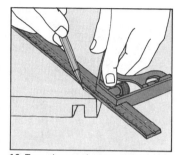

16 Turn the tread over; on the top, mark a 45 degree mitre at the outside corner where the side moulding will fit

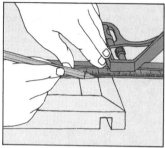

17 Measure the positions of the balusters on the old tread and mark them on the inside of the new mitre line

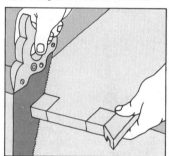

18 Cut out the mitre joint to accommodate the side moulding and saw along the lines of the baluster markings

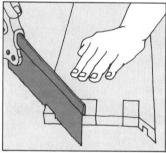

19 At the inner corner of the outside edge, cut off a piece to make a snug fit with the angled edge of the string

20 Use a wood chisel to remove the surplus between the lines which were cut for the baluster recesses

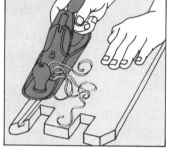

21 Turn the tread over and plane the front edge to match the shape of the existing tread nosings

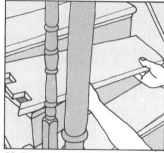

22 Try the tread in position. Plane angled corner of tread, if necessary, to get a flat, tight fit

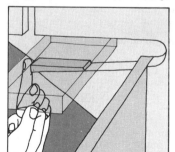

23 Fit an offcut from the tread into the inner string groove. Fit a filler piece underneath. Remove the offcut

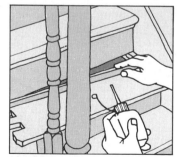

24 Glue the filler in place. While it dries, turn the tread over and glue the moulding in its groove

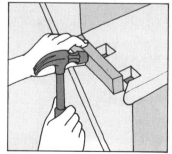

25 Glue the inner edge of the tread and fit it. Use a block of wood between hammer and tread to avoid damage

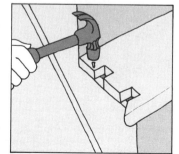

26 Nail the tread to the top of the outer string, not too near the edges to avoid splitting. Do not use glue

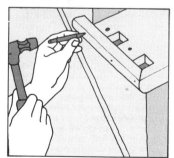

27 Nail on the old side moulding. Punch all the nailheads below the surface. Fill and paint

Staircases Treads and risers

Replacing treads and risers from below

When a staircase has closed strings (see p. 188) on both sides, damaged treads and risers have to be removed from underneath. But this is impossible without major structural work if the steps are supported by sloping beams, called carriages (see p. 189). It is important, therefore, to check whether there are any carriages beneath the length of the staircase.

Materials: softwood for the treads and risers; wood block for hammering; 1 in. (25 mm) softwood for wedges; PVA adhesive; 1½ in. (40 mm) screws; paint; 2 in. (50 mm) oval nails.
Tools: old wood chisel; mallet; panel saw; padsaw; power saw or plough-plane; wheelbrace and bit; ¼ in. (6 mm) drill; screwdriver; hammer.

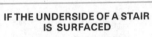

IF THE UNDERSIDE OF A STAIR IS SURFACED

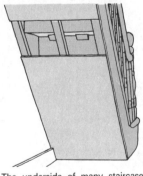

The underside of many staircases is surfaced with plaster or hardboard; in old houses the surfacing is by lath and plaster. To avoid having to remove the entire covering unnecessarily, check for possible carriages by taking off a strip only about 6 in. (150 mm) deep—but across the full width of the staircase. Use a chisel to remove plaster. If hardboard is fitted, drill a few small holes and cut out a panel.

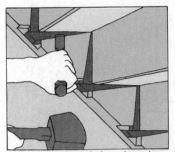
1 If the treads and risers have been wedged into the string, remove the wedges carefully with a chisel

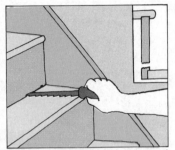
2 When the riser is jointed to the tread (see p. 190), drill a hole through the front and cut with a padsaw

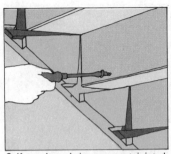
3 If treads and risers are not jointed, remove screws or nails holding them together from underneath stairs

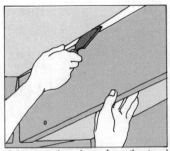
4 Lever a riser down from the tread with an old chisel. Work it down from side to side alternately

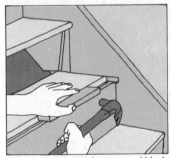
5 At the front, use a hammer and block of wood to tap back the tread. Pull it free from underneath the stairs

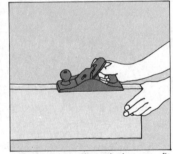
6 Cut new treads and risers to fit between the grooves. Plane the front tread edges to match the old ones

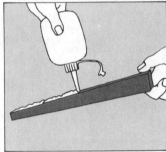
7 Cut and glue two wedges to fit in the grooves behind the riser. Make them slightly wider than the grooves

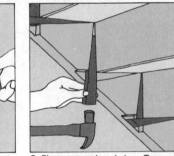
8 Fit new tread and riser. Temporarily nail riser at bottom. Drive vertical wedges tightly up against the riser

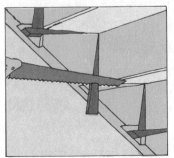
9 Remove nails and saw off at an angle the part of the wedge projecting below the new riser

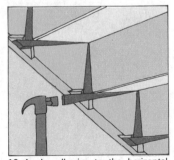
10 Apply adhesive to the horizontal wedges; drive them tightly into the grooves below the tread

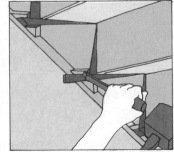
11 Chisel or saw off the part of the wedges still left projecting below the bottom edge of the string

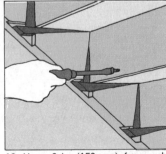
12 About 6 in. (150 mm) from each end, drill and fix 1½ in. (40 mm) screws through riser above tread centre

Curing creaks with tie-rods

When the wood of the treads has not been sufficiently seasoned before it is fitted, it may shrink and cause the stairs to creak.

Stairs which have one side against a wall must be repaired with blocks or brackets. But if the staircase is open on both sides, the simplest way to repair it is to fit a metal rod under every fourth or fifth tread up the length of the staircase. When they are securely fixed, tie-rods pull in both strings and compensate for the slight shrinkage of the tread wood.

Measure the width of the staircase from the outside of both strings. Order the required number of mild steel rods—about ½ in. (13 mm) diameter, and 1 in. (25 mm) longer than the staircase width—from an engineering workshop or garage.

Coat the rods, washers and nuts with polyurethane varnish for protection against rust.

Materials: rods with 2 in. (50 mm) thread at each end; washers; nuts; polyurethane varnish.
Tools: brace and ½ in. (13 mm) bit; open spanner; brush.

Mild steel rod with nuts and washers

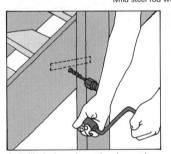

1 Drill holes through the strings below the centre of every fourth or fifth tread up the staircase

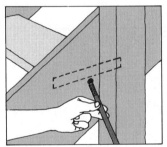

2 Push the rods through the holes and make sure that the same amount of thread is exposed at each side

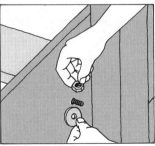

3 Fix a washer and nut to each thread and screw them up evenly by hand until they just touch the strings

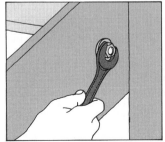

4 Tighten the nuts alternately with a spanner until the washers start to bite into the wood of the strings

Curing creaks with blocks and brackets

When one side of the staircase is closed (see p. 188), creaking treads can be repaired from underneath. This is a repair that is possible even if the stairs are supported by carriages underneath (see p. 189).

If the stair is open—or surfaced with hardboard which can easily be removed—fix triangular blocks of wood behind the tread and riser joints. Alternatively, use metal brackets.

To avoid removing a plastered surface, treads and risers which are not jointed may be silenced by squeezing PVA adhesive between them and nailing them from the top.

Materials: softwood 1¾ × 1¾ in. (45 × 45 mm), allowing about 6 in. (150 mm) for each tread; ¾ in. (20 mm) panel-pins; 2 in. (50 mm) oval nails; PVA adhesive; metal brackets and screws to fit if necessary.
Tools: hammer; panel or hand saw; chisel or screwdriver; nail punch; vice.

NAILING AND GLUING FROM THE TOP

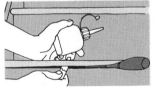

1 Part the tread and riser with a chisel. Apply PVA adhesive with a sliver of wood. Remove chisel

2 Angle two nails to go through the tread and the riser below. Punch below surface and fill

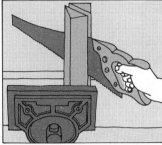

1 Hold a 1¾ × 1¾ in. (45 × 45 mm) piece of softwood in a vice and saw diagonally through its length

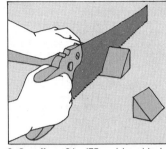

2 Cut off two 3 in. (75 mm) long blocks for each tread and riser joint underneath the staircase

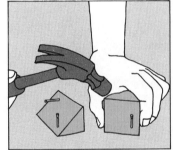
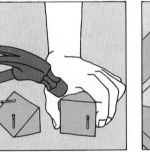

3 Check that each block fits the joint. Partly hammer in two pins to fix it to the tread and riser

5 Hammer in the panel-pins, making sure that one goes into a tread and one into a riser. Repeat at the other side

4 Put some PVA adhesive on the block and press it in position. Rub it firmly from side to side to expel the surplus

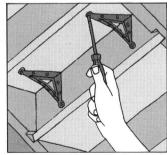

Metal brackets Obtain metal brackets a little shorter than the steps. Fix them 6 in. (150 mm) from each side

Staircases Treads

Repairing worn tread edges

When the edge, or nosing, of a stair tread becomes worn, it should be replaced as soon as possible. Damaged front edges are dangerous.

Although the entire tread should be replaced if possible (see p. 192), a cheaper and simpler alternative is to replace only the damaged part.

Make sure that the part of the tread exposed is sound before adding a new piece. If the damage to the nosing extends beyond the centre line of the riser, replace the entire tread.

Materials: $1\frac{1}{2} \times 1$ in. (38×25 mm) softwood slightly longer than the width of the treads; PVA adhesive; glass-paper; screws 1 in. (25 mm) longer than the depth of the replacement edge.

Tools: $1–1\frac{1}{2}$ in. (25–38 mm) wood chisel; wheelbrace or power tool and bit; combination square; hammer; nail punch; plane; pencil.

REMOVING A NOSING

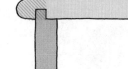

If a tread is butted to the riser, the nosing can be chiselled back to the centre of the riser

When tread and riser are jointed, chisel the nosing and the part of the riser jointed into the tread

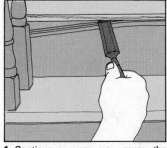

1 Continuous wear may cause the tread nosing to split along the edge. Remove any moulding underneath

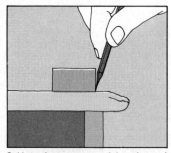

2 Use a batten as a straight-edge and draw a line $1\frac{1}{2}$ in. (38 mm) back from the line of the original front edge

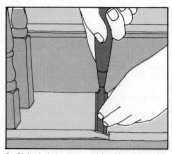

3 Chisel the worn nosing back to the line about the centre of the riser. Smooth the exposed edge

4 Cut the new nosing to the correct width. If the tread has a side moulding, mark and cut a mitre at one end

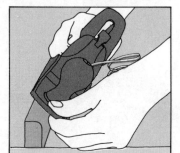

5 Plane off the front edges of the new piece to match the shape and angle of other treads on the staircase

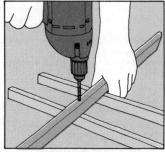

6 Drill and countersink holes in the nosing face, one centrally, the others 3 in. (75 mm) from each end

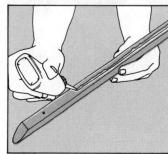

7 Apply PVA adhesive to the back of the new nosing, and insert three fixing screws in the drilled holes

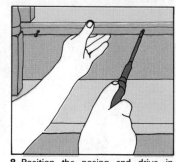

8 Position the nosing and drive in the screws, tightening each a little at a time and in turn to avoid strain

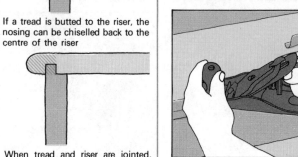

9 Wipe off any surplus glue and, if necessary, plane the top surface of the nosing flush with the tread

10 Nail through the mitred joint at the side to fix the nosing edge to the original piece of side moulding

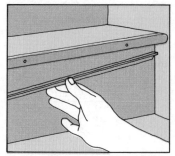

11 If a moulding was removed below the old tread, clean it and glue it on; or make and fix a new one

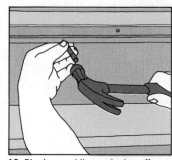

12 Pin the moulding and wipe off surplus glue. Punch in the heads and fill all screw and nail holes

Staircases Balusters

Securing loose balusters

If a flight of stairs sags, the bottom of the baluster rails may become loose. Longer replacement rails can be made, but it is usually less expensive to insert a strip of softwood between the top of the rails and the handrail or string above them. The thickness of the wood is slightly greater than the amount the stairs have sagged. Each rail is then removed and cut to fit.

Balusters are usually fixed by a nail at the top and are glued into a recess at the bottom

Materials: strip of softwood as required; small block of hardwood for hammering; nails.
Tools: claw hammer; mallet; spirit level; plane; nail punch; tenon saw; wood chisel; old chisel or screwdriver; cold chisel.

TWO-FLIGHT STAIRCASES

Staircase landings sometimes sag at one end only, causing unequal gaps beneath the loosened rails. The softwood insert should be slightly thicker than the biggest gap

1 Use a block of wood and a hammer to tap each rail from the handrail or string above. Remove the balusters

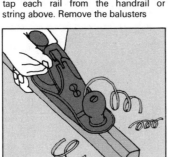

5 Plane along the softwood corners which will face down when the strip is fitted to the handrail or string

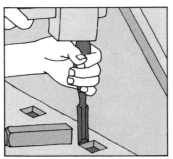

9 Use a chisel and mallet to clean out the recesses in the landing or steps where the rails are to be fitted

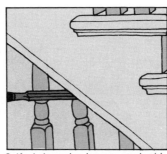

2 If a baluster has become stuck with paint, use an old chisel to prise it free. Take care not to damage the baluster

6 Nail the strip to the underside of the handrail or string and punch all the nailheads below the surface

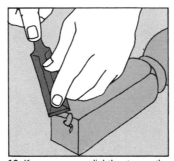

10 If necessary, slightly taper the bottom of the baluster rail so that it can fit into its recess

3 When all the loose rails are removed, clean along the fixing surface with a cold chisel or screwdriver

7 Hold the rail in its bottom recess, using a spirit level to get it vertical. Mark its outline on the insert strip

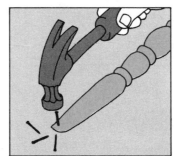

11 Hammer a nail at an angle into the top of the rail where it is to fit against the strip of softwood

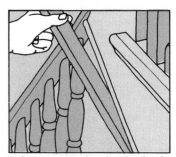

4 Cut an appropriate length of softwood slightly thicker than the biggest gap measured at the bottom of the rails

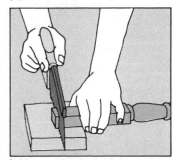

8 Measure the depth of the mark on the insert strip, and cut that amount from the bottom of the rail

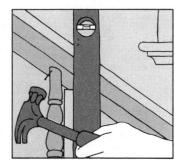

12 Check for vertical and hammer the nail in the top of the rail. Punch the head in and fill

Wall finishes Interior

Fitting ceramic tiles

If a wall tile becomes loose, remove it, clean the area behind it thoroughly and stick it back in place with a suitable adhesive (see p. 694).

If a tile breaks or cracks, cut it out and fit a new one. If several tiles are being replaced, use pieces of cardboard between them to act as spacers. Remove the cardboard when the adhesive is dry—about six hours later—and fill the joints with grouting cement.

Take part of a damaged tile for matching when buying replacements from a builders' merchant or do-it-yourself shop.

If a number of tiles on a wall are badly crazed, but the surface is otherwise sound, the wall can be tiled with one of the thinner types of do-it-yourself tiles without removing existing tiles. These tiles are $4\frac{1}{4}$ in. (106 mm) square and $\frac{5}{32}$ in. (4 mm) thick, and made with spacer lugs.

Before covering existing tiles, refix any which are loose and wash the surface of the wall with detergent and warm water. Rinse and dry the wall with an old towel.

Do-it-yourself ceramic tiles are available in various colours with plain or patterned surfaces.

If the grout between tiles becomes discoloured or cracked, scrape it out and fill with a fresh mixture.

Clean ceramic tiles with water and detergent. Use a nail brush and a little scouring powder to clean the joints—anything more abrasive may score the glazed surface on the tiles.

Materials: tiles; grouting material; thin lath; adhesive.
Tools: straight-edge; hammer; pincers; tile cutter; sponge; notched applicator; grouting stick; trowel.

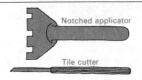
Notched applicator
Tile cutter

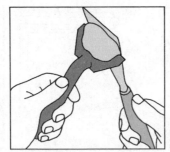
1 Make sure that the wall is clean and smooth. Put adhesive on an applicator with a small trowel

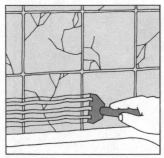
2 Apply the adhesive evenly. Work on about a square yard at a time to ensure that adhesive does not set

3 Press tiles into position on the adhesive. Check with straight-edge to ensure that they are even

Cutting tiles

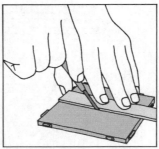
1 Lay a straight-edge in position and score a line on the glazed surface with a tile cutter

2 Lay the scored line over a thin lath or two matchsticks. Press down gently to break tile

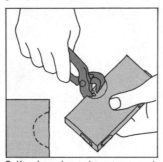
3 If a shape has to be cut out, mark and score the tile and nibble out the area with the pincers

Filling joints

1 Mix grouting cement in bowl to consistency of thick cream. With a clean rag, rub grouting over tiles

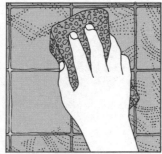
2 Press grouting well into joints. Use a damp sponge to wipe off excess grouting from face of tiles

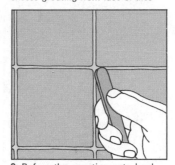
3 Before the grouting sets hard—after about five minutes—smooth the joints with a rounded stick

(see p. 694).

REMOVING A TILE

If a tile is broken, remove it carefully to avoid damaging the adjacent sound tiles.

Dig out as much of the old adhesive as possible to give a good key to fix the replacement tile.

Materials: tiles to match existing ones; adhesive cement (see p. 694); grouting cement.
Tools: pointed scraper; hammer; small chisel.

1 Dig out the grouting cement from all sides of the damaged tile with a sharp-pointed scraper

2 Chip away the damaged tiles with a hammer and chisel. Work from the centre to the corners

Wall finishes Exterior

Patching damaged rendering

If patches of rendering become loose and fall away from the brickwork of an outside wall, repair the rendering as soon as possible to ensure that the building remains weatherproof.

Add a little lime to the mortar mix to improve its workability and reduce the amount of shrinkage and crazing when it dries. In some cases a second layer may be necessary.

Materials: cement; sharp sand and lime (see p. 693); PVA bonding agent if necessary (see p. 693).
Tools: hammer and cold chisel; wooden hawk (see p. 120); steel float; wooden float; paintbrush; batten.

1 Chisel off any loose rendering round the damaged area. Rake out joints between the bricks

2 If bricks are smooth, brush on a bonding agent. If they are rough, brush on water

3 Place new mortar on a hawk held against the wall. Push mortar on to the bare area with a steel float

4 Cover with a layer ½ in. (13 mm) thick or until mortar is just thicker than adjacent old rendering

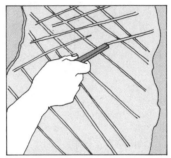

5 If old rendering was more than ½ in. thick, score the first coat deeply. Leave to dry for at least 24 hours

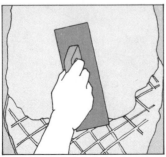

6 Mix fresh mortar and spread it on top of first coat until it is slightly higher than the surrounding area

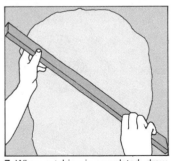

7 When patching is completed, draw a batten across the wet mortar in a sawing motion to scrape off surplus

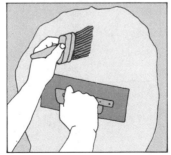

8 Leave for an hour to dry out, then dampen with a brush and water. Smooth with a steel float

MENDING CRACKS

Repair fine cracks in rendering as soon as they appear, to prevent more extensive damage. Do not try only to fill cracks: they must be opened out so that new mortar can be pressed under the edges of the old rendering.

1 Chisel along cracks and cut underneath edges with scraper. Brush out loose material

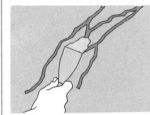

2 Brush undiluted bonding preparation (see p. 693) into cracks. Work in new mortar with scraper

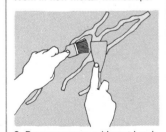

3 Remove excess with wet brush, and leave to dry. Dampen surface and smooth with scraper

PEBBLE DASH

To patch an area of pebble-dash finish, remove all the existing damaged mortar and pebbles. Rake out the brickwork joints and spread on fresh mortar. Throw pebbles on to the mortar before it has set.

1 Prepare brickwork and apply mortar. Cover area quickly and apply second layer if necessary

2 Drag a batten over mortar and dab edges with damp brush until they are flush with old surface

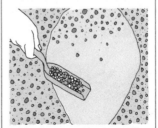

3 Throw matching pebbles against the fresh mortar. Press into surface with wooden float

Windows Sills

Repairing an external concrete sill

Concrete window-sills in old houses crack and flake because of prolonged weathering. But a sill will become damaged more quickly if there is movement in the walls surrounding it, or if it has been made of poor materials.

The easiest repair is to chip off the loose material and resurface the sill with sand-and-cement mortar. Use a small amount of lime (see p. 693) in the mix to reduce shrinkage.

Materials: 4:1 sharp sand and cement, hydrated lime (see p. 693); batten longer than window width.
Tools: hammer; cold chisel; bucket; trowel; steel float; wooden float.

1 Chip off the upper surface of the sill, to a depth of about 1½ in. (40 mm), with a hammer and cold chisel

2 Dampen the surface and lay 4:1 sand-and-cement mortar with lime. Push it into cracks and under the sill

3 Hold a batten against the front of the sill to give a straight edge. Fill to the batten with mortar

4 Remove batten. Slope mortar down to front with a steel float. Round the outer edge slightly

5 Flatten with circular movements of a wooden float. After two hours, polish with steel float and water

WOODEN SILLS

All wooden window-sills have a groove under their outer edge to keep rainwater away from the wall below. Clear the groove if it becomes blocked.

If gaps appear between the window frame and the outside wall, seal them before water can penetrate. Do not use ordinary putty: buy a mastic sealer from an ironmonger or builders' merchant. Although it hardens, it remains sufficiently elastic to allow for natural movement in the structure of the house.

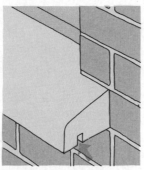

Grooves Scrape out dirt or paint to a depth of ¼ in. (6 mm)

Gaps Squeeze a mastic sealer into gap between frame and wall

Filling gaps inside windows

As the wood in a window dries, it shrinks and causes gaps to appear between the frame and the sill inside. This is common in new houses and in old houses when central heating has been later installed.

Do not try to fill the gaps with putty alone: it is likely to crack eventually. It is advisable to mix it with gold size or use whiting with gold size—obtainable from builders' merchants—to accelerate drying and reduce shrinking and cracking.

Materials: putty or whiting; gold size.
Tools: putty knife; paintbrush; dusting brush; cloth.

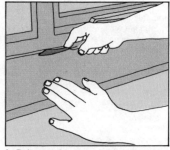

1 Rake out the gap with a putty knife and scrape off any ridges of hardened paint. Brush off loose particles

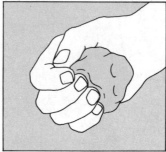

2 Wipe the area clean with a damp cloth. Knead a piece of putty in the hand and remove any lumps

3 Dip a putty knife into the gold size and work it into a small ball of putty on a tin lid

4 Brush gold size as deeply as possible into the gap. Work it well into the corners of the joint

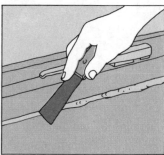

5 Press gold-size putty into the joint with a fingertip and trim off surplus with the knife

Windows Frames and sashes

Fitting a new casement-window sash and frame

A rotting casement window frame is dangerous and should be renewed immediately. Most casement frames are made in standard sizes and can be bought to fit. If the old one is a non-standard size, employ a builder to make a matching replacement.

Always renew sashes and metal fittings at the same time as the frame. Unscrew the sash hinges before removing the frame.

Treat any knots in the timber of the new frame and sashes with a knotting compound. Paint the frame with two coats of primer and leave it to dry for 24 hours before fitting.

Materials: new window frame and sash; glass to fit; glazing sprigs; putty; metal fittings if necessary; sand and cement; plaster; screws; cut nails. Tools: saw; hammer; cold chisel; wood chisel; crowbar; trowel; hawk; screwdriver; spirit level; punch.

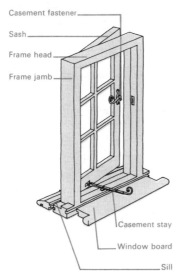

Casement fastener

Sash

Frame head

Frame jamb

Casement stay

Window board

Sill

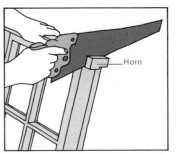

1 Cut off the horns from the new frame. Apply knotting compound and two coats of primer. Allow to dry

2 Cut away any external rendering from around the frame jambs and head with a hammer and cold chisel

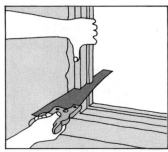

3 Saw through the old wood about 4–5 in. (100–125 mm) above the sill on both sides of the frame

4 Lever the sawn jambs away from the walls with a crowbar. Lever off the frame head

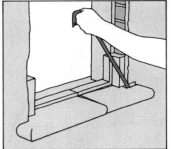

5 Cut through centre of window-sill and window board. Prise out sill, board and jamb studs with a crowbar

6 Place the new frame and sash assembly in position. Check that it is level and upright, using a spirit level

7 Secure the frame with wooden wedges at the top and bottom of each jamb. Make sure the sash opens easily

8 Open sash and hammer 4 in. (100 mm) cut nails into the wall at top and bottom of each jamb. Punch in heads

9 Make a mortar mix of 4 parts sand to 1 part cement. Push it well into the spaces round the frame

10 On the inside, make good the wall with plaster (see p. 120). Smooth it to match the wall surface

11 Outside, coat the tongued-and-grooved edges of the sill and frame with glue. Fit and secure with screws

12 Inside, fix the casement fastener to the sash. Outside, repair rendering (see p. 197) *(continued)*

Windows Frames and sashes

(continued)

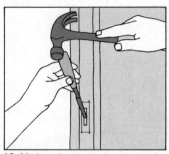

13 Mark and cut out the mortise for the fastener with a chisel. Cut out the centre part first

14 Cut out round the centre hole so that the fastener keep can be counter-sunk into the jamb

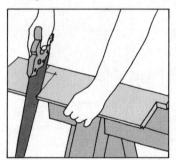

15 Mark and cut the window board to the correct length. Smooth off the overhang at both ends

16 Glue the tongued edge of the window board and the grooved edge of the sill. Fit the board in place

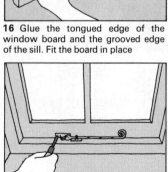

17 Support the window-board edge with timber until it is level. Hammer 3 in. (75 mm) cut nails through into wall

18 Fit the casement stay on the sash, and the locking peg on the frame base, with 1 in. (25 mm) screws

Fitting new sash cords

A box-framed window has an upper and a lower sash, each counter-balanced by a weight at each side of the window. The weights run up and down inside box sections as the windows are opened or closed.

If one of the cords supporting the weights breaks, it is advisable to renew the three others at the same time as the broken one.

To get access to the weights in the frame, remove the beading at the side of the frame and then take out the sashes. Open the pockets at the side of the box frame.

New sash cord is obtainable from most ironmongers: it is waxed, and is rot-proof and heat-resistant. Always buy clout nails to secure the cord to the sash framework.

Materials: sash cord; 1 in. (25 mm) galvanised clout nails; length of string; 1 in. (25 mm) panel-pins. Tools: claw hammer; pincers; wood chisel; knife.

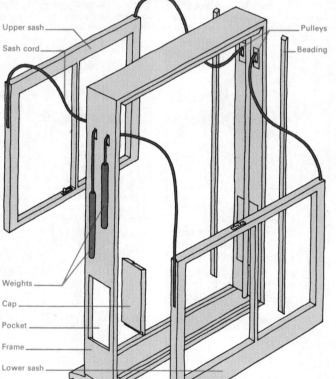

Upper sash

Sash cord

Pulleys

Beading

Weights

Cap

Pocket

Frame

Lower sash

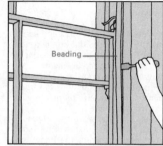

1 Use a wood chisel to prise off the interior beading fitted at both sides of the window

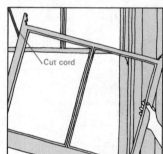

2 Lift out the bottom sash. Cut the sash cord if it is still intact, and lower the weight to the box bottom

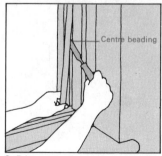

3 Prise out the centre beading between the sashes, cut cords and lift out top sash *(continued)*

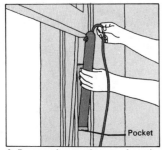

4 Remove the wooden caps from the pockets and lift the weights out of each box section in the frame

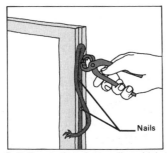

5 Pull out the clout nails which secure the cords to the sides of the sash. Discard the old cords

6 Tie string to a bent nail. Feed nail and string over pulley and lower nail out through pocket

7 Remove nail, tie end of the string to a new sash cord and pull it over pulley and out through the pocket

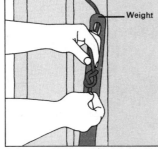

8 Remove string and tie the cord to a weight. Push weight in through the pocket and lower it in the box section

9 Tie a knot in the end of the cord. Hold the lower sash against the top and mark pulley position on side

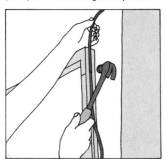

10 Lower sash. Pull cord tight and nail it in groove for 14 in. (355 mm) down from mark

11 Repeat other side. Lower upper sash cords over outside pulleys. Fix weight. Hold sash at bottom

12 Cut the cords to length and nail them to the sash at both sides. Refit the beading and the pockets

---

TEMPORARY REPAIR TO A LOOSE-JOINTED WINDOW

If the timber in a window shrinks, the joints may become loose and make it difficult to close. An inexpensive and simple solution is to wedge the window back into shape and secure the four corners with L-shaped galvanised brackets.

Materials: 3×3 in. (75×75 mm) brackets; 1 in. (25 mm) rust-proof sherardised screws; two softwood wedges.
Tools: hammer; saw; screwdriver; bradawl; plane.

1 Cut two wedges from a piece of softwood, 3 in. (75 mm) long and ½ in. (13 mm) wide at one end

2 Close window and drive the wedges in between window and frame until gaps in joints are closed

3 Put the bracket in position and mark the screw holes in the window with a bradawl. Fit the bracket

4 Do the same at the three other corners of the window. Check that all brackets are secure

5 Remove the wedges and open the window. If necessary, plane the opening edge of the window smooth

Windows Glass

Temporarily covering a broken window

When a window pane breaks, it may not be possible to repair it immediately. It can, however, be covered temporarily with a sheet of polythene. Nail the polythene, which must be large enough to cover the whole window frame, to softwood battens on all four sides.

The polythene provides protection against the weather and allows some light to enter.

Materials: sheet of polythene slightly larger than the window; softwood battens the size of the window frame; wire nails; drawing pins.
Tool: hammer.

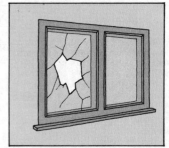

1 If the glass is broken, carefully remove all the pieces to ensure that they cannot cut the polythene

2 Fix the polythene in position with drawing pins along its top edge. Nail a batten along the top edge

3 Draw the polythene sheeting tightly and nail a batten over it on one side of the window frame

4 Draw the sheeting diagonally across the window and nail the other side batten to the frame

5 Stretch the polythene to the bottom to remove wrinkles, and nail the fourth batten

How to cut glass

For occasional household repairs, buy a good-quality single-wheel glass-cutter from a do-it-yourself shop. Always keep the wheel pivot clean and rust-free.

Before using a cutter, test it on a small piece of glass to make sure that it scores evenly. Ensure that the surface of the pane to be cut is free of grease. Start and finish cutting at the edges of each pane and use firm, but not heavy, pressure with the cutter.

When the glass has been scored, snap it over the edge of a wooden batten. Make sure the batten is level to avoid cracking the pane. Remove narrow strips of glass with pincers.

Materials: rag; glass; batten.
Tools: glass-cutter; pincers; pencil; straight-edge; crayon.

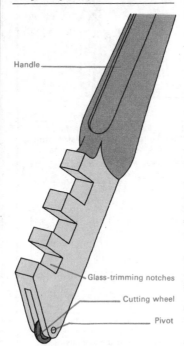

Handle

Glass-trimming notches

Cutting wheel

Pivot

1 Lay the glass on a flat surface and mark off the size to be cut with a crayon or china-marking pencil

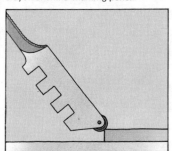

4 Apply an even pressure during the scoring, until the cutter runs off the other-side of the glass

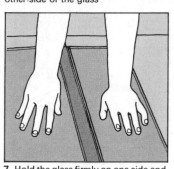

7 Hold the glass firmly on one side and exert gentle pressure on the other to snap off the surplus

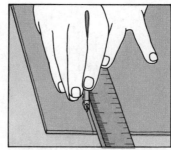

2 Hold the straight-edge firmly on the surface of the glass, close to the marked line. Score along it

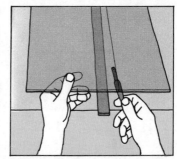

5 Lift the glass at one end and tap the underside gently with the cutter along the score mark

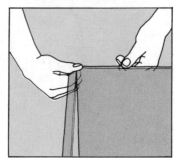

8 If only a small strip has to be trimmed, snap off the piece between thumb and forefinger

3 Start the scoring at the edge of the glass. Make sure that the cutting wheel turns freely and is undamaged

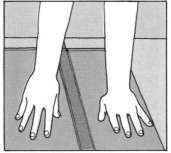

6 Lay the glass on straight-edge with the score mark on top and level with the edge of the batten

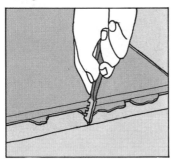

9 On very narrow edges, trim the glass along the scored line with pincers or the back of the cutter

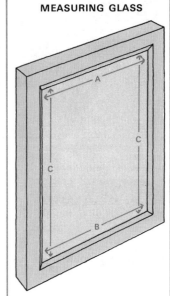

MEASURING GLASS

Panes of glass fit into rebates in the window sashes outside the house.

Measure the width of the rebate at the top (A) and bottom (B) of any frame to be filled.

If there is a difference in the two measurements, note the smaller of the two. Measure the height at both sides (C) and note the smaller figure.

Deduct $\frac{3}{16}$ in. (5 mm) from the width and height figures to allow for expansion and contraction of the glass when it is fitted in the frame. Have the glass cut to that final measurement.

When ordering glass, always state the width first, followed by the height.

If reeded glass is being used, make a sketch for the supplier to show the direction in which the reeds are to be fitted.

Cutting a circle in a pane of glass

To fit an extractor fan or louvred ventilator it is usually necessary to cut a circular hole in the window pane. This is done with a circular glass-cutter.

Find the centre-point of the pane and mark it with a crayon or china-marking pencil.

Measure the diameter of the hole required and add $\frac{1}{16}$ in. (2 mm). Set the arm of the cutter to half of that measurement.

Fix the suction pad of the cutter on the centre of the pane and run the cutting wheel to score the glass evenly round the whole circumference of the circle required. Do not try to remove the circle from the pane in one piece.

Score diagonally across it with a single-wheel cutter (see p. 202). Support one side of the pane with a hammer head and tap out the pieces of glass with the top or back of the glass-cutter.

The edges of the hole do not usually have to be cut clean, for the flanges of the unit being fixed overlap them.

Materials: glass.
Tools: circular glass-cutter; glass-cutter; hammer; crayon or china-marking pencil; pincers.

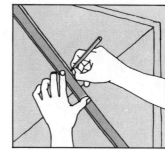

1 Mark diagonal lines on the existing pane with a crayon or china-marking pencil, to find the centre-point

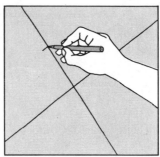

2 Mark the radius of the circle required, from the centre of the glass, on one diagonal line

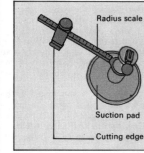

Radius scale
Suction pad
Cutting edge

3 Move the cutting edge along the scale of the cutter to the radius required for the circle

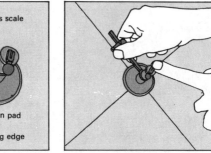

4 Fix the cutter suction pad at the centre of the pane. Make sure that the cutting wheel is on the mark

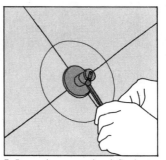

5 Press the cutter head firmly to score a circle. Tap the underside of the cut with a glass-cutter

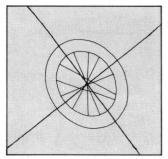

6 Move the cutter edge inwards about $\frac{3}{4}$ in. (20 mm) and score a second circle. Tap the underside

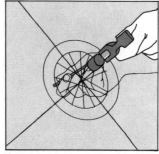

7 Score criss-cross lines in inner circle. Support scored glass with hammer and tap out segments

Windows Glass

(continued)

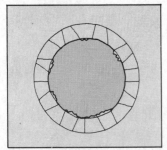

8 When all the glass in the inner circle is removed, score lines between the outer circle and the hole

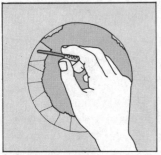

9 Gently tap out the remaining pieces of glass with the back or top of a single-wheel cutter

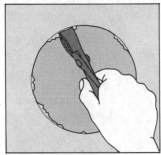

10 To clean the edges of the outer circle, break off any glass splinters with pincers

Replacing a pane of glass in a wooden window frame

On a wooden window frame the glass fits into a rebate in the sash. The rebate is usually on the outside and the glass is held firm by small sprigs and putty.

Always wear gloves to break out old glass. Start at the top of the window and work downwards, to reduce the risk of injury from falling pieces. Make sure that the rebate is completely clean; remove all traces of old putty, sprigs and glass.

Measure the glass size carefully and allow for expansion of the glass within the frame (see p. 202).

If the broken glass has a directional pattern, make sure the replacement glass is measured and cut to follow the same direction as the sound glass in the other windows.

Always use the correct type of glass: for windows up to 40 in. (1 m) square, use glass 3 mm thick; for small picture windows use 4 mm panes, and for very large windows buy glass 6 mm thick.

Always paint the rebate before fitting new glass. When laying on putty, make sure that its edge is just below the line of the sash rebate, so that when the putty is painted the paint line, which is taken on to the glass, is flush with the top of the rebate and cannot be seen from inside the window.

Square-ended filling knife

Putty knife

Materials: putty; glazier's sprigs; lead-based primer, oil undercoat or any matt oil paint; glass.
Tools: glass-cutter; hammer; wood chisel; pincers; rule; putty knife; square-ended filling knife; soft brush.

1 Score the broken pane with a glass-cutter about 1 in. (25 mm) inside the sash on all sides

2 With the window open, start at the top and tap out the broken pane. Remove the glass carefully

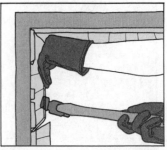

3 Score any pieces remaining at the edge. Tap and lever out these pieces, together with the old putty

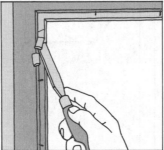

4 Close the window and remove the rest of the putty from the rebate of the window sash with a wood chisel

5 Pull out the sprigs with a pair of pincers, then clean the rebate of the sash carefully

6 Hold the new pane up to the frame rebate. Make sure that it fits freely with room for expansion

7 If the glass is slightly oversize, mark it in position in the frame and trim it to size (see p. 202)

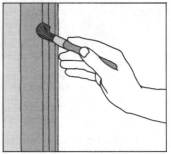

8 Brush the rebate clean and paint it with a lead-based primer. Allow to dry—about 4–5 hours

9 Mould putty in the hands until it is soft and pliable. Press it into the rebate angle *(continued)*

10 Place the glass in the sash rebate. Press its edges into the putty. Do not press the centre

11 Tap in sprigs with the side of a chisel. Slide the chisel along the glass to reduce the impact

12 Press more putty on to the edge of the glass. Shape it with a putty knife, level with the rebate inside

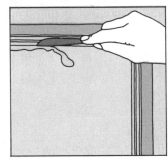

13 Mitre the putty at each corner of the sash with the blade of a square-ended filling knife

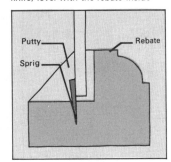

14 Trim any surplus putty from the surface of the glass with the edge of a putty knife

15 Make sure that putty is not above the rebate line, so that it cannot be seen from inside

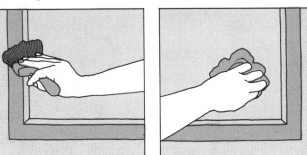

16 Seal all round the bevelled, trimmed putty with a damp brush. Use the brush gently

17 Clean the glass thoroughly with a soft dry cloth. If necessary, remove grease marks with detergent

18 Allow putty to harden for at least a week. Paint the putty. Take paint line a little above putty on to glass

Fitting glass in a metal window frame

In metal-framed windows, the glass is held in place by putty and wire clips. Though clip holes are provided all round the sash, it is not necessary to fit a clip into each one: only two or three are needed on each side of the frame. Use metal-casement putty, which is self-hardening—unlike the ordinary putty that is oil based and relies on absorption of the oil into the timber to dry. Make sure that all the old putty is removed and then immediately paint the metal sash with an aluminium-based paint.

Do not attempt to fit a new pane of glass to sliding metal windows. Engage an experienced glazier.

Materials: glass; metal-casement putty; aluminium paint; retaining clips.
Tools: putty knife; square-ended filling knife; glass-cutter; paintbrush.

Wire clip for metal window

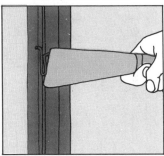

1 Remove the old putty from the sash and prise the old clips out of their holes in the sash

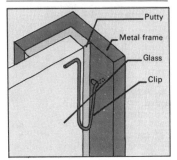

2 Fit the new pane. Press it against the putty bed and fit new glazing clips on each side

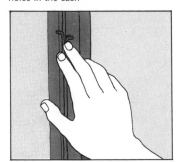

3 When the clips are fitted, push them fully home into the metal sash. If necessary, do this with the filling knife

4 Apply putty over the clips. Smooth the putty with a putty knife and mitre the corners

Windows Glass

Fitting new glass in leaded lights

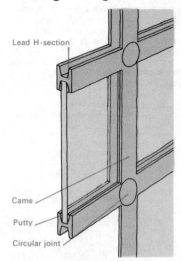

Lead H-section

Came

Putty

Circular joint

The individual panes of glass in a leaded light window are held by gold-size putty (see p. 198) in grooved strips of lead, called cames.

If cames are leaking, mark them during wet weather with a wax crayon. In dry weather, open the cames slightly, scrape out the old putty, fit new putty and press the cames back into place.

Always work on the outside of a window so that any disfigurement of the cames cannot be seen inside. If possible, leave the window in position while making a repair: leaded lights are easily distorted when removed from their frames.

If a window has bulged badly, however, remove it carefully. Lay it on a large flat board and gently press the cames flat.

Materials: gold-size putty cement; plumber's black; solder and flux; medium-grade glass-paper.

Tools: glass-cutter; ¼ in. (6 mm) wood chisel; brush; putty knife; hammer; soldering iron.

1 Chisel carefully through the soldered joints at both sides of the bottom of the damaged pane

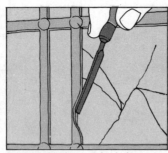

2 Use a chisel to turn back the cames down the sides and along the bottom of the pane

3 Tap out the glass from the inside of the window. Collect the pieces carefully and dispose of them

4 Scrape out any remaining cement with the edge of the chisel. Brush round all the empty cames

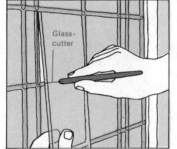

Glass-cutter

6 Push the strip of glass into the closed came at top. Score across at bottom came. Cut glass

7 Fill the cames with very soft gold-size putty cement. Press it well into the unopened came

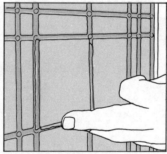

8 Slot the glass into the unopened came at the top and press it gently against the sides and bottom

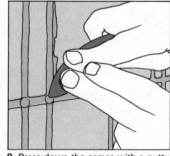

9 Press down the cames with a putty knife to ensure that they are all flat on the glass

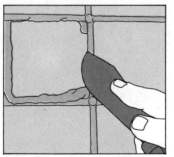

11 Carefully trim off surplus putty cement from both sides of the glass with a putty knife

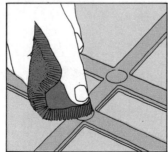

12 Burnish the broken joints with an abrasive pad or medium-grade glass-paper

13 Apply flux and place a little solder on each broken joint with a moderately hot iron (see p. 692)

14 To finish the joint neatly to match the others, rub the soldering iron round with a circular motion

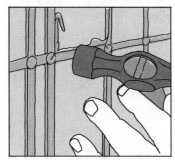

5 Measure across between open cames and cut glass slightly smaller than that width (see p. 202)

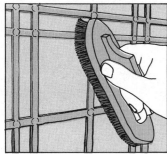

10 Gently tap the two broken joints back into position with a hammer. Take care not to damage any panes

Brush plumber's black, obtainable from builders' merchants, or any dark colouring into the putty cement

15 Brush plumber's black, obtainable from builders' merchants, or any dark colouring into the putty cement

Replacing an external glass block

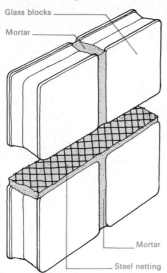

Glass blocks

Mortar

Mortar

Steel netting

When glass blocks are used in the external walls of a house they must be as weatherproof as the brickwork. Although glass blocks do not contribute to the structural strength of the wall, replace any damaged block as soon as possible to ensure that damp cannot enter the house.

When digging out the damaged block and mortar, direct the cold chisel away from the adjacent blocks to avoid cracking them.

Every third or fourth course of blocks is reinforced on one side of the opening with steel netting.

Set new blocks in a dry mix of 1:1:4 lime, cement and sand. This makes a weatherproof joint, and it can be pointed (see p. 18) in a colour to match the existing pointing.

Materials: glass block to match the damaged one; lime, cement and sand; colouring for pointing.
Tools: hammer; ½ in. (13 mm) cold chisel; stiff brush; large trowel; pointing trowel.

1 Carefully chip out the old block and mortar with a narrow cold chisel. Do not damage adjacent blocks

4 Spread mortar on the bottom and sides of the opening to match the thickness of adjacent joints

7 Tap the block lightly with the handle of the trowel until it is flush with the adjacent surface

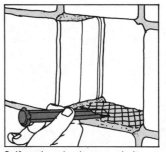

2 If steel netting is exposed, do not remove it, but chip away all mortar above and below it

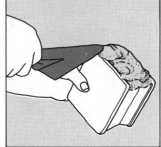

5 Spread the same thickness of mortar on the top of the glass block which is to be fitted in the hole

8 Use a pointing trowel to fill the joints. Trim all the surplus mortar from around the block

3 Clean the opening with a stiff brush until it is completely free of all dust and debris

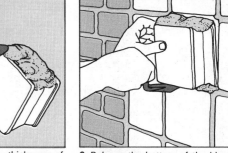

6 Balance the bottom of the block on a trowel, and ease it very gently into the opening

Colouring If preferred, point the joint with mortar tinted to match existing ones. Wipe new block clean

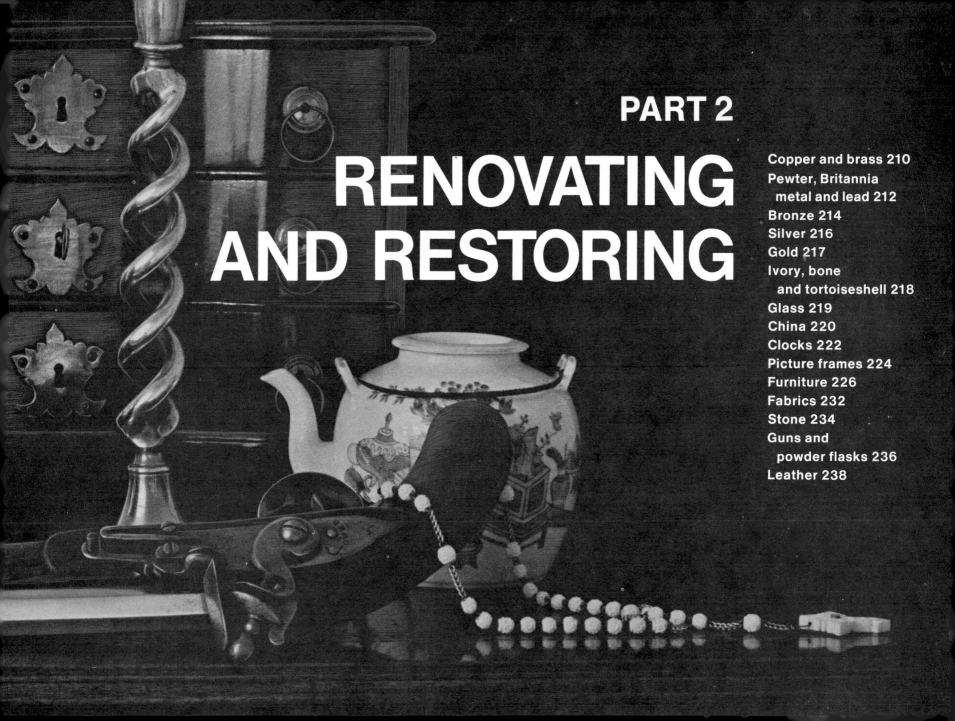

PART 2
RENOVATING AND RESTORING

Late-Victorian copper warming-pan. The pan was filled with hot cinders to warm beds

Victorian copper kettle. It was used on an open fire or coal-burning range

Brass hand-held oil lantern. Late-Victorian

Victorian clothes iron, heated either with coals or a metal slug

Victorian brass scale-weights, now used as ornaments or paper-weights

Late-Victorian brass luggage lock. Decorative as well as functional

Traditional copper jelly mould, used by Victorian cooks

Copper and brass

Copper and brass (which is an alloy of copper and zinc) need constant cleaning, but modern long-term polishes and lacquers have made this easy. Both metals are easy to repair.

Copper does not rust, but it stains easily, and water makes black spots on it. Soot in moist air reacts with the metal to produce a green deposit called verdigris.

Clean off verdigris and dirt by rubbing hard with a paste of powdered chalk and methylated spirit on a soft cloth. Use fine steel wool on stubborn areas. Do not use harsh abrasives, or the metal will be scratched. The final stage of polishing is to use a metal polish. A soft cloth buffing wheel on a power tool gives a deep shine, but over large surfaces polishing by hand with a soft cloth achieves a finer finish.

Clean brass by washing it in detergent, then rubbing it with a solution of 1 heaped tablespoon of salt and 2 tablespoons of vinegar to a pint of water. Clean old polish and dirt out of engraved brass with a solution of ammonia on a toothbrush, then with detergent, and finally with clean water.

Immerse badly corroded brass in a strong warm solution of washing soda for an hour, then wipe or brush it. If all the corrosion does not come off, repeat the process. Brush the stained parts with a glass brush, obtainable from a jewellers' supplier. Rub off spots of corrosion with scouring powder on a cloth or, if they are very bad, with fine steel wool. Polish out scratches with paste of whiting—a finely ground chalk obtainable at do-it-yourself shops. Dirty brass handles and fittings on furniture should, if possible, be removed before being cleaned. Otherwise, it will be almost impossible to work without getting cleaning fluids on to the surrounding wood.

Metal polish, a soft cloth and hard rubbing produce the best results on both metals, but shining up engraved brass is difficult. If the engraving is being rubbed away by polishing, do not use metal polish, which contains fine abrasives. Wipe the brass with vegetable oil on a cloth and rub it until it shines. On deeply engraved brass, use a medium-soft old toothbrush to get metal polish into all parts, then a soft brush inside a duster to get it out. Finish with a soft cloth.

There is no substitute for the sheen obtained on copper and brass by regular polishing. But clear lacquer, obtained from do-it-yourself and art shops, saves much of the work.

Because lacquer goes cloudy in cold weather and picks up dust in the atmosphere, it should be applied in a warm, dust-free room. Spray or brush the lacquer (using a new water-colour brush) on to the metal. Remove it with acetone if it begins to break up. If a pot has been mended with soft solder, paint on a coloured lacquer to match or approximate to the true colour of the metal. If the whole object is not clear-lacquered, however, this may make a brighter patch or strip which does not match the unlacquered metal.

Dents in copper and brass hollow-ware are best removed by pressing the metal against a short length of wood, shaped at one end to fit the curve of the damaged article. Hold the wood in a vice and put the damaged article over it. Press and rub against the shaped end until the dent is pushed out. Rub down with crocus paper, then with whiting and polish. Hammering is liable to make more dents than it removes, although hammering with a planishing hammer from the inside against a leather cushion is a professional method.

Fractures in brass and copper can be mended by soft soldering. But cast brass is heavy and hard soldering or brazing makes a much better job of such joins. Apply coloured lacquer over freshly soldered joints. If any rivets are broken or badly worn, remove them by nipping off the heads with cutting pincers, or centre-punch the heads and drill them out. Cut loose rivets with a jeweller's hacksaw, obtainable from a jewellers' supplier.

Insert a tight-fitting rivet from inside and hammer the head against a metal surface. If it is to be proud, use a concave punch; if it is to be countersunk, use a flat punch and file it down.

REMOVING A DENT

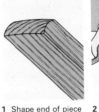

1 Shape end of piece of hardwood with a rasp and spokeshave to match the curve of the kettle. Fix the stake securely in a vice, shaped end uppermost

2 Put kettle over stake, fit shaped end to dented area and press. Continue to press and smooth dent over stake until kettle surface is smooth

3 Keep kettle on stake, and lightly hammer any remaining irregularities in surface. Move the kettle on the stake all the time. Finish by polishing

Late-Victorian brass scales of the type used by tea and coffee merchants. The scales, 2 ft 6 in. high and mounted on a mahogany base, were used with brass weights

Brass candle-holder, c. 1890

Pewter, Britannia metal and lead

Pewter, an alloy of tin and lead, was known to the Romans. In the Middle Ages it came into general use for domestic ware, and as time went on the pewtersmiths became as interested in design as the silversmiths, whose work they copied. Through Elizabethan and Stuart times, until the 19th century, pewter was widely used for table services, plates, salt and pepper pots, tankards, liquid measures and jugs.

Pewter cannot be used for cooking, as heat melts it. But it is durable, and can be mended easily. When it has been cared for and polished regularly, it glows with a deep, soft shine. If neglected, it collects a heavy, dull grey corrosion which is difficult to remove. Never store pewter in oak drawers or cupboards, because oak gives off fumes which can corrode the metal.

Rub off any light corrosion with crocus powder, or a powdered chalk called whiting, on an oily rag. The crocus powder and whiting can be obtained from do-it-yourself shops. Loosen bad corrosion with a bone, wood or plastic scraper, then rub hard with fine steel wool. To restore the surface polish, rub with whiting and then with metal polish or plate powder.

Dents can be pressed out on a shaped wooden stake held in a vice (see p. 211). Mend breaks in pewter with soft solder (see p. 692).

Take care that the soldering iron contacts only the solder, since pewter has a low melting point and is easily damaged by heat. A gas cooker lighter on a flexible lead is ideal, because its flame is not too fierce. Repair from inside if possible. Holes can be filled with solder. It does not matter if the surface is uneven, as the soft solder can be pared, filed or scraped into shape. To prepare a solder wire, melt 2 parts tin, 2 parts lead and 1 part bismuth in a ladle. Cut some grooves $\frac{1}{8}$ in. (3 mm) deep in a piece of wood and pour in the molten metal. When it is cool, prise out the wire, which is then ready for soldering.

Repairing a tankard

To renew the glass bottom in a pewter tankard, first remove the old glass and get a piece of toughened glass cut slightly smaller than the original. If the old glass was held by a flange, it may be possible to bend the flange to get the new one in. Make a bed of Araldite inside the flange, set the glass in and carefully bend back the flange. Wipe off any surplus Araldite before it sets with acetone on a swab. If the flange will not bend, file it out and cement the glass in place with fibre padding.

Britannia metal, a tin-antimony-copper alloy, looks rather like pewter but it can be polished until it shines almost like silver. Clean, mend and polish it as pewter.

Cleaning lead figures

Small ornamental lead figures may get a white deposit of carbonate of lead which can be removed by boiling them in several changes of water, and then placing them in a bowl containing 9 parts water and 1 part vinegar. Rinse in water containing a little washing soda and then in several changes of distilled water.

Broken lead figures, if they are solid, can be mended by rejoining the pieces and fitting them in a bed of sand. Cover with 1 in. (25 mm) of sand and apply heat from above with a blowlamp. Do not overheat: keep the flame moving but concentrate on the areas near the breaks. As the lead melts, the broken pieces fuse together. Do not use this method with hollow figures or they will end up as blobs of metal.

To clean large objects, such as window boxes, garden statues and troughs, scrub them with household scouring powder. Rinse thoroughly.

Hour-glass in pewter stand. Victorian copy of 16th-century English original

Chinese porcelain bowl set in pewter. Copy of an antique

Reproduction of 16th-century English serving-plate

Pair of English candlesticks of a design which appeared in 1820

One of a reproduction set of 16th-century English condiment pots

Quart tankard with lid, based on a design of 1800

Victorian pint beer tankard, dated 1850

Bronze

Bronze was the earliest alloy used by man. It is made from copper (more than 50 per cent) and tin, more recently with small additions of zinc, lead, nickel and phosphorus. Because it is relatively soft and easy to fabricate, it has been used for tools, weapons and utensils.

The early civilisations of China, Egypt, Greece and Rome made bronze coins and statues, and bronze was later used to cast bells and cannon—the original Victoria Crosses were made from bronze of Russian cannon captured in the Crimean War. It finally became extremely popular with British and Indian craftsmen in Victorian times for casting small statuettes and art objects.

Bronze ages well, and acquires its own fine patina in various shades of brown or blue-green. It needs no polishing, but wipe it occasionally with a soft, dry cloth. Corrosion, however, is common. Bright green spots—sometimes called bronze disease—start in a small area and spread swiftly like a rash to cover the whole object.

Remove the corrosion either by scraping carefully with a knife or by heavy rubbing with a brass brush. Do not use a steel or wire brush, which can damage the surface and cause the corrosion to reappear later.

Swab heavily corroded areas with a 10 per cent solution of acetic acid in water. After swabbing, wash the bronze in clean water and rub off any red discoloration with a soft cloth. If there is still discolouring, rub with a mixture of whiting and crocus powder, both obtainable from do-it-yourself shops.

Colouring soldered joins

If a bronze piece breaks off, soft-solder it (see p. 692). Colour the shiny solder joint with a bronze-coloured lacquer until it blends in with the adjacent bronze. It is also possible to use bronze wax gilt, but this is not as durable as lacquer. Soldered areas, and those parts which have been cleared of bronze disease, will not have the normal patina finish. To restore it, apply a bronze 'pickle', obtainable from art shops or some do-it-yourself shops. One alternative is to mix 3 parts basic copper acetate with 3 parts ammonium chloride and 1 part water. Boil the solution and submerge the bronze in it. Leave it in the solution until it is a rich brown colour. Another alternative, suitable for small bronze objects only, is to brush the piece with graphite and stand it in front of a fire or hair dryer to warm it while it absorbs the graphite. But it is difficult to get an even colouring over wide areas using this method.

Tiger. Oriental. One of a 19th-century pair

Oriental vase. One of a 19th-century pair

Warrior at bay,
19th-century
European

Victorian
ornamental
urn

Eastern warrior
on horse. The
man can be
dismounted and
the horse's head
and tail are
movable

Silver

Silver has been used for making jewellery, ornaments and utensils for at least 5000 years. It is valuable, so take it to a craftsman for repair or replating.

Silver is usually hard-soldered at the joints (see p. 692), but the soldering temperature, especially of the surrounding metal and the base metal under silver plate, is crucial. The work is tricky and much damage can be caused by inexperience. If, for example, a piece has been previously soft-soldered, hard-soldering involving high temperatures could damage the piece. Hammering out dents is also a craftsman's work as the thin metal may stretch or fracture in unskilled hands.

Both silver and silver plate tarnish and corrode quickly, especially near the sea: salt in the atmosphere causes silver chloride to form. Corrosion can be treated effectively with a proprietary silver dip. Alternatively, an effective home-made silver dip can be prepared by lining a large bowl with aluminium baking foil and laying the pieces of silver on it. Dissolve a cup of washing soda in 4 pints of hot water and pour the solution into the bowl. There will be much bubbling, caused by electro-chemical activity. Keep checking, and the moment the tarnish has gone remove the silver and wash it in running warm water.

Clean any remaining bad spots with a paste of French chalk and methylated spirit, or in water with a few drops of ammonia added.

Do not leave silver plate in a dip for too long, especially if any base metal is exposed. Just a quick in-and-out dip and rinse should clean it.

Green corrosion, which cannot occur on solid silver but may appear on the base metal of silver plate, can be removed by rubbing with a lemon or with a solution made by dissolving one teaspoon of citric acid in half a cup of water. Work on small spots at a time. Put the solution on and immediately wash it off, and repeat the process until the corrosion disappears.

For polishing it is best to use a long-term silver polish which will save having to do the job every few days. But first remove any scratches by rubbing with jewellers' rouge or fine crocus powder. Metal or plate polishes are slightly abrasive, and hard work brings up a fine shine.

A lacquer for silver ornaments can be obtained from a jeweller's. Before applying lacquer, wipe the object free of grease with white spirit and dry thoroughly. Apply the lacquer in a warm, well-ventilated room. It will last a year or so, but will eventually perish and must then be removed with acetone and the process repeated.

If silver is not in regular use or on display, wrap it in tissue paper, and put it in polythene bags: thus protected, it will stay bright and clean indefinitely.

Three-branched silver candelabra. 1830

Victorian silver teapot, hallmarked 1896

Silver sugar caster. Reproduction of a design of 1820

Silver creamer. The cow's tail is the handle: the cream is poured from the mouth

Georgian silver table-bell, hallmarked 1804

Silver-plate tray, based on a design of 1835

Gold

Gold was one of the first metals used by man, and the earliest known gold jewellery was found in Mesopotamia, in a burial hoard dating from 3000 BC. The purity of gold is expressed in carats. A carat is a 24th part, so 22-carat gold contains 22 parts of gold and 2 parts of other hardening metals. Because of the value of gold, its repair and restoration is best left to an expert. If gold gets dull, the shine can be restored by polishing with jewellers' rouge on a chamois leather. Small items such as rings can be burnished with a piece of polished steel, such as a knitting needle, but this method should not be used on engraved metal. Clean gold by washing it in warm, soapy water and polishing with a soft cloth or chamois leather.

Silver coffee pot. A reproduction of a Regency design

Silver-plate open-work cake or fruit basket. Reproduction of Georgian design

Silver fish knife and fork; part of a set made in 1861

Victorian gold heirlooms The box is a patch box, which held artificial beauty spots—an essential part of the fashionable woman's adornment. Lockets always carried pictures or mementoes of loved ones. The locket and the cross might have been carried on a gold chain. The thick gold wedding-ring is hallmarked 1900

Bone, ivory, tortoiseshell, horn and soapstone

Card cases, chessmen, statuettes, fans and other small objects made of bone, ivory, tortoiseshell or horn quickly collect dirt and grease and are liable to get broken or chipped. But they can easily be cleaned and repaired. The same methods can be used with soapstone, a variety of talc used for making ornaments.

Since all these materials absorb liquid and swell, never put them in water. To remove grease and dust, wipe with a swab or soft brush dampened in methylated spirit. Do not rub too hard, to avoid damaging the surface of the material.

Polish spots with whiting (a finely powdered chalk obtainable from art and do-it-yourself shops) and methylated spirit. Apply them with a small cotton-wool swab on the end of a cocktail stick or sharpened matchstick.

The yellowness which ivory and bone acquire with age may be thought attractive, but it can be removed by bleaching if necessary. Make up a stiff paste of whiting and hydrogen peroxide. Coat the piece thoroughly and stand it in sun and fresh air until the paste is dry. Wipe off the paste with a damp cloth and dry immediately with a soft cloth.

Restoration

Bone, ivory and soapstone objects which are breaking can be restored by sealing cracks with melted candle wax. Warm the object in an airing cupboard, then submerge it in a pan of melted wax for a few minutes. Lift it out, wipe off any surplus wax and allow to set. Note that after wax treatment, the object must always be kept away from heat.

An epoxy resin such as Araldite, diluted in acetone until it is liquid enough to run into surface cracks and holes, gives a smooth, strong fill for larger cracks. It can be coloured to match the ornament with powder pigments or oil paints, obtainable from art shops. Wipe off any surplus before it sets.

Make sure that any broken pieces are clean, and stick them together with Araldite. Bleach old glue stains with whiting and hydrogen-peroxide paste.

Small missing pieces can be remodelled directly on the object: mix Araldite to a very stiff dough with whiting and tint it to match the ornament. Support large pieces while the Araldite is setting, or they may sag before adhesion is effected.

An alternative fill can be made by mixing Caxamite glue, obtainable from art shops, and dental plaster. The mix should be the consistency of dough, with colouring added. The fill can be carved before it is quite set. Stick with Araldite.

Occasionally it may be possible to mould a missing part. If a piece from a chess set is chipped, for instance, take a Plasticine mould from its counterpart. Grease the Plasticine mould with a petroleum jelly before using an epoxy-resin filler. Dental plaster needs no such parting agent and is especially suitable for ornate carvings. Each one of these materials can be polished with fine abrasives, and finished with silicone polish. Rub linseed oil into horn objects with the palm of the hand.

Inlaid bone-and-ivory card case. Victorian

Victorian ivory bangle, inset with tortoiseshell

George II tobacco box—tortoiseshell mounted in silver

Georgian glass ointment bowl with silver-mounted tortoiseshell lid

Bone-handled silver fork —part of a Victorian table set

Glass

Hand-made glass dating from before the 19th century is rare and valuable and should be repaired only by experts. But glass objects made since then are less rare, and the amateur can confidently tackle small repairs.

Glass should be washed in warm water with a little liquid detergent, rinsed in clear water, then dried and polished with an impregnated silver wadding. Leave badly stained cut glass overnight in a mixture of water, detergent and a few drops of ammonia. If lime has become deposited, fill the glass with distilled water or rain water and leave it for a week before scrubbing the crust gently with a toothbrush.

Soak badly stained glass in a solution of 1 cupful of caustic soda in 4 pints of warm water, then wash the glass thoroughly. Metal polish on a soft cloth will rub off some spotty stains. If the insides of bottles or decanters have been stained and no brush can reach the marks, put in a tablespoonful of silver sand, obtainable from a gardening shop, with a weak solution of liquid detergent and warm water. Swirl the contents round and check frequently that the glass is not being scratched.

If a stopper is jammed in a decanter, apply a mixture of 2 parts white spirit, 1 part glycerine and 1 part salt to the join between bottle and stopper. Leave it for a day, then tap the stopper gently and try to remove it. If the stopper has broken off inside the neck, run hot water over the neck of the decanter so that it expands and releases the stopper.

Mend broken glass in the same way as broken china (see p. 221). But first roughen the smooth faces with glass-paper or an old glass-cutting tool to make a key for the adhesive. An epoxy resin makes a firm join. Use gummed paper to apply tension, as a very tight fit is essential. When the adhesive is set, clean off the surplus by rubbing with 00 or 000 steel wool.

To repair mouldings, use clear liquid plastic, such as Plasticraft. Make Plasticine backing moulds (see p. 221), but use only white Plasticine, which cannot stain the filler. Warm the glass before pouring the filler

REPLACING A PIECE

1 Find how the piece to be replaced should be fitted. Roughen edges with emery paper

2 Apply adhesive to the edges of the bowl and the broken piece. Fit and press together firmly

3 Brush surface with methylated spirit. Dry. Stick gummed strip over join and leave for 48 hours

Ivory knight on mother-of-pearl mount, from 18th-century Portuguese chess set

Ivory elephant—equivalent to a castle in a European chess set—from India, *c.* 1830

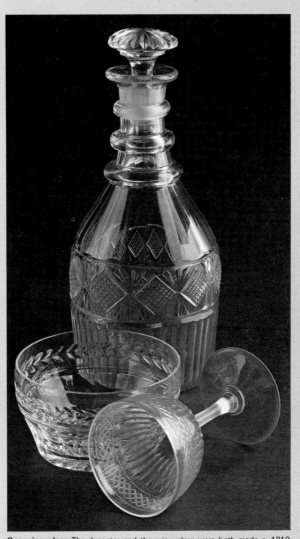

Georgian glass The decanter and the wine glass were both made *c.* 1810. The bowl is a reproduction of a design of the same period. Not all reproductions are genuine cut-glass: Georgian designs were often copied by moulding. Moulded glass can be distinguished by the blunt edges on its patterns. Cut-glass is ground on a wheel and its edges are sharp

English cake plate by Copeland, dated 1900

Early-Victorian Toby jug. The design first appeared in the mid-18th century

Victorian fireplace tile—these are now collected as colourful decorations

Dresden figurine of a country boy —part of a set with a matching shepherdess

Victorian stoneware mug—the everyday pottery of the period

Hand-painted porcelain ink-well from a Victorian lady's writing table

A Victorian present from Margate

Teapot from a small-scale children's tea service. Victorian

China

The term china includes all pottery made by firing clay in a kiln, from the finest porcelain to the coarsest earthenware. The differences are made by the clays used, the firing temperatures, and the qualities of glaze, decoration or design.

Valuable pottery—such as Meissen, Sèvres and Chelsea (which date from the 18th century)—is too rare and delicate to be restored by anyone other than an expert. But many other pieces of china, which probably have more charm than value, can be restored by anyone prepared to take the time.

Wash china in warm soapy water, then rinse and dry. Most domestic stains can be shifted by rubbing with bicarbonate of soda or common salt.

Grease and dust collect in cracks. Bleach with cotton-wool pads soaked in hydrogen peroxide. Coarse china is porous and often stains badly, but it can be cleaned by soaking for up to a week in neat domestic bleach.

In some cases, old joins may have to be taken apart. To soften old glue, soak in boiling water and detergent. Methylated spirit, amyl acetate and acetone are other softeners that can be tried. But remember that complete immersion softens *all* joints. In the last resort, pick away at old adhesive with a needle.

Broken surfaces must be clean and fit exactly or they will not join properly. Wipe with a piece of silk dipped in methylated spirit. Silk will not leave lint on jagged edges. Put the thinnest possible coat of epoxy resin (see p. 694) on each surface and press together. Remove any surplus adhesive before it dries, with a water-colour brush dipped in methylated spirit. Avoid touching the actual crack: any surplus on that must be removed by breaking the surface with fine glass-paper then by cutting it away with a razor blade.

To make a really good join of smooth surfaces, such as those on plates or cups, apply pressure by clamping or putting a weight on where possible, or by binding with a 1½ in. (40 mm) wide brown paper gummed strip (but not self-adhesive tape). Gummed strip shrinks as it dries, and exerts tension. Put strips that are wet, but not dripping, at right angles across the join: it is pointless to fix a strip along the line of the join. When the join has set, soak off the strips and remove surplus adhesive with glass-paper and a razor blade.

To repair a figure, bury it in a bowl of sand, with the broken surface just protruding and horizontal. Set it up so that the broken piece balances perfectly on its matching surface without adhesive. Glue it and keep checking to make sure that nothing slips. When the adhesive has set, remove any surplus along the join with fine glass-paper and a razor blade.

Chips can be filled with a mixture of epoxy resin (see p. 694) and finely powdered chalk, called whiting.

Missing parts on ornamental pieces can be replaced by modelling a new part out of epoxy-resin filler. If the missing part—of a plate, for example—is flat, make a backing of gummed strip. If the surface is curved, back it with dental impression compound, which can be bought from a dental materials supplier or from a dental mechanic. Mix a stiff dough of epoxy resin (see p. 694) with whiting and build it up against the backing. It sticks to the edges and, when dry, resembles unglazed china.

If the shape of the missing piece is part of a repetitive pattern, make a mould of a similar unbroken part with dental impression compound. Use this mould to make a new piece with a quick-drying filler, obtainable from a do-it-yourself shop. These pieces have to be cut and filed to fit when dry and stuck into place.

Large missing parts of a figure have to be cast. Model the missing part in Plasticine. Use calipers to check the length and thickness of similar parts. Study the pose to see how the missing part must have looked.

Build up a square with 'walls' of thick strips of Plasticine on a sheet of glass. Insert a wooden peg through one side of the square and into the model to hold it horizontally above the glass in the middle of the square. Mix plaster of Paris and water in a bowl, stirring until the mixture resembles thick cream. Pour this into the mould until it is half way up the model. Leave to set. Cut two wide grooves in the plaster as locating marks when the two sections are joined.

Coat the surfaces of the plaster with silicone grease, obtainable from hardware stores. Fill the rest of the frame with fresh plaster. When it has set, remove the Plasticine wall, ease the two sections apart, and take out the model.

This leaves a mould in which to cast the new piece. Smear silicone grease over the inside surfaces. Make up filler and pour into both halves. Bind them tightly together with wire, and ram more filler through the peg hole. Leave to set for two hours. If using epoxy resin, bake it for half an hour at 93°C (200°F). Remove from the mould, clean the casting and stick it into place. If a figure is hollow, broken pieces

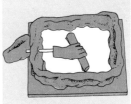
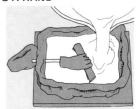

1 Model matching hand in Plasticine. Build Plasticine walls on sheet of glass. Fix hand horizontally in middle of box and peg it through one wall. Weight end of peg

2 Mix plaster of Paris and pour into box until it is half-way up hand. Let plaster set. Cut three deep grooves across it and coat all over with silicone grease

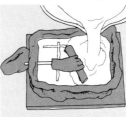

3 Mix fresh plaster of Paris and fill box with it. Leave overnight, to allow plaster to set hard. Next day separate the two sections of plaster and remove the hand

4 Put silicone grease on the insides of the plaster sections and fill them with filler paste. Tape the two parts of the mould together. Push more filler in peg hole and leave to set

can be dowelled together. Clean the broken edges and make sure they fit flush together. Then cut and bend a piece of half-hard brass wire to fit into both broken pieces. Roll out a ribbon of epoxy resin and whiting mix. Wind it round the piece of the wire which goes into the main part of the figure, and push it into the hole. Ram filler into the hole until it is full. When it is set, wind more filler round the other end of the wire and push the broken piece over it until the original edges come together.

Paint new parts with artists' oil paints mixed with a gel medium to make them runnier and heighten the gloss. For opaque colours use polymer paints mixed with their own glaze medium. Apply with fine water-colour brushes. First build up the whole area with ground colour matching the pot. This will probably contain a lot of white and be fairly opaque. When this has dried, build up further layers of more transparent colour until the original design is matched.

George III wall clock, made by Lowrie of London in 1795

Cuckoo clock made in the Black Forest area of Germany, c. 1800

American 30-hour wall clock of 1845. Many were exported to Britain

Alarm clock of 1790. It has no minute hand: the alarm is set by turning the inner dial

Trunk-dial wall clock, made by Moore of London in 1795

Pendulum clocks

Long-case clocks, which are worked by weights and a pendulum instead of springs, were made in thousands in the 19th century. Many are still ticking away, and will do so indefinitely if cared for.

Those that have stopped can often be made to work simply by cleaning and doing a few small repairs. Replacing broken parts is a specialist's job. But otherwise the clocks have simple movements and do not present many problems to an amateur.

Open the door in the trunk below the clock face. Lift the pulley off the gut and remove the weight. The top part of the clock, covering the movement and the face, is called the hood. Slide this forward, together with its glass door, to expose the movement. Lift off the pendulum, taking care not to bend or damage the suspension spring. Finally, remove the whole movement and clock face on its seat board. With some clocks it will be necessary to unscrew this from the cabinet.

Do not take the movement apart. To remove the hands, tap the small pin above the brass retaining washer, then pull it out with pliers. Remove any other pins or latches holding the dial to the front plate of the movement. Use a little rust remover on grade 00 steel wool or emery cloth on steel parts. Strip off old polish. Rub steel parts with black shoe polish. Replace old gut lines with new gut, non-stretch nylon or stranded steel.

The hands can be re-blued in any of three ways: with bluing fluid, by burying them in sand and heating with a gentle blowlamp flame, or by blackening them in the flame of a candle and then painting them with clear lacquer. If they have broken, mend with silver solder.

Having made sure there is no more dirt, old oil, damp or rust anywhere, reassemble the clock. First touch each bearing with a drop of light machine oil on a piece of copper wire. Never put oil on the teeth of cog wheels. Replace the hands. If they fall by their own weight, tap the outside brass washer lightly all round until the hands hold on their arbors.

To replace any infill which may have been polished out

MAKING A KEY

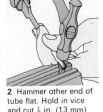

1 File the end of a cut nail to fit winding shaft. Insert about ¾ in. (20 mm) into 2 in. (50 mm) length of copper tube. Hammer tube round nail. Remove nail

2 Hammer other end of tube flat. Hold in vice and cut ½ in. (13 mm) deep slot along it. Hammer a screwdriver blade sideways into slot to open it slightly

Butterfly

3 Take a 1½ in. (40 mm) length of tube. Hammer flat to make butterfly

4 Hammer cut end tightly round butterfly: bond with epoxy resin

PENDULUM CLOCK MOVEMENT

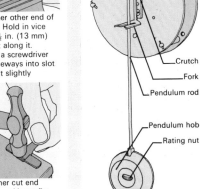

Back cock

Crutch

Fork

Pendulum rod

Pendulum bob

Rating nut

of the engraved lines on the dial, paint a mixture of shellac, methylated spirit and black powder pigment into the engraved parts. Let it set, and wipe off surplus with whiting on a soft rag. Polish well. Regilding or resilvering is specialist's work, but gilding waxes, which can be obtained at art shops, can be used to touch up small spots, provided the surface is to be lacquered and not polished.

Reassemble the clock (except for the pendulum) and be sure that the face is positioned centrally behind the glass door. Put the pendulum through the trunk door, the gap in the seat board, and the crutch. Feed the suspension spring through the slit in the back cock, and pull it down on its seating. The spring should swing freely with the pendulum block free in the crutch.

Check with a plumbline and spirit level that the clock is upright and level. Wind up the weight and swing the pendulum. The ticking should be even and solid. If the clock is not set right, the ticking will be uneven and will eventually stop. If so, face the clock and place the first finger of one hand at the top of the crutch on the side from which comes the louder tick. Place the first finger of the other hand at the bottom of the crutch on the other side. Bend the crutch gently with the lower finger, towards the louder tick, until both ticks are the same. If the clock either loses or gains time, adjust the rating nut on the pendulum. A pendulum length of 39½ in. (1005 mm) gives exactly one second between ticks.

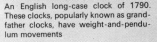

An English long-case clock of 1790. These clocks, popularly known as grandfather clocks, have weight-and-pendulum movements

Picture frames

A good period picture frame can cost £1000, and even a simple maple frame may cost more than £15. Old frames are, therefore, worth restoring, though work on valuable frames should be left to experts.

The corners of frames are the weakest points. If the original glue and pins no longer hold the corners together, take the frame to pieces, scrape off the old glue and remove the pins. Glass-paper the faces of the corners until clean wood is showing. Apply Scotch glue on both faces, and reassemble in a corner cramp, using enough pressure to make a good bond. If no corner cramp is available, square the corner with a tri-square and make a string tie to hold it.

Hold the corners tight and drive panel pins across the join through its thickest parts. An alternative is to drill small holes and tap in wooden pegs.

To strengthen corners without dismantling the frame, drill diagonally across the corners and glue in wooden dowels. Alternatively screw diagonal or triangular corner plates of plywood or metal to the back of the frame.

If the frame is to be used for a new, smaller picture, its size can be reduced by dismantling only two diagonally opposite

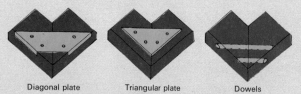

Diagonal plate   Triangular plate   Dowels

corners. Measure the opposite sides to the required length, use a mitre box to cut them, then rejoin.

When measuring, remember that the inside edge of the frame overlaps both glass and picture. Always measure from the inside of the groove into which the picture fits.

Frames which have been stained, varnished, lacquered, veneered or painted can be cleaned and retouched (see p. 231). Detergent, water and glass-paper should remove grease and grime; but keep water away from glued corners, and do not use it on plaster mouldings.

Remove varnish with a paint-stripping agent and glass-paper. Brush plaster mouldings carefully with a hog's-hair brush and a little methylated spirit. Frames can be regilded with gold leaf, but this is best done by an expert and can be expensive. Wax gilts, which come in various shades of gold and are obtainable from art shops, can be rubbed on with a finger or cloth. They will blend better with old gilding than will gilt paint or lacquer.

If the moulding on an otherwise sound frame is badly broken, strip it off with a chisel and scraper. Finish smoothing with glass-paper.

Replace small pieces of broken moulding with filler or plastic wood, and regild. If large chunks of moulding have gone, clean away crumbling plaster. Take an impression of a matching part with dental-impression compound, which can be bought from dental suppliers. Make a cast of the impression with filler paste (see p. 683) or gilders' compo, which can be bought from an art shop.

When the cast has set, take it from the mould. Clean the edges gently with a needle file and glass-paper and stick it on the frame with epoxy resin, such as Araldite. Paint with Gesso, a plaster primer obtainable from art shops. Mouldings made with gilders' compo need at least two coats of primer before being finished with gilt, gilt wax or gold leaf.

REPAIRING A MOULDING

1 Press impression compound on a piece of moulding which matches the missing part. Leave it to set for a few minutes

2 Lift compound from frame. File surplus from inner rebate of impression. Tack wood strip to filed edge. Fill with filler paste to top of strip

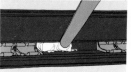

3 File new moulding to fit gap in frame. Apply adhesive

4 Stick moulding in place and colour with wax gilt (see p. 231)

Carved wooden photograph frame. Victorian, c. 1860

Maplewood frame, c. 1840

A Hogarth frame, 1860. Such frames have a gold-black-gold pattern and usually hold prints

Reverse Hogarth frame, 1800. Reverse frames are very thick and the picture is mounted at the front

Elaborately carved and moulded gilt frame. English, 18th century

Carved wooden frame. Dutch, 17th century

English gilt frame, 18th century

Carved wooden frame with inner band of moulding. Victorian

Oval gilt frame of plaster and compo on wooden base. Victorian

CLEANING AN OIL PAINTING

Years of grime or layers of old varnish can turn an oil painting into a dull, brown smudge. Careful cleaning can restore much of its original appearance (see p. 363)

Button-backed
elbow chair, 1860

Pedestal wine table
with gallery, *c.* 1780

Furniture: polished

Furniture that has lost its lustre but is unmarked can have its shine restored fairly easily. Rub the surface with a coarse cloth dampened with white spirit. This will loosen the accumulated wax and grime, which can then be removed with a clean rag. Restore the gloss by rubbing with a polish reviver or burnishing compound, obtainable from DIY shops, or even with a metal polish. Apply it with a soft mutton cloth or stockinet: cloth containing synthetic fibres will not produce a good gloss. Finish by rubbing vigorously with a clean soft cloth.

If the finish on a piece of furniture has been badly damaged, it will need to be removed so that a new finish can be applied. Use a solvent paint remover to take off a finish. Do not use caustic soda, which will darken many woods, or a sander, which will leave circular marks that will show through the finished film. Ideally stripping should be done out of doors, but if this is not possible stand the furniture on a large polythene sheet to protect the floor, and make sure that the room is well-ventilated.

Dab the paint-remover on liberally and, after a short while, remove as much as possible with a flat scraper. Dampen the wood again with the paint-remover and rub it, with the grain, using small pieces of No. 2 and 3 steel wool.

At this stage the wood can be lightened if necessary by bleaching; or it can be stained to a darker shade with wood stain. Naphtha-based stains are best as they are penetrating, do not raise the grain and are fast drying. Apply them evenly over the whole surface with a cloth. If the grain is very open, fill it before staining with a paste-type grain-filler, thinned if necessary with white spirit. Rub across the grain to fill the pores, and wipe off the surplus while soft with a clean cloth.

Holes and cracks should be filled with a paste-type wood-filler. Make good any broken edges or corners with plastic wood.

French polish can be used to provide a finish, but it requires a fair degree of skill in application and its surface is easily marked by heat, solvents and abrasions. A two-part plastic-coating lacquer will give just as good a finish and will be more resistant to marking.

Alternatively, a polyurethane finish is acceptable for many surfaces and is easily applied with a brush.

To get an antique finish, apply not less than two coats and rub the final coat, with the grain, with 000 steel wool and wax polish. Finish off with a clean soft cloth.

Removing water stains

A finish that shows heat and water marks is usually shellac or cellulose. Marks that have not penetrated right through to the wood can often be removed with a cutting compound, obtainable from DIY shops, or with metal polish rubbed in with a soft cloth. But if they have gone right through, stripping is necessary and the whole surface must be treated.

A grey or black stain usually indicates that water has penetrated to the wood itself. Take off the old finish and remove the stain with a two-part wood bleach, obtainable from DIY and paint shops, or with a solution of 1 tablespoon of oxalic acid, obtainable from a chemist, and 1 pint of water. This solution is not as strong as the bleach, but the acid is poisonous and must be used with extreme care. Again, treat the whole surface, not just the affected part. If bleaching has made the wood lighter than required, darken with a naphtha-type stain before applying the finish.

Scratches and burn marks

A scratch mark right through the polish to the wood can be eliminated only by stripping and re-finishing, but it can be made less noticeable by rubbing in wax shoe polish of the nearest shade. Alternatively, reduce a shellac varnish with methylated spirits to a thin solution and apply this carefully to the scratch with a small soft brush, or a toothpick. Repeat this application until the stain stands proud of the surface, then level it with fine glasspaper or wet-or-dry paper. Restore the gloss with metal polish or burnishing compound.

Burn marks are more difficult to repair. Scrape away the finish from the burnt area and from the charred wood underneath. Sand the bare wood with glasspaper and, if necessary, restain it. Then apply several coats of clear finish until the mark is proud of the surrounding surface and finish off as you would for a scratch mark. A deep hole can be filled with coloured beeswax (see p. 73).

If furniture has split or cracked, often caused by central heating, stripping is essential. Fill in cracks with paste wood-filler or, if very large, with slivers of wood and adhesive before applying the finish. Dents can be made less obvious by applications of clear finish, but stripping is usually necessary to remove them. After stripping, either sand the surrounding area until the dent is no longer apparent or apply a little water to the dented area to swell the wood fibres.

If a finish has become 'crazed', it is usually made of cellulose and cannot be restored, only replaced. Stripping is necessary, as it is with a finish that has faded through exposure to strong sunlight.

Carved Canterbury, for storing sheet music, c. 1780

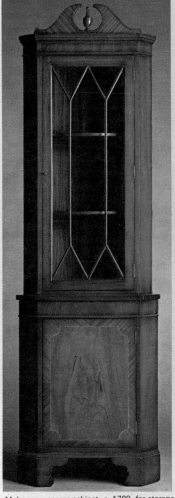

Mahogany corner cabinet, c. 1780, for storage and display. Mahogany was one of the more popular woods among furniture craftsmen in Britain during most of the 18th century. It first became fashionable in 1730–5, when it was found to be ideal for intricate carving, and was later used as a veneer

Furniture: veneer, inlay, marquetry and boulle

When furniture craftsmen of the 17th and 18th centuries designed a chair, they did not see it simply as something to sit on. They pictured their piece of furniture as a thing of beauty—a framework on which to blend together finely grained wood veneers and delicately hued mother of pearl, or to be embellished with bold marquetry patterns and extravagant designs in brass.

Their artistry fell into four main categories: *veneers*, strips of mahogany or walnut, waxed and polished to enrich their grain and colour; *marquetry*, patterns and pictorial designs built up from a variety of different woods; *inlay*, which achieved a similar effect using pieces of tortoiseshell, mother of pearl, ivory and ebony; and *boulle*, named after a French family of cabinet makers in the 17th and 18th centuries whose furniture was decorated with designs in brass, picked out in black pigment and filled in with inlay. The skills of these craftsmen linger on in many small individual firms.

No special skills are needed to repair general damage or wear to this kind of furniture decoration, but the work requires extreme care, and patience in tracking down suitable replacement materials.

Finding veneers to match

Wood veneers can be difficult to match. It is possible to buy new veneer strips, but they are generally thinner than the old hand-sawn veneers and do not always match in colour. It oftens pays to go to an auction to look for a broken oddment of furniture which has suitable veneers.

To remove a veneer from its backing, first clean off any old polish with white spirit and carefully scrape clean the varnish or wax. Place a damp cloth over the cleaned strip and press with a fairly hot iron. Keep the cloth damp. This melts the Scotch glue holding down the veneer, which then can be peeled off. The same technique is used to raise small areas, but use a soldering iron instead of an iron.

Wipe off all traces of the old glue while it is still warm. Dampen the veneer and flatten it between two pieces of wood for about 24 hours before use. Do not let it dry completely, for veneers must be relaid while still damp and pliable. The replacement strip of veneer should be slightly thicker than the existing one, to allow for sanding. If a new veneer is being used, build up a number of strips to get this thickness.

Stick the new strip down with Scotch glue. Apply a weight or clamp until the glue is completely set, with a strip of wood inserted between the strip and the weight as protection. Wax and polish to match the existing finish.

It is not always necessary to replace a new strip of veneer on a section which has blistered. Neatly cut the blister across the top and squeeze a little glue into the cut, pressing the veneer back into place.

Paper patterns for marquetry

The same hot-iron and gluing method is used in repairing marquetry. Lay a piece of paper over the missing section and rub with a soft pencil to get an outline of the area. Cut the paper roughly to the pattern and stick it to the replacement section of wood. Cut the wood slightly larger than the pattern and rub down the edges with glass-paper until an exact fit has been obtained. Stick it into place with glue.

Sometimes dampness causes a large area of marquetry to lift. If it has lifted only slightly, check that no dust has penetrated into the gap. Press the section down with a block of wood well warmed with an iron. The warmth of the wood, weighted or cramped over the raised portion, slightly melts the old glue and resticks the raised portion back into position as it cools.

If dust has got beneath the raised area, remove the section completely. Use a hot iron and damp cloth. Clean all dirt and glue from the base and refix the section with glue. Weight or cramp it.

Finding suitable replacement materials is an even greater problem with inlay and boulle, which use more complex and varied materials. Antique and second-hand shops often have boxes containing suitable oddments, and it is worth searching through them to find matching pieces. As a last resort, missing pieces of inlay can be built up with synthetic resins or wax (see p. 73), coloured to match. If boulle has lifted seriously or is bent, leave the

Walnut table, edged in marquetry, made in France in 1775. This form of decoration was introduced to England by the Huguenots, who were escaping from religious persecution in France, in the late 17th century

repair to an expert restorer; but if the lifting is only slight, carefully remove the section and scrape clean of all dirt. Stick with an epoxy-resin adhesive (see p. 694), and weight it down until the glue has dried.

Fitting new handles

A simple way to improve pieces of furniture, such as chests of drawers, is to fit new handles. The Victorians had a habit of replacing metal handles with round wooden knobs, often leaving the marks of the former back-plates showing. Sets of old handles can be picked up cheaply at antique and second-hand shops, but make sure that the back-plates are large enough to cover any existing indentations.

The existing knob handle may be set on a threaded wooden dowel screwed into the drawer, or on a plain dowel glued in place. Try unscrewing or tapping out. If the knob is set firm, split it from the top with a hammer and chisel, levelling off the dowel with the face of the wood.

Sometimes parts of knobs become split off along the grain. Replace these by cutting a matching block approximately to fit. Sand the broken surface level and, keeping the grain of the new piece running the same way as the old, stick and dowel it into position. Once the piece has set, shape the new block by hand until it blends in with the original knob. Broken mouldings can be dealt with in the same way. Refit loose knobs with epoxy resin (see p. 694) mixed with sawdust to act both as a glue and a filler.

PATCHING DAMAGED VENEER

1 Lay a matching veneer over damage. Line up grain and cut a boat-shaped piece, larger than damaged area, through both veneers

2 Cut scored piece out of old veneer. Remove old glue and any dust from wood beneath. Apply Scotch glue to patch and to hole

3 Press patch down with veneer hammer, the nose of an iron or similar hard object. Lay paper pad on patch and cramp or weight

Boulle on a box
made in France
in 1780

Mahogany
veneer cabinet
made in 1840

Chinese chair,
inlaid with
mother of pearl, 1860

Velvet-covered
stool with inlay
design, 1875

French gilt chair covered in cut velvet, 1780

French cabinet with ormolu mounting, 1820

Furniture: gilt, ormolu and painted

Some pieces of furniture have decorative finishes, such as gilding, patterns in gilded bronze—called ormolu—or simple oil-painted designs. Restoring faded or damaged finishes, or even adding a completely new finish to a particular piece of furniture, are tasks that require care and patience.

Gilding is the fixing of gold leaf to a prepared surface and rubbing it into place. Gold leaf will not tarnish: it lasts for years, giving a true gold look to any wood, metal or plaster base.

Old gold leaf can be cleaned with water containing a few drops of ammonia. New gold leaf can be bought in plain sheets, or in transfers which have a tissue backing. The transfer sheets are much easier to use than the plain sheets. When applying gold leaf to a new area, make sure that the surface is clean and dry. Paint the base with Japan gold size and leave it to get tacky.

Lay the sheets in place, slightly overlapping at the edges; rub them down carefully, following the direction of the overlap, with a clean cotton cloth until all the edges blend evenly together. The knack is to lay the sheets on the surface when the size has reached the correct degree of tackiness. If the size is too wet, the leaf wrinkles; if it is too dry, the leaf will not stick.

Wax gilt as an alternative

Gold leaf is pure gold. Because it is so expensive, various imitations have been tried. The best of these is wax gilt. The other popular alternative, gold paint, although simple to apply, produces a rather garish finish and lacks depth.

Wax gilts, available at most art shops, come in many tones of gold. They are ideal for touching-up damaged areas of gold leaf and for applying a broken gilt surface over white or coloured paint. They are simple to apply. On flat surfaces, use a soft rag or a finger; for crevices, use a small, stiff oil brush. Because wax gilt can easily be removed with turpentine substitute, protect it by covering the surface with a clear alcohol-based varnish, obtainable from art shops.

Another alternative is liquid leaf, again easy to apply. It can be brushed on, or drawn on with a pen. It is brighter than gold leaf and does not have the same 'antique' finish as wax gilt.

Cleaning tarnished ormolu

Ormolu is bronze, cast into decorative shapes which are gilded with gold leaf and attached to parts of furniture. A form of decoration which has developed from ormolu is brass alloy, with the same appearance as gold.

The surface of ormolu often becomes tarnished because the brass sweats through the gilding. Clean it by brushing the surface gently with soap and warm water containing a few drops of ammonia. To remove any obstinate dirt from the surface, add more ammonia. Always wear rubber gloves for this work.

Restoring painted furniture

To restore faded or damaged parts of painted furniture, scrape the paint down to the surface. Fill any deep scratches or holes with plastic wood, or Polymer texturing paste which can be bought at art shops. Rub the area with fine glass-paper and repaint, using matching artists' oil colours.

To achieve a matt finish, use only an undercoat paint; cover it when dry with a good-quality matt varnish. If an undercoat is left unvarnished, it discolours or turns

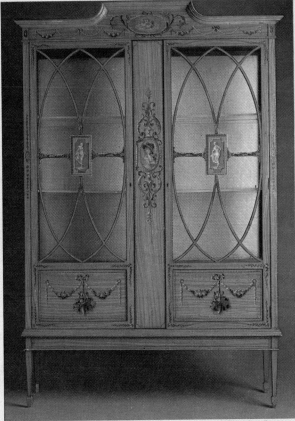

Sheraton satinwood cabinet, late 18th century. Satinwood followed mahogany in the 1780's as a popular wood for furniture. Because it was very expensive, however, it was mainly used only for small pieces

Detail from the cabinet shows the intricacy of the inlay which decorated early furniture

powdery after a time. Small areas of old paint texture can be matched by using white undercoat as the base. Apply matching colours with artists' oil paint, which should always be a tone lighter than the original. When the paint dries it will be the necessary tone darker and will match the existing tones.

A gloss finish can be matched by brushing on a coat of clear varnish; for a matt finish, use matt varnish. It is best to varnish the whole area rather than to retouch only the newly painted piece. This gives an overall even texture. New gloss varnish may be a little too shiny when dry; if so, rub it down gently with fine steel wool. Make sure the varnish has completely hardened: rubbing it down too soon will 'fur' the surface.

Victorian tea-cosy. Berlin-work —fine wool embroidery— decorated with beads

Framed Victorian sampler— alphabet theme indicates that it is a child's work

Victorian lady's parasol or sun-shade. Wild silk, decorated with lace

Embroidered belt for lady's dress or skirt

Decorated pincushion—these were often made by soldiers and sailors serving abroad

Fabrics

Christening robes, wedding dresses and pieces of embroidery often have a great sentimental value. Unfortunately, such fabrics are difficult to preserve and tend to discolour with age.

Before attempting to clean any fabric article, check it for colour fastness. Place a corner of the material on a sheet of white blotting paper and dab gently with cotton wool, dampened in water. Lift the fabric and check the blotting paper. If there is no colour stain on the paper, it is safe to wash the fabric.

Wash old materials in a weak, lukewarm solution of water and mild soap or liquid detergent: never use strong soaps or washing powders. Pour the solution into a flat container, large enough to take the fabric without folding.

With large items, such as a dress or a long tapestry, it may be necessary to use a bath as a container.

Rinsing and drying
Dabble the fabric gently up and down a few times. Drain off the solution and rinse at least three times in lukewarm water which has been boiled. Press the fabric gently in the rinsing water. Lay it flat in a warm place and allow to dry. Large items should be laid flat on a sheet of polythene and dried with a hand-held hair dryer set at 'cool'. Take care not to hold the dryer too close to the fabric. If the fabric is not colourfast, clean it with a patent cleaner, such as Genclean, or soak it in white spirit for an hour.

Work in a well-ventilated room with no naked flames, as white spirit is inflammable. Drain off the spirit and dab any particularly dirty spots with cotton wool and spirit. Lay the fabric flat to dry in a well-ventilated room.

If a fabric is too fragile for washing and rinsing, cover it with $\frac{1}{4}$ in. (6 mm) of potato flour, obtainable from health food shops, slightly warmed. Whisk off the flour with a baby's hairbrush before it cools. Soak cotton

and linen which has yellowed with age in a very dilute solution of domestic bleach (try just a few drops to start with, adding more if needed) and lukewarm water. Rinse thoroughly in clean, lukewarm water. Add blue bag to the final rinse.

Lace and muslin
To clean lace, detach it from its garment and soak it in lukewarm distilled water for 30 minutes. Remove the lace and dabble it in a weak solution of lukewarm water and detergent. Rinse it well and lay it on a sheet of white blotting paper. Pin the lace flat to prevent distortion while it dries. Cover with tissue paper and press with a barely warm iron.

Wash muslin garments, old dolls' clothes and baby clothes in the same way. When they are nearly dry, roll them in absorbent paper. Finally press flat through tissue paper with a cool iron.

Use French chalk to remove grease and dirt from fragile articles. Sprinkle the powder liberally over the garment. Leave it for a few minutes, then shake and brush it off carefully.

Remounting embroidery
Old samplers and other pieces of embroidery which have been mounted on frames can be remounted on ready-stretched artists' canvas, obtainable from art shops. Buy a piece of canvas slightly larger than the frame and back-stitch (see p. 278) the sampler or embroidery to it with a good-quality thread. Fit the canvas in the frame and tap the stretchers lightly so that they flatten the material on the canvas.

Fitting the glass
Make sure that the fabric cannot come into contact with the glass in the frame. Make a narrow 'window frame' of thick cardboard to fit between the glass and the fabric. Stick a piece of thin card or thick brown paper over the back of the frame and seal the edges with gummed strip to ensure that the backing paper cannot lift and allow dirt into the frame.

Free-hanging wall tapestries should be sewn to nylon or terylene net. Attach the hooks or rings used to hang them to the nylon or net, not to the tapestry.

Do not wash fabric fans. Many of their parts are held together with glue, and water may loosen the adhesion. First check for colour fastness with water and blotting paper. If the colour holds, dab any grease spots with a dry-cleaning fluid. Sprinkle fans that are not colourfast with French chalk and shake it off after a few minutes.

Victorian beadwork purse. Beadwork was a popular occupation with young ladies

Victorian child's christening robe, made of fine cotton and decorated with *broderie anglais.* Many such robes have survived as family heirlooms.

At best, cotton tends to yellow with age, and often the fibres weaken. Cleaning can prolong the life of cotton garments, but they must be treated with great care to prevent them breaking up.

Wash in a mild solution of warm water and detergent. Gently paddle the material up and down in the water: do not rub it. Rinse gently two or three times in distilled or boiled water. Dry it by wrapping in absorbent paper. Lightly iron the material with a cool iron when nearly dry

Granite figure of
seated Buddha,
carved in India.
Early 19th century

Wild boar in dark
green marble.
Unknown origin,
19th century

French pyramid
clock, mounted in
marble and
decorated with
ormolu, 1850

Alabaster
figure,
c. 1880

Oriental marble head,
probably brought to
Britain late 19th
century

Stone

Clean outdoor ornaments and stone garden furniture as little as possible. Natural weathering is often part of the beauty of such objects.

Porous stone, such as limestone and sandstone, develops a protective weathered crust over the years. If this is removed by harsh scrubbing, the stone may crumble. Hose the stone with a powerful jet of water and lightly clean with a stiff brush. This removes most dirt. Mildew stains can be removed with a simple 'blotting-paper' technique. Place sheets of clean white paper in hot distilled water and beat them into a pulp. Spread the pulp about 1 in. (25 mm) thick over the stain. The stone at first absorbs the water, but as the paper dries, it draws back the moisture—and the stain. Oil stains can be removed by the same method, but before the pulp is placed over the stained area it should be left to dry on its own and then be soaked in white spirit.

Oil stains can also be removed by spreading a paste of powdered kaolin and benzine over them and wiping it off after a minute or two. Repeat if stain is particularly stubborn.

Non-porous stone, such as granite and basalt, can be handled less gently. Use a brass-wire brush and scrub with detergent and water. Rub with white spirit to remove oil stains. Alabaster, on the other hand, is absorbent and will be stained by water. It should be wiped gently with white spirit, petrol, benzine or paint solvent.

Clean marble with soap and water; add half a teacup of ammonia to each bucket, and gently swab the marble. But note that when marble is cleaned it will lose its gloss and will have to be repolished.

Remove minor stains with a solution of 1 part oxalic acid (poisonous) and 19 parts water. Fungus stains can be bleached out by adding a drop or two of ammonia to a well-diluted solution of hydrogen peroxide. Never use strong, undiluted acids on marble. They can create unsightly patches which always show, however much the marble is polished.

Joining broken pieces

Breaks in limestone, sandstone, granite and basalt can be joined with an epoxy resin, such as Araldite (see p. 694). Thoroughly rub down the edges which are to be joined with coarse glass-paper, and clean with detergent and water. Make sure that the stone is completely dry before applying the glue. Small missing pieces can be built up by mixing resin with powdered stone. Alabaster can be mended by sticking broken pieces together with clear glue. Mix whiting with the glue to build up any missing or chipped pieces. This mixture has the same translucent appearance as alabaster. Araldite mixed with whiting and an appropriate colouring can be used to repair chipped marble pieces and holes and cracks in marble. First remove any grease with soap and water and a stiff-bristled brush. Rub down with fine glass-paper and clean with soap and water. Apply the Araldite-and-whiting mixture only when the marble

Granite mortar for kitchen use. Italian, 19th century

Green marble trinket box. European, mid-19th century

One of a pair of carved alabaster lions. Italian, 17th century

Garden urn, carved from sandstone. Victorian

is completely dry. Polish alabaster with a little beeswax dissolved in turpentine, or with a good-quality wax furniture polish rubbed on with a soft white cloth.

Use silicone furniture polish on marble. Flat surfaces can be rubbed with silicone wax and buffed with a lambswool pad on a power drill. If this treatment is repeated two or three times, the marble will have a mirror-like finish that will last for years, provided that it is occasionally dusted with a soft cloth.

Protective coatings for marble

To reduce the risk of staining, marble kept inside the house should be brushed occasionally with a mixture of white shellac and methylated spirit. Marble in the garden can be protected with a coating of white beeswax.

Mix the beeswax with white spirit until it has the consistency of butter. Warm the marble in front of a fire so that it absorbs the wax; wipe off any surplus.

Slabs of marble used as shelves or garden seats often chip at the edges and corners. It is difficult to build these up with the Araldite mixture, so use a fine sanding disc on a power tool and smooth them out. Do not apply too much pressure: friction may cause staining. Repolish with beeswax, but be prepared for a lot of hard work to restore the original shine unless a buffing wheel is used.

Guns and powder flasks

Most old guns are operated either by flintlock, in which the steel struck by the flint produces a spark to ignite the charge, or by percussion cap, where the hammer strikes a copper cap containing powder to produce the ignition flash. In good condition, these guns are valuable collectors' pieces. But others which are dirty or damaged can often be cleaned and restored by amateurs.

Cast-metal parts and wooden blanks, which can be shaped to replace damaged or missing stocks, can be obtained from specialist suppliers.

Even old gunpowder explodes, so be sure that any gun being repaired is not loaded. Insert the ramrod, or a length of wood, into the barrel to check if there is any obstruction. If there is, remove it with a modern shotgun cleaning rod which has a screw tip, or use an ordinary steel screw soldered to a piece of stiff wire. Screw the rod gently into the obstruction and pull it out like a cork. Wash the barrel repeatedly with hot water and dry it. To dismantle the gun, first half-cock it, then remove the screw which holds the cock (in the flintlock) or the hammer (in the percussion type) and slide it off.

Unscrew the pan-cover pivot and screw securing the spring beneath the pan: remove the parts. Unscrew the holding bolts or screws and remove the lock-plate. Several screwdrivers are needed: the blade must fit each screw slot exactly so as not to burr the screw. If the screws are hard to move, apply penetrating oil. To dismantle a flintlock mechanism, loosen the four screws which hold the mainspring, sear, sear spring and the bridle. Compress the mainspring (in a small hand vice if necessary), take out the spring screw and remove the spring. The pin at the rear of the mainspring engages in the lock-plate, and the other end of the spring engages in the toe of the tumbler. Take out other loosened screws and all will come apart.

Remove rust with fine emery paper or powder. Take care to remove all abrasive powder. Smear all parts with petroleum jelly and reassemble. Press the tumbler down to the fired position so that the end of the mainspring goes over it. Put the cock on and pull it back to the half-cocked position so that the tumbler toe compresses the mainspring. Refit the rest of the pieces in reverse order to removal.

To clean the barrel, first remove it from the stock. A metal extension of the barrel—the tang—runs into the stock. Remove the tang screws and any retaining bands or pins. The trigger guard, butt cap and ramrod pipes are screwed or pinned and must be removed with care. If screws do not yield to penetrating oil, leave them alone—it is an expert's job to drill them out.

Clean barrels and other metal parts with a mixture of oil and paraffin. Repolish all parts with progressively finer abrasives; finish with jewellers' emery or crocus paper.

Gun barrels may have been blued to prevent rust. Special bluing fluids can be bought from gunsmiths. To avoid leaving fingerprints, which cause rusting, jam a piece of wood into the barrel and hold the gun by it.

Clean the stock with steel wool and linseed oil. If it is broken, mend with epoxy resin (see p. 694) mixed to a paste with matching stained sawdust. To replace a large piece of wood, take a matching piece of old wood and carve it to fit. Dowel and glue it into place. Remove dents in the stock by steaming (see p. 297). If the stock is infested with woodworm, treat with an insecticide (see p. 186). If a stock is riddled with worm, or crumbling, dip it into synthetic resin, or inject resin into the holes with a syringe. Rub the stock thoroughly with raw linseed oil to preserve the wood and improve its colour and gloss.

Powder flasks were made in hundreds of designs and several materials. But the majority are pear-shaped and made of tin, brass or Britannia metal (see p. 212).

Metal powder flasks were usually made in halves soldered together. If the soldered seam has parted, find out which alloy the flask is made of before trying to re-solder it (see p. 692). A simple test is to put a few drops of water in a cup and carefully add an equal number of drops of nitric acid, obtainable from a chemist. Put a drop of this solution on the metal to reveal the colour. Red-brown indicates bronze; yellow and yellow-red, brass; dark grey, pewter; and bright silver-grey, Britannia metal.

To polish the flask, use the technique appropriate to the material it is made of. Never use a rag buffing wheel, which could easily damage the design.

To remove the cap and spring, unscrew it, or take out the retaining screws. If the screws are stiff, apply penetrating oil. If they still do not move, knock them inwards with a punch. Press the hole back to size from inside, and use a slightly larger screw when replacing the cap. Do not attempt to knock out dents before soldering, as this can distort the two halves and they may no longer match.

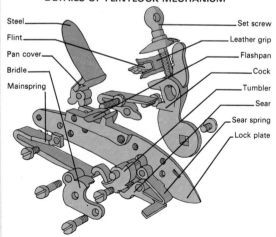

DETAILS OF FLINTLOCK MECHANISM

Steel
Flint
Pan cover
Bridle
Mainspring

Set screw
Leather grip
Flashpan
Cock
Tumbler
Sear
Sear spring
Lock plate

Single-barrelled flintlock sporting gun, made in Denmark, mid-18th century

Heavy-percussion holster pistol. British cavalry issue, 1853

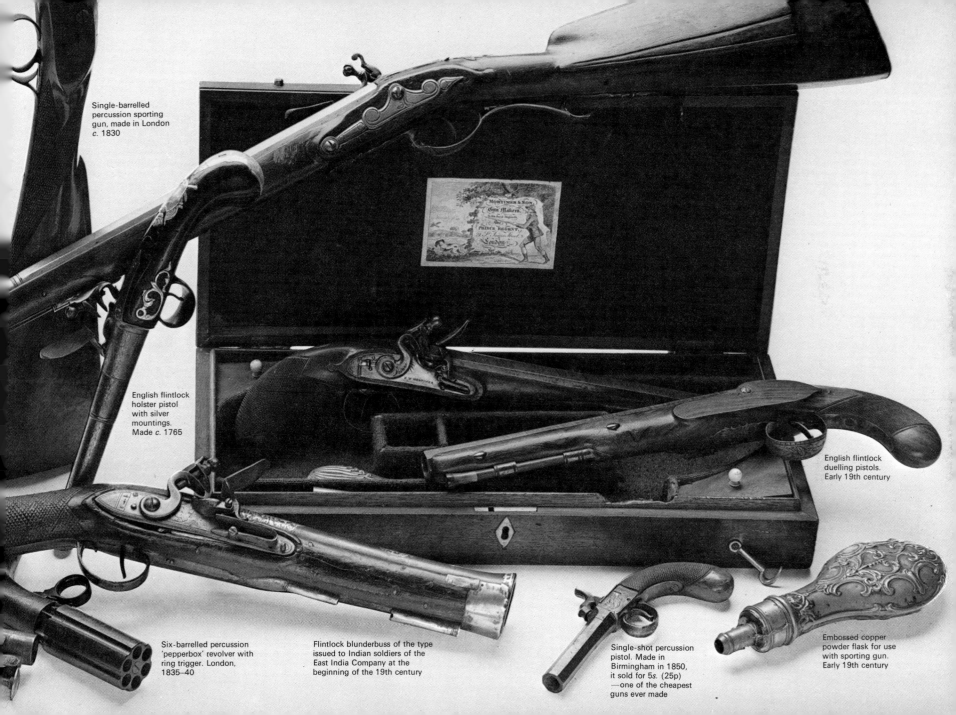

Single-barrelled percussion sporting gun, made in London c. 1830

English flintlock holster pistol with silver mountings. Made c. 1765

English flintlock duelling pistols. Early 19th century

Six-barrelled percussion 'pepperbox' revolver with ring trigger. London, 1835–40

Flintlock blunderbuss of the type issued to Indian soldiers of the East India Company at the beginning of the 19th century

Single-shot percussion pistol. Made in Birmingham in 1850, it sold for 5s. (25p) —one of the cheapest guns ever made

Embossed copper powder flask for use with sporting gun. Early 19th century

Leather

Leather can keep its looks and its suppleness for years, as long as it is treated regularly—say, every month or so. It can even improve with age. But if it is neglected, it is likely to become hard and look powdery. Even leather in this condition, however, can be revitalised—provided that it is not allowed to deteriorate for very long.

Before attempting any treatment, test the leather for colour fastness. Dampen a cloth in warm water, rub on some soap and wipe the leather. Do not soak the leather: pieces which have been stuck together may come apart. If no colour is removed, wipe on a mixture of 3 parts castor oil and 2 parts surgical spirit. Leave for 24 hours, then wipe with castor oil.

If the leather is thick and stiff, work in saddle soap or a hide cream with a soft brush or sponge. Treat daily until the leather becomes supple again.

If leather is stained, rub it with a soft rag dipped in white spirit or petrol—but do not use too much and do not rub too hard, or the leather may become discoloured. If there is a mould on the leather, treat it with a liquid fungicide, obtainable from a leather dealer or do-it-yourself shop. Leather which has been artificially coloured should be finished after cleaning with leather stain, obtainable from craft shops. Try some out on a corner that does not show, to test that the colour matches. To restore colour which has been rubbed off or scratched, retouch by stippling new stain with the tip of a watercolour brush. Make sure that only the bad spot and not the surrounding leather is dyed. If large areas need to be brightened, rub with leather polish in a matching colour.

Always finish leather work by polishing with a good wax dressing or cream on a soft cloth. Treat the leather about once a month with good-quality dressing.

To restick a leather desk top or box covering, use Scotch glue or a urea formaldehyde adhesive (see p. 694). If such coverings need treating in any way, carry out the work after they have been stuck down. Dressing applied before sticking may soak through the leather and prevent proper adhesion.

Cutting a new leather desk top

A new leather desk top can be cut from hide, skiver (made from sheepskin) or morocco. Cut a paper template to ensure a correct fit. When the leather is cut, lightly chamfer underneath its edges with a very sharp knife to ensure that they will not protrude above the surrounding wood. Peel off the old leather from the wood and scrape all old glue from the desk top with a knife. Rub with glass-paper until the surface is completely clean and smooth.

Coat both the new piece of leather and the base with glue. Lay one long edge of the new leather in position on the desk and insert a large sheet of greaseproof paper between the rest of the leather and the base. Press the leather gradually into place and withdraw the greaseproof a little at a time. Smooth with a cloth pad to remove air bubbles.

To re-cover a shaped object—for example, a leather handle—first peel off the old leather and remove all glue from the object. Make a paper pattern of the piece to be covered (if possible use the old removed piece as a guide) and cut a new piece of leather. Chamfer the joining edges underneath to avoid a ridge when they are stuck down.

Soak the new leather in water overnight, then smooth it into place round the object. Trim off any surplus edges. Bind it into place with a wide tape and leave it for 24 hours to dry.

When the binding is removed, the leather will have dried into the exact shape required. Fix with adhesive.

Sheraton writing table of 1770, with tooled-leather writing surface

RENEWING A DESK TOP

1 Cut leather to shape; lay it face down, edge to edge with work surface. Make a bevel cut to the edge

Greaseproof paper

2 Spread adhesive on wood and underside of leather. Lay greaseproof paper between. Match front edges of leather and table; gradually withdraw paper and press down leather

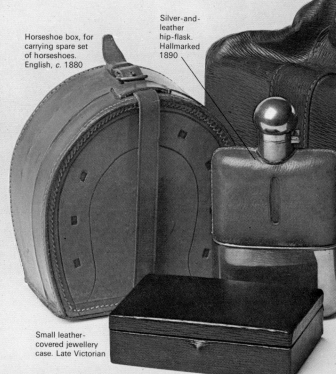
Horseshoe box, for carrying spare set of horseshoes. English, c. 1880

Silver-and-leather hip-flask. Hallmarked 1890

Small leather-covered jewellery case. Late Victorian

Leather water bottle. Spanish, early 19th century

Bull-whip—a long, heavy whip used by drovers to crack over the heads of their cattle. Victorian

Riding whip. 1890

Water bucket decorated with coat of arms. Early Victorian

Small leather grip—possibly a doctor's bag. Victorian

Mexican leather stirrups. Early 19th century

PART 3

AROUND THE HOME

Aquariums

General maintenance

A properly maintained home aquarium should not need a major clean-up more frequently than every other year; but as a weekly routine, remove any leaves that have fallen from the plants, wipe the inside of the glass and replace water lost by evaporation—usually about ½ in. (13 mm) a week. Disconnect electrical components from the mains before carrying out maintenance or adjustments.

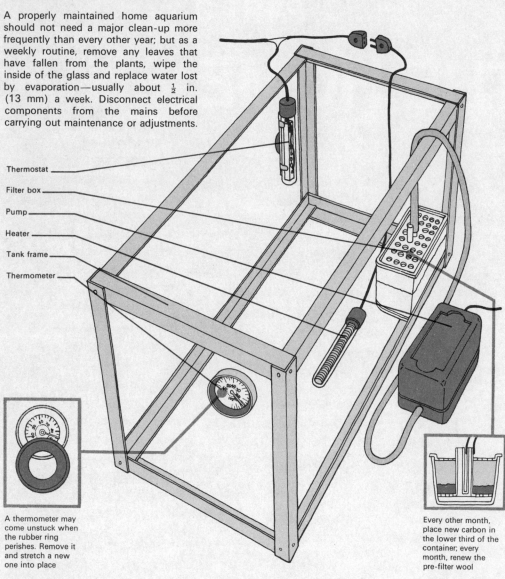

Thermostat

Filter box

Pump

Heater

Tank frame

Thermometer

A thermometer may come unstuck when the rubber ring perishes. Remove it and stretch a new one into place

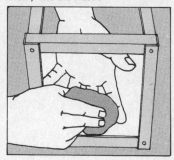

Every other month, place new carbon in the lower third of the container; every month, renew the pre-filter wool

Replacing broken glass

Bed the new glass on to glazing mastic: this is more suitable than putty as it has a higher resistance to water pressure. Knead the mastic first, then apply it liberally.

When bedding-in new aquarium glass, make sure that there are no gaps or air bubbles in the mastic and that it has an even thickness on all sides. Finish the repair with waterproofing adhesive which, like the mastic, is obtainable at any shop selling aquarium equipment.

Materials: matching glass (cut to size); waterproofing adhesive; glazing mastic. Tool: putty knife.

1 Remove the broken glass and clean the framework. With the tank up-ended, press the mastic in position

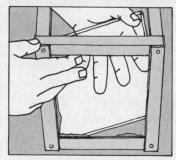

2 Position the new piece of glass in the frame so that it beds tightly and evenly into the mastic

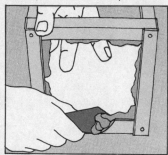

3 Trim off the surplus mastic from both sides of the glass. Avoid digging it out from underneath the glass

4 Clean the glass and wipe round the trimmed mastic, supporting the glass on the inside to prevent dislodging

5 Spread adhesive along the glass edges inside the tank. Allow 12–48 hours to dry, according to the adhesive

Adjusting a faulty thermostat

A thermostat controls the water temperature by means of make-and-break contact points. As the heater warms the water, expansion of a bi-metal strip causes the points to part, which switches the heater off. Contraction brings the points together, switching the heater on. A thermostat will fail if the points become welded together or do not make contact.

Welded points can be levered apart, but adjustment of points which remain open, for which a small screw is provided, needs professional attention, otherwise the temperature setting may not be accurate. Some dealers will adjust and reset thermostats, but it is often more satisfactory to replace a faulty thermostat with a completely new unit.

Tools: small screwdriver; fine file.

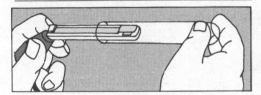

1 Push back the glass tube protective cap, unscrew the rubber bung, and remove the thermostat

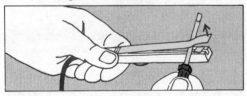

2 If the points are welded together, gently lever up the metal strip with a small screwdriver. Rub the contact surfaces with a fine file or emery paper. If an interference suppressor is included in the circuit, this may have failed and caused the weld. Replace the suppressor

3 Replace the thermostat in the tube, screw home the rubber bung, and put the glass tube protective cap back in place

Replacing a pump diaphragm

A noisy vibrator air-pump indicates that the rubber diaphragm has become worn and needs replacing with a new one. When fitting a new diaphragm, together with the circular spring clip holding it in position, ensure that the rubber is not perforated or folded. Use pliers to remove and replace the main holding nut, which should be only moderately tight.

Materials: new rubber diaphragm.
Tools: screwdriver; pliers; spanner to fit inner nut.

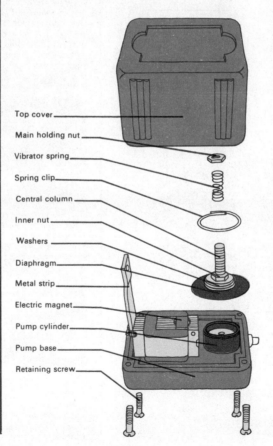

Top cover
Main holding nut
Vibrator spring
Spring clip
Central column
Inner nut
Washers
Diaphragm
Metal strip
Electric magnet
Pump cylinder
Pump base
Retaining screw

1 Remove the four screws securing the cover of the vibrator air pump and take off the cover

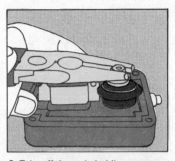

2 Take off the main holding nut, carefully lever up the metal strip and remove the vibrator spring

3 Lift up the metal strip and carefully lever off the spring that holds the diaphragm in position

4 Remove the worn diaphragm and its assembly of central column, washers and retaining nut

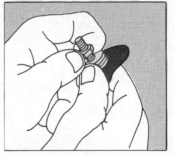

5 Unscrew the inner nut on the central column and remove the top spacing washers and the old diaphragm

6 Ensure that the lower washers are in position on the column. Fit the new diaphragm, washers and inner nut

Baskets

Materials and tools

All baskets made of cane should be washed and scrubbed regularly in warm water. Cane kept moist is stronger and more supple than if it is allowed to dry out. But if any part of the cane does break off, a basket can usually be repaired with matching cane.

The only exception is when the damage is caused by woodworm. Even if the broken part could be replaced, it is advisable to burn the basket, rather than allow the woodworm to spread elsewhere in the house.

Two useful basketwork repair tools are the bradawl and the bodkin, either of which can be used to make space for a cane during weaving.

Basket cane is available in 15 sizes from many large stores and handicraft dealers. The thinnest is size 1; the thickest size 15. When trying to obtain replacement cane, it is always advisable to take the damaged basket to the shop to match it exactly.

Heavy-duty or industrial baskets may require willow, which is thicker and shinier, instead of cane. If in doubt, get a dealer's advice.

Before starting a repair, it is important to get the cane supple and workable by soaking it in lukewarm water for 10–15 minutes. The thicker sizes of cane, and any that has already been lacquered, should be left in the water for at least an hour before being used.

Some baskets are made of plastic-covered cane. This, too, is generally available at handicraft shops.

Materials: cane to match the basket.
Tools: sharp knife; bodkin or bradawl; pincers.

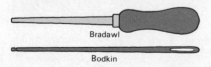

Bradawl

Bodkin

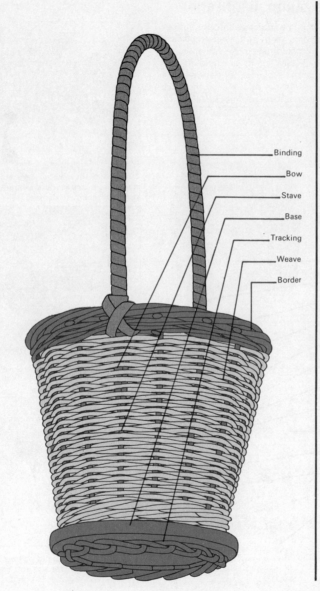

Binding

Bow

Stave

Base

Tracking

Weave

Border

Renewing a handle and binding

The handle of a basket is made from two different types of cane. It derives its strength and its shape from a stout cane, called the bow; wound round the bow is a binding cane, called lapping, which gives a more decorative finish and secures the bow to the basket. This lapping, which is available in several thicknesses, is made by splitting ordinary cane down the middle and flattening it.

Some baskets may have a plastic binder instead. Plastic can also be used to replace the original cane lapping if a more decorative finish is wanted. Make sure to obtain enough material before starting the repair.

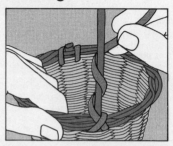

1 Strip off the old binding, pulling its ends from the weave on both sides. Check the length needed, allowing an extra few inches for working

2 Examine the bow. If it is broken or cracked, remove it. Use a pair of pincers to pull out a broken stub. Soak a new bow for at least an hour

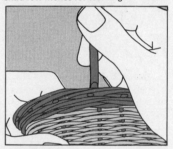

3 Sharpen the end of the new bow. Push one end through the border and depress it about 2 in. (50 mm) next to the stave

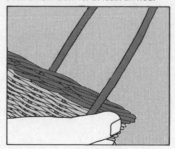

4 Bend the bow to the correct height and shape for the handle. If it cracks, secure another length of cane and soak it for longer to make it supple

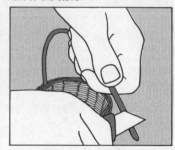

5 Cut the bow to length, allowing about 2 in. (50 mm) to push into the weave. Cut the free end to a point, the cut face outwards *(continued)*

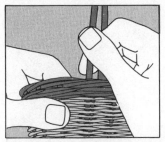

6 Push the second end into the border directly opposite the first. Push it about 2 in. (50 mm) down into the weave, against a stave

7 Push the binding in left of the bow. Cross the other end down, outside, right of bow. Push its end in below the third row of cane

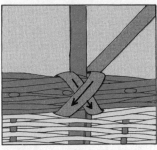
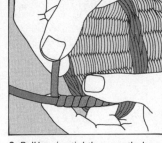

8 Pull the binding tightly up inside the basket, over the border and across the outside to the left of the bow. Push in below third row of cane

9 Pull lapping tightly across the bow. Starting close to the border, wind the lapping round the bow, its edges touching but not overlapping

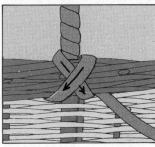
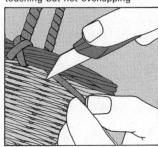

10 At the other end, take the lapping down across the outside of the bow and weave it through the basket as shown above

11 Inside, cross the lapping over to the other side of the bow and push it out against the side of the first stave. Cut it evenly at the stave

Repairing a hole in the weave

If the side of a basket is damaged, first cut out all the cracked and broken cane to determine exactly the size of the hole. It is not advisable to try to mend a hole across more than eight staves. Although repairs over a wide area may seem sound, the structure and strength of the basket are usually weakened and it is best discarded.

Make sure the new cane matches the existing cane in the basket in size and colour.

Cane damages easily when being worked. Keep it moist and taut. Do not jerk it, but press it down firmly to make sure that the repaired area is not bumpy or uneven when finished.

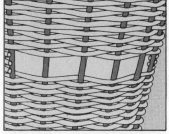
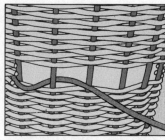

1 Undo the damaged pieces of cane and cut each one off at the centre of the nearest stave. Make sure that the ends rest on the staves

2 After soaking the cane, insert an end between the cut strand and the stave on one side. Leave a 2 in. (50 mm) tail inside and weave across the hole

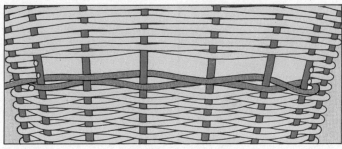
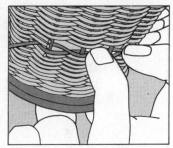

3 Gently bend the cane round the stave at the opposite edge of the hole and weave in the other direction above the preceding row. The weave of adjacent rows must alternate: one in front of a stave, the other behind it. Press the cane down frequently and keep the rows close together

4 At the end of each row, gently pull the cane to make sure that it is tightly woven. Take care, however, not to break the cane or distort the staves

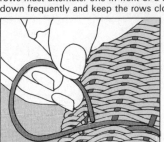
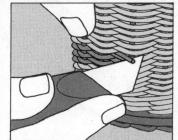
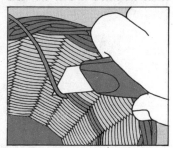

5 If the cane is too short, trim it after passing over an end stave. Start a row above it, and from behind that stave, with the new piece

6 Continue weaving in the new cane until the hole is filled. At the end of the last row, cut the cane diagonally where it meets the stave

7 Use a sharp knife to cut off the surplus tail or tails where new cane was started. Make the cuts flush with the original weave

Baskets

Replacing a stave or border

On most baskets the cane used for the upright staves is bent at the top and woven round to form the border. If, therefore, either the border or a stave is damaged, both parts need repair.

Make sure that the new cane is woven round the correct number of staves to give the same pattern as the existing border weave.

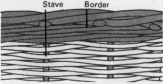

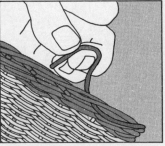

1 Find where the broken stave is woven into the border. Prise it up with a knife to free the broken end

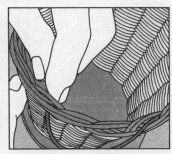

2 Remove the broken section. Cut back its stave to be at least 2 in. (50 mm) short of the border

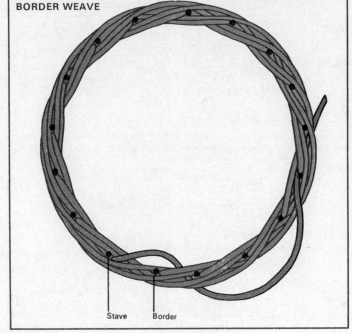

BORDER WEAVE

Stave Border

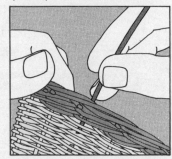

3 Sharpen a new cane and push it down through the weave to sit on top of the remaining piece of stave

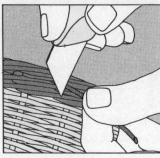

5 Make sure that the repair finishes against an upright and cut off the surplus piece of new cane

4 Bend the cane at the border. Check the pattern and count the number of staves between each weave. Then thread in the new piece, first one way and then another, making sure that the pattern is not distorted

Repairing broken tracking

The bottom ends of basket staves are woven underneath the base into a border, called tracking. This is the part most likely to be damaged by constant contact with rough surfaces. The principle is the same as for dealing with a broken top border: both the tracking and part of the stave affected have to be replaced.

1 Unwind the broken cane from the tracking and pull out its upright piece if the stave is broken

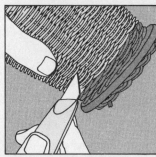

2 If the stave is unbroken in the weave, cut it with a sharp knife about 2 in. (50 mm) from the basket base

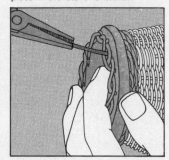

3 Use a pair of pincers to grip the stub of the stave below the base and pull out the cut section of stave

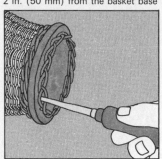

4 Push through the tracking weave with a bodkin or bradawl, to make room for the new cane

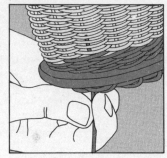

5 Sharpen the new cane and push it through the tracking until it meets the remaining stave *(continued)*

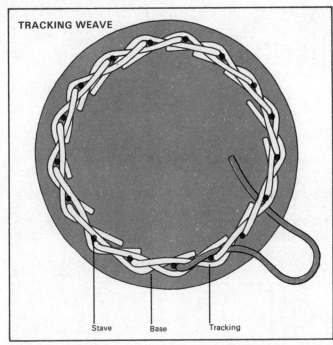

TRACKING WEAVE

Stave   Base   Tracking

6 Carefully bend the cane, as close to the base as possible. Study the pattern of the existing tracking and make sure that the new piece of cane is woven round the correct number of staves to maintain the design

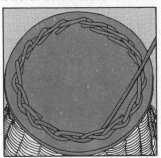

7 When enough cane has been woven, pull it tightly, but take care not to distort the shape

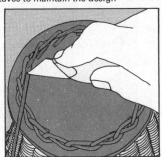

8 Make sure that the repair finishes against a stave and cut off the surplus cane at the upright

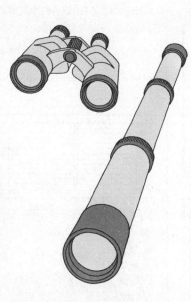

Binoculars should be cleaned only on the outside. Do not try to dismantle them to clean or repair the interiors. Telescope tubes can be removed and cleaned, but the lenses should not be taken out.

Clean the telescope or binocular casing with a clean, dry cloth: never use a cleaning fluid on the casing. Remove dust from the outer surface of a lens with cotton wool or a soft brush, then clean it with a recommended cleaning cloth, obtainable from a photographic dealer. Methylated spirit can be used to remove stubborn lens marks, but keep the cloth clean the whole time; a small speck of dust can scratch the lens.

Protect telescopes and binoculars from dust and damp by storing them always in their cases. If they are to be stored for a long period, wrap the case in polythene and make the package as airtight as possible.

Replacing a telescope felt

Inside each tube of a telescope is a pad of felt or cardboard wound round to ensure that when the telescope is extended it does not wobble. With considerable use, the pad is likely to become compressed, and it should be replaced with a new one. If cardboard is used to replace the pad, do not stick it to the tube. Adhesive is used only with felt pads.

It is advisable to renew all the pads on a telescope at the same time, even if only one is thin enough to require immediate attention.

Materials: cardboard or felt.
Tools: scissors; pencil; knife.

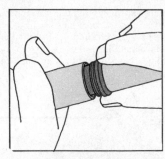

1 To remove a worn pad, unscrew the draw-tube stop-ring from the end of the next-larger tube

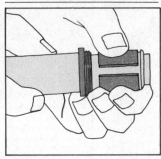

2 Pull out the tube and remove the pad at the end. Felt may have to be loosened with a knife

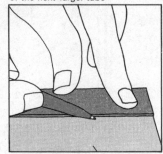

3 Mark the shape of the pad on new cardboard or felt. It should be thicker than the old pad

4 Cut out the new pad and bend it in position against the ridge at the end of the tube

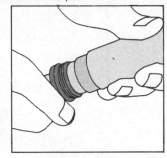

5 Reassemble the telescope and tighten the stop-ring. Check that the tube slides smoothly

Blinds Venetian blinds

Maintenance and adjustment

Venetian blinds require no lubrication, but it is important to make sure that the tilt mechanism and the cord lock in the head rail are kept clean. Make sure that the cords are replaced as soon as they show signs of fraying. Replacement is more difficult if they break.

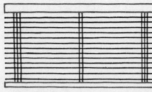

Tilt cord Bend the middle of the new tilt cord round the ratchet, and push its ends under the slots

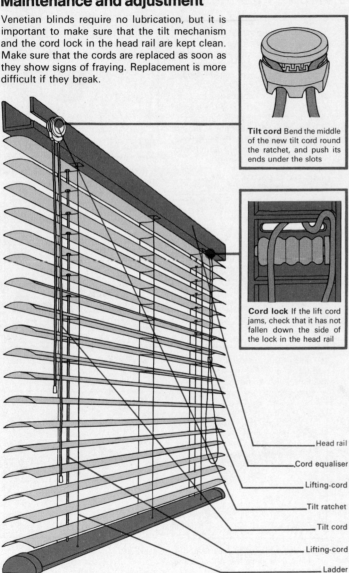

Cord lock If the lift cord jams, check that it has not fallen down the side of the lock in the head rail

Head rail
Cord equaliser
Lifting-cord
Tilt ratchet
Tilt cord
Lifting-cord
Ladder

Cleaning and replacing slats

The slats of a venetian blind should be removed occasionally and then sponged with warm water and detergent. Replace distorted slats.

Materials: slats as needed; rag, water and detergent.
Tool: screwdriver.

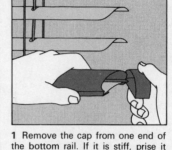

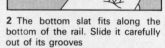

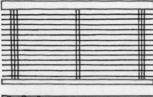

1 Remove the cap from one end of the bottom rail. If it is stiff, prise it off with a screwdriver

2 The bottom slat fits along the bottom of the rail. Slide it carefully out of its grooves

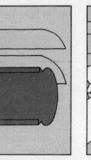

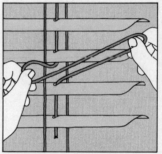

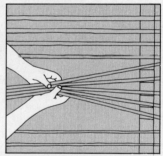

3 Undo the knot in the end of the lifting-cord at both ends of the rail. Do not untie the ladder knots

4 Pull both lengths of the lifting-cord out of the slats. Leave them hanging loosely from the head rail

5 Grip several slats together in the centre of the blind. Pull them down gently out of the ladders

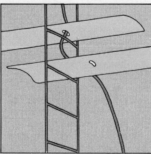

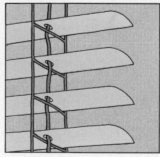

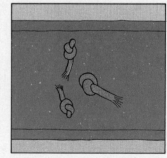

6 After cleaning, replace each slat separately. Thread the lifting-cord through each slat as it is fitted

7 Make sure that the lifting-cord is woven down alternate sides of the rungs of the ladders

8 Knot both ends of the cord and let the blind down. If it is not straight, readjust the equaliser

Renewing a frayed lifting-cord

A frayed lifting-cord can be replaced without removing the venetian blind from the window. Most have two cords, the larger ones sometimes three.

Materials: cord to fit blind; adhesive tape.
Tool: scissors.

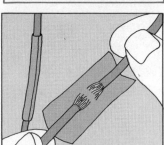

3 Butt the ends of the new cord to the cut ends of the old. Secure with adhesive tape

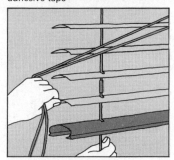

6 At the far side, hold the loop of the cord tightly and pull the cords through the bottom rail

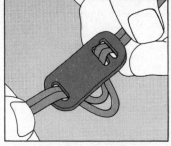

1 Slip the end of the lifting-cord out of the cord equaliser, which holds it evenly at the side of the blind

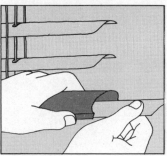

4 Remove the cap from one end of the bottom rail and slide the bottom slat out of its groove in the rail

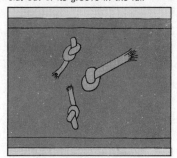

7 As each cord joint is pulled through the bottom rail, separate the old and new pieces and knot the cord

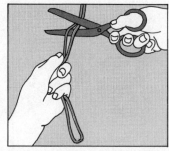

2 Hold the loop in one hand and cut through both pieces of cord, about 6 in. (150 mm) away from the loop

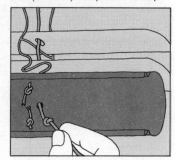

5 Release the lock, allow the blind to fall and draw the old and new pieces through the blind

8 Make sure that the blind is hanging straight. Hold the cord evenly and fit the loop through the equaliser

REPLACING A BROKEN CORD

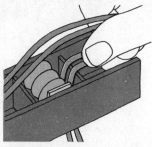

1 When a cord breaks, unknot the ends and pull the cord through the head rail

2 Feed the ends of the new cord up through the slot at the end of the head rail and over the cord lock

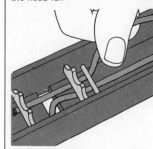

3 Pull the ends along the head rail and push one down the first cord slot. Take the other along the rail

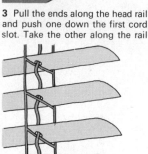

5 Open the blind and thread the cord through the slats. Weave round the ladder

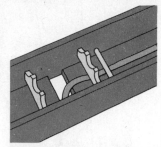

4 Pull the second end along the length of the head rail and push it down through the far slot

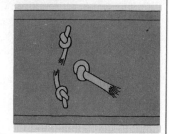

6 If there is a third cord, thread it down the centre slot and tie each cord end at the bottom rail

Blinds Roller blinds

Maintenance and adjustment

When a roller blind does not wind or stay in position correctly, it is probably because the ratchet is not properly tensioned. If no adjustment can be made, fit a new ratchet.

Materials: ratchet if needed.
Tools: hammer; pliers; screwdriver.

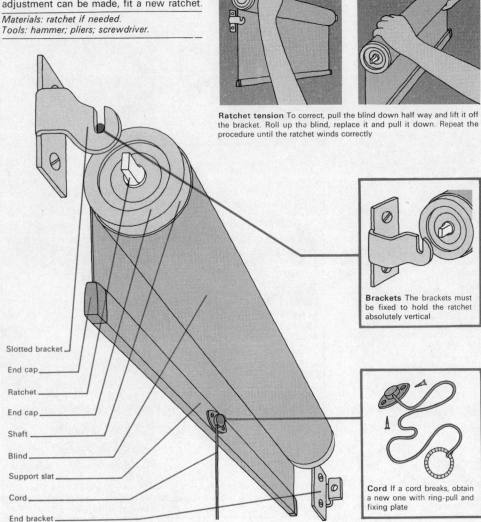

Ratchet tension To correct, pull the blind down half way and lift it off the bracket. Roll up the blind, replace it and pull it down. Repeat the procedure until the ratchet winds correctly

Brackets The brackets must be fixed to hold the ratchet absolutely vertical

Slotted bracket
End cap
Ratchet
End cap
Shaft
Blind
Support slat
Cord
End bracket

Cord If a cord breaks, obtain a new one with ring-pull and fixing plate

Fitting new material

Blind cloths are available from specialist dealers and large stores. Measure the width of the blind roller, and obtain a new blind 1 in. (25 mm) narrower. Make sure that it is long enough to cover the full length of the window.

The blind is usually stapled to the roller. If the staples are damaged when they are removed, and a suitable stapler is not available, tacks can be used to hold the new blind. But to avoid damage to the wood and the spring inside, make sure that the tacks are no longer than $\frac{1}{8}$ in. (3 mm).

Materials: tacks; blind cloth; staples.
Tools: hammer; screwdriver; pliers.

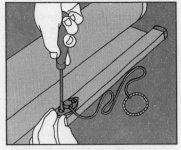

1 Take the blind off its brackets. Unscrew the cord fixture from the slat at the bottom of the blind

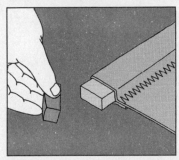

2 Pull the end caps from the support slat. If they are damaged, obtain replacements to fit the slat

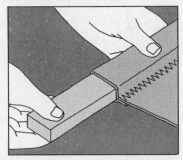

3 Slide the support slat out of the blind and fit it into the bottom of the new material. Replace the caps

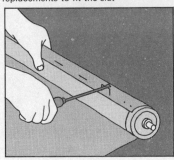

4 Prise the staples out of the roller gently, to avoid damaging the wood, and discard the blind

5 Hold the new blind evenly $\frac{3}{8}$ in. (10 mm) from the line on the roller. Staple or tack, then tension the blind

Blowlamps

Maintenance and fault-finding

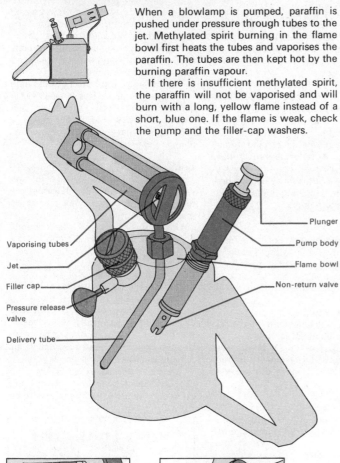

When a blowlamp is pumped, paraffin is pushed under pressure through tubes to the jet. Methylated spirit burning in the flame bowl first heats the tubes and vaporises the paraffin. The tubes are then kept hot by the burning paraffin vapour.

If there is insufficient methylated spirit, the paraffin will not be vaporised and will burn with a long, yellow flame instead of a short, blue one. If the flame is weak, check the pump and the filler-cap washers.

Plunger
Pump body
Flame bowl
Non-return valve

Vaporising tubes
Jet
Filler cap
Pressure release valve
Delivery tube

Jet If the flame splutters, the jet in the nozzle is obstructed. Clean it with a jet pricker

Filler cap If the flame is weak, check the filler-cap washer and renew it if it is worn

Fitting a pump washer

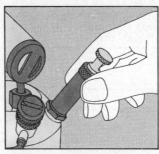

1 Unscrew the knurled cap on the top of the pump body. If it is tight, undo it with a spanner or pliers

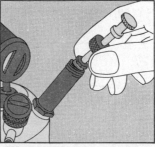

2 Carefully withdraw the plunger assembly from the pump. Do not force or lever the plunger shaft

3 To protect the shaft of the plunger assembly, wind on a few turns of plastic insulating tape

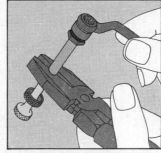

4 Grip the taped section with pliers and undo the shaft-retaining nut. Remove the washer assembly

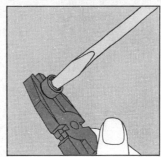

5 Holding the nut of the washer assembly firmly with pliers, use a screwdriver to undo the screw

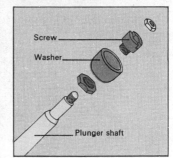

Screw
Washer
Plunger shaft

6 Soak the new pump washer in oil. Reassemble and remove the plastic insulating tape

Checking a valve

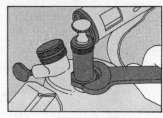

1 Use an open spanner to undo the nut securing the pump assembly

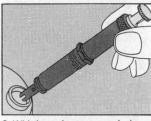

2 Withdraw the pump and plunger assembly from the blowlamp

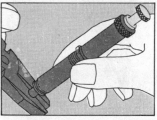

3 Unscrew the valve housing with pliers. Turn it anti-clockwise

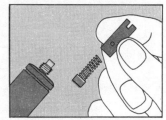

4 Lift out the spring and valve. If in poor condition, renew them

Books

The scope for repairs

Many simple book repairs can be attempted by an amateur—provided the book is still in reasonably sound condition. But if the stitching that holds the sections together has broken, and the book is sufficiently valuable to warrant the expense, get it repaired by a professional book repairer.

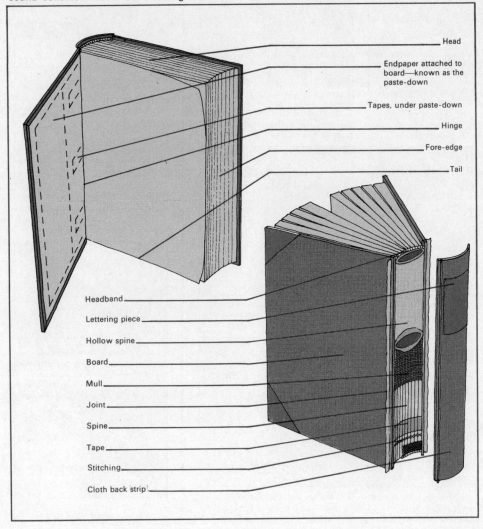

Head

Endpaper attached to board—known as the paste-down

Tapes, under paste-down

Hinge

Fore-edge

Tail

Headband
Lettering piece
Hollow spine
Board
Mull
Joint
Spine
Tape
Stitching
Cloth back strip

Caring for books

Before opening a book that has been standing for some time, blow along the head to remove any dust that may have settled on it. If necessary, use a soft cloth to brush away loose dust from the edges of the cover.

Surface dirt on the pages can be removed with a soft india-rubber. Use it gently, to avoid tearing the paper.

Fresh bread is also useful for removing dirt. Knead the bread into a ball and rub it gently over the paper, picking up any dirt as you go. Make sure that all traces of bread are removed from the pages or the growth of mould will be encouraged. Ingrained dirt, including thumb-marks, is impossible to remove.

Mould
This can be removed by brushing with a soft cloth—but the discoloration of paper affected by mould is permanent. Once the cause of the trouble has been removed, there is rarely a recurrence.

Serious damage
The more serious types of page damage —such as children's scribbling, damp and water stains—are impossible to treat at home. If the value of the book warrants treatment, leave the repair to an expert.

Handling a book
Never open a valuable book quickly or force the covers back to make it lie flat: this may break the spine. When turning the pages, smooth them outwards from the hinge.

Materials for repairs
An ideal adhesive is Resemul Emulsion 8101. If it is unobtainable, use a suitable PVA adhesive (see p. 694).

Also needed are: waste paper for pasting on (old newspapers are ideal); several sheets of waxed paper—the sort found in cereal packets, not grease-proof paper; strong brown paper of the type used for wrapping parcels; strong white or coloured paper for use as end-papers—good typing paper is ideal; and tissue paper for page repairs.

For covering, a proper book-binding cloth must be used. This is available in various colours and textures to suit individual tastes. For spine repairs a stiff, open-weave material, known as mull, is necessary.

Adhesive tape
Do not use self-adhesive tape for any type of book repair. The glue from the tape stains the paper and tends to make it brittle.

Once this happens, the original appearance cannot be restored.

Tools
Those needed to carry out a variety of repairs include: a steel ruler; a sharp knife with replaceable blades (a modelling knife, or a scalpel of the type available from art stores, is ideal); two adhesive brushes—a 1 in. (25 mm) paintbrush and a small watercolour brush; a plastic set square; a pair of scissors.

Bone folders can be bought, or one shaped from a bone letter-opener will be found suitable for the work to be carried out.

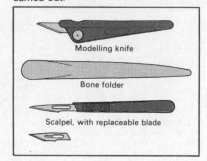

Modelling knife

Bone folder

Scalpel, with replaceable blade

Books Covers

Repairing damaged corners

Whether damaged corners on a book can be repaired depends on the quality of the binding. It is not possible, for example, to restore the corner of a paperback or cardboard cover; but when the cover is a board with a cloth covering, the corners can be restored.

It may be possible simply to stick down loose cloth. But if some of the cloth is torn away, make a more substantial repair by removing the old cloth corner and fitting a new one. To improve the appearance of the repair work, renew all four corners, even though only one is damaged. Use a material similar to that on the existing binding, but it is preferable to choose a contrasting colour.

If the corner of a board cannot be successfully repaired with adhesive, renew the entire cover (see p. 254).

REPAIRING A FRAYED CORNER

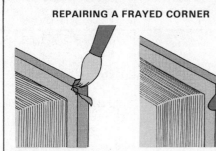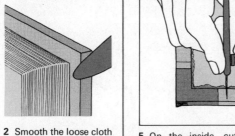

1 If the board itself is not damaged, brush a little adhesive on the corner and under the loose cloth

2 Smooth the loose cloth over the corner and press it with a bone folder. Hold it until it sticks

RESTORING A SPLIT CORNER

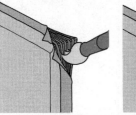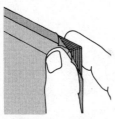

1 If the corner of the board is split, soak it with adhesive. Work adhesive with the fingers between the separated layers

2 Press the separations firmly together. Smooth the cloth over the board with a folder and hold it until it sticks

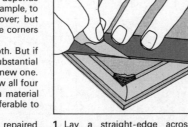

1 Lay a straight-edge across the corner to form an equal-sided triangle. Cut through the cloth, but take care not to cut and damage the board

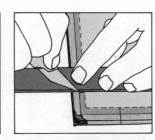

2 Open the cover of the book and continue the cuts over the edges of the board. Cut straight down to the edge of the cloth under the paste-down

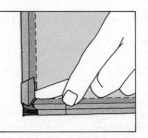

3 Cut along the inside edges of the cloth at the corner on the inside of the board and prise the cut piece up from the board with the folder

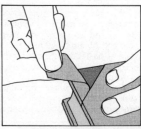

4 On the outside, peel off and retain for size the old corner. On the inside, scrape away the paste-down where it has been fixed over the turned-in cloth

5 On the inside, cut through the cloth, $\frac{1}{2}$ in. (13 mm) from the bared section, from the edge of the board to the edge of the cloth

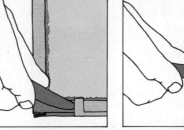

6 Cut along the cloth edge and carefully prise up the two $\frac{1}{2}$ in. (13 mm) tabs with the bone folder. Do not remove the tabs. Close the cover

7 Run the folder under the edge of the remaining cloth on the front of the board. Raise a strip $\frac{1}{2}$ in. (13 mm) deep and scrape it clean with a knife

8 Check the corner of the board. If it has separated, rub adhesive between its layers and hold the corner firmly until the layers are stuck together

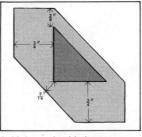

9 Make a six-sided paper template, as shown, round the removed corner cloth. Cut a new cloth corner to match the weave of the existing binding

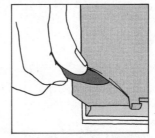

10 Spread adhesive on the bare board, under the loose cloth and on the back of the new corner cloth. Push the new cloth under the loose edge

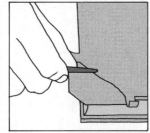

11 Press down the edge of the old cloth. Check the position of the new corner piece and rub it down carefully to stick it firmly into place

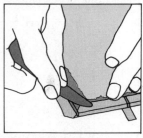

12 Open the cover and press the new cloth over the edges. Glue and fold down the two tabs. Renew the other corners. Fit new endpapers (see p. 256)

Books Covers

Fitting a new cover

If a hardback book cover is so badly damaged that it cannot be repaired by renewing the corners or the joints, remove the entire binding and fit a new one. Measure the book before starting the work and obtain cover material, a piece of mull and, if necessary, a piece of pasteboard to make replacement boards. The whole repair takes at least two days, to allow for drying. Do not try to cut down on the time.

It is advisable when stripping off the old covers to examine the book carefully in stages to see how it was assembled so that the same procedure can be followed.

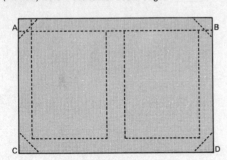

MARKING OUT THE COVER MATERIAL

1 Lay the new cloth flat, its underside upwards. Draw a line AB, $\frac{1}{2}$ in. (13 mm) from the top edge. Position one board (1) against AB, $\frac{1}{2}$ in. (13 mm) in from the left edge. Draw round the board. Place the second board (2) on AB, the width of the spine plus $\frac{3}{8}$ in. (10 mm) from (1). Draw round it. Draw a line $\frac{1}{2}$ in. (13 mm) from (2), from the top to the bottom of the cloth. Draw line CD $\frac{1}{2}$ in. (13 mm) below the lower board edges

2 Cut along line CD and along the line from D to the top of the cloth. Trim the corners $\frac{3}{16}$ in. (5 mm) from the board corners

1 Raise each cover in turn at right angles to the book. Cut along both joints to remove the back strip

2 Scrape off any paper or mull left on the spine. Do not cut the stitching. Coat with adhesive and leave for 24 hours

3 Tear out the free endpapers at front and back of the book. If the spine is damaged take the book to an expert

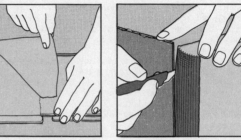

4 Remove and strip the boards. If damaged, cut new ones of the same size and thickness from a piece of pasteboard

6 Cut a new mull $2\frac{1}{2}$ in. (65 mm) wider and $\frac{1}{2}$ in. (13 mm) shorter than the spine. Glue to the spine

7 Cut brown paper to the length of the spine and four times its width. Fold each edge to the centre and unfold one side. Glue sides 1 and 3 and stick 1 on top of 2. Stick side 3 over outside. Glue one surface and stick it on the spine. Leave for 24 hours

8 Cut the new cloth to size and coat its inside surface with adhesive. Position the boards within the lines marked

10 Fold over and stick down the front edges of the cloth. Turn over the covers and rub the outside surfaces

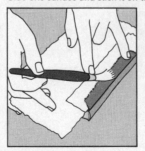

11 Put waste and wax paper between the edges of the mull and the book. Coat the mull outer surface with adhesive

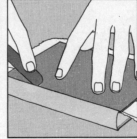

12 Glue the back strip and put the book between the new covers. Close it and rub the surfaces with the folder

13 Hold the covers at right angles. Remove the waste and rub down the mull. Retain the wax paper; leave for 24 hours

Books Pages

Repairing a tear

Torn pages can be repaired in two ways, depending on the type of paper and how it is damaged. With cheap paper or glossy, illustrated pages, it is advisable to fix the pieces together with a strip of tissue paper. A tear in a good heavy-quality paper is likely to leave some overlap. It is then possible to make a more satisfactory repair with adhesive and to strengthen the torn margin with tissue.

Fixing loose pages

When single pages of a book become loose, they can be glued back into place. Do not trim the inside, or hinge edge, of the loose page. Leave it uneven, but trim the other three edges square, if they have become frayed, before replacing the page in the book.

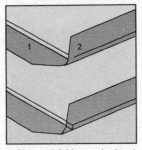

5 If the old boards are sound, scrape the paste-down away from the inside. Remove the mull inside each board

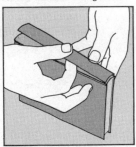

9 Glue and fold over the head (1) and tail (2) edges of the cloth to the boards. Press the corners flat with a fingernail

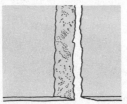

14 Make up and fix two new endpapers (see p. 256). Clean and stick the original back strip to the new spine

If there is even slight overlap, repair with adhesive

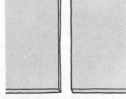

If the damage is a clean cut, repair with tissue paper

REPAIRING A CUT PAGE

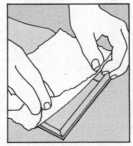

1 Place a piece of wax paper underneath the damaged page. Tear pieces of tissue paper about $\frac{3}{8}$ in. (10 mm) wide and about 1 in. (25 mm) long

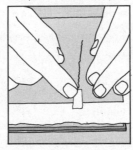

2 Fit the cut edges together. Paste a piece of tissue. Add pieces until the tear is covered. Place wax paper over the page and weight down

1 Lay a sheet of wax paper under the torn page. Thinly coat both edges of the tear with adhesive

2 Lay the torn page on the wax paper with the frayed edges fitting correctly together. Press them down

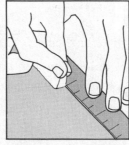

3 Place another sheet of wax paper on top of the repair. Close the book, put a weight on top and leave it to dry

4 Remove the top wax paper. Tear a strip of tissue $\frac{3}{8}$ in. (10 mm) wide and longer than the width of the margin

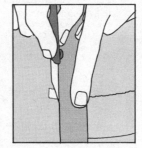

5 Stick tissue lengthwise over the torn margin on the even-numbered page to extend beyond the page edge

6 Place wax paper on top of the page. Weight down until dry. Remove wax papers and trim the tissue

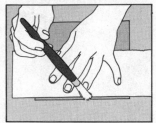

1 Thinly spread adhesive down the inside edge of the page. Do not glue more than $\frac{1}{8}$ in. (3 mm) wide

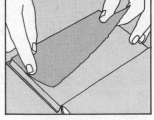

2 Line up the edges of the page with the rest of the book and carefully press it along the hinge

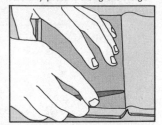

3 Rub the glued edge down. Put in wax paper on the unglued side. Close and leave for 24 hours

Books Hinges and joints

Repairing a broken hinge

The hinges on which the covers of a book open and close are the folds in the centres of the endpapers. If these are cracked or have given way, remove the endpapers and make new ones from a good-quality typing paper. Have wax paper and waste available to protect the pages when pasting.

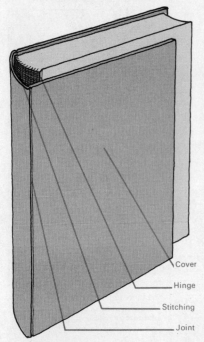

Cover
Hinge
Stitching
Joint

1 Support each cover in turn on a book. Tear away the free endpaper at the front and the back of the book

2 Use a kitchen knife to scrape the paste-down off the cloth edges inside the covers. Take care not to tear the cloth

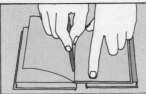

4 Position the endpaper on the board of the book and fold the endpaper at the hinge. Press along the crease with a bone folder

6 Line up the front endpaper with the page edges and press down the glued fold. Close the book and stick in the other endpaper

8 Smooth the paper to the board. Remove the waste but keep the waxed paper between the end-papers and close the book

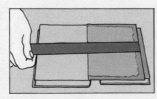

3 Measure the depth of the pages of the book, and add $\frac{1}{4}$ in. (6 mm) to the width of the opened covers. Cut two new endpapers

5 Protect the paper by holding a straight piece of scrap paper $\frac{1}{8}$ in. (3 mm) from the fold. Brush adhesive down the exposed endpaper

7 Insert a sheet of waxed paper and a sheet of waste between the free and paste-down endpapers. Glue the surface to be pasted

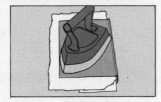

9 Stick the paste-down paper to the board at the other end of the book in the same way. Weight the book with an iron for 24 hours

Renewing damaged joints

The cloth joints which join the two covers of a book to the spine are likely to break as the cloth becomes brittle with age. If this happens, remove the back strip, on which the title is usually printed, and fit new joints. Replace the back strip when the repair has been completed.

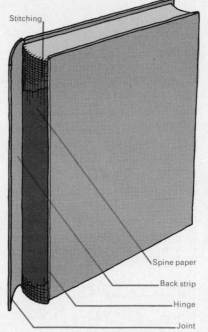

Stitching
Spine paper
Back strip
Hinge
Joint

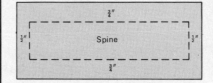

New cloth Choose a piece of new cloth to match or contrast with the existing binding. Cut it $1\frac{1}{2}$ in. (40 mm) wider and 1 in. (25 mm) longer than the spine

Spine
$\frac{3}{4}''$
$\frac{3}{4}''$
$\frac{1}{2}''$
$\frac{1}{2}''$

1 Open the book and cut along the edges of the back strip, but not deeply. Remove the strip and set it aside

8 Prise the $\frac{3}{4}$-in. tabs up with the point of the bone folder. Scrape them clean carefully with the sharp edge of a knife

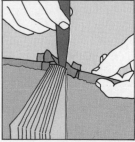

15 Open the boards to form a straight line. Fold the cloth over the head of hollow spine and boards. Repeat on tail

2 Lay a straight-edge $\frac{1}{16}$ in. (2 mm) from the cut edges of both boards. Trim the cloth with a sharp knife

3 If the spine paper is cracked or peels easily, scrape it off gently. Take care not to damage the stitching

4 Spread adhesive along the spine. Leave for a few minutes, then rub it in. Put on a second coat and leave overnight

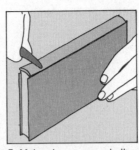

5 Make a brown-paper hollow spine (see p. 254). Glue one side of it and stick it firmly to the spine of the book

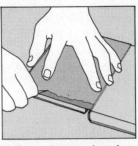

6 Scrape the paste-down from the cloth edges inside the boards. Take care not to damage the edges of the cloth

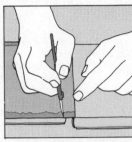

7 Cut in a straight line down the cloth edges, $\frac{3}{4}$ in. (20 mm) from the hinge, at the top and bottom of both boards

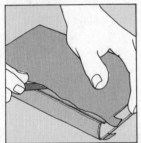

9 Close the book. Loosen a $\frac{3}{4}$ in. (20 mm) strip down each cloth edge. Turn the strips back and clean them

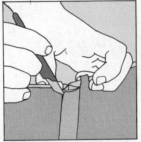

10 Open the book fully and cut $\frac{1}{2}$ in. (13 mm) down both sides of the new hollow spine at the top and bottom

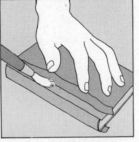

11 Brush adhesive under the cloth along the bared edge of one board and along the surface of the hollow spine

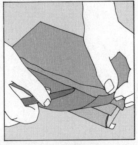

12 Spread adhesive on the inside of a new cloth. Push it under the loose cover cloth with the folder. Rub down

13 Protect the cover with waste paper and fold back the loose strip. Spread on adhesive; stick the strip on the new cloth

14 Rub the cloth firmly round the spine. Turn the book over. Use wax paper to protect it and glue the other side

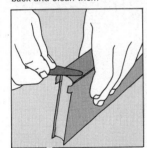

16 Smooth the cloth with the folder. Make sure the crease is straight and even across the spine. Close the book

17 With the folder, press gently down the joints to form a crease. Take care not to pierce the new cloth

18 Open each cover and glue the loose tabs back inside the boards. Prepare and fit new endpapers (see p. 256)

19 Lay the old back strip on the bench, with its inside upwards. Trim $\frac{1}{32}$ in. (1 mm) off both sides of the strip

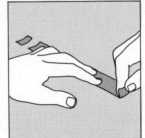

20 Peel back the cloth at both ends of the back strip and cut off at the creases. Remove any paper from the back strip

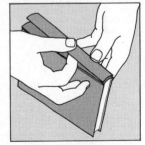

21 Brush adhesive on new spine cloth and back strip. Position the back strip right way up; rub it down carefully

Camping equipment Tents

Taking care of a tent

Always fold and store a tent cloth separately from the metal or wooden parts. Never store it when the cloth is wet; and keep it in a dry place. Before putting the tent away after a season, smear a little light oil on the metal parts to protect them from rust. When the tent is erected, make sure that the cloth is not over-strained at any section. Slacken the ropes when it rains and at night.

Most parts and accessories—for example, the runners and guy ropes, pegs, rubber rings and canvas tabs—are replaceable and can be obtained from a camping-equipment dealer if the make and size of the tent are specified.

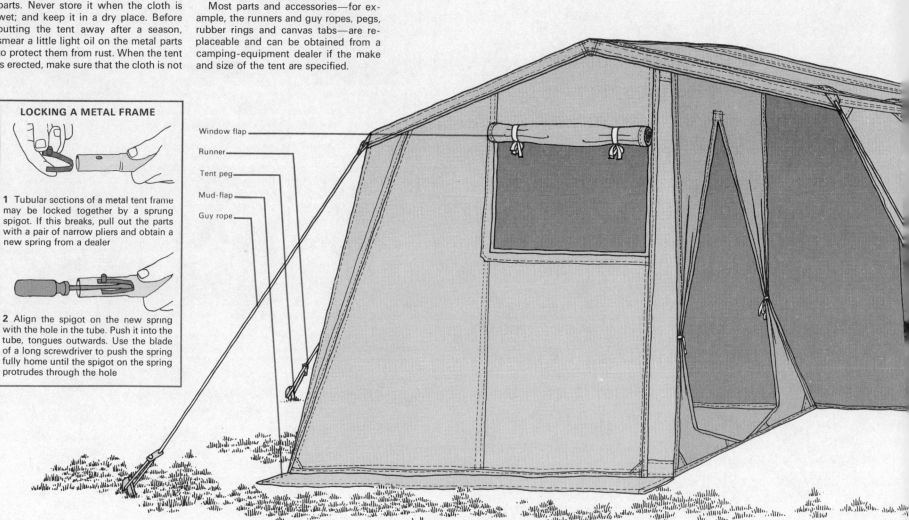

LOCKING A METAL FRAME

1 Tubular sections of a metal tent frame may be locked together by a sprung spigot. If this breaks, pull out the parts with a pair of narrow pliers and obtain a new spring from a dealer

2 Align the spigot on the new spring with the hole in the tube. Push it into the tube, tongues outwards. Use the blade of a long screwdriver to push the spring fully home until the spigot on the spring protrudes through the hole

Window flap

Runner

Tent peg

Mud-flap

Guy rope

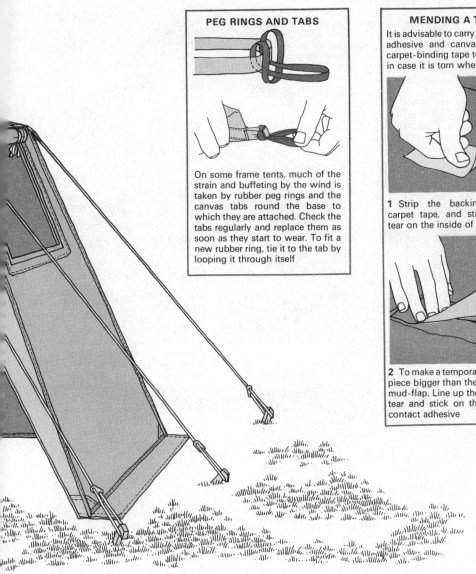

PEG RINGS AND TABS

On some frame tents, much of the strain and buffeting by the wind is taken by rubber peg rings and the canvas tabs round the base to which they are attached. Check the tabs regularly and replace them as soon as they start to wear. To fit a new rubber ring, tie it to the tab by looping it through itself

MENDING A TEAR

It is advisable to carry some contact adhesive and canvas patches or carpet-binding tape to repair a tent in case it is torn when being used.

1 Strip the backing from the carpet tape, and stick it on the tear on the inside of the tent

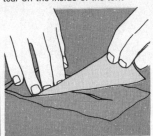

2 To make a temporary patch, cut a piece bigger than the tear from the mud-flap. Line up the edges of the tear and stick on the patch with contact adhesive

Re-proofing tent cloth

It is important to re-proof tent cloth— which is usually cotton—every three years. Do so before the start of a season and allow the cloth to dry before the tent is used.

When only small patches of the cloth develop leaks during use, spray them with an aerosol re-proofer.

Always treat the seams of the tent with a proprietary wax sealer when the tent is re-proofed. It is also advisable to do this at the beginning of each camping season.

Materials: re-proofing agent; wax sealer.
Tool: whitewash brush.

1 Lay the tent flat, outside upwards. Dip a whitewash brush into water, then into the re-proofer. Apply firmly

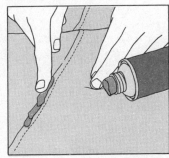

2 When the re-proofing solution has dried, rub wax sealer along the outside of all the seams. Work it in thoroughly

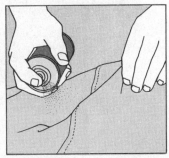

3 If small areas of the cloth later develop leaks, spray a proprietary re-proofing agent on the outside surface

REMOVING MOULD FROM A TENT

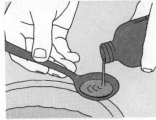

1 Mix 1 part of sodium hypochlorite —obtainable from most chemists— in 20 parts of warm water

2 Sponge the solution over the outside of the moulded areas. Allow it to dry, and wash with clean water

Camping equipment Tents

Repairing holes and tears

Small pieces of ready-proofed cloth for patching tent tears are obtainable from camping-equipment dealers. Do not stick pins in the tent to hold the patch in place before stitching.

Obtain matching 60-gauge thread, and use a large sewing needle to hemstitch the patch (see p. 278). The stitches must be tight and close together. Finish the hemstitch with three stitches on top of each other.

Always patch inside—except when the tear is near a seam. Rub wax sealer on the finished repair.

Materials: cloth; thread; wax sealer.
Tools: scissors, needle.

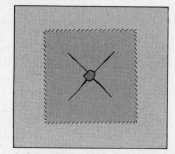

1 On the inside, cut and hemstitch a patch over the hole in the cloth. Outside, make four diagonal cuts

2 Turn under the four pieces of cloth formed by the cuts to leave a hem about ½ in. (13 mm) deep

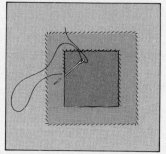

3 Hemstitch the folded edges to the cloth patch from outside. Wax the stitching when finished

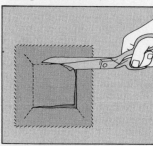

L-shaped tear Sew a patch over the tear inside. Outside, cut the L shape into a square, and cut diagonally at the corners. Tuck under and stitch

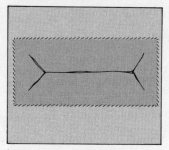

Long tear Sew on the patch. Cut two diagonal lines at each end of the tear. Tuck under and hemstitch the four pieces of cloth inside the tent

Patching at a seam

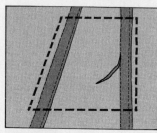

1 When the tear is on a seam, cut a patch to cover the torn area and the adjacent seam or seams. Allow an additional ¼ in. (6 mm) at each side of the patch for a hem

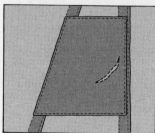

2 Turn under a ¼ in. (6 mm) hem on all four sides of the patch. Hemstitch it over the tear on the outside of the tent. Sew it to the outside edges of the adjacent seam or seams

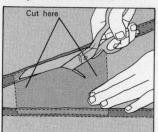

3 Inside the tent, cut the torn cloth along the seams to within 1 in. (25 mm) of each end. Cut across the cloth 1½ in. (40 mm) from each end. Fold ½ in. (13 mm) and sew

Fitting a new frame spring

The tubular, metal sections of a tent frame are usually kept in pairs, connected by a spring. With constant use, the spring may break or wear loose.

Replacement springs, and the tool required to fit them, are obtainable in packs for various frame sizes.

Materials: pack of new springs.
Tool: pliers.

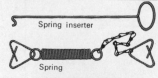

Spring inserter

Spring

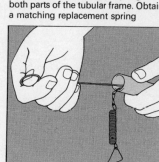

1 Pull out the damaged spring from both parts of the tubular frame. Obtain a matching replacement spring

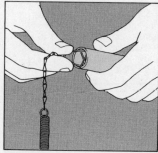

2 Compress the spring-clip at the end of the chain and push it into the narrower of the two tubes

3 Use the spring inserter to push the spring-clip down into the tube until the spring touches the tube

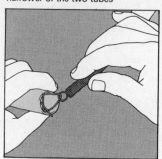

4 Compress the other spring-clip slightly and push it into the other and longer tube

5 Use the spring inserter to push it down as far as possible. When finished, the spring should be hidden

Camping equipment Accessories

Repairing a punctured air-bed

To find a puncture in an air-bed, blow it up and listen for escaping air. If that is not successful, half-inflate the bed and hold it in a bath of water until air bubbles are seen.

Repair kits for canvas beds contain rubber solution, those for plastic beds a liquid cement.

Never use lighter fuel or petrol on a plastic air-bed: clean the torn part first with a damp cloth, then with a dry cloth. Spread on only one coat of the liquid cement and leave the patch to dry for about five hours.

Materials: repair kit; rag; petrol or lighter fuel, or water.

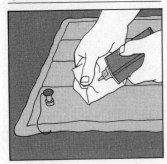

1 Clean the area round the torn canvas with petrol or lighter fuel. Use only water if the air-bed is plastic

2 Squeeze rubber solution on the torn canvas. Work it in, allow to dry and apply a second coat

3 Roughen the back of the patch with glass-paper. Apply solution, allow to dry and apply a second coat

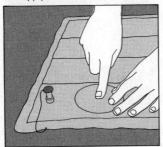

4 When the solution is dry, stick on the patch and press firmly from the centre. Leave to dry for 12 hours

Mending camping accessories

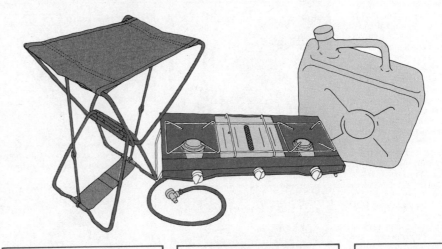

REPAIRING A STOOL

1 A canvas stool is most likely to tear at the side edge. Collapse the stool and fold ¼ in. (6 mm) surplus material underneath

2 Overstitch (see p. 278) along the folded edge. Open and check canvas is even

MENDING A GAS PIPE

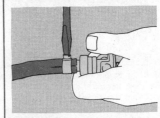

1 Before each season check all flexible pipes. If one is cracked, unscrew the clip and remove the pipe from the appliance

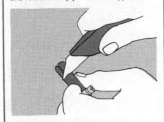

2 Lay it on a bench and cut straight across below the crack. Refit and tighten the clip

SEALING A CONTAINER

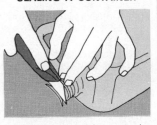

1 Polythene water-containers may spring a leak at a welded seam. To seal it, cut a thin sliver from the end of the nozzle

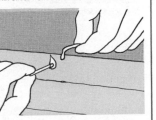

2 Hold it over the seam and melt it in a match or lighter flame. Touch in the hole

Carpets Fitting and moving

Moving a stair carpet

Before laying a stair carpet, check the direction of its pile. The carpet must be laid so that brushing towards the top of the staircase raises the pile, and brushing towards the bottom flattens it.

This means that if the carpet is patterned, the base of the pattern should be towards the bottom of the staircase. On a plain carpet, or where the pattern is less easy to follow, find the direction of the pile by rubbing the carpet with the fingers. In one direction the pile will be brushed up; in the other it will be flattened.

Never reverse a stair carpet unless it has been laid wrongly. Carpet wears more rapidly if the pile is in the wrong direction. If a carpet is becoming worn, lift it and re-lay it 3 in. (75 mm) higher. Place pads so that they overhang the nose of each tread.

When a carpet is lifted, remove all pads and tacks from the staircase and clean the steps thoroughly. If the pads are worn, obtain a roll of similar underlay material and cut new pieces about 10 in. (255 mm) deep. On a corner, fold and tack the surplus at the inside edge against the riser, not the tread.

Materials: tacks; underlay if necessary.
Tools: pliers; claw hammer.

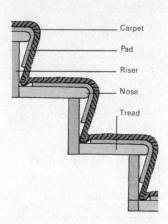

Carpet
Pad
Riser
Nose
Tread

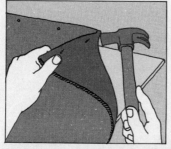

1 Remove a corner tack at the top of the staircase. Pull the carpet, and hammer behind it to remove the tacks

2 To remove riser tacks, pull the carpet firmly back and lever from behind it with a claw hammer

3 As each stair is stripped, roll up the carpet and lay it on the tread below the one being worked on

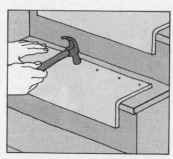

4 Lay underlay on each tread, ¾ in. (20 mm) from the riser above. Tack along the rear edge of the pads

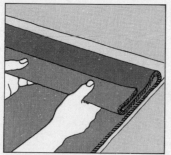

6 If the carpet was folded at the top, increase the fold by 3 in. (75 mm). If not, fold the edge 3 in. under

7 Butt the folded edge against the landing underlay. Hammer in one tack at the centre of the carpet

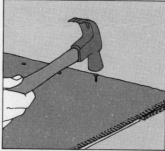

8 Hammer in a tack every 3 in. (75 mm) along the edge. Work outwards from the centre tack towards each side

9 At the nose of the first stair, hammer in a temporary tack, and press the carpet down and into the riser below

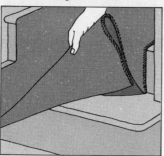

11 Secure the carpet on the other stairs. Make sure it is tight and straight. At the bottom, fold under the surplus

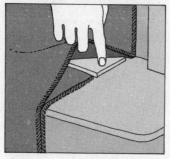

12 Straighten the fold. Cut and fit padding to fill the gap between the edge of the fold and the riser

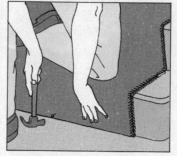

13 Hammer one tack in the centre of the bottom fold. Tack every 3 in. (75 mm) towards each side

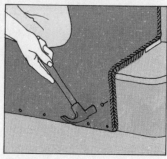

14 Hammer a tack close to each side edge of the staircase carpet, halfway up the bottom riser

5 Take the carpet to the top landing and pull it downstairs to unroll it. Roll it up from the bottom

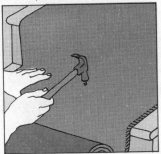

10 Hammer one tack upright, at the centre, close against the riser. Space four more tacks across the tread

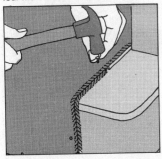

15 On the first tread, tack once at each side edge of the carpet through the double thickness

Re-laying a gripped carpet

Some stair carpets are held from behind by right-angled metal grip-rods nailed and screwed at the riser joints. The inner surfaces of the rods have small spikes to grip the carpet backing. The riser spikes point downwards, the tread spikes inwards. Take care when prising the carpet off the spikes. Make sure it grips firmly when it is re-laid.

Clean the staircase thoroughly and check the condition of the underlay pads and the spikes.

Materials: underlay and grip-rods, if necessary.
Tool: hardboard strip.

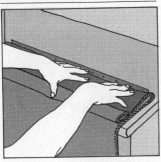

2 Press the carpet down off the riser spikes with the finger tips. Free it along the width of the rod

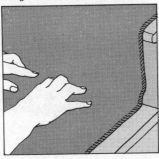

4 Fold under 3 in. (75 mm) at the top and press the carpet into each joint. Work from the middle to the sides

1 Remove any tacks along the top edge of the carpet, and fold it back on to the tread below

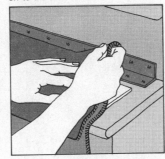

3 Push the carpet into the joint with one hand. With the other, ease it gently off the tread spikes

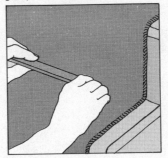

5 Use a piece of hardboard to crease each corner tightly on to the spikes before fitting the next step

Lifting and re-laying a fitted carpet

It is advisable to lift a fitted carpet before starting to redecorate a room. To re-lay the carpet, secure it first at the side of the room with the longest straight edge. Tack it from a corner. But at the opposite side, tack the carpet temporarily, first at the centre of the wall, then outwards to each corner. If it is tacked from the corner it is unlikely to lie flat and even. Finally, fix the carpet at the side walls.

Carpets held by grip-rods at the edge of the room can be lifted without removing the strips.

Materials: tacks.
Tools: screwdriver; pincers; hammer.

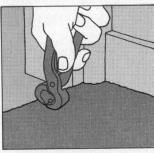

1 Probe under one corner edge of the carpet with a screwdriver to find a tack. Remove with pincers

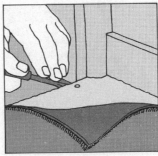

2 Lift up the carpet flap. Probe again with the screwdriver and remove the tacks in the underlay

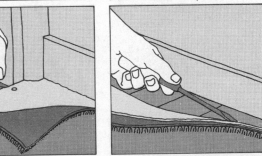

3 Hold back the carpet and underlay. With the screwdriver under the underlay, prise up the tacks

4 Fold back the carpet and underlay separately as each length is freed. Continue round the room

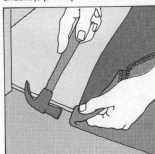

5 If the carpet edge is folded, pull it gently and hammer from behind to remove tacks   *(continued)*

Carpets Binding and joining

(continued)

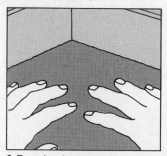

6 To re-lay the carpet, first position the underlay correctly from a corner along the longest wall

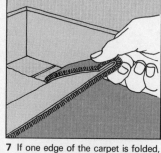

7 If one edge of the carpet is folded, set back the underlay exactly to butt against the turned-under edge

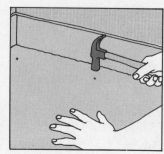

8 Hammer tacks through the underlay 3 in. (75 mm) from each wall and about 2 ft 6 in. (760 mm) apart

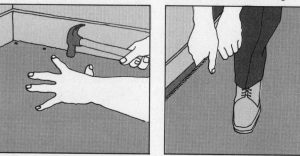

9 Tack the carpet along the longest wall. Space tacks 9 in. (230 mm) apart, 1 in. (25 mm) from the wall

10 In the middle of the opposite wall, grip the carpet and shuffle it towards the skirting board

11 Hammer in a temporary tack 18 in. (455 mm) from the wall. Repeat every few feet along the wall

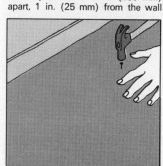

12 Check that the carpet is tight against the skirting board. Hammer in more temporary tacks if needed

13 Start at the middle of the wall, and press the carpet towards the skirting board. Fold under the edge

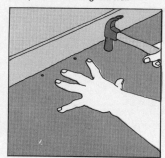

14 Hammer tacks 1 in. (25 mm) from the wall and every 9 in. (230 mm), working from the centre

Binding an Axminster or Wilton carpet

To prevent fraying after an Axminster or Wilton carpet has been cut, bind its edge with carpet tape. The tape should be pressed firmly up over the end of the carpet and into the base of the pile tufts to give a firm, round edge. Take care when applying adhesive not to get any on the tufts of the carpet.

Materials: latex adhesive; piece of old carpet or cloth; carpet binding tape. Tools: knife; scissors.

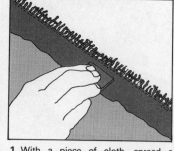

1 With a piece of cloth, spread a strip of adhesive, 1 in. (25 mm) wide, along the back of the cut edge

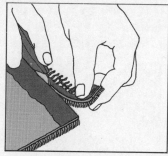

2 Find the second row of carpet weave from the cut edge. Cut straight across it with a sharp knife

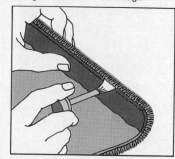

3 Dab adhesive along the edge of the weave—not the tufts. Rub it in with the fingers and leave to dry

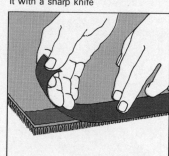

4 Cut binding tape longer than the carpet. Rub in adhesive and lay tape to overlap the edge by $\frac{1}{8}$ in. (3 mm)

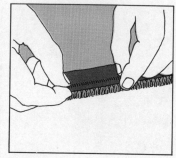

5 Wrap the tape up over the edge of the weave. Trim it at the tufts and cut off surplus at both ends

Joining carpet edges

Some carpets have edges—called selvedges—woven so that the fibres cannot unravel if they are cut.

To join two pieces of selvedge carpet, use a carpet needle and a waxed thread, doubled and knotted. If ready-waxed thread cannot be obtained, treat ordinary carpet thread with a stick of beeswax, which can be bought at a hardware shop.

To join carpet with no selvedge, use the Axminster or Wilton patching technique (see p. 266).

Materials: waxed thread; latex adhesive.
Tools: carpet needle; hammer.

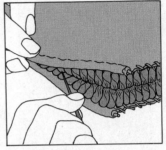

1 Line up the two pieces to be joined, pile to pile and edge to edge. Push in the tufts with a needle

2 Overstitch along the join to the end and back, pushing down the tufts with the needle as necessary

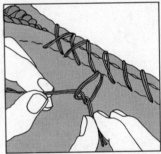

3 If the thread runs out, sew two reverse stitches. Knot and trim the thread. Start again with new thread

4 When the join is stitched, lay the carpet open upside-down. Flatten the join with the side of a hammer

5 Dab some latex adhesive along the stitching at the back. Rub it in with the fingers and leave it to dry

Binding a jute carpet

To bind the edges of a jute carpet, obtain a sharp carpet needle, a waxed thread and some binding tape.

The best binding is hessian in a colour matching or contrasting with the carpet.

Materials: hessian tape; latex adhesive; waxed thread.
Tools: large, heavy-duty scissors; carpet needle.

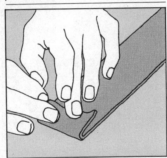

3 Rub in the adhesive and let it become tacky. Fold over and stick the tape 1 in. (25 mm) from each end

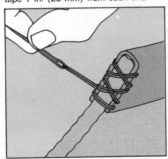

6 Secure the end with tight overstitching, to the fold in the tape. Sew back down so that the stitches criss-cross

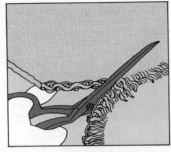

1 Trim the frayed edge of the jute with a large pair of heavy-duty scissors. Make sure it is neat and straight

4 Line up the end of the tape with the carpet. Fold the length of tape evenly down the edge of the carpet

7 Secure the whole length of tape by stitching in and out through the edges on both sides of the carpet

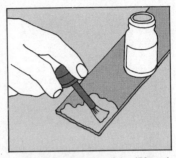

2 Cut a strip of hessian 2 in. (50 mm) longer than the carpet edge. Coat 2 in. at each end with adhesive

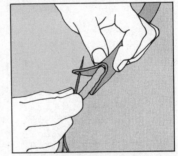

5 Hold the tape in place and stitch. Hide the knot in the thread by pushing through first from under the tape

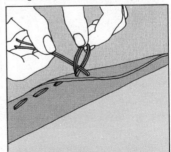

8 If thread runs out, tie a knot under a tape edge, trim, and continue with new thread. Overstitch the end

Carpets Joining and backing

Carpets Patching

Foam-backed

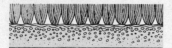

Pieces of foam-backed carpet can be joined with contact-adhesive tape. Make sure that the edges to be joined together are straight, and that the pile of each piece runs in the same direction. When the repair is complete, lightly hammer the join across the top of the carpet.

Materials: heavy-duty adhesive tape.
Tools: sharp knife or a strong pair of scissors; hammer.

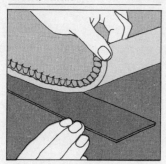

1 Cut tape longer than the carpet. Lay one foam piece along the centre of the tape length

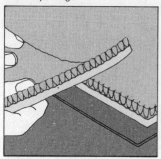

2 Butt the second piece of carpet and press it on the tape. Trim the tape at the top and bottom

Non-slip backing

It is possible to buy a ready-made non-slip backing for a rug, but a cheaper alternative is usually to buy plastic foam sheeting at a carpet or upholstery shop. Always cut the foam sheet ½ in. (13 mm) shorter and narrower than the rug which is to be backed. Make sure when sticking on the plastic foam that there is a ¼ in. (6 mm) margin all round between the edges of the foam backing and those of the rug.

Materials: ¼ in. (6 mm) plastic foam sheeting, cut to size; latex adhesive; rag.
Tool: scissors.

1 Cut the backing. Dab adhesive along its edges and in strips 6 in. (150 mm) apart across the width

2 Smear adhesive over the backing with a rag. Treat the back of the rug in the same way. Stick on the backing

Patching an Axminster or Wilton carpet

If an Axminster or Wilton carpet tears or becomes badly worn, it can be patched with a carpet remnant. If none is available, cut a patch from a part permanently covered by furniture, rather than leave the carpet looking unsightly. Make sure the direction of the pile matches that of the surrounding sound carpet.

Materials: latex adhesive; hessian tape; piece of wood; rag.
Tools: felt pen; sharp knife.

1 Untack and turn the carpet back. Use a felt pen to mark a square around the back of the damaged area

2 Coat adhesive across the square and extend it 1 in. (25 mm) on each side. Rub it in with a rag

3 Slide a piece of wood under the damage. Cut along the lines of the square with a sharp knife

4 Place the square upside-down on the back of a remnant. Match the patterns if possible. Mark and cut

5 Cut two strips of hessian tape, each 2 in. (50 mm) longer than the square. Coat with adhesive

6 Stick the tapes over the hole at the back of the carpet, overlapping by 1 in. (25 mm) at each end

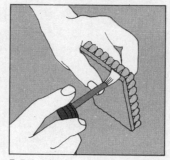

7 Dab adhesive on the back of the patch and on its edges—not the tufts. Rub in thoroughly

8 Press the patch into place. Gently squeeze round, and hammer down the edges lightly

Patching a foam-backed carpet

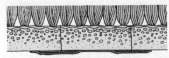

It is always advisable to keep any foam-backed remnants when the carpet is laid. If no surplus is available, it may be possible to cut a piece permanently covered by furniture.

The technique for patching a foam-backed carpet can also be used to repair damaged vinyl floor-coverings.

Materials: matching carpet-patch; tacks; strong contact-adhesive tape.
Tools: sharp knife; hammer.

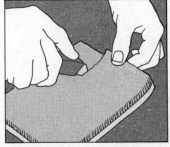

1 Measure a square round the damage and with a sharp knife cut a piece of matching carpet slightly larger

2 Lay the patch over the damage, with its pile matching. Hold it temporarily with two carpet tacks

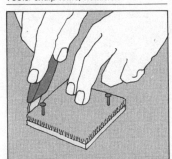

3 Cut through the carpet along the edges of the square. Make sure that the cuts are clean and straight

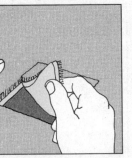

4 Pull out the tacks and lift off the patch. Remove and discard the square of damaged carpet underneath

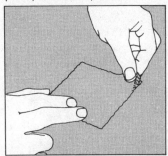

5 Test that the patch fits exactly and lay it aside. Cut a strip of adhesive tape 2 in. (50 mm) longer than the hole

6 Turn back the carpet. Stick on the strip to overlap the hole by half its depth and at each end by 1 in. (25 mm)

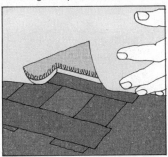

7 Cut three more strips of tape to the same length. Stick them in the same way on the other edges

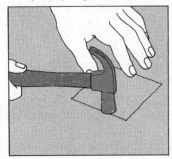

8 Turn down the carpet and press the patch on to the tape edges. Lightly hammer along the joins

Patching a woollen rug

Small holes in woollen rugs, such as those caused by cigarette burns, can be patched with 4-ply wool. Measure the hole and always cut a little more than may be needed. Before starting the repair, trim off any singed or damaged tufts with a pair of sharp nail scissors.

Materials: matching 4-ply wool; sharpened matchstick or toothpick; latex adhesive.
Tools: scissors; nail scissors; pin.

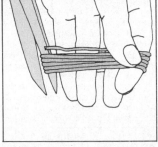

1 Wind enough wool for the repair round the fingers of one hand. Cut through both ends

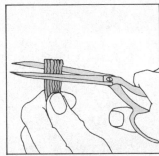

2 Bunch the strips tightly together and cut off enough ½ in. (13 mm) pieces to fill the hole

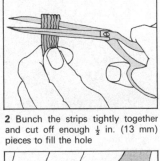

3 With a matchstick or toothpick, dab adhesive in the hole. Stand a bunch of strands in the adhesive

4 Use the toothpick or a sharpened matchstick to work the strands into position. Add more if necessary

5 Trim with nail scissors. When the adhesive dries, use a pin to blend the tufts with the surrounding wool

Carpets

Carpet sweepers

Fitting a metal strip

If a carpet starts to curl up at an edge, fix it to the floor with a spiked metal strip. This is sold in standard widths but can be cut to fit with a hacksaw. It is essential that the carpet fits snugly under the lip of the strip, and the foam backing or underlay must be cut away to form a recess for the strip.

Fitted carpets may be secured round the room by spikes attached to wooden rods which have no lip but are fixed in the same way as the strips.

Materials: metal strip; tacks; piece of wood.
Tools: hammer; felt pen; sharp knife; hacksaw.

1 Cut a metal strip to size and position it on the floor. Tack through the holes in its base

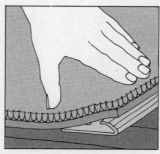

2 If the carpet is foam-backed, lay it on the top of the strip. Do not tuck it under the lip at this stage

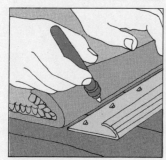

3 Fold the edge of the carpet back and mark along with a felt pen where it meets the strip

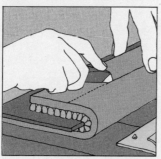

4 Insert a length of wood under the fold and score the foam along the line. Do not cut a fibre-backed carpet

5 Carefully peel off the foam backing from the carpet edge to the line scored by the knife

6 Tuck the carpet under the lip. Rest a piece of hardboard or wood along the lip and hammer the carpet down

7 With a fibre-backed carpet and underlay, mark and cut the underlay to butt against the edges of the strip

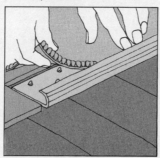

8 Tuck the carpet under the lip. Use a block of wood and hammer the lip down firmly on top of the carpet

Overhauling a sweeper

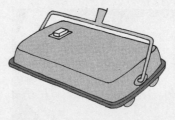

Carpet sweepers should be dismantled only to clean the brush or renew wheels or tyres. The brush may be held by the frame, by levers or by bails. The wheels can be removed easily for tyre replacement when the brush is freed

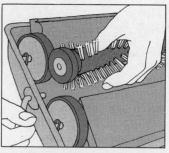

1 On some models the brush roller is held by the bail arms at the sides. Pull them out to free the brush

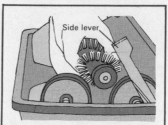

Levers Push in each side lever slightly. Lift them up and free the brush roller. Pull out the sides of the frame and remove wheels

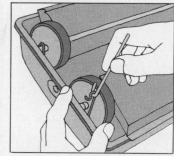

2 If the wheels are held by a spring, bend a piece of strong wire and hook it round the spring. Lift it out

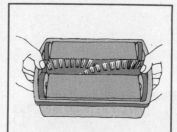

Frame The brush may be held by the frame of the sweeper. Pull the sides outwards gently and unhook the brush roller. Remove the wheels

3 Lift up each wheel in turn and pull it away from the wheel axle. Leave the axles in the sweeper

China

Handle
Bail
Wheel axle
Spring
Dust carrier
Brush roller
Wheel

Lubrication Apply a little light oil on a pipe cleaner to the wheels and brush roller

CLEANING THE BRUSH

Some sweepers have metal teeth which clean the brush as it is rolled. With other types, remove the brush and clean it with an old comb

FITTING A NEW TYRE

On some models the sweeper tyres are cemented to the wheels: pre-cemented replacements are available from the manufacturers. To remove a faulty tyre, immerse the wheel in boiling water for five minutes. Prise the tyre off with a knife. Use glass-paper on the rim to remove old cement. Do not touch the inside sticky surface of the new tyre. Fit it and immerse in boiling water for a minute. Take the wheel and fitted tyre out of the water and allow the cement to harden

Mending a porcelain dish

If a porcelain dish, cup or plate breaks, make sure that all the pieces are kept. Wash them in soapy water and dry them thoroughly.

Use one of the epoxy resins. The quick-drying type takes about one hour to set, the slow-drying type up to 12 hours. Cellulose resins do not withstand frequent washings.

Repairs to handles of china in use are unlikely to be strong enough. For repairs to decorative china, including restoring a pattern, see p. 221.

Materials: epoxy resin; whiting filler; 600–700-grade wet-and-dry paper. Tools: knife; sharp knife.

1 Lay out the pieces of the porcelain in order. First fit them dry. Mix resins and apply with a matchstick

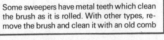

2 Fit the pieces together. Allow adhesive to go rubbery, then trim off any surplus. Place somewhere warm

3 Allow each piece to set before sticking in further pieces. Fill any chips with resin and whiting filler

4 Allow the filler and resin to set. Before completely hard cut off any surplus with a sharp knife

5 Dampen wet-and-dry paper and smooth the filled surface of the porcelain. Restore the pattern (see p. 221)

Cigarette lighters

Maintaining petrol and gas lighters

The wheel on a flint-operated cigarette lighter must be cleaned once a month to keep it working efficiently. If it becomes worn, it can be replaced readily on both petrol and gas-filled lighters.

Take care, however, to cover the valve on a gas lighter during repair work, to prevent gas leaking. Do not try to repair either inlet or outlet gas valves. Because they are under pressure, they may fly out, causing damage.

A new wick can be fitted to petrol lighters, and the rayon wool packing can be replaced if it no longer absorbs the petrol.

Check that the teeth of the plunger mesh tightly with the pinions. If either the plunger or a pinion is worn, fit a replacement part

Pinion   Plunger

Flint wheel

Ratchet spring

Pinion

Snuffer cap

Plunger

Pivot-pin screw

Plunger spring

Pivot pin

Wick tube

Use pliers to pull out extra wick as necessary. Do not damage the wick tube

Wick

Flint spring

Filler screw

Flint-spring screw

CLEANING

Flint wheel Press the plunger repeatedly and use a stiff brush to clean the wheel

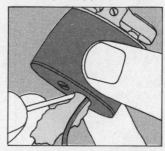

Escaping gas When cleaning a gas lighter, tape over the valve to contain gas

Side-operated lighters Turn the tap at right angles to the body. Lift the wheel out

Replacing a wick

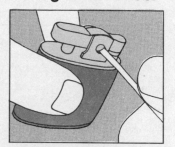

1 Remove wick and packing. Push wire of the new wick through the wick tube. Pull it out of the filler hole until 3 in. (75 mm) protrudes at tube

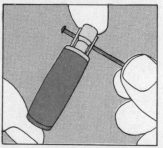

2 Cut off the wire and insert new packing. Use rayon wool, not cotton wool, to absorb petrol. Feed the wick in gradually with the packing

3 Use a wick inserter or straightened paper clip to push the wick further into the tube, leaving $\frac{1}{8}$ in. (3 mm) protruding. Refill the lighter

Fitting a flint wheel

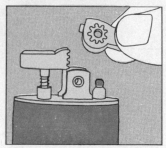

1 Remove the flint-spring screw at the bottom of the lighter. Use a small screwdriver to undo the pivot-pin screw at the top

2 Press down on both the plunger and the snuffer cap to ease the pressure on the pivot pin. Push out the pin with a matchstick

3 Remove the snuffer cap. Note the position of the wheel, ratchet spring and pinions. Fit a new flint wheel and reassemble the lighter

Clocks and watches

Maintaining clocks

Expensive clocks and watches should be maintained by a watchmaker. The cheaper type of alarm clock can be safely cleaned and lubricated without expert help, but do not try to dismantle the movement.

If possible, use benzine for cleaning. When petrol is used, allow it to dry and remove its sediment with a soft brush. Obtain special clock oil to lubricate the movement, and apply it sparingly, using a fine wire hammered flat.

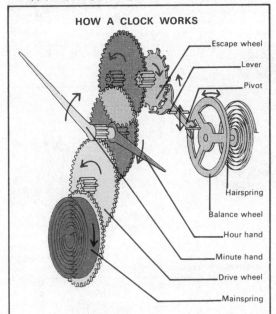

HOW A CLOCK WORKS

Escape wheel
Lever
Pivot
Hairspring
Balance wheel
Hour hand
Minute hand
Drive wheel
Mainspring

The accuracy of a clock or watch depends on a two-part mechanism: one turns the hands, the other controls their rate of turn. As the mainspring unwinds, it turns the drive wheel, which moves the hands clockwise round the face. The second part of the mechanism—called the escapement—regulates the speed of the hands. A balance wheel, which moves backwards and forwards continuously, is pushed anti-clockwise by the hairspring. This causes a lever to hold the escape wheel and stop the hand movement momentarily. But the escape wheel, driven clockwise from the drive wheel, pushes the lever and balance wheel back, turns one notch and allows the hands to move

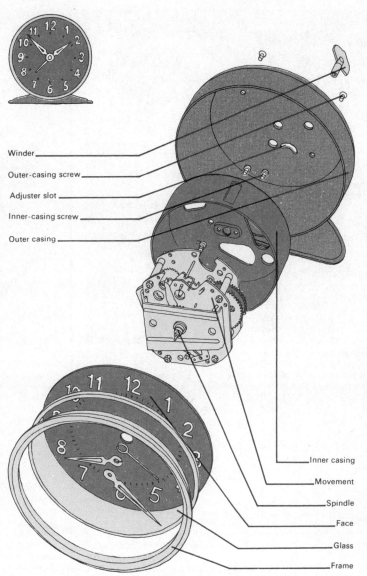

Winder
Outer-casing screw
Adjuster slot
Inner-casing screw
Outer casing

Inner casing
Movement
Spindle
Face
Glass
Frame

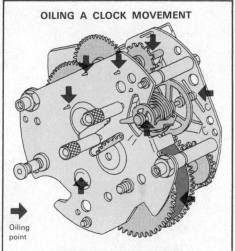

OILING A CLOCK MOVEMENT

Oiling point

Lubricate a clock movement every two years with clock oil. Apply one drop to each bearing end and to every alternate tooth of the escape wheel. Put a few drops on each spring

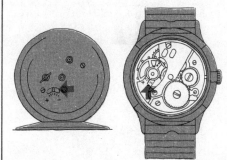

CORRECTING THE TIMING

Most clock and watch movements have an adjusting lever which can be moved along a scale marked F or + (faster) at one end, and S or − (slower) at the other, to alter the timing of the movement

Clocks and watches

Cleaning a clock movement

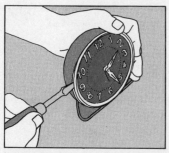

1 Carefully prise off the frame with a screwdriver and remove the glass from the front of the clock

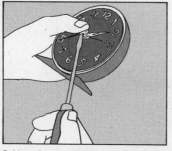

2 Use the screwdriver to lever the hands off the spindle. Take care not to twist or bend them.

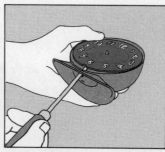

3 Prise the face off the clock, usually by levering up through a gap in the base of the clock

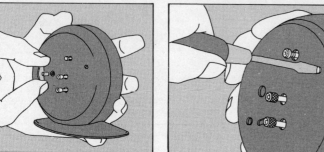

4 Remove any keys or knobs which are larger than their holes at the back of the clock casing

5 Unscrew the outer casing, either at the back or by removing the feet of the clock. Take out the inner casing

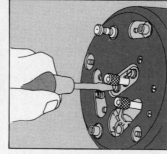

6 Undo the two screws securing the clock movement to the inner casing. Lift out the movement

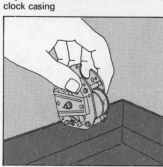

7 Immerse the movement in a tray of benzine or petrol. Leave it to soak for at least 15 minutes

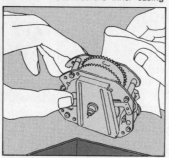

8 Take the movement out of the tray, shake off the surplus liquid and wipe the outside with a lint-free cloth

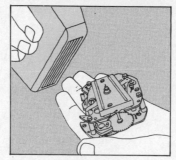

9 Use a hairdryer to dry the inside. If petrol was used, remove sediment with a soft brush. Oil the movement

Cleaning a watch case and bracelet

If the movement can be removed completely from the casing, immerse the case and bracelet, if they are dirty, in jewellery cleaner. Make sure, however, that a leather strap is detached from the watch before cleaning.

Do not try to rub away scratches on crystal and plastic fronts or on the face of the watch.

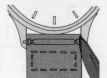

Strap pinions on a watch are spring-loaded at each end. Compress one spring on each to remove a leather strap

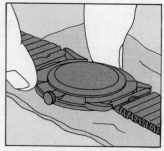

1 Apply metal polish to fine scratches on a glass front. Rub it briskly on a chamois leather

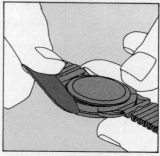
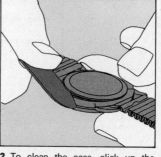

2 To clean the case, click up the winder if necessary; prise off or unscrew the back. Remove the movement

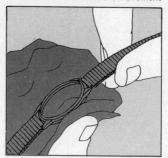

3 Immerse the case and bracelet in jewellery cleaner for ten minutes. Do not clean the movement

4 Shake and wipe off the surplus cleaner. Hold the case and bracelet under running water

5 Use a lint-free cloth or hairdryer to dry the case and bracelet. Replace the movement

Clothes airers Automatic lines

Replacing nylon cords—1

This type of compact two-line unit has a spring-operated rewind pulley mounted at right angles to the direction of pull. If the braided nylon line becomes frayed, it is easily replaced with new cord obtainable from hardware shops. Take the old cord to the shop for matching.

Materials: 27 ft (8 m) of nylon cord.
Tool: small cross-headed screwdriver.

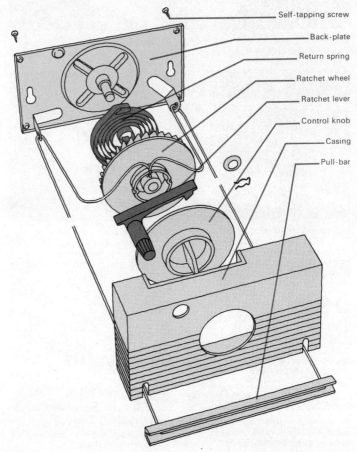

Self-tapping screw
Back-plate
Return spring
Ratchet wheel
Ratchet lever
Control knob
Casing
Pull-bar

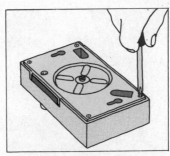

1 Lift the unit off the wall and undo the four self-tapping screws that secure the back-plate

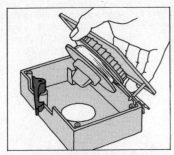

2 Remove the back-plate, complete with the control mechanism and old nylon line, from the casing

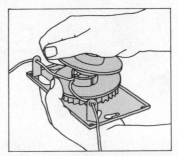

3 Push two fingers under the flange of the control knob and ease it off gently. Remove the old line

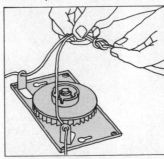

4 Thread the ends of the new line through the pull-bar and back-plate guides and tie them together

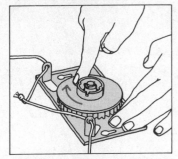

5 Before fitting the new line, tension the ratchet wheel by turning it clockwise 30 full rotations

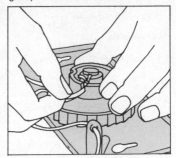

6 Slip the knotted end of the line into the slot so that the knot rests in the inner recess of the boss

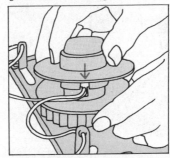

7 Line up the slot in the control knob with the slot in the boss and push the knob back into place

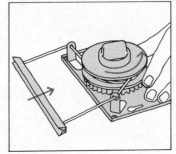

8 Release the ratchet wheel gently, allowing the new line to rewind itself evenly round the boss

9 Before refitting the mechanism in the casing check that the ratchet lever is in position

Clothes airers Automatic lines

Replacing nylon cords–2

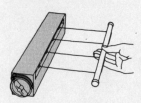

This four-line unit works in much the same way as a roller blind. If the braided nylon lines become frayed, it is easy to fit new ones which are obtainable at most hardware and do-it-yourself shops.

Materials: 62 ft (19 m) of nylon cord.
Tool: small cross-headed screwdriver.

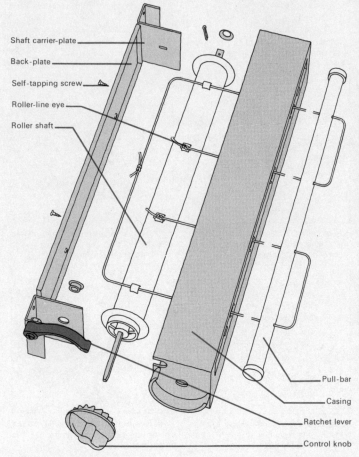

Shaft carrier-plate
Back-plate
Self-tapping screw
Roller-line eye
Roller shaft

Pull-bar
Casing
Ratchet lever
Control knob

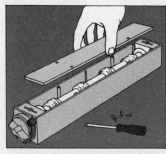

1 Remove the four self-tapping screws holding the back-plate, and lift the plate off the casing

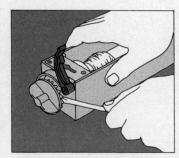

2 Prise the control knob off the shaft. This is secured only by friction and has no locking device

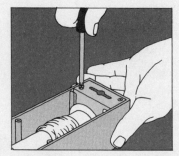

3 Undo the two screws that secure the shaft carrier-plate at the end opposite the control knob

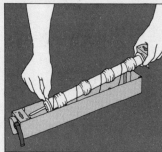

4 Lift the carrier-plate clear of the casing and draw out the complete roller and shaft assembly

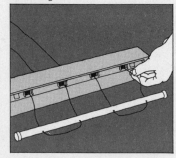

5 Thread two lengths of line, each 31 ft (9·5 m) long, through the pull-bar and the slots in the casing

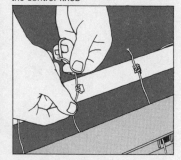

6 Pass the inner end of each line through a centre eye of the roller, and tie them round the eyes

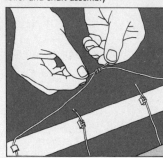

7 Thread the outer parts of the lines through the end roller-eyes and tie together in the centre of the roller

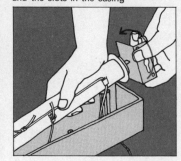

8 Holding the roller, turn the shaft carrier-plate clockwise through 52 rotations to tension the spring

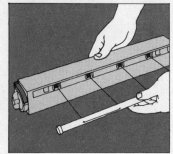

9 Draw the lines out to their full length to equalise the tension on each and let them run in again

Clothes airers   Hinged type

Fitting new hinges

The cloth hinges holding the frames of book-fold clothes airers are likely to wear or split in time.

New hinges can be made from 1½ in. (40 mm) jute webbing, which is available at most do-it-yourself or ironmongery shops. When fitting the new hinges, note that the centre hinge is wrapped round the frame uprights in the opposite direction to the hinges above and below it. Tack all the hinges to one upright, then fix them to the other. Use three tacks for each fixing to the upright.

Materials: good-quality webbing, about 1½ in. (40 mm) wide; tacks. Tools: claw hammer; knife.

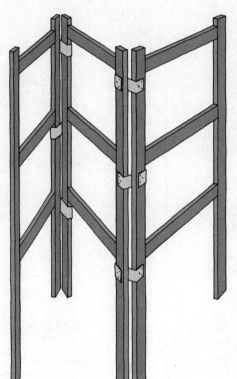

Top hinge

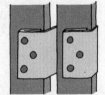

Centre hinge

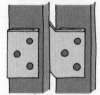

Bottom hinge

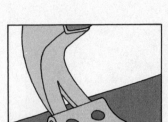

1 Use the hammer claw to remove old, torn hinges and tacks holding them in place. Cut new hinges

2 Double one end of each webbing strip and tack on to one upright. Stagger three tacks on each hinge

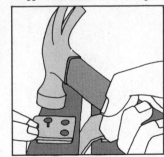

3 Wrap the hinges round second upright. Leave enough slack for movement. Double the ends and tack

Cutlery

Straightening blades

Knife blades may become bent, buckled or notched, or they may become separated from their handles.

Bent blades If a knife is bent at the tip, hammer it flat on a flat piece of steel —for example, the base of a flat iron. Smooth after hammering with a fine-grade slipstone and emery paper.

Buckled blades To straighten a buckled blade, fix it between two blocks of smooth hardwood in a vice and lever it back to its correct shape.

If no vice is available, lay the blade on a firm flat surface. Hold a smooth block of hardwood firmly on top of the buckled section and lever it straight.

Scalloped blades The point of a blade with a scalloped edge can be sharpened by honing the back of the blade, which has no scalloping. Never use a sharpener on the front of a scalloped blade. Such blades should be sent to the manufacturer for sharpening.

Saw-edged blades Do not try to sharpen saw-edged blades. Special equipment is needed to avoid damage. Take them to a hardware specialist.

Removing heat stains
If a blade is heat-stained, rub with fine-grade wet-and-dry abrasive paper, used wet, and a dry 3/0 or 4/0 emery paper.

SHARPENING BLADES

Sharpen kitchen knives weekly if they are in regular use.

Most are hollow ground by the manufacturer at an angle of 30 degrees. Hold them at this angle when sharpening.

A blade should be sharpened gradually, working first on one side, then on the other, then back to the first side.

When using a steel sharpener, hold the knife in one hand and draw the steel down the blade from the knife handle. Keep the knife pointing away from the body.

Using a stone Draw one side along the stone (top). Turn the blade and pull it back along the stone (bottom)

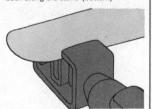

Using a hand sharpener Pull the blade firmly through the discs several times in the same direction. Do not saw backwards and forwards

Cutlery

Removing nicks

Hone away small nicks in unplated or stainless-steel knife blades with a fine-grade slipstone. For a bad nick use a fine hand file. Polish with grade 3/0 or 4/0 emery paper.

Materials: slipstone; fine file; emery paper.
Tool: vice.

1 Fix the knife blade—edge up—in a vice. Reduce nick with upward strokes of slipstone or file

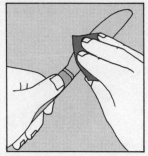

2 Hone the whole cutting edge back to the depth of the deepest nick. Polish with emery paper

Rebonding a knife handle

Many knife blades have a tang or spike which is glued into a bone handle. If the handle and blade come apart, they can be stuck together again, provided the tang of the blade is unbroken.

Materials: epoxy resin (see p. 694); cloth; adhesive tape.
Tool: screwdriver.

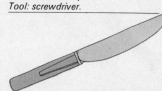

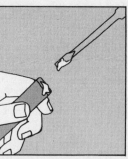

2 Push epoxy resin with the screwdriver into the handle. Pack it about two-thirds full

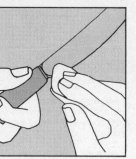

4 Use a soft cloth to remove any surplus resin which has oozed out of the handle

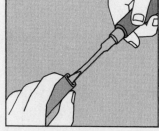

1 Use an old screwdriver to scrape out all the adhesive from the inside of the handle. Scrape gently

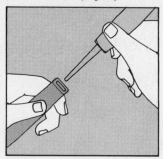

3 Push the tang firmly into the handle. Make sure that the butt of the blade touches the bone

5 Bind the blade to the handle with adhesive tape. Leave to harden for at least 24 hours. Remove tape

Mending forks

Most fork prongs—which are called tines—can be straightened if they become bent. But some repairs to forks cannot be done at home. If the spring guard of a carving fork becomes loose, for example, take it to a jeweller for repair.

Tools: vice; rule; cloth.

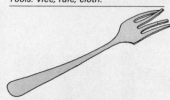

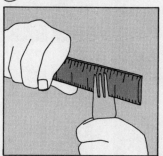

1 If the tines are bent towards each other, insert a wooden rule and lever them apart

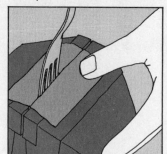

2 If the tines are out of line, lay a cloth in a vice and gently tighten it to clamp and realign the tines

Repairing spoons

Valuable silver spoons should be repaired only by an expert. But it is possible to restore ordinary household spoons which have been dented.

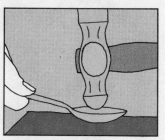

1 If a distortion bulges inwards, place spoon on a wooden surface and gently tap it with a domed hammer

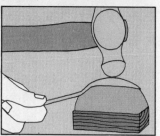

2 If the distortion bulges outwards, make a cast with filler (see p. 683), with the top shaped to the inside of the bowl. Allow the cast to set. Rub down the bump and stick the cast to a piece of wood.
  Rest the bowl on the cast and hammer the distortion gently with a domed hammer or fibre mallet

Fabrics and clothing Dyeing

Choosing and using fabric dyes

Always check the fabric to be dyed and make sure that the dye is suitable. If a garment comprises more than one type of material, follow the directions for the most delicate part.

Always wear rubber gloves when dyeing. If the clothes have to be stirred, use a spoon.

Make sure that the fabrics are weighed dry, and soak them thoroughly before putting them in the dye

Special finishes Do not try to dye any fabric which has a special finish—for example, if it is permanently pleated, crease-resistant,

flame-proof, mothproof or showerproof. Dye only fabrics which can be washed: do not treat material which has to be dry-cleaned.

Never dye swimsuits, foam-backed fabrics, electric blankets, sheepskin, fur, leather, suede, felt, plastic sponges or glass-fibre.

Faded colours Find out if the existing colour is fast by washing a small part of it. If the colour is removed, or if it has faded in parts, treat the garment first with a proprietary dye remover suitable for the fabric.

Drying After dyeing, wring or lightly spin the

fabrics. Dry them away from sunshine or direct heat. Clean the bowl or washing machine thoroughly with hot water, detergent and bleach. Rinse it before using again.

Types of dye There are four types of fabric dye. Make sure that they are suitable for the fabrics being coloured.

Cold dye is a powder which has to be mixed. It should not be used on most man-made fibres; but it is the only colourfast dye—which makes it suitable for articles frequently washed. Fabrics dyed by any other means

should not be washed with other clothes.
Wash 'n' Dye needs no mixing and cleans as it dyes. It does not act on some man-made fibres.

Liquid dye is ready-mixed and needs no heating. Use on any fabric that can be dyed.

Multi-purpose dye has the biggest choice of colours, is cheapest, and can be used on any dyeable fabric; but the powder must be carefully mixed. Except for very pale colours, a boiler or heatproof bowl is needed to heat the solution.

Fibre	Dye
Cotton, linen, wool	any
Silk	any
Rayon Viscose	any
Acetate	any except cold
Nylon (also Enkalon, Celon, Perlon)	any except cold
Terylene (also Crimplene, Dacron, Tergal, Terlanka)	only multi-purpose or liquid
Tricel	only multi-purpose or liquid
Acrylic (Orlon, Acrilan, Courtelle)	do not dye
Cashmere, Angora	do not dye
Mohair	do not dye

Approximate weight guide

		lb.
Candlewick bedspread	single	$2-3\frac{1}{2}$
	double	$3\frac{1}{2}-7$
Curtain, 9ft long	light	$2-3$
	heavy	7
Chair cover (linen)	light	$2-3$
	heavy	$3\frac{1}{2}-5$
Blanket	single	$2\frac{1}{2}-4$
	double	$3\frac{1}{2}-7$
Sheet	single	$1-2$
	double	$2-4$
Pillowcase		$\frac{1}{4}-\frac{1}{2}$
Towel	hand	$\frac{1}{4}-\frac{1}{2}$
	bath	$1-2$
Sweater	light	$\frac{1}{4}-\frac{1}{2}$
	medium	1
	heavy	$1\frac{1}{2}-2$
Slacks	light	$\frac{1}{2}$
	heavy	1
Cotton dress		$\frac{1}{2}-1$
Blouse		$\frac{1}{4}$
Nightdress		$\frac{1}{2}$
Slip		$\frac{1}{4}$
Shirt		$\frac{1}{2}$
String vest		$\frac{1}{4}$
Stockings	4 pairs	$\frac{1}{2}$

Method	Quantity per lb. fabric	Preparation	Dyeing
Multi-purpose dye: by hand	2 tins (4 if dyeing nylon or acetate black; 6 for Terylene or Tricel)	Wash fabrics. If clean, wet them Dissolve dye in boiling water (1 pint per tin) Fill fireproof bowl or boiler with very hot water to cover fabrics; add dye and 1 heaped tblspn salt per tin. Stir	Spread fabrics evenly in bowl or boiler. Keep submerged and moving. Simmer 20 minutes **Pastel shades** Do not simmer **Wool** Bring slowly to simmer; reduce immediately Stir gently for 10 minutes **Nylon, acetate, Terylene, Tricel** Stir 15 minutes Rinse until water clears
Multi-purpose dye: washing machine	2 tins (4 if dyeing nylon or acetate black, 6 for Terylene or Tricel). Half-load at a time	Wash and rinse fabrics Mask inside of lid with foil Dissolve dye in boiling water (1 pint per tin) Run very hot water into machine ($1\frac{1}{2}$ gal. per tin) Add dye and 1 heaped tblspn salt per tin. Agitate	Add fabrics and agitate for 20 minutes. Keep heater on if possible. If automatic, use hottest cycle **Wool** Do not agitate: stir gently for 10 minutes **Blankets** Agitate for only 5 minutes Rinse until water clears
Liquid dye: by hand	$\frac{1}{2}$ bottle (dark colours, 1 bottle)	Wash and rinse fabrics Fill bowl with very hot water to cover fabrics Add dye and 2 tblspns salt per $\frac{1}{2}$ bottle. Stir	Spread fabrics evenly in bowl. Keep submerged and stir for 20 minutes **Wool** Stir for only 10 minutes Rinse until water is clear
Liquid dye: washing machine	$\frac{1}{2}$ bottle (dark colours, 1 bottle). Half-load at a time	Wash and rinse fabrics Mask inside of lid with foil Run very hot water into machine Add dye plus 2 tblspns salt per $\frac{1}{2}$ bottle. Agitate	Add fabrics and agitate for 20 minutes. Keep heater on if possible. If automatic, use hottest cycle **Wool** Do not agitate: stir gently for 10 minutes **Blankets** Agitate for 5 minutes Rinse until water clears
Wash 'n' Dye: washing machine	$\frac{1}{2}$ jar. Half-load at a time	Mask inside of lid with foil Run in very hot water (3 gal. per $\frac{1}{2}$ jar) Add dye. Agitate	Add fabrics and agitate for 12 minutes. Keep heater on if possible. If the machine is automatic, use the hottest cycle **Wool** Wet before dyeing. Do not agitate: stir gently Rinse until water clears
Cold dye: by hand	2 tins	Wash and rinse fabrics Add warm water to dye (1 pint per tin). Stir Fill bowl with enough cold water to cover fabrics Add dye and 4 heaped tblspns salt per tin and either 1 sachet Cold Fix or 1 heaped tblspn soda dissolved in hot water. Stir **Wool** Fill bowl with hot water, but instead of salt and Cold Fix, use $1\frac{1}{2}$ cups vinegar	Spread fabrics evenly in bowl Stir constantly for 10 minutes. Keep fabrics submerged Rinse Wash in very hot water and detergent Rinse until water clears
Cold dye: washing machine	2 tins. Half-load at a time	Wash and rinse fabrics Mask inside of lid with foil Dissolve dye (1 pint of warm water per tin). Stir Run cold water into machine (1 gal. per tin) Add dye, and 4 heaped tblspns salt per tin and either 1 sachet Cold Fix or 1 heaped tblspn soda dissolved in hot water. Agitate **Wool** Fill machine with hot water, but instead of salt and Cold Fix, use $1\frac{1}{2}$ cups vinegar	Add fabrics and agitate for 10 minutes, then occasionally for 20 minutes. If the machine is automatic, consult a dealer **Wool** Do not agitate, but stir gently Rinse Wash in very hot water and detergent Rinse until water clears

Fabrics and clothing Washing

Washing, drying and ironing

Before washing any garment, check the fabric and find out how it should be treated. If a garment combines several types of fabric, treat it in the way recommended for the most delicate part.

Ironing Follow the temperature markings on the iron. Some may indicate the settings for specific fabrics; others may show only when the iron is hot, warm or cool. Many modern irons have dots to indicate the approximate temperature: 000 (very hot), 00 (warm), 0 (cool).

Washing	Temperature	Action	Water removal
Cotton, linen			
White	very hot	maximum	spin/wring
Fast colours	hot	maximum	spin/wring
Non-fast colours	warm	medium	spin/wring
Special finishes	hand-hot	medium	short spin/drip dry
Viscose rayon			
White and fast colours	hot	maximum	spin/wring
Non-fast colours	warm	medium	spin/wring
Special finishes	hand-hot	medium	short spin/drip dry
Acetate rayon, Tricel	warm	medium	short spin/drip dry
Permanently pleated	warm	hand-wash	drip dry
Nylon (also Enkalon, Celon, Perlon)			
White	hot	medium	short spin/drip dry
Coloured	hand-hot	medium	short spin/drip dry
Terylene (also Crimplene, Dacron, Tergal, Terlanka)	hand-hot	medium	short spin/drip dry
Acrylic	warm	medium	short spin/drip dry
Acrylic/cotton	hand-hot	medium	short spin/drip dry
Permanently pleated	warm	hand-wash	drip dry
Wool (inc. mixtures)	warm	minimum	spin
Silk Fast colours	warm	hand-wash	spin

Ironing	Condition of fabric	Temperature
Cotton, linen	damp	hot
Viscose rayon	damp	hot
Acetate rayon, Tricel	damp	warm
Nylon (also Enkalon, Celon, Perlon)	dry	warm
Terylene (also Crimplene, Dacron, Tergal, Terlanka)	dry	warm
Acrylic	dry	cool
Wool (inc. wool mixtures)	damp	warm
Silk (slub, crêpe)	damp / dry	warm / warm

Fabrics and clothing Stitches

Sewing materials and equipment

It is advisable to have two pairs of scissors for any kind of needlework. Buy heavy scissors—with 6–7 in. (150–180 mm) blades—and small nail scissors for clipping. Do not use wax sticks to mark fabrics. Have tailor's chalk—white and coloured—available.

Use a medium-size needle—size 3/7—for wool, flannel, and other firm fabrics: size 8/10 for silks. For embroidery—such as appliqué stitching—buy a crewel needle. Always use a thread to match the fabric but buy a shade deeper. Use Sylko thread for wool and cotton; silk thread for jersey and silk fabrics. Never use thread longer than 18 in. (455 mm).

Do not stoop over the work when sewing: keep the material on a flat surface at a height which allows the arms to rest comfortably.

Preparation and finishing are equally important to good repairs. Pin and tack the fabric carefully, and make sure it is pressed neatly when the repair has been made.

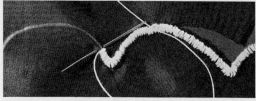

Appliqué stitch Used for decorative motifs. Use a crewel needle and embroidery silk. Sew very small overstitches close together. Cut along the outside of the shape when complete

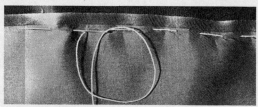

Tacking stitch Start on the right-hand side. Push needle through the fabric and bring it out again $\frac{1}{2}$ in. (13 mm) further along. Pass over $\frac{1}{2}$ in. and push needle in. Continue to the end

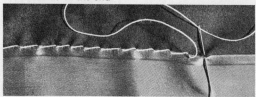

Hemstitch Start with the knot under the turn of the hem. Pull needle through and take up threads of garment as near hem as possible. Pull needle up through edge of hem. Keep stitches slanting

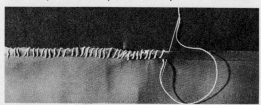

Overstitch Used for hems. Start with thread knot under the turned edge. Cross needle to the main part of material, pick up a few threads and take needle back up through the hem edge

Herringbone stitch Used to sew two edges without overlapping. Insert needle under one edge. Pull thread up and across to underside of other edge. Cross back over to first edge and push down

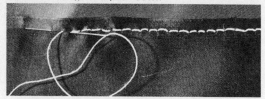

Backstitch Used for seams. Push needle through to right side of fabric and back again to make a small stitch. Push needle through behind last hole made and out just ahead of the previous stitch

Fabrics and clothing Shirts

Turning a worn cuff

The method of repairing worn shirt cuffs varies according to whether the cuff is a single or a double one.

With a single cuff, tuck the frayed edge inside itself and sew a new hem. With a double cuff, remove the whole cuff, turn it over with the frayed edge inside and re-attach it to the sleeve.

Materials: thread to match the shirt fabric.
Tools: small, fine scissors; pins; sewing machine; iron.

Tacking-stitch

Hemstitch

Overstitch

1 Before removing double cuffs, pin and tack-stitch the pleats just above the cuff

2 Use small, fine scissors to unpick the thread holding the cuff to the sleeve

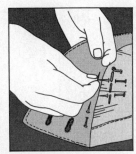

3 Turn the cuff over, worn edge on the inside. Pin in place along old stitching line

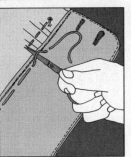

4 Use a tacking stitch along the old stitching line on the shirt cuff. Remove all the pins

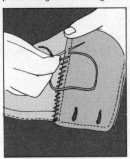

5 Iron the outside, machine stitch along the edge of the cuff. Remove the tacking

6 Turn the sleeve inside out and finish off by hemstitching along the other side

REPAIRING A SINGLE CUFF

1 Cut along bottom edge and up the sides for about 1 in. (25 mm)

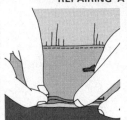

2 Turn in enough cuff to hide the edge that has become worn or ragged

3 Pin along the cuff near the folded edge. Tack-stitch and remove pins

4 Sew along cuff edge with small overstitching. Machine along original stitch line

Patching a worn collar

To mend a worn collar on a schoolboy's shirt, cut a piece larger than the tear from the tail of the shirt and sew it over the collar with matching thread. If there is only a slit or a slight tear in the collar, use 1 in. (25 mm) fabric tape instead. Ensure that the patch fits firmly over the repair and that there is no loose material that could ruck and form a fold.

Materials: thread.
Tools: scissors; needle; pins; iron.

Hemstitch

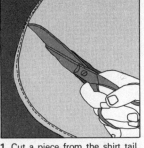

1 Cut a piece from the shirt tail. Turn in the cut end of the tail and hemstitch

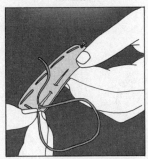

2 Trim the patch to fit over the worn area. Turn in and tack-stitch the edges. Press the patch

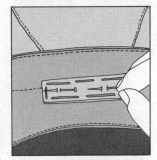

3 Trim any ragged edges on the collar. Place the patch over the worn part and pin it down

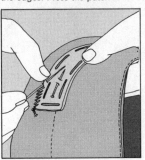

4 Hemstitch finely round the patch with a thread matching the colour of the shirt

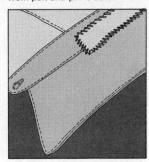

5 Remove the tacking. Press the patch smoothly against the collar with a warm iron

AROUND THE HOME 279

Fabrics and clothing Trousers

Replacing a broken zip

If a zip slider is worn or distorted, the teeth of the zip will not lock together when the slider is pulled across them. A new slider must be exactly the same size as the one it is to replace. To fit a new slider, see p. 335.

When buying a new zip for a pair of trousers, take the old zip to the shop as a comparison and make sure the shop assistant knows what it is for. Trouser zips are usually stronger than skirt zips.

Materials: zip; tacking and machine thread.
Tools: small, straight scissors; needle; sewing machine.

Overstitch

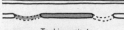
Tacking stitch

Backstitch

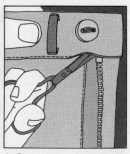
1 Cut away the stitches holding the waistband to the trousers at the top of the zip

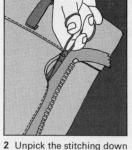
2 Unpick the stitching down both sides and at the bottom of the old zip

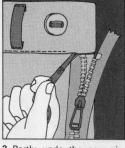
3 Partly undo the new zip and tuck one side of it into the trouser waistband

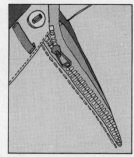
4 Line up the edge of zip tape with edge of zip flap. Tack-stitch it to the flap

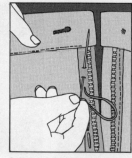
5 Machine-stitch down the tacked side parallel to the zip. Remove tacking

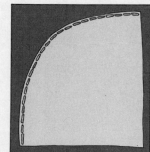
6 Turn trousers inside out. Tack-stitch the other side of zip, ½ in. (13 mm) from edge

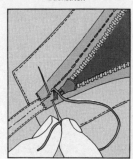
7 Stitch the ends of the zip tape together at the bottom. Check that it is straight

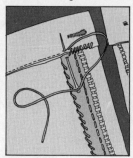
8 Backstitch the zip by hand, close to the teeth. Remove the tacking

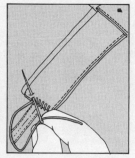
9 Overstitch the waistband of the trousers on both sides of the zip

10 Overstitch neatly across the ends of the flap inside the front of the trousers

Repairing a torn pocket

If there is a large hole in the pocket, the damaged area must be cut off and replaced. But if there is only a small hole, near the bottom of the pocket, stitch a new seam above the tear.

Materials: spare lining or ready-made pocket; tacking and machine thread.
Tools: scissors; sewing machine; needle; iron.

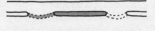
Tacking stitch

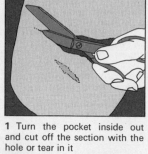
1 Turn the pocket inside out and cut off the section with the hole or tear in it

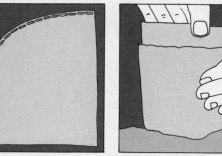
2 Fold over some new pocket material, cut to size and machine-stitch round edge

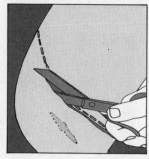
3 Fit the new piece upside-down into the turned-out pocket. Tack-stitch the edges together

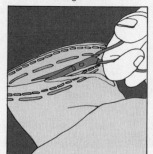
4 Machine-stitch round the join. Remove tacking. Trim the edge. Push pocket inside and press

Corner hole Machine above the tear in a slight curve. Trim below the new stitching

Fabrics and clothing Jackets

Patching with leather

Leather cuff strips and elbow patches can be bought in ready-made sets. If they are not already perforated for sewing, run them under an unthreaded sewing machine, ⅛ in. (3 mm) in from the edge of the leather.

Materials: leather cuffs and patches; strong thread.
Tools: pins; needle; scissors.

Overstitch

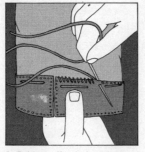

1 Fold a cuff strip lengthways. Pin it to the cuff. Tack and remove pins. Overstitch

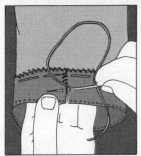

2 Sew the ends of the strip together over the whole width, again using an overstitch

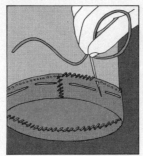

3 Turn the sleeve inside out, fold the patch over and overstitch edges. Remove tacking

REINFORCING AN ELBOW

1 Pin the patch over the elbow and tack-stitch it. Remove the pins

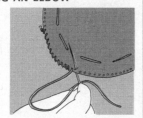

2 Push needle up through patch and overstitch all round. Remove the tacking

Mending tweed and flannel

To mend tweed or flannel, cut a piece from an unseen part of a seam or hem. Make sure that the pattern and weave of the patch match those of the torn area.

Materials: matching silk thread; tacking thread; damp cloth (for pressing completed repair).
Tools: scissors; needle; thimble; iron.

Tacking stitch

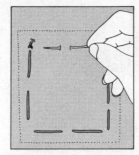

1 Match the pattern, and tack-stitch the patch to the underside of the tear

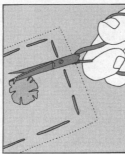

2 Trim the loose threads around the edge of the hole in the material

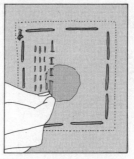

3 Use a thread to match the weave of the fabric and sew with a very small darn-stitch

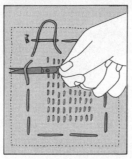

4 Turn the material over and remove the tacking stitches with a pair of scissors

5 Cut away surplus fabric round the repair. Press on right side with a damp cloth

Reinforcing buttons

To strengthen fastenings on clothes which get rough treatment—such as school jackets—sew a strip of matching tape inside the jacket, along the whole length of the buttoning.

Materials: matching cotton tape; thread.
Tools: scissors; pins; needle; thimble.

Hemstitch

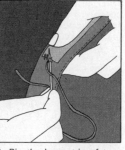

1 Pin the long strip of tape inside the jacket edge. Hemstitch it to the inside facing

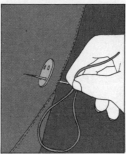

2 Use thread to match button thread and sew twice through tape and button

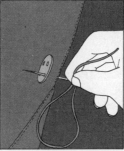

3 Push needle through near button and twist thread round button three times

4 Sew through between the button and the jacket and take thread through the tape

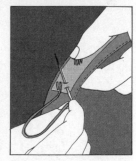

5 Overstitch three times behind the button. Cut thread and repeat on other buttons

Fabrics and clothing   Skirts

Fitting a new zip

Although a skirt zip is not covered by a flap, it is possible to conceal the zip by fitting the skirt edges precisely. Make sure before sewing in a new zip to a garment that the edges of the material meet, and then tack-stitch them together.

Materials: zip; tacking and machine thread.
Tools: small, straight scissors; pins; needle; sewing machine.

Overstitch

1 Unpick the skirt waistband with scissors for 1 in. (25 mm) on both sides of the zip

2 Unpick and cut the stitching down both sides of the old zip. Remove the zip

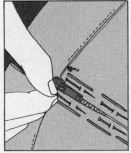

3 Pin new zip in place. Tack-stitch along both sides of zip and across line of zip

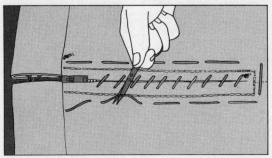

4 Remove pins and make sure that edges of the material are held lightly together with the tack-stitching. Machine down sides and across bottom of zip. Remove tacking

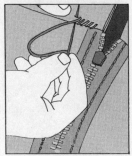

5 Turn skirt inside out. Slip the top of zip tapes under band and hem across bands

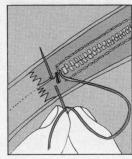

6 Overstitch across the bottom of the zip tapes. Trim inside of skirt at the tape

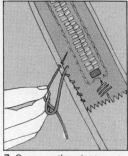

7 Oversew the zip tape to the skirt. Then iron zip through a damp cloth

Repairing a torn pleat

Stretching at the top of a pleat can cause wear and may even tear it. To repair a tear, place a triangular patch across the outside of the seam. If no other matching material is available, cut a patch from a seam.

Materials: matching material for patch; a small piece of Vylene; thread; damp cloth.
Tools: pins; dressmaking scissors; needle; iron.

Hemstitch

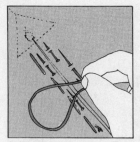

1 Lay the skirt flat and pin the edges of the pleat so that they meet but do not overlap. Tack-stitch and remove pins

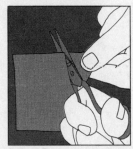

2 From a hem, cut a triangle with each side about 2 in. (50 mm). Cut a Vylene triangle with 1 in. (25 mm) sides

3 Pin the Vylene triangle in the centre of the triangle of material. Cut the points off the larger triangle

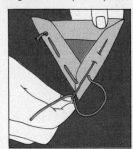

4 Fold the edges of the material over the Vylene. Tack them down. Press the triangle with a damp cloth

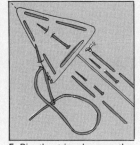

5 Pin the triangle over the pleat, with point on the seam. Hemstitch finely. Remove tacking and pins, then press

Replacing a loop

If the loop at a hook-and-eye fastening breaks, remove the existing eye or thread.

Make a new loop with buttonhole thread by tying a series of ordinary loop knots on top of each other until the thread builds up to form a thicker 'string'.

Materials: buttonhole thread.
Tool: needle.

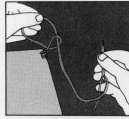

1 Sew four stitches at the same spot. On fourth, pull needle tightly through loop

2 Repeat the loop knot eight times until knots build up into a string

3 When the string is long enough, fold it over and sew the free end to the dress

Fabrics Elastic/Fur/Quilts

Fitting new elastic

If the elastic in a garment stretches and becomes unusable, measure a new piece against the old—unstretched—when it is still in the garment. Allow a 2 in. (50 mm) overlap for the join. Sew it to the old elastic and pull it through the hem.

Materials: elastic; thread.
Tools: safety pin; needle; scissors.

Overstitch

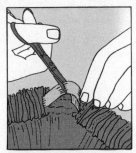

1 Unpick the hem. Cut through the old elastic and hold the two ends

2 Sew new elastic to end of old piece. Fix safety pin to loose end of new elastic

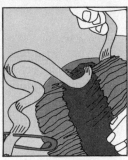

3 Pull the old elastic to drag new elastic through until the pin reaches the hem

4 Cut off the old elastic. Hold both ends of new elastic and remove the safety pin

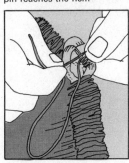

5 Overlap the two ends by 1 in. (25 mm) and sew them together. Overstitch the hem

ADDING ELASTIC

Do not try to remove elastic which is held by rows of machine stitching—for example in pyjamas or pants. If it becomes stretched, fit a 9 in. (230 mm) strip of new elastic over the old at the back. Buy elastic to match the garment. Stretch it when machining it.

Materials: 9 in. (230 mm) elastic strip; thread.
Tools: sewing machine; needle; pins; tape measure.

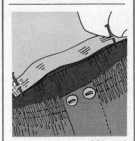

1 Measure 13 in. (330 mm) across the back. Pin the new strip at each end, then machine stitch

2 Stretch new elastic and tack it to the old. Machine along the top and bottom edges. Remove tacking

Mending fur

When the skin of a fur is torn it can be repaired from behind without damaging or disturbing the fur. When dealing with a coat, remove any lining and padding before beginning work on the skin.

To finish the repair, smooth the fur lightly down with the side of a pin.

Material: silk thread.
Tools: needle; pins; scissors.

Overstitch

1 Fold the skin along line of the split. Press down fur between the split with a needle

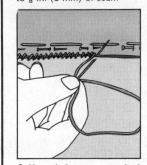

2 Start ½ in. (13 mm) before the split and sew with an overstitch to ½ in. past it

Re-covering a quilt

To re-cover a quilt, wrap it in new material such as cotton curtain fabric and sew around. Cut the covering material 2 in. (50 mm) wider and longer than the quilt.

Materials: re-covering material; thread; ½ in. (13 mm) buttons.
Tools: tape measure; scissors; pins; needle; sewing machine.

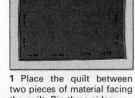

1 Place the quilt between two pieces of material facing the quilt. Pin three sides

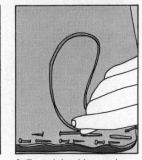

2 Remove quilt and machine round the three sides. Trim to ⅛ in. (3 mm) of seam

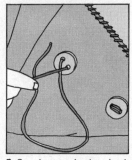

3 Turn right side out. Insert the quilt and turn in open end. Pin and tack

4 Hemstitch across tacked end, ⅛ in. (3 mm) from edge. Remove tacking stitches

5 Sew buttons back to back on both sides of the quilt where originally indented

Fabrics and clothing Sheets and pillowcases

Turning the sides to the middle

Sheets are more likely to wear in the middle than at the edge. If the sheet has been torn near the centre, cut it in two down its length at this point and put the outside edges in the centre. Stitch the edges together.

Materials: tacking and sewing-machine thread.
Tools: large pair of scissors; pins; sewing machine.

Tacking stitch

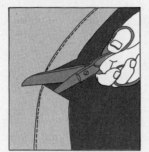

1 Cut through the hem of the sheet in line with the part that is worn or torn

2 Tear the sheet right down and cut through the hem at the other end

3 Align the two frayed edges. Pin them together and trim loose threads. Take out pins

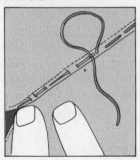

4 Overlap the original sides ½ in. (13 mm). Pin together and tack. Machine along join

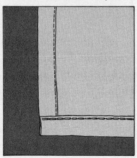

5 Fold in the outside edges ½ in. (13 mm). Pin and tack. Machine-stitch along new hem

Repairing a small hole

A hole in a pillowcase can be covered with a decorative appliqué patch instead of mended invisibly. This design can be a star—as here—or a flower, for instance, and in any contrasting colour.

Materials: paper; material for patch; tacking thread and mercerised or embroidery silk.
Tools: needle; pins; scissors.

Appliqué

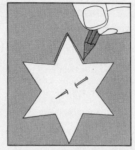

1 Cut a paper pattern in any shape. Pin it to a square of material and draw round it

2 Place the centre of the square over the hole. Tack round edge of the material

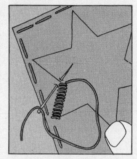

3 Appliqué-stitch round the edge of the design. Sew with no space between stitches

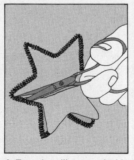

4 Turn the pillowcase inside out and trim the edges of the hole to the appliqué stitching

5 Turn pillowcase to its right side and trim excess material from patch

Mending a long tear

When a tear in a sheet or a pillowcase is long and fairly straight, mend it by patching with 1 in. (25 mm) wide white fabric tape.

Materials: 1 in. (25 mm) wide white fabric tape; tacking, cross-stitch and machine thread.
Tools: scissors; pins; needle; sewing machine.

Backstitch

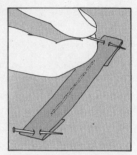

1 Cut the fabric tape 2 in. (50 mm) longer than tear. Turn in and pin over sheet

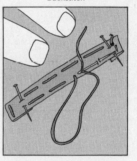

2 Check that the torn edges of the sheet meet behind the tape. Tack tape to sheet

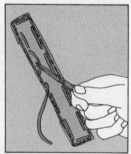

3 Machine-stitch or back-stitch round edges of tape and remove tacking stitches

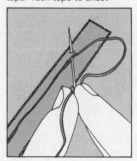

4 Turn sheet over and stitch edges of tear together, taking stitches through the tape

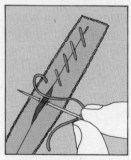

5 When stitching, make sure the material is smooth on each side of the tear

Making a square patch

A sheet or pillow with a large hole in it can be repaired with a patch of matching material. Obtain the material from a hem or an unwanted sheet. If the sheet to be patched is badly worn, make the patch much larger than the hole.

Materials: tacking, hemming and sewing-machine thread. Tools: scissors; needle; iron; sewing machine; pins.

Hemstitch

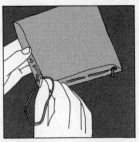

1 Cut the patch large enough to overlap the hole by 1 in. (25 mm). Turn in the edges, tack and press

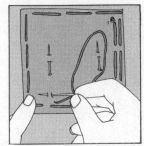

2 Remove the tacking. Place the patch on the hole, and tack it to the sheet. Press flat with an iron

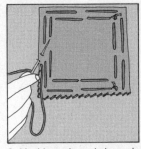

3 Machine or hemstitch evenly all round the edge of the patch, keeping the patch flat and even on the sheet

4 Turn the sheet over. Cut the raw edges of the hole to within ¼ in. (6 mm) of the stitching. Snip off the corners

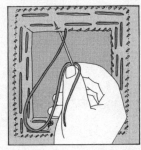

5 Turn in the raw edges. Pin and tack them down. Hemstitch the turns to the patch. Remove the tacking

Repairing a torn edge

If a sheet has been torn on the hem, the tear can be covered with a piece of ¼ in. (6 mm) wide fabric tape. Use matching tape when possible. If the stitching of a pillowcase has burst at the seam, simply re-sew the seam.

Materials: ¼ in. (6 mm) wide fabric tape; tacking and sewing-machine thread. Tools: scissors; pins; sewing machine; needle; iron.

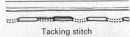

Tacking stitch

1 Trim the edges of the tear. Fold and pin the fabric tape along the edge of the sheet and over the tear

2 Tack-stitch the fabric tape to both sides of the sheet along the torn edge to hold it in position temporarily

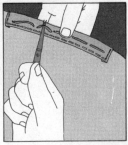

3 Machine along the edges with matching cotton. Take out the tacking and press with the iron

MENDING A FRAYED PILLOWCASE

1 Turn the pillowcase inside out and trim to clear the way for repairing loose edges of case

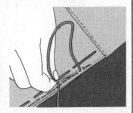

2 Tack the two edges together. Continue the existing line of stitching with a machine

Darning

In darning, rows of stitches are sewn first in one direction and then at a right angle. The repair should have a diamond shape. Leave small loops at the end of each row to allow for any shrinkage.

Materials: darning wool (or elasticated or double Terylene thread). Tools: darning mushroom or apple; darning needle.

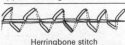

Herringbone stitch

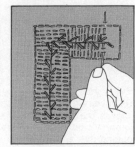

1 Use a herringbone stitch to draw edges of an L-shaped tear together without any overlapping

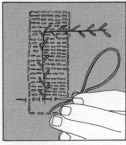

2 Darn thread back and forth on one side of tear only. Extend darning ½ in. (13 mm) beyond each end of tear

3 Repeat the darning stitch, at right angles to that already done, across the tear on the other side of the material

DARNING A HOLE IN A SOCK

1 Extend darning ¾ in. (20 mm) on either side of hole. At the hole, thread straight across

2 Work to a diamond shape. Then repeat stitch at right angles, weaving across wool at hole

Fishing tackle Cane rods

General maintenance

Clean all rods after fishing outings. After sea fishing, wash the rod in fresh water to remove all traces of salt. Dry it with a clean rag. After a freshwater outing, rub the rod first with a clean, damp rag, then with a dry one.

Smear all the exposed metal parts—ferrules and reel screw-fittings—with oil or light grease. Wipe this off before using the rod again.

Every three months

Check that the line has not grooved the rings. If the rings are porcelain, look for cracks. Fit new ones if necessary, and re-bind loose rings.

To clean inside the ferrules, dampen a rag in surgical or methylated spirit and wrap it round a small stick.

Clean a cork handle with warm water and a little washing-up liquid.

Every year

Remove all rings and bindings and varnish the rod. Although this is more important on cane rods—to stop water getting into and weakening the cane—it is useful also on glass-fibre, to improve the appearance.

Storing the rod

Always store fishing tackle in a dry place. Keep it out of sunlight, which could soften the varnish. For the same reason, do not carry tackle on the rear window-ledge of a car.

Make sure that all the ferrules are kept free from dirt during storage by plugging them with old bottle corks cut to fit them.

Keep the rod in a cloth cover. Tie it at the middle of the rod, but tie loosely to avoid bending the rod.

Materials: oil or grease; old corks; methylated or surgical spirit; rag; washing-up liquid; parts as necessary; varnish.

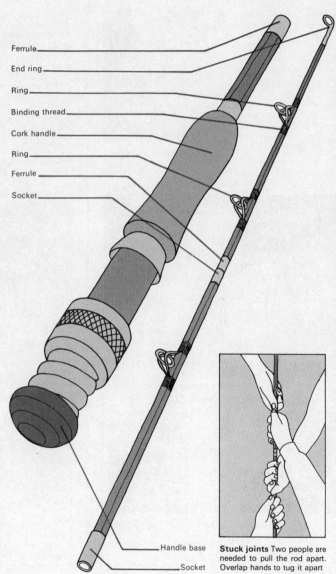

Ferrule
End ring
Ring
Binding thread
Cork handle
Ring
Ferrule
Socket
Handle base
Socket

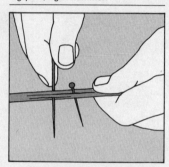

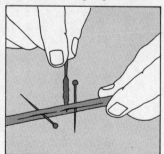

Stuck joints Two people are needed to pull the rod apart. Overlap hands to tug it apart

Repairing a splintered cane

If a cane rod splinters, glue and bind the pieces together. When there is more than one splintered area in the same section of rod, treat them in one operation. When the splinters are repaired, replace any rings and bindings which had to be removed and re-varnish the whole section.

Glass-fibre rods are unlikely to break. If they do, however, no repair is possible.

Materials: waterproof, resin-based glue; varnish; thin, cane-coloured thread; rag.
Tools: paintbrush; sharp knife; sewing pins; light hammer.

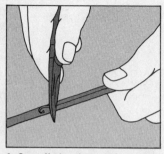

1 Cut off the rings with a sharp knife and scrape the varnish from the splintered section

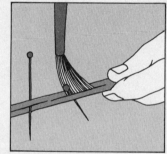

2 Push sewing pins carefully through the cracks to widen them a little before starting to glue them

3 With a small paintbrush, coat inside the cracks with a waterproof, resin-based glue

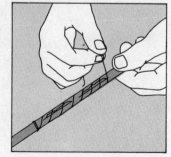

4 Prod the glue into the extreme ends of all the cracks with the tip of a sewing pin

5 Remove the pins. Do not wipe away surplus glue. Bind thread widely and diagonally *(continued)*

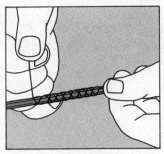

6 Bind tightly beyond the other end of the crack and back again, crossing the threads. Finish with a loop

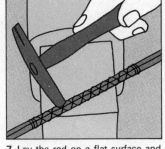

7 Lay the rod on a flat surface and tap lightly along the binding with a light hammer

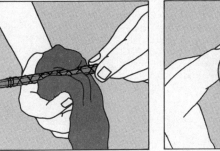

8 Wipe away any surplus glue with a clean, dry, lint-free rag. Try not to smear the glue up the cane

9 Look down the repaired section to ensure it is straight. Twist one end gently if necessary

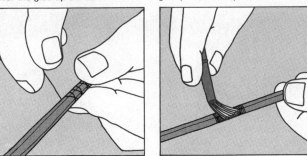

10 Leave the rod to dry for about 12 hours. When the glue is thoroughly set, unwind the thread

11 Scrape off surplus glue with a knife. Bind with cane-coloured thread and brush on varnish

Binding a ring

Binding thread is obtainable in different thicknesses: fine gauge for small, freshwater rods and stouter gauges for the bigger sea rods.

The binding technique is the same for all types of rod. Cut a 3 in. (75 mm) piece of thread for a loop before starting to bind. Make the new binding tight and neat by holding the reel of thread in one hand and twisting the rod with the other. Do not glue or varnish the new thread.

Materials: clear adhesive tape; new thread to suit the rod.
Tool: razor blade.

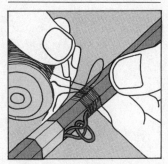

2 Bind without overlapping. Lay a doubled 3 in. (75 mm) thread across the binding at the side

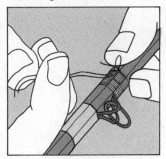

4 Pull the ends of the loop, to bring the loop and the thread end under the edge of the new binding

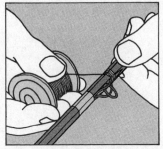

1 Tape one tongue to the rod. Start binding the other tongue, trapping the end of the thread

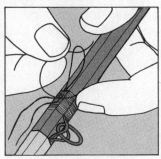

3 Bind four or five times over the loop. Cut the binding thread and push its end through the loop

5 Trim the thread end. Remove the clear tape and bind the other ring in the same way

Fitting an end ring

When the end ring at the tip of a rod is pulled off or lost, it is possible to fix a replacement, usually by gluing with Araldite. Only on sea rods, where the rings are bigger, is it necessary also to bind the tongue. Smooth the end of the tongue with a fine file before binding.

When the end ring has been glued and pushed on to the rod tip, twist it until it is in line with the other rings. Wipe off any surplus glue with methylated spirit.

Materials: Araldite; new end ring; rag; methylated spirit.
Tools: fine file; matchstick.

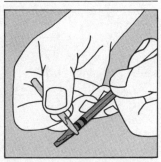

1 Dab some Araldite on the tip of the rod with a sliver of wood or a matchstick

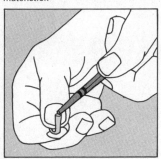

2 Trickle the surplus adhesive into the ring tube and fit the two together. Twist to align the ring

Fishing tackle Cane rods

Repairing a loose socket

A fishing rod should be straight. Check regularly by fitting the sections together and looking along the length of the rod. If one of the sections is out of alignment, the most likely cause is a faulty socket. In some cases, a simple repair is sufficient—heat the socket glue and twist the socket straight. If that is not successful, remove and refit the socket.

Materials: silk thread; binding thread; rag; Araldite; matchstick; methylated spirit.
Tools: sharp knife; gas ring; vice; fine file; glass-paper; hacksaw blade; small block of wood; hammer.

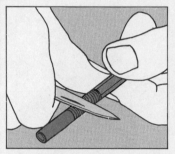

1 Cut off the old binding by scraping firmly with a sharp knife. Do not cut into the rod

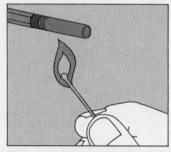

2 Heat the socket gently over a match flame to soften the adhesive inside. Take care not to overheat it

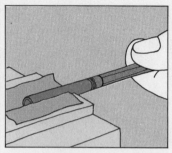

3 Protect the socket with a rag and secure it in a vice. Grip the rod section and pull it out of the socket

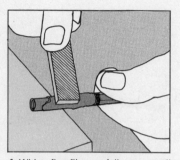

4 With a fine file, carefully remove all the old socket glue from the base of the rod section

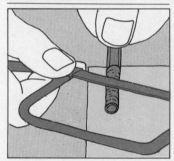

6 Roughen the surface of the rod with an old hacksaw blade or file to give a good key for the adhesive

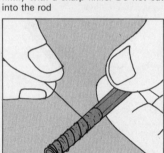

7 Build up the thickness of the rod to fit the socket tightly by binding the roughened section with silk thread

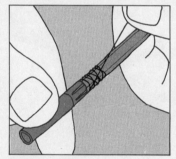

8 Slip the socket on the rod to test how they fit. Bind on more thread if it is still not tight

9 Use a matchstick to coat some Araldite on the new silk binding and inside the socket

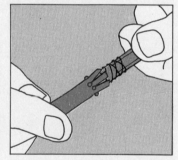

10 Allow the adhesive to become tacky. Push the socket as far as possible on to the end of the rod

12 With a cloth moistened with methylated spirit, wipe away any surplus adhesive forced out

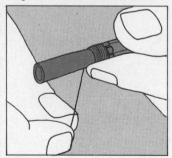

13 Bind the tongues of the socket with a strong binding thread. Bind straight and do not overlap the thread

14 Leave the socket to dry for 12 hours. Check that it is tight, and gently hammer down the tongues

15 Moisten a rag with methylated spirit and wipe away any soft glue around the binding or on the socket

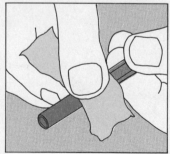

16 Cut and strip the binding off the socket tongues. Remove any hardened glue from the socket with glass-paper

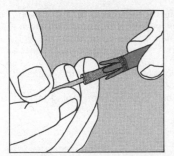

5 Wrap a strip of glass-paper round a matchstick and rub the inside of the socket clean

11 Wrap the rod in a rag and secure it in the vice. Tap the socket fully home with a small piece of wood

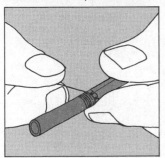

17 Re-bind the tongues with silk thread, preferably of a colour matching that of the rod

Re-varnishing a rod

When the varnish on a cane or glass-fibre rod is very badly damaged along the whole length of the sections, it is advisable to remove the rings and re-varnish.

If the varnish is cracked at a few small spots, it is possible to retouch only the faulty patches. If renewing tyings, treat the ring-binding thread with a colour preservative, made from acetone—which can be obtained from a pharmacy—and a clear adhesive mixed in equal parts.

Materials: clear adhesive; acetone; clear varnish; rag.
Tool: small paintbrush.

2 Allow sufficient time for the clear varnish to dry. Clean the rest of the rod with a damp rag

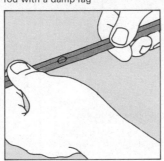

4 Hold the rod between thumb and forefinger and gently rub the varnish round the rod

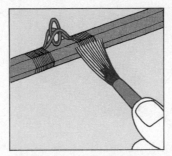

1 Apply colour preservative to the bindings with a small brush. When it is dry, apply clear varnish

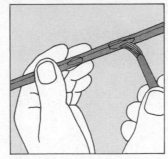

3 Use the small paintbrush to dab varnish on the spots where the old varnish is damaged

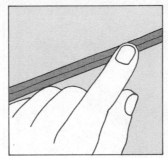

5 Rub the varnish along the rod with the fingers. Allow 24 hours for it to dry, then apply a second coat

Repairing a cork handle

The cork handle of a fishing rod consists of narrow strips called chives fitted on to the butt section of the cane or glass-fibre.

Chives, if they are damaged, must always be replaced from the top—which means that when the damaged area is near the handle base, several sound pieces have to be removed. Strip the rings and bindings from the rod section to allow the cork chives to be fitted.

Materials: chives; Araldite; rag; methylated spirit; thread; clear adhesive.
Tools: sharp knife; steel rule; medium, flat and round-edge files; small paintbrush; vice; glass-paper.

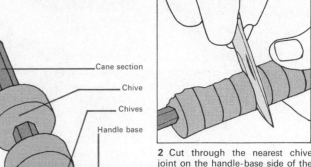

Cane section
Chive
Chives
Handle base

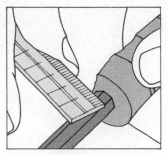

1 Measure the diameter of the cane or glass-fibre and obtain enough chives of the correct size

2 Cut through the nearest chive joint on the handle-base side of the damaged cork

3 Strip off all the old or damaged cork from the cut joint to the top of the handle *(continued)*

(continued)

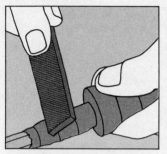

4 Remove any cork still sticking to the surface of the rod with a medium-grade file

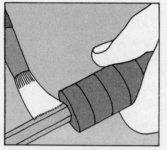

5 Brush a little Araldite around the handle and on the flat face of the first old cork chive

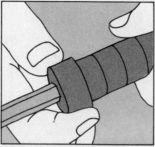

6 Glue and push the first new chive down the rod until it fits tightly against the old cork

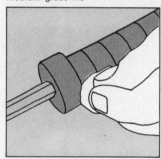

7 Dampen a rag in methylated spirit and wipe off surplus adhesive where the old and new chives join

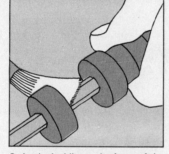

8 Apply Araldite to the faces of the other new chives and the handle. Fit them tightly together

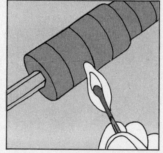

9 Hold a match flame under the chives to expand the cork slightly and seal the joins. Leave overnight

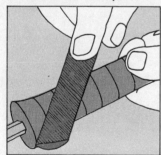

10 Use a file with a rounded edge to start shaping the new chives to match the rest of the handle

11 Finish the shaping with glass-paper—using a coarse grade first, then medium and finally fine

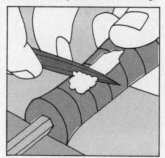

12 Fill any cracks in the cork with a mixture of clear adhesive and cork dust. Scrape on with a knife

Cleaning after use

After every freshwater fishing trip, separate the fly-reel halves, wipe inside with a dry rag, then lubricate with a rag damped in cycle oil. Regularly clean inside with a rag soaked in paraffin or petrol, and lubricate. When the reel has been used for sea fishing, wash it in fresh water. Dry it with a clean rag and lubricate.

Clean the inside of the spindle occasionally with several pipe cleaners bunched together.

Spare parts for fly-reel repairs can be obtained from fishing-tackle specialists or from the manufacturer.

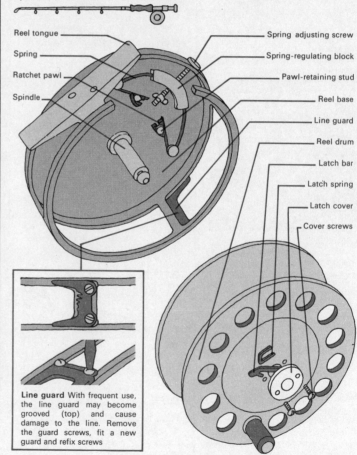

Reel tongue
Spring
Ratchet pawl
Spindle

Spring adjusting screw
Spring-regulating block
Pawl-retaining stud
Reel base
Line guard
Reel drum
Latch bar
Latch spring
Latch cover
Cover screws

Line guard With frequent use, the line guard may become grooved (top) and cause damage to the line. Remove the guard screws, fit a new guard and refix screws

Replacing a broken spring and pawl

Some fly reels are right-handed and have only one check spring and one pawl. On a few types, the manufacturer provides a spare spring and pawl in the reel base. Make sure when fitting a new pawl that its rounded edge is against the spring.

Two-handed reels have two springs and pawls. The pawl nearer the line guard has its long straight edge against the spring. The other—like the right-handed reel—has the rounded edge against the spring.

Materials: spring; pawl; cycle oil; paraffin; rag.
Tools: pliers; paintbrush.

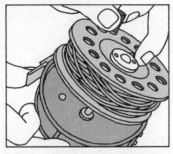

1 If the ratchet is faulty, press the latch bar back against its spring and pull the halves of the reel apart

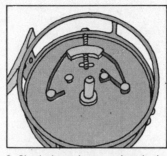

2 Check the spring or springs in the reel base. Make sure that the pawls are positioned correctly

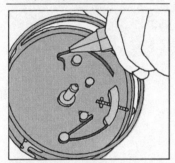

3 If a spring is broken, slide it off its stud with a pair of pliers. Here, a spring is broken and a pawl is missing

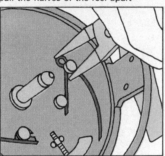

4 Wipe away oil and dirt with a paraffin rag. With the pliers, squeeze the head of a new spring on to its stud

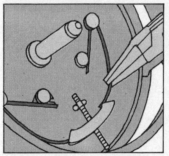

5 Use the pliers to slot the long tail of the spring in front of the regulating block and tension it

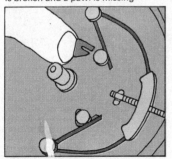

6 Slide a new pawl on to the retaining stud, with its long straight side against the spring

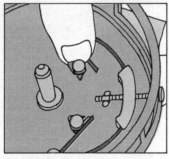

7 If the pawl is the nearer to the reel tongue, turn it clockwise to position the rounded edge against the spring

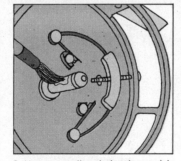

8 Use a small paintbrush to dab cycle oil on the spindle, the pawl and the regulating block

Replacing a latch spring

If a reel drum becomes very loose in the base, it is likely that the latch spring has broken or become so weak that it is not holding back the latch bar properly.

Unscrew the latch cover and remove the spring. Clean inside with a dry cloth and fit a new spring.

When replacing the latch cover, position it by gripping it first behind the latch bar's retaining stud. Press it down gently and make sure that neither the latch bar nor the spring has become displaced.

Materials: latch spring.
Tool: screwdriver.

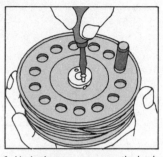

1 Undo the two screws on the latch cover. Take off the cover and remove the spring or broken parts

2 Make sure the latch bar is on its stud. Place the long side of the new spring against the bar

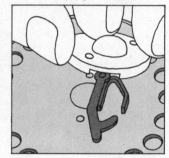

3 Replace the latch cover from behind the stud. There is an indentation in one side to fit the latch bar

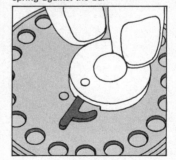

4 Make sure the cover lines up with the screw holes. Press it home without displacing the spring or bar

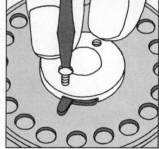

5 Hold the cover firmly in position to stop it slipping. Replace the two screws and tighten them

Fishing tackle Fixed-spool reels

Overhauling a fixed-spool reel

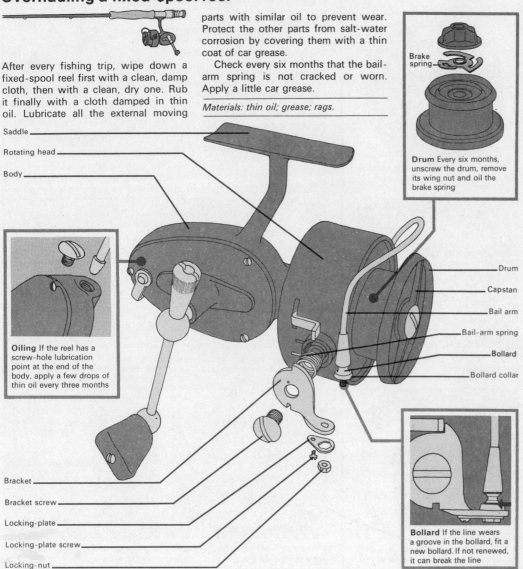

After every fishing trip, wipe down a fixed-spool reel first with a clean, damp cloth, then with a clean, dry one. Rub it finally with a cloth damped in thin oil. Lubricate all the external moving parts with similar oil to prevent wear. Protect the other parts from salt-water corrosion by covering them with a thin coat of car grease.

Check every six months that the bail-arm spring is not cracked or worn. Apply a little car grease.

Materials: thin oil; grease; rags.

Saddle
Rotating head
Body

Oiling If the reel has a screw-hole lubrication point at the end of the body, apply a few drops of thin oil every three months

Bracket
Bracket screw
Locking-plate
Locking-plate screw
Locking-nut

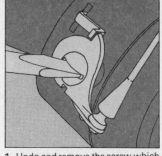

Brake spring

Drum Every six months, unscrew the drum, remove its wing nut and oil the brake spring

Drum
Capstan
Bail arm
Bail-arm spring
Bollard
Bollard collar

Bollard If the line wears a groove in the bollard, fit a new bollard. If not renewed, it can break the line

Replacing a bail-arm spring

The purpose of the bail arm on a fixed-spool reel is to wind the line quickly on and off the reel. When its spring breaks, the arm loses its tension and cannot be adjusted for casting or reeling in. The reel is unusable until a new spring is fitted. The spring housing may vary slightly from one type of reel to another. If necessary, consult the manufacturer's instruction booklet to identify the type of reel being used.

Materials: new spring, obtainable from fishing-tackle dealer.
Tools: screwdriver; steel knitting needle or pin.

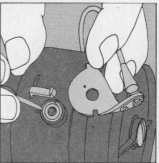

1 Undo and remove the screw which holds the bracket on the reel head

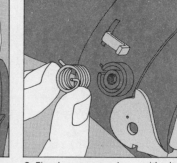

2 Remove the bracket and prise out the spring with a knitting needle

3 Fit the new spring, with its horizontal tail in the slot

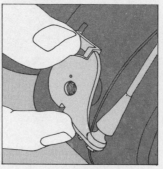

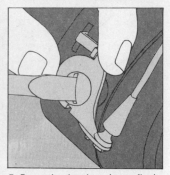

4 Replace the bracket and fit the vertical tail in the bracket hole

5 Press the bracket down firmly. Replace and tighten the screw

Fitting a new bail arm

The bail arm of a fixed-spool reel can break at either of the two ends where it is attached to the reel body. A new arm is obtainable from a tackle shop or direct from the reel manufacturer. Check the bollard and bollard collar before starting the repair, and obtain replacements if necessary.

Note that most pivot-screws cannot be undone with a conventional screwdriver. Pincers are usually a suitable alternative.

Materials: bail arm; bollard and bollard collar if necessary; rag.
Tools: pincers; small screwdriver; small spanner.

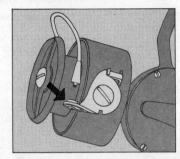

1 The bail arm of a fixed-spool reel usually breaks at its bracket, where it is subject to great stress

2 Loosen the bail-arm pivot-screw by fitting pincers at each end of its slot. A screwdriver is not suitable

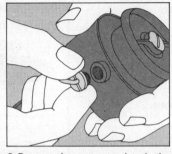

3 Remove the screw to detach the broken arm from the reel. Retain the bollard and collar if possible

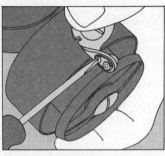

4 Undo the locking-plate screw, which is usually very small, with a screwdriver. Lay it aside carefully

5 Remove the locking-plate which is fitted over the hexagonal lock-nut. Clean it with a dry rag

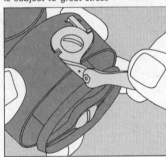

6 Loosen the lock-nut with a small spanner. Remove it by hand and set it aside carefully

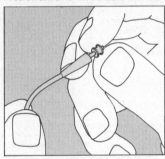

7 If the old bollard is not worn, fit it on the new bail arm. If it is grooved, obtain and fit a new one

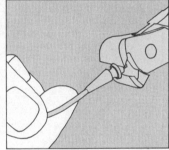
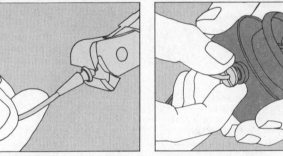

8 Slide the bollard collar on to the end of the bail arm and tighten it gently with pincers

9 Screw in the new arm at the side of the reel. Secure it as tightly as possible with the finger tips

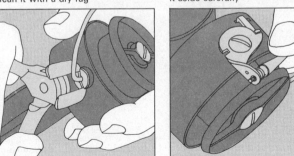

10 Tighten the pivot-screw with pincers. Take care not to break the bail arm by overtightening the screw

11 At the other side of the reel, push the end of the bail arm through its retaining hole in the bracket

12 Screw the small lock-nut on the end of the arm and tighten it with the spanner. Do not overtighten

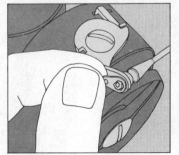

13 Refit the locking-plate, with its hexagonal hole in position over the top of the locking-nut

14 Replace the retaining screw of the locking-plate and tighten it with a small screwdriver

Fountain pens

Maintenance and repair

Do not try to repair an expensive fountain pen. If it is faulty, take it to a dealer or send it to the manufacturer. Less expensive pens, however, can be mended safely at home.

If any work is to be done to a pen nib, first identify the type of fitting. When the nib is screwed in, there is usually a gap between the nib and the pen finger grip. When the nib is pushed in, the finger grip fits closely round the body of the nib.

Make sure when fitting a new ink sac that no old rubber is left on the tube. Remove particles to prevent ink leakage.

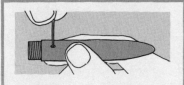

Erratic inking Unscrew the nib and sac unit from the pen. Prick the vent hole in the body with a small pin. Reassemble the sac unit and nib

FITTING A NEW INK SAC

1 Unscrew and remove the pen casing. If the sac is in a cartridge (bottom), pull off the cartridge. Remove the sac

2 Cut off the old sac. Fit a new one on the ink tube. Reassemble the pen

REPAIRING PEN CAPS

Some clips are fixed to the cap with bent tags. Fix a new tag with Araldite

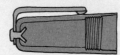

If a clip is secured with a rivet, fit a new rivet. Spread its tongues gently

FITTING A NEW NIB

Screw nibs can be removed with finger pressure. Do not try to force them with pliers. If a nib cannot be removed even after being held in hot water, consult the dealer.

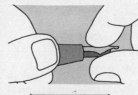

Screw nibs Unscrew the nib and ink feed from the pen casing (top). Clean inside the nib holder with a thin cloth (bottom). Fit new nib

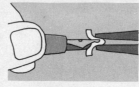

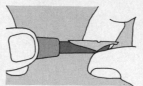

Pull-out nibs Wrap nib tip in cloth and pull off (top). Fit new nib on ink feed and slide into pen (bottom)

Cleaning a blocked pen

If the pen does not fill, there are three possible faults: a blockage at the ink feed under the nib; a twisted or perished sac; or a jammed filler mechanism. If the feed is blocked, clean it. If the sac is perished, fit a new one. Try to free a filler mechanism by manipulating it. If this fails, take the pen to a dealer for repair.

TYPES OF FILLER MECHANISM

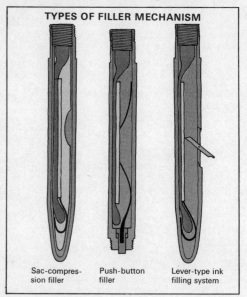

Sac-compression filler   Push-button filler   Lever-type ink filling system

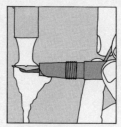

1 Hold the nib under cold running water and operate the filling mechanism. If the pen does not fill, try again in a weak solution of detergent and water

2 If it is still blocked, remove the nib unit and separate the nib from the ink feed. Scrape any hardened ink from the feed groove with a wood splinter. Reassemble

Furniture

Preparing to repair furniture

Many furniture repairs are within the scope of an amateur; but it is advisable to experiment on a piece of scrap timber similar to the damaged piece before attempting to work on a valuable item.

Plan the repair carefully and make sure that all the tools and materials required are available before starting work. Never try to use tools which are blunt or in a poor condition (see p. 380).

Do not try to hurry furniture repair work: a satisfactory result often depends almost entirely on patience and slow, but methodical, stage-by-stage work. If an adhesive is used, it is advisable to leave it to set overnight, before continuing the repair.

Using adhesives

Never use a contact adhesive to stick pieces of wood (see p. 694). Most old furniture will have been fixed originally with Scotch glue—an adhesive which eventually dries into brown crystals. Remove all traces of the old adhesive, and use the same type of glue—which must be heated before use—for the repair. Many modern synthetic adhesives do not bond properly when mixed with old Scotch glue.

If adhesives are used, it is essential to hold the work together with some kind of cramp while the glue sets. G cramps and sash cramps (see p. 296) can be bought in many sizes and strengths. But it is also possible to make cramps from scrap pieces of wood for particular jobs. In many cases, it may also be necessary to use string as an additional support for the pieces being joined.

If new wood is required for a repair, take care to match the original in type, colour and grain. Examine wood carefully to ensure that there are no faults (see p. 688). Buy it several days before the work is to be started and store it in a well-heated, damp-free place.

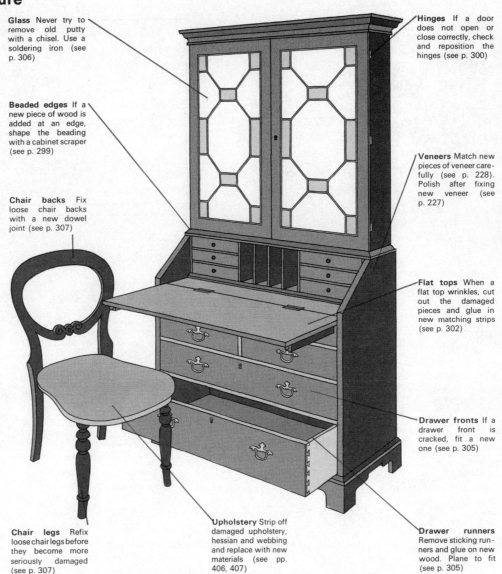

Glass Never try to remove old putty with a chisel. Use a soldering iron (see p. 306)

Beaded edges If a new piece of wood is added at an edge, shape the beading with a cabinet scraper (see p. 299)

Chair backs Fix loose chair backs with a new dowel joint (see p. 307)

Chair legs Refix loose chair legs before they become more seriously damaged (see p. 307)

Hinges If a door does not open or close correctly, check and reposition the hinges (see p. 300)

Veneers Match new pieces of veneer carefully (see p. 228). Polish after fixing new veneer (see p. 227)

Flat tops When a flat top wrinkles, cut out the damaged pieces and glue in new matching strips (see p. 302)

Drawer fronts If a drawer front is cracked, fit a new one (see p. 305)

Upholstery Strip off damaged upholstery, hessian and webbing and replace with new materials (see pp. 406, 407)

Drawer runners Remove sticking runners and glue on new wood. Plane to fit (see p. 305)

MAKING A CRAMP

Cramps for almost any kind of woodwork repair can be made from pieces of hardwood. Use wood about 1 in. (25 mm) thick for a cramp up to 20 in. (510 mm) long; $1\frac{1}{4}$ in. (30 mm) thick for up to 36 in. (915 mm); and $1\frac{1}{2}$ in. (40 mm) board for lengths up to 48 in. (1·2 m).

The base board should be no narrower than $2\frac{1}{4}$ in. (55 mm), and the two end pieces of the same width and thickness as the base board.

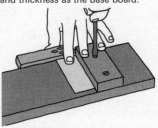

1 Glue and screw a stop block $1\frac{1}{2}$ in. from one end of the baseboard. Check that it is square

2 Mark and cut two wedges at least $1\frac{1}{2}$ times the length of the block. Taper them 1 in 8

3 Position wedges, with about half their length overlapping, against an end block. Place repair work against the wedges, glue and screw in second block

Furniture Tools

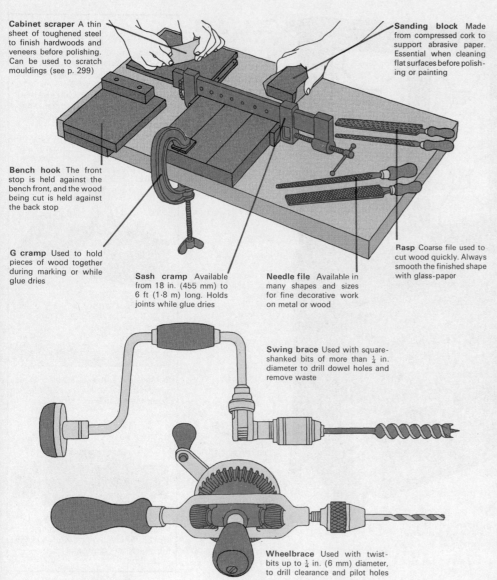

Cabinet scraper A thin sheet of toughened steel to finish hardwoods and veneers before polishing. Can be used to scratch mouldings (see p. 299)

Bench hook The front stop is held against the bench front, and the wood being cut is held against the back stop

G cramp Used to hold pieces of wood together during marking or while glue dries

Sash cramp Available from 18 in. (455 mm) to 6 ft (1·8 m) long. Holds joints while glue dries

Needle file Available in many shapes and sizes for fine decorative work on metal or wood

Sanding block Made from compressed cork to support abrasive paper. Essential when cleaning flat surfaces before polishing or painting

Rasp Coarse file used to cut wood quickly. Always smooth the finished shape with glass-paper

Swing brace Used with square-shanked bits of more than $\frac{1}{4}$ in. diameter to drill dowel holes and remove waste

Wheelbrace Used with twist-bits up to $\frac{1}{4}$ in. (6 mm) diameter, to drill clearance and pilot holes

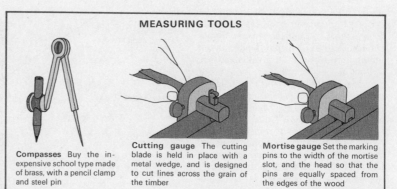

MEASURING TOOLS

Compasses Buy the inexpensive school type made of brass, with a pencil clamp and steel pin

Cutting gauge The cutting blade is held in place with a metal wedge, and is designed to cut lines across the grain of the timber

Mortise gauge Set the marking pins to the width of the mortise slot, and the head so that the pins are equally spaced from the edges of the wood

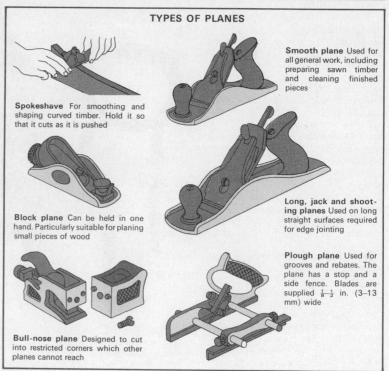

TYPES OF PLANES

Spokeshave For smoothing and shaping curved timber. Hold it so that it cuts as it is pushed

Block plane Can be held in one hand. Particularly suitable for planing small pieces of wood

Bull-nose plane Designed to cut into restricted corners which other planes cannot reach

Smooth plane Used for all general work, including preparing sawn timber and cleaning finished pieces

Long, jack and shooting planes Used on long straight surfaces required for edge jointing

Plough plane Used for grooves and rebates. The plane has a stop and a side fence. Blades are supplied $\frac{1}{8}$–$\frac{1}{2}$ in. (3–13 mm) wide

Furniture Techniques

REFITTING A LOOSE SCREW

If a screw is undamaged but does not tighten, either its hole has become too large or the timber round the screw is too damaged to hold it.

Check the timber first. If it shows signs of splitting, repair it (see pp. 298, 299).

If the hole has been enlarged, make a tapered wooden plug and fit it into the hole. An alternative is to drill out the hole and push in a standard fibre plug.

Glue the plug in position and allow to set before refitting the screw.

Materials: fibre plug; glue.
Tools: screwdriver; hammer; chisel; wheelbrace and bit; punch.

1 Shave the end of a piece of hardwood with a chisel to a blunt-pointed taper to fit the hole

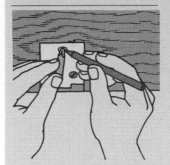

2 Push the plug into the hole and mark it $\frac{1}{8}$ in. (3 mm) above surface of timber. Cut off the surplus

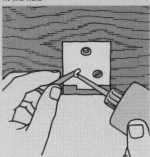

3 Glue both the hole and the plug. Drive the plug into hole, until it reaches the bottom. Trim off surplus

4 If the plug is being driven through a plate, use a punch to make sure it is below the surface

5 Allow the glue to harden. Drill a small pilot hole into the plug and then refit the screw

REMOVING STICKING WOOD SCREWS

To remove a tight screw, support the piece of furniture firmly on a bench or in a wooden vice. Brush the head of the screw with a wire brush to remove rust or dirt. If the screw slot is filled with rust or paint, clear it by driving the corner of a screwdriver blade along the slot with a wooden mallet. Sometimes a stubborn screw will turn if first it is turned slightly clockwise to tighten it more.

Use the longest screwdriver possible, with a blade which fits the screw slot.

Tools: screwdriver; mallet; hammer; punch; wheelbrace and bit; soldering iron.

1 Make sure the screwdriver is seated well in the slot. Apply as much pressure as possible and turn anti-clockwise

2 If the screw cannot be moved, place the screwdriver firmly in the slot and strike the head of the screwdriver firmly with a hammer.

Try to turn the screw half a turn in a clockwise direction. This may move the screw sufficiently to break its seal.

If the screw still does not move, hold the screwdriver blade at an angle against the edge of the screw slot. Tap it round in an anti-clockwise direction with a wooden mallet.

If that is not successful, heat the head of the screw with a soldering iron. This causes the screw to expand and compress the timber. When the screw cools, undo it

SCREWS WITH BROKEN HEADS

1 Hold a centre punch at an angle against the broken head and tap the punch anti-clockwise with a hammer

2 If it does not move, punch off the remaining half head. Drill out the screw with a metal twist bit

REMOVING DENTS

Do not leave dents in wood for any longer than necessary: they can be removed more easily when they are freshly made.

Steaming or damping are the best methods, but some woods with a high oil content or prominent pattern—for example, teak—may require professional polishing after treatment.

Materials: clean rag or cotton wool; water.
Tools: electric iron or soldering iron.

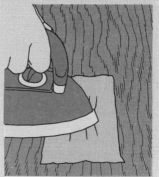

1 Place a damp cloth over the dent and heat it with an electric iron. If the area is small, use a soldering iron

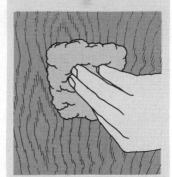

2 Alternatively, place a wet rag or cotton wool over the area and leave for several hours. Let the wood dry thoroughly

Furniture Techniques

PATCHING DEEP DENTS AND KNOT HOLES

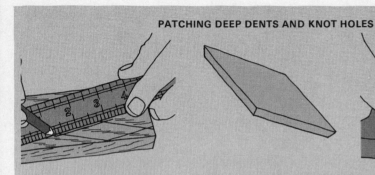

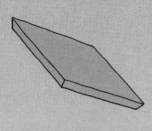

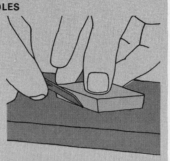

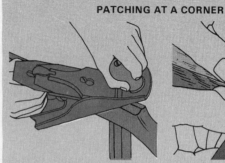

1 Choose a piece of wood to match the furniture. Mark a diamond shape along the grain larger than the hole

2 Cut out diamond with fine-toothed saw. Taper cuts so that top face of diamond is slightly larger than bottom

3 Hold the diamond over the hole. Score the furniture round the bottom edge of the diamond with a sharp knife

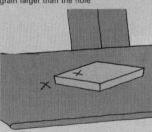

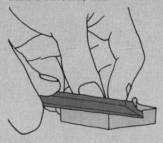

4 Make a mark on the diamond and another beside it on the furniture to identify how it is to be fitted

5 Cut out the hole marked on the furniture. Use a mallet and chisel, and remove all waste gradually

6 Test-fit the diamond in the cut hole. Remove it, and shave its bottom face until it fits level in the hole

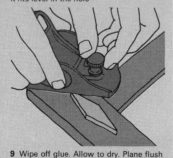

7 Squeeze glue into the hole in the furniture and spread it evenly on the bottom and sides of the diamond

8 Push the diamond into the hole. Hammer it home very gently to avoid splitting the wood of the furniture

9 Wipe off glue. Allow to dry. Plane flush with surface and rub with fine abrasive paper. Polish (see p. 227)

PATCHING AT A CORNER

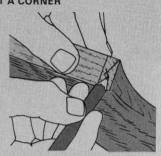

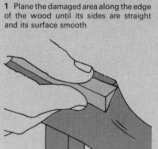

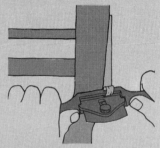

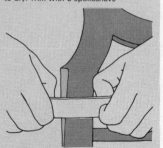

1 Plane the damaged area along the edge of the wood until its sides are straight and its surface smooth

2 Hold a piece of matching wood against the planed area and mark the shape of the missing wood on its end

3 Cut down the lines marked with a fine saw. Hold triangular piece against furniture and check that it fits

4 Spread hot Scotch glue on both surfaces and rub pieces together. Leave to dry. Trim with a spokeshave

5 When the patch is the correct size, match any edge carvings or special shape with a chisel and fine file

6 Finish with a cabinet scraper or fine abrasive paper held on a cork block. Polish to match the original wood

PATCHING ALONG AN EDGE

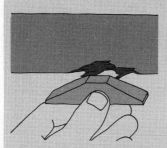

1 Match wood and grain of furniture. Cut a patch longer and deeper than damage. Taper it to the centre

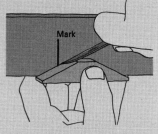

2 Hold patch over the damage and score round its edges with knife. Mark patch and furniture to identify

3 Hold a tri-square at lines marked for end of patch. Continue lines over edge to depth of damage

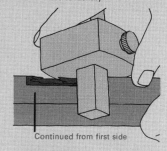

Continued from first side

4 Set a marking gauge slightly deeper than the damage. Score down second edge between the lines marked

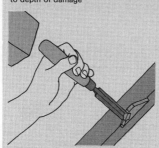

5 Carefully chisel out the waste. Do not go beyond lines marked. Keep chisel square and upright

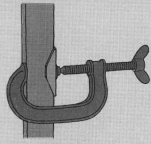

6 Glue with PVA adhesive (see p. 694). Cramp patch in place. When dry, plane flush with surface. Polish (see p. 227)

PATCHING A BEADED EDGE

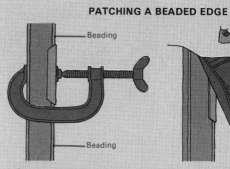

Beading

Beading

1 Cut a patch. Chop out the damaged area. Glue the patch and the edge, and cramp the patch in place

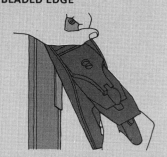

2 When the glue has set, remove the cramp. Plane the patch flush with the surface of the furniture

3 Cut a corner out of a cabinet scraper with a needle file to match the beading of the furniture exactly

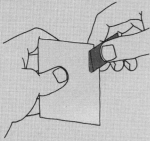

4 Rub each flat face of the scraper on an oil-stone. Hone the shaped edge with a slip-stone, to remove the burr

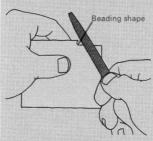

Beading shape

5 File the edge of the scraper above the beading shape, so that it cannot cut the surface of the wood when used

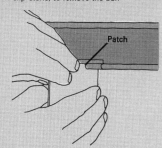

Patch

6 Hold scraper against edge of furniture. Draw it down grain to make a series of deepening cuts

DAMAGE AT HINGE

1 When wood has split round hinge screws, remove the screws in both hinges and take off door or flap

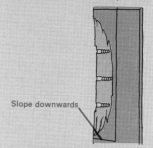

Slope downwards

2 Mark straight line down beyond damage. Mark second line at bottom. Slope it downwards from edge of wood

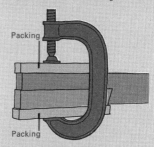

Packing

Packing

3 Cut out damage and cut patch to fit hole. Glue and cramp it in place. When set, cut and plane flush

Furniture Techniques

REPAIRING A SPLIT AT A HINGE

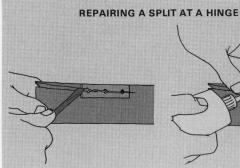

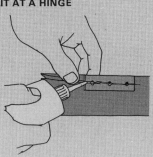

1 Remove the hinge from the split piece of wood. Prise split gently apart and blow out loose splinters

2 Squeeze a wood glue (see p. 694) into the split along its whole length. Rub it down the surface of crack

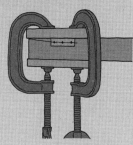

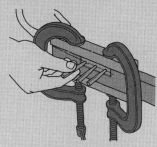

3 Place packing pieces of wood on both sides of the cracked piece and cramp the split firmly

4 While the glue is still wet, cut tapered wooden plugs and push them into the screw holes in the wood

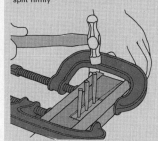

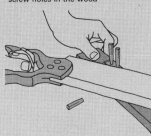

5 Make sure that the cramps are holding the wood tightly. Tap in the plugs as far as possible. Leave glue to set

6 When glue has set, remove cramps and packing wood. Saw plugs flush. Drill screw holes and refit hinge

ADJUSTING HINGES

When a door on a cabinet is not opening or closing correctly it is likely that its hinge is set too deeply in either the door or the cabinet. A typical symptom is that the door may tend to spring open. The simplest repair is to remove one or both hinges and fit a piece of a cigarette packet between the hinge and the wood.

If the door is springing open, fit a single layer of card behind the cabinet leaf of each hinge. When the door has dropped, fit card behind the cabinet leaf of the bottom hinge. If the top hinge is set too deeply, causing the top to bind, fit card behind its cabinet leaf.

Jamming of the hinge can be caused by screws not fitting flush with the countersink, i.e. the heads project. It may be necessary to fit a smaller gauge screw.

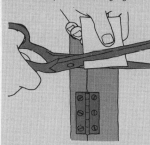

1 Cut a piece of cigarette packet slightly narrower and shorter than the measurements of the hinge leaf

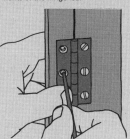

2 Remove the screws in the cabinet side of the hinge. Push in the piece of card and refit the screws

REPAIRING UNEVEN LEGS

Chairs and tables may rock on a floor because their legs are of uneven lengths through wear or because the floor itself is uneven.

First find out which is faulty. Turn the chair or table upside-down on a bench and lay flat, parallel pieces of wood across each pair of legs. Look across the top surfaces of the wood. If they are in line, the floor is uneven: several repairs are possible (see p. 78).

If the top surfaces of the wood are not in line, the fault is in the legs of the chair or table. Trim the longest leg until the piece sits evenly on a flat surface.

An alternative is to cut a scrap of wood and fix it with a countersunk screw to the short leg. Smooth it with glass-paper to match the other legs.

1 Stand chair or table on a flat board. Pack wood under short leg or legs until it is standing evenly

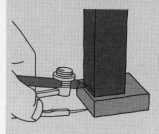

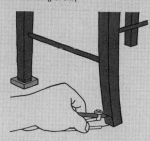

2 Set a pair of compasses to the distance from the board to just above the bottom of the shortest leg

3 Hold compasses on board and mark round the bottom of all four legs to the depth set

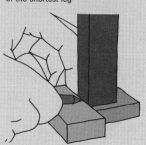

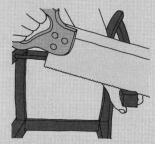

4 If compasses are not available, trim a piece of wood a little thicker than packing. Hold on board and mark legs

5 Saw all the legs at the lines marked on them. Rub down the cut edges with fine abrasive paper

Furniture Tables

Mending cracks

Table tops which are made of several pieces of timber may crack or split at the joins. The only repair is to separate the pieces, plane the edges and reassemble. A small filler strip may need to be inserted (see p. 302).

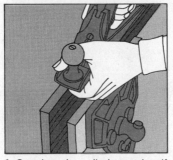

1 Complete the split by sawing if necessary. Plane the edge of one piece straight and to the angle of the break

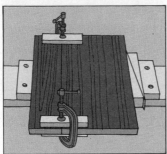

2 Set a sliding bevel to the angle and plane the other piece to match. Glue and cramp

Repairing a dowel-jointed frame

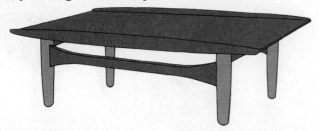

Many table frames are dowel-jointed. If not enough glue was used when the table was made, or if the dowels break under a severe impact, the frame may separate. To repair it, drill out the old dowels and fit new ones. If a mortise-and-tenon joint breaks, there is little an amateur can do to repair it. This is work best left to a professional repairer.

3 Cut off the dowel ends. Hold rail in vice and drill out stubs with a bit of the correct size

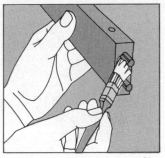

7 Taper dowel ends with chisel. Glue dowels and insert in rail holes. Glue rail and dowels

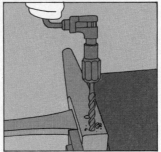

4 Hold leg in vice and drill out the dowel stubs. Do not drill right through the leg

8 If an old, sound dowel remains in the leg, clean away surplus glue and clear the glue channels

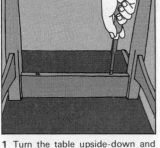

1 Turn the table upside-down and undo the long screws which hold the frame to the top

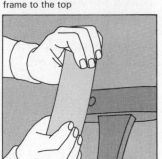

5 Remove old glue from the leg and the rail with a cabinet scraper (see p. 296) or small plane

9 Press the rail and its dowels into the leg. Hold block against join and tap with a mallet

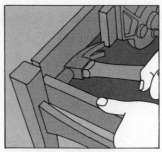

2 Hold the frame in a vice. Hold a softwood block against one side and hammer to separate the joint

6 Cut dowels $\frac{1}{8}$ in. (3 mm) shorter than the combined depth of holes. Cut slits down dowels with chisel

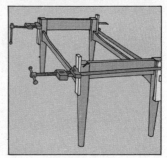

10 Use one cramp to secure each joint repaired. When the glue sets, fix the table top

Furniture Tables and trolleys

Mending the legs

Many table legs screw into metal plates fixed under the table. If the plates become loose, fit new and slightly longer screws.

If the table top is too soft for the screws to grip, glue on blocks of wood and screw the plates to them.

If a leg is knocked sharply, it may split around the dowel screw. Glue it.

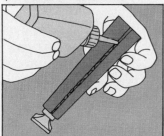

1 Remove the dowel screw and any loose splinters or timber. Squeeze glue into the split

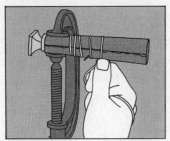

2 Hold leg top in vice. Cramp the bottom and wrap string tightly around rest of the leg

Mending a split at a castor

If trolley wheels are knocked sharply, they can split the ends of the legs which hold them.

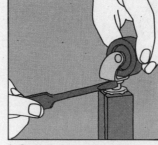

1 Carefully lever the castor out of its metal or plastic housing at the bottom of the leg with a screwdriver

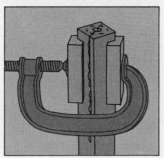

2 Push the screwdriver under the housing spikes and prise it up. Bend metal spikes if they are flattened

3 Push screwdriver into the castor hole and carefully lever the split open. Squeeze glue into crack

4 Saw a V in two softwood blocks to fit round leg. Place at opposite corners of the leg and cramp

5 When the adhesive has set, clean hole and gently hammer the housing home. Refit the castor

Repairing a distorted top

A solid-timber table top can become distorted across the grain if its underside is not supported by battens. The only successful repair is to cut out the wavy section. If the width is to be kept the same, new matching wood can be inserted.

1 Hold a rule against the table edge with its end at the centre of a rise or fall. Draw along and mark. Repeat at other wavy sections

2 Number the pieces and saw down lines. Plane edges square with face. Hold faces together in order and check that no light shows through

3 Cut a strip of matching wood to the width lost in planing. Glue edge of numbered piece, place strip on glue and glue other edge of strip

4 Glue all the joining edges of the other pieces and of the filler strips in the numbered order. Put them together carefully

5 Cramp the pieces (see p. 295) across width so that pieces are flat. Use G cramps to secure the ends of the joins. Trim and plane

Furniture Drop-flap stays

Making a new wooden stay

When the hinged wooden stays on a drop-flap table break or wear, they can be replaced by wooden or metal stays. If stays of the correct shape and size are unobtainable, make replacements from hardwood.

Materials: 1 in. (25 mm) hardwood; ¼ in. (6 mm) diameter mild-steel rod, 4 in. (100 mm) long; adhesive (see p. 694).

Tools: compasses; tenon saw; coping saw; marking and cutting gauges; chisel; mallet; rasp; wheelbrace and ¼ in. (6 mm) twist-drill; sash cramp; screwdriver; plane; tri-square; punch; vice.

1 Remove any retaining screws from the back of the adjacent rail. Chisel through the hinge tenon

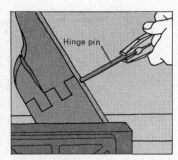

2 Hold the hinge-piece in a vice. Punch and pull out the metal pin which holds the hinge together

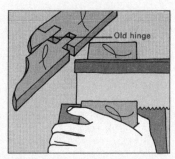

3 Mark the front and top edges to identify them. Cut hardwood to the sizes of the parts. Allow for tenon

4 Set a cutting gauge to the length of the hinge fingers on the old pieces. Mark the face and edges of new pieces

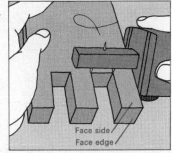

5 Set a marking gauge to the width of the old hinge fingers and gaps. Mark on the face side from the face edge

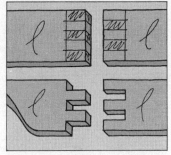

6 Mark both meeting ends of the new pieces up to the lines. Pencil in the areas to be cut (top)

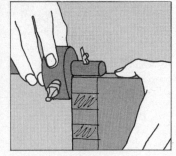

7 Set the cutting gauge to the centre of the old hinge-pin hole. Mark across new top and bottom edges

8 Measure the exact centre of the lines just marked across the edges. Mark the centre-point

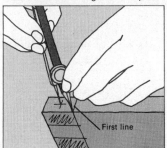

9 Set a pair of compasses from the centre-point just marked to the end of the base-line

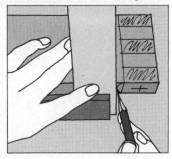

10 Draw an arc from the hole mark. Draw a line from the outside of the circle to back edge and down back

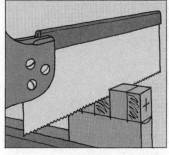

11 Use a tenon saw to cut out the waste inside the lines which mark the fingers of both halves

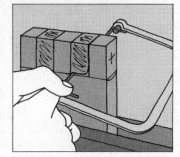

12 Cut across the waste between the fingers with a coping saw, just above the line marked for their base

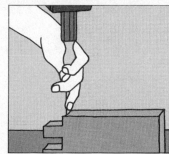

13 Chisel out the remaining waste to the marked lines and the arcs at top and bottom *(continued)*

Furniture Drop-flap stays

(continued)

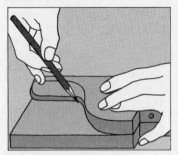

14 Lay the old moving arm over its matching new piece and mark the shape of the cut-away grip

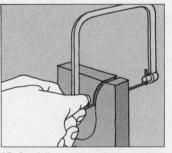

15 Carefully cut round the marked shape with a coping saw, just outside the pencilled line

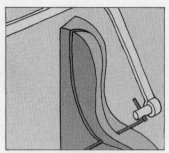

16 Mark the outline of the cut-away back of the moving arm and cut with coping saw. Finish with a rasp

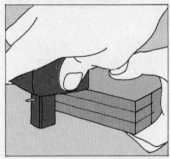

17 Mark width of mortise in table leg on end and edges of new fixed hinge. Mark depth on face and back

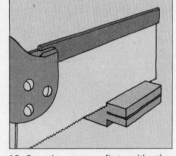

18 Cut the tenon—first with the grain, then across it—at the marks on new wood. Keep to waste side of lines

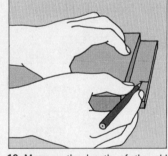

19 Measure the length of the old tenon. Mark and cut the new tenon shoulder to match

20 Push the hinge halves together and grip in a vice. Drill a $\frac{1}{4}$ in. (6 mm) hole from each side until the holes meet

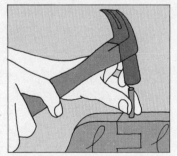

21 Clear the hole of chips. Taper the end of a $\frac{1}{4}$ in. (6 mm) steel rod and drive it into the hole

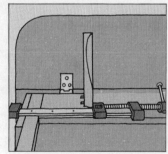

22 Glue and cramp the tenon into the mortise. Screw through adjacent rail into back of fixed section of hinge

Adjusting a drop-flap stay

If there is movement at the stays or table flap when it is unfolded, turn the table upside-down and check that the fixed top is fitted tightly.

To support the flaps correctly, the tips of the opened hinged stays should be in contact with the underside of the flap when it is level with the fixed top. If they are not, fit wedges to the flap if there are hinged wooden stays. If the stays are metal, wedge the underside of the hinged end of the stays.

Materials: hardwood scrap; countersunk wood screws.
Tools: plane; tri-square; screwdriver.

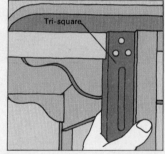

1 Open the hinged stays of the table at right-angles. Check that the tips contact the flaps evenly

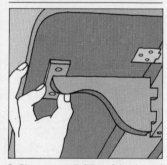

2 Plane a small fillet of hardwood until it raises the flap correctly. Fix to the flap with countersunk screws

METAL STAYS

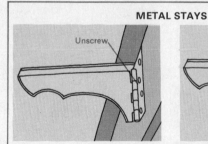

1 If the tip of a metal stay does not touch the flap, unscrew the stay from the side rail

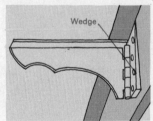

2 Fit a slim wedge—tapered to its top edge—to the side rail, then refix the stay

Furniture Drawers

Repairing a cracked drawer front

If a drawer front cracks or splits, check first that the split is clean and regular. If it is, squeeze glue into the split, and cramp the whole drawer front to press the pieces together.

But if the split is dirty or irregular—and with pieces missing—take the front off the drawer, plane the split edges and glue the pieces together. In this case it will be necessary to fit a filler piece of matching wood to make up the original depth of drawer front, and to repolish the new wood.

Materials: glue; scraps of wood.
Tools: plane; tri-square; chisel; hammer; rule; cramps; tenon saw.

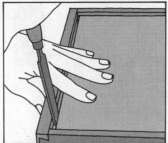

1 Turn drawer upside-down and unscrew back of bottom. Ease bottom free of front groove with a chisel

2 Drive the joints between the sides and front apart. If the joints stick, moisten with steam

3 Separate the split sections. Hold in a vice, and plane each split edge square and flat. Check with tri-square

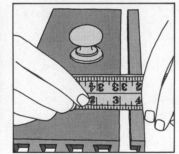

4 Lay drawer front flat to match the depth of the other drawers. Measure the gap in the centre

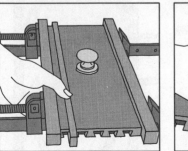

5 Plane matching timber to fit, and glue the edges. Insert a strip in the gap. Cramp together

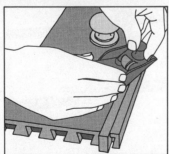

6 Allow glue to set. Plane the filler strip flush with both front and back of the drawer front

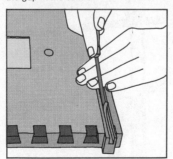

7 Chisel out drawer groove if necessary. Cut ends of strip flush with sides, then cut out dovetails

Mending a stiff drawer

Drawers may slide on side runners or on the bottom edges of their sides. If a side runner is damaged, screw new strips of hardwood on to the cabinet sides.

Drawers often tighten on furniture which is moved into a newly built house. It is best to leave them for some weeks, for as the house dries out, the timber in the furniture shrinks.

If a drawer should become completely jammed, switch on a fan-heater about 4 ft (1·2 m) away and leave it for a few hours.

When a drawer sticks because the bottom edges are uneven, fit a new wooden strip and plane to size.

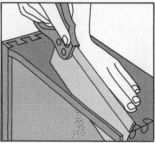

1 Mark a straight line as close as possible to the bottom edge. Cut along line, but do not cut the front of the drawer

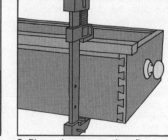

2 Plane the sawn edge flat and square. Cut a new strip $\frac{1}{16}$ in. (2 mm) wider than sides and thick enough to make up width of side

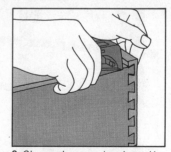

3 Glue and cramp in place. Use packing to ensure that cramps cannot damage wood or drawer sides. Wipe off surplus glue

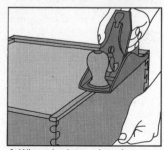

4 When glue is set, plane the excess from the sides and bottom until flush. Refit drawer and lubricate with candle grease

Furniture Glass-fronted cabinets

Fitting a new pane of glass

Many cabinet doors have small panes of glass which are mounted in shaped wooden beads.

The glass is usually held in place by putty mixed with gold size, which sets very hard. It must be removed with a hot soldering iron. Do not try to cut the putty away with a chisel, as this is likely to split the woodwork and may break the adjacent panes.

Heat a small area of putty at a time and keep the iron moving over the area, to ensure that the bead is not burnt. Take particular care when removing the putty at the edge where it meets the beading.

Even with great care, it is almost impossible to remove the putty without slight burning of the polished surface. Touch in any damaged area with French polish.

When the putty is removed, cut cardboard templates to fit inside the beading. Trim off $\frac{1}{16}$ in. (2 mm) round the edge of the card to allow clearance. Take the templates and a piece of the old glass to a glass dealer and have the new glass cut to match.

Fit and secure the glass with putty and gold size. Coat the new putty with oil paint to match the old.

The glass in some cabinets is retained by wooden strips fixed to the beads. Unscrew or prise them free with a chisel.

Materials: glass; putty and gold size; French polish: oil colour: No. 1 glass-paper.
Tools: putty knife: soldering iron: chisel: fine paintbrush: scraper.

1 Soften old putty with a heated soldering iron. Lift the soft putty out with a chisel or paint scraper

2 To avoid cutting the hands, wear gloves. Tap out the broken glass with the chisel handle

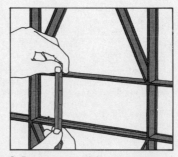

3 Remove remaining putty and measure inside the bead. Make a template $\frac{1}{16}$ in. (2 mm) less all round

4 If the bead has been scratched, rub it with No. 1 glass-paper. Apply French polish with a fine brush

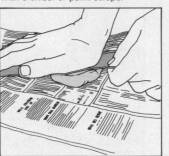

5 Knead new putty on newspaper, to remove any surplus oil. Press a hole in the centre of the putty

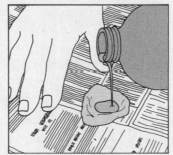

6 Fill the hole with gold size. Knead the putty until the gold size has been absorbed in it

7 Press a small amount of putty around the inside of the beading, to cover the horizontal and vertical edges

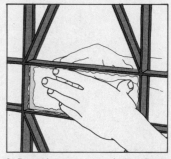

8 Press the new pane of glass firmly in position against the putty. Take care to leave no gaps in the putty

9 Support the glass from the inside and cut the surplus putty from the outside with a putty knife

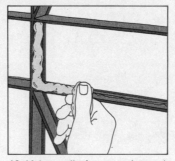

10 Make a roll of putty and press it firmly against the glass and the frame beading inside the door

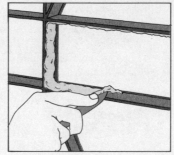

11 Use a putty knife to press and shape the putty filler at the correct angle between glass and beading

12 Make sure the height of putty is level with the beading edge through the glass. Paint with oil paint

Furniture Chairs

Repairing loose chair backs and legs

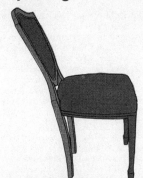

When a chair has no tie-rails between its front and back legs the joint between the back legs and the seat frame may become loose. If the chair is fully upholstered, it must be partly stripped before the work can be done.

If the original adhesive at the joint was Scotch glue—indicated by brown crystals—use Scotch glue for the repair: otherwise use a PVA adhesive (see p. 694).

Materials: $\frac{3}{8}$ in. (10 mm) dowel rod; adhesive.
Tools: screwdriver; mallet; drill or wheelbrace and $\frac{3}{8}$ in. (10 mm) bit; pencil; tenon saw; cramps.

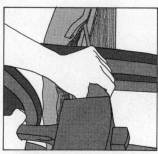

1 Remove gimp (see p. 410) and upholstery from back rail and rear 6 in. (150 mm) of both side rails

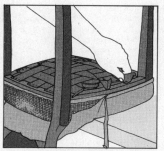

2 Prise out tacks holding bottom canvas and webbing. Discard canvas and webbing if worn (see p. 406)

Patching a chair rail

When a seat rail has been re-upholstered several times, it may begin to splinter where old tacks have been removed.

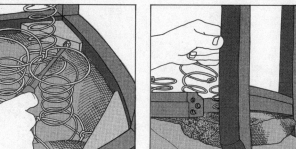

3 Undo screws which hold the two corner blocks. Tap blocks sharply with a hammer and remove them

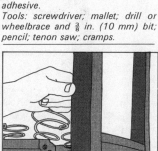

4 Remove the tacks which hold the stuffing canvas and spring ties to the back rail

5 Follow the angle of the side rail and drill the broken dowels from both back legs and the seat frame

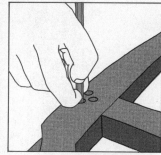

6 Measure the depth of the holes in each side of the frame and in each matching leg. Use a pencil as a gauge

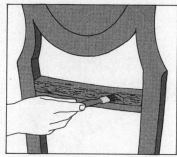

1 Coat the rail with adhesive. Cut a hessian strip to cover the front, top and back of the rail

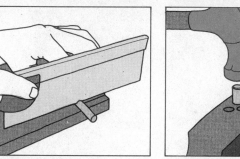

7 Cut dowels $\frac{1}{8}$ in. (3 mm) shorter than each depth measured. Number them ready for fitting

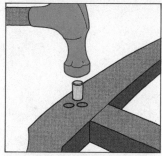

8 Glue and tap the dowels into the legs. Glue protruding dowels and holes in seat frame. Fix together

9 Cramp the frame with two sash cramps (see p. 296). Protect the polished frame with softwood strips

10 Refit the webbing and upholstery (see p. 406). Refix corner blocks or fit new ones if necessary (see p. 308)

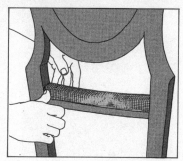

2 Lay hessian on rail and brush on a further coat of glue. Allow to set and re-upholster (see p. 405)

Furniture Chairs

Replacing a broken rail

If a chair rail breaks, buy a piece of timber to match the rest of the frame. Make sure that it is slightly wider and deeper than the existing rail. If the old rail is square or rectangular, plane the new one to shape. If it is circular, shape with a rasp and spokeshave.

Materials: matching timber, $\frac{1}{8}$ in. (3 mm) wider and deeper than measurements at centre of old rail, and slightly longer than overall length of the rail, plus the width of the chair legs; Scotch glue.
Tools: tenon saw; spokeshave; plane; compasses; pencil; rule; rasp or file; brace and bit; chisel; glass-paper.

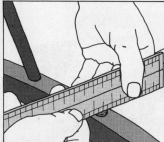
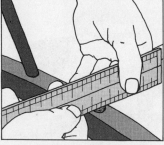

1 Cut off old rail at both legs. Measure diameter of stub in legs and fit a slightly undersized bit in brace

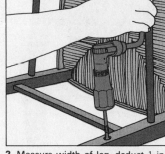

2 Measure width of leg, deduct $\frac{1}{2}$ in. (13 mm) and mark shank of bit with tape. Drill stubs to that depth

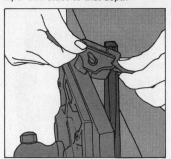

5 Hold wood in vice. If rail is round, trim with spokeshave from centre to circle at each end, all round wood

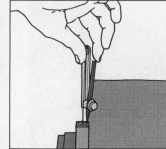

3 Remove remaining wood with small file. Measure between legs, add depth of holes and deduct $\frac{1}{4}$ in. (6 mm)

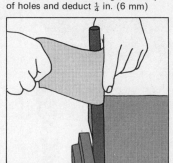

6 Finish shaping with a rasp or file and clean to an even form with medium and fine glass-paper

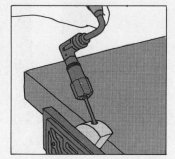

4 Cut new wood to length. Draw a circle with the same diameter as old stubs on each end

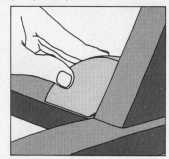

7 Test the size of the new rail in position. If it is still too wide, continue filing. Glue and fix

Fitting a new corner block

Corner blocks are used to strengthen the seat framework of most upright chairs. If an existing block becomes loose, or if it has to be removed for repair work, fit a new block of same size and approximate thickness.
Cut the block of hardwood in a triangular shape to match the existing pieces. Make sure that the grain of the wood runs parallel to the longest side of the triangle.

Materials: 1 in. (25 mm) hardwood; No. 10 wood screws; Scotch glue.
Tools: screwdriver; wheelbrace and $\frac{3}{16}$ in. (5 mm) bit; brace and $\frac{5}{8}$ in. (16 mm) bit; coping saw; plane.

1 Cut triangle. Drill longest side with $\frac{5}{8}$ in. (16 mm) bit—to within $\frac{3}{4}$ in. (20 mm) of other two sides

2 Use a wheelbrace and $\frac{3}{16}$ in. (5 mm) bit to drill through the centre of the holes already drilled

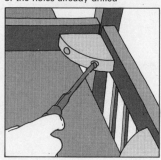

3 Hold the triangle in position and find shape required. Plane the two sides until the triangle fits exactly

4 Glue the block in place (see p. 694). Drive two No. 10 wood screws through the block and into the frame

Repairing a fretted chair back

Fretted chair backs are often old and brittle. If they are knocked or subjected to exceptionally hard wear, they are likely to break.

When fretwork is cracked or broken, check that no wood is missing. If none is, glue the parts together as soon as possible to prevent further damage to the chair or to clothing.

If some part of the fretwork has been lost, however, buy matching timber to patch the chair.

Materials: timber of suitable thickness; Scotch glue; stain; polish.
Tools: chisel; small tenon saw; pencil; rule; block plane; rasp; fine files; cramp.

1 Separate the split parts carefully. If no wood is missing, glue and cramp the pieces together (see Fig. 8)

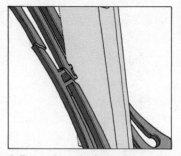

2 To replace broken pieces, cut through damaged parts of fretwork with a small tenon saw, and remove

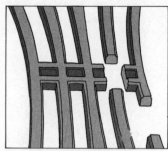

3 Examine the chair carefully. Buy timber to match the thickness and grain of the fretwork

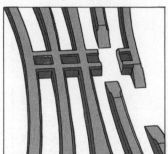

4 Taper the cuts in the long pieces of fretwork, from front to back of the chair, to increase the gluing area

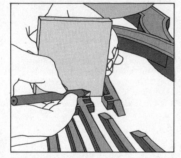

5 Hold the matching pieces of timber against the chair and mark the overall sizes of the gaps to be filled

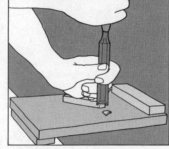

6 Cut pieces to fit and chisel the long edges to fit the tapers on the chair. Finish tapers with a block plane

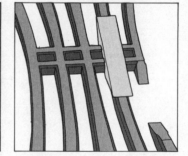

7 Fit all the pieces without glue as they are cut. Continue planing until they fit without gaps

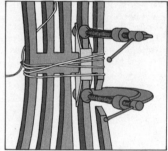

8 Glue the pieces of timber in position and cramp and tie them to the chair back. Leave to set overnight

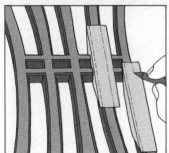

9 When the glue is set, remove cramps and mark the final shape required on the patches

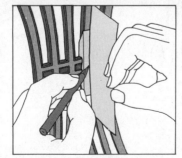

10 If frets are straight, draw cutting lines against a rule. If not, bend thin metal to shape and draw along it

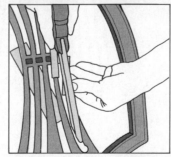

11 Support the fretwork on a block of wood on a bench and remove most of the excess patches with a tenon saw

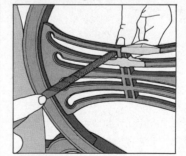

12 Remove the remainder of the excess with a sharp chisel, then use a rasp and fine files to achieve final shape

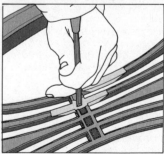

13 If the frets are carved, scribe the patches with a sharp chisel. Stain and polish the new wood (see p. 227)

Furniture Cane chairs

Fitting new cane to a seat

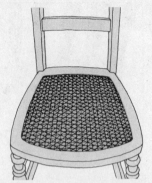

Re-caning a chair bottom is a seven-stage job.

Stage 1 Fitting cane from front to back
Stage 2 Fitting cane across the chair
Stage 3 Fitting a second layer from front to back
Stage 4 Fitting a second layer across
Stage 5 Fitting a diagonal layer
Stage 6 Fitting an opposite diagonal layer
Stage 7 Fitting an edging cane, called beading

Use No. 2 split cane for stages 1–4, No. 3 for stages 5 and 6 and Nos. 6 and 2 for stage 7. Use thicker basketwork cane to plug the holes at the end.

Soak all cane for five minutes before use and keep it in a polythene bag during use to preserve the dampness until the cane is fitted in the chair.

Buy about 20 golf tees to peg the cane temporarily during fitting.

Tools
File the point off an awl to clear the holes before starting to fit the new cane. Make sure that a bodkin is available for the later stages, when the holes may be obstructed by cane.

On straight edges, the edging cane is secured every second hole. On curved edges, secure it at every hole.

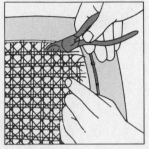

1 Remove the cane by cutting it all round the inside of the chair frame with side cutters

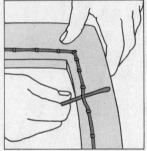

2 Use a screwdriver to prise up and remove the beading cane around the top of the frame

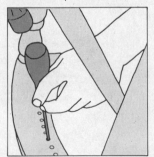

3 Hammer an awl—first from below, then from above—through each hole in the frame

STAGE 1

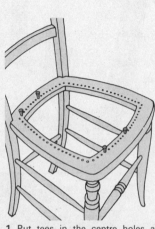

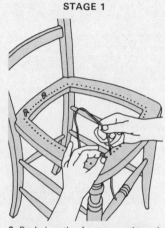

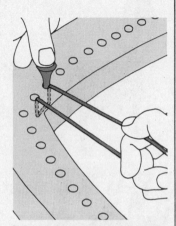

1 Put tees in the centre holes at back and front. Put a tee in left-hand back hole and count holes between two back tees. Count same number to left of front centre. Mark with tee

2 Push length of cane up through the front end hole. Leave about 3 in. (75 mm) below chair. Peg with tee. Take cane to end hole at back. Push down, tension, peg with tee

3 Bring cane up next hole to the right. Pull taut and move tee to secure it. Take cane to opposite hole at the front, pull taut and secure with a new tee

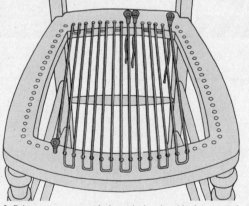

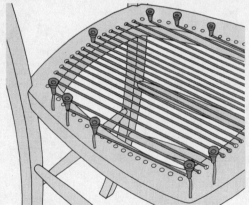

4 Bring cane up next hole and plug it with the second tee. Continue in same way to the front hole opposite the last back hole. When a new cane length is needed, push it up through the hole beside the end of the preceding piece. Pull both taut and peg with a tee

5 Fill the sides of the seat, keeping the cane at the sides parallel to that fitted in the centre of the seat. Use the side holes as needed but do not use any of the four corner holes. Secure loose ends by plugging the holes with extra tees

STAGE 2

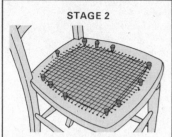

Fit cane across the chair in exactly the same way. Lay cane on top of first layer. Do not interweave

STAGE 3

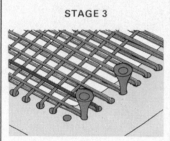

Fit second layer of cane from front to back. Do not interweave it with the first layer. Peg loose ends

STAGE 4

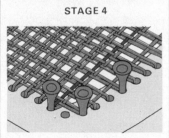

Fit the second layer across. Weave cane under the first front—back layer and over the second one

STAGE 5

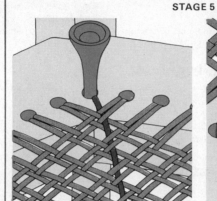 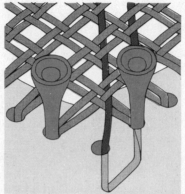

1 Fit the first diagonal cane from the back right corner. Weave cane under the side-to-side canes, over the front—back canes. Weave about 2 in. (50 mm) at a time and pull taut. Make sure cane is flat

2 Take the cane down diagonally through opposite hole and up next hole on the front. Tighten and peg. Continue until the right-hand triangular section is filled. From same corner hole, fill other section

STAGE 6

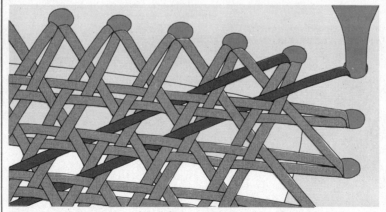

Fit the second diagonal layer from left to right. Reverse the weaving so that the cane goes over the side-to-side canes, and under the back—front rows

STAGE 7

1 Cut plugs of basket cane and, starting one hole in from each corner, plug every second hole if it has loose cane hanging below the chair

2 Use a hammer and a small peg of wood to knock the thick cane just below the surface of the chair frame. Trim cane ends under seat

3 Dampen a piece of No. 6 beading cane about 1 in. (25 mm) longer than the width of the seat front. Peg at two corner holes

4 Bring a dampened length of No. 2 cane up the first free hole. Take it up and over the beading cane: push it down same hole

 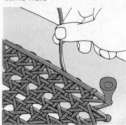

5 Pull it tightly and plug with basketwork cane from below. Cut short end, but leave the long piece of No. 2 cane to continue along front

6 Miss a hole; bring cane up next hole. Weave over beading cane and peg. Repeat along other sides. Remove tees and plug corner holes

Gas equipment

Safety and maintenance

Find the main gas tap, which is always adjacent to the meter, when first moving into a house or flat. When a leak is suspected, turn off the tap immediately. Call the local gas board, which operates a 24-hour emergency service. Never try to trace a gas leak with a naked flame. Rub a little liquid detergent around the suspect joint. If the liquid bubbles, there is a leak. Do not let any detergent get into burner parts or holes.

Do not try to install new gas equipment. Engage an officially approved installation firm which shows the registration mark of CORGI (Confederation for the Registration of Gas Installers).

Keep gas equipment clean, but do not try to improve its performance or modify it in any way. If there is any doubt about the efficiency of gas equipment, consult the gas board.

Cooker

Use a stiff bristle brush to clean the burner holes on a modern cooker: on round-holes use a matchstick.

Replacement burners for most cookers can be obtained from gas showrooms.

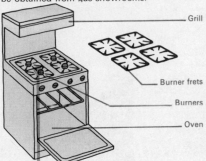

Grill
Burner frets
Burners
Oven

CLEANING A PILOT JET

Primus pricker

When the automatic ignition does not operate, it is likely that the pilot jet is blocked. Probe it clear with a pricker, available at gas showrooms. Do not use a pin or needle, which could damage the jet

Water heater

The front panel of most modern water heaters can be removed to allow the heater and jet to be cleaned or adjusted. On some older heaters, the pipes may have to be disconnected; have such a heater cleaned and adjusted by a professional gas fitter. If the pilot jet is blocked, use a Primus pricker to remove dirt and dust.

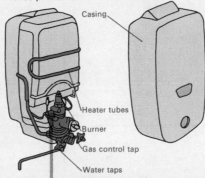

Casing
Heater tubes
Burner
Gas control tap
Water taps

ADJUSTING THE PILOT FLAME

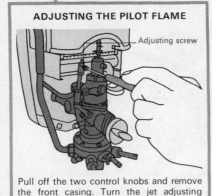

Adjusting screw

Pull off the two control knobs and remove the front casing. Turn the jet adjusting screw to obtain an adequate flame

Refrigerator

If the flue at the back of the refrigerator is removable, clean it every six months. If it is not accessible, refer to the makers' handbook or consult the local gas board.

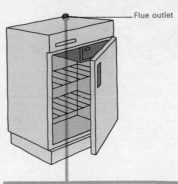

Flue outlet

REMOVING THE FLUE

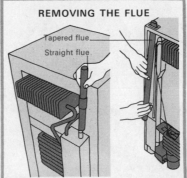

Tapered flue
Straight flue

If a flue tube is circular and untapered, lift it straight out. If it is oval, lift it to disengage the base and draw it down

Convector heater

Remove the front panel of a convector heater once a year. Prick the jet and clean inside the casing. The automatic ignition on many heaters is powered by a battery, which has to be replaced when it is exhausted.

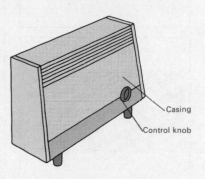

Casing
Control knob

REPLACING A BATTERY

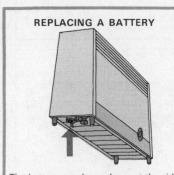

The battery may be under or at the side of the casing. To replace it on underside fittings, slip off the locating clip and remove the battery. On side mounted ones, pull off the covering panel

Hair clippers

Radiant fires

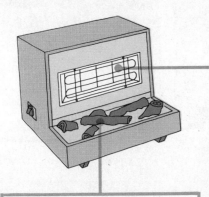

FITTING A NEW BULB

Remove the plug from the socket. Lift out the fire-effect panel. Remove metal spinners to give access to bulb. Unplug the bayonet fitting. Fit a new bulb and reassemble

FITTING A NEW BATTERY

Pull off the panel at the front of fire. Fit a new battery or batteries in the case and refit the panel

FITTING NEW BARS

The clay bars which glow and keep the heat of the burner jets are called radiants. If they become damaged, remove them and fit matching replacements, which can be bought at gas showrooms. Note that there are two types—box and bar radiants. On most fires a grille is sprung into slots at the side. Undo it to gain access to the radiants.

BOX RADIANT

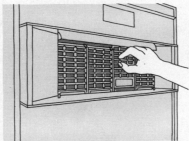

Lift up the broken radiant and ease the bottom out of the locating slot. Slide it out of the fire. Slot in the top of the new element first, then the bottom. Slide it down

BAR RADIANT

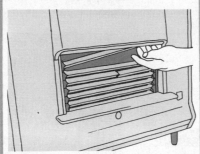

Lift up one end of the top bar. Slide the bar up and out of its slot. Remove all the bars until the broken bar is reached. Fit a new bar and slide the others back. Make sure that they sit horizontally in the framework

Sharpening and cleaning

When dismantling the clippers use pliers to remove the spring from its slot. This will release the moving handle. Sharpen the cutters as soon as they lose their fine edge. Unscrew the knurled nut to remove the lower cutter, then squeeze the handles tightly together to release the upper cutter.

Sharpen each of the cutters on an oil-stone or on glass coated with grinding paste. Keep them flat and rub with a circular motion

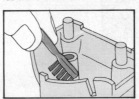

Clean hair clippers every few months with petrol and an old toothbrush. Oil lightly after cleaning. Wipe off any excess oil

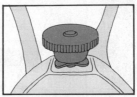

When assembling the clippers, replace the washer with its concave side facing down. Replace the knurled nut only finger-tight

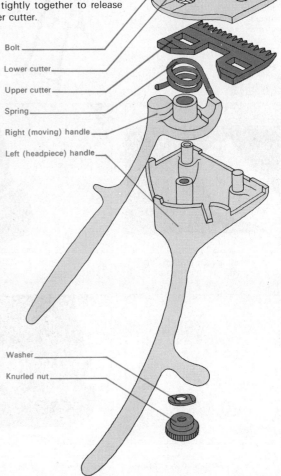

Bolt

Lower cutter

Upper cutter

Spring

Right (moving) handle

Left (headpiece) handle

Washer

Knurled nut

Ironing boards

Fitting a new asbestos pad

Old, frayed asbestos pads on ironing boards can be dangerous and should be replaced by new ones obtainable from hardware shops.

On some metal boards the pad is held in place by a retaining strip. On others it may be secured by a nailed flange or by hardwood beading. To remove a nailed edge round an asbestos pad, gently ease the strip out with a screwdriver, then pull out the nails with pincers.

Materials: asbestos pads to fit board; rivets.
Tools: hammer; drill; old screwdriver; pencil; pincers.

Cover

Asbestos pad

Retaining strip
(wood or metal)

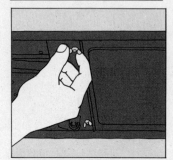

1 Unscrew the wing nuts holding the retaining strip on the underside of the ironing board. Lay them aside

2 If the asbestos is riveted to the board, hammer an old screwdriver round its tongue to remove the rivet

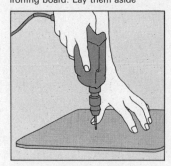

3 Dampen the new asbestos pad. Mark the rivet hole and drill through the new pad

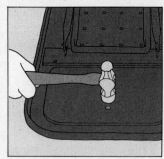

4 Push a new rivet through the asbestos and the board. Hammer the rivet tongue. Refit retaining strip

Making and fitting a new cover

A new ironing-board cover can be made from an old linen sheet.

Use the old cover as a pattern and fold over a seam for the cover elastic all round the new cover. Leave an opening in the seam where the elastic is to be tied.

Materials: bed sheet; pins; new cord elastic, if necessary; safety pin.
Tool: sewing machine or needle and thread.

1 Remove the metal or wooden strip which retains the edge of the damaged cover. Remove the asbestos pad and old cover from the board

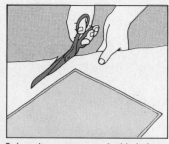

2 Lay the cover on a doubled sheet. Cut sheet with $\frac{1}{4}$ in. (6 mm) margin at the straight end and 1 in. (25 mm) margin round the sides

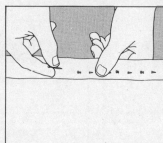

3 Fold the straight-end edge over $\frac{1}{4}$ in. (6 mm) and pin across. Fold the other edges over $\frac{1}{4}$ in., then a further $\frac{1}{2}$ in. (13 mm)

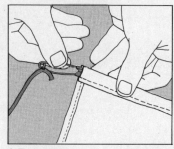

4 Tack-stitch (see p. 278) and machine the edges. Do not stitch across the seam ends. Thread elastic on a safety pin through the seam

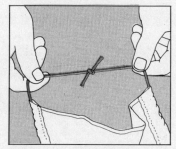

5 Hold the end of the elastic while it is being threaded. Remove safety pin and tie the two elastic ends together in a slip knot

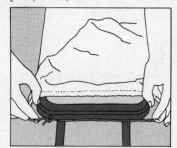

6 Take the knotted elastic over the straight end of the board. When it is in position, pull the cover tip over the tip of the board

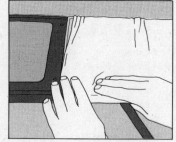

7 Smooth out the edges of the cover to eliminate creases. This may make it necessary to untie the elastic and adjust the tightness

8 Refit the asbestos. Fit and secure the retaining strip. Pull the elastic round the cover so that the knot can be pushed inside the seam

Jewellery Maintenance and cleaning

Tools for jewellery repairs

The special tools for jewellery repairs are smaller than those ordinarily used because of the scale of work involved. Pliers, for instance, whether taper, flat or round-nosed, have an overall length of $4\frac{1}{2}$ in. (115 mm). There is a range of needle files with profiles to fit most kinds of jewellery shapes. A lightweight hammer and an ordinary darning needle are also useful.

For straightening dents around the edge of a mount on a piece of jewellery, use flat-nosed pliers, another good general-purpose tool. When working round links and chains, use round-nosed pliers: their jaws fit the shapes of the links and chains closely.

Use a fine abrasive, such as emery cloth or crocus-paper, to smooth any metal after it has been roughened by filing. Obtain jewellers' rouge—an extremely fine polish —to clean and polish dull stones.

When a piece of jewellery requires a very hard surface during a repair job, use a metal block. If no block is available, a suitable makeshift working surface is the base of an old flat-iron. Grip the handle in a vice and see that the surface is clean and smooth.

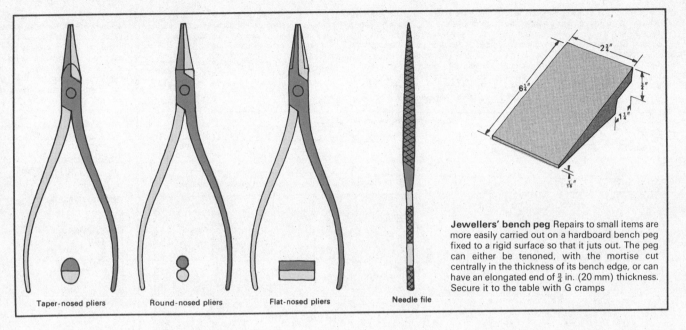

Taper-nosed pliers   Round-nosed pliers   Flat-nosed pliers   Needle file

Jewellers' bench peg Repairs to small items are more easily carried out on a hardboard bench peg fixed to a rigid surface so that it juts out. The peg can either be tenoned, with the mortise cut centrally in the thickness of its bench edge, or can have an elongated end of $\frac{3}{4}$ in. (20 mm) thickness. Secure it to the table with G cramps

Cleaning a piece of jewellery

Valuable pieces of jewellery should never be repaired by an amateur. If there is any fault, take them to a jeweller. Fashion jewellery, however, which is made of non-precious or semi-precious metal and stones, can be cleaned and maintained at home.

Almost all stones can be cleaned with a soft brush, water and washing-up liquid. In the case of opals, which are easily damaged, use only a dry soft brush.

Solid silver can be cleaned in a solution of hot water and household soda: use about a tablespoon for every pint (half litre). Heat the solution in an aluminium saucepan, which is likely to stain badly. Make sure that it is thoroughly scoured before it is used for cooking.

Do not, however, use this method for any piece which includes stones. Such pieces, whether set in gold, platinum or silver, are best cleaned by dipping them in a proprietary jewellery-care liquid, such as Goddard's.

Most fashion jewellery is made of a soft white metal which is later plated to give it its final finish. Replacement wire or metal to match is usually available from a jewellers' supply merchant or non-ferrous metal dealer. It is worth keeping old pieces of jewellery for use in repairs.

It is possible to retouch damaged surfaces or to colour replacement parts to match the old. Metallic paints are generally available to give a matt finish. For a gloss finish, however, it is advisable to obtain a proprietary lacquer and thinner.

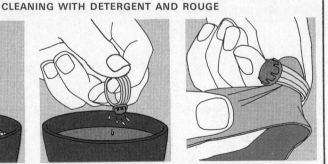

CLEANING WITH DETERGENT AND ROUGE

1 Remove grease and dirt with an artists' oil paintbrush, warm water and washing-up liquid

2 Rinse in cold water and check that no stones are missing before pouring the water away

3 Dry with towelling. Brighten and polish with jewellers' rouge and chamois leather

Jewellery Necklaces

Re-stringing a necklace

It is advisable to check a bead or pearl necklace regularly and to renew the string as soon as it becomes worn or perished. Special string can be obtained, but a strong matching thread is an adequate substitute. Use balsa cement to seal the ends of the new string before the clasps are fixed on them. Check how the beads are fitted. Some necklaces have the beads simply strung together; others have a knot at each bead or only one between groups of two or three beads. Re-string in the same way.

If the beads vary in size or colour, check the order in which they are strung and follow the original pattern when re-threading them.

Before removing all the beads from the original string, fold a sheet of newspaper in an M-shape. As each bead is cut from the old string, lay it in order in the V-fold of the paper.

Materials: new string or thread; balsa cement.
Tools: darning needle; sharp-nosed pliers with cutters; scissors.

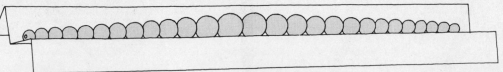

Lay the beads in order in a folded newspaper, if necessary blocking the ends

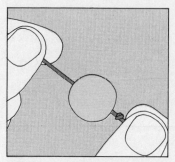

1 Tie a double knot 1½ in. (40 mm) from one end of the new string. Thread the first bead on the other end

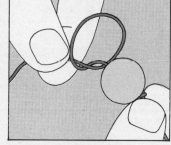

2 Slide the bead up to the knot, make a loop and put the free end of the string through the loop. Do not tighten

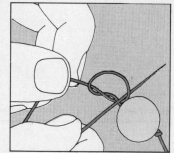

3 Push a needle through the loop beside the bead, so that the bead is hard against the first knot

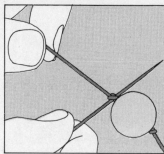

4 Slowly pull the string to tighten the loop. Use the needle to guide it into a knot tightly against the bead

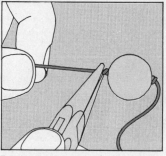

5 Use pliers to make sure that the knot is as close to the bead as possible. Re-string other beads the same way

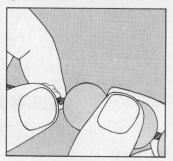

6 When all but the last bead are in place, rub balsa cement on the string end. Fit the bead and knot the string

Repairing a broken string

A necklace with a knotted string usually breaks between knots, and at least one bead falls off. Keep it carefully until the necklace can be repaired. If the whole string is in poor condition, re-thread it. But if the rest of it is strong, the two halves can be fitted together without removing all the beads and re-stringing the whole necklace.

Materials: thread; balsa cement.
Tools: darning needle; scissors.

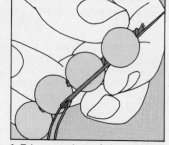

1 Take one piece of the necklace. Push a needle with double thread out through the last bead

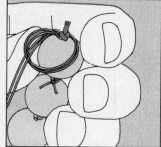
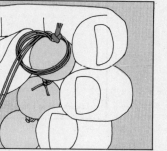
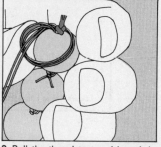

3 Pull the thread taut and knot it in front of the bead, but behind the knot at the break

4 Slip the loose bead on to the thread and push it back over the broken end of the original string

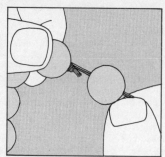

6 Draw the halves together and push the needle into the knot behind the first bead on the second half

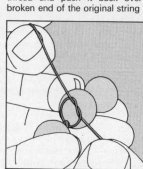

7 Draw the thread through the knot. Cut it from the needle and tie the thread with a reef knot

Jewellery Clasps

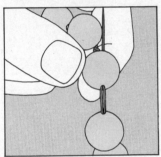

2 Wind the two ends of the thread around the string, behind the second knot, and tie in a reef knot

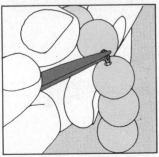

5 Take the second piece of the necklace and thread the needle through the first secure bead on it

8 Cut to leave ¼ in. (6 mm) thread. Put balsa cement on the end and push it into the nearest bead

KNOTTING A CLASP

Most necklace clasps have a small metal ring with which they are attached to the string of the necklace. To make sure that the clasp is neatly fixed, take care to tie it as close as possible to the last bead on the string. Hide the end of the string in the bead.

Materials: balsa cement.
Tools: scissors, tweezers.

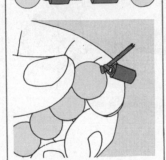

1 Tie each clasp close to each end bead with a reef knot. Cut the string, leaving the length of the bead plus the knot

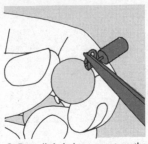

2 Put a little balsa cement on the end of the string and allow to dry. Push the string into the bead hole until only the knot shows

Bracelet clasps

If a clasp is loose, bend its engaging arm back into shape.

Tool: smooth-jawed pliers.

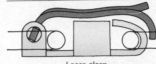

Loose clasp

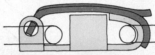

Correct shape

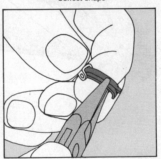

1 Undo the clasp. Gently bend the length of the arm back to its original shape with pliers

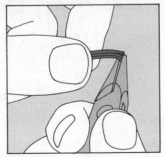

2 Adjust the hook of the arm until it engages again correctly with the rounded end of the clasp

Adjusting an ear-ring 1

Some ear-rings have a separate spring which is held at one end in a slot on the ear-ring mount. If the ear-ring does not grip the lobe, the spring is set too high.

Tool: round-nosed pliers.

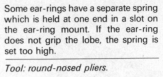

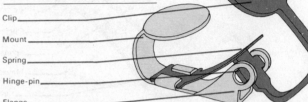

Clip
Mount
Spring
Hinge-pin
Flange

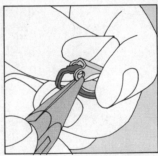

1 Gently open the flanges to an angle of about 30 degrees at each side using pliers

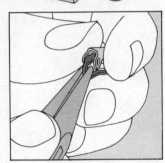

2 Turn the mount sideways and lift out the hinge-pins carefully, one at a time, with pliers

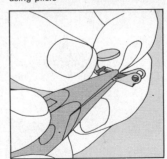

3 Squeeze the whole length of the spring until it is flat against the body of the ear-ring

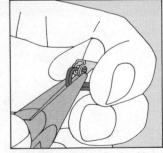

4 Lift the spring, refit the hinge-pins and gently press the flanges together. Do not force them

Jewellery Clasps

Adjusting an ear-ring 2

When the ear-ring spring is simply cut out of the clip, the ear-ring may become loose as the spring arches.

Tool: smooth-jawed pliers.

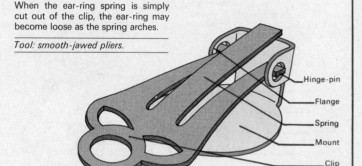

- Hinge-pin
- Flange
- Spring
- Mount
- Clip

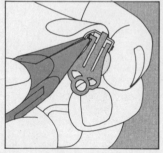

1 To readjust the spring, first bend the flanges of the ear-ring out to an angle of about 30 degrees

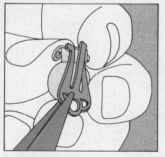

2 Remove the clip by twisting it sideways so the hinge-pins come out of their retaining holes

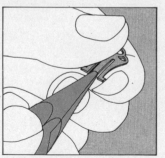

3 Grip the tip of the spring with the pliers and lever it down so that it lies flush with the clip

4 Refit the hinge-pins so that the spring tip is over the back of the flanges. Press flanges into position

Adjusting an ear-ring 3

Many ear-rings have a spring formed by bending back the end of the clip. To increase tension, widen the space between the clip and the spring.

Tool: smooth-jawed pliers.

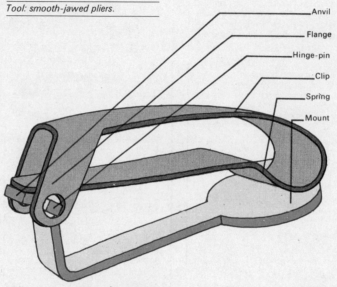

- Anvil
- Flange
- Hinge-pin
- Clip
- Spring
- Mount

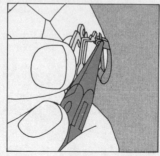

1 Pull one flange off its hinge-pin with the pliers. Hold the first flange and free the other pin. Hold the clip and spring halfway along both and pull apart until the tip of the spring is a little lower than the flanges

2 Hold one of the flanges with the pliers. Line up the end of the spring with the anvil, and compress it to the flange on its pin. Use the pliers to fit the other flange to its pin. Press the two flanges together

Mending a V-spring

Many clasps on bracelets and neck-laces have a V-shaped spring which fits into a flat sheath on the other side of the clasp. If the spring becomes loose, open slightly with a knife. If it breaks, take it to a jeweller for repair.

Tool: knife.

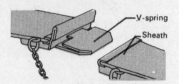

- V-spring
- Sheath

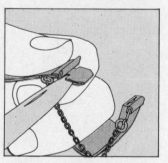

1 Turn a small knife blade between the leaves of the spring to open them slightly wider apart

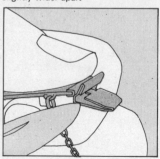

2 Check how the spring grips its sheath. Continue opening the spring until it engages with a click

Jewellery Pins

Straightening a brooch pin and hook

Straighten a bent brooch pin or hook before wearing it again.

Materials: wood with shallow saw cut.
Tools: smooth-jawed pliers; round-nosed pliers; fine file.

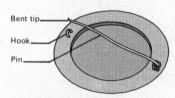

Bent tip
Hook
Pin

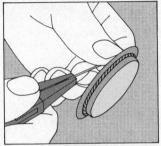

1 Straighten the pin with smooth-jawed pliers. Bend the hook on the brooch to fit over the top of the pin

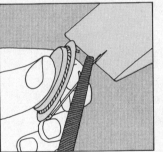

2 Lay the end of the pin in a groove in the piece of wood and file the bent tip smooth and straight

3 Spring the pin into the hook. If the pin touches the brooch when this is done, readjust the hook

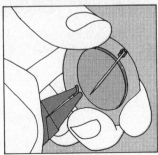

4 Hold the hook just above its root with round-nosed pliers and gently bend one side upwards

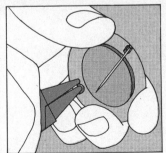

5 Even out the hook with a second bend. If the hook breaks off, solder it back in position (see p. 692)

Jewellery Chains and links

Making new links for a chain

When the links of a jewellery chain break, obtain a matching soft wire from a jeweller. To form circular links, wind the wire round a metal rod with the same diameter as the inside of the existing links. Wind elliptical rings on an oval nail of a suitable size.

Materials: soft wire.
Tools: vice; brace; jeweller's saw; two pairs of smooth- jawed pliers; rod.

Circular link   Elliptical link

1 To make a circular link, grip a brace in a vice. Secure the rod in the chuck and slide one wire end between the jaws

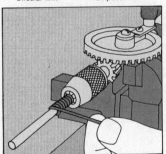

2 Hold the wire at 90 degrees to the rod. Turn the brace handle, and guide and tension the wire as it winds

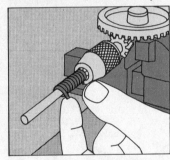

3 Keep each coil tight against the previous one. When enough rings are made, pull the coil off the rod

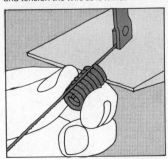

4 Cut the whole coil lengthways down one side with the blade of a jeweller's saw. Snip off the ends

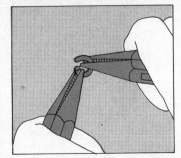

5 Use two pairs of pliers to open and close the ends of each link when attaching it to the chain

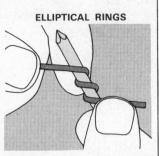

ELLIPTICAL RINGS

1 To make elliptical rings, wind the wire round an oval nail at an angle of more than 90 degrees

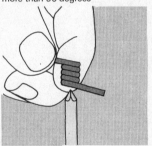

2 When enough rings are formed, push them together and pull the coil off the nail

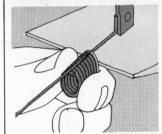

3 Cut down one side of the coil. Link the rings to the jewellery or to the chain and close the ends with the pliers

Mending single links

Many pieces of jewellery are made from individual, different or identical pieces held together by links. If the links are overstrained, they open and the jewellery falls apart.

Tool: smooth-jawed pliers.

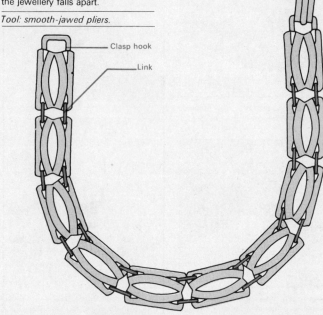

Clasp

Clasp hook

Link

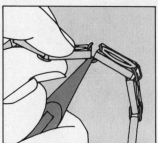

1 With a pair of pliers, thread the open link through the adjoining pieces of jewellery. Put a thumb behind the link to hold it in place, and turn the jewellery over carefully

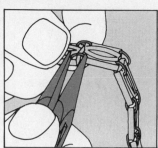

2 From the front, use the pliers to grip the open ends of the link. Squeeze them together gently until they butt closely. Squeeze the ring flat in the pliers to get an even shape

Repairing knuckle links

Some soft-metal necklaces have what are known as knuckle links. A spindle is cast into one end of each section of the necklace. In the end of the adjacent section there are twin knuckles, which are clenched together over the spindle to form a hinge joint.

Materials: crocus-paper.
Tools: taper-nosed pliers; needle file.

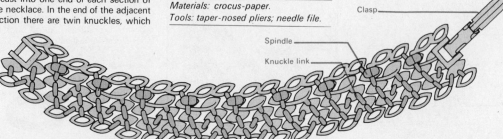

Clasp

Spindle

Knuckle link

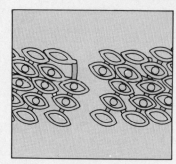

1 If two sections of a necklace are strained and break apart, lay them out on a flat, clean surface

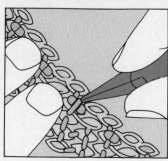

2 Push the ends together and use a pair of taper-nosed pliers to fit the spindle back through the knuckle

3 Fit the jaws of the taper-nosed pliers very carefully over the open ends of the twin knuckle

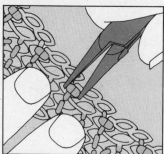

4 Gently pinch the knuckle together until its top ends are seen to butt straight against each other

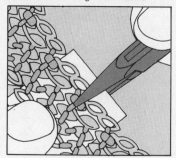

5 Put a piece of cloth over the face of the jewellery and pinch the knuckle across the width of the necklace

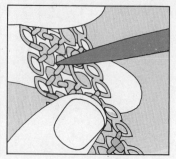

6 Use a needle file to remove any burr which may have built up over the repaired join. Finish with crocus-paper

Jewellery Cuff links

Safety chains

The weakest point in a safety chain is the linking ring between each end of the chain and the bracelet. If it is strained, the link opens at its joint and the chain is likely to fall off.

Tool: smooth-jawed pliers.

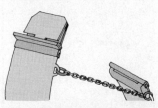

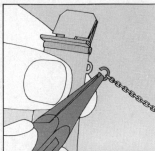

1 To refit the chain, hold the open link in a pair of pliers and feed it back through the bracelet eye

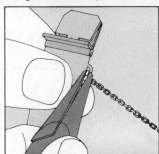

2 Hold the link and move the pliers to squeeze its ends. If the ring is lost, make another (see p. 319)

Bonding a broken link

If a riveted or soldered link breaks off a cuff-link mount, buy rocker-type links from a craft shop or a jewellers' supplier. They are available in plated metal and solid or plated silver or gold. Choose a type to suit the colour of the cuff link.

The rocker links can be used to convert chain cuff links to a more modern design.

Materials: Araldite; fine-grade glass-paper.
Tools: smooth-jawed pliers; needle file.

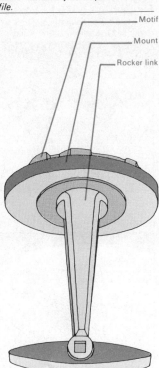

Motif
Mount
Rocker link

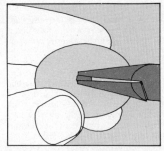

1 Use a pair of smooth-jawed pliers to straighten any distortion on the back of the cuff-link mount

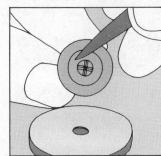

2 Scrape off any old adhesive with a needle file. Roughen the area and the face of the rocker link

3 Put a little Araldite on the face of the rocker link. Press the mount on to it. Leave to set for 24 hours

Soldering silver links

If an all-metal solid or plated-silver cuff link breaks or becomes loose, repair it with silver solder. If the heat of soldering discolours the back of the link, immerse it for a few seconds in a solution of 1 part sulphuric acid to 16 parts water. This can be bought at a chemist's.

Materials: flux; silver solder; ready-diluted sulphuric acid; asbestos; length of soft iron wire.
Tools: brazing torch; fine file; scraper; tweezers.

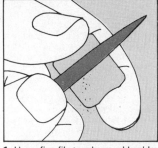

1 Use a fine file to rub any old solder off the back of the cuff-link mount. Make sure it is clean

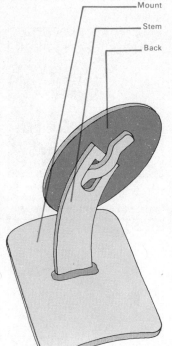

Mount
Stem
Back

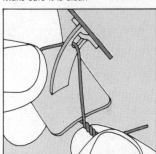

2 Position the stem on the mount and hold it in place with a piece of soft wire. Stand it on asbestos

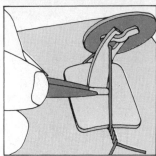

3 Solder the link (see p. 692). Clean it in the acid solution. Scrape off surplus solder with tweezers

Jewellery Dents and loose stones

Removing dents

Fashion jewellery is made of soft metal which dents or bends easily. To correct faults, use flat-nosed pliers and a lightweight hammer. Always work gently and use a metal block or the surface of an old iron as a base. A shaped piece of jewellery metal should be worked on a similarly shaped working surface. Make sure that all the tools are clean and smooth to avoid leaving permanent marks on the metal. Wherever possible, hammer from the back of the jewellery.

When removing burr marks after a repair, use crocus-paper as sparingly as possible to avoid damaging the finish. Touch up the repair with a suitable preparation (see p. 315).

Materials: crocus-paper.
Tools: flat-nosed pliers; lightweight hammer; metal block; fine file.

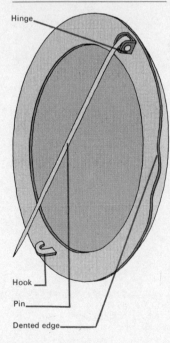

Hinge
Hook
Pin
Dented edge

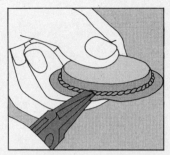

1 Use pliers at first to smooth out as many dents as possible. Squeeze the edges gently

2 When the edges are partly re-shaped, finish by hammering lightly from the back against a metal block

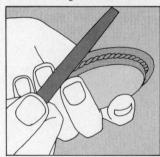

3 With a fine file, remove any marks from the repair area. Finish off with crocus-paper

Fixing a loose stone with adhesive filler

When a stone becomes loose or falls out of a piece of fashion jewellery, check the mounting. In most cases, the reason is simply that the adhesion has failed; but it is possible that the mounting has worn or become too loose to hold the stone.

If the stone can be re-stuck, roughen the back of it and the mounting in which it is to be set with a piece of emery cloth wrapped round a needle file. For very small areas, use only the tip of the file. Make sure that the file or cloth is rubbed in all directions to provide a good key.

Materials: emery cloth; Araldite; resin filler.
Tools: scraper; needle file; thin wire.

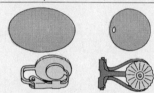

Ear-rings To make use of an old stone, buy a plain mount (left) or, if the stone is pierced (right), one with a spike, and stick the stone to the mount

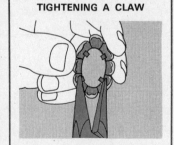

TIGHTENING A CLAW

If a claw breaks, get it replaced by a jeweller. A loose claw, however, can be tightened by an amateur. Use a pair of smooth-jawed pliers and squeeze very gently until each claw tip fits firmly against the stone.

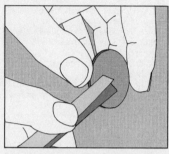

1 Scrape old adhesive from the stone and mount. Roughen the surfaces with emery cloth wrapped round a file

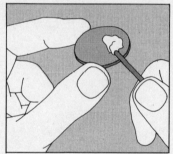

2 Mix a little Araldite and spread a thin coat on the meeting surfaces of the mount and the stone

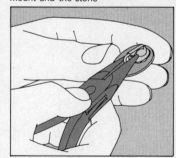

3 Place the stone on its mount and leave to dry. Position stones identically if repairing two ear-rings

SHAPED MOUNTS

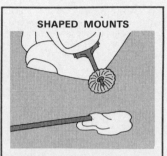

1 If the mount has a spike or shaped part to fit the stone, mix a filler paste with a thin wire

2 Scrape off any adhesive and put a little filler on the mount around the centre pin

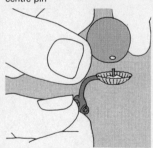

3 Gently bed the stone down on the mount. Allow the filler to dry before wearing the ear-ring

Kitchen equipment

Cleaning

Clean all kitchen equipment immediately after use. Dry thoroughly before storing and make sure that faults are repaired as soon as possible. A loose saucepan handle, for example, can often be repaired (see p. 324), but not if its condition is allowed to deteriorate.

Electrical equipment
Attempt only minor repairs on electrical appliances (see p. 521). Make sure that the equipment is disconnected from the power supply before starting work. If the fault involves testing the appliance with the power on, take the equipment to a dealer or repair shop.

Condensation
One of the main problems in a kitchen is condensation. If the ventilation is not good enough to disperse steam created when cooking or washing, treat the walls and ceiling (see p. 28). If the condensation remains, fit an extractor fan (see p. 30) as near the cooker as possible. Mount it in an outside wall or window.

Sinks
Make sure that the sink is firmly fitted. If the sealant between the sink and the wall is damaged, reseal the gap (see p. 148).

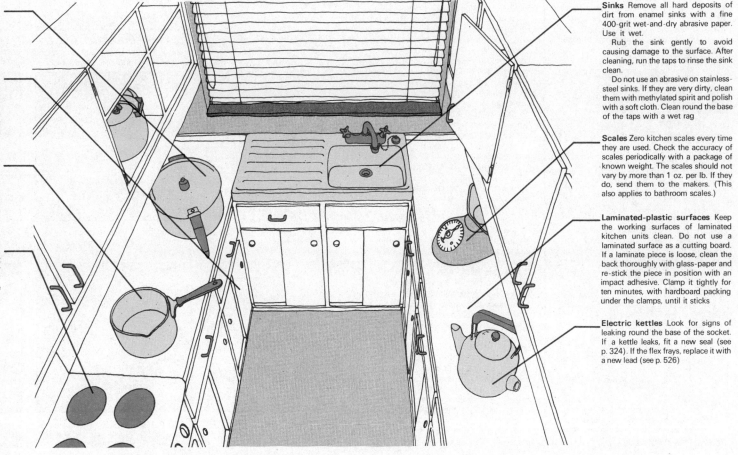

Pressure cooker Keep the pressure cooker clean, especially round the rim of the lid. Only minor damage can be repaired at home (see p. 325). Any major fault should be repaired by the manufacturer

Sliding doors Clean out the runners of sliding doors regularly to make sure that they operate easily. Clean runners and the door edges with detergent. Dry thoroughly and lubricate the door runners—fibre tracks with candle wax, metal tracks with oil. Paint both sides of the doors to avoid warping

Saucepans Clean aluminium saucepans with soap-impregnated steel wool or a nylon pot scourer. Make sure the handles are fitted tightly (see p. 324). Small holes can be repaired (see p. 324). Do not use an abrasive cleaner on a non-stick surface (see p. 325)

Cookers and ovens Keep the gas or electric rings clean. Remove spilt foodstuffs with a wire-wool scourer or oven cleaner, except on self-cleaning ovens, before they can be burnt into the surface

Sinks Remove all hard deposits of dirt from enamel sinks with a fine 400-grit wet-and-dry abrasive paper. Use it wet.
  Rub the sink gently to avoid causing damage to the surface. After cleaning, run the taps to rinse the sink clean.
  Do not use an abrasive on stainless-steel sinks. If they are very dirty, clean them with methylated spirit and polish with a soft cloth. Clean round the base of the taps with a wet rag

Scales Zero kitchen scales every time they are used. Check the accuracy of scales periodically with a package of known weight. The scales should not vary by more than 1 oz. per lb. If they do, send them to the makers. (This also applies to bathroom scales.)

Laminated-plastic surfaces Keep the working surfaces of laminated kitchen units clean. Do not use a laminated surface as a cutting board. If a laminate piece is loose, clean the back thoroughly with glass-paper and re-stick the piece in position with an impact adhesive. Clamp it tightly for ten minutes, with hardboard packing under the clamps, until it sticks

Electric kettles Look for signs of leaking round the base of the socket. If a kettle leaks, fit a new seal (see p. 324). If the flex frays, replace it with a new lead (see p. 526)

Kitchen equipment Saucepans and kettles

Saucepan handles

The most common fault with any saucepan is that its handle is likely to work loose. If the pan bears the British Standards kitemark, its handle is usually fitted to a metal bracket with a long screw, which can be tightened without difficulty if it works loose. On most older saucepans, the handle is riveted.

1 Secure the head of a hammer in a vice. Support the damaged pan, with the handle upwards, on the hammer head

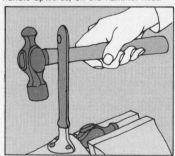

2 Use a second hammer to tighten all the rivets in the handle fixing. Rub smooth with emery paper

De-scaling and mending a kettle

In hard-water areas, kettles frequently develop a hard, thick coating of chalk—called furring—on their walls and base. This means that the kettle—even when it is heated internally by an electric element—takes longer to boil and wastes heat.

Several solutions to remove furring are available from hardware shops: use them with care. They are based on formic acid and contain strong burning agents which can be dangerous. Do not allow a de-scaling solution to come into contact with the eyes, skin, or any fabric.

Buy about 4 fl. oz. (113 ml) of the de-scaling solution for a 3 pt (1·5 litre) kettle. Fill the kettle two-thirds with clean, tepid water, and stand it in the sink. Pour in about half the de-scaling liquid and leave it to act on the furring. When the solution has stopped effervescing in the kettle, examine the walls inside—but take care not to feel inside with the hands. If furring is still visible, pour in a little more solution and leave again. Continue until the chalk deposits have been cleared completely.

If the de-scaling solution has little effect on the furring, empty the kettle and refill with a little water. Boil it for 10–15 minutes, until the chalk cracks and falls off in chunks. Remove the broken pieces and finish by using the de-scaling solution.

Before using the kettle after descaling, fill it with clean water. Boil, empty and rinse thoroughly in running water.

In some areas, it may be necessary to repeat the de-scaling treatment every few weeks to remove furring.

Most kettles are made of aluminium. If they develop a leak in the base, they cannot be soldered, because aluminium has a low melting-point. It is possible, however, to repair small holes with a tin and cork pot mender. If such patches are not readily obtainable, make one from a tin can and a flat piece of cork.

Materials: empty tin can; flat piece of cork; 10p coin; $\frac{1}{8}$ in. (3 mm) nut and bolt.
Tools: sharp scissors; hammer; metal rod; large nail; can opener; screwdriver.

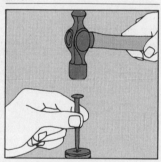

3 Hold a large nail in the centre of the top disc. Hammer firmly through all three discs

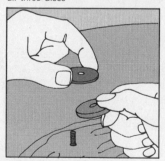

6 Fit the cork, then the tin disc over the bolt inside the kettle. If the bolt is loose, use a thicker one

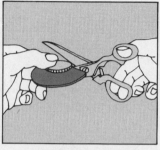

1 Cut out both ends of a tin can. Hold a 10p coin on both pieces of tin and cut round it with scissors

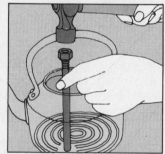

4 If the kettle base is ridged, hold a metal rod inside and hammer it flat, 2 in. (50 mm) round the leak

7 Inside the kettle, screw on the nut until it is fingertight. Check that the bolt is not loose in the hole

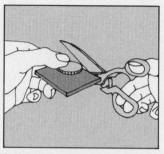

2 Hold the coin on a flat piece of cork and cut round it. Sandwich the cork between the tin circles

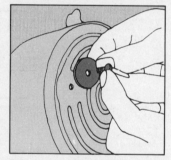

5 From the underside, insert a $\frac{1}{8}$ in. (3 mm) bolt through one tin disc and through the kettle

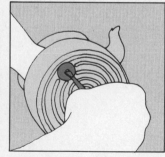

8 Hold the nut with the fingers inside. From the underside, tighten the bolt with a screwdriver

Kitchen equipment Pressure cookers and frying pans

Maintaining pressure cookers

The efficiency of a pressure cooker depends on two steam-tight rubber seals in the lid—the safety plug and the gasket which seals the lid. If either is faulty, or there is dirt under the gasket, steam can escape.

Safety plug

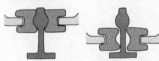

Closed   Blown

The rubber safety plug has a central metal pin which is forced upwards when the pressure inside the cooker becomes excessive because the centre vent has become blocked. If the rubber wears or perishes, however, the safety valve may open before the pressure is excessive, and the cooker therefore cannot operate.

To reset the plug, take the cooker off the heat and wait until no more steam is escaping. Lift off the weights or open the valve. Remove the lid and turn it upside-down. Put a thumb on each side of the plug and press firmly until the metal plug is forced back into place.

Do not return the cooker to the heat before checking the water level. Make sure the control valve is not blocked. If the safety plug continues to blow open, renew it.

Faulty gasket

Leaking moisture or steam around the rim of the cooker lid is usually a sign of a defective gasket. If there are dents on the rim of the base, smooth the metal with emery paper to ensure a proper seal.

FITTING A SAFETY PLUG

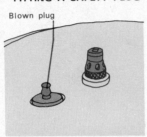

Blown plug

1 When the safety plug blows, reset it. If it continues to blow, obtain a new plug from a dealer

2 To remove the old plug, press back the pin. Pull out from the underside, then push out rubber

3 Turn the lid over. Fit the new plug in the hole with the nose of the pin upwards

REPLACING A GASKET

1 Turn the lid upside-down on a bench top. Pull the gasket out from the lugs round the rim

2 Wash inside the rim with soapy water. Dry it thoroughly and make sure it is not distorted

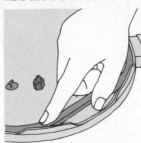

3 Tuck the gasket firmly round the rim under each lug. Make sure it fits snugly

CASSEROLE COOKERS

On casserole pressure cookers, the gasket is on the outside of the lid. When fitting a new gasket, press it well down and all round into the rim of the cooker lid

1 Lay one end of the crossbar on a table edge. Press and turn the centre knob to lock it open

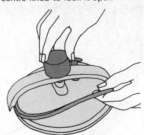

2 Remove the old gasket. Wash the lid and dry it. Press a new gasket firmly into place

Frying pans

Do not wash a stainless-steel frying pan with either detergent or washing-up liquid—which usually contains a grease solvent—but allow the metal to season with use. Wash only in clear, hot water, and rub the inside lightly with larded paper before storing.

Aluminium

Pans of aluminium are best washed with a soap/steel wool pad. Dry thoroughly. If an aluminium pan becomes discoloured, make a strong solution of cream of tartar and water, or vinegar and water. Pour it into the pan and allow it to simmer for 20 minutes.

Non-stick surfaces

Never use steel wool on a non-stick surface, but wash in hot water with washing-up liquid or detergent to make sure that grease is removed every time the pan is used. If grease is left in the pan, a film gradually builds up and makes the non-stick surface ineffective.

If a pan is discoloured, dissolve 2 tablespoons of baking soda in $\frac{1}{2}$ cup of bleach and 1 cup of water. Boil the mixture in the pan for ten minutes.

When a non-stick surface becomes damaged—for example, by using a metal slicer on it instead of a wooden or plastic spatula—treat it with a proprietary aerosol spray. Such a repair can be only temporary, and eventually the pan will have to be discarded and replaced with a new one.

Lampshades

Renewing a lining and cover

Washable lampshades—linen, crêpe, chiffon or plastic—can be cleaned in warm water and detergent. Rub with a soft cloth and rinse well under a cold tap. Pat dry with a towel and stand it near an open window to dry thoroughly.

To tighten a fabric shade after washing, rotate it near gentle heat. Never leave a plastic shade near a fire.

Never re-cover with a synthetic material if the lining is close enough to the bulb to be scorched.

Materials: lining; cover; trimming; 1 in. (25 mm) binding; thread; paper; wire wool; braid; solder.
Tools: scissors; needle; pencil; soldering iron; hammer.

SECURING FAULTY GIMBAL JOINTS AND STAVES

To tighten a gimbal joint, hold a metal block underneath and tap the rivet head gently with a small hammer

When a stave breaks off a ring, remove the cover, lining and tape and solder the fracture (see p. 692)

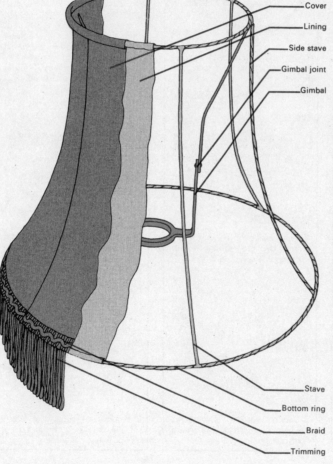

- Top ring
- Cover
- Lining
- Side stave
- Gimbal joint
- Gimbal
- Stave
- Bottom ring
- Braid
- Trimming

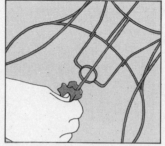

1 Strip off the old cover and lining and clean rusted or discoloured staves with wire wool

2 From the top, diagonally bind both side staves—to which the gimbals join—with fabric tape

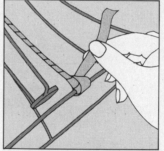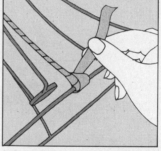

3 Finish each with a loop knot and cut off the surplus tape. Bind the rings in the same way

4 Use a narrow, plastic-coated adhesive tape to bind all the other staves vertically

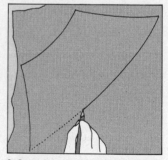

5 Wrap a piece of paper round half the frame. Fold it at the rings and the two side staves

6 Spread the paper on a flat surface and mark with a pencil along the fold marks. Cut out the shape (*continued*)

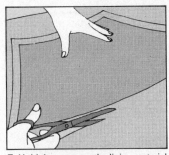

7 Hold the paper on the lining material. Allow an inch extra all round the shape and cut two pieces

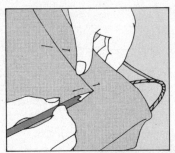

8 Pin one piece to the frame, around both side staves. Pencil in the lines of the side staves

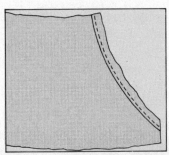

9 Unpin the material. Put the two pieces together, and stitch $\frac{1}{4}$ in. (6 mm) outside each line

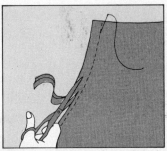

10 Cut and mark two cover pieces in the same way. Stitch along each line, not outside it. Trim the seams

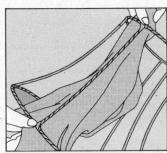

11 Place the lining inside the frame, with its seams lining up with the two side staves

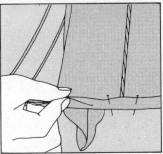

12 Fold the lining round the bottom ring and pin it. Smooth it out gently, up towards the top ring

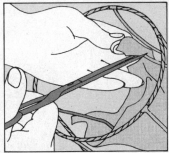

13 At the top ring, snip both seams and fold their flaps around the end of the gimbal

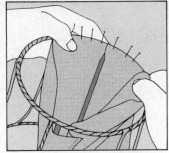

14 Pin the lining evenly round the top ring. Stitch it down the side staves and round both rings. Remove the pins

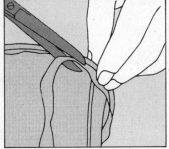

15 Trim off all the surplus lining material as close as possible to the rings and side staves

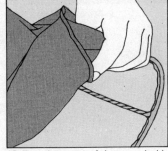

16 Turn the seams of the cover inside and fit them on the outside of the frame against the side staves

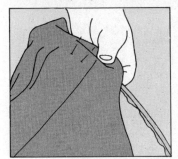

17 Pin the material carefully round the top and bottom rings and the two fabric staves

18 Tension the material to make a smooth fit. Stitch and trim off the surplus material

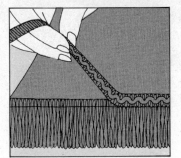

19 Stitch the trimming to the bottom ring and finish off the work by over-stitching braid to both rings

ALTERNATIVE TRIMMING FOR RINGS

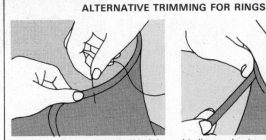
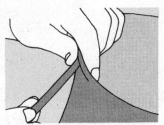

The rings can be covered with 1 in. (25 mm) bias binding. Fold and iron down the edges before stitching the binding to the rings (left) or sticking it on with latex adhesive (above) and stitching the join

Luggage and leatherware

Maintenance and repair

To keep leatherware supple and in good condition, sponge it occasionally with a leather dressing. Leave it to dry for 24 hours and polish it with a soft shoe brush or cloth.

The most common kinds of damage are broken fastenings—locks or zips—and torn or detached handles. Most repairs can be made without specialist help, but it may sometimes be necessary to obtain parts—such as a new suitcase hinge—from the manufacturer.

Two types of rivet are available for repairs. If both sides of the rivet are to be seen, use a capping rivet. If the teeth of the rivet are to be hidden inside the bag or suitcase, use a bifurcated rivet—which has no cap.

FITTING A NEW LOCK

1 Cut the lining inside the case behind the lock. Prise open the tongues of the lock

2 Remove the lock and fit a new one. Bend down the tongues inside and stick the lining

FITTING A NEW HANDLE

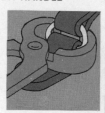

1 Open the D rings at each end with pliers. Remove the damaged handle from the case

2 Put the D rings through each end of the handle plate or chape and tighten with pincers

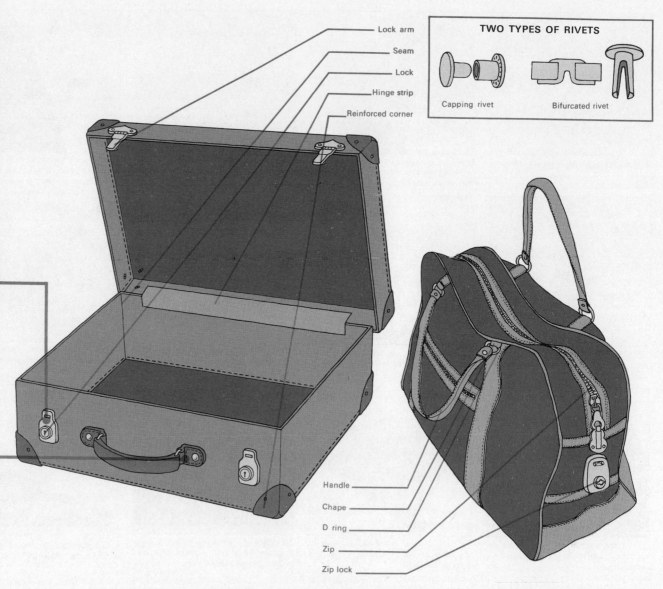

Lock arm

Seam

Lock

Hinge strip

Reinforced corner

TWO TYPES OF RIVETS

Capping rivet

Bifurcated rivet

Handle

Chape

D ring

Zip

Zip lock

Luggage and leatherware Corners and seams

Reinforcing worn corners

If the stitching of a corner piece on a suitcase is damaged, reinforce it by fitting new vulcanised fibre corner pieces, available from most shoe-repair or leatherware shops. Note, however, that they cannot be fitted on rounded corners.

Because the teeth of the rivet are hidden inside the case, it is enough to use the simple bifurcated type. Make sure that its teeth are hammered down to prevent damage to clothing when the case is packed.

Materials: corner pieces; rivets.
Tools: knife; centre punch; hammer; old flat iron or metal block.

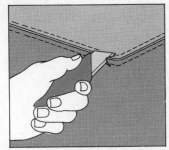

1 Cut away a small section at the corner of the case to allow for the inside rounding of the corner piece

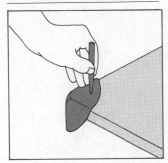

2 Hold the corner piece on a firm edge. Punch holes in the centre, ½ in. (13 mm) from each of its edges

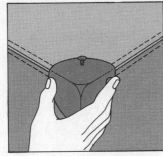

3 Push a rivet into the hole in the top face and place the corner piece in position on the case

4 Hold a metal block inside the case and hammer the top of the rivet firmly from outside the case

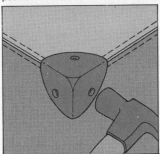

5 Hammer the remaining two rivets through the corner case. Make sure the teeth of the rivets are flat

Double-stitching luggage edges

When two surfaces or edges have to be sewn together at right angles to each other, use a double stitch. Its advantage over the backstitch (see p. 278) is that it looks neater when both sides of the stitch are visible.

The tool used by specialists to pierce leather is a sewing awl. If none is available, sharpen an ordinary bradawl down to a fine point as a substitute. To prevent the thread from fraying after the repair, rub it in beeswax.

Materials: 18-gauge linen thread; bees-wax.
Tools: knife; two harness needles; awl or bradawl filed to a sharp point.

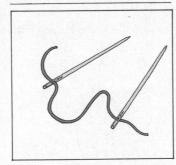

2 Taper the ends of the waxed thread and push them through the eyes of two blunted harness needles

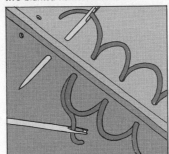

5 Push the awl from the left through the next two holes, and as it is removed push in the second needle

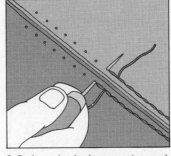

3 Push a bradawl or sewing awl through the holes before those of the last sound old stitch

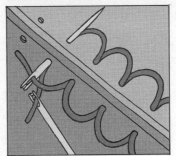

6 Push the awl and the first needle up through the second hole and the second needle into the third, and so on

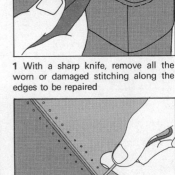

1 With a sharp knife, remove all the worn or damaged stitching along the edges to be repaired

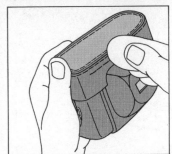

4 Pull out the awl with the right hand; with the left, push the first needle in from the left

7 When the stitching is complete, cut the threads and rub with a wooden handle along the new stitching

Luggage and leatherware   Seams and handles

Re-stitching a seam

When only one side of seam stitching can be seen, re-stitching can be carried out with one needle. For the sake of appearance, make sure that the longer, unsightly stitches are inside the case or bag.

Use a single thickness of linen thread, knotted at the end, for such repairs. Taper it with a sharp knife at one end, so that it can be threaded into the eye of the harness needle. Rub the thread in beeswax before using it, to make it waterproof.

Materials: linen thread; beeswax.
Tools: long-nosed pliers; harness needle; knife; bradawl.

1 Remove the broken stitching with long-nosed pliers. From outside push an awl into the first empty hole

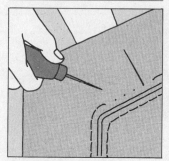

2 As the awl is removed, push the needle and thread through the hole from inside the case or bag

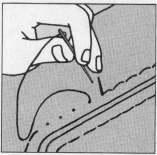

3 Go back one hole to sound stitching. Push the awl through from inside and the needle from outside

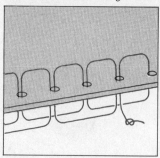

4 Go forward two stitches. Push the awl from outside and the needle from inside. Repeat along the seam

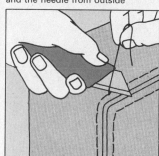

5 Continue sewing a few holes beyond the sound stitching. Cut the thread close to the case

Re-fixing a slotted handle

The handles on most travelling bags and holdalls have a D ring at each end, which is attached to a piece of leather slotted into the side of the bag. The leather piece—which is called a chape—can wear or break free from its rivet.

Try to obtain a matching piece of leather to make a new chape. If no identical leather is available, dye the piece obtained with shoe polish to match the old chape leather.

Materials: leather $\frac{1}{16}$ in. (2 mm) thick; shoe polish; bifurcated rivet and cap.
Tools: side cutters; knife; centre-punch; hammer; pliers.

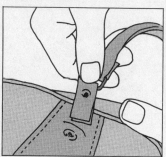

2 Pull out the chape. Lay it flat on a new piece of leather and cut round it with a sharp knife

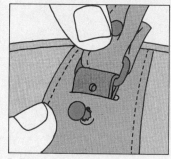

5 Slide the new chape into its slot, and push the head of a bifurcated rivet through the bag and the chape

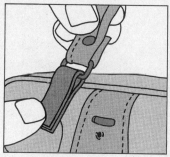

3 Stain the edges of the new piece with ink or polish to match, and fold it evenly round the D ring

6 Inside the bag, hammer open the tongues of the rivet and push the rivet into place

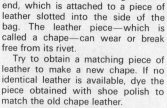

1 Remove the cap of the rivet which holds the damaged chape inside the bag. Remove the rivet with pliers

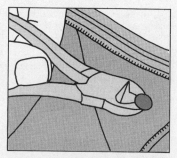

1 Remove the cap of the rivet which holds the damaged chape inside the bag. Remove the rivet with pliers

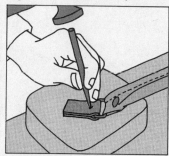

4 Centre-punch a hole in the middle of the doubled piece of new leather, just below the D ring

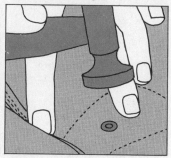

7 Make sure that the chape is straight in its slot. Hammer the rivet cap home inside the bag

Repairing a shopping-bag handle

Many handles have no D ring and chape holding them to the bag: they may instead be riveted in a slot in the leather or fabric sides. If the handle breaks away at this point, stick on a strengthening patch of matching leather and slot in the end of the handle.

When a handle breaks in the middle, cement a 4 in. (100 mm) strip of calf leather round the break. When the cement dries, back-stitch (see p. 278) through the patch and handle.

Materials: leather; neoprene cement; 9-gauge bifurcated rivet.
Tools: knife; steel rule; centre punch; tacking hammer; brush; bradawl.

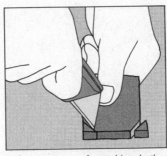

1 Cut a square of matching leather to cover the tear in the bag. Trim all four corners neatly with a knife

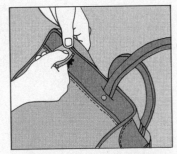

2 Lay the leather patch alongside the torn slot and find where the end of the handle should slot into it

3 With the point of the knife, cut a slot in the patch, only slightly longer than the width of the handle

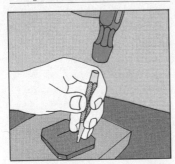

4 Lay the patch on a block of wood, and centre-punch a hole ½ in. (13 mm) below the middle of the slot

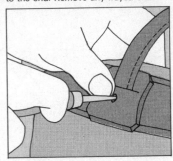

5 Lay the ragged end of the handle on the bench and trim as close as possible to the end. Remove any frayed ends

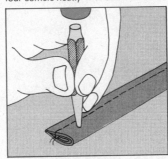

6 Lay the handle on the block of wood and punch a hole through the centre, ½ in. (13 mm) from the end

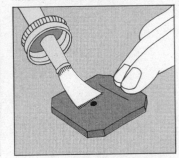

7 Turn the rough side of the leather patch uppermost and coat it with neoprene cement. Glue the bag surface

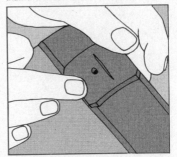

8 When the cement is dry, give both surfaces a second coat. Allow them to dry and press the patch in place

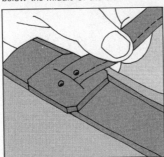

9 Before the cement dries and sticks, push the handle into the slot and line up the two holes

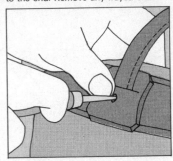

10 Use a bradawl to push through the two punched holes. Push through to the inside of the bag

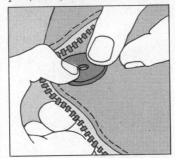

11 Cut a leather washer about 1 in. (25 mm) across. Punch a hole in the centre and position it inside the bag

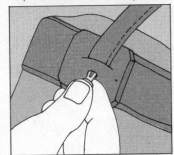

12 Push a 9-gauge bifurcated rivet from outside—through the patch, handle and the leather washer

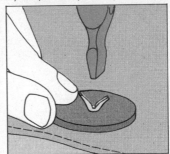

13 Open the bag and lay it on a hard surface. Use the end of a tacking hammer to open the rivet tongues

Luggage and leatherware Handles

Repairing a sports bag handle

The chape on an airline or sports bag is usually part of the strip of leather or fibre which runs down both gussets. If the chape tears, it is possible to fit a new piece outside the bag without taking off the whole strip.

Whatever the original material used, always use leather for a strong repair. A scrap of hide-side leather about $\frac{1}{16}$ in. (2 mm) thick can usually be obtained cheaply from leatherware or shoe-repair shops.

Materials: leather scrap: rubber solution: capping rivets.
Tools: steel rule: knife: centre-punch: hammer.

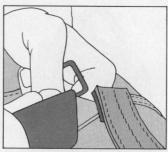

1 With a sharp knife, cut off the loose piece of chape where it is attached to the outside of the bag

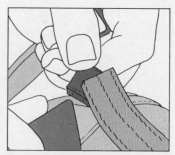

2 Cut the stitching holding the gusset strap to the bag to free about $1\frac{1}{2}$ in. (40 mm). Do not damage the bag

3 When the gusset strap is plastic or fibre, there is usually a reinforcing strip. Remove it with the knife

4 Lay the end of the strap on a flat, hard surface, and trim straight across to achieve a clean edge

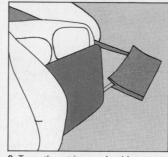

5 Take a strip of hide-side leather. Cut a 3 in. (75 mm) length (left) and trim it to the width of the handle

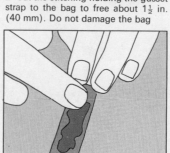

6 Turn the strip rough side uppermost. Gently taper one end of the strip and cut across all four corners

7 Spread a little rubber solution with the fingers along the strip. Make sure all of it is covered

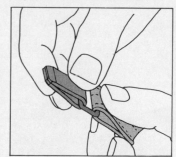

8 When the solution is tacky, push the new chape through the D ring and stick the ends evenly together

9 Lay the folded chape on a block of wood. Centre-punch a hole through the middle, just below the D ring

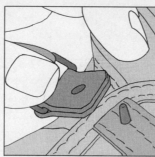

10 Open the bag and lay it on the wood. Punch a hole through the gusset, where the chape is to be fitted

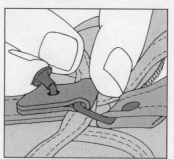

11 From the inside, push a rivet pin through the hole in the gusset. Fit the hole of the new chape on the pin

12 Hold the rivet in place from inside and lay the bag with the chape on a hard surface. Squeeze on the rivet cap

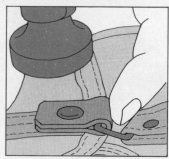

13 Gently hammer the rivet cap to secure it. Take care not to damage the new piece of leather when doing so

Fitting a brief-case handle

Replacement brief-case handles are available in varying sizes from most leatherware shops, but the metal rivets which retain the handle on the brief-case brackets cannot easily be replaced. Use instead blind-headed nails, available from do-it-yourself shops. Make sure that the size of nail obtained matches the holes in the brackets. If the nails are just a little oversize, widen the holes with a needle file.

Materials: new handle; two blind-headed nails to fit.
Tools: fine file; side cutters; hammer; needle file if necessary.

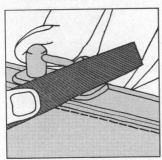

1 Use a fine file to remove the burred ends of the rivet pin at each handle attachment on the case

2 Pull out the pins with the side cutters—first at one side of the damaged handle, then at the other

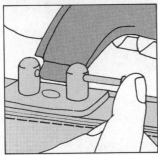

3 Obtain a matching handle and hold it in place above the brackets. Slide in the two new pins

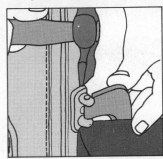

4 Hold the ends of the rivet pins against a hard surface and burr them with a hammer

Making a handbag handle

When the handle of a handbag breaks, try to obtain a ready-made matching replacement from a leatherware or shoe-repair shop. If that is not possible, obtain instead a strip of calf leather, double the width of the damaged handle and about 3 in. (75 mm) longer.

Turn the two outside edges in to meet at the back of the strip and stick them down with neoprene cement. Stain the leather to match the bag.

Materials: new handle or calf leather to fit the handbag; two capping rivets; stain; neoprene cement if necessary.
Tools: knife; centre punch; hammer; pliers.

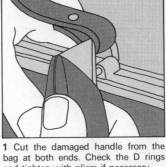

1 Cut the damaged handle from the bag at both ends. Check the D rings and tighten with pliers if necessary

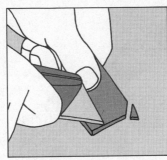

2 Take the new handle or the made-up strip of leather and trim the end corners neatly with a sharp knife

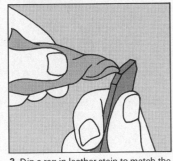

3 Dip a rag in leather stain to match the colour of the bag or handle, and stain the corners and edges of the strap

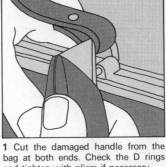

4 Turn each end back about 1¼ in. (30 mm). Allow for the D ring and punch a hole through both thicknesses

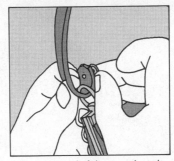

5 Loop one end of the strap through a ring on the bag so that the short end is underneath the strap

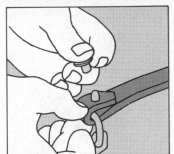

6 Push a rivet pin through from the top side of the strap and position the cap on the end of the pin

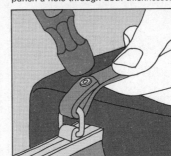

7 Hold the folded strap on a hard surface and hammer the rivet cap home. Fix and rivet the other end

Luggage and leatherware   Handles, locks and fastenings

Fitting a handle rivet

Some handles are simply riveted straight on to the outside of the bag. If a handle breaks off at the rivet without tearing or damaging the material in any way, it can be repaired by obtaining and fitting a matching rivet. Use a capping rivet if both sides of the rivet are to be seen. If it is necessary to cut round the lining inside the bag to secure the rivet, stick the lining back in place—usually to a card base—with neoprene cement.

Materials: capping rivet; neoprene cement if needed.
Tools: knife; side cutters; hammer.

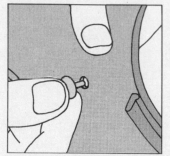

1 Remove the old rivet from the handle with cutters. Push a new rivet pin through from inside the bag

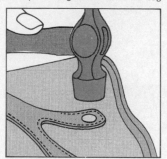

2 Lay the hole of the handle on the pin. Fit the rivet cap and hammer it home against a flat surface

Replacing a broken zip

If the zip in a bag or suitcase becomes stiff and tight, rub a candle along it to lubricate it. Work the zip up and down between the teeth several times until it moves freely. Make sure that bags and suitcases are not over-filled, to avoid strain on them.

When a zip has to be replaced, take the old one to the shop to make sure that the correct length and type is obtained. Several weights are available: for most kinds of luggage a medium-weight zip is adequate.

Materials: rubber solution; zip; linen thread.
Tools: knife; darning needle.

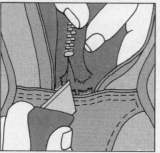

2 Cut across the tape at both ends of the zip. Leave the bag stitching intact underneath the cut

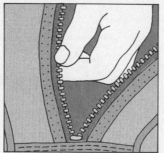

5 Open the zip and spread solution on the other edge of the zip tape and inside the bag. Stick together

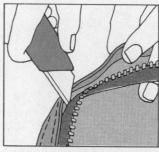

1 With a sharp knife, cut the stitching along both sides of the damaged zip. Do not cut the bag

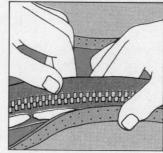

3 Remove any loose threads. Coat one edge of the zip and one edge inside the bag with rubber solution

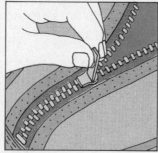

6 Open and close the zip several times before the solution sets. Make sure that it is correctly positioned

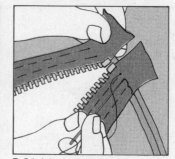

4 Allow to dry for ten minutes. Line the zip up with the bag and stick the two glued edges together

7 Stitch both edges of the zip through the existing stitch holes. Back-stitch at both ends (see p. 278)

Fitting a zip lock

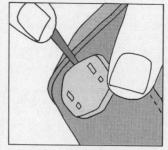

1 With a screwdriver, prise open the tongues securing the lock. Insert the blade between the lock and bag

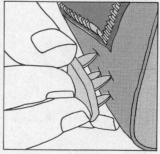

2 Prise the lock off the bag from outside. Take it to a dealer and obtain a new one to fit the zip

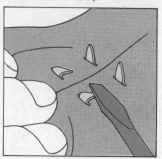

3 Push the tongues through the existing holes and bend them over inside. Hammer them flat

Renewing a zip slider

If the teeth of a zip pull apart when the zip is closed, and there is no visible damage to the teeth themselves, check the slider. The most likely fault is that its sides have become worn so that they no longer grip the zip teeth tightly. Alternatively, the top and bottom of the slider may have come apart slightly. Take the bag to a handicraft or needlework dealer and obtain a slider and zip stop to match.

If the handle of a slider breaks off, cut and fit a small curtain ring.

Materials: new zip slider.
Tool: small screwdriver.

Zip slider

Zip stop

1 Open the zip and use a screwdriver to prise off the stop at the closed end of the zip

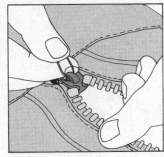

2 Pull the slider down out of the zip. Slip the new slider over the beads at the end of the zip

3 Partly close the zip and fit the tongues of the new stop into the old holes. Hold it in place with one hand

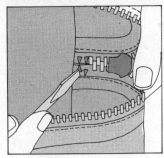

4 Inside the bag, use the blade of a small screwdriver to turn over and press down the tongues of the stop

Replacing a brief-case lock

If the spring of a brief-case or similar lock breaks, it is not usually possible to make any repair to it: fit a new part.

Although some locks have only one locking position, it is always advisable when fitting a new part to obtain a three-position replacement. This means, however, that extra holes may have to be cut in the case or bag for the tongues of the lock. Position it carefully and mark where the slots are needed.

If the case or bag is lined, cut the lining before starting the repair.

Materials: new lock; neoprene cement.
Tools: knife; screwdriver; pliers; old paintbrush.

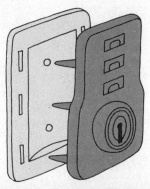

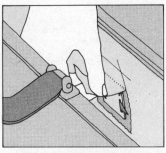

1 Inside the case, cut round three edges of the lining over the lock. Peel it back on the fourth edge

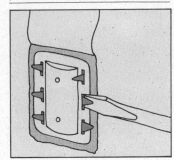

2 Prise up the tongues of the damaged lock with a small-bladed screwdriver. Do not pierce the leather

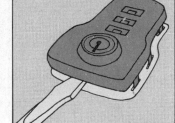

3 From the front, use a screwdriver to prise up the body of the lock. Remove it carefully from the holes

4 Position the new lock and cut new slots for the tongues if necessary. Fit the lock in place from the front

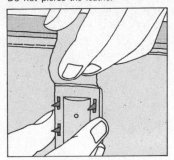

5 Inside, slip the back-plate over the tongues of the lock. Outside, make sure that the hasp will engage the lock

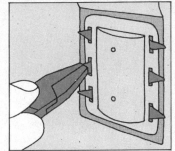

6 If it does not, adjust the slots in the leather. Push the tongues over with a small pair of pliers

7 Coat the back of the lining and the lock back-plate with neoprene cement. Allow to dry and stick together

Repairing a brief-case flap

The metal end of a brief-case flap, with the part which fits into the lock, is called the hasp. If the pin snaps off, obtain and fit a new hasp.

It is difficult to obtain the special pin or pins needed to hold the hasp on to the flap. As a substitute, use ½ in. (13 mm) fine brass nails. Take the brief-case to the dealer to obtain nails of the correct gauge.

When holding the hasp against a hard surface to rivet the nails, protect its surface with a cloth.

Materials: hasp; brass nails.
Tools: screwdriver; side cutters; pliers; hammer.

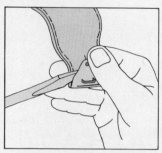

1 Prise the old hasp off both sides of the brief-case flap with the blade of a small screwdriver

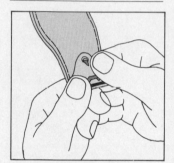

2 Slide on the new hasp and push ½ in. (13 mm) brass nails through the holes, from outside to inside

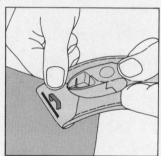

3 Use side cutters on the underside of the hasp to cut off the end of the brass nails

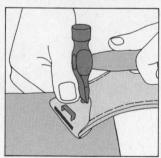

4 Hold the outside of the hasp against a flat surface. Protect it if necessary. Flatten the end of the nails

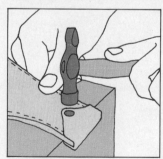

5 Turn over the hasp on the flat surface and hammer very gently on the head of the brass nails

Renewing a turn fastener

A turn fastener on a handbag usually has four parts: the top plate and fabric washer on the handbag flap, and the fastener and back-plate on the body of the bag.

If the top plate becomes loose, remove it, fit a thicker piece of fabric and stick it back with rubber solution. When the main part of the fastener is faulty, because the turn-button spring has broken or the turn button has snapped off, obtain a new one to fit the slot in the top plate.

Materials: fastener; rubber solution; neoprene cement.
Tools: screwdriver; pliers; knife.

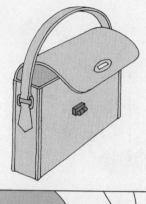

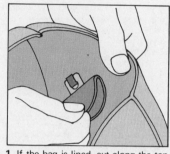

1 If the bag is lined, cut along the top of the lining with a knife. Remove the fabric patch behind the fastener

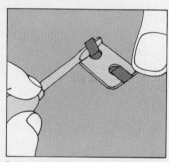

2 Use a small screwdriver blade to prise the tongues up from the back-plate of the damaged fastener

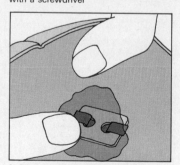

3 Lift off the back-plate. If it has been stuck to the bag, lever it off carefully with a screwdriver

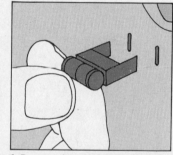

4 Remove the old fastener from the front and slot the tongues of the new one into the two holes

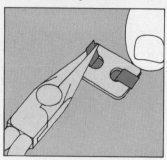

5 Put the backing-plate over the tongues inside and use pliers to bend the tongues down to the plate

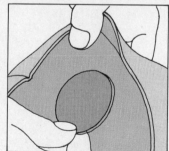

6 Coat the back of the old patch and the area round the back-plate inside the bag with rubber solution

7 When the rubber solution dries, stick the patch over the plate. Use neoprene cement to refit the lining

Repairing a hidden fastener

A hidden handbag fastener usually has a spring and washer fitted to the body of the bag, with a pin and washer on the flap. Because of the way in which the flap is pulled to open the bag, the fastening is more likely to tear off the flap than the body of the bag.

Before starting the repair, take the bag to a leatherware or specialist dealer and obtain the part of the fastener required. There is usually no need to buy a complete fastener.

Materials: leather; ink or shoe polish; neoprene cement.
Tools: screwdriver; pliers; steel rule; knife; pencil; hammer.

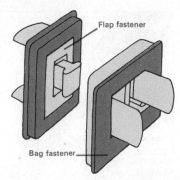

Flap fastener

Bag fastener

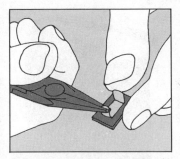

1 Prise up the two tongues of the invisible fastener with the blade of a small screwdriver. Remove the backing

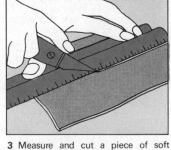

2 Straighten the tongues gently with a pair of pliers until they stand at right-angles to the fastener body

3 Measure and cut a piece of soft leather to cover the width of the handbag and the depth of the tear

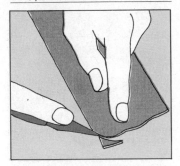

4 Lay the piece of leather on the handbag flap and mark the corners. Trim the patch to fit the flap

5 Lay the leather on the flap and hold the fastener on it. Mark the fastener's position by closing the flap

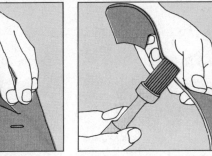

6 Remove the new piece and lay it on a flat surface. Cut the two slots marked by the tongues with a knife

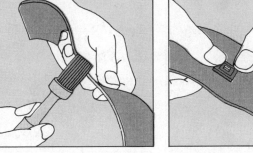

7 Dye the edges of the new strip of leather with ink or shoe polish to match the existing handbag flap

8 Fix the tongues of the new fastener in the cut slots so that the fastener is on the outside of the leather

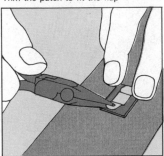

9 Put the backing over the tongues and use pliers to bend them down. Hammer them flat with pliers

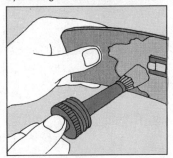

10 Lay the strip in position on the flap of the bag and make a pencil mark across the bottom of the leather

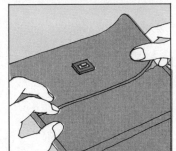

11 Coat the back of the strip and the surface of the handbag flap with neoprene cement

12 Lay the new piece of leather back in place on the flap. Adjust it until the corners match exactly

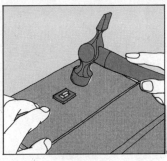

13 To make sure that the new leather sticks securely, tap lightly with a hammer across its whole surface

Luggage and leatherware Straps

Renewing a shoulder sling

If a new sling for a shoulder bag or satchel is difficult to obtain, buy a 54 in. (1·4 m) luggage strap of about the same width as the old strap. Do not buy a wider piece and attempt to cut it to size. Make a new strap band from a piece of the luggage strap. When fitting the new strap to the rings of the bag, make sure before riveting the ends that the smooth side of the strap will be uppermost on the shoulder.

Materials: 54 in. (1·4 m) luggage strap; shoe polish to match bag; capping rivets.
Tools: awl; knife; steel rule; centre punch; pliers; hammer.

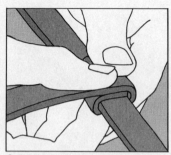

1 Remove the broken straps from the bag. Cut about 12 in. (305 mm) from the buckle end of a new luggage strap

2 Fold the longer piece of strap round the buckle end so that it overlaps to form a retaining band. Mark the length

3 Lay the marked strap on a flat surface and cut across the marked line with a sharp knife

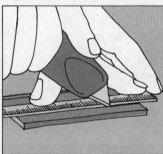

4 Measure the width of the strap and mark the band about two-thirds across its width. Cut down its length

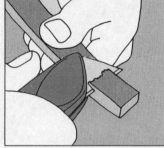

5 Turn the rough side of the band uppermost and taper about ¾ in. (20 mm) from each end of the leather

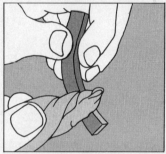

6 Dye the edges of the band piece with a rag and shoe polish to match the colour of the satchel leather

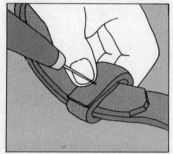

7 Lay the two pieces of strap on each other. Fold the retaining band round. Make a hole through it with an awl

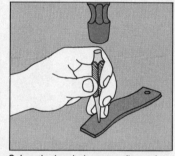

8 Lay the band piece on a flat surface and punch a hole at each end through the holes made by the awl

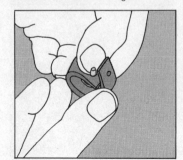

9 Push a rivet pin through from the underside of one end. Fold the other end over on to the rivet

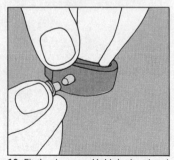

10 Fit the rivet cap. Hold the band and rivet carefully and squeeze the cap on to the rivet with pliers

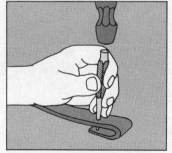

11 Fold over the cut ends of the two pieces of strap. Punch a hole through both thicknesses each time

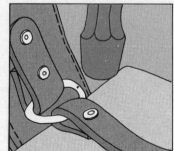

12 Fit the longer strap round the D ring at one side of the bag. Push a rivet through and hammer its cap

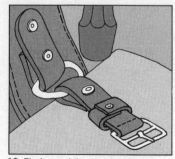

13 Fit the retaining band to the buckle end of the strap. Loop that end round the other D ring. Hammer the rivet

Mirrors

Replacing cracked glass

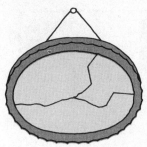

When a mirror breaks, it may be more expensive to replace the glass than to buy a complete new mirror. However, if the frame is to be kept, obtain new mirror glass, polished and bevelled at the edges, from a glass merchant. With a rectangular mirror, measure the straight edges inside the frame. If the broken mirror was circular or specially shaped, try to fit its edges together and make a template from cardboard.

Materials: cardboard; pencil; glass; $\frac{1}{2}$ in. (13 mm) panel-pins.
Tools: chisel; hammer; pliers; screwdriver.

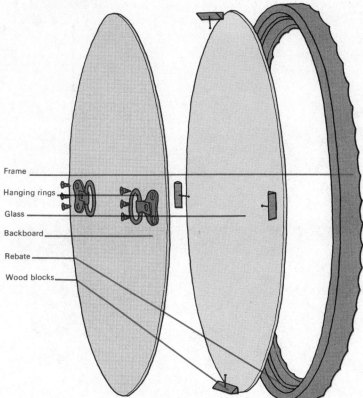

Frame
Hanging rings
Glass
Backboard
Rebate
Wood blocks

1 Lay the mirror on a cloth-covered surface. Remove the hanging cord and unscrew the hanging rings

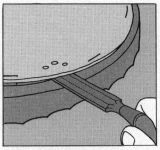

2 The backboard is usually stapled or tacked to the frame. Ease it off carefully with a chisel

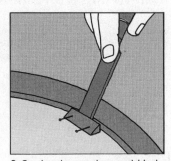

3 Gently prise out the wood blocks pinned to the inside of the frame. Keep them for reassembly

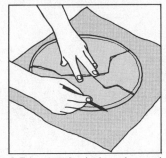

4 Take out the broken glass and reassemble on a piece of paper. Draw round the edge

5 Using the marked paper as a template, obtain new silvered glass and fit it on the rebate

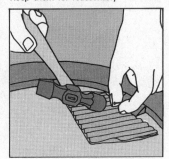

6 Protect the new glass with cardboard as you pin the wood blocks in position to hold the glass

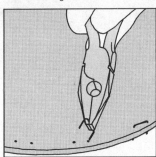

7 Remove the staples or tacks from the backboard with pliers. Cut a new backboard if necessary

8 Tack the backboard to the frame with $\frac{1}{2}$ in. (13 mm) panel-pins, angling them away from the glass

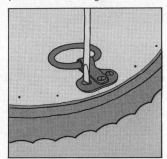

9 Screw the hanging rings in their original position. Replace and fix the hanging cord or chain

Musical instruments Violins

Maintenance and minor repairs

Simple repairs to relatively inexpensive violins can be carried out at home. More advanced jobs—and almost all repairs to valuable instruments—need expert attention.

Only basic household tools are required. Use Scotch glue for sticking: it can be dissolved with warm water if further repairs are needed later. Replacement parts can be obtained from musical-instrument shops. While working on a violin, rest the instrument on a soft surface, such as folded newspaper or a thick cloth.

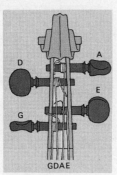

String positions This shows how the strings are ordered and fastened to the pegs at the scroll end

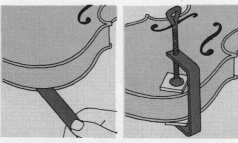

Fixing a loose belly Insert a little glue in the gap between the belly and rib. Clamp together, padding with hardboard to avoid damage. Clean off surplus glue and leave for 24 hours

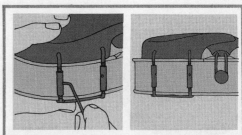

Fitting a chin rest Tighten the long nuts with a special key or with stiff wire. The rest must not touch the tail piece, or it will vibrate during playing

Scroll

Peg-box

Fingerboard

Belly

Purfling

Rib

'f'-hole

Bridge

Fine tuner

Tail piece

Chin rest

Saddle

End pin

Sound-post A hard knock may make this fall down. If it does, loosen the strings and remove the bridge. Replacement is a job for an expert

Fitting new strings

When changing a complete set of strings, deal with only one at a time; if all are removed before any are replaced, lack of pressure on the belly may cause displacement of the sound-post. Each string must protrude at least 1 in. (25 mm) through its peg: use tweezers if it proves difficult to pull them through. E and G strings are ready-looped for easy fitting. Gut strings are commoner but steel is more durable. If steel strings are fitted, lower the bridge about $\frac{1}{8}$ in. (3 mm) by trimming.

Materials: new strings as necessary.
Tool: tweezers.

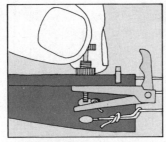

1 Fit the threaded end of the E-string adjuster through the hole in the tail piece. Screw on the knurled nut and the adjuster screw

2 Slip the loop on the end of the string on to the adjuster and position the plastic sleeve to protect the bridge from damage

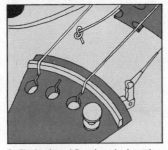

3 Fit the A and D strings by knotting the ends, slipping the knots through the holes in the tail piece, then drawing the strings into the slots

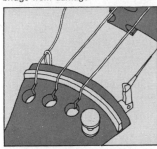

4 Fit the G string by pushing the looped end through the hole in the tail piece, then threading the string back through the loop

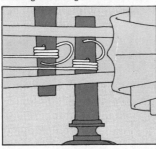

5 Wind the strings on to the pegs from the centre outwards. Turn each peg clockwise and do not allow the string to cross over itself

Fitting a new bridge

The vibrations from the strings are passed to the violin body through the feet of the bridge, so a new bridge must be fitted as closely as possible to the contours of the belly. Normally this involves glass-papering, but bridges with self-adjusting feet can be bought.

Materials: new bridge.
Tools: glass-paper; fine file; knife for cutting nicks.

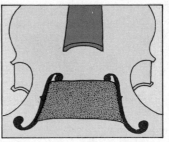

1 Place a piece of fine-grade glass-paper, rough side up, on the belly of the violin in the position where the new bridge is to be fitted

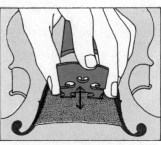

2 Rub the bridge up and down on the glass-paper in the direction shown. This will shape the feet of the bridge to the contour of the belly

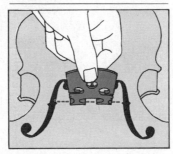

3 Remove the glass-paper and position the bridge in line with the cuts in the middle of the 'f' holes. Check that the feet fit the surface exactly

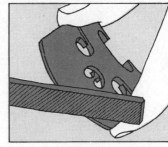

4 Using a fine file, trim the top of the bridge approximately to the contours of the fingerboard. Judge this by eye; finish with glass-paper

5 When viewed from the scroll, the G-string end of the bridge should be $\frac{1}{4}$ in. (6 mm) higher than the fingerboard, the E-string end $\frac{3}{16}$ in. (5 mm)

6 Cut nicks for the strings, the two outer ones $\frac{1}{8}$ in. (3 mm) from the ends of the bridge and the two inner nicks at equal spacing between them

7 The completed bridge, showing the curvature of the top and base, the positioning of the outer nicks and how the top is sloped to one side

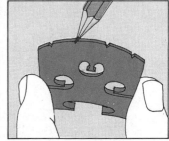

8 Rub a little pencil lead in the nicks. Check the sound-post again, place the bridge in position (do not glue it) and restring the violin

Musical instruments Violins

Replacing gut in the tail piece

The tail piece is held to the end pin with gut or wire—gut if the violin has gut strings, wire if they are steel. Replace worn or frayed gut with wax-impregnated tail gut; wire with stranded brass picture wire. If fastening with wire, knot the ends instead of burning them.

Materials: about 6 in. (150 mm) of gut or wire; thread (for gut).

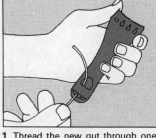

1 Thread the new gut through one of the holes in the tail piece. Burn the protruding tip with a lighted match to make it swell

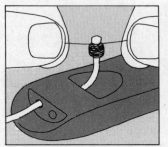

2 Bind the burnt end tightly with strong thread. This will make it larger than the tail-piece hole so that it cannot be pulled through

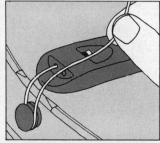

3 Loop the gut round the end pin. Measure the length needed to take the gut back through the tail piece, allowing $\frac{1}{8}$ in. (3 mm) for burning

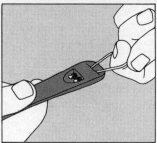

4 Cut off the surplus. Thread the loose end through the other tail-piece hole, burn and bind the tip. Check that the loop holds securely

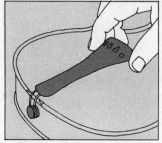

5 Replace the loop over the end pin and refit the tail piece so that it does not touch the saddle inset in the edge of the violin

Replacing a loose fingerboard

When refitting a loose fingerboard, free the strings from the peg-box end. Handle the instrument gently while the strings are loose; before replacing them, check that the sound-post is still in position. Have a damaged fingerboard replaced by an expert.

Materials: Scotch glue.
Tools: thin-bladed knife; clamps; glass-paper.

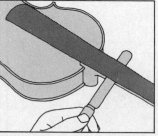

1 If the fingerboard is lifting away at only one point, use a thin knife blade to force glue between the fingerboard and violin neck

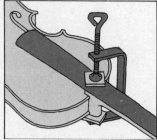

2 Press the surfaces together and clamp them, using packing under the clamp to avoid damaging the violin. Allow 24 hours to dry

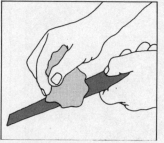

3 If the board has come off, sponge off the old glue with hot water. When the surfaces are dry, rub them lightly with glass-paper

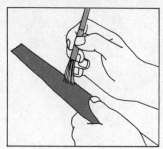

4 Gently warm the board near a fire or radiator, then spread a thin layer of Scotch glue on the underside down both edges

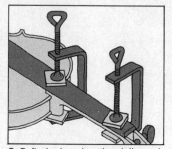

5 Refit the board to the violin neck and clamp them together, again using packing to avoid damage. Allow 24 hours for the glue to dry

Fitting a new peg

Fit a new peg when the old peg is so worn that it is no longer seating properly and the string is no longer held taut. A correctly fitted peg should turn easily in both holes without squeaking or jumping.

Materials: new peg to match.
Tools: fine file; glass-paper; vice; hand drill and $\frac{1}{16}$ in. (2 mm) bit; saw.

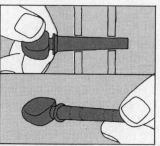

2 Put the peg in its hole and turn it several times to form two shiny rings. These are essential for correct fitting and smooth turning

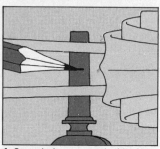

4 Smooth the sawn end with glass-paper, put the peg back in its hole, and mark it at the centre between the two sides of the peg-box

Musical instruments Guitars

Maintenance

To keep a guitar in good condition, wipe it every month with a soft cloth moistened in a little corn oil. Wipe the fingerboard under the strings with a clean, dry rag each time the instrument has been played.

About every three months, lubricate the cog mechanisms at the machine head with a little graphite or candle grease, but take care not to spill it on the body. If a cog sticks, use a graphite-based penetrating fluid to free it.

When cleaning or repairing a guitar, always lay it on a soft surface—an old blanket or layers of newspaper—to avoid scratching the varnished surface.

Take care when using a home-made clamp—say, to repair a crack in the belly of the instrument—that the main part of the body is protected by rags. If wedges are to be used, they should be cloth-covered, and they must be tapped gently. The ribs in the side of a guitar are very thin, and can crack easily if subjected to strain or force.

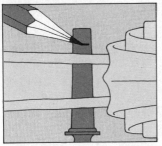

1 A new peg is usually thicker than required and needs shaping to fit. Reduce it with a fine file or rasp and finish with glass-paper

3 Refit the peg and mark the protruding end $\frac{1}{8}$ in. (3 mm) from the peg-box edge. Remove the peg and saw off the surplus

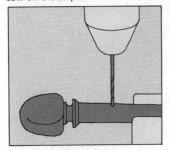

5 Take the peg out again and drill a hole $\frac{1}{16}$ in. (2 mm) in diameter through the marked centre to accommodate the string

Strings The correct position of the stringing on a Spanish guitar for a right-handed player. The stringing would be reversed for a left-handed player

E A D G B E

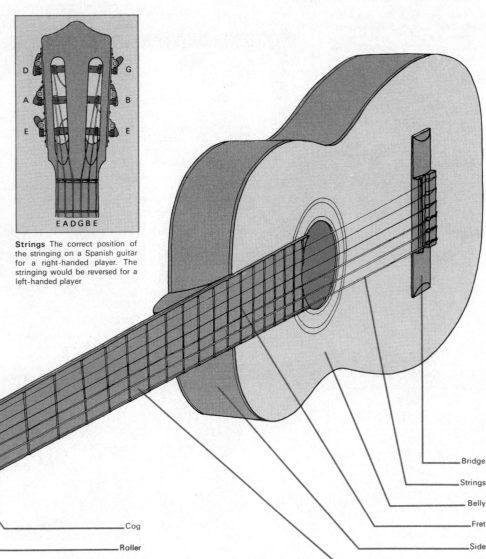

Bridge

Strings

Belly

Fret

Side

Fingerboard

Cog

Roller

Machine head

Musical instruments Guitars

Repairing a crack in the belly

A crack or gap in the belly of a guitar can be closed with glue under pressure, but care is needed if further damage is not to be caused during the repair. Remove or slacken the strings.

Make a wooden clamp to take the width and depth of the guitar body. It should be 1 in. (25 mm) longer than the width of the part of the belly being repaired and ½ in. (13 mm) deeper. Secure its corners by cross-nailing.

Cut three softwood wedges, each about 3 in. (75 mm) long and tapered from a maximum thickness of 1 in. (25 mm). Wrap them in rags.

Materials: wood; rags; glue; nails.
Tools: light hammer; paintbrush.

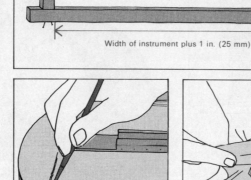

Depth of instrument plus ½ in. (13 mm)

Width of instrument plus 1 in. (25 mm)

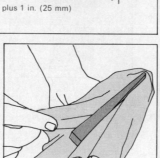

1 Make sure the crack is free of dirt. Use a fine paintbrush to apply hot Scotch glue along it

2 Position the clamp around the belly of the guitar and prepare the wedges by wrapping them in rags

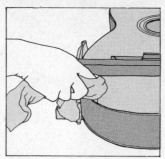

3 While the glue is hot, lightly drive in a wedge at each side. Tap them alternately and evenly

4 Remove any surplus glue with a cloth and hot water. Check that the edges of the crack do not overlap

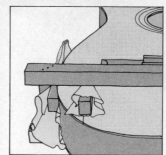

5 Tap in the third wedge above the crack to keep the edges flush. Allow 12 hours for the glue to dry

Fitting a new string

When obtaining new strings for a guitar, make sure that the dealer knows the type of instrument they are needed for. Electronic and cello guitars, for example, require steel strings with metal studs at one end. Spanish guitar strings, made of nylon or gut, have no studs, but are simply looped or knotted at the bridge.

Make sure also that the correct thickness of string is obtained. Keep spare strings labelled or in the packet in which they were supplied.

Take care when tightening a new string that the peg is not overwound.

Materials: new strings as needed.

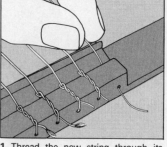

1 Thread the new string through its hole in the bridge. Knot the end if it is the finest—high E—string

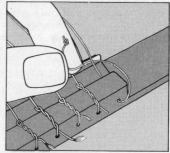

2 Cross the short—or knotted—end over the bridge, under the string, and under the loop thus made

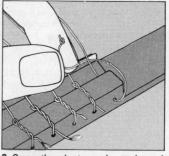

3 Push the end through the loop—several times if the string is not knotted. Pull the free string tight

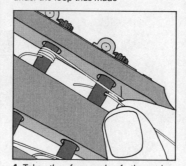

4 Take the free end of the string through the slot in the correct tuning roller. Turn the roller anti-clockwise

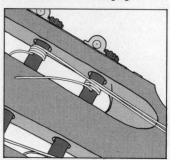

5 Wind the string four or five turns on its roller. To avoid wear, make sure that it does not overlap

Fitting a new fret wire

The wires across the fingerboard, against which the strings are pressed —called the frets—can work loose and cause a buzzing noise when the instrument is played.

Materials: fret wire; fine emery paper.
Tools: hammer; side cutters; fine file; straight-edge.

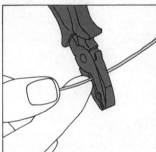

2 Cut the wire with side cutters. Take care not to eliminate the natural curve of the fret wire

4 Trim the fret wire with the side cutters so that it is flush with both edges of the fingerboard

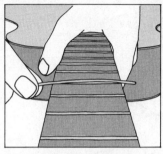

1 Free the strings and remove the old fret. Measure a new fret wire, allowing ½ in. (13 mm) extra

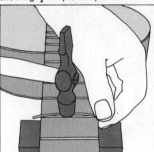

3 Support the fingerboard. Position the fret and lightly tap it home, working from the middle outwards

5 With a fine file, lightly rub the ends of the fret. Take care not to damage the fingerboard

RAISED FRETS

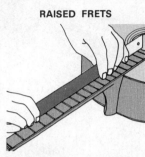

1 A raised fret can also cause buzzing. Free the strings and slide a straight-edge across the frets

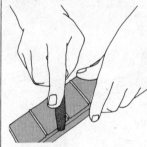

2 When a high fret is located, rub a fine file gently across its centre. Do not dislodge it

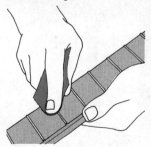

3 When it is filed down, remove the file marks by polishing the fret with fine emery paper

Repairing a machine head

The tuning roller and cog mechanism in the machine head of a guitar can be obtained only as a unit. Since rollers— which seldom break—and cogs are not available, it is advisable to keep an old replaced machine head for spare parts.

Materials: machine-head side.
Tools: screwdriver; hacksaw.

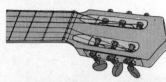

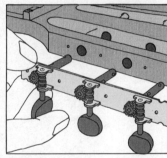

2 Obtain an identical head and fit it. Screw it up tightly and evenly. Refit the strings on their rollers

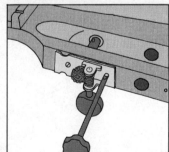

4 Saw a replacement roller and cog from the spare machine head and screw on to the guitar head

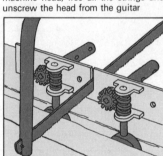

1 When a cog wears or breaks in the machine head, free all the strings and unscrew the head from the guitar

3 When a spare head is available, remove the damaged head and hacksaw off the faulty part

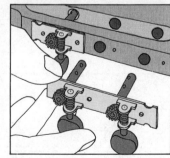

5 Refit the two remaining cogs and rollers from the head which has just been removed. Refit the strings

Musical instruments Pianos

Maintaining a piano

Major repairs to pianos should be done only by an expert. Regular maintenance can be carried out without difficulty to keep them in good condition.

Materials: bowl of water; 15-watt bulb; oil; washing-up liquid; methylated spirit; soft rag.
Tool: screwdriver.

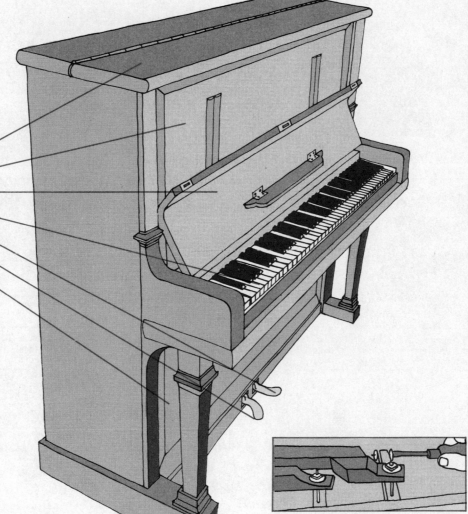

Top door
Fall
Lid
Keyboard
Loud pedal
Soft pedal
Bottom door

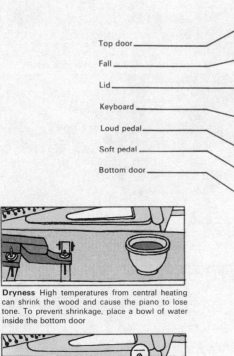

Dryness High temperatures from central heating can shrink the wood and cause the piano to lose tone. To prevent shrinkage, place a bowl of water inside the bottom door

Dampness If the piano is kept in a damp room, the wood and felt may swell and may not operate the hammers. Place a small lamp with a 15-watt bulb inside the bottom door. Keep it lit constantly

Pedals If the pedals squeak when operated, remove the bottom door and apply a few drops of light machine oil to the pedal screws. If the pedals are loose, tighten the screws

Renewing a key covering

On most older pianos, the keys are covered with ivory, which is stuck on with animal glue. It is more likely to come loose than the newer plastic coverings which are often pinned.

Ivory coverings are in two sections. When refitting, make sure that both are pressed tightly together.

Before starting the repair, ease the key out from under its hammer.

Materials: animal glue.
Tools: flat piece of wood; elastic band.

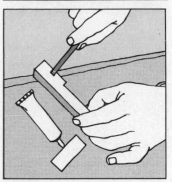

1 Clean the wooden surface of the key. Spread on a slow-drying animal glue, such as Seccotine

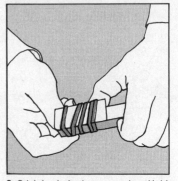

2 Stick back the ivory covering. Hold it in place to dry with an elastic band. Wipe off any excess glue

Freeing stuck keys

Piano keys sometimes stick when the balance and guide pins under the keys become wedged. The pins fit into small mortice holes which have cloth linings, called bushings. A damp room can cause the bushings to swell and trap the pins. The guide pins are at the front of the piano key; the balance pins are in the middle.

Tool: screwdriver.

Key bushing

1 Lift the key. Lift the hammer to take the pressure off the key. Ease the key out of the board

2 The guide pin fits into a hole at the front of the key. Check that the bushing is not swollen

3 The balance pin fits into the hole halfway down the key. Check that the bushing there is not swollen

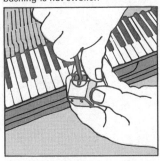

4 Use a screwdriver to push the bushing back in place at the guide-pin hole and the balance-pin hole

Cleaning Lift six keys at a time. Use methylated spirit for ivory, diluted washing-up liquid for plastic

Repairing a split shank

With age or heavy-handed playing, the shank of a key hammer is likely to break. If the break is clean through the shank, engage a professional to do the repair. If the shank is only split, however, mend it with glue and cord.

Materials: animal glue; cord or thread.
Tool: flat wooden stick.

Split hammer shank

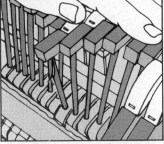

1 Push forward the hammers to find which shank has split. Make sure it has not broken right through

3 Apply the animal glue evenly to both inside edges of the hammer shank that is split

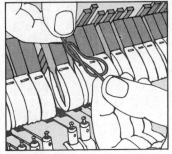

4 Take 6–8 in. (150–200 mm) of thread or thin cord. Tie a small loose loop at one end of it

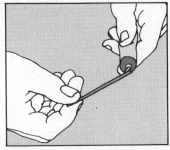

2 Squeeze some slow-drying animal glue—such as Seccotine—on to a long strip of wood

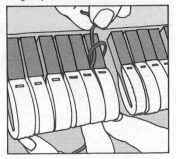

5 Slip the loose loop of thread or cord gently over the head of the hammer with the split shank

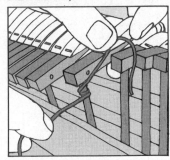

6 Tighten the loop above the split and then bind the cord or thread round the fracture

7 Wind the cord or thread tightly down the whole length of the fracture. Tie a knot at the end

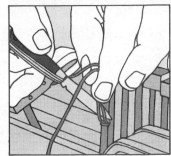

8 Allow the glue to dry for 24 hours. Cut off the loose ends of cord or thread. Leave the binding in place

Musical instruments Recorders

Cleaning and maintenance

A recorder should be cleaned each time it has been played. Attach a thread in a needle to a piece of silk large enough to fit loosely in the bore. Drop the needle down the bore and pull the silk through. Lubricate the instrument every two weeks by damping the silk in almond oil. To clean inside the head, use a rag wound round a small stick.

Materials: silk rag; almond oil; thread.
Tools: needle; cleaning brush; hammer.

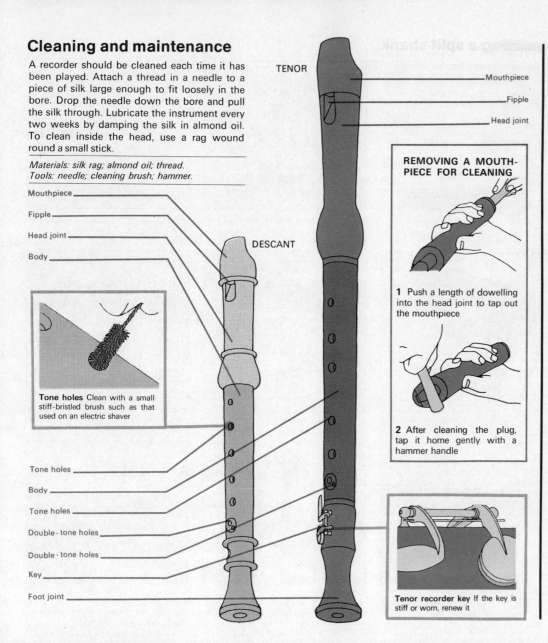

TENOR
Mouthpiece
Fipple
Head joint

DESCANT

Mouthpiece
Fipple
Head joint
Body

Tone holes Clean with a small stiff-bristled brush such as that used on an electric shaver

Tone holes
Body
Tone holes
Double - tone holes
Double - tone holes
Key
Foot joint

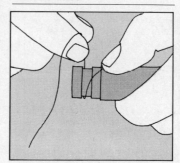

REMOVING A MOUTH-PIECE FOR CLEANING

1 Push a length of dowelling into the head joint to tap out the mouthpiece

2 After cleaning the plug, tap it home gently with a hammer handle

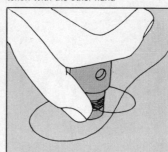

Tenor recorder key If the key is stiff or worn, renew it

Making the joints secure

The joints on a recorder must be tight and leakproof. When they are first bought, they have a special thread—called lapping—wound round the joint tenon, and some of the more expensive instruments may also have a cork covering on the joint.

If the lapping or cork wears, it is enough on an inexpensive recorder to wind ordinary thread round the joint. With more expensive instruments, however, it is advisable to use only the special lapping obtainable from a musical-instrument store.

Materials: lapping; tallow.
Tool: razor blade.

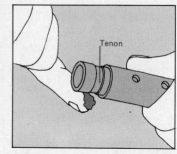

Tenon

1 Remove the frayed or cut lapping. Wipe the tenon clean and apply a thin coating of tallow to it

2 Hold down one end of the lapping thread and wind it evenly round the tenon with the other hand

3 When the tenon is fully covered, hold the free end with one hand and fit the head on the joint

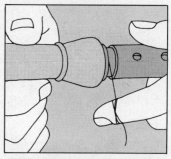

4 If it is not a tight fit, remove the head and wind on more thread. Tie the lapping with a single knot

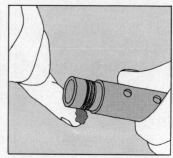

5 Cut both ends of the thread with a razor blade. Apply a good coating of tallow to lubricate the joint

Repairing a tenor key

The presence of a key at the foot of a tenor recorder makes it more prone to breakage than the descant instrument. If the spring wire breaks, the key rests on the hole. If the key pad becomes worn, it cannot sit correctly on the hole and the air seal is lost. If the cork on the tail of the key becomes worn or displaced, the key will be over-vented and a noisy action will result.

Materials: wire (to remove the axle); spring wire; $\frac{1}{16}$ in. (2 mm) cork sheeting; shellac; cork pad; impact adhesive; glass-paper.
Tools: pliers; hammer; knife; small screwdriver.

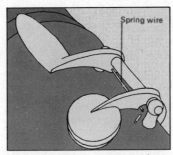

1 When the pad rests permanently on its hole, the spring wire is either broken or too weak to hold the key

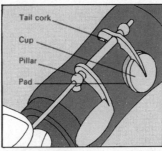

2 Use a piece of stiff wire to push the axle out of the pillar supporting the key. Lift off the key

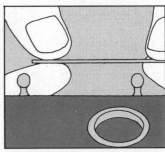

3 Fit new spring wire through the mountings. Measure accurately, remove it and cut to length required

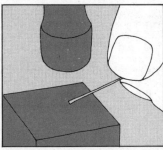

4 Temper one end of the cut wire in a match or lighter flame. Hammer it into an expanded wedge shape

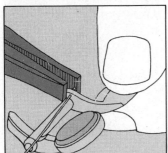

5 Fit the wire, using pliers to make sure that the wedge end is housed firmly in the hole in the key

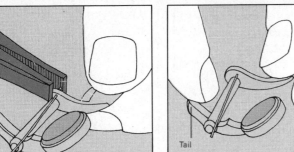

6 Check the cork on the tail of the key. If it is worn or missing, replace it with a new piece of cork

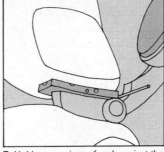

7 Hold a new piece of cork against the key. Cut it slightly larger than the tail. Fix with impact adhesive

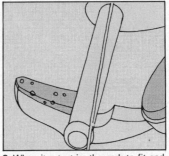

8 When it sets, trim the cork to fit and chamfer the edges with fine glass-paper. Taper it slightly at the end

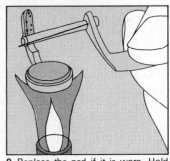

9 Replace the pad if it is worn. Hold the cup in a low gas flame to melt the shellac holding the pad

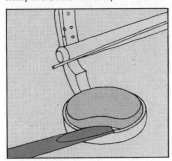

10 Prise the pad from the cup with a small screwdriver or knife. Clean the cup and put in a little fresh shellac

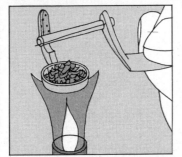

11 Return the cup to the gas flame. Hold it there until the shellac melts and starts to bubble in the cup

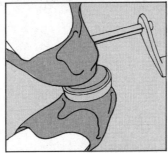

12 Wrap two fingers in a rag and press the new pad into the cup. Make sure the shellac is not spilt

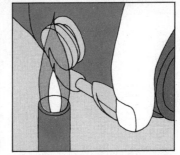

13 Remount the key on the instrument. Hold the cup over the flame for a moment to soften the shellac

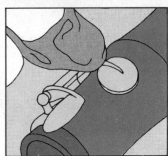

14 To seat the pad correctly, cover one finger and press the cup, while still warm, on to the tone hole

Oil heaters Convectors

Care and maintenance

A convector heater should be emptied when it is not to be used for some time. Let it burn until all the paraffin in the tank and on the wick has been used. For safety, it is advisable to do this with the heater in the open air. Make sure that it is protected from strong winds.

If parts of a heater become damaged, it is usually necessary to replace them: few repairs are possible. Some small faults, however, can be corrected. For example, the central tube may become distorted by heat. Remove it from the heater and apply gentle hand pressure to restore its shape.

In most cases, the only maintenance needed is to keep the heater clean and to trim or replace the wick when necessary.

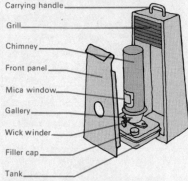

Carrying handle
Grill
Chimney
Front panel
Mica window
Gallery
Wick winder
Filler cap
Tank

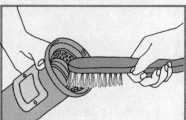

Gallery Remove the chimney complete with its gallery. Look for dust and carbon inside. Clean with a soft brush. Wash with soapy water

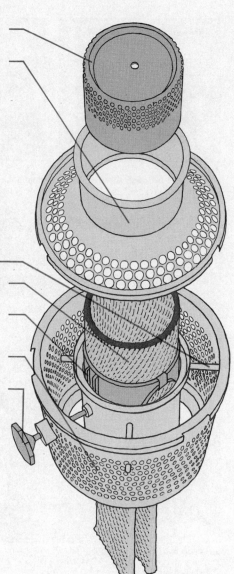

Flame spreader Check inside for fluff

Outer wick tube Clean fluff from the underside. Remove carbon below the upper rim

Tie-rods These are held in position by spring washers and need replacing when distorted

Wick Check that it is not contaminated (see p. 351)

Wick carrier Wash and dry the carrier before fitting a new wick

Burner base Remove any dirt inside the base

Wick winder If the winder is stiff, the cause is a mis-aligned centre tube or a contaminated wick

TRIMMING THE WICK

1 Detach the wick trimmer from the casing. Lay it on the top of the burner

2 Turn up the wick until it can be seen through the slots in the trimmer

3 Turn the trimmer clockwise until the wick is even and free of carbon. Readjust the wick

Fitting new mica

1 If the mica in a chimney window becomes discoloured or damaged by heat, fit new mica

2 Remove the top screw holding the mica panel frame and loosen the screws at the sides

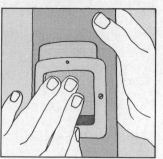

3 Slide out the old mica and fit a new piece. Replace the top screw and tighten all three

Wick faults

Do not allow the wick on a paraffin heater to become contaminated with oil, petrol or water. Make sure that the can used to store the paraffin and the heater tank are completely clean before they are filled.

If a wick does become discoloured or heavily encrusted with carbon, it cannot burn properly. Discard it and fit a new wick. Empty the fuel from the tank and pour it into the ground: it is illegal to pour it into the public drains. Clean the tank out with a dry rag before refilling.

Types of wick

Convector-heater wicks vary slightly from one model to another. To make sure that the correct replacement is obtained, give the dealer the name and type of the heater. Note that there are two principal types of Valor wicks: they are not interchangeable. The type is marked inside the heater.

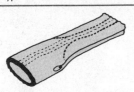

Contamination If a wick tail is contaminated by water, it becomes discoloured. Carbon on the rim shows oil contamination

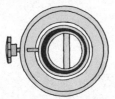

Buckled tube Constant heat may buckle the centre tube of the burner base. Remove the outer tube and re-align the centre tube with gentle hand pressure

Replacing Aladdin wicks

1 To fit a new wick to an Aladdin heater, remove the chimney. Unscrew the burner base nuts

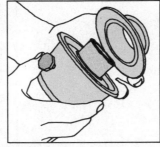

2 Remove burner and flame spreader. Unscrew the outer wick tube with a quarter-turn anti-clockwise

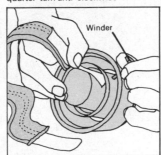

Winder

3 Turn up the wick until winder cogs disengage. Cut down the wick to free it if necessary. Pull it out

4 Hold the winder out and push a new wick between the winder cogs and the centre tube

5 Pull the wick ends down through the slots until the wick fits tightly over the centre tube

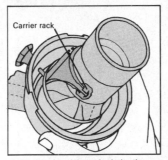

Carrier rack

6 Fit the old wick carrier in its slots on the wick. Fit the carrier rack on the winder cogs and lower the wick

Replacing Valor wicks

1 To fit a wick to a Valor heater, first remove the chimney. Lift the flame spreader from the centre tube

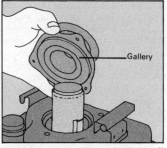

Gallery

2 Unscrew the gallery and take it off. If there is a sealing washer, check it. Replace it if it is damaged

3 Turn up the wick until the ratchet is free of the adjusting wheel. Pull the wick off the tube

4 With a Valmin wick, a plastic wick applicator is provided. Fit it on top of the centre tube

5 Place the new wick over the centre tube with the ratchet facing the wheel. Press it down gently

6 Turn the wick down below the applicator. Remove the applicator, refit flame spreader and gallery

Oil heaters Radiant heaters

General maintenance

Radiant heaters must be kept clean and dry. Make sure that the wick and burner are not allowed to become contaminated with oil or water, and clear away any fluff or dirt that may collect. If the heater starts to smoke, check the wick (see p. 350) and the control valve.

If the heater is glowing irregularly, or if soot is forming on the wire gauze above the burner, examine the spiral element. If it is overstretched at any point, fit a new one.

Once a year strip the heater completely and clean all the components with a soft, lint-free rag and warm, soapy water. Clean the gauze thoroughly with a wire brush. If it becomes dented, hammer it back to shape gently with the brush handle. If any part is worn or damaged, fit a replacement.

Make sure when obtaining new parts that the dealer is told the make and type of heater to which they are to be fitted. Wicks, especially, vary a great deal. Do not try to fit one which is intended for another heater.

Materials: parts as needed.
Tools: wire brush; water and lint-free rag; spanner; screwdriver; spirit level.

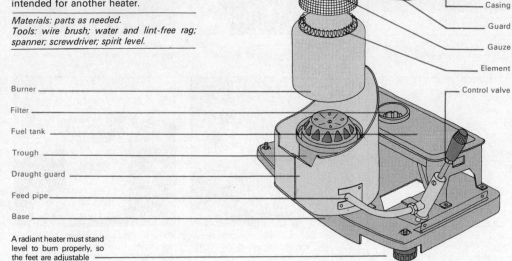

Casing
Guard
Gauze
Element
Control valve
Burner
Filter
Fuel tank
Trough
Draught guard
Feed pipe
Base

A radiant heater must stand level to burn properly, so the feet are adjustable

Overhauling a heater

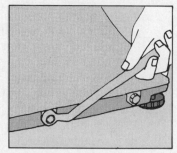

1 Undo the retaining bolts or screws round the bottom edge of the heater casing. Lift off the casing

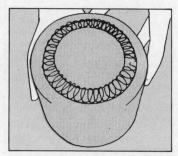

2 Remove the wire gauze and element unit. Make sure that the element is not stretched or brittle

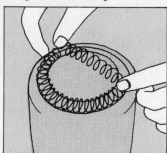

3 If necessary, fit a new element. Take care not to overstretch it. Press it down firmly all the way round

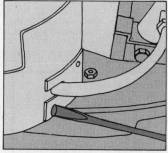

4 Unscrew the bracket at the side of the draught guard where the fuel feed pipe runs into the burner

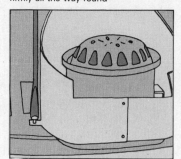

5 Remove the screws holding the draught guard to the base of the heater. Lift off the guard and wash it

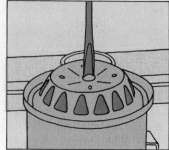

6 Undo the centre screw in the top of the burner trough. Remove it and clean with water and a brush *(continued)*

Oil lamps

Care and maintenance

All paraffin pressure lamps work on the same principle and should be cleaned and overhauled at least once a year. Never use pliers or a wrench for dismantling: all components can be unscrewed by hand. The mantle is very fragile: take care not to touch the mesh when removing it from the lamp.

Because the vaporiser gradually becomes clogged with carbon deposits during use, it is advisable to fit a replacement after every 500 hours of burning. Make sure every time the lamp is dismantled that new washers are fitted at the base of the vaporiser, at the base of the control gland, and on the pump.

Materials: washers; glass; mantle; vaporiser; machine oil.

7 Undo the nut holding the fuel feed pipe to the control valve. Push the pipe back gently

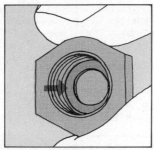

8 Turn the heater over and undo the nut holding the control valve. It is accessible only from underneath

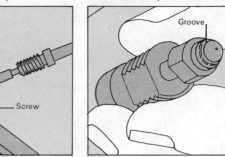

Groove

Screw

10 Undo the control-valve locking screw and pull out the spindle. Ensure it is clean and unworn

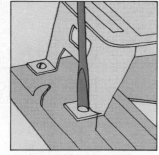

11 If the brass valve seating is worn, replace the spindle and screw it down hard until it seats correctly

9 Examine inside the control-valve nut. If the washer is worn, obtain and fit a replacement

12 Undo the union nut and screws to remove the tank trough from the base. Wash and dry the base

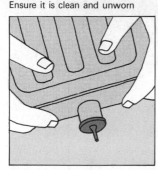

13 Check the fuel tank carefully before reassembling. Tip it towards its valve and look for leaking fuel

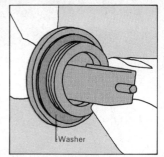

Washer

14 If fuel escapes from around the washer, reposition it correctly, or fit a new one if it is worn

Wick

15 Reassemble the heater. If the wick is contaminated or encrusted with carbon, fit a new one

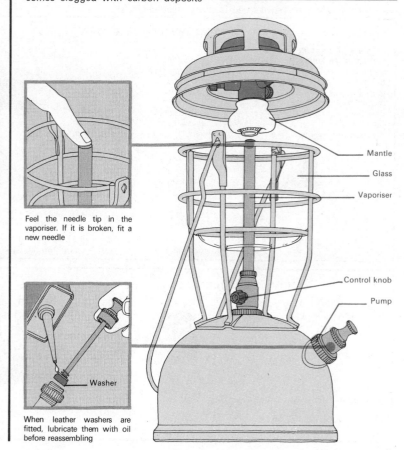

Mantle

Glass

Vaporiser

Control knob

Pump

Washer

Feel the needle tip in the vaporiser. If it is broken, fit a new needle

When leather washers are fitted, lubricate them with oil before reassembling

Photographic equipment Cameras

Looking after a camera

All photographic equipment must be kept clean and dry. When it is not being used, store it carefully in a dry place. Renew batteries in electrical equipment at least once a year—even if they are not exhausted—to ensure that they do not cause damage through corrosion.

If a camera fails when still loaded with unexposed film, open it in a changing bag if possible. If none is available, the camera can be opened safely during the day under bedclothes, but make sure that the sheets and blankets are packed tightly round the camera to keep out the light. After dark, it can be opened in a room or large cupboard, provided steps are taken to ensure that no light can filter in through the window or round the door.

If a camera is so damaged that the mechanism has to be dismantled, take it to a specialist. Never try to repair an electronic flash gun. Such equipment works with an electric discharge of thousands of volts, and tampering with it is a potential danger.

CLEANING THE OPTICAL SYSTEM

All parts of photographic equipment which transmit light must be kept clean to ensure that the pictures produced are of good quality. Remove dust with bellows or a puffer brush—obtainable from a photographic dealer. Wipe with either a proprietary cloth or lint-free rag dampened in lens-cleaning fluid obtained from a photographic dealer. Clean plastic optical components in the same way as glass, but handle them gently: they are easily scratched.

Puffer brush

1 Remove dust with bellows or a puffer brush

2 Lightly brush off any specks of dust or fibres

3 Dampen a rag with lens-cleaning fluid and wipe

REMOVING CORROSION CAUSED BY LEAKING BATTERIES

Chemicals from leaking batteries can damage the metal parts of photographic equipment. If possible, remove the battery compartment from the camera and brush off the corrosion. Wipe with a dry cloth and fit new batteries.

If a contaminated compartment cannot be cleaned, buy a new one. If the damage affects other parts of the equipment, take it to a repair shop.

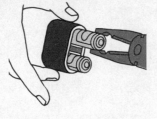

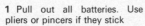

1 Pull out all batteries. Use pliers or pincers if they stick

2 Brush a removable compartment in hot running water

Repairing a faulty still camera

If a film jams, open the camera in the dark and try to free the film by unwinding it from the take-up spool and reloading it. If this is unsuccessful, cut the film where it has jammed. Wrap the exposed part for processing before reloading the unexposed part of the film. Photographs are likely to be patchy if light rays are reflected by surfaces inside the camera. Paint any shiny surfaces with matt black paint, obtainable from a photographic shop.

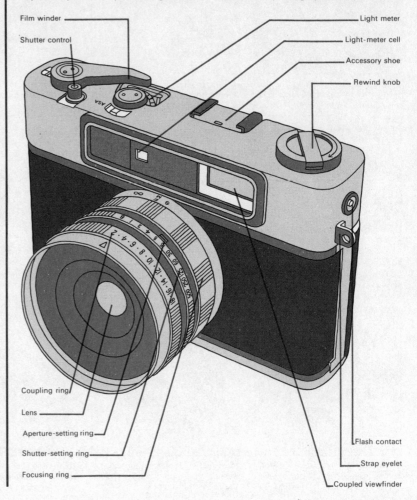

Film winder

Shutter control

Light meter

Light-meter cell

Accessory shoe

Rewind knob

Coupling ring

Lens

Aperture-setting ring

Shutter-setting ring

Focusing ring

Flash contact

Strap eyelet

Coupled viewfinder

If pictures are consistently out of focus, check the range-finder—which may be separate or part of a coupled viewfinder on the camera.

Set the range-finder or coupled viewfinder on the camera to infinity (∞), and look through the viewfinder at a very distant object —for example, a tree or house. If the range-finder is badly adjusted, the two images are seen to be separated horizontally, vertically, or in a combination of both. The horizontal and vertical alignments of the range-finder are adjusted by separate screws or knobs. If the adjuster is a screw fitting, use only a small screwdriver to turn it. Make adjustments gently, and check frequently that the images are being moved together correctly. Do not force the adjuster.

If, after adjustment, the range-finder does not operate correctly, take it to a photographic specialist. Do not try to dismantle it.

HORIZONTAL SEPARATION

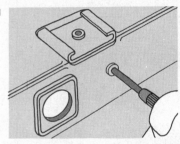

When two distant images are alongside each other with the viewfinder at ∞, make adjustment on the horizontal-alignment screw or knob on the back of the camera or on the distance-indicator dial

When separation is both horizontal and vertical, adjust one correctly before starting on the other

VERTICAL SEPARATION

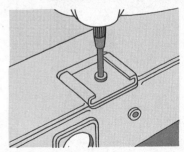

When one image is seen to be higher than the other, look for the adjustment point at the side of the range-finder or on top of the camera —usually under a plate or on the accessory shoe

Turn the knob or screw gently. Do not force it. Look through the viewfinder frequently to check the adjustment

Mending a hole in the camera bellows

If a bellows camera consistently produces photographs fogged or patched in one area, it is likely that the bellows have a small hole. To find the hole, move a small pen torch around inside the bellows, and look outside for chinks of light.

Try to obtain—from a photographic dealer—a black patching material with a rubber coating on one side. It must be thin enough to fold with the bellows. Use impact adhesive.

Materials: patching material; impact adhesive.
Tools: pencil or chalk; scissors; pen torch; matchstick; tweezers; spoon.

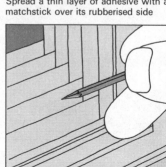

Patches indicate a hole in the bellows

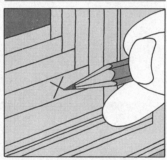

1 Find the hole in the bellows with a light. Mark it with chalk or pencil, but do not puncture the bellows

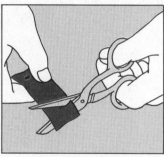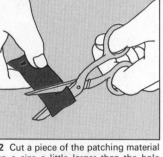

2 Cut a piece of the patching material to a size a little larger than the hole in the bellows

3 Hold the patch with tweezers. Spread a thin layer of adhesive with a matchstick over its rubberised side

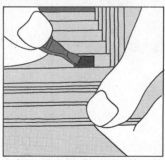

4 Support the bellows outside with the fingers of one hand. Inside, place the patch over the hole with tweezers

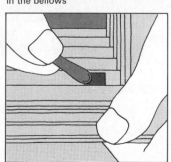

5 Hold outside, and press the patch firmly in place with the handle of a small spoon

Pin hole Fill a pin hole from the inside with black Bostik. Use a sharpened matchstick to apply it

Mending a flash-gun

When a flash-gun fails, fit a new bulb and try again. If it still fails, the fault must be in the power source or the contacts which carry the power.

If the gun is electronically operated, do not dismantle it: take it to a dealer. With a battery-powered gun, clean the contacts and make sure that they are correctly sprung. Fit a new battery if necessary. If the gun still does not work, take it to a specialist repairer.

Tools: tweezers; paintbrush; rag; pliers.

CLEANING THE CONTACTS

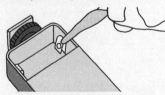

1 Remove the batteries and clean both ends of each with a dry rag. Make sure that they are leakproof

2 Clean the contacts with a rag wrapped round a paintbrush. Pull the contacts out slightly with tweezers

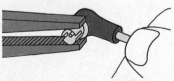

3 Clean the plug at the end of the gun connecting cable. Squeeze it gently with a pair of pliers

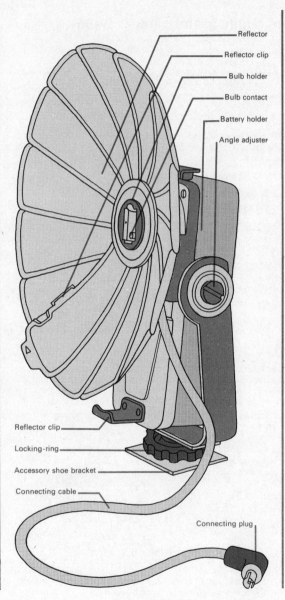

Reflector

Reflector clip

Bulb holder

Bulb contact

Battery holder

Angle adjuster

Reflector clip

Locking-ring

Accessory shoe bracket

Connecting cable

Connecting plug

Checking an exposure meter

Check the adjustment of an exposure meter every six months—or when it has been dropped or knocked. It should register zero when no light can enter it.

If the meter does not operate correctly, even when the adjustment is accurate, fit a new battery and clean the contacts. If it still does not work—or if it is not battery-powered—take it to a dealer for repair.

Materials: rubber or lightproof material.
Tool: small screwdriver.

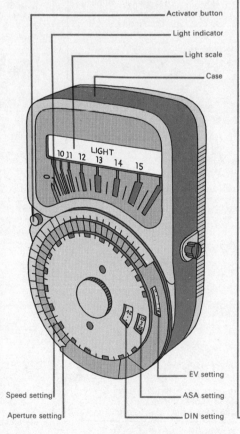

Activator button

Light indicator

Light scale

Case

LIGHT
10 11 12 13 14 15

Speed setting

Aperture setting

EV setting

ASA setting

DIN setting

ADJUSTING A METER

1 Fold a piece of rubber or light-proof material tightly over the light-sensitive cell

2 Providing that all light has been excluded, the meter should register zero

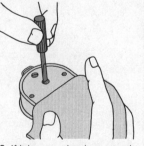

3 If it is not registering correctly, adjust the screw on the back with a small screwdriver

Photographic equipment   Ciné cameras

Cleaning and maintenance

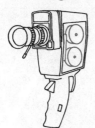

A ciné camera has two spools. As the camera is operated the film passes from one spool to the other through a moving gate. The drive spool can be powered by a clockwork or electric motor. A clockwork motor must be wound before each shot if the film is to travel at the correct speed. Make sure that the batteries in an electric motor are in good condition and that the battery contacts are clean (see p. 354). Do not leave film unused in the camera for more than a week or two. If left for long periods, the film is likely to bend away from the claw in the gate and may not run when the trigger is pressed.

If the movement of the film does not synchronise with the camera shutter, the film cannot be exposed correctly. Take the camera to a dealer.

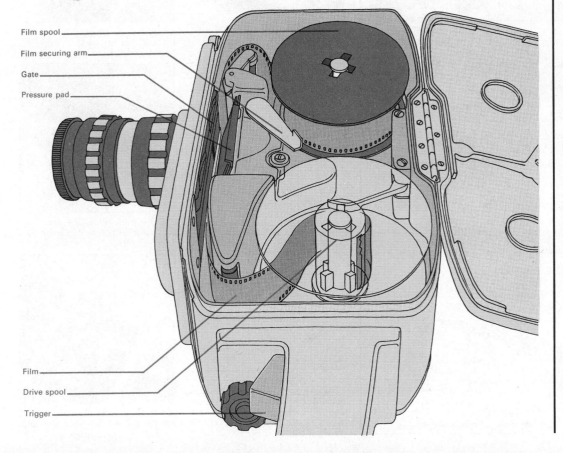

- Film spool
- Film securing arm
- Gate
- Pressure pad
- Film
- Drive spool
- Trigger

Cleaning the film path

Dust, dirt or emulsion from the film can build up in the gate and cause the film to jam. Always clean the film path—where it runs through the gate—after 12 films have been run through the camera. Use methylated spirit and a lint-free cloth.

1 Check that the pressure pad is removable. Draw it back and ease it out of the camera gate

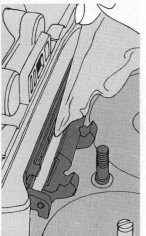

CLEANING A FIXED PAD

If the pressure pad cannot be removed from a ciné camera, clean the gate with a rag, dampened in methylated spirit and wrapped round a pointed stick. Make sure that all emulsion deposits are removed

2 Clean the pad with a rag and methylated spirit. Clean the gate with a fine-bristled paintbrush

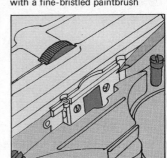

3 If there are any emulsion deposits on the gate, scrape gently with a thin pointed stick

Photographic equipment Ciné films

Freeing jammed film

If a camera jams while it is being used, open it in the dark to avoid wasting the unused film.

Check the drive spool. If it is not winding the film quickly enough, or if it has stopped running, the film is building up inside the film chamber and jamming the gate.

If the film has been damaged, cut out the broken piece before trying to rewind it on the drive spool.

Tool: tweezers.

SUPER 8 mm CASSETTES

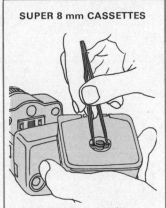

If a film cassette jams, do not try to dismantle it. Open the camera door and remove the cassette. Use a pair of tweezers to wind the boss clockwise. If the film cannot be freed, send the unopened cassette to the manufacturers

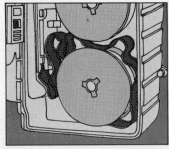

1 Open the camera in the dark and feel for the unwound film packed in the film chamber

2 Lift out the drive spool. Hold the film on it firmly to prevent the film continuing to unwind

3 If the film has been badly creased or torn, tear through it neatly. Keep the film on the spool for processing

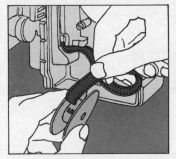

4 Take the end of the film still in the camera and thread it on to a spare drive spool. Fit the spool in the camera

CLEARING THE GATE

1 If the film jams but is correctly wound on the drive spool, draw back the gate and lift out the film

2 Move film onwards six holes. Squeeze the trigger. If the film does not move, consult a dealer

Cleaning and storage

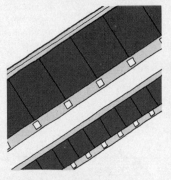

Developed ciné film must be handled carefully. Torn perforations or bad joins can jam the projector and cause irreparable damage to the film.

Clean and inspect films after every showing. Remove any marks when the film is being rewound. Use a rewinder, which will be slower than winding in the projector but will allow the film to be examined. Hold a dry, lint-free cloth in one hand and wind the film through it. If there are stubborn marks on the film, dampen the cloth in methylated spirit. To check the perforations, hold the sides of the film gently between the thumb and index finger. Repair any damage immediately: a temporary repair can be made with a V cut.

Place a light behind the film and look for scratching on the film surface. Cut out badly scratched frames and splice the ends of the sound pieces.

Storage

Keep old, inflammable films in a steel container. Modern films can be kept in plastic containers. Make sure that the container used is clean, to avoid scratching the film.

Never leave a film in the projector when it is not in use. The film may stretch into loops at the sprockets and break or jam as soon as the projector is used again.

1 Rewind the film slowly and feel for tears in the edges with the fingers of one hand

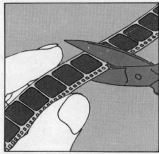

2 Cut into the side of the film at the torn sprocket hole with a small pair of sharp scissors

3 Cut at an angle at both sides of the hole. Continue rewinding and check for further damage

Photographic equipment Ciné projectors

Cleaning and lubrication

All ciné projectors are powered by mains electricity. Always unplug the projector from the current supply before attempting any cleaning or maintenance.

Clean the lens, condenser and mirror (see p. 354) regularly. If the reel-drive shafts are metal, lubricate them with a little thin oil after every 24 hours' running. If the shafts have nylon bearings, no lubrication is needed.

Clean the gate of the projector with a fine-pointed stick and a clean cloth dampened in methylated spirit. Ensure that the sprocket teeth are clean.

When loading the film, make sure that it engages the teeth of the gate sprocket correctly. Check that the film loops at the top and bottom of the gate, so that it is not over-tensioned.

SLOW RUNNING—PROJECTOR STOPS

If the projector runs slowly, or stops, check that the belt from the motor to the drive pulley is not slipping or broken. If a new belt is needed, remove rubber particles from the pulley surfaces before fitting it.

If the projector still runs slowly, take it to a dealer to have the motor checked or replaced

STREAKED PICTURE

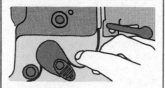

If the picture goes into vertical streaks, there is no loop at the projector sprocket. Repeated loss of loop can be caused by worn sprocket teeth. Take projector to a dealer for attention

NO LIGHT

Check that the bulb (left) is fully home in its socket. Push it down (right) until the socket rim grips the glass base

CHECKING AND CLEANING BULBS

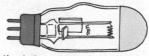

1 If a bulge appears in the glass of a bulb, replace the bulb immediately: if the bulge expands until it touches a condenser or the side of the projector, it can explode

2 Never handle a quartz-iodine bulb with bare fingers. Clean with a rag and methylated spirit

CLEANING THE GATE

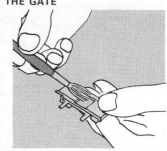

Clean the projector film gate before the projector is used. Jack the lens forward, to gain access to the gate, and remove or pull back the pressure pad. Clean the gate with a pointed stick and clean rag dampened in methylated spirit. If the pressure pad is removable, clean it with a soft brush and replace it

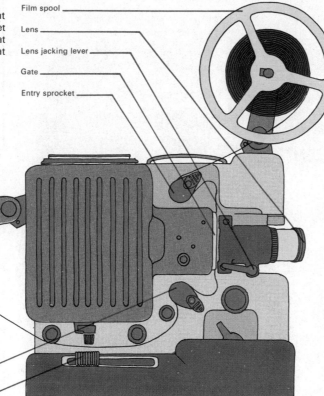

Film spool

Lens

Lens jacking lever

Gate

Entry sprocket

Shaft

Drive spool

Exit sprocket

Speed control

Photographic equipment Slide projectors

Maintaining a slide projector

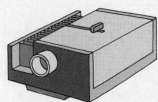

If the cooling fan stops when the light is on, switch off immediately to prevent overheating. If there is no loose wire, the fan motor may be faulty or the lamp may be out of alignment. Take the projector to a specialist repairer.

If the projector overheats when the fan is working, check that there is space underneath for air to enter. Make sure the fan blades are not bent flat. Check that the heat filter is in place.

Lighting and electrical system
If the light fails, check that the bulb is secure in its socket and that there are no loose wires. Check the fuse (see p. 519) or batteries (p. 354). If the projector works on batteries, take them out of the projector when it is not in use to prevent possible corrosion.

Jamming
A projector may jam if a slide is deformed or too thick. Free it by hand or with a small screwdriver. If an automatic changing mechanism jams, check the operating belt. If it is stretched, take it to a dealer.

Remote control
Do not try to adjust or repair the remote-control mechanism. If it is faulty, consult a specialist.

Optical system
Clean the lens, condensers, heat filter and mirror regularly (see p. 354). Replace any broken part.

Mending slides

Slides are likely to become buckled and difficult to focus if they are used in an overheated projector. Remove a damaged transparency and remount it. To prevent further trouble, it is advisable to use a plastic frame, with the transparency sandwiched between two pieces of glass. Mounting kits are available from photographic dealers.

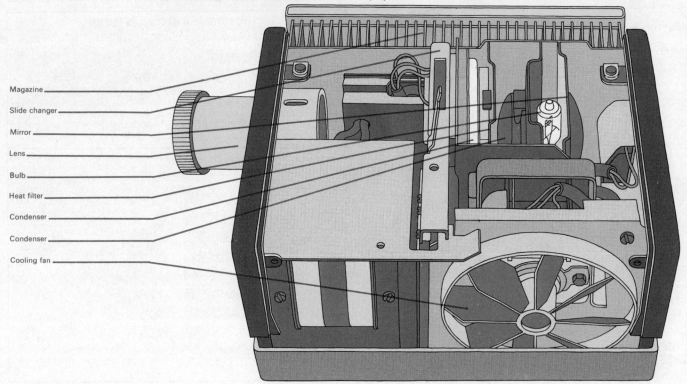

Magazine
Slide changer
Mirror
Lens
Bulb
Heat filter
Condenser
Condenser
Cooling fan

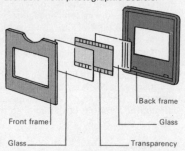

Front frame
Glass
Back frame
Glass
Transparency

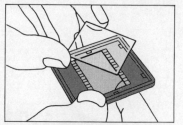

1 Clean the glass pieces and lay one in place in the back frame. Position the transparency accurately on the glass

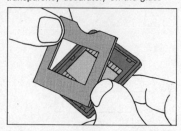

2 Cover the transparency with the second piece of glass. Position the front frame and snap it into the back frame

Pictures

Remounting and reframing

Many pictures should be cleaned and repaired only by specialists. Watercolours, for example, could be destroyed by the wrong cleaning methods: oil paintings, even on canvas, may be much more delicate than they appear. If there is any doubt about the type or condition of a picture, seek expert advice. Do not attempt to repair valuable pictures.

The jobs most likely to be within the scope of an amateur are remounting and reframing. To do any other work, especially cleaning, start at a part of the picture which could be hidden by its border. If colour comes off, stop work and consult an expert.

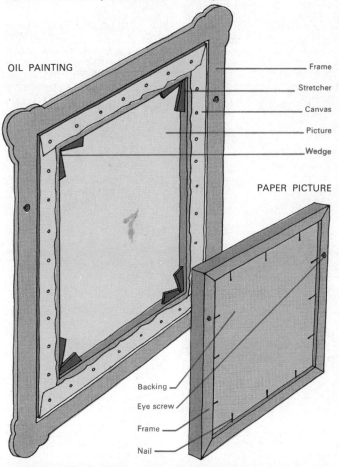

OIL PAINTING

- Frame
- Stretcher
- Canvas
- Picture
- Wedge

PAPER PICTURE

- Backing
- Eye screw
- Frame
- Nail

REMOVING OIL PAINTINGS

An oil canvas is usually tacked to an unjointed wooden frame—called a stretcher—which is itself mounted in an ornamental frame. Often the stretcher is nailed to the frame, but this method is wrong—hammering can loosen or crack the paint.

1 To remove a painting nailed into a frame, grip the frame near the top at each side. Press gently with the thumbs against the wood of the stretcher until it moves. Continue pressing down the sides until the canvas is free

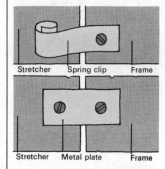

Stretcher   Spring clip   Frame

Stretcher   Metal plate   Frame

2 Do not nail the canvas back into the frame. Screw two spring clips to each side of the frame so that their free ends hold the stretcher tightly. Alternatively, screw two metal plates to each side of the frame to overlap the stretcher

Removing a print

Paper pictures are often mounted on a backing card, with a window-frame border of card at the front. If the picture is to be reframed, or if the card border has become discoloured, remove the picture from the card and remount it.

Most pictures are glued straight on to the backing card, in which case it may be possible to separate them with water (see p. 363). Sometimes the picture is fixed to the backing card with paper hinges. Take care when detaching such pictures from their backing, because the paper is likely to tear if handled roughly.

Tools: pliers; sharp knife.

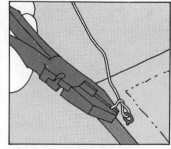

1 Use pliers to undo the hanging wire at the back of the picture. Remove the eye screws from the frame

2 With a sharp knife, cut round the backing paper against the inside of the frame. Remove the paper

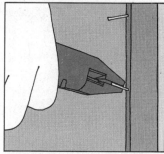

3 Use the pliers to remove the bent nails which secure the backing board to the wooden frame

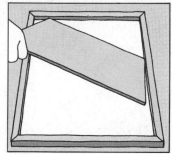

4 Lift out the backing board. If it is damaged or badly worn, cut a new piece for reassembly

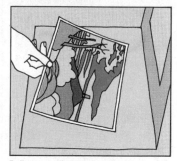

5 Remove the mounted picture. Lift up the window mounting and peel the picture hinges from the backing

Pictures Prints and water colours

Removing grease

Grease stains can be removed from a paper picture by dabbing them lightly with a ready-made acetone solvent—obtainable from a chemist or artists' dealer. Take care to use only a little of the solvent. When it has loosened the grease, cover the stained area with blotting-paper and press lightly with a warm iron. Make sure that the iron is just hot enough not to be able to be touched by hand. Do not leave it on the blotting-paper more than ten seconds at a time.

Materials: acetone; cotton wool; clean blotting-paper; saucer.
Tool: iron.

1 Lay the picture on some blotting-paper. Dab the stain with cotton wool moistened with a little acetone

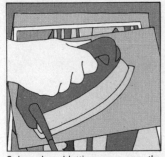

2 Lay clean blotting-paper over the stain and gently press with a warm iron until the stain has been removed

Mending a tear

If a paper picture has a small tear or hole, it can be repaired by pasting a good-quality artists' paper over the back of the damaged area.

The white paper of the repair can be touched in. But first check that the tints it is proposed to use match those in the picture.

If the tints of the picture cannot be matched, consult a specialist.

Materials: good-quality artists' paper; starch or flour glue; matching tints.
Tools: knife; glue brush; fine artists' brush.

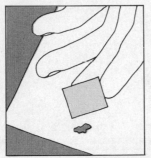

1 Cut a piece of paper larger than the hole. Apply glue around the back of tear. Stick on patch

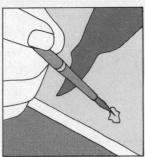

2 Use a matching tint to touch in the white paper of the patch showing in the picture

Removing stains from a print

Rust like stains on prints mounted on card can usually be removed by immersing the print in a bleach solution. Use 5 ml. of Chloromine T—it can be ordered from most chemists—in a pint ($\frac{1}{2}$ litre) of water. It is also possible to spot-bleach small areas of a print or painting, but the picture must later be retouched (see p. 362).

When bleach is used, test it on an obscure corner to make sure that the picture is colourfast. This is generally true only of prints. However, many oriental prints are not colourfast. If there is any doubt, consult a specialist.

Materials: tray; glass sheet; Chloromine T; two boards, 1 in. (25 mm) thick; blotting-paper.
Tools: palette knife; four G cramps.

SIMPLE CLEANING

Surface dirt on watercolours and pastel pictures should be removed only by a specialist, but it can be removed from prints at home.

1 Rub fresh breadcrumbs lightly over the picture. When they become dirty, use fresh crumbs

2 For stubborn dirt, use artists' putty rubber. Press it lightly on the dirt, then rub very lightly

1 Immerse the print in a tray of water until the mount begins to free itself at the corners or edges

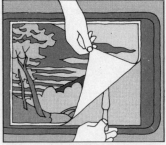

2 Do not try to hurry the removal process. As the picture soaks, ease it carefully with a palette knife

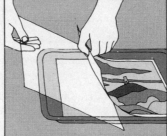

3 Slide a sheet of glass under the print. Lift it gently out of the water on top of the glass

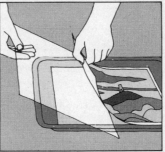

4 Slip the print carefully off the glass into the bleach. It can safely stay there for several hours

5 When the stains are removed, use the glass to lift the print out of the bleach. Rinse in a tray of clean water

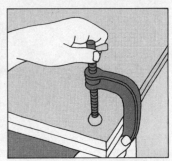

6 Lay print on blotting-paper. Cramp the picture between fresh blotting-paper and boards until it is dry

Re-mounting a print

If a paper picture has been cleaned, it can be stuck to a card mount. A simpler alternative, which avoids the risk of staining by glue, is to mount the picture with stamp hinges at only two or three points along its top edge. A second piece of card can be cut and fitted to make a border for the picture. When reframing a print or watercolour, it may be necessary to put extra card behind the backing board if the picture is too loose.

Materials: stamp hinges; good-quality card; self-adhesive tape; panel-pins. Tools: knife; straight-edge.

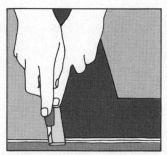

1 Measure and cut a new backing mount. If required, cut a front border to suit the picture

2 Lay the top edges of the two cards together. Stick tape along to form a hinge between the cards

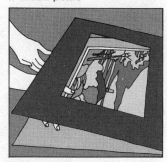

3 Fold the cards together. Position the picture correctly and mark its top edge on the mount

4 Fix the top edge of the picture securely in position on the back mount with two or three stamp hinges

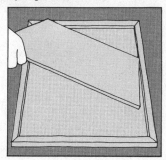

5 Fit the picture and the backing board in the frame. Drive in pins and bend over to hold the board

Cleaning and re-varnishing

Before starting to clean surface dirt from an oil painting, remove it on its stretcher from the frame (see p. 361). If the canvas is loose, tuck wads of cotton wool between the canvas and the slats and frame of the stretcher to prevent crease marks from the stretcher appearing on the canvas during cleaning of the painting.

Clean a small area at a time. Use only a little turpentine or white spirit; examine and change the cottonwool swabs frequently. There should be no danger of paint coming off on the swabs: this would occur only with a recently painted picture, which should not be cleaned. Never touch an oil painting with water as this can cause staining and discoloration.

Removing varnish
When a painting has been cleaned, examine the varnish carefully. If it is very old, it is likely to have become dark or milky, obscuring the painting.

The varnish can be removed with acetone. Note, however, that acetone is a powerful solvent. Use turpentine or white spirit to stop its dissolving action. To remove varnish, pour acetone into one saucer and a little turpentine into another. Start at an edge which is normally hidden by the frame.

Use an acetone swab to dissolve the varnish: take it off the painting with a turpentine swab which will stop the acetone working.

Check the swabs and the painting frequently. If any colours appear on the swabs, stop the dissolving action immediately with turpentine. On old paintings do not persist in trying to remove all the varnish as repeated treatment may damage the canvas.

Re-varnishing
Check the back of the canvas. If there are damp patches, allow the canvas to dry out. Never heat the canvas to speed the drying.

When the painting is dry, lay it face up on a flat surface and apply a picture varnish. Use a new 2 or 1½ in. (50 or 40 mm) paintbrush with best-quality bristles. Varnish thinly and evenly in both directions to avoid brushmarks.

To repair a hole or tear in a painting canvas, buy a piece of unprimed canvas. Cut it slightly larger than the damaged area. Lay the picture face down on several layers of greaseproof paper. Melt beeswax in a double saucepan. Dip the canvas patch in wax and apply directly to back of picture, smoothing it in with a palette knife.

Materials: acetone solvent; turpentine; picture varnish; cotton wool; beeswax; greaseproof paper; canvas. Tools: palette knife; paintbrush.

1 Tuck wads of cotton wool between the canvas and the frame and slats of the stretcher

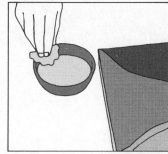

2 To remove varnish, use an acetone swab. Rub it with a circular motion, starting from the edge of the picture

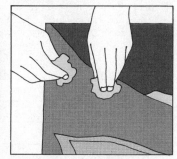

3 Keep a turpentine swab in the other hand to remove varnish and stop acetone action immediately if necessary

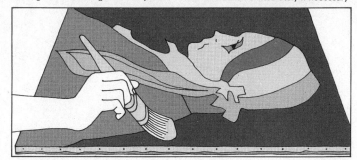

4 Allow the painting to dry. Apply a picture varnish. Do not lift the painting until the varnish has superficially dried (15 minutes), then stand it on edge, facing a wall to avoid dust settling on it. Never heat the painting to dry it

Prams and pushchairs

Care of wheels and hoods

Check all pram wheels, nuts and bolts regularly to make sure that they are secure. Ensure that the brake grips firmly when it is applied.

Although most pram wheels have nylon bearings which need no lubrication, it is advisable to apply a few drops of thin oil to the axles when the wheels are removed.

Take care when parking a pram to avoid scraping the hood against a wall. If the hood is becoming worn or torn, sew on metal corner shields to protect the hood from further damage.

Do not allow damage—especially to upholstery—to extend. It is always better to repair a simple fault or tear than to let it develop into major damage which requires specialist attention.

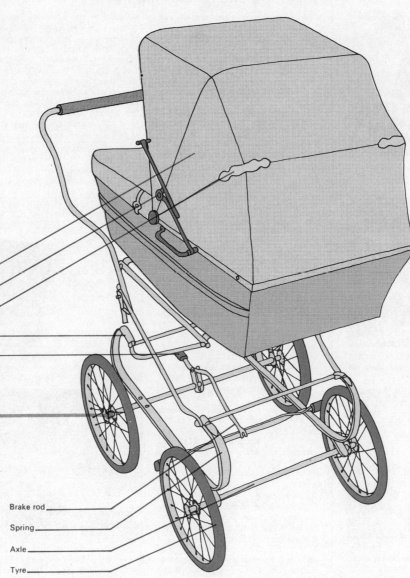

Hood

Hood hinge

Hood shield

Spring

Brake pedal

Lubrication If the wheels squeak when the pram is pushed, remove them and apply a few drops of thin cycle oil to the axles

Brake rod

Spring

Axle

Tyre

Removing pram wheels

The wheels of a pram are held in place either by simple clips or by devices known as sliders or plungers. All three types of lock fit into a groove in the axle shaft.

To fit a new wheel or tyre, take the damaged one to a dealer to obtain the correct type and size.

Materials: parts as needed; thin oil.

Clip   Slider   Plunger

Spring clip Push the ends of the clip apart with the thumbs and push it to the side to unhook its lug from the shaft groove. Remove wheel

Slider Some wheels are held to the groove in the shaft by a spring-loaded slider. Pull the slider out of its housing at the side of the wheel axle

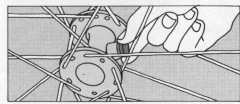

Plunger If the wheel is held by a plunger device—usually in the centre of the axle—pull it up and slide the wheel off the shaft

Removing pushchair wheels

If a pushchair wheel is damaged, take it to a pram specialist to have it repaired. If only the tyre is worn, however, remove it and fit a new one.

The wheels on most pushchairs are held by a star-lock washer under the hub cap. To remove a wheel, prise off the cap and lever off the star-lock washer with a screwdriver. It is unlikely that a washer can be removed and used again. Buy a replacement from a pram store.

Materials: star-lock washer; grease; new tyre.
Tools: screwdriver; tyre levers.

FITTING A NEW TYRE

If a pram tyre is worn, cut it off the wheel, clean inside the rim and fit a new tyre.

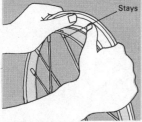

1 Place one side of the new tyre in the rim and work the remainder round with the fingers

2 Fit the last section over the rim with a tyre lever. Check that the tyre is evenly fitted

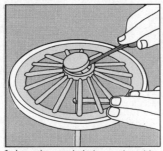

1 Lay the pushchair on its side. Prise off the wheel hub-cap with the blade of a screwdriver

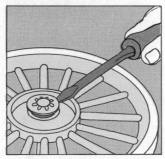

2 Ease the star-lock washer off the shaft with a screwdriver. Make sure a new one is available

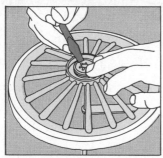

3 Refit wheel and press an inverted star-lock washer into place. Make sure it fits evenly on the shaft

Strengthening hood corners

Always make sure that a pram or pushchair hood is folded neatly and that no excess is allowed to bulge over the sides. In time, a badly folded hood is likely to fray.

Take care not to rub the hood corners against walls and check the corner pieces regularly to ensure they are secure and undamaged.

If a corner piece does become loose, or if the hood starts to fray at the edges of its joints, buy new metal shields, obtainable from most pram dealers, to prevent further damage. To sew on a shield, secure the hood lock on the other side of the pram. This ensures that one side is held stiffly while the side being worked on has enough slack to allow sewing.

Make sure during sewing that the needle cannot pierce the hood lining: it must pass through the holes in the metal shield, then round the stays of the pram hood and back through the outside fabric of the hood.

Materials: corner pieces; waxed thread (see p. 612).
Tool: spear-point needle.

1 Bend the shield to fit the hood corner. Knot the thread and pass it through an end hole

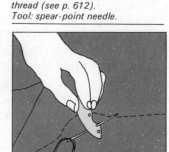

2 Sew the first six holes. Sew round the hood stay but not through the hood lining

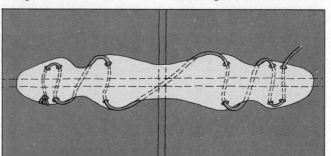

3 Draw the thread tight. Make sure that the corner piece fits the shape of the hood. Pass the thread round the back of the stay at the corner and continue stitching through the remaining six holes

Materials: corner pieces; waxed thread (see p. 612).

SPLIT UPHOLSTERY

Large splits or tears in upholstery should be professionally repaired. A small tear can usually be patched at home.

Materials: matching material; contact adhesive.
Tools: scissors; adhesive applicator.

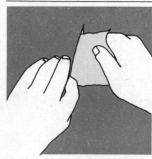

1 Cut a patch of matching material ½ in. (13 mm) larger all round than the actual tear. Work the patch gently inside the torn lining. Make sure that it is flat. Position it centrally under the split

2 Spread adhesive on the top of the patch and the underside of the torn lining. Keep the lining away from the patch until the adhesive is tacky. Press the surfaces together

Prams and pushchairs Upholstery

Fitting a new section of piping

If the piping in pram upholstery is damaged, cut it out and take it to a pram dealer to obtain matching material and matching cord. Buy a half-circle needle to stitch the piping to the upholstery.

Materials: PVC or leather cloth; piping cord; nylon thread.
Tools: sharp knife; razor blade; sewing machine; scissors; 3 in. (75 mm) half-circle needle.

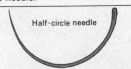

Half-circle needle

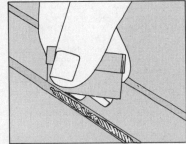

1 Cut with a razor blade along the threads holding the damaged piping to the pram upholstery. Cut out damaged piece

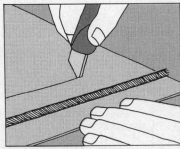

2 Cut a piece of material to the length of damage and about 1½ in. (40 mm) wide. Cut new cord to same length

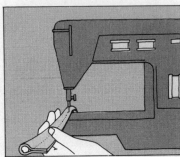

3 Fold material carefully round the cord. Machine-stitch the edges of the material together close to the piping cord

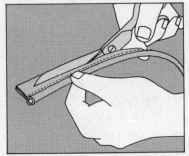

4 Trim the excess from the sewn edges with scissors. Leave only ¼ in. (6 mm) beyond the stitching

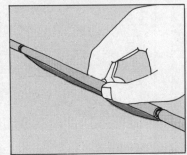

5 Prise the pram upholstery edges apart. Insert new piping between them and fold over the edges

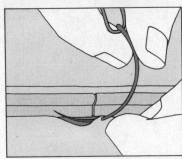

6 Thread a half-circle needle with double nylon thread. Push it into the bottom folded edge at left end of new piping

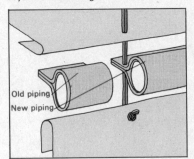

Old piping
New piping

7 Take the needle up through the piping flap and through the second piece of upholstery. Make sure piping hides knot

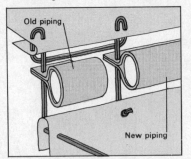

Old piping
New piping

8 Back-sew one stitch ½ in. (13 mm) along upholstery. Pass the needle through old piping and upholstery and pull tight

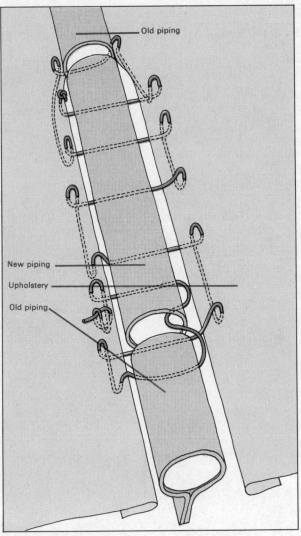

Old piping
New piping
Upholstery
Old piping

9 Take the needle ½ in. (13 mm) past the first stitch and push it through. Move along ½ in. and push it back. Continue along and finish by joining old and new piping as shown

Records

Storage and cleaning

Protect records from heat—fires, sunlight, radiators, hot-water pipes and electrical equipment. Do not leave a record on a stationary turntable if the record player is switched on: rising heat from an amplifier can warp the record.

Store records vertically in their polythene bags and sleeves, away from dust and preferably at a moderate uniform temperature.

Mono record players can be used to play stereo records provided that a stereo cartridge wired for mono is fitted. Heavier pick-ups may cause severe damage to stereo records. Stereo record players can, however, be used for mono records.

If the quality of reproduction deteriorates, check that the needle, or stylus, is not worn or broken. A sapphire stylus should play a hundred 12 in. record sides: a diamond one should last for a thousand sides. A worn stylus scratches every record it plays. If a new stylus is to be fitted (see p. 551) take the old one to the dealer when buying the replacement.

CLEANING RECORDS

1 Wipe the record gently with a soft cloth slightly dampened in a record-cleaning solution

2 Use a cleaner—called an ioniser—which has a velvet face to eliminate static and remove dust

NEEDLE CARE

Clean after every playing session with a soft brush or a velvet cleaner

HANDLING AND STORING RECORDS

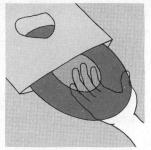

1 To remove a record from its bag, put fingers under centre label and thumb on the edge. Do not touch the grooves

2 Hold the sides between the hands to avoid touching the surface grooves when fitting or lifting the record

3 To store a record after playing, first place it in its bag. Then insert the bag, open end first, in the cardboard sleeve

Scissors

Sharpening and repairing

When scissors are not cutting efficiently, first check that the screw joint between the blades is not loose. Next make sure that the cutting edges have not been damaged or blunted. If the scissors do not cut after they have been sharpened, check that the blades have not lost their slight inward curve.

Materials: slip-stone; three small blocks of wood.
Tools: vice; hammer.

BLUNT EDGES

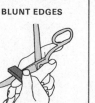

Sharpen with a fine slip-stone kept at right angles to the face of the blade

DAMAGED EDGES

Run a fine slip-stone, smeared with light oil, over the inner face of the blade

FLATTENED BLADES

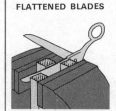

Hold blade in vice between three equally spaced blocks. Tighten the vice slightly

LOOSE JOINT

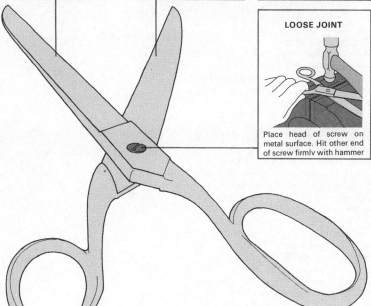

Place head of screw on metal surface. Hit other end of screw firmly with hammer

Sewing machines   Vibrating shuttle

Care and maintenance

A sewing machine is a finely balanced piece of machinery: do not try to dismantle it. If a major repair seems necessary, take the machine to a specialist dealer or repairer.

Maintain and use the machine carefully. Always follow the manufacturer's instructions when buying new needles, choosing the grade of thread to use or when fitting special attachments to the machine.

Use only good-quality thread suitable for the fabric being sewn. Cheaper threads are likely to tangle, knot or break. Ensure that needles are fitted correctly and securely. Do not try to sew with a bent or blunt needle.

Lubricate a machine once a week if it is in regular use. If a machine has not been used for some time, oil it before starting to sew.

Types of machine

There are two basic types of sewing machine. On the conventional type—called the vibrating-shuttle machine—the lower thread is wound on a bobbin which is housed in a shuttle under the needle plate. As the machine is operated, the shuttle moves backwards and forwards in time with the action of the needle. It is a simple mechanism, and the shuttle can easily be replaced if the spring breaks or becomes too weak. Vibrating-shuttle machines may be operated electrically or by hand or foot.

The second type of machine—called the central-bobbin machine—is usually electrically operated. It has an oscillating shuttle that moves round a static bobbin (see p. 370).

On both types of machine, the fabric is moved forwards automatically as it is sewn. The machine should feed the fabric through adequately. Guide it under the needle, but make sure that it is not pulled or held.

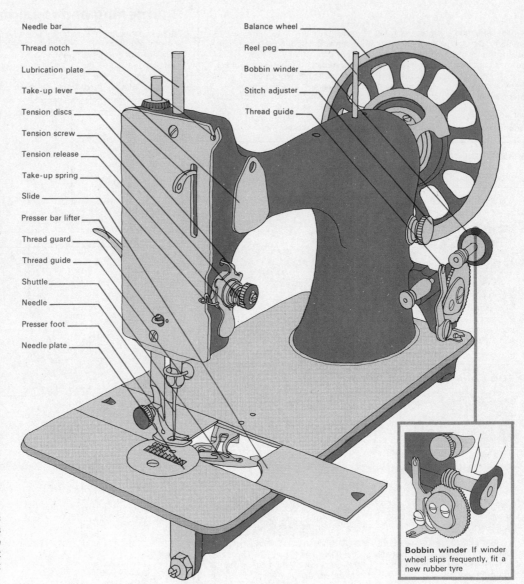

Needle bar
Thread notch
Lubrication plate
Take-up lever
Tension discs
Tension screw
Tension release
Take-up spring
Slide
Presser bar lifter
Thread guard
Thread guide
Shuttle
Needle
Presser foot
Needle plate

Balance wheel
Reel peg
Bobbin winder
Stitch adjuster
Thread guide

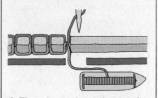

Bobbin winder If winder wheel slips frequently, fit a new rubber tyre

HOW THE MACHINE SEWS

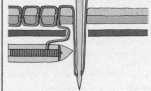

1 As the machine is operated, the needle and upper thread come down to penetrate the fabric

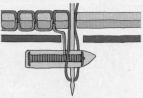

2 As the needle rises, it leaves a loop of thread under both the fabric and the needle plate

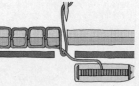

3 The shuttle, holding the bobbin of lower thread, goes through the loop to form the stitch

4 The take-up lever rises to the highest point and pulls the stitch tight. The fabric is moved forwards

Stitching and sewing faults

For normal sewing the tension of the two threads should be equal. If a thread breaks frequently or if the stitching is faulty, check both of the thread tension adjusters.

Broken threads

If the upper thread breaks, make sure that the needle is fitted correctly and that the thread is not tangled. If there is no obvious fault, turn the tension screw anti-clockwise to slacken.

If the thread still breaks, check the hole in the needle plate. When a machine is mis-treated, the needle may just hit the rim of the hole. Eventually the hole will become damaged and break the thread during sewing.

When the lower thread breaks, make sure that it is tightly wound on the bobbin. Check the thread tension. If it seems too tight, undo the shuttle-spring screw half a turn.

Puckered material

The most common fault when material puckers is that the upper thread is too taut. Undo the tension screw on the front of the machine.

Slipping stitches

If stitches slip frequently, make sure that the material is not being held or pulled back. Check that the needle is not bent or blunt. Make sure that it is the correct size for the machine and that it is fitted and threaded correctly. Check that the thread is not too heavy for the material.

If the fault cannot be found at the needle, make sure that the presser foot is tight against the fabric.

Lower thread looping

If the lower thread forms a large loop and makes a loose stitch, make sure that the upper and lower tensions are adjusted evenly. If they are correct, check that there is no thread caught in the tension discs. Make sure that the take-up spring is not damaged or worn. If a new spring is needed, take the machine to a dealer.

Upper thread looping

When the upper thread loops, check that the shuttle tension spring is not too tight. Make sure there is no thread remnant under the spring.

Needle plate

Check the needle plate frequently to see that no lint or pieces of thread have collected under it.

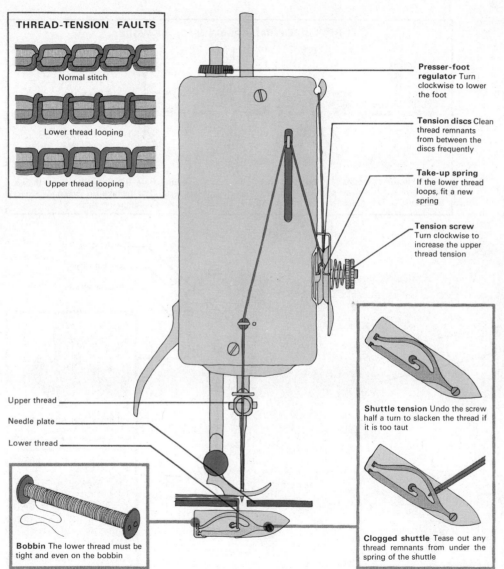

THREAD-TENSION FAULTS

Normal stitch

Lower thread looping

Upper thread looping

Upper thread
Needle plate
Lower thread

Presser-foot regulator Turn clockwise to lower the foot

Tension discs Clean thread remnants from between the discs frequently

Take-up spring If the lower thread loops, fit a new spring

Tension screw Turn clockwise to increase the upper thread tension

Bobbin The lower thread must be tight and even on the bobbin

Shuttle tension Undo the screw half a turn to slacken the thread if it is too taut

Clogged shuttle Tease out any thread remnants from under the spring of the shuttle

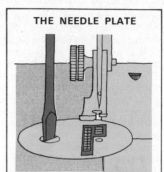
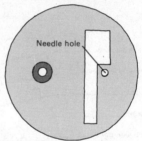
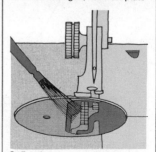

THE NEEDLE PLATE

1 Raise the needle and presser foot. Undo the screws on the needle plate

Needle hole

2 If the rim of the needle hole is worn or damaged, fit a new plate

3 Brush out any thread remnants which have collected under the plate

Sewing machines Central-bobbin

Care and maintenance

Always make sure that the sewing machine is disconnected from the power supply before making adjustments.

If a machine is in constant use, it should be lubricated once a week. Check in the instruction booklet to find the lubrication points, and use only an oil recommended by the manufacturer. Do not strip the electric motor on any machine and do not attempt any major repair. If the stitch-adjustment mechanism fails, for example, take the machine to a dealer.

Replacement belts, bobbins and bobbin carriers are available from most sewing-machine dealers. Ensure that new parts are suitable for the machine.

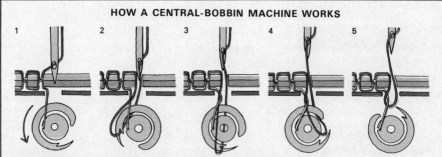

HOW A CENTRAL-BOBBIN MACHINE WORKS

1   2   3   4   5

As the needle descends (1), the hook advances: when it rises (2), it leaves a loop through which hook enters. The hook then pulls upper thread over bobbin (3) to link up with lower thread. The loop slips off as the take-up lever pulls excess thread (4), and tightens the stitch (5)

Sewing faults

The sewing and stitching faults likely to arise on a central-bobbin machine are similar to those found on the vibrating-shuttle type (see p. 368). But because the central bobbin is more complex, it is more likely to jam if lint and particles of thread collect in the bobbin carrier. Remove the carrier and brush it clean regularly.

It is possible to adjust the tension on a central bobbin, but do not try to repair it if it becomes damaged. Take the machine to a dealer who specialises in the particular machine model.

The upper-thread tension control is usually a knurled knob with figures marked on it to help adjustment. These are explained in the instruction booklet.

BOBBIN AND CARRIER

Make sure that the lower thread is wound tightly and evenly round the bobbin. If it strays over the flanges, the machine cannot operate

Screw

Brush the bobbin carrier to make sure that there are no lint or thread particles clogging it. Adjust the tension screw half a turn if necessary

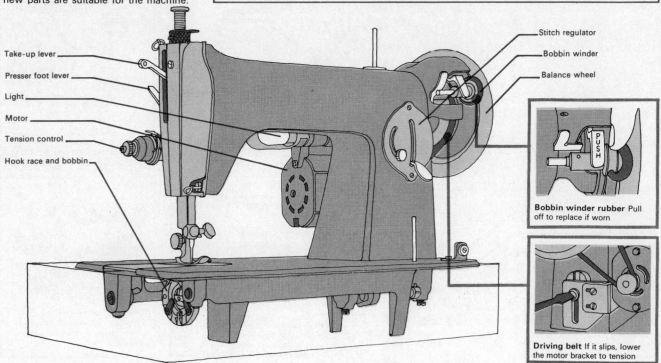

Take-up lever
Presser foot lever
Light
Motor
Tension control
Hook race and bobbin

Stitch regulator
Bobbin winder
Balance wheel

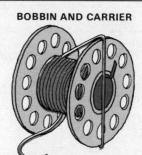

Bobbin winder rubber Pull off to replace if worn

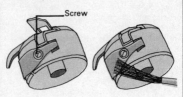

Driving belt If it slips, lower the motor bracket to tension

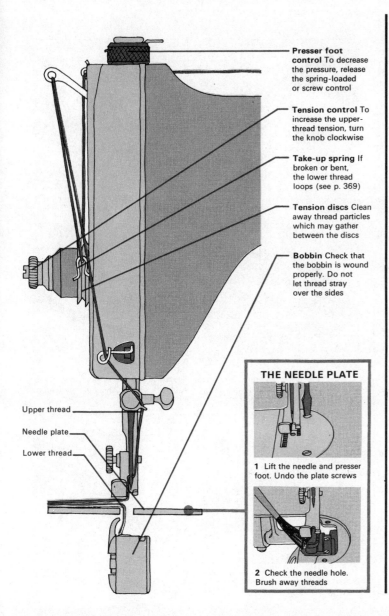

Presser foot control To decrease the pressure, release the spring-loaded or screw control

Tension control To increase the upper-thread tension, turn the knob clockwise

Take-up spring If broken or bent, the lower thread loops (see p. 369)

Tension discs Clean away thread particles which may gather between the discs

Bobbin Check that the bobbin is wound properly. Do not let thread stray over the sides

Upper thread
Needle plate
Lower thread

THE NEEDLE PLATE

1 Lift the needle and presser foot. Undo the plate screws

2 Check the needle hole. Brush away threads

Cleaning and freeing a hook race

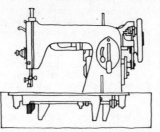

On a central-bobbin machine, the lower thread is wound on its bobbin in the same way as on a vibrating-shuttle type (see p. 368). Instead of a horizontal shuttle, however, the central-bobbin type has an oscillating hook to form the stitch. If the thread jams behind the hook, it stops the machine: dismantle the hook race to clean it. Make sure that the machine is not connected to the power supply.

If replacement parts are needed, use only those recommended by the manufacturer.

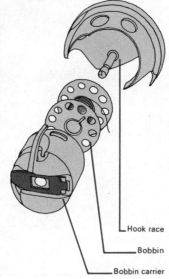

Hook race
Bobbin
Bobbin carrier

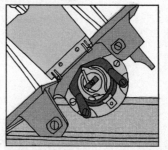

1 Tilt the machine and make sure the central-bobbin mechanism is clear of the wooden base

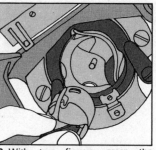

2 With two fingers, grasp the hinged latch on the bobbin case. Pull the carrier away from the race

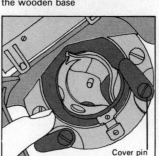

Cover pin

3 Push back the two cover pins or screws which hold the retaining ring securely against the hook race

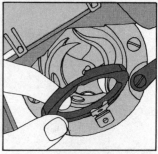

4 Prise up the retaining ring on its hinge until clear of the hook race. Brush the underside of the ring

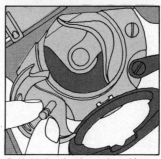

5 Hold the shuttle carrier with two fingers and pull it to lift the hook race out of the machine

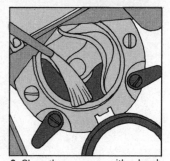

6 Clean the race-way with a brush. Use a toothpick to remove any packed lint or thread

Shoes

Because of the way most shoes are now made, home repairs are confined to such jobs as fixing stick-on soles, replacing leather or rubber heels and renovating scuffed toe-caps. Do not attempt to repair PVC soles or heels. PVC can be identified by touching the sole with hot copper wire and putting the wire back in the flame. If the wire burns green, the sole is PVC.

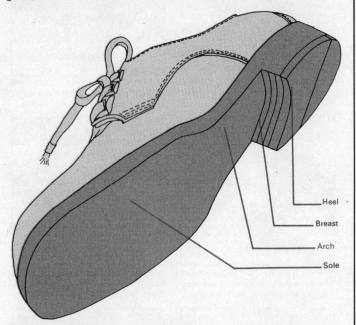

Heel

Breast

Arch

Sole

RENOVATING A SCUFFED TOE-CAP

1 Remove all the polish with methylated spirit and smooth the scuffed area with glass-paper

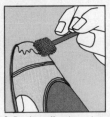

2 Brush off the dust and re-surface the area with a matching proprietary shoe colouring

3 Apply further coats of colouring until the area blends with the rest of the shoe

Fixing a stick-on sole

The method of fixing stick-on soles is the same for leather-soled and rubber-soled shoes, but different preparation is needed. Remove grease and dirt from a leather sole with a rasp to obtain good adhesion; clean a rubber sole with solvent such as lighter fuel, rub the sole with coarse glass-paper and brush off the dust. If the leather sole is porous enough to absorb the neoprene cement, apply a second coat when the first is dry. Though a shoe-maker's last is ideal for providing support when hammering the sole after sticking, a hand placed inside the shoe is satisfactory. Stick-on soles should be about $\frac{1}{16}$ in. (2 mm) inside the edge of the shoe sole.

Materials: two stick-on soles; neoprene cement; lighter fuel (if applicable).
Tools: hammer; tin grater; rasp; glass-paper and brush as applicable; pencil.

TRIMMING A SOLE

1 To trim an over-size sole, pencil the outline of the shoe sole on the stick-on sole

2 Trim the stick-on sole by cutting $\frac{1}{16}$ in. (2 mm) inside the drawn outline

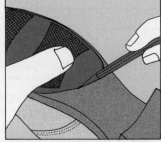

1 Position one of the soles and draw a pencil line round it on the sole of the shoe

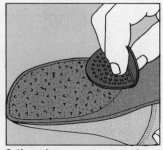

2 If you have no rasp to roughen a leather sole, use the grater which is supplied with the cement

3 Work cement well into the sole and beyond the drawn line. Apply cement to the stick-on sole

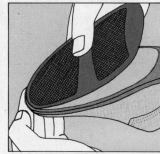

4 When the surfaces are tacky, fit the stick-on sole to the pencilled area, starting at the toe

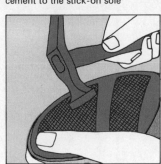

5 Press the sole down hard at the edges and hammer it down, working outwards from the centre

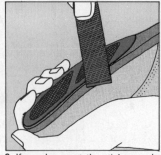

6 If you have cut the stick-on sole to shape, chamfer the edge with a rasp or glass-paper

Fitting rubber heels

When replacing a leather heel with a rubber one, it is necessary first to remove at least two thicknesses of leather, since a rubber heel is thicker than a layer of leather. Rubber heels are sold with nail holes already stamped in them and with metal washers fitted in the holes. Nails are generally supplied with the soles. When nailing, support the shoe with a last or block of wood held in a vice.

Materials: two rubber heels; piece of leather; ¾ in. (20 mm) flat-headed nails; neoprene cement; matching stain.
Tools: screwdriver; pincers; chisel; hammer; Stanley knife; medium-grade glass-paper; punch; rasp; vice; last.

FITTING LEATHER HEELS

1 When repairing a heel with leather, mark the shoe heel outline on the leather and trim to fit

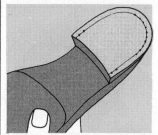

2 Fasten leather heels with closely located nails around the edge. Preparation and finishing-off are as for rubber heels

1 Prise up the worn heel's first layer with a screwdriver and peel it off with pincers. Remove the second layer in the same way

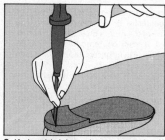

2 If the third layer is worn, mark off the worn area. Score along the mark with a chisel, penetrating only one layer of leather

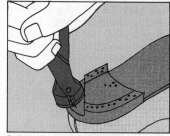

3 Remove the worn leather from the next layer with the pincers. Cut off any exposed nails with the pincers, but do not pull them out

4 Build up the cut-away, with the leather overlapping the heel. Hammer three nails in at an angle to push the piece towards the cut edge

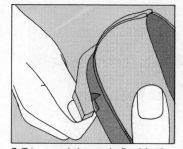

5 Trim round the newly fixed leather with a Stanley knife. Hammer in two more nails, almost upright, between those already hammered in

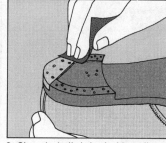

6 Clean the built-in heel with medium-grade glass-paper. Use the glass-paper to roughen the face of the new heel which is to be cemented on

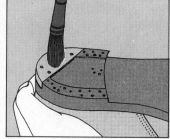

7 Coat the heel of the shoe with neoprene cement and work the cement well into the leather. Allow about ten minutes for the adhesive to dry

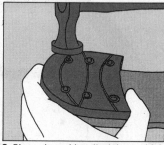

8 Place the rubber heel in position on the cement-coated leather and hammer in the nails just below the ridges of the holes

9 Use a punch and hammer to drive the nails below the surface of the heel, deep enough for their heads to contact the metal washers

10 Using a wet knife, trim round the newly fitted heel and along the breast of the instep, level with the rest of the heel

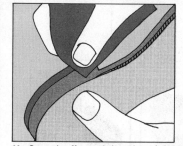

11 Smooth off round the edge of the heel, using in turn the rough and the fine sides of a rasp and then coarse and fine glass-paper

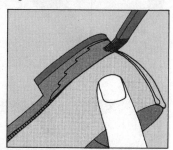

12 Colour the heel with wood stain or water-based ink. When it is dry, shine with several applications of shoe polish to get a good finish

Spectacles

Use a very soft cloth to clean spectacle lenses. If the frame is dirty, scrub it with a soft nylon toothbrush and soap under warm running water.

Check the hinge screws for tightness. Never overtighten the screws: the thread on the screw or in the hinge could be damaged. A broken frame can be temporarily repaired with adhesive tape, but it is advisable to have the spectacles mended by an optician as soon as possible.

Never attempt to repair a broken lens or to refit a lens which was held by adhesive: take the spectacles to a qualified optician.

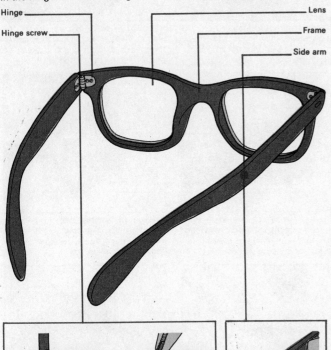

Hinge
Hinge screw
Lens
Frame
Side arm

Screws Use a small screwdriver to tighten the hinge screws

Lost screw Use a bent piece of paperclip as a temporary hinge

Broken arm If arm is wire-reinforced, use epoxy adhesive

Repairing with adhesive tape

The main stress point in a pair of spectacles is the bridge piece. It is one of the points most likely to break, but it can be temporarily repaired with clear adhesive tape. The same technique can be used to mend a break in a side arm which has no reinforcing wire in it.

Materials: dry cloth; clear adhesive tape.
Tool: sharp knife.

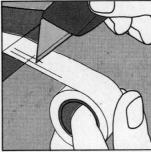

2 Cut six 1 in. (25 mm) strips of adhesive tape $\frac{1}{4}$ in. (6 mm) wide. Do not finger the adhesive side

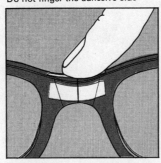

4 Rub the four pieces of tape firmly, to squeeze out any air between the tape and the frame

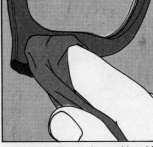

1 Clean the frame thoroughly with a dry cloth on and around the break to remove all grease and dirt

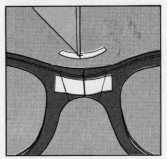

3 Hold the frame parts firmly together. Lay the strips across the back, front, top and bottom

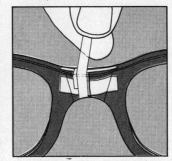

5 Wind $\frac{1}{4}$ in. (6 mm) strips of tape round the bridge piece to overlap each other by $\frac{1}{8}$ in. (3 mm)

Refitting a lens

Nylon thread

Only lenses which are partly rimless can be replaced without professional help. They are usually held in place by a taut nylon thread.

Materials: fabric tape.

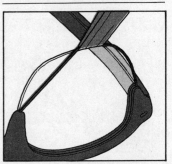

1 Place the lens in its groove in the frame top. Hook narrow fabric tape round the retaining thread

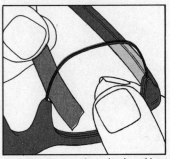

2 Pull the tape to draw the thread into the lens groove. Hold the lens firmly. Remove the tape

Sports equipment Footballs and football boots

Repairing a punctured bladder

Loss of air from a bladder may be due to dirt in the valve or to a puncture. Clear the valve by pumping the dirt into the bladder. Repair a puncture in the same way as a bicycle inner-tube (see p. 571).

Materials: puncture outfit; about 24 in. (610 mm) of new football lace. Tools: an old spoon (use the handle to loosen the old lace and tighten the new one); needle-valve adaptor; needle-eye lacing tool; pump; knife.

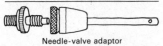

Needle-valve adaptor

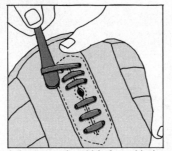

1 Lever out the old lacing with the handle of an old spoon or with a similar improvised tool

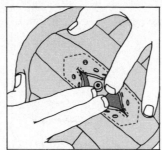

2 Open the lace-hole flaps to get at the bladder valve which protrudes through the casing tongue

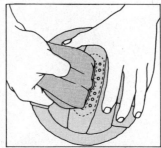

3 Before removing the bladder, insert the needle-valve adaptor in the valve and squeeze out any remaining air

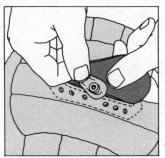

4 Repair the puncture and replace the bladder, putting the valve through the tongue hole

5 With the adaptor and pump, inflate slightly. Unscrew the pump, leaving the adaptor in the valve

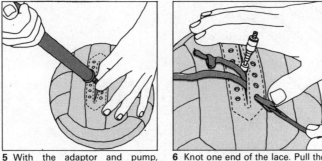

6 Knot one end of the lace. Pull the lace from the inside through an end hole with the lacing tool

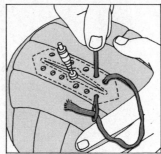

7 Draw the knot under the lip of the lace-hole flap. Pull the other end of the lace through two more holes

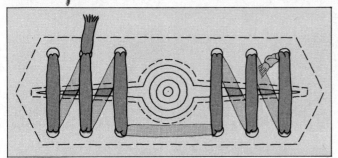

8 Continue the lacing as shown in the diagram above, pulling the lace down through the holes on one side and up through those on the other. After the last hole, take the lace up through a hole already used

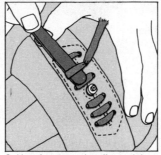

9 Use the spoon handle to tighten the lacing, which must lie flat and untwisted on the casing

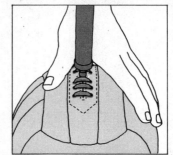

10 Pump up the ball, remove the adaptor, and poke the valve under the casing. Cut off the surplus lace

Replacing a stud

Two kinds of studs can be fitted to football boots: nylon for muddy conditions, rubber for hard ground. Nailed-in leather studs are no longer used. The studs are screwed into threaded inserts in the sole and heel of the boot and are easily replaced or changed. Nylon studs can be tightened with a spanner. An insert needs replacing only when it has worn loose or has a worn thread

Insert   Nylon   Rubber

1 To replace a worn stud-insert, remove the leather sock inside the boot and prise the insert out of the inner sole

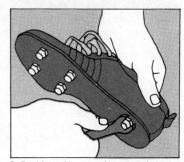

2 Position the new insert and use a spanner to screw the new stud into it from the underside of the boot

Sports equipment Skis

Water-skis and snow-skis

The general maintenance of snow-skis and water-skis is similar in many respects. But whereas some repairs can be made to water-skis at home, the job of repairing snow-skis is usually beyond the ability of the amateur. Take them to a sports-equipment specialist.

Clean both types of ski every time they have been used. Always rinse water-skis thoroughly in fresh water—particularly if they have been used in salt water. Rub snow-skis down with a clean, dry cloth. Do not throw the skis on the ground or bang them together: rough handling cracks the varnish. Seal any slight cracks or scuffs in the varnish by rubbing with a silicone wax on a soft cloth.

Do not leave skis exposed to the weather for longer than a couple of days, because frequent variations in humidity and temperature cause them to wear quickly: When they are not in use, store them in a dry place at room temperature. Rest them upright against a wall. Smear any metal edges with a protective coat of silicone grease and unbind the foot-bindings on snow-skis.

Revarnishing skis

Both types of ski should be revarnished once a year—water-skis in winter and snow-skis in summer—ready for the next season. Hold the skis on a flat, level surface and strip off the foot-bindings. Use wet-and-dry paper very wet, and rub the top surfaces of the two skis thoroughly to remove blemishes. Wipe them with a clean, wet rag and leave the skis to dry.

Give both the topsides a good coat of varnish and leave them to dry. Turn the skis over and rub down the undersides. Varnish them and leave to dry. Treat the side edges in the same way.

Materials: water; 320-grade wet-and-dry paper; clear polyurethane varnish.
Tools: paintbrush; glass-paper block.

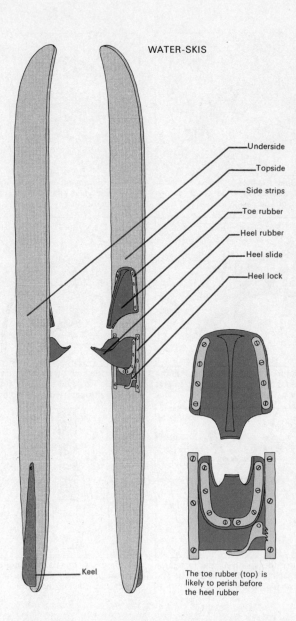

WATER-SKIS

- Underside
- Topside
- Side strips
- Toe rubber
- Heel rubber
- Heel slide
- Heel lock
- Keel

The toe rubber (top) is likely to perish before the heel rubber

Replacing a foot rubber on a water-ski

A water-ski has two foot rubbers—one at the heel, the other for the toe. The toe rubber, because of the extra strain it takes, usually perishes first: heel rubbers generally last much longer. It is not necessary to renew both when only one is damaged.

New rubbers and side strips can be bought at most boating, yachting and marine suppliers. Take the perished rubber, with its aluminium strips, to ensure that the correct type is obtained.

Materials: foot rubbers and aluminium strips as needed.
Tools: screwdriver; pencil; centre punch; hammer.

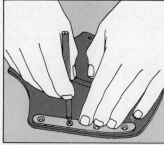

1 Remove the aluminium strips. Position them on the new foot rubber and mark the screw holes

2 Use a centre punch and hammer to make holes on the marks where screws will fit in the new rubber

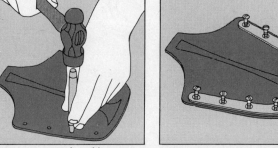

3 With the rubber on the bench, position the aluminium strips along the sides and push the screws firmly in

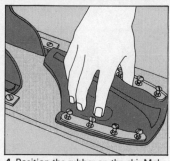

4 Position the rubber on the ski. Make sure that the screws line up with the existing holes in the top of the ski

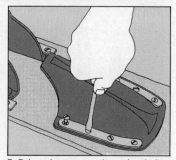

5 Drive the screws into the holes. Tighten all the screws on one side before securing those on the other edge

Fitting a new keel on a water-ski

If the keel of a water-ski is broken or warped, saw a wedge-shaped replacement from beech or mahogany. Cut it to the width and length of the old keel, and taper from $1\frac{1}{2}$ in. (40 mm) deep at the back to $\frac{3}{4}$ in. (20 mm).

Materials: beech or mahogany; latex-based contact adhesive; varnish; four brass or nickel-plated screws.
Tools: saw; plane or Surform; glass- and garnet-paper; drill; screwdriver; paintbrush; pencil.

Water-ski keel

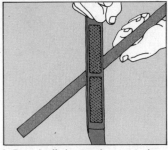

1 Round off the rough, sawn edges of the new keel piece with a small plane or Surform

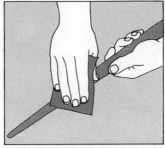

2 Smooth the edges and faces with glass-paper. Use garnet-paper to rub down the bottom edge of the keel

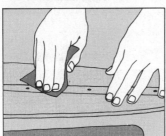

3 Remove any remaining pieces of old keel, and rub the keel area thoroughly with garnet-paper

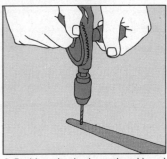

4 Position the keel on the ski and mark the screw holes. Drill two pilot holes, the front hole through the keel

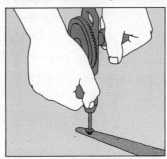

5 Countersink the front hole on the bottom of the keel enough to sink the screw head below the surface

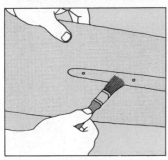

6 Brush a latex-based contact adhesive along the keel area of the ski and the meeting surface of the keel

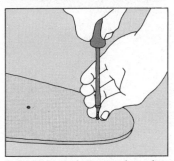

7 Stick the surfaces together when they are tacky. Drive screws in through the holes on the ski topside

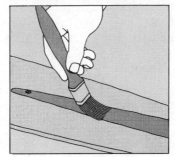

8 Drive a screw through the countersunk hole in the front of the keel into the ski and varnish the keel

Repairing a torn wet-suit

When a wet suit is torn, dry and clean the area. Tears less than 2 in. (50 mm) long need no reinforcement, but longer tears require backing with $\frac{3}{4}$ in. (20 mm) neoprene tape to strengthen the join. This tape is sold by shops and stores that supply diving equipment.

Where reinforcing tape is needed, place the tape over the tear and draw round it with chalk to show where the adhesive should be spread. Stick the patch to the outside of the suit.

Materials: dry rag; neoprene adhesive; neoprene tape; chalk; French chalk.
Tools: paintbrush; pinking shears or scissors; hammer.

Wet-suit

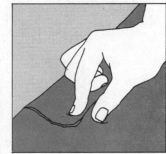

1 If the tear is small, brush a thin layer of contact adhesive along the edges. Allow it to become tacky

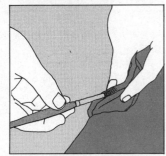

2 Close up the tear and pinch the edges firmly until they stick together to make a strong join

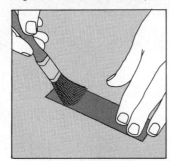

3 Spread adhesive on the chalked area. Cut tape longer than the tear and spread with neoprene adhesive

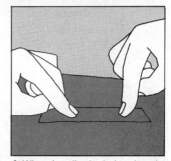

4 When the adhesive is dry, place the tape over the tear and firm with the fingers. Sprinkle with French chalk

Sports equipment Tennis rackets

Replacing broken strings

When more than six tennis-racket strings are broken, re-stringing is a job for a specialist. Smaller repairs, however, can be done without expert help.

The new string is fitted in one continuous piece. To get the correct tension, make a tightening rod by fixing two screws—slightly staggered—into opposite sides of a piece of broom handle (see Fig. 5). Use two knitting needles to hold the tension of the string in the racket while the next row is being woven.

Materials: gut or synthetic fibre.
Tools: knitting needles; wooden rod with staggered screws; knife; vice.

1 Wrap the shaft in a cloth and hold it in a vice. Cut off the last broken string 2½ in. (65 mm) from the frame

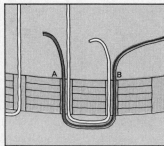

2 From inside, take one end of the new string (brown), push it out through hole A and through the hole behind (B)

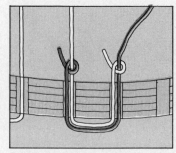

3 Loop the new string round the old row, close to the frame. Loop the end of the old string round the new

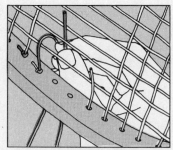

4 Tighten the loops and push them into their holes. Weave the string across and through its opposite hole

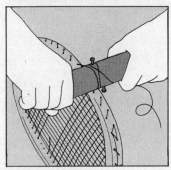

5 Wrap the string round the screws in the rod and turn it to tighten

6 Jam a knitting needle into the hole to ensure that the tension is not lost

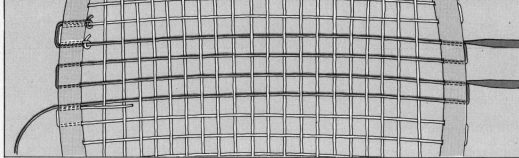

7 Continue threading. Tighten each row and keep a needle in the row just completed. Take the needle from two rows away to hold each new string. On the last row, push the string out through the hole containing the broken piece

8 Take the short end of the old string out of the frame. Tension it and hold the tension with a knitting needle

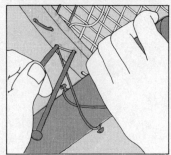

9 Push the short end back in the next hole and tension the free end of the new string. Push in a needle to hold it

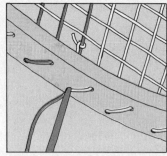

10 Loop the end of the old string round the new and tighten the loop. Remove needle and push knot into hole

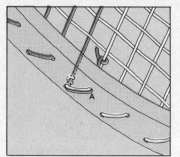

11 Push the end of the new string in through hole A and loop it. Remove the needle

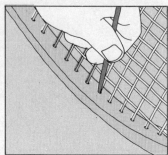

12 Tighten the loop round the old string and push it down into its hole with a needle. Cut off the surplus

Sports equipment   Table-tennis bats

Re-gripping a tennis-racket handle

Special adhesive tape for the handle of a tennis, squash or badminton racket is available from most sports-equipment specialists. It should be overlapped very slightly to give a good grip to the hand.

On some rackets, the end of the grip tape is held by a single strip of narrow adhesive, wound horizontally round the shaft. If a small tack is used instead, take care not to damage the handle of the racket when removing and replacing it.

Materials: handle tape; narrow adhesive tape.
Tools: sharp knife; pliers; hammer.

1 Remove the adhesive strip or tack holding the end of the grip tape. Unwind the grip tape

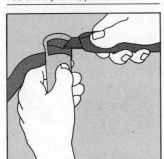

2 Stick new grip tape on the end of the handle. Make a long diagonal cut from below the top corner

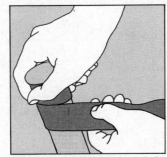

3 Discard the offcut and wind the tape on, following the line of the diagonal cut. Overlap tape slightly

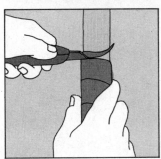

4 When the original grip area is completely covered, cut the tape. Trim it straight across the shaft

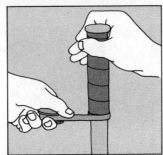

5 Seal the end with a narrow adhesive tape. Lightly tap in the fixing tack if one was removed

Re-facing a table-tennis bat

New facings for ordinary table-tennis bats can be obtained from sports-equipment dealers. Use narrow adhesive tape for edging. Strip off the old material, rub the surfaces with glass-paper, and stick on the new facings. Facings for sponge bats are too expensive to make repair worth while.

The edge of the bat is slightly rounded and the facings should just cover the curve. Do not allow the edging tape to overlap on to the face.

Materials: contact adhesive; two facings; edging tape; medium-grade glass-paper.
Tools: knife or razor blade; scissors.

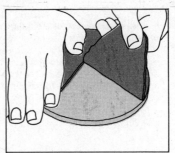

1 Peel off the old facing material. Trim with a sharp knife or razor blade around the handle of the bat

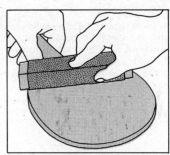

2 Rub the surface of the bat with medium-grade glass-paper to provide a good key for the contact adhesive

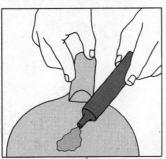

3 Spread a thin coat of adhesive evenly across the surface of the bat. Leave it to become tacky

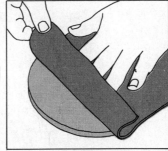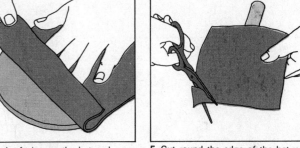

4 Lay the facing on the bat and press it firmly from the centre out to the edges. Apply more adhesive if needed

5 Cut round the edge of the bat with scissors. Allow the facing to overlap the curved edge very slightly

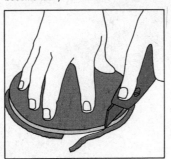

6 Lay the bat on a flat surface, with its new facing underneath. Cut carefully round it to trim the facing

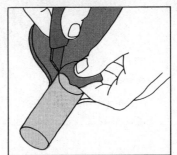

7 At the handle, use a sharp knife or razor blade to trim the material to fit with the remaining original rubber

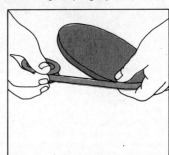

8 Press down the edges of the facing and bind with edging tape. It should not overlap the face of the bat

Tools Woodworking

Sharpening the cutting edges

New saws and bits can be used without sharpening. Check, however, that the cutting edge has not been damaged in transit. When tools are bought second-hand, they almost always require sharpening before they can be used with any effect.

Chisels and plane irons require sharpening before use, and some time may have to be spent initially in honing their backs perfectly flat. Flatness can be seen as a highlight of polished metal after honing.

Always work on a flat, steady surface when sharpening tools. Do not remove any more metal than is absolutely necessary to obtain the correct cutting angle.

When tools are to be stored, smear a little thin oil over their metal surfaces.

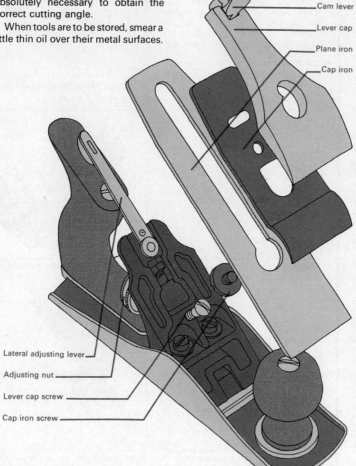

Cam lever
Lever cap
Plane iron
Cap iron

Lateral adjusting lever
Adjusting nut
Lever cap screw
Cap iron screw

PLANE AND CHISEL BLADES

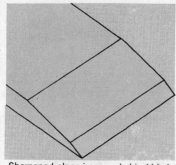

Sharpened plane irons and chisel blades have two angled faces: a steep, honed edge at an angle of 30 degrees, and a longer, ground face sloping back from it at an angle of about 25 degrees. Plane irons are made from two qualities of steel bonded together: a hard steel, which stops just short of the cut-away slot, and a softer steel which forms the upper part of the iron. After considerable use, the hard steel is completely honed away and the iron must be replaced.

MAINTAINING AN OIL-STONE

Sharpen chisels and planes on an oil-stone at least 6×2×1 in. (150×50×25 mm)—one with a length of 8 in. (200 mm) is best. Combination stones have one side fine, the other medium. Keep the stone in a wooden box. If the stone becomes oil-clogged, heat it in an old baking tin in a moderate oven for about an hour.

Materials: paraffin; rag; glass; light machine-oil; fine carborundum powder. Tool: steel rule.

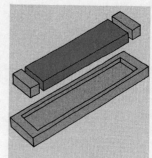

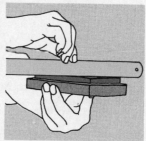

1 Lay a steel rule across the length and width of the oil-stone. If it is not flat, regrind it

2 Lay glass flat and sprinkle on carborundum powder and water. Rub the stone round on it

3 Examine the stone frequently. Continue grinding until powder clings evenly to the whole surface

4 When the powder clings to the whole stone, it should be level. Check again with a steel rule

Tools Planes and chisels

Checking the blades for wear

Check chisels and planes before they are used. If the blades are blunt, worn or chipped, hone them to a keen edge on an oil-stone.

Make sure that no more metal is removed when honing than is necessary to restore a sharp edge to the cutting tip of the blade.

When sharpening the first few times, only the steep cutting angle need be ground. Eventually, however, it will become necessary to grind back the longer angle of the blades.

It is essential, to obtain sharpness, to hone the backs of all flat blades carefully every time the blades have been sharpened until they are perfectly flat at the cutting edge.

Materials: oil-stone; oil; paper.
Tools: steel rule; tri square; old chisel or knife; leather strop; screwdriver.

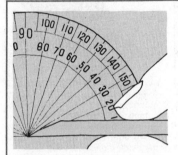

Check the angles Lay a protractor flat. Hold the side of the blade against the protractor so that its flat back is on the bottom line and its tip exactly at the centre point. Measure the honed and ground angles

Test for sharpness The most effective way to test a plane or chisel blade for sharpness is with the hand. Stroke the edge of the blade very carefully with a thumb. A sharp blade drags the skin

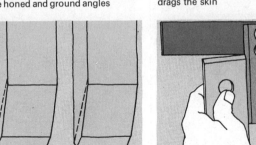

Chipped or worn blades If a blade has become chipped or worn to less than 30 degrees, regrind it to 25 degrees on a carborundum or sandstone wheel. Hone afterwards

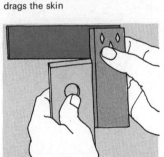

Plane iron Hold the handle of a tri square against the side of the blade. If the cutting edge slopes away from the blade of the square, the cutting iron is no longer true

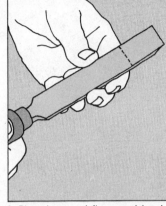

1 Plane irons and firmer and bevel-edge chisels are all sharpened in the same way. Check the back of the blade. At least the lower 1½–2 in. (40–50 mm) should be flat, with no high spots along the cutting edge

2 Apply a little oil to the oil-stone. Take care not to flood it: three or four spots about the size of a 5p coin are enough at a time. The oil will spread evenly over the stone with the first sharpening movements

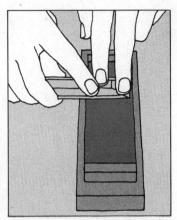

3 If high spots exist along the cutting edge of the back, hone the back of the blade. Use a medium-grade stone if high spots are prominent: hold the blade under two fingers across the width. Finish on a fine stone

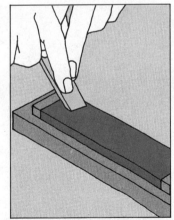

4 When the back of the blade is flat, work on the front of the 30-degree edge. Hold the chisel in line with the arm and rub it up and down the stone. To use the stone evenly, work diagonally in both directions

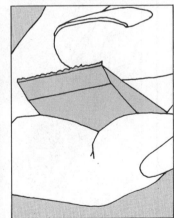

5 The tip of the blade wears into a thin burr which bends over on to the flattened back surface. The burr should run the whole length of the edge: it can be felt by carefully stroking along the back of the blade

6 Hold the blade across the oil-stone and hone on the back edge. After a few passes, the burr wears very thin and turns over to the front edge again. Continue rubbing each side until it wears off *(continued)*

Tools Planes and chisels

(continued)

7 Where super sharpness is required, finish sharpening against a leather strop, preferably one bonded to a wooden block. If the burr continues to turn over and does not wear off, the chisel may be too soft; it is then of little use

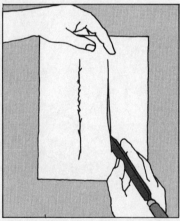

8 Finally, test the blade. Hold up a sheet of newspaper or typing paper and draw the full edge of the blade along it. A properly sharpened edge should make a clean cut down the paper. A blunt edge tends to tear the paper (left)

Refitting and adjusting a plane iron

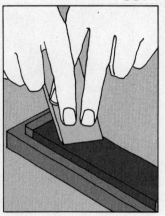

1 Plane irons are sharpened in the same way as chisels (see p. 381), but because they are often wider than the oil-stone, they should be held at an angle across the stone so that all the edge is honed

2 When the plane iron is honed, fit it against the top of the cap iron. Make sure that they fit evenly so that the iron can break and push shavings aside. Check that the front edge of the cap iron is not arched

3 If the cap iron arches away from the blade, rub its front meeting edge lengthways along the oil-stone. Do not remove any more of the metal than is necessary to fit the iron flat against the top surface of the blade

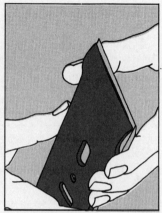

4 When the cap iron is correctly ground, place it on the back of the cutting iron and slot the screw in the mating hole. Slide the cap iron down until about $\frac{1}{16}$ in. (2 mm) of the blade projects beyond its end

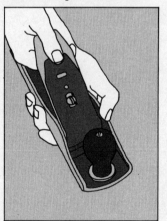

5 Tighten the cap iron screw and check that the blade still projects $\frac{1}{16}$ in. (2 mm). Insert the irons with the cap iron uppermost, and engage the slot in the cap iron over the blade adjustment pin

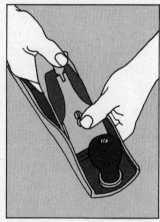

6 Slide the lever cap over the fitted blade and cap iron. Press down the cam to lock them. If they are loose when the cam is locked, remove it and tighten the lever cap screw. Relock them

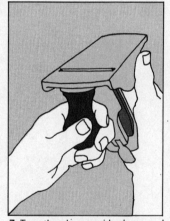

7 Turn the plane upside-down and look along the bottom. Move the adjusting lever until the edge of the iron is parallel with the mouth. If it cannot be adjusted, check the blade for squareness (see p. 381)

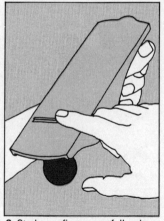

8 Stroke a finger carefully down the underside of the plane from the front. The blade should just protrude for most work. If a deeper or shallower cut is required, adjust it with the knurled knob at the back

Sharpening gouging chisels

There are many kinds of chisel gouges, including firmer, turning and scribing. All have a honed angle (see p. 380) of 30 degrees, and a ground angle of 25 degrees. The difference is that the firmer and turning tools have the angled faces on the outside face of the chisel, and the scribing gouge is angled on the inner face.

A tapered slip-stone is needed for sharpening. It can be obtained from an ironmonger or tool merchant. Keep it dry in a tin or wet in a jar of paraffin.

Materials: paraffin; light oil.
Tools: slip-stone; oil-stone.

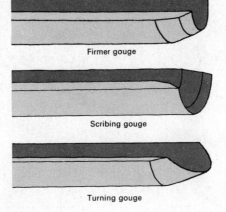

Firmer gouge

Scribing gouge

Turning gouge

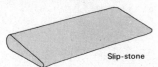

Slip-stone

SHARPENING A TURNING GOUGE

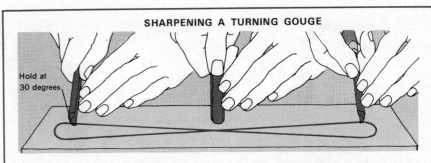

Hold at 30 degrees

Turning gouges are sharpened in the same way as firmer gouges; but to maintain the double rounding of the cutting edge, it is essential to hone the back or outside angle through a figure-of-eight movement at an angle of 30 degrees on the oil-stone.

SHARPENING A FIRMER GOUGE

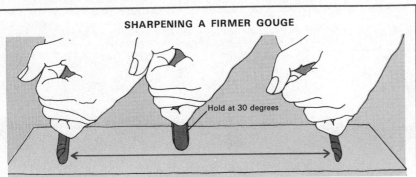

Hold at 30 degrees

Rub the end, honed face of a firmer gouge at 30 degrees along the oil-stone. Rock it at the same time to hone the whole cutting edge.

When a burr forms inside, apply a little light oil. Hold the chisel steady and rub and swivel the slip-stone inside. Repeat on both sides until the burr wears off.

SHARPENING A SCRIBING GOUGE

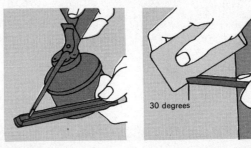

30 degrees

To sharpen a scribing gouge, first oil inside the blade and rub with a slip-stone held at 30 degrees. When a burr forms, rub the outside flat against the oil-stone. Repeat on both sides until it is sharp.

Extremely blunt edges can be honed on a coarse stone before being sharpened on a fine stone; but a badly chipped gouge will need regrinding on a conical stone.

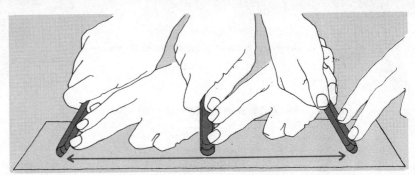

Tools Saws

Sharpening the teeth

Panel saw

Tenon saw

Handsaws used in the home can be divided roughly into two types: flexible saws and the smaller rigid saws that are braced along their backs with folded metal sections.

Flexible saws are used for cutting timber to rough overall dimensions; backed rigid saws, which have finer teeth, are used for more accurate work such as joint cutting.

The panel saw is the most common of the flexible type, which also includes cross-cut and rip saws. It is usually about 20 in. (510 mm) long and has 10 points (9 teeth) to the inch. The more popular of the rigid saws—they have 14 or more teeth to the inch—are the tenon, which is frequently 10 in. (255 mm) long, and the dovetail, usually 8 in. (200 mm) in length. Handsaws should always cut freely under

their own weight on the forward thrust. Any tendency to ride over the wood, instead of cutting keenly through it, indicates the need for sharpening. If the saw veers to one side, it is an indication of bluntness on one side of the blade or of the need to re-set the teeth.

Saw teeth are set at an inclined angle to the face of the blade and alternate from side to side. This gives a cut wide enough to allow the blade to move without jamming and permits the path of the saw to be corrected if it should wander away from the line to be cut.

Tools: two pieces of wood; vice; saw set; medium flat file and a double-ended saw file to suit large saws; fine flat file and a needle file for tenon and dovetail saws.

TOOLS FOR SHARPENING SAWS

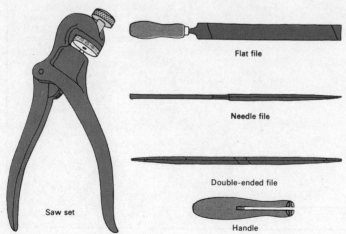

Saw set

Flat file

Needle file

Double-ended file

Handle

Side view

Top view

1 Support the saw in a vice between two wood strips. The wood must clench the saw evenly no more than $\frac{1}{4}$ in. (6 mm) below the teeth. Clamp long saws at each end to prevent them whipping

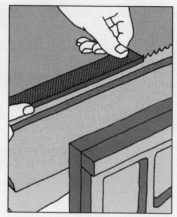

2 On uneven well-worn saws, run a fine flat file down the length of the blade once or twice to level off all the teeth. This will create a shiny 'flat' on the teeth; eliminating the flat serves as a guide when sharpening

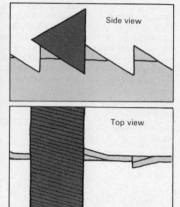

Side view

Top view

3 On a rip saw, first file the back of the teeth angled away from you. Start from the handle and hold file horizontally straight across blade. Use long, light strokes. Reverse the saw and sharpen the other teeth

4 File a cross-cut or panel saw in the same way as a rip saw, but holding the file at 60 degrees to the flat surface of the blade. Sharpen the teeth leaning away from you. Reverse the saw to sharpen the others

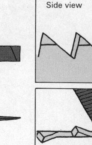

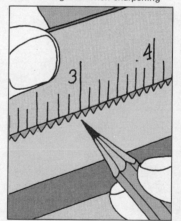

5 Set the teeth of large handsaws and tenon saws with a saw set after sharpening. Count the number of teeth per inch—usually 9 on a large saw, 14–16 on a tenon. Dovetail saws do not have to be set

6 Set the number of teeth per inch on the saw set. Work along from the handle end, and clench all the teeth pointing away from you. Reverse the saw in the vice and repeat the process to set the other teeth

Tools Wood drills

Sharpening a centre bit

Centre bits are one of the more common patterns of wood drill. The steel from which they are made is relatively soft and can easily be sharpened with a fine file.

The bits are made with a raised wing which scribes the outer circumference of the circle just before the second cutting edge, which is at 90 degrees to the centreline of the bit, and cuts away the circumscribed waste. It is essential that both edges be sharp for clean drilling.

No metal should be filed away from the outer faces of the wings or from the underside of the second cutting edge when sharpening.

Materials: block of wood.
Tool: fine needle file.

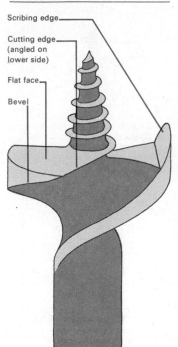

Scribing edge

Cutting edge
(angled on
lower side)

Flat face

Bevel

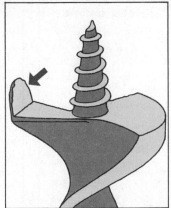

1 Examine the scribing edge carefully. Its tip may be blunted by frequent use or may have been chipped or burred by an obstruction in the wood. If the scribing edge is worn as low as the cutting edge, the bit cannot work

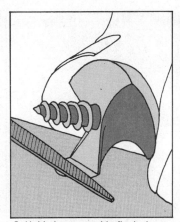

2 Hold the centre bit firmly in one hand on a block of wood. With a fine needle file in the other hand, sharpen the sloping inside face of the scribing edge. Use long, light strokes and remove as little of the metal as possible

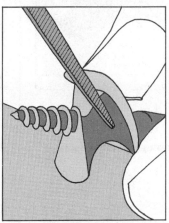

3 Turn the centre bit and stroke lightly with the needle file along the outside of the scribing edge to remove any rough, burred metal. If this is not done, the diameter of the drilling bore may be enlarged slightly

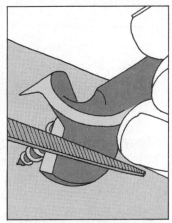

4 Sharpen the cutting edge carefully. Use long, light strokes and keep the file to the angle of the face. As soon as the edge is restored, stop filing. Never remove any more metal than is absolutely necessary

Tools Hammers

Fitting a hammer handle

If a new hammer handle is needed, choose it carefully. The more even and straight the grain in the wood of a handle, the stronger it is.

Take the hammer head to a do-it-yourself shop or builders' merchant to make sure that the replacement fits. If it is not possible to buy an exact fit, get a larger size and trim it.

Handles are sometimes pre-cut to take one or two securing wedges, which can be cut from softwood.

Materials: handle: wedges.
Tools: hammer; small saw; punch; $\frac{1}{4}$ in. (6 mm) wood bit: electric drill or wheel brace; pliers; vice.

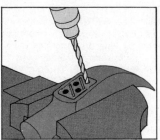

1 Grip the hammer head in a vice. Drill into the handle with a $\frac{1}{4}$ in. (6 mm) bit on each side of the wedge. Drill the holes close to each other

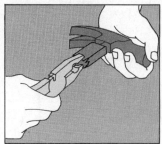

2 Pull the handle out with pliers. Punch it out if it sticks. If steel wedges are fitted, keep them for use in the new handle

3 If the new handle is not cut to take the wedges, grip it in a vice and saw cuts down the handle $\frac{1}{4}$ in. (6 mm) deeper than the wedge

4 Fit the handle into the head. Tap the end of the handle on the ground firmly several times to drive the head down on to the handle

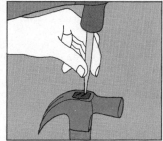

5 Saw off any excess wood protruding above the hammer head. Drive in the wedges until they are flush with the face of the handle end

Torches

Care and maintenance

Torches and cycle lamps should be kept clean and dry. Never leave the batteries in a torch or lamp which is not to be used for some time: they may leak and corrode any metal parts. If this happens, rub the damaged area with fine glass-paper. If the case is plastic, wipe off battery leakage with a damp cloth.

There is usually a choice of two types of battery, both readily available, to fit each size of torch: a high-power (HP) battery and a super-power (SP) one. An HP battery is for use with heavy-duty bulbs, of ·5 amp or more, which provide a powerful beam. It has a relatively short life. An SP battery is for use with bulbs up to ·5 amp.

Bulbs and reflectors

Voltage and amperage rating are marked on every bulb; make sure that replacement bulbs match the old ones. It is advisable to use bulbs which have a slightly lower rating than the batteries to ensure that they provide a strong beam even when the batteries are partly exhausted. A bulb of too low a rating will burn out; one of too high a rating will provide a poor light.

Bulbs of the same voltage may have a different ampère rating, which indicates the strength of beam and so the amount of power they consume. The higher the rating of the bulb, the sooner the battery is exhausted.

Torches usually have a reflector. Do not try to clean it, even with a soft rag, for the metal surface is very sensitive and easily damaged.

Some mini-torches and pen torches have no reflector, but are fitted instead with a special type of bulb, called a lens-end.

On some relatively expensive torches, the entire head—reflector, lens, bulb holder and bulb—is a sealed unit, and there is no alternative but to fit a new unit if the bulb fails.

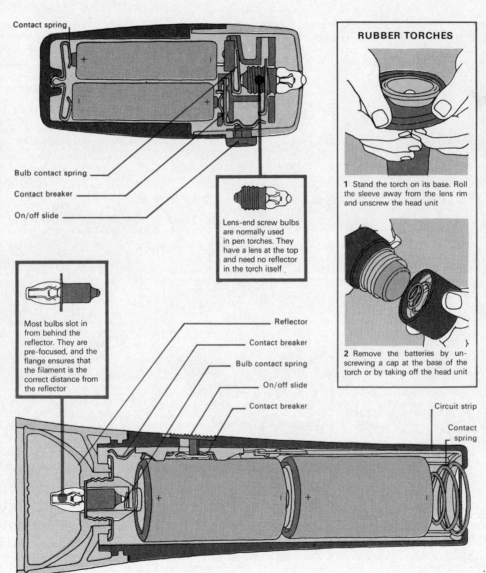

Contact spring

Bulb contact spring

Contact breaker

On/off slide

Lens-end screw bulbs are normally used in pen torches. They have a lens at the top and need no reflector in the torch itself.

Most bulbs slot in from behind the reflector. They are pre-focused, and the flange ensures that the filament is the correct distance from the reflector

Reflector
Contact breaker
Bulb contact spring
On/off slide
Contact breaker
Circuit strip
Contact spring

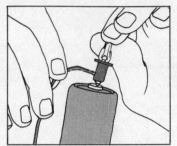

RUBBER TORCHES

1 Stand the torch on its base. Roll the sleeve away from the lens rim and unscrew the head unit

2 Remove the batteries by unscrewing a cap at the base of the torch or by taking off the head unit

Finding the fault

Fault-finding is relatively simple when a torch is in regular use. Battery failure is a gradual process: bulb failure is sudden and unexpected.

When the torch has not been used for some time, however, it may be more difficult to decide whether the battery or the bulb has failed. Remove both from the torch. Hold them together and test with a piece of wire such as a straightened paper clip. If the bulb lights, the fault is in the torch itself.

If that is not successful, test the battery of the faulty torch with a bulb known to be good from another torch. If it lights, obtain a new bulb; if it does not, buy a new battery.

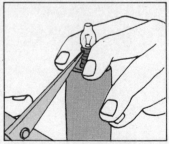

1 Hold the bulb contact on top of the battery contact. Use a straightened paper clip to connect the bulb to the battery base

2 If no stiff wire or paper clip is available, a pair of all-metal scissors can be used to complete the circuit between the battery and the suspect bulb

Toys Wheeled toys

Care and maintenance

Pedal toys for very young children usually have moulded plastic parts riveted to metal sub-frames and forks. If a plastic part breaks, obtain a replacement from the manufacturer. Drill out the existing rivets and fit the new part with nuts and bolts. Lubricate the pedals, wheels and fork bearings with light oil every two months. Check and tighten all nuts and bolts on the toy every few months.

Frame rivets
Rear axle
Stabiliser wheel
Head-bearing box

Plastic moulding
Front forks
Pedal crankshaft
Pedal block

Fitting new rear wheels

Many rear wheels are held in place by small dot-cap fasteners. The caps, which grip the axle with two stressed spring clips, are easy to fit, but they have to be broken when the wheel is to be removed.

Materials: dot-cap fasteners; emery cloth; oil.
Tools: pincers; hammer; file.

Dot-cap
Axle
Spring clip

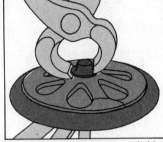

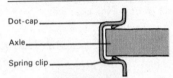

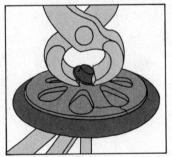

1 Place one jaw of the pincers behind the nipple of the cap, and the other under the rim

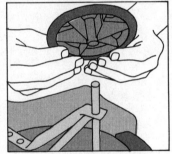

2 Squeeze the pincers and lever up the cap to break the clips. Remove the cap from the axle

3 Clean the end of the axle shaft with a fine file to remove any burrs. Pull the wheel off the axle

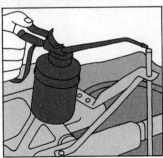

4 Clean the axle shaft with emery cloth to remove rust stains. Lubricate with light oil and fit the new wheel

5 Place a new dot-cap fastener on the axle. Strike the cap sharply with a hammer to force the clip on the shaft

FITTING A FRONT WHEEL

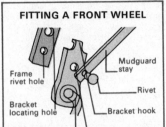

Frame rivet hole
Bracket locating hole
Pedal crankshaft
Mudguard stay
Rivet
Bracket hook
Bracket rivet hole

Replacement front wheels are made with the pedal crankshaft attached. Drill out the bracket rivet and slide the brackets off the old shaft. Use a spring washer with a $\frac{1}{4}$ in. (6 mm) bolt and nut to fit the new wheel assembly. Note that the wheel rivet secures the mudguard stay to the front fork.

Materials: wheel; spring washer; $\frac{1}{4}$ in. bolt and nut.
Tools: drill; punch; hammer; spanner; screwdriver.

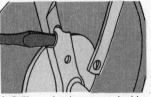

1 Drill out the rivets at each side. Tap them through with a hammer and punch. Lever off the bracket

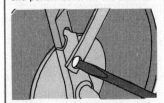

2 Fit the new wheel and hook the bracket to the frame. Make sure end of bolt does not touch wheel

Fitting a new pedal

Many pedals are secured with dot-cap fasteners which fit into a recess in the plastic pedal mould. If the pedal is damaged, cut around the fastener, and then remove it with pincers. If the plastic cannot be cut, hammer the pedal until the clip in the fastener breaks.

Materials: new pedals; dot-cap fasteners; wooden or steel block. Tools: hammer; pincers.

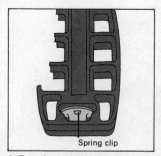

1 Turn the pedal on the shaft until the spring clip in the fastener can be seen

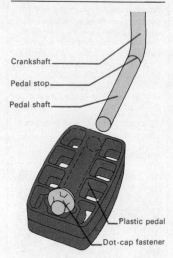

2 Support the pedal on a block. Strike the pedal until the clip breaks. Remove the pedal

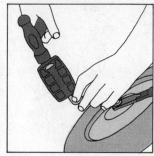

3 Fit a new dot-cap fastener in the new pedal recess. Slide on pedal and tap the end with a hammer

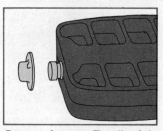

Dot-cap fastener The clip of the fastener clamps on the axle

Mending a treadle

Most pedal cars and go-karts are fitted with sturdy treadle and steering mechanisms designed to withstand violent impacts. The most vulnerable parts of the system are the drive rods and the plastic linkage brackets which are riveted to the drive rods at the rear. If the drive rods buckle, remove and straighten them. If rods or brackets cannot be repaired, fit new parts: they are obtainable from the manufacturer.

Materials: brackets; drive rods if necessary. Tools: drill; hammer; punch; spanner.

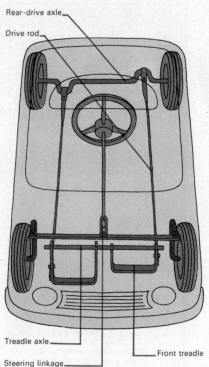

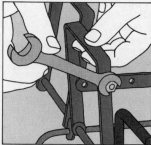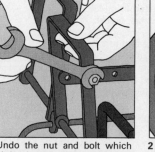

1 Undo the nut and bolt which hold the damaged drive rod to the foot-treadle assembly

2 Drill out the rivet which holds the drive rod to the plastic bracket on the rear axle

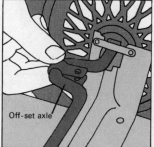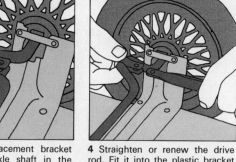

3 Spring a replacement bracket over the rear axle shaft in the centre of the off-set axle

4 Straighten or renew the drive rod. Fit it into the plastic bracket so that their holes are in line

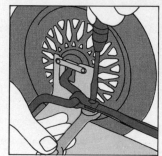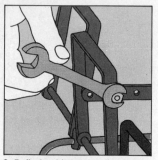

5 Fit a bolt through the bracket and drive rod. Tighten, but ensure the bracket can turn on the shaft

6 Refit the drive rod to the treadle mechanism with nut and bolt through the same hole as before

Toys Tricycles

Repairing the freewheel

A child's tricycle should be maintained and oiled as regularly as an adult's bicycle (see p. 570). Adjust the front brakes and fit new brake blocks when necessary (see p. 576).

If the freewheel sticks, remove the rear axle and take off the sprocket. Clean, and lubricate with light oil.

Materials: new freewheel unit; new bolt for the rear wheel.
Tools: spanners; punch; hammer; screwdriver; vice.

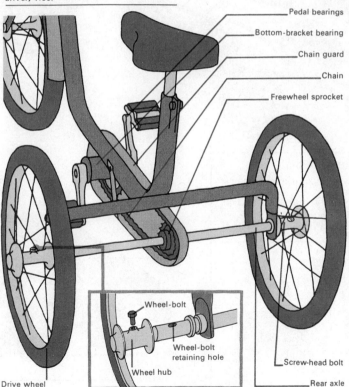

Pedal bearings
Bottom-bracket bearing
Chain guard
Chain
Freewheel sprocket

Wheel-bolt
Wheel-bolt retaining hole
Wheel hub
Screw-head bolt
Rear axle

Drive wheel

Drive wheel This is held on the axle by a hexagonal bolt which screws through the wheel hub and fits into a hole in the shaft

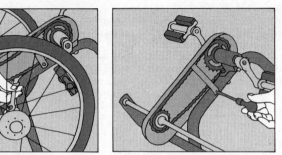

1 Loosen the bolt on the rear drive wheel. Remove the bolt and slide off the wheel and the washer

2 Loosen the bolt on the other wheel. Remove the wheel. Undo the screws holding the chain guard

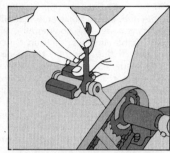

3 Undo the pedal shaft on the chain-guard side. Turn it anti-clockwise with a spanner

4 Loosen the nuts holding the bottom-bracket assembly to the frame. Slide the assembly backwards

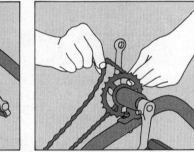

5 Lift the slack chain off the front chain wheel. Let the chain hang at the side of the guard on the rear axle

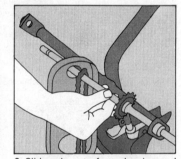

6 Slide axle out of one bearing and then back to free it from the other. Remove chain guard and chain

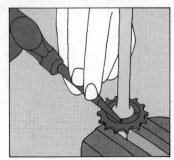

7 Hold the axle sprocket in a vice with the four holes uppermost. Tap it anti-clockwise with a punch and hammer

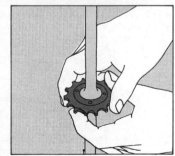

8 Unscrew the loosened sprocket by hand. Clean shaft and shaft threads. Refit sprocket and tighten by hand

9 Refit chain assembly. Slide bottom bracket forwards until chain has $\frac{1}{2}$ in. (13 mm) slack in it. Tighten

Toys Electric cars

Maintenance and repairs

Electric cars must be kept clean and lightly lubricated. Make sure that all the electrical parts—the commutator, armature, carbon brushes, pick-up braids—are free of fluff and dirt. Use a pin or knife blade to clean carbon from the commutator slots, but do not scratch the surface to avoid excessive wear on the carbon brushes.

Check the heads of the carbon brushes and the ends of the braids. Make sure that the crown wheel and pinion—which drive the car—mesh securely. Do not try to repair a transformer or faulty armature. Take the car to a model shop or send it to the makers.

Lubricate the car sparingly with thin oil. The most important parts are the felt pads at each end of the armature and the crown wheel and pinion. Do not spill oil on carbon brushes or commutator.

Tools: small screwdriver; thin-nosed pliers; cutters; tweezers.

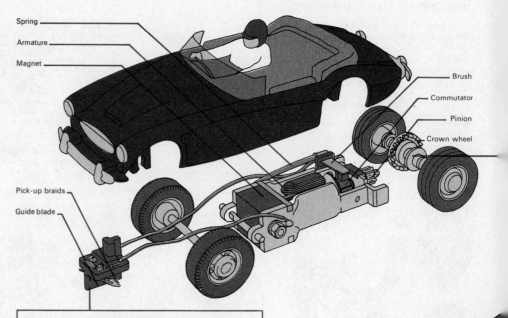

OVERHAULING THE MOTOR

When a car stops working, first check that the commutator is clean: even a single hair caught on it can stop the car.

Remove the two carbon brushes to reach the commutator. Renew both brushes even if only one is worn.

Materials: carbon brushes; rag; spirit.
Tools: tweezers; pin or knife; screwdriver.

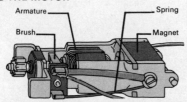

1 Unclip the motor from the chassis. Press in the brush clips, and use tweezers to pull the carbon brushes free

2 Use the tweezers to remove any hair from the commutator. Take care not to damage the surface

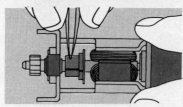

3 Clean carbon from the slots with a knife or pin. Wipe with lint-free rag and methylated spirit

4 Fit new carbon brushes with the tweezers. Secure with the brush spring and ensure the lead is correctly positioned

CONTACT BRAIDS

If the contact braids are worn or damaged, the car motor does not receive power and cannot operate efficiently. To remove a braid, it is necessary to take out the guide blade, which may have a pin that slots into the car body. On some models, the guide-blade assembly is held by a nut.

Materials: two braid pieces; methylated spirit.
Tools: toothbrush; tweezers; cutters.

1 Clean the braids with a brush and methylated spirit. Trim frayed ends

2 If worn, remove braids with tweezers. Fit replacements in same way

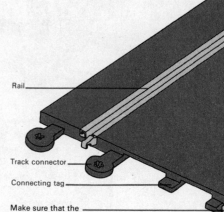

Make sure that the contact tag is not bent up. Reshape with a screwdriver to fit the hole in the adjacent track

RENEWING A CROWN WHEEL

The crown wheel on the rear axle engages with the pinion at the end of the armature and drives the car. To renew a crown wheel, first remove a track wheel. Fit the crown wheel so that its teeth mesh with the pinion.

Materials: crown wheel; track wheel.

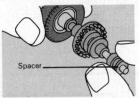
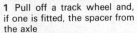

1 Pull off a track wheel and, if one is fitted, the spacer from the axle

2 Press the crown wheel off the axle. Fit a new one and replace spacer and wheel

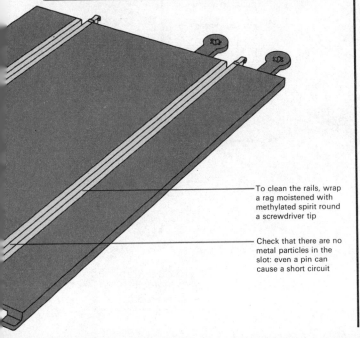

To clean the rails, wrap a rag moistened with methylated spirit round a screwdriver tip

Check that there are no metal particles in the slot: even a pin can cause a short circuit

Fitting a throttle-resistance mat

If the hand-controller throttle fails, check that the wiper arm on the trigger is clean. If it is, the most likely fault is that the resistance mat has become so worn that the wiper arm is no longer making adequate contact.

Always unplug the connecting leads from the hand controller before starting to dismantle it.

Materials: fine emery cloth; rag; methylated spirit; core solder.
Tools: soldering iron; small screwdriver; tweezers.

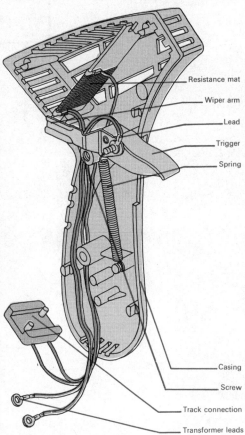

Resistance mat
Wiper arm
Lead
Trigger
Spring
Casing
Screw
Track connection
Transformer leads

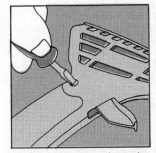

1 Undo and remove the casing securing screw. Remove the top part of the casing carefully

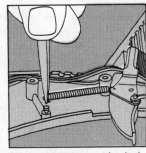

2 Use tweezers to unhook the tension spring from its pin in the handle. Do not stretch it

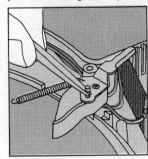

3 With tweezers, remove the pin holding the lead eyelet. Take off the wiper arm

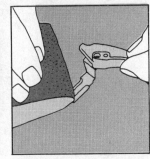

4 Clean the arm with emery cloth and wipe it with a rag dampened with methylated spirit

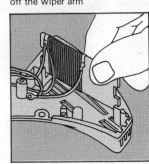

5 If the resistance mat is worn, pull it out of its slot. Unsolder it (see p. 692) from its leads

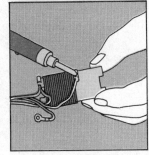

6 Solder (see p. 692) a new mat on to leads. Reassemble the arm, eyelet and spring. Refit casing

Care and maintenance

Most electric trains have several lubrication points: check the manufacturer's instruction sheet, and lubricate with a light machine oil as often as necessary. Take care not to drop oil on the commutator and carbon brushes: they should be dry at all times.

Do not attempt to make any repair to the armature, wheels, the valve-gear assembly or the power unit. If any one of these components is faulty, send the train to the manufacturer for attention.

RENEWING A COLLECTOR

An electric train receives its power through pick-ups in contact with the wheels. The power is then transmitted to the collector screwed to the base of the engine. A lead from the pick-ups connects with the leads for the carbon brushes and smoke unit. If pick-ups are damaged, fit a new collector.

Materials: collector; core solder.
Tools: soldering iron; screwdriver.

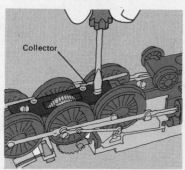

1 Turn the chassis upside-down. Remove the two screws holding the collector

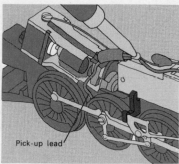

2 Unsolder (see p. 692) the pick-up lead from the others. Free the collector

3 Thread the new collector lead up through the chassis, between the first two wheels

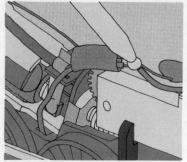

4 Re-solder the new lead to the others. Fit and tighten the collector screw

FITTING A NEW SMOKE-UNIT ELEMENT

When the smoke unit on an electric train fails, it is likely that its electric element has burnt out. The fibre wad which produces the smoke cannot usually wear out. When buying a new element, tell the dealer the make and type of engine to which it is to be fitted.

Materials: element.
Tool: small screwdriver.

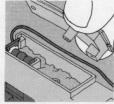

1 Undo the single securing smoke-unit screw and lift off the lid

2 Lever out the element. Fit a new one, press it down firmly and replace the lid and screw

Carbon brushes To fit new brushes, compress the spring clip and take out the old brushes. Fit new ones with the tag on the same side as the insulating sleeve

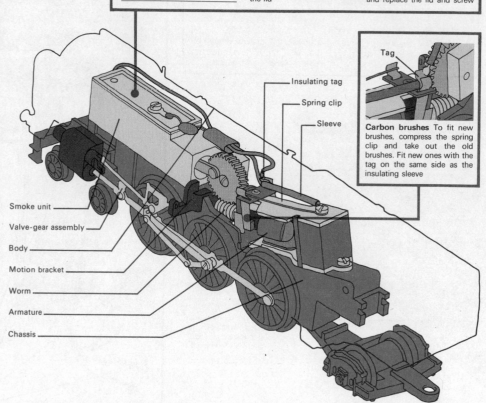

Tag
Insulating tag
Spring clip
Sleeve
Smoke unit
Valve-gear assembly
Body
Motion bracket
Worm
Armature
Chassis

Renewing the motion bracket

The valve-gear assembly which drives the wheels of an electric train is held in place under the smoke unit by a plastic piece called the motion bracket. The bracket slots into the chassis between the smoke unit and the worm at the end of the armature. Two slots at each end of the bracket engage with tags that are located at the top of the valve-gear assembly.

If the motion bracket breaks, the valve-gear assembly may fall away. Remove the smoke unit and fit a new motion bracket.

Materials: motion bracket.
Tool: small screwdriver.

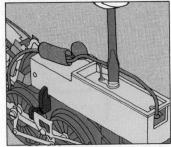

1 Use a small screwdriver to undo and remove the long screw holding the smoke unit to the chassis

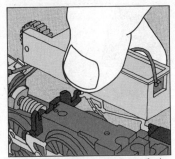

2 Lift the smoke unit clear of the engine. Make sure that its leads are not damaged or pulled out

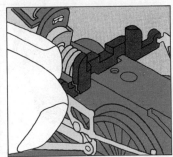

3 Hold the bracket at each side and lift it up a little while it is still attached to the gear assembly

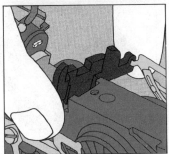

4 Note how the bracket fits. Unslot the assembly pieces one at a time from it. Do not strain the gear assembly

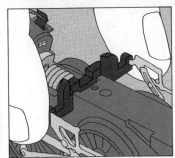

5 Fit a new bracket and slot in the assembly. Replace the smoke unit and screw back its holding screw

Track maintenance

Clean the rails periodically with a rag and a little methylated spirit. When a track is very badly damaged repairs are impracticable, and it must be renewed: but repairs can be carried out to minor damage. If the rails slide off their sleepers, fit new fishplates. The hair spring on a points-change unit can also be replaced.

Materials: methylated spirit; rag.
Tools: thin-nosed pliers; tweezers.

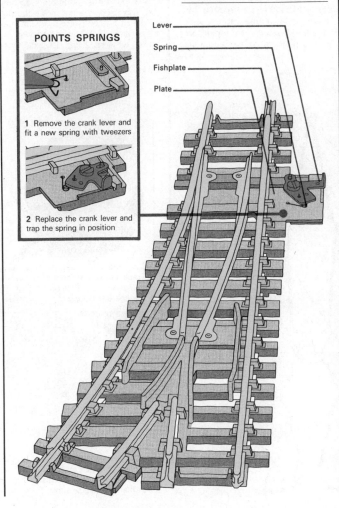

POINTS SPRINGS

1 Remove the crank lever and fit a new spring with tweezers

2 Replace the crank lever and trap the spring in position

Lever
Spring
Fishplate
Plate

Fitting fishplates

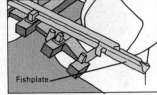

Fishplate

1 Press down on the sleeper at the damaged fishplate end and gently ease out the rail with the fishplate

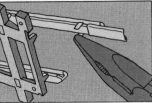

2 With pliers, carefully widen the fishplate tags holding the rail's underside and remove the fishplate

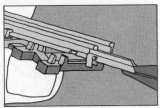

3 Slide on a new fishplate with the pliers and press in the tags so that they grip the rail firmly

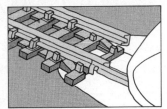

4 Slide the rail back into place. Slot the tags into the hole in the second sleeper from the end

Toys Dolls

How dolls are constructed

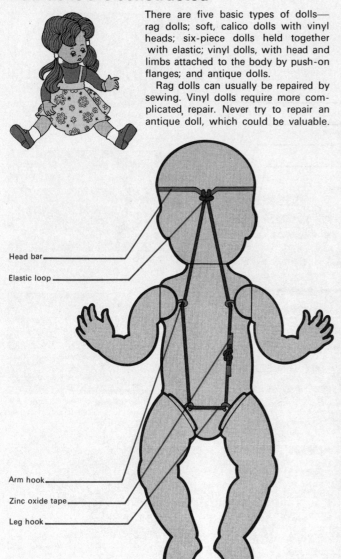

There are five basic types of dolls—rag dolls; soft, calico dolls with vinyl heads; six-piece dolls held together with elastic; vinyl dolls, with head and limbs attached to the body by push-on flanges; and antique dolls.

Rag dolls can usually be repaired by sewing. Vinyl dolls require more complicated repair. Never try to repair an antique doll, which could be valuable.

Head bar

Elastic loop

Arm hook

Zinc oxide tape

Leg hook

Re-stringing a doll

When the elastic breaks inside a strung vinyl doll, all the limbs and the head are freed from the body and the doll falls to pieces. These pieces can be reconnected, however, with a length of elastic $\frac{1}{4}$ in. (6 mm) thick.

The elastic is tied into a loop which is then fixed to a bar inside the doll's head. It is then passed through hooks connected to the arms and legs or is fixed, without being looped, over a metal latch attached to the bar.

Materials: $\frac{1}{4}$ in. (6 mm) thick, round elastic; zinc-oxide tape; pieces of strong fence wire.
Tool: scissors.

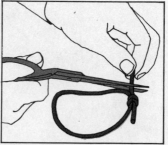

1 Cut a piece of elastic double the length of the doll's body section. Tie its ends in a reef knot

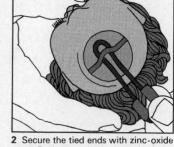

2 Secure the tied ends with zinc-oxide tape. Push the elastic loop into the doll's head and past the metal bar

3 Hook the end of the elastic over the bar and out of the head through the other side of the loop

4 Push the free side of the elastic loop into the neck hole of the doll's body. Push the head and body together

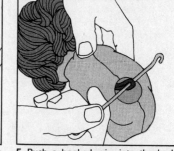

5 Push a hooked wire into the body through a leg hole. Catch the elastic and pull it out through the hole

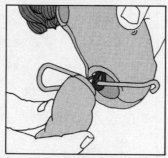

6 Hook the leg on to the loop and pull out the wire. Catch the elastic through the other leg hole and fix

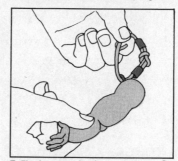

7 Fit the arms in the same way. On big dolls, make a separate small loop to fix the arms

Metal latch If the doll has a metal latch from the head bar, fit the elastic over the latch, not round the bar

Toys Teddy bears

Toys Vinyl balls

Tightening the limbs

If the limb of a teddy bear becomes very loose, the pin or wire may have become stretched or the fabric may have been torn away at the pin.

To tighten the joint it is necessary to unstitch the main body seam and remove the stuffing temporarily.

When the joint has been repaired, replace the original stuffing and add new kapok if required. Sew the edges of the body seam together, pulling the seam tight every three or four stitches.

Materials: kapok stuffing; needle and thread to match toy.
Tools: long-nosed pliers; scissors.

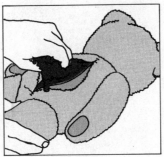

1 Unpick the main body seam. Remove the stuffing until loosened joint can be seen inside the body

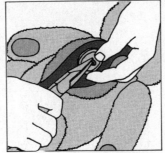

2 Push the limb against the body. Grip joint-plate with one hand and tighten pin with long-nosed pliers

Wire joint If the joint has only one piece of wire, use the pliers to increase and tighten the curl

Split-pin If the joint has a split-pin, curl both ends up to tighten it. Flatten the loops with the pliers

Mending a leak

A leaking valve or minor puncture in a vinyl ball can be repaired without special equipment.

To find the leak, screw the adaptor into the valve and inflate the ball with a cycle pump. Move the ball in a bowl of water and look for air bubbles rising from the leak.

If the valve itself is leaking, fit a new valve rubber. If the ball is punctured, repair it by heat moulding.

Materials: bowl; valve rubber; chalk.
Tools: adaptor; cycle pump; old screwdriver or chisel.

Adaptor

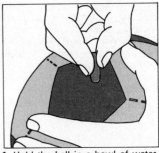

1 Hold the ball in a bowl of water and turn it to find the puncture. Mark the puncture with chalk

REPLACING THE VALVE

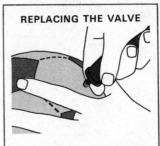

1 Screw the adaptor into the valve and fit the pump to the adaptor. Pull the pump to remove the valve from the ball

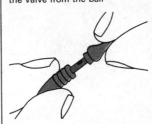

2 Pull off the old valve rubber. Lubricate the valve stem with soap and slide the new valve rubber on to the stem. Reassemble

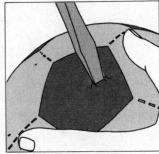

2 Heat a screwdriver blade on a gas ring. Rub the hot blade gently over the puncture to mould the vinyl

3 Allow the vinyl to harden for five minutes. Fit the adaptor to the valve and inflate the ball

Typewriters

Stripping a typewriter

All typewriters, whether portable or standard, have similar basic components. Although there are individual differences—for example, there may be a hinged top-plate instead of the lift-off type, or combined base and side-plates instead of separate parts—the procedure for cleaning, repairing and maintaining typewriters does not vary greatly. Store screws and small parts in a tin.

Materials: thin oil; impact adhesive; methylated spirit; cloth.
Tools: screwdriver; small knife; pliers; soft paintbrush; stiff toothbrush.

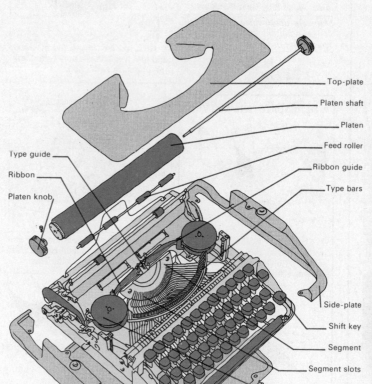

- Top-plate
- Platen shaft
- Platen
- Feed roller
- Ribbon guide
- Type bars

Type guide
Ribbon
Platen knob

- Side-plate
- Shift key
- Segment
- Segment slots
- Spool
- Shift key
- Base-plate
- Side-plate

1 Pull off the top-plate. If it is the hinged type, undo the screws attaching it to the side-plate

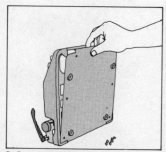

2 Stand the typewriter on its back edge, undo the screws in the base, and remove the base-plate

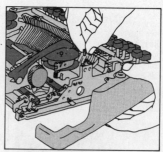

3 If the side-plates have not been detached by the removal of the base, unscrew and remove them

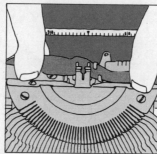

4 Lift the ribbon free of the slots near the type guide. Some ribbon holders have to be pushed aside

5 Release the sprung retaining arm with one hand and lift off the ribbon spool with the other

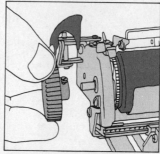

6 Slacken, but do not remove, the screw in the left-hand platen knob. Remove the knob and washer

7 Loosen the two inner screws at the other end of the platen. Pull the knob to remove the platen shaft

8 Push carriage to the right. Ease platen out, if necessary first removing the plastic paper guides

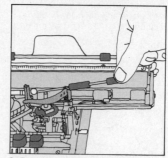

9 Free the right-hand end of the feed roller, which is now exposed, and remove the roller carefully

Cleaning and oiling

Clean the platen with a cloth dampened in methylated spirit

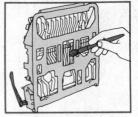

Clean all parts accessible from underneath with a soft brush

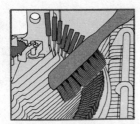

Use a stiff toothbrush to remove dirt from the type bars

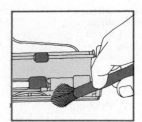

Clean the typewriter carriage with a soft, dry paintbrush

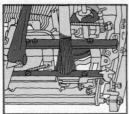

Move the carriage to each side and brush along its track

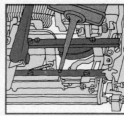

Apply a little thin oil to each end of the carriage track

Gently bend any type bar which hits the type guide off-centre

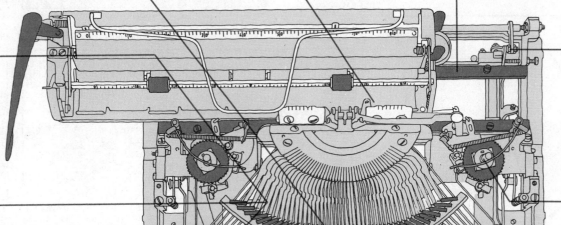

Apply thin oil to the shift-key pivot screw at each side

Lubricate each ribbon shaft with thin oil. Wipe off excess oil

Depress as many keys as possible and brush beneath the type bars

Remove dirt from the segment slots with a fine knife blade

Use a soft brush to remove remaining dirt from the slots

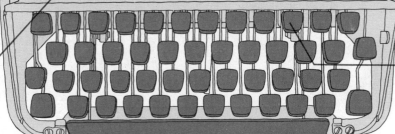

Apply impact adhesive to any loose key tops and replace them

Typewriters

When the carriage does not move

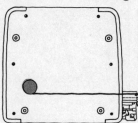

The movement of a typewriter carriage is controlled by a spring and drawband. The band, attached to one end of the carriage, winds round the spring at the other. As a key is pressed, the carriage is activated and the band pulls the carriage along. If the carriage does not move, the band has become detached from the carriage or the spring has lost its tension.

Tools: screwdriver; steel knitting needle.

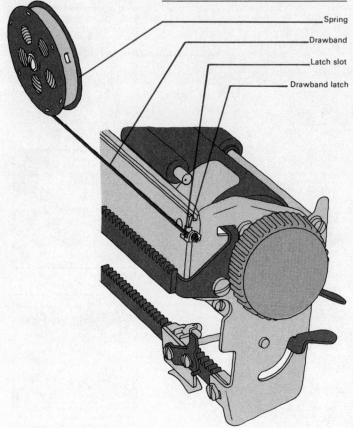

Spring

Drawband

Latch slot

Drawband latch

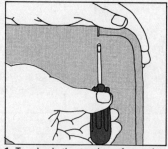

1 To check the tension of a spring or fix a loose drawband, first unscrew the base-plate of the typewriter

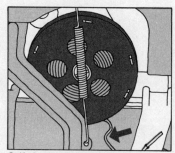

2 If the band (arrowed) is dangling loosely, its latch must be replaced in the slot at the other end of the carriage

3 Bend the tip of a steel knitting needle, and tie a loose loop in the drawband near the latch end

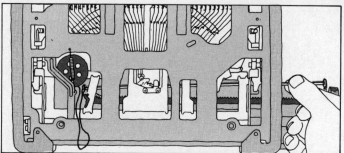

4 Push the carriage to the right and unwind the band entirely from the spring. From the opposite end, push the needle along the carriage until it reaches the spring. Attach the loop in the drawband to the needle hook

5 To set the tension of the spring, keep the loop on the hook and wind the spring back six full turns

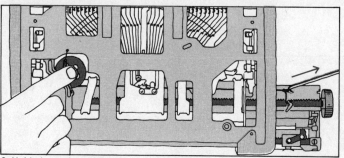

6 Hold the spring with one hand and pull the needle, with the drawband attached, along the carriage. If the spring should slip, the tension must be reset by releasing the band and again turning the spring six times

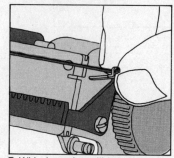

7 With the spring still held, undo the loop in the drawband and fix the latch in its slot in the carriage *(continued)*

8 To check that the spring tension is correct, set the right-hand margin as far right as possible

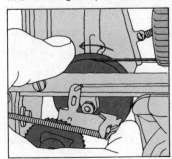

9 Move the carriage to the left almost as far as it will go. The keys should lock when the margin stop is reached

10 If the carriage does not lock, detach the band, wind the spring one more turn, hold it and refix the latch

When the ribbon does not reverse

If the ribbon mechanism gives trouble, first check that both spools fit the drive shaft. If a wrong ribbon has been fitted, the shaft may not operate its spool. If the ribbon cannot move at all, check the vibrator and operating links. When only the reverse operation is affected, check the ribbon reverse links and spring.

Tool: long-nosed pliers.

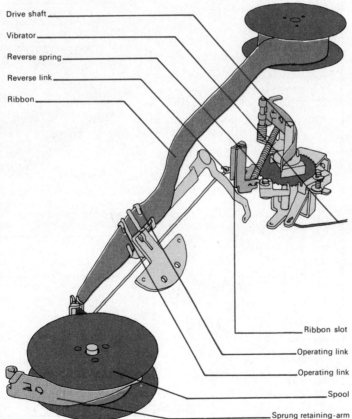

Drive shaft

Vibrator

Reverse spring

Reverse link

Ribbon

Ribbon slot

Operating link

Operating link

Spool

Sprung retaining-arm

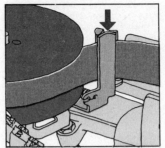

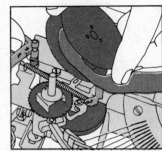

1 Check first that the ribbon is threaded through the ribbon slots at both spools

2 If the fault persists, remove both spools (see p. 396) and free the ribbon from the operating link

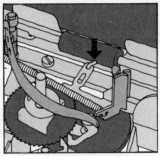

3 If one of the reverse links is making contact with the feed roller, straighten it with pliers

4 Make sure the reverse spring is attached to the link and its lug. Replace it if it is broken

WHEN THE RIBBON DOES NOT MOVE

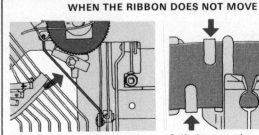

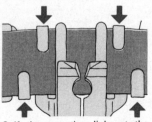

1 If the ribbon vibrator is bent, straighten it with gentle finger pressure. Do not use force

2 If the operating links at the ribbon guide are bent, straighten them carefully with the fingers

Typewriters

When the bell does not work

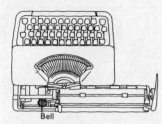

Bell

A warning bell is fitted to most typewriters to indicate that the carriage is reaching the right-hand margin. If it stops working, its striking hammer may be bent, or the operating spring may have broken. When this happens, make a new hook on the spring with a pair of long-nosed pliers.

Tool: long-nosed pliers.

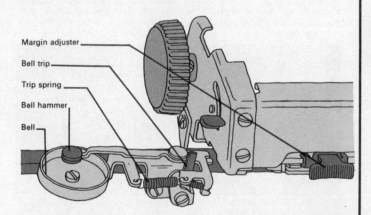

Margin adjuster

Bell trip

Trip spring

Bell hammer

Bell

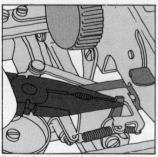

Bell trip A bent bell trip may not make contact with the margin adjuster. Straighten it with thin pliers

Trip spring Pull the end of a broken spring with pliers and gently shape a new hook. Attach it to its hole

When the characters are out of alignment

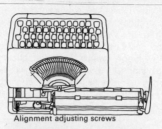

Alignment adjusting screws

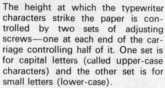

This is an example of characters out of alignment

The height at which the typewriter characters strike the paper is controlled by two sets of adjusting screws—one at each end of the carriage controlling half of it. One set is for capital letters (called upper-case characters) and the other set is for small letters (lower-case).

To align the characters, first decide which side of the carriage and which characters are affected. It may be unnecessary to adjust all the screws.

Tools: screwdriver; small spanner; pliers.

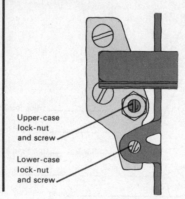

Upper-case lock-nut and screw

Lower-case lock-nut and screw

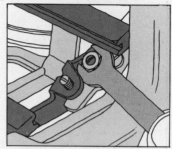

1 If the capitals are striking the paper unevenly, undo the upper-case lock-nut on the side affected

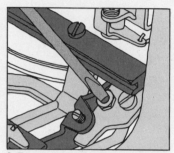

2 Turn the screw and keep trying the keys until the setting is correct. Hold the screw and tighten the nut

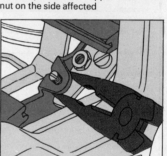

3 To adjust lower-case characters, loosen the lock-nut on the lower-case adjusting screw with a pair of pliers

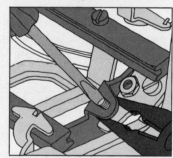

4 Find the right setting and hold the screw with the screwdriver while tightening the lock-nut underneath

CAPITALS BADLY ALIGNED

When capital letters are only occasionally out of line, at different carriage positions, it may be because of the speed of typing rather than because of a fault in the machine. Capitals are brought into position by the shift key on the keyboard. But if the typist releases the key before the type bar strikes the paper, the capital falls out of alignment. To compensate adjust the spring on the shift key.

Tools: spanner; thin pliers.

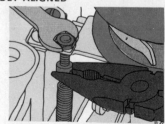

Hold the lock-nut near each shift-key lever with a spanner and use pliers to turn the adjuster clockwise twice

When the margin is inconsistent

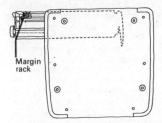

Margin rack

This is an example of an inconsistent margin

If the left-hand margin shows a ragged edge, it can be corrected by adjusting the margin rack.

Tool: screwdriver.

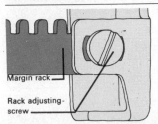

Margin rack

Rack adjusting-screw

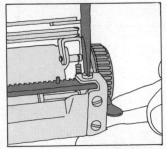

1 The margin rack is located just behind or below the carriage. Undo the screw at each end

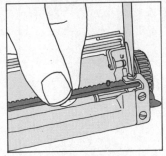

2 Slide the rack a fraction to the right. Hold it in its new position and tighten the two screws

IF THE MARGIN-RELEASE KEY DOES NOT WORK

The margin-release key operates through a lever spring

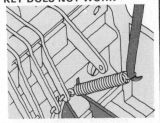

If the spring becomes detached, use a bent knitting needle to replace it correctly

When the space bar is faulty

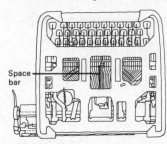

Space bar

This is an example of the space bar jumping two spaces

If the arms of the space bar are bent, they may wedge against the side plate or catch on the type bars under the keys. They can be straightened with gentle finger pressure if necessary. When the bar causes the carriage to jump two spaces instead of one, correct the fault by adjusting the space-bar trip-mechanism. A small spanner—for example, a magneto spanner—is required for the adjustment.

Tools: two small spanners.

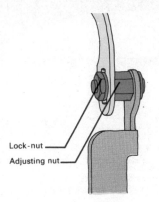

Lock-nut

Adjusting nut

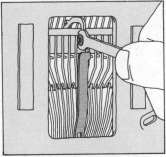

1 With the machine upright, slacken the space-bar lock-nut

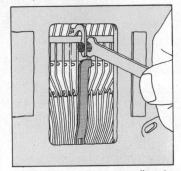

2 Use a second spanner to adjust the lock-nut one way or the other

3 Use the space bar to find the correct setting. Tighten the lock-nut

TIGHTENING THE SPACE BAR

If the space bar wobbles when it is pressed, or if it operates noisily, the rubber stop beneath it may have become displaced. It may be inside the base-plate.

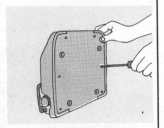

1 Remove the base-plate and find the loose rubber stop

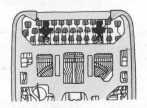

2 Locate the slots to which the rubber stops should be fitted

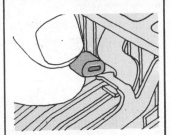

3 Replace the stop on the space bar leg. Check that the stop is in position on the other leg

Umbrellas

General wear and tear

Repairs can be made to many umbrellas, but in general it is not possible to get parts for foreign-made or telescopic types. Also, it is sometimes impossible to remove broken parts. When the tip of a walking-length umbrella, for example, is metal, it is part of the stem and cannot be replaced if it becomes worn or damaged. On the other hand, wooden tips can usually be pulled off. If there is any doubt, take the umbrella to a specialist dealer and ask for advice.

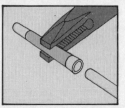

Damaged wooden tip Remove with pliers. Coat the stem with Araldite and twist on a new tip

Patching To mend a hole, cut a nylon patch. Apply clear adhesive to one side of the patch. Fix the patch inside with the cover taut. Stick down any loose threads from the outside

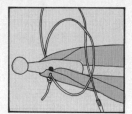

Sewing When sewing the cover to a rib tip, stitch through the hem. End with a slip-knot

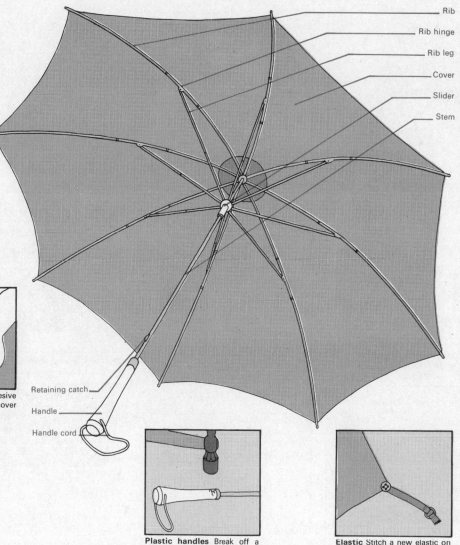

Rib
Rib hinge
Rib leg
Cover
Slider
Stem

Retaining catch
Handle
Handle cord

Plastic handles Break off a damaged handle. Secure the new one with epoxy-resin glue

Elastic Stitch a new elastic on an outside fold, near a crease, through one cover thickness

Removing and replacing

Measure the rib of an umbrella to ensure that replacements are of the correct length. Sizes vary from 18 in. (455 mm) to 20 in. (510 mm).

The wire needed to tie the ribs and their rib legs to the notches may be difficult to obtain, but florist's wire is an adequate substitute. Note that on some inexpensive umbrellas the notches may be plastic. As a result, the new ribs may be difficult to fit. Use a hacksaw to extend the notch slots.

On some older umbrellas the rib tips cannot be detached from the ribs. Cut the thread holding the cover to them and remove the whole rib.

Although spare parts for umbrellas are normally sold in large quantities, mainly to repair shops, some specialists may be willing to sell them singly. If parts cannot be bought, try to use parts from an old umbrella.

When the cover has to be sewn back on to the ribs after a repair, take care to stitch only through the seam, not the material itself. Work close to the rib hinge.

Materials: ribs as necessary; florist's wire; thread.
Tools: pliers; hacksaw; knife; needle.

TESTING THE HINGES

Umbrella ribs usually break at the hinge. Before replacing a broken rib, check all the others by bending them back slightly against their hinges. Any that are in poor condition will break under the test, and they can be replaced at the same time

broken umbrella ribs

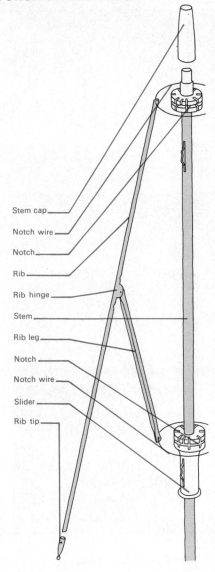

Stem cap
Notch wire
Notch
Rib
Rib hinge
Stem
Rib leg
Notch
Notch wire
Slider
Rib tip

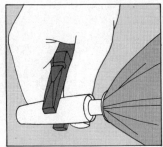

1 If the umbrella has a plastic cap at the tip, hold the handle and twist off the cap with a pair of pliers

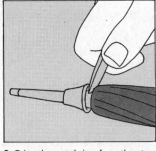

2 Prise the metal ring from the stem of a full-length umbrella. Do not damage the cover

3 Push off at least six rib tips by sliding the pliers between the cover and the ribs. Do not unstitch the tips

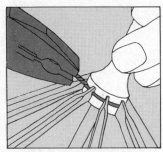

4 Find the wire securing the rib legs to the slider. Prise it out with a knife and untwist it with pliers

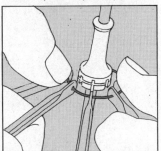

5 Open the wire gently so that it can be removed from the slider notches with the legs still on it

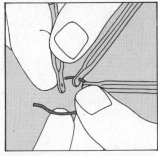

6 Remove all the rib legs from the wire. Do not allow them to drop on the umbrella cover

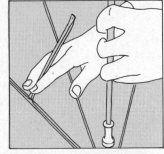

7 Fold the legs back against their ribs and slide the broken pieces out from the threads in the cover

8 Turn the umbrella inside out, so that the remaining ribs and legs hang down from the stem notches

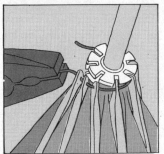

9 Prise out and unwind the wire holding the ribs near the tip. Bend back the ends to hold the ribs in place

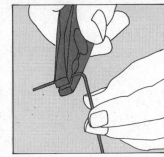

10 Take two wires, each about 4 in. (100 mm) long. Bend both at right angles 1 in. (25 mm) from one end

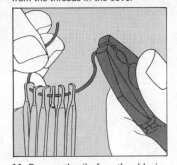

11 Remove the ribs from the old wire and place them in order on the new piece. Replace any broken ribs

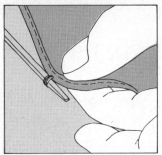

12 Remove the broken rib pieces from the cover. Slide in the replacement ribs carefully   *(continued)*

Umbrellas

(continued)

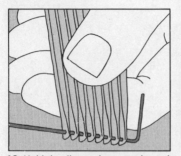

13 Hold the ribs on the new wire and check to ensure that they have been fitted in the correct order

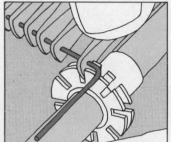

14 There is a groove in one side of the notch. Hold the 1 in. (25 mm) tail of the wire in it and fit each rib in its slot

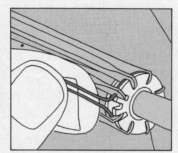

15 With the ribs firmly in place, bend both ends of the wire so they are parallel with the stem

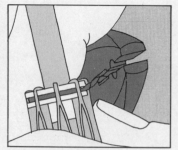

16 Use the pliers to twist the ends of the wire, but take care not to break it by overtightening

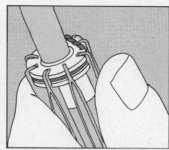

17 Cut the twisted wire to leave about $\frac{1}{4}$ in. (6 mm). Press it down against the stem in the direction of the handle

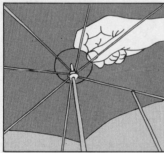

18 Fold the cover and ribs back to their normal position. If there was a protective rosette, replace it

19 Close the umbrella and smooth down the cover. Replace the plastic cap or metal ring

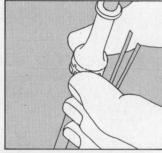

20 To reconnect the legs to the slider, first ensure that the slider is held on the catch nearer the handle

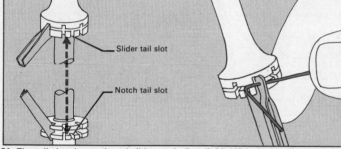

Slider tail slot

Notch tail slot

21 The tail slots in notch and slider are in line (left). With the handle upwards, take the rib on the right of the notch tail slot and thread its leg on to the other piece of new wire which was cut. Put wire tail and leg in their slider slots (right)

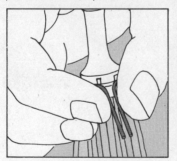

22 Hold the wire in place and thread each leg in order. Place the legs in their slots as they are threaded

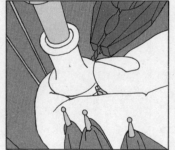

23 When all the ribs are located correctly, bend the ends of the wire down over them, and twist with pliers

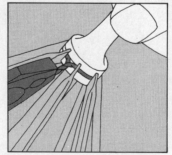

24 Cut the wire to leave about $\frac{1}{4}$ in. (6 mm). Press it down inside the ribs, against the stem of the umbrella

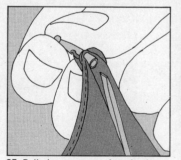

25 Pull the cover so that the loose tips can be replaced on the ribs to which they belong

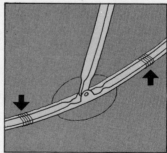

26 Check that all the threads holding the cover on the ribs are intact. If any have broken, replace the stitching

Upholstery Sprung dining chairs

Tools and equipment

It is always advisable to repair upholstery on a flat surface covered with blankets to ensure that materials and frame are not damaged. Most materials are readily available from furniture dealers; hessian and needles from most do-it-yourself or needlework stores. Hessian is available usually in two widths, 36 in. (915 mm) and 72 in. (1·8 m). For dining chairs buy the 36 in. size.

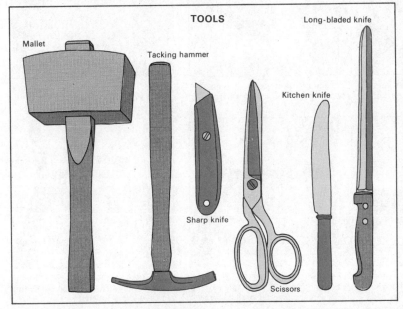

TOOLS

Mallet

Tacking hammer

Long-bladed knife

Sharp knife

Kitchen knife

Scissors

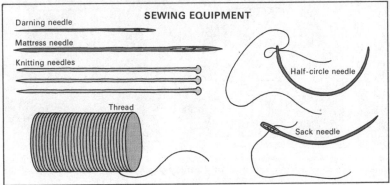

SEWING EQUIPMENT

Darning needle

Mattress needle

Knitting needles

Half-circle needle

Thread

Sack needle

Re-upholstering a sprung dining chair

Upright wooden chairs may be sprung or unsprung. If there are no springs, the work that can be done to repair damaged coverings is straightforward (see pp. 411, 412). With a sprung chair, repair is more complicated, for when the work is completed the springs must be firm in their correct positions.

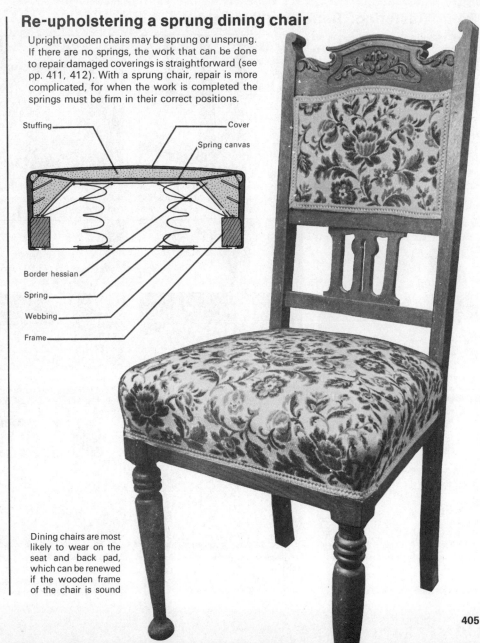

Stuffing

Cover

Spring canvas

Border hessian

Spring

Webbing

Frame

Dining chairs are most likely to wear on the seat and back pad, which can be renewed if the wooden frame of the chair is sound

Upholstery Sprung dining chairs

Re-upholstering: Renewing the webbing

When repairing a sprung chair, make sure that its springs are sewn upright to the webbing.

Materials: 2½ yds × 2 in. (2·3 m × 50 mm) webbing; ⅝ in. (16 mm) upholstery tacks; parcel twine.
Tools: knife; sack needle; tacking hammer; mallet; old chisel.

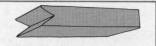

Tensioning Webbing can be tensioned with a length of 2×1 in. (50×25 mm) wood with a deep V across one end

1 With the seat upside-down, use an old chisel and mallet to remove the tacks. Knock in direction of wood grain

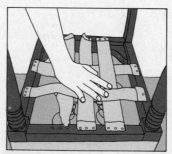

2 Remove the hessian. Press firmly down on the webbing to check its condition and strength

3 If any of the webbing is damaged, use the mallet and chisel to knock out the tacks holding it

4 With a sharp knife, cut the twine which holds the springs upright to the old webbing. Discard the webbing

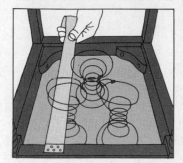

5 Turn up the new webbing end ¾ in. (20 mm). Fix with two rows of tacks at front and stretch across the seat

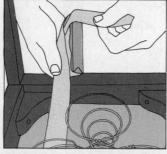

6 Hold the tensioner on the back edge. With the strip being fitted on top, wrap the surplus webbing round it

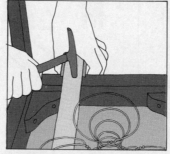

7 Lay the V shape against the chair edge. Press down to tension the webbing. Fix with one row of three tacks

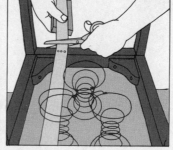

8 Remove the tensioner and cut the webbing ¾ in. (20 mm) beyond the frame. Fold over and fix with two tacks

9 Fix two more strips of webbing down the length of the chair where the old ones were located

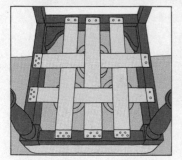

10 Weave and tack two strips across the chair. Push each spring under a double thickness of webbing

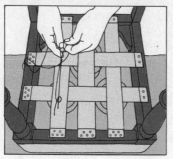

11 Push needle and single thread in and out round the top loop of a front spring. Secure with a knot

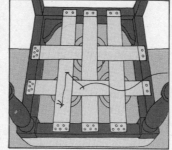

12 Stitch the opposite side of the spring loop and tie a slip knot. Repeat at the inside edge of the spring

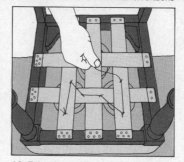

13 Take the needle and thread across to the nearest point on the adjacent spring. Stitch in a triangle, as before

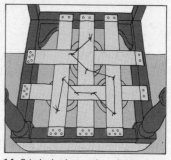

14 Stitch the last spring also at three points. To finish, tie a double knot and trim the twine

Re-upholstering: Fitting new hessian

On most upright chairs the springs are covered with hessian before padding is fitted. But on antique chairs and the more expensive modern ones there may also be a layer of wadding between the springs and the hessian.

Two types of hessian are required for repairs: 10 oz. (280 gr.) for the centre-piece, over the springs, and 7 oz. (195 gr.) for the edges.

Materials: hessian; twine; $\frac{5}{8}$ in. (16 mm) tacks; thread.
Tools: mallet; old chisel; knife; scissors; tacking hammer; steel knitting needles; $4\frac{1}{2}$ in. (115 mm) half-circle needle; 10 in. (255 mm) mattress needle.

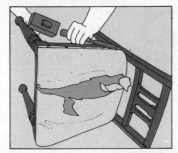
1 Use the chisel and mallet to remove the nails holding the binding. Knock in the direction of the grain

2 Remove the tacks holding the cover. Take care not to split the wood at the corners of the chair

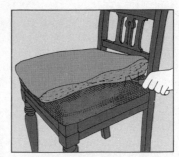
3 Cut the twine securing the padding to the top of the old hessian. Lay the padding aside

4 Check the centre and border pieces of hessian. If any is damaged, buy new hessian to cover the tear

5 Fit a piece of 10 oz. (280 gr.) hessian, 2 in. (50 mm) wider and longer than the old hessian centre-piece

6 At the back, turn up 1 in. (25 mm) of hessian and secure with $\frac{5}{8}$ in. (16 mm) tacks, $1\frac{1}{2}$ in. (40 mm) apart

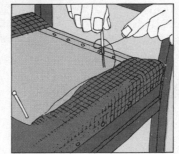
7 Fold under 1 in. (25 mm) along the three other edges. Secure the two front corners with steel knitting needles

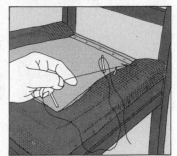
8 Push a half-circle needle and single thread through both hessians at a corner. Secure with a knot

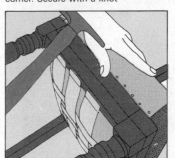
9 Stick the needle through the hessian, $1\frac{1}{2}$ in. (40 mm) along the edge; pull twine tight across its half-circle

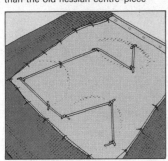
10 Complete stitch, pulling needle through its loop. Repeat every $1\frac{1}{2}$ in. (40 mm). Stitch springs (see p. 406)

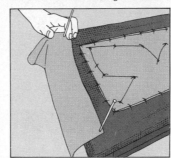
11 Cut border hessian 3 in. (75 mm) longer and wider than the damaged area. Fold under $\frac{1}{2}$ in. (13 mm) at top

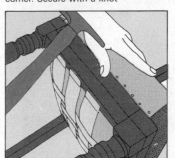
12 Position the new piece of border hessian and hold its two top corners with steel knitting needles

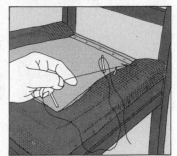
13 Tuck under the bottom edge to line up with the hessian at either side. Fix tacks $1\frac{1}{2}$ in. (40 mm) apart

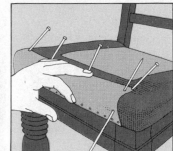
14 Secure top with two more needles. Push threaded needle through front and top of patch *(continued)*

Upholstery Sprung dining chairs

(continued)

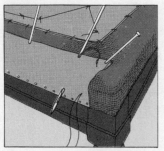

15 Leave a 12 in. (305 mm) tail of twine. Push eye end of needle back, about 1 in. (25 mm) along

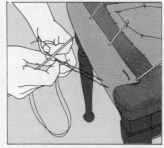

16 Pull the needle free and tie a slip knot with the two pieces of twine hanging from the border hessian

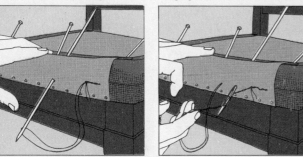

17 Push the needle up through the hessian, 2 in. (50 mm) along. Leave a large loop of twine at the front

18 Bring the needle back 1 in. (25 mm) towards the start. Push the tip through and wind tail round it twice

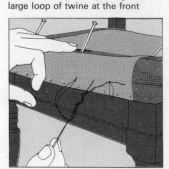

19 Pull the needle through the wound twine. Make sure it forms a tight knot—called a roll stitch

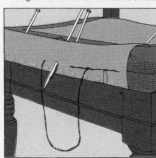

20 Continue stitching across the patch. Remove knitting needles and finish with a double roll stitch

Re-upholstering: Padding and re-covering a seat

When the covering of a sprung dining chair is renewed, it is advisable to fit new padding—usually a $\frac{1}{2}$ in. (13 mm) plastic-foam square.

Most covering materials can be bought in 48 in. and 50 in. widths (about 1·2 m). Special binding tape—called gimp—and pins to hold it can be bought in many colours to match the covering material.

Materials: $\frac{1}{2}$ in. (13 mm) plastic foam; cover material; $\frac{5}{8}$ in. (16 mm) tacks; gimp; gimp pins; latex-based adhesive. Tools: tape measure; scissors; felt-tip or ballpoint pen; tacking hammer; sharp knife.

1 Lay the old stuffing on the new hessian. Do not stitch it. Measure its width and length

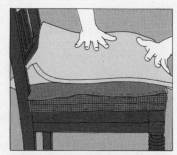

2 Cut plastic foam 2 in. (50 mm) wider and longer than the stuffing. Lay it evenly on the stuffing

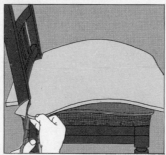

3 Cut diagonally at the two back corners, then cut them square to fit against the back legs

4 Mark the chair shape down both sides of the foam. Allow enough foam to roll over the stuffing edge. Trim it

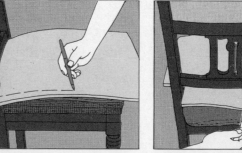

5 Measure from 1 in. (25 mm) below the tack holes at the back of the chair to 1 in. below the holes at the front

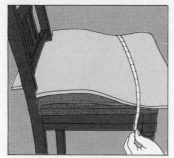

6 Measure the width from 1 in. (25 mm) below the tack holes at one side to 1 in. below the holes on the other

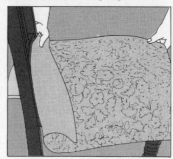

7 Cut the covering material to these measurements. Lay it on the seat and make sure the pattern is centred

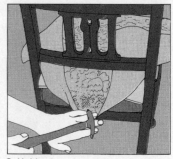

8 Hold the cover temporarily in position by fixing a tack lightly at the back of the chair *(continued)*

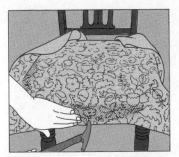

9 Smooth the cover to the front and hammer in another temporary tack at the centre of the tacking line

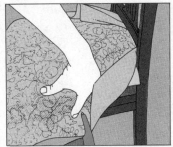

10 Smooth the cover to each front corner. Tack lightly. Smooth to the centre of each side. Tack lightly

11 Fold the back corners over against the legs. Cut diagonally from each tip to within ¼ in. (6 mm) of its leg

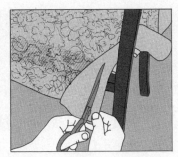

12 Cut each back flap to overlap the legs by ½ in. (13 mm). Cut no higher than the top edge of the chair rails

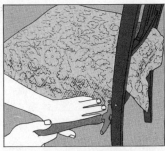

13 At each back corner, push surplus material into the chair with scissors. Tack both sides at the back leg

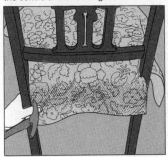

14 At the back, fold under the side edges and tack the material down the old tacking line

15 On all four sides, fix tacks 1 in. (25 mm) apart along the old tacking line. Hammer in the temporary tacks

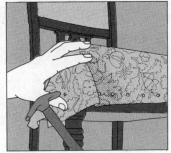

16 At the front corners, pull down the material tightly and tack in the centre on the old tacking line

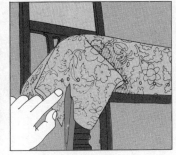

17 Fix a tack 1½ in. (40 mm) on each side of the first corner tack. Cut the cover up to the centre tack

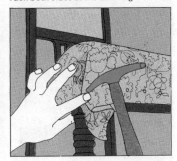

18 Pinch the surplus material between the fingers. Fold it in towards the chair leg and secure with three tacks

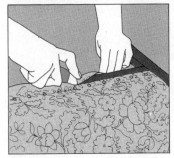

19 With a sharp knife, carefully trim the material all round the chair just below the tacking line

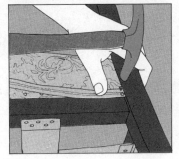

20 To fit the gimp, fold under ½ in. (13 mm) at the end and secure it with two gimp pins at one back leg

21 Coat the gimp with a latex-based adhesive. Apply only enough to stick to one side of the chair at a time

22 Stick the gimp down along the trimmed edge round the chair. Pinch each corner and fix with a gimp pin

23 At the other back leg, fold under ½ in. (13 mm) of gimp. Stick it down firmly and fix with two gimp pins

Upholstery Sprung dining chairs

Fitting a new back pad

When re-covering the back pad of a dining chair, choose a material that does not clash with the seat cover. Gimp (trimming) and gimp pins should match the material used. Note, however, that the material at the back of the chair is not usually bound with gimp. Fit two layers of flock stuffing to give the back pad a slightly domed surface.

Materials: $\frac{3}{8}$ in. (10 mm) tacks; flock; gimp; gimp pins; cover material; latex-based adhesive.
Tools: mallet; screwdriver or an old chisel; tape measure; tacking hammer; knife; scissors.

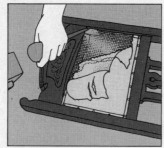

1 Knock out all the old tacks—in the direction of the grain—with a mallet and screwdriver or old chisel

2 Remove the covering. Undo two adjacent edges of hessian, pull taut and re-tack every 1 in. (25 mm)

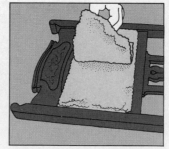

3 Lay on a flock strip the size of the pad, then a second strip 1 in. (25 mm) shorter and narrower

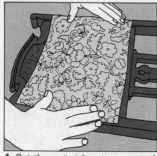

4 Cut the material, pattern centred, 1 in. (25 mm) wider and $\frac{1}{2}$ in. (13 mm) deeper than the panel

5 Lay the cover against the bottom rail. Pin at centre, then every 1 in. (25 mm) along the edge

6 Smooth the cover to the sides and top. Hammer in pins 1 in. (25 mm) apart. Trim cover in line with wood

7 Fix the first end of the gimp with two pins; do not fold it. Coat the underside with adhesive

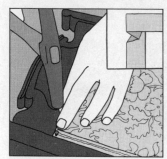

8 Press gimp along each side. Fold it at each corner and pin. At end, tuck under $\frac{1}{2}$ in. (13 mm) and pin

9 Remove the old covering at the back of the chair. Cut new material 1 in. (25 mm) wider and deeper

10 Lay material on the pad. Make sure the pattern is centred. Fold under $\frac{1}{2}$ in. (13 mm) all round

11 Secure the back cover along the old tacking lines. Use gimp pins spaced 1 in. (25 mm) apart

New seat hessian

Fit new hessian under a chair seat only after all other re-upholstering work is finished. Lay down several sheets of paper on the table or bench, to make sure, when the chair is turned upside-down, that the new seat covering is adequately protected against dirt and rough surfaces.

Cut a patch of 7 oz. (195 gr.) hessian 2 in. (50 mm) wider and longer than the widest and longest parts of the chair bottom, to fold under.

Materials: 7 oz. (195 gr.) hessian; $\frac{1}{2}$ in. (13 mm) tacks.
Tools: tape measure; tacking hammer; scissors; knife.

1 Fold the edge under 1 in. (25 mm). Hammer in tacks every 2 in. (50 mm) to within 2 in. of the corners

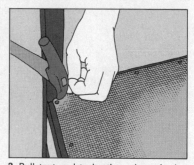

2 Pull taut and tack other edges. At the corners, fold the material to shape and tack close against the legs

Upholstery Unsprung chairs

Re-covering the loose seat of a dining chair

When the loose seat of a dining chair is re-covered, it is advisable also to lay in new flocking to give the seat a properly rounded surface. Use two pieces of flock, one larger than the other, with the smaller piece on top of the larger.

Make sure that the flocking does not slip over the edge, even slightly. When this happens the seat can no longer fit in the frame of the chair. If the seat is a difficult fit, gently tap along the edges with a mallet to remove any bumps or ridges.

Materials: ⅜ in. (10 mm) tacks; flock or wadding as required; cover material.
Tools: mallet; screwdriver; tape measure; tacking hammer; knife; scissors.

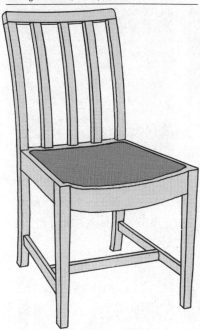

Seat covering The loose seat of an unsprung dining chair is usually covered with vinyl. Other materials can be used, however, to match the rest of the furniture in the room

1 Lay the seat upside-down on a flat surface. Remove the tacks with a mallet and screwdriver

2 Pull off the cover. Pack in new pieces of flock to give a domed surface, then add the smaller layer

3 Measure across the widest and longest parts. Add 2 in. (50 mm) to each measurement and cut new cover

4 Replace the flock and fit the new cover. Stand the seat on one edge, making sure the cover is taut

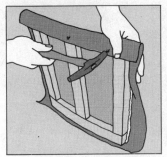

5 Hammer in a temporary tack under the front edge. Smooth the cover and lightly fit two corner tacks

6 Turn the back edge up. Pull the cover tight and hammer in three temporary tacks, matching the front

7 Turn the seat right side up. Use the side of the tacking hammer to tap any bumps or ridges on the top

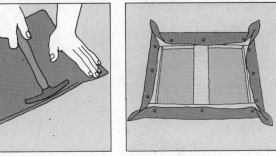

8 Turn the seat over and secure the remaining two sides with three temporary tacks in each

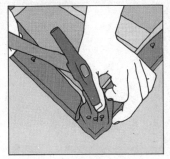

9 Stretch the longest part of the corner over the seat and hammer in three tacks to secure it

10 Use a sharp knife to slit the cover, beyond the tacking line, from one end tack to the other

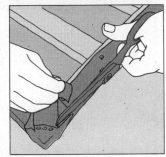

11 Take the flap at each side of the line of tacks. Cut the top surface of each fold to its nearest tack

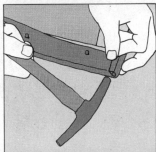

12 Fold one cover flap over the seat edge. Secure it with a tack. Lightly hammer seat edge fold *(continued)*

Upholstery Pipe-edged chairs

(continued)

13 Fold the other flap over in the same way and tack it. Repeat at the three other corners of the seat

14 Space tacks every 1 in. (25 mm) along all four sides. Hammer home all the temporary tacks

15 Use a knife to trim along all the surplus covering as close as possible to the lines of tacks

Repairing a tear along a seam

Many types of chairs and cushions have piped edges. Although they can be completely re-covered (see p. 408), a simple alternative is to sew a torn area with matching mattress twine. Although materials and shapes may vary from chair to chair, the method of repair is basically the same.

The stitch recommended—which is called Frenching—can also be used to re-attach loose piping.

Materials: fine mattress twine.
Tools: darning needles; 1½ in. (40 mm) half-circle needle.

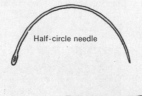

Half-circle needle

Damage to pipe-edged chairs
The most common damage to occur is a split or tear in the covering material near the piping

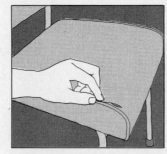

1 Take the torn edge further from the piping and fold it under ¼ in. (6 mm). Pull towards piping

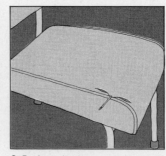

2 Push a darning needle into the stuffing through the torn top cover. Make sure that the tear is closed

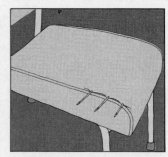

3 Use as many darning needles as necessary to hold all the torn edge close to the piping

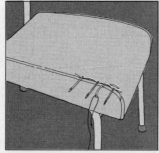

4 Thread a half-circle needle, knot the twine and push the needle up and down through the cover

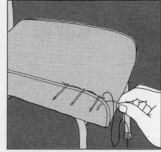

5 Pull twine tight then take the needle back ¼ in. (6 mm). Push it through to the outside under the piping

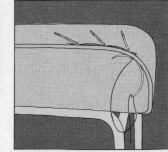

6 Push the needle through the side cover close to the piping. Pull the twine tightly to close the tear

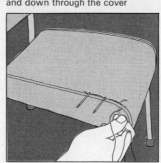

7 Push the needle back up under the piping, without stitching the seat cover. Pull the twine tightly

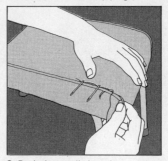

8 Push the needle into the covering. Pull tightly, then push it under the piping, ready for the next stitch

9 Continue stitching until the whole tear is sewn. Extend the stitching ½ in. (13 mm) beyond the tear

Upholstery Armchairs

Care and maintenance

The most common faults with padded armchairs are that their springs may wear or break or that the fabric may tear. Springs and webbing can be replaced (see p. 406), but make sure that the correct size of spring is bought. In some cases, fabric can be stitched together almost invisibly (see p. 412); in others, stitching may be unnecessary (see p. 414). When the chair is structurally sound but its fabric is badly damaged, buy a loose cover to fit it.

REPAIRING A DAMAGED SPRING HOOK

Many armchairs which have wooden arms and removable cushions are sprung only by a criss-cross pattern of rubber webbing. If it wears or breaks, fit new webbing (see p. 406).

Other chairs have metal springs, attached to plates along the side rails of the chair. In some cases, the springs stretch right across the chair; in others they are fixed to the ends of webbing pieces. If a webbing piece breaks, replace it with a spring.

Tools: side cutters or wire cutters; pincers; power drill if necessary.

1 Unhook the spring from the metal side plates. If its hook is stretched or broken, cut it off with cutters. To make a new hook, pull the end with pincers and stretch it open. Grip the end of the spring and bend it carefully at right angles

2 Check the metal plate and the hole in which the spring hook should fit. If it is worn or split, fit a $\frac{1}{4}$ in. (6 mm) metal bit in a power drill and make a new fixing hole about $\frac{1}{4}$ in. (6 mm) to one side of the old hole. Hook the spring securely in position

Replacing decorative buttons

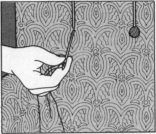

1 Use a 10 in. (255 mm) mattress needle and mattress twine. Leave one twine end only 3 in. (75 mm) long. Do not knot. Insert the needle

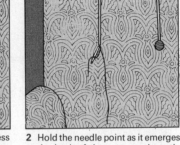

2 Hold the needle point as it emerges at the back of the settee and gently pull it until the eye passes through the front fabric

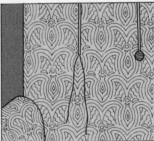

3 Push the eye back through to the front, close to its insertion point, holding the thread tight in the eye. Unthread the needle

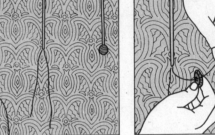

4 Pull the tails tight and to even length; trim them so that they are each about 6 in. (150 mm) long. Thread the button on to one of the tails

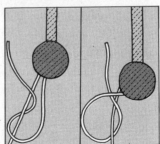

5 Tie a slip-knot with the tail ends (left). Pull tight. Push the button into its recess in the chair fabric and tie a half-hitch knot (right). Pull tight

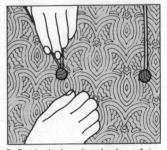

6 Cut both thread ends about 1 in. (25 mm) from the button. Wind them round the button and use the needle to push them into the fabric

Upholstery Armchairs

Repairing a torn arm

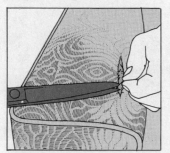

1 Examine the tear carefully. Snip off any loose threads along it, but do not cut back the cover material

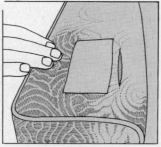

2 Cut a piece of fabric longer and wider than the tear. It does not have to match the cover

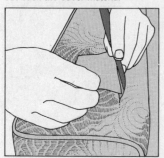

3 Use a kitchen knife to tuck the fabric patch gently under the tear. Manoeuvre it into position

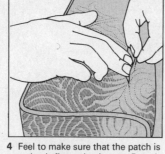

4 Feel to make sure that the patch is completely flat under the tear. Press it down firmly

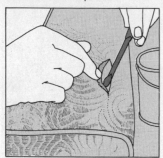

5 Pull back the tear. Apply PVA adhesive with an old knife to the patch and underside of the fabric

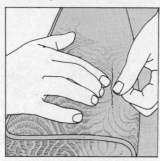

6 Keep the tear open until adhesive is tacky. Press down one edge at a time. Press the edges together

Mending a foam cushion

Foam-rubber or latex cushions are likely to wear first at the front edge. Although the life of the cushion can in some cases be extended by turning it round, the only satisfactory solution is to replace the worn edge of the foam with a new piece.

When cutting foam to size, mark the edge with a needle or felt-tip pen. Any sharp knife can be used on foam, but the cleanest cut is usually made with a newly sharpened carving knife.

Materials: PVA adhesive; foam rubber; fine mattress thread.
Tools: sharp knife; carving knife; half-circle needle; scrap wood.

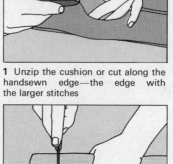

1 Unzip the cushion or cut along the handsewn edge—the edge with the larger stitches

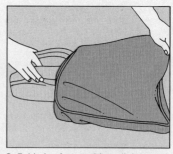

2 Fold the foam rubber slightly and pull it carefully out of the cover. Do not tear the other stitching

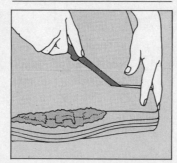

3 Cut straight across the foam rubber with a carving knife, about 2 in. (50 mm) back from the damage

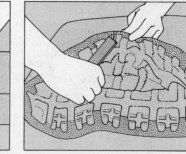

4 Measure the damaged piece. Cut a replacement the same width and length but ½ in. (13 mm) deeper

5 Use a piece of wood to coat the edges of the two pieces with a PVA adhesive. Coat inside the edges

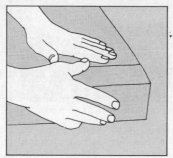

6 Lay the new strip against the end of the original piece on a flat surface, compressing to make a level join

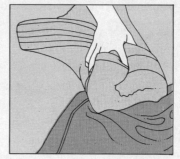

7 When the adhesive has set, fold the cushion at right angles to the stuck edge. Push it into its cover

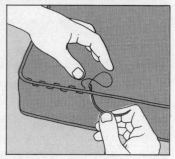

8 Ensure that the cover fits neatly. Sew with a 1½ in. (40 mm) half-circle needle and fine mattress thread

Upholstery Rubber webbing

Fitting new webbing

Rubber webbing for the seats and backs of chairs is available in 1 in. and 2 in. (25 mm and 50 mm) widths. Use the 2 in. width to re-web armchairs and settees: 1 in. webbing is usually strong enough for most chair backs.

Five strips are needed to re-web an armchair seat, more for a settee. Always start with the centre strip and go on to fix the pieces on each side of it.

Materials: rubber webbing; ⅝ in. (16 mm) tacks.
Tools: hammer; old chisel or screwdriver; sharp knife.

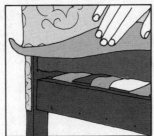

1 Use a hammer and an old screwdriver or chisel to remove the tacks in the cover at the front and back of the seat. Peel back the cover

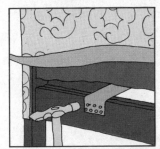

2 Remove the damaged webbing. Fit a new 2 in. (50 mm) strip of webbing over the back edge of the seat. Hammer in seven tacks

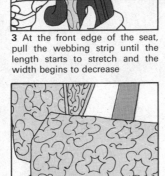

3 At the front edge of the seat, pull the webbing strip until the length starts to stretch and the width begins to decrease

4 Fix the strip about 2 in. (50 mm) over the front edge. Secure with seven tacks and trim the webbing just beyond the tacks

5 Fix the other strips in the same way. Lay old webbing under the new at the front and back of the chair and tack it in place

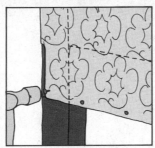

6 Fold the loosened cover material back into place at the front and back of the seat. Tack securely every 2 in. (50 mm)

7 Examine the cover flaps at each corner. Fit extra tacks wherever there is a loose edge at a corner of the covering material

Vacuum flasks

On older vacuum flasks, the most common problem is likely to be rusted metal—which makes it difficult to unscrew the flask to clean or repair it. Modern vacuum flasks are usually made of plastic.

Flasks used to carry food should always be left unstoppered when they are not being used. If a flask is to carry cold drinks or food, cool it first in a refrigerator. If hot liquid is to be carried, warm the liner with boiling water.

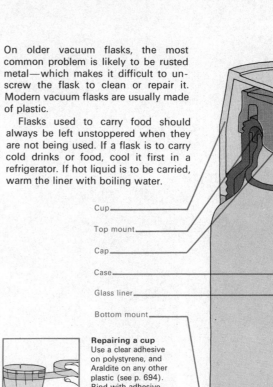

Cup
Top mount
Cap
Case
Glass liner
Bottom mount

Repairing a cup
Use a clear adhesive on polystyrene, and Araldite on any other plastic (see p. 694). Bind with adhesive tape while setting

Fitting a liner
Unscrew the top of the flask and remove the old or broken liner. Fit the new liner on the bottom mount. Replace the top mount and screw on the top of the flask body

Mending a bottom mount If the bottom cracks or splits, the liner may move about. Mend with a suitable adhesive (see p. 694). Bind until dry

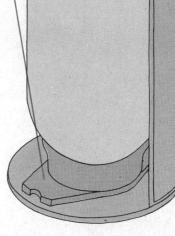

PART 4
IN THE GARDEN

Clothes lines

Maintaining a rotary clothes dryer

Do not leave a rotary clothes dryer permanently outside. If it gets wet, wipe it dry as soon as possible. Lubricate the moving parts with light machine oil every three months. If rust develops, clean the affected area down to bare metal with emery cloth and coat with zinc-galvanising paint.

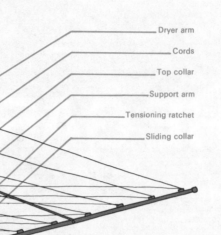

Dryer arm

Cords

Top collar

Support arm

Tensioning ratchet

Sliding collar

FITTING A PERMANENT CLOTHES POST

Dig a hole 12 in. (305 mm) square and 24 in. (610 mm) deep. Set the post in the hole and make sure that it is upright. Fill in around it with hardcore and concrete (see p. 693). Leave the concrete for a week before using the clothes line.

Materials: hardcore; concrete mix.
Tools: spade; shovel; plumbline or spirit level; wheelbarrow.

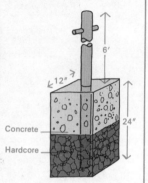

6'

12"

24"

Concrete

Hardcore

FITTING A NEW CAPPING RIVET

All rotary dryers have a sliding collar which raises and lowers the arms.

The arms are secured at the collar by capping rivets. If a rivet comes out, a new one can be obtained from the manufacturers. Secure it with the star-lock capping piece.

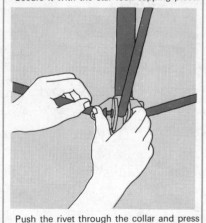

Push the rivet through the collar and press on the star-lock cap

TENSIONING THE CORD

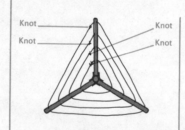

Knot

Knot

Knot

Knot

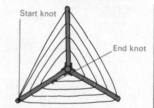

Start knot

End knot

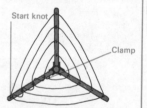

Start knot

Clamp

Separate cords Undo the knots in each length of cord. Pull the cord tightly round the sides of dryer and re-tie each length

Continuous cord Start at the outer knot and pull cord tightly to the knot on inside row. Undo the knot and re-tie it

Clamp fitting Pull cord from knot on outside arm. Undo clamp screw at centre. Pull surplus through and retighten clamp

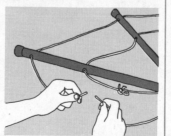

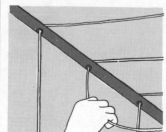

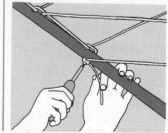

Cultivators Wheel-driven

Maintenance

There are two main types of cultivators—those in which the engine drives both the wheels and the blades, and those in which it drives the blades only. In the first type, power is transmitted through a V belt, which may wear or break.

Check the engine and transmission oil levels each week. Drain, flush and refill the transmission every 250 working hours or six months. For safety, disconnect the spark-plug before working on the machine.

Materials: belt; blades; French chalk; petrol; rag.
Tools: spanners; emery paper.

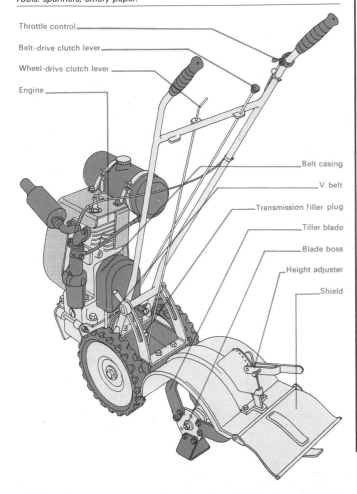

Throttle control

Belt-drive clutch lever

Wheel-drive clutch lever

Engine

Belt casing

V belt

Transmission filler plug

Tiller blade

Blade boss

Height adjuster

Shield

Replacing the belt drive

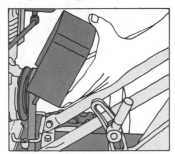

1 To remove the casing, pull its two pegs from the tubes mounted on the chassis frame of the cultivator

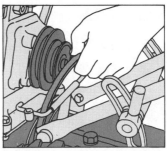

2 Release the belt-drive clutch lever. Lift the belt off the top pulley and draw it out below the machine

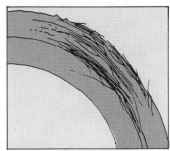

3 Examine the belt. If it is cracked or the plies have begun to separate, obtain a replacement to fit the machine

4 Clean the top and bottom pulleys with a rag and petrol. Remove any roughness with emery paper

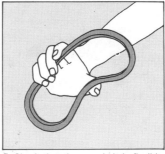

5 Check that the new belt is flexible. Coat the inside face of the belt and the pulleys with French chalk

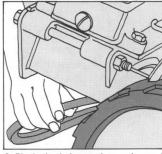

6 Pinch the belt together and pass it through the machine from below. Fit it on the bottom pulley

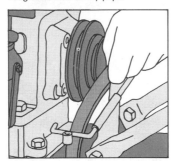

7 Draw the belt up through the machine and slide it into position on the engine drive pulley

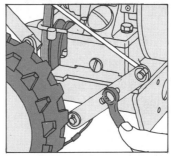

8 To ease the belt fitting or adjust its tension, undo the tensioner cam nut on the clutch arm

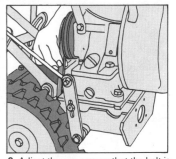

9 Adjust the arm cam so that the belt is fully tensioned when the engine is raised by the clutch lever

Cultivators Wheel-driven   Cultivators Blade-driven

Fitting new blades

1 Tip the machine forwards so that the blades are clear of the ground. Lift the shield on its hinge

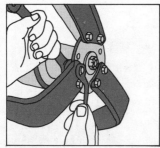

2 Check and, if necessary, replace the blades one at a time. Two spanners are needed to release the blades

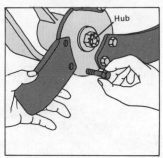

Hub

3 Undo the nuts on the two bolts holding the blade to the hub and remove the bolts and spring washers

Check for wear

4 If a blade is worn or badly damaged, obtain a new one. Do not try to sharpen a well-worn blade

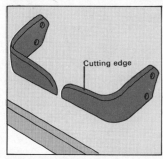

Cutting edge

5 Fit the blades with the cutting edge facing the direction they travel and pointing towards each other

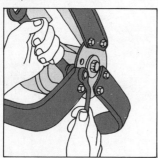

6 Bolt the blades firmly back into position. Always use new bolts, nuts and spring washers

Maintenance

On some cultivators the engine drives only the blades, but these also propel the machine forwards. The drive is taken from the engine through a belt or chain to the blades. Usually, the transmission assembly is filled with oil and sealed when the machine is made; it should need no attention unless a leak occurs. Check the engine-oil level regularly and make sure that the belt is correctly tensioned and in good condition.

Materials: parts as needed.
Tools: spanners; screwdriver.

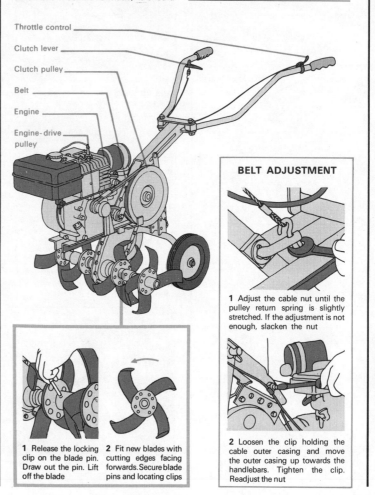

Throttle control
Clutch lever
Clutch pulley
Belt
Engine
Engine-drive pulley

BELT ADJUSTMENT

1 Adjust the cable nut until the pulley return spring is slightly stretched. If the adjustment is not enough, slacken the nut

2 Loosen the clip holding the cable outer casing and move the outer casing up towards the handlebars. Tighten the clip. Readjust the nut

1 Release the locking clip on the blade pin. Draw out the pin. Lift off the blade

2 Fit new blades with cutting edges facing forwards. Secure blade pins and locating clips

Fitting a new belt

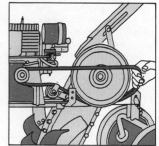

1 Release the clutch so that the belt is slack. Lift the belt off the large reduction pulley

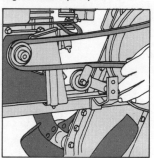

2 Hook the belt off the clutch pulley first, then remove it from the engine drive pulley

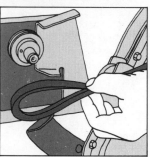

3 To replace the belt or fit a new one, pinch it together and fit it first to the engine drive pulley

Fencing Maintenance

Taking care of garden fences

To keep fences in good condition, treat them regularly with a preservative (see p. 508) and ensure that soil does not build up against the gravel boards.

Examine posts for signs of rotting (see p. 508) so that they can be replaced or reinforced in good time: repairs are more difficult and costly when a section has collapsed. Buy only pressure-impregnated posts.

To straighten a leaning fence, prop it upright temporarily and bolt the posts to concrete spurs (see p. 424).

If arris rails are broken, but not rotted, repair them with galvanised brackets or extensions.

Lapped fencing

Interwoven or lapped fencing is usually supplied in 6 ft. (1·8 m) panels. Even slight damage usually means that the whole panel has to be renewed—unless there is another damaged panel which can be stripped.

Tall panels are very likely to be buffeted by wind. In soft ground: reinforce the posts with concrete spurs.

If a fence is being renewed, set the panels on a single course of bricks with a strip of roofing felt between the bricks and the panel base to prevent rotting at ground level.

Palings

Fences which have slats attached to rectangular rails are usually painted. Re-paint every three years so that the existing coat cannot deteriorate. Use rust-proofed nails to fasten loose slats.

Other fences

Similar maintenance is needed for ranch-type fencing with broad, horizontal boards fastened directly on their posts.

Metal chain-link and plastic mesh cannot be repaired easily. Renew it if it is seriously damaged.

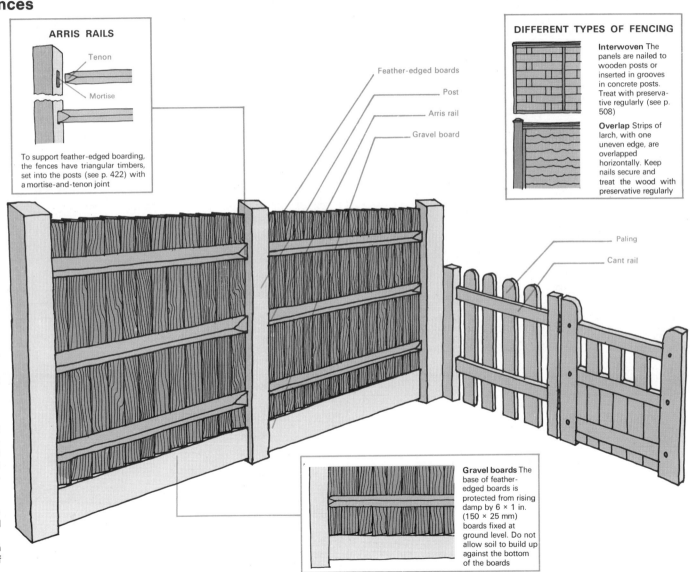

ARRIS RAILS

Tenon

Mortise

To support feather-edged boarding, the fences have triangular timbers, set into the posts (see p. 422) with a mortise-and-tenon joint

Feather-edged boards

Post

Arris rail

Gravel board

DIFFERENT TYPES OF FENCING

Interwoven The panels are nailed to wooden posts or inserted in grooves in concrete posts. Treat with preservative regularly (see p. 508)

Overlap Strips of larch, with one uneven edge, are overlapped horizontally. Keep nails secure and treat the wood with preservative regularly

Paling

Cant rail

Gravel boards The base of feather-edged boards is protected from rising damp by 6 × 1 in. (150 × 25 mm) boards fixed at ground level. Do not allow soil to build up against the bottom of the boards

Fencing Gravel boards and arris rails

Fitting a new gravel board

Fit gravel boards with their outer surfaces flush with the posts. On some fences they fit into recesses cut in the posts; on others they are nailed to blocks that are attached to the inside of the posts.

Cut new blocks, if necessary, from 2 × 2 in. (50 × 50 mm) hardwood. Fix the pegs so that their tops are in line with the bottom of the boarding, and set them back from the front of the post to allow for the thickness of the new gravel board.

Materials: gravel boards; hardwood blocks; galvanised nails.
Tools: shovel; hammer; saw.

1 Remove any rotted or damaged gravel boards. Clear away soil where new boards are to be fitted

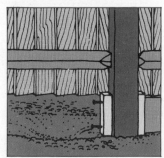

2 Cut 2 × 2 in. (50 × 50 mm) blocks, 6 in. (150 mm) long, if the old ones are broken. Nail inside posts

3 Cut the gravel boards to fit and nail them to the surface of the blocks. Replace soil

CONCRETE POSTS

1 Cut 2 × 2 in. (50 × 50 mm) pegs 24 in. (610 mm) long. Drive them 18 in. (455 mm) into soil at posts

2 Get a helper to support the pegs. Cut gravel boards to length and nail them to the pegs

Mending a broken arris rail

If an arris-rail tenon (see p. 421) has broken, but the rest of the rail is in good condition, secure the rail with either a wooden chock or a metal extension available from hardware and do-it-yourself shops. If the post is concrete, fit a new rail.

To fit a new arris rail to firmly set wooden posts, tenon one end and insert in the mortise of one post. Fix the other end, without a tenon, to the second post with a chock or bracket. If either of the posts is loose, pull it out of line slightly so that the tenons at both ends can be housed in mortises. Push the post straight after fixing again and secure it (see p. 424). When ordering new arris rails, measure the distance between the posts when they are upright. Add 3 in. (75 mm) to the measurements to allow for tenons. Treat the arris rails with preservative after shaping the tenons and before fixing them to the posts.

When a rail is broken or rotted, the adjacent rails may be in poor condition and it is often best to renew all of them at the same time.

Materials: arris rails; metal extension brackets or wood for chocks; galvanised nails and screws; preservative.
Tools: axe; saw; brace and bit if needed; brush; screwdriver.

WOODEN CHOCKS

1 Cut four 1 × ¾ in. (25 × 20 mm) strips, long enough to fit round the mortise. Screw on three

2 Brush with preservative. Drop the rail into the slot and secure with the fourth strip on the top

METAL BRACKETS

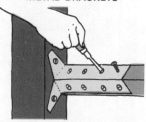

Extension To fit a metal extension bracket, secure the arms to the post with galvanised screws, then screw both faces to the arris rail

Bracket Use galvanised screws to fasten a bracket to one side of a broken rail. Get a helper to push the two pieces of rail tightly together and screw through the bracket into the other side

FITTING TENONS

1 Use an axe or billhook to shape the ends of a new arris rail if they are to fit into mortises

2 Brush preservative liberally into the mortises. Treat the faces and the tenon of the new rail

3 Insert the rail and secure the joint by a galvanised nail through the post into the tenon

Fencing Posts

Removing a wooden post

In wet or clay soil, an old wooden post may be difficult to remove, even after the topsoil around it has been loosened and dug out. The easiest way to remove a post that seems to be stuck is to use a strong rope and a stout piece of timber to lever it out. Remove at least one board on each side of the post to allow a rope to be passed round the post.

Support the run of fencing on each side of the post and free the arris rails before lifting the post.

Materials: 4 in. (100 mm) nails; stout rope; bricks; timber for levering. Tool: hammer.

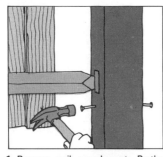

1 Remove soil round post. Partly drive a 4 in. (100 mm) nail into each side 12 in. (305 mm) from ground

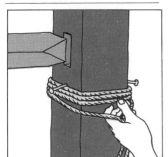

2 Tie a length of stout rope several times round the post immediately beneath the two nails

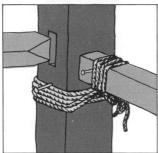

3 Hammer two nails 1 in. (25 mm) from the end of the levering timber. Tie rest of rope round timber

4 Build bricks or stone slabs about 3 in. (75 mm) higher than the nails in the post. Lever down to ease the post out of the ground. If necessary, adjust the height and position of the bricks

Fitting a new fence post

If a new wooden post has to be fitted, fasten the existing rails to it with chocks or metal extension brackets (see p. 422).

Posts usually measure 4 × 4 in. (100 × 100 mm) or 6 × 6 in. (150 × 150 mm). Fit the larger size for fencing in very exposed areas and for all fences over 5 ft (1·5 m) high. Dig a hole not less than 18 in. (455 mm) deep for the posts of a 4½ ft (1·3 m) fence.

Materials: new post; support battens; hardcore; cement, sand and aggregate (see p. 693); creosote.
Tools: claw hammer; saw; shovel; spirit level.

1 Tack a batten to the top of the arris rails on each side of the post to support the fence during repair

3 Saw through the old rails close against the post to be removed. Dig around the base and lift out the post

6 When the concrete is hard, attach the rails to the posts (see p. 422). Remove battens

2 Remove one feather-edged board on each side of the post and remove both gravel boards

4 Dig out soil to make a hole 12 in. (305 mm) square. Fit new post and ram in 6 in. (150 mm) of hard core

7 Cut the top of the post at an angle, sloping down towards the arris rails, and creosote the top

5 Mix enough concrete (see p. 693) to fill the rest of the hole. Shovel it in evenly and tamp down

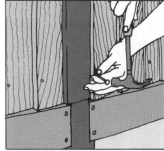

8 Refix the feather-edged boards on both sides of the new post and fasten the two gravel boards

Fencing Posts

Fencing Feather-edged boards

Supporting a post with a spur

If a post has rotted at or below ground level but is otherwise sound, fit a spur to support it. Concrete spurs can be bought with fixing holes already made. If a wooden spur is used, treat it with preservative (see p. 508) before fitting it.

Fix the spur to the rotted post with 6 in. (150 mm) coach screws or 8 in. (200 mm) coach bolts, obtainable from builders' merchants.

Materials: spur; coach screws or bolts; cement, sand and aggregate, hard core (see p. 693).
Tools: shovel; spirit level; hammer; spanner.

1 Dig a hole about 12 in. (305 mm) square and 24 in. (610 mm) deep around the post

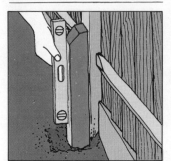

2 Set the spur in the hole, with its longer straight face against the post. Check that it is upright

3 Ram some hard core round the base of the spur, and fill the hole with concrete (see p. 423)

4 A week later, partly hammer in coach screws or drill holes through the spur and post and fit bolts

5 Use a spanner to tighten the screws or to secure the nuts, pulling the post tightly against the spur

Fitting new boards

Feather-edged boards are most likely to rot at the top and bottom where damp can penetrate the grain. After many years they may also warp and split if they have not been treated regularly with preservative.

One or two boards can be replaced without disturbing the whole section of fencing. But if several boards are damaged in different parts of a section, renew the whole run.

Push the thin edge of each feather-edged board under the thicker edge of the board next to it. To fit single boards, loosen the nails holding the adjacent thick edge. Always use galvanised or non-ferrous nails to fix the boards and hammer them into the centre of the arris rail.

When replacing a whole section of fencing, make sure that the feather-boards overlap each other by at least ½ in. (13 mm).

To achieve even overlapping along a run, use a gauge made of a piece of wood ½ in. narrower than the individual boards. At the end of the run, increase the overlap of the last three boards, if necessary, so that the final board fits closely against its post.

Materials: boards; galvanised nails.
Tools: claw hammer; punch; spirit level; improvised gauge.

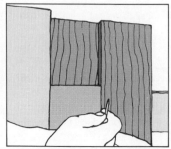

1 Nail the first board with its thick edge against the post. Position next board with gauge

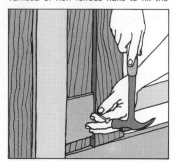

2 Nail through the overlap at top. Check the position of the lower end. Nail board to lower arris rail

3 Continue fixing the boards. Always hold the gauge against the wide edge of one board to position the next

4 Every fourth or fifth board, check with a spirit level that the boards are upright. Adjust if necessary

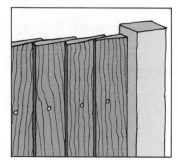

5 If the last gap is very narrow, reverse the final board so that its thick edge is against the post

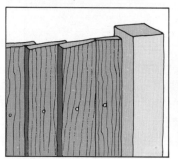

6 An alternative way to fill a small gap is to cut a strip to fit from the thicker side of a board

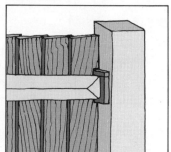

7 If an arris rail is fixed with a wooden chock, cut away the edge of the last board to fit round the chock

Fencing Woven and lapped panels

Fitting new panels or slats

It is usually possible to fit slats in a woven fence panel only if some are available from an old panel. New slats are difficult to obtain, even from the panel manufacturers, and often the only repair possible is to fit a complete new panel. Before doing so, however, find out if a local supplier has a damaged panel which could be dismantled.

Standard panels are 6 ft (1·8 m) wide. If a smaller panel has to be fitted, cut a standard one to length.

The panels are bordered by rails at top and bottom, with vertical battens on each side at both ends. The vertical battens on one side of the panel are joined to the top rail, and for this reason are longer than the battens on the other side.

Posts for woven or lapped fencing are usually 3 × 3 in. (75 × 75 mm). Use thicker posts on exposed sites. Buy wood which has been pressure-impregnated against rot (see p. 508).

Do not allow soil to pile up against the base of the panels. Keep grass growing against it trimmed. The relatively thin wood is liable to rot if exposed to constant damp.

Materials: new panel; galvanised nails.
Tools: saw; claw hammer; spirit level.

---

see p. 508

FITTING A SINGLE BOARD

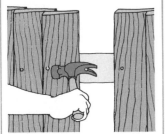

1 To fix a single board, first remove or punch in any nails on the exposed arris rails

2 Punch the nails securing the thick, outer edge of the adjacent board right through into the rail

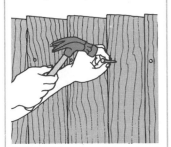

3 Slide thin edge of new board under thick edge of old. Nail through overlap

3 Use a claw hammer to remove the upright batten on each side of the surplus end of the panel

7 Saw off the surplus ends of slats and rails on the outside of the repositioned battens

4 Reposition and nail the battens inside the drawn lines. The longer batten should project at the bottom

8 Position the panel and align it with the adjacent section. When it fits tightly, hammer into place

1 To replace an odd-length panel, hold the new panel in the gap with one end overlapping the post

5 Nail the battens together through each slat. Place a slab under the panel to turn the ends of the nails

9 Nail the panel to the uprights with 3 in. (75 mm) galvanised nails. Insert three or four at each end

2 Mark the amount of overlap on both sides of new panel. Allow for depth of mortises on concrete posts

6 Support the panel evenly to avoid straining the frame and saw off the protruding end of the longer batten

Protecting posts Screw a hardwood cap to the top of the post to protect the exposed end grain

Flexible-drive units

Overhauling the cable

The extent to which a flexible-drive unit can be repaired or overhauled depends on the type of dogs fitted to both ends of the inner cable. If neither can be unscrewed, no repair is possible. If one dog can be unscrewed, the dog and inner cable can be replaced. On some models, however, it may be necessary to renew the whole inner cable when only one dog is worn or damaged. Always obtain spare parts and suitable grease from a recommended dealer who specialises in the model being overhauled.

Materials: parts as needed; grease.
Tools: Mole grips; vice.

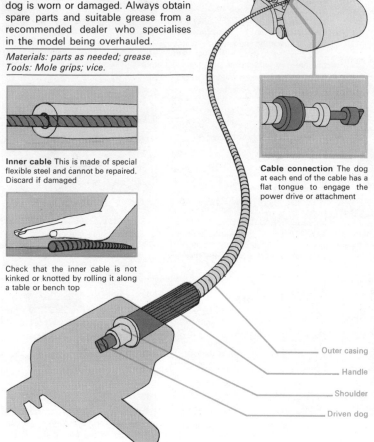

Inner cable This is made of special flexible steel and cannot be repaired. Discard if damaged

Check that the inner cable is not kinked or knotted by rolling it along a table or bench top

Drive end of cable

Cable connection The dog at each end of the cable has a flat tongue to engage the power drive or attachment

Outer casing

Handle

Shoulder

Driven dog

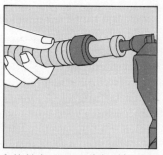

1 Hold the tongue of the drive dog in a vice and pull back the casing to expose the shoulder of the inner cable

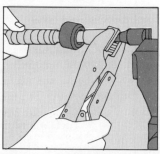

2 With the tongue still in the vice, grip the inner-cable shoulder with Mole grips. Turn it anti-clockwise

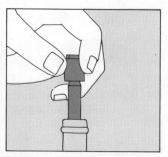

3 When it is loosened, unscrew the drive by hand. Lift off the spacing washer between dog and outer casing

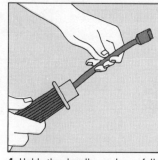

4 Hold the handle and carefully pull the entire length of inner cable from its outer casing

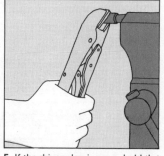

5 If the driven dog is worn, hold the shoulder in a vice to unscrew it. If it cannot be unscrewed, discard the cable

6 The inner cable is of woven steel. If it is broken or damaged, obtain a new cable

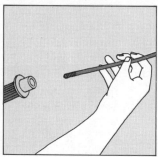

7 Fit the driven dog on the new cable. Lubricate the other end and feed it into the casing at the handle

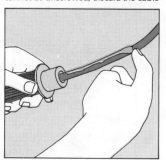

8 Keep smearing the cable with grease, about 18 in. (455 mm) at a time, and feed it into the casing

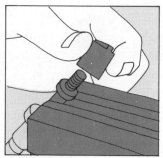

9 Hold back the free end of the casing and grip the cable in the vice. Refit the washer and drive dog

Garden drainage

Improving the drainage of a garden

Drainage can be improved easily in any garden where there is a ditch, stream or low-lying area near by: lay a system of pipes to take away the surplus water. In most town gardens, however, this is usually not possible.

Soil texture

Mix coarse sand or ashes with the soil and give annual dressings of compost. To improve the texture of clay, apply 6–8 oz. of ground lime-stone per sq. yd (250 gr per sq. m). Allow a month or two for the rain to wash in the lime and rake 8 oz. of gypsum per sq. yd (290 gr per sq. m) into the topsoil.

Raised garden

Build raised beds with side walls of brick or stone. Leave drainage holes in the walls at ground level and lay in rubble before the soil.

Rock garden

To build a rock garden on wet soil, lay rubble over the area. Top with smaller stones before placing the soil and rocks.

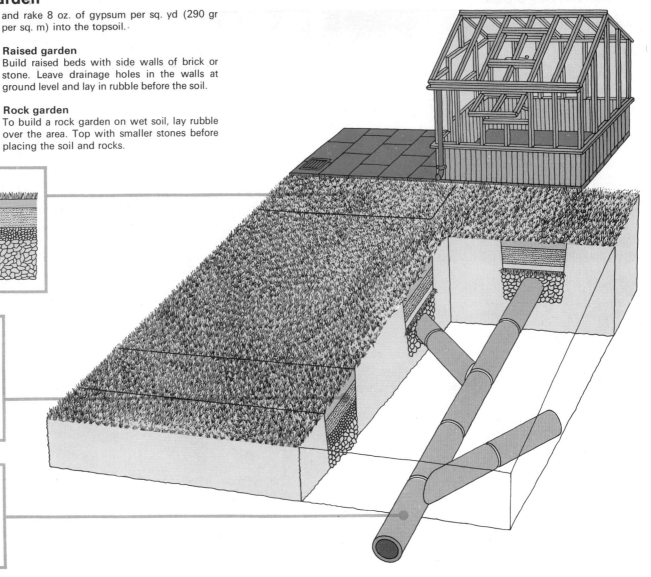

BUILDING A SOAKAWAY

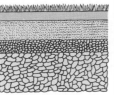

Water can be drained to a rubble-filled pit—called a soakaway—through a rubble trench or pipes.

The size of the soakaway depends on the area and nature of the soil. A pit 3 ft (915 mm) deep and 3 ft square, for example, is adequate for the run-off from a greenhouse or terrace or to drain a ground area of approximately 150 sq. ft (14 sq. m)

DIGGING A RUBBLE TRENCH

If a garden floods occasionally, dig a trench across it, about halfway down its length. If there is a slope, dig a second trench at the foot of it.

Make the trenches about 3 ft (915 mm) deep. Lay about 2 ft (610 mm) of rubble in the trench and cap it with small stones or gravel. Turn turfs upside-down on top of the gravel, or cover it with polythene sheeting

LAYING DRAINAGE PIPES

Pipes are the most efficient drainage system, but they can be laid only if there is a ditch or stream near the garden. The bottom of the trench must be slightly sloped to give a drop of about 1 ft in 30 yds (305 mm in 27 m). Allow for a 6 in. (150 mm) covering of soil or turf at the top end of the system. For example, if the trench is 130 ft long the fall must be about 18 in. (455 mm) and the outlet at the ditch end about 24 in. (610 mm) deep

Garden drainage

Laying drainage pipes

In most gardens, 3 in. (75 mm) diameter pipes are sufficient for the drainage, but a herringbone system will need 4 in. (100 mm) pipes for the central spine.

If the lower end of the trench is significantly higher than the normal water level in the stream or ditch, dig out more soil. Lay pipes slightly apart for water to enter the system.

Materials: agricultural drainage pipes; gravel or small hardcore; polythene sheeting or turfs to cover the pipes. Tools: garden line; planks; broom; turf cutter or sharp spade; wheelbarrow; spirit level.

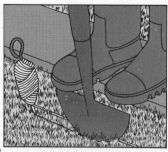
1 Fix a garden line as a guide and cut along it. Make a second cut about 7 in. (180 mm) from the first

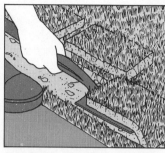
2 On a lawn, lift turfs in 12-in. (305-mm) sections. Keep them in the same order at the side of the trench

3 Pile soil in a barrow. Keep the darker topsoil separate from sub-soil for correct replacement

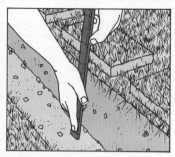
4 Check that the depth is within the limits needed to give the necessary drop along the trench

5 Brush loose soil from the grass into the trench as it is dug, otherwise the lawn surface may become caked

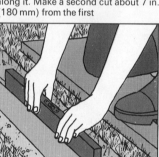
6 Check the slope by placing a spirit level on the edge of a plank. Keep the bubble just off centre

7 Lay 1 in. (25 mm) of gravel or small hardcore in the trench as a base for the drainage pipes

8 Lay the pipes centrally. Leave a gap of $\frac{1}{16}$ in. (2 mm) between them and bed them securely in the gravel

9 Check with the spirit level that the pipes are being laid in line—with the bubble just off centre

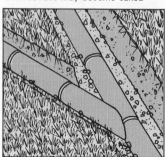
10 Slant any branch pipes down to the spine and chip the end pipe to fit. Make an entry hole in the spine

11 Place a further layer of gravel or small hardcore over the pipes. Cover with inverted turfs if possible

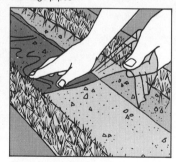
12 Alternatively, lay polythene sheeting to stop loose soil filtering into the gravel over the pipes

13 Replace the soil and firm it with the foot. Rake the top loose and re-lay the turfs slightly proud

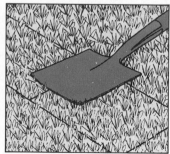
14 Firm the turfs with the back of a spade. Sweep any loose soil from the surrounding grass

Garden furniture

Care and maintenance

Allow fabric-covered garden furniture to dry naturally if possible before storing. Keep it in a well-ventilated shed or garage during the season. It is advisable in winter—because of increased dampness—to store it in the house.

Lubricate all pivots and hinges occasionally with a little thin cycle oil. Make sure that all the screws are tight. To tighten a rivet, support one side on a hard surface and hammer its head firmly.

Treat any wooden parts with a colourless preservative once a year—preferably during dry weather when the wood is absorbent.

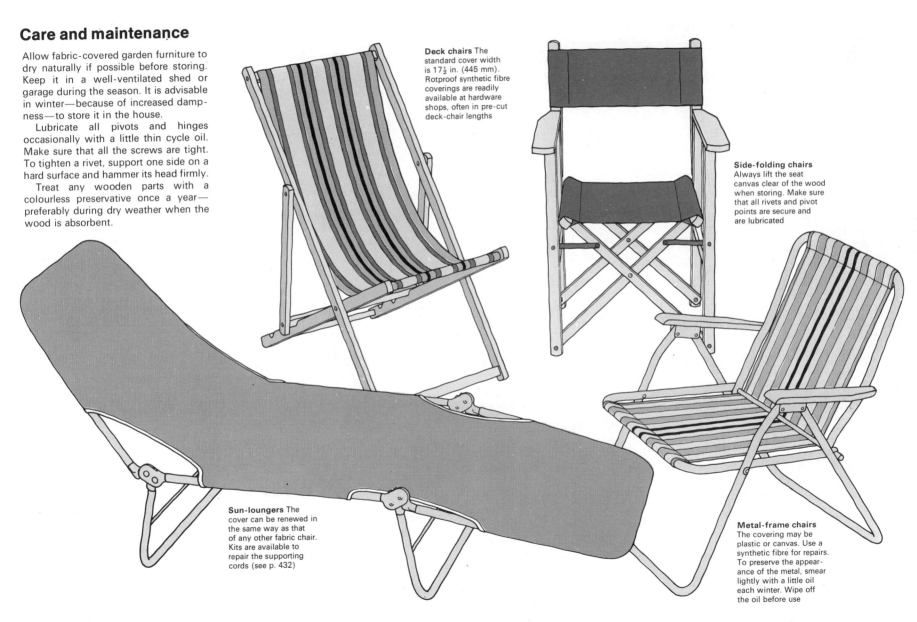

Deck chairs The standard cover width is 17½ in. (445 mm). Rotproof synthetic fibre coverings are readily available at hardware shops, often in pre-cut deck-chair lengths

Side-folding chairs Always lift the seat canvas clear of the wood when storing. Make sure that all rivets and pivot points are secure and are lubricated

Sun-loungers The cover can be renewed in the same way as that of any other fabric chair. Kits are available to repair the supporting cords (see p. 432)

Metal-frame chairs The covering may be plastic or canvas. Use a synthetic fibre for repairs. To preserve the appearance of the metal, smear lightly with a little oil each winter. Wipe off the oil before use

Garden furniture Covers

Re-covering a metal collapsible chair

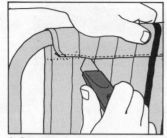

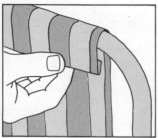

Materials: new cover strip to fit; 60-gauge matching thread.
Tools: sharp knife; tape measure; darning needle; pins.

1 Cut through the existing stitching and remove the damaged chair cover. Buy a new one to fit. Allow 1 in. (25 mm) on the length for turns

2 With the chair open, fold the new cover strip over the top bar. Make sure that it is straight. Fold under ½ in. (13 mm) of the strip

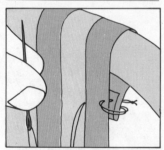

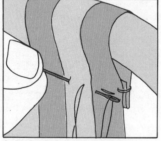

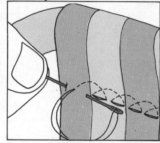

3 Double and knot thread. From the back, push needle through the fold and front of cover. Take it ½ in. (13 mm) along and push through

4 Go back ¼ in. (6 mm). Push the needle through to the front. Pull thread tightly. Take needle forwards ½ in. (13 mm) and push through

5 Go back ¼ in. (6 mm) and push through. Continue backstitching to the end of the cover strip. Finish with a double stitch at the back

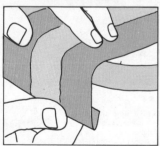

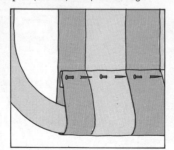

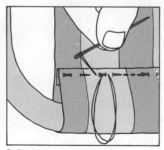

6 Take cover down behind bar at back of seat and over the top of the front bar. Fold under ½ in. (13 mm) of the front edge

7 Pin every 1½ in. (40 mm) across the folded edge. Fold and unfold the chair to check that the cover is correctly fitted

8 Backstitch across the front hem in the same way as at the top of the chair. Finish with a double stitch. Remove the tacking pins

Re-covering a deck chair

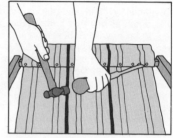

Materials: length of cover canvas.
Tools: hammer or mallet; screwdriver or old chisel; ⅜ in. (10 mm) tacks.

1 Push a screwdriver under the existing canvas and prise out tacks. Use a hammer or mallet if necessary. Remove the canvas from the chair frame

2 Measure the length of the cover and buy a new one to match. Fold one end under 1 in. (25 mm) and tuck it round the top rail of the chair

3 Hammer a tack to hold the centre of the cover on the underside of the top rail. Hammer in tacks at each end, then two more midway between

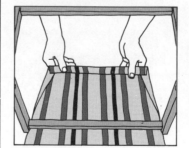

4 Take other end of cover to bottom rail, which is shorter than the top. Taper each side until it fits and fold the edge under 1 in. (25 mm)

5 Align the edge of the fold with the inside edge of the rail underneath. Tack first at the centre, then at the edges, then midway between

Re-covering a side-folding chair

Materials: $\frac{3}{8}$ in. (10 mm) tacks; cover material.
Tools: hammer or mallet; old chisel; sewing machine; knife; tape measure.

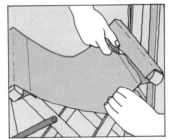

1 Use a sharp knife to cut through the old canvas along both seat edges. Take care not to damage the wooden rails with the knife

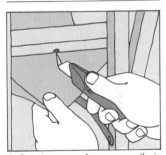

2 Cut the cover from any nails in the rails, but do not remove them. If they protrude, hammer them home gently. Do not split the frame

3 Open the chair. Measure from the outside edge of one rail and across the chair to the outside of the other. Add 2 in. (50 mm)

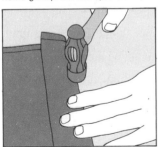

4 Turn $\frac{1}{2}$ in. (13 mm) at each long cover edge. Machine-stitch. Fold 1 in. (25 mm) at both ends and hammer the folds

5 Lay one folded end on the outside of one rail. Collapse the chair and fix the cover with six tacks. Repeat at the other rail

---

FITTING A NEW BACK SUPPORT

1 Use a hammer or mallet and an old chisel to knock out the tacks holding the cover in position on the back supports

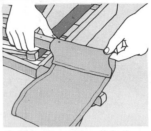

2 Slide the cover off both uprights. Use deck-chair fabric for the new back. It has selvedged edges which cannot unravel

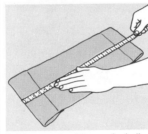

3 Measure the old cover, including the turned-over ends. Add 2 in. (50 mm) to the length and 1$\frac{1}{2}$ in. (40 mm) to the width

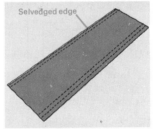

Selvedged edge

4 Use a selvedged edge for one of the longer sides. Fold it over $\frac{1}{2}$ in. (13 mm); make two $\frac{1}{2}$ in. folds on the other long side

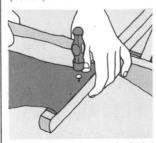

5 Machine-stitch along the folded edges. Fold one end under 1 in. (25 mm) and fix it to the inside of the back-post with four tacks

6 Wind the cover round the post and across the front of the chair. Fold the other end under, and fix to the inside of the other post

---

Fixing fitted covers

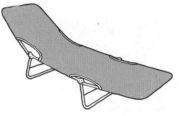

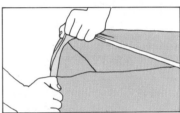

1 If a sun-lounger cover tears, partly fold the chair. Undo the retaining cords and remove the material

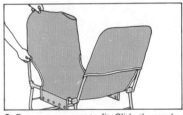

2 Buy a new cover to fit. Slide the ready-made pockets over the tubular ends of the sun-lounger

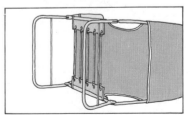

3 Lay the lounger on its side and refit the cords underneath (see p. 432) through the lacing holes in the flaps

Garden furniture Cords and tears

Replacing a broken support cord

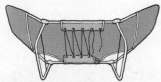

Most of the strain on a sun-lounger cover is taken by the support cord under the metal frame. If the cord breaks, it is not usually possible to make a satisfactory repair with any other kind of cord. Special repair kits are, however, obtainable from hardware shops and department stores selling garden furniture.

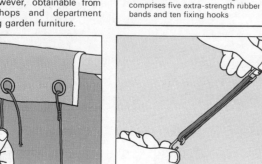

REPAIR KITS

Hook

Rubber band

The repair kit for a sun-lounger comprises five extra-strength rubber bands and ten fixing hooks

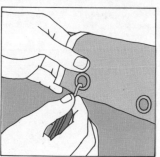

1 Remove the broken or worn cord from the eyes in the cover flaps. Check that the cover is sound

2 Fix a hook at each end of each rubber band in the sun-lounger repair kit. Leave the hooks open

3 Locate one hook in each eye of one flap. Make sure that the cover is straight

4 Working from the centre hook, stretch the bands and secure with the free hooks in the other flap

Repairing a tear at a side flap

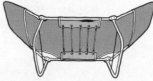

When the cover of a piece of garden furniture tears, it may be possible to repair it without discarding the whole cover. It is, however, usually necessary to remove the cover to stitch the tear.

Materials: 60-gauge thread.
Tools: scissors; darning needle.

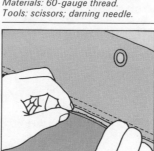

2 Fold the torn canvas about $\frac{1}{4}$ in. (6 mm) under. Taper to the edges. Butt the fold against the flap

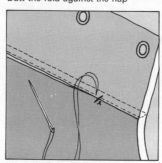

4 Pull the thread tightly and bring it down. Push it through the cover and up through flap

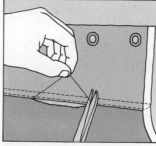

1 Cut the loose threads from the tear and pick back the stitching about $1\frac{1}{2}$ in. (40 mm) on each side

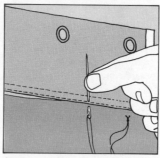

3 Use a needle with thread doubled and knotted. Start sewing $\frac{1}{2}$ in. (13 mm) from one end of the tear

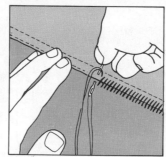

5 Overstitch (see p. 278) to $\frac{1}{2}$ in. (13 mm) beyond the folded edge. Knot and cut the thread

Patching a tear

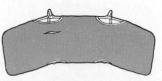

When the cover of a piece of garden furniture is torn some distance from a seam or side flap, stitching is unlikely to provide a satisfactory repair. Try to obtain a similar piece of canvas or synthetic fabric to use as a patch. If none is available, use a double thickness of an old sheet for the repair.

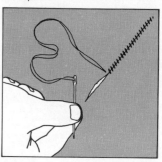

2 Fold under $\frac{1}{4}$ in. (6 mm) of the edges and overstitch (see p. 278). Do not overlap the edges

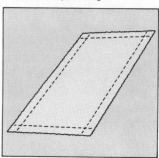

4 Fold under $\frac{1}{2}$ in. (13 mm) round the edges of the patch. Tack-stitch (see p. 278) the edges

Garden tools Shears

Sharpening and setting blades

Garden shears can cut efficiently only if their blades are correctly set and sharpened.

The blades should bow slightly away from each other along their length, but the tips should overlap. If they do not bow correctly, grip each blade in turn in a vice and bend it gently. If the points do not meet, file the heel of the shears.

Blades cannot be sharpened adequately by the amateur if they are distorted or badly chipped. Take them to a specialist.

Smear the blades with a little light oil before storing the shears for the winter.

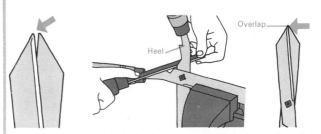

Blade tips If the tips of the blades do not overlap slightly (left), hold each blade in a vice and file the heel (centre). Check frequently and continue to file until the blades overlap slightly (right) when fully closed

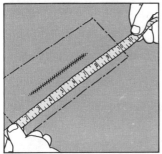

1 Remove the cover. Start stitching $\frac{1}{2}$ in. (13 mm) from the tear. First push the needle up from below

3 Finish stitching $\frac{1}{2}$ in. (13 mm) beyond the tear. Cut a patch to overlap 2 in. (50 mm) all round

5 Lay the patch on the underside of the tear and overstitch it tightly to the cover of the chair

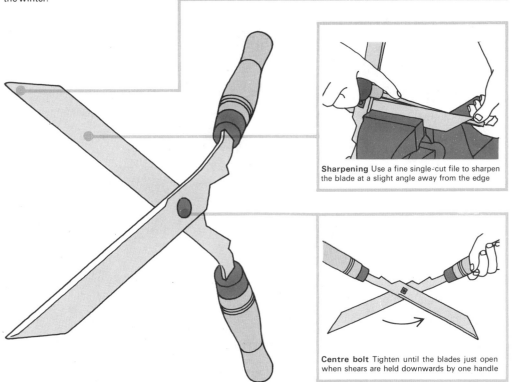

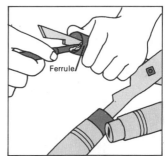

Sharpening Use a fine single-cut file to sharpen the blade at a slight angle away from the edge

Centre bolt Tighten until the blades just open when shears are held downwards by one handle

Fixing a handle

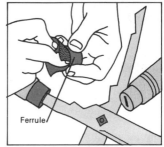

1 If a handle is loose, shake out any loose wood particles and clean the ferrule with emery cloth

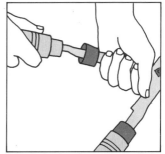

2 Clean the shaft and position the ferrule. Apply epoxy-resin adhesive to the shaft and the handle

3 Push the handle on to the shaft. Make sure that it seats in the ferrule. Tap it home with a mallet

Garden tools Spades and shovels

Fitting a new handle

The handles of spades, shovels or forks are replaceable. In most cases the handles have a standard diameter and any tool supplier can provide a replacement.

A new handle is likely to be longer than needed. Cut it to size and taper the shaft to fit the tool socket—which may be cylindrical or have two straps.

Most modern spades or forks have the handle secured by a single countersunk screw. Older types have riveted handles.

Materials: new handle; 6 in. (150 mm) wood screw.
Tools: screwdriver; handbrace and wood bit; wheelbrace and steel drills; hammer; punch; wooden mallet; plane or Surform; chisel; glass-paper; vice; saw.

REMOVING RIVETS

If the handle is riveted into the spade socket, remove the rivet.

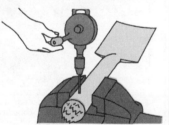

1 Centre-punch the rivet in the socket. Drill out the rivet head

2 Use a hammer and punch to drive the rivet through the handle

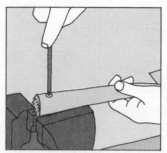

1 Rest the socket of the spade on a partly open vice. Undo the locating screw with a screwdriver

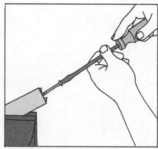

2 Screw a 6 in. (150 mm) wood screw well down into the broken end still in the socket

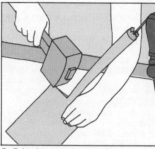

3 Grip the wood screw firmly in the vice and strike the blade top with a mallet. Draw out broken end

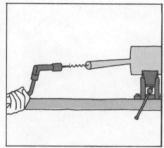

4 If the shaft still sticks, drill two $\frac{7}{8}$ in. (22 mm) holes in the end with a wood bit

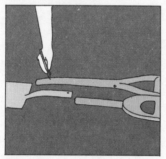

6 Lay the broken handle and spade together, next to the new handle. Mark required length on new shaft

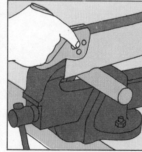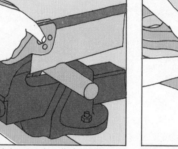

7 Hold the new handle in a vice and saw off the surplus shaft. Make sure that it is cut squarely

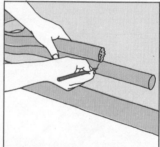

8 Lay the top section of the old handle on the new. Mark the position of the socket top on the new handle

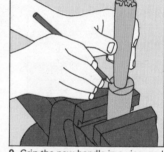

9 Grip the new handle in a vice, end uppermost. Hold the old tapered end on to it and mark the thickness

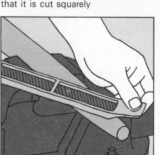

11 Grip the shaft in the vice again. Mark the end thickness on the unplaned side. Plane down

12 Use a plane or Surform to round off the squared taper to match the socket of the spade

13 Fit the shaft in the socket with handle parallel with socket top. Strike blade on wood block

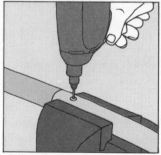

14 Drill a pilot hole and fit the locating screw. If riveted, fit a new rivet. Make sure it is flush

Garden tools Rakes and brooms

Fitting a handle on a rake or hoe

Always buy a good-quality ash handle for a rake or hoe. Softwood, although less expensive, is likely to strip and splinter.

Never try to fit the straight end of a shaft into the rake or hoe socket without shaping it: it eventually tears away from the securing screw.

Taper the end of the handle to fit the socket of the rake or hoe, drill the handle, and secure it by fixing a round-headed screw through the hole in the socket.

Materials: handle; wood screw.
Tools: pencil; plane; drill; vice; screwdriver.

Fitting a new broom handle

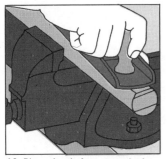

5 Remove spade from vice. Hold socket downwards and tap with a mallet to dislodge shaft

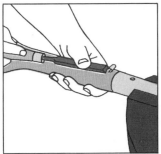

10 Plane the shaft at an angle, from the line round the shaft, to the thickness lines marked on the end

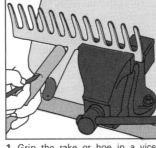

1 Grip the rake or hoe in a vice. Place the handle against it and mark the socket depth

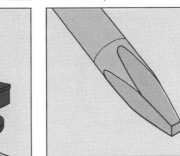

2 Plane at an angle from the mark round the handle to the end of the shaft to taper it

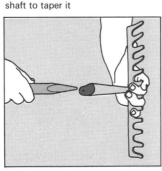

15 Shave the shaft with a chisel to get a slight taper up from the socket. Polish with fine glass-paper

3 Make sure that the taper slopes in evenly to the centre. Round off the corners to fit the socket

4 Fit the tapered end of the handle firmly into the socket. Tap the end on the ground to drive it home

5 Grip the socket in the vice. Drill a pilot hole in the handle and fit a screw through the socket hole

1 Measure the depth of the socket in the broom head in which the new handle is to be fitted

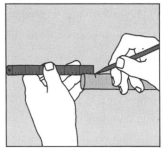

2 From the straight end of the handle measure the amount which is to be inserted in the broom head

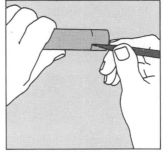

3 Continue the mark round the outside of the new broom handle. Check that line is straight

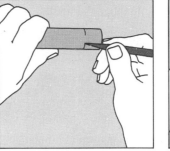

4 Measure the diameter of the broom socket and mark it in the centre of the handle end

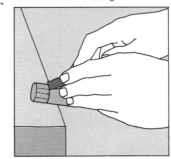

5 Use a chisel to shave down all round from the mark on the outside to the mark on the end

6 Fit the handle into the broom-head socket. Tap the handle firmly on the ground. Fit screw

IN THE GARDEN 435

Gates

Care and maintenance

When a gate is not shutting correctly, or if it is sagging or dragging along the ground, first make sure that its posts are upright and secure. Check that the hinges and screw-holes are sound. If the hinges are loose, unscrew them—or break off the screws with a cold chisel if necessary—fill the holes and fit new screws to hold the hinges. Fit new timber in place of any that is unsound, and check that the joints of the gate itself are sound. If the woodwork is parting at the joints, strengthen the gate and restore its shape with metal brackets, galvanised if possible. Several types are made; buy the heaviest gauge possible.

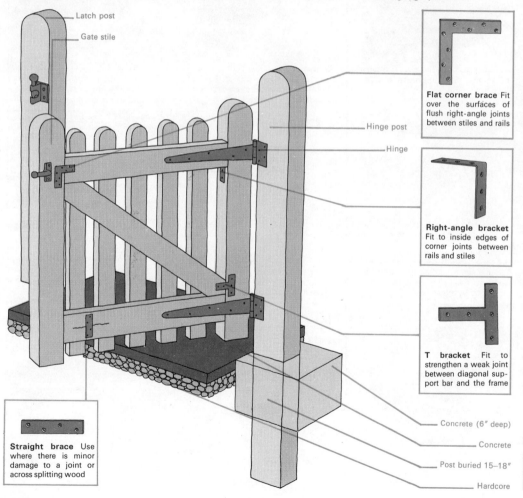

Latch post

Gate stile

Hinge post

Hinge

Concrete (6″ deep)

Concrete

Post buried 15–18″

Hardcore

Straight brace Use where there is minor damage to a joint or across splitting wood

Flat corner brace Fit over the surfaces of flush right-angle joints between stiles and rails

Right-angle bracket Fit to inside edges of corner joints between rails and stiles

T bracket Fit to strengthen a weak joint between diagonal support bar and the frame

Fitting a new post

Treat all gate posts once a year against rot (see p. 508). Occasionally push a penknife into the timber near the ground. If it penetrates easily and deeply, remove gate and post and buy a new impregnated post.

To fit the new post, dig a hole about 12 in. (305 mm) square and 15–18 in. (380–455 mm) deep. Position the post and check that it is upright with a spirit level. Nail a plank of wood on each side to support it. Adjust the supports if necessary and secure them with pegs. Cover the base with at least 9 in. (230 mm) hardcore. Top with a 6 in. (150 mm) layer of concrete.

1 If the rotted post is a hinge post, take off the gate. Dig out the post. Adjust the sound post if it is not upright and firm

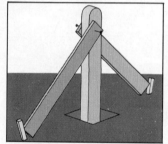

2 Dig a hole 12 in. (305 mm) square and 15–18 in. (380–455 mm) deep. Position post and nail on supports to keep it upright. Fill the hole

3 When the concrete has set, remove the supports. Wedge the gate in place and mark hinge holes on post. Drill. Pack old holes with filler

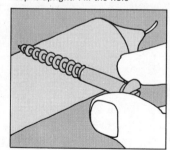

4 Roll new screws along a candle to wax them. Drive them into the filled holes to within $\frac{1}{8}$ in. (3 mm) of the surface of the wood

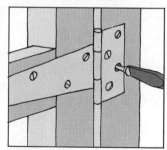

5 When the filler has set, remove the screws. Position hinges on gate and drive in screws. Wedge gate in place and screw hinges to stile

Greenhouses

Maintenance and repair

The amount of maintenance needed on a greenhouse depends on the material from which the frames are made.

Wooden frames
Wooden greenhouses need more regular and thorough maintenance than any other type. Strip and repaint softwood frames every three years. Coat red cedarwood with a water repellent every four years, and treat oak every two.

Steel frames
If a galvanised-steel greenhouse rusts, strip the paint off the affected area, treat with a rust-remover and paint on a coat of zinc primer immediately. Apply an undercoat of paint as soon as the primer has dried, then a topcoat.

Aluminium frames
Aluminium greenhouses are the easiest to maintain. They never need to be painted. When white oxide develops on the metal, leave it as a form of protection. If it is too unsightly, wash the frames with hot soapy water.

Choice of glass
Clean the glass in the greenhouse regularly with soapy water and use a syringe to force out algae from between overlapping panes.

Try to get horticultural glass for glazing: it is cheaper than the glass used in house windows. Cut each pane (see p. 202) to allow a gap of not less than $\frac{1}{16}$ in. (2 mm) each side of the frame.

Putty
Use linseed-oil putty on wooden frames; butyl or metal-casement putty on metal.

Always remove and knead all the putty from a tin at once. If there is putty left after a repair job, put it back in the tin, press it down firmly and cover with cold water to keep it soft and pliable.

ACCESS TO THE ROOF

Most side panes in a greenhouse can be reached from the ground or by using step-ladders. A ladder, however, is usually needed to repair high roof panes. Never lean it directly on the glass or on the glazing bars.

If possible—for example, if there is a convenient ventilator—work from inside on a step-ladder.

1 Screw long battens to the gable ends of a timber greenhouse. If the frame is metal, tie the boards in place. Position the ladder and make sure that it follows the angle of the roof. Secure the foot of the ladder

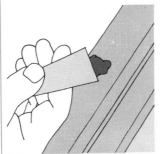

2 On a wooden greenhouse, remove the boards after the repair and fill the screw holes

---

Glazing methods

On most timber-framed greenhouses the glass is bedded on putty and secured by headless pins. On the roof, the bottom of one pane overlaps the pane below. On the walls of the greenhouse, the panes are butted together.

Use brass or galvanised pins; rust on plain steel pins can crack the glass.

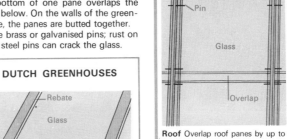

DUTCH GREENHOUSES

Rebate

Glass

Wooden stop

Some timber greenhouses are glazed without putty: the wood is grooved to hold the glass

Pin

Glass

Overlap

Roof Overlap roof panes by up to $\frac{1}{2}$ in. (13 mm). Pin at bottom of each pane to prevent sliding and to secure top of pane below

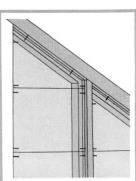

Walls Follow the original method. If the frame is rebated, use pins only if the pane is a loose fit

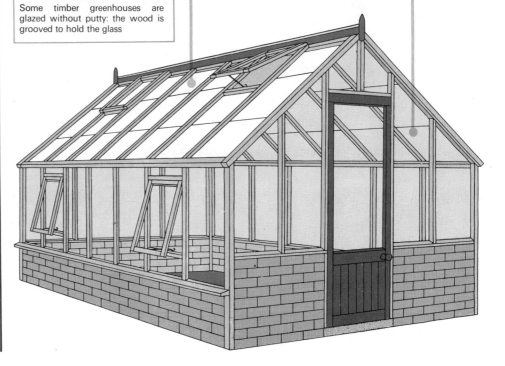

Greenhouses Timber frames

Glazing with putty

Replace panes only in dry weather: putty does not stick to wet wood. If the frame is softwood, always paint on a coat of white-lead paint before applying new putty.

When hammering in pins, slide the hammer across the glass to avoid breaking it. If the hammer head is rounded, use a punch to tap in pins at the overlaps.

Materials: glass; brass or galvanised pins; putty.
Tools: hammer; pliers; old screwdriver or chisel; punch, if hammer head is rounded; steps or ladder; cloth; putty knife.

1 Remove the pins and broken glass. Take off the old putty with a blunt screwdriver or chisel

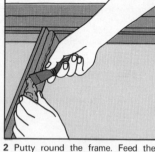

2 Putty round the frame. Feed the putty on with one hand and press it home with a putty knife

3 Lay the glass in place. Bed it firmly, but press only where it is backed by putty

4 Fix one pin tightly against the bottom of the pane at each side to ensure that the pane cannot slip

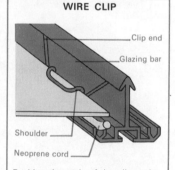

5 Fix pins just above the overlap at each side to keep the pane pressed firmly against the putty

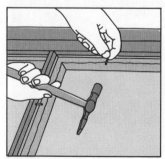

6 If a top pane is not held in a rebate, secure it at the ridge with two pins to prevent it lifting

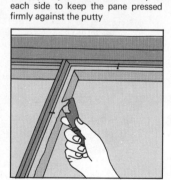

7 On the outside, hold the blade of a putty knife flat against the glass and remove excess putty

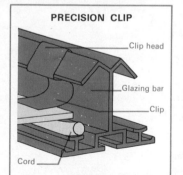

8 Inside, hold the blade against the side of the glazing bar and slide it along to remove putty

Greenhouses Metal frames

Glazing methods

Some metal-framed greenhouses are glazed with putty (see p. 439), but in most the glass rests on neoprene or foam-rubber strips. In all cases the glass is held by clips—pliable aluminium, sprung wire or metal strips. Buy clips to match those on the rest of greenhouse glazing.

When fitting a new pane, position the clips to match the positions of those on adjacent panes.

WIRE CLIP

Clip end
Glazing bar
Shoulder
Neoprene cord

Position the ends of the clip under the glazing bar. Press the shoulder over the edge of the glass

PRECISION CLIP

Clip head
Glazing bar
Clip
Cord

Push the lower part under the glazing bar against the glass. Press the head over the bar

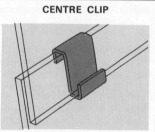

CENTRE CLIP

To reduce the risk of glass breakage, slide the clips to the edges of each new pane. Slide them back when the glass is fitted

CENTRE-LEG CLIP

Centre leg

1 Fit the clip under the bar with the legs resting on top of the glass

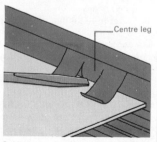

Centre leg

2 Use a screwdriver blade to push the centre leg into the gap between the frame and the glass

Glazing with putty

The pliable aluminium clips used for holding glass may be unserviceable if they have been straightened. If new clips are not available, cut replacements from a thin sheet of zinc.

Materials: glass; butyl or metal-casement putty; clips or thin zinc.
Tools: wire brush; putty knife; stepladder; cloths; side cutters; screwdriver.

Straight clips Use straight clips to hold each pane at the centre of its bottom edge and at the sides and top of the frame

T clips Use T clips to support the sides of each pane at the bottom of its overlap

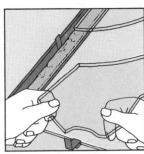

1 Straighten the clips on the broken pane with a putty knife. Remove the remaining glass

2 Scrape out the old putty and remove all clips. Clean metal with a wire brush

3 Apply butyl or metal-casement putty round the frame. Bed it well down into the angle of the frame

4 Press straight clips into frame angle. Bend to shape with a screwdriver and cover with putty

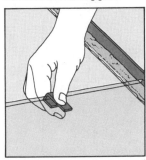

5 Bend a clip over the centre of the top edge of the existing pane below the gap

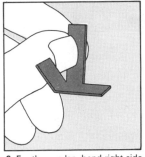

6 For the overlap, bend right side of one T clip and left side of another. Bend up legs of both

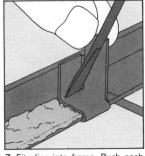

7 Fit clips into frame. Push each bent leg against top of panel below. Bend legs on to the glass

8 Position the new pane in the frame. Press it firmly but gently down on to the putty bed

9 Bend up the end of the straight clip which was previously fixed at the centre of the pane below

10 Wipe off any putty from the vertical faces of the clips at the top and sides of the frame

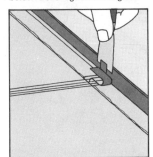

11 Bend the side clips up over the overlapping glass. Bend the remainder of T shape over the leg

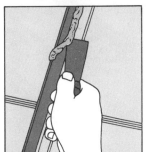

12 Trim surplus putty from both sides (see p. 438). Wipe off finger marks with a damp cloth

Hedge trimmers

Maintenance and lubrication

A hedge trimmer may be powered either by its own electric motor or by a flexible drive from a mower or cultivator. On most trimmers, only one blade moves and there is one gear unit: where both blades move, each has its own unit. Always disconnect the trimmer from its power source before attempting to overhaul it. Keep it well lubricated. Clean it after use.

Materials: parts as necessary; grease as specified by maker; oil; screws or rivets.
Tools: screwdriver; spanner to fit blade bolts; wire brush; fine single-cut file; oil-stone; vice.

Replace the blade-driving block if the slot is worn. Pack it with grease

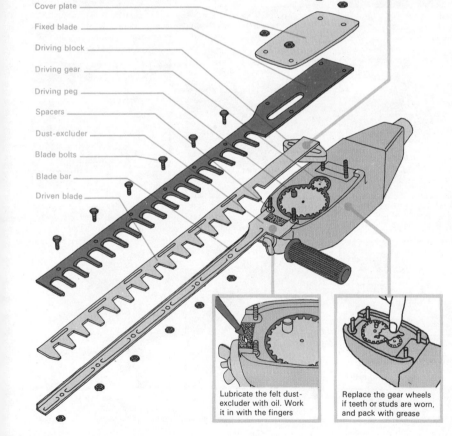

Cover plate
Fixed blade
Driving block
Driving gear
Driving peg
Spacers
Dust-excluder
Blade bolts
Blade bar
Driven blade

Lubricate the felt dust-excluder with oil. Work it in with the fingers

Replace the gear wheels if teeth or studs are worn, and pack with grease

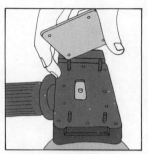

1 Undo and remove the four nuts holding the gearbox cover. Lift the cover off the trimmer

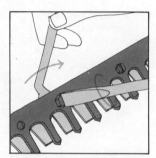

2 Remove the blade bolts. Note the position of the concave washers under the blade bar

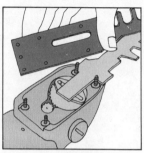

3 Carefully lift the fixed blade from its four studs. Do not dislodge the spacers on the studs

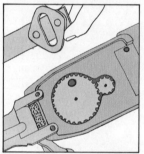

4 Lift the driven blade off the peg on the driven gearwheel. Lay the gear unit aside for the time being

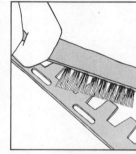

5 Remove any congealed clippings from the surfaces and teeth of both blades with a wire brush

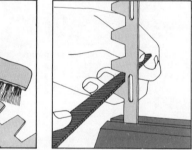

6 Grip the driven blade in a vice. File its teeth sharp. Do not alter the angle of the teeth edges

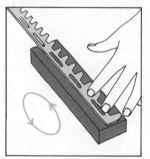

7 Remove burrs from the back of the teeth by rubbing round and round on an oil-stone

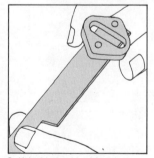

8 If the blade-drive block is worn, remove it. Obtain a replacement part and screw or rivet it in place

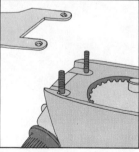

9 Remove the spacers from the two front studs. Prise up and remove the blade *(continued)*

Hoses

10 Brush the blades and bar thoroughly with paraffin. Leave them wet, as a protection against sap

11 Replace the blade bar and spacers. Fit the driven blade in position, its slot on the drive peg

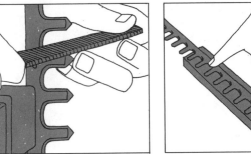

12 With the fixed blade in a vice, sharpen the teeth with a file. Retain the original angle

13 Remove any burrs from the fixed-blade teeth by rubbing the back of it on an oil-stone

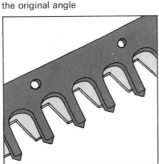

14 Fit the fixed blade, flat face downwards. Line up the bolt holes in the two blades and the bar

15 Tighten the nuts, then undo them slightly so that the bolts can just be turned by hand in their holes

Fitting a hose union

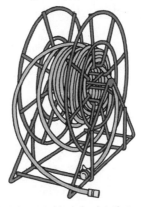

To make a good, leak-free joint between lengths of plastic or rubber hose it is advisable to use interlocking connectors, called compression joints. Some joints have a snap connection; others have a screw fitting.

As an alternative to using a compression fitting for repairing a damaged hose, cut out the faulty section and rejoin it with a piece of copper tubing which has the same outside diameter as the internal bore of the pipe. Secure joint with two screw-adjusted clips.

Materials: fittings as necessary.
Tool: sharp knife.

1 To join two lengths of hose, first trim squarely across the ends of the hose with a sharp knife

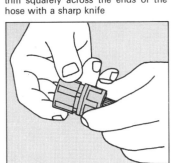

3 Push the parts together and screw the threaded ring on to the connector body. Repeat with the other length

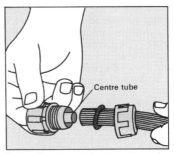

2 Fit the threaded ring, then the expansion ring on to one length. Push connector centre tube into hose

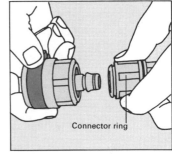

Snap connectors To connect two fittings, push together. To release, twist and pull the connector ring

TYPES OF HOSE CONNECTORS

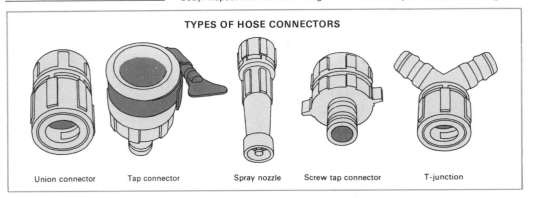

Union connector   Tap connector   Spray nozzle   Screw tap connector   T-junction

Ladders

Lawn-edge trimmers

Care and maintenance

Do not attempt any major repairs which affect the strength and safety of a ladder—for example, the replacement of rungs or stiles. Special repair techniques are required for such work.

Proper maintenance, however, is important. Do not leave a ladder outdoors: store it on the wall of a damp-free shed or garage. If it has not been used for some time, buy some wood preservative and saturate the ladder woodwork. Allow it to dry for at least 24 hours and apply a coat of clear varnish. Never paint a ladder, for this hides defects which could cause an accident.

If the ladder has aluminium rungs, dampness is less likely to damage it. But check for splits at the stiles where the wood may swell or contract. If the sliders and brackets of an extending ladder work loose frequently, have the ladder checked by an expert: the wood may be rotting.

Materials: wood preservative; clear varnish.
Tools: hammer; screwdriver; spanner; paintbrush.

Rung On an old or second-hand ladder tap each rung with a hammer. Engage an expert to replace any faulty rungs

Slider Check the sliders and brackets in summer, when the wood has contracted. Tighten their nuts or screws if necessary

Tie rod Tighten loose rod nuts with a screwdriver. If the rod is held by rivets, tap them firmly with a hammer

Stile Even small splits are potentially dangerous, especially those near rungs. They must be repaired by an expert

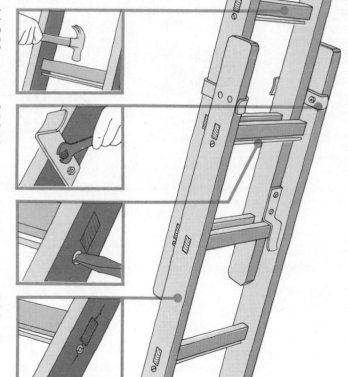

Fitting a new blade

Lawn-edge trimmers have a bar blade with a cutting tip at each end. Always switch off the battery master switch and the operating switch at the handle before attempting any repair.

1 Make sure that both switches are off. Undo the knurled screw on the cover

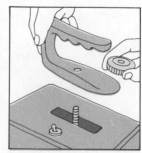

2 Remove the blade cover. Undo the top screw securing the handle and battery cover

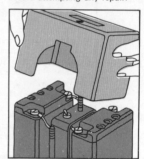

3 Lift the cover away from the machine. Check that the batteries are undamaged

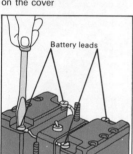

Battery leads

4 Undo the four battery terminal screws. Bend back the leads to both batteries

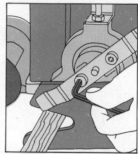

5 Place a piece of wood in the guide bar to stop the blade turning. Undo blade bar screws

6 Remove the blade. Check that the screws holding the guide bar are tight

7 Fit a new blade with its cutting edge facing the machine and away from the cover

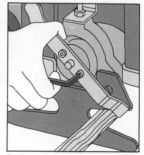

8 Use a piece of wood to stop blade turning and tighten blade screws. Do not overtighten

Lawn mowers Cylinder cutters

Maintenance and lubrication

The same general rules for maintenance apply to all types of cylinder mowers—sidewheel and roller-driven, hand-pushed and powered. For additional advice on maintaining powered machines, see p. 450 onwards.

Lubrication varies according to the make of mower. Some require grease, some oil; others need little or no lubrication, as the bearings are lubricated during manufacture and sealed for life. Consult the maker's handbook for identification of the lubrication points and information on the correct materials to use.

Generally, a mower should be oiled or greased after every eight hours of mowing. Lubricate the machine thoroughly before storing it for the winter.

Never put a mower away without at least cleaning the blades, wiping them with an oily rag and cleaning the deflector plate. Ideally, clean the whole machine.

Materials: oil and grease.
Tools: oil-can or grease gun; screwdriver or spanner to remove the drive casing; scraper to remove grass; straight-edge and hammer.

The cutting mechanism of a cylinder mower. For that of rotary mowers, see p. 459

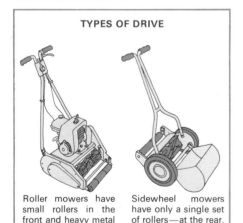

TYPES OF DRIVE

Roller mowers have small rollers in the front and heavy metal rollers at the rear which drive a cutting cylinder

Sidewheel mowers have only a single set of rollers—at the rear. The cutting cylinder is driven directly from the wheels

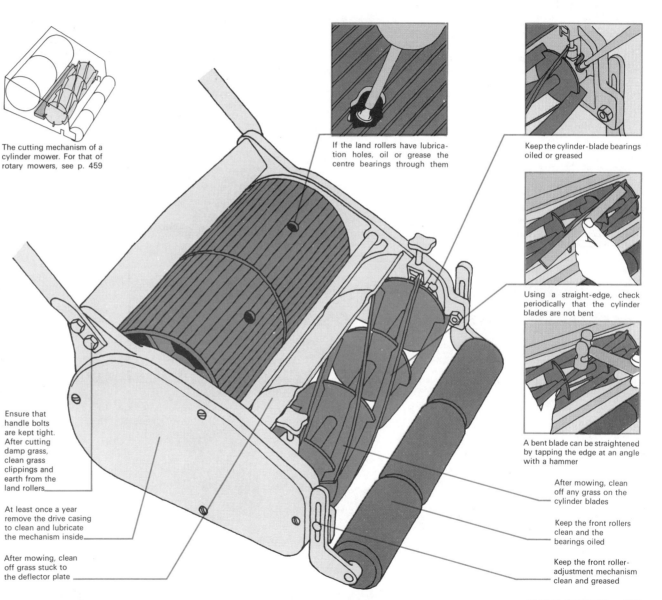

If the land rollers have lubrication holes, oil or grease the centre bearings through them

Keep the cylinder-blade bearings oiled or greased

Using a straight-edge, check periodically that the cylinder blades are not bent

A bent blade can be straightened by tapping the edge at an angle with a hammer

After mowing, clean off any grass on the cylinder blades

Keep the front rollers clean and the bearings oiled

Keep the front roller-adjustment mechanism clean and greased

Ensure that handle bolts are kept tight. After cutting damp grass, clean grass clippings and earth from the land rollers

At least once a year remove the drive casing to clean and lubricate the mechanism inside

After mowing, clean off grass stuck to the deflector plate

Lawn mowers Cylinder cutters

Adjusting the height of cut

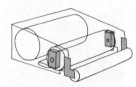

The height at which a lawn mower cuts grass depends on the distance between its fixed bottom blade and the ground. This is governed by an adjustment on the mower's front roller bracket. If the mower is pivoted downwards on the brackets, the blades are nearer the ground and the grass is cut short. If it is pivoted upwards, the bottom blade is lifted from the ground, allowing the mower to tackle longer grass.

On some machines it is possible to make the adjustment accurately on a calibrated scale. On others the adjustment has to be made by trial and error, or by measuring the roller height accurately each side.

Tool: spanner.

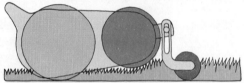

1 When grass is very long, it should be cut twice. Mow first with the bracket adjustment at the top calibration

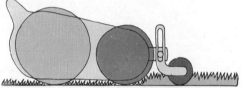

2 Move the mower downwards on the adjusting bracket and cut again to get the grass at the required height

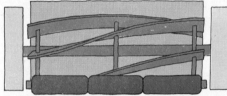

3 Make sure that the mower cuts the grass evenly. The front roller must be parallel to the bottom blade

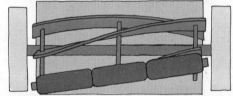

4 If the roller is higher at one side than the other, the mower cuts in ridges. Loosen the bracket and straighten

FOUR WAYS TO ADJUST FRONT ROLLERS

The roller brackets may be held at each side by bolts. Slacken them with a spanner

Undo the lock-nut at each end and adjust the roller with the thumb screws

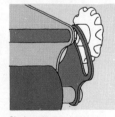

Slacken the knurled knob and pivot the roller bracket on its support bar

Turn the hand screw to operate the adjusting lever that is connected to the roller

Adjusting the blades

To cut efficiently, the cylinder and bottom blade of a lawn mower must be adjusted correctly—either by pivoting the bottom blade or by raising or lowering the cylinder. If the blade and cylinder are too far apart, they cannot cut the grass. If they are too close, the cylinder may not turn. When the blades are adjusted, ensure they are sharp. If they are badly chipped, fit new blades. When the blades have to be removed on a powered mower, drain off the petrol and oil before turning it over, and disconnect the plug lead.

Tool: spanner.

METHODS OF ADJUSTMENT

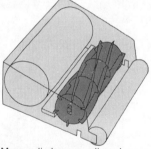

Many cylinders are adjusted on a shaft by a screw at each side

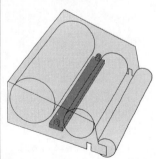

On some mowers, the bottom blade can be pivoted

1 Slacken the lock-nut on the adjusting screw at each end of the cylinder. Undo the two screws slightly

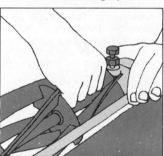

2 Pull the cylinder up and down. If there is excessive play, replace the cylinder bearings (see p. 446)

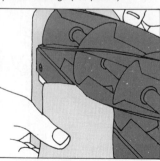

3 Gradually tighten both adjusting screws until the blades can cut cleanly through paper. Tighten the lock-nuts

Sharpening the blades

There is a comparatively inexpensive fitting on the market that can be used to sharpen the cylinder blades of hand and powered mowers.

You clip the fitting on to the static bottom blade of the mower, stick a strip of self-adhesive abrasive paper on to the fitting, and raise the mower off the ground. Rotation of the cylinder blades against the abrasive will give a uniform sharp edge along the length of each blade.

The fitting can be obtained for 10, 12, 14, 17 and 18 in. widths, and replaceable abrasive strips are available for all sizes of the fitting.

Back-lapping

Without such a fitting, sharpening is best done by back-lapping – turning the blades backwards in order to grind them against the static bottom blade. Do not attempt to sharpen a cylinder against a badly worn bottom blade.

Remove the drive casing before starting work and stand the mower on wooden blocks to raise the blades clear of the ground. Readjust the blades from time to time to ensure continuous contact with the static blade.

If the mower has a belt drive, the belt can be left in place, provided the clutch is disengaged. Turn the cylinder with a wheel-brace, or with a speed-brace and socket, fitted to the end bolt. For turning the cylinder of a side-wheel mower, make an improvised tool by cutting slots in a box spanner as shown on p. 449.

Materials: coarse grinding paste.
Tools: screwdriver to remove the drive casing; bolt to fit the gear wheel, or speed-brace and socket or wheel-brace to fit the nut on the cylinder shaft.

HOW TO TURN THE BLADES

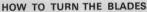

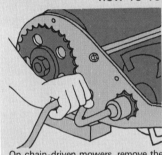

On chain-driven mowers, remove the chain (see p. 450). Use a brace and socket to turn the sprocket nut on the end of the cylinder shaft

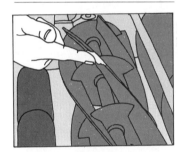

Some gear-driven mowers have a specially tapped hole in the roller gear. Screw in a bolt to make a handle and secure it with a nut

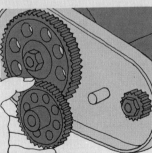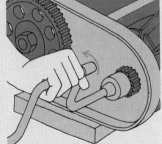

For easy turning on a gear-driven mower, slide the central idle gear off the shaft to prevent the roller assembly turning. Fit a brace and socket to the nut on the end of the shaft; turn the blades in the direction shown

1 Adjust the blades until they touch. Apply grinding paste to each blade and sharpen by rotating the cylinder backwards, grinding the blades together

2 When grinding is finished, wipe each blade, including the bottom one, to clean off the paste. Adjust the cylinder as shown on opposite page

Fitting a new bottom blade

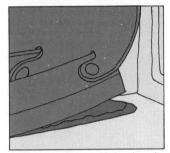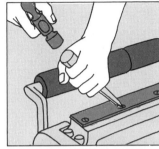

1 Fit a new bottom blade when the old blade becomes rounded and is beyond resharpening

2 To loosen a tight screw, place a punch in the slot of the screw-head and strike it with a hammer

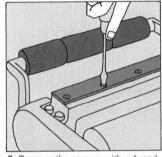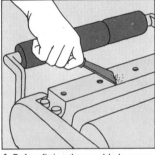

3 Remove the screws with a broad-bladed screwdriver and lift the bottom blade off the blade block

4 Before fitting the new blade, scrape the blade block clean to give it a smooth, flat surface

5 If the new blade is coated with a protective paint, clean off to bare metal before fitting it

6 Use new securing screws to fit the new blade to the block, tightening them as much as possible

Lawn mowers Cylinder cutters

Replacing cylinder bearings

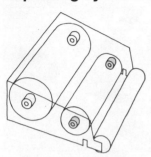

If a cylinder mower cuts unevenly or makes a grating noise when used, the cylinder-shaft bearings may be worn. Slacken the cylinder-adjusting screws (see p. 444) and lift the blades. If there is play, fit new bearings. Always remove the spark-plug before working on a power mower.

Materials: two ball-races; two felt seals; grease; oil.
Tools: screwdriver; spanner; mallet; hammer; punch; levers; vice.

Land roller
Bearing assembly
Spacer
Tension spring
Cylinder gear
Idler shaft
Idler gear
Gear casing
Dowel key
Roller gear

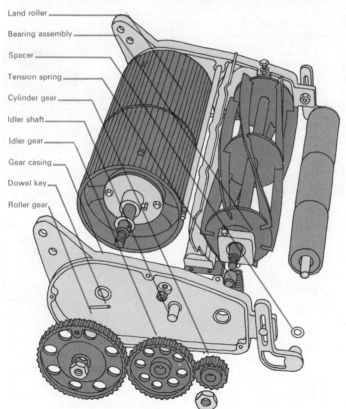

1 Undo the screws or bolts securing the cover at the side of the mower. Remove the cover

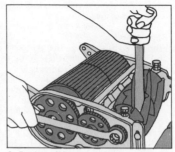

2 Push a hammer handle into the blades to lock them. Undo the cylinder and roller gear nuts

3 Some roller and gear shafts have dowel keys. Punch them out and remove the three gear wheels

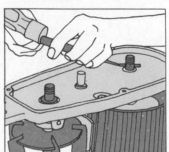

4 The roller shaft may have a dowel key beneath the wheel. Use a hammer and punch to tap it out

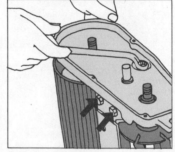

5 Undo the retaining nuts on the casing and also remove the bolts holding the bottom blade block to it

6 Remove the casing and, if one is fitted, the spring between the casing and the bearing assembly

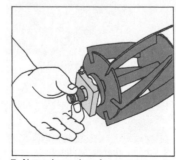

7 Note the order of any spacers or washers on the shaft near the bearing assembly. Remove them

8 Holding the bearing assembly with one hand, tap the shaft gently with a mallet to free it

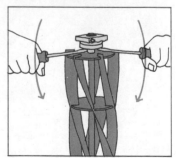

9 At the other end, use two levers to prise the bearing assembly off the cylinder blade shaft *(continued)*

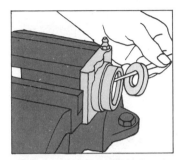

10 Put each bearing assembly in a vice and tap off the cap. Prise out the felt seal and discard it

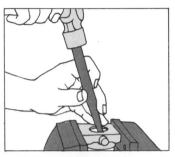

11 Hold the assembly in the top of the vice and use a hammer and punch to tap out the ball-race

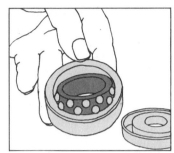

12 Push the inner ring of the ball-race upwards to check the ball bearings for signs of wear

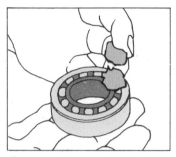

13 When refitting or replacing a ball-race, smear grease between the balls and the two rings

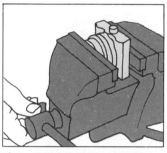

14 Position the ball-race with care and use the vice to squeeze it back into the bearing unit

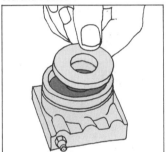

15 Use a new felt seal. Soak it thoroughly in clean oil and fit it into the bearing assembly

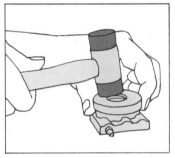

16 Clean the bearing seal cap, position it and tap it gently back on to the bearing assembly

17 Tap the bearing assemblies back on to the ends of the shaft from which they were removed

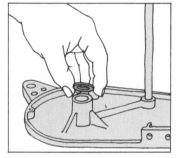

18 Start to reassemble the mower by replacing any spacers and washers removed from the casing

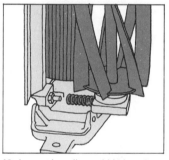

19 Lower the roller and blade unit on to the casing, making sure the spring is in position

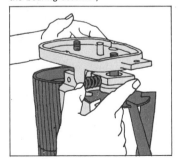

20 At the other end, fix the spring to the bearing assembly, compress it and fit the casing

21 Align the bolt holes on the casing with the holes in the bottom blade block. Replace the bolts and tighten

22 Screw down the cylinder adjusters to get the shaft central in its hole. Replace the spacers

23 If a dowel key is fitted on the roller shaft, replace it and position the gear wheel on it

24 Refit the other gears. Lock the blades with a hammer. Tighten the nuts and secure the casing

Lawn mowers Cylinder cutters

Overhauling the freewheel on a roller mower

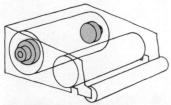

The blades of a roller mower are driven by a shaft inside the roller. As the mower moves forwards, pawls engage with a ratchet to turn the shaft. When the mower is pulled back, the pawls slip over the ratchet and the shaft does not turn. If the blades fail to turn, the freewheel is faulty.

Materials: ratchet; pawls and springs; oil; rag.
Tools: spanners; mallet; thin pliers; punch; screwdriver.

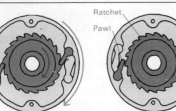
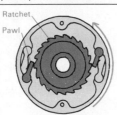

Forwards: ratchet engaged   Backwards: ratchet free

Ratchet
Pawl

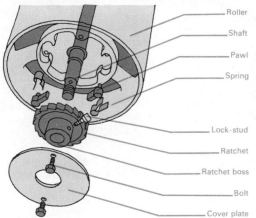

Roller
Shaft
Pawl
Spring
Lock-stud
Ratchet
Ratchet boss
Bolt
Cover plate

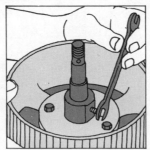

1 Remove the roller (see cylinder bearings, p. 446). Unscrew the driving shaft lock-stud

2 Hold the roller in one hand and tap the end of the shaft with a mallet to free it

3 Set aside the half of the roller containing the shaft. Unbolt the cover plate on the other half

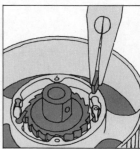

4 Remove the pawls and their springs with pliers. The ratchet should then lift off easily

Check for wear

5 If the ratchet or the pawls are worn, or if the springs are cracked or weak, obtain new parts

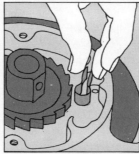

6 Fit the spring with its head away from the pawl-peg hole and its long tongue nearer the ratchet

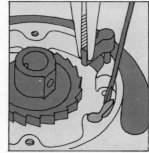

7 Hold the spring back with a screwdriver, and fit the pawl with its peg in the hole

8 Apply some oil to lubricate the mechanism. Never use grease; it may cause the pawls to stick

9 Clean the inside of the cover plate and replace it. Tighten the two retaining bolts

10 Refit the roller on the shaft. Use a punch to turn the shaft until the stud holes are in line

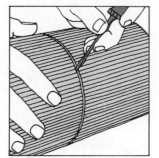

11 Check that the two rollers are close together. They should be able to turn independently

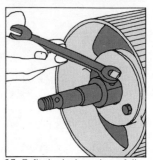

12 Refit the lock-stud carefully. Overtightening may cause the ratchet boss to crack

Overhauling the freewheel on a side-wheel mower

Inside each wheel is a gear ring which meshes with a pinion on the blade shaft. As the wheel moves forward, the pinion turns. A pawl is so fitted in the blade shaft that it falls against a flat edge inside the pinion, causing the shaft to turn also. When the wheel moves back, the pawl falls the other way, and slips over rounded edges. If the wheels do not drive the blades, the freewheel is faulty. The shaft does not turn in the pinion.

Materials: pinion or pawl; oil; rag; grease.
Tools: pliers; screwdriver.

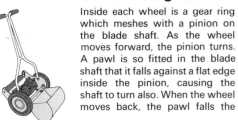

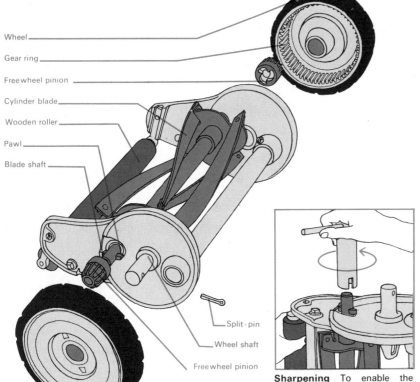

Wheel
Gear ring
Freewheel pinion
Cylinder blade
Wooden roller
Pawl
Blade shaft

Split-pin
Wheel shaft
Freewheel pinion
Wheel cap

1 Prise off the wheel cap with a screwdriver. Pinch the split-pin ends and push it out

2 Remove the wheel from the shaft and check that its gear ring is not chipped or damaged

3 Use a screwdriver to scrape the congealed grease and grass-cuttings from the cogs

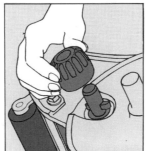

4 Pull or unclip the freewheel pinion from the blade shaft. Clean and examine its cogs

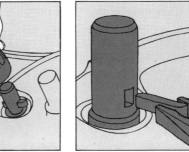

5 Use a pair of pliers to remove the pawl from its housing slot in the cylinder

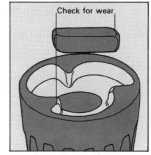

Check for wear

6 If the sharp edges of the pawl or the lugs inside the pinion are worn, as here, replace the pawl

Sharpening To enable the blades to be turned (see p. 445) for sharpening, make up a tool from an old box spanner, cutting slots in one end with a hacksaw to engage the pawl

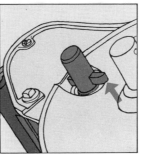

7 Refit the pawl in its slot, with a rounded end facing forwards and downwards

8 Correct fitting of the pawl determines whether its flat edge meets the flat pinion lug

9 Replace the pinion and check by hand that it operates the blade shaft. Replace the wheel and cap

Lawn mowers Cylinder cutters

Adjusting chains and replacing sprockets

Most powered mowers—and some hand-operated machines—are chain driven. In time the chains are likely to wear or stretch and knock against the chain case. On powered machines, the chain which drives the cylinder shaft can be adjusted by moving a tensioner bracket. With other types, the only repair possible is to remove the chain and shorten it by removing a link (see p. 573). Special half-links can be bought if the correct length cannot be obtained by removing full links.

Check the sprockets when the chains are removed from a mower. If they are worn or distorted, they are likely to damage the chain.

Materials: chain, links, sprockets and nylon tensioner pad, if needed; two wooden blocks.
Tools: pliers; spanner; rivet extractor, if necessary.

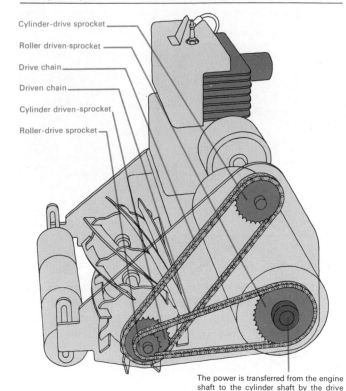

Cylinder-drive sprocket
Roller driven-sprocket
Drive chain
Driven chain
Cylinder driven-sprocket
Roller-drive sprocket

The power is transferred from the engine shaft to the cylinder shaft by the drive chain. A separate clutch usually engages the driven chain to operate the roller and move the mower forwards

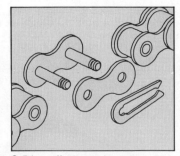

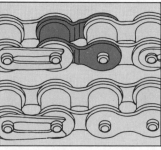

1 The chain should fit tightly on the sprockets (left). If there are gaps (right) the chain needs tightening

2 Prise off the spring clip which secures the chain connecting link. Separate the two parts of the link

3 Take out one link and refit the chain (bottom). If it is now too short, fit a half-link (top)

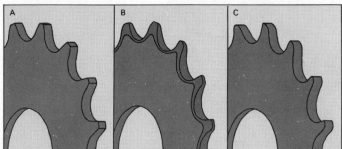

4 Check that the sprocket teeth are sharp and flat (A). If any sprocket face has worn near the teeth (B), or if the tips of the teeth have become rounded (C), obtain a new sprocket to fit the mower. Remove the chain

5 Remove the sprocket and fit a new one. It may be held by a split-pin or by a nut and spring washer

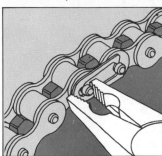

6 Fit the chain round one sprocket and position the ends on the other. Refit the connecting link (see p. 573)

7 On a powered mower, loosen the nut holding the tensioner bracket. If the nylon pad is worn, fit a new one

8 Press the tensioner down against the chain until the chain is just taut. Tighten the bracket nut

Maintaining pulleys: replacing a belt

When a new mower belt has to be fitted, make sure that it matches the old one in width, length and thickness. If necessary, take the belt to the dealer for positive identification. If one part of the old belt is excessively worn, check the pulleys before fitting the replacement. Adjust the tension spring so that the blade pulley turns freely within the belt when the clutch is disengaged.

Materials: belt; emery cloth; French chalk.
Tools: spanners; scraper; screwdriver.

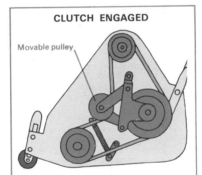

CLUTCH ENGAGED

Movable pulley

The belt runs round three fixed pulleys. When the mower is operated, the belt is held taut by a movable pulley

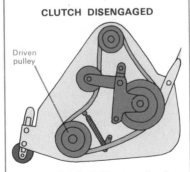

CLUTCH DISENGAGED

Driven pulley

Releasing the clutch lifts the pulley from the belt, allowing the driven pulley to revolve freely within the belt

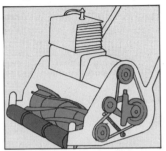

1 Remove the belt cover. Make sure the clutch is released to disengage the movable pulley

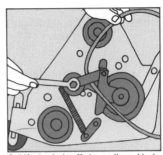

2 Lift the belt off the pulleys. Undo the bolt securing the movable pulley and remove the pulley

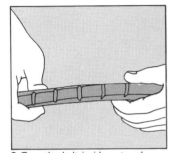

3 Turn the belt inside-out and examine the running surface. If it is cracked or worn, as here, replace it

4 If the plies have stripped and the belt starts to come apart, examine each pulley for rough surfaces

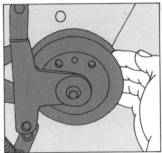

5 Run the fingers inside the pulleys to feel for roughness on the sides and in the base

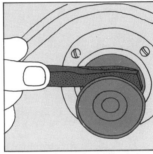

6 Fold a piece of emery cloth to fit and clean thoroughly around the inside of each pulley

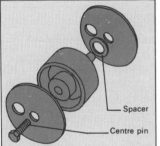

7 Examine the movable pulley. If its sides are loose, take out the centre pin and fit new spacers

Spacer

Centre pin

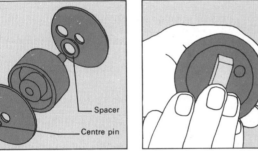

8 Clean the sides and hub of the pulley with an old chisel. Reassemble, and refit the centre pin

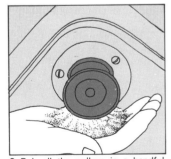

9 Rub all the pulleys in a handful of French chalk to enable the drive to run free when disengaged

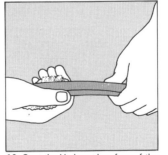

10 Coat the V-shaped surface of the belt by pulling it through a handful of the French chalk

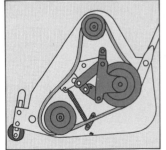

11 Loop the belt round the three fixed pulleys. Refit the movable pulley and tighten the centre bolt

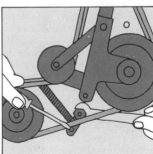

12 Engage the pulley. Undo the adjusting nut and push the bracket to tension the belt correctly

Types of clutches

A lawn-mower clutch is designed to transmit power from the engine to the cutting and roller mechanisms—and to disconnect the power when necessary.

Most mowers have more than one clutch. The main one, near the engine, drives the cutting cylinder. It is controlled by a lever on the handlebars (multi-plate clutches, see p. 456) or by the speed of the engine (centrifugal clutches, see p. 454).

A secondary mechanism, called the dog clutch (see p. 453), usually connects the drive from the main clutch of the mower to the rear roller to drive the mower forwards.

A third—called the overrun clutch (see p. 457)—may be fitted on the end of the cylinder. It operates automatically as a freewheel unit to allow the mower to be drawn backwards while power is still being transmitted to the cylinder.

Belt drive

The clutch on a belt-driven mower is a pulley system (see p. 451) which can be moved up and down to tension or slacken one of the belts. When it is released, the pulleys revolve freely without driving the belt and the roller.

How to check for a faulty clutch

If the mower roller or cutting cylinder is not being driven efficiently, it is likely that one or more of the clutches is worn and faulty.

Some faults which appear to be at the clutch, however, may be caused by a broken chain or drive belt. Remove the casings protecting them and check that they are in good condition. If the chain or belt is broken, fit a new one (see pp. 450, 451).

Before trying to trace a fault, disconnect the spark-plug lead from the plug so that the engine cannot start if the cylinder or roller is turned with a clutch engaged.

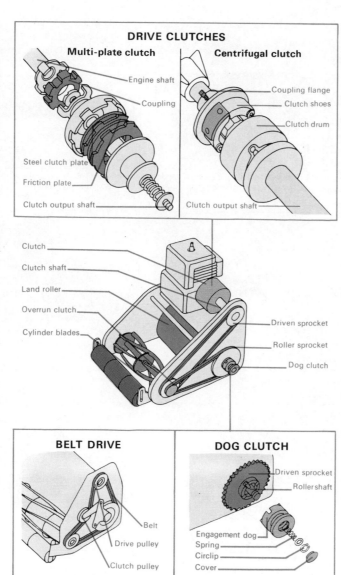

DRIVE CLUTCHES

Multi-plate clutch — Engine shaft, Coupling, Steel clutch plate, Friction plate, Clutch output shaft

Centrifugal clutch — Coupling flange, Clutch shoes, Clutch drum, Clutch output shaft

Clutch, Clutch shaft, Land roller, Overrun clutch, Cylinder blades, Driven sprocket, Roller sprocket, Dog clutch

BELT DRIVE — Belt, Drive pulley, Clutch pulley

DOG CLUTCH — Driven sprocket, Roller shaft, Engagement dog, Spring, Circlip, Cover

FINDING THE FAULT

Symptom	Checking order	Action
Engine starts, but the clutch shaft does not revolve	Worn coupling between the engine crankshaft and the clutch shaft	Fit a new rubber coupling (see p. 456)
	Loose or missing locking-bolt at the coupling	Fit a new locking-bolt if the threads are stripped
	Cracked flange	Renew the coupling flange
	Broken engine crankshaft or clutch shaft	Renew shaft on engine or clutch (see p. 456)
Clutch shaft turns, but the blades are not driven	Slipping clutch	Adjust the clutch (multi-plate clutch, see p. 456); (centrifugal clutch, see p. 454)
	Worn clutch plates or shoes	Fit new metal and friction clutch plates (see p. 456) Fit replacement clutch shoes (see p. 454)
	Faulty chain or belt drive	Fit new chain (see p. 450) Fit new belt (see p. 451)
	Faulty overrun clutch	Overhaul (see p. 457)
Blades turning but not being driven	Dog clutch not correctly engaged	Engage the dog clutch on the end of the roller drive shaft (see p. 453). Check that the clutch engagement dogs are not damaged. Fit new parts if necessary
	Broken drive shear-pin	Fit new pin (see p. 453)
	Slack belt	Re-tension the pulley (see p. 451). Fit a new belt if necessary
	Faulty chain or belt drive to the dog clutch	Renew chains or belts if necessary (see pp. 450, 451)
	Broken dog-clutch shear-pin	Fit new shear-pin (see p. 453)

Overhauling a dog clutch

On some mowers the clutch is operated by pushing in a knob at the chain belt cover. This meshes a part called the operating dog with a driving dog and pin on the shaft. They are held together as the shaft turns. If they separate, the mower stops. When this happens in normal running, check the faces for wear. Normally, the dogs are forced apart when the blades strike a stone. If they are not, the pin holding the sprocket to the shaft is designed to shear, which will prevent damage to the engine.

Materials: shear-pin; dogs; circlips.
Tools: screwdriver; circlip pliers; pliers; hammer; punch.

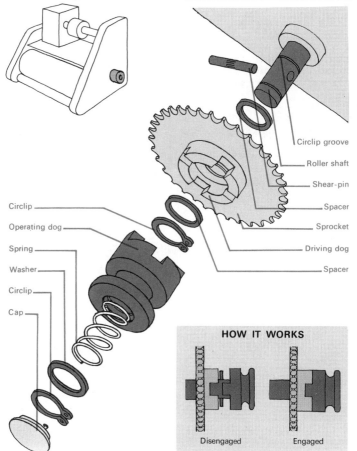

Circlip groove
Roller shaft
Shear-pin
Spacer
Sprocket
Driving dog
Spacer

Circlip
Operating dog
Spring
Washer
Circlip
Cap

HOW IT WORKS

Disengaged   Engaged

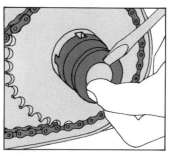

1 Remove the chain cover (see p. 446). Use a screwdriver to prise the centre cap off the clutch knob

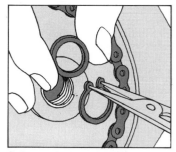

2 Open and remove the circlip with the circlip pliers, holding the washer and spring in place. Remove them

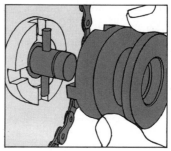

3 Pull the operating dog off the roller shaft. Store all the parts in order, to help with reassembly

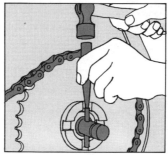

4 Punch out the shear-pin—or, if it is broken, the remaining part of it—from the slot in the shaft

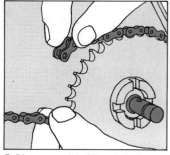

5 Disconnect the drive chain (see p. 450) and remove the chain from the sprocket. Retain the connecting link

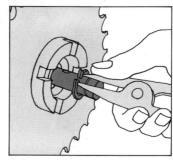

6 Remove the second circlip from its groove on the shaft and take the spacer from the inside of the driving dog

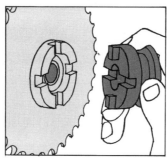

7 Examine the edges of both dogs for wear. If the operating dog is damaged, it must be replaced

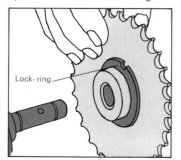

Lock-ring

8 A worn driving dog can be replaced if secured by a lock-ring. If not, replace the complete sprocket assembly

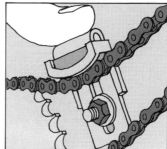

9 Fit a new shear-pin if the previous one was broken. Replace the chain and adjust its tension (see p. 450)

Overhauling a centrifugal clutch

On some mowers, the clutch engages automatically as the engine speed increases. A carrier plate, driven by the engine, revolves inside a drum on the roller shaft. As the throttle opens, two shoes on the plate are flung outwards by centrifugal force. They engage the drum and drive it and the roller shaft. If the blades turn irregularly, check the shoes for wear.

Materials: clutch shoes; bushes; pivot-pins; petrol. Tools: spanner; pliers; screwdriver; hammer; punch; mallet; fine glass-paper.

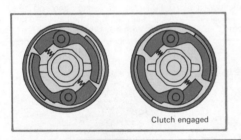

Clutch engaged

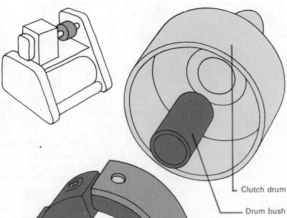

The spring adjusting screws have a screwdriver slot at each end. The countersunk head must be fitted from inside the shoe

- Clutch drum
- Drum bush
- Shoe lining
- Clutch shoe
- Tension spring
- Spring adjusting screw
- Carrier bush
- Washer
- Shoe pivot-pin
- Split-pin
- Carrier plate
- Lock bolt
- Hub keyway
- Shaft key
- Engine shaft

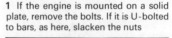

1 If the engine is mounted on a solid plate, remove the bolts. If it is U-bolted to bars, as here, slacken the nuts

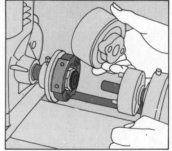

2 Gently tap the engine back along its mounting with a mallet to separate the clutch drum and shoe assembly

3 The clutch drum is held by two studs. If there is excessive play at the shaft, remove the drum

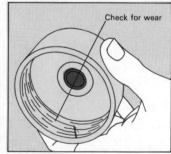

Check for wear

4 Clean the drum thoroughly in petrol. If the inside is seen to be scored or worn, fit a new drum

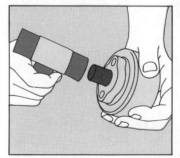

5 If there is play at the shaft or if the drum bush is worn, tap out the bush and fit a replacement

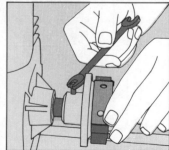

6 Remove the lock bolt which holds the shoe carrier plate in place on the end of the drive shaft *(continued)*

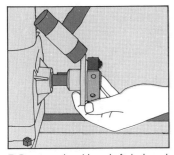

7 Because the drive shaft is keyed, the carrier plate may be a tight fit. Gently tap it free with the mallet

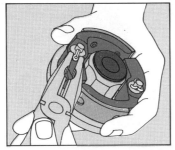

8 Use pliers to close the ends of the split-pins holding the shoes on the pivot-pins. Remove the split-pins

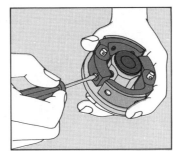

9 To ease the tension on the adjusting springs, undo the screws as far as it is possible

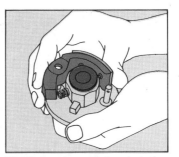

10 Lift the shoes off the pivot-pins, easing them off carefully so that the springs do not get lost

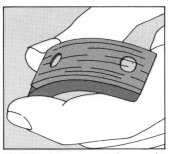

11 If the shoes are worn down to the rivets, remove the adjusting screws on the underside and keep them

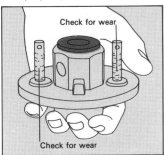

12 If the pivot-pins have been worn by the movement of the shoes, punch them out and rivet in new pins

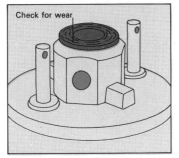

13 If the bush on the carrier plate is worn, it should be replaced. Tap it out with a hammer and punch

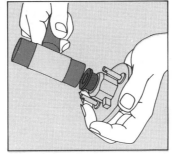

14 Position a new bush on the carrier plate boss and tap it home firmly and evenly with a mallet

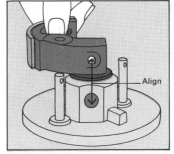

15 Fit adjusting screws into the new shoes. Put one shoe on its pin, with the hole and screw aligned

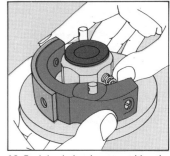

16 Push back the shoe to position the spring between the adjusting screw and the hole in the boss

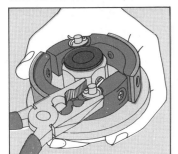

17 Fit the other shoe and spring. Replace the washer on each pivot-pin. Fit the split-pins holding them

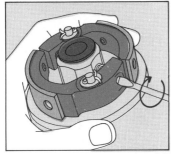

18 Give the adjusting screws one full turn. They may have to be readjusted if the clutch slips when it is used

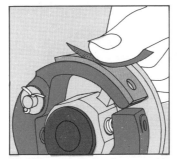

19 Refit and lock the shoe assembly on the shaft. Clean the shoe linings with fine glass-paper to remove dirt

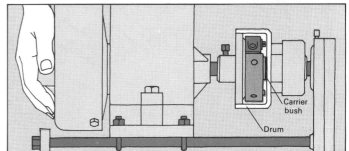

20 Refit the drum on its two studs on the drive shaft. Slide the engine until the carrier bush is hard against the inside of the drum. Draw the engine back slightly, so that the drum can revolve freely. Refit the bolts

Lawn mowers Clutches

Overhauling a multi-plate clutch

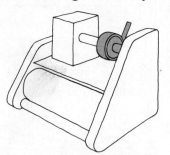

A multi-plate clutch has two steel plates and two friction plates. The friction plates rotate all the time the engine is running, but they cannot turn the blades until the clutch is engaged and they are pressed against the steel plates fixed to the driven shaft.

If the steel plates become rusted or oily, or the linings of the friction plates wear, the clutch slips.

Materials: clutch plates; rubber coupling; shaft key; emery cloth; petrol.
Tools: spanners; feeler gauge; pliers.

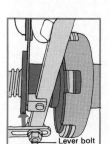

Clutch adjustment
Engage clutch and slacken lever bolt. Place a ·010 in. feeler between the thrust ring (arrowed) and pad. Move lever until pad and ring are pinching the feeler. Tighten the lever bolt

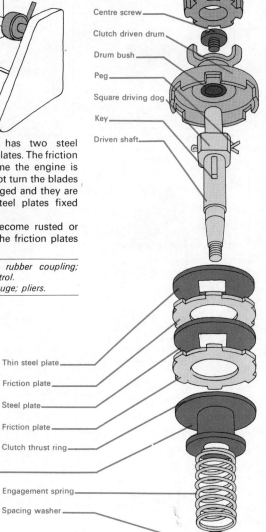

Rubber drive coupling
Centre screw
Clutch driven drum
Drum bush
Peg
Square driving dog
Key
Driven shaft

Thin steel plate
Friction plate
Steel plate
Friction plate
Clutch thrust ring

Engagement spring
Spacing washer

1 Undo the engine mounting bolts. Gain access to the clutch by removing or sliding back the engine

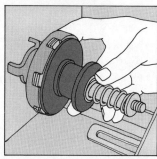

5 Pull the clutch assembly out of the bearing housing. Remove the washer at the spring end

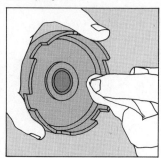

9 Clean the inside of the drum with a petrol-soaked rag. Renew the hub bush if it is worn (see p. 454)

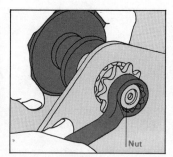

2 Remove the drive chain (see p. 450). Hold the clutch unit and take off the sprocket unit

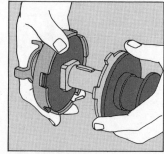

6 To dismantle the clutch, remove the spring and thrust ring. Pull out the four clutch plates

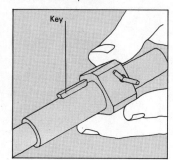

10 If the key on the driven shaft is worn or bent, pull it out with pliers and fit a new one

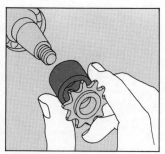

3 Remove the spring washer and slide the sprocket and its collar off the end of the shaft

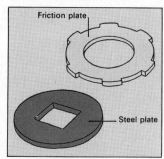

Friction plate
Steel plate

7 Clean the steel plates with emery cloth. Renew the friction plates if they are worn or chipped

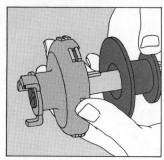

11 Replace the drum on the shaft and reassemble the unit, fitting the thin steel plate first

4 Undo the adjusting bolt and re-move the lever. If its thrust pad is worn, rivet on a new one

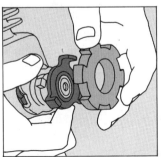

Drum

8 Undo the centre screw at the end of the driven shaft. Remove the clutch drum from the shaft

12 Before replacing the engine, check the rubber drive coupling on the engine shaft. Renew it if perished

Overhauling an overrun clutch

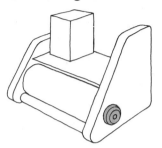

Most powered mowers have a free-wheel unit—called an overrun clutch —on the drive end of the cylinder shaft. When the mower moves for-wards, with the engine running, the chain turns the blades. When the mower is pulled backwards, the over-run mechanism frees itself automati-cally and—although the engine still drives the chain—the cylinder stops.

If the freewheel stops working, the most likely cause is that its parts have become worn or dirty.

Materials: parts as needed.
Tools: spanner; hammer.

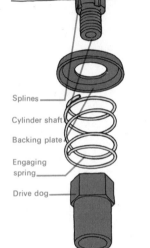

Splines

Cylinder shaft

Backing plate

Engaging spring

Drive dog

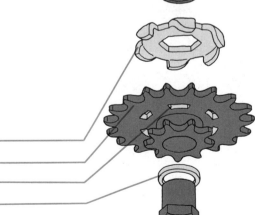

Overrun dog

Sprocket

Web

Washer

Sprocket nut

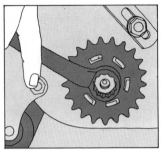

1 Remove the chain and jam the blades with a hammer handle. Undo the sprocket nut

2 Remove the nut and its washer. Slide the sprocket and overrun dog off the drive dog

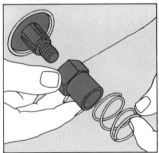

3 Remove the engaging spring and drive dog. Clean the splines on the end of the cylinder shaft

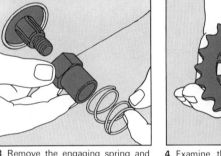

4 Examine the sprocket teeth and webs. If they are worn, fit a new sprocket unit

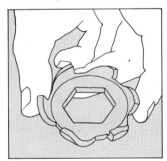

5 Check the overrun dog. If its flat edges are worn or rounded, fit a replacement part

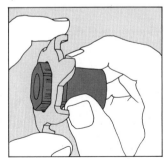

6 Make sure that the overrun dog fits tightly on the drive dog. Renew them if there is movement

Lawn mowers Rotary cutters

Maintenance and lubrication

All rotary mowers are power driven—by an engine, battery or mains electricity. Basic maintenance is the same for all types, but check the handbook for any variation in adjustment or lubrication requirements.

Clean the underside of the mower thoroughly each time it is used. Do not allow grass cuttings to congeal with the engine oil. Make sure that the machine is evenly adjusted, and that there is no excessive vibration as the blade rotates.

Materials: oil; petrol; new cord.
Tools: screwdriver; brush; spanner.

Adjusting the height of cut The height of individual wheels is adjusted on most rotary mowers by turning an adjusting screw (left)

or moving a lever (centre). On some models a single lever adjusts all four wheels through connecting linkages (right)

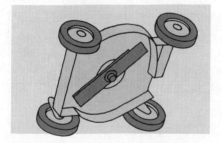

Cleaning After use, remove the spark-plug lead, tilt the machine and remove grass clippings from the underside and exit passage

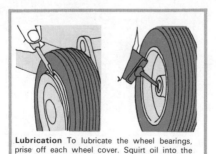

Lubrication To lubricate the wheel bearings, prise off each wheel cover. Squirt oil into the spindle until it overflows, then replace the covers

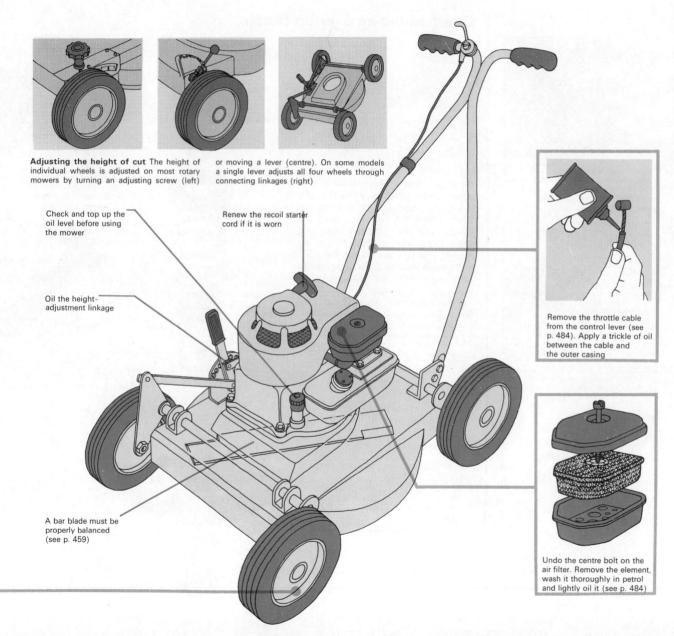

Check and top up the oil level before using the mower

Oil the height-adjustment linkage

A bar blade must be properly balanced (see p. 459)

Renew the recoil starter cord if it is worn

Remove the throttle cable from the control lever (see p. 484). Apply a trickle of oil between the cable and the outer casing

Undo the centre bolt on the air filter. Remove the element, wash it thoroughly in petrol and lightly oil it (see p. 484)

Sharpening rotary bar blades

On some rotary mowers the blade is a bar with two sharp edges and two corners turned up towards the machine. As the blade rotates, the bent corners create a draught to disperse the grass cuttings.

Bar blades must be correctly balanced. If one end is heavier than the other, the blade vibrates excessively and could damage the engine. File down the heavier end and keep checking the balance. If too much metal is removed, file the other end to restore the balance.

Tools: spanner to fit blade centre bolt; fine single-cut file; knife; vice.

1 Tilt the mower, with the lead disconnected and the spark-plug uppermost to prevent oil seepage

2 Undo the blade-securing bolt. Remove the flat washer and spacer in the centre of the blade

3 With the blade in a vice, file its cutting edges. Follow the original cutting angle

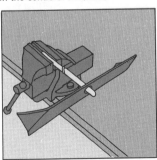

4 Hold a knife in the vice, and slide the bar on to the blade. If one end of the bar drops, it is out of balance

5 File the side of the bar—not the cutting edge—at the heavier end, until it balances evenly

Fitting new blade ends

A variation of the simple type of rotary bar blade is one with detachable cutting edges bolted at each end. They cannot easily be sharpened and should be renewed if they become worn or blunt. It is not necessary to remove the bar itself from the mower to replace the blade ends.

Always renew the blade ends in pairs, and fit new nuts and bolts, otherwise the bar will be out of balance and may damage the engine.

Materials: two new blade ends; nuts and bolts.
Tool: spanner to fit blade bolts.

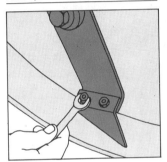

1 Undo the blade bolts and remove the blades. Brush or scrape the bar before fitting the new blade ends

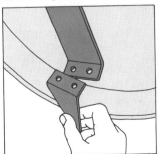

2 Use new nuts and bolts to fit the blade ends, the cutting edge pointing in the direction of rotation

Renewing disc blades

On many rotary mowers, the blades are circular or rectangular strips of metal bolted to the edge of a large rotating disc. Circular blades cannot be sharpened, but as they lose their sharpness they can be turned to expose a fresh cutting edge. When the edges of circular blades have been used, fit new ones. It is not possible to move or sharpen rectangular blades: replace them if they are worn. At the same time renew the two blower blades bolted to the top of the disc.

Materials: blades as needed.
Tools: spanner to fit bolts; knife.

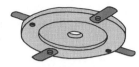

The underside blades cut the grass; upper (blower) blades disperse it

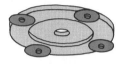

Circular blades can be turned to expose an unused cutting edge

1 Undo the bolt holding the disc on to the mower. Remove the whole disc assembly from the machine

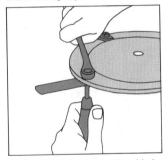

2 Unbolt the two cutting blades from the bottom of the disc. Remove the blower blades from the top

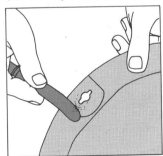

3 Scrape the surface of the disc clean, so that the new blades can be bolted evenly

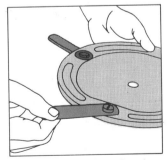

4 Use new nuts, bolts and washers. Do not over-tighten: each blade should be able to move on its bolt

Lawn mowers Pawl-type recoil starters

Pawl-type recoil starters—on which a metal arm engages a ratchet to turn the engine shaft—are used on most mower engines. One exception is the Briggs and Stratton (see p. 462). Wear in the pawl mechanism, or a broken cord or mainspring, generally involves dismantling the complete starter assembly.

Note how the pulley and spring are fitted: they must be replaced in the same way. To make sure that the strain of starting the engine is taken on the cord, the spring must be accurately tensioned. Wind it up as tightly as possible and, in doing so, note how many turns are required before the cord disappears into the pulley housing. When the spring is fully wound, let it uncoil by one more turn than was taken by the cord in winding up.

Materials: cord; recoil spring; pawl and pawl spring.
Tools: spanner; screwdriver; hammer; punch; pliers.

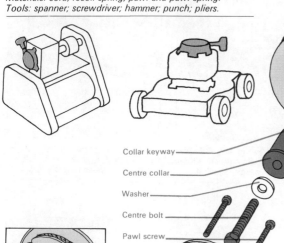

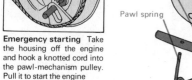

Emergency starting Take the housing off the engine and hook a knotted cord into the pawl-mechanism pulley. Pull it to start the engine

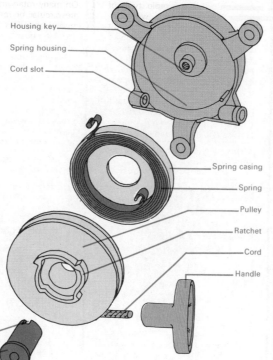

Housing key
Spring housing
Cord slot

Spring casing
Spring
Pulley
Ratchet
Cord
Handle

Collar keyway
Centre collar
Washer
Centre bolt
Pawl screw
Pawl housing
Pawl
Pawl spring

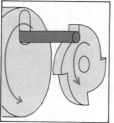

How it works When the cord is pulled, a straight edge on the ratchet engages the pawl which rotates the engine shaft

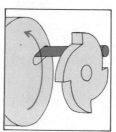

Immediately the engine fires, the pawl is thrown outwards and rides over the rounded teeth of the pulley ratchet

Replacing the cord and spring

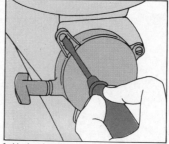

1 Undo the three screws which hold the starter housing on the side of the engine block

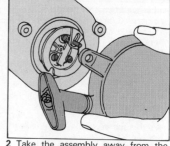

2 Take the assembly away from the block. Slide the handle down the cord and undo the knot (see p. 463)

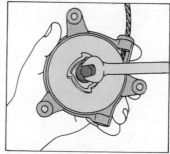

3 Remove the handle and release the cord gently to unwind the spring. Undo the centre bolt

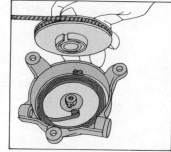

4 Remove the bolt, washer and centre collar. Take the pulley unit out of the spring housing

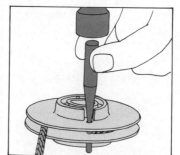

5 Remove the cord if it is broken or frayed. If it is fixed with a pin, punch the pin out

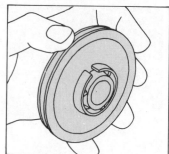

6 Check the lugs which engage with the ends of the spring. If they are worn, fit a new pulley *(continued)*

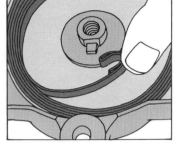

7 If the spring is broken, unhook it from its locating peg and remove it in its casing from the housing

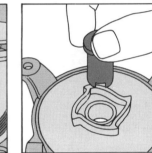

9 Fit a new cord if needed and replace the pulley so that the slot (arrowed) engages the end of the spring

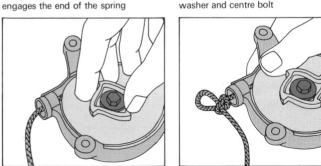

11 Wind the pulley and count the turns until the cord disappears. Wind on until the spring is tight

8 Fit the new spring on its locating peg and bend its inner end towards the hub of the housing

10 Replace the centre collar to fit against the housing key. Refit the washer and centre bolt

12 Release pulley by one more turn than counted earlier. Thread cord through eye, and knot. Fix handle (see p. 463)

Overhauling the pawl mechanism

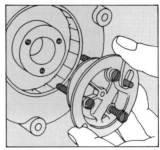

1 Remove the spring and pulley assembly. Undo the three screws holding the pawl unit. Remove it

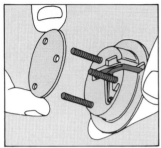

2 Take off the back-plate and remove the screws. If thin washers are fitted, replace them when assembling

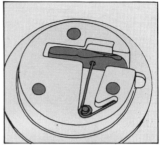

3 Check that the spring which fits into the pawl is not broken. If it is, obtain a replacement spring

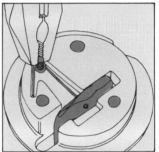

4 Remove the spring. If a rivet is used, tap it out from the front and use pliers to pull it free

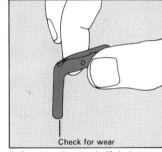

5 Remove the pawl. If it is worn where it engages the pulley ratchet, it should be renewed

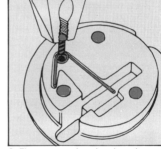

6 Fit a new stud or rivet into the eye of the spring and screw or tap it into the pawl housing

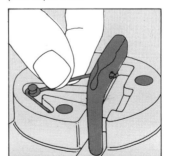

7 Gently raise the long end of the spring and push it into the hole in the pawl. Position the pawl

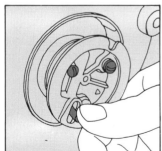

8 Replace the screws, washers and back-plate and fit the assembly on the engine block. Tighten evenly

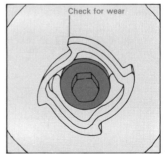

9 Examine the pulley ratchet. If it is worn, fit a new pulley. Replace the housing on the engine

Replacing the cord and spring

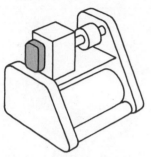

To fit a new recoil starter cord to Briggs and Stratton engines, only the cowling has to be removed. If the recoil spring breaks, however, complete dismantling is necessary. Use only the maker's recommended parts: no others are suitable.

Materials: new cord, 42 in. (1·1 m) long; new spring; plastic retaining caps.
Tools: screwdriver; pliers; spanner to fit the cowling bolts.

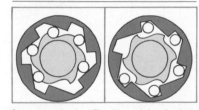

Starter mechanism The drive unit has five balls which can fall into any of the six slots. When the balls are in the slots, the starter unit is locked on the engine shaft (left). As soon as the engine fires, the balls are thrown outwards (right) and the starter mechanism is then free to idle

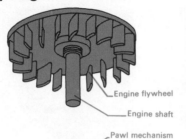

Engine flywheel
Engine shaft
Pawl mechanism
Engagement shaft

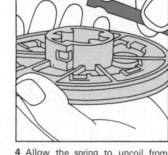

Pawl cover
Screen
Pulley unit
Spring
Cowling

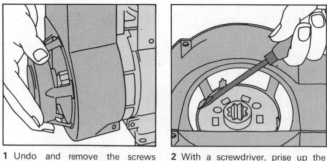

1 Undo and remove the screws holding the cowling on the engine. Carefully remove the cowling

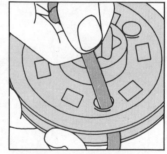

4 Allow the spring to uncoil from the pulley and unhook its other end from the pulley centre boss

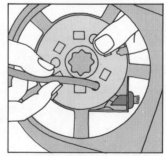

7 Refit the pulley and its clips. Turn it anti-clockwise 13¼ turns to wind up the spring

2 With a screwdriver, prise up the clips holding the pulley unit inside the cowling

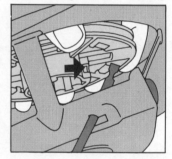

5 If a new cord is needed, pull out the old one. Tie a knot in one end of the new piece. Do not fit it

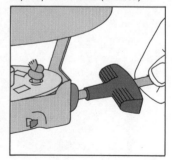

8 Hold the pulley and push the unknotted end of the new cord through the pulley slot and cowling

3 Lift the pulley up and unhook the end of the spring from the slot (arrowed) in the side of the cowling

6 Feed the straight new spring through the cowling slot. Engage end at pulley centre boss (arrowed)

9 Hold the cord tightly and tie a loop knot in it. Fit the handle, and knot or seal the cord

Overhauling the drive mechanism

Failure of the drive mechanism to engage may be caused by the five engagement balls sticking in the release position. Strip the unit and thoroughly clean the balls, ratchet and housing in petrol. Reassemble dry. Never lubricate this mechanism as oil or grease will only pick up dust, which will cause the balls to stick.

Replacement parts for the drive mechanism of a Briggs and Stratton starter are not readily available. If a fault cannot be corrected by cleaning, remove the unit and fit a new one.

Materials: petrol; lint-free rag.
Tools: screwdrivers; hammer; punch.

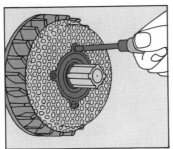

1 Undo the four screws holding the protective screen over the pawl mechanism. Remove the screen

2 To loosen the mechanism on the shaft, replace one screw. Tap the lug with a hammer and punch

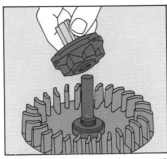

3 When the mechanism has started to unscrew from the engine shaft, remove it by hand

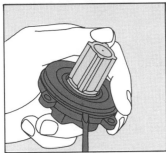

4 If the engagement shaft is worn, obtain and fit a new mechanism. If it is not, prise off the pawl cover

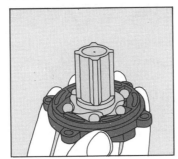

5 Clean the five balls in petrol. Dry them and reassemble the mechanism. Screw it on the engine shaft

Fitting a new handle

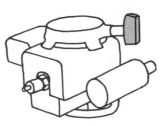

There are three basic ways in which a recoil starter handle can be fitted to the cord. Make sure that the knot holding it is firmly tied.

Knot The simplest fitting is a knot at the end of the cord, recessed in a countersunk hole in the handle

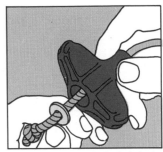

Push the cord through the hole in the handle. Fit the washer and tie a loop knot. Pull it into the recess

Box-plate On some types, the cord is tied to a steel box-plate which fits into a cut-out handle

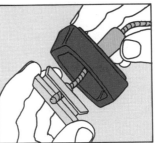

1 Push the box assembly out of the handle. Feed the cord through the handle and the hole in the box

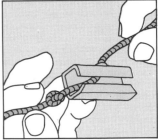

2 Knot the cord and draw it with the box into the handle recess. Make sure that it fits tightly

Bar To avoid strain on one part of the handle, some types have a bar fitting for the cord

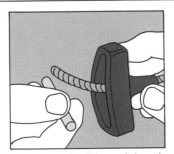

1 Feed enough of the cord through the hole in the handle to be able to tie it to the bar

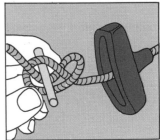

2 Tie a loop knot. Double the cord end back under the bar and fit the bar in the slot in the handle

Lawn mowers Impulse starters

Overhauling the starter mechanism

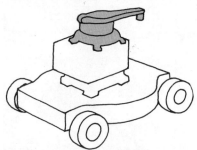

Impulse starters are operated by a handle-wound spring. Most have a mainspring which is double-wound, with its ends slotted in the centre of the ratchet housing. Others use a boxed spring, removed in the same way as those on recoil starters (see p. 460). All the other parts, and the method of dismantling, are the same for both types.

When an impulse starter fails to operate, it is likely that one or more of its components has worn. The parts most likely to fail are the pawls, the springs and, in time, the ratchet teeth. Dismantle and check the mechanism. Replacement parts are available from most gardening-machinery dealers.

Materials: pawls, pawl springs, mainspring; brake bands as required.
Tools: spanner; $\frac{11}{16}$ in. (18 mm) socket and bar, or ratchet; pliers; screwdrivers.

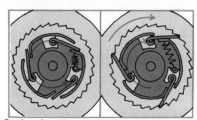

Pawl action When the starter is wound up, the pawls are held in their cover (left). When the mechanism is released, the cover moves against its spring and throws the pawls out to engage starter cup

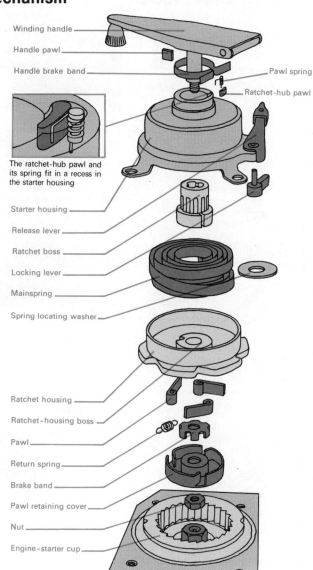

The ratchet-hub pawl and its spring fit in a recess in the starter housing

- Winding handle
- Handle pawl
- Handle brake band
- Pawl spring
- Ratchet-hub pawl
- Starter housing
- Release lever
- Ratchet boss
- Locking lever
- Mainspring
- Spring locating washer
- Ratchet housing
- Ratchet-housing boss
- Pawl
- Return spring
- Brake band
- Pawl retaining cover
- Nut
- Engine-starter cup

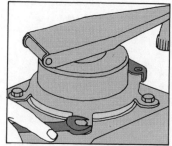

1 Undo and remove the four bolts holding the starter housing on the engine casing

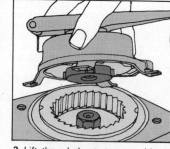

2 Lift the whole starter assembly out of the starter cup, which is bolted to the end of the engine shaft

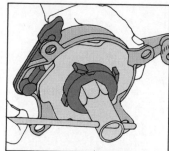

3 With an $\frac{11}{16}$ in. (18 mm) socket and bar, or ratchet, undo the centre nut holding the pawl retaining cover

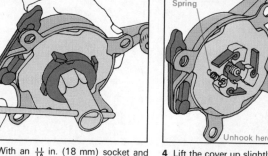

Spring

Unhook here

4 Lift the cover up slightly and unhook the return spring from the cover hook. Remove the cover

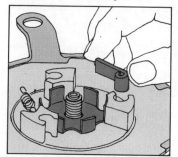

5 Take the three pawls out of the ratchet housing and unhook the return spring from its peg

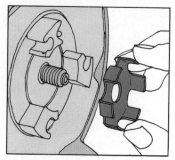

6 If the brake band has not been removed with the pawl retaining cover, lift it off the centre boss *(continued)*

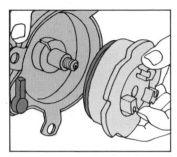

7 Remove the ratchet housing and mainspring from the starter housing. Set the ratchet housing aside

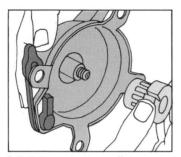

8 Pull the ratchet boss off the starter housing. If its splines are worn, obtain a replacement part

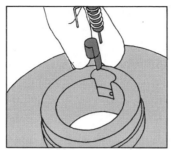

9 Turn over the housing and remove the handle. Renew the ratchet hub pawl and spring if they are worn

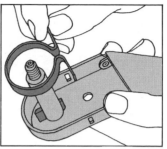

10 Make sure that the handle pawl is unworn and that it slides freely. Remove the brake band and fit a new one

11 Now check the ratchet housing. If it is fitted with a double-wound spring, remove the central washer

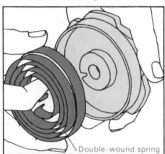

12 Unhook the spring from its slot in the ratchet-housing boss. Remove it from the housing

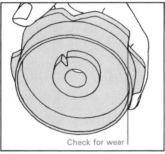

13 Check the ratchet teeth and boss. If they are worn or damaged, fit a replacement ratchet housing

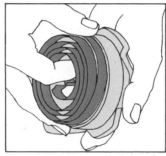

14 Engage the lower end of the spring in the boss. Wind it in until it fits in the ratchet housing

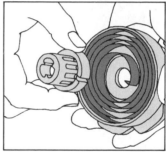

15 Position the spring locating washer, and fit the ratchet boss to engage the upper end of the spring

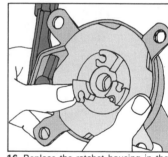

16 Replace the ratchet housing in the starter housing. Make sure that the washer is centred inside

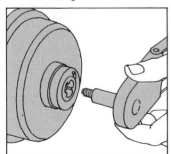

17 Hold the reassembled unit securely in one hand, and refit the handle with the other

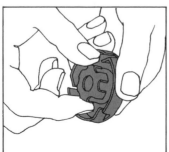

18 Fit a new brake to the pawl retaining cover. If necessary, pinch the lugs in, by hand, to obtain a tight fit

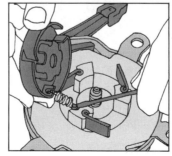

19 Renew the pawls where necessary and fit them in place. Fit the spring and hook it to the cover

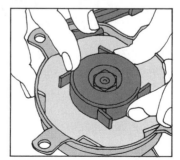

20 Refit the cover and tighten the centre nut. Turn the cover by hand to check that the pawls work

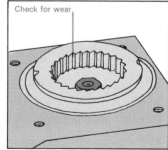

21 Check the engine starter-cup teeth. If they are worn, fit a new cup. Refit the starter unit tightly.

Lawn mowers Engines

Regular maintenance

A lawn-mower engine should be maintained regularly. Clean the spark-plug at least twice a year (see p. 644). Remove the flywheel cover-plate and check the contact-breaker points once a year (see p. 485). Make sure the fuel system is in good working order (see pp. 478–83). Check the carburettor air filter and remove any grass cuttings. If the fuel line has a filter, make sure it is clean, and if no fuel filter is fitted, clean the float bowl and jets twice a year.

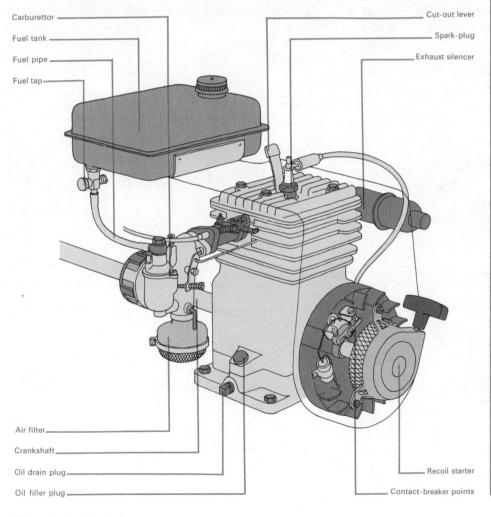

Carburettor
Fuel tank
Fuel pipe
Fuel tap

Cut-out lever
Spark-plug
Exhaust silencer

Air filter
Crankshaft
Oil drain plug
Oil filler plug
Recoil starter
Contact-breaker points

HOW TO START AN ENGINE

When starting a lawn-mower engine from cold, turn the starter rapidly to ensure that the fuel/air mixture in the combustion chamber is sufficiently compressed. Make routine checks before starting, to ensure that the engine can be used safely.

If the engine is a two-stroke, make sure the petrol-oil mix is to the maker's recommendation. If in doubt, mix 16 parts of petrol to 1 of oil.

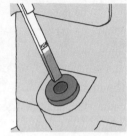

Oil level Check the level of the oil in a four-stroke engine (see p. 468)

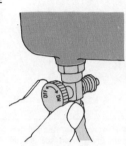

Fuel supply Make sure the fuel tap is turned on and the tank is not empty

Choke control On a fixed-jet carburettor (see p. 478) ensure the choke is closed (left). On a slide carburettor (see p. 482) pull the knurled knob up to close the choke. Diaphragm carburettors (see p. 480) have no choke control. Prime with button (right)

Throttle control Ensure that the throttle lever is in the 'start' position

Ignition switch If an ignition switch is fitted, make sure it is switched on

Recoil starter Pull cord sharply to obtain enough speed to start engine

Finding the fault when a mower does not start

ENGINE WILL NOT START

Check the spark-plug
Disconnect plug lead and remove the spark-plug. Reconnect the lead to the plug and lay the plug on the engine. Operate starter mechanism. **B**
If the plug does not spark, check the plug gap with a feeler gauge. **A**

Spark at the plug
Check that the tap under the petrol tank is turned on. **C**
Remove fuel pipe from the carburettor to check the fuel flow; and eliminate any air-lock. **D**
Clean the fuel filter. **L**
If petrol reaches carburettor, strip it and clean jets **E** or diaphragm (see p. 480)

No spark at plug
Remove high-tension lead from the spark-plug. Hold it close to, but not touching, the engine block and operate starter. **G**
If a spark is seen between the lead terminal and engine block, fit new plug
If there is no spark, check the contact-breaker points. **H**

Check the condenser. **I**
Check wiring for breaks. Fit new cables if necessary. **J**
Fit a new radio suppressor to the high-tension cable. **K**

ENGINE FIRES BUT WILL NOT CONTINUE TO RUN

Electrical system
Remove spark-plug and check that it is not wet
Check contact-breaker points gap. **H**
Check condition of condenser, by fitting a replacement. **I**
Check insulation of high-tension lead. **J**
Fit a new radio suppressor to the high-tension cable. **K**

Fuel system
Check that tap is turned on. **C**
Check flow to carburettor. **D**
Clean the carburettor float bowl. **E**
Clean the carburettor air filter (see p. 484)
Make sure the choke is in the correct position for starting: if the engine is hot it must be in 'off' position

ENGINE RUNS FOR A FEW MINUTES THEN STOPS

Electrical system
Check spark-plug. **A**
Check contact-breaker points gap. **H**
Fit a new condenser. **I**
Fit new suppressor. **K**
Check high-tension lead for cracked insulation. **J**

Fuel system
Remove the fuel pipe from tank. Open fuel tap and blow through it. If it is blocked, fit new tap. **C**
Blow through the fuel-tank breather vent to make sure

it is clear. Check if the engine runs with the filler cap off
Make sure that the choke is not set in the start position —usually indicated by black smoke as the engine fires
Remove and clean or replace the air-filter element (see p. 484)
If there is too much oil in the two-stroke mixture, drain and refill with correct mixture

ENGINE STOPS SUDDENLY AFTER CONSIDERABLE USE

Electrical system
Spark-plug may be overheating: fit new one (see p. 644)
Check high-tension lead for spark. **G**
If no spark, check contact-breaker points. **H**
Fit a new condenser. **I**
Check high-tension leads for signs of cracking. **J**
Fit new high-tension lead suppressor. **K**

Fuel and mechanical
Refill the petrol tank
Check carburettor air filter (see p. 484)
Strip and clean carburettor (see p. 478)
Check compression. **F**
Remove spark-plug and place thumb over hole
Turn engine and check that cylinder sucks in
If there is no compression, overhaul the engine (four-stroke, p. 468; two-stroke p. 474)

STARTER WILL NOT TURN ENGINE

Engine faults
If starter does not operate at all, the engine has seized up
Overhaul the engine (see pp. 468 and 474)
If starter pulls freely with no resistance, mechanism spring is broken
Fit a new spring (see p. 460)
If there is resistance or spring tension, the starter pawl or engagement mechanism is faulty. Overhaul (see p. 461)

ENGINE STARTS BUT MACHINE WILL NOT OPERATE

Mechanical faults
Faulty drive mechanism
Overhaul (see p. 450)
Faulty clutch. Overhaul (see pp. 452–7)

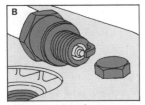

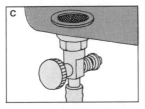

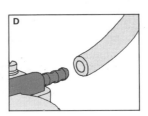

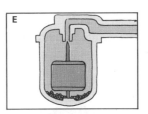

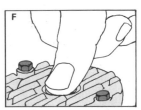

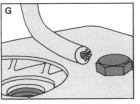

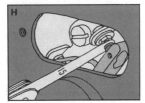

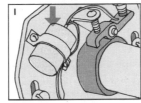

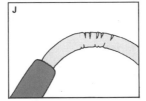

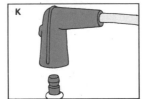

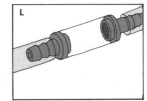

Lawn mowers Four-stroke engines

Differences in construction

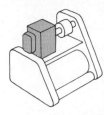

All four-stroke engines work on the same basic principle, but their construction varies. Many, for example the Suffolk, have a cast-iron cylinder block and crankcase with an aluminium cylinder head and sump. Others, such as the Briggs and Stratton, are all aluminium. Run the point of a screwdriver along a cylinder-block vane: if the block is cast iron, it will show only a surface scratch, but if it is alloy the screwdriver will have made a definite scoring.

HOW A FOUR-STROKE ENGINE WORKS

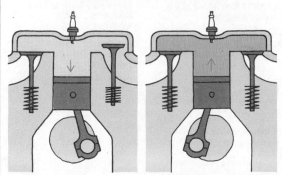

Induction The inlet valve opens and the piston descends, drawing in the air/fuel mixture

Compression The inlet valve closes and the piston rises to compress the mixture

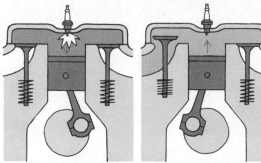

Power The compressed gas, ignited by a spark, expands and pushes the piston down

Exhaust The exhaust valve opens. The flywheel pushes up the piston to expel the burnt gas

Maintaining a Suffolk

The only routine maintenance on a Suffolk engine is to change the oil at recommended periods. Continual use, however, results in a build-up of carbon deposits in the combustion chambers, on the piston crowns and on the valves inside the engine. If the engine is not operating efficiently, dismantle it and de-carbonise all affected parts.

Materials: gaskets; valves and springs; grinding paste; rag; oil. Tools: spanners; grinding stick; 2p coin; screwdriver; sockets and ratchet; mallet; pliers.

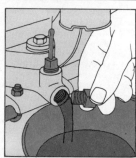

1 Drain the oil at the start of the year. Unscrew the drain plug and tilt the mower

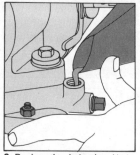

2 Replace the drain plug. Undo the filler plug, pour in ½ pint of oil and replace the plug

The crankcase breather unit has a spring, cover, valve, valve carrier, fibre washer

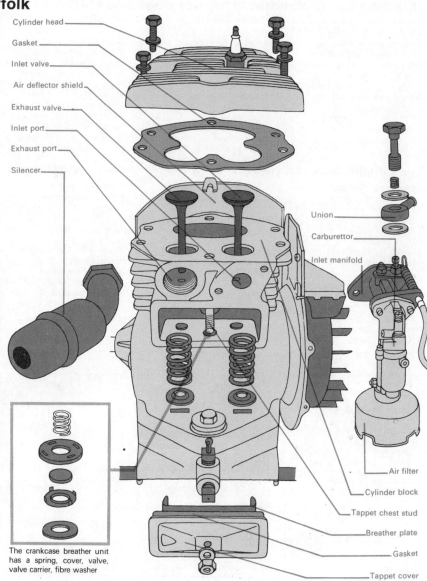

Cylinder head
Gasket
Inlet valve
Air deflector shield
Exhaust valve
Inlet port
Exhaust port
Silencer
Union
Carburettor
Inlet manifold
Air filter
Cylinder block
Tappet chest stud
Breather plate
Gasket
Tappet cover

Dismantling a Suffolk

1 At the carburettor, remove union bolt, filter and two fibre washers. Disconnect fuel line

2 Undo the bolts holding the cowling at the side and on the cylinder head

3 Undo the inlet manifold bolts. Lift the carburettor off and hold it in one hand

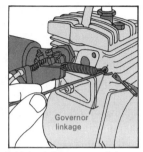

4 Unhook the governor linkage from the flap. Do not bend it. Remove the carburettor

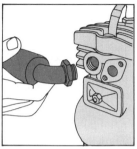

5 Loosen the lock-nut on the exhaust pipe and unscrew the pipe from the exhaust port

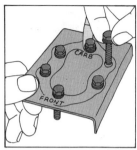

6 Remove the head bolts and cut-out lever. Push them into a marked piece of card

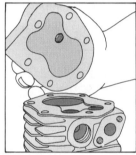

7 Tap the sides of the cylinder head lightly with a plastic or hide mallet. Lift it off

8 Peel off and discard the head gasket. Make sure that all particles of gasket are removed

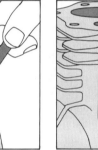

9 Undo the nut on the tappet cover below the exhaust and inlet ports. Remove the cover

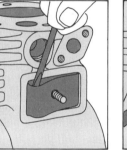

10 Use a screwdriver to prise out the sprung plate which protects the valves

11 Prise out the crankcase breather-assembly spring under the tappet chest stud

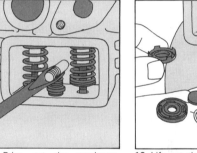

12 Lift out the breather components. Obtain a new valve and fibre washer

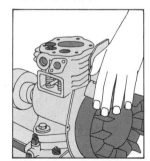

13 Turn the flywheel until one valve is pushed fully up. This ensures that the other is closed

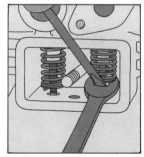

14 Prise up the closed valve's collar and spring. Lever back the cotter with a screwdriver

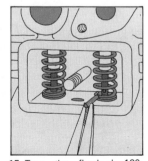

15 Turn the flywheel 180 degrees. Twist the valve until the cotter can be pulled out

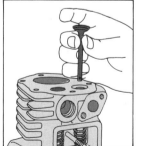

16 Lift the valve out of its guide, leaving the retaining cap and spring in place

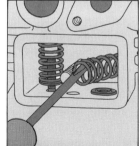

17 Prise out the spring and renew it if it is worn or cracked. Remove the valve cap

18 If a valve cannot be lifted out, clean the stem by turning the valve against a file

Lawn mowers Four-stroke engines

Decarbonising and valve grinding on a Suffolk

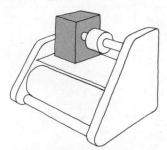

To improve the engine performance, scrape the carbon from the valves and regrind them about every two years. If they are badly pitted, use coarse paste; if not, fine grinding paste is suitable for regrinding.

Head

Valve face

Valve stem

Cotter peg

Spring

Retaining cap

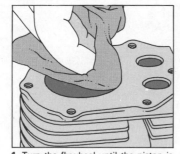

1 Turn the flywheel until the piston is at the bottom of the cylinder. Clean the cylinder with a petrol-damped rag

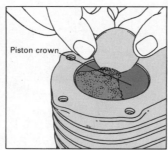

Piston crown

2 Move the piston up and use a soft scraper—for example, a 2p coin—to remove carbon from the crown

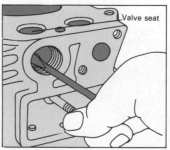

3 Clean carbon from the inlet and exhaust ports with a screwdriver. Do not touch the valve seats

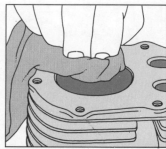

Valve seat

4 Wipe the piston crowns, ports, cylinder face and bore with a petrol-damped rag to remove carbon dust

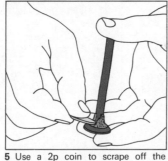

5 Use a 2p coin to scrape off the carbon on the head of the valve and at the base of the stem

6 Fix the head of the valve on a grinding stick and dab a little grinding paste around the valve face

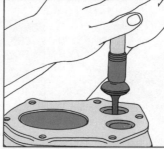

7 Hold the stick between the palms, and turn the valve in its seat. To grind evenly, lift the stick occasionally

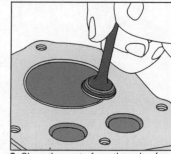

8 Clean the paste from the valve face and seat. Check that the face is smooth. Regrind if necessary

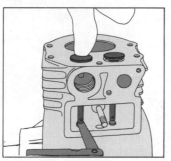

9 Refit valves. Close each in turn by rotating the flywheel. Press the closed valve and measure the gap at the base

10 The inlet clearance should be ·007 in., exhaust ·015 in. Grind the end of the stem on an oil-stone if necessary

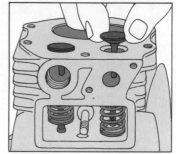

11 Reposition the valve springs and caps in the tappet chest. Drop the valves gently into place

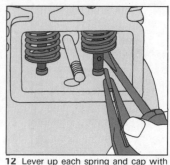

12 Lever up each spring and cap with a screwdriver. Use pliers to push the cotter peg through the stem

Reassembling a Suffolk

1 Obtain a new fibre washer and valve and reassemble the crankcase breather unit in the tappet chest

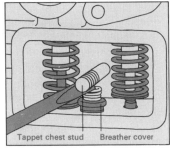

2 Compress the spring and ease it into place between the tappet chest stud and the breather cover

Tappet chest stud   Breather cover

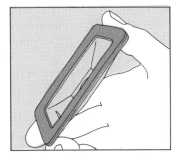

3 Smear on a little grease to seal a new cork gasket to the tappet cover. Replace the spring plate

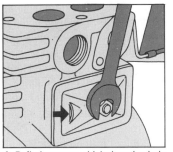

4 Refit the cover, with its breather hole (arrowed) below the exhaust port. Take care not to overtighten the cover nut

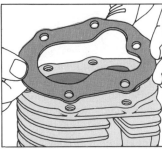

5 Fit a new cylinder-head gasket. Replace head and bolts. Fit the spark-plug cut-out lever

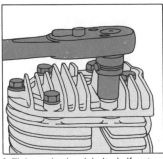

6 Tighten the head bolts half a turn at a time. Start with the centre bolts and work diagonally

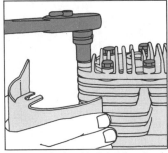

7 Loosen the head bolt holding the air deflector shield. Fit the shield and retighten the bolt

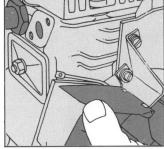

8 Make sure the governor flap pivots freely on its spindle. When lifted, it should fall under its own weight

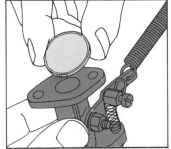

9 Use a 2p coin to remove any remaining gasket material from the inlet manifold at the carburettor

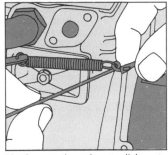

10 Connect the carburettor linkage to the governor flap. Make sure that the rod is not bent

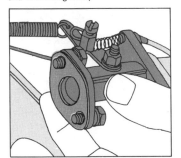

11 Use a new manifold gasket. Fit the carburettor to the engine and tighten the two bolts evenly

12 Loosen the head bolt (arrowed) that secures the cowling bracket. Fit the cowling and retighten the head bolt

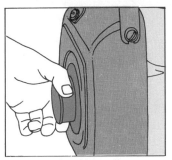

13 Tighten the side cowling screws. Make sure the flywheel can turn without rubbing against the cowling

14 Adjust the spark-plug gap by bending the earth electrode. Check the gap (·025 in.) with a feeler gauge

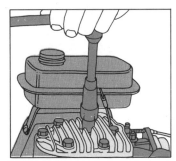

15 Fit the plug to the cylinder head. Tighten gently with a plug spanner. Overtightening may strip its thread

Lawn mowers Four-stroke engines

Overhauling a Briggs and Stratton

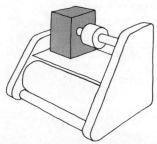

Decarbonising and valve-grinding on the Briggs and Stratton engine are the same as for any other engine (see pp. 470–1). But because even the cylinder bore is alloy, special care is needed when scraping away the carbon. The recommended tappet clearances are: inlet ·005 to ·007 in., exhaust ·009 to ·011 in.

Materials: gasket set; grinding paste; valves and springs; clean rag; oil; abrasive paper.
Tools: ring and open-ended spanners; grinding stick; 2p coin; screwdrivers; sockets and bar; hide mallet; hammer and punch; pliers.

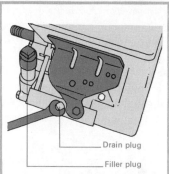

To drain the oil, remove the drain plug at the base of the crankcase. The filler plug is to the left of the drain plug

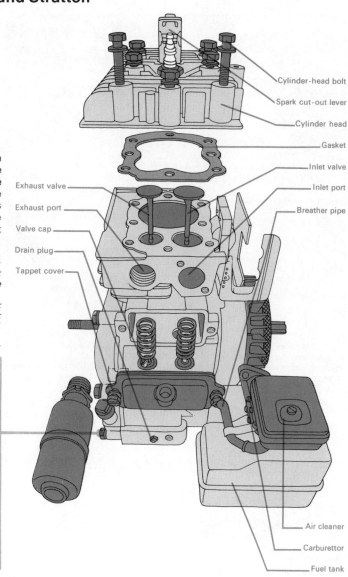

Cylinder-head bolt

Spark cut-out lever

Cylinder head

Gasket

Inlet valve

Inlet port

Breather pipe

Exhaust valve

Exhaust port

Valve cap

Drain plug

Tappet cover

Air cleaner

Carburettor

Fuel tank

Dismantling a Briggs and Stratton

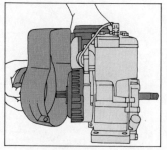

1 Undo and remove all the bolts holding the cowling on the engine. Lift off the cowling

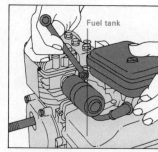

Fuel tank

2 Undo the bolts holding the combined carburettor/fuel tank assembly at the cylinder inlet port

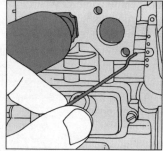

3 Remove the carburettor. Disconnect the governor link from the control flap. Note which hole it fits in

4 Tap the exhaust pipe lock-ring loose with a hammer and punch. Unscrew it from the exhaust port

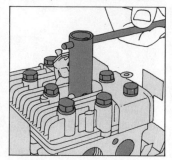

5 Unscrew the spark-plug. Clean it with an abrasive paper and check the gap (·025 in.) with a feeler gauge

Cut-out lever

6 Undo the cylinder-head bolts half a turn at a time. Note which holds the spark-plug cut-out   *(continued)*

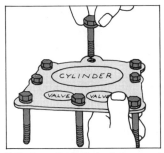

7 To keep the bolts in their correct order for reassembly, fit them through a marked piece of card

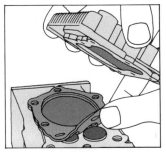

8 Tap the cylinder head lightly with a hide mallet. Remove it and peel off the old gasket

9 Undo the two screws securing the tappet cover. Remove the cover plate and peel off its gasket

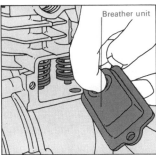

10 If the tappet cover contains the crankcase breather unit, press the valve in to check that it moves freely

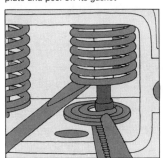

11 Prise up the valve spring with a screwdriver. Use pliers to slide the slotted cap off the valve-stem groove

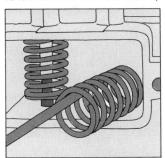

12 Lift out the valve. Use a screwdriver to prise the spring out of the tappet chest. Replace it if broken

Reassembling a Briggs and Stratton

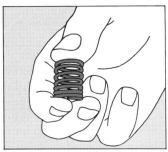

1 The inlet-valve spring coils are closer at one end. The tight coils should fit at the bottom of the chest

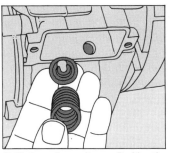

2 Fit the spring on its cap. Position the two in the tappet chest with the cap slot facing inwards, towards the engine

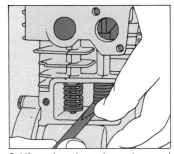

3 Lift up the valve spring and cap and insert the valve. Engage the stem of the valve in the cap slot

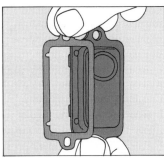

4 Fit a new gasket on the tappet cover, lining up its breather holes with the holes at the bottom of the cover

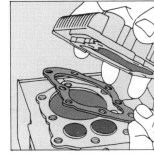

5 Make sure the faces of the cylinder head and block are clean. Fit a new head gasket and replace the head

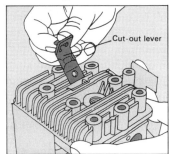

6 Locate the spark-plug cut-out lever in its slot in the cylinder head. Fit the eye under the rear head bolt

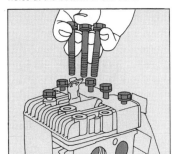

7 The three long bolts fit the exhaust corner. Tighten all the bolts diagonally, working from the outside inwards

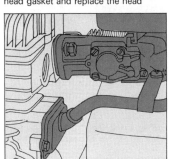

8 Fit a new gasket and replace the carburettor. Connect the governor linkage and fit the breather pipe

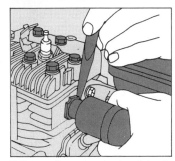

9 Screw the exhaust pipe into its port, hand-tight only. Tighten its locking ring with a hammer and punch

Lawn mowers Two-stroke engines

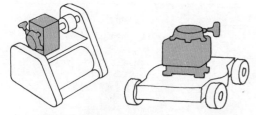

A two-stroke engine is so named because a complete operating cycle, from the fuel entering the cylinder to the exhaust gases being expelled, requires only two movements of the piston. The main design difference between a two-stroke and a four-stroke is that a two-stroke has no separate sump or filler plug for oil. Oil is mixed with the petrol when the tank is filled.

The engine shown is an Aspera, but all two-strokes work on the same basic principle.

HOW A TWO-STROKE ENGINE WORKS

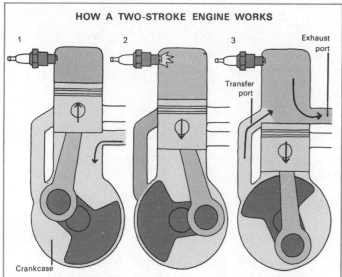

(1) The rising piston compresses the fuel mixture above it while sucking mixture into the crankcase. (2) The fuel is ignited, driving the piston downwards. This partially compresses the new charge that has been drawn into the crankcase. (3) Fresh mixture is forced into the cylinder through the transfer port, uncovered by the piston's downward stroke, and this helps to expel burnt gases through the exhaust port

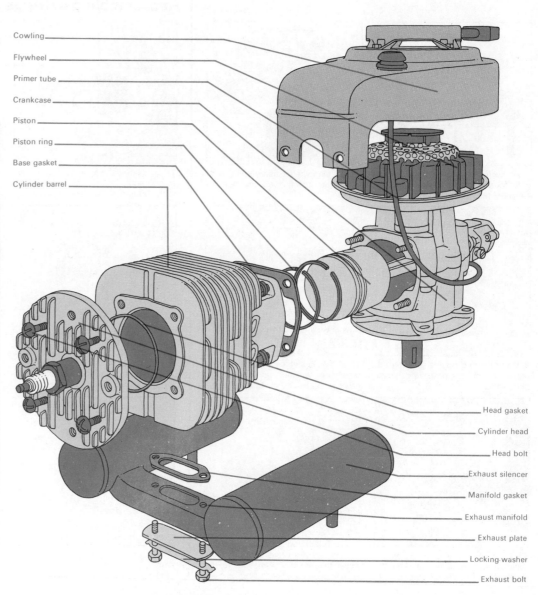

Cowling
Flywheel
Primer tube
Crankcase
Piston
Piston ring
Base gasket
Cylinder barrel

Head gasket
Cylinder head
Head bolt
Exhaust silencer
Manifold gasket
Exhaust manifold
Exhaust plate
Locking washer
Exhaust bolt

Dismantling the engine

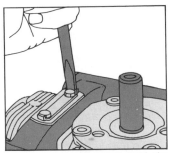

1 Take a screwdriver and bend the tabs of the locking-washer back from the bolts holding the exhaust assembly

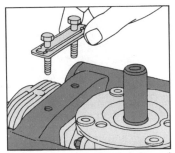

2 Undo the two exhaust bolts and remove the locking-washer and exhaust plate beneath them

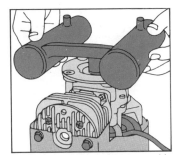

3 Lift the complete exhaust assembly —which consists of the pipes and manifold—off the engine block

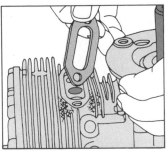

4 Brush or scrape dirt from the vanes close to the exhaust ports. Peel off the old exhaust manifold gasket

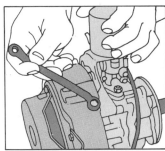

5 Undo the two bolts which hold the carburettor bracket underneath the cowling on the engine

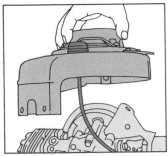

6 Gently lift the cowling off the engine. Do not force it, because the fuel primer pipe is still connected

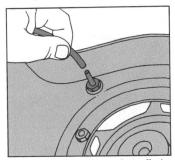

7 Pull the fuel primer pipe off the button tube inside the engine cowling. Check that the lock-nut is tight

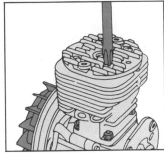

8 Remove the spark-plug from the cylinder head and undo the head bolts half a turn at a time until they are free

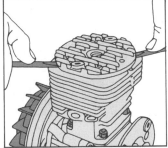

9 Use two screwdriver blades under opposite edges of the cylinder head and lever it upwards

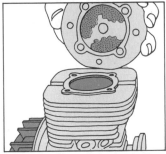

10 Remove the cylinder head. Never hammer it free. It is recessed into the cylinder barrel and can be damaged

11 Prise out the head gasket—a copper ring, which sits in the recess in the top of the cylinder barrel

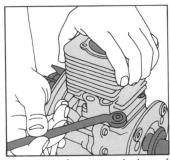

12 Undo the four nuts at the base of the cylinder barrel. Remove the nuts and the spring washers

13 To remove the cylinder barrel, lift it straight up to avoid damaging the piston and rings

14 Prise the piston rings outwards and lift them out of the piston grooves. Have new rings available

15 Remove and discard the fibre gasket at the base of the cylinder. Obtain a new one to fit when reassembling

Lawn mowers Two-stroke engines

Decarbonising the engine

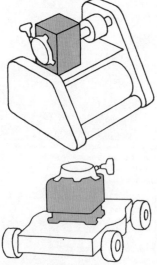

When decarbonising a two-stroke engine, examine also the silencer. Excessive carbon formation can suppress a two-stroke engine. Place the silencer in a fire for 15 minutes. Remove it, let it cool and then tap along the silencer with the handle of a hammer to loosen the burnt carbon. Shake the carbon out of the silencer.

Never sand-blast the spark-plug of a two-stroke engine. The abrasive particles stick to the inside surface of the plug and become loose when the engine operates. They can damage the engine when they drop inside it.

Always check the piston rings when decarbonising a two-stroke engine. The compression of the air-fuel mixture, and the expulsion of the burnt exhaust gases, rely on a perfect fit between the rings and the cylinder bore. If necessary, fit new piston rings.

Materials: new piston rings; gasket set; clean, lint-free rag; paraffin.
Tools: soft scraper; screwdriver; hammer; wire brush.

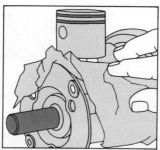

1 Cover the crankcase opening round the piston with a rag to keep out carbon particles

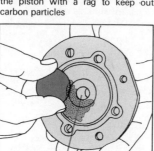

4 Scrape the carbon off the head with a 2p coin. Clean the spark-plug hole thread with a wire brush

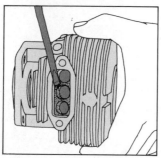

7 Scrape any carbon from the exhaust port, but do not scratch the bore. Wash the barrel in paraffin

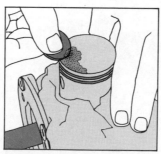

2 Use a soft scraper—a 2p coin, for example—to remove the carbon from the crown of the piston

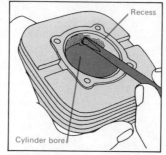

5 Remove the carbon from the gasket recess in the cylinder barrel and the cylinder bore with a screwdriver

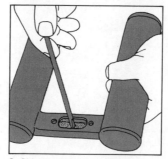

8 Chip the carbon out of the exhaust entrance on the silencer. If it is clogged, lay the silencer in a fire

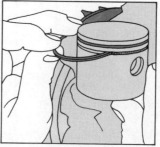

3 Break an old piston ring and use the end to scrape carbon from the ring grooves in the piston

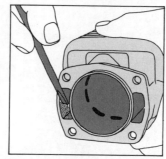

6 Use the screwdriver to clean out the transfer ports at the base of the cylinder barrel

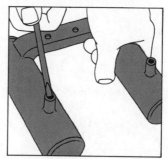

9 Use a screwdriver to chip out any hard carbon blocking the ends of the exhaust pipes

A DIFFERENT DESIGN

Some two-stroke engines—for example, the Villiers—have a combined cylinder head and barrel which is removed in one piece.

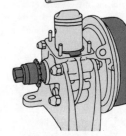

1 Remove the carburettor and spark-plug from the cylinder. Undo the four base nuts and lift the complete cylinder head and barrel off the piston

2 To clean a combined cylinder head and barrel, reach into the head from the base of the barrel with a long, soft brass or copper scraper

Although there are several types of piston fitted on two-stroke engines the cleaning is basically the same.

1 A piston may have a half-round cut in the base of the skirt where it meets the transfer port

2 In some designs, the transfer port is cut out of the piston skirt

3 A domed piston usually has lugs in the ring grooves to locate the piston rings

Ring-gapping and reassembly

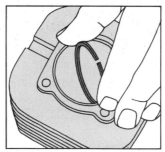

1 Push each new piston ring edgeways into the bore in turn. Twist it parallel to the top of the barrel

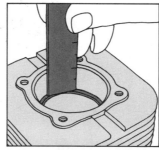

2 Measure from the top to the ring. It must be exactly 1 in. (25 mm) from the top. Make sure the ring is level

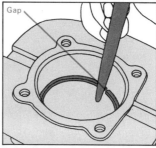

3 Check with a feeler gauge that the gap in the ring is exactly that recommended by the manufacturer

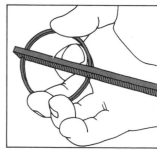

4 If the gap is too small, draw a double-sided file across it and check again with the feeler gauge

5 Fit the ends in the piston groove first. Spring the ring over the piston crown. Fit the second ring

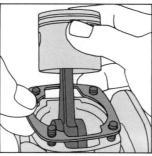

6 Clean the top face of the crankcase with paraffin and fit a new gasket. Do not use gasket cement

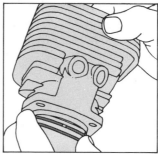

7 Make sure the ring gaps are on opposite sides of the piston. Compress and slide on the barrel

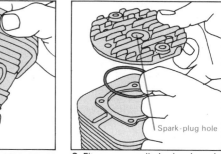

8 Fit a new cylinder-head gasket and replace the head. Tighten the bolts evenly around the head

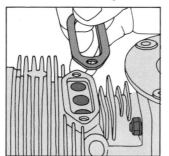

9 Fit a new gasket on the exhaust manifold. Make sure it lines up with the exhaust port

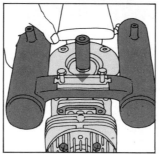

10 Refit the exhaust with a new tab locking-washer (arrowed). Tighten the bolts and bend tabs over them

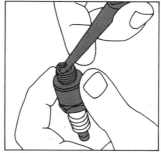

11 Fit a new spark-plug. Set the gap to ·025 in. by bending the earth electrode. Check with a feeler gauge

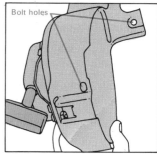

12 Check the cowling bolt holes. If more than one is split, fit a new cowling to the engine

Lawn mowers Carburettors

Adjusting and maintaining a fixed-jet carburettor

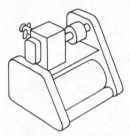

A carburettor is a mechanical device which mixes air and petrol and controls the flow of the mixture to the engine combustion chamber. If the carburettor is badly adjusted, the engine runs unevenly and may stop every time it is left to idle.

Find out what type of carburettor is fitted to the mower. If there is a float chamber, the carburettor may be either a fixed-jet or a slide type. The difference between them is that a slide carburettor has a cable leading directly into the top of it (see p. 482). The control cable on a fixed-jet carburettor attaches to the governor assembly. The third type—the diaphragm carburettor—has no float chamber (see p. 480).

To adjust a fixed-jet carburettor, start the engine and run it until it reaches normal working temperature. Set the throttle adjusting screw to a fast idling speed. Turn the main-jet screw until the engine sound is even. Undo the air-bleed screw until the engine falters and screw it back one full turn. Readjust the throttle control to normal idling.

If the engine does not run smoothly after adjustment, dismantle the carburettor and check its components.

Materials: parts as needed.
Tools: screwdriver; spanners; pliers.

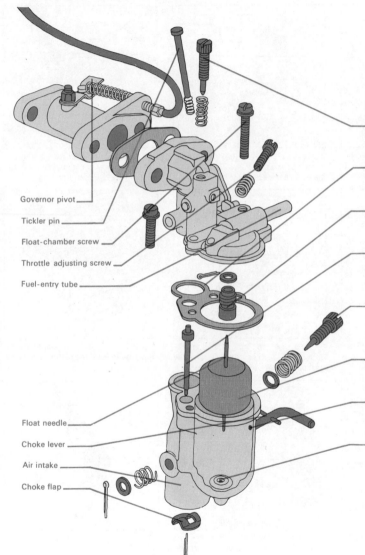

Governor pivot

Tickler pin

Float-chamber screw

Throttle adjusting screw

Fuel-entry tube

Float needle

Choke lever

Air intake

Choke flap

Air-bleed screw Fit a new one if the tapered point is grooved. Blow through the drilling, where the screw fits, to make sure it is clear

Gasket Always fit new gaskets at the inlet manifold and carburettor flange when the carburettor is dismantled

Needle seating Unscrew the assembly from the body of the carburettor. If the needle is pitted or grooved, fit a complete new assembly

Slow-running tube Never push wire into it. If a blockage cannot be cleared with an air line, obtain and fit a new tube

Jet-adjusting screw Screw right in. Count the number of turns. Remove it and check the needle point. If it is grooved or worn, fit a new screw

Float-chamber bowl Clean out sediment. If the varnish on the float itself is worn or cracked, renew the float

Vent hole Make sure that the vent hole in the side of the float-chamber bowl is clear to allow air to leave the chamber

Bore hole Make sure the small bore hole inside the base of the float chamber is clean and that the float spigot fits in it

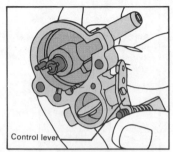

Control lever

Governor link Some governor linkages have more than one possible position. Note the hole in the control lever in which the governor link fits. Replace the link in the same hole to give correct governor speeds

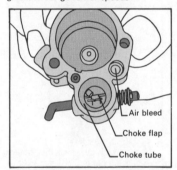

Air bleed

Choke flap

Choke tube

Choke flap Check that the choke tube and air-bleed hole are clear. Make sure the flap opens and closes fully when the lever is operated

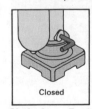

Closed

Open

Choke lever To close the choke, turn the lever horizontal to the carburettor body. To open, turn it downwards

Dismantling a fixed-jet carburettor

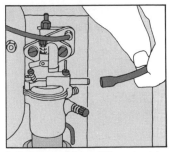

1 Pull the fuel line off the entry tube at the side of the carburettor above or beside the float chamber

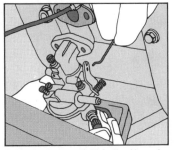

2 Undo the manifold bolts. Note the governor linkage or spring position and remove it from the carburettor

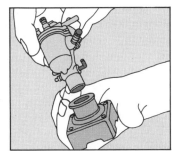

3 Lift the carburettor off the inlet manifold. Pull the air-filter assembly from the carburettor air intake

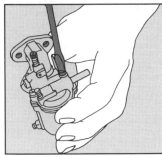

4 Undo the screws holding the float chamber. Note their correct positions if they differ in length

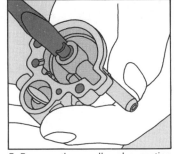

5 Remove the needle-valve seating from the top of the carburettor with a screwdriver wider than the slot

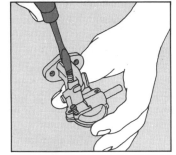

6 Undo the air-bleed screw. Renew it if it is worn or grooved. Screw it in fully. Turn it back three-quarters of a turn

7 Remove the float and check the needle seat. If it is worn, or if the float is damaged, renew it

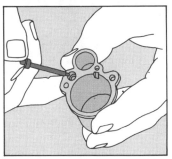

8 Lift out the slow-running tube. Blow through it to clear the bore. Use an air line if possible. Do not use wire

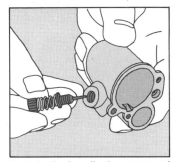

9 Undo the jet-adjusting screw and check that the needle is not bent or grooved. If damaged, fit a new one

Reassembling the carburettor

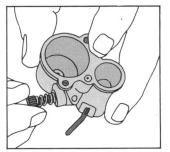

1 Refit the jet-adjusting screw. Screw it fully into the body, then unscrew it one-and-a-quarter turns

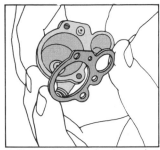

2 Renew the float-chamber gasket. Make sure that it fits over the head of the slow-running tube

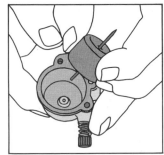

3 Fit the float assembly. Make sure that the square shaft of the needle fits correctly into the housing hole

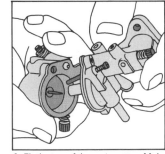

4 Fit the top of the carburettor. Make sure the float needle enters the needle seat. Tighten the bolts

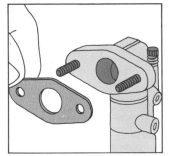

5 Clean up the flanges of the inlet manifold and the carburettor. Obtain and fit a new flange gasket

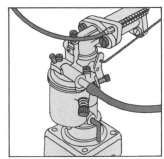

6 Refit the carburettor. Tighten the flange bolts, then refit the air cleaner, governor link and fuel line

Lawn mowers Carburettors

Maintaining a diaphragm carburettor

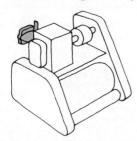

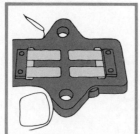

Reed valve Wash the unit in petrol. Check the reeds carefully. If any are not flat against the face of the unit, obtain and fit a complete new valve assembly

The most distinctive feature of a diaphragm carburettor is that it has no float chamber (see p. 478). It is normally fitted straight on to the engine crankcase with a non-return reed valve between the carburettor body and engine. This valve must be in sound condition to prevent the crankcase pressure blowing back.

At the base of the carburettor unit there is a round, flat plate with a small breather hole in it. It is through this hole that the atmospheric pressure pushes the diaphragm—a thin membrane of composition rubber and canvas. As the diaphragm rises, it lifts a needle valve to allow petrol to flow into the chamber above the diaphragm.

Before starting the engine, pump the small priming handle at the side of the carburettor. This pushes air in through the primer hole in the diaphragm cover to lift the needle valve and allow petrol to pass into the carburettor.

The main jet controls the amount of fuel entering the engine. To increase or lessen the flow, turn the main-jet adjusting screw. A non-return valve at the base of the jet prevents fuel escaping back down into the diaphragm chamber.

If the engine is not running smoothly, first try to adjust the throttle control and main jet. If this is not successful, dismantle the unit and examine the components for signs of wear. Renew bent or damaged needle valves.

Materials: parts as needed.
Tools: screwdrivers and spanners to suit carburettor; scriber.

THE DIAPHRAGM

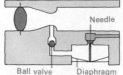

Needle

Ball valve   Diaphragm

While the engine is stationary the diaphragm is held down by the fuel and air pressure and the non-return ball valve is closed

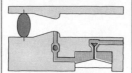

When the engine is running, suction lifts the ball off its seating and draws air and fuel from the chamber above the diaphragm. Atmospheric pressure pushes the diaphragm upwards, lifting the needle off its seating and allowing more fuel to flow. The fuel is metered according to engine speed by the difference in pressures between the chambers

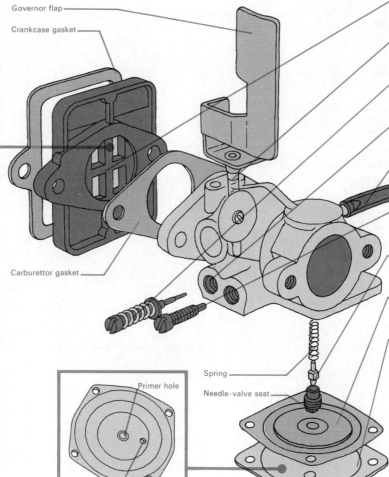

Governor flap

Crankcase gasket

Carburettor gasket

Spring

Needle-valve seat

Primer hole

Breather hole

Diaphragm cover Make sure that the breather hole in the diaphragm cover is clear. Blow through it with an air line

Reed valve The reeds of the valve should always face the engine. New gaskets must be fitted on both faces of the valve

Throttle spindle Check the throttle control spindle for wear. If it is worn, ask a dealer to fit a new one

Throttle adjustment If the needle point is worn or bent, renew it. Turn it to adjust the idling speed of the engine

Throttle-adjustment jet After removing the adjustment screw, blow through its drilling to make sure it is clear

Fuel line Remove fuel line from tank, not from carburettor. Blow and suck through pipe to check non-return valve is open

Main jet Blow through the small delivery hole in the end of the main jet. If it is blocked, renew the jet

Needle valve Check the point on the needle valve and the condition of its spring. If either is damaged, fit a new valve

Diaphragm Hold the diaphragm up to the light to see if it is damaged. If it is even slightly perforated renew it

Diaphragm cover Clean any sediment from the fuel chamber and diaphragm cover

Needle valve If its seat is grooved, obtain a new unit. If the spring is worn, fit a new one and ensure it moves freely

Removing the carburettor assembly

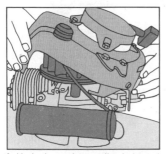

1 Undo the engine cowling bolts and remove the cowling. Disconnect the primer tube from the cowling button

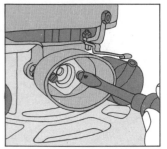

2 Pull the end off the air cleaner and remove the element. Lift out the rear gauze and undo the two screws

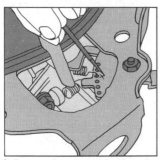

3 Remove the return spring from the governor linkage. Mark the hole it fits into with a scriber

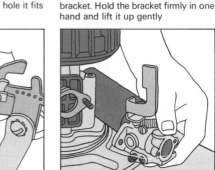

4 Undo the bolts holding the steady bracket. Hold the bracket firmly in one hand and lift it up gently

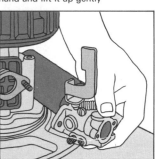

5 With the other hand disconnect the magneto earth lead which is attached to the bracket. Remove the bracket

6 Undo the nuts holding the carburettor to the engine. Remove the carburettor and reed valve behind it

Overhauling a diaphragm carburettor

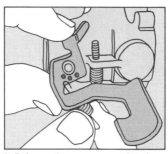

1 Remove the governor spring from the carburettor linkage. Mark the hole that the spring fits into

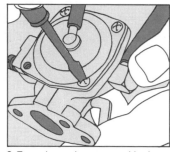

2 Turn the carburettor upside-down and remove the four screws holding the diaphragm cover plate

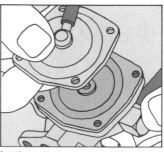

3 Lift the diaphragm cover off the body of the carburettor. Discard the gasket under the diaphragm lip

4 Remove the diaphragm. Hold it up to the light. If it is perforated, discard and renew it

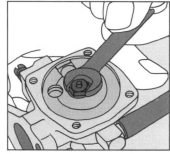

5 Use a small spanner to unscrew the needle-valve assembly seat from the centre of the carburettor body

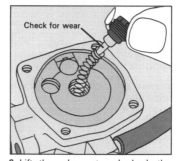

6 Lift the valve out and check the needle for wear. If the spring is bent, renew the complete valve unit

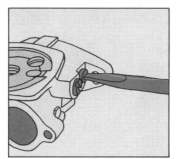

7 Turn the adjusting screw clockwise. Count the number of turns needed to unscrew it completely from the body

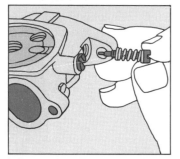

8 Remove the adjusting screw. Check the needle point for wear or bending. If it is damaged, renew it

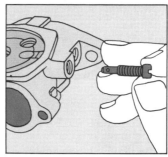

9 Unscrew the main jet. If it is blocked, blow through it with an air line. Reassemble the unit

Maintaining a slide carburettor

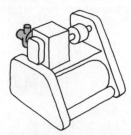

If the throttle cable runs directly from an operating lever on the mower handlebar into the top of the carburettor, the carburettor is a slide type. This means that, as the control lever is operated, a slide in the top of the carburettor body rises to allow air to enter the intake chamber. At the same time a needle at the bottom of the slide lifts and allows the appropriate amount of fuel to enter and mix with the air.

The float should be able to rise in its chamber to cut off the supply of petrol until more is needed.

A float is made of either copper or plastic. If it is copper, shake it and listen for fuel inside, which indicates that the float is perforated.

If a solid plastic float looks dull instead of shiny, it is probably absorbing petrol and so is too heavy to lift and operate as a cut-off mechanism.

Materials: parts as necessary.
Tools: screwdriver; spanners; pliers.

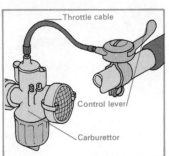

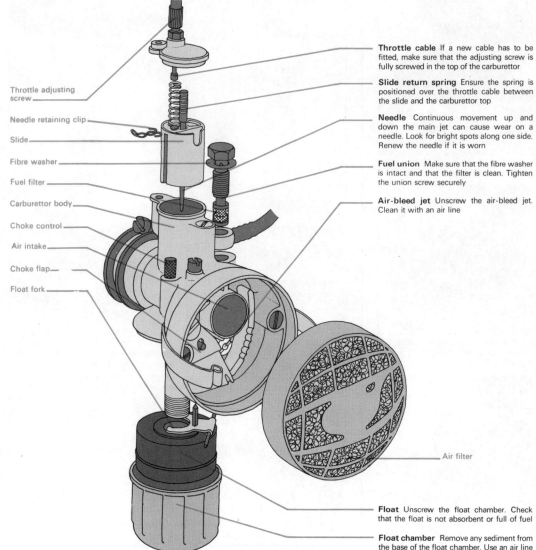

Throttle adjusting screw

Needle retaining clip

Slide

Fibre washer

Fuel filter

Carburettor body

Choke control

Air intake

Choke flap

Float fork

Air filter

Throttle cable If a new cable has to be fitted, make sure that the adjusting screw is fully screwed in the top of the carburettor

Slide return spring Ensure the spring is positioned over the throttle cable between the slide and the carburettor top

Needle Continuous movement up and down the main jet can cause wear on a needle. Look for bright spots along one side. Renew the needle if it is worn

Fuel union Make sure that the fibre washer is intact and that the filter is clean. Tighten the union screw securely

Air-bleed jet Unscrew the air-bleed jet. Clean it with an air line

Float Unscrew the float chamber. Check that the float is not absorbent or full of fuel

Float chamber Remove any sediment from the base of the float chamber. Use an air line to blow through any jets in the bottom

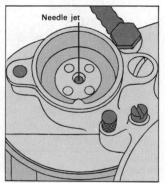

Needle jet Blow through the jet to make sure it is not blocked. If it cannot be cleared, take it to a dealer for replacement. A special tool is needed to remove and replace it

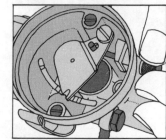

Choke flap Push and pull the choke control button on top of the housing. If the flap is stiff, lubricate the linkage with light oil

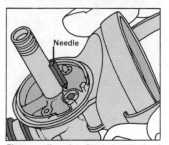

Float needle valve Check that the tip of the needle is not grooved. If it is worn, fit a complete new needle-valve assembly

Overhauling a slide carburettor

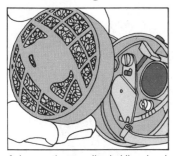

1 Loosen the two clips holding the air filter to the front of the carburettor. Wash the filter in petrol

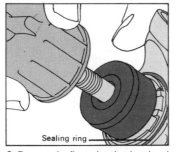

Sealing ring

2 Remove the float-chamber bowl and check the sealing ring in the carburettor body. Renew it if it is perished

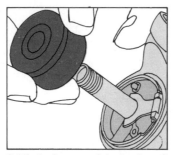

3 Lift the float out of the bowl or off the shaft. If it is punctured or absorbent, fit a new float

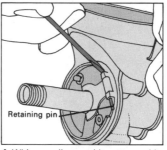

Retaining pin

4 With a small screwdriver at one side, push the retaining pin as far as possible out of the float fork

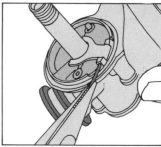

5 Grip the pin with a pair of pliers and pull it free. Hold the carburettor upside-down and remove the float fork

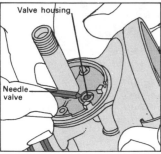

Valve housing

Needle valve

6 Lift out the needle valve. If it is worn, unscrew the valve housing and fit a complete new assembly

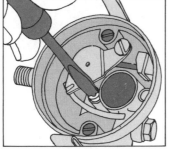

7 Turn the carburettor on its side. Un-screw the air-bleed jet and blow through it to make sure it is clear

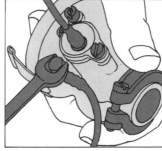

8 At the side, undo the fuel-union nut, clean the filter in petrol and fit new fibre washers each side of the union

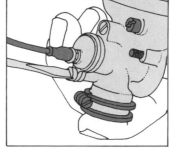

9 Undo the screw holding the car-burettor top to the body. Some threaded tops are screwed on the body

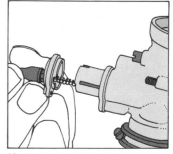

10 Draw the top and slide assembly from body. Keep the assembly straight to avoid damaging the needle

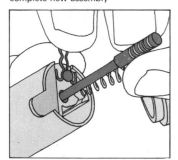

11 If the needle point is worn, fit a new needle. Note in which groove the securing clip is fitted

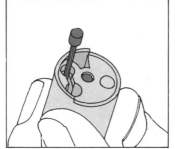

12 If the throttle cable is worn or frayed, turn over the top and push the cable nipple out of the slide base

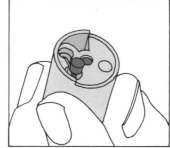

13 Gently pull the nipple across the elongated slot in the slide. Push it out through the larger hole

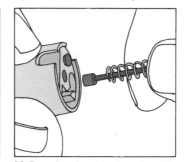

14 From the other side, draw the cable and the return spring out of the slide. Fit a new cable

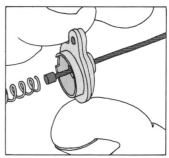

15 Fit the spring over the cable and push the nipple through the slide to locate it in the stop hole. Reassemble

Lawn mowers Throttles

Most petrol-engined mowers have a friction throttle lever, which can be set in any position. If the lever is not holding, undo the centre bolt and fit new friction washers.

Centre bolt
Washer
Cover
Tension spring
Friction plate
Friction washer
Lever
Lever housing

Cable nipple
Inner cable
Outer casing

Cable replacement Fit the nipple into the hole in the lever and turn the cable down into the cable slot. Make sure that the nipple moves freely in the lever, as it has to turn when the lever is operated

Lawn mowers Air filters

Cleaning and maintenance

If a lawn-mower engine is emitting heavy black smoke, it is likely that the air filter is blocked. This restricts the flow of air into the carburettor and results in too rich a mixture, which eventually stops the engine. Check and clean the filter every time the machine is serviced.

Materials: filter element; engine-oil; petrol.

OIL-FILLED FILTER

Some filter units have an oil-filled bowl and replaceable element. Fill the bowl to the recommended level.

1 Pull back the two spring-loaded clips to release the oil-filled filter bowl

2 Pull down the bowl to remove the element. Clean the element and half fill the bowl with oil

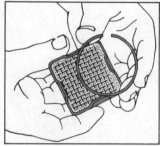

1 If a sponge filter is fitted, remove the assembly from the carburettor. Pinch and lift out the circlip

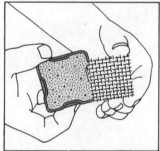

2 Pull off the protective filter gauze from the body. Wash the gauze thoroughly in clean petrol

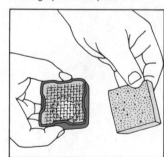

3 Lift out the sponge. Wash in petrol and squeeze dry. Soak in oil and squeeze out the surplus

PAPER ELEMENT

A dry paper filter can be cleaned by tapping it against a firm surface. Under no circumstances should it be cleaned by washing: fit a new one if it is in bad condition.

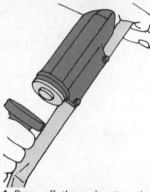

1 Draw off the carburettor air-delivery tube attached to the body of the air-filter assembly

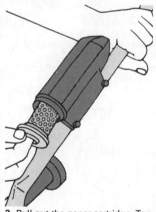

2 Pull out the paper cartridge. Tap it to remove dust and dirt. If it is very dirty, fit a new element

Lawn mowers Ignition

Cleaning contact-breaker points

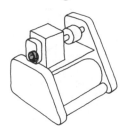

If the engine is running badly, disconnect the lead from the spark-plug and hold it against the engine body. Turn the engine. If there is a good spark, fit a new plug (see p. 644). If the spark is weak, check the contact-breaker points. Renew them if re-facing does not leave a level surface. The contact-breaker gap on all but Aspera and Briggs and Stratton engines can be reset through a panel in the flywheel, but if the points have to be replaced, remove the flywheel. If the flywheel is not located by a key on the crankshaft, note the timing marks to help with reassembly.

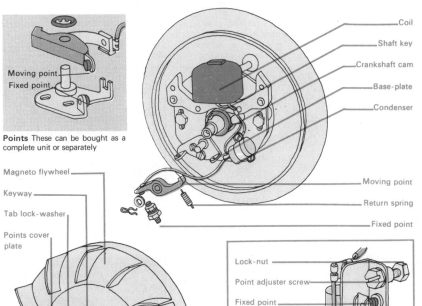

Moving point
Fixed point

Points These can be bought as a complete unit or separately

Magneto flywheel

Keyway

Tab lock-washer

Points cover plate

Coil

Shaft key

Crankshaft cam

Base-plate

Condenser

Moving point

Return spring

Fixed point

Lock-nut

Point adjuster screw

Fixed point

Moving point

Condenser

Return spring

Briggs and Stratton On this engine, points have one adjusting screw and a lock-nut. When new points are fitted, coat the threads of the mounting screws and the points cover with mastic sealer

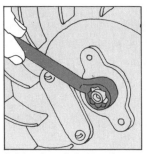

1 Prise the tab lock-washer up and undo the flywheel nut until it is flush with the shaft end

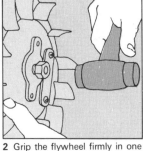

2 Grip the flywheel firmly in one hand. Strike the nut at the shaft end with a mallet

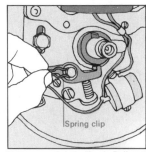

Spring clip

3 Remove the flywheel. Pull out the spring retaining clip to free the moving point

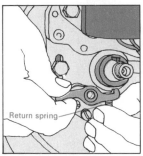

Return spring

4 Hold the return spring in place with one hand and lift out the moving point

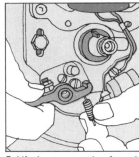

5 Lift the return spring from the holes in the moving point and the base-plate

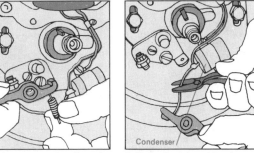

Condenser

6 If the lead is soldered, cut it about ¾ in. (20 mm) from the condenser. If not, unscrew

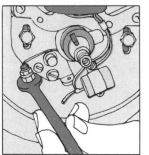

7 Undo the nut which holds the fixed point on the base. Remove the nut and two flat washers

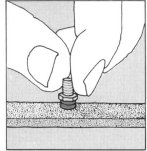

8 Re-face the surface of the fixed point by rubbing it on a dry emery stone. Hold it upright

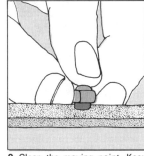

9 Clean the moving point. Keep the arm of the point off the emery stone. Replace (see p. 486)

Lawn mowers Ignition

Fitting new points and adjusting the gap

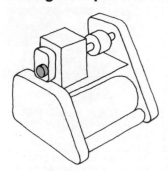

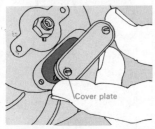
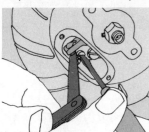
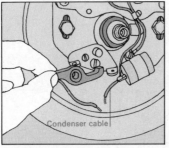

1 Strip the insulation off the ends of the new moving-point lead and off the short condenser lead

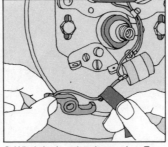

2 Wind the bared ends together. Tape them securely with a small piece of plastic insulating tape

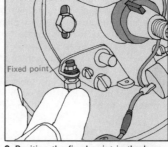

3 Position the fixed point in the base-plate with a flat washer on either side of the plate. Screw on the nut

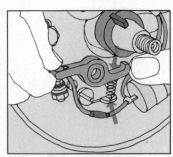

4 Fit the return spring in the arm of the movable point and in the hole in the base-plate bracket

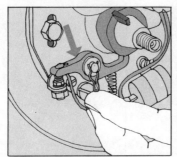

5 Locate the movable-point arm on its shaft. Fit a flat washer and the spring retaining clip

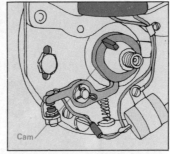

6 Turn the engine until the high point of the cam is against the moving point. The points will then be open

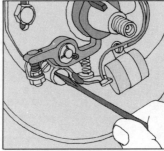

7 Undo the base-plate securing screw, then tighten it just enough to hold the plate in position

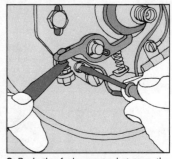

8 Push the feeler gauge between the points. Move the base-plate by turning the adjusting screw

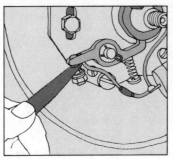

9 Spin the cam on the shaft and check again with the feeler. It should be a close fit between the points

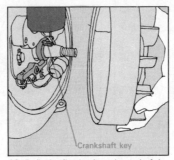

10 Refit the flywheel on the end of the shaft. Make sure the crankshaft key is located correctly

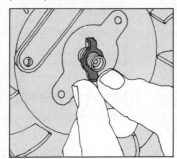

11 Use a new tab lock-washer. Make sure that it fits in the keyway. Fit and tighten the nut

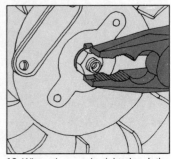

12 When the nut is tight, bend the tab of the lock-washer over the edge of the nut

Lawn mowers Electric

Maintenance of batteries

Many battery-operated mowers have a built-in charger. If one is not fitted, a charger can be bought separately. Put the battery on charge every time the machine is used.

Most chargers are 1½ amp. If the machine is used for, say, 30 minutes, the battery must receive a 12-hour charge to bring it back to a fully charged state (see p. 528).

Never let the battery on a mower become completely discharged. If this is allowed to occur, a domestic battery charger is not strong enough to recharge it fully; take the battery to a garage for attention.

The drive and cutting mechanism of a battery-operated mower are similar to those on hand-pushed and petrol-engined mowers.

Materials: distilled water; Vaseline.
Tools: wire brush; spanner; clean rag.

BATTERY CARE

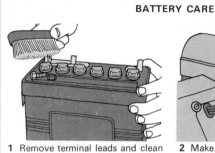 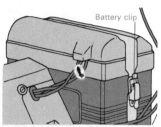

Battery clip

1 Remove terminal leads and clean posts with wire brush. Wipe the case dry and coat the posts and terminal-lead ends with Vaseline

2 Make sure the battery-case top is fitted properly. Tighten the securing clips, to prevent battery moving when machine vibrates

Topping up Top up the battery with distilled water. The water must just cover the plates. Clean and dry battery top with a rag

Battery clip

Battery

Cylinder

Front roller

Chain cover

Electric motor

Height-adjusting lever

CLUTCH ADJUSTMENT

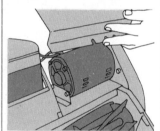

1 Lift cover off motor to gain access to clutch-adjusting screw

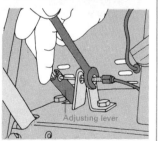

Adjusting lever

2 Loosen lock-nut and undo cable adjuster until there is at least ⅛ in. (3 mm) free play

Cable care of mains-powered mowers

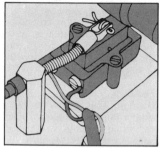

Do not attempt any maintenance work on a mains-powered lawn mower until the plug has been disconnected from the power supply.

Maintenance of the drive and cutting mechanism is the same as for any other type of cylinder or rotary mower (see p. 443).

Electrical maintenance consists mainly of cable care. If a longer cable is needed, use a manufacturer's recommended non-crushable waterproof connector. Never use a standard domestic connector: it could cause a short circuit when used on a damp or wet lawn. Check the handlebar switch control cable regularly. If it is worn, renew it.

Materials: waterproof non-crushable connector; control cable; split-pin.
Tools: electrician's screwdriver; pliers.

EXTENSION CABLE

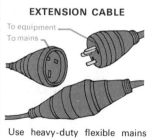

To equipment

To mains

Use heavy-duty flexible mains cable and a waterproof plug and socket of the type recommended by the mower manufacturers

1 Remove the motor cover from the machine to gain access to the switch control cable

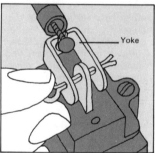

Yoke

2 Squeeze the ends of the split-pin together. Pull out the pin to free the yoke from the switch lever

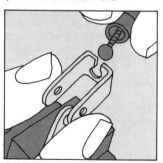

3 Slip the cable nipple out of the yoke and remove the cable from its stop. Fit a new cable

Lawns

Looking after a lawn

Cut the grass at least once a week throughout the growing season. On a lawn which receives a lot of wear, set the blades $\frac{1}{2}$–$\frac{3}{4}$ in. (13–20 mm) high. Ornamental lawns of fine grass should be more closely cut—say $\frac{3}{8}$ in. (10 mm).

Feeding

On light soils, yearly or twice-yearly applications of fertiliser, preferably mixed with sifted compost, are essential. Lawns on even the most fertile soils benefit from an annual dressing.

As a mild stimulant, apply $\frac{1}{2}$ oz. sulphate of ammonia, mixed with 4 oz. of dry sand, per sq. yd (18 gr. mixed with 140 gr. per sq. m). Such a stimulant, however, should never be used after July, when it would produce too lush a growth in the autumn. For a more balanced, long-lasting effect, use a proprietary lawn fertiliser and follow the manufacturer's recommendations. Most are intended to be used during the growing season. Water the lawn thoroughly if rain does not fall within a few days of application.

Weeds

It is possible to destroy most lawn weeds, without harming the grass, by using proprietary selective weedkillers. Some are effective against a wide range; others are more specific. Use a broad-action killer first, and treat weeds which persist with a suitable specific mixture.

Moss

Treat moss patches with a proprietary killer, following the manufacturer's instructions. An alternative is to sprinkle with $\frac{1}{2}$ oz. sulphate of iron mixed with 4 oz. sand per sq. yd (18 gr. mixed with 140 gr. per sq. m). If the moss was caused by bad drainage, rectify the fault first (see p. 427). In all cases, feed the lawn with fertiliser after treatment.

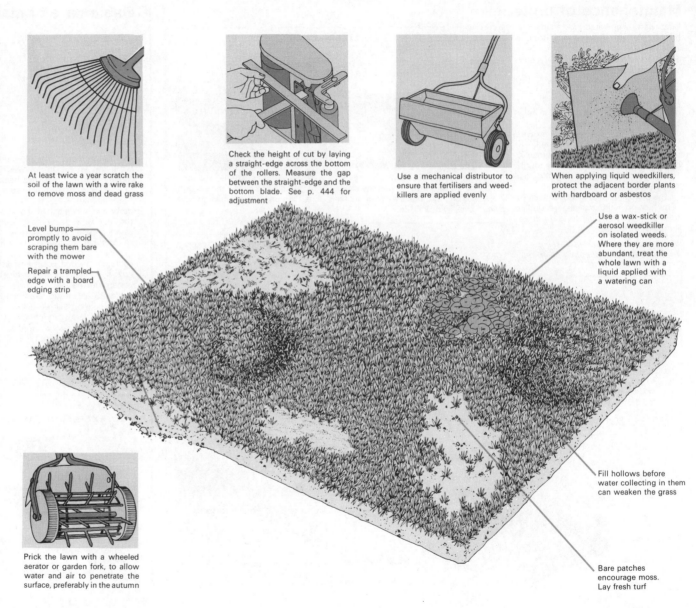

At least twice a year scratch the soil of the lawn with a wire rake to remove moss and dead grass

Check the height of cut by laying a straight-edge across the bottom of the rollers. Measure the gap between the straight-edge and the bottom blade. See p. 444 for adjustment

Use a mechanical distributor to ensure that fertilisers and weed-killers are applied evenly

When applying liquid weedkillers, protect the adjacent border plants with hardboard or asbestos

Level bumps promptly to avoid scraping them bare with the mower

Repair a trampled edge with a board edging strip

Use a wax-stick or aerosol weedkiller on isolated weeds. Where they are more abundant, treat the whole lawn with a liquid applied with a watering can

Prick the lawn with a wheeled aerator or garden fork, to allow water and air to penetrate the surface, preferably in the autumn

Fill hollows before water collecting in them can weaken the grass

Bare patches encourage moss. Lay fresh turf

Levelling humps and hollows

Replacing a worn patch

1 With a spade, cut two lines at least 2 in. (50 mm) deep at right angles across the bump or hollow

2 Continue each line 12 in. (305 mm) beyond the fault; cut round the outside to form four squares

3 Undercut each square about 2 in. (50 mm) and lift it out. Place the squares aside in matching positions

4 If the fault is a hump, dig away the surplus soil and any large stones. Remove any tree roots visible

1 Obtain sufficient new turfs to cover the worn area. Remove the worn turfs, loosen and level the soil, then firm it

5 If the lawn is hollowed, sift enough topsoil to level it and pour the soil in the depression

6 Rake the surface level and loosen the top 2–3 in. (50–75 mm) with a fork to help re-establish the turf

7 Remove any large stones. Cut a board the width of the hole and tamp the soil firm with its edge

8 Replace each turf in its original position. Butt the edges firmly against the unlifted turf

2 Add or remove soil if necessary. Place the new turfs with their edges firmly butted against the old

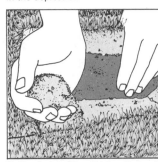

9 Check that the re-laid turf is level. If necessary lift the pieces again and add or remove soil

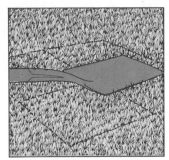

10 Firm the turf with the back of a spade. Keep the blade flat to avoid damaging the turf

11 Alternatively, use a square of wood, 1 in. (25 mm) thick, nailed to a 2×2 in. (50×50 mm) handle

12 Sprinkle a little sifted soil along the joins and brush it in lightly with a stiff broom

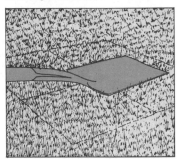

3 Firm the new turf evenly. Sprinkle sifted soil along the joins and brush it in with a broom

Lawns

Leaf-sweepers

Repairing a damaged edge

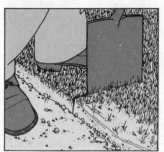

1 With a spade, cut a line 1½ in. (40 mm) deep at both ends of the damaged edge

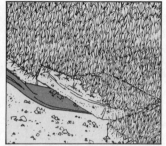

2 Cut a third line to form a square or rectangle. Undercut and lift the turf from the lawn

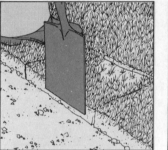

3 Turn the turf with its damaged edge inwards. Re-lay it and tap the outside edge to line with the border

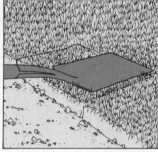

4 Firm the turf evenly with the back of the spade. Do not move it out of alignment with the border

5 Fill the damaged area, now inside, with sifted soil. Firm it and sprinkle grass seed over the new soil

6 Sprinkle fine soil over the seed. Push in small canes to mark the area until the grass is established

How a leaf-sweeper works

All garden leaf-sweepers have a set of brushes which can move in only one direction. Leaves are thrown up at the front to hit a shield which deflects them into a basket. This is usually pivoted so that the leaves can be discharged without tipping the machine.

Some sweepers have four separate brushes, each mounted on a backing board: others have two boards with two brushes on each.

Axle shaft

Pinion

Wheel

Frame bracket

Basket

Handle

Brushes

Deflector shield

Height-adjustment screw

Bearing

Changing the brushes Remove the nuts holding each brush board on the axle

shaft (left); tap the bolts through the board and lift off the old brushes (above)

Freewheel mechanism

Each wheel on a leaf-sweeper has a freewheel mechanism which works in the same way as the freewheel on a lawn mower (see p. 448). If the wheels do not turn the brushes when the sweeper is pushed forwards, it is likely that the pawls are broken and are no longer engaging the pinion.

If the brushes turn when the sweeper is pulled backwards, one of the mechanisms has jammed and needs repairing.

Materials: pawl; pinion; light oil; grease.
Tools: spanners; pliers; screwdriver.

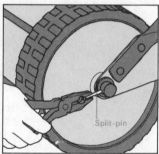

Split-pin

1 Pinch up the ends of the axle split-pin with pliers. Draw the pin out of the axle

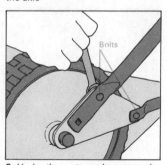

Bolts

2 Undo the nuts and remove the bolts holding the handle to the frame bracket. Remove handle *(continued)*

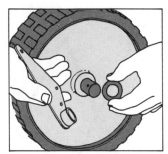

3 Slide the frame bracket off the axle and remove the washer between the wheel and bracket

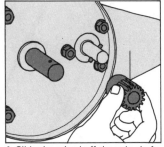

4 Slide the wheel off the axle shaft. Remove the driving pinion from the end of the brush shaft

Check for damage

5 Clean the end of the brush shaft. Pull out the pawl. Make sure the pawl and pinion are not damaged

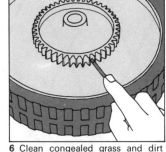

6 Clean congealed grass and dirt from the gearwheel teeth with a screwdriver. Do not grease the teeth

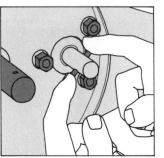

7 Fit the pawl in its slot on the axle shaft. Oil it lightly and make sure it slides. Refit the pinion

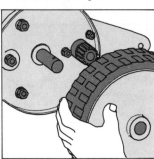

8 Clean the axle shaft. Smear a little grease on the shaft. Fit the pinion and refit the wheel

Fitting new brush-shaft bearings

A leaf-sweeper brush shaft rotates on a ball-race mounted at each end of the shaft. When the shaft moves up and down excessively, check the bearings. If they are worn, renew them.

Remove both wheels and the pinion and pawl mechanism to gain access to the two side-plates on which the bearings are fitted. Only one side-plate need be removed to dismantle the brush gear: remove only the bearing housing on the second side-plate.

Materials: two new ball-races; high-melting-point grease.
Tools: spanners; punch; hammer; vice; mallet.

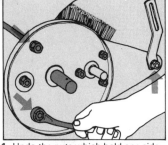

1 Undo the nuts which hold one side-plate on the crossbars of the leaf-sweeper. Remove the nuts

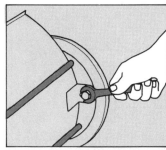

2 Undo the deflector-shield bolt which is screwed into a nut welded on the side-plate

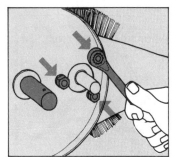

3 Remove the nuts from the bolts which hold the bearing housing on the side-plate. Remove side-plate

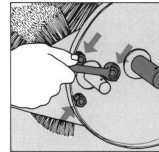
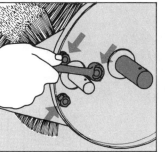

4 At the other wheel undo the nuts which hold the bearing housing on the side-plate

6 Support the bearing housing and strike the shaft with a hide mallet to remove the bearing

7 Slide off the bearing tension spring which is fitted behind the bearing housing at one end of the shaft

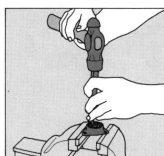

5 Pull the brush shaft out of the second wheel and lift off the bearing covers at both sides

8 Hold the bearing housing in a vice. Tap a steel punch on the centre ring to remove the ball-race *(continued)*

Leaf-sweepers

(continued)

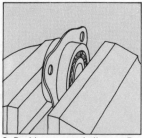

9 Position a new ball-race. Put the housing in a vice and tighten the vice to press the race into the housing

10 Make sure the ball-race is fully home. Pack grease into the housing and work it between the ball bearings

11 Fit the shaft spacing washers. Refit the spring on the correct end. Tap the two bearing assemblies on to the shaft

12 Replace the bearing cover and slide the complete brush-shaft assembly into the sweeper side-plate

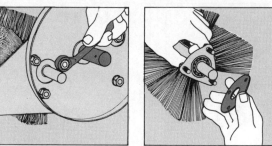

13 Fit the housing bolts, spring washers and nuts. Tighten the nuts firmly to hold the bearing housing in place

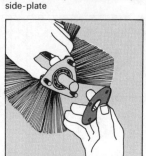

14 Refit the other side-plate. First fit and tighten the shaft bearing bolts, then tighten the crossbar nuts

Nets

Knots used in repairs

A net is usually one continuous piece of string or cord, woven and knotted to make a pattern of meshes.

There are two types of net: square-mesh and diamond-mesh. The knots are the same in each; only the pattern and edges are different (see p. 493).

When a net is made, only one basic knot, called the sheet-bend, is used. This is also used in repair with two others—the figure-of-eight, for starting a repair, and the side knot.

Materials: cord or twine to match thickness of net.
Tools: netmaker's needle; gauge; scissors; rod or broom handle.

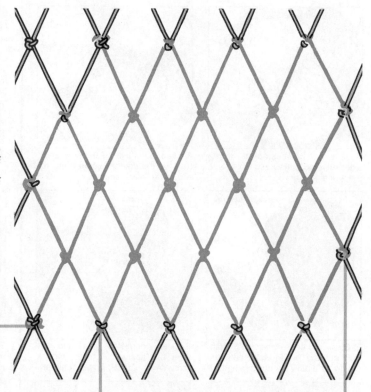

FIGURE-OF-EIGHT KNOT

To start a net repair, join the new twine to an old mesh with a figure-of-eight knot

SHEET-BEND KNOT

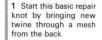

1 Start this basic repair knot by bringing new twine through a mesh from the back

2 Pass the twine up, then take it round the back of the mesh so that it forms a loop

3 Pass the twine down, to cross behind the loop just formed, but in front of the mesh

4 Pull the twine to tighten the knot so that it is in the centre at the bottom of the mesh

SIDE KNOT

At the end of a row, loop the twine from behind, round and up into the old mesh. Finish with the sheet-bend technique

Tools required

If a large area of net has to be repaired, buy a netmaker's needle from a handicraft dealer. Two types are available: show the dealer what thickness of cord is being repaired.

Thread the twine on to the needle as shown below. As it is woven into the meshes, it is unwound from the needle.

To ensure that the new meshes match the old in size, make a gauge. Cut a thin strip of wood just less than half the depth of the meshes and long enough to cover at least three mesh widths.

Cut-out needle Used for heavy nets. Thread on the cord as shown

Simple needle Made of plastic, this is best for fine-mesh nets

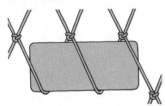

Gauge Hold it against knots of meshes above the repair. Pass new cord or twine round bottom edge of gauge and knot at top

Mending a hole in a net

Before starting a repair, find out which is the top side of the net. This can be determined by loosening any one of the existing knots. The net is the right way up when a sheet-bend knot (as shown on p. 492) is at the top of the mesh from which it is made.

To support the net, push a rod or broom handle horizontally through the meshes just above the damaged area. Hang the net from a wall at a convenient working height.

If more than one row of meshes is damaged, a gauge will be needed to keep the mesh at the right size.

Take a piece of the damaged net to a hardware store or ships' chandler to obtain matching cord or twine.

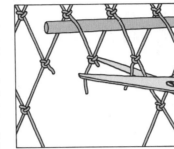

IDENTIFICATION

Unpick any knot and hang net so that knots are at top of their meshes

Diamond-mesh nets have cord attached to top of each edge mesh

Square-mesh nets have double or triple cords round all four edges

1 To repair a diamond-mesh net, hang it and cut out damage. Round its edge cut off all loose strands at the knots

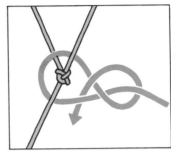

2 Start at the top row on left of hole. Tie the new twine in a figure-of-eight round the old knot

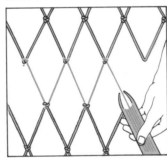

3 If only one row is needed, zigzag the twine between the old meshes, tying in a sheet-bend at each turn

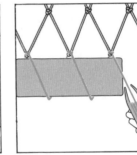

4 If more than one row is needed, hold gauge as indicated. Wrap twine round it, knotting at the top

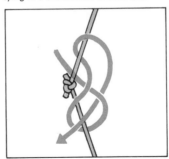

5 When the end of a row is reached, tie the cord with a side knot. Continue back along the row below

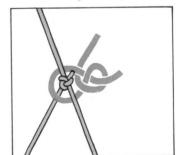

6 At the end of the repair, tie the cord in figure-of-eight to the knot in the nearest old mesh

SQUARE-MESH NETS

Always hang a square-mesh net diagonally to repair it.

The techniques used are the same as those for diamond-mesh, except at the edges.

Work the first row from right to left. When at the end of each row, double the cord back on itself, as in lower picture, to start the row below. To keep the net square, make an extra mesh at each left-hand side and reduce each row by one mesh on the right of the net. Use sheet-bends to start and fill the hole: finish with a figure-of-eight knot.

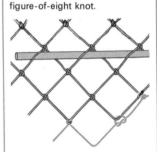

Right-hand side Tie the new cord at the edge of the net. Start row below one mesh to the left

Left-hand side Double back cord to make additional mesh on the left of the row below

Paths and drives Concrete

A concrete path may develop holes or cracks because it has been badly laid—perhaps with a poor bed of rubble which allows subsidence—or because the mixture was inadequate (see p. 693). Because similar damage is likely to occur later at some other part of the path, the only fully satisfactory solution is to break up the path and re-lay it.

If, however, this is not possible, the faulty areas can be patched or filled with fresh concrete.

Concrete consists of water, cement and a mixture of stone and sand, called aggregate. Cement and aggregate may not be available in small loose quantities, but it is possible to buy them ready-mixed in varying proportions for different types of work. Always add a PVA bonding agent to the mix to ensure a sound bond between the new and old concrete.

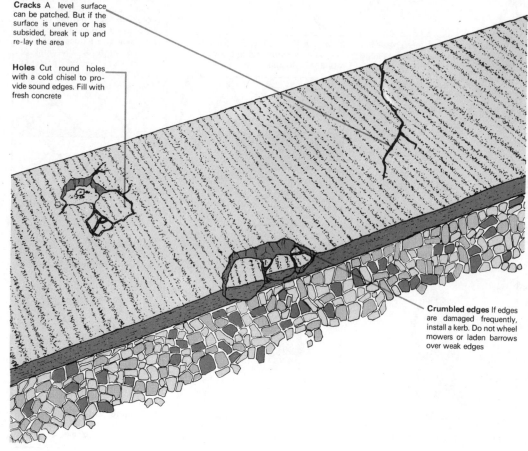

Cracks A level surface can be patched. But if the surface is uneven or has subsided, break it up and re-lay the area

Holes Cut round holes with a cold chisel to provide sound edges. Fill with fresh concrete

Crumbled edges If edges are damaged frequently, install a kerb. Do not wheel mowers or laden barrows over weak edges

Filling a crack

If a path develops a crack because of subsidence, it is difficult to achieve a smooth, satisfactory repair without breaking up the sunken area and re-laying it on a sound foundation. If, however, the surface of the path is quite even, although the concrete is cracked, it is a simple matter to fill it with mortar—a mixture containing no stones. If the path is coloured, make sure that the fresh mixture is similarly tinted (see p. 693).

Materials: sharp sand and cement (3:1); PVA bonding agent; water.
Tools: hammer; cold chisel; wire brush; trowel or float; broad brush; board.

1 Chip along both sides of the crack with a hammer and cold chisel to form a V groove about 1 in. (25 mm) wide

2 Use a wire brush to remove all the dirt and loose concrete chippings along the widened crack

3 With a broad brush spread a priming coat of PVA bonding agent along the surfaces of the concrete groove

4 Mix cement, sand and water with PVA bonding (see p. 693) on a board. Pack the mortar into the groove

5 Make sure the mixture is well packed against the edges of the groove. Level it with a trowel or float

Repairing a crumbling edge

The edges of a solid concrete path may crumble and break off if they are subject to rough wear. Avoid trundling lawn mowers and wheelbarrows over unprotected edges: lay a board across the edge if it has to be crossed by wheeled equipment.

Clear a damaged edge thoroughly and make sure that the foundations are sound before filling with new mortar. Use a mixture of 4 parts sand to 1 part cement.

Materials: sharp sand and cement (4:1); water; PVA bonding agent.
Tools: spade; edging board; float or trowel; hammer; chisel; broad brush.

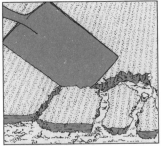

1 Lever out all the broken pieces. Chip back with a chisel if necessary and strengthen the foundations

2 Lay a board along the edge and hold it with bricks. Brush bonding agent in the hole

3 Mix the mortar as dry as possible (see p. 693) and shovel it into the hole at the edge

4 Make sure that the mortar is packed against the edges. Firm it with the back of a spade

5 Smooth with a trowel or float. Remove the board after 48 hours, but leave for seven days before use

Replacing a flagstone

Flagstones are available from a builders' merchant in many shapes, sizes and colours. To obtain a matching stone, take the merchant a piece of the one to be replaced.

Two mortar mixtures are required. Fix the flagstones in place with a wet mixture of 3 parts sand to 1 part cement: fill the gaps between the slabs with a barely damp mixture of 6 parts sand to 1 part cement. Make sure that the stone is level with adjacent stones, and brush off any surplus concrete.

Materials: sand; cement; water.
Tools: spade; trowel; tamping timber; straight-edged length of wood.

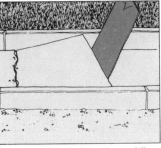

1 Lever out the broken pieces of flagstone with a spade. Remove about 1 in. (25 mm) of the base

2 If the base has sunk, firm it and shovel in a little dry-mix mortar (6:1). Level with a trowel

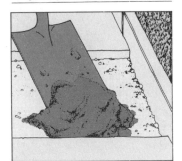

3 When the base is at the same level as the surrounding area, fill with the wet-mix mortar (3:1)

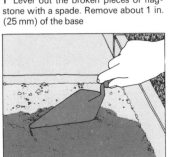

4 Use the trowel to smooth the mortar. Add more until it is flush with the bottom of the other stones

5 Place the edge of the new flagstone on the edge of an adjacent stone. Lower it gently into the open space

6 Tamp the stone down gently at each corner with a length of strong timber. Take care not to crack it

7 Check the level of the stone with a straight-edged length of wood. If necessary remove it and fill the base

8 Mix a little more dry mortar (6:1). Use the edge of the trowel to tamp the mixture down between the flagstones

Paths and drives Concrete

Replacing a kerbstone

Kerbstones are available from builders' merchants in many standard sizes. It is advisable to remove the damaged stone from the path and take part of it to the dealer to make sure that he has a replacement of matching colour and texture.

Check the foundations before fitting a new kerbstone. If the original stone broke because of subsidence, add more rubble to the foundation to bring the kerbstone in line.

Materials: matching kerbstone; sharp sand and cement (3:1); water.
Tools: mallet or club hammer; spade; trowel; straight piece of wood.

1 Use a mallet or club hammer to tap the broken pieces of kerbstone. Do not damage the adjacent paving

2 Carefully prise out the pieces with a spade. Remove about 2 in. (50 mm) of the old base

3 Loosen and level the base. Mix mortar (see p. 693) and spread it in the base, 2 in. (50 mm) deep

4 Ease the new kerbstone into place. Use the end of the hammer handle to tap it down very gently

5 Lay a straight piece of wood over the kerb and along the sides to make sure that the new stone is in line

Casting a new kerbstone

If a kerbstone of the correct shape, height and width cannot be obtained, cast a replacement stone in position in the kerb from wet concrete. The mixture required is 4 parts sandy aggregate to 1 part cement.

It is unlikely that the new stone will ever match the rest of the kerb exactly, especially if the original concrete is coloured. One solution is to treat the whole kerb with a cement paint.

Materials: ¾ in. (20 mm) all-in aggregate; cement; water.
Tools: mallet or club hammer; shovel; trowel; float or length of wood; edging boards.

1 Remove the damaged stone. Tap a length of wood into the soil outside. Support with pegs if necessary

2 Lay a thinner strip inside the kerb and hold it in position with bricks. Make sure the wood is flush with the kerb top

3 Mix the concrete (see p. 693) and pack it into the gap in the kerb. Use a shovel if the gap is very large

4 Make sure that the concrete is forced against the boards and that it is tightly packed. Push it down several times

5 Use a piece of wood longer than the stone being cast to ensure that the concrete is flush with the other stones

6 Smooth the top of the concrete with the trowel. If the other stones have rounded edges, shape the wet concrete

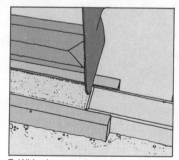

7 With the trowel, mark the division between the concrete and the adjacent stones. Remove surplus concrete

8 Leave the concrete to set for at least 48 hours. When it is hard, remove the two edging boards

Paths and drives Asphalt

Repairing a broken edge

If a path or drive shows signs of wear, buy ready-mixed macadam from a builders' merchant. Use an edging board to make sure that the repaired edge is straight and neat.

To compress the macadam over a large area, use a lawn roller. Keep it wet to avoid lifting patches. If only a small part is being repaired, however, it may be better to make a special tamping tool —called a punner. Nail a piece of 1 in. (25 mm) wood, about 6 × 6 in. (150 × 150 mm), on the end of a 2 × 2 in. (50 × 50 mm) wooden handle.

Materials: macadam; water.
Tools: hammer; chisel; broom; punner or roller; spade; edging board.

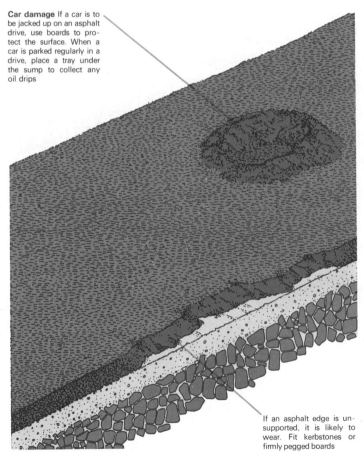

Car damage If a car is to be jacked up on an asphalt drive, use boards to protect the surface. When a car is parked regularly in a drive, place a tray under the sump to collect any oil drips

If an asphalt edge is unsupported, it is likely to wear. Fit kerbstones or firmly pegged boards

1 Lay a straight piece of timber on the path parallel to the edge. Score a new edge line behind the damage

3 Remove all the soil and debris with a spade, level with the base of the sound asphalt

5 Spread macadam mixture into the hole until it is proud of the surrounding surface. Roll or tamp it firm

2 Chip out the asphalt between the marked line and original edge. Extend the chipping beyond the worn area

4 Lay a board along the edge. Tap it into the soil until it is flush with the asphalt. Support with pegs if necessary

6 When the patch is solid and level, carefully remove the edging board. Leave for 24 hours before use

Filling a hole

1 Use a hammer and chisel to chip a square or rectangular section out of the path around the hollowed area

2 Dig out the asphalt and base. Make sure that the enlarged hole is at least 1½ in. (40 mm) deep

3 Sweep the hole clean. If it is not deep enough, dig out a little more base or soil *(continued)*

(continued)

4 Shovel in enough macadam to stand a little above the surrounding surface. Keep it off the old asphalt

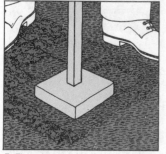

5 Firm the macadam patch with a wooden punner. Use a lawn roller if the repaired area is extensive

6 If the firming creates indentations in the surface, shovel in more macadam and firm it. Leave for 24 hours

Filling a hollow

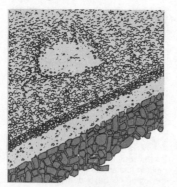

Most loose-stoned paths and drives are laid with rounded ⅜ in. (10 mm) pea shingle. Gravel, which is also used, is a coarser angular stone, ungraded in size. Another alternative is hoggin—a mixture of gravel and clay.

Sweep the drive clear of gravel and shingle every three years. Discard worn stones and mix the remainder with a fresh supply of matching stone.

It may be difficult to obtain gravel or shingle in quantities of less than ½ cu. yd (0·4 sq m). It can, however, be kept to restore worn areas.

Materials: gravel, shingle or hoggin.
Tools: shovel; spade; rake; roller.

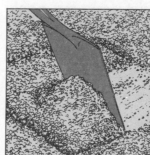

1 Use a spade to mark a square or rectangular area round the hollow in the gravel or shingle

2 Scrape off all the loose stones until a sound, firm base is reached. Level it with the back of the spade

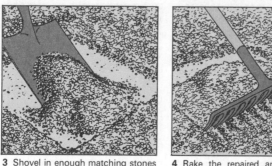

3 Shovel in enough matching stones to cover the whole cleared area to the depth of the rest of the drive

4 Rake the repaired area to blend with the surrounding surface. Turn the head of the rake and tamp down

Replacing a broken brick

For safety, remove and replace bricks in a path or drive as soon as they break. Take a piece of damaged brick to a building supplier to make sure that the replacement bricks match those of the pathway.

Do not attempt to hammer the brick level. If it does not fit flush with the surrounding surface, remove it and add to or take away some of the mortar mix underneath the brick to get it at the correct height.

Materials: bricks; sand and cement (3:1); water.
Tools: trowel; straight-edged timber; spirit level.

1 Use a trowel to prise out the broken pieces of brick. Do not disturb the surrounding bricks

2 Remove all the debris from the hole and lay in a 1 in. (25 mm) bed of 3:1 mortar mixture (see p. 693)

3 Fit a new brick in position and tamp it down gently with the trowel handle. Remove surplus mortar

4 Check the repair by laying a spirit-level or a straight piece of timber over the area

Pools Swimming and ornamental

Repair techniques

A fall in the water level of a swimming or ornamental pool does not necessarily indicate that the pool is leaking. Because of evaporation, a pool can be considered watertight if the level does not drop more than about $\frac{1}{2}$ in. (13 mm) in a week.

Concrete pools

There are two main causes of damage to the structure of a sunken concrete pool. If the original cement was badly mixed, the surfaces may be excessively porous. Alternatively, the concrete may crack under the pressure or movement of the earth around the pool. This is particularly likely if the pool is left without water for a long period. In winter, however, there is the additional hazard of ice. Float a number of polystyrene slabs on the water to absorb the expansion of the water as it freezes.

It is unlikely that a successful permanent repair can be achieved without special tools and expert help, but an amateur may be able to seal a crack or porous surface temporarily. Never use ordinary cement mortar. A waterproof mastic cement can be used for a single crack, but it is advisable to obtain instead a proprietary liquid plastic and coat the whole inside. Make sure, however, if the pool is ornamental that the plastic is not harmful to the fish and plants.

Drain the pool and apply the plastic solution, following the manufacturer's instructions, to the sides and bottom. Cover the pool with a sheet of polythene to ensure that rain cannot fall on it while the plastic cures. The time required for the curing process depends greatly on temperature and the type of solution used. Leave it for the maximum time recommended by the manufacturer on the container.

It is not necessary to drain an ornamental pool if the only damaged area is a watercourse or waterfall feeding it. Simply switch off the pump and dry the cracked surface before sealing it with liquid plastic.

Removing plants and fish

If, however, an ornamental pool does have to be completely drained, a temporary storage pool must be provided for the plants and fish. Do not use any kind of metal container. Plastic buckets or very large basins may be sufficient for a small number of plants and fish, but make sure that the total surface area of any containers used is not less than a quarter of the area of the pool. The water should not be less than 12 in. (305 mm) deep.

When a large number of plants and fish have to be stored, make a temporary pool from a doubled sheet of polythene. It can be used to line a suitable hole in the garden, but if there is no convenient area available build a rough wooden frame to support the polythene above the ground.

Store plants and fish separately to make sure that the disturbed oxygenating plants do not foul the water. Cover the fish container with a net to protect the fish from cats, and place it in a shaded part of the garden—particularly in summer.

Glass-fibre pools

Rigid, high-quality glass-fibre pools are unlikely ever to be damaged by sharp rocks or moving earth, but the cheaper, flexible type can develop a leak if it is not accurately fitted into its hole in the garden. If it is damaged, drain the pool to below the split area and carry out the repair with a glass-fibre kit, following the maker's instructions.

Electric pumps

It is dangerous for an inexperienced amateur to attempt any electrical repair on a water pump. Check only that the filter is not clogged with weeds. Have any other fault repaired professionally.

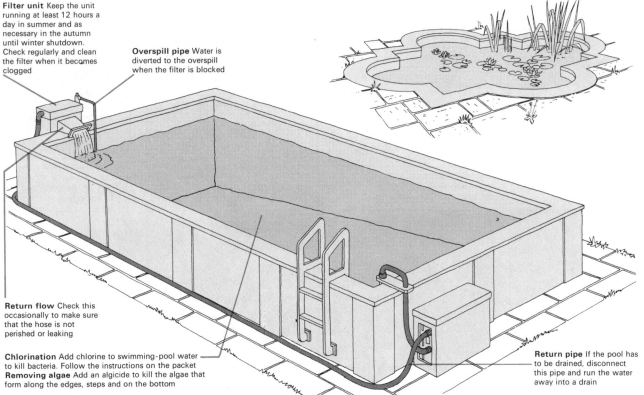

Filter unit Keep the unit running at least 12 hours a day in summer and as necessary in the autumn until winter shutdown. Check regularly and clean the filter when it becomes clogged

Overspill pipe Water is diverted to the overspill when the filter is blocked

Return flow Check this occasionally to make sure that the hose is not perished or leaking

Chlorination Add chlorine to swimming-pool water to kill bacteria. Follow the instructions on the packet
Removing algae Add an algicide to kill the algae that form along the edges, steps and on the bottom

Return pipe If the pool has to be drained, disconnect this pipe and run the water away into a drain

Pools Swimming and ornamental

Repairing pool liners

The lining of prefabricated pools—both swimming and ornamental—is usually of PVC or butyl. Repair kits are available for these materials. If polythene has been used to line a small ornamental pool, it is not advisable to try to repair it: replace the entire lining with PVC or butyl. Similarly, if a concrete pool cannot be successfully repaired with liquid plastic, the inside can be lined with PVC or butyl.

In most cases, when there is only one leak in a lined pool, the damaged part of the liner can be found at the level of the water. It is advisable, however, to check the rest of the liner for possible damage.

To find a leak in the bottom of the pool, feed a little permanganate of potash or blue ink down a pipe to the bottom of the pool. If the water is seeping away through a tear, the colouring will flow towards it.

To repair a tear less than $\frac{1}{2}$ in. (13 mm) long, it is not necessary to drain all the water from the pool. Apply a waterproof adhesive—such as Titebond—only to the patch, and stick it over the tear under water. No adhesive is needed on the torn liner. This simple repair is not practicable, however, on an ornamental pool which has a layer of soil on top of the liner, or on a pool where a considerable amount of the sand base under the liner has been washed away.

Where the tear is longer, adhesive must be applied to both surfaces and it is necessary to remove the water. Clean the torn area and the patch with methylated or surgical spirit, both of which evaporate quickly.

On some pools it may be possible to make a stronger repair by removing the liner completely and patching the tear on both sides.

Materials: PVC or butyl repair kit to suit the liner; methylated or surgical spirit; cloth; permanganate of potash or blue ink; tube to reach the bottom of the pool; funnel; dry sand.
Tools: scissors; broom.

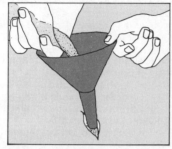

1 Lift the bottom liner and stick the funnel through the tear. Pour in enough dry sand to replace any washed away

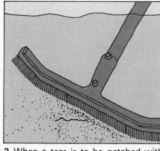

2 When a tear is to be patched with the water still in the pool, brush away any sand round the hole

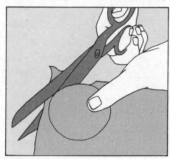

3 Cut a circular patch from the repair kit, about twice the size of the hole or tear in the liner

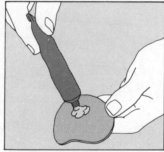

4 Clean the patch with spirit and apply adhesive. Do the same to the damaged area if it is above the waterline

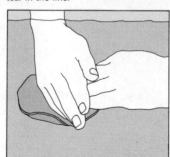

5 Allow the adhesive to become touch-dry and place the patch on the tear. Smooth out any air bubbles

6 Weight the patch down while it sets. If it is under water, lower a bag of sand on a rope

Patching a split seam

When a welded seam splits, repair it with two patches. One butts on the seam edge, the other sticks over both. Cut the first about $1\frac{1}{2}$ in. (40 mm) wide and 8 in. (200 mm) longer than the split. Cut the second 3 in. (75 mm) wide and a little shorter than the first: round off its corners.

Materials: repair kit.
Tools: scissors; straight-edge; knife.

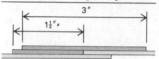

1 Cut two patches. Cut the smaller one with a straight edge to butt against the seam edge

2 Round off the two corners of the smaller patch opposite the straight edge. Coat the patch with adhesive

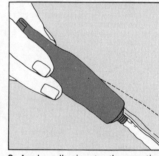

3 Apply adhesive to the meeting surfaces of the seam and the small patch. Stick the seam together

4 Fix the smaller patch so that its straight edge butts tightly against the seam edge

5 Glue and fix the larger patch on top so that a small area of the first is seen on three edges. Weight down

Pools Swimming pools

Replacing a pump seal

If water is allowed to seep back along the shaft of a centrifugal pump, the motor, impeller and housing may be damaged. Fit a new pump seal, which can be obtained from the pump manufacturer or a recommended dealer.

Some impellers can be removed by releasing a nut on the shaft; others can be freed only by holding the shaft with a spanner and turning a lever in the impeller anti-clockwise. When refitting the housing, tighten the nuts diagonally to get it evenly sealed.

Materials: seal assembly; brown paper; boiled linseed oil.
Tools: file; adjustable wrench and spanner; ring spanner; hammer.

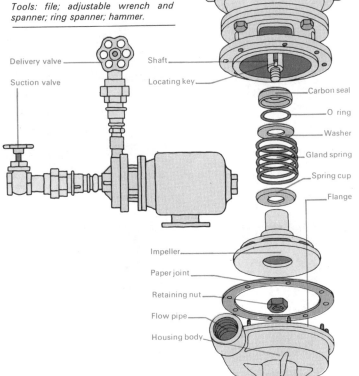

Delivery valve
Suction valve
Shaft
Locating key
Carbon seal
O ring
Washer
Gland spring
Spring cup
Flange
Impeller
Paper joint
Retaining nut
Flow pipe
Housing body

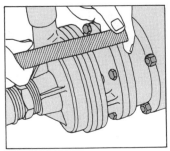

1 Turn off suction and delivery gatevalves. File a line across the flanges to provide a guide for reassembly

2 Disconnect the suction and delivery pipes by unscrewing the unions or couplings with an adjustable wrench

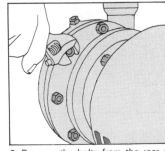

3 Remove the bolts from the rear of the pump housing with an adjustable spanner. Release the housing body

4 When the housing body is removed, examine the paper joint inside the flange. Discard it if it is damaged

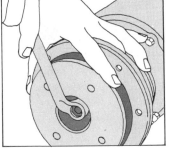

5 If there is a centre nut, undo it to free the impeller. If not, use a spanner on the shaft and lever on the impeller

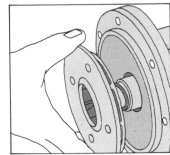

6 Withdraw the impeller with the seal assembly. Lay out the parts carefully in order to help reassembly

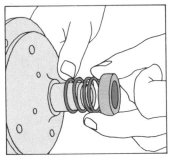

7 Fit the new seal assembly so that the wider carbon surface faces away from the housing body

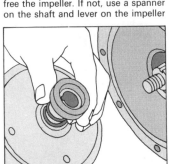

8 Make sure that the locating key on the shaft is in position on the keyway. Replace the impeller

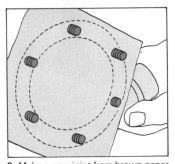

9 Make a new joint from brown paper the same thickness as the original. Seal it with linseed oil

Pools Swimming pools

Replacing a gland valve

If water escapes from a gland valve in a swimming-pool's filling system, tighten the gland nut to compress the packing round the shank. After a time, the packing can be compressed no more and it should then be replaced.

Materials: asbestos rope; grease or graphite.
Tools: spanner; screwdriver; hammer; blunt nail.

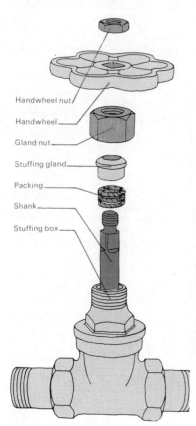

Handwheel nut
Handwheel
Gland nut
Stuffing gland
Packing
Shank
Stuffing box

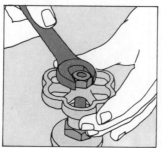

1 Cut off the water supply. Undo the handwheel nut above the handwheel and lift off the wheel

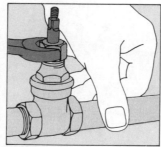

2 Remove the gland nut from the shank by turning it anti-clockwise with a spanner

3 Lift off the stuffing gland. If it is a tight fit, prise it out of the housing with a screwdriver

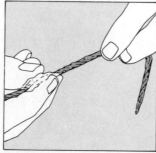

4 Cut a strand of asbestos rope to make new packing. Smear it with graphite or water-pump grease

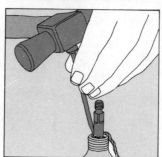

5 Coil the new packing round the shank and hammer it down with the end of a blunt nail

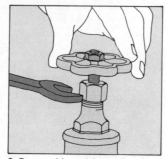

6 Reassemble and leave the gland nut hand-tight. Switch on the pump; tighten the nut until there is no leak

Adjusting the starter motor

If a newly installed pump starter motor functions only intermittently, check that the amperage setting is a little above the rate given on the motor cover. Always switch off the current before removing the cover. Adjustment may be by a knurled knob and calibrated scale or by clips pushed in to reduce the amperage and pulled out to increase it.

Tool: screwdriver.

ADJUSTMENT METHODS

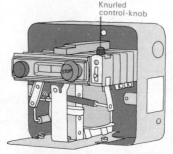

Knurled control-knob

Calibrated adjustment A graduated setting can be obtained by adjustment of the knurled knob on larger motors

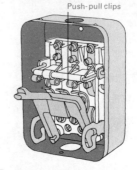

Push-pull clips

Push-pull clips Only two settings are possible—clips all in or out

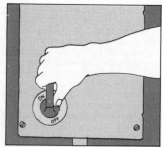

1 Switch off the current and isolate the motor by turning the control handle to the OFF position

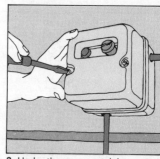

2 Undo the cover-retaining screw or screws and lift the cover from the motor body

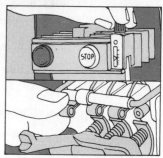

3 Set the indicator $\frac{1}{2}$ amp more than required. If push-pull clips are fitted, they should all be at the same setting

Sheds

Re-covering a felt roof

Inspect roofing felt regularly and coat it with bitumen paint every three or four years. When the felt begins to rot, re-cover the roof. The heavier the grade of roofing felt, the longer will be its life.

If the edges of the roof are inadequate for secure nailing, fasten battens to the eaves and roof ends before starting to fix the new felt.

Allow for this additional overhang when measuring and cutting the felt. After cutting, leave the felt outdoors to weather for a few days before fitting it to the roof.

Materials: 12×1 yd (11 m×914 mm) roofing felt; ½ in. (13 mm) large-headed galvanised clout nails; 1×1 in. (25×25 mm) battens, if needed, for the eaves and roof ends; 1½ in. (40 mm) wood screws, to secure the battens. Tools: ruler; pencil; knife; straight-edge; saw; hammer.

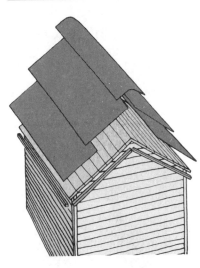

Garden sheds Five strips of felt are usually needed—two on each side of the roof, and a 12 in. (305 mm) wide strip for the ridge. If the two main strips on either side overlap by 15 in. (380 mm) or more, cut the ridge strip from the surplus. Overlap the strips by at least 3 in. (75 mm).

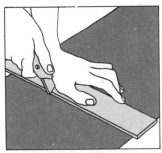

1 Use a straight-edge and cut four main strips the length of the roof plus 1 in. (25 mm) at each end

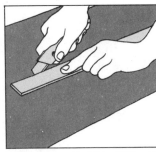

2 Cut a ridge strip 12 in. (305 mm) wide and the same length as main sheets. Leave a few days to weather

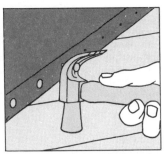

3 Strip the existing felt from the shed roof. Pull out or hammer flat any protruding nails

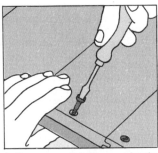

4 Screw or nail battens under the eaves. When hammering, hold a weight under the batten

5 Lay one lower strip carefully to overhang eave and each end of roof by 1 in. (25 mm)

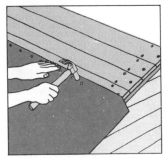

6 Hammer in nails 6 in. (150 mm) apart, 3 in. (75 mm) from the upper edge—to be covered by the overlap

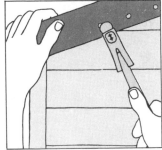

7 Make sure that the felt is flat. Secure it at the eaves and ends with nails spaced 2 in. (50 mm) apart

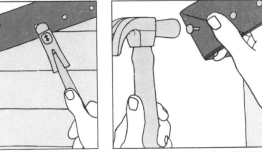

8 Fold the surplus over at the corners and secure it by nailing through both thicknesses of felt

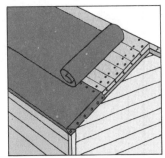

9 Lay the second strip to overlap the first by 3 in. (75 mm). It must be within 3 in. of the ridge

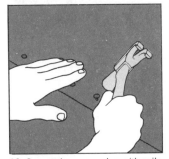

10 Secure the upper edge with nails 6 in. (150 mm) apart. Fix nails in lower edge and ends 2 in. apart

11 Nail the felt on the other side in the same way. Secure the ridge strip with nails 2 in. apart

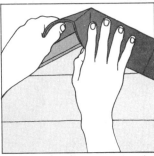

12 Fold the overhang at each end of the ridge strip. Nail it securely against the ends of the roof

Sprayers Hand-operated

Maintaining a hand syringe

There are two main types of hand-operated sprayer. The simple single-action syringe is filled by immersing the nozzle in liquid and pulling the plunger out. When the plunger is pushed in, the liquid is sprayed out. It has to be filled again before it can be used—unlike the types which fill themselves during spraying or have an attached container (see pp. 505–6).

Jets, nozzle-holes and non-return ball valves must be kept clean. If they become blocked, do not try to clear them with any tool or wire. Use a bicycle pump or air line to force dirt through from the outside to the inside of the nozzle. Never try to clear a nozzle by blowing through it. It may still retain traces of poisonous insecticide or fungicide.

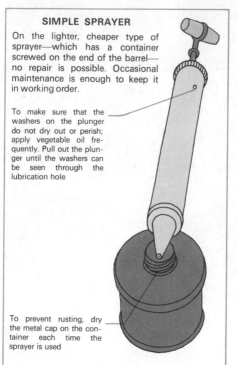

SIMPLE SPRAYER

On the lighter, cheaper type of sprayer—which has a container screwed on the end of the barrel—no repair is possible. Occasional maintenance is enough to keep it in working order.

To make sure that the washers on the plunger do not dry out or perish; apply vegetable oil frequently. Pull out the plunger until the washers can be seen through the lubrication hole

To prevent rusting, dry the metal cap on the container each time the sprayer is used

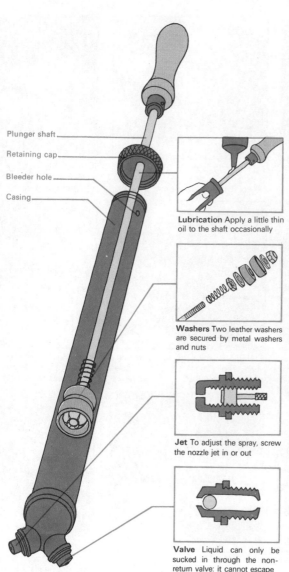

Plunger shaft

Retaining cap

Bleeder hole

Casing

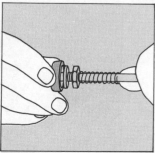

Lubrication Apply a little thin oil to the shaft occasionally

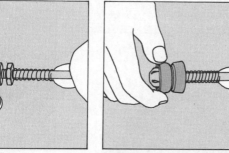

Washers Two leather washers are secured by metal washers and nuts

Jet To adjust the spray, screw the nozzle jet in or out

Valve Liquid can only be sucked in through the non-return valve: it cannot escape

Fitting new washers and packing

The two leather cup washers in a single-action syringe are fitted base to base on the end of the plunger shaft. If they become worn, liquid can escape up the barrel—indicated by leaking at the bleeder hole in the casing. New washers must be well greased to allow the plunger to be fitted into the outer casing.

Some syringes also have a leather washer at the retaining cap. It should be kept well greased. If liquid escapes through the cap, fit a new packing.

Materials: washers; vegetable oil or grease; string.
Tools: knife; spanner.

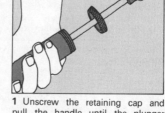

1 Unscrew the retaining cap and pull the handle until the plunger washers are freed from the barrel

2 Remove the first plunger nut and metal washer. Take the two cup washers off the end of the shaft

3 Make sure the upper metal washer has not been removed. Fit two new washers, base to base

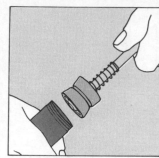

4 Fit the lower metal washer and nut. Do not overtighten. Grease the washers, and replace the plunger

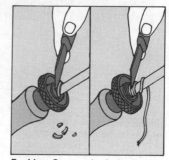

Packing Cut out the faulty washer. Wind a greased string round the shaft and pack it into the cap

Strainers and hoses

Some hand-operated sprayers have their own container with a trigger-controlled suction valve. Others are filled from a bucket, but, unlike a single-action hand syringe, the barrel and hose take in liquid continuously as the plunger is operated. The most common fault is that the strainer becomes blocked with dirt or sediment. Always clean the strainer either with running water or with an air line from the inside outwards.

Make sure that the sprayer is used only with suitable liquids. For example, a plastic hose used to spray on a winter tar-oil wash will harden and need to be replaced. Always clean the sprayer with clean water after use.

Strainer Remove the strainer from the hose. Hold it inside upwards under running water. If clogged, use an air line

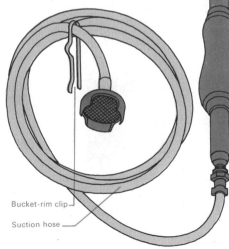

Bucket-rim clip

Suction hose

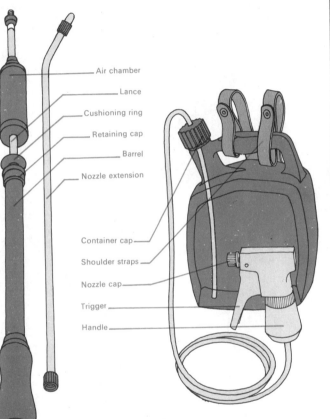

Air chamber

Lance

Cushioning ring

Retaining cap

Barrel

Nozzle extension

Container cap

Shoulder straps

Nozzle cap

Trigger

Handle

Internal strainer When a strainer valve is fitted inside the end of the suction hose, cut it out to clean it. Blow through with an air line. To refit it, soften the end of the hose in warm water. Push the strainer home with a matchstick

Replacing sealing washers

The most likely fault with any sprayer is that the sealing washer on the plungers has worn or become perished. Spare washers—cork or leather—are obtainable from shops or from the manufacturer.

The rubber cushioning ring between the barrel and the air chamber may also perish after long use. Although it does not affect the operation of the sprayer, a new one can be fitted if necessary when the washer has to be renewed.

Materials: washer; ring; rivet.
Tools: hammer; centre punch; spanner.

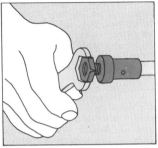

1 Unscrew the cap at the end of the barrel. Pull out the plunger and undo the washer retaining nut

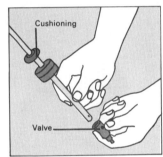

Cushioning

Valve

2 Remove the old seal. If the cushioning ring is perished, knock out the valve rivet to remove it

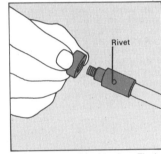

Rivet

3 Fit a new cushioning ring. Fit the plunger valve and a new seal. Tighten the screw and reassemble

RUBBER-COVERED VALVES

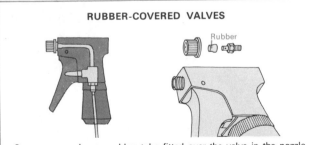

Rubber

Some sprayers have a rubber tube fitted over the valve in the nozzle cap. When the sprayer has been stored for some time, unscrew the nozzle and take out the valve. Renew the rubber if it is perished

Sprayers Compressed-air

Maintenance and fault-finding

All compressed-air sprayers work on the same principle. Air is first compressed in the container by pumping the plunger. When the discharge valve is operated—either by a trigger or a press-button—the pressure of the air forces out the liquid through a nozzle where it is atomised. Liquid continues to flow out until the pressure of the air or the liquid in the container is exhausted.

In some compression sprayers the plunger is a leather cup washer, which should be greased or lubricated regularly with a vegetable oil. Replace it if it becomes worn. Other sprayers have neoprene O rings instead of washers. They, too, must be replaced if they are worn.

If the spray is unsatisfactory, it is likely that the air pressure is inadequate. Find out if the pump cup washer is worn or if air is escaping past a sealing washer. Check that there is no blockage at the nozzle. Make sure that the spray is not distorted because the nozzle cap has been screwed on loosely. If there is a bubbling sound in the container, or if liquid escapes at the handle, check the non-return air valve; it is likely to be blocked or broken.

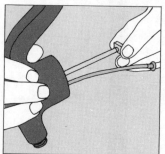

O ring · Washers

If the O ring or neoprene washers in the plunger outlet wear, water may leak from the nozzle joint

Large shoulder-slung compression sprayers are suitable if high trees need treatment

Smaller hand-held sprayers are sufficient for low trees and shrubs

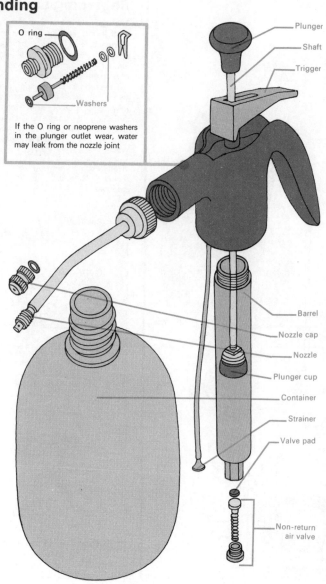

Plunger
Shaft
Trigger
Barrel
Nozzle cap
Nozzle
Plunger cup
Container
Strainer
Valve pad
Non-return air valve

Renewing washers and valves

Washers and O-ring seals should last for several years, but they may in time become soft and spongy—which makes it impossible to pressurise the air in the container.

The non-return air valve usually has a small spring and either a ball or a rubber disc. Check the spring each season. If it is rusty or worn, renew it. Rubber discs may become ingrained with small pieces of grit, or be so heavily impressed in their seating that they cannot make a seal. Replace them if necessary.

Materials: parts as needed.
Tool: spanner.

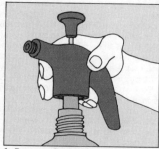

1 Remove the nozzle assembly. Unscrew the trigger and handle; lift them free of the compression chamber

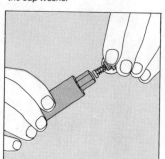

3 Make sure that the upper metal washer has not been removed with the cup washer

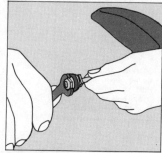

4 Fit a new cup washer with its base towards the plunger handle. Replace the lower metal washer and nut

6 When refitting the valve, place the spring on the retainer and the rubber pad towards the pump barrel

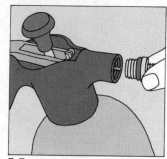

7 To renew the neoprene O ring on the discharge body, unscrew the valve from the trigger casing

Steps   Brick and concrete

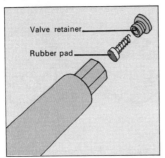

2 Unscrew the pump barrel and withdraw the plunger. Remove the plunger nut and cup washer

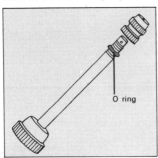

5 To replace a non-return valve rubber pad, unscrew the valve retainer on the end of the pump barrel

(labels: Valve retainer; Rubber pad)

8 The nozzle is sealed with a small O ring. Make sure that it is correctly located in its groove

(label: O ring)

Replacing a broken brick

If the brickwork in garden steps is damaged, remove the broken bricks and fit new ones as soon as possible. Before obtaining matching bricks from a builders' merchant, check all the steps carefully to find out whether any further bricks are in poor condition.

Two mortar mixes are required (see p. 693). Fix the bricks into position with a 4:1 mix, leave it to dry for 24 hours, then use a 3:1 mix for pointing.

Materials: sand; cement; water; bricks.
Tools: trowel; wire brush; straight-edged timber; hammer; cold chisel.

1 With a hammer and cold chisel, chip out the damaged brick. Take care not to disturb adjacent bricks

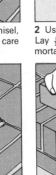

2 Use a wire brush to clean the hole. Lay ½ in. (13 mm) thickness of 4:1 mortar mix

3 Set the new brick in position and tap it down gently with the handle of a trowel. Remove surplus mortar

4 Check with a board that the surface is level. Leave for 24 hours and point with a 3:1 mix

Repairing damaged concrete

If the edge of a concrete step cracks or crumbles, it is possible to repair it by casting fresh concrete to the shape of the step. Use a mix containing 3 parts shingle, 2 parts sand and 1 part cement. Add PVA bonding adhesive (see p. 693).

Trowel in the mix gradually and firm it down thoroughly to make sure that there are no air pockets. Leave the step for at least seven days before using it.

Materials: sand; cement; shingle; water; PVA bonding agent.
Tools: hammer; chisel; trowel; float; paintbrush; edging board; wire brush.

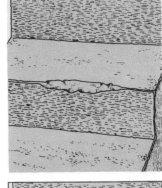

1 Chip away 2–3 in. (50–75 mm) of concrete around the damaged part of the step. Brush it clean

2 Cut an edging board the height of the step and wider than the damage. Hold it in place with bricks

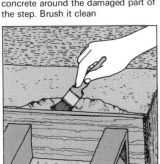

3 Brush a coating of PVA bonding agent on the surface. Fill the hole with the concrete mix

4 Tamp the concrete with the edge of the trowel. Smooth it. Leave the board in place for at least 24 hours

Timber Preservation

Protecting timber against rot and decay

Timber used in the garden must be treated with preservative to protect it from fungus infections and wood-boring insects. It is advisable to buy timber which has been impregnated under pressure with a protective solution. If there is any doubt about whether the wood has been treated, prepare the parts which are to be fixed in the soil by soaking them in preservative for several days.

Creosote

The most effective tar-oil preservative is creosote, which is available from most hardware stores in any quantity over half a gallon. Several grades are made: always use British Standard 144.

The major disadvantage of creosote is that it darkens the wood and cannot be painted over.

Like other tar oils—for example, pitch and bitumen—creosote cannot penetrate moist timber. Always apply it on a warm, sunny day when the timber is likely to be dry. It may take several days to dry completely.

While it is still wet, creosote can kill plants. Cover nearby plants and bushes and make sure that children and animals cannot come into contact with the wet timber.

Never use tar-oil preservatives on garden swings or climbing frames which are to be used by children.

Organic solvents

Where the appearance of the timber is important, do not use creosote. There are available several types of organic solvent—preservative chemicals dissolved in white spirit or petroleum oil. Their advantage is that paint can be applied over them. But they are likely to be more expensive than tar oils.

Some mixtures contain a colouring, which means that they can be used to improve the appearance of the wood as well as act as a preservative. Organic solvents are particularly useful for application to timber already attacked by fungi or insects.

Read the manufacturer's instructions carefully. Some solvents are poisonous to plants and animals. Make sure that nearby plants are covered if necessary.

Organic solvents should never be used on bird trays, nesting boxes or kennels.

Preservatives rarely penetrate more than $\frac{1}{8}$ in. (3 mm) when applied by brush, and the treatment should be repeated every other year. Water-repellent preservatives, clear or coloured, are preferable.

Varnishes

Garden furniture can be varnished to improve or keep its natural appearance. Varnishes are not preservatives, although they do provide some protection against the weather. A water repellent is often better as it will not crack or blister.

PROTECTION AT SOIL LEVEL

To reduce the risk of soil-level rot in posts that have not been impregnated, drill a hole at an angle halfway through the post. Pour creosote in and plug with wood or cork. Renew annually

Trees

Removing branches

Dead and diseased branches are sources of infection and may eventually break off and cause damage. Remove them as soon as possible.

Employ a professional to deal with heavy branches which are more than step-ladder height from the ground or which might do damage when they drop.

Use a bow saw for thick branches, a pruning saw for thinner ones. As soon as a branch is removed, coat the cut with a proprietary sealer, white lead or grafting wax, all of which are obtainable from garden shops.

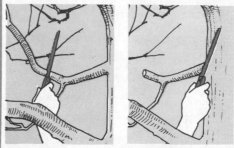

Small branches First cut through the branch about 18 in. (455 mm) from the trunk. Saw off the remainder cleanly at the trunk. Paint the face of the cut with sealing compound

Moss Cover any plants and grass growing near the foot of the tree with polythene sheeting. Spray the moss on the tree during the winter with a tar-oil wash. Stand to windward to avoid spray

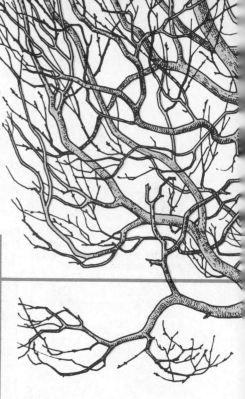

Removing snags If a tree has been left with a protruding snag, cut back close to the trunk and apply a sealing compound

Large branches

Remove large branches during the winter while the tree is dormant, and seal the cut immediately afterwards. If a branch is so awkwardly placed that it might swing dangerously and cause damage or injury, rope it to another one higher on the tree before sawing. Make the final cut as close to the tree as possible: protruding snags look unsightly and may become diseased. If the branch removed is already diseased, burn it without delay to prevent it spreading spores or harbouring pests.

Materials: sealing compound.
Tools: bow saw; knife; paintbrush.

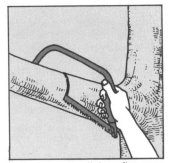

1 To prevent splitting, first saw 18 in. (455 mm) from the trunk

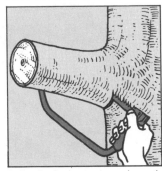

2 For the final cut, saw underneath the branch, close to the trunk

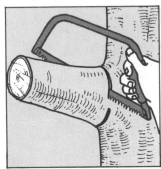

3 Saw from the top to the lower cut. Make sure the cut surface is flat

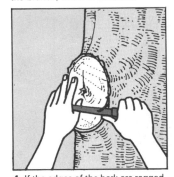

4 If the edges of the bark are ragged, trim them with a sharp knife

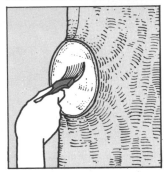

5 After sawing, apply a sealer to protect the cut from disease

Canker Paint sunken and cracked parts of the trunk with a proprietary compound

Trimming To remove part of a branch, first saw a few inches from the final cut

Make the final cut from underneath at a joint. Trim with a knife and apply sealer

Walls

Rebuilding a brick wall

A garden wall is most likely to be damaged at the entrance to a gate or drive. If it is pushed over, knock down the whole damaged section and rebuild it. Use as many of the old bricks as possible. If any new bricks are needed, buy second-hand ones to match the colour of the wall.

Older stone, flint or brick walls may originally have been bonded with lime mortar. Repair them with a 1:1:6 mixture of lime, cement and sand. Recently built walls have cement mortar. Choose the correct mixtures for repairs and repointing (see p. 693).

Materials: sand and cement for mortar; water, lime and bricks or tiles as necessary.
Tools: bolster chisel; hammer; shovel; trowel; spirit level; string.

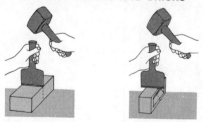

CUTTING BLOCKS AND BRICKS

Lay bricks or stone blocks on a flat surface and cut them with a hammer and bolster chisel. Use light taps on lightweight and soft blocks, heavier blows on concrete

1 Use a hammer and bolster chisel to remove all old mortar from the wall and any bricks which can be used again

4 Build up the end to the top level of the wall at the centre. Check with a spirit level that it is upright

7 When the wall is complete, build the pier to the original height. Check for vertical and horizontal with a spirit level

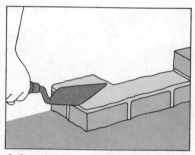

2 Spread a smooth, flat layer of mortar about ⅜ in. (10 mm) thick on top of the end section of the wall

5 Stretch a string between the end and the centre of the wall. Spread a layer of mortar on the existing bricks

8 Cut roof or quarry tiles to overhang the pier and lay them on a ⅜ in. (10 mm) bed of mortar. Remove excess mortar

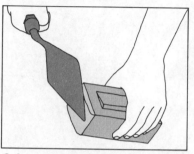

3 Spread the mortar ⅜ in. (10 mm) thick over one end of the brick to be laid at the outside end of the end section

6 Lay a course of bricks, their tops level with the string. Continue to lay bricks course by course, with string as a guide

9 Finish the pier with bricks. Spread on an angled layer of mortar between the brick edges and the tile tops

Wheelbarrows

Care and maintenance

Ideally, clean a metal wheelbarrow every time it has been used. Always store it in a garage or shed. Remove the body and paint frame, after cleaning off any rust, once a year.

Load a barrow carefully. If heavy loads are dropped into it, the metal body is likely to be dented or split; it should then be replaced.

Most bodies are bolted to the frame, but if they are riveted drill out the rivets and use bolts and nuts to fit the new body.

Never bump a barrow up a kerb or step, as this may damage the tyre. Only pneumatic tyres can be replaced: with others the complete wheel assembly must be renewed.

The wheel bearings are nylon and require no lubrication after fitting. Dust and sand, however, can gradually destroy them. If the barrow is to be used on gritty or sandy surfaces, lay boards and keep the barrow on them. If bearings are damaged or worn, remove wheel and fit new bearings and spindle.

Materials: new bearings; grease.
Tools: screwdriver; spanner; mallet.

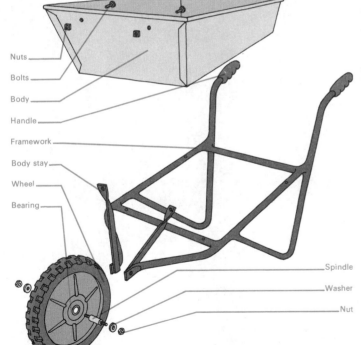

Nuts
Bolts
Body
Handle
Framework
Body stay
Wheel
Bearing

Spindle
Washer
Nut

1 To fit new bearings to a wheelbarrow, remove the nut and washers at each side of the wheel spindle

2 Spring the frame forks and body stays apart. Slide the wheel out of the barrow framework

3 Draw the bearing spindle out of the hub centre. If the spindle is badly scored, fit a new one

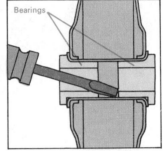

Bearings

4 Push a screwdriver into the wheel hub to force the nylon bearings out of the hub

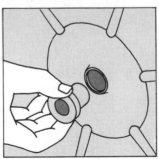

5 Fit the new bearings to the hub centre. Tap them fully home with a hide or plastic mallet

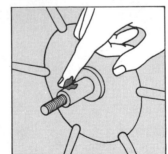

6 Grease the bearing centre and the spindle. Refit the spindle in the wheel, and reassemble

Handcart wheels

On two-wheeled handcarts, regularly tighten the mounting bolts, especially those securing the handlebars to the body. Remove the wheels and lubricate the axle with grease at least twice a year. Check that the washers behind the wheels are not worn.

Materials: split-pins; grease.
Tool: pliers.

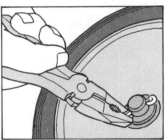

1 Straighten the ends of the split-pin with a pair of pliers. Pull out split-pin

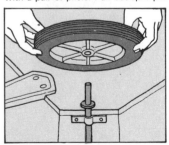

2 Lift off the wheel. Clean and grease washers and axle. Reassemble

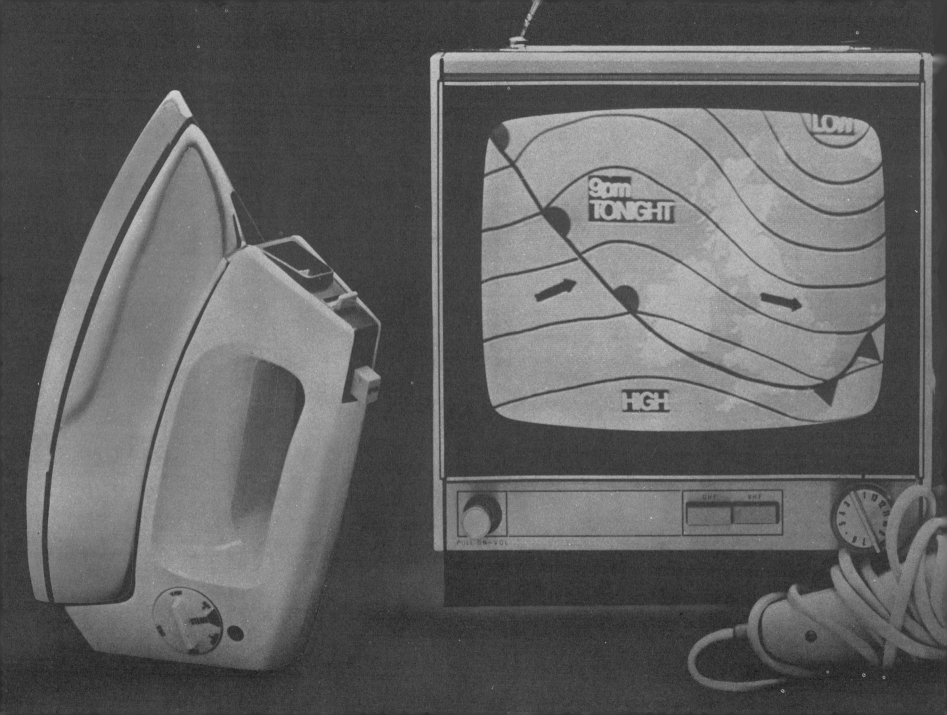

PART 5

ELECTRICAL EQUIPMENT

Understanding electricity

Terms used in electricity

The flow of electricity through wires and cables from the mains supply can be compared with the flow of water through pipes from a tank. When there is no tap open, the water is motionless: but when a tap is opened, the height of the tank water exerts pressure on the water in the pipes and forces it through the outlet. This water pressure is comparable with the *voltage* in electricity.

The rate of the water flow—similar to the flow of current—is determined partly by pressure and partly by the size of the outlet. For example, a very narrow spray or nozzle allows less water to flow than a wide pipe. Similarly in electricity a very thin wire restricts or *resists* the flow of current. Electricians measure this resistance in *ohms* and the flow of current in *ampères* (amps).

The higher the resistance of a piece of electrical equipment, the lower the amperage. To find the strength of electricity required for any equipment, divide the voltage of the household supply by the resistance of the equipment. For example, if an electric fire has a resistance of 16 ohms and the voltage is 240 volts, the amperage is 15 amps: if an electric light bulb has a resistance of 1000 ohms, the amperage is 240 divided by 1000, or approx. $\frac{1}{4}$ amp.

The amount of electricity used at any moment by equipment is measured in *watts* and is calculated by multiplying the amperage by the voltage. A fire supplied with 240-volt current at 12·5 amps has a consumption of 3000 watts or 3 kilowatts (3 kW). Most equipment has its wattage indicated—for example, fires may have a label (3 kW) and light bulbs have a rating (for example, 100 W) stamped on them.

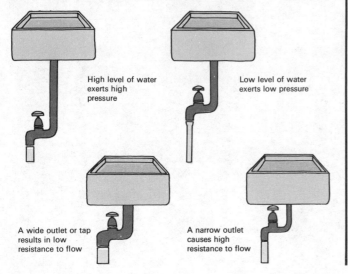

High level of water exerts high pressure

Low level of water exerts low pressure

A wide outlet or tap results in low resistance to flow

A narrow outlet causes high resistance to flow

How electricity comes into a house

Electric power comes into the home through a service cable to a fuse unit sealed by the electricity board. The live supply wire has a red sheath: neutral is black. A third wire, usually bare—the earth—connects the casing of the main fuse box to the ground.

Never try to open the sealed fuse. If there is a power fault, check all the other fuses in the house (see p. 519). If no fault is found, call the emergency service of the local electricity board.

From the sealed fuse, the live and neutral wires run through an electricity board meter, which records the amount of electricity used, to the mains switch. In houses wired since 1947, the mains switch is usually part of the consumer's fuse unit: in houses wired before that date, the mains switch may be separate from the fuse box. If the switch is part of the fuse unit, the house will have ring-mains wiring; if it is separate from the unit, the house usually has radial wiring (see p. 515).

The total amount of electricity which can be used at any one time in a house is determined partly by the wiring (see p. 515) and partly by the rating of the electricity board's sealed fuse. If more power is required, a new supply cable or new wiring can be fitted: consult the electricity board.

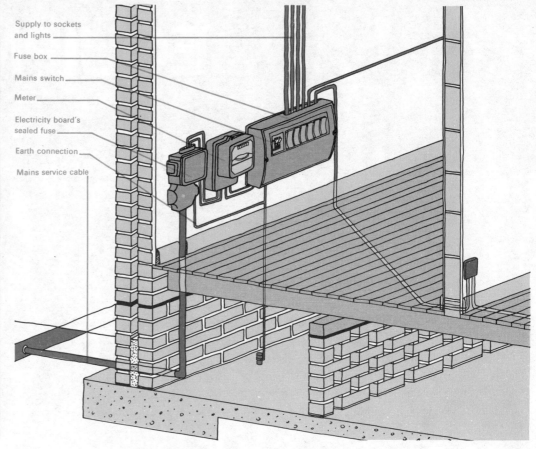

Supply to sockets and lights

Fuse box

Mains switch

Meter

Electricity board's sealed fuse

Earth connection

Mains service cable

Electrical wiring in older houses

In houses wired before 1947, power is distributed separately to each wall socket. This system, called radial wiring, requires as many fuses as there are sockets, and it has been replaced in new installations by ring wiring.

In a radial system, all the power sockets are supplied from one fuse box with its own mains switch: but there are separate boxes, each with a mains switch, for the lighting circuits and for large fixed equipment—for example, cookers and immersion heaters.

The wiring from each fuse to its socket is usually two-core—live and neutral—carried in a metal pipe, called a conduit, which provides an earthing connection. In some houses, however, there may be no conduit: instead a third bare wire is used as the earth. Whatever the type of wiring, all sockets and light fittings are usually earthed.

Some sockets are large enough to take 15-amp round-pin plugs; others may take only the smaller 5-amp or 2-amp types. This is usually an accurate indication of the strength of the wiring between the fuse and the socket. Never fit a fuse of a higher rating than its socket (see p. 519) and do not try to operate heavy equipment—for example a 3-kW fire—from a 5-amp or 2-amp socket.

Although it is possible to draw 12,000 watts (12 kW) at any time without blowing the electricity board's sealed 50-amp fuse, this is unlikely to happen in practice since all the appliances in the house will not be used at the same time.

Ring-mains wiring

In houses wired since 1947, many or all wall sockets are connected by a continuous single loop of cable, called a ring circuit. In most cases one ring serves the upstairs power sockets, and a second supplies those on the ground floor. Lighting and heavy-loading equipment have separate circuits and fuses, but there is usually only one fuse box and one mains switch.

Each ring is fused at the mains box—30 amps for power circuits, and 5 amps for lighting. Individual sockets, however, are not separately fused, and if a fault in a piece of equipment does not blow the cartridge fuse in its own 13-amp plug (see p. 519), the whole circuit may be affected.

The mains fuse for a ring limits the amount of power that can be drawn from it. For example, a power circuit with a 30-amp fuse can supply only 7200 watts (7·2 kW) at any time. If the ring is overloaded, the mains fuse blows and cuts the supply to all its sockets.

Branch cables, called spurs, are connected to the ring cable to supply outlying sockets. But any power drawn from the spur is also drawn from the ring: when heavy equipment is used on the spur, less power is available for the other sockets. Such equipment as immersion heaters and cookers are on separate circuits and have their own fuses in the mains fuse box.

Do not try to install a new circuit or take a spur cable from an existing ring. Engage a qualified electrician and have the work inspected by the local electricity board to make sure that it is satisfactory.

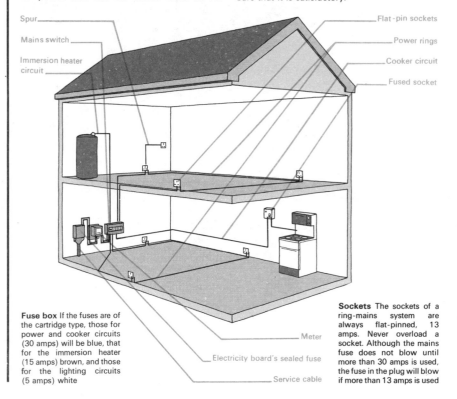

Immersion heater circuit

Round-pin sockets

Power-circuit fuses

Cooker-circuit fuses

Service cable

Lighting-circuit fuses

Meter

Electricity board's sealed fuse

Spur

Mains switch

Immersion heater circuit

Flat-pin sockets

Power rings

Cooker circuit

Fused socket

Meter

Electricity board's sealed fuse

Service cable

Fuse boxes Power is distributed from the electricity board's sealed fuse through a meter to separate mains switches and fuse boxes from sockets, lights and heavy equipment

Fuses The fuses are fine pieces of wire secured in porcelain holders. Lighting fuses are normally 5 amps: power fuses may be 5, 15 or 30 amps

Fuse box If the fuses are of the cartridge type, those for power and cooker circuits (30 amps) will be blue, that for the immersion heater (15 amps) brown, and those for the lighting circuits (5 amps) white

Sockets The sockets of a ring-mains system are always flat-pinned, 13 amps. Never overload a socket. Although the mains fuse does not blow until more than 30 amps is used, the fuse in the plug will blow if more than 13 amps is used

Understanding electricity

How lighting circuits are wired

In many houses built before 1966, the wiring for lighting circuits runs from the fuse box to a series of junction boxes above the ceilings. Separate cables are taken from each junction box to the ceiling roses and light switches. The cables are sometimes enclosed in metal conduits and are difficult to replace if they become worn or damaged. Nowadays, a simple loop-in system, using a four-terminal ceiling rose, is almost always used.

The three-core wiring is continuous and runs from the fuse box to each ceiling rose in turn. Separate cables are taken from each rose to its switch and the lampholder.

Lighting circuits are always fused with a 5-amp wire or cartridge (see p. 519). Never fit a fuse of a higher rating, and never try to use a lampholder as the outlet for a piece of equipment, such as a fire. Employ an electrician to extend lighting circuits or to replace old wiring.

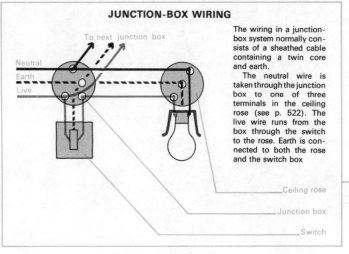

JUNCTION-BOX WIRING

The wiring in a junction-box system normally consists of a sheathed cable containing a twin core and earth.

The neutral wire is taken through the junction box to one of three terminals in the ceiling rose (see p. 522). The live wire runs from the box through the switch to the rose. Earth is connected to both the rose and the switch box

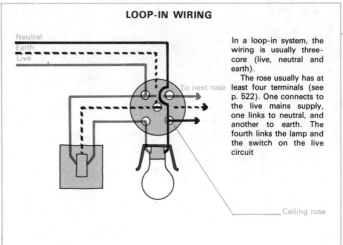

LOOP-IN WIRING

In a loop-in system, the wiring is usually three-core (live, neutral and earth).

The rose usually has at least four terminals (see p. 522). One connects to the live mains supply, one links to neutral, and another to earth. The fourth links the lamp and the switch on the live circuit

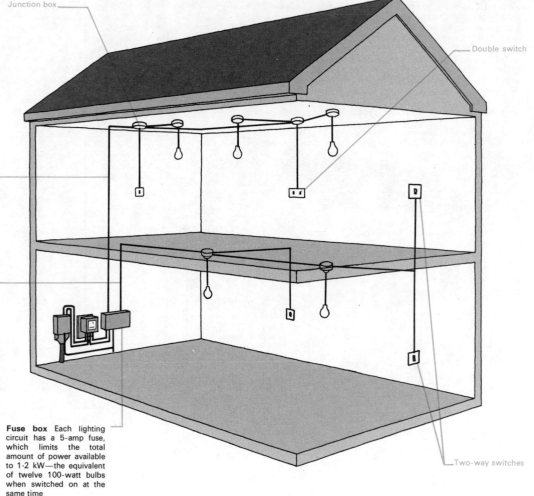

Fuse box Each lighting circuit has a 5-amp fuse, which limits the total amount of power available to 1·2 kW—the equivalent of twelve 100-watt bulbs when switched on at the same time

(continued)

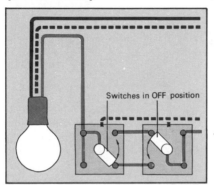

Two-way switches Lights may be controlled from more than one point in a house—from a hallway or an upstairs landing, for instance—by fitting two-way switches. A live wire is connected to one switch; the switch return from the rose to the other. The two switches are connected by strapping wires

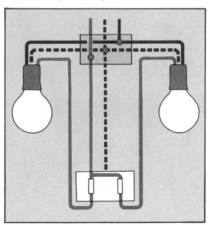

Double switches Two lights can be controlled independently from a single point by fitting a double switch unit. The live wire is taken from the junction box to the two switches in the unit, then to the two ceiling roses. Neutral and earth are taken from the box to both roses, and the earth to the switch. Double switches are often fitted in large rooms

What the colours mean

Current is carried from the power supply to the appliance through a plug and flexible cord. Government regulations now specify a new colour-coding for all flexible cords supplying household equipment. These colours have been standardised throughout Europe to reduce the danger of making a wrong connection to plugs on imported appliances.

Always make sure that the live lead—which was previously red and is now brown—is connected to the fused or live side of the plug. If it is connected to the unfused side, the equipment is still live even if the fuse in the plug blows.

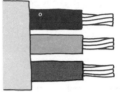

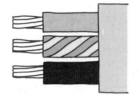

Old flex Black is neutral, green is earth, and red is the live wire

New flex Light blue is neutral, green/yellow is earth and brown is live

FLEX RATINGS AND CONNECTORS

Always use flex or cable of the correct gauge; the higher the current needed for equipment the thicker the cable should be.

0·5 mm² (3 amp) Two-core flex. Load up to 700 watts. Used for lamps, radios, TV sets and blankets

0·75 mm² (6 amp) Two-core sheathed flex. Load: up to 1400 watts. For lighting and non-earthed equipment

0·75 mm² (6 amp) Three-core flex. Load: up to 1400 watts. Used for spin dryers, refrigerators, single-bar fires

1·0 mm² (10 amp) Three-core flex. Load: up to 2400 watts. Used for kettles and two-bar radiant fires

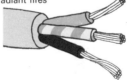

1·5 mm² (15 amp) Three-core sheathed flex. Load: up to 3000 watts. Used for large fires and washing machines

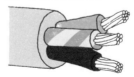

4·0 mm² (25 amp) Heavy three-core cable. Used for cookers up to 6000 watts

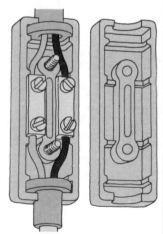

5-amp enclosed connector Use to lengthen flex

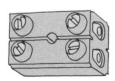

Block connector Use to join concealed cables, never to lengthen flex

Stripping flex

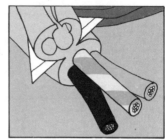

1 Carefully cut down the sheathing by amount required for the plug or equipment. Cut it off. Do not cut into the insulation

2 Remove the insulation from the wires with a wire stripper, baring only enough wire to fit the terminal. Do not cut through wires

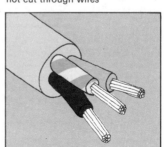

3 Twist the strands of each wire. When fitting into a screw hole push it fully home. Wrap it clockwise round terminal posts (see p. 525)

Understanding electricity

How much current a circuit can carry

LIGHTING CIRCUITS (5 AMP)

Lighting circuits—whether junction box or loop-in (see p. 516)—have 5-amp fuses. Many houses have more than one circuit, each of which can carry a maximum current of 1200 watts (1·2 kW) as the power supply is 240 volts.

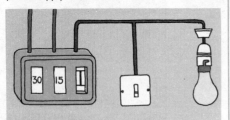

If there is a fault at any light or switch, the entire circuit fuses. No light is fused separately

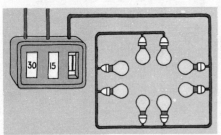

Maximum load on a lighting circuit is 1·2 kW, equivalent to twelve 100-watt or eight 150-watt bulbs

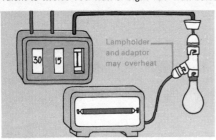

Never plug an electric fire into a lighting circuit. Although a one-bar fire (1 kW) does not blow the 5-amp fuse, it can overheat the lampholder

POWER CIRCUITS (5 AND 15 AMP)

In a house which has radial wiring (see p. 515) the power sockets are round-pin. A 5-amp circuit can carry 1·2 kW and a 15-amp circuit can carry 3·6 kW. Each circuit is individually fused; in a fault, the rest of the system is not affected.

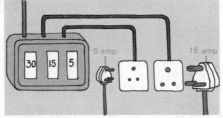

A radial circuit has 15-amp round-pin plugs (equipment) and the smaller 5-amp type (lighting)

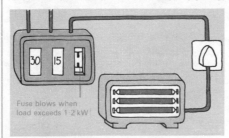

A 5-amp circuit can take a one-bar (1 kW) fire, but not a 3 kW type

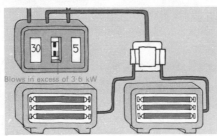

Never overload a 15-amp socket by using an adaptor. Two 3-kW fires, for example, would blow the fuse at the mains fuse box

POWER CIRCUITS (13 AMP)

A ring circuit (see p. 515) has power sockets that accept only flat-pinned 13-amp fused plugs. Circuit current rating is 30 amps and maximum load is 7·2 kW, but the fuse may not blow until twice this load is switched on. Take care not to overload the circuit wiring.

It is advisable to check which sockets are on the same ring. Switch off at the mains, remove one 30-amp fuse and switch on the power. Plug a piece of equipment into each socket. Those which have no power are on the same ring.

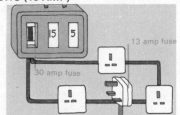

Any number of sockets can be fitted on to a circuit in a ring-mains wiring

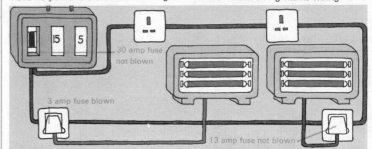

One 3-kW fire does not overload a ring circuit, but it must be connected to a plug with a 13-amp fuse (right). If the fire plug has a fuse of a lower rating (left), it blows when the fire is switched on. The mains fuse is not affected

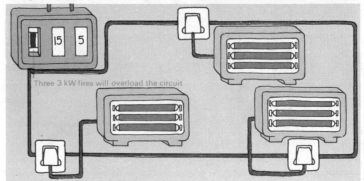

Three 3-kW fires consume 9000 watts—more than the total available on a ring circuit. If additional power is needed in a house, consult the electricity board

What a fuse does

Every electric circuit is protected by a fuse, which is designed to melt and break the circuit if too much current is passed through it.

For example, a 3-kW fire used at 240 volts draws current at the rate of 12½ amps. If it is plugged into a circuit with 5-amp fuse and wiring, the fuse blows to break the circuit and to protect the wiring. A fuse will also blow if a piece of equipment develops a short circuit—for example, if the live wire makes contact with neutral or touches an earthed part of the equipment. Extra heavy current flows through the wiring and the fuse blows.

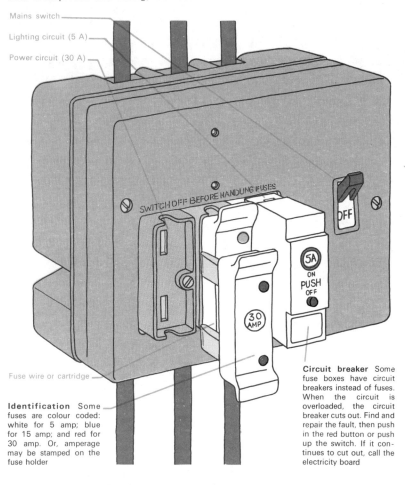

Mains switch

Lighting circuit (5 A)

Power circuit (30 A)

SWITCH OFF BEFORE HANDLING FUSES

OFF

5A
ON
PUSH
OFF

30
AMP

Fuse wire or cartridge

Identification Some fuses are colour coded: white for 5 amp; blue for 15 amp; and red for 30 amp. Or, amperage may be stamped on the fuse holder

Circuit breaker Some fuse boxes have circuit breakers instead of fuses. When the circuit is overloaded, the circuit breaker cuts out. Find and repair the fault, then push in the red button or push up the switch. If it continues to cut out, call the electricity board

Fitting a new circuit fuse

When a fuse blows, switch off at the mains and look for and repair loose or bare wires and broken connections. If no fault can be found, replace blown fuse. (If not identified inside fuse box, examine each fuse in turn.)

If a fuse keeps blowing after it has been replaced, do not try to make the equipment work by fitting a fuse of a higher rating: call the local electricity board's emergency service.

CHECKING FUSES

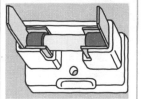

Cartridge fuse Check with a circuit tester (see p. 526) or fit a substitute

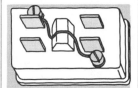

Bridge fuse When it is not blown, a thin wire can be seen over the porcelain bridge

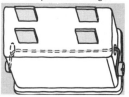

Protected fuse To check, try to prise out wire at one end with small screwdriver

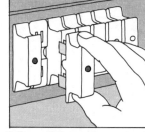

1 Turn off the power supply at the main switch. Open the fuse box and pull out fuses until the blown one is found

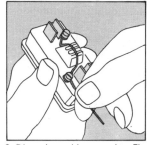

2 Discard cartridge or wire. Fit new cartridge or wrap new wire clockwise round one screw. Tighten the screw

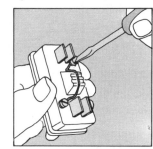

3 Draw wire across and wrap it clockwise round other screw. Leave a little slack, then tighten screw. Cut off surplus

FITTING A PLUG FUSE

Never use a fuse of a higher rating than is needed to safeguard the appliance to which the plug is fitted.

Although other fuses are available, it is recommended officially that only 3-amp or 13-amp fuses be fitted.

Use a 3-amp fuse for equipment such as blankets, record players, tape recorders, clocks and lighting up to 700 watts.

Most other domestic equipment requires a 13-amp fuse. Colour TV and some appliances with motors may need a 13-amp fuse, even when rated below 700 watts. Follow the maker's instructions.

1 Remove plug cover and pull out cartridge fuse

2 Push new cartridge into holder. Refit cover

Understanding electricity

Reading a meter

There are two types of electricity meters: one with a set of dials and the other with a row of figures, like the mileometer on a car. Both types measure electricity consumption in units called kilowatt hours (kWh)—the amount used by 1000-watt equipment in an hour.

Dial meter Ignore the small dial marked 1/10. Read the other five dials from left to right.

If the hand on any dial is between figures, read the figure before it. If a hand is on a figure, check the next dial to the right. If the hand of that dial is between 0 and 1 write down the figure indicated. If it is before the 0, write down the figure before it. The reading shown on the meter below is 43299 kWh.

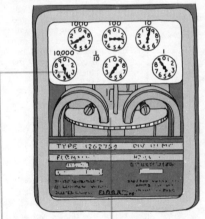

Dials Start reading the meter from the dial on the left and work to the right of the meter

Recorder The disc turns as electricity is consumed. It operates the dial hands through gears

Figures-only meter Read five figures from left to right: consumption here is 21673 kWh

Basic tool kit

The most important repair equipment required is fuse wire—or cartridge fuses—to match the power installation in the house (see p. 519). Always keep a torch beside the fuse box to provide light when a fuse replacement becomes necessary.

At least two screwdrivers are needed—one with a ¼ in. (6 mm) and the other with a ⅛ in. (3 mm) tip. A small screwdriver with a neon tester can be used to check whether a terminal is live by touching the terminal with the tip of the screwdriver and the end of the handle with a finger. If the neon glows, the terminal is live. Do not use a tester with damaged insulation; take care not to touch the bare blade while testing.

Have a sharp knife available, and buy a pair of electrician's cutters and pliers with insulated handles. Do not try to strip the insulation from wires and cables with pliers or a knife: use a wire stripper.

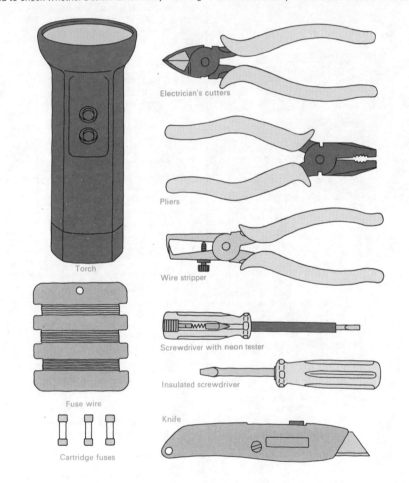

Torch

Electrician's cutters

Pliers

Wire stripper

Screwdriver with neon tester

Insulated screwdriver

Knife

Fuse wire

Cartridge fuses

MAKING A CIRCUIT TESTER

Never attempt to repair any wires connected to the power supply, and always try to check repaired equipment before using it.

To check that circuits and earth connections are unbroken (see p. 526) make a small circuit tester from a torch battery and bulb. Do not try to use it on live wires or on equipment which is plugged in to the power supply.

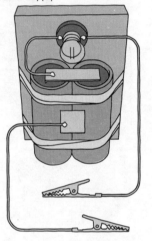

Cut a piece of wood a little longer and wider than a 3-volt torch battery. Buy a small torch bulb and holder, and solder a piece of wire to each terminal of the bulb holder. Screw the bulb holder to the top of the piece of wood.

Secure a battery to the wood with elastic bands. Solder one of the wires from the bulb holder to the top battery terminal. Solder the other wire to a crocodile clip. Solder a third piece of wire to the terminal on the front of the battery and to a second crocodile clip.

Safety

Using electricity safely

Electricity, used carelessly, can kill. The too-hasty connection of electrical equipment, forgetfulness which causes an earth wire to be overlooked, or the 'temporary' flex which is allowed to become permanent are all dangers. At the least, they can result in a shock or a burn: at the worst, a fatal accident or a fire.

Make sure that electrical repair work is carried out properly. Some minor repairs (see pp. 522–67), if undertaken with care, are within the scope of most householders. More involved electrical work, however, including permanent wiring, should be carried out only by a qualified electrician.

Dangers of fire

Slipshod electrical work is one of the most common causes of home fires.

Never assume that flex lasts for ever: it frays with use. Check all flex regularly and renew it immediately if it shows signs of wear.

Never secure flex with staples along the top of a skirting board, and never place flex under a carpet. A staple which bites too deeply, or continuous treading on a carpet, can eventually fray the wire and cause a serious fire.

Never use an electric heater without a guard over the bars. A fire can be started if clothing comes into contact with the element.

Always make sure that fuses of the correct rating (see p. 519) are used. A 13-amp plug, for example, usually has a 13-amp fuse already fitted when it is bought. Always check the amperage of the equipment to which the plug is to be connected and fit a fuse of the correct rating before using the plug. It is dangerous to fit a fuse with a rating higher than that of the equipment to which the plug is to be fitted: if the equipment overloads the circuit, the fuse would not blow and wiring could overheat and catch fire.

Do not risk overloading a radial circuit (see p. 515) by using adaptors on a power socket. Where necessary, have an extra socket fitted by a qualified electrician.

Dangers of shocks

Bodily contact with wiring, or with a metallic fitting in contact with the power supply, produces a shock, which is at least unpleasant and may be fatal. All exposed metal parts should be earthed.

Make sure that all equipment with a three-core flex is properly earthed (see pp. 525, 526). If in any doubt, consult an electrician or ask the electricity board to inspect it.

Some hand tools have an earth terminal, and require a three-pin plug and three-core flex connection. Double-insulated hand tools need not be earthed: use two-core flex, correctly connected to the L and N terminals (see pp. 525, 526).

Never touch electrical equipment with wet hands: if contact is made with earthed pipes or taps with wet hands, the danger is all the greater.

Flexible cords can cause shocks if not enough care is taken to gather every strand when making connections to terminal points.

Never connect wires to the wrong terminal points—the live wire to neutral or neutral to live. Equipment connected in this way can function correctly when switched *on* but be dangerous even when switched *off*. The switch should be on the live side of cable or cord.

Make sure that the earth wire is never connected to the L or N terminal.

Electricity in the garden

Many gardens use electricity: to floodlight trees, light and heat greenhouses, provide power for water pumps in pools and fountains, and to heat the soil under glass.

Do not try to install fixed electrical wiring of this kind. Specialised knowledge and skill are needed.

When fitting an extension lead, ensure that the socket part of the connector is fitted on the lead from the power supply.

WARNING!

Always disconnect electrical equipment from the power supply before inspecting or repairing it. As a reminder, each repair described in the following pages shows a plug removed from its socket.

To work on switches or sockets linked to the supply, turn off the supply at the mains. For added safety, remove the fuse of the circuit concerned at the mains fuse box (see p. 519).

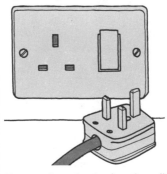

Always pull out the plug from the wall socket before inspecting any piece of electrical equipment

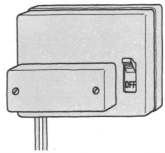

Some equipment has no removable plug. Switch off the current at the mains fuse box

THE SIGNS OF SAFETY

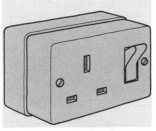

Power socket The safest type of wall socket is one which incorporates a switch

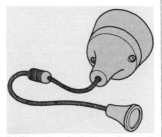

Pull-cord switch Never fit a wall switch in a bathroom. Fit pull-cord switches

Rubber connector Use rubber connectors to extend cables outside the house. Rubber helps to keep out dampness

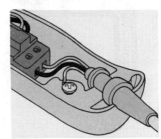

Earth wire Equipment which is not double-insulated must always have three-core cable, including an earth wire

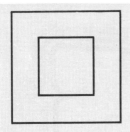

Double-insulated Modern equipment which is double-insulated is marked with a square within a square. No earth is needed

Insulated lamp-holder Use only moulded lamp-holders in bathrooms or kitchens, where condensation creates a shock hazard

Types of ceiling rose

The type of light rose fitted to the ceilings in a house depends on whether the loop-in or junction-box system of wiring is used.

Loop-in wiring

In the loop-in system, each rose has at least four terminals (see p. 516). Note the position of each wire before trying to fit a new rose. If the lampholder is metal, a three-core flex is used from rose to light.

Junction-box wiring

In the junction-box system, the rose need have only three terminals: live, neutral and earth. The earth connection may end at the rose or, if the lampholder is metal, it must be taken down to the light.

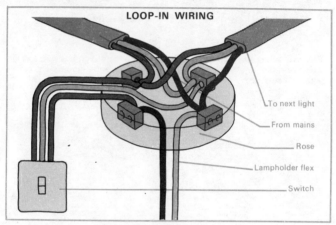

LOOP-IN WIRING

To next light
From mains
Rose
Lampholder flex
Switch

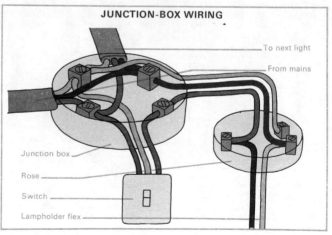

JUNCTION-BOX WIRING

To next light
From mains
Junction box
Rose
Switch
Lampholder flex

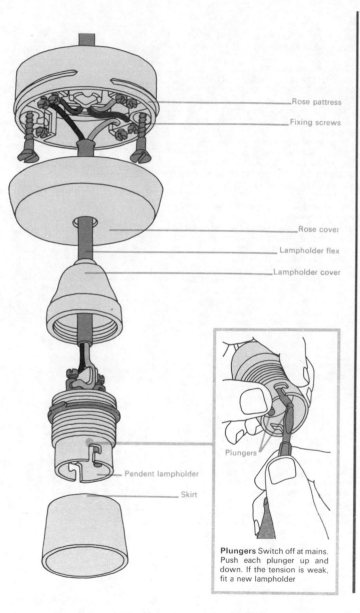

Rose pattress
Fixing screws
Rose cover
Lampholder flex
Lampholder cover
Pendent lampholder
Skirt

Plungers

Plungers Switch off at mains. Push each plunger up and down. If the tension is weak, fit a new lampholder

Fitting a new rose

Switch off at the mains before starting work on a rose or pendent lampholder: it is not safe enough to switch off only at the wall.

A modern ceiling rose has an enclosed, non-combustible base and can be fixed direct to the ceiling. Old-type roses with open bases, and most replacement lighting fittings, are suspended from open-backed ceiling plates which must be mounted on plastic or metal pattresses.

Always fit new lampholder flex when renewing a rose. In kitchens and any other rooms where temperatures are likely to be higher than average, use a heat-resisting flex.

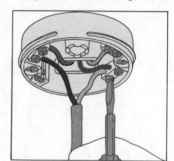

2 Note how the wires are fitted. Unscrew all the terminals and remove the two-core lampholder flex

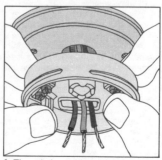

4 Thread the cable wiring into the new pattress and secure the individual wires in the rose terminals

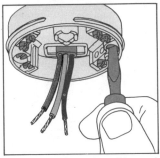

1 Switch off at the mains. Unscrew the rose cover by hand and let it slide down to the lampholder

3 Straighten the mains wiring and unscrew the rose pattress from the ceiling or mounting

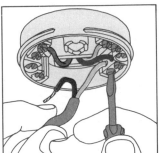

5 Thread the lampholder flex into the rose cover. Screw flex into correct rose terminals. Screw on cover

Fitting a lampholder

To fit a lampholder on flex from a ceiling rose, make sure that the power is switched off at the mains. Cut the flex so that both wires are equal length.

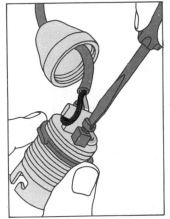

1 Thread flex through lampholder cover and strip off insulation. Fit wires to terminals

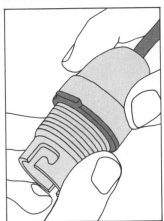

2 Screw on lampholder cover and check that flex hangs straight. Fit lampshade and bulb

How switches are wired

Do not try to install new switches and wiring: it is specialist work and should be done by an experienced electrician. It is possible, however, for a householder to fit replacement switches.

Always make sure that the wires are connected to the correct terminals in the switch unit. In a simple one-way switch there are two wires from the live terminals in the rose to the terminals in the switch.

In a two-way switch, which allows the power to be switched on or off from two different points—a hall and a landing, for instance—there are three terminals and at least three wires plus an earth. One, at the common terminal, is either the live or the switch return wire; the other two are strapping wires linking the two two-way switches and completing the circuit. Sometimes three-core (and earth) cable is used to link the two switches, the conductor colours being red for the common wire, yellow and blue.

WARNING Turn off the power at the main switch before carrying out maintenance or repairs. Do not attempt jobs other than those suggested

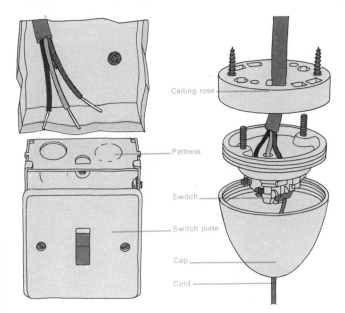

Ceiling rose

Pattress

Switch

Switch plate

Cap

Cord

Wall switch

Pull-cord switch

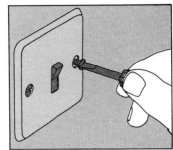

Dismantling Switch off at the mains or remove the fuse. Undo the screws holding the switch plate

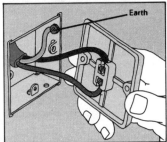

Earth

One-way switch Fit the earth wire to the terminal on the mounting box and the other two wires to the terminals on the switch

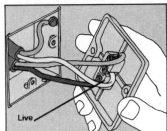

Live

Two-way switch Fit the live or switch return wire to the common terminal, the strapping wires to the other two and the earth to the box. Replace the switch plate

Fittings Sockets

Types of sockets

Wall sockets may have a switch for electricity to be switched off before plugs are removed or be without a switch, which means that the power can be cut only at the fuse box. If a socket is to be replaced, it is always safer to choose one with a switch. Where several appliances are to be used at any point, it is advisable to fit a twin socket instead of using an adaptor on one socket. Existing earth wires are usually bare, but green sleeves should be placed over the ends of new installations.

Sockets can be fitted flush with the wall or mounted on the surface, depending on the box used. The twin socket illustrated is suitable only for surface mounting.

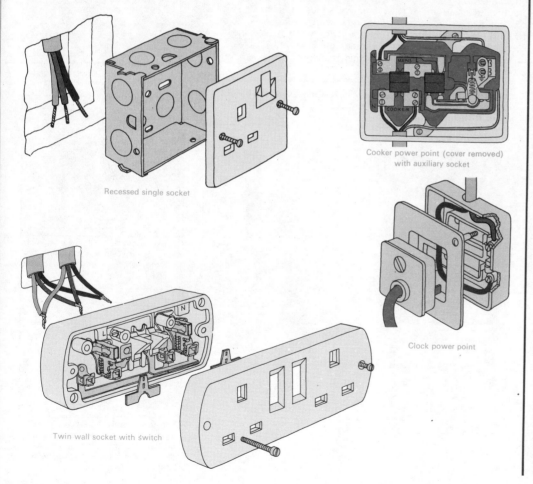

Recessed single socket

Twin wall socket with switch

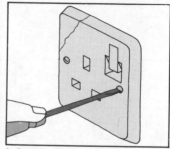

Cooker power point (cover removed) with auxiliary socket

Clock power point

Fitting a new socket

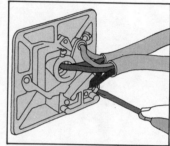

1 Switch off at the mains fuse box (see p. 519). Undo the screws holding the socket plate

2 Ease the socket plate from the wall. Undo the terminal screws and remove wires to release plate

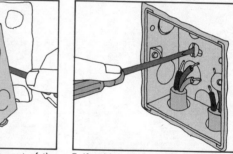

4 Prise the damaged box out of the recess in the wall with a chisel or with a screwdriver

5 If cables are damaged, have new ones fitted by an electrician. Screw new box into recess

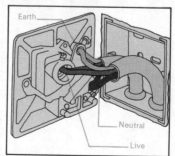

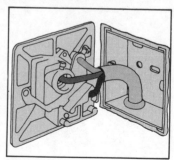

Earth

Neutral

Live

7 Connect the three sets of wires to the socket terminals: red to L, black to N, earth to E

8 If it is a radial circuit or a spur with only three wires, connect the red to L, black to N and earth to E

Fittings Plugs

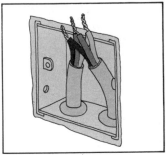

3 Examine the socket box for damage. If any part is broken, buy and fit a new box

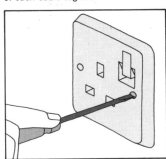

6 If the circuit is a ring main (see p. 515), twist the two matching wires of each cable together

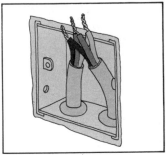

9 Ease or turn the socket plate into position. Make sure no wires are trapped. Screw on to box

Moving a socket

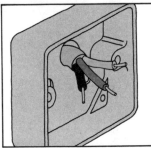

1 If a wall-mounted socket becomes loose, switch off at the mains and disconnect wires from terminals

2 Unscrew the socket box from wall, and drill and plug screw holes slightly lower or higher, avoiding the cable

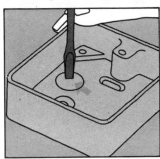

3 If new box is needed, push out moulding (arrowed) to thread in cable. Screw to wall and connect

Types of plugs

The type of plug that can be fitted to any electrical equipment is determined mainly by the size of socket available.

On a ring-main circuit (see p. 515), use 13-amp plugs. These do not vary in pin design: 13-amp sockets are uniform. Check the rating of the equipment (see p. 514) and fit a cartridge fuse of the correct amperage. On a radial circuit, use a two or three-pin plug to fit the socket.

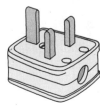

13-amp (flat pins)

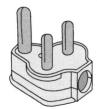

15-amp (round pins)

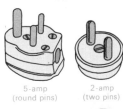

5-amp (round pins)   2-amp (two pins)

5-amp flex connector

Wiring a plug

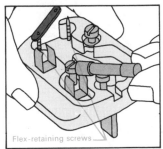

Flex-retaining screws

1 Open plug. Undo one flex-retaining screw and loosen the other. Remove the fuse from the plug

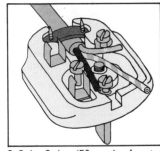

2 Strip 2 in. (50 mm) of outer insulation from cable. Fit into plug: tighten flex-retaining screws

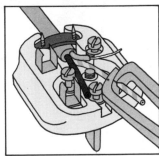

3 Check that wires reach terminals correctly. Strip $\frac{5}{8}$ in. (16 mm) insulation from each wire

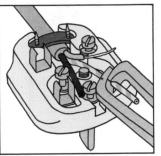

Alternatively, if the plug has screw-hole terminals, strip only $\frac{1}{4}$ in. (6 mm) from the wires of the flex

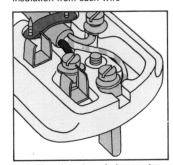

4 Push wires into holes or loop clockwise round terminals: brown to L, blue to N, green/yellow to E

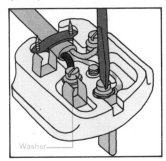

Washer

5 Make sure there are no loose strands. Tighten screws and refit fuse and cover

Fittings Connections and fault-finding

Fitting new flex

If the flex on a piece of equipment is frayed or damaged, remove it and fit new flex as soon as possible. Most household equipment has three-core flex, although some low-amperage fittings—for example, lights—and double-insulated items (see p. 521) have two-core, with no earth wire. Buy only new colour-coded flex (see p. 517) and make sure when fitting it that the wires are connected to the correct terminals. If there is any doubt about which terminals are live and neutral, consult an electrician before fitting the flex: a trial-and-error attempt is dangerous.

Terminal	Possible descriptions	Symbol	Colour
Earth	Green or green/yellow	E	or
Live	Red or brown	L	or
Neutral	Black or blue	N	or

Equipment terminals may be identified by words, letters, symbols or colours

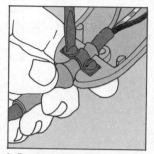

1 Remove the casing or cap from the equipment and undo the two screws holding the flex

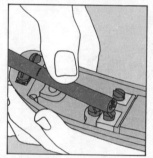

2 Loosen terminals and remove old cable. Remove any rubber sleeve and fit to new flex

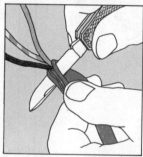

3 Hold flex on terminals and make a mark on sheathing near inner edge of cable clamp

4 Cut through sheathing. Take care not to damage the insulation on the wires

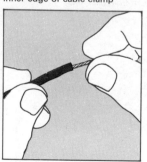

5 Remove ½ in. (13 mm) insulation from wires with stripper. Do not cut through strands

6 Twist strands of each wire carefully together. Do not mix the wires

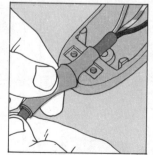

7 Connect the wires. Slide rubber sleeve into place, secure clamp and refit casing

Testing wires and circuits

When a piece of equipment is not operating, although power is available at the socket, check its flex and plug with a circuit tester (see p. 520). Do not try to test wires connected to the power supply; always unplug equipment before testing.

If the equipment has a high resistance (see p. 514)—for example a fire element—it cannot be tested with a circuit tester but should be tested by a dealer.

To test live and neutral, connect the test leads to both ends of each wire in turn. To check earthing, connect one clip to a metal part of the equipment and the other to the earth pin of the plug.

Double-insulated units (see p. 521), are not fitted with an earth return.

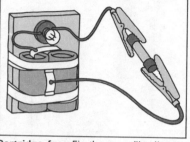

Cartridge fuse Fix the crocodile clips to each end of the fuse. If the bulb does not light, the fuse has blown

Flex Connect the test clips to the ends of each wire in turn. Shake the flex. If the bulb flickers or does not light, discard the flex

Switch Remove the switch from the wiring. Connect clips to its terminals. Bulb should light only when switch is on

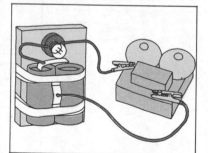

Bell Attach the clips to the two terminals on the bell. If the circuit is sound, the bulb should light or glow, even if only dimly

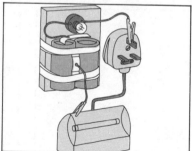

Earth Connect clips to a metal part of the equipment and earth pin of plug. If bulb does not light, the earth connection is faulty

Electric motors

Two types of motors

An electric motor consists of two sets of electro-magnets: an outer, fixed set, called the stator, or field coil, and an inner set, free to revolve, called the armature.

The shaft of the motor is connected to the armature, so that when the armature spins the shaft spins with it, driving the piece of equipment to which the motor is fitted.

When the electricity supply is switched on, the coils of wire making up the stator and the armature become magnets, each with a north and south pole. The north poles of the stator attract the south poles of the armature, setting it in motion and so turning the shaft. The armature is kept spinning in one of two ways, depending on the type of motor.

Brush motors

In a brush motor, there is a switching device, called a commutator.

This shuts off the current from a pair of armature coils as soon as a north and a south pole come together and switches the current to the next pair of coils, so creating two new magnets to be attracted by the magnets of the stator. This type of motor can be used with alternating current from the mains, or with direct current from a battery.

Induction motors

An induction motor needs alternating current, which automatically reverses its flow many times a second.

As a north and a south pole come together in this type of motor, the current flow is reversed, turning what was a north pole in the stator into a south pole. This reversal repels the south pole of one armature magnet and attracts the north pole of the next.

Fitting brushes

If a brush motor stops and starts frequently, or if sparks can be seen at the commutator, remove and check the condition of the brushes. If they are badly pitted or worn, buy matching replacements. Tell the dealer the make and model to which they are to be fitted, or write to the manufacturer. Never try to use brushes which are not designed for the equipment.

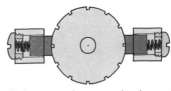

Each motor has two brushes at opposite sides of the commutator. They are spring-fitted and may be held by screws or clips.

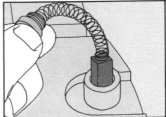

1 Unscrew or unclip the brush. Note the position of any guide marks

2 Clean commutator with methylated spirit. Fit the new brushes carefully, following any guide marks. Refit the clip or screw

---

BRUSH MOTOR

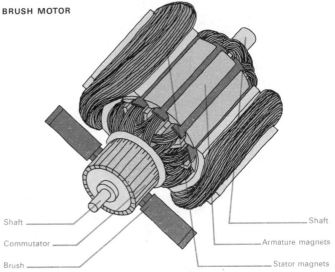

Shaft

Commutator

Brush

Shaft

Armature magnets

Stator magnets

A brush motor can be readily identified by its shape: its length is greater than its width. Induction motors, on the other hand, usually have approximately the same length and width.

A brush motor can be used either with alternating current from the mains or with direct current from a battery, because of the operation of its switching device, the commutator.

This is made up of copper segments on one end of the rotor shaft. Each strip is connected to a winding in the armature and is supplied with electricity through two stationary pieces of graphite, called brushes, which are in contact with the commutator but are not fixed to it.

When the motor is switched on, current flows to the stator coils and through the brushes to the two segments of the commutator with which they are in contact. This magnetises the armature coils, and the armature starts turning, bringing the next two commutator segments into contact with the brushes. The operation is repeated many times a second.

INDUCTION MOTOR

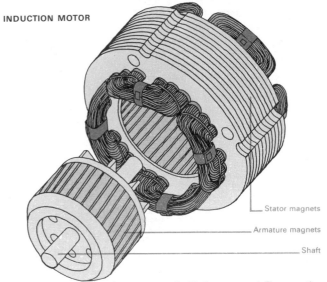

Stator magnets

Armature magnets

Shaft

Motors which can operate only on alternating current—that is the mains supply—are called induction motors. They have no commutator and no brushes, and their armature is not connected directly to the electricity supply.

Power is fed only to the stator coils, but by an electrical process called induction the armature also becomes magnetised, because it is in the middle of the stator's magnetic field.

When the current is switched on it reverses the magnetic field in the stator coils 50 times a second. The magnetism induced in the armature stays constant. As a result the stator attracts, then repels, the armature strips 50 times a second.

Induction motors are simpler in design and construction than the brush type. Little maintenance is needed, but make sure that the motor is kept clean. If it is operating spasmodically, disconnect the equipment from the power supply and check that the armature can turn freely inside the stator. If it does not, take the equipment to a dealer.

Batteries

How a battery works

A battery consists of a number of cells, each of just over two volts. Six-volt batteries have three cells; 12-volt batteries have six.

In each cell, there are positive and negative plates—the electrodes—immersed in diluted sulphuric acid—the electrolyte. One electrode is made of spongy lead, the other of lead dioxide.

The acid reacts with the plates to convert chemical energy into electrical energy. This builds up a positive charge on the lead-dioxide electrode and a negative charge on the other. Current flows from the negative plates to the positive plates through the electrolyte. As the chemical reaction goes on, lead sulphate forms on the surface of both electrodes and the sulphuric acid enters the plates, weakening the solution. When the surfaces of both plates have turned completely to lead sulphate, the battery is flat.

Once the cell has been re-charged with an electric current, the electrodes are restored to their original condition.

On some cars the earth strap is connected to the negative terminal, on others to the positive terminal. Check carefully before removing the leads.

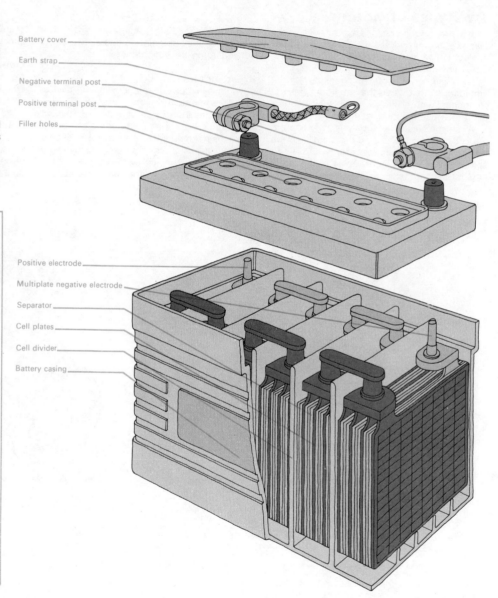

Battery cover
Earth strap
Negative terminal post
Positive terminal post
Filler holes

Positive electrode
Multiplate negative electrode
Separator
Cell plates
Cell divider
Battery casing

FINDING THE FAULT

Symptom	Checking order	Action
Starter motor failing to crank engine properly: battery mower lacks power	Flat battery	Top up with distilled water and trickle charge
	Dirty terminals or bad earth connections	Clean and reconnect
	Battery unable to give high current	Re-charge, and take battery to dealer for heavy-discharge test
Corrosion on terminals and retaining clamps	Acid leakage, due to:	
	overfilling. This may not be apparent as the corrosion will have been caused by the excess acid spilling out	Top up until plates are just covered
	overcharging. A mist of escaping acid can be seen through the air vent of the filler cap during re-charging or while the motor is running	Have the charging rate of the battery checked at garage
	cracked case	Take to dealer for possible repair or buy new battery
	loose terminal post	Smear terminal post with petroleum jelly (Vaseline)
Battery requires frequent topping up	Overcharging. A mist of escaping acid can be seen through the air vent of the filler cap during re-charging or while the motor is running	Have charging rate of the battery checked at garage
	Cracked case	Take to dealer for possible repair, or replace battery

Care and maintenance

A battery should be kept dry and clean. It must be fixed firmly to its mountings so that it cannot vibrate and spill the electrolyte.

The terminals and leads are likely to become corroded with acid, particularly if the electrolyte level is too high or if the battery is over-charging. When this happens, the current can leak or discharge across dirty and damp surfaces. More seriously, spilled electrolyte can damage the brackets securing the battery.

Materials: ammonia; Vaseline; lint-free rags; emery paper.
Tools: ring spanner; screwdriver.

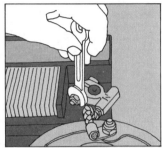

1 Disconnect the terminals with a spanner. If the terminals are tight, tap with a screwdriver handle

2 Use a ring spanner to undo the nut holding the strap to the body of the car

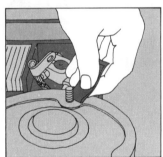

3 Clean the earthing point and the earth-strap tag with a piece of fine emery paper

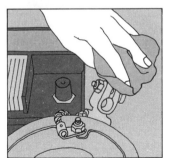

4 Remove any acid from the earth strap with a rag and ammonia. Dry with a clean rag

5 Smear the terminals with petroleum jelly (Vaseline) to prevent corrosion. Refix and tighten the screws

Checking the battery condition

The condition of a battery depends on the strength of the electrolyte. It becomes weaker as water forms during discharge and stronger as acid forms in charging.

Check the battery condition every week, by taking a sample of the electrolyte from each cell with an instrument called a hydrometer.

The hydrometer measures the strength—called specific gravity—of the acid in the cells. The specific gravity of the electrolyte should be at least 1·260. If the hydrometer reading is 1·260–1·280, the battery is fully charged. If the reading is 1·100 or below, the battery is without charge.

The readings for each cell should be within 50 points of each other. If there is any greater difference, it is likely that a cell is defective. Take the battery to a garage or a specialist.

Some hydrometers, instead of being marked with a gradation, show in words whether the battery is fully charged, half charged or dead.

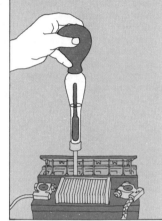

1 Squeeze the bulb on the hydrometer. Insert the nozzle into a cell. Release the bulb to draw up electrolyte into the hydrometer

TOPPING UP

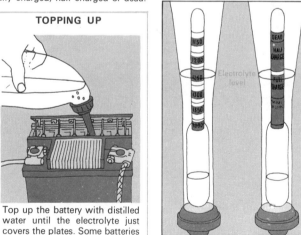

Top up the battery with distilled water until the electrolyte just covers the plates. Some batteries have a separate filling hole for each cell; others have a common filling trough

2 Check the reading as the hydrometer scale floats on the electrolyte. Return fluid to cell, and check the other cells

MAINTAINING A BATTERY

Never allow a battery to remain flat for more than a week: crystals quickly form and the plates become buckled beyond repair. Always store a battery fully charged, and re-charge it once a month while it is not being used.

To prolong the life of a battery, keep it topped up and fully charged. Never use a booster charge—which can buckle the plates—except when the battery has to be re-charged in an emergency. If a battery has to be taken to a garage for re-charging, take it to one with a trickle charger: others will use only a booster charge.

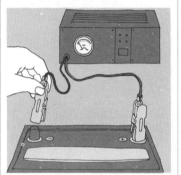

Charging at home To bring the battery up to full charge with a trickle charger, disconnect the leads from the battery and top it up with distilled water. Make sure that the air vents in the filler caps are unblocked. Connect positive (+) lead from charger to positive terminal on battery and negative (−) lead to negative terminal.

The dial on the charger indicates the rate at which the battery is accepting the charge. Charge until the reading falls to 1 amp.

Never use a naked flame near a battery under charge; the gases given off are explosive. Switch off the charger before disconnecting the leads from the battery.

Bells and chimes

Blankets

How bells and buzzers operate

The electric circuit in many bell and chime units is operated by an electro-magnetic solenoid. As current passes through the electro-magnet a plunger is pulled down to strike the gong. When this happens, a contact spring on the plunger moves away from a contact screw in the solenoid and breaks the circuit momentarily so that the plunger springs back. This cycle is repeated many times every second to give a continuous ringing or buzzing for as long as the bell-push is pressed.

If the unit is powered by the mains through a transformer, always switch off at the mains before carrying out any maintenance.

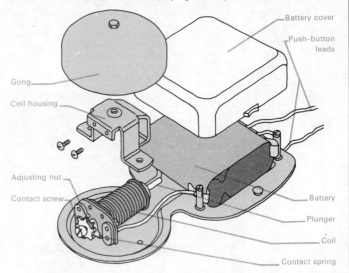

Battery cover
Push-button leads
Gong
Coil housing
Adjusting nut
Contact screw
Battery
Plunger
Coil
Contact spring

Maintaining chimes

When the bell-push on a set of chimes is pressed, current flows to the solenoid and the plunger strikes the first chime bar or tube. The circuit is broken when the bell-push is released and the plunger returns under spring pressure to strike a second chime bar or tube. This action is repeated every time the bell-push is depressed and released. Do not fit a set of chimes in a kitchen, as condensation can cause the plunger to rust. If it does become contaminated, remove it from the solenoid and clean it with fine emery cloth. On chimes with tubes, the batteries may fit into the centre tube: note the position before removing the old batteries.

When chimes are operated through the mains, always switch off at the mains before doing any maintenance.

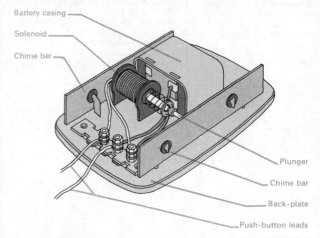

Battery casing
Solenoid
Chime bar
Plunger
Chime bar
Back-plate
Push-button leads

Blanket safety

Electric underblankets are only bed warmers: always switch off before getting into bed.

To ensure that an underblanket cannot move and become crumpled, eyelet holes or tapes must be fitted to allow the edges to be tied. Any not so fitted should be returned to the maker for attention.

Electric overblankets are intended for use over the bedclothes and can be left switched on during the night.

Some blankets have only a simple on-off switch: others have more complicated thermostatic controls which can regulate blanket heat according to body and room temperature.

Never try to repair an electric blanket: send it to the manufacturer. Have it serviced at least every two years.

Most blankets cannot be laundered, but if the blanket is washable follow the manufacturer's instructions.

Never dry-clean an electric blanket: the chemicals used damage the insulation wires.

An electric blanket should never be switched on if it is wet. Stretch carefully to full size over a drying rail until dry. The blanket and flexible lead should be examined frequently for signs of wear.

WARNING Remove plug from socket before carrying out maintenance or repairs. Do not attempt jobs other than those suggested

---

FINDING THE FAULT

Symptom	Fault	Action
No heat	Fuse blown	Fit new fuse (see p. 519)
No heat or intermittent heat	Loose flex connections at plug	Reconnect (see p. 525)
	Broken flex between plug and switch, or switch and blanket	Return to manufacturer
	Faulty switch	
	Faulty element or sealed flex connector	

To clean the contact spring and screw, rub a piece of cardboard between them. Do not use emery cloth

FINDING THE FAULT

Symptom	Fault	Action
No sound	Battery faulty	Fit new battery
	Loose connections	Reconnect (see p. 526)
	Leads broken	Fit new leads
	Bell push faulty	Fit new one
Intermittent ringing	Leads not making good contact at bell-push, battery (or transformer) or bell	Reconnect leads (see p. 526)
	Dirt on gong	Remove

CLEANING

Clean dirt from the solenoid spring and plunger with a soft brush. Make sure plunger moves freely

POWER SUPPLY

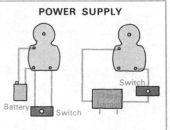

Battery
Switch
Transformer
Switch

Bells, buzzers and chimes operate on low voltage supplied either by a battery or a mains transformer. Always follow manufacturers' instructions for wiring

Cookers

Replacing cooker parts

An electric cooker has separate elements to heat the hot-plates, grill and oven. Each element has an individual electric circuit which operates at a different wattage from the others. The temperature which can be reached by the elements is pre-set during manufacture and is maintained by a thermostat.

All hot-plate elements are replaceable. Older models may have a plug fitting which enables them to be fitted without tools. Oven and grill elements, however, can be replaced only by a service engineer.

WARNING Switch off power at the mains before carrying out maintenance or repairs. Do not attempt jobs other than those suggested

FINDING THE FAULT

Symptom	Checking order	Action
No heat	Fuse blown in plug, fuse box or cooker box	Fit new fuse of correct amperage (see p. 519)
	Loose or broken flex connections. (Check with circuit tester see p. 526)	Remove back of cooker and inspect connections. Renew if necessary (see p. 526). Do not attempt to test a fixed supply cable. Do not try to fit a new fixed cable
Oven over-heating or boiling ring glowing continually	Short circuit in controller	Call service engineer or electricity board
One element fails to heat	Fault in sub-circuit to that element, or broken element	Call service engineer or electricity board
Fluorescent cooker light fails to work	Broken fluorescent light	Fit new light of the correct rating (see p. 539)
	Broken fluorescent light starter	Fit new starter of the correct rating (see p. 539)
Oven light fails to work	Broken bulb. (Check with circuit tester, see p. 526)	Fit new bulb of correct rating (see p. 532)
	Faulty switch	Have a new switch fitted by an electrician

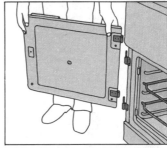

Cooker control switch This must be separate from, but within 6 ft of, the cooker

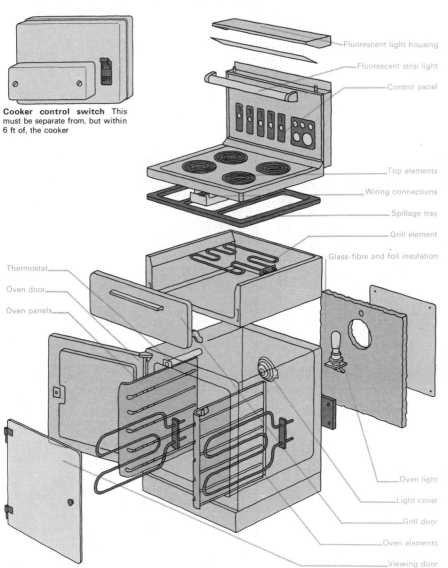

- Fluorescent light housing
- Fluorescent strip light
- Control panel
- Top elements
- Wiring connections
- Spillage tray
- Grill element
- Glass-fibre and foil insulation
- Thermostat
- Oven door
- Oven panels
- Oven light
- Light cover
- Grill door
- Oven elements
- Viewing door

Cleaning

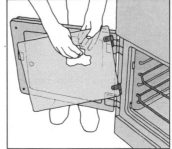

1 Clean an oven thoroughly once a week. If the outside door can be lifted off its hinges, remove it

2 If there is a glass door on the oven, clean it with a strong solution of detergent and hot water

3 Slide out the interior side panels and wash in detergent and hot water. Rinse and dry thoroughly. Reassemble

Cookers

Fitting a new element

A ring element is completely enclosed in a metal sheath, so it cannot be repaired. But it can be replaced. If one fails, take it to an electrical-supply shop or electricity-board showroom. Buy a new element of the same type, loading and voltage.

Tools: screwdriver and small box spanner.

Ring element

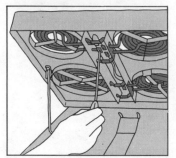

2 Undo the terminals of the faulty element, using a screwdriver or a box spanner as necessary

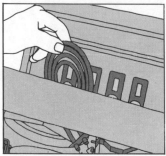

4 Lift out the old element from the top. Fit the new one in reverse order and tighten the terminals

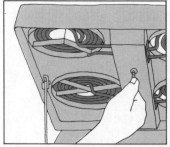

1 Lift the hinged top-plate of the cooker. Remove the screws holding the element-terminal cover plate

3 With a box spanner, unscrew the nuts holding the element support bracket on the side of the terminal box

Solid metal Some cookers have solid plates. Pull out the element plug and fit a new one

Fitting a control-panel light

Many cookers have a fluorescent light to illuminate the control panel. If either the light or its starter unit fail, new parts can be fitted.

Always switch off at the cooker and at the mains.

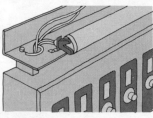

2 Slide the glass panels out of the framework. Wash them in hot water and detergent

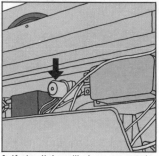

4 If the light still does not work, trace the wires from the terminals to the starter unit, usually at the back

1 Unscrew and remove the light-unit casing carefully. Do not damage the glass panelling

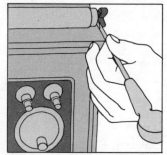

3 Prise the push-on terminal tabs off the pins at each end of the fluorescent tube. Fit new tube

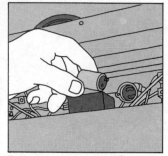

5 Unplug the starter and buy a new unit of the same type. Fit it and refit the cover

---

FITTING AN OVEN LIGHT

The oven light is operated by a switch when the door opens and closes. Fitting a new bulb may entail removing the back panel.

Tool: screwdriver.

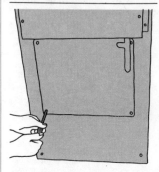

1 Undo the screws holding the back panel in position. The panel may have a lip which fits into a panel above or below it. Remove it, but do not force it out of its slot

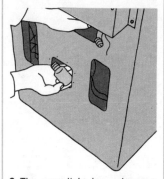

2 The oven light has a bayonet fitting. Remove it and fit a new one. Take care not to damage any of the wiring connected to the oven elements

Dishwashers

How a dishwasher works

Automatic dishwashers have a heater element in water in the base of the machine. When the water reaches the correct temperature it is pumped through the rotor, where it is flung off by an impeller or rotor on to the dishes. At the end of each pre-wash, wash and rinse programme, dirty water is drained through an outlet hose.

The entire operation, including pre-wash and several rinses, may take as much as $1\frac{1}{2}$ hours; but the average time, starting with a cold fill, is between 40 and 50 minutes. The operation can be shortened by starting further along the programme and setting the control switch to particular cycles. If dishes are not very dirty, for example, the pre-wash and one of the rinse cycles can be omitted.

Note that older dishwashers cannot remove burnt food deposits from dishes or cutlery.

WARNING Remove plug from socket before carrying out maintenance or repairs. Do not attempt jobs other than those suggested

FINDING THE FAULT

Symptom	Checking order	Action
No power	Fuse blown at plug	Fit new fuse (see p. 519)
No power or intermittent power	Loose flex connections at plug or appliance	Reconnect (see pp. 525, 526)
	Broken flex. Check with circuit tester (see p. 526)	Fit new flex if necessary (see p. 526)
	Burnt-out windings	Consult service engineer
Dishes not clean	Water not heating because element or thermostat is defective	Consult service engineer
	Water not circulating because rotor is blocked	Clean in running water
	Water not circulating because pump is defective	Consult service engineer
	Control unit defective	Consult service engineer
Dishes not dry	Faulty blower motor or element	Consult service engineer

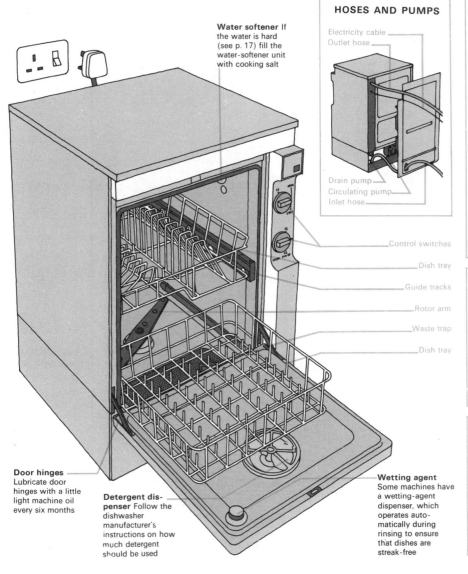

Water softener If the water is hard (see p. 17) fill the water-softener unit with cooking salt

Control switches

Dish tray

Guide tracks

Rotor arm

Waste trap

Dish tray

Door hinges Lubricate door hinges with a little light machine oil every six months

Detergent dispenser Follow the dishwasher manufacturer's instructions on how much detergent should be used

Wetting agent Some machines have a wetting-agent dispenser, which operates automatically during rinsing to ensure that dishes are streak-free

HOSES AND PUMPS

Electricity cable

Outlet hose

Drain pump

Circulating pump

Inlet hose

WASTE TRAP AND FILTER

Waste trap

Many machines have a perforated metal or plastic waste trap at the base of the wash chamber. Lift it out and empty it after each wash

Inlet filter

If the machine is emptying slowly, disconnect the inlet hose at the back. Prise out the waste filter and rinse it in running water

TRAY TRACKS

Tray roller

Dish trays have nylon rollers which fit into two metal guide tracks. If the tracks become distorted, consult a service engineer

CLEANING THE ROTOR

Hub cap

If the machine has a rotor and the holes in it become clogged, unscrew hub cap, lift off rotor and wash it under a tap

Extractor fans

The basic parts of an extractor

Extractor fans are usually fitted in outside walls or windows (see p. 30). The fan blades, which may be driven by an induction or brush motor (see p. 527) are housed between two grilles. The inner grille is usually shuttered, so that as the fan is turned off, the shutter closes and protects the room from draughts.

Always disconnect the fan socket from the power supply or switch off at the mains before trying to clean or repair the equipment.

FINDING THE FAULT		
Symptom	Checking order	Action
No power	Fuse blown at plug	Fit new fuse (see p. 519)
No power or intermittent power	Loose or broken flex connections at plug or fan	Reconnect (see pp. 525, 526)
	Broken flex. Check with circuit tester (see p. 526)	If necessary fit new flex (see p. 526)
	Burnt-out motor	Call a service engineer

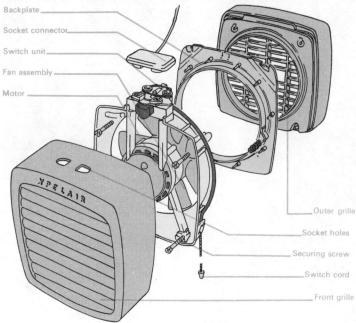

Backplate
Socket connector
Switch unit
Fan assembly
Motor

Outer grille
Socket holes
Securing screw
Switch cord
Front grille

Fitting new cord

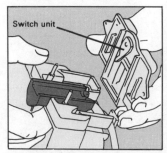

Switch unit

1 Disconnect the fan and remove front grille. Undo the screws holding switch unit. Remove unit

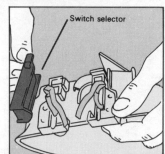

Switch selector

2 Slide the switch selector from between the metal contacts. Avoid damaging the contacts

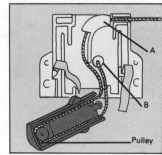

A

B

Pulley

3 Use a needle to push cord through sleeve, under curved part (A), round pulley and knot it in hole (B)

Cleaning a fan

1 Disconnect the flex socket from the fan assembly. Undo the screws holding the front grille

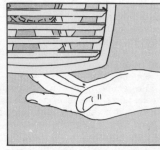

2 Press the release button, if there is one, and gently pull the grille off the front of the fan

3 Wash the shutter grille in warm water and detergent. Dry thoroughly with clean cloth

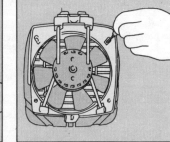

4 Undo the four screws holding the motor and fan assembly to inner clamp plate. Remove the motor unit

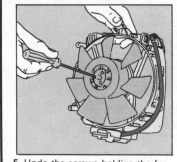

5 Undo the screws holding the fan blades on the motor shaft. Lift the fan impeller off the motor

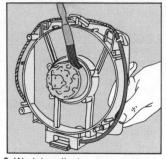

6 Wash impeller in soapy water and dry it. Clean motor, and holes in motor support arms, with dry brush

Fan heaters

Care and maintenance

Some fan heaters have only one fan, others have two. To reduce the risk of burning out or overheating, the heating element cannot be switched on independently of the motor. Most models have a cut-out device to operate if the fans stop or the air-vents are obstructed.

The continuous draught of air from the fans is designed to keep the element 'black'. If a section does begin to glow, and the air vents are not obstructed, the fan speed may be lower than it should be. Lubricating the motor bearings may restore the fan speed to normal. If not, take the heater to a dealer.

WARNING Remove plug from socket before carrying out maintenance or repairs. Do not attempt jobs other than those suggested

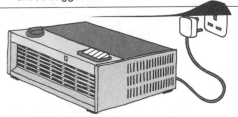

FINDING THE FAULT

Symptom	Checking order	Action
No power	Blown fuse at plug	Fit new fuse (see p. 519)
No power or intermittent power	Loose flex connections at plug or appliance	Fit new flex connection (see pp. 525, 526)
	Broken flex. Check with circuit tester (see p. 526)	If necessary, fit new flex (see p. 526)
	Broken element	Consult dealer
	Burnt motor (may not be apparent by visual check)	Consult dealer
Motor speed too low	Dry bearings	Lubricate with machine oil

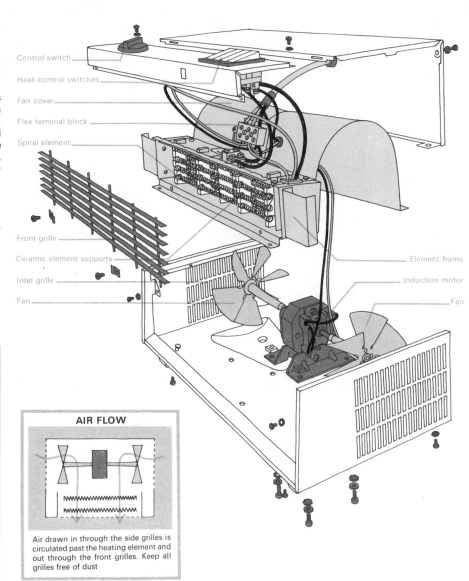

Control switch

Heat-control switches

Fan cover

Flex terminal block

Spiral element

Front grille

Ceramic element supports

Inlet grille

Fan

Element frame

Induction motor

Fan

AIR FLOW

Air drawn in through the side grilles is circulated past the heating element and out through the front grilles. Keep all grilles free of dust

CLEANING AND LUBRICATION

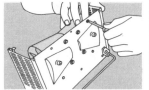

1 Unplug the heater. Undo and remove the screws holding the base or back

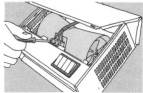

2 If the motor is housed behind a fan cover, disconnect the flex connections

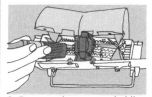

3 Remove the screws holding the fan cover. Clean the motor with a soft brush

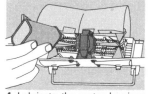

4 Lubricate the motor bearings with one or two drops of light machine oil. Reassemble

Fires

Types of electric fires

The element in an electric fire is a coil of fine wire with a very high resistance (see p. 514). When current passes through it, the wire glows.

An element may be exposed or protected. Exposed types are wrapped round a rod-shaped insulator or across a rectangular piece of fireclay. Protected elements are enclosed in silica-glass tubing. Both types can be removed and replaced.

Flame effect

Fires with a hot-coal or flame effect have a low-wattage bulb under the element unit. A mirror or piece of polished metal is rotated by the heat from the bulb and reflects the bulb light on to a translucent or metal surface. Both the bulb and the metal or mirror piece can be replaced if they fail.

Keep the polished reflector clean. Remove the fire from the power supply and take off the fireguard. Clean the reflector with a damp cloth—never use an abrasive, which will damage the surface—then dry it and replace the fire guard.

Never light cigarettes or paper from an exposed element: ash can drop down, solidify and damage the element or reflector; lighted paper will raise the temperature and damage the element.

Always test the earth return (see p. 526) after a fire has been repaired and before plugging it into the socket of the power supply.

WARNING Remove plug from socket before carrying out maintenance or repairs. Do not attempt jobs other than those suggested

FINDING THE FAULT

Symptom	Checking order	Action
No heat	Fuse blown at plug or at main fuse box	Find and repair fault (see p. 519) and fit new fuse of correct rating
	Broken or burnt element (check visually)	Fit new element of same type and size
No heat or intermittent heat	Broken flex. Check with circuit tester (see p. 526)	Fit new flex if necessary (see p. 526)
	Loose connections at plug or at fire	Renew connections (see pp. 525, 526)

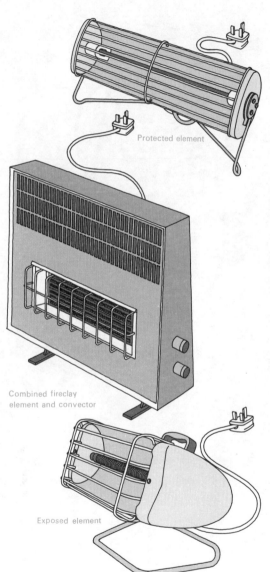

Protected element

Combined fireclay element and convector

Exposed element

Fitting a new element

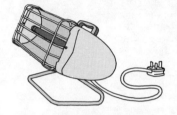

Exposed and glass-enclosed rods can be removed and replaced if they become faulty. The exposed type—where the element is simply a bare wire wrapped around an insulator—is more easily examined for damage.

1 Undo the securing screws or squeeze the bars gently inwards to prise the guard free from the casing of the fire

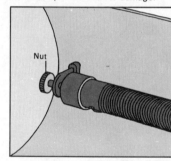

Nut

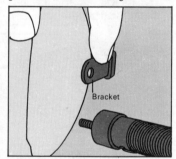

Bracket

2 Unscrew the milled nuts at each end of the element. Use a pair of pliers if necessary

3 The element is usually housed in brackets. Push one outwards, pull out element and fit a new one

ENCLOSED-ROD ELEMENT

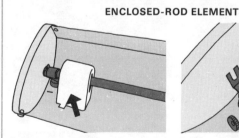

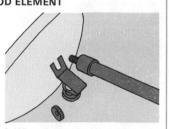

1 The terminals are usually covered by sleeves (arrowed). Squeeze front and back to free them

2 When the terminal is visible, undo the milled nut. Lift out the element and fit a new one

Renewing fireclay elements

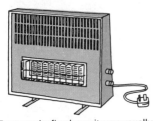

Rectangular fireclay units can usually be bought to replace damaged ones; but if a new unit cannot be obtained, buy a new wire element and fit it to the old backing. Take the fireclay unit to the shop.

FITTING A NEW FIRECLAY UNIT

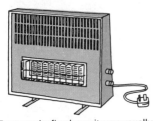

1 Undo back of fire and unscrew fireclay terminal screws. Remove nuts holding fireclay bar

2 Fit new bar and attach its wires to the terminals. Refit asbestos washer, metal washer and nut

---

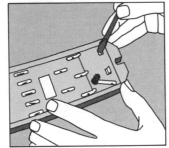

1 To fit a new element, first undo the top terminal screw and remove wire ends from fire

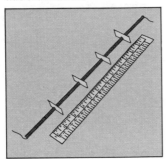

3 Lay the new element alongside a ruler. Mark equal parts to correspond with the rows of the fireclay

5 Secure one end of the element to the top terminal. Stretch it along the top row and fasten it at the end

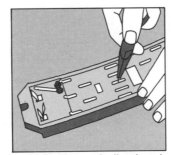

2 From behind, push clips through and remove them at the front with pliers. Straighten the clips

4 Uncoil and straighten about $\frac{1}{2}$ in. (13 mm) of wire at each point marked on the element

6 Stretch the element round the other rows of the fireclay and fit it at each end and in middle with clips

Bowl reflectors

If a reflector-bowl fire does not operate after the flex and plug connections have been checked (see pp. 525, 526) it is probable that a new element is needed.

1 Remove the fireguard and undo the two retaining screws beside the element on the reflector bowl

2 Ease off the lead box at the back. Disconnect the terminals, fit a new element and reassemble

Convection fires

A convection heater has a heavy-duty spiral element in the base. If the fire fails, ask a dealer to fit a new element. Clean the grid and inside the heater every few months.

1 To clean, undo the screws holding the grid at base of the heater. Clean the grid with a vacuum cleaner

2 Clean inside the heater to ensure that no fluff or dust remains. Do not dislodge the spiral element

Floor polishers

How a floor polisher works

Floor polishers have a brush motor (see p. 527) to drive the shafts to which the polishing mops or brushes are attached. Some models also have a polish or shampoo distributor which releases a small amount of polish or cleaning liquid on to the floor to be spread by the brushes.

A polisher has two or three circular mops or brushes. In time these wear and should be replaced. The method of fitting depends on the type of machine. Take an old brush or mop to a dealer to ensure that the correct replacements are bought.

WARNING Remove plug from socket before carrying out maintenance or repairs. Do not attempt jobs other than those suggested

FINDING THE FAULT

Symptom	Checking order	Action
Motor will not run	Blown fuse in plug	Fit new fuse (see p. 519)
	Faulty connection in plug or at polisher	Reconnect (see pp. 525, 526)
	Carbon brushes worn	Fit new brushes (see p. 527)
	Faulty switch	Take to dealer
	Faulty capacitor	Take to dealer
Motor runs intermittently	Faulty connections	Reconnect (see pp. 525, 526)
Whine, rattle or rumbling sound	Loose driving-shaft screw causing vibration	Tighten screw

FITTING RUBBER SKIRT

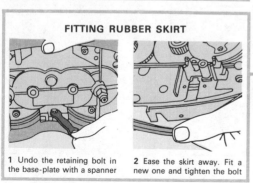

1 Undo the retaining bolt in the base-plate with a spanner

2 Ease the skirt away. Fit a new one and tighten the bolt

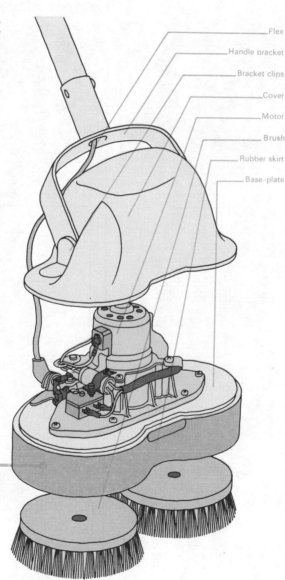

- Flex
- Handle bracket
- Bracket clips
- Cover
- Motor
- Brush
- Rubber skirt
- Base-plate

Cleaning the mechanism

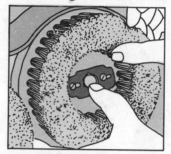

1 To remove polishing brushes, place the fingers behind the mop and press the shaft with the thumb

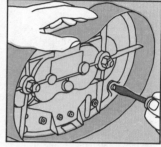

2 Remove the four screws which secure the top cover of the polisher to the base-plate

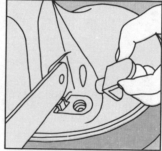

3 Spring the clips which hold the handle bracket on the top cover out of their housing

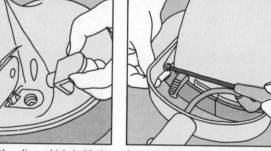

4 Undo the small screws—usually two of them—which hold the switch lever on the handle bracket

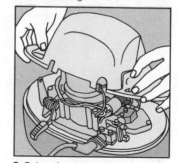

5 Raise the spring-loaded switch lever to a vertical position. Remove the polisher cover

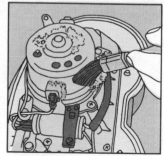

6 Clean the motor and surrounding mechanism with a soft brush. Make sure all fluff is removed. Reassemble

Fluorescent tubes

Maintenance and replacement

Fluorescent tubes have a working life of from 5000 to 7000 hours, so lasting about three to five years.

When a new lamp is first switched on, the light is likely to give a swirling effect along the tube. This should soon disappear, but if it persists, the starter may be faulty.

If an old tube starts to blacken about 2 in. (50 mm) from its end, the electrode material in the tube is evaporating and the light will soon fail.

If a tube is faulty, it can cause the starter (an automatic switch) to fail: fit a new tube immediately.

The gas-filled tube has a heater filament at each end. When the lamp is switched on, high voltage from the choke starts a flow of electrons between the heated filaments. These impinge on the fluorescent coating of the glass and produce light.

> **WARNING** Switch off power at mains before carrying out maintenance or repairs. Do not attempt jobs other than those suggested

FINDING THE FAULT

Symptom	Checking order	Action
Tube will not light	Fuse blown	Fit new fuse (see p. 519)
	Loose or broken connections	Reconnect
	Broken lamp electrode	Fit new tube
Electrodes glow at each end, but tube will not start	If the glow is white, the starter is faulty	Fit new starter
	If the glow is red, the lamp is nearly dead	Fit new tube
Tube glows at one end only	Lamp holder connection at dead end of tube short-circuiting	Fit new lamp holder
Tube flickers when switched on, but will not start	Faulty starter	Fit new starter
	Old tube	Fit new tube
Tube lights for a few seconds, then goes out, then repeats	Faulty starter	Fit new starter
	Old tube	Fit new tube
Tube lights up at half brightness	Old tube	Fit new tube

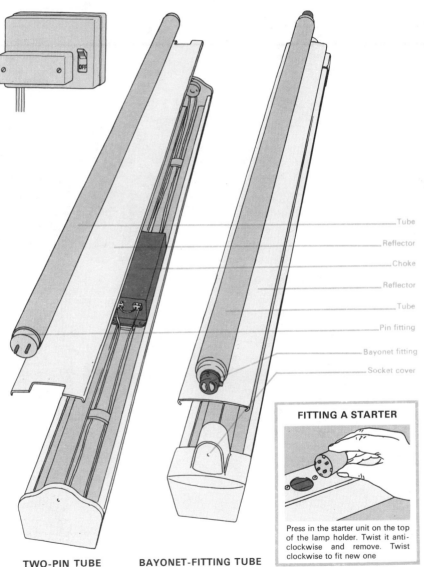

Tube
Reflector
Choke
Reflector
Tube
Pin fitting
Bayonet fitting
Socket cover

TWO-PIN TUBE   **BAYONET-FITTING TUBE**

FITTING A STARTER

Press in the starter unit on the top of the lamp holder. Twist it anti-clockwise and remove. Twist clockwise to fit new one

Fitting a tube

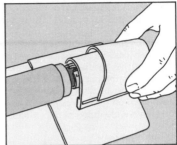

1 On a bayonet-fitting tube, slide the socket covers back to reveal the bayonet lamp holder at each end

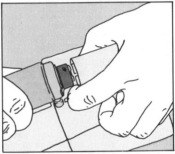

2 Press the tube at each end against the spring-loaded holders. Twist and remove. Fit new tube

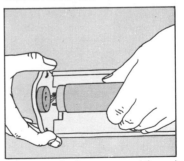

Two-pin tube Ease out one of the end brackets, which are hinged, to disconnect the tube pins. Remove tube

Food mixers

Care and maintenance

Food mixers are powered by electric motors, usually of the brush type (see p. 527). The beaters fit into one or two sleeves which are driven, through gear wheels, by a worm on the end of the motor spindle. Some models have an accessory drive-socket, which is an extension of one of the sleeve shafts. A fan at the back of the motor keeps the mixer cool when it is being used.

Large models with integral stands have a more powerful motor for heavy work. Consequently they can take a wide range of accessories.

Speed control

Some models have a variable-speed control. When it is operated, an electrical contact activates a governor on the armature shaft. In this way the selected speed is kept constant, even if the load on the motor varies during mixing.

Other models may vary the speed by switching resistances in the motor circuit or by switching selected tappings on the motor field winding.

Speed settings for many mixing processes are usually recommended in the manufacturer's instruction book. If higher speeds are used, the motor may overload and burn out. Never try to use accessories which are not manufactured specifically for the mixer.

WARNING Remove plug from socket before carrying out maintenance or repairs. Do not attempt jobs other than those suggested

---

FINDING THE FAULT

Symptom	Checking order	Action
No power	Blown at plug	Fit new fuse (see p. 519)
No power or intermittent power	Loose connections at plug or at appliance	Reconnect (see pp. 525, 526)
	Broken flex. Check with circuit tester (see p. 526)	If necessary, fit new flex
	Worn carbon brushes	Fit new brushes (see p. 527)
	Burnt motor windings	Take mixer to a dealer

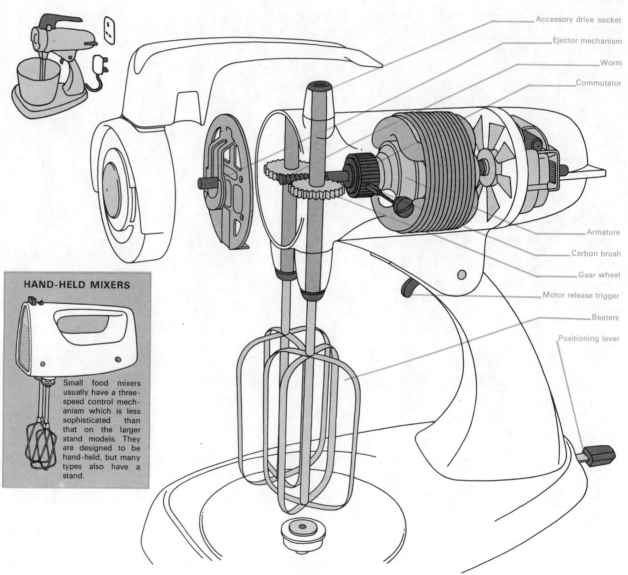

HAND-HELD MIXERS

Small food mixers usually have a three-speed control mechanism which is less sophisticated than that on the larger stand models. They are designed to be hand-held, but many types also have a stand.

Accessory drive socket
Ejector mechanism
Worm
Commutator
Armature
Carbon brush
Gear wheel
Motor release trigger
Beaters
Positioning lever

Hair dryers

Care and maintenance

Hair dryers may be hand-held, fitted on a stand, or may have a hose-and-bonnet attachment.

In all types, a small electric motor turns a fan which drives air across a spiral wire—the heating element— on to the hair. Most have a switch to allow the dryer to be used with the heating element on or off.

Never switch on the element independently of the motor. It is possible to do this on the older types of dryer, but it is dangerous, for the dryer will rapidly overheat. In most types, however, the element cannot heat unless the motor is running, and an automatic cut-out device switches off the element if it overheats.

Do not hold the dryer too close to the hair: in the absence of any instructions from the manufacturer, hold it about 12 in. (305 mm) away from the head.

WARNING Remove plug from socket before carrying out maintenance or repairs. Do not attempt jobs other than those suggested

FINDING THE FAULT		
Symptom	Checking order	Action
No power	Blown fuse in plug	Fit new fuse (see p. 519)
No power or intermittent power	Loose or broken connections at plug	Renew connections (see p. 525)
	Loose or broken flex connections in appliance	Renew connections (see p. 526)
	Broken flex. Check with circuit tester (see p. 526)	Fit new flex, if necessary
	Motor burnt out	Return to dealer or manufacturer
No heat	Broken element terminals	Fit new terminals or take to dealer
	Broken element	Fit new element or take to dealer
	Element cut-out tripped	Reset safety cut-out button
Flashing detectable through casing	Carbon deposits on switch contacts	Clean contacts with fine emery paper
Buzzing noise	Carbon deposits on switch contacts	Clean contacts with emery paper

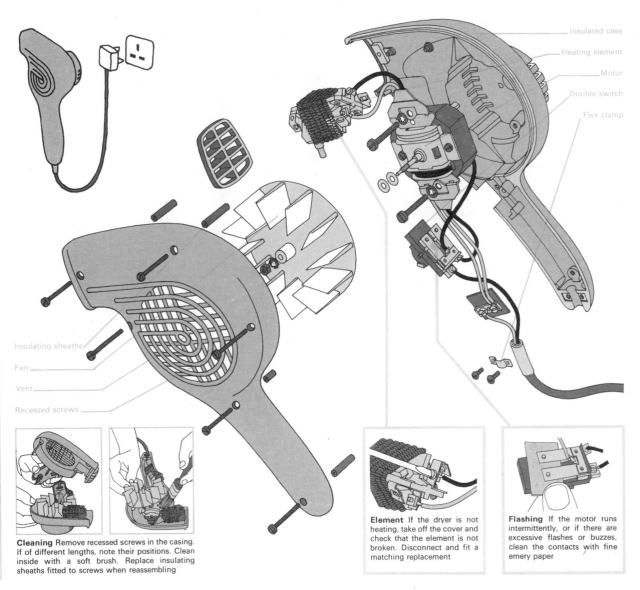

Insulated case

Heating element

Motor

Double switch

Flex clamp

Insulating sheaths

Fan

Vent

Recessed screws

Cleaning Remove recessed screws in the casing. If of different lengths, note their positions. Clean inside with a soft brush. Replace insulating sheaths fitted to screws when reassembling

Element If the dryer is not heating, take off the cover and check that the element is not broken. Disconnect and fit a matching replacement

Flashing If the motor runs intermittently, or if there are excessive flashes or buzzes, clean the contacts with fine emery paper

Irons

Construction

The element on most dry electric irons is clamped to the sole-plate between sheets of mica—a material which can withstand extremely high temperatures. A sheet of asbestos fitted above the element prevents heat radiating upwards, and a pressure plate bolted on top of the asbestos ensures that the heat is evenly distributed through the sole-plate.

In some irons the element is incorporated in the sole-plate; if the element fails, the entire sole-plate assembly must be renewed. Do not attempt to repair a faulty element. Take the iron to a dealer.

Checking the flex

The flex on an iron wears quickly because it is subjected to considerable twisting and friction. As soon as the fabric sheathing begins to fray or wear, fit a new flex. Some irons have removable flexes attached by a flex coupler similar to those used on electric kettles (see p. 544).

> **WARNING** Remove plug from socket before carrying out maintenance or repairs. Do not attempt jobs other than those suggested

FINDING THE FAULT

Symptom	Checking order	Action
No heat	Fuse blown at plug	Fit new fuse of correct amperage (see p. 519)
No heat or intermittent heat	Loose connections at plug	Reconnect (see p. 525)
	Loose connections at iron	Reconnect
	Broken flex (check with circuit tester)	Fit new flex (see p. 526)
	Broken element	Take iron to dealer or manufacturer
	Faulty thermostat	Ask dealer or manufacturer to check
Iron frequently too hot or too cold	Faulty thermostat	Take iron to dealer
Thermostat indicator light does not work	Broken bulb	Fit new bulb on a dry iron. Take a steam iron to a dealer

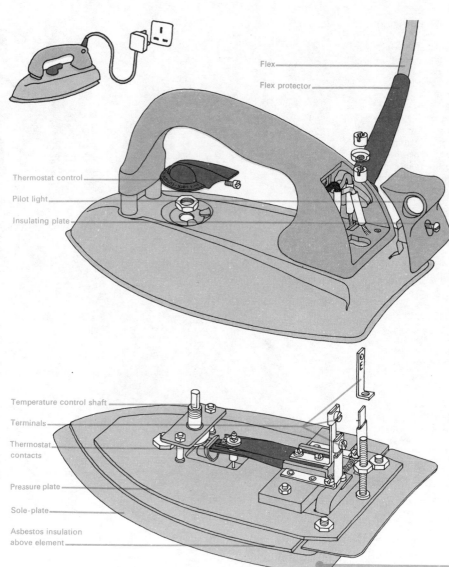

Flex

Flex protector

Thermostat control

Pilot light

Insulating plate

Temperature control shaft

Terminals

Thermostat contacts

Pressure plate

Sole-plate

Asbestos insulation above element

TEMPERATURE CONTROL

If the temperature control knob breaks, remove it and buy a matching replacement.

1 Undo the screw holding the knob on the thermostat spindle. Pull off the knob and discard it

2 The spindle and hole on the control knob both have one flat side. Tighten screw on to this

Sole-plate Do not iron over zips or buttons, as this can scratch the sole-plate. Remove stains with a detergent or special cleaner

Fitting a new bulb

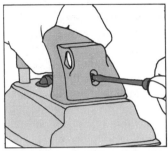

1 Undo the screw holding the insulating plate at the back of the iron handle. Take off the plate

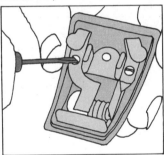

2 Loosen the screw which holds the terminal across the cap of the bulb. Leave the terminal in place

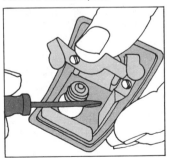

3 Swivel the terminal aside. Prise out the bulb and fit the new one. Refit the terminal and insulating plate

Maintaining a steam iron

Always use distilled water or soft water in steam irons: the scale left by ordinary tap water can rapidly clog the vents in the sole-plate. Do not over-fill. Empty the water tank immediately after use.

Store the iron on its heel to ensure that any remaining drops of water do not stain the sole-plate.

To clean a stained sole-plate, use a damp cloth and special cleaner, obtainable from hardware shops. Never use a metal polish or an abrasive.

On old irons it may be necessary to empty the tank if it is to be used dry. Newer types, however, usually have a valve which controls the flow of water. Some models also have a mechanism to project spray in front of the iron to provide additional dampness for creased materials. If the water system is faulty, take the iron to a dealer.

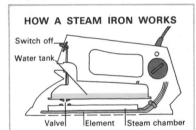

HOW A STEAM IRON WORKS

Switch off
Water tank

Valve | Element | Steam chamber

Switch Steam is released from a steam iron when the water-tank switch is pushed down. This opens a valve in the top of the steam chamber

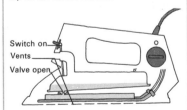

Switch on
Vents
Valve open

Steam Water flows through the valve and is turned into steam by heat from the element. The steam escapes through vents in the sole-plate

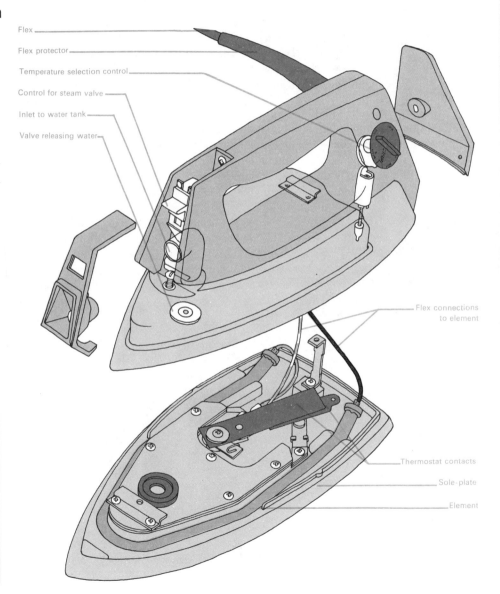

Flex
Flex protector
Temperature selection control
Control for steam valve
Inlet to water tank
Valve releasing water
Flex connections to element
Thermostat contacts
Sole-plate
Element

Kettles

Care and maintenance

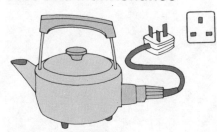

The heating element in an electric kettle consists of a spiral wire cushioned in magnesium oxide and covered by a non-corroding alloy.

An automatic kettle also has a thermostat which breaks the current flow when the water boils, so that the kettle cannot boil dry or overheat. On some models, the thermostat is designed to open and close continuously to keep the water simmering.

New elements can be fitted to most types of kettle without difficulty. But do not try to renew the element and thermostat in an automatic kettle. Take it to a dealer or send it direct to the manufacturer if there is a fault.

Never empty a kettle while it is still switched on. And never pour water into one which has just boiled dry: the result will be a scalding cloud of steam which—apart from the danger to users—may damage the element.

WARNING Remove plug from socket before carrying out maintenance or repairs. Do not attempt jobs other than those that are suggested

FINDING THE FAULT

Symptom	Checking order	Action
No power	Blown fuse at plug	Fit a new fuse of the correct amperage (see p. 519)
No power or intermittent power	Loose or broken flex connections at plug	Renew connections (see p. 525)
	Loose or broken flex connections at appliance	Renew connections (see p. 526)
	Broken flex. Check with circuit tester (see p. 526)	Fit new flex, if necessary
	Broken element. Check with tester	Fit a new element, if necessary
Flex coupler will not push home	Ejected coupler	Push back the spring-loaded ejector
Slow heating	Hard-water scale	De-scale
Leakage at the shroud	Perished sealing at the plug port	Remove the element and fit new washers

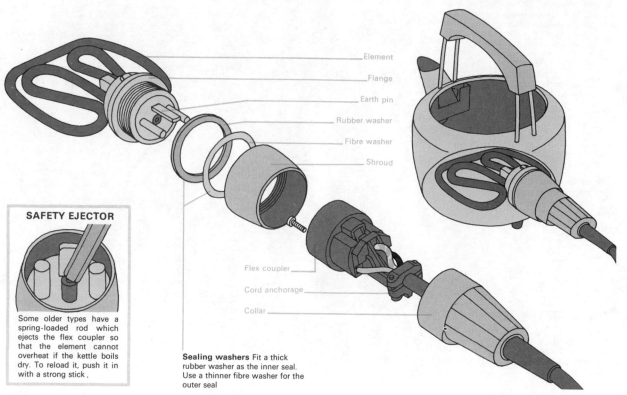

Element
Flange
Earth pin
Rubber washer
Fibre washer
Shroud
Flex coupler
Cord anchorage
Collar

SAFETY EJECTOR

Some older types have a spring-loaded rod which ejects the flex coupler so that the element cannot overheat if the kettle boils dry. To reload it, push it in with a strong stick.

Sealing washers Fit a thick rubber washer as the inner seal. Use a thinner fibre washer for the outer seal

EARTHING

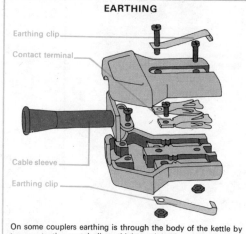

Earthing clip
Contact terminal
Cable sleeve
Earthing clip

On some couplers earthing is through the body of the kettle by two contacting metal clips which are joined together through the body of the coupler by a nut and screw

Fitting a new element

If a new element is needed, take the old one to a dealer to make sure that the replacement is of the correct design and wattage. Take care to fit new washers at the coupler housing in the correct order.

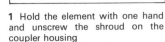

1 Hold the element with one hand and unscrew the shroud on the coupler housing

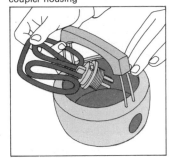

3 Twist the element assembly inside the kettle and pull it out gently through the top

2 Slide out the outer fibre sealing washer. Discard it and use the new washers supplied with the element

4 Remove stubborn scale around the plug port with detergent and a rag, or with a blunt knife

5 Put an inner sealing washer, usually rubber, on the new element. Fit the element and reassemble

Fitting new flex or a flex coupler

Electric kettles have flex couplers so that they can be disconnected both at the mains plug and at the appliance. With regular use the flex is likely to wear (see also p. 526).

Materials: flex; coupler.
Tools: screwdrivers; wire stripper.

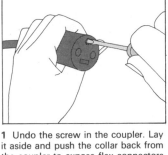

1 Undo the screw in the coupler. Lay it aside and push the collar back from the coupler to expose flex connectors

2 Loosen the screws which tighten the anchorage around the flex. Do not remove the screws

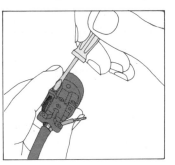

3 Loosen the screws holding the three terminals. Disconnect the terminals and pull out the flex

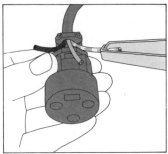

4 Fit new flex first through the collar, then the anchorage. Strip $\frac{1}{2}$ in. (13 mm) from the ends of the flex

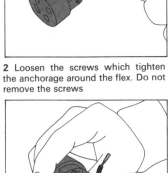

5 Make the earth lead longest to ensure live and neutral leads will be the first to pull out if flex is strained

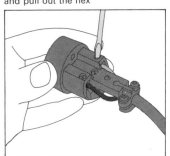

6 Screw the three leads to the correct terminals (see p. 526). Tighten the anchorage screws

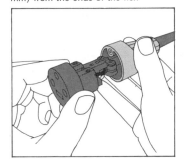

7 Slide the coupler collar along the flex. Align it carefully on the socket and screw it on firmly

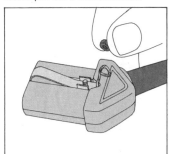

Earthing If the coupler has a metal earthing clip along the side, fit the earth wire and tighten nut

Power tools

How a power tool works

The chuck of a power tool is driven, through a gear system, by a small shaft at the end of the motor armature. As the motor operates, it turns the shaft at a very high speed. The gears reduce the speed so that the chuck revolves more slowly.

Some tools have a speed-selector mechanism, which provides a fast speed for working on soft materials and a slower speed for hard materials. A small fan fixed on the armature shaft is designed to keep the motor cool in normal working conditions. Never force a power tool: allow the motor to do the work. Never use blunt drills or accessories.

WARNING Remove plug from socket before carrying out maintenance or repairs. Do not attempt jobs other than those suggested

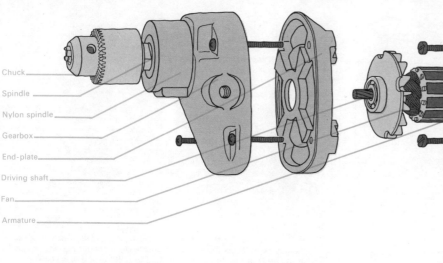
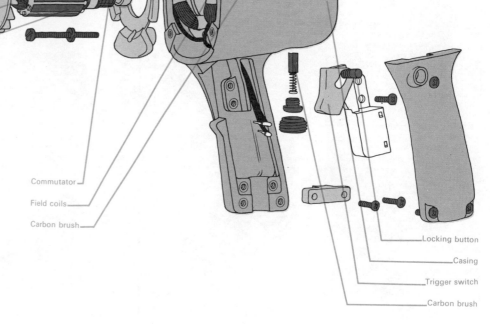

Chuck

Spindle

Nylon spindle

Gearbox

End-plate

Driving shaft

Fan

Armature

Commutator

Field coils

Carbon brush

Locking button

Casing

Trigger switch

Carbon brush

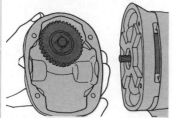

GEAR LUBRICATION

The gear wheel, which may be made of nylon, is packed in grease. Clean and repack with a high-melting-point grease once a year

REMOVING DUST

To clean grit and dust from inside the motor, hold a vacuum cleaner or a compressed-air line against the casing vents of the power tool

CENTRALLY SPLIT CASING

Chuck

Reduction gears

Switch

Field coils

Casing

Fan

The casings on some drills divide along the centre to give easy access to the motor and bearings. The two pieces of the casing are secured together with screws

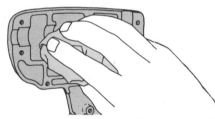

Cleaning the motor Undo the casing and wipe inside around motor carefully with a clean, dry rag

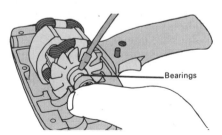

Bearings

Bearings If the bearings are sealed, no lubrication is needed. If not, use light oil and pack races with grease

---

FINDING THE FAULT

Symptom	Checking order	Action
No power	Blown fuse at plug	Fit new fuse (see p. 519)
No power or intermittent power	Loose connections at plug	Reconnect leads (see p. 525)
	Broken flex. Check with circuit tester (see p. 526)	Renew flex
	Worn or sticking carbon brushes	Fit new carbon brushes (see p. 527)
	Faulty switch	Fit new switch
	Broken windings	Return tool to dealer.
Excessive flashing at carbon brushes	Worn or sticking carbon brushes	Fit new carbon brushes (see p. 527)
	Broken motor windings. The wires may be scorched	Return tool to dealer or manufacturer
	Uneven wear on commutator	Return tool to dealer or manufacturer
Motor overheating or smoking	Motor overloaded	Switch off immediately
	Air vents blocked	Clean air vents
	Broken motor windings	Return tool to dealer or manufacturer

CHECKING BEARINGS

Ball type Hold the commutator and rock the bearing race. If there is considerable movement, pull off bearing race and gently tap on a new one

Bush type Bearings of porous phosphor-bronze absorb oil and require less frequent lubrication. Apply light oil once a year. If worn, fit a new bush

---

Fitting a new trigger switch

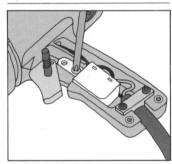

On some drills it is possible to undo the hand grip to gain access to the switch unit. If a switch is faulty, it is usually possible to fit a new one.

Materials: new switch unit.
Tools: screwdriver; soldering iron; paper clip.

1 Remove the screws in the hand grip. Note where longer screws fit. Separate the sections of the handle

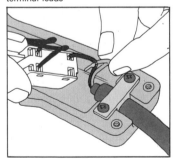

2 Undo the switch mounting-screws. Lift up the switch to gain access to the terminal leads

Lead channel

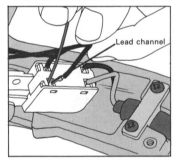

3 Push a straightened paper clip into the terminal lead channels to open the clamps holding them

Locking button

4 Note position of leads and pull them out. Fit new switch unit. Solder the lead ends and clamp them in channels.

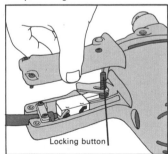

5 Reassemble the hand grip. Make sure that it fits over the locking button. Fit the screws

Power tools

Cleaning the motor

Dismantle a power tool and clean it thoroughly once a year.

Materials: clean, lint-free rag; strips of softwood.
Tools: hide mallet; screwdriver; thin-nosed pliers; soft brush.

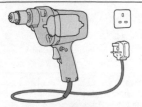

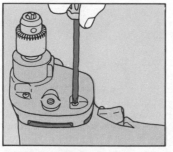

1 Undo and remove the screws holding the chuck assembly and gearbox on the drive body

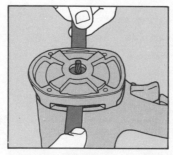

2 Use two small pieces of softwood to lever the motor assembly carefully out of the body casing

3 Slide the motor out of its housing. If it has an end-plate containing the gearbox assembly, tap it free

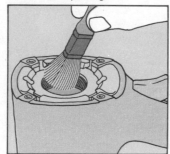

4 Inspect the commutator. If there is an uneven black line round its surface, have the commutator reground

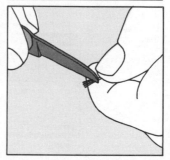

5 Clean motor housing and switch assembly with a soft brush. If necessary, remove switch unit (see p. 547)

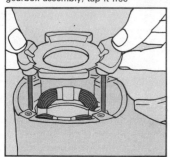

6 If the motor is very dirty, undo the securing screws and lift off the field-coil retaining plate

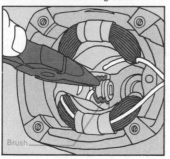

7 Use thin-nosed pliers to unhook the terminal clips holding the carbon brushes. Note their positions

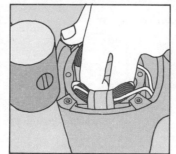

8 Slide out the field coils. If tight, gently tap the body with a mallet. Clean and reassemble

Radios

Soldering terminal leads

Continued replacement of the battery in a transistor radio may weaken the soldered connections between the leads and the terminal block which fits on to the battery. These leads can be resoldered. Before reconnecting, apply a hot soldering iron to the old solder on the terminal block to remove the broken wire. When soldering electrical connections, use only a cored solder.

Materials: cored solder.
Tools: soldering iron; pen-knife.

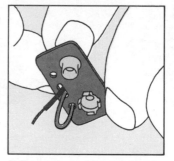

1 Remove $\frac{1}{4}$ in. (6 mm) of insulation from the broken wire and clean the bared surface with a knife

2 Wind any loose strands together, apply solder to the iron and tin the end of the wire (see p. 692)

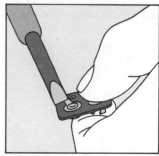

3 Thread the lead through the slot and back through the hole so that the bared end lies against the terminal

4 Apply a little solder to the iron and press the iron against the wire and terminal, fusing them together

Renewing a radio tuning cord

Most modern radios use transistors and printed circuits which cannot be repaired without specialised knowledge or skill. Home maintenance is confined to ensuring that the batteries, if any, are in good condition and that the set is kept dry and clean. If serious faults develop, take the radio to a dealer or mechanic.

If a battery transistor set is not to be used for a long period, remove the batteries: a discharged battery may ooze highly corrosive fluid which can damage the printed circuit beyond repair.

On some sets, it may be possible to renew the tuning cord if it becomes slack or frayed. Buy a new cord or a length of 30 lb. nylon fishing line and check the existing fitting carefully before removing the old cord.

When the cord is fitted, turn the control until the radio tunes into a known good station. Move the cursor (wave-length indicator) along the cord until it lines accurately with the scale of the station on the dial.

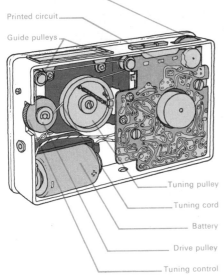

Volume control
Printed circuit
Guide pulleys
Tuning pulley
Tuning cord
Battery
Drive pulley
Tuning control

1 Remove the broken cord from the drive pulley. Count the number of turns it is wound round the spindle

2 Pass the replacement cord through the hole in the tuning pulley and tie a knot in the end of the cord

3 Wind round tuning pulley, over guide pulleys, correct number of times round drive pulley, and back to tuning pulley

4 Pass cord through slot in tuning pulley. Position spring on cord near to slot and tie the spring to the cord

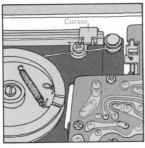

5 Before locating the spring, turn tuning knobs to end of the scale and clip the cursor on to the cord

6 Pull the spring and hook the end over the locating pin. Switch on and check cursor position with known station

Replacing amplifier fuses

Many modern amplifiers use two types of fuse: a 1 amp mains supply fuse and a 100 milli-amp high-tension fuse. The latter is designed to protect the transistors in the unit. If two amplifiers are installed in a single case, there will be two high-tension fuses fitted.

If the amplifier fails to work, check the mains fuse first. If a pair of amplifiers, servicing two speakers, is installed in one case and one of the speakers fails, one of the high-tension fuses has probably blown. If a high-tension fuse blows as soon as it is fitted, have the amplifier checked by a radio mechanic.

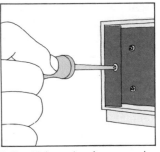

1 The high-tension fuses may be located behind a cover plate at the rear of the unit

MAINS FUSE

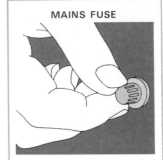

1 Unscrew the mains fuse holder. This is usually situated at the rear of the amplifier unit

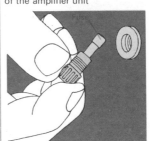

2 Draw the holder out, remove the cartridge fuse and fit a new one of the correct value

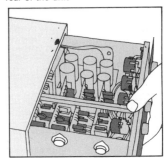

2 If they are located in the amplifier chassis, carefully draw the chassis out of its casing

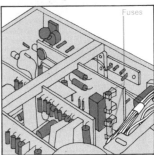

Fuses

3 The fuses may be set in holders or clips on the circuit panels. Replace as necessary

Record players

Maintenance

Most record players are pre-lubricated and their bearings are sealed for the life of the player. But if the action of the turntable seems sluggish, remove the table and lubricate the mechanism below it. Place a little oil on the top of a screwdriver blade and trickle it down the spindle. Keep oil away from any of the rubber components.

WARNING Remove the plug from the wall socket before carrying out maintenance or repairs. Do not attempt jobs other than those suggested

FINDING THE FAULT

Symptom	Checking order	Action
No power	Fuse blown at plug	Fit new fuse (see p. 519)
No power or intermittent power	Loose flex connections at plug or at record player	Fit new connections (see pp. 525, 526)
	Broken flex. Check with circuit tester (see p. 526)	If necessary, fit new flex (see p. 526)
	Worn brushes—if not an induction motor (see p. 527)	Fit new brushes if easily accessible, or take record player to repair shop
	Windings burnt out on motor—check visually	Take record player to repair shop
	Faulty switch	Consult repairer
Scratching noise	Worn stylus	Fit new stylus (see p. 551)
Rumble	Suspension springs screwed into chassis, which causes vibrations from motor	Loosen screws on deck
Crackling sound caused by static electricity	Dirty record	Clean record (see p. 367)
	Worn stylus	Fit new stylus (See p. 551)
	Faulty cartridge	Fit new cartridge (see p. 551)
	Loose connections to amplifier	
	Amplifier faulty	Take record player to repair shop
	Faulty speaker connections	
	Faulty speaker	
No sound	Leads disconnected between cartridge and amplifier	
	Faulty amplifier and speaker	Take record player to repair shop
	Cartridge not functioning	
Tone fluctuations	Faulty idler wheel	Check if wheel is worn or greasy. Sprinkle some talcum powder on the wheel. If no improvement, take record player to repair shop
Automatic changer not working	Faulty mechanism	Take record player to repair shop

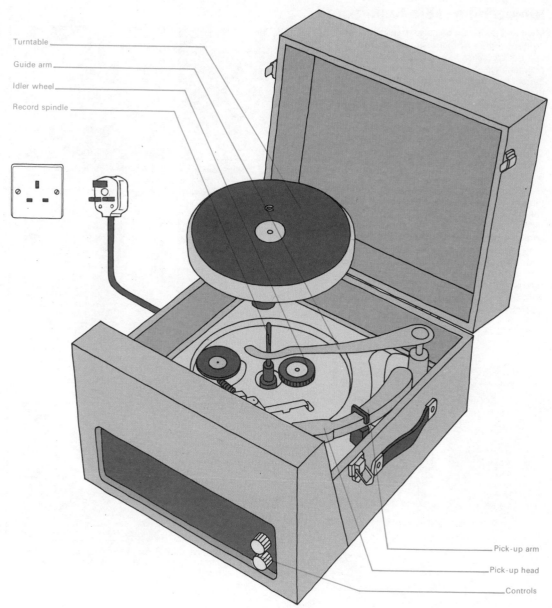

Turntable

Guide arm

Idler wheel

Record spindle

Pick-up arm

Pick-up head

Controls

WHEN THE AUTOCHANGE IS FAULTY

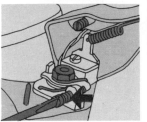

If the pick-up arm misses the record, loosen the adjusting screw (arrowed). If it moves too far in, tighten screw slightly

GROOVE JUMPING

Groove jumping can be caused either by a faulty turntable or by a badly adjusted pick-up arm.

If the turntable is uneven, fit a new one. If the table is flat, the jumping is caused by a fault in the pick-up arm.

1 Lift the arm and move the spring to a higher or to a lower hole to reduce or increase the pick-up arm pressure

2 For extremely fine adjustment, turn screw clockwise to reduce the pick-up arm pressure, anti-clockwise to increase it

FITTING A STYLUS

The stylus of a record player may be held in position by a plastic sleeve or by a small retaining screw. If a new stylus is to be fitted, always replace the old one with a matching stylus.

Tool: small screwdriver.

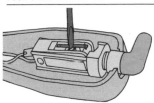

Plastic sleeve Prise the stylus out of its sleeve and gently press the new one into position

Screw fitting Undo the screw securing the stylus, lift out the stylus and fit a new one

FITTING A CARTRIDGE

The vibrations from the stylus are turned into sound by a cartridge in the pick-up head.

A faulty cartridge will cause a deterioration of the sound quality, and the cartridge should then be replaced with a matching one. On older sets it is possible to unplug the pick-up head from the arm, making cartridge changing easier.

Tool: small screwdriver.

Cartridge Remove the small screw from the top of the pick-up head. Tip the cartridge out. Note the colours of the leads and their respective positions. Disconnect them and fit a new cartridge, with the leads in the same positions as they were on the old cartridge

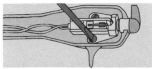 

Pick-up head Where it is possible, unplug the pick-up head from the arm. Undo the screws holding the cartridge in position, and pull out the leads, noting their positions so that they can be replaced correctly. Remove the faulty cartridge and fit the new one

Checking turntable speed

Place a record on the turntable and put a strobe disc, obtainable from record shops, on the centre of the record. Start the record player with the pick-up arm in the play position and place a mains-powered lamp close to it. If the speed is correct, the lines on the strobe disc corresponding with the selected speed will appear to stand still. If the lines appear to move forwards, the turntable is too fast; if backwards, it is too slow.

A worn idler wheel may affect speed or quality of reproduction and should be replaced.

Materials: strobe disc; idler wheel.
Tools: small screwdriver; pliers.

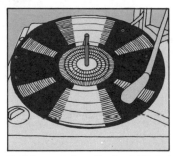

1 Put a record on the turntable and lay the strobe disc on the record. Select the speed and look at the same speed circle on the strobe disc

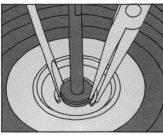

2 If the lines on the strobe show that the speed is incorrect, prise off the circlip holding the turntable to the boss of the spindle

3 Lift the turntable straight up, off the spindle. Take care when doing this not to damage the spindle of the guide arm

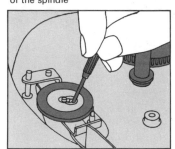

4 Use a small electrical screwdriver to lever off the circlip securing the idler wheel. Remove the washer between the circlip and the wheel

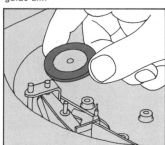

5 Lift the idler wheel off its shaft. Fit a new wheel, with a washer below and above it. Replace the turntable and circlip

Refrigerators

How refrigerators work

When a liquid evaporates it absorbs heat: if it is converted back to liquid form, called condensation, it gives off any heat it has absorbed.

Refrigerators and freezers are cooled on this principle. A liquid, known as the refrigerant, circulates round the refrigerator. As it passes through the cooling or frozen-food compartment it is evaporated so that it can absorb any heat in the compartment. It is then recondensed to give off the heat it has absorbed—usually through an exhaust pipe at the back of the equipment. Never position a refrigerator or freezer tightly against a wall; there is

often a spacer at the rear to prevent this.

In some refrigerators, the refrigerant is circulated by a motor-driven pump called a compressor; in others a heating element and absorption unit are used instead. On the compression type of refrigerator, the motor can be heard when the cooling system is operating. Absorption refrigerators operate silently.

A thermostatic control switches on the motor or heater when the temperature in the cooling compartment rises.

The cooling system cannot be repaired by an amateur. But it is possible to fit a new light bulb and door seal on many

models. Do not, however, try to fit a new door seal if it is clipped into a recess.

If a refrigerator does not automatically defrost the cooling compartment, switch it off once a week. Allow the ice to melt naturally; do not scrape it away. Dry inside thoroughly before switching on again. Defrost freezers in the same way at least once a year.

> **WARNING** Remove plug from the wall socket before carrying out maintenance or repairs. Do not attempt jobs other than those suggested

INTERIOR LIGHT

If a light bulb fails, disconnect at socket, remove protective shield, unscrew bulb and fit new one. Push in switch on door frame to check that bulb lights

DOOR SEALS

Lift up edge of damaged seal and remove screws holding seal flap on door. Fit new seal and tighten top screws. Adjust fitting and tighten remaining screws

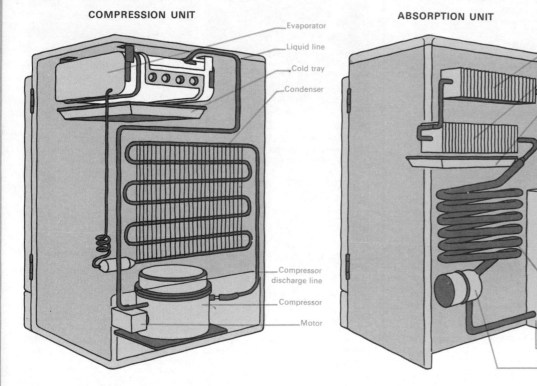

COMPRESSION UNIT

- Evaporator
- Liquid line
- Cold tray
- Condenser
- Compressor discharge line
- Compressor
- Motor

ABSORPTION UNIT

- Condenser
- Evaporator
- Cold tray
- Absorber
- Heat-exchanging unit
- Absorber vessel

FINDING THE FAULT

Symptom	Checking order	Action
No power	Fuse blown at plug	Fit new fuse (see p. 519)
No power or intermittent power	Loose connections at plug or refrigerator Broken flex (check with circuit tester, see p. 526) Heavy build-up of ice	Reconnect (see pp. 525, 526) If necessary, fit new flex (see p. 526) Switch off and allow refrigerator to defrost
Power is reaching the appliance, but it is not cooling adequately	Feel condenser-evaporator assembly: it should be warm if refrigerant system is working	**Absorption** Move temperature selector to a colder setting. If it still does not work, have heating element checked by a dealer **Compressor** Leave door open for a few minutes and check that motor starts. If it still does not work, have motor checked by a dealer

Shavers

Cleaning and lubrication

Electric shavers may be mains or battery operated. Some types have a brush motor (see p. 527); others have two coils which are magnetised and de-magnetised continuously as the current flows. They operate like solenoids (see p. 530), making a spring-loaded arm vibrate and drive the cutting head of the shaver.

If a brush motor fails, check and fit new brushes if necessary (see p. 527). If a vibrator fails, return the shaver to a dealer and have the whole unit replaced.

Cutting heads for all types of shavers are available from dealers. Always take the shaver to the shop so that the size of head required can be identified.

Most shavers should be lubricated occasionally with a little light machine oil.

> **WARNING** Remove plug from socket before carrying out maintenance or repairs. Do not attempt jobs other than those suggested

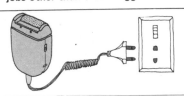

FINDING THE FAULT

Symptom	Checking order	Action
Motor not operating	Flat battery	Fit new battery
	Faulty connections	Reconnect (see pp. 525–6)
	Broken lead. Check with circuit tester (see p. 526)	Renew cable if necessary
	Burnt-out coil	Return to manufacturer
Intermittent operation	Break in flex. Check with circuit tester (see p. 526)	Fit new flex if necessary
	Loose wire in shaver	Reconnect

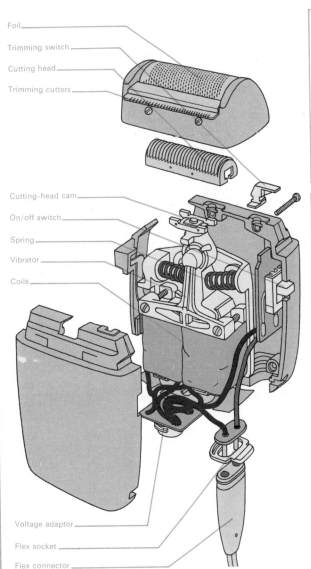

Foil
Trimming switch
Cutting head
Trimming cutters
Cutting-head cam
On/off switch
Spring
Vibrator
Coils
Voltage adaptor
Flex socket
Flex connector

SHAVING FOIL

Occasionally smear liquid paraffin on the shaving foil. If it becomes damaged, buy and fit a new one

RECHARGEABLE SHAVERS

If the terminals or contacts on a rechargeable battery shaver corrode, scrape clean and blow away the dust

REMOVING DUST

Clean lightly round the motor or vibrator unit with a small soft brush. Do not damage connections

ROTARY SHAVERS

Always clean a rotary shaver after use. Once a week remove the cutters for thorough cleaning. Refit the cutters in their original positions. If they become worn, fit new ones: this must be expected to be necessary after about two years.

1 Use a soft, fine-bristled brush to clean dust and hair from the head of a rotary shaver

2 Every week lift off the shaving head and brush dust or dirt from the motor or vibrator unit

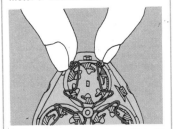

3 Compress the spring clips to remove the rotary cutters. Clean and replace the cutters.

Spin dryers

Maintenance

Spin dryers have a perforated drum which is rotated by a motor. Centrifugal force throws the clothes against the side of the drum and forces water out through the perforations. Some spin dryers are emptied by gravity, others are emptied by a pump.

The motor is fitted with a brake connected to the dryer lid. As the lid is opened the motor is switched off and the rotating drum automatically braked.

If a brush motor is fitted, it is possible to renew the brushes (see p. 527). If an induction motor fails, return it to the manufacturer.

WARNING Remove plug from socket before carrying out maintenance or repairs. Do not attempt jobs other than those suggested

FINDING THE FAULT

Symptom	Checking order	Action
No power	Fuse blown at plug	Fit new fuse (see p. 519)
No power or intermittent power	Windings burnt out	Return to the manufacturer
	Loose flex connections at plug or dryer	Reconnect (see pp. 525 and 526)
	Broken flex (check with circuit tester, see p. 526)	If necessary fit new flex (see p. 517)
	Push-rod switch faulty	Fit new one if broken. If not return machine to manufacturer
Drum revolves noisily and hesitantly	Brake binding	Adjust cable
	Clothing between drum and jacket	Retrieve clothing
Drum fails to brake	Brake cable slack	Adjust cable
	Brake lining worn	Renew brake shoe and lining
Motor runs but drum fails to revolve	Belt broken or slack on belt-driven machines	Adjust or fit new belt
Pump fails to operate	Belt broken or slack on belt-driven machines	Adjust or fit new belt
	Pump blocked	Remove, unblock
	Hose kinked	Straighten hose
Excessive vibration	Worn bearings	Call dealer
	Clothes not evenly loaded	Press down firmly

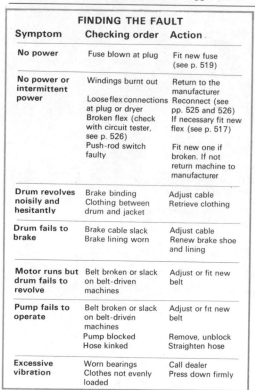

Brake operating pad
Catch
Motor
Drum drive belt
Pump drive belt
Pump

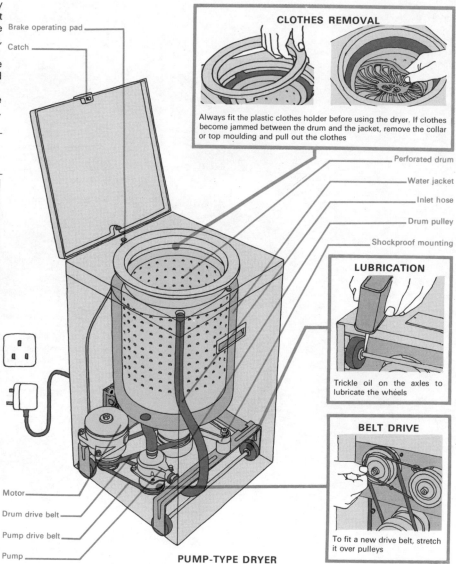

Perforated drum
Water jacket
Inlet hose
Drum pulley
Shockproof mounting

PUMP-TYPE DRYER

CLOTHES REMOVAL

Always fit the plastic clothes holder before using the dryer. If clothes become jammed between the drum and the jacket, remove the collar or top moulding and pull out the clothes

LUBRICATION

Trickle oil on the axles to lubricate the wheels

BELT DRIVE

To fit a new drive belt, stretch it over pulleys

ADJUSTING BRAKES

If the brake assembly—usually located at the base of the drum—is accessible, the brake cable can be adjusted.

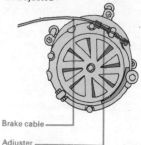

Brake cable
Adjuster

1 Hold the adjuster nut with one spanner and loosen the locknut with another

2 If brake binds and prevents drum revolving, slacken cable: if the drum does not brake quickly, tighten the cable

Fitting a pump gasket

Some spin dryers have a pump to drain the water from the drum. If it leaks, check the cork or soft-rubber gasket on the flange. If it is damaged, fit a new one.

If a gasket cannot be bought to fit the pump, cut a piece of cork or soft rubber $\frac{1}{16}$ in. (2 mm) thick to match the flange faces.

If the leak is caused by a faulty gland or worn impeller shaft, it is advisable to have a new pump fitted.

Materials: gasket cork; gasket cement. Tools: spanner; Phillips and bladed screwdrivers; pliers; centre punch; hammer; compasses; scissors; scraper.

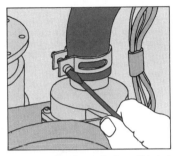

1 Loosen the clip on the hose fitted at the pump, then pull the hose off the end of the pump body

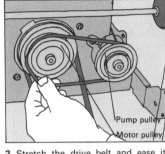

2 Stretch the drive belt and ease it over the edges of the motor and the pump pulleys

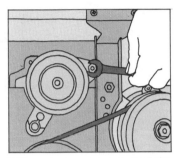

3 Use a spanner to undo the bolts which hold the pump to the frame of the spin dryer

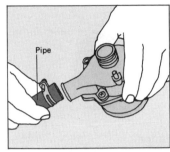

4 Lay the bolts aside carefully and remove the complete pump assembly from the machine

5 Undo the screws which hold the halves of the pump body together. Lay them aside

6 Carefully push a bladed screwdriver between the flanges and prise the parts open. Do not scratch flange faces

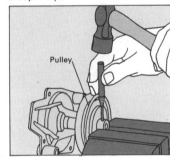

7 Carefully scrape any gasket particles off the flange faces with a scraper or blunt screwdriver

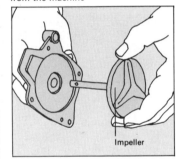

8 Punch the pin through the pulley collar with a hammer and centre punch. Lay it aside carefully

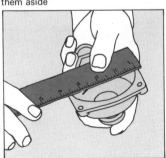

9 Remove pulley, file burrs off pin hole, and pull out impeller assembly. Check shaft for wear

10 Measure the internal diameter of the pump body where the impeller is to be refitted

11 Draw a circle with a radius of the internal diameter measurement on a sheet of thin cork

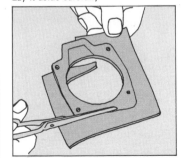

12 Cut out the circle and place the gasket material centrally on the pump body. Mark shape on cork

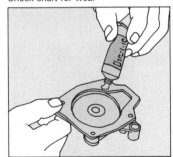

13 Carefully cut the shape out of the cork. Make sure that the screw holes are accurate

14 Coat both flange faces with gasket cement. Fit the gasket and reassemble the pump

Spin dryers

Storage heaters

Fitting a brake cable

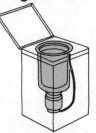

If a brake cable is stretched, broken or badly corroded, fit a new one.

Materials: new brake cable.
Tools: spanner; screwdriver.

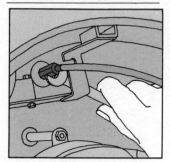

2 Undo the top adjuster nut from the button-release mechanism on the machine with a spanner

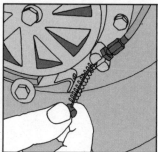

4 At the brake-band end, undo the lock-nut and screw in the adjuster. Remove cable from brake arm

1 Press down the brake-release button on top of the machine and free the cable from its stop

3 Free the cable nipple from the brake-release button and lift the cable away from the mechanism

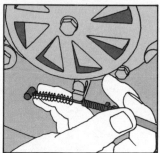

5 Slide the cable out of the stop bracket and remove it from the machine. Fit the new cable

Fitting linings

On a spin dryer the brake linings are forced inwards against the outside of a drum. If the brake is not slowing the drum quickly enough, remove the brake cable and disconnect the brake band from the drum. Fit a new brake band in the reverse order of removing the old one.

Make sure that the band is adjusted so that the drum stops revolving the moment the lid of the dryer is opened.

Materials: new brake band and lining.
Tools: spanners.

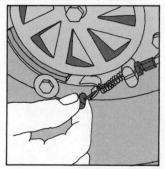

1 Loosen the cable adjuster and remove the brake-cable end from the brake-band mechanism

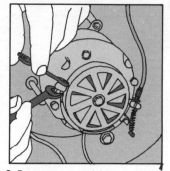

2 Remove nuts and bolts at each end of the brake band. Lift brake band off drum. Fit new one

How a storage heater works

The heating element in a storage heater is embedded in special firebricks inside a metal case. The case is aluminium-lined to reflect heat inwards, but it is also insulated with glass wool to allow a predetermined leakage of heat.

Storage heaters are wired to a two-rate meter and time switch, set to supply current to the heaters overnight when electricity is cheaper. The amount of heat can be varied by operating an input controller.

Some models have a manually operated fan to provide heat only when required or, on some models, to give an extra boost of heat. The fan can be wired to a room thermostat.

Do not try to repair a faulty heater: call an electrician.

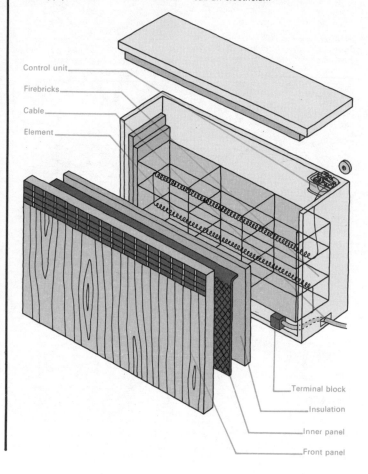

Control unit
Firebricks
Cable
Element
Terminal block
Insulation
Inner panel
Front panel

Tape recorders

Cleaning and lubrication

Recording tape is made of plastic, with a coating of iron oxide which can be magnetised. When the record button is pressed, the tape is held against a special erasing head which demagnetises it and ensures that no sounds remain on it. From the erase head, the tape is wound past a small electro-magnet, called the recording head. The sounds being recorded are converted into minute electrical impulses and are transferred by the recording head as a magnetic pattern on to the tape. When a tape is played back, at the speed it was recorded, the magnetic pattern causes minute voltage changes in the playback head—an electro-magnet similar to the recording head. These impulses are converted back to sound.

WARNING Remove plug from socket before carrying out maintenance or repairs. Do not attempt jobs other than those suggested

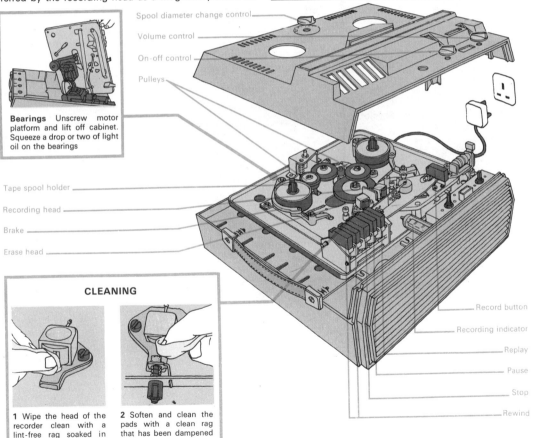

Bearings Unscrew motor platform and lift off cabinet. Squeeze a drop or two of light oil on the bearings

Spool diameter change control
Volume control
On-off control
Pulleys
Tape spool holder
Recording head
Brake
Erase head

Record button
Recording indicator
Replay
Pause
Stop
Rewind

CLEANING

1 Wipe the head of the recorder clean with a lint-free rag soaked in methylated spirit

2 Soften and clean the pads with a clean rag that has been dampened in methylated spirit

FINDING THE FAULT

Symptom	Checking order	Action
No power (indicator not lit up)	Fuse blown at plug or mains	Fit new fuse (see p. 519)
No power or intermittent power	Loose connections at plug or tape recorder	Reconnect (see pp. 525 and 526)
	Broken flex. Check with circuit-tester (see p. 526)	If necessary, fit new flex
Power on, but tape does not wind	Brake locked or motor faulty	Consult dealer
Tape winds at erratic speeds	Pulleys sticking	Lubricate spindles
	Worn brushes in motor	Fit new brushes to the motor (see p. 527)
	Brakes faulty	Consult dealer
Wow or flutter (tone fluctuations)	Take-up spool pulley is too tight	Clean capstan. Fit new bearings on take-up pulley
Distortion in loud passages of recording	Recorded at too high volume	Check recording indicator level. If no fault is shown, consult dealer
	Amplifier faulty	Consult dealer
Distortion and low volume	Dust on playback head	Clean with soft brush or scrape the head with a matchstick
Background noise	Recorded at too low volume	Re-record with microphone nearer sound source: increase volume. If no improvement, consult dealer
Noise from previous recording	Erase-head pad faulty	Clean pad. Fit new spring if necessary
	Erase head faulty	Consult dealer
Tape breaks frequently	Brakes faulty	Consult dealer
No sound on recording	Broken wiring between microphone and tape recorder. Check wiring with circuit-tester (see p. 526)	Fit new wiring
	Microphone or recording head faulty	Consult dealer

Tape recorders Cassettes

Recording on a cassette

Cassette tape recorders do not use individual reels of tape, but have easy-fitting packs, which slot into two guides. The tape is automatically brought into contact with the drive mechanism and recording/play-back head. Some models are battery operated only; others can be operated on batteries or on the mains power. Apart from cleaning, there is little maintenance that can be attempted by an amateur.

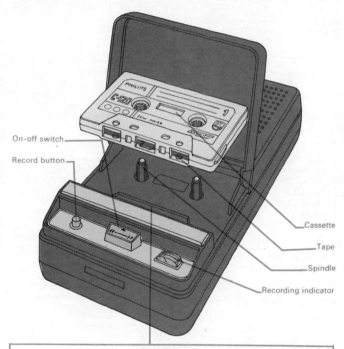

On-off switch

Record button

Cassette

Tape

Spindle

Recording indicator

CLEANING A CASSETTE RECORDER

Capstan

1 Remove tape. Push the control switch to the recording position

2 Brush away dust and clean the head with methylated spirit

3 Switch off record button. Apply oil lightly to the capstan bearing

Television sets

Installation

Television receivers should be installed only by qualified television technicians. A temporary installation may be made on a programme transmission, but final adjustments should always be made on a test-card transmission, which provides a standardised pattern for all adjustments of the set.

Focusing

The pictures should be sharply focused and free from interference. The circles, squares and rectangles shown on the test card must not be distorted.

There should be uniform gradations from black to white, with no shading at the right-hand edges of black or white areas.

Never accept a colour installation which has not been made on a test card.

In addition to securing perfect circles, squares and rectangles—as for black and white sets—accurate adjustment is needed for convergence and colour balance (see p. 560).

Aerials

However good the television set, a picture can be only as good as the signals passed to it by the aerial. If possible, site the aerial outdoors on the roof; the second-best position is in the attic or loft; the third possibility, on top of the set, may be reasonable in areas relatively close to the transmitter, but the picture is rarely perfect.

Except for a set-top type, aerial installation requires professional knowledge. When moving house to another part of the country, do not take the aerial: it is unlikely to be suitable for the new area.

Fitting an aerial plug

The signal received by the aerial is fed to the back of the television set by a cable and plug. Never pull out the aerial plug in a thunderstorm: the cable may accumulate high voltages and cause a serious shock or burn if the plug is held.

If a picture flashes when the aerial cable and plug are moved, remove the plug and fit a new one. When assembling the new plug be sure that no straids of braid can make contact with the centre wire of the cable. Always solder the centre wire to the pin before fitting it into the plug.

Materials: cored solder (see p. 692); emery cloth; plug.
Tools: wire cutter and stripper; soldering iron.

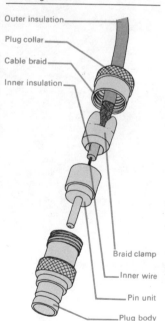

Outer insulation

Plug collar

Cable braid

Inner insulation

Braid clamp

Inner wire

Pin unit

Plug body

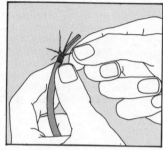

1 Remove 1½ in. (40 mm) of outer insulation. Loosen braid and fold it back, leaving about ¾ in. (20 mm) of inner insulation clear

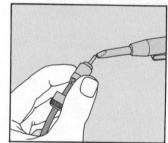

2 Remove inner insulation ¼ in. (6 mm) from the braid. Fit plug collar and braid clamp. Fit pin unit and solder centre wire to pin

3 Cut off the surplus wire from the end of the pin. Screw on the plug body, which will compress the braid clamp on the braid

How black-and-white TV works

Any television picture is a series of lines. All along the invisible chain from the camera in the studio to the television receiver, only one small piece of information is being transmitted and received at any instant.

The television camera does not take a complete picture: it scans the scene in the studio line-by-line and transmits what it sees in the form of minute electrical voltages. When the picture reaches the television receiver, these voltages are translated back into lines which are beamed on to the front of the cathode-ray tube, so that a picture can be seen.

The number of lines used in scanning in television cameras and receivers depends on the system used. In the United Kingdom, two standards are in use: 405 and 625 lines.

Every camera and receiver scans half of each picture twice: first the odd-numbered lines are scanned from top to bottom, then the even lines.

The whole scanning process happens 50 times a second, so that 25 complete pictures are built up every second.

Besides the electronic information which makes up each picture, the television station adds synchronisation pulses, which ensure that the scanning process on the television set starts at precisely the same point in the picture as the scanner on the TV camera in the television studio.

This ensures that the picture does not become jumbled or out of sequence.

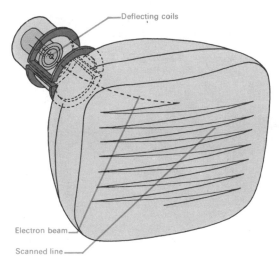

Scanning Each picture is scanned twice: first odd-numbered lines from top to bottom, then the even-numbered lines. The top and bottom scans are each half lines

Black-and-white picture faults

The electron beam that scans the scene in a television studio creates tiny electrical voltages according to the lightness or darkness of the part of the picture it is seeing. If a television set is correctly adjusted, these differences in light and shade—through the whole range from white to black—should be accurately represented. All the other information received by the television set must be correctly reproduced. For example, the line-hold control should ensure that the electronic beam scans the cathode-ray tube perfectly horizontally, and the vertical-hold control should ensure accurate vertical positioning of the beam at any time.

Adjust a television receiver only when the television station's test card is showing and make sure that all parts of it are clear (see p. 558). If a picture cannot be correctly adjusted with the controls outside the set, do not try to dismantle the set to repair it. Call a television technician.

Contrast A common fault with television reception is incorrect adjustment of brightness and contrast controls. These should be carefully adjusted together to get a picture of the required brightness which shows the correct gradations of grey between full white and black. Remember that a bright room light will reduce the contrast.

Sound faults The sound and picture in television are produced and transmitted separately. They are received by the same aerial but they are then separated and sent to the cathode-ray tube and the loudspeakers. Do not try to correct sound faults: no adjustment is possible. Call a service engineer.

Underscan The picture does not completely fill the screen from side to side. Adjust with the line-width or amplitude control, if one is fitted. If one is not fitted to the set, call a service engineer to make the adjustment

Vertical distortion and overscan The edges of the test card cannot be seen and the squares of the card are reproduced as rectangles. Adjust the line-width control, if fitted. If not, call an engineer to make the adjustment

Horizontal distortion Some rectangles are squeezed up; others are opened out. Adjust the horizontal or line control until the rectangles are reproduced as squares. If no control is fitted, call an engineer to make the adjustment

Television sets

The basic principles of colour TV

The picture is built up from three primary colours—red, green and blue. Both the camera and the receiving set use three electronic beams, one for each colour, to scan the picture, instead of a single beam as for black-and-white television (see p. 559). But the basic principle is otherwise the same, with the camera scanning the scene in front of it line by line and the set reproducing it in corresponding lines.

When a colour camera is directed at a scene, one electron beam picks up only the red areas, another the green parts and a third the blue parts. These electronic signals are coded and sent through the transmitter, and are received and decoded separately through the television receiver.

Mixtures of the three colours can reproduce the whole range of colours in the spectrum.

The receiver has a phosphorescent screen coated with over a million dots, arranged in threes—red, green and blue: behind the screen, a very fine mesh, called a shadow mask, filters the beams from three electron guns. The beams from one gun are directed at the red dots, those from the second gun at the green dots and those from the third at the blue dots. Provided that the mesh and the screen are in perfect alignment, an accurate colour picture will be reproduced by activation of the dots. White and all shades of grey can also be reproduced by correct mixtures of the three primary colours, and any colour set will reproduce black-and-white transmissions as black-and-white.

For good colour reproduction, free from interference, the receiver must have a signal of adequate strength. This requires a suitable aerial installation, which cannot as a rule be provided by the type placed on top of the set.

Colour shades may vary slightly between different programmes and between channels, but once adjustments have been made to give good reproduction, further adjustments should not be necessary. Adjust a colour set only when the colour test card is being shown. Do not accept a newly installed set if reproduction is below standard.

TELEVISION SAFETY

A faulty television set should be repaired only by a technician. Never remove the back of the set, even if it is switched off and the plug removed. A black-and-white set generates 10,000 volts or more; a colour set uses 25,000 volts. These voltages may be present for some time after the set has been switched off, and they can kill.

All receivers must be operated from a three-pin plug and socket, even though the mains lead has only two wires. The wires must be correctly connected to the L and N plug pins (see p. 525), and no other equipment should be used from the same socket.

Never place on a set anything which might spill liquid, for example a vase of flowers. If there is any sign of smoke or burning, switch off and pull out the plug immediately.

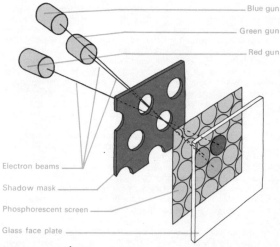

Blue gun
Green gun
Red gun

Electron beams
Shadow mask
Phosphorescent screen
Glass face plate

Colour reproduction Each electron gun directs its beams through tiny holes in the shadow mask, and each beam can hit only a correspondingly coloured dot in front of each hole

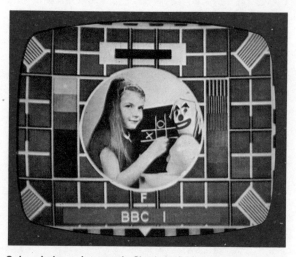

Colour balanced correctly Check the flesh tones carefully: they should be pure and unexaggerated. Make sure that the white, black and grey areas show definite gradations and are not coloured

Colour cast A predominance of any one colour is called colour cast. If the set has an external colour-intensity control, adjust it to reduce the colour cast: otherwise, call a service engineer

Divergence The white lines and lettering on the test card have broken into the three primary television colours—red, green and blue. Call a service engineer to adjust the convergence controls

Toasters

When a toaster goes wrong

The element in an electric toaster is wound on asbestos or mica sheets. A thermostat control or heat-sensing device measures the heat reflected from the bread and shuts off the toaster when the bread is ready. When the pre-set heat is reached, the thermostat operates the pop-up mechanism —either by an electrical impulse from a device called a solenoid or by a metal strip which gradually heats and bends to contact a tripping plate. Only simple repairs are possible by the amateur.

WARNING Remove plug from socket before carrying out maintenance or repairs. Do not attempt jobs other than those suggested

FINDING THE FAULT

Symptom	Checking order	Action
No power	Fuse blown at plug	Replace fuse (see p. 519)
	Loose connections at plug or toaster	Reconnect (see pp. 525, 526)
	Broken flex. Check with circuit tester (see p. 526)	If necessary renew connections
	Broken element. Remove crumb tray. Inspect element	Take toaster to dealer
Intermittent power	Loose connections at plug or toaster	Reconnect (see pp. 525, 526)
	Broken flex. Check with circuit tester (see p. 526)	If necessary renew flex
	Broken element. Remove crumb tray. Inspect element	Take toaster to dealer
Toast does not brown correctly	Broken thermostat	Return to dealer or manufacturer
Toast does not pop up	Broken mechanism	Return to dealer or manufacturer

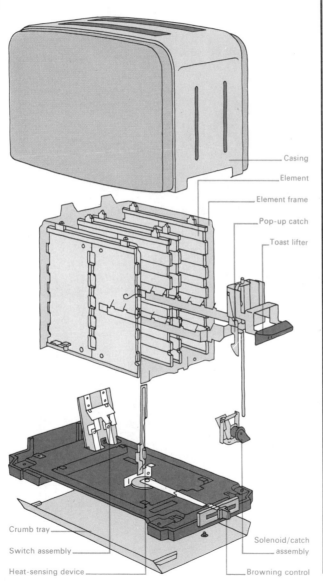

Casing
Element
Element frame
Pop-up catch
Toast lifter
Crumb tray
Switch assembly
Heat-sensing device
Solenoid/catch assembly
Browning control

Cleaning the crumb tray

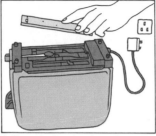

1 Remove the plug from the socket and unclip or unscrew the crumb tray from the underside of the toaster

2 Shake gently and clean the tray with a damp cloth. Do not touch inside toaster

HOW THE POP-UP MECHANISM WORKS

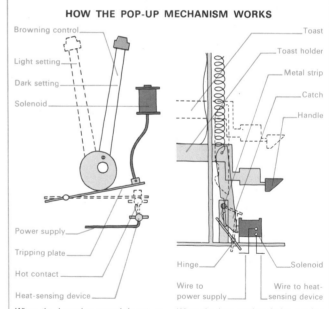

Browning control
Light setting
Dark setting
Solenoid
Power supply
Tripping plate
Hot contact
Heat-sensing device

Toast
Toast holder
Metal strip
Catch
Handle
Hinge
Solenoid
Wire to power supply
Wire to heat-sensing device

When the browning control is set at 'light', a tripping plate is moved towards the heat-sensing device; when set to 'dark', the plate moves away from it. This controls the length of time that it takes for the heat-sensing device to contact the tripping plate

When the heat-sensing device touches the plate, an electrical impulse is transmitted to the solenoid through a connecting wire. The solenoid, which is an electro-magnet, is activated and attracts a metal hinge, which releases the catch holding the toast carrier

Tumble dryers

How a tumble dryer works

Most tumble dryers are powered by induction motors (see p. 527), which drive a perforated clothes drum and a fan. Heat generated by an electric element is directed into the drum, and on to the clothes, by the fan. Most dryers have a door-operated switch which stops the drum if the door is opened before the drying cycle is completed. Controls can be pre-set to dry the clothes completely or damp-dry them for ironing.

On some machines, moist air extracted can be directed outside through a fitting in the wall.

Most faults must be repaired by a skilled mechanic. Day-to-day maintenance, however, can be carried out by the owner.

WARNING Remove plug from socket before carrying out maintenance or repairs. Do not attempt jobs other than those suggested

FINDING THE FAULT

Symptom	Checking order	Action
No power	Fuse blown at the plug	Fit new fuse (see p. 519)
No power or intermittent power	Loose flex connections at plug or dryer	Reconnect (see pp. 525–6)
	Broken flex. Carry out battery and bulb test (see p. 526)	If necessary, fit new flex
	Windings burnt out	Check visually for burning. Return to dealer or manufacturer for service
	Faulty switch assembly	Call a service engineer
Motor runs, but no heat produced	Element burnt out	
	Thermostat not working	Call a service engineer
	Faulty switch assembly	
Motor runs, but the drum fails to revolve	Belt broken or too slack	Call a service engineer
Excessive vibration	Worn bearings	Call a service engineer

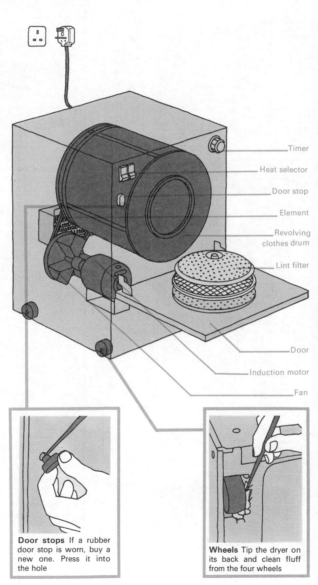

- Timer
- Heat selector
- Door stop
- Element
- Revolving clothes drum
- Lint filter
- Door
- Induction motor
- Fan

Door stops If a rubber door stop is worn, buy a new one. Press it into the hole

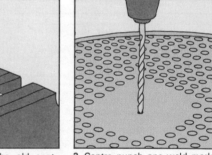

Wheels Tip the dryer on its back and clean fluff from the four wheels

Mending a loose filter

Clean the filter each time the machine is used. On the inside of the filter shield on one popular model a T-shaped nut fits into a clip. With constant cleaning the nut may break at its weld points. Drill out the old welds carefully to avoid damaging the enamel. Check regularly that there are no snags round the new rivets to damage clothes.

Materials: small brass rivets; metal block; rag.
Tools: hammer; spanner; pliers; wheelbrace and bit; vice; wire cutter; punch; centre-punch.

1 Wrap the loose T nut in rag. Grip it with a pair of pliers and undo its screw and nut

2 Centre-punch the old spot-weld marks. Hold the nut in a vice and drill $\frac{1}{8}$ in. (3 mm) holes

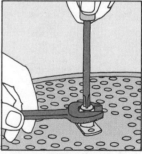

3 Centre-punch one weld mark on the shield and drill out to the same size

4 Lay T nut in position. Fit rivet and burr with hammer and punch. Drill, and fit second rivet

5 Fit the screw and hexagon nut. Adjust them until they fit the filter-retaining clip

Vacuum cleaners

The two types of cleaner

There are two basic types of vacuum cleaner: upright, with a handle; and cylindrical or spherical, with a hose. In an upright cleaner, the motor has two functions: to drive a rotating brush which dislodges dirt and dust from the floor; and to operate a fan or impeller to create the suction which draws the loosened dirt into the cleaner bag. Most cylindrical and spherical types have no moving brush: the motor drives only a suction fan.

In upright models the air sucked in escapes through the fabric of the cleaner bag: in cylindrical models it is pushed by the fan through an exhaust hole: and in spherical models, which operate similarly to the cylindrical types, the air is expelled from below the base to create a cushion which makes the cleaner more manoeuvrable.

Some vacuum cleaners have plastic, double-insulated casings and, therefore, are fitted with two-core flexes (see p. 521). Other models have earthed supply cables.

WARNING Remove the plug from the wall socket before carrying out maintenance or repairs. Do not attempt jobs other than those suggested

---

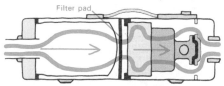

Cylindrical Air is sucked through the hose inlet into the dust bag. A filter pad ensures that dust is not expelled through the exhaust

Upright A belt links the motor to a roller which has spiral brushes. Dust, beaten up by the brush, is sucked over the motor into the dust bag

FINDING THE FAULT		
Symptom	**Checking order**	**Action**
No power	Fuse blown at plug	Fit new fuse (see p. 519)
No power or intermittent power	Loose or broken flex connections at plug or cleaner	Reconnect (see pp. 525, 526)
	Broken flex. Check with circuit tester (see p. 526)	Fit new flex if necessary (see p. 526)
	Worn, loose or sticking carbon brushes	Fit new brushes (see p. 527)
	Motor windings burnt out	Consult dealer
Poor cleaning	Overfull dust bag	Empty bag
	Split hose	Make a temporary repair by binding with tape and consult dealer
	Bad connection with hose end	Repair with adhesive (see p. 694)
	Worn roller brush	Fit new brush (see p. 564)
	Damaged fan	Consult dealer
Smell of burning rubber	Loose belt drive	Fit new belt (see p. 564)
	String around impeller	Remove obstruction

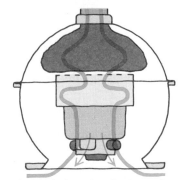

Spherical Air is drawn into the cleaner through the hose and expelled through the base to create an air cushion and make the cleaner more manoeuvrable

Maintaining a cylinder cleaner

Most vacuum cleaners are operated by a brush motor. If it fails, or if it is operating only intermittently, check the brushes (see p. 527).

Most other repairs should be left to a dealer or electrician. To avoid unnecessary breakdowns, however, empty the dust bag regularly and make sure that the cleaner is not used to pick up sharp objects. Replace the filter if it becomes clogged or damaged.

Hose Make a temporary repair to a frayed or split hose by binding with masking or plastic insulating tape

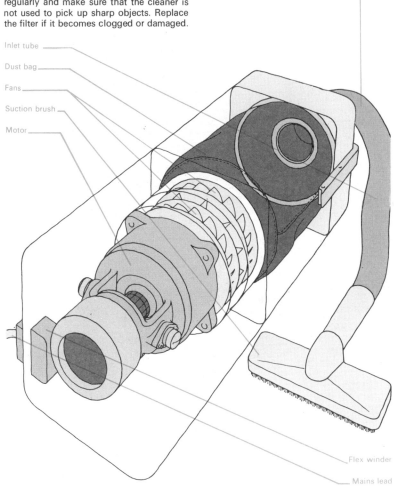

Inlet tube

Dust bag

Fans

Suction brush

Motor

Flex winder

Mains lead

Vacuum cleaners

Maintaining an upright cleaner

Maintenance of an upright cleaner and its motor is similar to that for the cylindrical type (see p. 563). Most faults cannot be repaired in the home, but it is possible to minimise the number of repairs necessary by emptying the dust bag regularly and ensuring that the belt and brushes are changed as soon as they begin to wear.

If the cleaner has a protective rubber strip round the base, do not try to renew it: take the machine to a dealer.

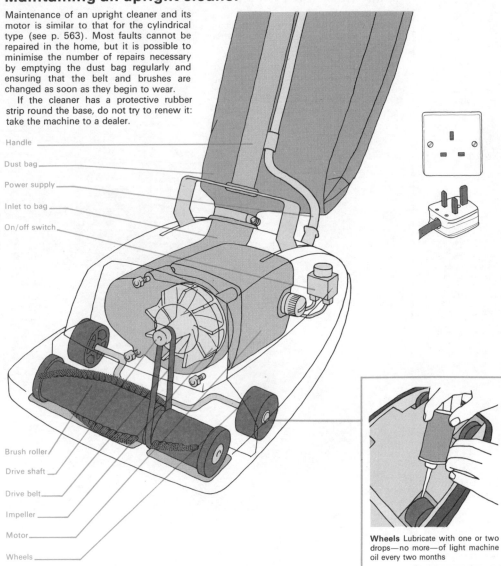

Handle

Dust bag

Power supply

Inlet to bag

On/off switch

Brush roller

Drive shaft

Drive belt

Impeller

Motor

Wheels

Wheels Lubricate with one or two drops—no more—of light machine oil every two months

Fitting a new drive belt or roller brush

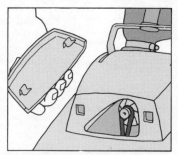

1 Remove the cover plate from the front of the cleaner. Pull the belt off the pulley

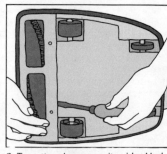

2 Turn the cleaner on its side. Undo the screws which secure the metal shield behind the brush roller

3 If there is a catch beside the roller, free it. Lift out the brush and belt. Discard belt if worn

4 Fit a new belt round the slot in the centre of the roller. Refit the roller and the metal shield

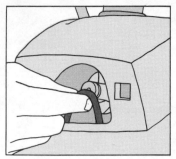

5 Turn the cleaner upright. Twist the belt clockwise and stretch it over the pulley

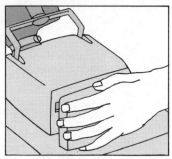

6 Fit cover plate. If it is not a slide fit, it is usually fitted in one side then sprung in the other

Washing machines

How washing machines work

Home maintenance of a washing machine is limited to lubrication and minor repairs to hoses. Do not attempt to fit new belts: they must be tensioned accurately, which needs special equipment.

The spin-dryer in a twin-tub machine is identical in principle to individual spin-dryers (see p. 554).

WARNING Remove plug from socket before carrying out maintenance or repairs. Do not attempt jobs other than those suggested

FINDING THE FAULT

Symptom	Checking order	Action
No power	Fuse blown at plug or mains	Fit new fuse (see p. 519)
No power or intermittent power	Loose connections at plug or machine	Reconnect flex. The earth, live and neutral connections are not marked. Note the position of the connections before removing old flex
	Broken flex. Check with circuit tester (see p. 526)	Fit new flex if necessary
	Faulty switch	Consult dealer
	Motor windings burnt out	Consult dealer
	Brushes on a brush motor	Fit new brushes if worn (see p. 527)
Power, but drum not turning	Broken or slack belts	Consult dealer
Leaks	Split hose	Repair hose
	Faulty pump	Fit new gasket to pump (see p. 555) If pump still leaks, have a new pump unit fitted
Spin dryer revolving erratically	Clothes caught between revolving drum and watertight case	Look for obstruction (see p. 554)
	Faulty brake cable	Adjust or fit new cable (see p. 556)
	Worn brake lining	Fit new lining (see p. 556)
Power, but no heat	Faulty element	Consult dealer

WASHING ACTION

Tumbler A drum revolves horizontally. The clothes are lifted out of the water on baffles and tumble back again

Agitator A flanged structure mounted vertically on a spindle moves the clothes clockwise and anti-clockwise more than 60 times a minute

Pulsator A flanged disc on the side of the washing tub revolves clockwise. Its speed is usually about 600 revolutions per minute

Single-tub machines with a wringer

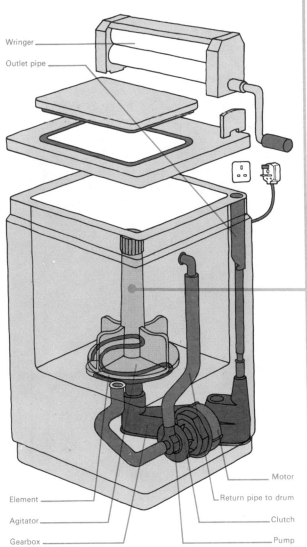

Wringer

Outlet pipe

Element

Agitator

Gearbox

Motor

Return pipe to drum

Clutch

Pump

GREASING A SPINDLE

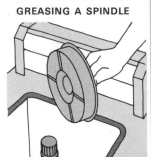

1 If the agitator is fitted with a filter dish on top, unscrew or pull it off the spindle

2 Unscrew the spindle from the motor drive shaft, then draw out the spindle

3 Spread a little light grease along the spindle thread and refit tightly in the shaft

Washing machines

Twin-tub machines

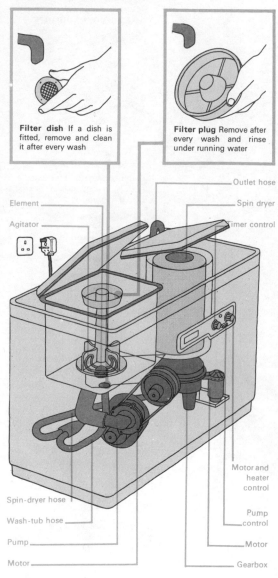

Filter dish If a dish is fitted, remove and clean it after every wash

Filter plug Remove after every wash and rinse under running water

Element

Agitator

Outlet hose

Spin dryer

Timer control

Spin-dryer hose

Wash-tub hose

Pump

Motor

Motor and heater control

Pump control

Motor

Gearbox

REPAIRING A HOSE

Replace a damaged part of an inlet or outlet hose with copper tubing that has exactly the same internal diameter as the hose.

Materials: copper tube to fit tightly in hose; jubilee clips. Tools: small hacksaw; screw-driver.

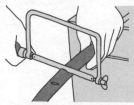

1 Cut out the damaged part with a hacksaw. Fit a length of copper tube in one side

2 Slide a clip $\frac{1}{2}$ in. (13 mm) on to the hose. Tighten the clip to secure hose on tube

3 Fit clip on other section of hose. Push in tube and tighten clip

Automatic single-tub machines

Outlet hose

Springs

Drive belt

Motor

Washing and spin-drying tub

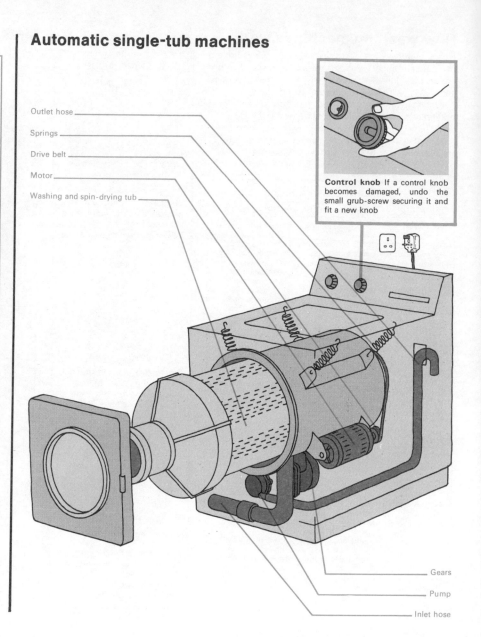

Control knob If a control knob becomes damaged, undo the small grub-screw securing it and fit a new knob

Gears

Pump

Inlet hose

Waste disposers

Faults and their symptoms

Waste disposers which rotate in one direction only have an On-Off switch: those that can also rotate in the reverse direction are controlled by a switch marked Forward and Reverse.

There are two cables at the box of the reversing type, a three-core flex connected to the mains, and a five-core lead to the disposer motor. If one is broken or disconnected, the motor may run in one direction and not the other, or may not run at all.

On some models, a perforated-metal saver mounted at the top of the unit, but below the sink plug, ensures that cutlery cannot fall into the disposer. To use the equipment, remove the saver, turn on the cold-water tap and switch on the machine. Push the waste down the outlet past the rubber petals. Leave it running until the sound of grinding stops.

WARNING Turn off at main switch before carrying out maintenance or repairs. Do not attempt jobs other than those suggested

FINDING THE FAULT

Symptom	Checking order	Action
Motor will not turn or reverse	Grinder jammed	Switch off. Dismantle and clean grinder
	Fuse blown in control box	Fit new fuse (see p. 519)
		If fuse blows again, check for faulty connections
		If connections satisfactory call service engineer
	Loose connections at control box or motor	Reconnect (see p. 526)
	Broken lead. Check supply to machine with circuit tester (see p. 526)	If necessary, fit new lead (see p. 526)
Intermittent running	Loose connections at control box or motor	Reconnect
	Broken lead. Check with circuit tester (see p. 526)	If necessary, fit new lead (see p. 526)
Slow-running motor and burning smell	Coils burnt out	Call service engineer

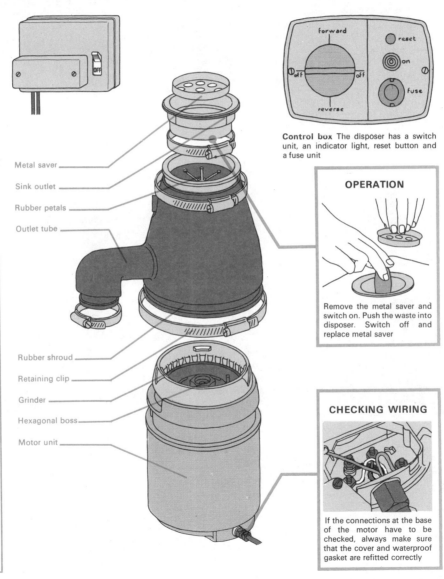

Metal saver

Sink outlet

Rubber petals

Outlet tube

Rubber shroud

Retaining clip

Grinder

Hexagonal boss

Motor unit

Control box The disposer has a switch unit, an indicator light, reset button and a fuse unit

OPERATION

Remove the metal saver and switch on. Push the waste into disposer. Switch off and replace metal saver

CHECKING WIRING

If the connections at the base of the motor have to be checked, always make sure that the cover and waterproof gasket are refitted correctly

Unjamming

If a waste disposer jams, it switches off automatically. Switch off at the main switch and reach into the unit to try to clear the obstruction. If this fails, use the release tool to free the blockage. Press the reset button and switch on. If the machine has a reversing control, minor jams can be cleared by switching to reverse.

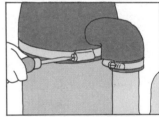

1 Fit the release tool through the sink outlet on to the hexagon nut. Turn it backwards and forwards

2 If the motor cannot be freed, undo the screw holding the clip round the base of the rubber shroud

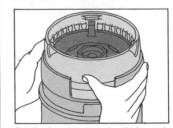

3 Lift the motor and grinder unit out of the rubber shroud. Remove the obstruction and reassemble

Bicycles

Lubrication

When a bicycle is in regular use, lubricate the bearings and chain every fortnight with cycle oil. Apply a few drops at the places indicated, taking care to keep oil off the tyres.

On some cycles there are no oiling points on the bottom bracket, pedals or hubs; the bearings have been packed with grease during manufacture and need no further attention.

For lubrication of bicycles fitted with variable gears, see pp. 584 and 586.

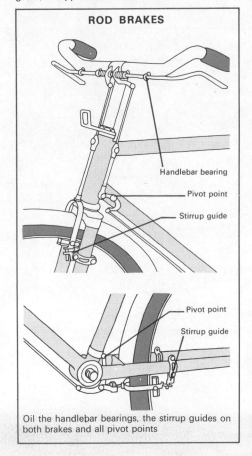

ROD BRAKES

Handlebar bearing

Pivot point

Stirrup guide

Pivot point

Stirrup guide

Oil the handlebar bearings, the stirrup guides on both brakes and all pivot points

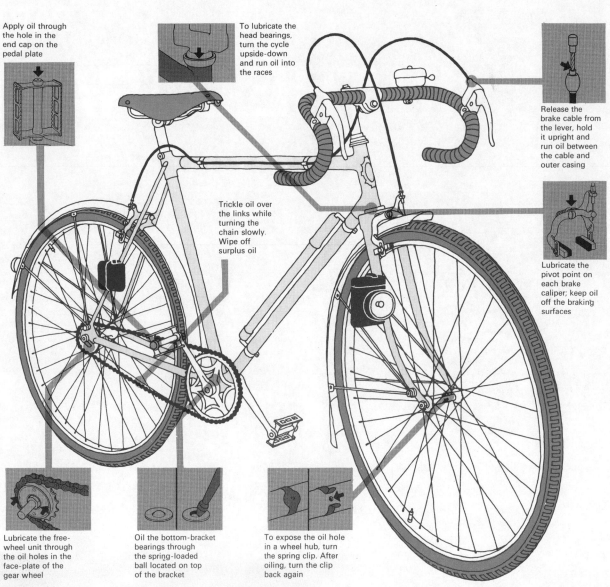

Apply oil through the hole in the end cap on the pedal plate

To lubricate the head bearings, turn the cycle upside-down and run oil into the races

Release the brake cable from the lever, hold it upright and run oil between the cable and outer casing

Trickle oil over the links while turning the chain slowly. Wipe off surplus oil

Lubricate the pivot point on each brake caliper; keep oil off the braking surfaces

Lubricate the free-wheel unit through the oil holes in the face-plate of the gear wheel

Oil the bottom-bracket bearings through the spring-loaded ball located on top of the bracket

To expose the oil hole in a wheel hub, turn the spring clip. After oiling, turn the clip back again

Bicycles   Valves and inner tubes

Mending a puncture

If you have a flat tyre, first check the valve (see below). If that is sound, see if there is a flint or nail in the outer cover that can give you some indication of where the puncture might be. Whenever you remove an inner tube, check that the rim tape is properly covering the spoke nipples.

Materials: puncture-repair outfit containing an indelible pencil, glass-paper or an abrasive stick for cleaning the tube, rubber solution, rubber patches and French chalk; petrol.
Tools: three tyre levers.

Checking a valve

To check whether a valve is leaking, turn the wheel until the valve is at the top and submerge it in an egg cup or similar container filled with water.

The inserts of Woods type valves can be removed when faulty. The plunger type must be replaced: the rubber type need have only the rubber renewed. Repairs cannot normally be made to Schrader and Presta valves.

A larger pump connector is required for the Schrader valve. A knurled nut on the plunger of the Presta, which is used mainly on sports machines, must be loosened for air to pass through.

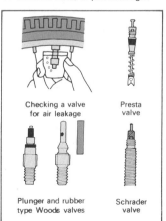

Checking a valve for air leakage   Presta valve

Plunger and rubber type Woods valves   Schrader valve

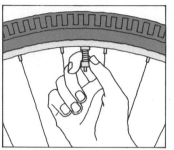

1 Unscrew the nut that retains the valve assembly and withdraw the valve from the inner-tube stem

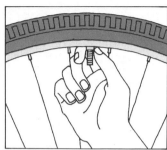

2 Remove the lock-ring and push part of the valve stem up inside the wheel rim to free the cover

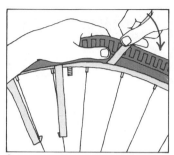

3 Insert the levers between the rim and tyre. Lever the tyre off, hooking each lever in turn round a spoke

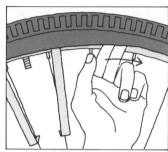

4 When a quarter of the tyre has been levered off, run the fingers round the rim to free the remainder

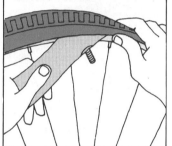

5 With one edge of the cover removed, draw the tube out. Press it to the rim to ease it past the brake blocks

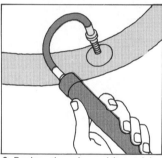

6 Replace the valve and its retaining nut and inflate the tube just sufficiently for it to adopt its natural shape

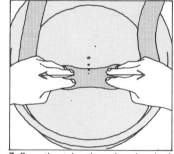

7 Pass the tube through a bowl of water, stretching it slightly to enlarge any small punctures

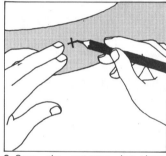

8 Once the puncture has been located, mark its position with the indelible pencil in the kit

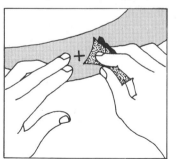

9 Deflate the tube and clean the area with glass-paper, a moistened abrasive stick or a petrol-soaked cloth

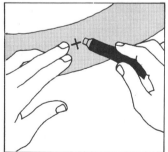

10 Spread the adhesive thinly over the surface around the mark and leave it until it is practically dry

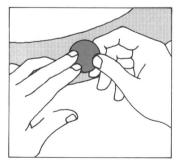

11 Peel off the backing from a patch and press the patch, tacky side down, firmly over the puncture

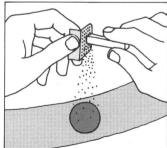

12 Dry any surplus adhesive with French chalk. If solid chalk is provided in the kit, powder it on the grater

Bicycles Wheels

Fitting a new rim tape

A rim tape is fitted to protect the inner tube from possible puncture by the spoke nipples. When a tyre and tube have to be removed for any reason, it is as well to examine the tape for signs of misplacement or deterioration. This often starts with rust stains, developing eventually into fraying or splitting.

There are two types of tapes—one made of a thin webbing material, the other of rubber. Rubber tapes, used mainly on sports cycles, cost more but are less trouble to fit. They must be bought to fit the wheel, whereas webbing tapes are adjustable. Tools are not needed in either case.

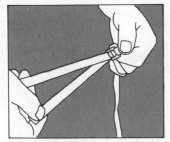

1 To fit a webbing tape, open it with the convex side of the eye downwards and pass the free end through the slot from the top

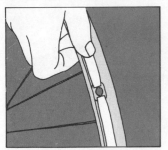

2 Loop the tape round the rim, aligning the metal eye with the wheel-rim valve hole. Make sure that the tape is not twisted

3 Keeping the eye and valve hole aligned, draw the tape tight. Tuck the surplus material under the main run of the rest of the tape

4 Fit a rubber tape convex side downwards. Align the tape's valve hole with the wheel-rim valve hole, then feed the tape round the rim

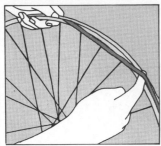

5 To avoid twisting the tape, draw a finger under it as it springs over the rim. See that it sits centrally in the well of the rim

Refitting a tyre and tube

1 Slip one entire side of the tyre over an edge of the wheel rim, taking care as you do so not to push the rim tape out of position

6 Draw the free edge of the tyre into the rim well, finishing with a small section of tyre overlapping the rim across the valve stem

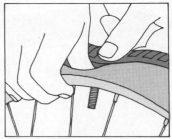

2 Pull back the tyre's free edge over the valve hole in the rim and insert the valve stem; then draw the tyre back over the inner tube

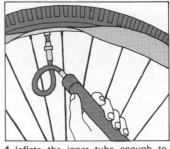

4 Inflate the inner tube enough to give it its natural shape. Avoid over-inflation, as this makes it difficult to refit the tyre

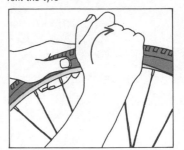

7 Press the cover into the rim centre, working from both sides towards the area still to be fitted. Roll the last part on with the balls of the thumbs

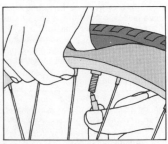

3 Screw the valve lock-ring finger-tight. Replace the valve, checking the rubber in older-type valves, and tighten the valve retaining nut

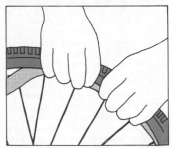

5 Roll the tube into the centre of the rim well. Adjust the fitted edge of the tyre if necessary to ensure that the tube is positioned correctly

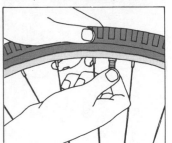

8 Loosen the valve stem lock-ring and push the stem into the rim. Pull the stem out again, tighten the lock-ring and inflate the tyre

Bicycles Chains

Testing a chain: fitting a new one

Grit, lack of oil or wrong tensioning will cause chain wear. In use, a worn chain makes a grating sound.

Each link of the chain is made up of two side plates riveted at one end to a central roller. Generally, the ends of the chain are joined by a connecting link, the closed end of which must face the direction of travel. The endless Derailleur gear chain has no connecting link.

Most new chains need shortening by removing one or two surplus links. This is easiest with a rivet extractor, but a fine punch and hammer will do. Follow the same procedure to shorten an old chain. Replace worn sprockets (see p. 588) with new ones when fitting a new chain.

Materials: new chain; paraffin.
Tools: rivet extractor, or a fine punch and a hammer; pliers; spanner; wire brush.

CHAIN WEAR

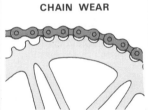

Worn Some of the chain links can be seen to ride over the top of the chain-wheel teeth

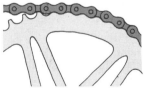

Unworn The chain 'beds down' between the chain-wheel teeth without any lifting

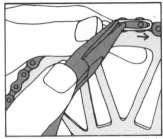

1 Remove the connecting-link spring clip by closing the pliers across one of the rivet heads and the ends of the clip

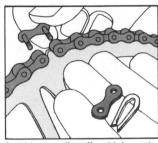

2 With the clip off, withdraw the end plate and slide the main body of the connecting link from the ends of the chain

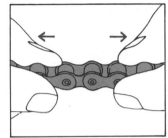

3 Pull two adjacent chain links in opposite directions. If there is much play between them a new chain must be fitted

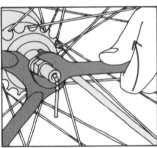

4 To allow full adjustment of the chain, loosen the rear-wheel nuts and move the wheel forward as far as it will safely go

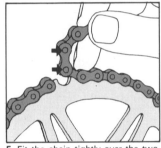

5 Fit the chain tightly over the two sprockets. The arrows indicate the two rivets that must be removed to make the chain fit

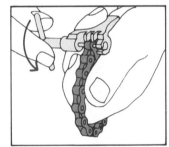

6 With one of the rivets in the rivet-extractor jaws, give the handle six full down-turns. Repeat with the other rivet

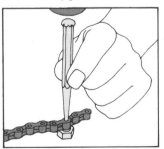

7 If you have no extractor, put the rivet over the centre of a small nut and tap the rivet flat. Drive it out with a fine punch

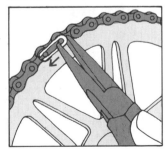

8 Replace the chain. Fit the connecting link, placing the clip over one rivet and pressing it over the other into the rivet grooves

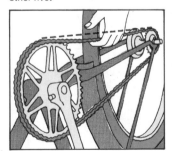

9 Adjust the rear wheel to give the chain ½ in. (13 mm) of free play. Position the wheel centrally and tighten the securing nuts

Cleaning a chain

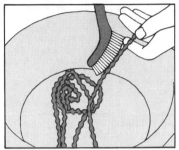

1 Soak the chain for 12 hours in a bowl of paraffin. Then remove sand and grit with a wire brush

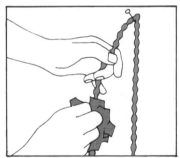

2 Hang up the chain to let the paraffin run off. Dry it with a clean rag, ensuring that no cloth is caught in the links

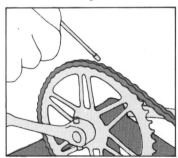

3 Refit the chain, adjust the tension, and oil each link with a proprietary cycle lubricant

Bicycles Wheels

Renewing spokes and straightening a wheel

Just one faulty spoke can throw a wheel out of true, causing erratic braking and a tendency to wobble. Spokes are easy to replace, though on the gear side of the rear wheel the freewheel or fixed sprocket must first be removed (see pp. 588–9). An alternative in this case is to make a special spoke-head, as shown.

Spokes are fitted in alternate directions on each side of the hub. Below, in detail, are the spoke arrangements on a front and a rear wheel. If several spokes are missing, it is essential to 'lace in' the new ones correctly.

Materials: replacement spokes of correct length; nipples.
Tools: spoke spanner; screwdriver; fine file; chalk; straight-edge.

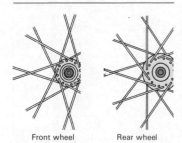

Front wheel   Rear wheel

Wheel faults
A wheel may be out of true in two ways. A radial distortion makes the rim uneven, with the hub slightly off centre, and can give a bumpy ride. A lateral distortion causes side-to-side movement, leading to wobbling.

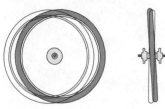

Radial (left) and lateral (right) distortion

1 Remove the tyre and replace the wheel. Take out both ends of a broken spoke; unscrew the nipple to release a bent spoke

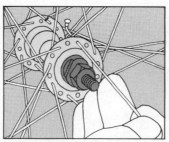

2 Feed a new spoke through the hub hole. The head must be on the opposite side of the hub to the spoke-heads on either side of it

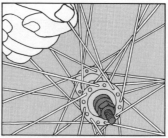

3 Draw out and swing up the spoke to the wheel-rim hole, making sure that it laces across the correct number of fitted spokes

4 Fit the spoke through the rim hole and screw the spoke nipple on to the threaded end. Tension the spoke with a screwdriver

5 To avoid removing a rear-wheel sprocket, a special spoke-head can be made. Start by drilling a $\frac{1}{8}$ in. (3 mm) hole in a thin cycle spanner

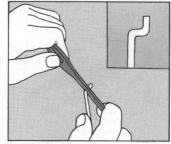

6 Take a spoke 1 in. (25 mm) longer than the length needed, cut off its head, and bend it to the shape shown in the inset diagram

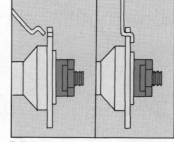

7 This shows how the shaped spoke end fits the hub. Push it in and twist it upwards so that it hooks round the hub flange

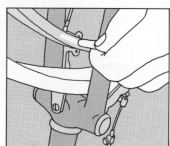

8 To correct lateral distortion, hold chalk close to the rim, spin the wheel and mark where the chalk touches

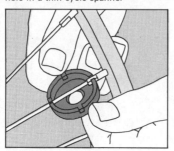

9 Within the marked area tighten only the spokes which lead to the opposite side of the hub. Adjust half a turn at a time until the wheel is true

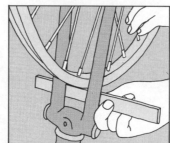

10 To correct radial distortion, remove the mudguard and place a straight-edge across the forks column at right angles to the rim. Spin the wheel

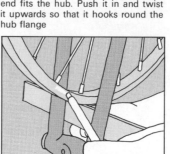

11 Raise the edge so that it just touches out-of-true rim areas. Mark those areas with chalk and tighten all spokes at these points

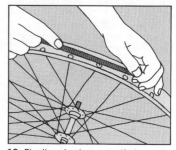

12 Finally, check to see if there are any spokes protruding from their nipple-heads. File them off flush with the nipples

Checking and replacing bearings

Wheel-bearing wear is caused by dirt, lack of oil, or over-tightening. It can be felt as a roughness if the wheel is spun while the spindle is hand-held. The ball bearings and cones are most likely to be affected; the two cups, generally integral parts of the hub, seldom wear. If they do, replace the wheel.

Materials: new cones and bearings as necessary; grease; paraffin.
Tools: spanners, including cone spanner; vice.

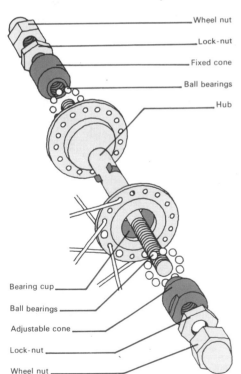

Wheel nut
Lock-nut
Fixed cone
Ball bearings
Hub

Bearing cup
Ball bearings
Adjustable cone
Lock-nut
Wheel nut

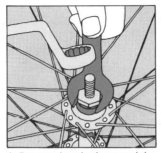

1 Remove the wheel nuts and the wheel. If it is the rear one, remove the chain from the sprocket

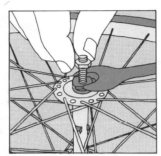

2 Holding the spindle in a vice and the adjustable cone with a spanner, undo the lock-nut

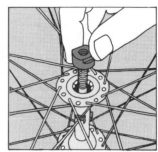

3 Unscrew the cone. It should be only finger-tight, but a cone spanner may be needed

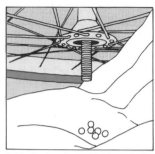

4 Undo the vice, with the spindle in position. Invert the wheel to release the ball bearings

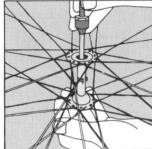

5 Draw out the spindle and shake out the other ball bearings from beneath the wheel hub

6 Clean the ball bearings and adjustable cone with paraffin. Replace any parts that are worn

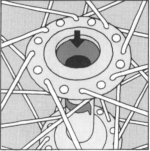

7 Remove all old or hardened grease from the hub cups: clean and check for signs of wear

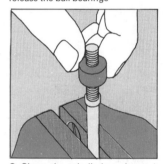

8 Clamp the spindle in a vice and replace the fixed cone. Fit a new one if the old one is worn

9 Tighten the new cone down to the stop. Replace and tighten the lock-nut if one was fitted

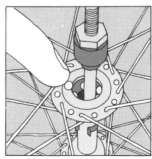

10 Loosely position the spindle, grease the hub cups, and fit the ball bearings to one cup

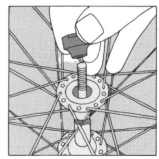

11 Reverse the wheel, hold the spindle in the vice, and refit the other ball bearings and cone

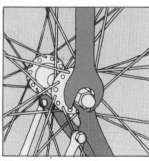

12 Adjust the cone so that the wheel turns under the weight of the valve. Replace the lock-nut

Bicycles Cable brakes

Adjusting brakes and fitting new blocks

The kind of cable brake shown is the one most commonly used today. Other kinds work on the same principle—a split caliper is operated by an inner and outer cable. Adjustment, and the fitting of new blocks, is the same for all types; but choose new blocks that will fit the shoes. Adjust brakes so that the blocks are about $\frac{1}{8}$ in. (3 mm) from the rim. To draw the shoes closer to the wheel, turn the knurled adjuster anti-clockwise.

Materials: a set of brake blocks.
Tools: spanner to fit brake-shoe nut; screwdriver; hammer; pliers; vice.

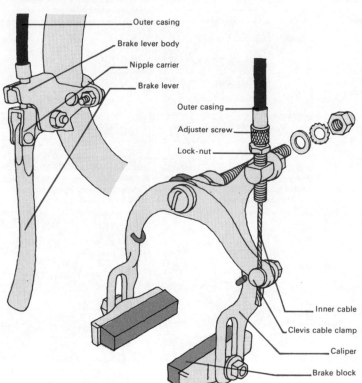

Outer casing
Brake lever body
Nipple carrier
Brake lever
Outer casing
Adjuster screw
Lock-nut
Inner cable
Clevis cable clamp
Caliper
Brake block
Brake shoe

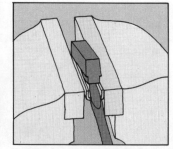

1 Undo the nut holding the brake-block shoe to the caliper base and slide out the shoe assembly

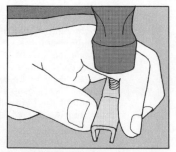

2 With the shoe held securely in a vice, lever out the worn block with a screwdriver

3 If the shoe jaws are too tight for the new block, lightly hammer the shoe base to spread the jaws

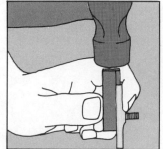

4 Stand the shoe upright on a hard surface and tap in the block, firmly holding the block in the shoe

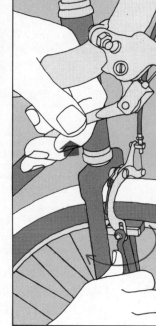

5 To hold the block firm in the shoe, pinch the open shoe ends together with a pair of pliers

6 Line up the fitted shoes evenly with the rim and hold them firm *with the brake on* when tightening up

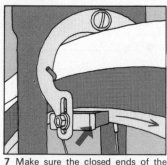

7 Make sure the closed ends of the shoes face in the same direction as the rotation of the wheel

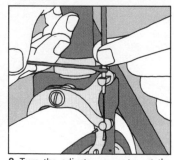

8 Turn the adjuster screw to get the correct brake position. Lock the screw with the lock-nut

Mending a broken cable

Brake cables are subject to hard wear and in time may fray and break, almost always close to the brake lever. If sufficient inner cable remains, resolder the nipple to the cable. To fit a new cable, follow the method shown in the two final illustrations.

There are two basic types of inner cable. The one shown has only one nipple, at the brake-lever end; the other end is held in a clamp on the brake caliper. The second type, which should be left in the outer casing during repair, has a nipple at each end: it may be necessary to shorten the outer cable slightly, by cutting with a junior hacksaw, to expose sufficient inner cable.

Provided it is undamaged, the original nipple can be used again. If you have to buy a new one, choose one to match from the several types available (see below).

Materials: solder; flux; nipple.
Tools: small flame torch (the Ronson butane type is ideal); emery cloth; spanner; hammer; fine file; pliers.

Types of nipples for soldering

Solderless nipples

In an emergency a broken inner brake cable can be repaired temporarily by fitting a solderless nipple. There are two basic designs—barrel-shaped and bell-shaped—to fit different types of nipple carriers on the brake lever. This is recommended as an emergency repair only, not as a permanent cure.

Barrel-shaped   Bell-shaped

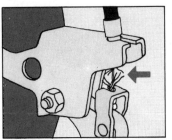

1 Most cables break just in front of the brake lever, generally because the nipple carrier on the lever has not been pivoting freely on its shaft

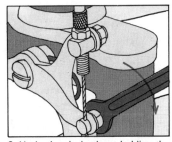

2 Undo the clevis clamp holding the inner cable to the brake caliper straddling the wheels. Withdraw the cable from its casing

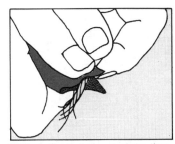

3 Wash the broken end of the inner cable in petrol to remove any oil and then clean it thoroughly with a piece of fine emery cloth

4 Melt the solder in the nipple and remove the cable end. Shake the nipple while it is still hot to get rid of old solder and clear the hole

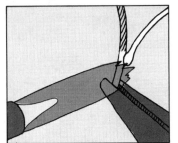

5 Hold the broken end of the cable right at its tip with the pliers. Heat it, apply flux and then tin the final inch of cable with solder

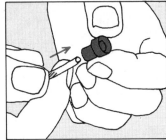

6 Snip the tinned end clean with the side cutter on the pliers and slide the cable nipple, narrow end first, on to the trimmed end of the cable

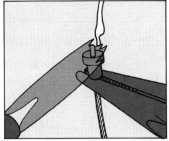

7 Leave a short length clear of the nipple, hold the cable in the pliers, apply flux, heat it and run solder into the head of the nipple

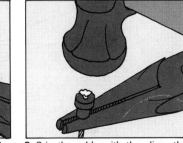

8 Grip the cable with the pliers, the base of the nipple against their jaws, and burr the cable end over by tapping it with a hammer

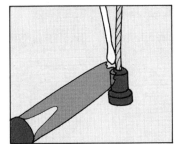

9 Put flux on the cable and nipple, hold them upside-down in the flame and let the solder run down to fill the nipple body and head

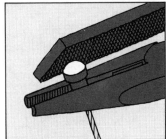

10 Use a fine file to clean off any surplus solder from the head of the nipple, leaving a neat dome of solder holding the cable

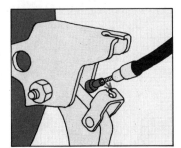

11 Oil the whole length of the inner cable and slide it back into its outer casing. Fit the inner cable nipple back on the brake lever

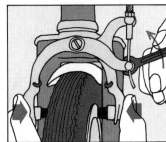

12 Slide the other end of the inner cable through the clevis clamp on the brake caliper and tighten the clamp bolt. Adjust the brake

Bicycles Rod brakes

Brake adjustment

Before adjusting the brakes, check that the pivot points on the rod linkage are lubricated and move freely. Straighten any bent rods. Fit new blocks by the method given for cable brakes on p. 576.

Tools: spanners to fit lock-nut on rear stirrup and clevis nuts; screwdriver.

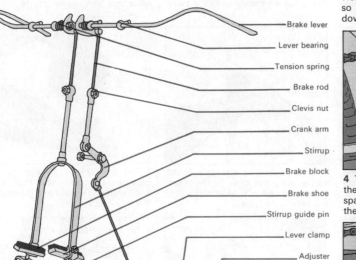

Brake lever

Lever bearing

Tension spring

Brake rod

Clevis nut

Crank arm

Stirrup

Brake block

Brake shoe

Stirrup guide pin

Lever clamp

Adjuster

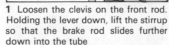
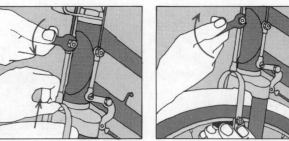
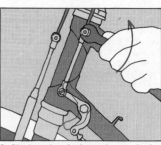

1 Loosen the clevis on the front rod. Holding the lever down, lift the stirrup so that the brake rod slides further down into the tube

2 Raise the stirrup to bring the brake blocks about $\frac{1}{8}$ in. (3 mm) clear of the rim of the wheel. Tighten the clevis nut to secure

3 Slacken the clevis on the rear brake. Adjust the rod to bring the top of the crank arm in line with the down tube of the cycle-frame

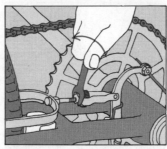

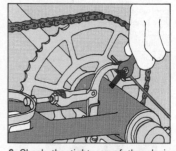

4 Turn the cycle upside-down, loosen the lock-nut on the adjuster with a spanner, and run the nut to the end of the thread

5 Move the stirrup until the blocks are about $\frac{1}{8}$ in. (3 mm) from the rim. Screw the adjuster to secure it, then tighten the lock-nut

6 Check the tightness of the clevis that secures the down-tube brake rod to the stirrup. It should not require any adjustment

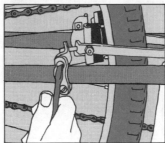
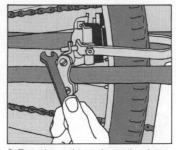
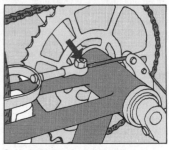

7 After brake adjustment, the stirrup guides may also need adjusting. The first step is to loosen the screws on the clamp

8 Tap the guides along the frame tubes, with the stirrup pins in the guide holes, until the guides are about $\frac{1}{4}$ in. (6 mm) away from the stirrup

9 If the rear brake is similar to the front brake, adjust it by loosening the nut and sliding the stirrup along the brake rod

Bicycles Hub brakes

Fitting new front shoes

Brake shoes on a hub-brake assembly need replacing if they are worn down to the rivets or have become oily from a leak in the bearings. In the latter case, a new bearing sealing-ring must be fitted. It is not worth spending time re-lining the shoes; instead, buy replacement shoes or, for rear wheels, a complete new assembly. To fit new shoes the wheel must be removed and the hub brake stripped down. A new assembly is needed for rear wheels because the smaller size of the drum makes it impracticable to fit replacement shoes.

Materials: front-brake replacement shoes, or a complete brake assembly for rear hub; grease.
Tools: spanners to fit hub wheel-nuts, brake-arm nut and shoe pivot bolt; screwdriver; vice.

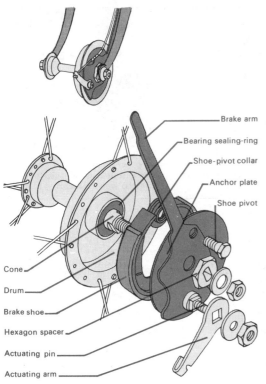

Brake arm
Bearing sealing-ring
Shoe-pivot collar
Anchor plate
Shoe pivot
Cone
Drum
Brake shoe
Hexagon spacer
Actuating pin
Actuating arm

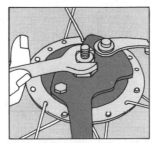

1 Take off the front wheel and hold the spindle in a vice, brake drum uppermost. Remove the lock-nut and washer

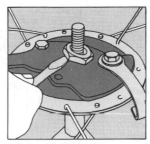

2 Prise the hexagon spacer off the shaft with a screwdriver. The spacer fits over the flattened edges of the cone

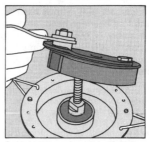

3 Hold the anchor plate by either the brake arm or the actuating arm and lift up to remove the complete assembly

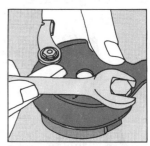

4 Start dismantling the brake shoes by undoing the bolt holding the shoe pivot. This is on the outside of the brake plate

5 Hold the brake shoes together in one hand to prevent them opening, and undo the nut securing the actuating arm

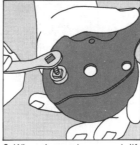

6 When the nut is removed, lift off the actuating arm. It fits over a squared spindle, so note how it is positioned

7 Now draw away the complete brake-shoe assembly, together with the actuating pin, from the anchor plate

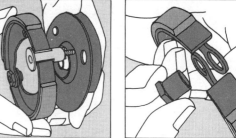

8 Press the shoes together to remove the pivot collar from the shoe eyes. Renew the collar if it is showing signs of wear

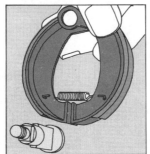

9 Overlap the eyes, spreading the lower end against the spring pressure. Remove the pin

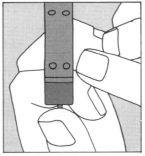

10 Fit new brake-shoe linings if they are dirty from oil or worn down to the rivets

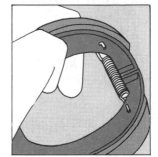

11 Before fitting shoes, hook the return spring into the shoe holes to bring the shoes together

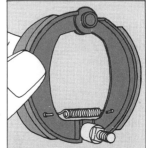

12 A reassembled shoe. Lightly grease the actuating pin and pivot collar before replacing

Bicycles Front forks

Checking and replacing bearings

If the handlebars turn with a harsh or clicking sound, the fork bearings need replacing.

The assembly below has bearing cups as an integral part of the cup housing fitted to the forks frame tube; another kind has separate cups sitting freely in the frame-tube housing.

Materials: ball bearings and bearing cups; grease.
Tools: spanner for handlebar centre bolt; thin-nosed pliers; spanner for locking-ring; hammer; long steel punch for bearing-cup removal; length of steel tube to fit over forks column; small steel punch; hide or plastic mallet if available.

Locking-ring
Lamp bracket
Adjustable bearing cup
Ball bearings
Integral bearing cup
Forks column
Forks frame tube
Ball bearings
Base bearing cup
Integral bearing cup
Front forks

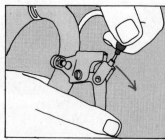

1 Apply the brakes. While releasing the lever, free the outer cable by withdrawing it from its stop in the head of the brake handle

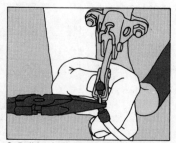

2 Pull back the outer cable to unhook the inner-cable nipple. With rod brakes, slacken the clevis adjusters and withdraw the rods (see p. 586)

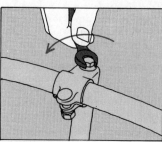

3 Undo the bolt in the centre of the handlebar stem anti-clockwise until it stands $\frac{1}{4}$ in. (6 mm), but no further, above the handlebars

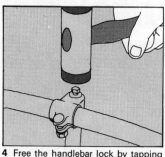

4 Free the handlebar lock by tapping down the centre bolt with a plastic mallet until it is flush with the top of the stem of the handlebars

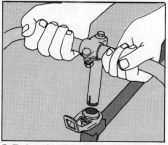

5 Twist the handlebars backwards and forwards, lifting them at the same time, until they are removed from the forks column

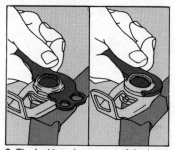

6 The locking-ring on top of the head bearing, which is either a hexagonal nut or a slotted C nut, can now be unscrewed with a suitable spanner

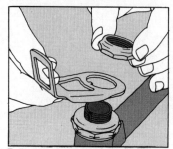

7 Remove the locking-ring, and the cycle-lamp bracket if one is fitted, to gain access to the adjustable bearing cup at the top of the column

8 Keeping the cycle upright and steady, carefully unscrew the top adjustable bearing cup in an anti-clockwise direction

9 Take out the ball bearings from the integral cup and clean both cups. If the bearings show signs of wear buy new ones of the same size *(continued)*

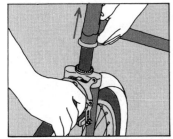

10 Lift the cycle frame off the forks tube. Take particular care not to disturb or lose the ball bearings in the lower race

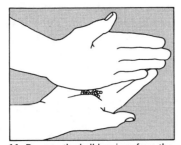

11 Remove the ball bearings from the lower race and wash them, with those from the upper race, in paraffin. Dry between the palms of the hands

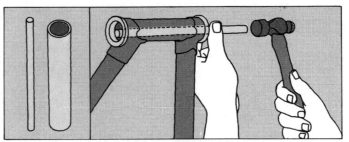

12 Two items are needed for removing and replacing bearing cups: a solid punch longer than the cycle-frame tube and a hollow tube, longer than the forks column, to fit over the column. Place the solid punch against the cup flange and hit with a hammer to expel either of the frame-fitted cups

13 Fit the new integral-type bearing cup into the cycle-frame tube. It must sit squarely to avoid causing damage to the frame

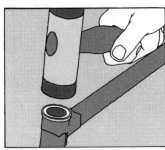

14 Use a hide or plastic mallet, or a hammer and hardwood block, to drive the bearing cup into the tube. Even seating is essential

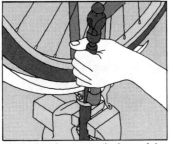

15 The bearing cup at the base of the front forks fits tightly over a shoulder on the column. Drive off the cup with a hammer and punch

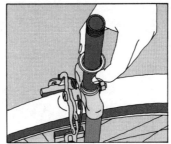

16 Clean the forks column, in particular the boss on which the bearing cup fits. Drop the new cup over the column and on to the boss

17 To fix the cup, slip the tubing, which should not be wide enough to slip into the bearing cup, over the column and tap with the mallet

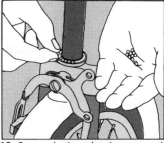

18 Grease the base bearing cup and replace the balls. If fitting new ones, check that they are correct in size and number

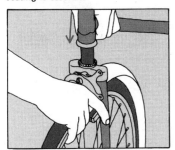

19 Grease the upper base bearing cup and lower the cycle frame over the forks column, taking care not to disturb the ball bearings

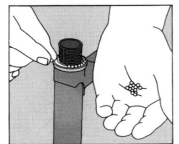

20 With the bearing cup on the upper fork greased, replace its ball bearings, again taking care to fit the right size and number of balls

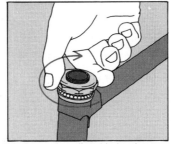

21 Screw the adjustable bearing cup on to the forks tube. Tighten until there is no more play and the fork bearings are moving freely

22 Replace the lamp bracket, with its tongue slotted in the column groove. Hold the adjustable cup firm and replace the locking-ring

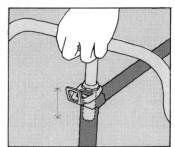

23 Replace the handlebars with at least $2\frac{1}{2}$ in. (65 mm) of their stem inside the forks column. Tighten the handlebar nut; replace the brakes

Bicycles Bottom bracket

Checking and replacing bearings

A worn bottom-bracket bearing gives a rough or grating sensation when turned. Replace the balls as soon as this is noticed, otherwise the rest of the assembly may be damaged.

The bearing has two cups, a spindle with cones, a lock-ring and ball bearings. The fixed right-hand cup, behind the chain wheel crank, slackens in a clockwise direction: the other cup, which is adjustable and held by a lock-ring, is slackened anti-clockwise. The bearings are generally, but not always, ¼ in. (6 mm) in diameter. Bottom-bracket spindles are not standard in length, so take the old parts along for comparison when buying replacements.

Materials: a replacement spindle; left and right-hand cups; bearings; grease.
Tools: hammer; hardwood block; thin punch; spanner for cotter-pin nuts; hide mallet; C spanner for bearing lock-ring; cone or peg spanner.

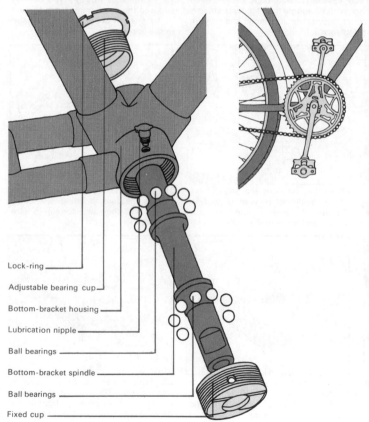

Lock-ring
Adjustable bearing cup
Bottom-bracket housing
Lubrication nipple
Ball bearings
Bottom-bracket spindle
Ball bearings
Fixed cup

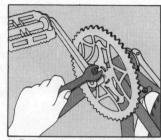

1 Remove the chain by freeing its connecting link. Undo the nuts of the two crank cotter pins and remove the nuts and their washers

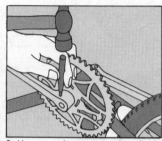

2 Hammer the cotter pins flush, using the wood block to avoid damaging the threads. Drive out each pin with a thin punch

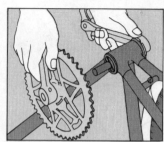

3 Take off the crank wheel. If it is tight, hold the other crank lever and twist the wheel off the bottom-bracket spindle

4 If the left-hand crank lever is tight, tap it off with a soft-headed hammer or mallet, striking the lever close to its centre boss

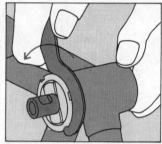

5 Use a C spanner, hooked into the notches of the lock-ring, to undo the ring. This unscrews in an anti-clockwise direction

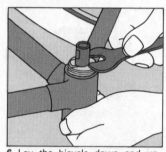

6 Lay the bicycle down and un-screw the adjustable cup. Hold the spindle against the cup as the cup is being removed

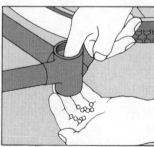

7 Draw out the spindle and cup, using one hand to catch the ball bearings. If any balls are stuck inside the hub, poke them free

8 Undo the fixed cup on the right-hand side of the bracket in a clock-wise direction. Remove the lubrica-tion nipple if one is fitted

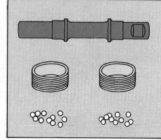

9 Examine the cones fixed to the spindle, the two cups and the ball bearings. Renew any parts that show signs of wear   *(continued)*

Bicycles Crank assembly

10 Refit the fixed cup and grease it. With a finger in the hole, replace the right number of bearings to sit evenly inside the cup

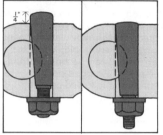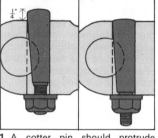

11 Grease the adjustable left-hand cup and replace the ball bearings. Place the shorter end of the spindle in position in the cup

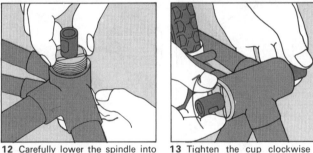

12 Carefully lower the spindle into the housing, making sure that the ball bearings at the other end are not disturbed. Screw the cup home

13 Tighten the cup clockwise to eliminate end play of the spindle, while still allowing it to revolve freely in the bearing

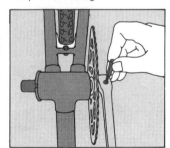

14 When the cup has been adjusted to its correct position, hold it with the spanner and tighten up the lock-ring to secure it

15 Refit the crank levers: the one with the chain wheel fits the longer right-hand side of the spindle. Replace the cotter pins

Adjusting and replacing cotter pins

A cotter pin needs adjusting or replacing if the crank lever is a loose fit on the spindle. This shows when riding if the lever drops forward slightly as it passes the upper vertical position.

Adjust by tapping the pin further in, filing it if necessary. If, after adjustment, the unthreaded end of the pin is about flush with the crank lever, so that at the other end the thread sticks out too far for the nut to be tightened, fit a new cotter pin.

Materials: new cotter pin (standard size), with washer and nut.
Tools: spanner to fit nut; file; hammer; hardwood block; vice.

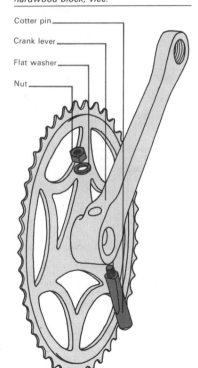

Cotter pin
Crank lever
Flat washer
Nut

1 A cotter pin should protrude about $\frac{1}{4}$ in. (6 mm) from the crank (left). The pin on the right cannot be adjusted and must be replaced

2 Supporting the crank with a block, hit the new pin with a hammer. Enough thread must be exposed to take the washer and fit the nut

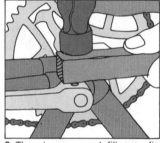

3 The pin may need filing to fit. When tapping it out, a hardwood block held between the pin and the hammer safeguards the thread

4 Score marks on the flat side of the cotter pin, caused by friction inside the crank when driving in the pin, will indicate where to file the pin

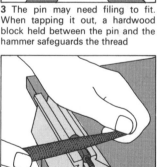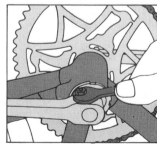

5 With the pin in a vice, flat face uppermost and just clear of the vice jaws, file evenly to remove the score marks. Refit the pin in the crank

6 Fit the washer and nut on the replaced pin, tightening the nut clockwise. Make sure the thread of the pin fits the nut

Bicycles Hub gear cables

Renewing a trigger-control gear cable

Hub gears are generally controlled by a trigger on the handlebars. This seldom gives trouble if oiled regularly, but the connecting cable may wear and need replacing. A new cable, complete with outer casing, can be bought from any cycle dealer. Fitting is straightforward if the stages are followed correctly. Oil the rear hub fortnightly—the oil hole is generally protected by a sprung cap—and occasionally oil the cable pulley.

Materials: new trigger-control cable; oil.
Tool: screwdriver.

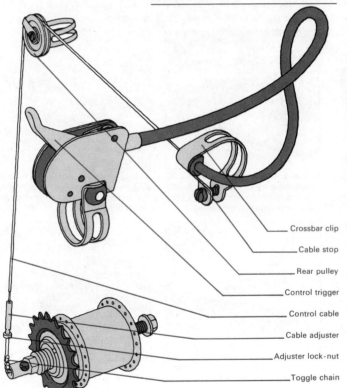

Crossbar clip

Cable stop

Rear pulley

Control trigger

Control cable

Cable adjuster

Adjuster lock-nut

Toggle chain

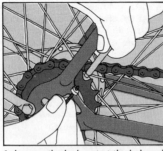

1 Loosen the lock-nut at the hub end and separate the cable adjuster and hub toggle chain

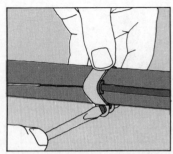

2 Use a screwdriver to loosen the crossbar bracket clip enough to let it turn on the bar

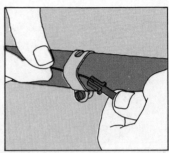

3 Take the gear cable and stop from the clip. The stop is split, so the cable can be slipped out

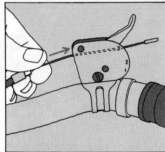

4 Push the inner cable towards the control trigger to free the nipple, and draw out the cable

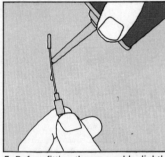

5 Before fitting the new cable, lightly lubricate the control end of the inner cable with bicycle oil

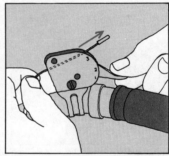

6 Depress the trigger to allow the cable nipple to be pushed through the front of the unit

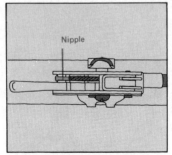

Nipple

7 Check that the cable runs over the trigger-control slot and that the nipple is located correctly

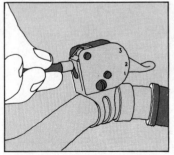

8 Slip the outer cable stop into the wider part of the slot, then slide the cable upwards

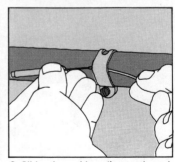

9 Slide the cable adjuster through the crossbar clip before fitting the outer cable stop *(continued)*

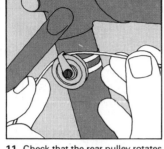

10 Fit the inner cable into the channel of the stop. Tighten the clip on to the stop against the crossbar

11 Check that the rear pulley rotates freely, apply oil, then feed the inner cable over it

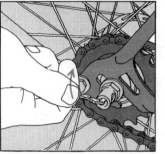

12 Tighten the toggle by cranking it at 90 degrees to the hub spindle. Finally, unwind half a turn

13 Set the trigger at the number two position before connecting the cable to the chain

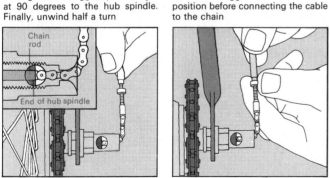
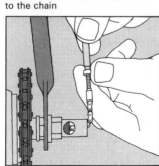

14 Turn the adjuster until the end of the chain rod is level with the end of the hub spindle

15 After adjustment, set the gear in third position and screw the adjuster lock-nut upwards

Renewing a twist-grip control gear cable

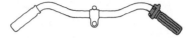

Twist-grip gear changes are nowadays often fitted to cycles which have Sturmey Archer hub gears. Before replacing a cable, the unit has to be removed from the handlebars; but in other respects the job is similar to replacing a trigger-control unit. Take particular note of how the components are positioned, as correct assembly is essential for smooth working.

Materials: twist-grip control cable.
Tool: screwdriver.

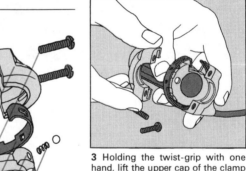

Lower cap
Upper cap
Securing screws
Cable retaining ring
Selector body
Selector ball and spring
Twist-grip

1 Undo the twist-grip's two securing screws one full turn and remove the grip from the handlebars

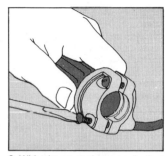

2 With the control removed, start dismantling it by taking out the two securing screws

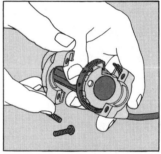

3 Holding the twist-grip with one hand, lift the upper cap of the clamp off the body of the grip

4 Slide the cap's lower half down the cable. Slip the cable out through the slot in the cap's side

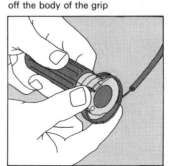

5 Take the cable retaining ring off the grip and slide the cable out through the slot in the ring

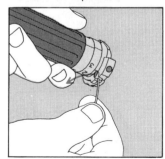

6 Remove the cable nipple from its housing. Fit the new cable and reassemble in the reverse order

Bicycles Derailleur gears

Replacing a gear cable

A Derailleur gear consists of a multi-sprocket freewheel unit and a carrier mechanism to direct the chain from one sprocket to another. Gear is changed with a control lever mounted on the frame tube. The most likely faults are a broken control cable and a badly adjusted guide mechanism. A new chain has to be riveted together—a job best left to a dealer.

Materials: new inner control cable; plastic protector sleeve for the cable.
Tools: small screwdriver; pliers; spanner to fit the cable clevis nut; screwdriver for the control lever centre bolt.

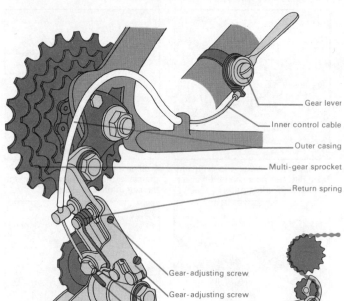

Gear lever
Inner control cable
Outer casing
Multi-gear sprocket
Return spring
Gear-adjusting screw
Gear-adjusting screw
Clevis nut
Protector sleeve
Chain wheel
Chain-wheel carrier

The chain runs over the sprocket and round the carrier wheels

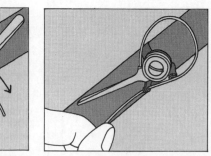

1 Remove the old cable, put the gear lever in the halfway position, and insert the new cable

2 Pull the lever right back—this avoids kinking the cable—and feed the cable through the guide eye

3 Feed the cable through the guide channel just above the bottom bracket of the cycle frame

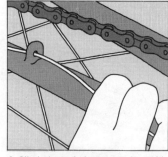

4 Slip it through the eye on the multi-gear sprocket side of the horizontal rear-fork stay

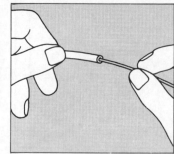

5 Slip the short length of outer casing over the cable. This casing will butt against the eye on the rear-fork stay

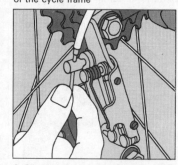

6 Slide the cable through the guide on the carrier mechanism. The casing must rest in the stop

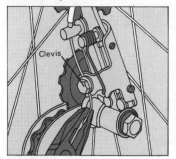

Clevis

7 Put the gear lever right forward and fit the cable to the clevis. Pull tight and tighten the clevis nut (arrowed)

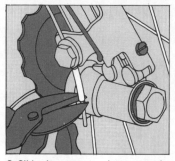

8 Slide the protector sleeve over the cable, up to the clevis, and cut off the surplus cable below it

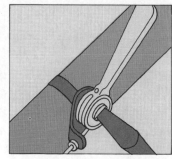

9 Check that the centre bolt on the gear lever is tight, so that the lever holds in any position

Adjusting a five-speed gear

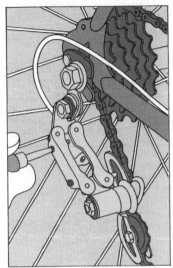

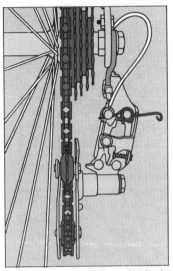

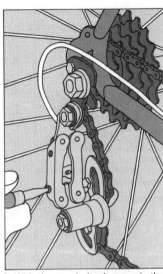

1 Put the gear in 'bottom'; screw in the top adjuster until the chain rides centrally on the largest sprocket without slipping over (overriding) the top

2 With the gear still in 'bottom', check the clearance between the carrier mechanism and the spokes. As little as $\frac{1}{8}$ in. (3 mm) is sufficient

3 With the gear in 'top', screw in the bottom adjuster until the chain rides the smallest sprocket centrally, but without overriding it

Removing a Derailleur-gear rear wheel

1 Holding the wheel with one hand to prevent it moving, loosen the wheel nuts with a spanner

2 Still holding the wheel, draw the guide mechanism back against the spring pressure and hold it there

3 Move the wheel forwards and lift it off between the upper and lower parts of the chain

Adjusting a ten-speed gear

By using the normal five-sprocket rear-hub gear and a double-chain wheel on the front, ten speeds are available. Adjust the rear carrier mechanism in the same way as a five-speed gear. The chain-guide mechanism at the front must be correctly set to prevent the chain overriding when the gear selection is made.

Tools: small screwdriver; steel straight-edge.

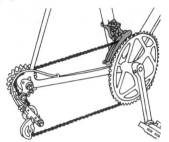

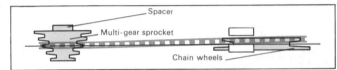

1 Check the alignment of the front and rear sprockets. The rear centre sprocket must line up centrally between the two front sprockets. If necessary, insert spacers between the hub and rear sprocket to give alignment

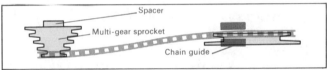

2 In this intermediate gear, with the chain riding on the rear outside sprocket and the front inside sprocket, see that the chain guide does not foul the chain while preventing it overriding the chain wheel

3 Two screws on the top of the chain-guide mechanism provide for adjustment of the guide

4 Turn each screw until the chain does not override the sprockets and is free of the guide

Bicycles Freewheel sprockets

Replacing a sprocket

Though it is possible to dismantle a freewheel sprocket, spare parts are difficult to obtain. If the sprocket starts to slip—the first sign of failure—it must be replaced. The sprocket also has to be removed for replacement of a wheel spoke on the gear side of the hub. In both cases a sprocket extractor is needed; as there are patterns to suit the several different types of freewheel unit, take the wheel to the shop when buying one. If a new sprocket is needed, choose one with the same number of teeth as the sprocket being replaced.

Materials: new freewheel sprocket.
Tools: wheel-nut spanner; sprocket extractor; vice or spanner to fit extractor nut.

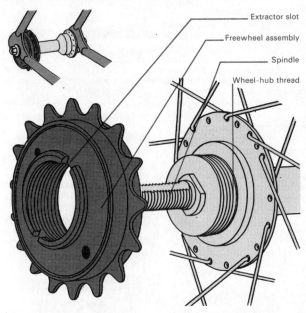

Extractor slot
Freewheel assembly
Spindle
Wheel-hub thread

TYPES OF SPROCKET EXTRACTORS

1 Take off the nuts and remove the wheel from the frame. Secure the wheel spindle in a vice, freewheel upwards

2 Place the sprocket extractor over the spindle and make sure its pegs engage in the slots of the freewheel unit

3 With the extractor in position, screw one of the wheel nuts down the spindle until it touches the extractor

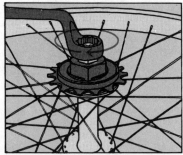

4 Tighten the wheel nut with a spanner to the same tightness as is needed to hold the wheel in the cycle frame

5 Take the wheel from the vice, turn it over, then tighten the jaws of the vice on to the extractor tool

6 Grip the wheel rim and turn the wheel anti-clockwise just enough to loosen the gear unit on the wheel-hub thread

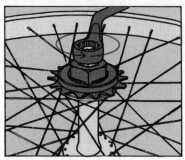

7 Remove the wheel, turn it over and grip the spindle in the vice. Undo the wheel nut above the extractor

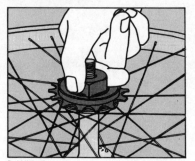

8 With the nut removed, use the extractor to unscrew the freewheel unit so that it can be lifted off the hub

9 Fit the new freewheel sprocket and tighten it by hand. The normal action of pedalling will tighten it fully

Bicycles Fixed wheels

Bicycles Pumps

Removing and replacing a fixed wheel

On racing cycles fitted with a fixed-wheel instead of a freewheel sprocket, the cranks and pedals are always rotating when the cycle is moving. The sprocket screws on to the hub and is held there by a lock-ring. The ring tightens anti-clockwise, so preventing the sprocket from unscrewing because of backward pressure against the pedals while slowing down. One of the many jobs for which a sprocket must be removed is replacement of a damaged wheel spoke on the sprocket side of the hub.

Materials: new sprocket and lock-ring.
Tools: hammer; punch; chain-tool sprocket re-mover; C spanner for lock-ring.

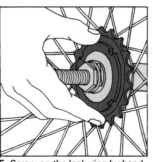
Hub
Sprocket thread
Lock-ring thread
Sprocket
Lock-ring

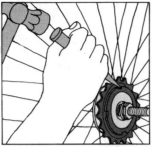
1 Use a C spanner, or a hammer and punch, to undo the lock-ring in a clockwise direction

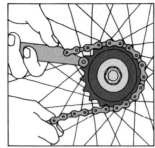
2 Hook a chain tool round the sprocket, the head between two teeth. Unscrew anti-clockwise

3 Once the sprocket has been loosened on the hub threads, un-screw by hand

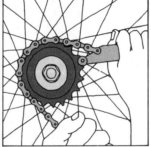
4 First screw the new sprocket on by hand, then use the chain tool to tighten it fully

5 Screw on the lock-ring by hand, with the boss facing the hub and against the sprocket

6 Hook the C spanner into the slots of the lock-ring and tighten the ring anti-clockwise

Fitting a new washer

1 Pull out the pump handle and unscrew the threaded cap

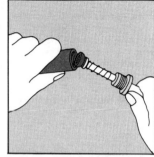
2 Remove the complete plunger assembly from the pump body

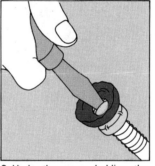
3 Undo the screw holding the washer to the pump shaft

4 Soften the new washer by working oil into it with the fingers

5 Replace the backing-plate and washer, convex sides together

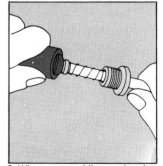
6 When reassembling, twist the washer into the barrel at an angle

Bicycles Coaster hubs

Renewing the bearings

Coaster hubs—or back-pedalling brake hubs as they are more commonly called —seldom give trouble. The freewheel mechanism inside the hub is sturdily made, but the bearings and cones may occasionally need replacing. This is a fairly easy job once the hub has been stripped. The main difference between coaster-hub bearings and conventional bearings is that the ball bearings of the former are caged while those in conventional bearings are loose.

Materials: new ball-bearing cages; bearing cones; new brake mechanism if the present one is worn.
Tools: hammer; punch; C spanner for locking; tube to fit over the drive-clutch boss; screwdriver; hardwood block.

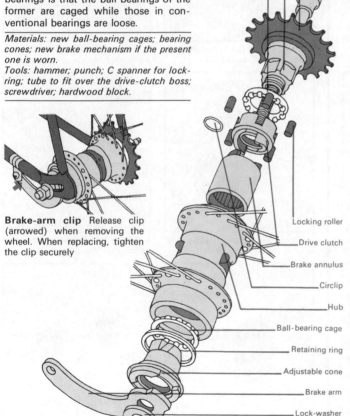

Brake-arm clip Release clip (arrowed) when removing the wheel. When replacing, tighten the clip securely

Spindle
Fixed cone
Sprocket
Freewheel mechanism
Ball-bearing cage

Locking roller
Drive clutch
Brake annulus
Circlip
Hub
Ball-bearing cage
Retaining ring
Adjustable cone
Brake arm
Lock-washer
Lock-ring

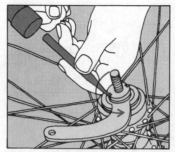

1 Use a C spanner, or a hammer and punch, to loosen and remove the lock-ring from the shaft

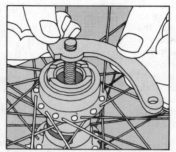

2 Remove the brake arm from the slots in the adjustable cone head, tapping the arm free if it is tight

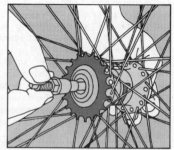

3 Hold the adjustable cone firm and unscrew the spindle, drawing it out of the hub as you unscrew it

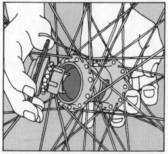

4 With the spindle removed, lift the sprocket and freewheel mechanism from the hub as a single unit

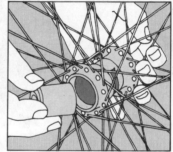

5 Tilt the open end of the hub towards your hand and collect the brake annulus and lock mechanism

6 Tilt the hub the opposite way and empty out the adjustable cone from the other end of the hub

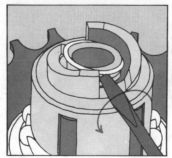

7 To start renewing bearings on the freewheel side, lift the circlip off the drive clutch with a screwdriver

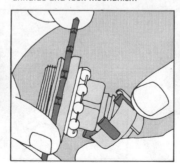

8 Slide the drive clutch off the boss, taking care not to lose any of the five locking rollers that may drop out

9 Lift the ball cage, which is part of the freewheel mechanism, off the cone. Check the cone for wear *(continued)*

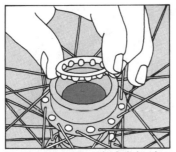

10 With a screwdriver handle, tap out the other ball cage and retaining ring from inside the hub

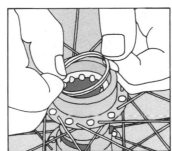

11 Clean and grease the hub-bearing cup and fit the new ball cage with the ball bearings towards the cup

12 Fit a new retaining ring, recessed side away from the cage. Tap in with a hammer and hardwood block

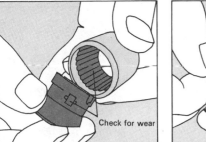

13 If the brake annulus grooves or lock mechanism are worn, refit a complete new brake mechanism

Check for wear

14 Grease the freewheel-mechanism cone and roller slots. Fit a new ball cage and refit the rollers

15 Slide the drive clutch over the freewheel-mechanism boss, each slot locating over a roller

16 Place the sprocket face down. Tap the circlip into its groove with a hammer and tube

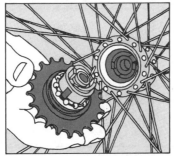

17 Refit the mechanism to the hub so that the clutch driving dogs engage with those on the annulus

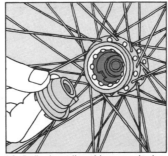

18 Refit the adjustable cone, its key in the annulus keyway. Screw in the spindle and adjust the bearings

Fitting new grips

Most handlebar grips are made from plastic or rubber. It is sometimes possible to slide the old grips off, but if they are firmly stuck to the handles they must be cut away. Use a knife to cut rubber grips, a small hacksaw to cut the harder plastic ones. Some plastic grips are in the form of a spiral: by twisting the grip one way, the spirals will open enabling it to be fitted easily. Rubber grips are stuck to the handles.

Materials: new handlebar grips; rubber solution.
Tools: junior hacksaw or a sharp knife; emery cloth.

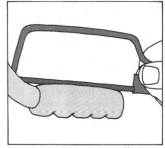

1 Use a hacksaw to cut off plastic handlebar grips, taking care not to scratch the chrome

2 Use a sharp knife to split a rubber grip down the middle; then peel it back off the handlebar

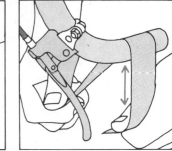

3 Clean old adhesive off the bars with emery cloth to just less than the length of the new grip

4 Squeeze rubber solution into the end of the grip. This helps it to slide on easily and holds it firm

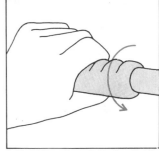

5 Twist the grip on to the bar, finishing with the finger grooves under the bar. Wipe off surplus solution

Bicycles Pedals

Renewing the bearings

Pedal bearings wear in time if not oiled regularly. In use, their action begins to feel rough to the feet.

A pedal has a spindle with a fixed cone at the inner end, an adjustable cone, a lock-washer and a lock-nut. Because the ball bearings sit in cups which are an integral part of the pedal, new pedals must be fitted if the cups become worn.

Materials: medium-grade grease; new components as necessary.
Tools: pedal spanner; spanner for the lock-nut; screwdriver; vice.

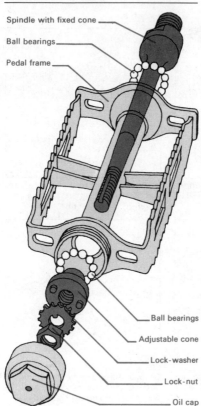

Spindle with fixed cone
Ball bearings
Pedal frame
Ball bearings
Adjustable cone
Lock-washer
Lock-nut
Oil cap

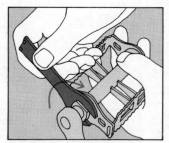

1 Remove the pedals from the crank levers. The right-hand pedal is undone as shown; turn the other pedal spindle the opposite way

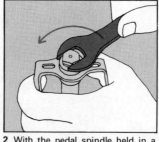

2 With the pedal spindle held in a vice above the threaded end, remove the oil cap from the outside plate with a spanner

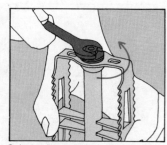

3 Immediately below the oil cap is the outer bearing lock-nut. Remove this nut and the lock-washer beneath the lock-nut

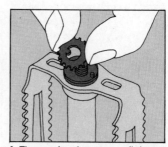

4 The washer has a peg fitting a groove in the spindle and serrations that lock over two pegs on the face of the adjustable cone

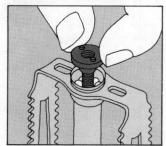

5 Unscrew the adjustable cone, using its two pegs as lever points for a rigid edge if the cone has been secured more than finger-tight

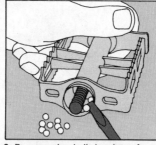

6 Remove the ball bearings from the outer cup, holding the spindle in place to secure the rest of the ball bearings at the other end

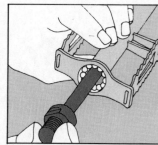

7 Withdraw the spindle and take the ball bearings from the inner cup. Count the balls from both cups as a guide to replacement

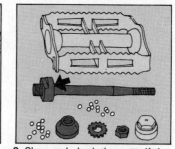

8 Clean and check the parts. If the fixed cone is worn, replace the spindle. Renew the balls if they are pitted or rusted

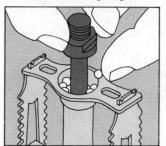

9 Grease the inner cup, partly insert the spindle, and replace the balls. Push the spindle home and invert the pedal

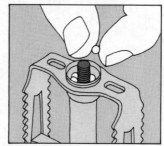

10 Grease the outer cup and refit the other ball bearings in the cup, making sure that they fit snugly and evenly round the spindle

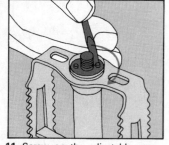

11 Screw on the adjustable cone, tightening until the pedal is stiff. Then ease it off slightly until the pedal turns freely

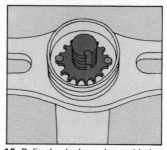

12 Refit the lock-washer, with its serrations locked against the pegs of the adjustable cone. Replace the lock-nut and oil cap

Replacing the rubbers

Pedal rubbers need replacing when they become slippery to the feet. Sets of four rubber replacement blocks can be bought from any cycle dealer. Though the pedal shown here has been removed from the cycle, the job can be done just as easily with the pedals still fixed to the crank levers.

Materials: set of pedal rubbers; rubber solution.
Tools: spanner to fit lubrication cap; two spanners to fit pedal end plate nuts, or one spanner and a vice; fine emery cloth.

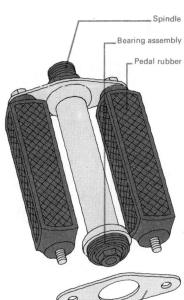
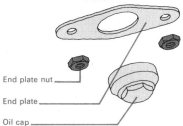

- Spindle
- Bearing assembly
- Pedal rubber
- End plate nut
- End plate
- Oil cap

1 Unscrew the lubrication cap and an end nut on each spindle. A vice or second spanner may help

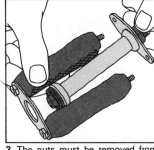

2 The nuts must be removed from the same end so that one plate and the pedal centre can be withdrawn

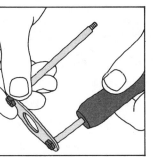

3 Remove the old rubbers and clean rust or rubber particles from the spindles with emery cloth

4 Squeeze rubber solution into each rubber bore to lubricate when fitting and to secure the rubbers when set

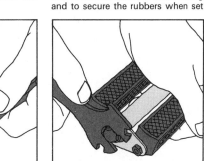

5 Fit the new pedal rubbers firmly against the end plate and square with each other

6 Reassemble the pedal, tightening the end plate nuts and finally screwing back the oil cap

Replacing a tape

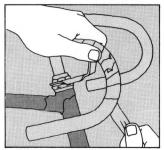

1 Remove attachments such as brake levers from the handlebars and peel off the old tape

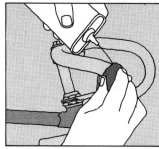

2 Clean dirt and any old adhesive off the handlebars. Petrol is an effective cleaning fluid

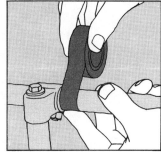

3 Start retaping at the centre of the handlebars—square at first, then at a slight angle to the bar

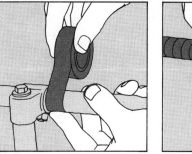

4 Press the tape into place as it is wound. Half cover each coil to get a flat even surface

5 Avoid creases and ridged edges when winding round curves, if necessary stretching the tape

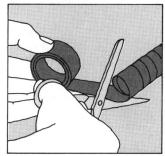

6 Overlap the handlebars by about $\frac{1}{4}$ in. (6 mm). Cut off neatly and tuck the surplus tape inside the tubing

Bicycles Mudguards

Fitting new mudguards

Mudguards on sports cycles are generally made of plastic; those on roadsters are usually steel. The method of fitting is basically the same; but whereas the stays on a plastic mudguard (shown in the picture sequence) fit lugs on the sides of the cycle frame, those on a steel mudguard (below) are usually secured on the wheel spindles inside the washers of the wheel nuts.

Materials: pair of mudguards to suit the wheel diameter.
Tools: spanners to fit mudguard nuts; small hacksaw; pliers; screwdriver.

STEEL MUDGUARDS

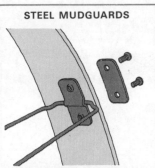

1 A steel guard has a single one-piece stay held on the inside by a plate and bolts

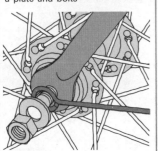

2 The stay fits under the wheel-hub nuts, with a washer between the nut and stay

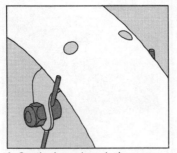

1 On plastic mudguards the stays are fixed to the guard brackets by small clevis pins and nuts

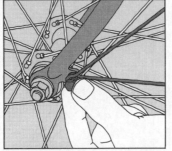

5 Fit the guard stays on each side to the fork bolt and screw the bolt finger-tight into its lug

9 Now slide the rear mudguard through the forks. Take off the brake caliper if more room is needed

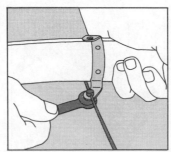

2 Fit the pins to the brackets, with the nuts on the outside and the stay holes on the inside

6 With the clevis nuts loosened, adjust the mudguard to get it parallel with the tyre. Tighten all nuts

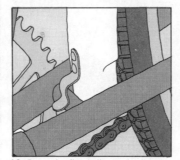

10 Press the fixed clip on the bottom of the guard over the tube between the horizontal forks

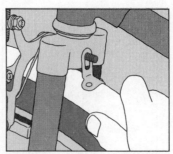

3 Slide the front guard through the forks until the clip fits on the bolt at the rear of the forks

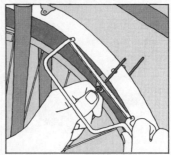

7 Cut two-thirds of the way through the protruding stays about 1 in. (25 mm) above each clevis pin

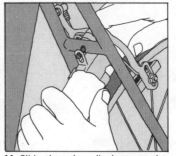

11 Slide the other clip between the vertical frame tubes. The clip eye fits the brake-caliper centre bolt

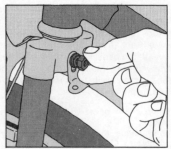

4 Fit a flat washer and a star lock-washer to the bolt. Screw on the nut but do not tighten yet

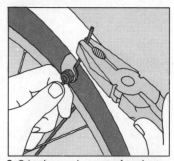

8 Grip the surplus part of each stay with a pair of pliers and bend at the cut to make a clean break

12 Tighten the nut, adjust and tighten the stays, then bend the clip ends round the mudguard edges

Bicycles Dynamos

Checking a tyre-driven unit

A conventional tyre-driven dynamo must be correctly positioned if it is to work well without wearing the tyre unduly. If, after adjustment, it fails to work, test both bulbs with a battery and test-leads. If these are sound, test the dynamo and cycle wiring and clean the bulb contacts.

Materials: bulbs and wire, as necessary.
Tools: spanner for dynamo bracket bolts; small screwdriver; test lamp made up from 6v bulb, bulb holder, bell wire and crocodile clips; ruler; straight-edge; fine emery cloth; battery.

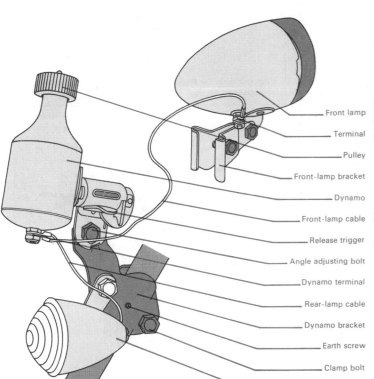

Front lamp
Terminal
Pulley
Front-lamp bracket
Dynamo
Front-lamp cable
Release trigger
Angle adjusting bolt
Dynamo terminal
Rear-lamp cable
Dynamo bracket
Earth screw
Clamp bolt
Rear lamp

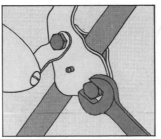

1 Loosen the two clamp bolts on the dynamo bracket, and the earth screw, just enough to allow the dynamo unit to be moved

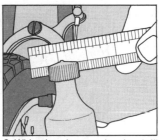

2 With the dynamo in the 'off' position, clearance between tyre and dynamo pulley should be ⅝ in. (16 mm). Adjust if necessary

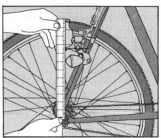

3 An imaginary centreline on the dynamo body should align with the hub centre. Adjust at the angle-adjusting bolt

4 Raise or lower the dynamo so that the centre of the pulley contacts the tyre at a point slightly above the centre of the tyre wall

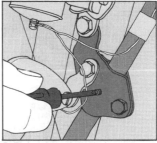

5 Tighten the clamp bolts and earth screw. If the unit still does not work, undo the leads on the two terminals at the base of the dynamo

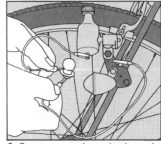

6 Connect one lamp lead to the bracket, the other to the dynamo terminal. The bulb should light when the wheel is spun with the dynamo on

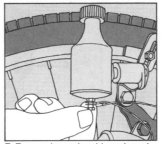

7 To test the cycle wiring, clean the terminals on the front and rear lamps. Refit the two leads to the terminal at the base of the dynamo

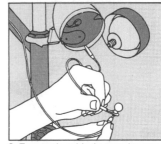

8 Test each cable in turn by connecting it to the test lamp and earthing the lamp's other wire. Test by spinning the wheel

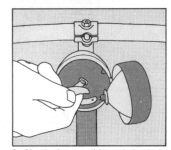

9 Check the condition of the bulb contacts in both lamps. If they are dirty, rub the contact area with fine emery cloth

Bicycles Dynohub lighting

Testing and cleaning

A Dynohub generator is built into the front or rear-wheel hub. The unit should never be dismantled; this causes demagnetisation, even if the armature is removed for only a short period. If the unit includes batteries, remove them as soon as they are exhausted, otherwise they may cause corrosion.

When tracing a fault, check the bulbs first with a battery and test lamp. Check that all contacts are clean. If the unit still does not work, check the Dynohub, the switch contacts and the wiring. When testing the wiring, check that the switch is on.

Materials: bulbs, cables, batteries, as necessary. Tools: spanner for terminal nuts; test lamp made up of bulb, bulb holder, bell wire and crocodile clips; fine emery cloth.

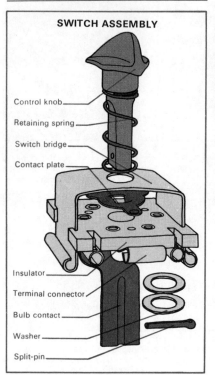

SWITCH ASSEMBLY

Control knob

Retaining spring

Switch bridge

Contact plate

Insulator

Terminal connector

Bulb contact

Washer

Split-pin

1 Clean all terminals and ensure that their shanks are fitted with plastic sleeves to prevent shorting

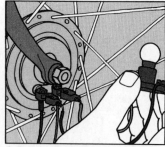

2 To test the Dynohub, connect the test leads as shown. The bulb should light when the wheel is spun

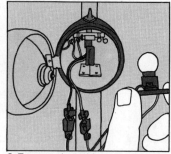

3 To test the wiring, connect the front and rear lamps in turn to the test leads and spin the wheel

4 To dismantle the switch unit so that the switch contacts can be cleaned, withdraw the small split-pin

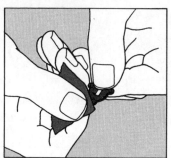

5 Lift up the switch control knob to free the three-point contact plate. Clean the plate with emery cloth

6 Lay the plate on the insulated terminal block with the pips facing downwards. Reassemble the unit

Wiring for plastic lamps

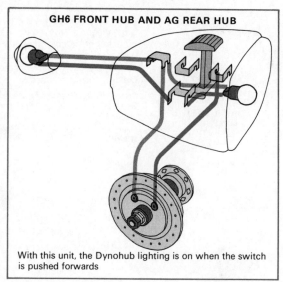

GH6 FRONT HUB AND AG REAR HUB

With this unit, the Dynohub lighting is on when the switch is pushed forwards

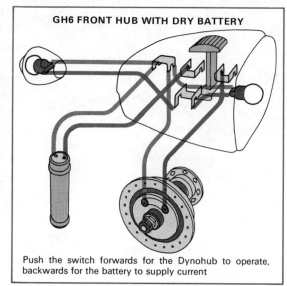

GH6 FRONT HUB WITH DRY BATTERY

Push the switch forwards for the Dynohub to operate, backwards for the battery to supply current

Wiring for metal lamps

AG REAR HUB WITH FILTER-SWITCH UNIT

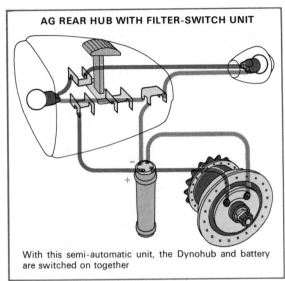

With this semi-automatic unit, the Dynohub and battery are switched on together

AG REAR HUB WITH DRY BATTERY

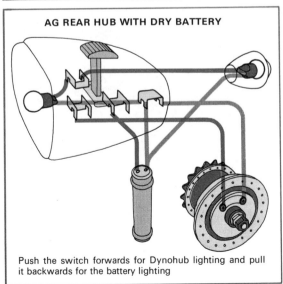

Push the switch forwards for Dynohub lighting and pull it backwards for the battery lighting

GH6 FRONT HUB AND AG REAR HUB

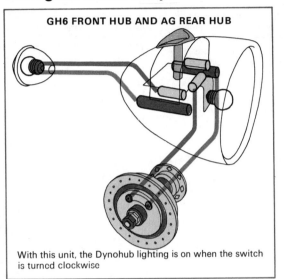

With this unit, the Dynohub lighting is on when the switch is turned clockwise

GH6 FRONT HUB WITH DRY BATTERY

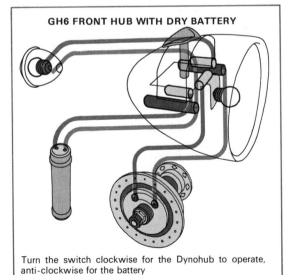

Turn the switch clockwise for the Dynohub to operate, anti-clockwise for the battery

AG REAR HUB WITH FILTER-SWITCH UNIT

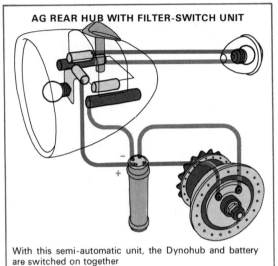

With this semi-automatic unit, the Dynohub and battery are switched on together

AG REAR HUB WITH DRY BATTERY

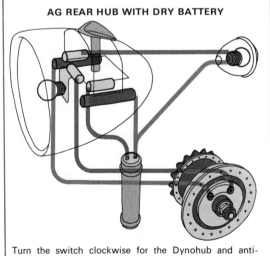

Turn the switch clockwise for the Dynohub and anti-clockwise for the battery

Boats

Laying up a boat for the winter

Before storing a boat for the winter, make sure it is thoroughly dry. Check that all the drain passages through the ribs of the vessel are clear. Remove any congealed dirt that might block the exit path for water when the boat is stored.

The pre-storage treatment depends on the construction of the boat. Some clinker hulls are designed so that the slight swelling of the wood when it is in the water seals the joints between the planks: do not try to fill any cracks that become apparent when the boat is out of the water. Other boats, however, have sealer or caulking between the planks. Examine this carefully. If it is unsound or soft, dig it out and spread in new sealer (see p. 609).

Check under the deck planking—especially when it encloses a space where air cannot circulate. The wood is likely to rot in a damp, airless atmosphere. Always cover a boat for the winter. Lay blocks of wood on the deck to raise the covering off the boat to prevent sweating. If possible, use a boat cover ready-made to fit the boat. However, if such a cover is not available, use black polythene sheeting. Make sure that it is a loose fit but clear of the hull and anchored to the ground.

In the spring

Check the boat carefully before it is first used after being laid up. Rigging, especially, should be checked at the beginning of the season—and at least once more during the year.

Make sure that all deck and rigging fittings are tight. If a screw or bolt turns easily, it is likely that the threads have become damaged. Fit a new one.

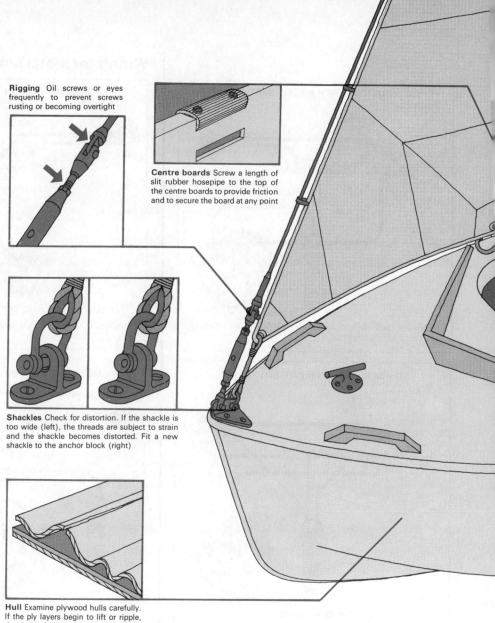

Rigging Oil screws or eyes frequently to prevent screws rusting or becoming overtight

Centre boards Screw a length of slit rubber hosepipe to the top of the centre boards to provide friction and to secure the board at any point

Shackles Check for distortion. If the shackle is too wide (left), the threads are subject to strain and the shackle becomes distorted. Fit a new shackle to the anchor block (right)

Hull Examine plywood hulls carefully. If the ply layers begin to lift or ripple, the timber is likely to rot underneath. Replace if necessary (see p. 602)

TREATING WORN SURFACES

The paint or varnish on a boat is likely to wear rapidly at the gunwales, where passengers get in and out frequently, and at the seat and the toe boards. Such areas can be treated without revarnishing or painting the whole boat. Rub each coat down with water-soaked abrasive paper.

Materials: wet-and-dry 400-grade abrasive paper; paint or varnish.
Tool: paintbrush.

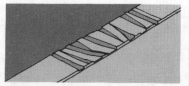

1 Areas that become worn or 'scuffed' should be treated to prevent damp getting into the grain of the timber

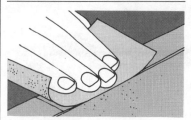

2 Rub the surface down with dry 400-grade abrasive paper. Feather and taper the edges of the damaged area

3 Apply several coats of paint or varnish. Extend each coat over the adjacent finish at each end of the worn area

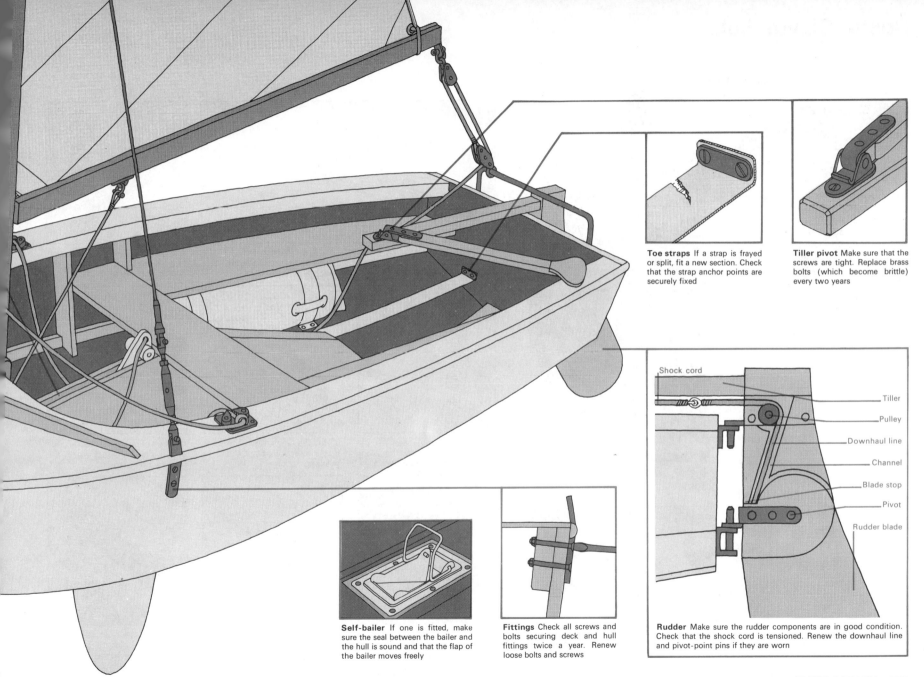

Toe straps If a strap is frayed or split, fit a new section. Check that the strap anchor points are securely fixed

Tiller pivot Make sure that the screws are tight. Replace brass bolts (which become brittle) every two years

Shock cord

Tiller

Pulley

Downhaul line

Channel

Blade stop

Pivot

Rudder blade

Self-bailer If one is fitted, make sure the seal between the bailer and the hull is sound and that the flap of the bailer moves freely

Fittings Check all screws and bolts securing deck and hull fittings twice a year. Renew loose bolts and screws

Rudder Make sure the rudder components are in good condition. Check that the shock cord is tensioned. Renew the downhaul line and pivot-point pins if they are worn

Boats Clinker hulls

Replacing a damaged plank

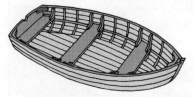

The neatest way to repair a damaged plank is to cut out the part which has been holed and fit a new piece of matching wood. If the damaged section is long, curved or twisted, engage a professional boatbuilder.

Materials: wood to match the damaged plank; rivet nails and roves; synthetic resin glue; glass-paper; paint.
Tools: keyhole and tenon saws; drill; punch; hollow punch; chisel; plane; hammer; cutting pliers.

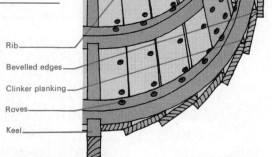

- Joint cover
- New plank
- Gunwale
- Rib
- Bevelled edges
- Clinker planking
- Roves
- Keel

SECURING A RIVET NAIL WITH A ROVE

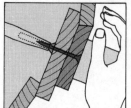

1 Insert the nail. While someone holds an iron block at its head, drive on the rove with a hammer and hollow punch

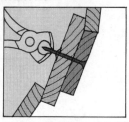

2 With cutting pliers, remove the point of the nail to leave just $\frac{1}{16}$ in. (2 mm) projecting above the head of the rove

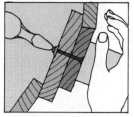

3 Lightly hammer the end of the nail to burr it over. Do not use force, which would result in bending the nail in the wood

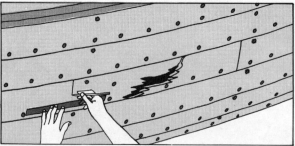

1 Mark the section to be cut. Draw the lines midway between the ribs of the hull—so that the new plank can be secured to them—and about 12–18 in. (305–455 mm) from each end of the hole

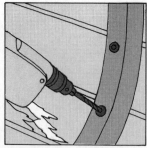

2 Inside the boat, drill and punch out the rivet nails holding the damaged plank to the ribs

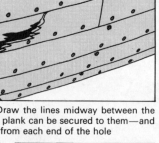

4 Tilt the keyhole saw to cut through the part of the plank hidden by the overlap above

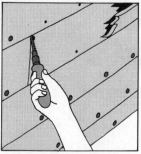

5 Pull the plank down and away from the section above. Clean the overlapping edge

6 Use a chisel to square the ends of the planks against which the new section is to fit

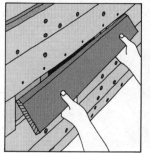

8 Cut the new section. Bevel its top outer edge. Make sure its ends fit the existing planks

9 Glue all the meeting surfaces of the plank and fit it. Drill and fix three rivet nails at each end

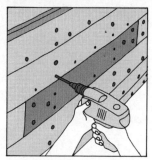

10 Follow the rivet line of the rib and drill holes. With help, fix all nails and roves securely

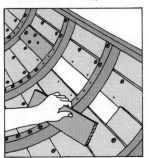

3 Drill ½ in. (13 mm) holes just inside the lines. Use a keyhole saw to cut down the plank

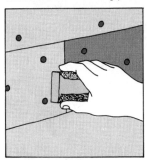

7 Cut two joint covers to fit exactly between the ribs. Glue and rivet them to existing planks

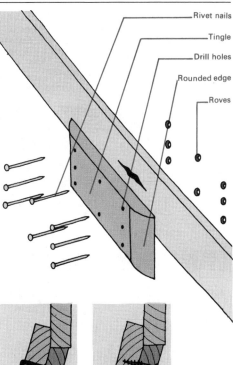

Rivet nails

Tingle

Drill holes

Rounded edge

Roves

Nailing In light planking, use copper nails and clench them over inside the boat

Screwing Use brass screws to secure hard-wood planking thicker than ½ in. (13 mm)

Patching a damaged hull

A simpler but less attractive way to repair a split in a plank is to fix a patch of matching wood—called a tingle—over it. If the damage is on a curved section, fix canvas between the hull and the tingle.

Materials: wood to match the hull; synthetic resin glue; canvas; jointing compound; copper nails; brass screws; rivets and roves; glass-paper.
Tools: saw; plane or Surform; drill; screwdriver; light hammer; iron block; hollow punch; cutting pliers.

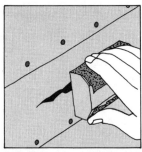

1 Remove paint or varnish with glass-paper about 3 in. (75 mm) round the hole. Cut a tingle

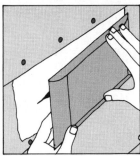

4 When the glue is tacky, position the tingle and press it firmly against the plank

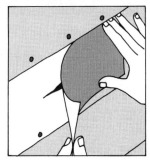

7 Place the canvas over the hole and press it firmly. Coat the surface with jointing compound

2 With the tingle in a vice, round off three edges—but not the one which meets the plank above

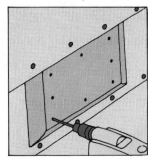

5 Drill holes smaller than the nails or screws to be used. Secure the tingle with screws or nails

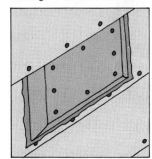

8 Position the tingle and drill undersize holes. Secure with nails, screws or rivets and roves

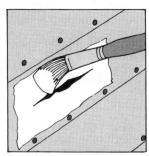

3 Coat the damaged plank and the meeting surface of the tingle with synthetic resin glue

6 If the damage is on a curve, cut a canvas patch. Coat it and the plank with jointing compound

9 Remove surplus compound and canvas when the tingle is tightened against the plank

11 Glass-paper dried glue. Paint or varnish the new timber to match the surrounding area

Boats Plywood hulls

Repairing a hole or small crack

Inspect a plywood hull regularly for signs of blistering. If water enters and freezes in the ends of the grain, the wood may become cracked and distorted.

When renewing plywood use only the correct grade of wood—BSS 1088. Any other type will be unsuitable. Fit the new plywood either to a rib in the hull or to a jointing cover fixed inside the boat (see p. 600). Make sure that the grain ends are sealed with polyurethane paint or varnish.

Glass fibre can also be used to repair plywood cracks, but this method is not advisable for racing dinghies, where balance is critical to the boat's performance.

Materials: BSS 1088 plywood or veneers; $\frac{3}{4}$ in. (20 mm) brass nails; synthetic resin glue.
Tools: saws; plane or Surform; hammer; chisel; pincers; file; drill.

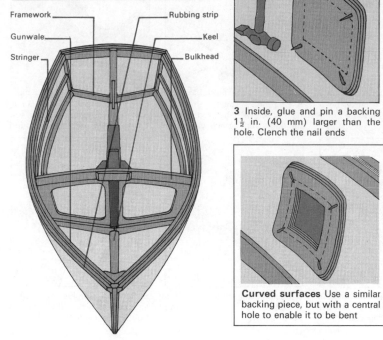

Framework — Rubbing strip
Gunwale — Keel
Stringer — Bulkhead

1 Drill four holes. Cut round their outside edges with a keyhole saw to remove the damaged area

2 If the plywood has separated, cut until sound edges are reached. Bevel them outwards with a file

3 Inside, glue and pin a backing $1\frac{1}{2}$ in. (40 mm) larger than the hole. Clench the nail ends

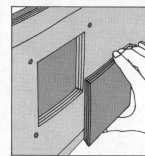

4 Cut a patch, bevel the edges to match the hole, and glue and pin it against the backing piece

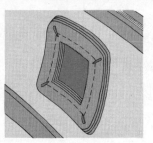

Curved surfaces Use a similar backing piece, but with a central hole to enable it to be bent

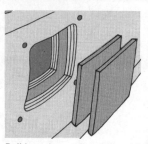

Build up the patch outside with glued veneers. Pin through the final layer into the backing piece

Renewing a plywood section

When the damage to a plywood hull is extensive, or when even a small crack is caused near one of the rubbing strips, remove the strip with the damaged plywood. To make a good joint, cut the old and the new rubbing strip at an angle of about 1 in 7—that is, with the length of the cut about seven times the thickness of the strip. This is known as scarf jointing.

Materials: BSS 1088 plywood or veneers; $\frac{3}{4}$ in. (20 mm) brass nails; synthetic resin glue.
Tools: saws; plane or Surform; hammer; pincers; file.

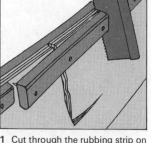

1 Cut through the rubbing strip on both sides of the damage. Take care not to cut the inside frame

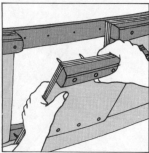

2 Cut round the hole with a keyhole saw and remove the plywood. Bevel the edges outwards

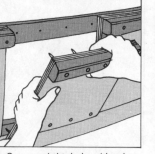

3 If there is no rib or stringer to which the patch can be nailed, fit jointing covers (see p. 600)

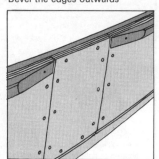

4 Cut and bevel the patch. Glue and nail it in place. Cut the rubbing strip to a 1-in-7 angle

5 Cut a new piece of rubbing strip to fit. Glue and nail it through the plywood to the inside frame

Boats Veneered hulls

Replacing a layer of veneer

When a hull is made from veneer or thin plywood bonded with synthetic resin glue, repairs can be made to one or two layers without cutting completely through the hull. Make sure when obtaining new veneers that they match the original, and take care to fit them so that the grain runs in the opposite direction to that of the layer underneath.

Materials: veneers; synthetic resin glue.
Tools: dovetail saw; sharp knife; chisel; hammer; pliers; screwdriver; trigger stapler; scraper; straight-edge; sander.

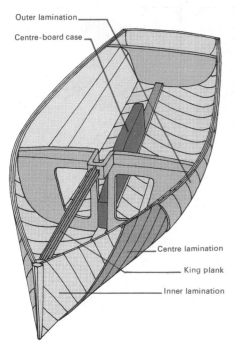

Outer lamination
Centre-board case
Centre lamination
King plank
Inner lamination

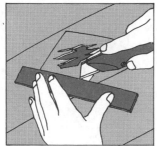

1 Mark a diamond shape round the damaged area. Cut through one layer with a sharp knife

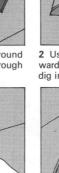

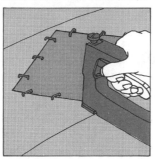

3 Scrape the inside edges clean. If a second layer has to be removed, cut it smaller than the top layer

5 With a trigger stapler, punch staples round the edge of the final patch; or secure with weights

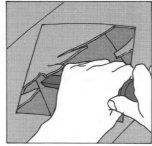

2 Use a chisel, bevel side downwards, to strip the veneer. Do not dig into the lower layers

4 Cut veneers and glue them with their grains in the opposite direction to the one underneath

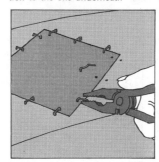

6 When the glue sets, remove the staples. Sand the patch and wipe with hot water to close staple holes

Repairing a hole

When a veneered hull has been holed, it should be repaired in three layers. Cut through the damaged area completely; but on the outside and inside cut the layers larger than the hole. When the new veneers are glued in place, with their edges staggered, the repair will be strong and waterproof. If, when the glue has set, there is a small gap round the outside layer, fill with marine-resin glue.

Materials: veneers; marine-resin glue.
Tools: knife; chisel.

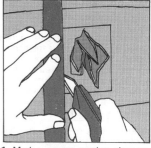

1 Mark a square section close to the hole. Use a knife to cut out the section marked

2 Inside, cut out a layer larger than the hole and with two V-shaped ends. Trim the edges

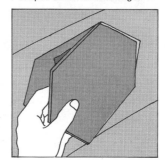

4 Glue the outside patch with its grain running in the same direction as the existing layer

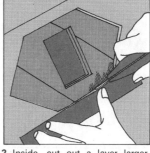

3 Outside, cut a larger layer. Check the grain of each veneer and cut new matching pieces

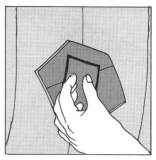

5 When the first layer is set, glue the square veneer. When it sets, glue in the inside layer

Boats Polystyrene hulls

Filling a surface scar

Polystyrene hulls are robust, but surface damage can be caused by dragging the boat over a rough shingle beach, or even by using rope instead of webbing to tie the boat to a trailer. In most cases it is unlikely that the damage will need anything more than surface filling to restore the smooth face of the polystyrene. To prevent further damage, repair the scar before using the boat again.

Materials: exterior-quality Polyfilla; emulsion paint; fine glass-paper; clean rag.
Tools: plaster knife; paintbrush; sanding block.

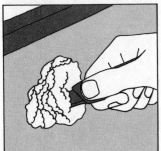

1 To get a good key for the filler, dig out more polystyrene with a sharp blade. Clean thoroughly

2 Follow the maker's instructions to mix the filler. Force it into the hole with a plaster knife

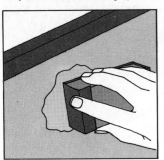

3 Leave the filler for six hours to harden. Rub the surface smooth with fine glass-paper on a block

4 Check that the contour of the hull is not distorted, and paint the patch with emulsion paint

Repairing a hole

If a polystyrene hull is holed, a replacement section can be glued into the damaged area. Polystyrene is available in blocks of many thicknesses. Obtain a piece thicker than the hull, and shape it with a Surform to fit the contour.

Use only epoxy-resin adhesive to fix it in position. Impact adhesive destroys polystyrene.

Materials: a polystyrene block; epoxy-resin adhesive; clear adhesive tape; fine glass-paper; emulsion paint; exterior-quality Polyfilla.
Tools: fine wood saw; paintbrush; cutting knife; plaster knife; Surform; sanding block.

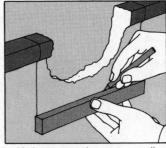
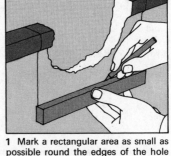

1 Mark a rectangular area as small as possible round the edges of the hole in the polystyrene hull

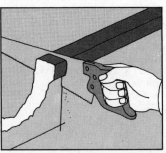

2 Cut down the vertical marks with a fine-toothed wood saw. Use a sharp knife to cut horizontally

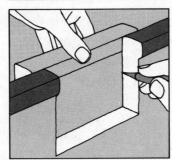

3 Square the edges of the cut area. Hold the replacement block behind and mark the shape of the hole on it

4 Cut the polystyrene to fit the hole and shape it to the hull contours. Spread on epoxy-resin adhesive

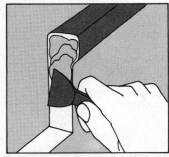

5 Make sure the edges of the hole are free of polystyrene particles. Spread on epoxy-resin adhesive

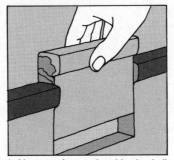

6 Line up the patch with the hull surface and press it firmly into position. Remove any surplus adhesive

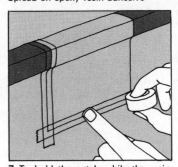

7 To hold the patch while the resin sets, fix clear adhesive tape on both sides of the joint. Remove afterwards

8 Use fine glass-paper to smooth the surface. Fill any small cracks with Polyfilla and brush on emulsion paint

Boats Rubber dinghies

Repairing a puncture or tear

Punctures and very small tears in a rubber hull can be repaired simply by patching. When the tear is more than about 2 in. (50 mm) long, it should be sewn, with a herringbone stitch, before patching. The advantage of the herringbone stitch is that it pulls the torn edges together but prevents the material from overlapping.

When the damage is more serious—for example, holes or tears in a rubbing strip, seam, rope supports or transom—do not try to mend it by sewing and patching. A special repair technique is needed. If there is no specialist repair shop close at hand, mark the damaged area and return the boat to the maker.

Materials: puncture repair kit; stitching twine; detergent.
Tool: sailmaker's needle.

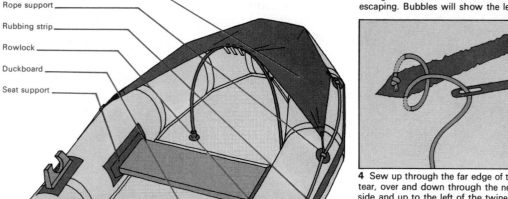

Canopy
Rope support
Rubbing strip
Rowlock
Duckboard
Seat support
Seam strip
Transom

1 To find a small puncture, spread detergent over the area where air is escaping. Bubbles will show the leak

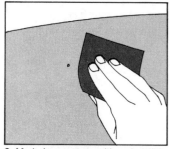

2 Mark the puncture with an indelible pencil. Deflate the boat. Rub the area with emery cloth before patching

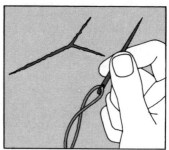

3 When the tear is more than 2 in. (50 mm), sew with a sailmaker's needle and twine

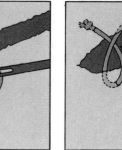

4 Sew up through the far edge of the tear, over and down through the near side and up to the left of the twine

5 Bring the twine across the stitch already made and up from below the far side of the tear

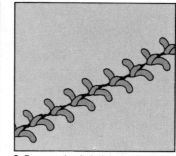

6 Draw each stitch tight as it is made. Make sure the two edges do not overlap. Continue until the tear is repaired

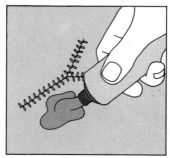

7 Spread adhesive on the repair area. Allow the solution to dry and then apply a second coat

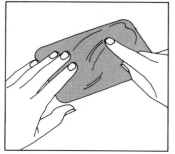

8 Cut a patch about 1½ in. (40 mm) wider and longer than the tear or puncture. Apply adhesive

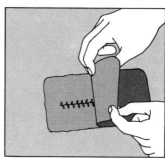

9 When the second coat is tacky, press on the patch. Leave to set for 24 hours before inflating the boat

Boats Glass-fibre hulls

Glass-fibre hulls are constructed of several layers of glass mat or cloth bonded together by a synthetic resin. When making any repair—even to surface scoring—make sure that the hull is completely dry. All work should be carried out in a temperature of 16–24°C (61–75°F). Do not work in direct sunlight. Follow the maker's instructions for mixing the resin. Because it sets quickly, do not mix too much at one time.

Materials: glass-fibre repair kit; filler powder; release agent; acetone to clean brushes; cardboard; polythene; adhesive tape; aluminium or hardboard if necessary.
Tools: mixing containers; scissors; brushes; abrasive paper and glass-fibre polish; sander; file; hacksaw; drill; screws.

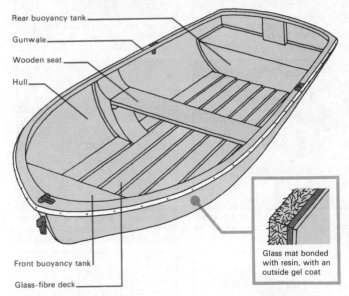

Rear buoyancy tank
Gunwale
Wooden seat
Hull
Front buoyancy tank
Glass-fibre deck

Glass mat bonded with resin, with an outside gel coat

SURFACE SCRATCHES

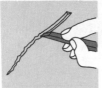

1 Use a sharp point to scrape out a V-shaped groove along the scratch

2 Mix the resin and filler, and press it firmly into the enlarged groove

3 Leave the repair for a day, then rub down with 320-grade paper

Repairing impact damage

Any severe impact damage, whether holed or not, weakens the fibres of the hull. It is always advisable to cut out the whole area affected and rebuild it with glass mat and resin. Do not cut more than is necessary.

It is difficult to match the colour of the hull by adding pigment to the resin mixes. Paint the surface with a matching polyurethane paint after the repair is made.

Because most resins start to harden within 30 minutes of mixing, make up only small amounts which can be used within that time. There is no way to soften resin once it has started to set.

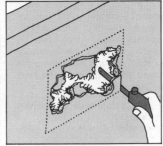

1 Cut round the damaged area with a hacksaw, to remove as small a piece of hull as possible

2 Use a file or disc sander to bevel the edges of the cut from both sides of the hull (inset)

3 Provide a key for the backing mat by cleaning the inside of the hull with a coarse disc sander

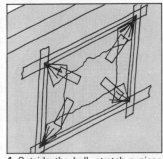

4 Outside the hull, stretch a piece of polythene over cardboard and tape it against the edges of the hole

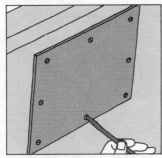

5 For a larger hole, bolt or screw a piece of aluminium or hardboard outside. Coat it with release agent

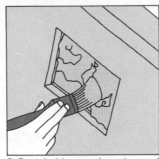

6 From inside, spread a gel coat of resin on to the polythene, hardboard or aluminium

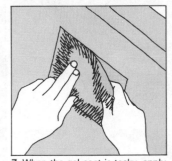

7 When the gel coat is tacky, apply layers of resin and glass mat. Build up to the thickness of the hull

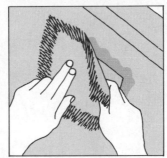

8 Fix a backing mat over the patch inside. Leave for 24 hours, remove the outside support, fill the bolt-holes

Boats Painting and varnishing

Repairing a blind hole

When a boat is holed at a point where it is not possible to work on both sides of the damaged section— for example, at a buoyancy tank— a patch can be built up against a hardboard backing. The effectiveness of the work depends on how securely the hardboard is fixed inside the damaged section. Do not start building up the outside with glass fibre until the resin holding the hardboard has set firmly. If the glass fibre is put on before the backing is secure, the patch will eventually work itself loose; then water will be able to enter and the repair will have to be done again.

1 Cut out the damaged area in a rectangular shape and bevel the edges outwards with a file or sander

2 Rub with glass-paper inside. Cut a hardboard backing bigger than the hole. Drill two holes in the centre

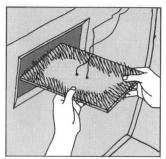

3 Insert a piece of wire in the holes. Spread three coats of resin on the board. Push it into the hole

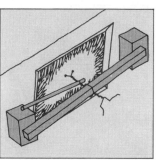

4 Pull the wire round a wooden bridge outside. Tighten with a stick between the backing and wood

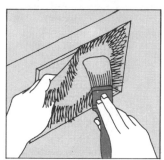

5 When the resin sets, cut the wire to remove the bridge piece and fill the hole with glass mat and resin

Restoring the paintwork

To achieve a good finish when painting or varnishing a hull, make sure that the preparation is carried out carefully. Clean the existing paint or varnish with detergent or sugar-soap. Rinse and wash thoroughly afterwards with plenty of clean water. Allow the surface to dry.

Examine the paint or varnish. If any gloss remains, rub it with a medium-grade wet abrasive paper, and wash again with clean water.

If parts of the paint or varnish are in poor condition, remove them with a chemical paint-stripper. Remove all traces of the stripper with detergent and rinse with clean water. It may be possible to strip the paintwork more quickly by burning; but use this method only on wooden or steel hulls, never on glass fibre, polystyrene or canvas. Do not burn varnish.

Ask a dealer for a stopper, for filling irregularities in the timber, suitable for the paint or varnish to be used. Find out if the wood should be primed before using the stopper. Fill all holes or cracks in the hull; when the stopper dries, smooth it level with the surface with abrasive paper.

When varnish is applied to bare wood, thin the first coat to give a better penetration. Subsequent coats should be normal strength.

For glass-fibre hulls, use only polyurethane paint or varnish. Ordinary paints may be used for other materials, but polyurethane finishes are always more waterproof and durable.

When painting a polystyrene hull, use only a good-quality waterproof emulsion paint. Conventional oil-based synthetic paints will attack polystyrene and destroy the texture of the material.

Materials: marine-quality paint or varnish, with maker's recommended stoppers, fillers and thinners.
Tools: wet-and-dry abrasive paper— various grades; putty knife; sanding block; paintbrushes—3 in., 2 in. and ¾ in. are the most useful.

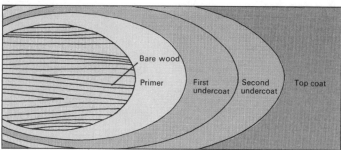

1 The primer bonds to the bare surface and provides a base for the other coats. If thin primer is used, put on two coats. Paint on one or two undercoats to provide a matt surface on which to paint the top coat

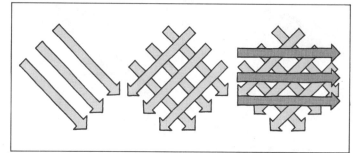

2 Brush on the undercoats diagonally. The direction of the strokes should be at right angles to that of the coat below. This reduces the risk of paint runs when the top coat is brushed horizontally across the hull

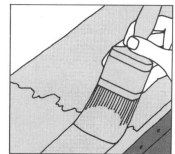

3 Avoid brush marks by overlapping the area just painted. Ease up the brush as it completes the stroke

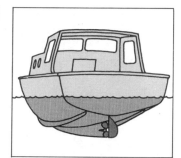

4 If the boat is permanently in the water, use anti-foul paint below the water line. Float before the paint dries

Boats Ribs and corner supports

Replacing a breasthook or knee

Most boats have shaped parts fixed inside the corners to strengthen the structure. With the exception of the piece in the bow, which is known as a breasthook, these supports are called knees. If they break, they can be renewed—either from a solid block of oak or by laminating mahogany strips. Choose the method to match the existing supports.

Materials: oak block or mahogany veneers; synthetic resin glue; copper nails and roves; glass-paper.
Tools: coping saw; plane; chisel; saw; flat and curved Surforms; drill; hammer; cutter; hollow punch.

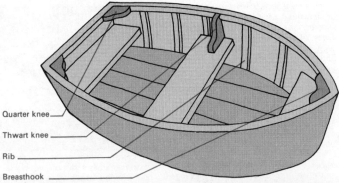

Quarter knee
Thwart knee
Rib
Breasthook

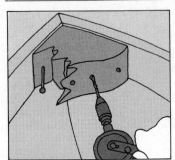

1 Drill out the old roves and nails. If the knee or breasthook is glued, prise it carefully away from the side

2 Clean the surface with glass-paper. Hold the new wood on top and from below mark the corner shape on it

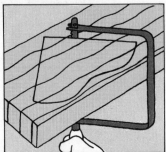

3 Make sure the grain runs diagonally across the knee. Cut the wood and trim its outside edge to shape

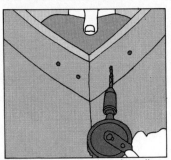

4 Use a bit smaller than the nails to drill holes through the bow. Drill horizontally into the knee

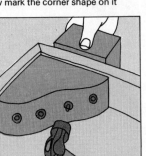

5 Glue the block and nail it in place from outside. Inside, cut the nail ends and fit roves (see p. 600)

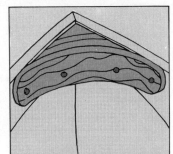

Lamination Fix a small block in the corner. Glue and nail veneers until the last veneer bends along the sides

Repairing a rib

If a boat rib cracks or breaks, strengthen the hull as soon as possible by fixing a new piece of rib alongside the damaged part. This is called doubling. Use either a solid timber which can be bent to the shape of the hull—for example, rock elm or ash—or make a laminated repair with mahogany veneers.

Materials: rock elm or ash, or mahogany veneers; synthetic resin glue; copper nails and roves; glass-paper.
Tools: tenon saw; plane; flat and curved Surforms; hammer; iron block; hollow punch; drill.

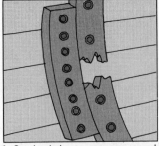

1 Cut the timber to pass over several planks. Glue it against the rib and fix with nails and roves

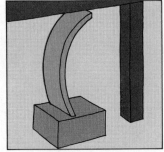

2 For a tighter curve, soak timber for several hours. Shape it and jam it under a bench until it sets

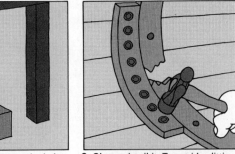

3 Glue and nail it. To avoid splitting planks, ensure nails are not in line with existing rib nails

4 For a laminated rib, make a card template, allow for thickness of laminations, and cut wood to shape

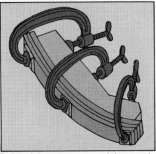

5 Bend the veneers round the wood, then glue and grip with clamps. Fix to the hull when the glue sets

Boats Decks

Maintaining and caulking

Inspect the underside of a deck regularly for signs of leaking. The caulking between the planks can easily be renewed. If a plank is rotten, cut it out and fit a new one.

Materials: marine glue; mouldings and planks if needed; paint; copper tacks or nails.
Tools: saw; plane; chisel; melting-pot; hammer; screwdriver; paintbrush; old file.

Fix strengthening pieces of wood under the deck where fittings—for example, cleats—have to be screwed on

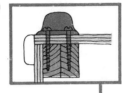

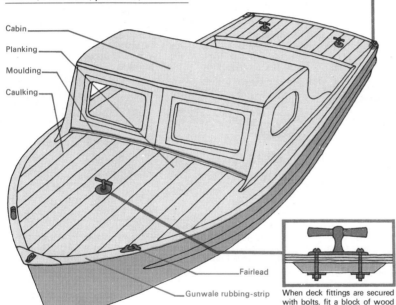

Cabin
Planking
Moulding
Caulking

Fairlead
Gunwale rubbing-strip

When deck fittings are secured with bolts, fit a block of wood and large washers underneath

CAULKING

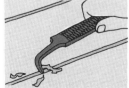
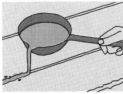

1 Scrape out the old caulking with the bent tang of a file

2 Melt marine glue—not resin glue —and pour it between the planks

3 When set, trim off the surplus glue with a sharp wood chisel

Renewing a deck canvas

When a deck is canvas-covered, check the plywood underneath carefully before re-covering. If the wood is blistered or cracked, cut out the damaged section and fit a new piece of plywood (see p. 602). Do not fit new canvas to rotting wood. Renew any moulding strips that are damaged or distorted.

Materials: 12 oz. canvas; paint or jointing compound; copper nails or tacks; plywood or mouldings if needed.
Tools: pliers; hammer; screwdriver.

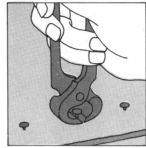

1 Remove any mouldings or deck beading and strip out the old canvas. Pull out nails or tacks

2 Renew damaged plywood (see p. 602). Apply paint or jointing compound to the section

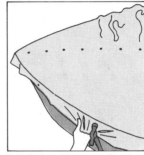
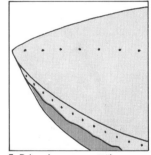

3 Drape the canvas evenly over the deck. Nail every 3 in. (75 mm) down the centre

4 Nail the sides at a few key points to ensure that the canvas lies flat without creases

5 Drive in copper tacks every 3 in. (75 mm) along the edge of the canvas

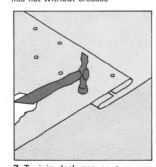
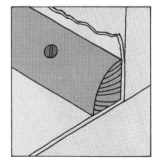

6 Refit the hull mouldings just below the level of the deck. Screw into existing holes

7 To join deck canvas, turn one edge up and the other down. Tack through both, close together

8 Where the canvas meets the cabin, turn up the edge, fix with a moulding and trim off

Boats   Canoes

Renewing a fabric covering

Make sure, before attempting to re-skin a canoe, that the framework is sound. Remove all the external wood and the metal protective strips. Strip off the old material and remove tacks. Clean the framework with fine glass-paper, re-varnish and rub down (see p. 607). Two pieces of material are required. Measure the length and depth of the framework and the deck and buy material a little larger all round.

Materials: PVC-coated fabric or proofed canvas, about 120 oz. grade; lighter material for decking; $\frac{3}{8}$ in. (10 mm) copper tacks; adhesive to suit material (see p. 694); gloss paint; glass-paper.
Tools: scissors; pliers; hammer; knife; screwdriver.

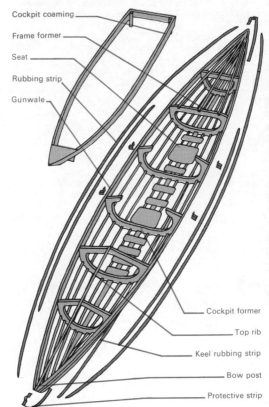

Cockpit coaming
Frame former
Seat
Rubbing strip
Gunwale

Cockpit former
Top rib
Keel rubbing strip
Bow post
Protective strip

1 Turn the frame upside-down on trestles. Drape the skin over the frame, with equal surplus all round, and put an electric heater under the canoe to make the material easier to work. Drive three tacks into the post at one end. Stretch the material and tack to the post at the other

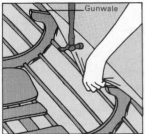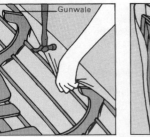

Gunwale

2 Turn canoe over. Draw material taut at the centre over the gunwales and tack firmly to the inside of the canoe frame

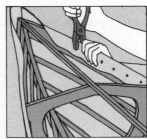

3 Pull the material up tightly and fix tacks 2 in. (50 mm) apart. If a hammer cannot be used, press the tacks in with pliers

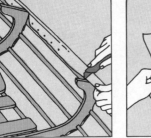

4 Trim the fabric as it is tacked. Cut notches to fit it round the ribs and formers. If the fabric puckers, heat it and pull firmly

5 At both ends, draw the fabric tightly against the posts. Allow $\frac{1}{2}$ in. (13 mm) overlap and cut off the surplus

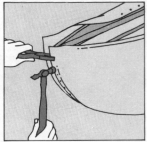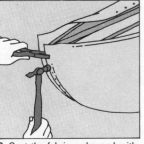

6 Coat the fabric and wood with a suitable adhesive. Draw fabric over the ends with pliers and fix tacks 1 in. (25 mm) apart

7 Cut four pieces of fabric 2 in. (50 mm) wide to cover the posts, and bend over the top. Glue and tack two to each post

8 PVC-coated fabric need not be painted, but if canvas is used apply a coat of paint before fixing the keel strips. Screw from inside

9 Stretch the deck fabric tautly over the frame. Tack it at each end and on both sides, $\frac{1}{2}$ in. (13 mm) down the gunwales

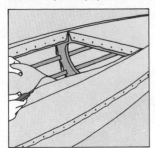

10 Fix tacks along the gunwales 2 in. (50 mm) apart. Cut out the cockpit shape. Tack down the edges of the covering

11 Fit the cockpit coaming in position and replace any remaining rubbing strips. Screw the metal end-pieces to the framework

Boats Spiling

Measuring a deck piece

If it is impossible to hold wood in place to find the shape required for a repair, use the traditional boat-building method called spiling.

There are two variations. To find the shape of a curved beam or plank, fit a long, narrow strip of wood in the section to be filled. Mark off the measurements on it.

To measure a large open space, use scrap timber and a pointed stick long enough to reach from the board to the furthest edge.

Materials: plywood or timber scraps; lath (for spiling stick); hardboard. Tools: saw; hammer; nails; pencil.

Spiling stick
Spiling board

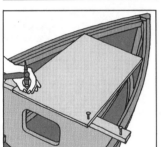

1 Nail a wood strip across the space for which a board is to be cut. Lay scrap hardboard over the area and nail it to the wood

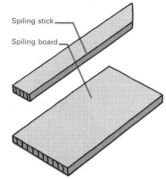

2 Cut a pointed stick. Hold it on the board, so that its point touches the inside edge of the boat. Mark round the end of the stick

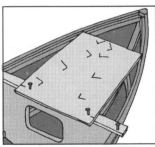

3 Move the stick round the inside of the boat, repeating the marking every few inches. Mark round the same corner of the stick each time

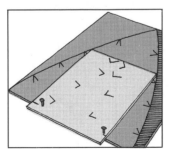

4 Nail the marked board on the piece to be cut and lay the stick against the pencil marks. Mark its point each time and join up the marks

Marking out a plank

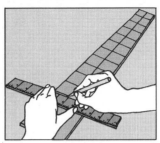

1 Cut a wood strip longer and narrower than the section to be filled. Draw a centreline. Mark lines across it 3 in. (75 mm) apart

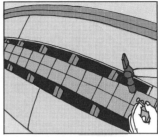

2 Position the marked strip over the section for which a new plank is to be cut. Nail it lightly at each end to hold it in place

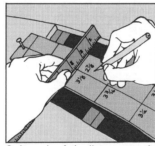

3 At each of the lines across the strip, measure from the centreline to the edge of the existing wood. Mark the measurement on the strip

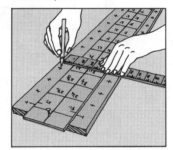

4 Remove the strip and lay it on the plank to be shaped. At each line across, measure out the distance shown and mark the plank

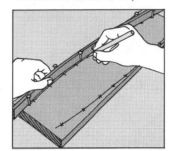

5 Lightly tap in nails on both sides of the marks. Bend a lath between the nails and draw the shape of the measured edge

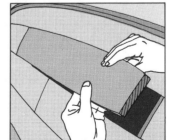

6 Do the same at the other markings and cut along the lines. The plank should fit exactly. Fix it in place (see p. 600)

Cutting a bulkhead

1 Mark an irregular shape in two stages. To measure each half, nail a board with one edge against the centreline of the area to be filled

2 Cut a pointed stick long enough to reach from the board to the furthest edge being measured. Mark around the end of the stick

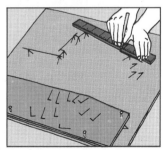

3 Lay the board on the wood to be cut. Mark off distances and join the marks. Measure the other half of the bulkhead in the same way

Boats Sails and rigging

Looking after the ropework

Check the ropes and rigging of a boat regularly, but especially before the start of a season when the boat has been laid up. Replace frayed ropes immediately. If a wire is found to have loose strands, tape it at once to avoid tearing the canvas. Replace it with new wire as soon as possible.

Make sure that the ends of all ropes are sealed—either by binding or whipping them, or by melting the ends in a flame if the rope is synthetic.

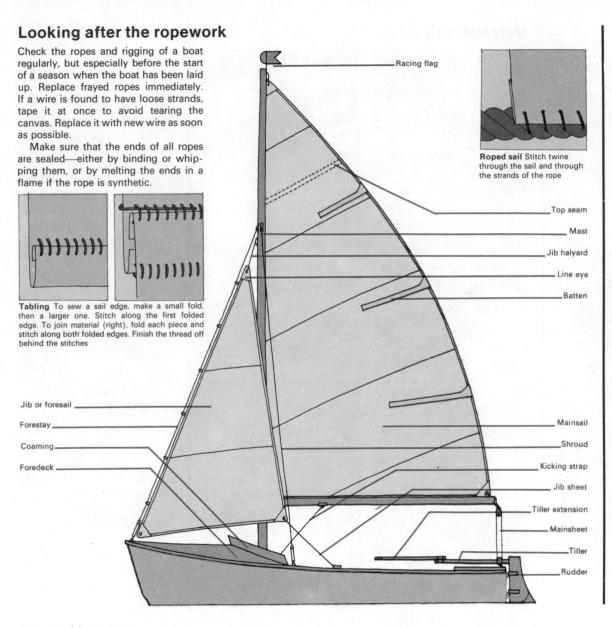

Tabling To sew a sail edge, make a small fold, then a larger one. Stitch along the first folded edge. To join material (right), fold each piece and stitch along both folded edges. Finish the thread off behind the stitches

Racing flag

Top seam

Mast

Jib halyard

Line eye

Batten

Mainsail

Shroud

Kicking strap

Jib sheet

Tiller extension

Mainsheet

Tiller

Rudder

Jib or foresail

Forestay

Coaming

Foredeck

Roped sail Stitch twine through the sail and through the strands of the rope

Stitching a tear

Small tears in a sail can be stitched; patch a larger tear. Use a sailmaker's palm to push the needle through.

Materials: fabric, matching the sail; twine; beeswax.
Tools: scissors; sailmaker's needle; sailmaker's palm.

Sailmaker's palm

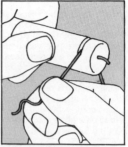

1 Draw the twine through a candle to seal and lubricate the fibres. Use twine doubled

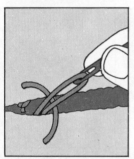

2 Push the needle up one side of the tear, down the other and through the tear

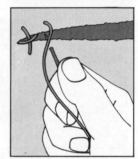

3 Take the thread across the stitch and under the canvas to start the next stitch

4 When it is completed, the herringbone stitch should be flat and tight

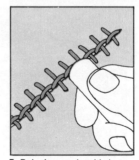

5 Rub the repair with beeswax or a candle to protect it from wind and water

Patching a tear

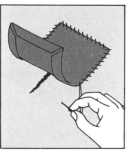

1 Slit the corners of a patch and turn the edges under. Sew it on with a hemstitch

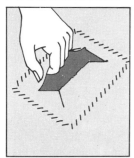

2 Turn the sail and cut the corners of the tear at an angle. Tuck the edges under

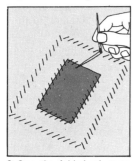

3 Sew the folded edges to the patch, using about five hemstitches per inch

Sealing the end of a rope

The ends of all ropes used on a boat should be sealed to prevent fraying. With conventional ropes, the most common method is to fix twine in the strands and bind it around the rope—called whipping the end. The depth of the whipping should normally be about the same as the thickness of the rope.

Synthetic ropes can be sealed by melting their ends in a flame.

Materials: twine or thread to suit ropes.

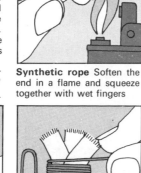

Synthetic rope Soften the end in a flame and squeeze together with wet fingers

1 With natural rope, open the end strands. Loop the twine over one strand

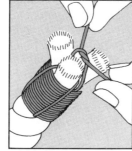

2 With the loop and its short end protruding, wind the twine round the strands

3 Lift the loop over one strand and pull the short end of the twine to tighten it

4 Take the short end up outside the binding and tie it to the long end

Splicing a rope

When two ropes have to be joined, unwind the strands at the meeting ends and weave the strands of one with the corresponding strands of the other. The advantage of this method—called splicing—is that the join never parts. Every pull on the rope only helps to tighten the splice.

The same method can be used to form an eye at the end of a rope. Unwind the strands at the end and twist the rope open where it is to be spliced.

To get a good working length for splicing, unwind the strands for about ten times their thickness. The strands of natural fibre rope should be interwoven at least three times. Nylon rope needs at least four or five weaves. When a splice is complete, cut off the surplus ends of the woven strands and pull ends of rope.

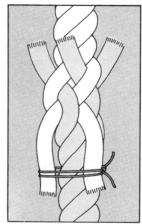

1 Unwind the strands of the two ropes. Push the ends together to interweave each strand into the other rope. Tie down the ends of one rope

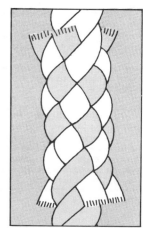

2 Weave the free ends through the strands of the other rope three or four times. Untie the other ends and weave them into the splice. Trim off surplus

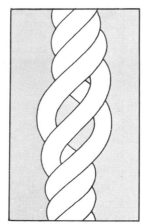

1 To make an eye splice, unwind the end strands of the rope. Untwist the rope to open three strands at the point where the loop is to be made

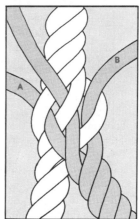

2 Weave the middle end strand with the middle rope strand. Weave A through the highest rope strand and B through the lowest open rope strand

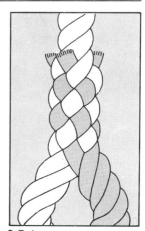

3 Twist more rope strands open and weave in the end strands, each passing over and under one main strand three or four times

Boats Oars and paddles

Repairing a broken blade

To prevent the most common form of damage to an oar or paddle—a split or broken blade—a protective copper strip can be fitted to the blade end. If, however, the blade does become damaged, build up the broken area with a new piece of wood and then fit the copper.

Materials: wood of the correct type, usually hemlock or ash; synthetic resin glue; copper sheet; ¾ in. (20 mm) copper nails for oar tips; copper tacks for leather; leather.
Tools: plane or Surform; saw; tin-snips; drill; pliers; sharp knife; mallet; hammer; centre punch.

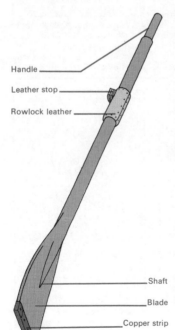

Handle
Leather stop
Rowlock leather
Shaft
Blade
Copper strip

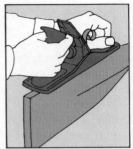

1 Use a plane or Surform to straighten the split or broken edge of the oar blade

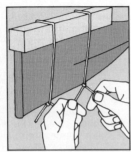

2 Glue on a slightly oversize piece of wood. Secure it with string until the glue sets

3 Use a plane or Surform to trim the wood to the correct contour round all its faces

4 Mark the shape of a protective strip on paper, with an overlap at the edges

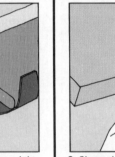

5 Cut the template shape out of a sheet of thin copper, about 20 gauge

6 Bend the copper round the tip of the blade. Overlap the short edges last

7 In the centre of the overlap corners, punch and drill holes smaller than the nails

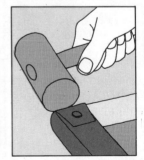

8 Drive in the nails, cut the ends to leave stubs of $\frac{1}{16}$ in. (2 mm), and burr them over

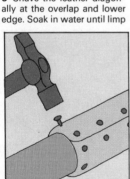

9 Use a mallet to tap and round off any sharp edges on the copper strip

Renewing rowlock leather

1 Remove tacks and strip off the old leather. Clean and varnish the stripped shaft

2 Cut a new piece of leather to go round the shaft and overlap by ¾ in. (20 mm)

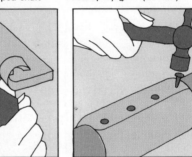

3 Shave the leather diagonally at the overlap and lower edge. Soak in water until limp

4 Stretch the leather round the shaft and fix with copper tacks ¾ in. (20 mm) apart

5 Hammer the lower edge of the leather and tack. Leave the upper edge square

6 Make a stop—¾ in. (20 mm) thick—from strips. Nail it round a third of the shaft

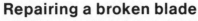

Boats Outboard motors

Maintenance

Nearly all outboard motors are two-stroke engines, with either one or two cylinders. Although different makes of engine vary slightly in detail, the basic maintenance is the same. If an engine is running well, only routine servicing need be done. But if the engine requires decarbonising or a more thorough overhaul, follow the method for two-stroke lawn-mower engines (see p. 476). Always follow the manufacturer's instructions when dismantling and repairing an engine. Keep strictly to the maker's recommended clearances.

If an engine falters, fit a new spark-plug. Never have the plug pressure-cleaned. The abrasive particles used in pressure-cleaning stick inside the plug, and can later fall off and foul the engine, causing severe damage.

The propeller may have a shear-pin, which is designed to break if the propeller jams. It is advisable always to carry a spare. If the propeller is spring-located, check the spring regularly and renew if it becomes worn or weak. Many of the more powerful engines have friction-drive propellers which do not need any maintenance.

When an engine is not to be used for some time, mount it on a bench or bar with the propeller in a drum of fresh water. Run the engine until the fuel is used. Never leave fuel in the tank over a long period. The petrol content of the two-stroke mixture soon evaporates and leaves only oil. This makes starting very difficult when the engine is first used again. Lubricate all the moving parts every three months, but take care not to leave oil near any electrical components.

Materials: manufacturer's recommended shear-pins or springs; spark-plugs.
Tools: spark-plug spanner; pin punch; centre punch; hammer; pliers; feeler gauge; files; screwdrivers; wire brush.

Spark-plug Set the gap to the maker's recommendation by bending the electrode

Testing the spark-plug Remove the plug and reconnect its lead. Hold the plug body against the engine to check that a spark is produced. When the engine is to be stored, take out the plug and squirt upper-cylinder lubricant down the bore

Shear-pin
Split-pin
Lock-nut
Washer

Propellers Many have a shear-pin which breaks if the propeller jams. Always fit a new split-pin in the lock-nut when the shear-pin is replaced. Check the propeller regularly for damage. File off any cuts on the edges of the blades

Gearbox If the gearbox is oil-filled, hold the engine horizontal to lubricate. Fill until the oil overflows. If it is grease-filled, squeeze grease in the lower plug-hole until it exudes

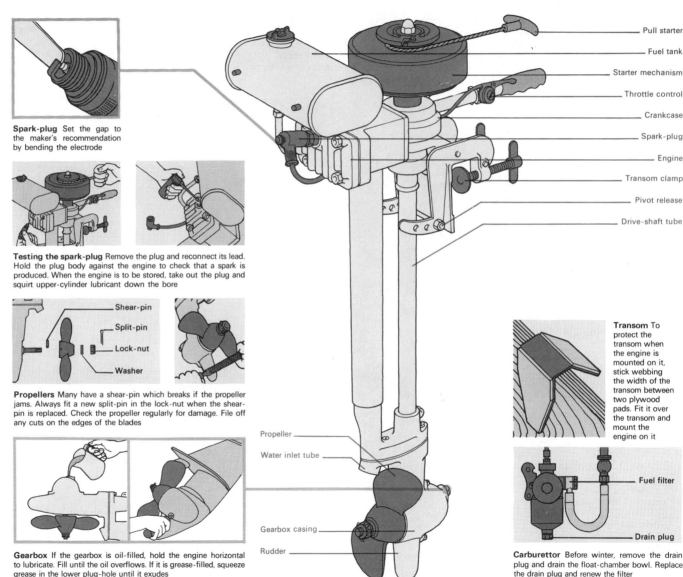

Pull starter
Fuel tank
Starter mechanism
Throttle control
Crankcase
Spark-plug
Engine
Transom clamp
Pivot release
Drive-shaft tube

Propeller
Water inlet tube

Gearbox casing
Rudder

Transom To protect the transom when the engine is mounted on it, stick webbing the width of the transom between two plywood pads. Fit it over the transom and mount the engine on it

Fuel filter

Drain plug

Carburettor Before winter, remove the drain plug and drain the float-chamber bowl. Replace the drain plug and renew the filter

Caravans

Interior maintenance

Check the inside of the caravan thoroughly before the start of each touring season. In particular examine gas connections for tightness, and make sure that mantles are sound. Look for signs of water penetration on the walls and roof. Any leaks are indications of faults in the bodywork or window seals. Cushions are best removed and stored for winter; if they have been left in the van, take them out and air thoroughly. Adjust or renew catches on drawers and cupboard doors if they do not lock securely, to prevent the contents being spilt during towing.

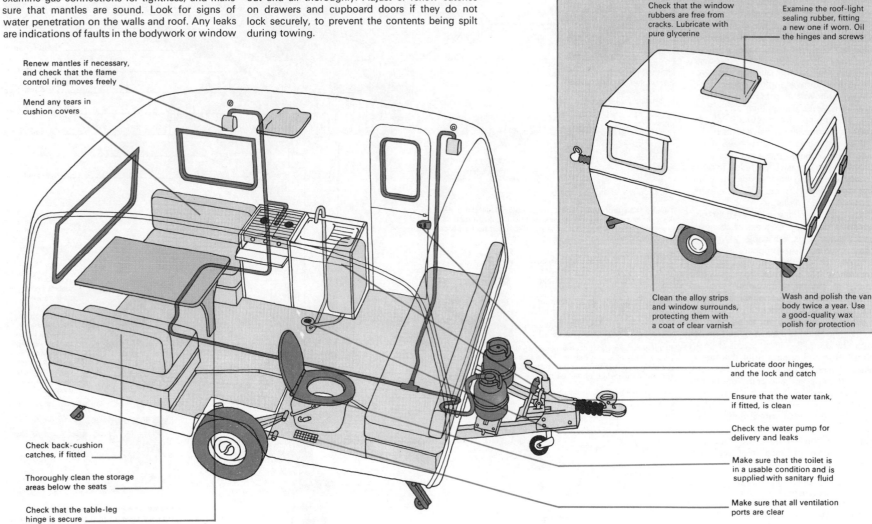

Renew mantles if necessary, and check that the flame control ring moves freely

Mend any tears in cushion covers

Check back-cushion catches, if fitted

Thoroughly clean the storage areas below the seats

Check that the table-leg hinge is secure

EXTERIOR MAINTENANCE

Check that the window rubbers are free from cracks. Lubricate with pure glycerine

Examine the roof-light sealing rubber, fitting a new one if worn. Oil the hinges and screws

Clean the alloy strips and window surrounds, protecting them with a coat of clear varnish

Wash and polish the van body twice a year. Use a good-quality wax polish for protection

Lubricate door hinges, and the lock and catch

Ensure that the water tank, if fitted, is clean

Check the water pump for delivery and leaks

Make sure that the toilet is in a usable condition and is supplied with sanitary fluid

Make sure that all ventilation ports are clear

Chassis maintenance

Regular maintenance of the chassis and running gear on a caravan is as important as the routine servicing of a car. There are recommended servicing periods for certain components; but because most caravans remain idle during the winter, a spring pre-touring check is advisable, even if the van has not covered the recommended mileage for servicing.

The parts requiring most care are the brakes, wheel hubs, suspension and towing gear. For safety, these parts must be maintained in perfect condition at all times.

Adjust Lockheed brakes by inserting a screwdriver through the drum and turning the adjuster screw

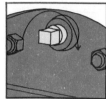

Adjust Girling brakes by turning the square peg on the brake back-plate, using a spanner

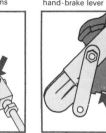

Lubricate the pivot-points and compensator arms

Oil the pivot-point of the hand-brake lever

Tyre care

Caravan tyres are subject to the same regulations as car tyres. To help to preserve them, keep the wheels covered and jack them clear of the ground if the van is out of use for more than a week. Maintain the tyre pressure advised by the caravan manufacturer.

1 Check that tread depth is at least 1 mm—the minimum required by law

2 At regular intervals, remove flints and stones from the treads

3 During storage or prolonged parking, shield the tyres from sunlight

Clean the corner-steady threads regularly. Lubricate with light oil for touring, with grease before storage

Check that the regulator seal is sound (see p. 622)

Lubricate the threads on the gas-bottle carrier

Lubricate the grease nipples on the towing coupling every 1000 miles (1600 km) or every six months

Strip and grease wheel-hub bearings every 5000 miles (8000 km) (see p. 621)

Check wheel nuts for tightness every 1000 miles (1600 km). Keep the threads well greased

Keep the stem and axle of the jockey wheel lightly greased

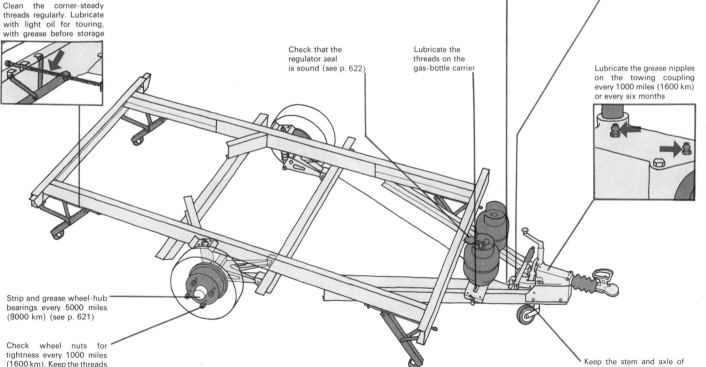

Caravans Tow hitches

General maintenance

For safety, the tow-hitch braking mechanism on a caravan must be adjusted correctly. The car's own brakes are not designed to take the extra load.

The reverse catch knock-off device, now fitted to nearly all caravans, must also be in good condition. It consists of a steel ring attached to the end of the tow-hitch shaft and is designed to release the reverse lock-clip when the caravan is drawn forwards. Without it, the reverse catch has to be worked by hand. Knock-off rings should be checked periodically as they will occasionally crack.

Knock-off ring To fit a new ring, use a file to smooth the end of the shaft. Tap the new ring into place, flush with the shaft, and tighten the Allen screw

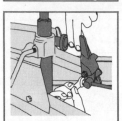

Handbrake With the lever fully released, adjust the brake rod until two fingers can be placed between the top of the brake arm and the end of the shaft

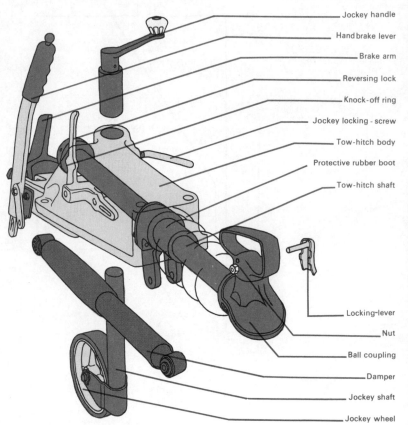

Jockey handle

Hand brake lever

Brake arm

Reversing lock

Knock-off ring

Jockey locking - screw

Tow-hitch body

Protective rubber boot

Tow-hitch shaft

Locking-lever

Nut

Ball coupling

Damper

Jockey shaft

Jockey wheel

Servicing a lock-lever

The lifting handle, which locks on to the ball, is kept in place by a spring-loaded lock-lever. In time, this lever may break or become jammed, or the plunger may wear out. The locking device is an essential safety feature, so before each outing check it by lifting the handle up and down after the caravan is attached.

Materials: lever spring; plunger.
Tools: spanner; hammer.

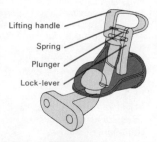

Lifting handle

Spring

Plunger

Lock-lever

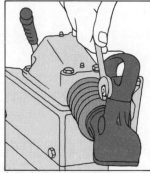

1 Undo the nut on the end of the lock-lever bolt. The bolt is fixed by a pivot to the lever mechanism

2 Tap the bolt through the head of the tow-hitch lifting handle. The bolt need not be removed

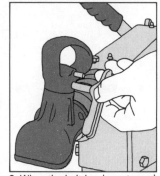

3 When the bolt has been tapped out far enough, turn the lock-lever through 90 degrees

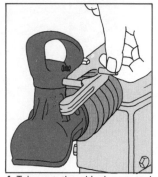

4 Take out the old plunger and spring. Refit, in reverse order, with a new spring and plunger

Fitting a new damper

If a caravan jerks or bumps during acceleration, deceleration or gear-changing, the most likely cause is a worn hydraulic damper.

The damper is situated just below the hitch. It is attached at one end to the body of the tow hitch and at the other end to the sliding tow-hitch shaft. The tow-hitch assembly must be removed before the damper unit can be replaced. New parts can be obtained from an authorised caravan dealer. If a riser bracket is fitted, leave the riser attached to the tow bar. Do not remove it with the tow-hitch assembly.

Materials: damper unit; front damper bolt.
Tools: spanners to fit tow-hitch bolts and damper bolts; hammer and punch.

HOW A DAMPER WORKS

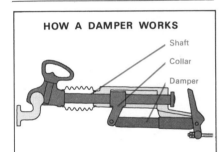

- Shaft
- Collar
- Damper

Acceleration When towing, the collar on the sliding shaft is drawn against the tow-hitch body and the damper is drawn out to the rebound position

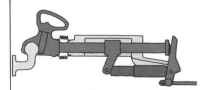

Deceleration When stopping or slowing down the shaft slides back through the tow-hitch body, compressing the damper and applying the caravan brakes

---

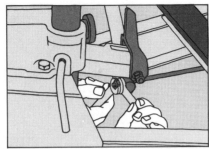

1 Turn down the corner steadies. Free the brake rod from the tow-hitch brake lever by unscrewing the nuts at the end of the brake rod

2 With the corner steadies screwed down, undo the four bolts that hold the tow-hitch assembly to the tow-bar riser bracket

3 Remove the tow-hitch assembly. This gives access to the front damper bolt which is otherwise shielded by the riser bracket

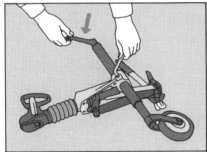

4 Turn the jockey handle (arrowed) anti-clockwise and unscrew the shaft. Release the lock-screw and remove the jockey-wheel body

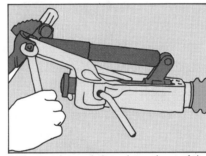

5 The rear damper bolt, an integral part of the brake lever, is held by a lock-nut and main nut beneath it. Undo these nuts next

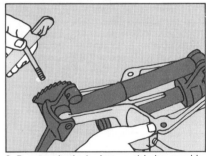

6 Remove the brake lever and bolt assembly. Note how the brake lever engages with a pawl connected to the brake arm

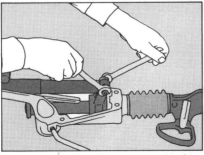

7 Undo the self-locking nut on the front damper bolt and tap out the bolt. The damper can now be released at the front end

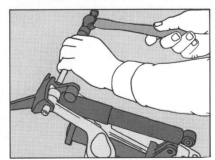

8 The rear of the damper is still held in place by an internal sleeve. Using the punch, tap the sleeve out sufficiently to free the damper

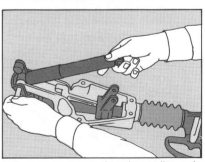

9 Fit the new damper, the colour coding on its front eye facing upwards. Replace the sleeve and reassemble in reverse order

Caravans Brakes and wheel bearings

Brake drum and hub assembly

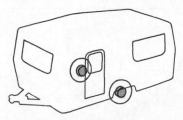

A caravan brake assembly is usually one of two makes, Lockheed or Girling. These are similarly constructed, but adjustment of the shoes is different.

Both types have combined brake-drum and wheel-hub assemblies. Strip annually to clean the inside of the drums, to examine brake linings and to lubricate the brake mechanism.

Fit new brake shoes if the linings have worn down to their rivets. It is inadvisable to renew one side only, so fit a complete set of shoes.

Materials: set of service exchange brake shoes; brake grease; split-pins; high-melting-point hub grease; seals; paraffin. Tools: brake-adjusting spanner (Girling); screwdriver; spanner to fit hub nuts; hammer; old chisel or screwdriver; wheel brace; car jack (bottle type); pliers.

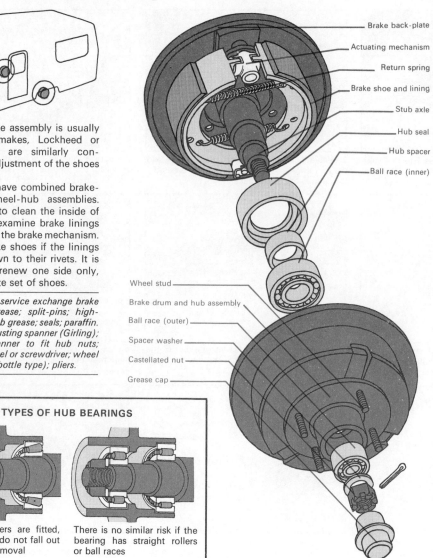

Brake back-plate
Actuating mechanism
Return spring
Brake shoe and lining
Stub axle
Hub seal
Hub spacer
Ball race (inner)

Wheel stud
Brake drum and hub assembly
Ball race (outer)
Spacer washer
Castellated nut
Grease cap

TYPES OF HUB BEARINGS

If tapered rollers are fitted, take care they do not fall out during drum removal

There is no similar risk if the bearing has straight rollers or ball races

Replacing brake shoes

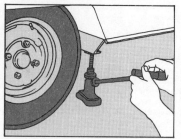

1 Jack up the caravan on a car jack, not on the corner steadies. Use wooden blocks to prevent tipping. Remove the wheel plate, nuts and road wheel

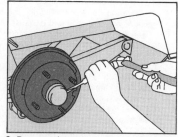

2 Remove the grease cap on the end of the axle shaft. It is a press-fit and can be tapped free with a hammer and an old screwdriver or blunt chisel

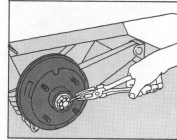

3 Straighten and withdraw the split-pin through the slots in the castellated nut and the hole in the axle shaft. Use a new pin when reassembling

4 To slacken off the shoes on Girling brakes (as here) turn the adjusting nut anti-clockwise; on Lockheed brakes release the adjusting screw

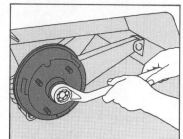

5 Remove the hub nut and the thick spacing washer behind it on the end of the axle shaft. Clean them as they are removed, ready for reassembling

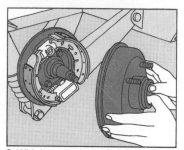

6 Withdraw the drum assembly from the shaft. Hold one hand at the hub centre; otherwise, if tapered rollers are fitted they may fall out *(continued)*

7 Clean off dust and rust from the inside surface of the brake drum. Replace the drum with a new one if it has been badly scored

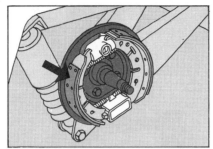

8 If the brake linings are worn down to the rivets, or are badly scored, fit a set of service exchange relined shoes

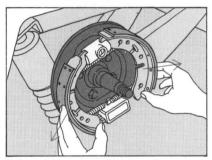

9 Spread the shoes against the spring pressure and prise out the shoes. Note the positions of the return springs

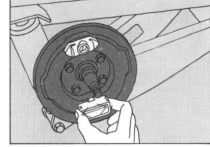

10 On leading and trailing shoe brakes, the lower shoe carrier slides in an elongated slot. Ensure that movement is free, then grease

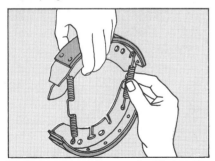

11 Some return springs can be fitted to the shoes before the shoes are fitted to the backplate. Others are hooked into place afterwards

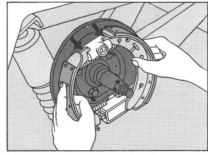

12 The linings are not central on the shoe platforms. Fit the shoes with the longer and shorter uncovered areas (arrowed) adjacent

Greasing wheel bearings

1 Prise the grease cap off the hub assembly and remove the inner race from the centre of the hub

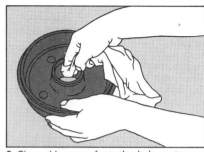

2 Clear old grease from the hub centre and from the bearings. Clean with paraffin. The bearings should revolve smoothly

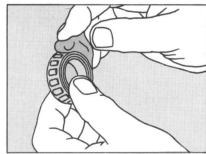

3 Wash and dry your hands and apply fresh grease. Knead it well into the race between the rollers and the cage

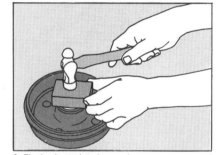

4 Fit the inner bearing and a new grease seal with the flat face outwards. Hammer it in, using a wood block across the seal face

5 Pack the inside of the hub with grease, forming the sides to leave a central passage. Overpacking will result in a pressure build-up

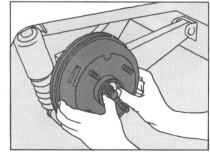

6 Refit the hub. Tighten the castellated nut until the split-pin holes line up and the wheel spins freely without any play. Fit a new split-pin

Caravans Gas fittings

Checking for gas leaks

The butane gas provided in portable canisters is naturally odourless. But it is given an unpleasant smell to enable users to detect a leak. Never use a naked flame if a leak is suspected. Check and tighten all loose joints before starting a tour. Replace flexible tubing as soon as it shows signs of wear. Special composition tubing is obtainable. Do not use rubber hoses, which perish quickly in contact with gas.

Materials: liquid detergent; composition tubing.
Tool: spanner.

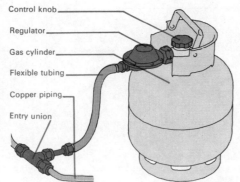

Control knob
Regulator
Gas cylinder
Flexible tubing
Copper piping
Entry union

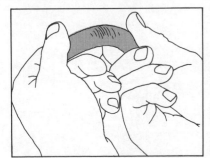

1 Examine the flexible tubing from the cylinder regulator. If it cracks when it is bent, replace it with new composition tubing

2 To confirm a leak, smear on liquid detergent and turn on the gas. The detergent will bubble as gas escapes at the leak

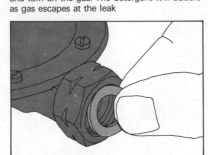

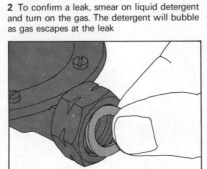

3 If there is a leak at the cylinder regulator, unscrew the outlet plug. Remove the washer and fit a new one

4 Some regulators have no plug. Prise out the old seal, and press a new one over the collar inside the neck

Maintaining light fittings

Strip and clean the parts of a caravan gaslight to remove dirt. Do not prod a blocked jet with wire. If it cannot be cleared by blowing through it, fit a new jet.

If the gas flow is still faulty when all the parts have been cleaned, fit a new control valve. Do not try to repair it.

Materials: mantles; replacement jet; asbestos washer.
Tool: small adjustable spanner.

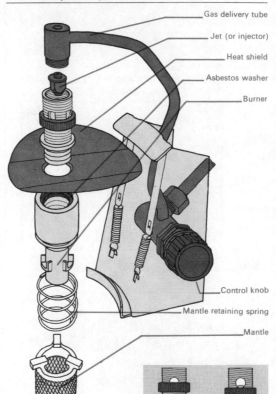

Gas delivery tube
Jet (or injector)
Heat shield
Asbestos washer
Burner
Control knob
Mantle retaining spring
Mantle

Air regulator Butane gas must mix in the correct proportion with air. Move the threaded screw up or down the air regulator to vary the amount of air entering

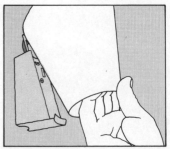

1 Push the light globe up against its retaining spring and remove it. Take care not to touch the mantle

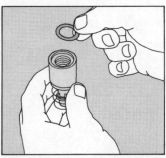

4 Check the burner and the asbestos washer. If they are brittle or cracked, obtain new parts before assembly

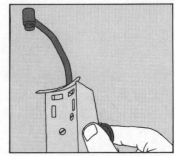

7 With all the parts removed, turn the gas on briefly to check the flow. Fit a new control valve if necessary

Caravans Electrical wiring

2 When removing a mantle, do not touch its mesh. Hold the lugs, push up and turn until the mantle neck is freed

3 Unscrew the burner by hand. If the spring is damaged, twist it free and fit a new heat-resistant part

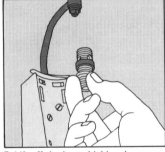

5 Lift off the heat shield and unscrew the regulator nozzle by hand. Check that the threaded screw moves freely

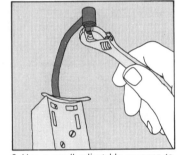

6 Use a small adjustable spanner to unscrew the jet. Blow through the jet. If it is blocked, replace it

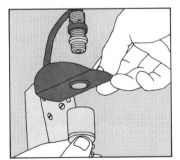

8 Refit the jet and regulator. Position the heat shield with its wide edge facing the wall. Fit the burner

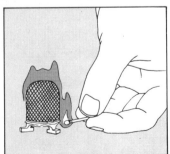

9 To avoid fouling the lamp with soot, burn the coating off a new mantle before fitting it to the lamp burner

Identifying wiring by colour

The electrical connections between a car and its caravan are made through a seven-pin plug and a socket designed to fit together in only one way. For identification, each wire has a coloured covering, and each plug terminal is marked with identifying letters and numbers.

COLOUR CODE

31 (white):
earth return

R54 (green):
offside flasher

54 (red):
stop lights

L54 (yellow):
nearside flasher

52 (blue):
interior light

58C (black):
nearside rear and
front sidelights

58 (brown):
offside rear and
front sidelights;
number-plate lights

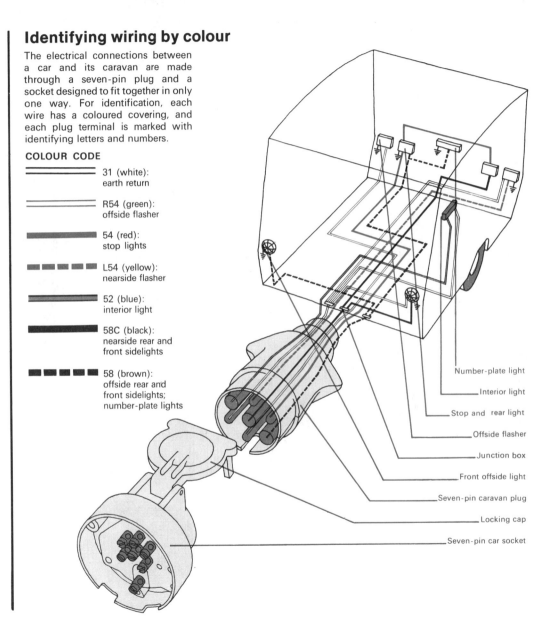

Number-plate light

Interior light

Stop and rear light

Offside flasher

Junction box

Front offside light

Seven-pin caravan plug

Locking cap

Seven-pin car socket

Caravans Windows

Replacing sealing strips

The window-frames of modern caravans are constructed of aluminium. The hinge at the top of each frame is in the form of a hook, the top bar of the window having a C-shaped section which slides into a similarly shaped lip on the top hinge bar. This bar is secured to the body with self-tapping screws. The easiest way to remove a caravan window is to slide the frame out of the hinge bar.

Sealing between the window-frame and bodywork is made with a specially shaped neoprene strip which is slid into a groove round the outside edge of the frame, behind the overlapping frame lip. This seal is compressed, to prevent seepage of water, when window is drawn against caravan body.

A second neoprene seal, between the glass and the window-frame, has a U section. It is fitted into an internal groove round the frame, and the glass is fitted into the centre of the U section. The neoprene fitting must be continuous for complete sealing.

If either of these neoprene seals shows signs of cracking, renew it with a similar one obtained from a dealer. Before renewing the seals, it is necessary first to remove the window, following the method shown.

Materials: external and glazing neoprene sealing strips of the correct sections; hinge plugs; masking tape.
Tools: screwdrivers (bladed and cross-head); pliers.

ALUMINIUM SURROUNDS
Neglect of the aluminium frame, leading to progressive corrosion, spoils the appearance of the caravan. Unfortunately, this process often passes unnoticed until it has reached an advanced stage.

Keep the window fully open when cleaning the aluminium surround, to prevent damage to the body paintwork by the cleaning and polishing material. If necessary, use a wire brush to remove loose particles from the frame surface. Clean off surface contamination on the alloy frame with ordinary cellulose thinners, and polish with a good-quality silver polish, or a proprietary solvent such as Autosol.

A coat of clear marine varnish will give added protection to the metal.

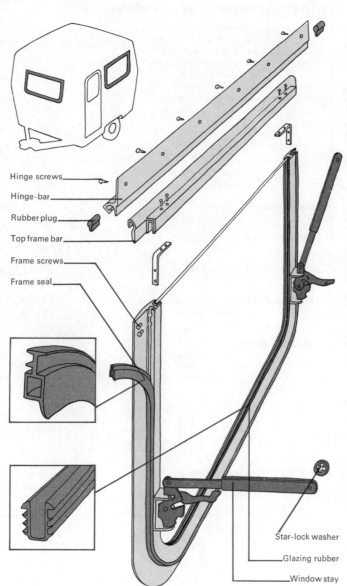

Hinge screws
Hinge-bar
Rubber plug
Top frame bar
Frame screws
Frame seal

Star-lock washer
Glazing rubber
Window stay

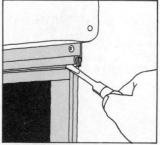

1 To avoid disturbing the hinge-bar seal when removing a window, prise open the channel ends

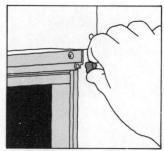

2 This will loosen the plastic plugs blanking off the ends of the channel. Remove the two plugs

3 Undo the two end screws in the top hinge-bar. Pull out the frame-sealing strip trapped beneath it

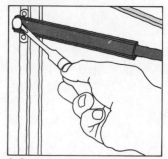

4 Open the windows fully, prise off the star-lock washers on the support stays, and remove the stays

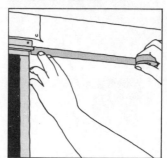

5 Apply masking tape in line with the hinge to avoid scratching the paint when removing the frame

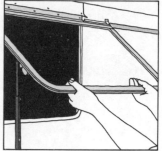

6 Check that the sealing strip is free of the hinge screw ends, then slide out the frame *(continued)*

Caravans Roof lights

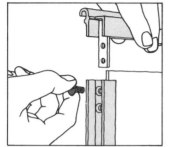

7 Peel back the outer seal to gain access to the frame screws that hold the top of the frame to the sides

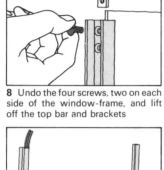

8 Undo the four screws, two on each side of the window-frame, and lift off the top bar and brackets

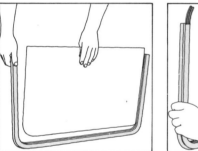

9 Carefully part the frame uprights slightly and lift out the glass. Remove the glazing strip

10 Fit a new seal, leaving a 1–2 in. (25–50 mm) surplus at each end. This will shrink if left for half an hour

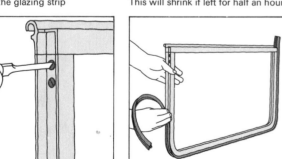

11 Trim off any remaining surplus, then replace the glass, the top frame bar, the brackets and the screws

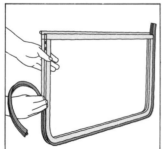

12 Fit a new sealing strip round the frame. Leave 3 in. (75 mm) at each end to tuck under the hinge-bar

Fitting a new roof light

Repeated opening and closing of the roof light may eventually cause cracking round the hinge bolt holes; and an insecure roof light, left open in a high wind, is likely to be torn off. Replace the light at the first sign of cracking, before this can occur.

The scissors-movement fitting has a left-hand and a right-hand hinge. It is essential when fitting a new roof light to fit these hinges with their elongated slots facing the same way.

Materials: new roof-light panel; neoprene sealing strip.
Tools: cross-head screwdriver; hand drill and bit; scriber.

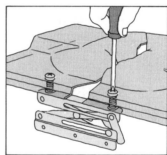

2 From inside the caravan, lift up the roof light, turn it corner to corner, and lower it through the opening

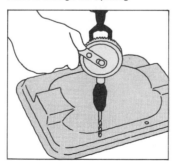

5 Carefully mark the centres of the new bolt holes and drill them, exerting only minimum pressure

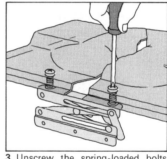

3 Unscrew the spring-loaded bolts holding the hinges to the panel. Some are held by nylon locking-nuts

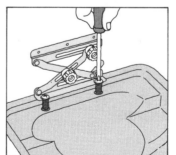

6 Correctly position the two hinges and bolt them to the new panel with a little sealer under each bolt head

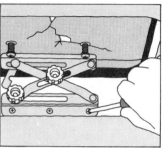

1 Undo the three self-tapping cross-head screws holding each of the two hinge-plates to the van body

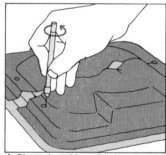

4 Place the old roof-light panel on top of the new, and use the old one as a template to scribe the new holes

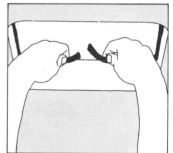

7 Before fitting the roof-light panel to the caravan body, renew the neoprene sealing strip round the rim

Caravans Water pumps

Servicing a foot pump

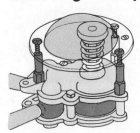

Overhaul kits containing seals and washers are available for all foot-operated pumps. The pump shown is a Jupiter Jet, but others are constructed on basically similar lines. The exploded illustration below shows the main components. Poor water delivery is an indication that the pump needs attention.

Materials: overhaul kit; tallow or Vaseline.
Tools: spanners to fit the body piston bolts and assembly nuts; screwdriver.

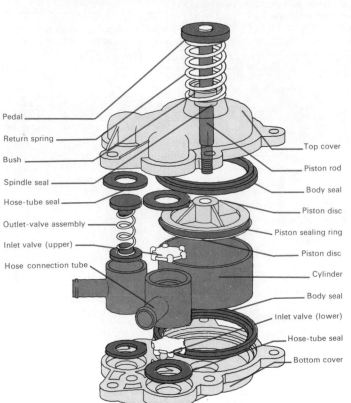

Pedal
Return spring
Bush
Spindle seal
Hose-tube seal
Outlet-valve assembly
Inlet valve (upper)
Hose connection tube

Top cover
Piston rod
Body seal
Piston disc
Piston sealing ring
Piston disc
Cylinder
Body seal
Inlet valve (lower)
Hose-tube seal
Bottom cover

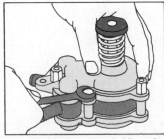

1 Undo the five nuts holding the pump together, including the three longer nuts that hold it to the floor. Draw the body apart

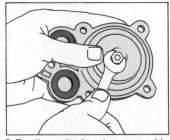

2 To dismantle the piston assembly from the top of the pump body, undo the brass nut on the end of the pump piston rod and remove the piston

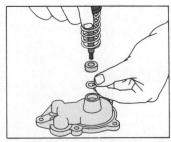

3 When the piston assembly is dismantled, it is advisable to renew both the spindle seal—a rubber O ring—and the piston-rod bush

4 The rubber piston ring is held firmly between the piston discs. Make sure it seats properly before beginning to reassemble the pump

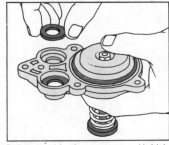

5 Reassemble the pump top. Hold it as shown above, and fit the new body seal and the inlet and outlet-hose connection tube seals

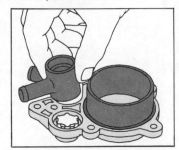

6 Refit the outlet-hose connection tube. Fit the inlet-hose tube over the lower inlet valve. Set the ends of the tubes at an angle as shown

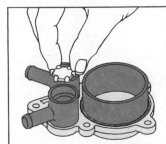

7 Refit the upper inlet valve, with the smooth side downwards, on to the shoulder in the body of the hose connection tube

8 Fit a new rubber outlet valve at each end of the light valve spring. Drop the assembled unit into the body of the outlet-hose connection tube

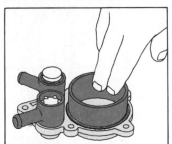

9 Lightly lubricate the pump cylinder with a smear of tallow or Vaseline. Refit the piston assembly and other parts of the pump body together

Overhauling a hand pump

Poor water delivery shows that worn glands and seals need replacing. An angled Whale unit is illustrated, but all plunger-type pumps have basically the same construction. Comprehensive pump overhaul kits containing glands, washers and seals can be obtained from dealers.

Materials: pump overhaul kit.
Tools: screwdriver; spanner for the stud on the plunger assembly.

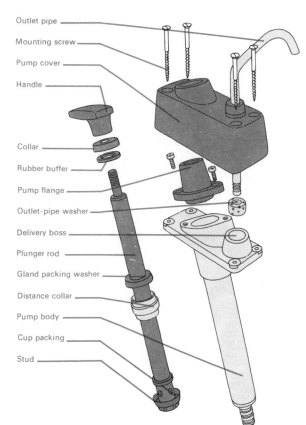

Outlet pipe
Mounting screw
Pump cover
Handle
Collar
Rubber buffer
Pump flange
Outlet-pipe washer
Delivery boss
Plunger rod
Gland packing washer
Distance collar
Pump body
Cup packing
Stud

1 Pull out the outlet pipe. Unscrew the pump handle and remove the collar and buffer

2 Undo the mounting screws holding the pump cover to the base and lift off the cover

3 Remove the screws holding the pump flange collar. Slip the flange off the assembly

4 Withdraw the plunger rod and complete pump assembly from the body of the pump

5 Slip the gland packing washer and distance collar off the plunger rod

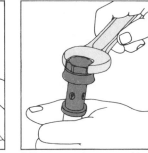

6 To remove the cup packing at the base of the plunger rod, unscrew the end stud

7 Removal of the stud and cup packing releases the ball valve in the plunger-rod base

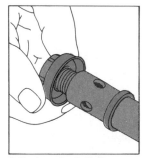

8 Replace the ball, fit a new cup packing on the stud threads and replace the stud

9 Fit the distance collar, short boss upwards; fit the packing washer, cup downwards

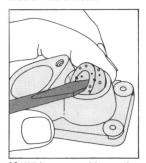

10 With a screwdriver, prise out the washer from the delivery boss on the pump body

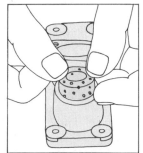

11 Insert a new cork washer, pressing it down firmly into the well of the delivery boss

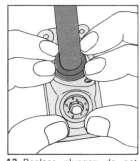

12 Replace plunger: do not let the gland washer turn up. Refit the flange and cover

Realigning a badly fitting door

A badly fitted interior cabinet can distort the body panel to which it is secured. If that panel is next to a stable-type door, the distortion will cause a wider opening between the door sections at one end than at the other when the door is open. To correct the fault, re-site and secure the cabinet while the panel is under pressure from the outside.

1 The bulging of the caravan panel next to the door will cause the two sections of the stable door to part unevenly in the middle when it is opened

2 To make the doors open evenly, reposition the fitted cabinet. First remove any plastic trim or fittings joined to the cabinet. Put them on one side for replacement

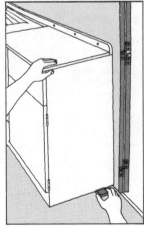

3 Remove the back strip if there is one and free any interior strips at the rear of the cabinet. Do not loosen the floor screws at the front of the cabinet

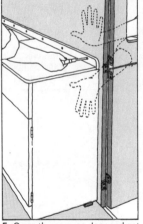

4 Tilt the unit forwards and pack wood under the rear corners to hold the top of the cabinet permanently away from the caravan panel

5 Open the caravan door and get a helper to push against the outside panel level with the centre hinge. Refit and tighten all cabinet screws. Replace the trim

Replacing a damaged corner steady

Corner steadies are provided as supports for the standing caravan. Using one as a jack to change a wheel will damage the support stays, which will then need replacing.

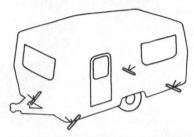

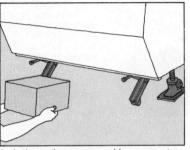

1 Jack up the caravan with a screw-type car jack. Place blocks of timber under each end of the caravan to prevent tipping

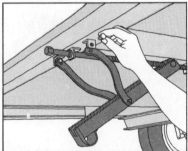

2 Clevis pins secured by split-pins hold the support stays to the chassis. Withdraw the split-pins to remove the clevis pins

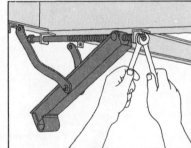

3 There are two nuts at the inner end of the steady jacking screw. Undo them by using two spanners together

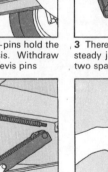

4 Withdraw the jacking screw from the trunnion in the top of the jack leg by turning the screw anti-clockwise

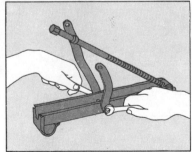

5 Take off the bent stays by removing the retaining nut, fit new stays, reassemble the steady and fit back on the caravan

Cars Bodywork

Care and maintenance

The body of a modern saloon car is made from stamped and pressed sections of thin-gauge metal. These are vulnerable to rust, especially in places where moisture tends to collect or which gather large amounts of corrosive dirt. There are several rust-inhibiting compounds available, but they are fully effective only when applied to bare metal.

The best and cheapest way to minimise corrosion is to wash and dry the car once a week. Most cars have drain holes on the lower edges of the doors and door sills. Make sure they are not blocked. Do not allow caked mud to build up on the underside of the body, especially under the wheel arches. Check paintwork weekly, and repair any damage immediately it is seen.

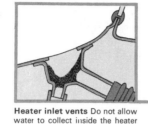

Heater inlet vents Do not allow water to collect inside the heater vents. Check that the drain tube is clear

Trim Check that the bright trim is fixed securely (see p. 638). Remove rust, apply a rust inhibitor and paint over it

Guttering Clear out any debris and dirt. Fill holes immediately

Mirrors Clean rear-view-mirror locating points every week. Smear grease on the fixing occasionally

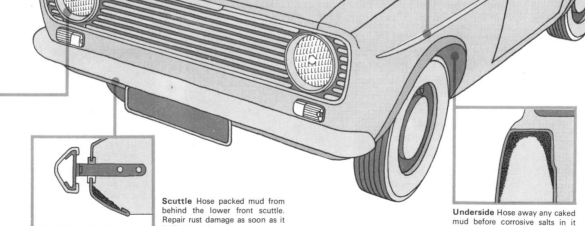

Lights Dry headlamps and side-lamps after washing them. Check regularly that water is not trapped behind the trim

Scuttle Hose packed mud from behind the lower front scuttle. Repair rust damage as soon as it is discovered

Underside Hose away any caked mud before corrosive salts in it can damage the bodywork

Doors and sills Do not let dirt lodge in the bottom of doors or in the door sills. Clean drain holes

Cars Bodywork

Riveting a split in the bodywork

If part of a car bodywork splits or tears, it may be possible to repair the damage with a patch of new metal and a riveting kit. Make sure before attempting any work, however, that the damaged area does not affect the strength or structural rigidity of the car. If there is any doubt, take the car to a garage and seek expert advice. Riveting kits are readily available at tool stores and car-accessory shops.

Materials: aluminium strip.
Tools: riveting kit; mallet; pliers; electric drill; wrench; wire brush; wood block.

USING A RIVETING KIT

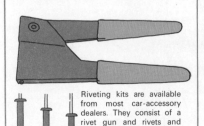

Riveting kits are available from most car-accessory dealers. They consist of a rivet gun and rivets and nails of different sizes

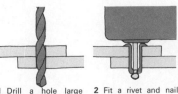

1 Drill a hole large enough for the rivet to be used through the two pieces of metal

2 Fit a rivet and nail together. Push into the gun and hold them firmly in the hole

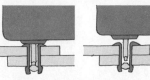

3 Squeeze the trigger of the gun. This will draw the nail up through the rivet

4 The gun squashes the bottom of the rivet outwards and breaks the nail

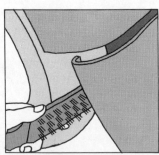

1 Thoroughly clean the inside surface of the damaged area of bodywork with a stiff wire brush

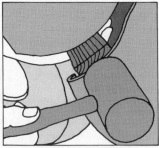

2 Hold a wood block inside the split. Hammer the edges to remove any distortion in the metal

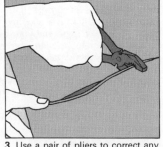

3 Use a pair of pliers to correct any slight metal distortion remaining at the edges of the split

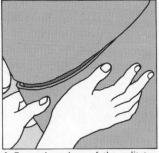

4 Force the edges of the split together. Find out how much metal is needed for a patch behind the gap

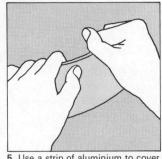

5 Use a strip of aluminium to cover the split. Bend it to the approximate contour of the wing

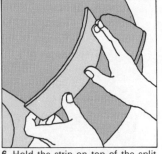
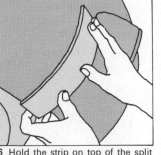

6 Hold the strip on top of the split wing. Adjust the strip to fit the curve of the wing

7 Fit the strip inside the wing. Hold it in position on one side with an adjustable wrench

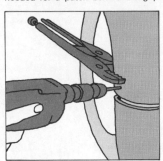

8 On the outside edge of the wing, drill a hole through the edge and the strip behind it

9 Fit a rivet and nail in the hole. Set the rivet with the gun. Rivet every 1 in. (25 mm) along the split

10 When one edge is completely riveted, drill and rivet back along the other edge

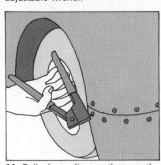

11 Pull the split together as the second edge is riveted. Fit rivets staggered with the first set

Repairing a dent or crease in a wing

Minor creases and dents in the bodywork of a car can be easily and inexpensively repaired with a two-part proprietary filler paste. There are several on the market.

Follow the manufacturer's instructions carefully when mixing and applying the paste. Take care not to use the applicator —supplied with the kit—to scoop paste out of the can when it has been in contact with the other part, the catalytic agent. If the two are mixed, the paste immediately starts to harden.

Glass-fibre repair kit

Extreme temperatures affect the setting and quality of the filler mixture. Do not use it in very hot or cold weather. Always work in a dry, draught-proof but well-ventilated place.

The quality of the finished repair depends greatly on the preparation. Keep the area clean and make sure that the bare metal is smooth before mixing the paste. Wear gloves to feel for smoothness. Fingermarks are likely to prevent a good bonding between metal and filler. The only specialist tool needed is a body file, which can be adjusted to the contours of the wing of the car.

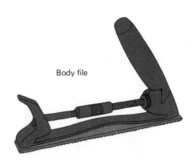

Body file

Use the file carefully and make sure that the repaired area is not rubbed down too much. Apply more filler if necessary.

Paint the finished repair to match the existing paintwork of the car. Matching aerosol paint kits are available in most accessory shops.

Materials: sanding disc; coarse and medium grades of wet-and-dry abrasive paper; body-filler kit, which should include paste, catalyst, aerosol primer, aerosol paint and paste applicator.
Tools: screwdriver; sanding disc; rubbing block; body file; power tool.

1 Use the power tool to sand the damaged part and surrounding area down to the bare metal

2 Rub the area with medium-grade abrasive paper. Do not touch the bare metal with the fingers

3 Scoop out a quantity of paste from the can. Spread it evenly on a smooth, clean surface

4 Add catalytic agent from the tube— about half a tube to half a can of paste are the correct proportions

5 Mix the paste and catalyst. Take care to remove air bubbles which may be trapped in the mixture

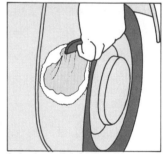

6 Apply a little paste at a time, pushing it hard on to the metal. Build up gradually in thin layers

---

USING A POWER TOOL

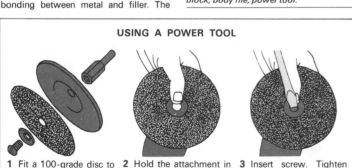

1 Fit a 100-grade disc to the sanding attachment of the power tool

2 Hold the attachment in the power tool. Place washer in position

3 Insert screw. Tighten with screwdriver. Make sure paper does not crinkle

7 Allow the filler to harden. Remove the high spots from the surface of the hardened filler with a body file

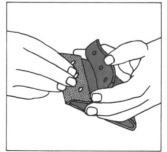

8 Fit a medium-grade abrasive paper to a rubbing block to rub down the repaired area

9 Make sure edges of the repaired area are feathered to meet the surrounding undamaged bodywork

Cars Bodywork

Repairing major rust damage

If the metal bodywork of a car becomes rusted, repair it with filler, resin and glass-fibre matting. Make sure that the damaged area is not in a part that makes a contribution to the car's structural strength. If there is any doubt, take the car to a garage for repair. Remove all traces of rust. Spray a rust-inhibiting agent on to the cleaned area before applying the glass-fibre and filler paste.

Materials: rust repair kit containing resin, hardener, glass-fibre matting, filler paste; perforated metal sheeting if necessary; rust inhibitor; mixing bowl; wet-and-dry paper.
Tools: power tool; screwdriver; light hammer; sanding disc; rubbing block; heavy file; cold chisel; brush; knife; hacksaw blade.

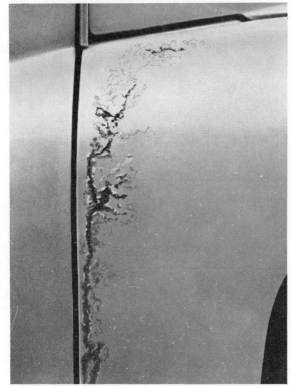

Rust Corrosion of the steel panels is first indicated by the formation of small blisters on the paint surface

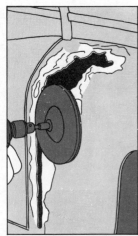

1 Scour the damaged area with a power tool and a sanding disc. Sand the paintwork around the affected part

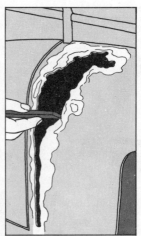

2 Use a cold chisel to break heavy rust deposits. Make sure that no traces of rust remain on the metal

3 Turn in the edges of the metal slightly, by tapping with a light hammer. Apply a proprietary rust inhibitor

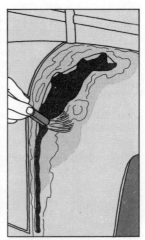

4 Mix the resin and hardener in a bowl. Soak a brush in the resin mix and saturate the damaged area

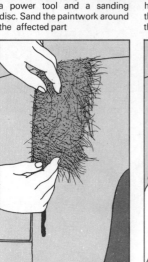

5 Lay a piece of pre-cut glass-fibre matting larger than the damaged area of the bodywork on top of the resin

6 Make sure the glass-fibre matting is thoroughly impregnated by using a stippling action with a resin-soaked brush

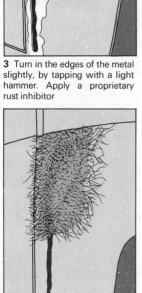

7 When the matting is fully saturated allow it to set for about an hour. Check that it is firm and hard

8 For splits in the bodywork, use perforated metal sheet instead of glass-fibre. Measure amount required *(continued)*

9 Mark the width needed (twice the width of the split) and bend the metal to a V shape over the bench edge or piece of wood

10 Bend the metal sheet backwards and forwards until it weakens along the line which was marked on it

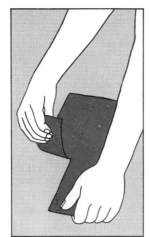

11 Tear off the perforated metal sheet. Check that the torn-off piece is about twice the width of the split

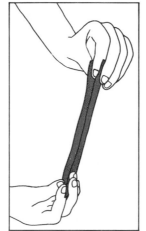

12 Bend the piece of metal sheet along its length and about halfway across its width to form a wide V shape

13 Fit the bent piece of sheet into the split in the body. Adjust the V so that the metal fits snugly in the split

14 If the repair involves the use of both matting and metal, make sure that the two materials meet over the hole

15 Use a heavy file, a sharp knife or a hacksaw blade to cut the excess matting from around the repair

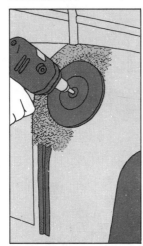

16 Use the power tool to sand round the edges of the glass-fibre and metal insert. Feather into the undamaged areas

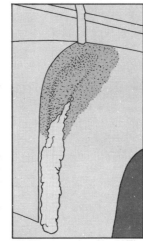

17 Mix a quantity of body filler according to the manufacturer's instructions. Apply to the prepared area of the bodywork

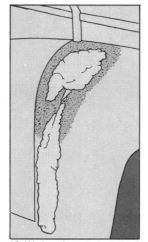

18 Work up from the bottom of the repair area. Make sure that the whole area of the cavity is packed with filler

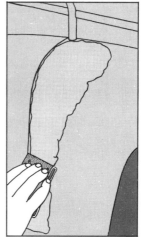

19 Ensure that the filler paste is not blocking drain holes in the body. Rub down with wet-and-dry paper. Feather the edges

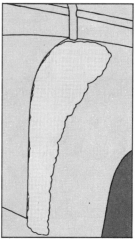

20 When the filled area is smooth, allow it to harden before applying finishing coats (see p. 634)

Cars Bodywork

Applying a finishing coat

To produce a smooth finished surface which can be painted, allow the body filler paste to harden thoroughly for at least a week.

The purpose of the final skim coat is to cover any small—and possibly unnoticeable—holes in the surface of the filler. Apply it so thinly to the hardened repair that the original filler can be seen through it. When rubbing down the skim coat, always make sure that the fine-grade wet-and-dry paper is kept thoroughly soaked with water.

Materials: body filler; medium and fine wet-and-dry paper; medium sanding disc for a power tool.
Tools: power tool with sanding attachment; filler applicator; rubbing block.

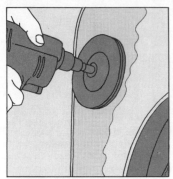

1 Buff the surface of the repaired area with a medium sanding disc fitted on a power tool. Feather the edges into the undamaged metal

2 Mix a small amount of body filler. With a clean applicator, apply a very thin skim coat to cover the surface of the repair

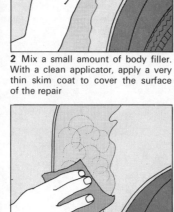

3 Allow the skim coat to harden. Fit a medium-grade wet-and-dry paper to a rubbing block. Use dry and rub with a circular movement

4 Put fine-grade paper on the block. Use dry and smooth further. Finish with fine-grade paper, used wet, without the block

Using an aerosol paint

Use aerosol primer and paint to finish a bodywork repair. Wash and dry the area to be sprayed. Use brown paper and adhesive tape to mask off at least 24 in. (610 mm) around the part of the bodywork to be sprayed.

Shake aerosol primers and paints for about five minutes before using them. Apply the primer first. Allow it to dry and wash the surface with clean, cold water. Rub the area with water-soaked wet-and-dry paper. Apply several light top coats.

Three weeks after applying the paint, give the surface a final polish with compound paste.

Materials: aerosol primer and paint to match car colour; brown paper; adhesive tape; fine-grade wet-and-dry paper; compound paste.

SPRAYING FAULTS

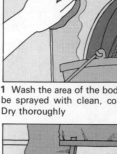

Running The paint may run if the aerosol is not shaken enough, if too much is applied, or if the can is held too close to the surface

Overspray Insufficient masking results in new paint extending to existing paintwork

---

1 Wash the area of the bodywork to be sprayed with clean, cold water. Dry thoroughly

2 Mask around the repair with brown paper and adhesive tape. Mask the wheels of the car if necessary

3 Apply the primer. Hold the aerosol about 12 in. (305 mm) from the bodywork. Spray from left to right

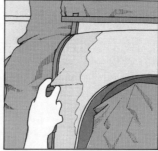

4 Rub the primer when it is dry. Wash and dry thoroughly before applying a finishing coat

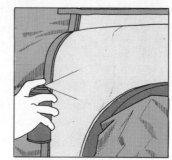

5 Apply the finishing coat. Release the aerosol button at the end of each horizontal stroke

6 Do not rub the final coat of paint. Polish with compound paste after three weeks

Types of door latch

Car latch mechanisms are operated by rods, cables or bars from the door handles. There are many different types, but they can all be removed for overhaul in the same way.

Take off the inner handle, armrests, window winder and door trim (see p. 667). Disconnect the connecting rods or bars which run from the handles to the mechanism.

Make a sketch of how the various linkages are connected to the latch mechanism, to help when reassembling. Some of the rod types are fitted through nylon bushes. It is essential to refit the bushes to eliminate rattle.

While the door panel is removed, check that the door drain hole is clear. Latches can become damaged if water lodges inside the door frame.

Lock mechanism Most is hidden inside the car door. All that can be seen are the pawl or disc and striker plate

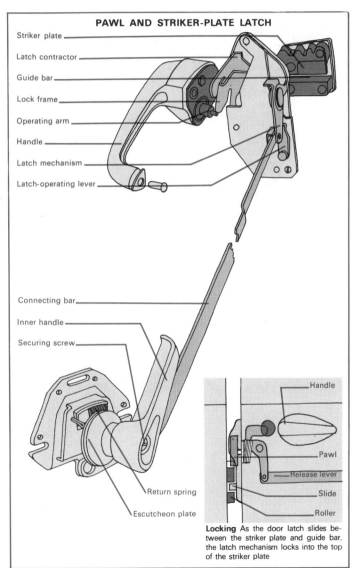

PAWL AND STRIKER-PLATE LATCH

Striker plate
Latch contractor
Guide bar
Lock frame
Operating arm
Handle
Latch mechanism
Latch-operating lever
Connecting bar
Inner handle
Securing screw
Return spring
Escutcheon plate

Handle
Pawl
Release lever
Slide
Roller

Locking As the door latch slides between the striker plate and guide bar, the latch mechanism locks into the top of the striker plate

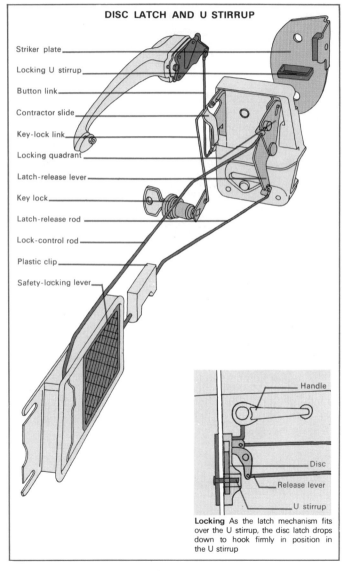

DISC LATCH AND U STIRRUP

Striker plate
Locking U stirrup
Button link
Contractor slide
Key-lock link
Locking quadrant
Latch-release lever
Key lock
Latch-release rod
Lock-control rod
Plastic clip
Safety-locking lever

Handle
Disc
Release lever
U stirrup

Locking As the latch mechanism fits over the U stirrup, the disc latch drops down to hook firmly in position in the U stirrup

Cars Bodywork

Maintaining and lubricating a lock

HOW A SAFETY LATCH WORKS

Disc latches are designed to withstand the impact of a crash without allowing the doors to burst open. When the door is closed, a rotating disc drops down into a U stirrup on the door pillar striker plate. The lock is secured by a pawl.

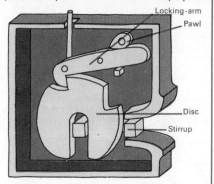

Locking-arm
Pawl
Disc
Stirrup

Door closed The disc in the safety latch is turned into the locking position when the stirrup makes contact with it. It is secured in the closed position by the pawl

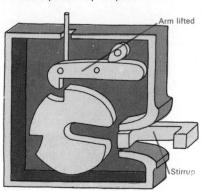

Arm lifted
Stirrup

Door open As the door button or lever is operated, the disc turns under spring pressure. This lifts the disc out of the U stirrup and releases the door

For safety, door locks must be kept correctly adjusted. Check the alignment of the parts regularly.

If a lock becomes stiff and difficult to operate, lubricate with a thin lock oil, available from car-accessory shops. Squirt the oil into the keyholes, where it not only lubricates the lock but also helps to prevent freezing during the winter months. Grease the lock mechanisms inside the door at least once a year.

Oil or grease spilt on the bodywork can soil passengers' clothes: wipe off any excess immediately with a dry clean rag.

LUBRICATION

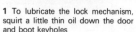

1 To lubricate the lock mechanism, squirt a little thin oil down the door and boot keyholes

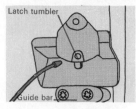

Latch tumbler
Guide bar

2 Open the door. Some cars have a lubrication hole in the latch. If not, oil around the latch tumbler

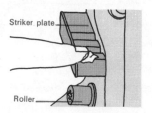

Striker plate
Roller

3 Lubricate the striker plate and roller below it with a medium-grade grease. Wipe off excess grease

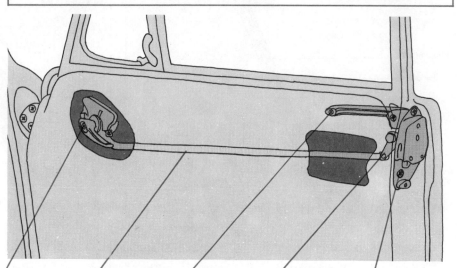

Interior handle If a handle is secured by a single centre-screw, tighten it with a screwdriver every 10,000 miles

Connecting bar If a stiff handle cannot be eased by lubricating, remove the trim and straighten the connecting bar

Exterior handle If a door handle is loose, remove the trim and tighten the retaining screws in the door panel

Pivot If an interior handle mechanism is slack, remove the pivot and fit a new nylon bearing bush or tighten the bolt

Screws Every 10,000 miles, tighten the screws holding the lock mechanism on the door panel behind the trim

Adjusting a latch

The alignment of a car door can be adjusted by moving the latch striker plate on the door pillar. If the door has a tendency to lift when it is closed, the striker plate is too high. If the door drops when closed, the plate is too low. Similarly, the position of the striker plate determines whether the door fits flush in line with the rest of the bodywork.

Adjust the plate so that the door can close correctly without forcing. If a striker plate is worn, fit a new one.

Materials: striker plate, if necessary.
Tools: pencil; screwdriver to suit striker-plate screws.

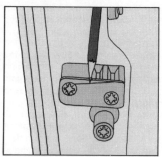

2 Close door so that pencil marks striker plate. The line should be parallel with the top of the plate

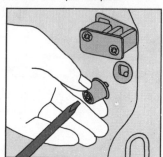

4 If the striker plate and roller are worn, remove roller. Refit its screw to hold the back plate in door

Fitting a new door-latch mechanism

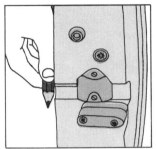

1 Open door and window. From outside, hold pencil inside the door, in line with the striker plate

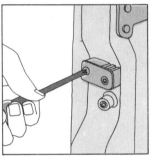

3 If line is at an angle, loosen striker-plate screws and move plate. Check again with pencil

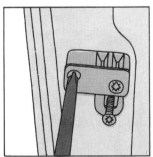

5 Remove the striker plate and fit a new plate. Remove the roller screw and fit a new roller

1 Remove the window-winder handle. It may be fitted with a central screw, circlip or peg (see p. 667)

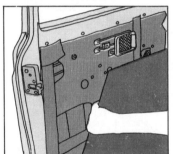

5 When all the retaining clips are freed, carefully lift the trim panel away from the door

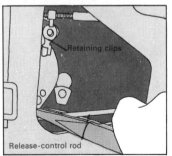

9 Remove the retaining clip on the lower rod—the release control. Disconnect the rod

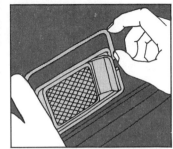

2 Remove a lever-latch handle in the same way. If it is a flush fitting, slide it off the trim

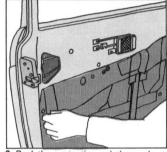

6 Peel the protective polythene sheet down from the top of the door panel to expose the latch mechanism

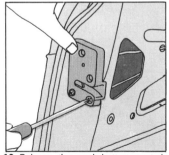

10 Release the push-button control rod from the latch bush inside the panel screws and lift out the latch unit

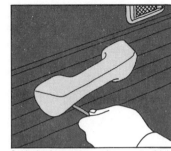

3 Undo the screws or box nuts which secure the arm rest to the door at the panel. Remove arm rest

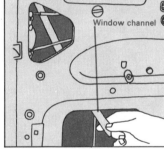

7 Pull back the window channel (see p. 667) inside the door, so that it does not obstruct the latch mechanism

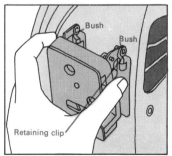

11 Fit the small plastic bushes and rod retaining clips first. Position and fix the new latch unit

4 Slide a screwdriver blade behind the door trim. Prise off the retaining clips round the edges

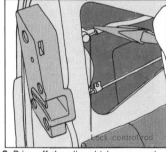

8 Prise off the clip which secures the lock control rod on the latch assembly. Lift the rod out of the latch bush

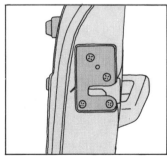

12 Tighten the four screws securing the latch. Make sure the unit is in line with the striker plate

Cars Bodywork

Adjusting bonnet and boot latches

If a bonnet or a boot latch is not operating correctly, it is likely that the locating plate and catch are out of alignment. Both can be loosened and moved fractionally to fit exactly.

Tool: spanner.

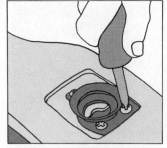

1 Loosen the striker-plate locating screws and move the plate to align it with the bonnet catch above it

BOOT LATCHES

1 Loosen the bolts on either side of the boot-latch clasp until it can be moved by hand

2 When the latch clasp is freed tap it gently to a new position and retighten

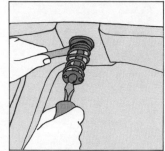

2 Hold the nut with a spanner and turn the locking bolt in or out to adjust the bonnet closing position

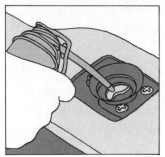

3 Once the bonnet striker plate has been adjusted, lubricate with thin oil to ensure easy bonnet closing

Door sealing

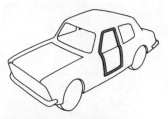

Car doors are usually sealed with a rubber strip. If it seems inadequate, apply adhesive (see p. 694).

Materials: contact adhesive.
Tool: screwdriver.

1 Dab a few touches of adhesive along the frame lip with a scrap of wood. Push the seal on the lip

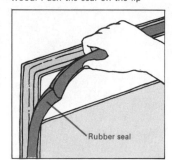

Rubber seal

2 Some cars are fitted with a sealer which usually snaps into place round the door frame

Fixing exterior trim

The bright exterior trim on a car is usually a chrome strip with a double lip on the underside. It is held in position by spring clips.

Tools: screwdriver; hammer.

PLASTIC CLIPS

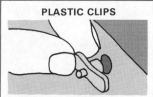

1 Push the new plastic clip into place in the hole in the car-body panel

2 Hold the clip level and tap the centre peg into the clip with a lightweight hammer

3 Once the clips have been fitted, slide the chrome trim into position from front or back of car

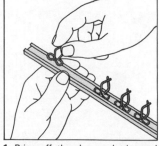

1 Prise off the damaged trim and count the locating holes in the body. Fit enough clips into new trim

2 Hold the trim against the body and slide the clips to the correct position in the trim strip

3 Locate the first clip. Do the same with all the other clips along the trim and push them home

Cars Cooling system

How a water-cooled system works

A car engine operates most efficiently when it is very hot. If it becomes too hot, however, the engine seizes up. For this reason, all engines have a cooling system to maintain the best possible operating temperature.

In most cooling systems, water is circulated round the engine and through the radiator by a pump which is belt-driven by the engine crankshaft pulley. The pulley belt also drives a fan which pushes or pulls cold air through the radiator to cool the hot water which has been pumped round the engine block. When the water is cooled, it is returned to the engine by the pump and back to the radiator for further cooling.

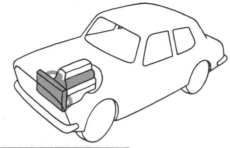

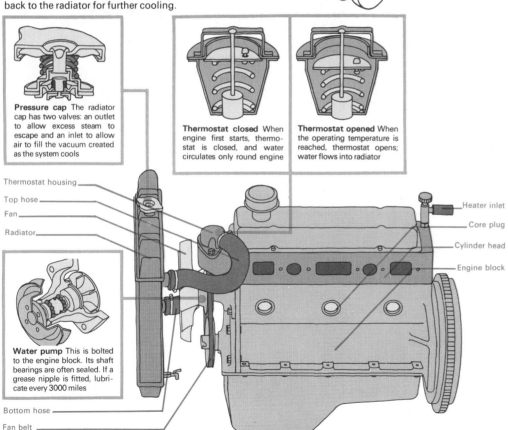

Pressure cap The radiator cap has two valves: an outlet to allow excess steam to escape and an inlet to allow air to fill the vacuum created as the system cools

Thermostat closed When engine first starts, thermostat is closed, and water circulates only round engine

Thermostat opened When the operating temperature is reached, thermostat opens; water flows into radiator

Water pump This is bolted to the engine block. Its shaft bearings are often sealed. If a grease nipple is fitted, lubricate every 3000 miles

Thermostat housing

Top hose

Fan

Radiator

Bottom hose

Fan belt

Heater inlet

Core plug

Cylinder head

Engine block

Fitting a new thermostat

When an engine overheats—indicated on the temperature gauge on some instrument panels—it is likely that the cooling-system thermostat has failed in the closed position.

Each thermostat has its correct opening temperature stamped on the rim. Remove it from its housing and support it in a pan of warm water. Heat the water with a thermometer in it, and check the temperature at which the thermostat opens. If it is above the figure on the thermostat, fit a new one.

Materials: thermostat; gasket; housing gasket; liquid detergent; grease.
Tools: screwdriver; spanner; scraper.

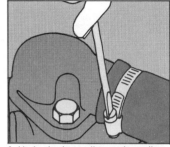

1 Undo the hose clips at the radiator top and at the thermostat housing. Draw the hose off the two tubes

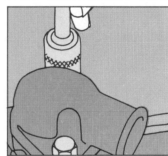

2 Undo the bolts securing the thermostat housing on the engine. Some engines have two; others have three

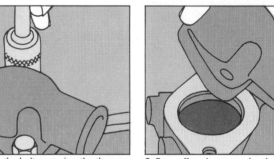

3 Ease off and remove the thermostat housing. If it is tight, do not lever under it. Tap the sides to free it

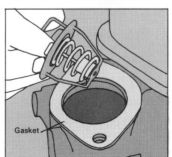

Gasket

4 Lift out the thermostat from the housing. Remove the thin gasket from the recess, if fitted

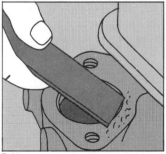

5 Use a scraper to remove any bits of the old gasket which may be stuck to the cylinder-head housing *(continued)*

Cars Cooling system

(continued)

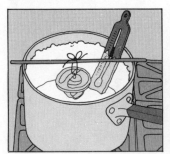

6 Support thermostat in water so that it does not touch pan. Heat water, check when thermostat opens

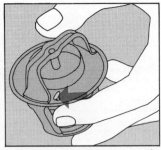

7 If the thermostat opens correctly, check that the bleed valve (arrowed) is free. Clean with air line

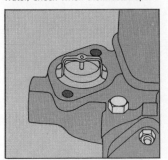

8 Fit a new recess sealing ring, if one is used, and position the thermostat. Some are marked 'FRONT'

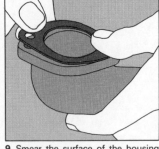

9 Smear the surface of the housing flange with grease and position the cork gasket so that the holes line up

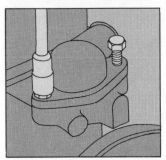

10 Refit the housing. Tighten the bolts sufficiently to compress the cork gasket and make a watertight joint

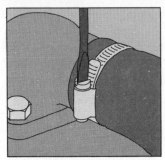

11 If the hose shows signs of wear, fit a new one. Smear the tubes with liquid detergent to make fitting easier

Fitting a new water pump

Water is driven round the engine and radiator by a pump (see p. 639) driven by the fan belt. Poor cooling is usually caused by a fault in the pump.

To check, remove the radiator cap and run the engine until the normal working temperature is reached. When the thermostat is open, water should be seen circulating in the radiator. If not, fit a new pump. If the pump is leaking, remove and check the gasket. If there are no leaks, fit a new pump.

Materials: pump flange gasket; gasket cement.
Tools: spanner; screwdriver; scraper; cleaning brush.

3 Undo the four bolts holding the fan to the water-pump centre boss. Remove the fan blades and the pulley

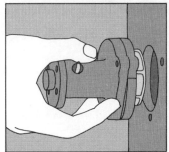

6 Pull off the water pump and remove the flange gasket. Thoroughly clean the engine-block face

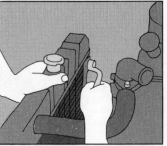

1 Drain radiator and free top and bottom hoses from engine. Undo bolts holding radiator to bodywork

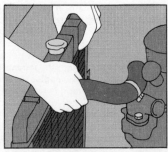

2 Lift the radiator straight up to remove it. Take care not to catch the radiator core on the fan blades

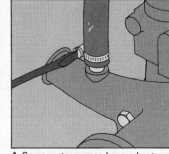

4 Some water pumps have a heater or by-pass hose fitted to them. Loosen the clip and remove the hose

5 If the pump-fixing bolts are secured by tab washers, bend up the tabs. Undo all the bolts

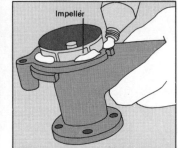

Impeller

7 Spread a light film of gasket cement round the new pump flange. Do not touch the impeller with cement

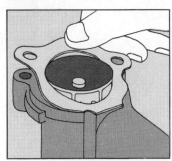

8 Lay a new gasket carefully on the pump flange. Make sure that any cutouts match the flange *(continued)*

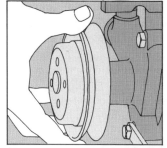

9 Coat the engine surface with gasket cement. Fit the pump and tighten all the bolts evenly

10 Refit the fan-belt pulley to the pump centre boss. Ensure that pulley and flange holes align

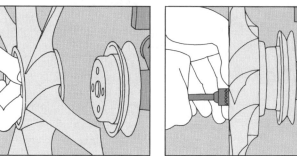

11 Line up the holes of the fan against the pump. Fit the securing bolts finger-tight

12 Tighten the fan-blade bolts half a turn at a time, so that they pull the fan and pulley together evenly

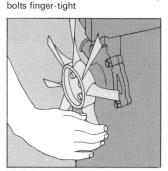

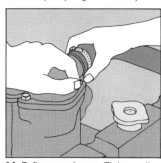

13 Spin the fan and water pump by hand. If the bolts are correctly tightened and the fan is true, refit the belt

14 Refit water hoses. Tighten clips and fill radiator. Start the engine and check for leaks

Back-flushing a radiator

Water in the cooling system causes corrosion which can build up and restrict the flow of water.

To clean a system thoroughly, water must be pushed under pressure through the system in the opposite direction to the way it normally travels—called back-flushing. This removes any debris lodged in the cooling tubes of the radiator and the water passages in the cylinder block.

Keep the water running until it appears clear. If a radiator core cannot be cleared, fit a new radiator.

Materials: water.
Tools: screwdriver; hosepipe.

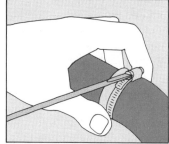
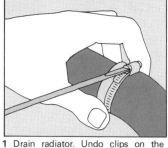

1 Drain radiator. Undo clips on the hoses and remove them from the radiator tubes

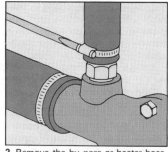

2 Remove the by-pass or heater hose, if fitted, from the water-pump body to prevent restriction when flushing

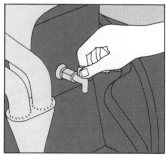

3 Open the drain tap, which is located near the bottom of the engine block at the rear of the engine

4 Close the radiator tap so that the flushing water can get out only from the filler and top hose tube

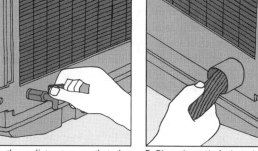

5 Place the end of a hose in the bottom hose tube. Turn on water and flush it through the radiator

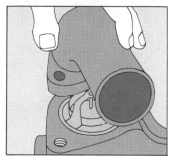

6 Remove thermostat-housing cover and lift out the thermostat to give outlet for the water from the block

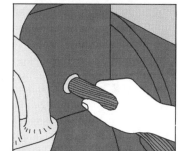

7 Remove engine drain tap. Place hose into engine-block water gallery. Turn on water and flush out

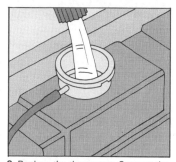

8 Replace the thermostat. Connect the hoses and refill the radiator with water. Start engine and check for leaks

Cars Electrical system

How a distributor works

The distributor is designed to deliver high-voltage current to the spark-plugs at the precise moment when the air-fuel mixture in the combustion chambers is ready to be ignited.

The accurate timing of the spark at the plugs is controlled by the setting of the contact-breaker points. If they are too close, the spark-plug receives the current too late, causing the engine to be under-powered. This is known as retarded ignition. If the points are too far apart, the plugs receive the current too soon, causing a knocking sound in the engine. This is advanced ignition.

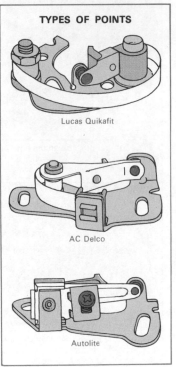

TYPES OF POINTS

Lucas Quikafit

AC Delco

Autolite

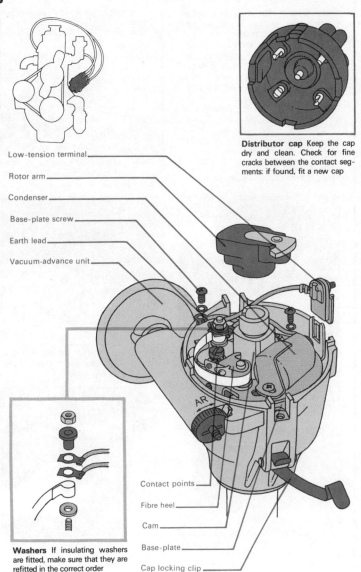

Low-tension terminal

Rotor arm

Condenser

Base-plate screw

Earth lead

Vacuum-advance unit

Contact points

Fibre heel

Cam

Base-plate

Cap locking clip

Washers If insulating washers are fitted, make sure that they are refitted in the correct order

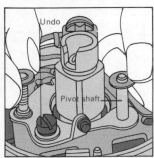

Distributor cap Keep the cap dry and clean. Check for fine cracks between the contact segments: if found, fit a new cap

Fitting new points

If the contact-breaker points in the distributor become badly burnt or pitted, they operate inefficiently and weaken the strength of the spark at the plug. Check the points gap every time the car is serviced. Note that if points are pitted, the gap cannot be set accurately. As a temporary repair, remove points and rub the faces on an emery stone.

Fit new points every 8000–10,000 miles.

Materials: contact-breaker points; emery stone.
Tools: 4 BA spanner; small-bladed screwdriver; feeler gauges.

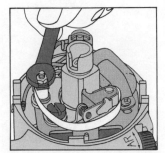

1 Undo the nut on the pillar. Remove the plastic insulator, the condenser and low-tension leads

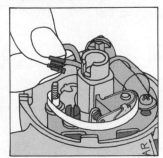

3 Remove insulating washers from the pillar and pivot shaft. Undo the large flat-headed screw

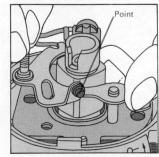

4 Lift off the fixed contact point. Rub both points on emery stone. If badly burnt, buy new points

6 Fit the moving point and the washers and terminal leads. Replace and tighten the nut on the pillar

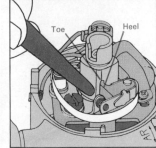

7 Turn cam until its toe touches the heel of the moving point. Place correct feeler between points

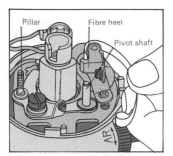

2 Lift the moving-point spring arm off the pillar. Remove the fibre heel from the pivot shaft

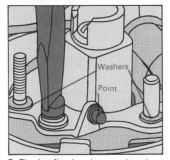

5 Fit the fixed point on the pivot shaft. Tighten screw and replace the insulating washers

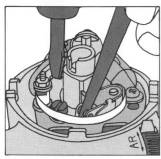

8 Slacken fixed-point screw. Move points with screwdriver in adjusting slot. Tighten screw

Correcting the ignition timing

To advance the ignition timing when the engine starts, the distributor has a device called the vacuum-advance unit. This unit is attached by a tube to the inlet manifold. When the engine is started, the vacuum in the manifold moves the diaphragm of the distributor unit. This turns the base-plate of the distributor and results in advanced ignition.

If the engine performs poorly at idling speed, but improves with acceleration, check the vacuum-advance unit.

Materials: diaphragm assembly.
Tools: screwdriver; thin-nosed pliers.

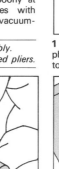

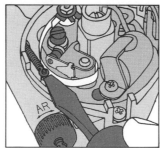

1 To check the vacuum-unit diaphragm, push distributor base-plate towards the unit with a screwdriver

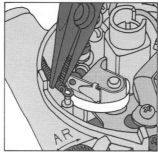

2 Press a finger against the suction hole. Release base-plate. If there is no suction, the unit is faulty

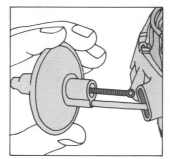

4 Remove circlip from the diaphragm shaft. Undo adjuster, counting the number of turns. Remove spring

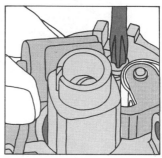

3 To remove the unit, lift the return spring with pliers from the pillar on the base-plate

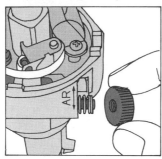

5 Draw out diaphragm assembly. Fit a new one. Reassemble and tighten adjuster the same number of turns

Fitting a new condenser

The condenser is a small, barrel-shaped component housed in, or close to, the distributor. It is designed to store the electrical charge, when the contact-breaker points are open, and to reduce sparking across the points. If there is not a regular spark, examine the points for any indications of burning.

If the points are very badly burnt, it is possible that the condenser is faulty. It cannot be repaired but must be replaced with a new one.

Materials: new condenser.
Tools: 4 BA spanner; Phillips screwdriver.

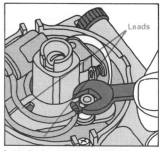

1 Undo the contact-points pillar nut. Remove the insulator and condenser and low-tension leads

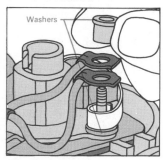

3 Fit new condenser. Tighten earthing screw. Fit the leads and insulating washer. Tighten pillar nut

2 Remove the earthing screw which holds the condenser to the distributor base-plate

FITTING NEW HIGH-TENSION LEADS

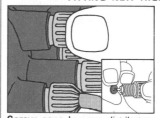

Screw caps In some distributors the leads are held by screw caps. Bare the wire. Push it through the cap and a washer. Bend tip over

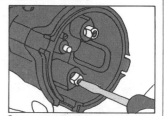

Segment screws In another type the leads are held by screws in the segments inside the cap. A third type of lead is simply pushed on

Cars Electrical system

How spark-plugs work

High-voltage current, delivered through leads from the distributor (see p. 642), flows down the centre electrode in each spark-plug and jumps a small gap to the earth electrode. This creates a spark which ignites the petrol-air mixture in the engine combustion chamber. If a spark-plug corrodes, or if deposits build up, this will result in poor engine performance. Clean the plugs every 3000 to 5000 miles, and make sure that the gap between the electrodes on each plug is correct according to the manufacturer's recommendations.

Tools: stiff-bristled brush; plug spanner; clean rag.

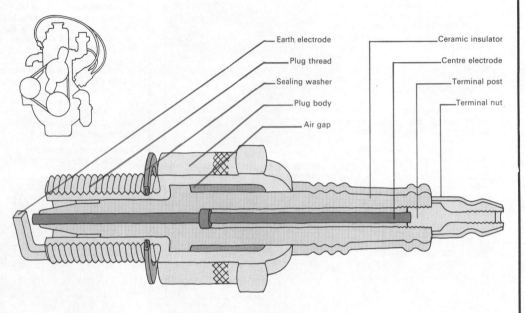

Earth electrode
Plug thread
Sealing washer
Plug body
Air gap
Ceramic insulator
Centre electrode
Terminal post
Terminal nut

REMOVING A SPARK-PLUG

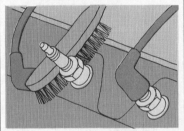

1 Clean around seating with a stiff brush (not wire) to ensure dirt cannot enter engine when plug is removed

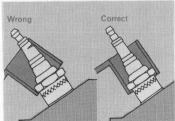

Wrong   Correct

2 Make sure that the plug spanner fits squarely (right) over the plug. If tilted (left) it may break the insulator

SPARK-PLUG FAULTS

The condition of an engine can often be determined by the appearance of the plugs

Oil Heavy deposits of oil on a spark-plug are usually an indication of serious engine wear. Have the engine compression tested by a garage to find if the oil is passing the pistons. If the compression is good, have the valves and guides checked by a mechanic

Carbon When carbon has built up on a spark-plug, suspect that the petrol-air mixture is over-rich. Check and tune the carburettor (see pp. 654–62). Make sure that the air cleaner is not dirty. Check and clean the contact-breaker points and condenser (see p. 642)

Burning When a spark-plug appears badly burnt, this is an indication of overheating, often caused by too weak a petrol-air mixture. Tune the carburettor (see pp. 654–62). Check the points gap (see p. 642). Check the cooling system (see p. 639)

Powdery deposits Small particles left after combustion are not harmful at first, but they can eventually form a hard glazing which cannot be removed: the plugs must then be discarded. Clean plugs which have powdery deposits every 2000 miles

Cleaning plugs

To adjust the plug gap, bend the earth electrode. Never attempt to move the centre electrode.

Never use a wire brush to clean plugs, as pieces of wire may foul the plugs. Scrape off carbon with a plug file or knife. If the electrodes are badly worn, fit new plugs.

Tools: knife; plug feeler gauges; bending tool; plug file.

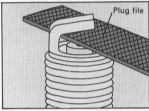

Plug file

1 Scrape carbon deposits from the plug surface. Clean the centre and earth electrode with a plug file

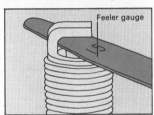

Feeler gauge

2 Fit a feeler gauge of the correct thickness between the faces of the two electrodes to measure the gap

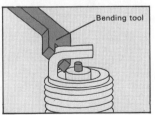

Bending tool

3 Bend the earth electrode with a bending tool to adjust the gap until the feeler just slides in

How a dynamo works

The function of a car dynamo is to generate current to keep the battery charged.

A dynamo does its job only when the engine is running at more than tick-over speed. It consists of a barrel-shaped outer casing with two electro-magnets (also known as field coils) inside it. Between the magnets are a number of separate windings of copper wire which make up the armature. The ends of each winding are joined to copper segments which together make up the commutator.

When the armature revolves, driven by the fan-belt, a current is generated in its windings. This current passes from the commutator into two pieces of carbon known as carbon brushes, which are in contact with the commutator, and from the brushes to the battery. If the brushes wear, or the fan-belt is slack or broken, the dynamo will not work.

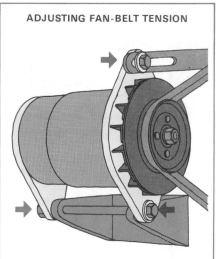

ADJUSTING FAN-BELT TENSION

To prevent the belt slipping, adjust it as recommended in the handbook. Slacken the three dynamo mounting bolts and pivot the dynamo away from, or towards, the engine

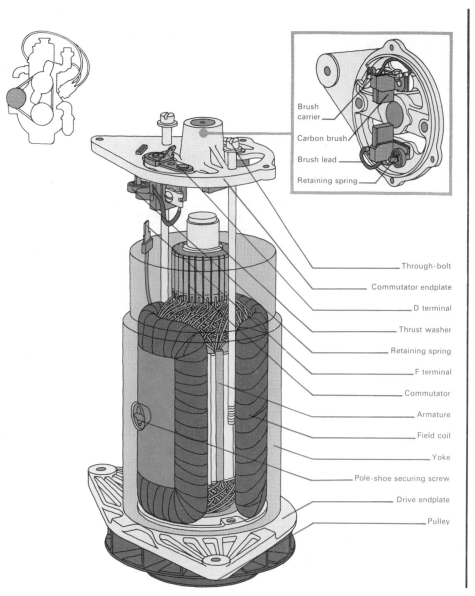

Brush carrier
Carbon brush
Brush lead
Retaining spring

Through-bolt
Commutator endplate
D terminal
Thrust washer
Retaining spring
F terminal
Commutator
Armature
Field coil
Yoke
Pole-shoe securing screw
Drive endplate
Pulley

Fitting new brushes

If the ignition light remains on when the engine is accelerated, the dynamo is not charging the battery. If the belt is already correctly tensioned, dismantle the dynamo. Clean the brush carriers and renew the brushes if they are worn or damaged. Clean the commutator and polish it with fine glass-paper. Cut between the commutator segments with an old hacksaw blade so that they are $\frac{1}{32}$ in. (1 mm) deep.

Materials: brushes; petrol-moistened rag; glass-paper.
Tools: vice; hacksaw blade; BA or box spanner; spring hook; screwdriver; mallet.

1 Secure the dynamo in a vice. Undo and remove the two through-bolts from the commutator endplate

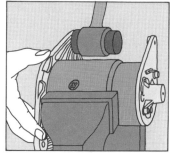

2 Gently tap the inside face of the drive endplate with a mallet to ease it from the housing *(continued)*

Cars Electrical system

(continued)

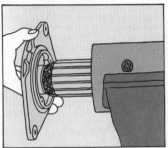

3 Pull out the endplate and armature assembly. Check that the thrust washer is on the end of the shaft

4 Hold the commutator endplate. Tap the inside face, top and bottom, to ease it from the housing

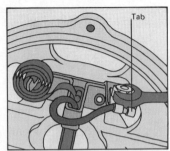

5 Undo the nuts or screws holding the brush leads in position. Do not bend the retaining tabs

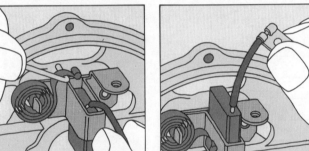

6 Bend a piece of stiff wire and hook the retaining spring upwards and away from one carbon brush

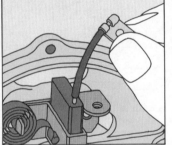

7 Remove the brush and fit a new one. Take out the second brush and fit a replacement

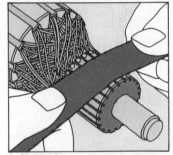

8 Clean the commutator segment surfaces with a petrol-moistened cloth. Polish with glass-paper

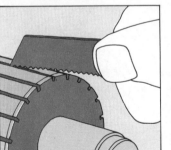

9 Undercut segment channels with a well-used hacksaw blade. Clean and refit assembly in the dynamo casing

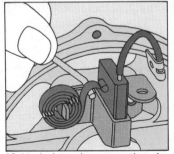

10 Hook the springs up against the brushes to hold them partly out of the holders. Reconnect the brush leads

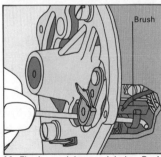

11 Fit the endplate and bolts. Push the hook through the ventilation hole to slip the springs over the brushes

Refitting a dynamo pulley

When a dynamo is bought, it will usually be without a pulley, and the pulley must be removed from the discarded unit to be fitted to the replacement.

The pulley is fitted on the end of the armature shaft—which is keyed to the shaft. The modern dynamo is usually fitted with a pulley made of plastic. Never attempt to remove this type of pulley with a puller, as used for metal pulleys.

An effective method of removing a plastic pulley is to tap the end of the shaft with a mallet.

Tools: spanner; mallet.

1 Use a spanner to undo the dynamo-pulley retaining nut. Remove the nut and turn it over

2 Refit the nut so that its flat face is outwards, flush with the end of the armature shaft

3 Support the underside of the pulley. Give a sharp, strong blow with a mallet to the face of the nut

4 Make sure that the join between the pulley and the shaft is broken. Remove the retaining nut

5 Remove the pulley from the shaft. Fit it on the new dynamo. Refit and tighten the retaining nut

Cars Engines

Fitting a new headlamp bulb

When a bulb fails, remove the lamp unit and disconnect the leads from the bulb holder. Make a note of how each terminal is connected.

Take the old bulb to a car-accessory shop and buy an identical replacement. There are two types: tungsten and quartz-halogen. Tungsten requires no special care; but when replacing a quartz-halogen bulb, try not to touch the glass with bare hands. Natural acid on the fingers causes it to fail as soon as it is switched on. If it is touched, clean it with methylated spirit before fitting.

Always make sure that the leads are refitted to the correct terminals.

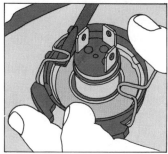

1 Remove the lamp unit from the car. Lift up the spring clips holding the bulb holder to the lamp

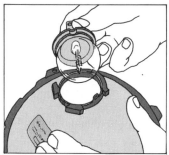

2 Remove the bulb holder. Fit a new bulb and replace the holder. Reassemble the unit in the car

SEALED-BEAM UNITS

In a sealed-beam unit, the headlamp glass is equivalent to the glass in an ordinary bulb. The whole unit can be removed by unscrewing the headlamp rim.

On some units, the leads are connected to a single plug at the back: on others they have to be fixed to individual terminals. Make a note of how they are fitted before disconnecting the unit.

To fit the new unit, make sure that the three lugs are correctly located. This ensures that the beam is correctly set.

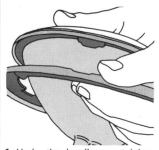

1 Undo the headlamp retaining ring and lift out the unit. Disconnect the leads and discard the unit

2 Connect the leads to the new lamp unit and fit it in position. Refit the lamp rim securely

Finding the fault

Symptom	Checking order	Action
Engine will not turn	Headlights	**If they are dim** Check the battery: recharge (see p. 529)
	Battery-lead terminals	**If corroded** Scrape corrosion off terminals. Clean the battery terminal posts with fine emery cloth. Remove earth lead to chassis: clean and refit
	Jammed starter, indicated by a loud click as starter is engaged	Switch off ignition. Select first gear, release the handbrake and rock the car backwards and forwards to free jammed starter
Starter motor whines when operated, but will not turn the engine	Bendix unit on the end of the starter-motor shaft (see p. 649)	Disconnect the starter-motor lead and remove the starter motor. Clean the Bendix unit in petrol. Lubricate with light oil and spin the Bendix by hand to make sure it moves along the motor shaft **When it moves freely** Refit the motor **If it cannot be freed, or if the pinion teeth are worn** Fit a new starter motor
Engine turns slowly, but will not start	Battery	Recharge (see p. 529) **If not holding charge** Fit a new battery
	Engine-chassis earth connection	Remove earth strap at chassis connection. Clean the strap eye and chassis to bare metal. Refit
Engine spins over on the starter, but will not start	Spark-plugs and the ignition system	**If no spark** Unscrew the spark-plugs. Check plug condition. Clean and re-gap (see p. 644)
	Supply to plug leads	Remove the plug leads and hold them, one at a time, about $\frac{1}{4}$ in. (6 mm) away from the engine block Operate starter to see if lead produces spark **If the lead sparks** Renew plugs (see p. 644)
	Current output from the coil	Place a screwdriver blade on a good earth point with the end of the blade close to the centre brush in the distributor cap Operate starter with ignition on **If there is no spark** Fit new coil
	Distributor cap and leads	Examine the distributor cap for signs of small cracks between the segments (see p. 642) **If cracked** Fit a new cap **If damp** Dry and refit **If the leads are cracked** Fit new leads (see p. 643)
	Fuel in the tank	Remove filler cap and rock car. Listen for fuel in tank **If empty** Refill with correct-grade petrol
	Fuel pump	**Electric pump** Turn on the ignition and listen to hear electric fuel pump ticking **If not** Tap pump lightly with a screwdriver handle **If still faulty** Disconnect inlet and outlet pipes. Remove power lead; unbolt pump unit and fit new pump **Mechanical pump** Operate the starter **If it does not deliver fuel** Overhaul pump (see p. 652)
	Fuel at carburettor	Remove the fuel line to the carburettor **Electrical pump** Turn on the ignition switch. **If there is no ticking sound** Check power supply (see p. 649) Check petrol flow from pipe *(continued)*

Finding the fault (continued)

Symptom	Checking order	Action
Engine spins over on the starter, but will not start *(continued)*	Fuel at carburettor	**Mechanical pump** Operate starter. Look for fuel at pipe **If none** Fit new pump
	Carburettor	Strip and clean the carburettor (see pp. 654–662)
Engine fires, but fails to keep running	Ignition and fuel	Remove the fuel line to the carburettor **Electrical pump** Turn on the ignition switch **If there is no ticking sound** Check power supply (see p. 649) **Mechanical pump** Operate starter. Check for fuel at pipe **If none** Fit new pump Make sure choke is working correctly for cold starting (see p. 649)
Engine stalls when idling, engine cold	Carburettor tuning	Tune the carburettor by regulating the volume and throttle-control screws (see pp. 654–662)
	Choke	Make sure the choke opens and closes fully when the choke control lever is used. Oil the choke-flap spindle and any connecting links for a smooth operation (see p. 649)
Engine stalls when idling, engine hot	Engine idling speed	Adjust throttle screw (see pp. 654–662)
	Idle fuel mixture	Adjust volume-control screw (see pp. 654–662)
	Slow-running jets (on fixed-jet or twin-choke carburettor)	Strip and clean the slow-running jet (see pp. 654–662)
	Choke	Remove air cleaner and make sure the choke is releasing (see p. 649). Oil the choke-spindle and controls
	Contact-breaker points	Clean and adjust the contact-breaker points **If they are badly pitted** Fit new points (see p. 642)
	Fuel coming out of carburettor float-chamber	Remove needle valve, clean and refit (see pp. 654–662) **If float not rising** Fit a new float
	Leak at intake manifolds	Tighten inlet manifold bolts and carburettor flange bolts **If no improvement** Fit new manifold and carburettor gaskets (see pp. 654–662)
Engine has uneven idle	Volume control and throttle stop screws	Run engine to normal temperature: tune (see pp. 654–662)
	Contact-breaker points	Check gap. Clean and reset (see p. 642) **If pitted** Fit new points
	Spark-plugs	Clean and reset spark-plug gap (see p. 644) **If worn** Fit new plugs
	Inlet manifold or carburettor flange	Tighten inlet manifold bolts and carburettor flange bolts **If no improvement** Fit new gaskets

Symptom	Checking order	Action
Engine stalls on acceleration	Air-cleaner element	Strip and clean element **If it is paper** Fit new element
	Choke	Remove air cleaner and make sure the choke opens and closes fully when the choke control is operated **If not** Adjust and oil choke controls (see p. 649)
	Fuel in tank	Remove filler cap and rock car, listen for sound of fuel **If empty** Refill with correct-grade petrol
	Fuel at carburettor	Remove fuel pipe from the carburettor and check the fuel output by operating the fuel pump (see p. 652) **If fuel flows** Check carburettor
	Needle valve stuck	Remove and clean the needle valve (see pp. 654–662)
	Accelerator pump	Overhaul (see pp. 654–662)
	Piston (constant-depression carburettor)	Overhaul (see pp. 657–659)
	Diaphragm (constant-depression carburettor)	Fit new diaphragm (see pp. 657–659)
	Distributor points	Check and fit new points if necessary (see p. 642)
Engine has poor acceleration and initial pick-up	Fuel at carburettor	Clean needle-valve assembly (see pp. 654–662). Check float level
	Accelerator linkage	Remove air cleaner and look down the air intake to make sure throttle butterfly is opening fully when the accelerator pedal is depressed **If not** Adjust the linkage
	Intake manifold	Tighten manifold and carburettor bolts. Fit new gaskets if necessary
Engine runs unevenly when accelerating	Spark-plugs	Remove and clean spark-plugs and re-gap (see p. 644)
	Distributor	Look for small cracks between the cap segments (see p. 642) Look for cracks in high-tension leads Clean and re-gap contact-breaker points
	Carburettor jets and filter	Strip and clean carburettor jets and filters (see pp. 654–662)
	Fuel pump	Clean pump filter (see p. 652) **Mechanical pump** Overhaul **Electrical pump** Fit a replacement if faulty
	Fuel flowing down side of float bowl	Clean needle-valve assembly. Renew if necessary (see pp. 654–662) Check float for puncture
	Exhaust system	Repair or fit a new exhaust system (see p. 651)

Symptom	Checking order	Action
Engine lacks power	Distributor vacuum-advance	Check suction of the vacuum diaphragm (see p. 643) **If faulty** Fit new one
	Intake system	Tighten the inlet manifold and carburettor flange bolts Fit new gaskets if necessary
	Fuel at carburettor	Clean and check the needle-valve assembly. Check the carburettor jets (see pp. 654–662)
	Throttle linkage	Remove air cleaner and look down the air intake to check the opening of the throttle **If faulty** Adjust linkage
Engine stops running when the vehicle is stopped	Throttle-stop screw	Adjust the screw to give the correct idling speed (see pp. 654–662)
	Slow-running jet	Strip carburettor and clean slow-running jet (see pp. 654–662)
	Inlet manifold	Tighten inlet manifold bolts and carburettor flange bolts. Fit new gaskets if necessary. Check distributor vacuum connection to carburettor
Engine runs on when the ignition is turned off	Engine temperature	Check cooling system and thermostat (see p. 639) Check that fan belt is turning the water pump (see p. 639) Make sure fuel-air mixture is correct (see pp. 654–662)
	Spark-plugs	Clean, and re-gap or renew (see p. 644)
Pinking (metallic knocking) from engine when accelerated	Grade of fuel	Remove fuel-tank plug. Drain off old fuel Fill with correct-grade petrol
	Engine temperature	Check cooling system (see p. 639)
	Spark-plugs	Clean and re-gap the plugs or renew if wrong type (see p. 644)
Engine misfires at high speeds	Ignition system high-tension lead and SW and CB connections at coil	Remove all connections Clean the terminal posts and tabs and replace
	Contact-breaker points	Clean and re-gap the contact-breaker points (see p. 642) **If burnt or pitted** Fit new points
	Spark-plugs	Remove and clean the spark-plugs and re-gap (see p. 644) **If pitted** Fit new spark-plugs
	Carburettor	Clean carburettor (see pp. 654–662)
Engine falters and stops when hot, but restarts after a period of time	Vapour in fuel line	Remove fuel pipe from the carburettor. Operate the fuel pump to feed petrol

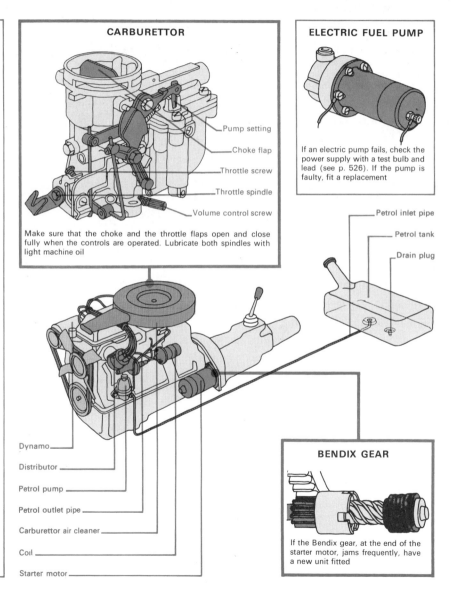

CARBURETTOR

Pump setting
Choke flap
Throttle screw
Throttle spindle
Volume control screw

Make sure that the choke and the throttle flaps open and close fully when the controls are operated. Lubricate both spindles with light machine oil

Dynamo
Distributor
Petrol pump
Petrol outlet pipe
Carburettor air cleaner
Coil
Starter motor

ELECTRIC FUEL PUMP

If an electric pump fails, check the power supply with a test bulb and lead (see p. 526). If the pump is faulty, fit a replacement

Petrol inlet pipe
Petrol tank
Drain plug

BENDIX GEAR

If the Bendix gear, at the end of the starter motor, jams frequently, have a new unit fitted

Cars Exhaust system

Ensuring that an exhaust system is safe

A faulty exhaust system is not only noisy and illegal; it is dangerous, because leaking fumes can filter into the car. Fit a new system immediately.

Start the engine and run a hand close to the exhaust pipework and silencer box to feel for escaping gases.

Some silencers are one-piece units; others are in sections, and it may be possible to replace only the faulty section. It is, however, advisable to renew the whole of the section. Always fit new gaskets between the manifold and the exhaust front pipe.

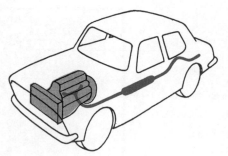

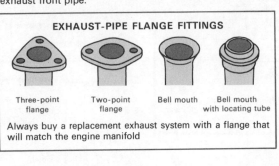

EXHAUST-PIPE FLANGE FITTINGS

Three-point flange

Two-point flange

Bell mouth

Bell mouth with locating tube

Always buy a replacement exhaust system with a flange that will match the engine manifold

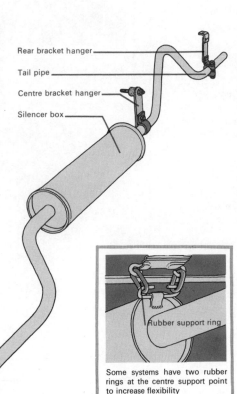

Rear bracket hanger

Tail pipe

Centre bracket hanger

Silencer box

Exhaust manifold

Manifold/pipe clip

Bell flange

Front pipe

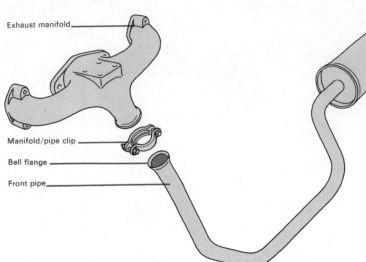

Some systems have two rubber rings at the centre support point to increase flexibility

Rubber support ring

Fitting a new silencer box

It may be possible to fit only a new silencer box, even on a one-piece exhaust system.

Cut through the silencer pipe on the engine side. Clean the cut end of the pipe thoroughly and remove any rust from the surface so that the new silencer can be fitted to the pipe easily and smoothly.

Make sure that the hanging straps and securing clips are in good condition. Fit new ones if necessary.

Materials: new silencer box and tail-pipe assembly.
Tools: screwdriver; hacksaw; file; emery cloth; spanner.

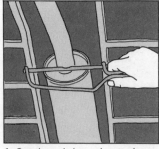

1 Cut the existing exhaust pipe as close to the silencer box as possible on the engine side

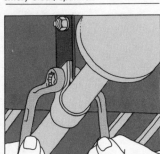

2 Undo the clip which holds the centre hanger, and free the hanger from the silencer assembly

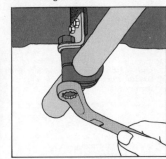

3 Undo the tail-pipe hanger. Carefully check the hangers. If they are worn, fit new ones

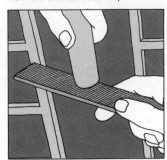

4 Clean the cut end of the old pipe with a sharp file and piece of emery cloth to make fitting easier

5 Fit the new silencer and tail-pipe unit. Push it well home on the old pipe. Refit hangers and tighten

Fitting a complete new system

If an exhaust system is badly rusted, renew it completely. Soak the manifold-flange bolts with penetrating oil for 24 hours before starting the job. Buy new hangers and support brackets if necessary. If a gasket is fitted between the pipe and the exhaust manifold, buy a new one.

When fitting a new system, hang it all in position before finally tightening any hanger. Start at the manifold and work backwards.

Materials: new exhaust system; hangers if necessary; emery cloth; exhaust-pipe retaining clips.
Tools: spanners; screwdriver; file.

COMMON FAILURES

Most exhaust systems fail near the silencer box or in the silencer end plate. Check when car is serviced

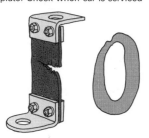

If the hanging straps are of webbing, look for splits. If they are rubber, check for deterioration

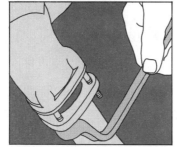

1 Undo the bolts holding the exhaust flange at the manifold. Find out if a gasket is fitted at this joint

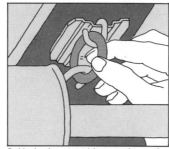

2 Undo the central hanger. It may be rubber rings (above), a webbing strap or a moulded-rubber buffer

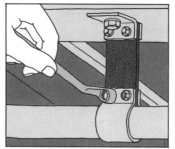

3 Undo the strap which holds the tail-pipe section to the car bodywork. Check that the strap is sound

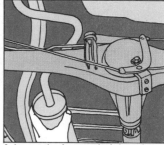

4 Lower the front end of the exhaust system far enough to clear the bodywork. Twist it sideways

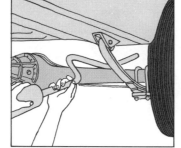

5 Draw the whole of the old exhaust away from the car towards the front to clear the car's rear axle

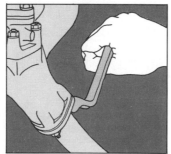

6 Fit the complete new assembly in position. Tighten the manifold nuts just enough to hold it in place

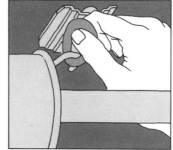

7 Connect the central hangers. If they are rubber, make sure they are in good condition. Renew if necessary

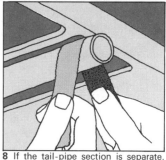

8 If the tail-pipe section is separate, clean the end of the pipe with emery cloth to ease the fitting

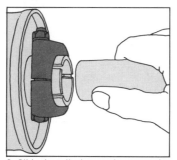

9 Slide the tail-pipe section on to the exhaust pipe. Make sure it is fully home. Screw up the retaining clip

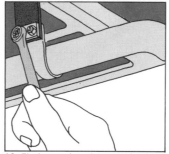

10 Fit the rear hanging strap in place, but do not tighten it until the whole system has been aligned

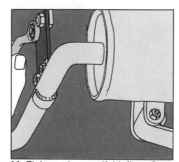

11 Tighten the manifold first. Centralise the centre brackets, then tighten the clips round the silencer box

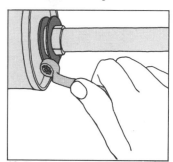

12 Finally tighten the tail support. Make sure that it hangs squarely, with no strain on the strap

Cars Fuel systems

How a mechanical fuel pump works

The mechanical type of fuel pump, which is operated by the engine camshaft, can be identified by its dome-shaped top. When a rocker arm on the pump is moved by the camshaft, it moves a diaphragm inside the pump. Petrol is sucked from the petrol tank, then pumped out to the carburettor as a spring pushes the diaphragm back to its original position.

Some cars have an electrically operated pump: if it fails fit a new one.

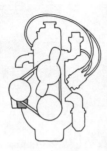

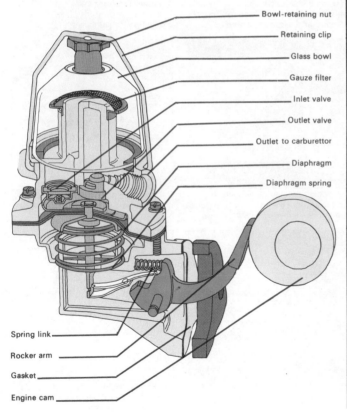

Bowl-retaining nut
Retaining clip
Glass bowl
Gauze filter
Inlet valve
Outlet valve
Outlet to carburettor
Diaphragm
Diaphragm spring

Spring link
Rocker arm
Gasket
Engine cam

Cleaning the filter bowl

If an engine falters or hesitates frequently during normal running, the fuel pump may be faulty. First check its filter bowl, which may have become clogged.

On most mechanical pumps the filter can be taken off and cleaned without removing the pump. Because the flow of petrol at the pump is controlled by the action of the diaphragm, no fuel escapes when the filter is removed. It is not necessary to disconnect any of the fuel pipes.

Materials: gauze filter; sealing ring; rag; petrol.
Tools: pliers; pin driver; soft brush.

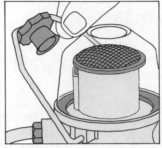

1 Undo the bowl-retaining nut with pliers. If it has an arch clamp, swing the clamp aside

2 Remove the filter bowl. Wipe thoroughly inside with a clean rag soaked in petrol. Set aside to dry

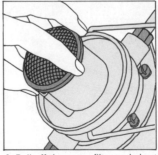

4 Pull off the gauze filter and clean it with petrol. If it is damaged, buy and fit a new one

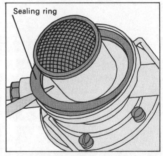

Sealing ring

3 Use a pin driver to hook the sealing ring from its recess in the filter bowl. Discard the ring

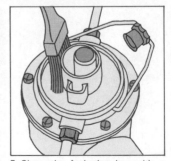

5 Clean the fuel chamber with a soft brush. Fit a new sealing ring. Refit bowl and tighten nut

Stripping and overhaulin[g]

If the fuel supply to the carburettor is still faulty when a fuel-pump filter has been removed and cleaned, it is possible that the pump valves or diaphragm are dirty or damaged.

Remove the fuel pump from the engine. Overhaul kits, containing all the parts likely to be required for replacement, are available from car-accessory shops. Make sure that the kit matches the pump on the car.

Materials: overhaul kit for pump; wood blocks; petrol; rag.
Tools: screwdriver; socket spanner; vice; $\frac{3}{4}$ in. (20 mm) tubing; punch; hammer; fine saw.

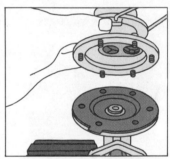

6 Undo the set screws holding parts together. Remove the top of the fuel pump. Set screws aside

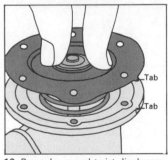

Tab
Tab

12 Press down and twist diaphragm. Remove and fit the spring to new one. Replace so that tabs meet

mechanical fuel pump

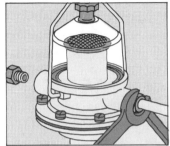

1 Disconnect the fuel lines from the pump. Some types can be pulled off without unscrewing

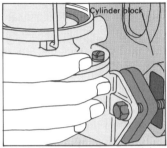

2 Undo the two fuel-pump retaining bolts with a socket spanner. Ease the pump away from the engine

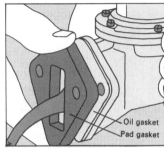

3 Remove the pad gasket and the oil gasket. Clean both gaskets thoroughly in petrol. Lay aside to dry

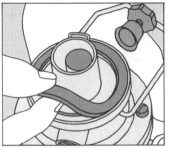

4 Remove the fuel filter bowl and sealing ring. Secure the pump in a vice between wooden blocks

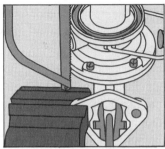

5 Lightly score down side of pump with a fine saw as a guide to positioning when reassembling

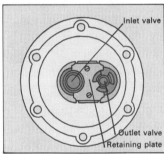

7 Find out how valves are secured. If there is a metal retaining plate, unscrew and remove it

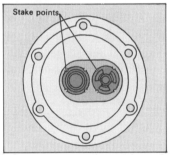

8 On some pumps, the metal round the valves is punched to overlap the edge. This is called staking

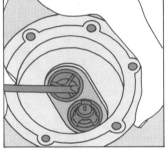

9 Lever out staked valves with a screwdriver. Remove only one at a time. Note fitting position

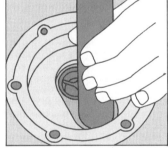

10 Fit new valves. Use a piece of $\frac{3}{4}$ in. (20 mm) tubing and tap them into position the correct way up

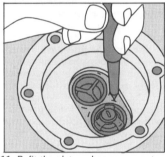

11 Refit the plate or hammer a centre punch firmly on the old stake marks to secure the valves

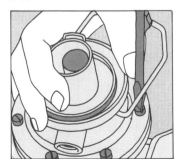

13 Refit the top of the pump. Line up scored marks and loosely fix the six retaining screws

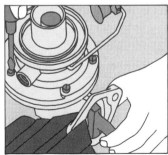

14 Hold down the rocker arm at the side of the pump. Tighten the six screws firmly to secure the diaphragm

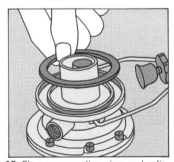

15 Fit a new sealing ring and refit filter bowl. Remove pump from vice. Fit new pad and oil gaskets

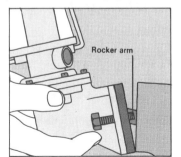

16 Hold rocker arm up to clear the pump cam and fit on engine. Rock to and fro, checking pump action

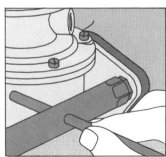

17 Refit and tighten the securing bolts with a socket spanner. Refit fuel lines from carburettor and tank

Cars Fuel systems

How a carburettor works

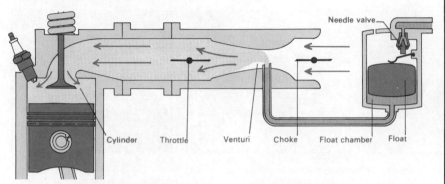

Needle valve

Cylinder   Throttle   Venturi   Choke   Float chamber   Float

The petrol used by an engine passes through the carburettor, where it is vaporised and mixed with air to form an emulsion which can be ignited in the cylinders.

Atmospheric pressure pushes air into a narrow section of the carburettor—called the venturi—where suction draws petrol out of one or more jets to provide a suitable mixture.

When the engine is started from cold, the mixture needed is 4 or 5 parts air to 1 part petrol. This is provided by the operation of a choke, which either restricts the amount of air in proportion to the petrol being used or, in some cases, increases the amount of petrol in proportion to the air. When the

engine is running normally the mixture is usually 14 or 15 parts air to 1 part petrol—whatever the speed of the engine. When the accelerator is pressed, more air and petrol are allowed into the venturi.

As the petrol is drawn through the jets, the level in the carburettor reservoir—called the float chamber—falls. A float drops with the level of the fuel and causes a needle valve to open. This allows more petrol to be pumped into the float chamber from the petrol tank. When the level has been restored, the float rises, the needle valve closes, and the supply from the petrol tank is momentarily stopped.

TYPES OF CARBURETTOR

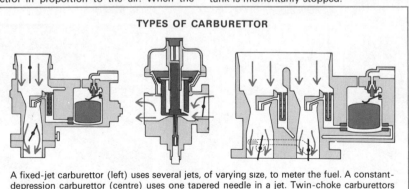

A fixed-jet carburettor (left) uses several jets, of varying size, to meter the fuel. A constant-depression carburettor (centre) uses one tapered needle in a jet. Twin-choke carburettors (right) are fixed-jet units with two chokes

Overhauling a fixed-jet carburettor

If a carburettor is faulty (see p. 647), check that the float chamber is not flooded and blow through the jets to check that they are clear. Make sure that the volume-control screw is not worn.

It is not necessary to remove the carburettor from the manifold for such routine checking. Make sure, however, that the bolts securing the carburettor are tight. If air leaks into the manifold, the air-petrol mixture is weakened and the engine lacks power.

Materials: overhaul kit, or parts as required.
Tools: spanner; screwdriver; pliers.

Volume-control screw If the screw is bent or ridged round the tapered seat, fit a new one

Float-chamber retaining screws
Accelerator linkage
Float-chamber flange
Pump jet
Economy unit

Accelerator-pump piston
Float pivot pin
Float arm and pivot
Slow-running jet plug
Float
Emulsion block
Float chamber

Second gasket
Diaphragm
First gasket

Overhauling a float chamber

The flow of petrol into the float chamber is controlled by a needle valve housed in the top of the chamber. If petrol floods from the float chamber, the needle valve or its seating is damaged. If the chamber is not filling correctly, check the float. Shake it to see if petrol has leaked into it.

If the float-chamber bowl is leaking, check that the gasket is not worn. When a new gasket is fitted, use new screw nails—called Parker-drive screws—to secure it.

Materials: gasket; float; needle valve; Parker-drive screws; washers.
Tools: screwdriver; hammer; spanner.

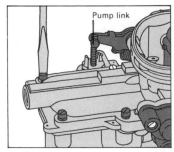

1 Undo the four screws on top of the float-chamber flange. Disconnect the accelerator-pump link if necessary

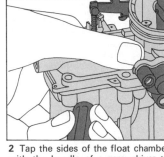

2 Tap the sides of the float chamber with the handle of a screwdriver to break the seal of the gasket

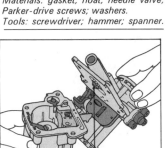

3 Separate the float-chamber assembly from the carburettor body. Take care not to damage the needle valve

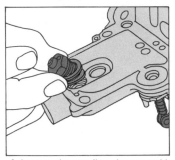

4 Loosen the needle-valve assembly with a spanner, then remove it from the underside of the float-chamber top

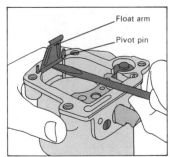

5 Use a screwdriver to hook out the float arm and its pivot pin from the slot in the carburettor casing

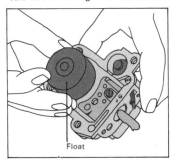

6 Ease the float out of the chamber. Shake it and listen for petrol inside. Renew the float if it is damaged

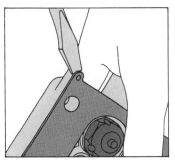

7 Use a screwdriver to prise the float-chamber gasket and its retaining nails from the float-chamber top

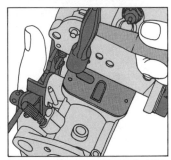

8 Fit a new gasket. Check that it is positioned correctly, and secure it with new screw nails

Removing the jets

A fixed-jet carburettor has more than one jet. The most common type, the Zenith, has four: main jet, compensating jet, slow-running jet and pump jet.

Jets can become blocked by impurities in the fuel. Never clean a jet by probing the hole with a piece of wire. This can enlarge and distort the drilling in the jet. To remove dirt, blow through the jets with an air line or foot pump. If the jet cannot be cleared, fit a new one.

Materials: emulsion-block gasket; jets as necessary.
Tools: screwdrivers.

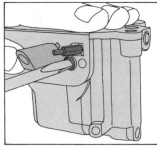

1 Remove the float chamber. Undo the two screws securing the emulsion block

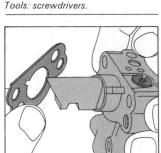

2 Remove the emulsion block from the float chamber. Pull off and discard the emulsion-block gasket

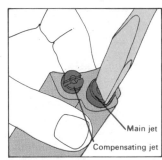

3 Use a screwdriver to remove the main jet and compensating jet from the base of the emulsion block

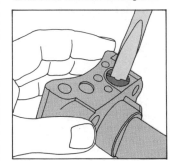

4 The slow-running jet is under a plug on top of the emulsion block. Unscrew the plug

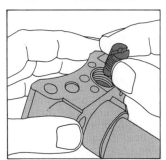

5 Use a small screwdriver to reach into the plug hole and undo the slow-running jet. Lift the jet out

Cars Fuel systems

Cleaning the accelerator pump

Most fixed-jet carburettors have an accelerator pump which increases the flow of fuel when a sudden extra effort is demanded from the engine. It is usually set in action by a linkage, which operates only when the accelerator pedal in the car is pushed down briskly.

If the car is not accelerating smoothly at high speed, check the pump and its linkage. Make sure that the pump jet is not blocked and that the piston and linkage can move freely.

Materials: petrol; light oil.
Tools: screwdriver; brush.

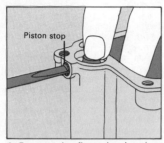

1 Remove the float chamber (see p. 655). Press the pump piston down into the fuel well on the chamber flange and unscrew the piston stop

2 Remove the pump piston and its spring. Renew the spring if it is worn or broken. Coat the piston thinly with light oil

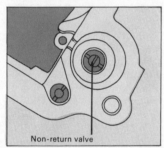

3 Check that the non-return valves at the bottom of the fuel well move freely. If they stick, unscrew them and fit new parts

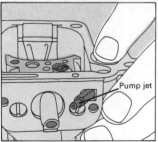

4 Half fill the well with petrol. Push the piston down and check that petrol squirts out of the pump jet. Blow through it if necessary

5 Clean the pump-control linkage with a petrol-soaked brush. Lubricate with light oil and check that it moves freely

Fitting a new diaphragm

Most fixed-jet carburettors are fitted with an economy device to weaken the air-fuel mixture when the car is travelling at cruising speed. In Zenith carburettors, the device is usually a rubber diaphragm which opens or closes an air-bleed circuit at certain stages of the engine's operation to change the mixture.

If the rubber stretches or is punctured, the diaphragm cannot work efficiently and the car uses more petrol than is necessary to maintain a cruising speed.

Materials: diaphragm and gaskets.
Tools: screwdriver; air line.

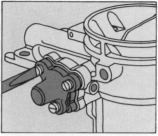

1 Identify the economy unit diaphragm (see p. 654) and undo the three screws holding it on the side or base of the carburettor body

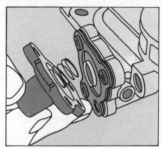

2 Carefully pull the diaphragm cover—which houses the first gasket and the diaphragm spring—from the carburettor casting

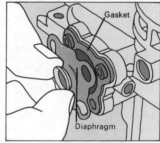

3 Remove the composition-rubber diaphragm from the casting. Take out the second gasket which is located behind the diaphragm

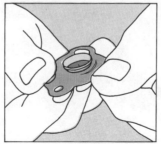

4 Stretch the diaphragm carefully between the fingers. If it is worn or split, buy and fit a matching replacement diaphragm

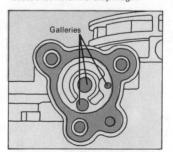

5 Blow through the galleries of the diaphragm housing with compressed air. Never prod them with wire. Reassemble and fit the unit

Tuning

The correct engine-idling speed depends on the amount of fuel drawn through the idling jet of the carburettor. This is governed by throttle-control and mixture-control screws. When reassembling, screw mixture control right in by hand, then out one-and-a-half turns.

Tool: screwdriver.

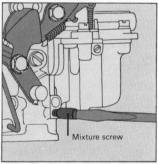

1 Start and run the engine until it reaches normal operating temperature. Turn the throttle screw until the engine is running fast. Adjust the mixture-control screw until the engine is running smoothly

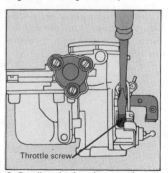

2 Readjust the throttle-control screw until the engine is running at normal tick-over speed, so that the ignition warning light on the fascia inside the car is just flickering

How a constant-depression carburettor works

A constant-depression carburettor can be readily identified by the plastic screwtop, generally black, of the dashpot damper.

A suction chamber, which is sealed on the Stromberg carburettor by a flexible diaphragm, controls the movement of a piston. Air is drawn out of the suction chamber as the engine operates, creating a partial vacuum into which the piston rises. As it rises, the piston pulls a needle in its base out of the carburettor jet. Because the needle is tapered, the higher it rises out of the jet the more fuel is allowed into the venturi (see p. 658).

Dashpot damper

Suction-chamber screw

Diaphragm

Guide rod

Diaphragm retaining screw

Throttle-control stop

Float-chamber gasket

Jet assembly

Float pivot

Jet

Jet holder

Adjusting screw

Jet To raise the jet—and decrease the fuel flow—turn the adjusting screw clockwise. Turn anti-clockwise to increase the supply

Retaining ring

Diaphragm

Air valve

Needle retaining screw

Metering needle

Suction chamber If the diaphragm is damaged, too much air is allowed into the chamber and the engine performance is likely to be poor

Needle valve

Float pivot

Twin float

Float chamber A badly seated needle valve or damaged floats in the float chamber can cause flooding and fuel wastage

Fitting a diaphragm and needle

If the engine is sluggish when it is accelerated, unscrew the damper and check that the dashpot is full of oil. The oil should restrict the rate of travel of the piston assembly.

If the oil level is correct, check the diaphragm. If it is perforated, air can enter the suction chamber and upset the rate at which the piston rises. When the piston diaphragm assembly is dismantled, check that the needle is not polished on one side. If it is, re-centre the needle.

Always check the piston return spring when the diaphragm is renewed. Springs are colour-coded to help identify the correct size.

1 Unscrew the dashpot damper and withdraw it from the cover of the suction chamber

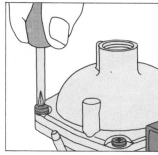

2 Undo the four cross-headed screws holding the suction-chamber cover on the carburettor

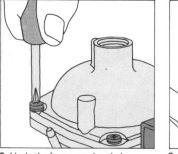

3 Remove the cover and the piston return spring. Buy a new spring of the same colour code

Needle

4 Withdraw the piston assembly from the carburettor. Take care not to damage the piston needle

5 Use a cross-head screwdriver to undo the four screws holding the retaining collar *(continued)*

Cars Fuel systems

(continued)

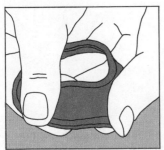

6 Remove the diaphragm. Stretch it between the fingers to check for splits. Buy a new one if necessary

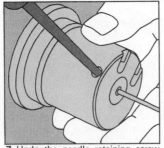

7 Undo the needle retaining screw recessed into the side of the piston. Remove the needle

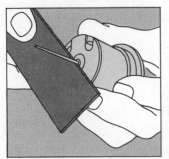

8 Fit a new needle. Use a straight-edge to ensure that the needle shoulder is flush with the piston base

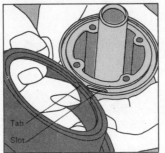

9 Fit the diaphragm. Make sure that the tab on the inner rim locates with the slot on the piston

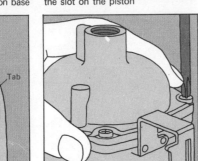

10 Refit the piston, with the tab on the diaphragm outer rim in the suction-chamber slot

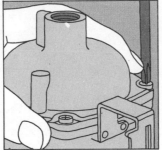

11 Fit the new piston spring. Refit the suction-chamber cover. Tighten the four retaining screws

Checking the float chamber

Two components—both situated in the float chamber—control the flow of petrol into the carburettor.

The float—which falls or rises with the level of the petrol in the chamber—causes a needle valve to open and close, to maintain the necessary level of petrol.

If an engine runs unevenly, or if its petrol consumption rises abnormally, it is likely that either the float or the valve is faulty. To check these components, it is necessary to dismantle the float chamber.

Materials: gasket; float if necessary.
Tools: screwdriver; rule.

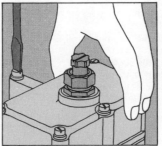

1 Turn the carburettor upside-down. Remove the six float-chamber retaining screws. Remove cover

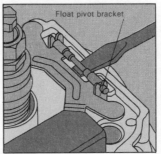

2 Use a screwdriver to hook the float assembly out of the pivot bracket at the side of the chamber

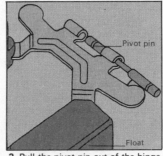

3 Pull the pivot pin out of the hinge. Shake the float to see if it is damaged. If it leaks, fit a new one

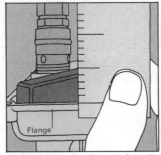

4 Check that the distance from the top of the float to the flange conforms with manufacturer's recommendations

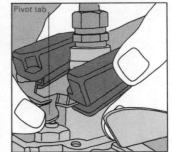

5 To adjust the float height, remove the float and gently bend the pivot tab. Check again

Cleaning the jets

All carburettor components must be clean. If the jet, for example, becomes obstructed, it may not feed enough petrol into the venturi. This causes the engine to run unevenly and it may eventually stop.

If the needle valve becomes contaminated by impurities in the petrol, it may stick and cause the float chamber to flood or be completely starved of fuel. In each case the engine would eventually stop.

Materials: needle valve and float-chamber gasket if necessary.
Tools: ring spanner; open spanner; long-bladed screwdriver; air line.

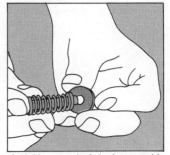

4 Hold one end of the jet assembly and turn the other to separate the parts. Clean in petrol

8 Fit a new float-chamber gasket. Position the float chamber and tighten the chamber retaining screws

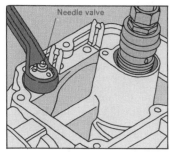

1 Use a ring spanner to unscrew the needle valve at the chamber flange. If it is sticking, fit a new one

2 Hold the carburettor sideways. Slacken the jet assembly holder which protrudes from the casting

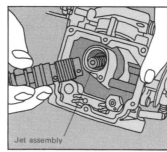

3 Remove the holder carefully. Turn carburettor right way up so that the jet assembly drops out

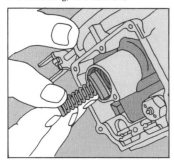

5 Reassemble and turn the O ring to lock the assembly. Slide the assembly into the carburettor

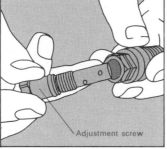

6 Undo the adjustment screw in the end of the assembly holder. Clean with an air line and refit it

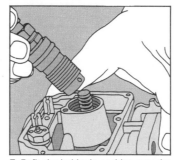

7 Refit the holder in position over the jet in the carburettor. Screw it almost completely home

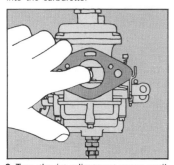

9 Turn the jet adjustment screw until the jet opening is felt to be level with the bridge of the jet

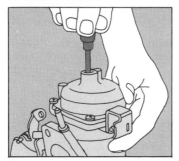

10 To make sure that the jet is centred, push the piston down from the top with a screwdriver

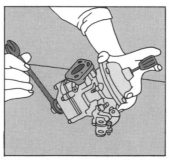

11 To centre the piston needle, lower and release the piston several times when tightening the jet holder

Tuning a CD carburettor

A carburettor should be tuned only after the engine has run long enough to reach a working temperature.

To check that it has been adjusted correctly, raise the piston with the tip of a screwdriver blade. If the engine stops immediately, the air-petrol mixture is too weak.

If the engine gains speed appreciably, the fuel mixture is too rich. Make a very slight adjustment to the jet screw and check again until the engine neither falters nor races when the piston is raised $\frac{1}{32}$ in. (1 mm).

Materials: light oil.
Tool: screwdriver.

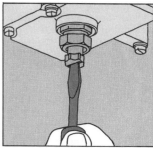

1 Turn the jet screw back three turns. Run the engine until it has reached normal operating temperature

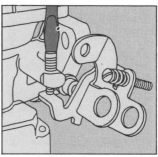

2 Adjust throttle screw until engine idles quickly. Adjust jet until idle is smooth; slacken throttle until normal

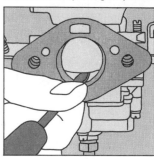

3 Check tuning by using tip of a screwdriver blade to raise piston a little. Readjust jet screw if necessary

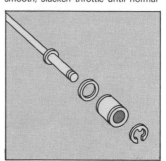

4 Unscrew the dashpot damper assembly. Inspect carefully. If bent or damaged, fit a new assembly

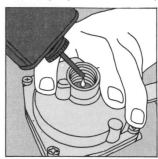

5 With the piston fully closed, fill dashpot with light oil until oil is $\frac{1}{4}$ in. (6 mm) from top. Refit damper

Cars Fuel systems

How a twin-choke carburettor works

To improve engine performance some motor manufacturers use fixed-jet carburettors which have two choke barrels fed with fuel from a common float chamber. These units work on the same basic principles as single-choke fixed-jet carburettors (see p. 654).

On some twin-choke units, one choke barrel is smaller than the other. The smaller barrel provides an economical fuel mixture for when the car is cruising or only lightly loaded. The second and larger barrel operates only when full performance or quick acceleration is required.

Most twin-choke carburettors have duplicate sets of jets for each choke barrel. A special pump jet is usually fitted to this type of carburettor to provide the extra fuel for acceleration.

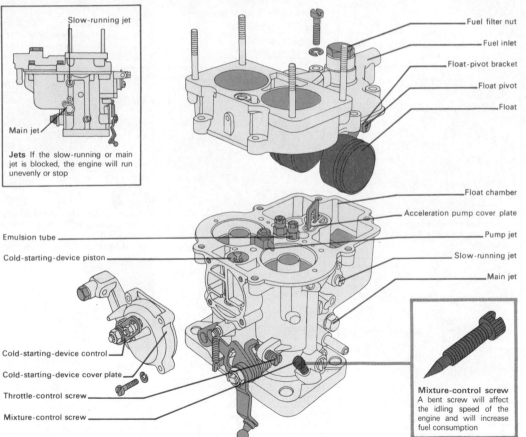

Slow-running jet

Main jet

Jets If the slow-running or main jet is blocked, the engine will run unevenly or stop

Fuel filter nut

Fuel inlet

Float-pivot bracket

Float pivot

Float

Float chamber

Acceleration pump cover plate

Pump jet

Slow-running jet

Main jet

Emulsion tube

Cold-starting-device piston

Cold-starting-device control

Cold-starting-device cover plate

Throttle-control screw

Mixture-control screw

Mixture-control screw A bent screw will affect the idling speed of the engine and will increase fuel consumption

Dismantling the float chamber

A brass float controls the flow of petrol into the float chamber. If it becomes damaged, the engine may run unevenly or stop.

Check that the float-adjustment tab (see Fig. 6) is not bent out of position —which could affect the smooth running and fuel economy of the car.

If the needle valve becomes worn or sticks, the float chamber may flood, or the carburettor may be starved of fuel, and the engine will stop.

Materials: float-chamber gasket; needle valve; brass float; fuel filter.
Tools: spanner; screwdriver; pin driver; box spanner; metric rule.

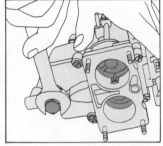

1 Undo the fuel filter-cover nut from the top of the carburettor with an open-ended spanner

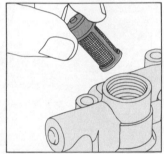

2 Take out the gauze fuel filter. Clean with an air line. If the filter is damaged, fit a new one

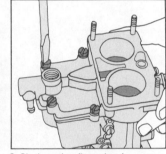

3 Slacken the float-chamber cover retaining screws, working at opposite corners. Remove the screws

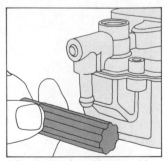

4 Tap the chamber with a screwdriver handle to break the seal. Lift off the cover of the chamber

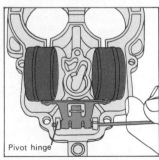

Pivot hinge

5 Use a pin driver to push out the float pivot hinge from the slotted end of the pivot brackets   *(continued)*

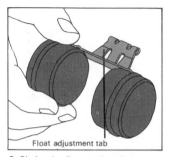

Float adjustment tab

6 Shake the float to find if fuel has entered it. Fit a new float if there are signs of wear or leaks

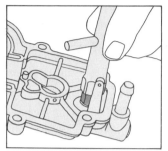

7 Use a small box spanner to undo the needle valve from the underside of the carburettor cover

Retaining eye

8 Remove the needle valve carefully. Do not touch the retaining eye on the needle valve

Ball bearing

9 Check that the ball bearing has no worn spots. If the bearing is worn, fit a new valve

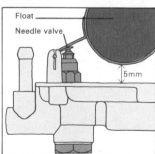

Float
Needle valve
5mm

10 Refit the needle valve and float. Make sure top of float rests $\frac{3}{16}$ in. (5 mm) from top of flange

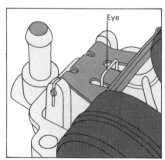

Eye

11 Refit the float. Make sure that the hinge fits under the locating eye of the needle valve

Overhauling a cold-starting device

Because a starter motor turns an engine at only approximately 100 rpm, not enough vacuum is created by the engine to draw in the amount of fuel needed for a rich starting mixture (see p. 654).

On most carburettors, a cold-starting circuit in the carburettor enriches the mixture when the driver pulls out the choke knob. Twin-choke carburettors have a more complicated, separate cold-starting device, which is also controlled by the driver through a choke cable leading from the dashboard. If the engine does not start easily, overhaul the cold-starting device.

Tool: screwdriver.

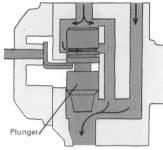

Plunger

Cold-starting device This provides a richer fuel mixture when the choke cable raises the plunger, as here

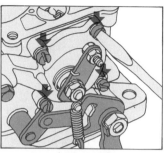

1 Unscrew the cover-plate retaining screws (arrowed) on the side of the carburettor. Remove the cover plate

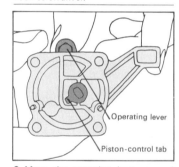

Operating lever
Piston-control tab

2 Move the operating lever up and down and check that the piston control tab moves freely

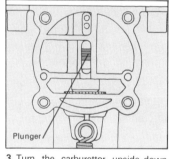

Plunger

3 Turn the carburettor upside-down and check that the plunger slides smoothly in its gallery

4 If the plunger does not slide smoothly, hook out its sprung retaining plate with a screwdriver

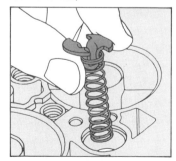

5 Shake the carburettor to free the plunger. Clean piston and gallery with an air line. Reassemble

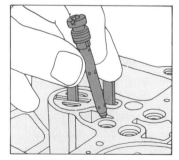

6 Unscrew the air corrector and starter jet from behind the emulsion tubes. Check that they are undamaged

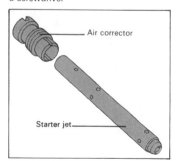

Air corrector
Starter jet

7 Unscrew the air corrector from the starter jet. Clean both thoroughly with an air line. Reassemble

Cars Fuel systems

Cleaning the jets on a twin-choke carburettor

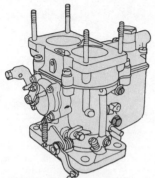

A twin-choke carburettor is fitted with more jets than a single-choke fixed-jet, but the operating principle is the same (see p. 654). Vacuum created by the engine draws fuel in the required quantity into the auxiliary venturi through the calibrated jets. It mixes with air to form a vapour which ignites in the engine combustion chambers.

If the jets become obstructed, the engine runs hesitantly and may eventually stop. Remove the jets and clean them with an air line.

Tools: box spanner; screwdriver; pliers; spanner; footpump (air line).

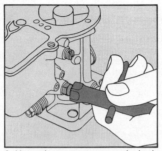

1 Use a box spanner to undo both main-jet holders—usually placed one on each side of the carburettor

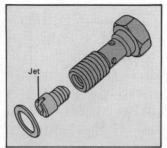

2 Unscrew the main jet from its holder. Clean the components with compressed air from a footpump

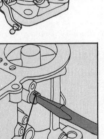
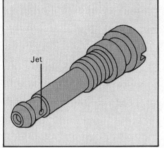

3 Unscrew the slow-running jets which are above the main jets on th side of the carburettor

4 There is no need to take the jet assemblies apart. Clean each jet with compressed air

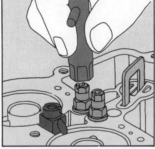

5 Undo the emulsion tubes and air-correction jets on each choke. Clean with compressed air

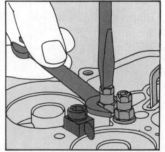

6 Hold the emulsion tubes with a spanner and refit the air-corrector jets with a screwdriver

7 Grip the top of the accelerator-pump rod with a pair of pliers. Pull it out of the carburettor

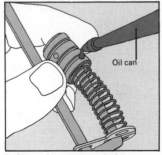

8 Clean the pump and the pump-well with air. Lubricate the piston with light oil and reassemble

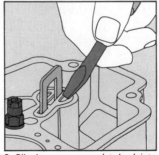

9 Clip the pump cover plate back into position on the carburettor with the blade of a screwdriver

10 Unscrew the pump jet, which is fitted between the two chokes. Clean it with air and refit

Tuning

When the carburettor is reassembled, tighten the mixture-control screw until the spring is fully compressed. Turn the screw back two-and-a-half turns. Fit the carburettor on the engine. Start the engine and run it to obtain normal operating temperature.

Note that it is dangerous to look down the chokes of the carburettor while tuning: excess petrol in the chokes can ignite if the engine is started.

Tool: screwdriver.

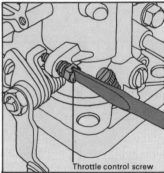

1 Adjust throttle screw until engine idles quickly. Adjust mixture-control screw until engine runs smoothly

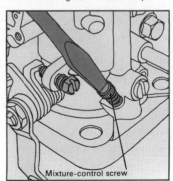

2 Screw in mixture control one complete turn. Turn the throttle screw anti-clockwise to get normal idling speed

Cars Upholstery

Mending damaged upholstery

Two repairs are possible if car upholstery is torn or damaged.

Torn seams can be sewn together; or an area can be patched with a matching piece of material —a wide range of colours and materials is available at car accessory shops.

If matching material cannot be obtained, examine the underside of the seat to see if there is sufficient surplus to allow some to be cut off for the repair.

If possible, remove the cover so that the seam can be stitched from the underside. Use a good-quality nylon thread and a half-circle needle, and make the repair with small overstitches (see p. 278).

Avoid stitching on any other parts of the upholstery. Sewn areas are not only unattractive, but may be extremely uncomfortable for passengers sitting on the repair.

Half-circle needle Use a fine upholstery needle to repair the damaged seams in car upholstery

---

REPAIRING SPLIT PIPING

If the piping around the edge of a seat splits, repair it immediately before the tear can extend to the seat covering.

The most effective repair is to push a thin piece of wood such as a matchstick or a piece of dowelling into the hollow ends of the split piping. Stick the two parts of the piping together and let the adhesive (see p. 694) harden before using the seat.

Materials: matchstick or thin dowel to fit the piping; contact adhesive.

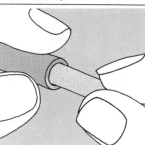

1 Apply contact adhesive to matchstick or thin dowel and push it into one side of the split piping

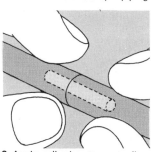

2 Apply adhesive to protruding stick and work other piece of piping on to it. Leave to set

---

Patching a torn seat cover

To repair a tear, buy a piece of material to match the upholstery of the car. Allow plenty of material to overlap the edges of the tear and cut it to shape.

Cover the patch with adhesive and push it into place as soon as the adhesive is applied, to ensure that it does not become tacky and stick to itself when it is folded.

Do not press the patch too firmly. If too much pressure is applied, the tear will be parted slightly and cause a bump when the adhesive sets.

Materials: patching material; contact adhesive (see p. 694).
Tool: scissors.

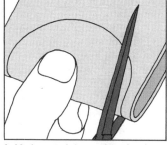

1 Mark a patch larger than the shape of the tear. Fold the new material and cut out the patch

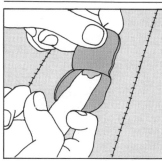

2 Carefully lift the torn piece of seat covering and apply adhesive all round the underside of the tear

3 Lay out the piece of patching material and spread adhesive on its top side. Do not let it become tacky

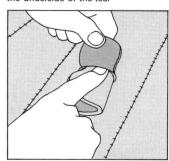

4 Fold the patch material and push it under the tear in the upholstery. Spread it out evenly under the tear

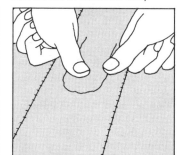

5 Press the covering gently on to the patch, but keep the torn edges together. Leave to set

---

SEWING A SPLIT SEAM

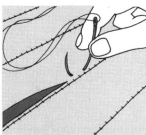

1 Start stitching beyond the end of the split. Sew from underneath, so that the knot is hidden

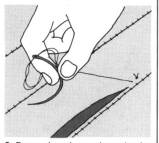

2 Draw thread up through the material and sew across the split seam with overstitching (p. 278)

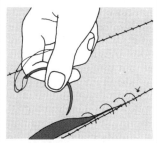

3 Sew the stitches about $\frac{1}{4}$ in. (6 mm) apart. Pull tightly after each stitch. Finish on underside

Cars Upholstery

Patching a carpet

If a car carpet tears, stick a canvas backing patch underneath it. Always make sure that the carpet is clean and dry before patching.

One of the most common areas of damage is round the edges of the carpet-securing studs, usually because a sharp edge on a fixing clip has cut into the carpet.

Find out what backing there is on the carpet and choose an adhesive to suit it (see p. 694).

Materials: patching material; carpet stud; adhesive.
Tools: thin-nosed pliers; light hammer; scissors.

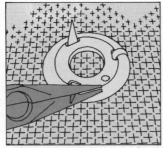

1 Remove carpet from car. Bend open the retaining tangs of the carpet stud clip and remove the stud

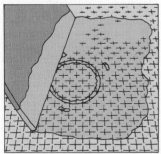

2 Clean the back of the carpet thoroughly and apply adhesive over the damaged area

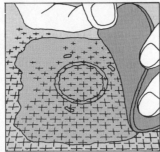

3 Cut a patch large enough to overlap the damaged area by 1 in. (25 mm). Spread adhesive on patch

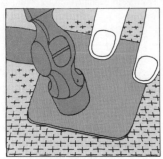

4 When the adhesive is tacky, press the patch firmly on to the carpet. Lightly hammer the surface

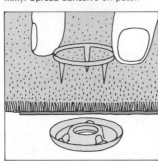

5 Push the stud clip through the patch at the correct position. Fit the stud and bend over the clip tangs

Repairing hoods and tonneau covers

Splits and tears in car hoods and covers can be repaired by patching.

Use an adhesive suitable for the material (see p. 694). Make sure that the patch is large enough to overlap the edges of the tear by at least $\frac{3}{4}$ in. (20 mm).

If possible, remove the torn cover and lay it flat on a bench or table. If the hood cannot be removed, erect it so that it is as taut as possible for the patch to fit evenly.

Materials: patching material; adhesive; French chalk.
Tools: scissors; hammer; wood block; adhesive applicator.

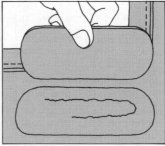

1 Cut a patch of material large enough to overlap the tear by $\frac{3}{4}$ in. all round. Mark the area inside the hood

2 Apply adhesive within the marked area, spreading it thinly and evenly up to the line

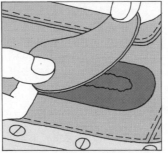

4 Stick patch to the hood. Press firmly from the centre outwards. Dust round patch with French chalk

3 Spread adhesive on the back of patch with a piece of hardboard. Allow adhesive to become tacky

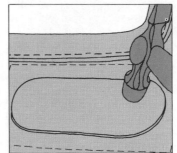

5 Hammer round patch. If the hood is not removable, hold a wooden block beneath the edge while hammering

MENDING SIDE TEARS

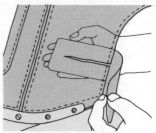

1 If the edge of a hood is torn, cut a patch to fold round and cover both back and front

2 Spread adhesive on both sides of the tear and on the underside of the patch

3 Allow the adhesive to become tacky and fit the patch round the split. Press firmly in place

Cars Radios

Improving reception

When a car radio is faulty, specialised equipment and techniques may be needed to trace the fault, but some simple tests and repairs can be tried before engaging a professional radio mechanic.

Earthing is one of the more common faults. Some receivers rely on the contact between the securing nuts and the fascia bracket to supply an earth. Although this may be adequate when the set is first installed, the contact can deteriorate.

Remove the fascia and the nuts and clean the area behind them with emery paper. As an additional earth, run a length of insulated cable between one of the radio retaining nuts and the car bodywork. Refit and tighten the nuts.

Never check the performance of a radio receiver if the bonnet is open. The bonnet acts as a screen: when it is opened, the aerial can pick up interference from the ignition system.

This fault may also occur if the bonnet does not earth properly with the rest of the bodywork. The earth between the two is usually through the bonnet hinges. If grease or oil is allowed to collect on the hinges the contact is lost.

Fit a braided earth strap to one of the bonnet hinge screws and to any convenient bolt on the bodywork. Make sure that the strap does not foul anything when the bonnet is closed.

Most car aerials rely on direct contact with the bodywork for their earth. If the contact is suspect, remove the aerial and clean the underside of the wing down to bare metal. Fit an additional earth strap to the aerial securing nut and to a bolt on the bodywork. Do not allow the aerial to become rusted: dry it when the car has been used in wet weather. Smear with petroleum jelly.

The quality of sound may be distorted if the speaker becomes loose on its mountings. If it is fitted to a panel thin enough to vibrate under the volume of sound, fit a more substantial baffle board.

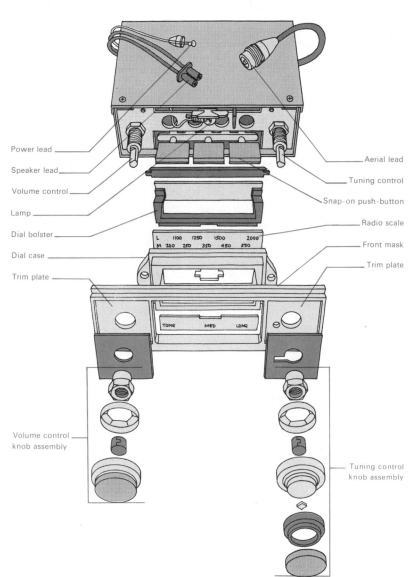

Power lead
Speaker lead
Volume control
Lamp
Dial bolster
Dial case
Trim plate
Volume control knob assembly

Aerial lead
Tuning control
Snap-on push-button
Radio scale
Front mask
Trim plate
Tuning control knob assembly

FINDING THE FAULT		
Symptom	**Checking order**	**Action**
Set does not light up or work wheh switched on	Blown fuse	Replace if necessary
	Poor connection at fuse in flex to radio	Clean and renew connection
	Bad earth connection	Clean and refit earth connection
	Faulty bulb	Fit new bulb
Set lights up but no reception	Faulty connection between aerial and set	Refit connection
	Faulty or damaged aerial cable	Fit new aerial
	Damaged speaker cone	Fit new speaker
	Faulty connection between set and speaker	Refit connection
Set crackles when the engine is accelerated	Bad aerial earth under the wing	Clean underside of wing: remount aerial
	Faulty suppressor at the SW terminal on coil	Fit new suppressor (see p. 666)
	Faulty instrument stabiliser suppressor	Fit new suppressor (see p. 666)
Set whines as engine is accelerated	Faulty aerial earth connection under the wing	Remove, clean and remount aerial
	Faulty suppressor on D dynamo terminal	Fit new suppressor (see p. 666)
Weak signal	Faulty aerial connections	Check aerial connections to set
	Aerial inadequately trimmed	Tune to a weak station and adjust trimming screw (see p. 666)
Distorted sound	Faulty speaker connections	Renew connections
	Damaged speaker cone	Fit new speaker

Cars Radios

Trimming an aerial

A car radio aerial should be adjusted to the set it supplies. This is called trimming and makes the set more sensitive to weak signals

On most receivers, there is a small trimming screw located at the side of the set or behind the tuning knob. Select a station from which the reception is known to be weak and adjust the trimming screw until the best possible reception is achieved.

Tools: small electrical screwdriver; spanner.

1 Switch on the radio and tune to a weak station—somewhere in the 200-metre band

2 Pull off or unscrew the tuning knob. Turn up the volume control as far as possible

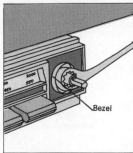

3 Remove the nut behind the tuning knob. Remove the bezel to expose the trimming screw

4 Adjust the screw, turning to left or right until the best reception is received

5 Refit the securing nut and bezel. Refit the tuning control knob and test reception

Fitting a suppressor

Crackling on a car radio is often interference caused by electrical impulses from another component. Suppress it by fitting a condenser between the component feed wire and an earth point.

Check a radio for interference with the engine running but do not open the bonnet. When closed, the bonnet itself provides an interference screen between ignition and aerial.

Common interference is:

Constant clicking which increases with engine speed
Action Fit a 1 microfarad condenser between the coil SW terminal and an earth point

Constant frying sound
Action Fit a 1 microfarad condenser between input terminal (B) on the instrument voltage stabiliser (see below) and earth

High-pitched whine which increases with engine speed
Action Fit a 1 microfarad condenser between the dynamo D terminal and the dynamo mounting bolt

Rhythmic ticking sound
Action Fit a 1 microfarad condenser between the power-supply terminal and earthing point

Frying sound which increases during braking
Action Fit special suppressors—obtainable from accessory dealers—to the drums or discs. of brakes

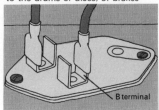

Voltage stabiliser This, if fitted, is found behind the instrument panel on the back of the speedometer or under the bonnet

SUPPRESSING THE COIL

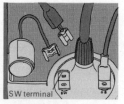

1 Fit condenser earth tag to the coil mounting bolt. Remove the lead from the coil SW terminal

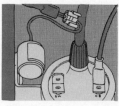

2 Slide back the insulating sleeve on the SW lead and fit the lead into the condenser tag

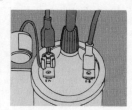

3 Refit the combined leads on the coil terminal. Push home and slide rubber sleeve over them

SUPPRESSING THE DYNAMO

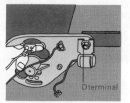

1 Bolt the condenser earth tag to the dynamo mounting bolt. Remove the dynamo D terminal lead, which is the larger of the two

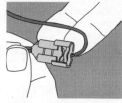

2 Slide the protective sleeve a little way up the removed dynamo lead and fit the end of the lead into the tag that is on the condenser

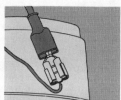

3 Push the protective sleeve carefully back over both terminal tags and push the pair of leads firmly on to the dynamo D terminal

FITTING A BONNET EARTH STRAP

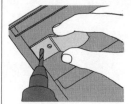

1 Bend a piece of thin steel and drill a hole in it. Hold it in place against the bonnet lip and drill through the hole into the bonnet lip

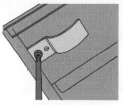

2 Fix the steel to the lip of the bonnet with a washer and a self-tapping screw. Then tighten the screw to ensure a good earth

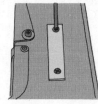

3 Position a plate on the body to meet the earth strap when the bonnet of the car is closed. Drill and fit screws to secure it

Cars Windows and windscreens

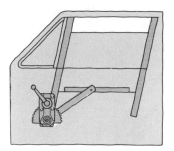

If a car window is stiff, or seems to be stuck so that it does not move at all, remove the winder mechanism for lubrication or replacement. The winder and door handles may be secured in one of three ways—by a pin, circlip or a screw.

Materials: winder mechanism if necessary; grease.
Tools: cross-head screwdriver; screw-driver; knitting needle; pliers.

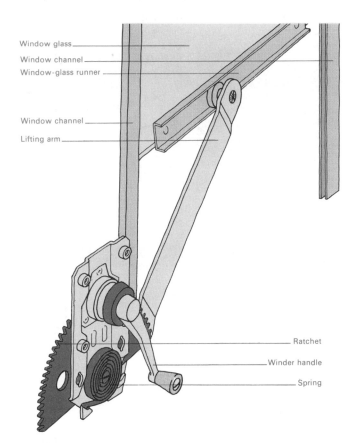

Window glass
Window channel
Window-glass runner

Window channel
Lifting arm

Ratchet
Winder handle
Spring

Lubricating and fitting a window winder

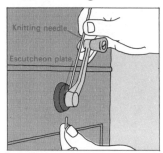

Knitting needle

Escutcheon plate

1 Push the escutcheon plate back against the trim. Push out the pin between the plate and the handle

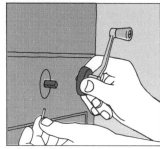

2 Pull off the winder handle. Remove the escutcheon plate from the winder mechanism shaft

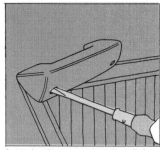

3 Undo the screws, or small box nuts, which hold the arm-rest on the door trim. Pull off the arm-rest

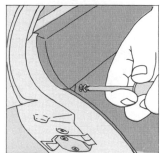

4 Check to see if the trim is secured by small screws, usually in the top corners. Remove the screws

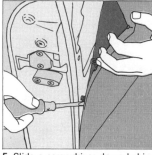

5 Slide a screwdriver down behind the trim until a clip is felt. Prise the clip out of the door

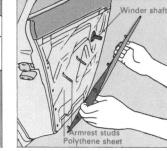

Winder shaft

Armrest studs
Polythene sheet

6 Continue prising the clips out of the door until the trim is free. Lift off the trim and remove polythene

7 Some doors may have a capping above the trim panel. If so, unscrew it and remove it from the door

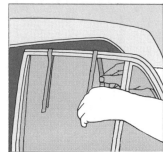

8 Make sure that the window is fully closed. Tape it over the top edge of the door so that it cannot fall

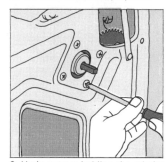

9 Undo screws holding the winder mechanism on the door panel. Push mechanism inside *(continued)*

Cars Windows and windscreens

(continued)

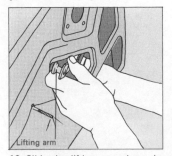

10 Slide the lifting arm along the window-glass runner and slip it out of the end of the runner frame

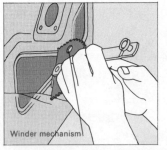

11 Support the winder mechanism underneath and work it out through one of the cut-outs in the door

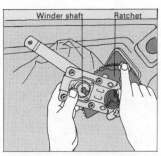

12 Grease the ratchet teeth and work the arm up and down with the handle to loosen it

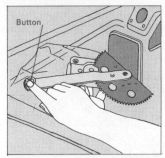

13 Grease the button at the end of the lifting arm so that it can run freely in the window runner

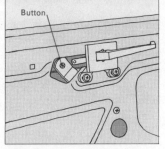

14 Slide the mechanism back in place so that the lifting-arm button locates in the window-glass runner

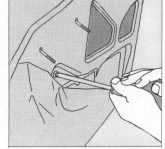

15 If the window glass is stiff in its side channels, loosen the securing screw, move screw and tighten

16 Refit the polythene sheet and tuck it securely into the bottom of the door frame and round the shaft

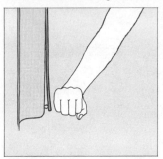

17 Refit trim panel by locating the clips in the holes and striking the panel, over the clip, with the hand

18 Make sure that the drain hole in the bottom of the door is clear, to allow internal moisture to run out

Cleaning a windscreen

If a windscreen cannot be cleaned adequately by normal wiper action, it is likely that impurities in the air have caused the surface to change so that it retains grease and repels water.

Clean both sides of the glass with a liquid detergent or a proprietary cleansing solvent to restore the surface. Pay attention to the lower corners where dirt and grime accumulate after being washed down the glass.

Avoid wetting the windscreen with water containing silicone additives used to clean the car body.

Materials: cleansing solvent or liquid detergent; lint-free rags.

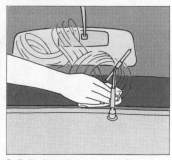

2 Squirt cleansing solvent or detergent over the windscreen. Start at the top so that the solvent runs down

4 Spread some of the solvent on a rag and wipe the rubber window surround to remove collected dirt and dust

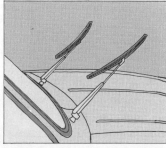

1 Start the wipers. Turn off the ignition to stop them centrally on the screen. Pull away from the screen

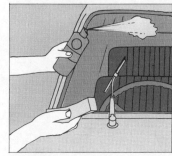

3 Rub the solvent on to the screen with a rag. Polish the screen with a clean rag as the solvent starts to dry

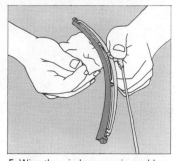

5 Wipe the windscreen-wiper rubbers with solvent on a rag. Reposition wiper blades correctly (see p. 669)

Wiper blades

A windscreen wiper on a car in average use can work efficiently for no more than about a year, during which time it wipes about 20 acres of glass. Fit new blades every autumn.

Several types of blade fitting are available. As a guide when buying new ones, check the type of windscreen and the age of the car.

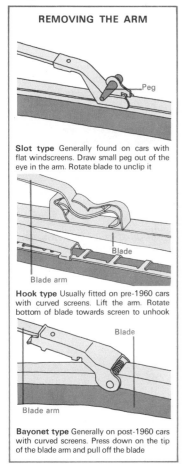

REMOVING THE ARM

Slot type Generally found on cars with flat windscreens. Draw small peg out of the eye in the arm. Rotate blade to unclip it

Hook type Usually fitted on pre-1960 cars with curved screens. Lift the arm. Rotate bottom of blade towards screen to unhook

Bayonet type Generally on post-1960 cars with curved screens. Press down on the tip of the blade arm and pull off the blade

Where wipers wear

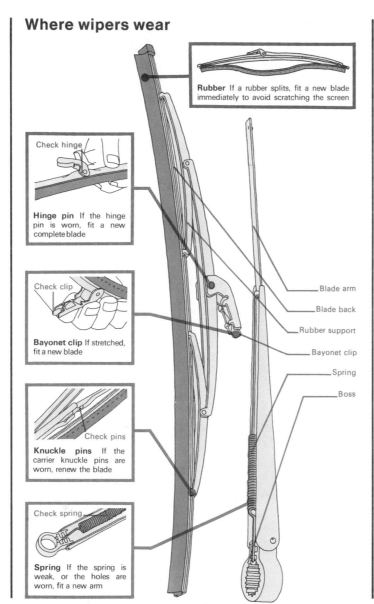

Rubber If a rubber splits, fit a new blade immediately to avoid scratching the screen

Check hinge

Hinge pin If the hinge pin is worn, fit a new complete blade

Check clip

Bayonet clip If stretched, fit a new blade

Check pins

Knuckle pins If the carrier knuckle pins are worn, renew the blade

Check spring

Spring If the spring is weak, or the holes are worn, fit a new arm

Blade arm
Blade back
Rubber support
Bayonet clip
Spring
Boss

Maintaining the blade arm

Never bend a blade arm to try to increase the wiper pressure on the screen. When the arm is distorted, the action of the wiper is even less efficient. If a wiper is working unevenly, check the condition of the spring and the boss pin.

Many wiper faults can be corrected without removing the arm from the car. But if an arm has to be removed, make sure that the wipers are in the parked position.

Materials: new blades and arms if necessary.
Tools: screwdriver or coin; adjustable spanner.

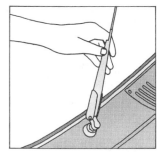

Boss pin Move the wiper arm up and down. If it is loose at the boss pin, fit a new arm

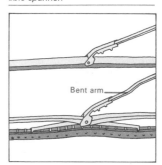

Bent arm Check that the arm is not bent (bottom). Bend it back to shape (top) or renew it

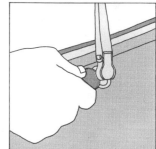

Removing arm Use a coin or the tip of a screwdriver to prise the boss off the wiper spindle

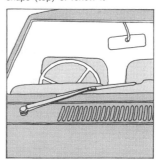

Wiper position Fit arm with the wipers parked. Fix arm 1 in. (25 mm) above windscreen rubber

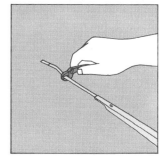

Blade judder Remove the blade with the arm upright. Gently twist arm until it is flat against screen

Cars Windows and windscreens

Types of windscreen washer

Windscreen washers are compulsory on all cars from September 1972. The pump unit may be operated manually by a push button, by vacuum from the inlet manifold or by the car's electrical system.

If the washer operates by vacuum, overhaul and clean the equipment every autumn. Make sure that the filter unit in the bottom of the inlet tube is unblocked. All other types of windscreen washer have a non-return ball valve in the tube. Check that it is not stuck. Renew the valve if necessary.

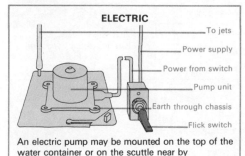

ELECTRIC

- To jets
- Power supply
- Power from switch
- Pump unit
- Earth through chassis
- Flick switch

An electric pump may be mounted on the top of the water container or on the scuttle near by

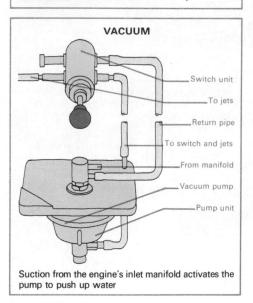

VACUUM

- Switch unit
- To jets
- Return pipe
- To switch and jets
- From manifold
- Vacuum pump
- Pump unit

Suction from the engine's inlet manifold activates the pump to push up water

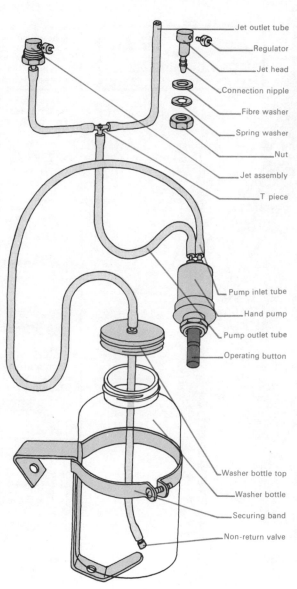

- Jet outlet tube
- Regulator
- Jet head
- Connection nipple
- Fibre washer
- Spring washer
- Nut
- Jet assembly
- T piece
- Pump inlet tube
- Hand pump
- Pump outlet tube
- Operating button
- Washer bottle top
- Washer bottle
- Securing band
- Non-return valve

General maintenance

EASY-CLEAN JETS

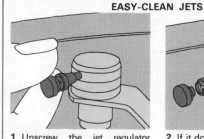
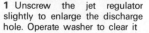

1 Unscrew the jet regulator slightly to enlarge the discharge hole. Operate washer to clear it

2 If it does not clear, remove the regulating nozzle and unblock it with a pin

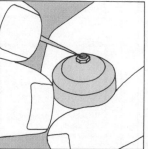
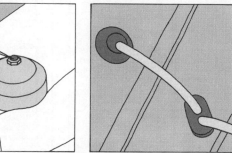

Ball jet Press the ball in with a pin and get a helper to operate the washer to clear it

Tubes Check the washer delivery tubes. If they are stretched, collapsed or damaged, fit new tubing

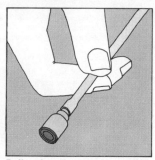

Filter Vacuum-operated washers have a filter in the tube in the container. Blow through it to clean

Ball valve Non-vacuum washers have a non-return ball valve in the tube. If it is stuck, renew the valve

Mopeds Maintenance

Lubricating a moped

The general maintenance of a moped is basically the same as that for an ordinary pedal cycle (see p. 570).

Some manufacturers fit pre-packed wheel bearings which need no lubrication during the life of the machine. But if a cup-and-cone bearing is fitted, strip it down every 5000 miles and repack with fresh grease.

Transmission

If the moped has a four-stroke engine (see p. 468), change the oil every 1000 miles. On two-stroke engines (see p. 474), there is no oil sump: the engine is lubricated by the petrol-oil mixture. Lubricate the automatic gear drive and chain to the rear wheel on all machines.

Controls

The brake cables, speedometer drive, throttle control cables and clutch cable will become difficult to operate if not lubricated regularly.

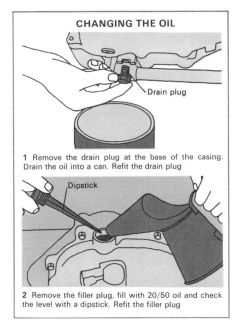

CHANGING THE OIL

Drain plug

1 Remove the drain plug at the base of the casing. Drain the oil into a can. Refit the drain plug

Dipstick

2 Remove the filler plug, fill with 20/50 oil and check the level with a dipstick. Refit the filler plug

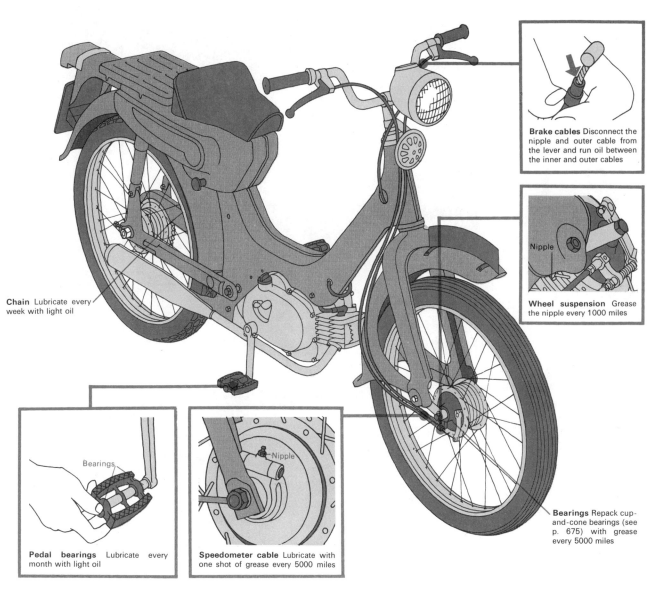

Brake cables Disconnect the nipple and outer cable from the lever and run oil between the inner and outer cables

Nipple

Wheel suspension Grease the nipple every 1000 miles

Chain Lubricate every week with light oil

Bearings

Pedal bearings Lubricate every month with light oil

Nipple

Speedometer cable Lubricate with one shot of grease every 5000 miles

Bearings Repack cup-and-cone bearings (see p. 675) with grease every 5000 miles

Mopeds Maintenance

TWO-STROKE LUBRICATION

The main lubrication point on a two-stroke engine is the automatic transmission unit. Keep the oil topped up and change it every 2000 miles.

Materials: 20/50 oil; filler can.
Tools: spanner; screwdriver.

1 Remove the transmission drain plug. Stand the moped over a can

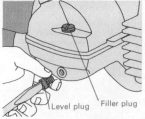

2 Replace the drain plug and undo the filler and level plugs

Level plug   Filler plug

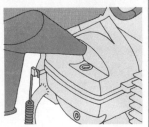

3 Fill with oil until it comes out of the level plug. Refit plugs

Cleaning an air filter

A carburettor air filter cleans the air drawn into the engine of dust and dirt. It is always near the carburettor, but its precise location depends on the make and type of moped.

If the filter system becomes blocked with dirt, too little air enters the carburettor and the machine uses more fuel.

Strip the filter unit every time the machine is serviced. Remove the element from the filter box and wash it in clean petrol. It should be soaked in oil before reassembly.

Materials: bowl; petrol; clean rag.
Tools: screwdriver; cleaning brush.

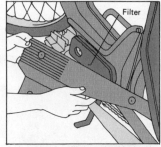

1 Locate the filter unit. Undo the screws and remove any covers protecting the filter

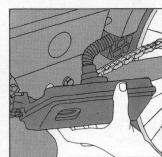

Filter casing
Carburettor

2 Remove the screws which hold the filter casing to the carburettor and the cycle-frame tubes

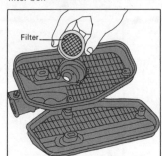

4 Undo the screws which hold the two sections of the filter box together. Separate the sections

Filter

3 Lift off the air-filter casing. Disconnect the intake tube from the filter box

Filter

5 Remove the filter. Wash it and the casing in petrol. Soak filter in oil, shake off surplus and reassemble

Adjusting the headlamp beam

It is dangerous to use a moped if the headlamp beam is not correctly set. Check the angle of the beam regularly and reset it if necessary.

Make sure that the light is dipping correctly. Never ride with only the main beam working. If the dipped-beam element of the bulb is faulty, fit a new bulb. Take the old one to an accessory shop, to buy the correct replacement.

Always keep the headlamp glass clean to ensure that the maximum amount of light can pass through it.

Materials: new bulb if necessary.
Tools: screwdriver; spanner.

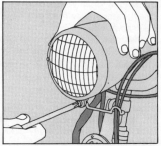

Filter

1 Undo the single screw at the base of the headlamp rim. Lift off the reflector and light unit

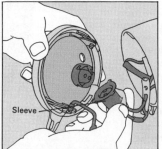

Sleeve

2 Slide back the rubber sleeve on the bulb holder. Press in the holder and twist to remove it

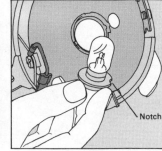

Notch

3 To fit a new bulb, make sure that the notch on the flange locates in the holder. Reassemble

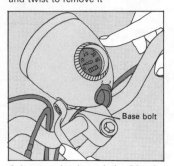

Base bolt

4 Loosen the base bolt. Dip the beam and adjust the light to strike the road 20 yds (18 m) ahead

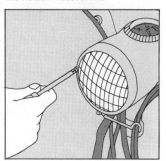

5 Adjust the side screw so that the main beam is pointing towards the kerb and not into the road

Mopeds Wheels and brakes

Checking the ignition system

The current to start and keep an engine running is generated by electro-magnets on the flywheel. As the moped is pedalled, the flywheel turns and the magnets rotate round an armature.

Contact-breaker points in the flywheel open and close to provide current at the exact moment it is required to ignite the fuel in the engine combustion chamber.

If there is a knocking sound in the engine, the contact gap may be too wide. If the engine regularly over-heats, the points may be too close.

Tools: screwdriver; feeler gauge.

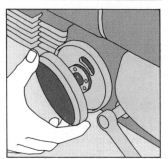

1 Remove flywheel cover. It may be secured by a spring fit, when it is simply pulled off, or by screws

2 Turn the flywheel until the F aligns with the static timing mark and the points can be seen

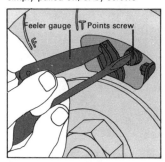

3 Loosen the points screw. Insert the correct feeler gauge between the points and tighten the screw

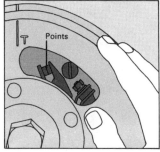

4 Turn the flywheel until the T lines up with the timing mark. Check that the points are just open

Fitting brake shoes to the rear wheel

If the rear wheel grates or wobbles, renew the bearings. If the brakes do not operate even after adjustment, fit new shoes.

On some models the chain has to be split. On others it is possible to loosen the wheel and spin the chain off the sprockets.

For both repairs, it is necessary to remove the wheel. When dismantling, note any spacers on the rear-wheel spindle, and make sure that they are replaced correctly later.

Materials: set of rear brake shoes and linings.
Tools: spanner; mallet; screwdriver.

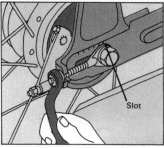

1 Note the position of the chain adjuster slot against the calibrated frame. Loosen the adjusting nut

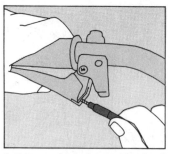

2 Draw up the brake trigger and pull the outer casing away from the handle. Disconnect the cable

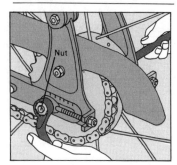

3 Hold one spanner on the spindle bolt and another on the spindle nut on the other side. Remove the nut

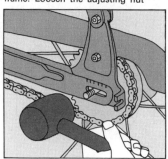

4 Lift off the adjuster on the nut side of the spindle and tap in the spindle with a hide mallet

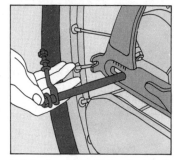

5 From the other side draw the spindle —with the chain adjuster on it—out of the wheel hub

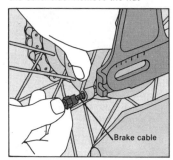

6 Push the wheel forward so that the brake cable can be released from the brake back-plate arm

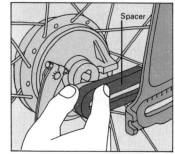

7 Lift the heavy spacer from between the wheel and the cycle frame to free the rear wheel

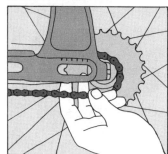

8 Push the wheel forward and lift the chain off the sprocket on to the spindle *(continued)*

Mopeds Wheels and brakes

(continued)

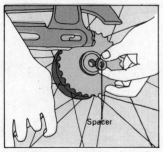

9 Lift the wheel out of the forks. Do not lose the small spacer which fits in the wheel sprocket

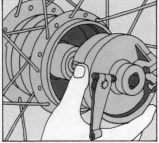

10 Lift the brake plate, which holds the brake shoes, out of the centre of the wheel hub

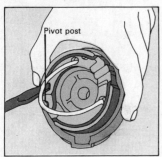

11 To remove brake shoes, lever the spring clip off the pivot post with a screwdriver and pull it clear

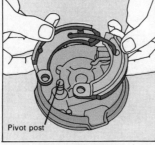

12 Lift the combined linings and shoes off the pivot post. Fit a new unit and reassemble

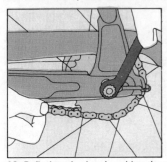

13 Refit the wheel and position the chain on the adjuster to allow about ¾ in. (20 mm) slack

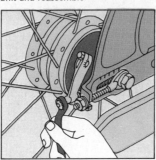

14 Fit the brake cable to the handle-bar lever and adjust at rear so that wheel can spin freely

Removing the front wheel on a Honda

If the front wheel of a Honda moped grates or wobbles, remove it and pack the bearings with grease or fit new ones. The only other time the wheel has to be removed is when the tyre is to be replaced or repaired.

The front wheels have quick-detachable (QD) spindles, which are easy to handle. When removing a wheel for the first time, note any spacing washers and make sure they are put back in the correct order.

Materials: brake linings if necessary; high-melting-point grease.
Tools: spanners; screwdriver; hide mallet.

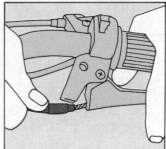

3 Slip the brake outer cable out of the brake lever to give more free play at the brake-drum arm

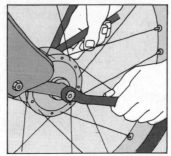

6 Use two spanners to undo the front-wheel spindle. Take off the nut and tap in the spindle

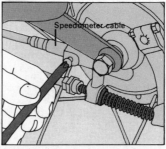

1 Undo the speedometer-drive retaining screw and draw the speedometer cable out of the wheel-drive unit

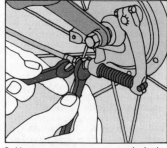

2 Use two spanners—one on the lock-nut and the other on the adjuster—to slacken the brake adjuster

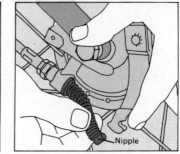

4 Push the brake arm towards the frame of the moped and slip the cable nipple out of its retaining socket

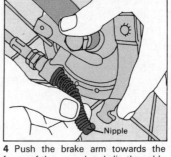

5 Draw the adjuster screw out of its housing. Slide the inner brake cable through the housing slot to remove it

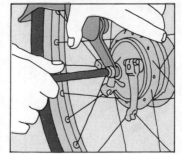

7 Draw the spindle through the hub and lay it aside. Draw the wheel out of the frame of the moped

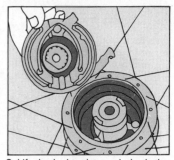

8 Lift the brake plate and check the brake linings. Grease the bearings. Renew if worn. Reassemble

Removing the front wheel on a Puch

Many mopeds do not have quick-detachable spindles (see p. 674) on the front wheels. On the Puch machines, for example, the fitting is the same as on ordinary bicycles.

The cup-and-cone bearings should be repacked with high-melting point grease every 5000 miles.

Check the bearing adjustment each time the moped is serviced. Never over-tighten bearings. The wheel has to be removed to replace a damaged speedometer drive unit or to fit a replacement brake shoe.

Materials: high-melting point grease.
Tools: spanners; cone spanner; pliers.

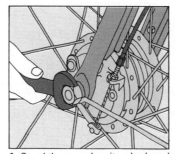

1 Stand the moped on its wheels and loosen the nuts on both sides of the wheel spindle

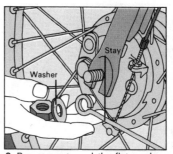

2 Remove nuts and the flat washers between the nuts and mudguard stays. Pull the stays off the spindle

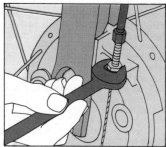

3 Undo the top lock-nut on the brake adjuster. Let the adjuster drop to free the cable at the brake arm

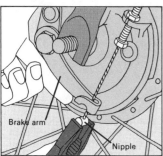

4 Grip the brake nipple firmly in a pair of pliers and pull it out of the brake-arm socket

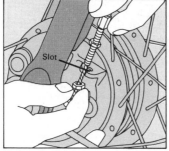

5 Run the lower lock-nut down and off the end of the adjuster thread. Slip the cable out of the holder slot

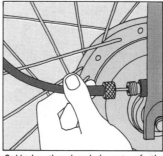

6 Undo the knurled nut of the speedometer drive cable. Draw cable out of wheel-drive mechanism

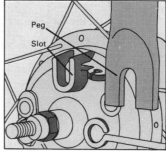

7 Pull up the forks. For reassembly, engage the slot in the brake plate with the peg on the forks

8 Remove wheel. Note spacers on the spindle between the hub and the forks of the machine

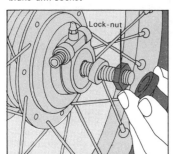

9 Remove spacers and undo the lock-nut which holds the speedometer drive unit in position on the spindle

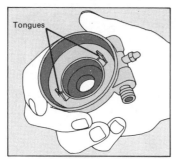

10 Pull the speedometer drive mechanism off the hub. If the locating tongues are broken, renew the unit

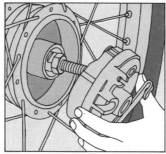

11 Undo the brake-plate retaining nut and remove the brake assembly. Strip, clean and repack the hub with grease

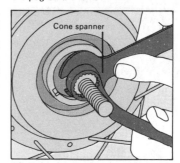

12 Hold the bearing cone in a thin cone spanner. Use a ring spanner to undo the cone lock-nut

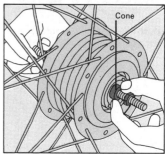

13 Hold the spindle and tighten the cone to eliminate free play. Hold cone and tighten the lock-nut

Mopeds Chains

Fitting and adjusting

The chain of a moped must be kept thoroughly lubricated, but it is not enough to apply oil in the normal way. Remove the chain every 1000 miles and soak it for a day in molten grease or a proprietary mixture available at accessory stores.

A chain should have $\frac{3}{4}$ in. (20 mm) slack on its bottom length: check the adjustment once a week. If the chain is too tight, it causes unnecessary wear on the sprockets; if it is too slack, full driving power is not transmitted to the back wheel.

TYPES OF CHAIN ADJUSTER

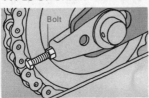

Pull adjuster Tighten the bolt to pull back the rear wheel

Push adjuster Tighten nut against the lug to move the wheel back

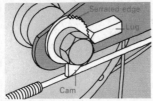

Cam adjuster Turn the cam against the lug to move the wheel

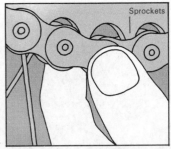

1 Try to pull the chain away from the rear-wheel sprocket. If it is loose on the teeth, fit a new or spare chain

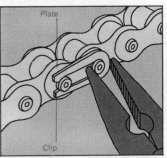

4 Fit the plate. Refit the link clip so that its rounded end faces the way in which the chain is to travel

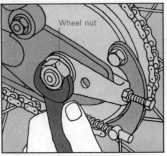

7 Refit the connecting plate and the link clip. Undo the rear-wheel retaining nut with a spanner

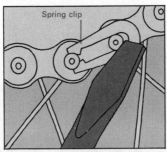

2 Find the spring clip and prise it off with a screwdriver. Remove the link and the link plate

5 Hold the free end of one chain in each hand. Pull the old chain out through the casing

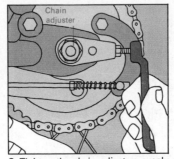

8 Tighten the chain adjusters evenly on each side until the chain has only $\frac{3}{4}$ in. (20 mm) slack along the bottom

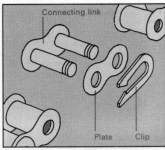

3 Fit the end of the replacement chain to one end of the old chain. Push the connecting link through both

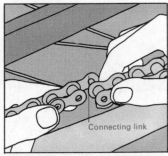

6 Undo the old chain from the new one. Join the two ends of the new chain with the connecting link

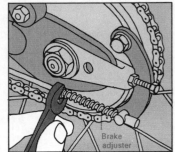

9 Tighten the wheel nut. Check that the rear brake is working correctly. Adjust if necessary

KEEPING A SPARE CHAIN

It is always useful to keep a spare chain, which can be fitted to the moped when the existing one is being lubricated.

When a chain is removed from the machine, examine it carefully to see if it can be repaired and kept as the spare.

The most common faults are that the chain may have stretched or that one or two links only may be damaged. Remove the extra or worn links and, if necessary, fit new ones (see p. 573).

1 Push the links together at the side of a ruler, then pull the ends of the chain. If there is more than $\frac{1}{4}$ in. (6 mm) movement over 12 in. (305 mm), discard the chain

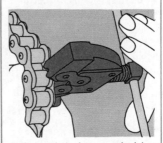

2 If the chain has stretched but is otherwise in good condition, use a link extractor to remove one of the links. Reconnect the chain (see p. 573)

Mopeds Engines

Finding the fault

A moped engine is started by pedalling. At speed, the centrifugal clutch engages and turns the engine, which should fire and start. If the engine does not start, check that the fuel tap is open and that there is fuel in the tank.

If the machine has a two-stroke engine (see p. 474) the fuel-oil mixture must be in the correct proportions. If in doubt, drain the tank and refill with the correct mix.

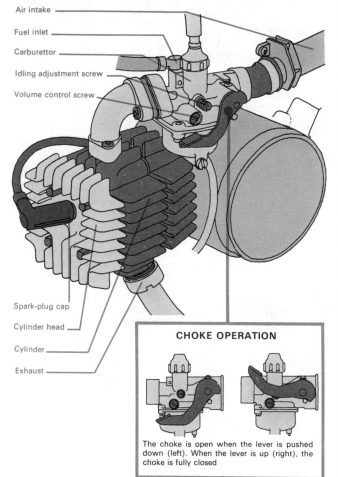

Air intake
Fuel inlet
Carburettor
Idling adjustment screw
Volume control screw

Spark-plug cap
Cylinder head
Cylinder
Exhaust

CHOKE OPERATION

The choke is open when the lever is pushed down (left). When the lever is up (right), the choke is fully closed

Symptom	Checking order	Action
Engine will not start	**Spark-plug** Remove the plug and reconnect the lead. Lay the plug on the engine block, spin the engine flywheel by hand and see if the plug sparks	**If the plug sparks** Check the fuel system **If the plug does not spark** Remove the spark-plug lead and hold it near engine block. Spin the engine and see if there is a spark **If lead sparks** Fit a new spark-plug **If lead does not spark** Bend the lead and look for cracking. Fit a new lead. Reset the contact-breaker points gap (see p. 673)
	Fuel system Disconnect fuel pipe at carburettor, turn on the fuel tap	**If no fuel** Clean fuel tap with stiff wire **If fuel flows** Check the carburettor
	No fuel in carburettor Remove the float chamber bowl	Turn on the fuel tap to see if fuel is passing the needle valve **If not** Clean the valve assembly (see p. 679) **If fuel reaches carburettor** Check jets (see p. 679)
	Engine flooded Turn off fuel supply, open the throttle fully and try to start the engine	**If engine starts** Turn on fuel. Clean and dry spark-plug (see p. 644) **If the carburettor continues to flood** Clean needle valve (see p. 679). Shake float. If fuel inside, fit new float
Engine starts but cuts out	**Fuel supply partially blocked** Remove fuel pipe from carburettor; turn on the tap	**If no fuel** Clean tap and filters **If fuel flows** Check needle valve (see p. 680). Clean jets (see p. 679)
Engine starts but kicks back	Ignition timing inaccurate	Check that the points gap is correct **If not** Regap (see p. 673) **If correct** Remove the flywheel cover and make sure the contact points open just as the flywheel timing marks line up (see p. 673) **If not** Reset the timing or have it done by a skilled mechanic
Difficult starting when cold	Ignition system	Check that the spark-plug is of the correct grade for engine **If wrong** Fit new plug of correct grade **If right** Clean and regap (see p. 644)
	Contact-breaker points gap	**If wrong** Regap (see p. 673)
	Choke in correct position Close throttle then open it slightly	**If it still fails** Strip and clean carburettor jets (see p. 679)
Difficult starting when warm	Mixture strength	Check that the choke is not in the cold start position
	Carburettor flooding	Make sure needle valve is not stuck (see p. 680) **If stuck** Free and clean, or renew if necessary
Engine will not idle or stops when throttle is opened	Carburettor faulty	Strip and clean the carburettor (see p. 680)
Engine misfires when accelerated	Ignition system	Remove spark-plug and clean and regap (see p. 644) Bend the spark-plug lead and check for signs of cracking. If damaged, fit a new lead Check contact-breaker points gap, clean and regap (see p. 673) Fit new points if necessary

Mopeds Engines

De-carbonising a two-stroke engine

A moped two-stroke engine should be overhauled and decarbonised when there are indications that the engine is not operating efficiently—for example, if the moped has to be pedalled to get up hills, or if there are oily deposits at the end of the exhaust pipe. It may also be possible to tell from a change in the sound of the exhaust—say, if it becomes muffled—that carbon has built up in the combustion chambers.

Materials: gasket set; piston rings if necessary; 2p coin; rags.
Tools: plug spanner; ring and open-ended spanners; old hacksaw blade; pliers; screwdriver.

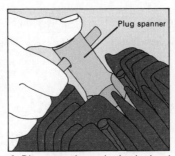

1 Disconnect the spark-plug lead and remove the spark-plug. Clean the plug and reset the gap (see p. 644)

2 Undo the cylinder-head retaining nuts half a turn at a time until they are loose. Remove them

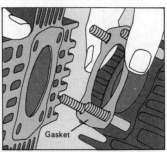

3 Pull the cylinder head off the engine. Remove the cylinder-head gasket and discard it

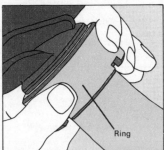

4 Unscrew the ring holding the exhaust pipe. Remove and discard the gasket between the flanges

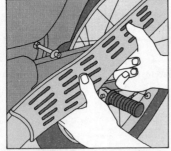

5 Undo the other bolts securing the exhaust system to the machine. Lift off the exhaust

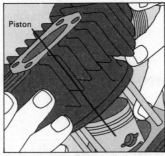

6 Gently pull off the cylinder barrel. Support the piston with the fingers as the barrel comes free

7 Push the piston down as far as it will go. Pack clean rags between the piston and the crankcase

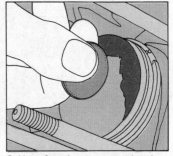

8 Use a 2p coin to scrape carbon from the top of the piston crown. Do not scratch deeply

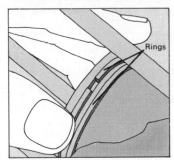

9 Check that the piston rings are free in their grooves. If they are worn, fit new rings (see p. 475)

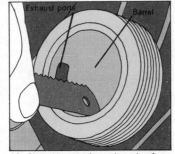

10 Clean any carbon deposits from the exhaust ports inside the barrel with the back of an old hacksaw blade

11 Carefully scrape away the carbon from the cylinder head. Use a 2p coin to avoid damaging the alloy head

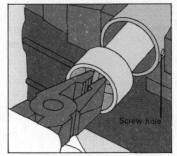

12 Undo the single screw holding the baffle in the silencer. Draw the baffle out with a pair of pliers

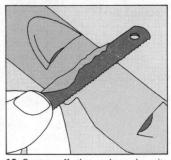

13 Scrape off the carbon deposits from the baffle and from inside the silencer box. Reassemble

Mopeds Carburettors

Care and maintenance

Worn components in the slide carburettor (see p. 482) of a moped can cause difficult starting and high fuel consumption. Regular tuning ensures economical fuel consumption.

If a moped is not to be used for a long period, drain the float-chamber bowl. This is especially important with a two-stroke engine. Fuel can evaporate and leave neat oil which fouls the spark-plug when the engine is eventually started.

Never probe a carburettor jet or drilling with wire—blow out any obstructions with a foot-pump. If a blockage cannot be cleared, fit new jets.

TWIST GRIP

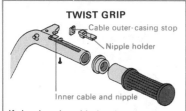

Cable outer-casing stop
Nipple holder
Inner cable and nipple

If the throttle cable breaks, remove the twist grip. Loosen the grip screw, pull off the handle, release nipple and draw out old cable. Fit a new one and reassemble

TUNING THE CARBURETTOR

To keep the engine running evenly, the fuel-air mixture must be correct. Balance the mixture by the two control screws at the side

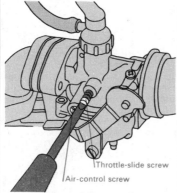

Throttle-slide screw
Air-control screw

1 Screw in the throttle-slide screw. This lifts the throttle slide and allows more air to enter the carburettor to give a fast idling speed

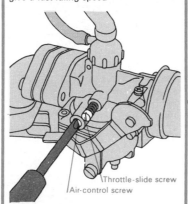

Throttle-slide screw
Air-control screw

2 Adjust the air-control screw until engine runs faster and evenly. Unscrew throttle-slide screw to reduce to normal tickover speed

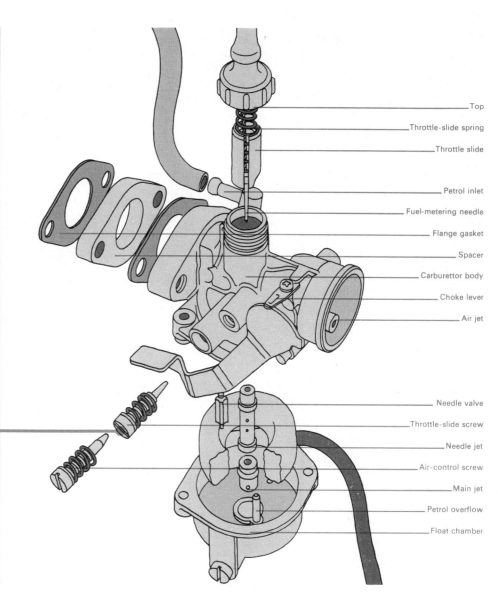

Top
Throttle-slide spring
Throttle slide
Petrol inlet
Fuel-metering needle
Flange gasket
Spacer
Carburettor body
Choke lever
Air jet
Needle valve
Throttle-slide screw
Needle jet
Air-control screw
Main jet
Petrol overflow
Float chamber

Mopeds Carburettors

Dismantling and overhauling

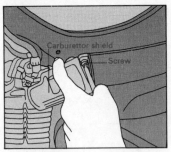

1 Undo all the screws which hold the carburettor shield on to the side of the moped

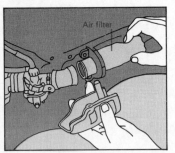

2 Lift off the shield to expose the carburettor. It may also be necessary to remove the air-filter box

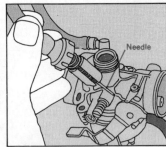

3 Unscrew the top of the carburettor to remove the throttle-slide assembly with the fuel-metering needle

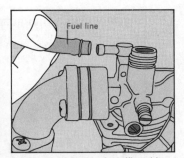

4 With the fuel tap in the 'off' position, release the fuel-line clip and pull the line off the carburettor

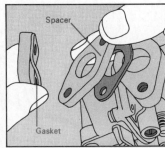

5 Undo the screws holding the carburettor to the manifold flange. Discard gasket and spacer

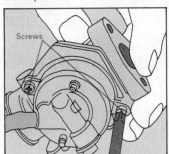

6 Remove the two cross-headed screws holding the float chamber to the carburettor body

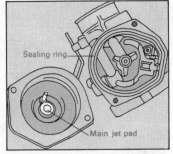

7 Remove the chamber bowl. Check the sealing ring on the float-bowl flange and the main jet pad

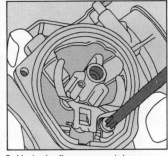

8 Undo the float-arm retaining screw. Lift the arm out to gain access to the needle valve

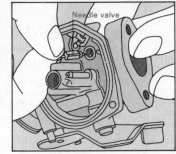

9 Lift the needle valve out and inspect its seating. If it is ridged or worn, fit a new valve assembly

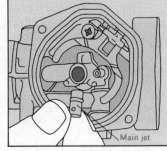

10 Remove the main jet from the base of the needle jet. If it is blocked, clean with an air line

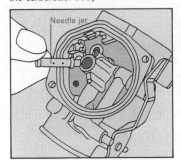

11 Lift out the needle jet. Check that it is clean and unblocked. If necessary clean with an air line

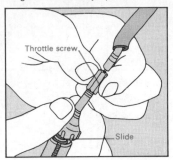

12 Screw the throttle-adjustment screw down to leave enough slack in the cable to remove the throttle slide

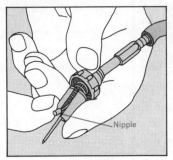

13 Slip the cable nipple out of the throttle slide. If the needle is worn, fit a new one in the same setting

14 To refit the throttle slide in the carburettor body, make sure that the slot is in line with the locating peg

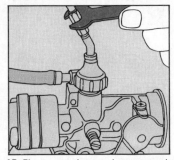

15 Fit new gaskets and spacer and refit the carburettor. Take up slack on the throttle cable by the adjuster

PART 7

REFERENCE

BUYERS' RIGHTS

If an article breaks soon after it has been bought, do not start to repair it: first complain to the dealer and ask to have the fault put right. Home repairs may invalidate a guarantee.

Anyone who pays for goods or services has certain rights and protection under the law. If the goods purchased are found on examination to be faulty, or the repair work that has been carried out is inadequate or even likely to be dangerous, the householder may be able to claim compensation for any loss or damage to himself or his property.

A buyer's most valuable rights are normally against the person or shop which sold him the goods or provided the service. Normally, it is the *seller*, not the manufacturer, who is legally obliged to ensure that any goods sold are not defective.

These transactions are covered by the Sale of Goods Act, 1979.

No substitute

When a buyer describes to the shopkeeper exactly what he wants—for example, if he asks for a specific type or make of paint—the shopkeeper cannot legally substitute some other kind.

Even if the buyer does not notice at the time of buying that he has not been given what he wanted, he is entitled to return the goods later to the shop and to ask for his money to be refunded.

Unsuitable goods

The buyer can claim against the seller if the goods are unsuitable for his purpose. If he asks the shopkeeper's advice or tells him what the goods are to be used for, it is the shopkeeper's responsibility to ensure that the goods are suitable.

When a buyer purchases a proprietary brand *with the advice of the shopkeeper*, he can claim against the shopkeeper if the goods are found to be unsuitable.

Always consult a shop assistant before buying an item as to its suitability for the purpose for which it is required.

Faulty goods

The buyer has the right to expect that anything he buys is of a certain standard—called, in law, *merchantable quality*. This means that goods must be in working order and in a condition which would be acceptable, considering the price paid, to a reasonable private or trade buyer. A television set, for example, must be able to receive both sound and pictures: a colour television set must be able to receive colour pictures.

There is, however, an important condition. The buyer may lose his legal protection—his claim against the seller—if he has inspected the goods before buying them. When the fault is one which should have been seen in a reasonable examination, he cannot claim his money back if he later decides that he is not satisfied.

Many goods are so packaged that the buyer has no opportunity to examine them. If he is shown a demonstration model or sample in a shop but later finds that the article he has bought is defective, he is

EXCLUSIONS

Shopkeepers can no longer avoid their obligations under the Sale of Goods Act, provided the goods purchased by the buyer are for private use and are purchased from someone who sells them in the course of a business.

A notice or order that says 'We accept no liability for any breach of any statutory or other conditions' is now invalid and should be ignored by the customer. The Sale of Goods Act, 1979, has changed the law to extend protection to the purchaser and the consumer.

entitled to make a claim against the shopkeeper.

There is no specific time limit on the buyer's right to demand a refund for faulty goods, but he is not protected indefinitely.

Second-hand goods

A buyer has the same protection in principle with second-hand goods, but the standard expected of the goods is lower. They must, however, conform to the seller's description.

Hire-purchase transactions

The buyer has similar rights buying goods on hire purchase to those when buying goods outright. But the responsibility for their quality rests upon the owner of the goods—usually the hire-purchase company.

The owner cannot avoid responsibility by contract or agreement. Any clause in a hire-purchase contract that tries to exclude the owner's obligations is invalid, provided the transaction is one where the owner hires goods out in the course of business and the hirer is hiring goods for his private use.

Trade Descriptions Act

Buyers are also protected under the Trade Descriptions Act 1968, which makes it an offence for a shopkeeper to describe goods falsely or to claim that he is selling them at a bargain price if he has made no reduction.

A dissatisfied customer can complain to the local council's weights and measures department, which is responsible for prosecuting. Sometimes when the department successfully prosecutes a shopkeeper, the court will compensate the buyer.

The protection of the Trade Descriptions Act, 1968 also applies to services.

Damage or loss

When a householder is injured or suffers some loss as a result of defective goods or workmanship, it is usually advisable to claim against the manufacturer, who is responsible in law for any damage caused by *negligence* during manufacture. Always consult a solicitor as soon as possible after suffering loss or injury.

How to complain

If goods are faulty, first complain to the manager or owner of the shop from which the goods were bought and ask for them to be exchanged or repaired.

If that is not enough, write to the shop and keep a copy of the letter. If further action is needed, complain to the appropriate local trade association, of which the shopkeeper or contractor is likely to be a member. If this does not produce results, consult a solicitor about taking action through the courts.

GUARANTEES

The Sale of Goods Act 1979 invalidates any agreement or clause to exclude the buyer's rights against the seller, provided the goods are sold in the course of a business and are bought for private use.

Many manufacturers still invite buyers to complete a reply-paid 'Guarantee' postcard and enter into an agreement with the manufacturer. Such guarantees no longer exclude the buyer's general legal rights: even if he does sign, the buyer can still claim against the seller.

Rarely are the benefits given by such guarantees greater than those provided by the buyer's general legal rights. Often a buyer invoking a guarantee must pay the cost of sending the goods to the manufacturer, and he may also be charged for labour costs. Often the manufacturer agrees to replace only defective parts 'which in their opinion are due to faulty workmanship .

PUBLIC SERVICES

Drains The householder is responsible for his own drains (except on council estates), but the engineer and surveyor's department gives free advice and, if there is a health threat, free assistance.

Pests Consult the local council pest officer for free advice and help in dealing with rats, mice, pigeons, wasps, flies, maggots, Dutch elm disease and other pests (see p. 696).

House renovation grants can be obtained to modernise old houses.

Improvement grants are made for improving the standards of houses and the conversion of large properties into flats. *Intermediate grants* are for provision of basic amenities, such as a fixed bath or shower, and any associated repairs. *Special grants* cover installation of basic amenities in houses in multiple occupation. *Repair grants* are for repair or replacement—not improvement or conversion—in houses in 'housing action' and general improvement' areas where owners cannot meet the cost of the work themselves.

All these grants have an upper limit and the local council should be consulted in all cases before any work is undertaken.

Electricity All electricity boards offer a contract maintenance service for cookers: fees are paid quarterly. They operate emergency breakdown services for all appliances and provide an inspection service on request. Electricity board fitters are available to re-wire a house. Inquire at the local electricity showroom.

Gas Contract maintenance is provided for all gas equipment, including central heating. Each gas board operates an emergency repair service.

Telephones Faulty or damaged receivers are repaired or replaced free of charge, unless the damage has been deliberately caused. Persistent problems or disputes about telephone service can be reported to the local Advisory Committee for Postal Services. Inquire at a post office.

Water Leaking taps and ball valves are repaired by some water boards. The service is usually available during weekday working hours and only if no private plumber can be engaged. Some boards make a nominal charge for the work.

INSURANCE

When a house or its contents are insured, find out before starting to make repairs whether the cost can be recovered under the terms of the policy. Always inform the insurance company as soon as damage occurs and submit an estimate of the likely repair cost.

Except where an immediate emergency repair is necessary, the company may refuse to meet a claim if an estimate has not been submitted and approved by the insurance company before repair work is started.

Household policies
Insurance of the house structure is usually a condition of the granting of a mortgage.

Such household policies normally cover the house and any garage or outbuildings. Permanent fixtures which would not normally be removed when changing houses, for example, baths, radiators, windows and doors, are also usually included.

Most policies cover damage by fire or explosion, vehicle impact, objects which have fallen from an aircraft, by burglary, central-heating oil leaks, malicious damage by a third party, and accidental damage to baths and fittings. Special cover is needed for woodworm and rot.

New houses In addition to the normal insurance cover, any new house constructed by a firm that is registered with the National House' Building Council has a ten-year guarantee. If a registered builder refuses to repair defects, write to the council at 58 Portland Place, London W1N 4BU.

Contents policies
Personal belongings which are insured under a normal contents policy may be covered even if they are damaged when they have been temporarily removed from the house.

Some policies exclude items stored in a garage or outhouse.

GLASS-FIBRE

Glass-fibre kits, such as Isopon, which can be used for many repairs, are available in two forms—filler paste and resin with fibre matting.

Filler paste To repair a crack or fill a very small hole, use a filler kit which contains a tin of paste with a tube of hardener. Always follow the manufacturer's instructions. Rub damaged surfaces with glass-paper to get a rough, matt finish.

If filler paste has to be laid thickly, criss-cross the surface with a file. If rotting wood is to be filled with paste, fix protruding screws in damaged area to provide a good key.

When the paste has hardened—usually after 45 minutes—it can be rubbed down with glass-paper, chiselled, sawn, painted or varnished.

Mat and resin When the area to be repaired has a hole which cannot be successfully mended with paste, use a resin-and-mat kit. This consists of a tin of resin, a bottle of liquid hardener and sheets of bonded glass-fibre strands.

Clean the damaged area thoroughly and cut the matting to overlap about 1 in. (25 mm) on each side. Pour resin into an old tin and add the hardener according to the manufacturer's instructions.

Spread the mixed resin on to the repair area and press the matting on to it immediately. Stipple the matting with a paintbrush until it is thoroughly impregnated with resin from below. Always work from the centre outwards to eliminate any air bubbles.

Stains Use acetone, obtainable from a chemist, to remove resin stains on clothing. To remove resin from the hands, wash them in clean warm water.

Danger Glass-fibre materials are poisonous in their unhardened state. Keep them away from the mouth and eyes and always work in a well-ventilated room. Never work in rain or strong sunshine.

FIXTURES AND FITTINGS

When screws in a plaster wall become loose, the most likely fault is that they are not long enough. Plaster, which is not itself strong enough to support most fittings, is about ¾ in. (20 mm) thick on most house walls and for that reason screws should be at least 1¼ in. (30 mm) long to penetrate the brickwork which is underneath the plaster covering.

If, however, the fitting is particularly heavy or likely to be under strain, make sure that the screw is longer than that minimum so that it will remain firm.

Filling holes When a fitting becomes loose, undo and remove all its screws. Brush out the screw holes and check that they are long enough to take the new screws required. If they are wide and shallow, but long enough to take the new screws, fill them with a paste—for example, Polyfilla. Fix the new screws—without the fitting—immediately. Remove them when the filler has set, position the fitting and refit the screws. If the old holes are not long enough to take the new screws, allow the filler to set and drill new holes with a masonry bit.

When the holes are oversize or distorted, use a special compound filler—for example, Rawlplastic. Ram it firmly into the hole and position and screw on the fitting immediately, before the filler sets.

1 Brush out the holes and push filler paste firmly into them. Smooth the filler at the surface of the wall with a putty knife

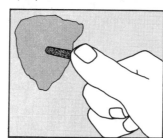
3 Push a proprietary wall plug or tapered piece of wooden dowel rod into the new screw hole until the end is just below the wall surface

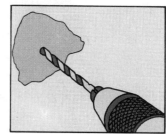
2 If a hole deeper than the filled one is needed, allow the filler to set. Drill a slightly oversize hole with a masonry bit

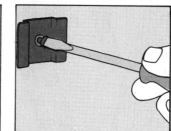
4 Position the fitting and insert the screw. If there is more than one screw, tighten them in rotation to avoid distortion

DISTORTED HOLES

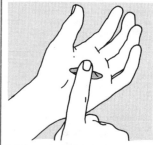
1 When the old hole is too distorted for a normal plug, dampen a little of the compound filler and roll it in the palm of the hand

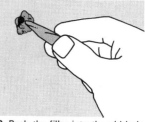
2 Push the filler into the old hole in the wall. Ram it in firmly and roll more filler and push it into the hole if necessary

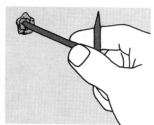
3 Ram filler home with tool provided with kit. Make shallow pilot hole with point of tool and screw on fitting

LADDERS

The choice of ladders for household repairs is governed by two factors—the amount of covered storage space available and the maximum height that the ladder may have to reach. It is dangerous to overstretch when working at the top of a ladder: buy one which, when extended, is at least as tall as the highest point to be reached when using it.

Push-up extending ladders can be difficult for one person to manoeuvre into place. If the ladder has to be extended by more than 16 ft (5 m), obtain one that is rope-operated.

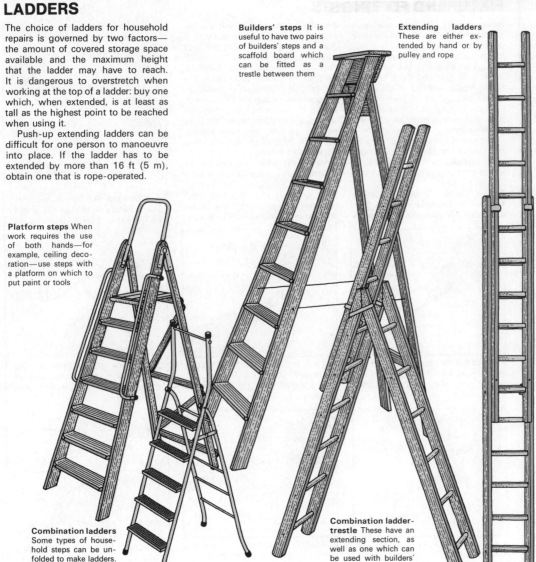

Platform steps When work requires the use of both hands—for example, ceiling decoration—use steps with a platform on which to put paint or tools

Combination ladders Some types of household steps can be unfolded to make ladders. They are not suitable for very high work

Builders' steps It is useful to have two pairs of builders' steps and a scaffold board which can be fitted as a trestle between them

Combination ladder-trestle These have an extending section, as well as one which can be used with builders' steps and a scaffold board to form a trestle

Extending ladders These are either extended by hand or by pulley and rope

LADDER SAFETY

Always examine a ladder for cracked or rotten rungs and for any loose joints.

Never rest a ladder against glass, glazing bars or plastic guttering.

Never overstretch to one side of a ladder: it may slide sideways.

Never stand on the top rungs of a ladder. The minimum safety position is about four rungs down.

Always leave at least a two-rung overlap between sections on a 14 ft (4·3 m) extension ladder; three rungs on a 16 ft (4·9 m) ladder.

Always wear shoes: boots make it difficult to feel the rungs, and wearing plimsolls can be painful.

Carrying Grip the ladder with one hand and support it above shoulder level with the other

Lifting Push the foot of the ladder against the wall. Work hands down the rungs to push it upright

Positioning Pull out the bottom. The ideal distance from the wall is about one quarter of ladder height

Uneven ground If the ground is uneven, cut and position wood blocks at the lower side of the ground

Soft ground Stand the foot of the ladder on wide board, with a batten screwed across to prevent slipping

Securing on soft ground Drive stakes into the ground and tie the sides of the ladder to them

Securing on a hard surface Place a bag of sand or soil against the foot of the ladder

Securing at top Tie ladder to a downpipe bracket or a ring bolt screwed to the soffit

Climbing Always look straight ahead —not down or up. Be prepared for flexing on ladders that are very long

Painting Hang the tin of paint on to a metal S hook (see p. 33). Always try to hold the ladder with one hand

Wide overhangs Fix a stay, obtainable from builders' merchants, to position the ladder further out from the wall

CRAWLING BOARDS

Do not attempt any major roof repairs without using crawling boards: they are essential to safety and make the work much easier.

Some suppliers hire sets containing a top section—known as the headboard—with extension lengths. A useful-sized set is a 10 ft (3 m) headboard with three 3 ft 9 in. (1·1 m) extensions, which can be assembled easily by one person.

Stand on scaffolding or a tower (see p. 686) when fitting crawling boards: do not work from a ladder.

Double sets are useful when extensive work is being done: one set can be used to hold materials the other for working.

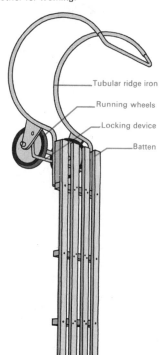

— Tubular ridge iron

— Running wheels

— Locking device

— Batten

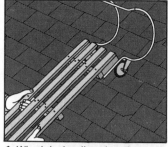

1 Wheel the headboard section partly up the roof. Hold it level to ensure that slates or tiles are not damaged

2 Slot extension-length flanges over the headboard end. Turn over boards and lock joint (inset)

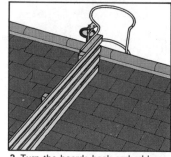

3 Turn the boards back and add sections. When ridge is reached, turn boards over to hook irons over ridge

4 Check that the boards are securely anchored. When climbing, use hands on crossbars for additional support

5 Do not lay tools or materials on the roof. Secure them between the crossbars of the crawling boards

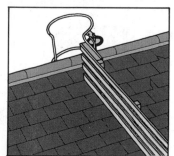

6 To move the crawling boards, return to the scaffold. Push boards up from ridge and turn over twice

685

Reference

SCAFFOLDING: SINGLE TOWERS

The cheapest and simplest form of scaffolding that can be erected easily by one person is a sectional tower. The tower has castors on the bottom frame so that it can easily be moved along to new positions.

It costs more to hire than a ladder, but it is safer to use provided the surface on which the tower is to be used is smooth and level. Its height should not exceed three times the minimum base dimension.

Many do-it-yourself shops and plant-hire firms hire out sectional towers on a weekly basis. They are generally available up to 31 ft 8 in. (9·6 m) high and the platform size is usually 8×4 ft (2·4×1·2 m).

Guard rail

Toe board

SPIGOT PIN

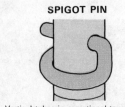

Vertical tubes in a sectional tower are sometimes held together by a spigot pin pushed through both tubes

FINGER-FLICK BRACELOCK

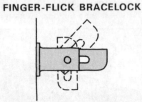

The cross braces of the tower are held in place by a finger-operated locking mechanism

Cross brace

H frame

Castor

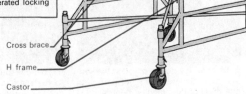

1 To erect a tower scaffold, first connect one frame and cross brace. Secure finger-flick bracelocks

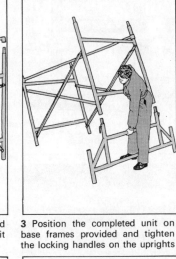

2 Repeat on the opposite frame and cross brace. Join frames and fit horizontal cross brace to corners

3 Position the completed unit on base frames provided and tighten the locking handles on the uprights

4 Fit two braces diagonally to the four corners of the tower base and lock in castor wheels or base plates

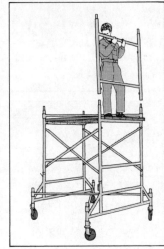

5 Lay temporary boards to stand on. Add further frames and cross braces, then lock in place with spigot pins

6 At the height required, add decking boards, guard rails, guard posts and toe boards

SCAFFOLDING FOR LARGER AREAS

Prefabricated scaffolding, formed by end frames that are tied with cross braces, is the simplest type of scaffolding to cover a large span. It can be erected and dismantled quickly and easily by two people.

The frames are designed in the form of an H—often with an additional horizontal bar to give extra support. The frames slot into each other on a spigot-and-hole principle, and additional frames can be fitted to increase the working width.

On level surfaces fit base plates under the legs of the bottom frame; on uneven surfaces ask the supplier for a set of adjustable base plates.

When building up the height, lay bars, called ledgers, horizontally across the top of each frame to take transom units and boards. This makes a temporary platform from which to build the next section.

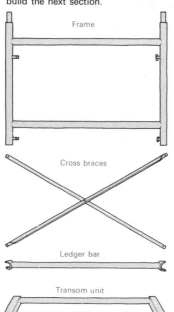

Frame

Cross braces

Ledger bar

Transom unit

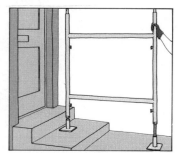

1 On uneven surfaces, adjust base-plate legs to approximate level. Fit wood blocks if necessary

2 If the ground is soft, set out wooden planks 8 ft (2·4 m) apart. Make sure that they are level

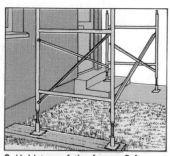

3 Hold two of the frames 8 ft apart and secure them together with a pair of diagonal braces

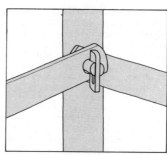

4 To add to the width, fix additional braces to the second frame to secure a further frame 8 ft away

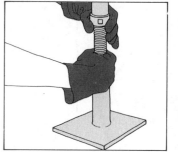

5 When these first frames are in position, check carefully that they are level and upright. Adjust if necessary

6 Ease ledger bars horizontally across the top of the frames centrally between the side transom bars

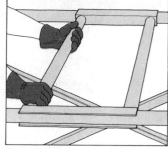

7 Place the transom unit in position. Fit the three-sided end first. The two-sided end rests on the ledger

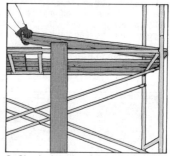

8 Check that the fittings are secure. Place two boards on to the frame ends and transom-unit section

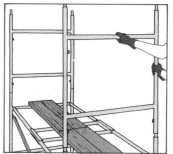

9 Work from one temporary platform. Lift the next frames into position over the spigots

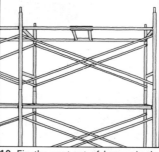

10 Fix the next set of braces in the same way as the first. Add ledger bars, transom units and boards

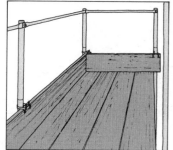

11 Slot in guard-rail fittings and boards for a working platform. Fit toe boards to the bottom of the platform

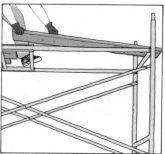

12 Dismantle in reverse method of construction. Lift off boards first and take away the frames last

Reference

TIMBER

When timber has been felled and cut into planks it should be allowed to season—that is, to dry naturally—under cover but in the open air. Never buy freshly cut wood: ask the timber merchant for an assurance that softwood—for example, pine or spruce—has been seasoned for at least a year. Hardwoods such as oak, teak or walnut should be kept for one year for every inch of their thickness.

Do not buy very wide boards: it is likely that they have been cut from the heartwood of the tree, and as a result will dry unevenly and crack or warp down the centre. If wide wood is needed, buy several narrow planks and joint them (see p. 302).

Always examine timber carefully when choosing it. Look for serious faults and bad discoloration: but be prepared to buy boards a little longer than needed and to cut off the faulty areas. If timber has been properly seasoned for the correct length of time, no further serious faults are likely to develop after it has been put to use.

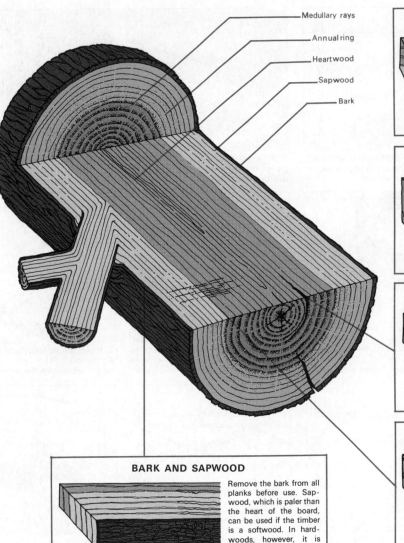

Medullary rays
Annual ring
Heartwood
Sapwood
Bark

DEAD KNOT

A star shape surrounded by a black ring indicates a dead knot, which may drop out of the timber as it dries. It is advisable not to buy wood with this fault; but if it is unavoidable, cut out the knot area and patch it (see p. 298)

LIVE KNOT

Knots that have no star shape are usually live. If the timber has been adequately seasoned it is unlikely that the knot will shrink more than the board in the future. Live knots have little appreciable effect on the strength of timber

BARK AND SAPWOOD

Remove the bark from all planks before use. Sapwood, which is paler than the heart of the board, can be used if the timber is a softwood. In hardwoods, however, it is open to worm attack

WARPING

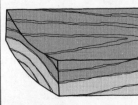

When timber is warped or twisted down the length of the grain, cut it into shorter lengths and plane to an even thickness.

If the warping is across the grain, cut and square the wood into strips: glue together and plane (see p. 302)

CUP SHAKES

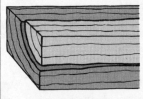

The heartwood of timber may dry more quickly than the rest of the tree and may, in time, start to split. If the edge or centre of a seasoned board shows signs of splitting, do not use it. Saw off and discard the whole of the faulty area

END SHAKES

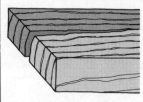

If the ends of a board dry more quickly than the rest, they may split or crack. The fault, called end shakes, is unlikely to affect the rest of the timber. Cut across the plank about 2 in. (50 mm) beyond the end of the split

BRITTLE HEART

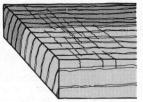

Lines, cracks or splits across the grain in the timber are called brittle heart. The fault, most common in hardwoods, reduces the strength of the timber. It is advisable to cut out the damaged area if the wood is to be used in any form of structural work

TYPES OF MANUFACTURED BOARD

Plywood is made from an odd number of layers of veneer, each laid with its grain at right angles to the one below and above it. They are bonded together under pressure with glue. The more veneers in plywood, the greater is its strength. For outside, use an external-quality plywood with weatherproof adhesive.

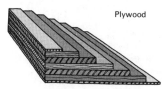

Plywood

Fibreboard This is pressed from wood pulp or fibre, with a bonding agent and fillers. The standard quality is available $\frac{1}{8}$ in. and $\frac{1}{4}$ in. (3 mm and 6 mm) thick.

Fibreboard is extensively used for room insulation.

Hardboard Made from softwood pulp, pressed into sheets ranging from $\frac{1}{12} - \frac{1}{2}$ in. (2.4–13 mm) thick. Standard hardboard has one smooth finished face and a rough mesh texture on the reverse. Other types are available.

Blockboard Made from strips of softwood about 1 in. (25 mm) wide laid edge to edge and sandwiched between veneers, usually of birch.

Blockboard is suitable for making such items as doors, table tops, shelving and room dividers.

Blockboard

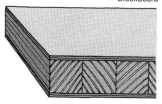

Battenboard Like blockboard, but the core strips are usually about 3 in. (75 mm) wide. Difficult to obtain.

Battenboard

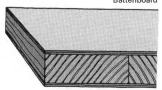

Laminboard Similar to blockboard but the core is made from wood strips about $\frac{1}{4}$ in. (6 mm) wide glued together before the veneers are bonded on the outside. One advantage of laminboard over blockboard is that the pattern of the core is less likely to be registered on the surface veneer.

Laminboard

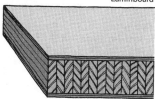

Chipboard This is made from wood particles bonded together with resin at high pressure and temperature. Most chipboard has coarse particles at the centre and fine particles on the surface.

Chipboard is cheaper than blockboard but can be used for much the same purposes.

Chipboard

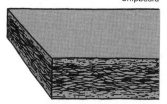

WORKING WITH SHEET MATERIALS

When a manufactured board is to be cut across the grain, lay a straight-edge on the line to be cut and score with a sharp-bladed knife. Score only once, but deeply enough to ensure that the surface will not chip or splinter when sawn. Support the board carefully and cut it with a fine-toothed saw on the waste side of the score mark. Smooth the cut edge with glass-paper.

If a board is faced with laminated plastic, cut it first with a glass-cutter to prevent splitting.

Gluing

If a surface is to be glued, roughen it with a file or rasp to provide a key. Ordinary wood glues (see p. 694) are adequate for most boards, but the surfaces must be cramped together until the glue sets. Resin or PVA adhesives are best for chipboard: always follow the manufacturer's instructions carefully.

Screwing and nailing

Fix screws or nails through the face of chipboard, never through wood and into the board. Make sure that any screws and nails used are long enough to give an adequate hold in the board. Do not screw or nail into the edge of chipboard or the end grain of blockboard and laminboard.

Always drill pilot holes for screws to prevent splitting.

Preparing hardboard

To avoid distortion it is advisable to season hardboard by wetting it on its rough side at least 24 hours before fixing it.

Use a pint of water for each 8×4 ft (2.4×1.2 m) sheet and lay sheets back to back on a flat surface. Allow them to dry in the place where they are to be used.

If a board is to be painted with oil-based paints, prime both sides with a suitable wood primer.

If it is intended to use blockboard indoors, leave it in the room where it is to be used for four weeks before painting. This will considerably reduce the chances of the board and the paint cracking.

WORKING WITH TIMBER

Timber, when it is bought, usually has about 17 per cent moisture content; but most modern adhesives are ineffective if there is more than 12 per cent moisture in the wood. Store wood in a dry, warm room or workshop for a month or more before use.

Never lean timber against a wall: it may curve under its own weight. Cut $\frac{3}{4} \times \frac{3}{4}$ in. (20×20 mm) sticks to the width of the wood and lay them 15 in. (180 mm) apart on a floor. Lay timber on top and place the same number of sticks exactly above the first ones. Continue piling the wood with sticks positioned between each board.

Softwoods

Most merchants sell softwood rough-sawn or planed ready for use. If the wood is not to be exposed when the work is complete, use it rough-sawn. If it is to be visible, buy it planed or finish it in the workshop.

Always allow for the loss in planing when ordering wood: for example a 6×1 in. (158×25 mm) board is in fact $5\frac{3}{4} \times \frac{7}{8}$ in. (147×22 mm) when it is prepared.

Hardwoods

It is not usually possible to buy hardwoods ready planed. Most are rough-sawn, and the bark and sapwood may not have been removed. Always allow for cutting and planing.

When ordering hardwood, state the purpose for which it is required, as this may have some bearing on the timber selected.

USING A MITRE BOX

Mitre boxes, with which wood can be sawn at an angle, are intended for use with a tenon saw. If a box has metal saw guides, always adjust them to the thickness of the saw being used.

Each box has two slots so that left and right mitres—sometimes called internal and external angles—can be cut. Always grip a mitre box in a vice or secure it with cramps so that one hand is free to hold the wood being cut.

Hold the work face uppermost and with its outer edge tight against the back of the box. Support wood which extends beyond the ends of the box on small blocks, so that the work remains level at all times.

1 If the wood being cut is narrower than the inside of the box, hold it by hand or fix it with wedges

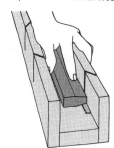

2 If the wood has a bevelled underside, pack it underneath so that it can be cut evenly

ADHESIVES FOR PLASTICS

Many types of plastics are used for common household articles. Before any article can be repaired, it is essential to identify the type of plastic. If it is practicable, cut a small piece from the damaged article and test it by burning (see p. 691). If it is not possible to make such a test, assume that the cheaper the article, the more likely it is that the plastic is polythene or polystyrene. High-quality goods are usually made of acrylics, nylon, acetal or GRP (see p. 691). Those listed against each item are in the order they are most likely to be found.

Three basic types of adhesives are enough to deal with most plastics repairs: contact, clear and epoxy.

Contact adhesives
Apply contact adhesives to both surfaces. Leave the adhesive to dry, then press the surfaces to form a strong bond immediately on contact.

A major disadvantage is that the join cannot be moved easily after contact. Dunlop Thixofix will allow limited adjustments to be made, provided the surfaces are brought together gently when the adhesive is touch-dry; test by touching with a knuckle.

Clear adhesives
If the surfaces are non-absorbent hard plastic, spread clear adhesive on both. If one surface is absorbent—for example cloth, felt or canvas—spread adhesive only on the plastic surface.

With some cheap types of flexible PVC, chemicals in the plastic and the adhesive may react together and gradually soften the bond.

Epoxy adhesives
Epoxies are more expensive than most other adhesives and have to be mixed before use, but they do provide a stronger bond, especially when the join is to be exposed to heat, strain or frequent immersion in water. They have many household applications.

	Plastics (see p. 691)
Kitchenware	
Aprons	9,5
Beakers	2,5,1
Bowls and basins	5,2,3
Bread bins	5
Brooms and brushes	5,2
Buckets and dustpans	5,2
Cabinets	2,5
Canisters	5,2,3
Carpet shampooers	5,2
Chairs	5,12
Colanders	5
Condiment sets	5,2
Cups, saucers, plates	1,2,3,5
Door and drawer handles	2,4,5
Drainers	11,7
Egg cups	5,2,1
Jugs	3,2,5
Knife handles	6
Refrigerator fittings	2,3,5
Scales (pans)	5,2
Shelves	11,7
Shopping bags	9
Sink tidies	5,2
Stools	5
Table and bench tops	11
Table cloths	9,5
Taps	8
Tumblers	3
Vacuum flasks	5
Vegetable and crockery racks	5,9
Waste bins	5
Work surfaces	11
Bathroom fittings	
Baby baths	5,6
Bath panels	11,6,14
Bath racks	2
Baths	6
Cabinets	2,5

	Plastics (see p. 691)
Curtains	9
Laundry baskets	5
Lavatory seats	1
Mirror frames	2,5,7,4
Taps	8
Toilet-roll holders	1,8
Towel rails	2,5
House construction	
Ceiling tiles	15
Corrugated roofing	7,12
Curtain tracks	7,8
Decorative panels	11,6,14
Door facings	11,7
Door finger-plates	3,6
Door handles	8
Floor tiles	9
Guttering and drainpipes	7,5
Letter boxes	1
Louvres	2,7
Skirting	7
Wall tiles	2,9
Garden and garage	
Air beds	9
Bicycle mudguards	10,7
Boat and car covers	9,5
Car anti-mist panels	7
Car upholstery	9
Cloches, flexible	5,9
Cloches, rigid	7,3,6
Dashboard panels	2,4
Dashboard switches	1,5,2,4
Fencing and trellis	7,9
Flower pots and bowls	2,5
Flower tubs	12,5
Garden baskets	9
Garden chairs	5,12
Garden ornaments	12,5
Greenhouses	7,3,6
Hoses	9,5

	Plastics (see p. 691)
Motorcycle screens	6
Paddling pools	
flexible	9
rigid	12
semi-rigid	5
Tools, garage	10,8
Tools, garden	5
Watering cans	5
Sports, toys and games	
Binoculars	2,5,4,8
Cameras	2,5,4,8
Chess sets	6,2
Dolls, flexible	9
Dolls, rigid	5,2
Dolls' furniture	2
Fishing reels	8
Fishing rods	12
Footballs	9
Golf-club heads	4,10
Model cars and tracks	5,2
Model kits	2,3,5
Paintboxes	2,5
Pencil cases, flexible	9
Pencil cases, rigid	2,5
Photograph album covers	9
Toy spades	5,2
Train sets	2,5,12
Clothing	
Belts	9
Gumboots	9
Overalls	9
Overshoes	9
Rainwear	9,5
Sandals	9
Miscellaneous	
Ashtrays	1
Book covers	9,10
Brief-cases, flexible	9

	Plastics (see p. 691)
Brief-cases, rigid	5
Chairs	5,6,12,14
Cigarette boxes	6,2,3
Clock and watch faces	10,6,3
Clock cases	5,2
Clothes hangers	3,2,6,9
Coal scuttles	5,7
Cushions and pillows, foam	13
False teeth	6
Fountain pens	2,3,5,10
Furniture edges	7
Furniture handles	2
Hair dryers	1,5
Handbags and purses	9
Hold-alls	9
Insulation wood panels	14
Lampshades	2,6,10
Maps	10,9
Money boxes	5,2
Ornaments	6
Picture frames	2,5,7,4
Satchels	9
Slide rules	6,10,7
Spectacle cases	9,5
Spectacles and sun glasses (frames)	10,4
Suitcases, flexible	9
Suitcases, rigid	4,5
Transistor radios	2,5
Umbrella handles	1,5,2,6
Upholstery covers	9
Vacuum cleaners	4
Vases	5
Wallets	9

Electrical
Never repair broken electrical fittings such as plugs, adaptors, junction boxes, switches or plates. Always replace them with new ones.

Plastic	Identification	Adhesive	Brand names
1 Thermo-setting plastics	Hard, brittle and heat-resistant—for example, bakelite. Only powdery chips can be cut from thermo-setting plastics	**Epoxy** Contact adhesives may be a suitable alternative, but not when area of contact is small	Araldite, Borden Superfast Power Pack, Bostik 7,
2 Polystyrene, high impact	Rigid and brittle. Makes a metallic noise when dropped on a hard surface. Complete sliver can be cut from edge. Burn sliver and blow out flame—sweet, aromatic smell	**Clear**	Bostik 1, Evostik Clear and Clean
3 Polystyrene, clear	Transparent, glass-like and very brittle. Makes tinny noise when dropped on a hard surface	**Clear** The solvents in many adhesives other than that given will dissolve polystyrene	Bostik 1 GA186
4 ABS	Tough, rigid. Sliver can be cut. Melts if touched with hot metal. Sinks in soapy water and makes metallic noise when dropped. When burnt gives off odour of burning rubber	**Contact**	Borden Superstik, Bostik 3, Clam 3, Dunlop Thixofix, Evostik Impact or Clear and Clean, Tretobond 404, Unistik
5 Polythene and polypropylene	Tough and brightly coloured. Both make a dull noise when dropped and both float in soapy water. Polypropylene is glossier and more rigid than polythene but it has similar uses	**Cannot be stuck.** Can only be heat welded	
6 Acrylics	Usually transparent—for example Perspex. Make dull sound when dropped on hard surface. Burn with yellow flame: smell of methylated spirit when flame is extinguished	**Acrylic-based only** Clear adhesives stick acrylics but may crack or craze them	Perspex Cement
7 PVC, rigid	Hard, glossy and weather-resistant. Usually light coloured. Difficult to burn; greenish flame gives off acrid vapour when extinguished	**Contact**	Borden Superstik Bostik 3, Clam 3, Dunlop Thixofix, Evostik Impact, Tretobond 404, Unistik
8 Nylon and acetal	Tough, rigid moulding materials. Difficult to burn. Acetals have blue flame and pungent smell; nylons have yellow flame and smell of burning hair	**Epoxy** Clear adhesives can be used, but give poorer bond	Araldite, Borden Superfast Power Pack, Bostik 7
9 PVC, flexible	Burns with small, bright yellow flame, immediately self-extinguishing: acrid smell	**Clear** ✱	Borden Superstik, Bostik 1, Clam 58, Evostik Clear and Clean
10 Cellulose	Highly inflammable—for example celluloid	**Clear or Contact** Soften surfaces to be bonded with nail-varnish remover	Consult dealer. Some types not suitable for cellulose
11 Decorative laminates	Hard, heat-resistant and scratch-resistant—for example Formica, Arborite, Warerite	**Contact**	Borden Superstik, Bostik 3, Clam 3, Dunlop Thixofix, Evostik Impact, Tretobond 404, Unistik
12 Glass-reinforced plastics (GRP)	One side smooth, the other rough. Fibre strands show clearly	**Contact** ●	Borden Superstik, Bostik 3, Clam 3, Dunlop Thixofix, Evostik Impact, Tretobond 404, Unistik
13 Polyurethane foam, flexible	Brown, sponge-like honeycomb	**Contact** ●	Borden Superstik, Bostik 3, Clam 3, Dunlop Thixofix, Evostik Impact, Tretobond 404, Unistik
14 Polyurethane foam, rigid	Lightweight, firm and usually brown	**Contact** ●	Borden Superstik, Bostik 3, Clam 3, Dunlop Thixofix, Evostik Impact, Tretobond 404, Unistik
15 Polystyrene, expanded	White, rigid foam. Easily crushed	**Water-based or specialised solvent-based adhesives** Multi-purpose adhesives dissolve polystyrene	Clam 24, Dunlop Ceiling Tile, Evostik Polystyrene Ceiling Tile, Unibond E.P.A.

● Rub surfaces lightly with medium-grade glass-paper before bonding

✱ Clear tape can be used in some cases—for example, maps. Use coloured cloth-backed tape on PVC upholstery

SOLDERING

One of the most effective ways to join pieces of metal is soldering—running a molten alloy over the joint. When the alloy sets, it forms a hard, rigid bond between the two pieces of metal.

For joints which are unlikely to be subject to severe strain or heat, the soldering can be done at a low temperature of 120–240°C (250–480°F). This is called soft soldering. A second method, called hard soldering, produces joints as strong as some solid metals and has a resistance to stress and strain. But this soldering must be done with a blowlamp at 590–900°C (1100–1650°F).

Tinned iron, brass, copper, zinc, Britannia metal, lead, pewter and gilding metal can be joined by either method. But even these may require hard soldering if the pieces are very thick. Nickel and wrought ironwork must always be hard soldered, brazed or welded. Welding is best left to a specialist with the necessary equipment.

Both methods require a special soldering alloy and a chemical compound, called flux, which keeps the joint clean and helps the solder to flow. The type of solder and flux required is determined by the metals being joined and the method used. Aluminium, cast iron and most types of steel cannot be soldered. Use nuts and bolts or rivets to join pieces together.

Soft soldering

Soft solder, an alloy of tin and lead, is available in sticks or wire. Several types of all-purpose fluxes can be obtained, and it is advisable to ask a do-it-yourself dealer for advice on the most suitable for the soldering work which is to be done.

Some wire solders have a core of flux which flows with the solder as it melts. Because they eliminate the need for a separate fluxing stage during a repair, cored solders are particularly useful for intricate radio and electrical work.

The heat for most soft soldering can be supplied by a soldering iron, which has a copper tip called a bit. Some have to be heated over a flame, but it is usually more convenient to use an electric or blowlamp iron.

A wide range of soldering irons is available. Always make sure that the bit is large enough for the work being done. For example, sheets of metal and large pieces of copper absorb heat quickly and need larger bits. If a bit is too small, it loses heat too quickly.

Hard soldering and brazing

Hard soldering is done with silver solders, which are expensive alloys of silver, copper and zinc. A similar high-temperature process—brazing—uses an alloy of copper and zinc, which is known as spelter.

Both types are available in wires or strips, and spelter may also be bought in granulated form. The flux required for both brazing and hard soldering is borax: it is used in either powder or paste form.

In both processes the parts to be joined must be pre-heated to an extremely high temperature. Do not try to use a soldering iron: a blowlamp is essential for the work.

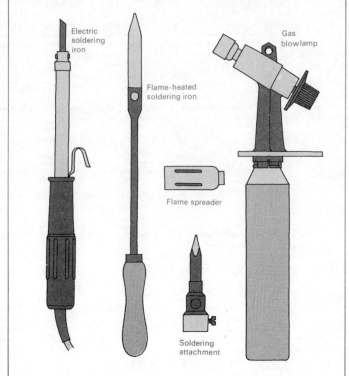

Electric soldering iron

Flame-heated soldering iron

Gas blowlamp

Flame spreader

Soldering attachment

SOFT SOLDERING

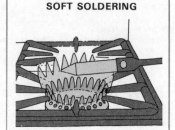

1 Clean the bit and the metal to be joined. Heat the bit in a flame and apply flux to it and to the pieces of metal

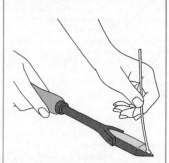

2 Melt solder on the bit. Hold the metal parts together and draw the soldered bit along the join. Leave to set

Intricate work A self-heating iron and cored solder are convenient for intricate work. Do not use flux separately

HARD SOLDERING

1 Clean the parts to be joined with emery cloth or a coarse file. Coat them with borax flux, in paste or powder form

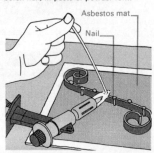

Asbestos mat

Nail

2 Clamp the two edges and heat them with a blowlamp until the metal glows. Press solder strip along the joint

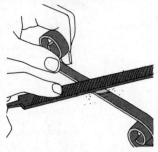

3 Leave the joint to cool and set. Wash off flux with hot water and clean the joint with a fine, flat file

CONCRETE

Concrete has three ingredients: cement, water, and a mixture of stones and sand called aggregate. The aggregate provides bulk and strength; cement bonds the aggregate together; and water makes the mixture plastic and workable at first, then causes a chemical reaction to harden the cement.

Ask for all-in aggregate, in which sand and stones are ready-mixed. Portland cement, available in several colours, is suitable for most jobs. Rapid-hardening cement is advisable, however, when there is a risk of frost, because concrete laid in cold weather can disintegrate if there is night frost before the hardening is complete. Ready-mixed aggregate and cement, available in bags from builders' merchants, is convenient for small jobs.

Choosing the mixture

Aggregate and cement are mixed in different proportions—by volume—for different purposes. Three basic mixes are enough to deal with most repair jobs.

For foundations, driveways where cars are to be used, floor slabs, gate and fence posts and other heavy-duty repairs, use 1 part cement to $4\frac{1}{2}$ parts all-in aggregate ($\frac{3}{4}$ in. (20 mm)

max. size). For paths use 1 part cement to $3\frac{1}{2}$ parts all-in aggregate ($\frac{3}{8}$ in. (10 mm) max. size).

To fill small cracks and holes, use 1 part cement to 3 parts coarse sand.

Mixing and drying

Always mix concrete with tap or spring water: river and sea water may contain impurities which could affect the setting. Use just enough water to keep the mix workable: excess water escapes by evaporation and leaves tiny pores that weaken the concrete.

Drying takes about four days in warm weather, and up to ten days in winter. Cover new concrete with damp sacks or polythene sheets to control its drying. If it is left exposed, especially in hot weather, the surface dries more quickly than the interior, and the concrete is likely to crack.

Repairing concrete

To repair cracks and holes in concrete, clean all loose material and dust from the damaged section with a stiff-bristled brush. Coat it with a polyvinyl-acetate (PVA) adhesive and leave it overnight. Next day mix 1 part cement and 3 parts coarse sand and add PVA adhesive. Follow the manufacturer's instructions carefully when using PVA.

HOW TO MIX CONCRETE

1 Heap aggregate and add cement on top. Shovel from bottom of heap until colour is even. Make a crater and add a little water. Shovel dry mixture from edge into crater. Do not allow crater to collapse

2 Turn until heap is evenly moist. Make new crater, add more water and mix again. Flatten heap and jab several times with shovel. If ridges disappear, the mix is too wet. A correct mix should hold firm ridges

MORTAR

Mortar has three ingredients: clean graded sand, a binding agent—usually Portland cement or hydrated lime—and water.

Choose a fine grade of sand, which is easier to work than coarse sand and dries out to a smooth finish.

A mixture of fine sand and cement sets quickly and forms strong mortar, but settling and shrinkage in drying can cause it to crack. Lime–sand mortar sets slowly and is weak, but it does not crack in settling and shrinkage cracks are small. Cement and hydrated lime are often used together, therefore, to make a mortar which combines the strength of cement and the shrink-resistant properties of lime. Such mortars are easy to work.

Another binding agent less commonly used is masonry cement. When mixed with sand it is slow drying and is especially suitable for bricklaying or blocklaying.

Special aerating compounds, or plasticisers, can be added to ordinary cement–sand mortar to form air pockets into which the water expands when it freezes. This prevents the mortar cracking if it is laid down in winter. Plasticisers also result in smoother mortar, which is easier to mix and point.

Preparation

Mix the dry ingredients thoroughly, then make a crater. Add a very little water at a time and turn the mixture over continuously. Do not use too much water. Good mortar should hold the impression of a trowel: if it crumbles, it is too dry; if it levels out, it is too wet.

If a plasticiser is added, follow the manufacturer's instructions.

Mortar should be neither stronger nor weaker than the materials with which it is used. Consequently a wide range of mixes is needed for different purposes.

A number of different mixes may be suitable for any given job (see table).

USING THE CORRECT MORTAR MIXTURE *(see also lower table)*

Foundations	A3, A4, D2
Sandstone: dense	A1
Sandstone: porous and limestone	A5
Rubblestone Frost risk, if laid in cold weather No frost risk	A1 A2
Granite	A4
External bricklaying and pointing Frost risk, if laid in cold weather No frost risk	A1, B1 A2, B2
Internal bricklaying and pointing	A2, B2
Engineering bricks	D1
External blocklaying	A1, B1, C1
Internal blocklaying	A2, B2
Earth-retaining walls, garden walls	A3
Rendering on dense strong materials Top coat, exposed position Top coat, sheltered position or moderate exposure to frost and rain Undercoat, exposed position Undercoat, sheltered position or moderate exposure to frost and rain	A1, C1 A1, A2, B1, B2 A3, C2 A1, C1
Rendering on strong porous materials Top coat, exposed position Top coat, sheltered position or moderate exposure to frost and rain	A1, C1 A1, A2, B1, C3
Rendering on weak porous materials Top coat, exposed position Top coat, sheltered position or moderate exposure to frost and rain	A1, C1 A1, A2, B1, C3
Grouting between tiles	D2

MORTAR MIXTURES

		1	2	3	4	5
A	Portland cement: lime: sand	1:1:6	1:2:9	2:1:9	1:2:4	1:3:11
B	Portland cement and plasticiser: sand	1:6	1:8			
C	Portland masonry cement: sand	1:5	1:4	1:6		
D	Portland cement: sand	1:3	1:4			

GENERAL-PURPOSE ADHESIVES

When two materials are to be stuck together, the more similar they are the stronger will be the bond between them. For example, when a piece of metal is stuck to metal of the same type, the chemical reaction caused by the adhesive is exactly the same on both surfaces. With the correct adhesive, the bond is so strong that pressure of 1000 lb. per square inch would be required to pull them apart.

But when two materials are very dissimilar—for example, rubber and metal—the chemical reactions in each are very different and the strength of the bond is almost nil.

Types of adhesive
Although some materials cannot be stuck together, most manufacturers produce a range of compound adhesives which are designed to cause the most effective chemical reactions in different types of material. Three types are enough for most household repairs.

Epoxy resins The strongest and most versatile of all general-purpose adhesives is epoxy resin, a two-part compound which has to be mixed immediately before use.

Most take about six hours to set in normal room conditions, but if the materials being bonded are themselves resistant to heat, setting can be accelerated by placing the articles in a warm oven or near a radiator.

Contact adhesives A cheaper and more convenient type of adhesive for amateur use is the contact type, which requires no mixing. Spread the adhesive on both surfaces to be joined and leave them until the solvent evaporates enough to leave the adhesive tacky. In most cases, the two surfaces cannot be moved after they have been joined (see p. 690).

Clear household adhesives For small repairs to certain materials (see p. 695) or for emergency work when no other adhesive is available, use a clear household adhesive. If neither surface is absorbent, spread the adhesive on both. If one is absorbent,

spread adhesive only on the other.
Other types Traditional animal, blood and casein glues, including Scotch glue, are being superseded, particularly for bonding wood. PVA adhesives are common nowadays for carpentry work; but make sure that all traces of the old glue are removed when resticking a joint. PVA adhesives are also used to bond concrete (see p. 693).

For certain work, special adhesives are available, such as rubber latex solutions for carpet and fabric repairs.

How to choose an adhesive
If one of the surfaces to be joined is movable and the other fixed, first find the movable material in the left-hand column on p. 695. Find the second material at the top of the page. The intersection of the columns across and down will show the correct adhesives as numbered on this page. If both surfaces are movable it does not matter which line is read first.

Some materials have different top and bottom surfaces—for example wall and floor tiles and certain plastics. If a material has a sticking surface of a different finish or texture from its top area—for example plastic or rubber tiles—look in the left-hand column.

When more than one adhesive is recommended on p. 695, consult the chart on this page. Choose the adhesive whose properties are most suited to the work.

The figures in heavy type on p. 695 indicate the adhesive most suitable for any work subject to extreme conditions.

Preparation
Always make sure that the surfaces to be bonded are clean and dry.

Read the manufacturer's instructions before mixing or applying an adhesive. Make sure that any for use outdoors is weather resistant. Solvent-based adhesives may be inflammable: do not smoke or work near a flame.

Some adhesives may be harmful to the skin. Rub barrier cream on the hands before attempting a large repair.

Type	Resistance to stress	Resistance to moisture	Resistance to mould	Resistance to heat	Gap filling	Life in container or after mixing	Examples
1 Epoxy Extremely versatile resin adhesives. Very strong and durable	Very good	Very good	Very good	Very good	Yes	$\frac{1}{2}$ hour to 8 hours	Araldite, Borden Superfast Power Pack, Bostik 7
2 Contact Made from rubber and a solvent which evaporates to leave tacky bonding surface	Good	Good	Good	Good	No	Months unless left open	Bostik 3, Clam 3, Durofast, Dunlop Thixofix, Evostik Impact, Gloy Contact, Tretobond 404, Unistik
3 Clear household All-purpose rubber solution	Fair	Good	Very good	Good	No	Months unless left open	Bostik 1, Durofix, Evostik Clear and Clean, Gloy Clear, Uhu
4 Natural latex Tough and flexible. Designed for textile repairs	Good	Poor	Fair	Good	No	Months unless left open	Clam 5, Copydex, Jiffybind, Jiffytex, Surestick
5 PVA (polyvinyl acetate) Bonding and general purpose adhesive	Good	Poor	Very good	Poor	No	Months unless left open	Borden Wood Glue, Bostik Woodworking, Clam 7, Dunlop Woodworker, Timbabond 606, Unibond
6 Urea (urea formaldehyde) Gives strong wood bond for exterior use. Lasts 5–10 years	Very good	Good	Very good	Good	Yes	$\frac{1}{2}$ hour to 24 hours	Aerolite, Cascamite
7 Animal glues Low cost but have been superseded by chemical adhesives	Very good	Poor	Fair	Poor	No	Weeks but may putrefy	Certofix
8 Casein Good adhesion to wood, but stains many hardwoods	Very good	Fair	Fair	Good	No	2 to 24 hours	Cascomite
9 Starch, dextrine, water-soluble cellulose Paper-hanging adhesives	Poor	Very poor	Poor	Poor	No	Weeks, but may putrefy	Clam, Dextrine, Polycell
10 Specialised ceiling adhesive	Good	Fair	Good	Good	Yes	Months unless left open	Clam 24, Dunlop Ceiling Tile, Evostik Polystyrene Ceiling Tile, Tretobond 282, Unibond E.P.A.
11 Specialised floor adhesive	Good	Fair	Good	Good	No	Months unless left open	Dunlop Flooring, Evostik Flooring
12 Specialised wall adhesive	Good	Good	Good	Good	Yes	Months unless left open	Clam 2 or Clam 143

	Acoustic tiles	Bricks and concrete	Carpets	Ceramic tiles	Cork (except tiles)	Cork tiles and sheeting	Fabrics and cloth	Glass, china, pottery	Hardboard	Leather	Leathercloth	Metal	Paper and cardboard	Plaster	Plasterboard	Plastics, soft flexible	Plastics, hard rigid	Plastics, laminated (Formica, etc.)	Plastics, floor tiles and sheeting	Plastic tiles	Polystyrene foam	Rubber	Rubber floor tiles and sheeting	Stone	Wood
Acoustic tiles	2	2	–	2	4,2	2	4	–	2	2	–	2	5,2	2	2	3	–	–	3	–	10	2	2	2	2
Bricks and concrete	–	–	–	2	–	–	–	–	–	–	–	1	–	–	–	–	–	–	–	–	–	–	–	1	–
Carpets	–	4,2	4	2	4	4	4	–	5,2	4	4,2	2	4	5,2	5,2	3	3,2	2	–	–	5	2	–	4,2	5,2
Ceramic tiles	12	12	–	2,1	2	2	12	2,1	12	2	2	2,1	12	12	12	3	2,1	2,1	3	–	12	2	2	12	12
Cork (except tiles)	4,2	3,2	4	2	3,2	3,2	4,2	3	5,2	2	3,2	2	5	5,2	5,2	3	3	2	11,3	–	10	2	2	3,2	5,2
Cork tiles and sheeting	2	11	–	2	3,2	2	4	3	11	3	–	2	3	11	11	3	2	2	11	–	–	2	2	11	11
Fabrics and cloth	4	4,2	4	12	4,2	4	4	3,7,8	5,7,8,2	4,7,8,2	4,2	3,2	4	5	5	3	2,1	2	3	–	4	2	2	4,2	5,7,8,2
Glass, china, pottery	–	3,1	–	2,1	3	3	3,7,8	3,1	–	3,7,8,1	3	3,1	3	3,1	3,1	3	3,1	2,1	3	–	–	2	3	3,1	–
Hardboard	2	5,2	–	2,1	5,2	2	5,2	–	5,1	2	5,2	2,1	5,2	2	2	3	2	2,1	3	–	5	2	2	2,1	5
Leather	2	3	4	2	2	3	4,7,8,2	3,7,8,1	2	2,7,8	3	2	3	2	2	3	3,2	2	3	–	4	2	2	2	2,7,8
Leathercloth	–	3	4,2	2	3,2	–	4,2	–	5,2	3	3	3	3	3,2	3,2	3	3,2	2	–	–	–	3	3	3	5,2
Metal	2	2,1	–	2,1	2	2	3,2	3,1	2,1	2	3	2,1	3,2	2,1	2,1	3	2,1	2,1	3	–	–	2	2	2,1	2,1
Paper and cardboard	5,9,2	5,9,2	4	3,2	5,9	3	4	3	5,9,2	3	3	3,2	5,9	5,9	5,9	3	3	2	3	–	5,9	2	2	3	5,9,2
Plaster	–	–	–	–	5,2	2	5,2	3,1	2	2	3,2	2,1	5	5	5	3	2	2,1	3	–	–	2	2	–	5,1
Plasterboard	–	2	–	–	5,2	2	5,2	3,1	2	2	3,2	2,1	5	5	5	3	2	2,1	3	–	–	2	2	2	5
Plastics, soft flexible	3	3	3	3	3	3	3	3	3	3	3	3	3	3	3	3	3	3	3	–	–	3	3	3	3
Plastics, hard rigid	–	2,1	3,2	2,1	3	2	3,2	3,1	2,1	3,2	3,2	2,1	3	2,1	2,1	3	3,1	2,1	3	–	–	2	2	2,1	2,1
Plastics, laminated (Formica, etc.)	2	2,1	–	2,1	2	2	2	2,1	2	2	2,1	2	2	2,1	2,1	3	2,1	2,1	3	–	5	2	2	2,1	2,1
Plastics, floor tiles and sheeting	3	11	–	3	11	11	3	3	11	3	–	3	3	11	11	3	3	3	3	–	–	3	3	11	11
Plastic tiles	–	12	–	–	–	–	–	12	–	–	–	3	–	12	12	–	–	–	–	12	12	–	–	12	12
Polystyrene foam	10	10	–	10	–	4	–	10	4	–	–	5	10	10	–	–	–	–	10	10	–	–	–	10	10
Rubber	2	2	–	2	2	2	2	2	2	2	2	2	2	2	2	3	2	2	3	–	–	2	2	2	2
Rubber floor tiles and sheeting	2	11	–	2	2	2	2	3	11	2	–	2	2	11	11	3	2	2	3	–	–	2	2	11	11
Stone	–	1	–	2	–	2	–	–	–	–	–	1	–	–	–	–	2,1	–	–	–	–	–	–	1	–
Wood	2	2,1,6	–	2,1,6	5,2	2	5,7,8,2	–	5,6	2,7,8	5,2	2,1,6	5,2	5,6	5,6	3	2,1	2,1,6	3	–	5	2	2	2,1,6	5,6

HOUSEHOLD PESTS

Use chemicals against insects and household pests sparingly: the pests may eventually become resistant. Store containers safely out of the reach of children—many of the chemicals used for this purpose are poisonous—and follow the manufacturer's instructions when using them.

If a pest cannot be identified from the table on this page, send a specimen in a sealed tin to Rentokil, Felcourt, East Grinstead, W. Sussex RH19 2JY.

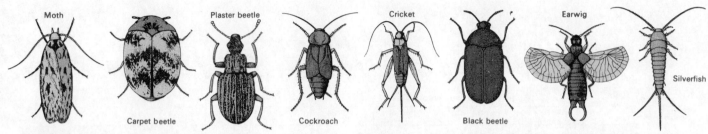

Moth · Carpet beetle · Plaster beetle · Cockroach · Cricket · Black beetle · Earwig · Silverfish

Pests	Likely damage	Where pest is found	What to do
Ants	Contaminate sweet foods. Nuisance indoors	Most common in spring and summer **Pharaoh ants** In warm places—for example, cracks or panelling near radiators or boilers **Black ants** Enter house from garden or foundations	Use proprietary ant bait in jelly form which workers take back to nest **Chemicals** Aerosols, puffer pack of insect powder, special lacquer to paint thresholds, shelves and pipe holes
Carpet beetles	Eat wool, fur and feathers	Behind skirtings, under fitted carpets and in birds' nests under eaves or in roof	Clean airing cupboard, skirtings and floor cracks and fill if necessary Dislodge birds' nests Vacuum underside of carpet and both sides of underfelt **Chemicals** Insect-killers for carpet edges; mothproofing aerosols
Clothes moths and house moths	Larvae eat wool and hair, including carpets and upholstery	Most common in summer. Eggs, which turn into larvae, found in woollens in warm dark places during winter	Shake out woollens regularly or store in sealed plastic bags Move furniture and vacuum carpets often **Chemicals** Aerosols, to mothproof for three months
Cockroaches and black beetles	Spread disease by excreting on food	Dark, warm, damp crevices, especially in kitchens; come out at night to eat	Cover all food. Wrap refuse and put in tight-lidded dustbin To find source, search at night with a torch **Chemicals** Powder or aerosol for crawling insects If unable to find the source, apply same insecticide every week along base of walls and cupboards. Call local council public health inspector when infestation cannot be cleared
Crickets	Soil food, may damage fabrics. Make irritating chirruping noise	In rubbish or in cracks of old houses in winter	Cover food **Chemicals** Aerosol or powder insecticide
Earwigs	Harmless	On floors and window ledges, seeking shelter	Cover food **Chemicals** Insecticidal spray or powder for windows and doors

Pests	Likely damage	Where pest is found	What to do
Flies and bluebottles	Spread disease from body hairs and feet on to food	Ceilings, windows and light fittings. Maggots hatch from eggs on meat, fish, garbage, etc.	Cover all food. Wrap scraps before putting in tight-lidded dustbin When suspected source of infestation is a poultry farm, sewage works or slaughterhouse, contact local council public health inspector **Chemicals** Aerosols, hanging strips and dustbin powders
Mice and rats	Spread disease and gnaw woodwork, pipes and wiring. Eat food	Enter house from under floor along plumbing or through heating and ventilation ducts. Often breed in outhouses	Fill rodent holes with cement and coarse wire wool **Chemicals** Use special bait, such as Alphakil for mice and Rodine for rats; call local public health inspector if rat menace persistent
Plaster beetles	Harmless	In houses decorated before plaster has dried or in damp sheds and cellars	Heat and air room **Chemicals** Insecticidal sprays
Silverfish	Eat paper, crumbs and wallpaper pastes	Active at night in damp, warm places in kitchen or bathroom—usually floor cracks	Air and dry room. Fill cracks in skirtings and floors (see p. 82). Do not use flour paste for paper-hanging **Chemicals** Powder and aerosol for crawling insects
Spiders	Harmless	In dark corners or baths	Spiders may enter a bath through the waste pipe if the trap dries out. Run the taps occasionally if the bath is not in use **Chemicals** Powder or aerosol for crawling insects
Wasps	Eat jam and fruit and spread disease. Can sting repeatedly, but are also beneficial because they eat insects	Nest in banks, walls, hedgerows, attics and sheds	If nest outdoors, use a proprietary wasp nest killer. If nest indoors, call local public health inspector or pest control firm Half-fill a jar with jam and beer to trap and drown wasps **Chemicals** Fly-killing aerosol or wasp nest killer

REMOVING STAINS FROM FABRICS AND CARPETS

Most stains yield to detergent in hot water: the adjacent chart deals with those that may not.

Take action immediately fabric or a carpet is stained: a stain may be permanent if allowed to dry.

Some colours or fabrics—for example, acetate rayon—are harmed by certain solvents and spirits, so first test an inconspicuous corner. Leave it to soak for 15 minutes.

Stain-removing solutions can rot or eat away the backings of carpets. Use only the minimum required.

Work inwards from the edge of a stain. Blot the material: then apply treatment. On non-washable fabrics, use a minimum of water-based remedies. Always rinse the fabric thoroughly or rub with a damp cloth to remove all solvent.

If the treatment recommended does not succeed, leave the material wet, with paper tissues above and below it to absorb the stain, or repeat the process several times.

When more than one treatment is suggested, use the more convenient.

If a colour stain persists, bleach or Dygon may remove it. But never use bleach on wool or silk: use perborate, obtainable from chemists.

Take stained suede to a specialist cleaner.

Thinners for paint, and for removing stains, are generally specified on the tin. For instance, use white spirit for oil-based paint, water for emulsion paint.

Most chemicals are poisonous: always keep them away from children's reach. Note also that some chemicals are inflammable, some give off a harmful vapour and some cause burns.

CHART KEY
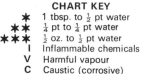

✱	1 tbsp. to ½ pt water
✱✱	¼ pt to ¼ pt water
✱✱✱	½ oz. to ½ pt water
I	Inflammable chemicals
V	Harmful vapour
C	Caustic (corrosive)

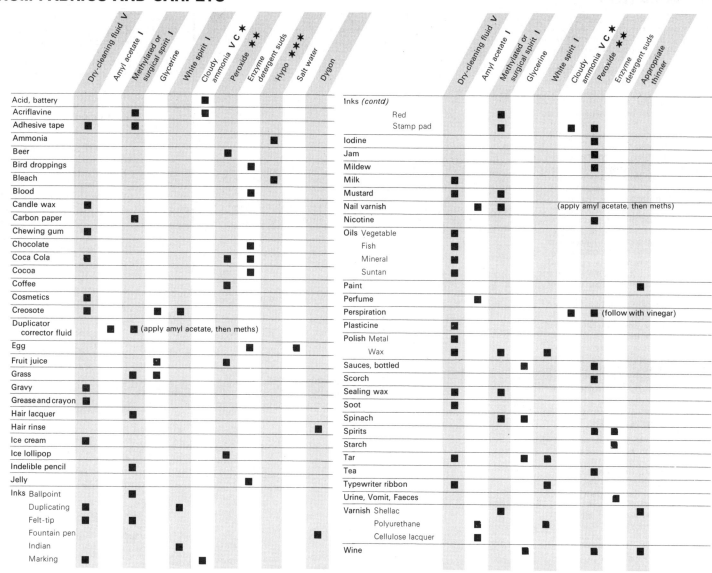

Stain	Dry-cleaning fluid V	Amyl acetate I	Methylated or surgical spirit I	Glycerine	White spirit I	Cloudy ammonia V C	Peroxide ✱✱✱	Enzyme detergent suds	Hypo ✱✱✱	Salt water	Dygon
Acid, battery						■					
Acriflavine		■				■					
Adhesive tape	■	■									
Ammonia									■		
Beer					■						
Bird droppings								■			
Bleach									■		
Blood								■			
Candle wax	■										
Carbon paper			■								
Chewing gum	■										
Chocolate							■				
Coca Cola	■					■	■				
Cocoa							■				
Coffee						■					
Cosmetics	■										
Creosote	■			■	■						
Duplicator corrector fluid		■	■									(apply amyl acetate, then meths)
Egg							■			■	
Fruit juice				■		■					
Grass			■	■							
Gravy	■										
Grease and crayon	■										
Hair lacquer			■								
Hair rinse											■
Ice cream	■										
Ice lollipop						■					
Indelible pencil			■								
Jelly					■						
Inks Ballpoint			■								
Duplicating	■			■							
Felt-tip	■		■								
Fountain pen										■	
Indian											
Marking	■				■						

Stain	Dry-cleaning fluid V	Amyl acetate I	Methylated or surgical spirit I	Glycerine	White spirit I	Cloudy ammonia V C	Peroxide ✱✱	Enzyme detergent suds	Appropriate thinner
Inks (contd)									
Red				■					
Stamp pad				■		■	■		
Iodine							■		
Jam							■		
Mildew							■		
Milk	■								
Mustard	■			■					
Nail varnish		■		■						(apply amyl acetate, then meths)
Nicotine							■		
Oils Vegetable	■								
Fish	■								
Mineral	■								
Suntan	■								
Paint									■
Perfume				■					
Perspiration						■	■			(follow with vinegar)
Plasticine	■								
Polish Metal	■								
Wax	■				■				
Sauces, bottled						■		■	
Scorch							■		
Sealing wax	■	■							
Soot	■								
Spinach					■	■			
Spirits						■	■		
Starch								■	
Tar	■				■	■			
Tea								■	
Typewriter ribbon	■					■			
Urine, Vomit, Faeces								■	
Varnish Shellac			■						■
Polyurethane		■			■				
Cellulose lacquer		■							
Wine						■	■	■	

METRICATION

Many countries are changing from the imperial system of weights and measures to one agreed throughout Europe—the metric System International (SI).

Unlike the decimalisation of British currency in 1971, however, the changeover is gradual and no fixed timetable has yet been set.

Industry has been asked by the government to plan its own timing, with the intention of completing the transition by about 1981.

The building trades have meanwhile been among the first to metricate their measurements. Wood is cut and prepared to metre and millimetre widths, lengths and thicknesses. Paints are sold in litres, half-litres and quarter-litres but, for the present, the tins must also show the quantity in imperial. Cement is now sold in 50-kilogramme bags instead of by the hundredweight; and builders' merchants supply sand and ready-mix for concrete in cubic metres instead of in cubic yards or bushels.

Pipes and fittings for plumbing are now available in metric sizes, but in some cases conversion pieces are necessary with their use.

Although these changes have been made, most suppliers are still prepared to accept orders in imperial measures. But when the goods are supplied, they may be shown on the invoice as part of a metric measurement.

CONVERSIONS

Both the metric and imperial equivalents on this page are correct to three places of decimals.

Elsewhere in the book, however, metric equivalents are calculated to the nearest 5 mm, except where the measurement is critical.

The abbreviations for the most common metric measurements are: mm, millimetre; cm, centimetre; m, metre; cl, centilitre; l, litre; g, gram; kg, kilogramme.

CONVERSION TABLES

Length

1 mm	0·039 in.	$\frac{1}{64}$ in.	0·397 mm
2 mm	0·079 in.	$\frac{1}{32}$ in.	0·794 mm
3 mm	0·118 in.	$\frac{1}{16}$ in.	1·587 mm
4 mm	0·158 in.	$\frac{1}{8}$ in.	3·175 mm
5 mm	0·197 in.	$\frac{1}{4}$ in.	6·350 mm
6 mm	0·236 in.	$\frac{1}{2}$ in.	12·700 mm
7 mm	0·276 in.	$\frac{3}{4}$ in.	19·050 mm
8 mm	0·315 in.	1 in.	25·400 mm
9 mm	0·354 in.	12 in. (1 ft)	304·800 mm
10 mm (1 cm)	0·394 in.	36 in. (1 yd)	914·400 mm
1000 mm (1 m)	39·370 in.		

Area

1 sq. cm	0·155 sq. in.	1 sq. in.	6·452 sq. cm
1 sq. m	1·196 sq. yds	1 sq. ft	929·030 sq. cm
		1 sq. yd	0·836 sq. m

Volume

1 cu. cm	0·061 cu. in.	1 cu. in.	16·387 cu. cm
1 cu. m	1·308 cu. yds	1 cu. ft	0·028 cu. m
		1 cu. yd	0·765 cu. m

Capacity

1 cl	0·352 fl. oz	1 fl. oz.	2·841 cl
1 l	1·760 pints	1 pint	0·568 l
		1 gallon	4·546 l

Weight

1 g	0·035 oz.	1 oz.	28·350 g
1 kg	2·205 lb.	1 lb.	0·454 kg
1 metric ton	0·984 tons	1 cwt.	50·802 kg
		1 ton	1·016 metric tons

TIMBER IN METRIC SIZES

All softwood is sold in standard metric lengths, beginning at 1·8 m and increasing by stages of 300 mm. As it loses about 1·5 mm from each face when planed, a prepared 150×25 mm piece is actually about 147×22 mm.

Hardwood

Basic metric thicknesses for sawn hardwood are 19, 25, 32, 38, 50, 63 and 75 mm, then rising in 25 mm stages.

Manufactured boards

Plywood, blockboard and other manufactured boards (see p. 689) are sold in the old imperial sizes, but the dimensions are expressed in millimetres instead of in metres. For example, a 96×48×$\frac{1}{4}$ in. manufactured board is described as 2440×1220×6·5 mm.

SAWN SOFTWOOD: AVAILABLE SIZES

Thickness	Width in millimetres								
	75	100	125	150	175	200	225	250	300
16 mm	●	●	●	●					
19 mm	●	●	●	●					
22 mm	●	●	●	●					
25 mm	●	●	●	●	●	●	●	●	●
32 mm	●	●	●	●	●	●	●	●	●
38 mm	●	●	●	●	●	●	●		●
44 mm	●	●	●	●	●	●	●	●	●
50 mm	●	●	●	●	●	●	●	●	●
63 mm	●	●	●	●	●	●	●		
75 mm	●	●	●	●	●	●	●	●	●
100 mm		●		●		●		●	●
150 mm			●		●				●

Lengths	
1·8 m	(5 ft 10$\frac{7}{8}$ in.)
2·1 m	(6 ft 10$\frac{5}{8}$ in.)
2·4 m	(7 ft 10$\frac{1}{2}$ in.)
2·7 m	(8 ft 10$\frac{1}{4}$ in.)
3·0 m	(9 ft 10$\frac{1}{8}$ in.)
3·3 m	(10 ft 9$\frac{7}{8}$ in.)
3·6 m	(11 ft 9$\frac{3}{4}$ in.)
3·9 m	(12 ft 9$\frac{1}{2}$ in.)
4·2 m	(13 ft 9$\frac{3}{8}$ in.)
4·5 m	(14 ft 9$\frac{1}{8}$ in.)
4·8 m	(15 ft 9 in.)
5·1 m	(16 ft 8$\frac{3}{4}$ in.)
5·4 m	(17 ft 8$\frac{5}{8}$ in.)
5·7 m	(18 ft 8$\frac{3}{8}$ in.)
6·0 m	(19 ft 8$\frac{1}{8}$ in.)
6·3 m	(20 ft 8 in.)

PLUMBING

Pipes and fittings in metric sizes are now gradually replacing those in imperial sizes. The sizes of metric pipes refer to outside diameters, those of imperial pipes refer to the bores.

The nearest equivalent of a $\frac{1}{2}$ in. pipe, for instance, has become 15 mm, not 12 mm as might be expected. Capillary fittings (see p. 137) with imperial measurements cannot be used on metric pipes, and vice versa, but conversion pieces are made for linking different systems.

Compression fittings are interchangeable for the $\frac{3}{8}$ in., $\frac{1}{2}$ in., 1 in. and 2 in. imperial sizes with their metric counterparts—12 mm, 15 mm, 28 mm and 54 mm. Fittings and pipes with bores of $\frac{3}{4}$ in., 1$\frac{1}{4}$ in. and 1$\frac{1}{2}$ in. are not interchangeable with the replacement sizes of 22 mm, 35 mm and 42 mm.

Index

Fire

If you can tackle the fire yourself

Use water on most fires, including oil heaters.

Do not use water on fats and oils other than heaters. Smother fire with a lid, plate, damp cloth, earth or sand.

In all fires involving electricity, switch off the power at the mains or remove the plug from the supply to the faulty appliance. Water or a fire extinguisher can then be used on the appliance, except on a televison set. If a television set catches fire, smother the fire with a blanket.

Chimneys

Do not attempt to put out the fire yourself. Call the fire brigade immediately.

Remove rugs, carpets and furniture from around the fire-place.

Close doors and windows to reduce ventilation to the room in which the chimney is on fire.

If a serious fire breaks out

1 Get everyone out of the house, closing doors and windows to isolate the fire

2 Call the fire brigade as quickly as possible

3 If trapped, get into a room (facing the street if possible). Shut door and block off gap at bottom of the door. Shout for help, but do not jump from windows except as last resort

In an emergency, dial 999 or call the operator

Electricity

Blown fuses

1 Turn the power off at the main fuse box. Never try to trace an electrical fault with the power switched on

2 If trouble is caused by faulty equipment, disconnect it from the supply and fit new fuse of correct value. Have appliance checked and repaired

3 If fault cannot be located, switch off at mains and call an electrician to isolate and repair the fault. Restore supply

Electricity board (telephone number) ....

Wiring or appliances not working correctly

It is possible for wiring or appliances to have a short circuit which is, however, insufficient to blow a fuse. This can result in overheating, or shocks from wiring, appliances, water pipes or taps

1 If an appliance is causing trouble, unplug it and have it checked and repaired

2 In all other cases, turn off power at mains and call an electrician or the local electricity board

EMERGENCY

Gas

Safety precautions

Make sure you know where the main gas tap is situated and how to use it. In most cases it is near the gas meter. It is turned off when the score line, on top of the valve, is at right angles to the gas pipe. In most cases, the lever or handle will also be at right angles to the pipework in the 'off' position. If the mains supply has to be turned off, remember to relight gas pilot light when supply is restored.

If gas smell is strong

1 Turn off the main gas tap

2 Call the local board immediately, day or night

3 Do not attempt to trace the escape with a naked flame

4 Extinguish any naked flames in the area and switch off electric fires

5 Do not enter a room where the smell of gas is very strong: the build-up of gas may have reached an overpowering stage

6 Carry anyone overcome by gas fumes into the open air and send for ambulance. Give the kiss of life

If a gas smell is slight

Often, cause of escape will be obvious—for instance, a pilot light or cooker burner which has gone out

1 Turn off the pilot light or burner concerned

2 Switch off and remove an electric fire if used in same room as the escape

3 Extinguish naked flames

4 Open all windows and wait for smell to go

5 Relight pilots or burners

6 If smell does not go, turn off gas supply at main tap

7 Call local gas board immediately: a round-the-clock service is provided. Do not attempt repairs

Gas board (telephone number)

K

How to give the Kiss of Life

If a casualty has stopped breathing (but not otherwise) give the kiss of life immediately. Continue—for up to four hours if necessary—until there is normal breathing or help arrives.

1 Place victim on his back. Clear any obstruction from his mouth

2 Pull his head back and lift his chin up

3 Pinch his nostrils together (except in the case of a child)

4 Cover his mouth with your own (in the case of a child cover the mouth and nostrils)

5 Blow gently into mouth. Check that chest rises

6 If it does not, pull his head further back and blow again into his mouth

7 Remove your mouth and wait until chest falls

8 Repeat procedure every five seconds until the person breathes normally or medical help arrives

Doctor (telephone number)

Ambulance (telephone number)

EMERGENCY

Plumbing

Burst pipes and joints

1 Cut off the flow to the burst pipe by turning off the nearest control valve. This valve is generally in the kitchen for the rising main (the pipe that supplies the cistern and the cold-water tap in the kitchen) and in the attic for pipes supplied from the cistern

2 If a control valve is not fitted on a cistern-supplied pipe, wrap a cloth round a broomstick and hold it against the appropriate outlet pipe inside the cistern

3 Get someone to wrap rags or sacking round the damaged pipe, put a bowl underneath to catch the drips and turn off the boiler or immersion heater. Drain the cistern by opening the taps supplied by it

4 Repair the joint or damaged pipe or send for a plumber. For a temporary repair, use Tacki-tape, which is obtainable from hardware merchants

Leaks

1 Place a bowl under the leak. Trace the source of the leak

2 Cut off the flow by turning off the control valve nearest to the leak. This valve is generally in the kitchen for the rising main (the pipe that supplies the cistern and the cold-water tap in the kitchen) and in the attic for pipes supplied from the cistern

3 Repair the leak or call a plumber

Plumber (telephone number)

Water board (telephone number)

Frozen pipes

1 Feel for bursts or loose compression joints around any likely trouble spots, such as near cold draughts or against an exposed wall

2 If the pipe is damaged, turn off nearest control valve. Repair damage or send for a plumber

3 If the pipe is undamaged thaw it out with a hot-water bottle, cloths soaked in hot water or a hair dryer

Overflows

4 Cut off water supply by turning off the control valve to the cistern, or lift the ball-valve and tie it to stick placed across cistern

5 Fit a new washer to ball valve or bend ball-valve arm to lower water-level

Blockages

For drains, see p. 61. For basins and lavatories, see pp. 158, 159

Published by The Reader's Digest Association Limited, 25 Berkeley Square, London W1X 6AB; The Reader's Digest Association Limited, 9th Floor, Nedbank Centre, Strand Street, Cape Town

Printed by Waterlow Ltd and bound by Dorstel Press Ltd